ARCHITECTURE
RESIDENTIAL DRAFTING AND DESIGN

by

CLOIS E. KICKLIGHTER, CSIT
Dean Emeritus, School of Technology and Professor Emeritus of Construction Technology
Indiana State University
Terre Haute, IN

JOAN C. KICKLIGHTER, CFCS
Coauthor of *Residential Housing* and *Upholstery Fundamentals*
Naples, FL

Publisher
The Goodheart-Willcox Company, Inc.
Tinley Park, Illinois
www.g-w.com

Goodheart-Willcox Company, Inc., and the authors make no warranty or representation whatsoever, either expressed or implied, with respect to any of the software or applications described or referred to herein, their quality, performance, merchantability, or fitness, for particular purpose.

Further, Goodheart-Willcox Company, Inc., and the authors specifically disclaim any liability whatsoever for direct, indirect, special, incidental, or consequential damages arising out of the use or inability to use any of the software or applications described or referred to herein.

Library of Congress Cataloging-in-Publication Data

Kicklighter, Clois E.
Architecture: residential drafting and design/by Clois E. Kicklighter,
Joan C. Kicklighter.
p. cm.
ISBN-13:978-1-59070-699-2
ISBN-10: 1-59070-699-4
1. Architecture, Domestic–Designs and plans. 2. Architectural design.
I. Kicklighter, Joan C. II. Title

NA7115.K46 2006
728—dc22   200641177

Goodheart-Willcox Publisher Brand Disclaimer: Brand names, company names, and illustrations for products and services included in this text are provided for educational purposes only, and do not represent or imply endorsement or recommendation by the author or the publisher.

The Goodheart-Willcox Company, Inc., Safety Notice: The reader is expressly advised to carefully read, understand, and apply all safety precautions and warnings described in this book or that might also be indicated in undertaking the activities and exercises described herein to minimize risk of personal injury or injury to others. Common sense and good judgment should also be exercised and applied to help avoid all potential hazards. The reader should always refer to the appropriate manufacturer's technical information, directions, and recommendations; then proceed with care to follow specific equipment operating instructions. The reader should understand these notices and cautions are not exhaustive.

The publisher makes no warranty or representation whatsoever, either expressed or implied, including but not limited to equipment, procedures, and applications described or referred to herein, their quality, performance, merchantability, or fitness for a particular purpose. The publisher assumes no responsibility for any changes, errors, or omissions in this book. The publisher specifically disclaims any liability whatsoever, including any direct, indirect, incidental, consequential, special, or exemplary damages resulting, in whole or in part, from the reader's use or reliance upon the information, instructions, procedures, warnings, cautions, applications or other matter contained in this book. The publisher assumes no responsibility for the activities of the reader.

Trademarks: All trademarked products, company names, and other items appearing in this text have trademarks registered by their respective owners. No other trademark ownership is implied by the publisher.

Introduction

Architecture: residential drafting and design provides the basic information necessary for planning various types of dwellings. It presents basic instruction in preparing architectural working drawings using traditional (manual) as well as computer-based methods. Further, the text was developed to serve as a reference for design and construction principles and methods. It is intended to help build the necessary technical skills to communicate architectural ideas in an understandable, efficient, and accurate manner.

Architecture: residential drafting and design is organized so that the content is presented in the logical order of use. The functional organization and layout of the text, the step-by-step procedures, and its easy-to-understand discussions make it easy for learners to learn and for teachers to teach.

Architecture: residential drafting and design is highly illustrated with the very latest products and building techniques. The text is printed in full color throughout to increase communication and add interest. In addition to providing information on architectural drafting, design, and construction, the text includes excellent coverage of computer-aided drafting and design (CADD) and architectural CADD applications, steel framing, EIFS, engineered wood products, insulated concrete wall forms, insulated concrete block systems, welded-wire sandwich panels, handicapped access (ADA), multifamily housing, industrialized housing, tradework specifications, and career opportunities. It also contains an extensive reference section. Topics on entrepreneurship, work ethics, GFCIs, ground-source heat pumps, in-house water treatment devices, job site safety, brick paving, water conservation, handrail and guardrail requirements, and span tables for joists and rafters are also included.

Topics that address issues related to handicapped access are clearly identified throughout the text. Whenever the icon shown here in the margin appears, the text next to the icon discusses an issue related to providing for the disabled. This may include allowing for clear space, providing lower countertops, planning extra light, and so on.

Many of the end-of-chapter activities are designed to be completed using computer-aided drafting and design (CADD) systems. These activities are clearly identified with an icon of a CD-ROM and drafting triangle. This icon appears here in the margin. While these problems are intended to be completed with CADD, most can be completed using traditional drafting methods for those who do not have access to a CADD system.

This text is intended for architectural drafting and design classes in high schools, vocational and technical schools, community colleges, universities, adult learner curriculum, and apprenticeship programs. A complete learning package for diverse classes in architectural design is available. The package includes a comprehensive workbook that is designed for use with the text and software packages to be used with most CADD packages. This is a *complete* teaching/learning package. This text will also serve as a valuable reference for builders, carpentry classes, skilled tradeworkers, interior designers, appraisers, and building departments.

About the Authors

Dr. Clois E. Kicklighter is Dean Emeritus of the School of Technology and Professor Emeritus of Construction Technology at

Indiana State University. He is a nationally known educator and has held the highest leadership positions in the National Association of Industrial Technology including Chair of the National Board of Accreditation, Chair of the Executive Board, President, and Regional Director. Dr. Kicklighter was awarded the respected Charles Keith Medal for exceptional leadership in the technology profession.

Dr. Kicklighter is the author or coauthor of *Drafting for Industry*; *Modern Masonry: Brick, Block, and Stone*; *Residential Housing and Interiors*; *Upholstery Fundamentals*; and *Modern Woodworking*.

Dr. Kicklighter's educational background includes a baccalaureate degree from the University of Florida, a master's degree from Indiana State University, and a doctorate from the University of Maryland. His thirty-seven years of experience includes industrial, teaching, and administrative positions.

Joan C. Kicklighter is the coauthor of *Residential Housing and Interiors*, *Upholstery Fundamentals*, and instructional materials in family and consumer sciences. She taught classes in business and family and consumer sciences at the high school and adult levels. Mrs. Kicklighter's educational background includes a baccalaureate degree from Indiana State University and graduate work at Eastern Michigan University. She is certified in Family and Consumer Sciences.

Autodesk Authorized Publisher Program Description

Autodesk
Authorized Publisher

The Autodesk Authorized Publisher Program is a program offered by the Autodesk Developer Network. It is designed to help authors and publishers produce and market materials that support Autodesk software products, such as AutoCAD and Architectural Desktop. Authors and publishers produce books, multimedia training materials, tutorials, newsletters, journals, and training seminar tools. To participate in the program, authors and publishers must have an Autodesk-approved agreement to market their materials and must register with the Autodesk Developer Network. Visit the Autodesk website at www.autodesk.com for more information on the Autodesk Developer Network.

Brief Contents

Section I
The World of Architecture

1 The World of Architecture 17
2 Basic House Designs 37
3 Primary Considerations 51

Section II
Architectural Drafting Fundamentals

4 Drawing Instruments and Techniques 67
5 Introduction to Computer-Aided Drafting and Design 91
6 CADD Commands and Functions 109

Section III
Room and Space Planning

7 Room Planning—Sleeping Area and Bath Facilities 129
8 Room Planning—Living Area 149
9 Room Planning—Service Area 189

Section IV
Plot Plans and Foundations

10 Plot Plans 217
11 Footings, Foundations, and Concrete 233
12 The Foundation Plan 259

Section V
Construction Systems

13 Sill and Floor Construction 273
14 Wall and Ceiling Construction 297
15 Doors and Windows 319
16 Stairs 353
17 Fireplaces, Chimneys, and Stoves 369

Section VI
Formulating a Design

18 The Floor Plan 389
19 Roof Designs 409
20 Elevations 431

Section VII
Electrical, Plumbing, and Climate Control

21 Residential Electrical 449
22 Information, Communication, and Security Wiring 465
23 The Electrical Plan 483
24 Residential Plumbing 491
25 The Plumbing Plan 505
26 Residential Climate Control 515
27 Climate Control Plan 539

Section VIII
Alternative Construction, Products, and Methods

28 Solar Space Heating 549
29 Nontraditional Structures 565
30 New Products and Methods of Construction 579
31 Modular Applications 597

Section IX
Presentation Methods

32 Perspective Drawings 607
33 Presentation Drawings 637
34 Architectural Models 661

Section X
Specifications and Estimating

35 Material and Tradework Specifications 675
36 Estimating Building Cost 685

Section XI
Remodeling, Health, Safety, and Careers

37 Architectural Remodeling, Renovation, and Preservation 695
38 Designing for Health and Safety 715
39 Career Opportunities 739

Reference Section 749
Acknowledgments 808
Glossary 810
Index 831

Expanded Contents

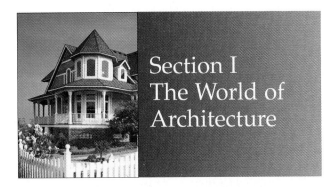

Section I
The World of Architecture

Chapter 1
The World of Architecture   17

People and Their Structures   17
> The Cape Colonials • The New England Gambrel • The Garrison • The Salt Box • The Southern Colonial

Contemporary Structures   24
> The Contemporary Style • The Ranch Design

Trends In Architecture   29

Multifamily Housing   32
> Cooperatives • Condominiums • Rental Apartments

The Americans with Disabilities Act (ADA)   34

Internet Resources   35

Review Questions   35

Suggested Activities   36

Chapter 2
Basic House Designs   37

One-Story Ranch Designs   37

One-and-One-Half-Story Designs   41

Two-Story Designs   42

Split-Level Designs   44

Traffic Circulation   47

Internet Resources   49

Review Questions   49

Suggested Activities   49

Chapter 3
Primary Considerations   51

Site Considerations   51

The Community   52

Cost and Restrictions   53

Zoning and Codes   54

Topographical Features   54

Family Needs   54

Budgeting for Housing   57

Other Considerations   57
> Modular Aspects • Quality of Living

Drawings Included in a Set of Plans   58
> Brief Plan Descriptions • Other Plans

Internet Resources   64

Review Questions   64

Suggested Activities   65

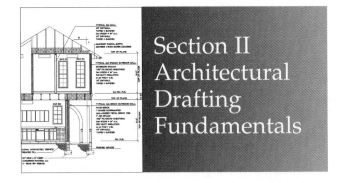

Section II
Architectural Drafting Fundamentals

Chapter 4
Drawing Instruments and Techniques   67

Orthographic Projection   67

Three Principal Views   67

Architectural Drafting Equipment 68
Pencils • Erasers • Erasing Shields • Paper •
Drawing Boards • T-Square • Triangles •
Protractors • Scales • How to Use a Scale •
Dividers • The Compass • Lettering Guides •
Irregular Curves • Case Instruments • Lettering
Devices • Technical Pens • Templates • Grids

Freehand Sketching 77
Sketching Technique • Sketching Horizontal
Lines • Sketching Vertical Lines • Sketching
Inclined Lines and Angles • Sketching Circles
and Arcs • Sketching Ellipses • Sketching
Irregular Curves • Proportion in Sketching

Computer-Aided Drafting and Design 81
CADD Hardware • CADD Software • Output
Devices

Lines Used In Architectural Drawing 83
Border Lines • Object Lines • Hidden Lines •
Centerlines • Extension Lines • Dimension
Lines • Long and Short Break Lines • Cutting-
Plane Lines • Section Lines • Guidelines •
Construction Lines • Line Type Application

Architectural Lettering 87
Some Notes On Developing a Style of Lettering •
Letter Spacing • Word Spacing • Letter Size

CADD Symbols Library 88

Internet Resources 89

Review Questions 89

Suggested Activities 90

Chapter 5
Introduction to Computer-Aided
Drafting and Design 91
What Is CADD? 91
Why Use CADD? 92
Productivity • Flexibility • Uniformity • Scale
Architectural CADD Applications 95
Schedule Automation • Renderings •
Animations
CADD Workstation 97
Computer Components • Storage Devices •
Display Types and Sizes • Input Devices •
Output Devices
Selecting a CADD Package 99
General Purpose CADD Packages • AEC CADD
Packages

Internet Resources 108
Review Questions 108
Suggested Activities 108

Chapter 6
CADD Commands and
Functions 109
Drawing Commands 110
Line • Double Line • Circle • Arc • Rectangle •
Polygon • Text • Hatch
Editing and Inquiry Commands 113
Erase • Undo • Move • Copy • Mirror • Rotate •
Scale • Fillet • Chamfer • Extend • Array •
List/Properties • Distance • Area
Display Control Commands 117
Zoom • Pan • View • Redraw/Regenerate
Dimensioning Commands 119
Drawing Aids 119
Grid • Snap • Ortho
Layers 121
Colors and Linetypes 122
Blocks and Attributes 122
3D Drawing and Viewing Commands 123
Isometric Drawing • 3D Modeling • 3D Views
3D Animation and Rendering Commands 125
Internet Resources 127
Review Questions 127
Suggested Activities 127

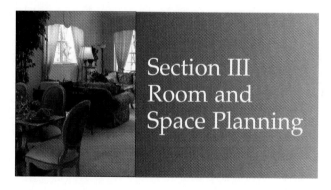

Section III
Room and
Space Planning

Chapter 7
Room Planning—Sleeping Area
and Bath Facilities 129
Areas of a Residence 129
Designing with CADD 130

Sleeping Area 131
    Bedrooms • Bathrooms
Internet Resources 146
Review Questions 146
Suggested Activities 147

Chapter 8
Room Planning—Living Area 149
Designing With CADD 150
Living Rooms 150
    Size • Location • Windows and Doors • Decor
Dining Rooms 158
    Plan • Size • Location • Decor
Entryway and Foyer 164
    Entryway • Foyer
Family Recreation Room 169
    Size • Decor • Applications
Special-Purpose Rooms 175
Patios, Porches, Courts, and Gazebos 177
    Patios • Porches • Courts and Gazebos •
    Applications
Internet Resources 187
Review Questions 187
Suggested Activities 187

Chapter 9
Room Planning—Service Area 189
Designing with CADD 189
Kitchen 189
    Kitchen Planning • Straight-Line Kitchen •
    L-Shaped Kitchen • Corridor Kitchen • U-Shaped
    Kitchen • Peninsula Kitchen • Island Kitchen •
    Cabinets and Appliances • Location and
    Ventilation • Decor • Applications • Kitchen
    Eating Areas
Clothes Care Center 205
Garage or Carport 207
    Size and Location • Design • Doors • Driveway •
    Applications
Internet Resources 214
Review Questions 214
Suggested Activities 214

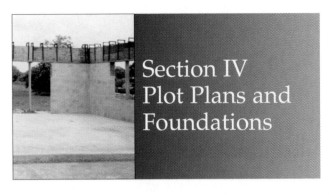

Section IV
Plot Plans and Foundations

Chapter 10
Plot Plans 217
Property Lines 217
Contour Lines 219
Topographical Features 220
Location of the Structure on the Site 222
Procedure For Drawing a Plot Plan—
    Manual Drafting 223
Landscape Plans 224
Procedure For Drawing a Plot Plan—CADD 225
Internet Resources 231
Review Questions 231
Suggested Activities 231

Chapter 11
Footings, Foundations, and
Concrete 233
Staking Out House Location 233
Excavation 235
Footing Shapes and Specifications 236
Foundation Walls 237
    T-Foundations • Slab Foundations • Pier and Post
    Foundations • Wood Foundations
Concrete and Masonry Basement Walls 245
Beams and Girders 248
    Weight Calculations • Beam Calculations •
    Post Calculations • Lintels
Concrete and Masonry 253
Concrete Blocks 254
Paving 255
Internet Resources 256
Review Questions 257
Suggested Activities 257

Chapter 12
The Foundation Plan   259

Preliminary Steps to Drawing a Foundation
  Plan   260

Drawing a Foundation Plan   261

The Basement/Foundation Plan   262

Procedure For Drawing a Basement Plan   265

Using CADD to Draw a Foundation and
  Basement Plan   267

Internet Resources   271

Review Questions   271

Suggested Activities   271

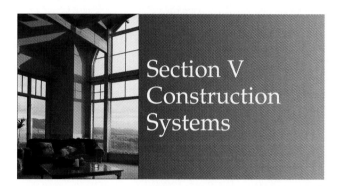

Section V
Construction
Systems

Chapter 13
Sill and Floor Construction   273

Platform Framing   273

Balloon Framing   274

Joists and Beams   275

Floor Trusses   278

Subfloor   280

Cantilevered Joists   282

Framing Under Slate or Tile   283

Engineered Wood Products   283
  Oriented Strand Board (OSB) • Parallel Strand
  Lumber (PSL) • Laminated Veneer Lumber (LVL) •
  Glue-Laminated Lumber • Wood I-Beams or Joists

Post and Beam Construction   290

Internet Resources   294

Review Questions   294

Suggested Activities   296

Chapter 14
Wall and Ceiling Construction   297

Frame Wall Construction   297
  Plates • Headers • Exterior Corners and Bracing •
  Interior Walls

Steel Framing   302
  Advantages of Steel Framing • Disadvantages of
  Steel Framing • Steel Framing Components •
  Wall and Roof Systems

Ceiling Construction   306

General Framing Considerations   306

Masonry Wall Construction   306
  Stonework • Masonry Veneer

Brick Names and Sizes   312

Traditional Three-Coat Stucco   312
  Preparing for Stucco • Moisture Barrier and
  Flashing • Lath (Reinforcement) • Scratch or
  Foundation Coat • Brown Coat • Finish Coat

Internet Resources   317

Review Questions   317

Suggested Activities   318

Chapter 15
Doors and Windows   319

Designing With CADD   319

Interior and Exterior Doors   320
  Interior Doors • Exterior Doors

Specifying Doors   327

Door Details   327

Windows   330
  Window Types • Window Schedules

Internet Resources   350

Review Questions   350

Suggested Activities   350

Chapter 16
Stairs   353

Types of Stairs   353

Stair Terminology   355

Designing With CADD   359

Stair Design   359
  Stringers • Treads and Risers

10

Stair Calculations and Drawing Procedure   362

Structural Details   363

Code Requirements For Handrails and
Guardrails   364

Adaptations for Special Needs   366
Stairlifts/Elevators • Ramps

Internet Resources   367

Review Questions   367

Suggested Activities   368

Chapter 17
Fireplaces, Chimneys, and Stoves
369

Fireplace Design Considerations   369

Fireplace/Chimney Terms   370

Designing With CADD   371

Hearth and Fire Chamber   371

Damper and Smoke Shelf   374

Flue   374

Framing Around Fireplace and Chimney   375

Fireplace Specifications   377
Single-Face Fireplace • Two-Face Opposite
Fireplace • Two-Face Adjacent Fireplace •
Three-Face Fireplace • Prefabricated Metal
Fireplaces and Stoves

Stoves   380

Internet Resources   386

Review Questions   387

Suggested Activities   387

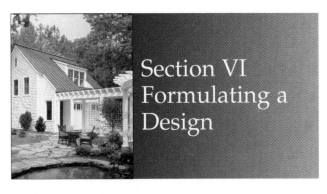

Section VI
Formulating a
Design

Chapter 18
The Floor Plan   389

Required Information   391
Location and Size of Walls • Location and Size
of Windows and Doors • Cabinets, Appliances,
and Permanent Fixtures • Stairs and Fireplaces •
Walks, Patios, and Decks • Room Names and
Material Symbols • Dimensioning • Scale and
Sheet Identification • Metric System of
Dimensioning

Drawing a Floor Plan   396
Procedure—Manual • Drafting Procedure—CADD

Internet Resources   407

Review Questions   408

Suggested Activities   408

Chapter 19
Roof Designs   409

Types of Roofs   409
Gable Roof • Winged Gable • Hip Roof • Dutch
Hip • Flat Roof • Shed Roof • Mansard Roof •
Gambrel Roof • Butterfly Roof • A-Frame Roof
• Folded Plate Roof • Curved Panel Roof •
Contemporary Roof Types

Traditional Frame Roof Construction   413
Rafters • Cornice • Rake or Gable End • Roof
Trusses • Ventilation • Flashing • Gutters and
Downspouts • Roof Sheathing and Roofing

New Roofing Materials   426
Asphalt Laminate Shingles • Metal Roofing

Internet Resources   429

Review Questions   429

Suggested Activities   429

Chapter 20
Elevations 431

Required Information 431
Elevation Identification • Grade Line, Floors, and Ceilings • Walls, Windows, and Doors • Roof Features • Dimensions, Notes, and Symbols

Drawing a Typical Wall Section 436

Procedure For Drawing an Elevation—Manual Drafting 439

Procedure For Drawing an Elevation—CADD 442

Internet Resources 446

Review Questions 447

Suggested Activities 447

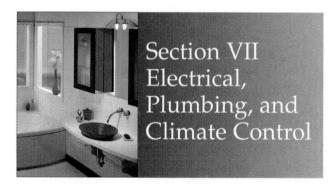

Section VII
Electrical, Plumbing, and Climate Control

Chapter 21
Residential Electrical 449

Electrical Terms 449

Service Entrance and Distribution Panel 450

Branch Circuits 452
Lighting Circuits • Special Appliance Circuits • Individual Appliance Circuits

Circuit Requirement Calculations 454

Outlets and Switches 454
Outlets • Switches

Ground-Fault Circuit Interrupter (GFCI) 458

Low Voltage Exterior Lighting 459
Planning Low Voltage Exterior Lighting • Low Voltage Wiring Considerations

Internet Resources 462

Review Questions 462

Suggested Activities 463

Chapter 22
Information, Communication, and Security Wiring 465

Introduction 465
Monitoring Functions • Switching (Activating) Functions • Programming Functions • Communication/Recording Functions • Alarm Functions

Information and Communication Wiring 467

Signaling Circuits 467

Data and Video Conductors 468
Structured Wiring • Radio Grade 6 Cable

Security Wiring 470
Systems to Protect Property • Systems to Protect Occupants and Property • Wiring for Security

Home Automation 472
Types of Home Automation Systems • Home Automation Summary Questions

Low-Voltage Switching 479

Internet Resources 480

Review Questions 480

Suggested Activities 481

Chapter 23
The Electrical Plan 483

Required Information 483
Service Entrance • Switches • Convenience Outlets • Lighting • Other Devices • Branch Circuits

Procedure For Drawing an Electrical Plan—Manual Drafting 487

Procedure For Drawing an Electrical Plan—CADD 488

Internet Resources 490

Review Questions 490

Suggested Activities 490

Chapter 24
Residential Plumbing 491

Water Supply System 491

In-House Water Treatment Devices 495

Water and Waste Removal 495

Plumbing Fixtures 498

Water Conservation 498

Private Sewage Disposal System 499
Septic Tank • Disposal Field • Disposal Field Soil Tests • Calculation of Disposal Field Size

Internet Resources 503

Review Questions 503

Suggested Activities 504

Chapter 25
The Plumbing Plan 505

Required Information 505
Waste Lines and Vent Stacks • Water Supply Lines • Drain Locations • Size and Type of Pipe • Plumbing Fixture Schedule • Symbols and Legend • Notes

Procedure For Drawing Plumbing Plan— Manual Drafting 509

Procedure For Drawing Plumbing Plan— CADD 511

Internet Resources 513

Review Questions 514

Suggested Activities 514

Chapter 26
Residential Climate Control 515

Temperature Control 515

Humidity Control 518

Air Circulation and Cleaning 520

Programmable Thermostats 520

Cooling Systems 522

Types of Heating Systems 523
Forced-Air Systems • Hydronic Systems • Electric Radiant Systems • Heat Pumps

Ground-Source Heat Pumps 530

Carbon Monoxide Detectors 530

Heat Loss Calculations 531
Calculation Procedure • Example of Heat Loss Calculation

True Window R-Value 536

CADD Heat Loss Calculations 536

Internet Resources 537

Review Questions 537

Suggested Activities 537

Chapter 27
Climate Control Plan 539

Required Information 539

Distribution System 539
Planning Outlet and Inlet Locations • Planning Ductwork • Planning Piping for a Hydronic System

Thermostats and Climate Control Equipment 542

Schedules, Calculations, and Notes 543

Procedure For Drawing Climate Control Plan— Manual Drafting 543

Drawing Climate Control Plans Using CADD 543

Internet Resources 547

Review Questions 547

Suggested Activities 547

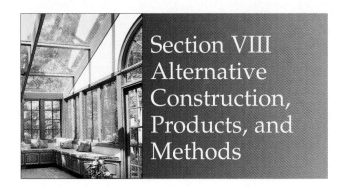

Section VIII
Alternative Construction, Products, and Methods

Chapter 28
Solar Space Heating 549

Insulation 549

Passive Solar Systems 549
Direct Gain Systems • Indirect Gain Systems • Isolated Gain Systems • Summary of Principles

Active Solar Systems 554
Warm Air Solar Systems • Warm Water Solar Systems

Advantages of Solar Heating 559

Disadvantages of Solar Heating 560

Calculation of Btus Possible for Any Given Location 560

Internet Resources 562

Review Questions 562

Suggested Activities 563

Chapter 29
Nontraditional Structures   565

Earth-Sheltered Dwellings   565

Site Considerations • Design Variations of Earth-Sheltered Dwellings • Advantages of Earth-Sheltered Housing • Disadvantages of Earth-Sheltered Housing

Dome Structures   571

Dome Variations • Typical Dome Construction • Advantages of Domes • Disadvantages of Domes

Internet Resources   577

Review Questions   577

Suggested Activities   578

Chapter 30
New Products and Methods of Construction   579

Introduction to Products and Methods   579

Exterior Insulation Finish Systems (EIFS)   580

Advantages of EIFS • Disadvantages of EIFS • Installation/Application

Structural Foam Sandwich Panels   581

Advantages of Structural Foam Sandwich Panels • Disadvantages of Structural Foam Sandwich Panels • Installation/Application

Concrete Wall Systems   584

Insulated Concrete Wall Forms • Insulated Concrete Wall Systems • Welded-Wire Sandwich Panels

Insulated Concrete Block Systems   589

Integra™ • Therma-Lock™

Frost-Protected Shallow Foundation   591

Weather-Resistant Deck Materials   592

Weather-Resistant Tropical Hardwoods • Synthetic Decking

The Hebel Wall System   595

Internet Resources   595

Review Questions   596

Suggested Activities   596

Chapter 31
Modular Applications   597

Standardization   597

Modular Components   600

Industrialized Housing   600

Internet Resources   604

Review Questions   604

Suggested Activities   604

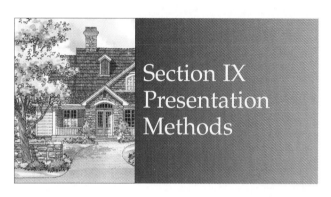

Section IX
Presentation Methods

Chapter 32
Perspective Drawings   607

Perspectives   609

Terminology • Two-Point Perspectives • Two-Point Perspective Drawing Sequence • One-Point Perspectives • One-Point Perspective Drawing Sequence • Computer-Generated Perspectives

Perspective Grids   631

Complex Features in Perspective   632

Internet Resources   634

Review Questions   634

Suggested Activities   635

Chapter 33
Presentation Drawings   637

Rendering   637

Pencil Rendering • Ink Rendering • Watercolor Rendering • Tempera Rendering • Colored Pencil Rendering • Felt-Tipped Pen Rendering • Scratchboard Rendering • Appliqué Rendering • Airbrush Rendering • Computer-Generated Renderings

Shading and Shadows   645

Entourage   646

Types of Presentation Plans   647
  Exterior Perspectives • Rendered Elevations •
  Presentation Plot Plans • Presentation Floor
  Plans • Rendered Sections • Walkthrough
  Animation
Internet Resources   659
Review Questions   659
Suggested Activities   659

Chapter 34
Architectural Models   661
Types of Models   661
Materials Used in Model Construction   663
Constructing a Balsa Model   664
Laser-Cut Model Parts   670
Internet Resources   671
Review Questions   671
Suggested Activities   672

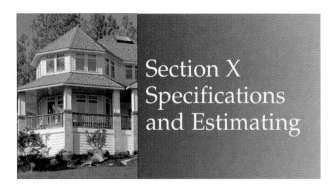

Section X
Specifications
and Estimating

Chapter 35
Material and Tradework
Specifications   675
Purpose of Specifications   675
Specification Formats   676
Examples of Specifications   676
Internet Resources   684
Review Questions   684
Suggested Activities   684

Chapter 36
Estimating Building Cost   685
Preliminary Estimates   685
  Square Foot Method • Cubic Foot Method
More Accurate Estimates   686
Internet Resources   693
Review Questions   693
Suggested Activities   693

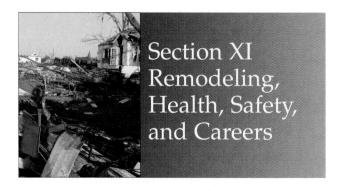

Section XI
Remodeling,
Health, Safety,
and Careers

Chapter 37
Architectural Remodeling,
Renovation, and Preservation   695
Choosing to Remodel   696
Types of Remodeling   697
  Changing Lived-In Areas • Making Unused
  Space Livable • Adding On • Buying to
  Remodel
Renovation   707
Historic Preservation   707
  Restoration • Preservation Through Remodeling •
  Adaptive Reuse
Preparing Remodeling, Renovation, and
  Preservation Plans   710
  Interior Designer • Architect • Contractor
Internet Resources   713
Review Questions   713
Suggested Activities   713

Chapter 38
Designing for Health and Safety 715

Introduction   715

Smoke and Fire Detection   715

Fire Prevention • Smoke Detectors • Fire Safety Code Requirements • Fire Extinguishers

Carbon Monoxide (CO) Detection   717

Carbon Monoxide Poisoning • CO Detectors

Radon Detection   719

Radon in the Home • Radon Testing • Radon Mitigation

Moisture and Mold Problems   722

Migration of Water Vapor • Sources of Water Vapor • Preventative Measures • Ventilation • Health Hazards Associated with Mold • Mold Prevention and Removal

Weather- and Nature-Related Safety   726

Earthquakes • Floods • Tornadoes • Hurricanes

General Home Safety   736

Internet Resources   737

Review Questions   737

Suggested Activities   738

Chapter 39
Career Opportunities   739

Careers in Architecture and Construction   739

Architect • Architectural Drafters • Architectural Illustrators • Specifications Writer • Estimator • Surveyor • Teaching Architectural Drafting • Construction Technologist • Residential Designer

Keeping a Job and Advancing a Career   743

Model Ethics Code • Work Ethic • Job Site Safety • Leadership on the Job

Entrepreneurship   745

Internet Resources   747

Review Questions   747

Suggested Activities   747

Reference Section   749

Building Material Symbols • Topographical Symbols • Plumbing Symbols • Climate Control Symbols • Electrical Symbols • ANSI Architectural Symbols • Vanity Sizes and Designs • Wall Cabinet Sizes and Designs • Base Cabinet Sizes and Designs • Double-Hung Window Sizes • Horizontal Sliding Window Sizes • Casement Window Sizes • Awning Window Sizes • Hopper Window Sizes • Picture Window Sizes • Glass Sliding Door Sizes • Design Data for Trusses • Span Data • Beam Data • Resistivity to Heat Loss of Building Materials • Metric System • Conversion Tables • Weights of Building Materials • Brick and Block Courses • Rafter Conversion Diagram • Plywood Grades and Specs • Asphalt Roofing Products • Concrete Reinforcement • Gypsum Wallboard Data • Reinforcing Bar Sizes • Foot Candle Levels - Design Temperatures and Degree Days • Wood Foundations Fire and Sound Ratings • Wall System Selection • Clearance Requirements • Building Requirements • Abbreviations • TJI Joists, LVL Headers, and LVL Beams • Radon Detection • Carbon Monoxide Detection • Earthquake Zones • CSI Specification • Rigid Foam Comparison • International Residential Code

Acknowledgements   808

Glossary   810

Index   831

Section I
Architectural Basics

1 **The World of Architecture**

2 **Basic House Designs**

3 **Primary Considerations**

The World of Architecture

Objectives

After studying this chapter, you will be able to:

➤ Identify the historical influences that helped shape today's home designs.

➤ Recognize and describe the elements of contemporary dwellings.

➤ Discuss current trends and influences in architecture.

➤ Identify types of multifamily housing.

Key Terms

Americans with Disabilities Act (ADA)
Apartment
Cape Ann
Cape Cod
Condominium
Contemporary (Modern)
Cooperative
Garrison
Multifamily housing
New England Gambrel
Postmodern Architecture
Ranch
Salt Box
Southern Colonial

The fascinating study of architecture encompasses a sensitivity to design, skill in drawing techniques, and a knowledge of the latest construction materials. It is the combination of these abilities that yields today's outstanding architects. These architects design the massive high-rise buildings, quaint lakeshore cottages, modern churches, and family homes required to meet the needs of our society.

The world of architecture is all around us. It has been one of the major achievements of humankind to design structures that bring the thrill of lasting beauty to the eye of the beholder. Whether it is a symbolic monument or a long awaited residence, a rewarding experience and years of pleasure belong to the architect and to those who view the structure, Figure 1-1. Some structures are designed for commercial and industrial use while others are planned for organizations or private living, Figure 1-2. The emphasis of this book is on the design, architecture, and study of residential structures. However, the relationships of line, form, and material of almost any structure has an impact on home construction.

People and Their Structures

Over the years, a number of architectural styles have been developed for house construction. Many of these styles developed so that structures would be suited for the climate and needs of families in various parts of the country. Others were planned especially for luxurious living, Figure 1-3. All of the factors that led to development of various styles provide a historical background that still

Figure 1-1. This computer-generated rendering shows a contemporary home that makes a strong statement through its interesting roof and strong architectural lines. (Helmuth A. Geiser, Member AIBD)

influence the design of today's homes. Some house styles became so popular that they took on names related to their shape, period of time, or area of the country in which they were built. The emphasis in this chapter is given to the design qualities that people have used over many years and now are imitated or incorporated into modern homes.

Figure 1-2. This multifamily dwelling, reminiscent of an earlier architectural style, was planned and designed by an architect.

Figure 1-3. This large, expensive home was designed for luxurious living with accommodations for an occasionally harsh environment. It is a seafront residence with a seawall to protect the landscaping and house from wave surges.

The Cape Colonials

Two very popular home styles developed over 200 years ago are the Cape Cod and Cape Ann. These traditional homes have influenced structural design since they were first conceived. People have enjoyed them for their aesthetic appeal. They provide a comfortable and livable atmosphere with large and functional rooms.

The *Cape Cod* is one of the earliest and best known of the traditional Colonial styles. It originated as a fairly small house with a steep roof and little overhang. A chimney accommodated the necessary room fireplaces. These homes were normally built as one- or one-and-one-half-story buildings. However, the same features have been incorporated in two-story styles. The eaves line is always near the top of the windows, ending with a gable roof. Narrow trim lines of the siding, which appealed to New Englanders many years ago, are still used on these homes. Shutters are generally used on all windows, giving emphasis to the white or yellow painted siding that was preferred in earlier times. Many variations of the Cape Cod are used in today's structures, Figure 1-4.

Another example of the Colonial style used in modern construction is the *Cape Ann,* Figure 1-5. This differs from the Cape Cod in many respects. The chimney is centrally located and is usually larger. The tapering gambrel roof encloses an attic that is often converted into extra rooms. A growing family may take this into consideration when planning their first home. Modern use of the Cape

Figure 1-4. This is a refined version of the traditional Cape Cod style. Later Cape Cod houses have dormers on the second floor. Many also have shutters.

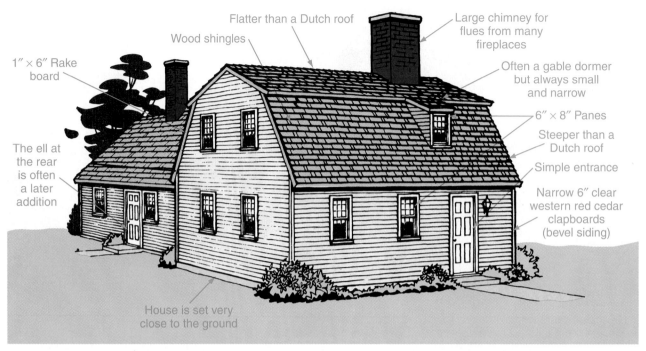

Flatter than a Dutch roof

Wood shingles

1″ × 6″ Rake board

Large chimney for flues from many fireplaces

Often a gable dormer but always small and narrow

6″ × 8″ Panes

Steeper than a Dutch roof

Simple entrance

The ell at the rear is often a later addition

Narrow 6″ clear western red cedar clapboards (bevel siding)

House is set very close to the ground

Figure 1-5. This rendering of a traditional Cape Ann style shows some of the differences between it and a Cape Cod style. Many modern homes are distinguished by features taken from this early structure. (Western Wood Products Association)

Ann characteristics provides a house with simple lines, sound construction, and a feel of colonial atmosphere. It makes a particularly attractive house along a tree-shaded avenue or in a wooded development.

The New England Gambrel

The *New England Gambrel* is a variation of other colonial styles, Figure 1-6. It features the gambrel roof where the pitch is abruptly changed between the ridge and eaves. Inherently American, the style is now used in most every section of the country. An advantage of the gambrel roof is the extra headroom and usable space. The shorter rafter lengths required can result in lower cost. Many adaptations of this architectural style provide pleasing and enduring homes for today's families.

The Garrison

A modern presentation of the traditional *Garrison* is an attractive house that includes a number of special features, Figure 1-7. A distinguishing feature is the overhanging second story. This construction technique includes a number of advantages. (1) The separate corner posts on each floor make it possible to use shorter, stronger posts. (2) The short, straight lines provide an economy in framing materials. (3) Extra space is added to the second level by the overhang at very little extra cost. The steep pitch roof adds attic space. Figure 1-8 shows the traditional Garrison from which modern design features have been developed. Narrow siding helps maintain the traditional styling in modern homes.

The Salt Box

An interesting and easily recognized Colonial style is the *Salt Box*, Figure 1-9. It is a direct offshoot of the basic colonial half house, which results in a long roofline sloping gently from the ridge to the eaves. Many of today's beautiful homes have borrowed from this distinctive style, developed by master builders of early America. The Salt Box house gets its name from the shape of coffee, tea, cracker, and salt boxes found in Colonial stores. The

Figure 1-6. The typical New England Gambrel style is adapted to this contemporary house.

side elevations of these containers had the same general shape as this fascinating architectural style. Variations of this style are used to enhance many new homes.

The long, low roofline at the rear of the Salt Box house came about by the addition of "lean-to" structures to add more living space. The low slanting roof was also helpful in

Figure 1-7. A contemporary Garrison home retains the straight-line features and overhanging second story of the original style.

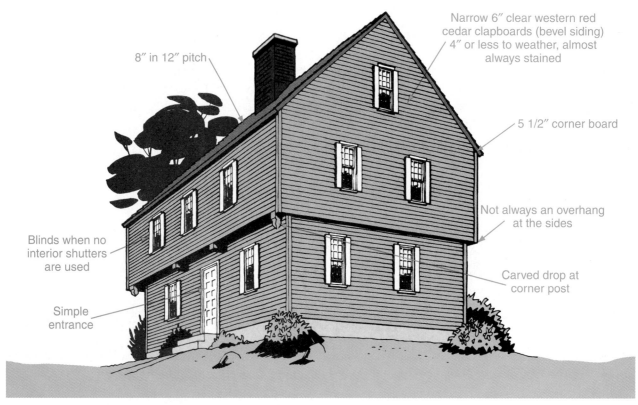

8" in 12" pitch

Narrow 6" clear western red cedar clapboards (bevel siding) 4" or less to weather, almost always stained

5 1/2" corner board

Not always an overhang at the sides

Carved drop at corner post

Blinds when no interior shutters are used

Simple entrance

Figure 1-8. The distinguishing characteristics of the traditional Garrison home. (Western Wood Products Association)

Figure 1-9. The style of this modern home is a beautiful representation of the early New England Salt Box home.

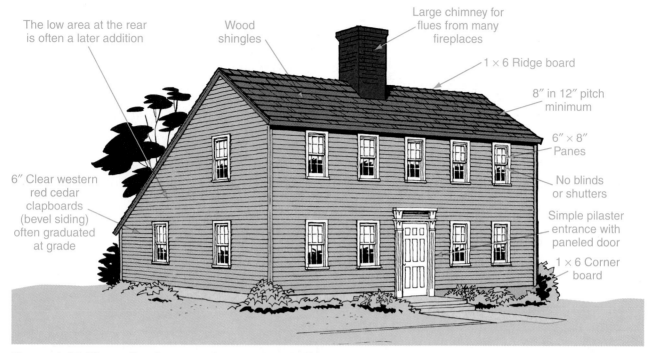

Figure 1-10. The styling features of the original Salt Box home with wood roof shingles, narrow wood siding, and no shutters. (Western Wood Products Association)

combating the bitter winds common to New England winters. The basic original style of the Salt Box house is shown in Figure 1-10.

The Southern Colonial

One of the most gracious of all the Colonials is the traditional *Southern Colonial.*

The style reflects the warmth, quaintness, and hospitality of the old south, Figure 1-11. Modern examples borrow many of the fine details of the Southern Colonial to express a mood of elegance and traditional charm. The outstanding architectural features are the front colonnade and the giant portico. The extended portico shelters the front entrance from the

Figure 1-11. The most gracious of all Colonial home styles is the Southern Colonial.

weather and keeps direct sunlight from glaring into the first and second story rooms. These homes were usually massive with upper and lower balconies, three-story chimneys for bedroom fireplaces, ornate woodwork and iron trim, and a roof over the driveway to protect persons using the side entrance. Many of these features of the Southern Colonial may be adapted to create esthetically pleasing qualities in modern homes.

Contemporary Structures

It is evident that the influences of the past, both in beauty and function, have had a profound effect on modern home designs. On the other hand, many new materials, appliances, and modes of living have caused the architect to "think out" ways to plan homes for all styles of modern living. The modern American home is a combination of many of these factors.

The Contemporary Style

The style of home that is generally called **contemporary** is the result of years of architectural planning, design, and evolution. Many are well planned, yet others lack imagination or design balance. Some inexpensive homes are functionally satisfactory for a family, yet the exterior styling may have to be quite conservative in the use of a variety of materials for economical reasons. See Figure 1-12. The ability of the architect and the needs or finances of the family are factors that generally dictate the type of construction being planned. Figure 1-13 shows the use of various materials and expensive detailing in a modern home.

The term "contemporary" or "modern" does not denote any one particular architectural style. Most modern homes borrow some distinctive features from more traditional structures, while others appear almost independent of past designs, Figure 1-14. However, to an architect it is not important to determine what defines a contemporary style. The most

Figure 1-12. An economical contemporary home built using standard materials.

Figure 1-13. Multiple materials, coordinated lines, and intricate details give an architectural flair to this contemporary style home. These same factors also result in this house being expensive to construct. (Photo Courtesy of James Hardie® Siding Products)

Figure 1-14. Unique styling is featured in this contemporary residence. Notice the strong vertical lines and bold use of curved glass block.

important job for the architect is to design homes that satisfy the customers; homes they can live in with pride and joy. In today's society, individual tastes vary to the extent that many people desire a house that is distinctly different from other houses. The owner may feel that the house represents a particular style of living and individuality, Figure 1-15. One

owner may enjoy the warmth of natural wood, Figure 1-16; another owner may like the solid structural design of a brick home, Figure 1-17.

The rapid developments of new construction materials and methods of fabrication have made it possible to design homes that require minimal maintenance, Figure 1-18. An architect can easily make extensive use of glass for appearance and interior light, Figure 1-19. An architect may also choose to place emphasis on exposed structural members to create a distinctive style, Figure 1-20.

The Ranch Design

One prominent modern architectural residential style is the *ranch home.* This is basically a long, low, one-story house style that developed from the homes built by ranchers in the southwestern US, Figure 1-21. The basic ranch design generally has a low-pitch roof with gables and overhanging eaves. A ranch house is traditionally built on a concrete slab with no basement. However, over the years, ranch homes have taken on many newer features, Figure 1-22. They now usually have a one- or two-car attached garage and a basement.

Figure 1-15. Individuality is emphasized in this home through the unique treatment of space.

Figure 1-16. This attractive home makes use of wood siding with a natural finish combined with large areas of glass. (AGS&R Studios)

Figure 1-17. A traditional brick home communicates the feeling of permanence.

Figure 1-18. Homes can be designed to require minimal maintenance. Materials such as vinyl or solid aluminum siding, gutters, downspouts, ornamental shutters, fascia, and soffits are attractive and easy to clean and maintain. (Norandex/Reynolds Building Products)

Figure 1-19. Large areas of glass are used extensively in this contemporary home.
(California Redwood Association)

Figure 1-20. Visible roof supports are part of a dominant design element in this home.
(Cultured Stone by Stucco Products, Inc.)

Figure 1-21. This rendering is of a ranch-style home with Spanish design influences. (Ken Hawk)

Many modern ranch-style homes have an L-shape layout to add interest and break up the straight-line effect. Skylights and cathedral ceilings are other variations found in some modern ranch homes.

New design concepts and additions to the basic ranch style have probably added more to the development of contemporary or "futuristic" homes than any other major factors, Figure 1-23. The ranch has twists, turns,

Figure 1-22. This thoroughly modern ranch home exhibits architectural detail designed to set it apart from traditional ranch homes. (Arthur Rutenberg Homes, Inc.)

Figure 1-23. This home contains the basic elements of the ranch style yet incorporates many contemporary architecture details.

angles, and curves added from the imagination of the architect of today and tomorrow.

Trends in Architecture

It is interesting to note that future home styles give the architect a freedom of design seldom known in the past. As indicated earlier, the multitude of individual preferences, materials, and structural techniques predicts a variety of unique expressions for architectural designing. Many new homes are designed for stately or dramatic effects, Figure 1-24 and Figure 1-25. Others are styled for particular settings, such as hillsides, seashores, and even cliffs, Figure 1-26 and Figure 1-27.

Figure 1-25. The complex layout of this home creates a dramatic effect.

Figure 1-24. The stately appearance of this two-story home is achieved with use of various building materials and interesting designs.
(Photo Courtesy of James Hardie® Siding Products)

Figure 1-26. This modern residence was designed for a seashore setting.

Figure 1-27. The roof design, use of glass, and structural materials of this residence are particularly suited for the arid climate. (Cultured Stone by Stucco Stone Products, Inc.)

Figure 1-29. This house, reminiscent of traditional architectural design, fits comfortably on a small city lot.

The trends in architecture appear to be leaning toward dramatic, yet comfortable, living styles. Homes that complement the site, provide a feeling of openness, and still retain the required privacy are always being developed. Figure 1-28 shows a residence designed to both convey spaciousness and take advantage of the natural surroundings of the site. Figure 1-29 shows a home designed to provide a vertical solution to a small city site.

A current trend in architectural design that is receiving strong support is called *post-modern architecture.* This trend or "style" combines traditional and contemporary influ-

ences into designs for truly modern structures that are strongly reminiscent of popular styles of the past. See Figure 1-30 and Figure 1-31. However, modern materials and building techniques are used to produce energy-efficient and weather-resistant homes.

Another trend in residential architecture is the renovation of older homes. Many older homes are structurally solid and may be

Figure 1-28. Attention to detail in every aspect of this modern home blended together with a sense of unity produces a superb family residence.

Figure 1-30. An example of postmodern architecture that combines traditional and contemporary influences. (Armstrong World Industries, Inc.)

Figure 1-31. An example of a postmodern structure that is strongly reminiscent of Georgian architecture. (Photo Courtesy of James Hardie® Siding Products)

restored to their original beauty with some care and attention. Figure 1-32 shows an historic early Victorian home that was saved from demolition. Figure 1-33 shows a restored late Victorian home that is still very functional today. The photos in Figure 1-34 illustrate the dramatic impact that thoughtful restoration can have even on less-dramatic traditional homes.

Experimentation with new materials and design concepts continues to produce radically new structures. Earth-protected homes and dome structures are two categories of homes that have resulted from experimentation with new ideas. A dome home that uses triangular sections bolted together to enclose a large interior space free of support partitions is shown in Figure 1-35. This structure is very energy efficient and flexible in terms of interior space utilization. The basic structure can be erected in a very short time since the modules are prefabricated and hauled

Figure 1-32. A restored early Victorian home that maintains the strong design influence of the past.

Figure 1-33. Elements of Victorian architecture, as shown in this restored structure, still show elegance today. (Norandex/Reynolds Building Products)

Figure 1-34. These two homes have undergone restorations. A—Before restoration. B—Restored home. C—Before restoration. D—Restored home. (Norandex/Reynolds Building Products)

Figure 1-35. This dome home is constructed from manufactured triangular sections assembled on-site to produce the roof and walls of the structure. (Linda Lindeman)

to the site. The exterior skin may use traditional roofing materials such asphalt shingles.

Multifamily Housing

The homes discussed to this point in the chapter are single-family residences. This means that a single family "unit" resides in the structure. However, there are other types of housing that are considered *multifamily housing*. This means that more than one family "unit" lives in the structure. Examples of multifamily dwellings include cooperatives, condominiums, and rental apartments, Figure 1-36. Other "dense" residential dwellings include tract houses, some manufactured houses, and mobile homes. These are considered "dense" because many structures are placed close together with little or no yard space.

Figure 1-36. This apartment building houses about a dozen families in one structure. The apartment management is responsible for the maintenance of the building, landscaping, and common areas. (Norandex/Reynolds Building Products)

Cooperatives

The term *cooperative* or "co-op" refers to a type of ownership, not a type of building. Cooperative ownership is most common in multifamily dwellings. Each family's living space is usually called an apartment.

Cooperative ownership combines the advantages of home ownership with the convenience of apartment living. Under a cooperative, an apartment building is managed and run as a corporation. The buyer purchases stock in the corporation that runs the building and, as an owner, receives an apartment. The value of the apartment determines the amount of stock purchased. The buyer receives a lease that grants them exclusive right to possession of the apartment.

Since the buyer owns the apartment, they do not pay rent. The buyer does, however, pay a monthly fee that is used to pay the property taxes and maintenance costs of the building. The corporation takes care of maintenance and repairs with the money collected from the stockholders.

Owners have a voice in how the co-op is run. This is an advantage over a rental apartment. Owners also have a say in who their neighbors are to be. Residents generally vote on whether or not a family should be allowed to purchase an apartment (stock) in the building. The major disadvantage of a co-op is that each member must abide by the wishes of the total group. If the group makes a bad decision, then all suffer.

Condominiums

Unlike the owner of a cooperative who buys stock, the owner of a *condominium* buys the apartment and a share of the common ground. The owner receives a deed to the apartment and pays taxes on it just as though it is a detached house. Owners of units in a condominium building have joint interest in all the shared property and facilities. These may include hallways, laundry areas, parking lots, sidewalks, lawns, tennis courts, and swimming pools. Common property is maintained with money collected from monthly assessments, as it is under cooperative ownership.

An owner of a condominium unit may sell the unit without consent or approval of other owners. In matters relating to common property, each owner has a vote in proportion to the original value of the unit they own.

A condominium complex may consist of a single building or a group of buildings and surrounding property. It may even include a mixture of apartments, townhouses, and duplexes. The special feature of a condominium is that each unit is owned individually with a joint interest in common property.

Rental Apartments

Any type of dwelling may be rented, but **apartments** are by far the most common rentals. In many cases, several apartment buildings are planned and built at the same time in a group. This makes good use of the land and helps provide greater security.

Rental apartments have definite advantages for large segments of the population. They offer a variety of lifestyles and are readily available. Apartments are especially popular among young singles, newly married couples, elderly couples or singles, and low income families. This probably stems from the fact that rental apartments usually require less expense and effort in upkeep than other types of housing. In addition, rental apartments provide housing for those who do not have the money for a down payment on a purchase or have less than perfect credit and cannot qualify for a mortgage.

In recent years, many new apartments have been built in attractive settings with conveniences to meet almost any need, Figure 1-37. Choices are unlimited in terms of style, size, price range, and facilities. Apartments are often conveniently located near public transportation, shopping centers, and recreation areas. Another advantage is that they require little time or effort from the renter for upkeep and maintenance.

Figure 1-37. Rental apartments have definite advantages for certain segments of the population.

Disadvantages of rental apartments relate mostly to loss of control over the living space. Renters have little or no voice in how the apartment building is managed or maintained—although this has improved in recent years. Neighbors may move in and out so often that no true neighborhood spirit is developed. Also, money spent on rent is not applied toward ownership nor is it tax deductible. After paying rent for years, renters have no property to show for their payments. A home owner, on the other hand, has ownership of property and can take mortgage interest and property taxes as income tax deductions. In spite of the disadvantages, the rental apartment is the best answer to the housing needs of many people.

The Americans with Disabilities Act (ADA)

On July 26, 1990, the **Americans with Disabilities Act (ADA)** became law. The ADA makes it illegal to discriminate against disabled persons in the areas of employment, public and private transportation, and access to public and commercial buildings. The physical access requirements of the ADA affect both existing places of public access as well as new construction. However, the ADA is not a building code—rather it is a civil rights statute. The ADA is enforced in the courts.

Title III of the ADA is the section of the law regarding public accommodations. The term "public accommodation" refers to privately-owned entities only. These include such places as hotels and motels; restaurants and bars; theaters; convention centers; shopping centers; banks; insurance offices; hospitals; professional offices of health care providers, lawyers, and accountants; museums; places of education; and daycare, senior, and recreation centers. Public accommodations do not include multifamily housing, which is covered under the Federal Fair Housing Act of 1988; private clubs; religious organizations; and public entities such as state or local governments or divisions thereof, which are governed by different standards under Title II of the ADA.

For those establishments affected by the ADA, reasonable modifications may be required to remove architectural and communication barriers. Some typical modifications may include installing ramps and curb cuts, widening doors, eliminating turnstiles, installing raised toilet seats and grab bars, installing flashing alarm lights and telecommunications devices for persons who are deaf, adding raised elevator buttons for persons who are blind, and providing parking that will accommodate people in wheelchairs. In addition, depending on the use of the area, the paths of travel to bathrooms, telephones, drinking fountains, and other facilities may also need to be made accessible.

Internet Resources

www.aia.org
American Institute of Architects

www.architectural-ornament.com
Architectural Ornament, Inc., manufacturer of polyurethane architectural molding

www.builderonline.com
Builder Magazine Online

www.concretehomes.com
Portland Cement Association

www.culturedstone.com
Cultured Stone, a producer of manufactured stone veneers

www.designbasics.com
Design Basics, Inc., a home design service

www.homesofelegance.com
Homes of Elegance

www.saterdesign.com
The Sater Design Collection, Inc.

www.wwpa.org
Western Wood Products Association

Review Questions — Chapter 1

Write your answers on a separate sheet of paper. Do not write in this book.

1. The needs of families and suitability for the local _____ have contributed to the structural styles of homes.

2. List the three major factors that the study of architecture includes.

3. Which of the following factors led to the name Salt Box for that particular style home?
   a) Implement sheds.
   b) Containers in village stores.
   c) Early churches.
   d) The shape of barn roofs.

4. What are three advantages of a Garrison style house?

5. What are the outstanding architectural features of the Southern Colonial home?

6. What is unique about the shape of the roof on a Gambrel style home?

7. Why do the terms contemporary and modern not describe a particular architectural style?

8. The basic ranch home is a low, long one-story house with a _____ _____ roof, gables, and overhanging eaves.

9. New design concepts and additions to the basic _____ style have probably added more to the development of contemporary or "futuristic" homes than any other major factors.

10. List four factors that appear to be influencing new trends in architectural design.

11. A trend or "style" that combines traditional and contemporary influences is called _____ _____.

12. How does a condominium differ from a cooperative?

13. What aspects of rental property might persuade a person to rent rather than buy a house?

14. How is the ADA enforced?

15. What is the basic purpose of the ADA?

Suggested Activities

1. Call on an architect and ask the following questions. Write a brief report on the responses the architect has given you.

   a) What particular style home is most in demand today?

   b) How does one become an architect and why?

   c) In what way does one communicate with clients to provide the style home they desire?

   d) How does one determine from a client just what design features will be most appealing to them?

2. From magazine and newspaper clippings, make an architectural design folder illustrating as many home styles as you can find. Indicate on each home any design feature that has been borrowed from the past or gives an indication of a futuristic trend.

3. Visit a local contractor and ask about materials currently used for exterior structural features. Ask for an explanation of each product and how each is used. Make a list of these materials and relate your findings to your class.

4. Select a particular traditional style home. Cut out and glue together a cardboard model of that design. Sketch in doors, windows, siding, etc., and put the model on display in your classroom.

5. Make a collection of catalogs from lumber dealers and suppliers. From this material, prepare a list of new materials that are available to replace older exterior structural devices. An example might be the use of aluminum or plastic gutters that replace galvanized iron gutters. Present this as a discussion with your class.

Basic House Designs

Objectives

After studying this chapter, you will be able to:

➤ List the four basic house designs.

➤ Explain the chief advantages of each house design.

➤ List disadvantages of each house design.

➤ Explain traffic circulation in a floor plan.

Key Terms

Intermediate Level
Living Level
One-and-One-Half Story
One-Story Ranch
Sleeping Level
Split-Level
Traffic Circulation
Two-Story

A residential home designer has four basic designs to choose from: one-story ranch, one-and-one-half-story, two-story, and split-level. Each of these styles has strengths and weaknesses that should be considered before making a choice. Factors such as space available for the house "footprint," site contour, climate, convenience, cost, surroundings, personal preference, and personal needs should all play a role in the final decision.

One-Story Ranch Designs

The *one-story ranch* style house has all the regular living space on one level, Figure 2-1. It may have a basement, depending on the section of the country in which it is built and preference of the prospective owner. Otherwise, it will sit on a crawl space or slab floor. A one-story ranch house is often simply called a ranch house.

Figure 2-1. A typical one-story ranch house has all of the normal living space on the main level. (Ken Hawk)

One of the chief advantages of the ranch design is that it lends itself beautifully to indoor-outdoor living, Figure 2-2. Patios, porches, and terraces can be added off of virtually any room. With lots of glass, it is possible to visually bring the outdoor surroundings inside to make the house appear even larger than it is. Another advantage of this design is the absence of stairs when the house is on a crawl space or slab. The ranch without a basement is popular with many older and handicapped people.

The ranch usually has a low-pitched roof, since no headroom is necessary above the ceiling, and wide overhangs. The low-pitched roof and short walls make outside maintenance easy. Cleaning the gutters, removing the screens, and painting do not require long ladders or other special equipment. Low height also simplifies construction. See Figure 2-3. The ranch easily lends itself to expansion and modification. A great number of variations is possible. See Figure 2-4.

The low and long appearance of the ranch is pleasing to most people, Figure 2-5. The ranch may be built with a full basement, Figure 2-6; crawl space, Figure 2-7; or on a slab, Figure 2-8.

A ranch house is not without disadvantages. One disadvantage of a ranch house is that it usually costs more to build than other designs of the same square footage. This stems from the fact that there is more roof area and more foundation length, Figure 2-9.

Figure 2-2. The quality of this outdoor space greatly enhances the living area of the home.
(The Oshkosh, WI private residence of Chancellor Richard H. Wells and family—formerly the Alberta Kimball Home)

Figure 2-3. This computer-generated rendering shows a large ranch house that combines simplified construction and minimal maintenance. (Helmuth A. Geiser, Member AIBD)

Figure 2-4. The ranch can be easily modified. In this duplex, the design has been expanded vertically to provide extra space.

Another negative aspect of the ranch is that it requires a larger lot, since it spreads out rather than up. Furthermore, the large "footprint" sometimes causes heating problems for certain areas of the house because of the distance from the furnace. There is generally no problem with electric heat. However, electric heat may be more expensive to operate than gas or oil.

Maintenance costs may be more on a ranch because of the large roof and exterior wall surfaces, Figure 2-10. Considerable hall space

Figure 2-5. The low, long design of this ranch home in Florida is attractive to most people.

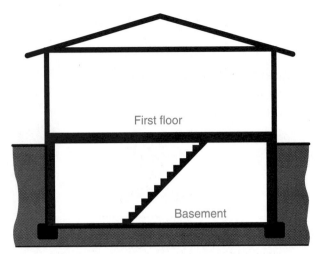

Figure 2-6. Including a full basement in the design adds valuable usable space to a ranch house.

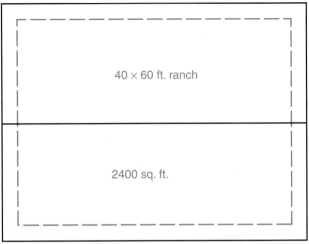

Foundation length = 200 ft.
Roof area = Between 2600 and 2800 sq. ft.

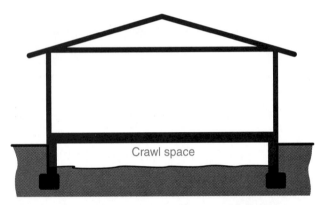

Figure 2-7. A crawl space under a ranch house adds accessibility for service and maintenance.

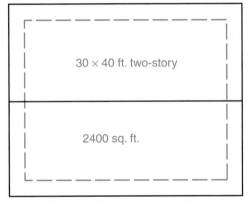

Foundation length = 140 ft.
Roof area = Approximately 1300 sq. ft.

Figure 2-9. A comparison of the foundation length and roof area of a ranch and a two-story house having the same square footage of living area reveals why a ranch is usually more expensive to build.

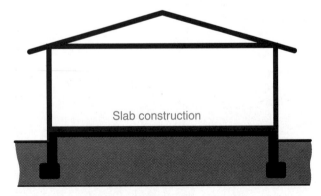

Figure 2-8. A ranch design with a concrete slab floor reduces cost and simplifies construction.

Figure 2-10. This spacious ranch house has extensive roof and wall areas that may produce maintenance problems.

may be required in a large ranch style house to provide access to all rooms, Figure 2-11. Careful planning should be done to keep hall space to a minimum.

One-and-One-Half-Story Designs

The *one-and-one-half-story* style house, sometimes called a Cape Cod, is essentially a one-story ranch with a steeper roof that allows for expansion of the attic, Figure 2-12. Dormers are usually added to provide additional light and ventilation in the attic space, Figure 2-13. A one-and-one-half-story house has two distinct advantages. The cost per unit of habitable living space is low. Also, there is built-in expandability since the attic space can be, and often is, finished.

When the attic space is finished, it generally contains bedrooms and a bath. Since any space with less than five feet of headroom is considered unusable, the total square footage in the attic is about one-half that of the first floor. Notice the unused side portions of the attic in Figure 2-12.

Dormers, stairs, and a slightly steeper roof are the principal sources of the additional costs required to build a one-and-one-half-story house over a one-story house. Additional costs will also be incurred if the design is adapted for disabled-accessible housing.

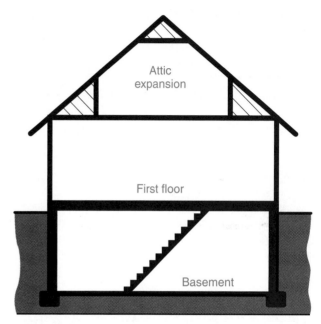

Figure 2-12. A section view of a typical one-and-one-half-story house with a basement.

Figure 2-11. An excessive amount of hall space is required to make this ranch design serviceable. Better planning is desirable.

Figure 2-13. Three dormers on this attractive one-and-one-half-story house provide natural light and ventilation to the finished attic area. (Photo Courtesy of James Hardie® Siding Products)

The one-and-one-half-story design is quite versatile. It can be constructed as a two-bedroom, one-bath house with the upper area left unfinished. This "minimal" house will meet the needs of a single person, married couple without children, or retired couple. As the family grows, the attic can be finished to provide more livable room.

Heating costs are minimized due to the small outside wall area compared to the amount of interior space. Cooling may be accomplished through the use of louvered ventilators at each end of the structure and a generous application of insulation. Adequate ventilation and insulation are necessary since about one-third of the ceiling area is directly under the roof. This area tends to be quite warm in the summer.

Care must be taken when designing the one-and-one-half-story structure to best accommodate the number of persons it can ultimately house. The electrical and plumbing systems should be planned with expansion in mind. Failure to consider expansion at the outset can greatly reduce the efficiency of these systems after expansion or may prevent the expansion all together. Other areas of the house, such as the kitchen, dining, and living rooms, should also be planned for the maximum number of occupants.

Two-Story Designs

Compared to one-story ranch and one-and-one-half-story houses, the *two-story* house is more economical to build, Figure 2-14. A two-story house requires a smaller lot and has a smaller roof and foundation area compared to interior space of most other designs. Figure 2-15 shows a typical example. It may be built with a basement, on a crawl space, or on a slab.

Heating and cooling a two-story house is simple and comparatively economical. Heat from the first floor naturally rises to the second floor. Even though the second floor is usually far from the furnace, it is usually easy to heat. Ventilation is easy and effective when an ample number of windows is included in the design. Cooling is also facilitated due to the fact that the ceiling is not directly under the roof, rather under an attic space.

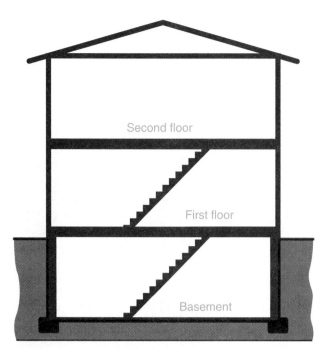

Figure 2-14. A section view of a typical two-story house.

Second floor

First floor

Basement

Figure 2-15. This attractive two-story house will fit comfortably on a narrow lot.

Figure 2-16. Two-story houses like this one were once very common throughout the midwestern states. Modern variations are still popular in some areas. (Shouldice)

In many areas, the two-story design is not as popular today as it was in the past, Figure 2-16. This is probably a result of the turn to more contemporary styles and the readily available inexpensive land in these areas. Two-story houses built in an ornate traditional style may appear to be out of place unless located among other similar styles, Figure 2-17. On the other hand, in some areas of the country, almost all new houses are an updated version of the traditional two-story design, Figure 2-18.

Figure 2-17. This house is an ornate traditional two-story house often found in the southern states.

Figure 2-18. The basic two-story house takes on a contemporary appearance with an overhanging porch roof, dormers, and a small room addition. (Photo Courtesy of James Hardie® Siding Products)

General exterior maintenance is usually more difficult and costly for a two-story house because of the height. For some people, the necessity of climbing stairs from level to level is considered a disadvantage. However, some styles may be adapted to include a stairway lift or elevator to provide greater accessibility. The two-story does not lend itself to variations in style as well as some other designs. However, architects have added a contemporary flair and, as a result, have improved the overall appearance and demand for two-story homes.

Split-Level Designs

The *split-level* was conceived to solve the problems presented by a sloping or hilly lot. It takes advantage of what might otherwise prove to be a troublesome difference in elevation, Figure 2-19. As a general rule, a split-level should not be built on a flat lot. Mounding up soil in front of the high section to give the appearance of a hill usually yields poor results.

Figure 2-19. This contemporary split-level house is well integrated within a steep hill on the site. (Cultured Stone by Stucco Stone Products, Inc.)

A split-level makes efficient use of space. The general arrangement of the split-level separates sleeping, living, and recreation areas on different levels, Figure 2-20. Little or no hall space is required in a split-level house due to its basic design. This is a positive factor to consider when selecting a house design.

Figure 2-20. This split-level house illustrates a standard arrangement of living quarters.

At the lowest level, there may be a basement that houses the heating and cooling equipment, storage, and perhaps a shop or washroom, Figure 2-21. This area is the usual depth of a basement on a ranch house. The basement "footprint" is about 40 to 60 percent of the house "footprint." This is usually enough for efficient use without wasted space.

In some instances, a basement may not be desired. In these cases, a crawl space is provided for maintenance and ventilation.

The next level up from the basement is the *intermediate level.* It generally houses the garage and recreation area, Figure 2-21. This area is ground level and thus lends itself to these functions. Patios and terraces may be

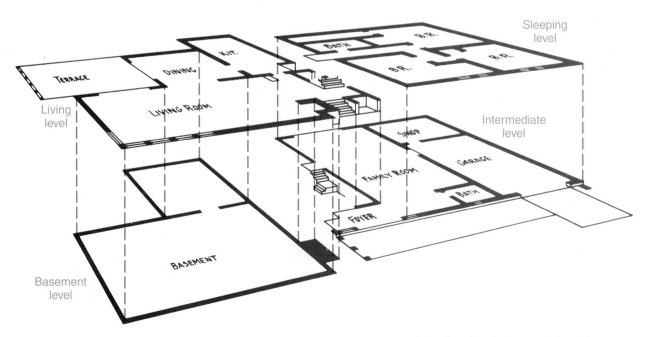

Figure 2-21. This three-dimensional drawing shows the arrangement of the four levels in a split-level house.

attached to the recreation area that further enhances its use. The intermediate level may also have a large foyer, mud room, or family room.

Slightly higher than the intermediate level is the *living level*, Figure 2-21. Generally, this area is located at ground level also; the sloping grade makes this arrangement possible. The kitchen, dining room, living room, and a full or half bathroom are normally located on the living level. The foyer, mud room, and washroom may also be located at this level, depending on the layout or preference.

At the highest elevation in the house is the *sleeping level.* This area contains the bedrooms and one or two bathrooms, Figure 2-21. The half-level difference between the living and sleeping levels affords greater privacy and quietness.

Split-level houses do have some negative aspects. They are generally more expensive to build than a two-story house. In most cases, however, they are cheaper than a ranch. Heating may be a problem if not handled properly. The use of zoned heating will usually solve the heating problem. This method of heating uses separate thermostats for various areas or "zones" of the house. Providing access to the different levels for an older or handicapped person can be a costly and difficult problem associated with a split-level house.

Variations of Split-Level Designs

There are basically three variations of the split-level design. These are the side-by-side, front-to-back, and back-to-front styles. The variation best suited for a given application is determined by the grade or slope of the lot.

Lots sloping from one side to the other side are suited for the side-by-side design. This design places the living area opposite the sleeping and intermediate areas, Figure 2-22.

The front-to-back variation of the split-level is suited for lots that are high in front and low in the back, Figure 2-23. This house looks like a ranch from the front and a two-story from the rear. The living area faces the street

and the bedrooms are on the second level to the rear.

The back-to-front variation of the split-level requires a lot that is low in front and high in back, Figure 2-24. The intermediate level faces the street at grade. The bedrooms are above and also face the street. The living level is at the rear. This model looks like a two-story in front and ranch in the rear.

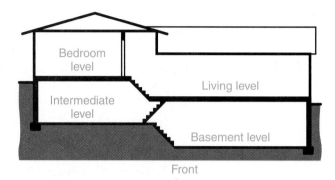

Figure 2-22. This is a front view section of a side-by-side split-level house.

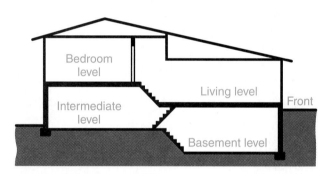

Figure 2-23. This is a side view section of a front-to-back split-level, which adapts to a lot that slopes down to the back.

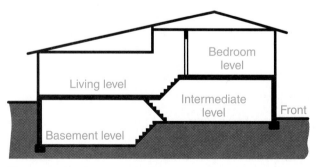

Figure 2-24. This is a side view section of a back-to-front split-level, which adapts to a lot that slopes down to the front.

Figure 2-25 shows another style that is often called a split-level. However, this is nothing more than a ranch with a raised basement, which causes it to be taller than a ranch yet not as tall as a two-story. It has a split entry where the foyer is halfway between levels. This is probably the reason for it being identified as a split-level. This house is perhaps better called a split-entry house.

Traffic Circulation

A primary consideration in designing a functional plan is traffic circulation. *Traffic circulation* is the movement of people from one area or room to another. Circulation must be planned for maximum efficiency of movement. Travel should be short and, if possible, not pass through other rooms. The pattern shown in Figure 2-26 is an example of a well-planned arrangement. The distance from the garage to the kitchen is short and direct. The foyer is centrally located and convenient to all parts of the house. All bedrooms are close to a bath. This design has few rooms with traffic patterns through them. The family room and eating nook are exceptions. An analysis should be made of traffic circulation to determine if the plan is as functional as it could be. Frequently, a slight change in the floor plan can smooth the flow of traffic to desired locations.

Figure 2-25. This simple design has a split entry to take advantage of a raised basement to add height and better lighting. (Alside)

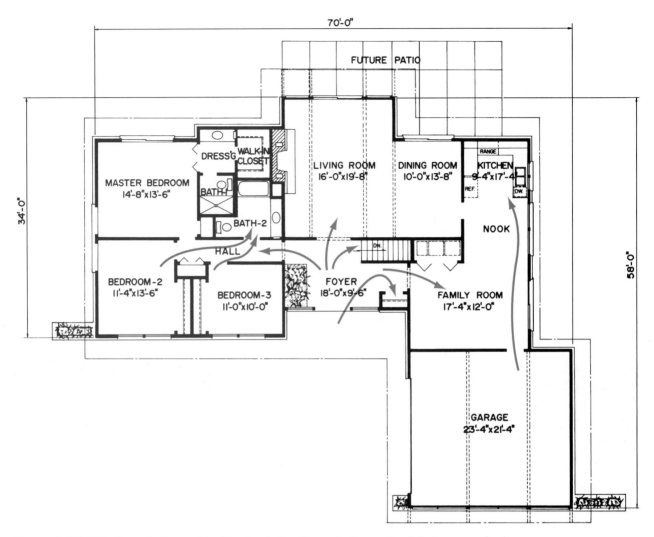

Figure 2-26. This is well-planned traffic circulation through the major living areas of a home.

Internet Resources

www.boralbricks.com
Boral Bricks

www.buildsoft.com
Buildsoft Construction Scheduling and Estimating Software

www.designgroupstudio.com
Eric Brown Design Group, designers of The Palladian Design Collection

www.gp.com/build/index.html
Georgia Pacific Corporation, supplier of building products

www.masonite.com
Masonite International Corporation, a door manufacturer

www.meltonclassics.com
Melton Classics, Inc., a producer of millwork

www.owenscorning.com
Owens Corning

www.reynoldsbp.com
Reynolds Building Products

www.softplan.com
SoftPlan Architectural Design Software

www.studerdesigns.com
Studer Residential Designs

Review Questions — Chapter 2

Write your answers on a separate sheet of paper. Do not write in this book.

1. List the four basic residential home designs.

2. Identify five advantages of the ranch-style house.

3. List five disadvantages of the ranch-style house.

4. A one-and-one-half-story house can be recognized by its _____ _____, which often has _____ to allow light into the attic.

5. The one-and-one-half-story house has two distinct advantages— _____ and _____.

6. One of the most economical houses to build is a _____ design.

7. List three negative aspects of the two-story house.

8. The _____ design was developed to solve the problem of a sloping or hilly lot.

9. Name the four levels of the split-level design.

10. List three variations of the split-level.

11. Why are dormers usually added to the one-and-one-half-story house?

12. In a split-level house, the basement "footprint" usually equals what percentage of the house "footprint?"
    a) 10 to 20 percent.
    b) 20 to 40 percent.
    c) 40 to 60 percent.
    d) 60 to 80 percent.

13. Which house design variation looks like a two-story from the front and a ranch from the rear?

14. Traffic circulation must be planned for maximum efficiency of _____.

Suggested Activities

1. Look through magazines and find a photo of each of the basic house designs (one-story, one-and-one-half-story, two-story, and split-level). Make color copies of the photos and mount the copies on illustration board for display.

2. Identify houses in or near your community that are examples of the basic house designs. Make a sketch of the house. Write descriptions of the materials used, colors, and location of each house.

3. Obtain a floor plan of a house from a magazine, newspaper, or other source. Determine the basic design and compile the following information about the house.
    a) How many square feet of living space is in the house?
    b) List the rooms identified in the house.
    c) How many sets of stairs are there in the house?
    d) Does the house have a basement, crawl space, or slab?

4. Visit a contractor or architectural firm and ask for prints of basic house designs. Bring these to class and discuss the advantages and disadvantages of each in respect to the families of different members of the class.

5. Invite an architect to your class to discuss how basic house designs are selected for various areas of your community.

6. Prepare a simple sketch of your own home showing the various levels for living and the contour of the property. Indicate what basic design your house resembles. If you live in a duplex, indicate which wall is shared and attempt to sketch the floor plan of the adjoining residence. If you live in an apartment or townhouse, sketch the home of a neighbor or friend.

7. Using your local newspaper for reference, read through the "houses for sale" section and make a list of the styles advertised. See if there seems to be a trend toward a particular basic design.

8. Using a computer-aided drafting and design (CADD) system, draw the floor plan shown in Figure 2-26 using single lines. Draw simplified doors and windows, as described by your instructor.

9. Using a computer-aided drafting and design (CADD) system, draw a top view of the floor plan pictorial shown in Figure 2-21 using single lines. If your CADD system supports layers, place each level on a different layer. Draw simplified doors and windows, as described by your instructor.

Primary Considerations

Objectives

After studying this chapter, you will be able to:

➤ Discuss key site considerations, restrictions, zoning, and codes.

➤ Evaluate a site with respect to important considerations.

➤ Record topographical features of a site.

➤ List family needs that should be considered when planning or purchasing a dwelling.

➤ Develop a budget for purchasing or constructing a house.

➤ Describe the basic construction drawings used to build a structure.

Key Terms

Building Codes
Construction Details
Deed
Electrical Plan
Elevations
Equity
Expansion Plan
Floor Framing Plan
Floor Plan
Foundation Plan
Furniture Plan
Gross Annual
  Income
Heating and Cooling
  Plan

Landscaping Plan
Modules
Pictorial
  Presentation
Plot Plan
Plumbing Plan
Roof Framing Plan
Roof Plan
Site
Specifications
Take-Home Pay
Title
Topography
Zoning

Most people have a "dream home" in the back of their mind that they hope to build some day. However, few people think beyond the house itself and look at the site location and characteristics, community attributes, zoning restrictions, family lifestyle, and quality of living. These considerations, in many instances, are just as important as the size and room arrangement of the house.

Site Considerations

The *site* is more than just a plot of land—it is part of a larger community, Figure 3-1. It is located in a certain school district and is a

Figure 3-1. A homesite is always a part of a larger community—subdivision; village, borough, or city; and state. This map shows major roads, apartments, schools, parks, and minor streets within a school district. (Midwestern Consulting, Inc.)

certain distance from shopping areas. An airport or major traffic artery may be nearby. The community in which the site is located may be growing or stagnant. In addition, the topography is important. *Topography* is the characteristics of the land on the site. The topography may be rolling or flat, high and dry or low and wet, big or small, wooded or treeless. It is located in a warm or cold climate. The site, next to the house itself, is probably the most expensive item. It must be evaluated carefully to realize its potential as a vital part of the home and its setting.

The characteristics of a site frequently indicate the basic type of house that would be best suited for that site. For example, flat topography lends itself to a ranch or two-story house. A hilly or sloping site is ideal for a split-level home. A site that has many trees may be ideal for a house with large windows and generous use of natural materials. Every effort should be made to take full advantage of site characteristics in planning the home. The structure should appear to be part of the site. It should blend in with the surroundings rather than stand apart from them.

The Community

The community and neighborhood should be evaluated on the following points. These and many other factors relate to the site selection and eventually to the happiness of the owner.

- Is the neighborhood a well-planned community, as shown in Figure 3-2? Or, has the neighborhood developed with no central theme or forethought, as shown in Figure 3-3?
- Are the existing homes in the community in the price range of the house you are considering buying or building?
- Are the neighbors in about the same social and economic categories as you?
- Is the community alive and growing or is it rundown and dying?
- Does the community have room for growth or is it restricted?
- Are the residents of the community people who take pride in their homes and keep them well maintained? Or, are there homes in disrepair?

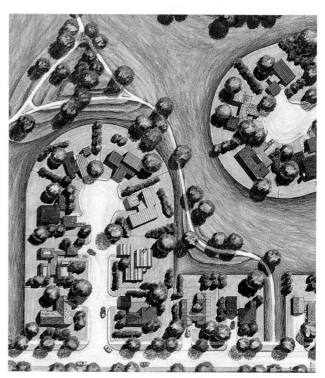

Figure 3-2. A well-planned community neighborhood takes advantage of the natural site characteristics. (Midwestern Consulting, Inc.)

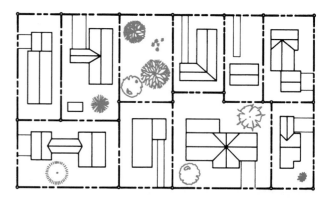

Figure 3-3. This block of homes shows little planning and has no central theme. Notice the different lot sizes and shapes and the different styles of homes.

- Does the community have modern churches, quality schools, and shopping areas?
- Are such facilities as fire protection, water, sewer, natural gas, and garbage collection available in this community?
- Is the site near where you work?
- Is public transportation available and close by?
- Is there a high rate of turnover in the neighborhood due to the resale of homes?

Cost and Restrictions

It is not possible to state exactly what percentage of the total cost of a home should be allowed for the site. This depends on many considerations. The site price, however, should be examined carefully to determine if it takes into consideration needed improvements, such as grading, fill, tree removal, and drainage. The cost of the lot should also take into account the amount of frontage it has and whether or not it is a corner lot. Any future assessments for road, sewer, or other improvements are usually proportional to length of frontage. Therefore, corner lots will have higher assessments.

Ownership of the property is transferred through a legal document called a ***deed,*** Figure 3-4. A ***title*** provides evidence of ownership and is where any liens, easements, or restrictions on the property are listed. A title

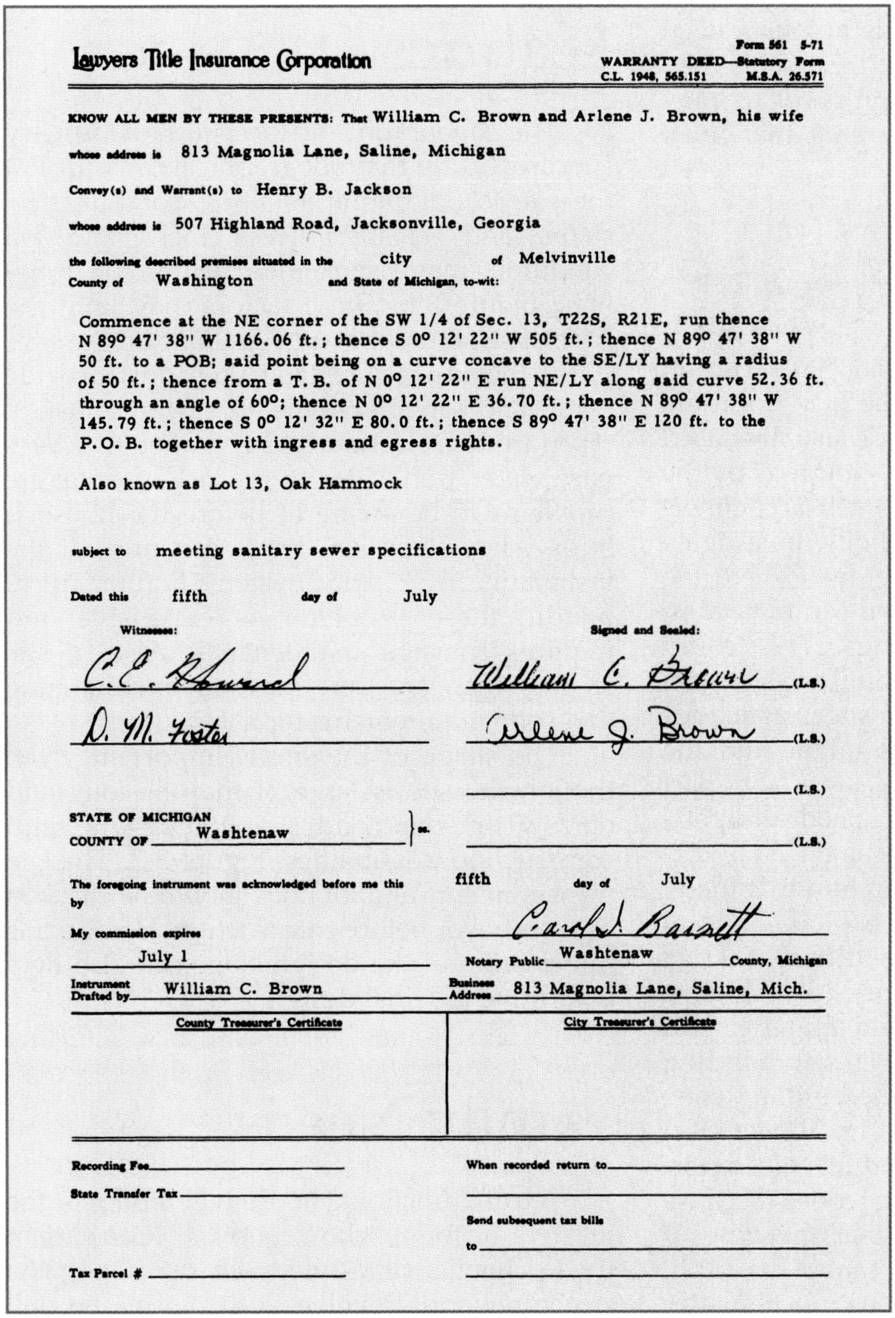

Lawyers Title Insurance Corporation

Form 561 5-71
WARRANTY DEED—Statutory Form
C.L. 1948, 565.151 M.S.A. 26.571

KNOW ALL MEN BY THESE PRESENTS: That William C. Brown and Arlene J. Brown, his wife

whose address is 813 Magnolia Lane, Saline, Michigan

Convey(s) and Warrant(s) to Henry B. Jackson

whose address is 507 Highland Road, Jacksonville, Georgia

the following described premises situated in the city of Melvinville
County of Washington and State of Michigan, to-wit:

Commence at the NE corner of the SW 1/4 of Sec. 13, T22S, R21E, run thence N 89° 47' 38" W 1166.06 ft.; thence S 0° 12' 22" W 505 ft.; thence N 89° 47' 38" W 50 ft. to a POB; said point being on a curve concave to the SE/LY having a radius of 50 ft.; thence from a T. B. of N 0° 12' 22" E run NE/LY along said curve 52.36 ft. through an angle of 60°; thence N 0° 12' 22" E 36.70 ft.; thence N 89° 47' 38" W 145.79 ft.; thence S 0° 12' 32" E 80.0 ft.; thence S 89° 47' 38" E 120 ft. to the P.O.B. together with ingress and egress rights.

Also known as Lot 13, Oak Hammock

subject to meeting sanitary sewer specifications

Dated this fifth day of July

Witnesses: Signed and Sealed:

C. E. Howard William C. Brown (L.S.)

D. M. Foster Arlene J. Brown (L.S.)

(L.S.)

STATE OF MICHIGAN
COUNTY OF Washtenaw } ss. (L.S.)

The foregoing instrument was acknowledged before me this fifth day of July
by

My commission expires Carl J. Barrett
July 1 Notary Public Washtenaw County, Michigan

Instrument Drafted by William C. Brown Business Address 813 Magnolia Lane, Saline, Mich.

County Treasurer's Certificate | City Treasurer's Certificate

Recording Fee ______ When recorded return to ______

State Transfer Tax ______

Send subsequent tax bills to ______

Tax Parcel # ______

Figure 3-4. A typical property deed containing a legal description of the site.

search is required by law in many areas before a deed can be transferred to a new owner to determine if there are any legal claims against the property. Even if not required by law, a title search should be conducted for your own protection. Until a property is paid for, a bank or mortgage lender will have a legal claim to the property. The deed and title are very important documents and should be examined carefully by a competent attorney before the property is purchased.

Restrictions on the property may specify the style of house that may be built on the lot, size of the house, type of landscaping, or even the overall cost of the house. Easements may allow utilities to cross the property or may prevent the filling of a low area that must remain for drainage purposes.

Zoning and Codes

Zoning creates areas that have certain building requirements for the size, location, and type of structure. Zoning is usually based on local building codes and "grouped" by the type of business or residence, such as commercial, single family, or multifamily. Investigate the zoning ordinances in the area where the site is located. It may be zoned commercial or for multiple-family dwellings. This could prohibit building a single-family residential structure. Even if the selected site is zoned for single-family structures, you might find the large open area nearby that plays a large part in the selection of the site is zoned for apartment buildings. Check the zoning!

Another area for consideration that many prospective buyers fail to explore is local building codes. Codes are different from zoning. *Building codes* specify requirements for construction methods and materials for plumbing, electrical, and general building construction. For example, the building code in a particular area may require all electrical wiring to be in grounded conduit. It is important to understand building codes because they may be so restrictive that the type of house planned for the site cannot be built. Also, construction costs may be much greater than for a different location because of code

requirements. On the other hand, the codes may be so lax that the quality of homes in the area is poor.

Generally, all construction and remodeling requires a building permit from the town, city, or village. Talk with a local building inspector to determine the cost of permits, required inspections, and other building regulations. Figure 3-5 illustrates a typical building permit form.

Topographical Features

The topography of the site is a primary concern. Study the topographical drawings of the site to determine its slope, contour, size, shape, and elevation. Trees, rocks, and soil conditions may also be indicated on the drawings, Figure 3-6. These factors may limit the type of structure that may be built on the site.

If the site is rural and you must provide water and septic systems, extra care must be taken in the selection of the proper site. Very hard water, iron water, or the lack of water are problems to be aware of before the house is built. Also, some soil types can prevent the installation of a septic system. Equipment to handle these problems is expensive and requires constant maintenance. Also, a site smaller than one acre may not meet zoning and code requirements for a rural site.

The shape of the site is important. Even though the site is large, it may be long and narrow or some odd shape that will limit construction possibilities, Figure 3-7. The site measurements and lot lines should be checked by a surveyor before construction. Having this information at the design stage can also help determine the final design.

Family Needs

A truly functional house will represent the lifestyle of those who occupy it. Rather than try to change a lifestyle to fit the house, the structure should evolve to fit those who will use it.

VIGO COUNTY
BUILDING PERMIT APPLICATION
VIGO COUNTY BUILDING INSPECTION DEPARTMENT
201 CHERRY STREET, TERRE HAUTE, INDIANA 47807

Applicant to complete numbered spaces only. This form must be signed by owner and/or contractor.

1 JOB ADDRESS				
LOT NO.	BLK	TRACT		
2 OWNER	MAIL ADDRESS	ZIP	PHONE	
3 CONTRACTOR	MAIL ADDRESS	PHONE		
4 ARCHITECT OR DESIGNER	MAIL ADDRESS	PHONE		
5 ENGINEER	MAIL ADDRESS	PHONE		
6 LENDER	MAIL ADDRESS	BRANCH		
7 USE OF BUILDING	PRESENT	PROPOSED		
8 Class of work: NEW	ADDITION	REMODEL	REPAIR	MOVE · REMOVE (WRECKING)
9 Describe work:				
10 Valuation of work: $				

PLEASE DO NOT WRITE IN SHADED AREAS

SPECIAL CONDITIONS:	Required	Received
RE-ZONING		
BOARD OF ZONING APPEALS		
HEALTH DEPT.		
FIRE DEPT.		
APPLICATION ACCEPTED BY	PLANS CHECKED BY	APPROVED FOR ISSUANCE BY

PLUMBING
NEW OR ALTERED SEWER LINES NECESSARY YES ☐ NO ☐
PLUMBING NECESSARY: ☐ YES ☐ NO | PLUMBING PERMIT FEE:
Number of fixtures to be installed ______
Sewers must be approved by Board of Health.

ELECTRICAL
NEW SERVICE: Required ☐ YES ☐ NO
Number of circuits to be installed ______
NEW SERVICE: Amperage ______
Electrical Permit Fee: $

NOTICE
THIS PERMIT BECOMES NULL AND VOID IF WORK OR CONSTRUCTION AUTHORIZED IS NOT COMMENCED WITHIN 120 DAYS, OR IF CONSTRUCTION OR WORK IS SUSPENDED OR ABANDONED FOR A PERIOD OF 120 DAYS AT ANY TIME AFTER WORK IS COMMENCED.

I HEREBY CERTIFY THAT I HAVE READ AND EXAMINED THIS APPLICATION AND KNOW THE SAME TO BE TRUE AND CORRECT. ALL PROVISIONS OF LAWS AND ORDINANCES GOVERNING THIS TYPE OF WORK WILL BE COMPLIED WITH WHETHER SPECIFIED HEREIN OR NOT. THE GRANTING OF A PERMIT DOES NOT PRESUME TO GIVE AUTHORITY TO VIOLATE OR CANCEL THE PROVISIONS OF ANY OTHER STATE OR LOCAL LAW REGULATING CONSTRUCTION OR THE PERFORMANCE OF CONSTRUCTION.

11 ______
SIGNATURE OF CONTRACTOR OR AUTHORIZED AGENT (DATE)

12 ______
SIGNATURE OF OWNER (IF OWNER BUILDER) (DATE)

ENGINEERS DEPT.

DRAINAGE			
SET BACK LINES			
ENTRANCE & EXITS			
PARKING SURFACE			
OFF STREET PARKING	SPACES AVAIL.	SPACES NEEDED	

AREA PLANNING
ZONED
OTHER:

Figure 3-5. A building permit must be obtained before construction may begin.

Family size is a major consideration in a house design. Future family growth should also be considered. Ample space should be provided for each member of the family to perform their chosen activities. Consideration should be given to providing space for:

- Accommodating Guests
- Bathing
- Dining
- Dressing
- Entertaining
- Family Recreation
- Hobbies
- Housekeeping
- Laundering
- Planning
- Preparing Food
- Relaxing
- Sleeping
- Storage
- Studying
- Working

These activities should not be thought of necessarily in relation to specific rooms. Some activities are performed throughout the house while others are restricted to certain areas. The

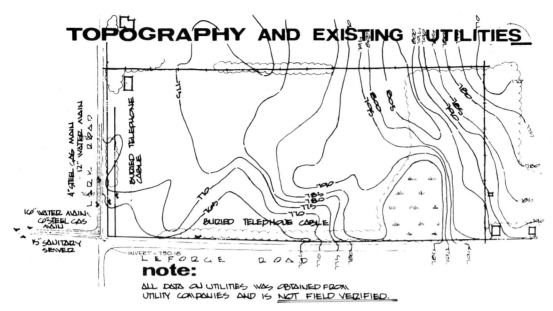

Figure 3-6. This site plan shows topographical features such as contour, elevations, trees, and property lines. (Midwestern Consulting, Inc.)

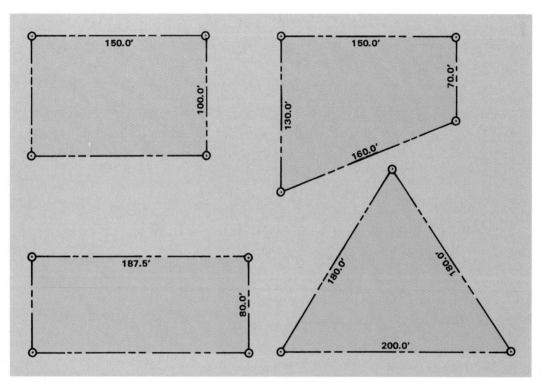

Figure 3-7. The shape of the site is important in determining the size and style of the house to be designed. Each of these sites has 15,000 sq. ft. of area, yet the triangular site appears the largest.

important point is to provide for activities in which the family will be engaged. Let the structure take the shape and arrangement that best serves these needs.

Budgeting for Housing

Whether building or buying a home, it is the most expensive item an individual or family will buy. When choosing a house to build or buy, you need to determine how much you can spend on housing. The amount you can afford will depend on several factors—income, other expenses and obligations, housing needs, and expected future income.

Since housing is generally a monthly expense, you might begin by calculating how much you can afford to spend on housing over a long period of time. Most financial advisors recommend that monthly housing costs amount to no more than one-third of your monthly take-home pay. *Take-home pay* is your earnings after taxes and other deductions have been subtracted. In other words, it is the amount of the check or direct deposit.

Housing cost is not limited to the monthly mortgage or rent payment alone. It also includes utility costs, property taxes for an owned residence, and insurance. To arrive at a rough estimate of the amount you can afford for housing, add all monthly nonhousing expenses. These include food, clothing, transportation, recreation, loans, insurance, taxes, and so on. Be sure to include scheduled savings and retirement planning expenses. Next, find the amount you have to spend each month. Be sure to include all income and earnings. Finally, subtract the monthly nonhousing expenses from the total monthly income. This is the maximum amount you can afford to spend for housing each month. You will probably want to keep your housing costs under the maximum that you can afford.

A rule-of-thumb for determining how much you can spend on the purchase of a home is a sale price that is no more than 2-1/2 times your gross annual income. *Gross annual income* is the amount of money you earn before taxes and other deductions. For example, if your gross annual income is $25,000 or about $12.25 per hour, you should be able to afford a $62,500 home.

Mortgage lenders may have more specific rules. In general, most lenders will not provide a mortgage that requires payments of higher than 28% of your gross monthly income. The actual amount of the mortgage payment is determined by the sale price of the house, the amount of money paid as a down payment, and the current interest rate. Most mortgage lenders require between 3% and 5% of the sale price as a down payment. In addition, until the owner has 20% equity in the home, most mortgage lenders require private mortgage insurance (PMI). *Equity* is the amount the house is worth minus the amount owed. The remainder is the amount of "cash" a homeowner will get from the sale of the house. PMI is insurance against the owner defaulting on the mortgage so the lender will not lose money.

Other Considerations

A house should not be planned entirely from an "inside-out" approach. Consideration should be given to the exterior design, size, and materials, Figure 3-8. The modular aspect of many materials should be considered to keep costs down. The ability to resell the house and the quality of living the home presents should also be considered. These factors add a unity to the structure and enhance its overall appearance.

Modular Aspects

When designing a house, it is important to understand standard sizes of construction materials. A house is a combination of many parts and these must fit together to form the whole. These parts are basic construction materials that are produced in standard sizes. Construction materials are available in different size increments or *modules*.

Home designers should know what standard sizes are available and plan structures

Figure 3-8. Design is important. Notice how the lines and use of materials complement each other in this unique house. (The Atrium Door and Window Corporation)

around these "modules" to reduce constructing costs. Costs are kept down by wasting less material and reducing the required custom work. For example, it would probably cost no more to build a house with overall dimensions of 40' × 60' than a house of 39' × 59'. The 40' × 60' house has considerable extra floor space. Yet, the same standard size construction materials are used for it as the 39' × 59' house. In fact, the cost may even be lower since there will be less custom work involved.

The following list is a quick survey of some representative construction material sizes. These should provide some guidelines for the designer.

- Plywood – 4' × 8'
- Paneling – 4' × 8'
- Construction Lumber – lengths of 8', 10', 12', 14', 16'
- Concrete Blocks – modules of 4"

Typical guidelines:
1. Exterior walls should be modular lengths in multiples of 4', or at least multiples of 2'.
2. Plan for the use of materials with as little waste as possible.
3. Plan rooms with an eye on standard sizes. For example, carpet is produced in 12' and 15' widths.

4. Walls should be modular heights in multiples of 2'.

Quality of Living

The location of the site, the characteristics of the site itself, the size and layout of the house, and many other factors all add up to a certain quality of living, Figure 3-9. It is the designer's job to take advantage of as many aspects as possible to increase the quality of living in the structures being designed. The quality of living provided by the structure is a measure of the success of the designer in solving a problem.

Drawings Included in a Set of Plans

A set of plans or drawings is the collection of all drawings and related specifications needed to construct a house. Most sets of plans for residential construction include:

- Plot Plan
- Foundation Plan
- Floor Plan

- Elevations
- Electrical Plan
- Construction Details
- Pictorial Presentations

Brief Plan Descriptions

The *plot plan* shows the location of the house on the site, Figure 3-10. It usually shows utilities, topographical features, site dimensions, and any other buildings on the property.

A *foundation plan* illustrates the foundation size and material, Figure 3-11. The foundation plan gives information pertaining to excavation, waterproofing, and supporting structures. It may also include the basement plan if the house has a basement.

The *floor plan* shows all exterior and interior walls, doors, windows, patios, walks, decks, fireplaces, mechanical equipment, built-in cabinets, and appliances, Figure 3-12. A separate plan view is drawn for each floor of the house.

Elevations are drawn for each side of the structure, Figure 3-13. These plans are typically

Figure 3-9. Imagine the site and design considerations necessary to construct this home designed by Frank Lloyd Wright. The natural surroundings add to the quality of life in the home.
(Western Pennsylvania Conservancy)

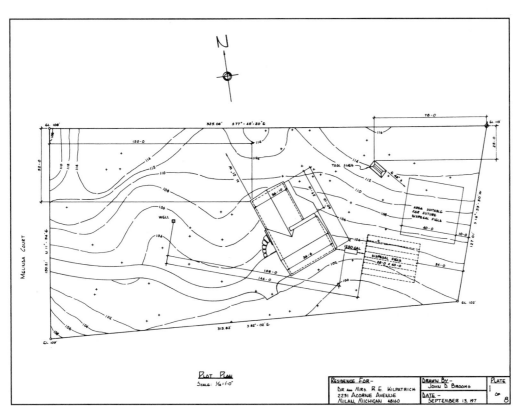

Figure 3-10. A typical residential plot plan.

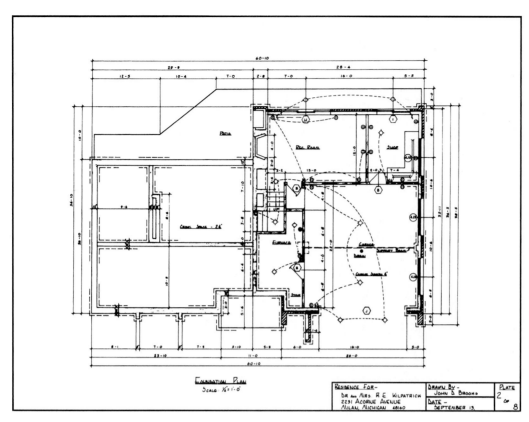

Figure 3-11. A basement/foundation plan for a residence. Notice how there are also some electrical components shown on this plan.

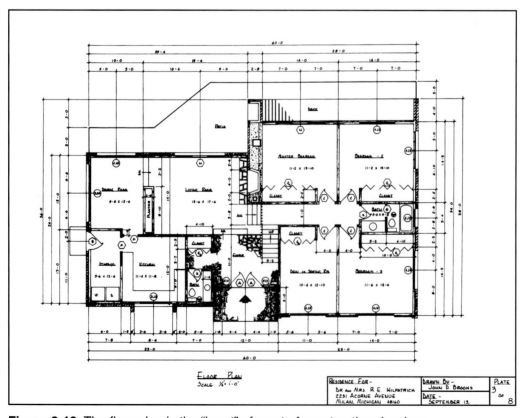

Figure 3-12. The floor plan is the "heart" of a set of construction drawings.

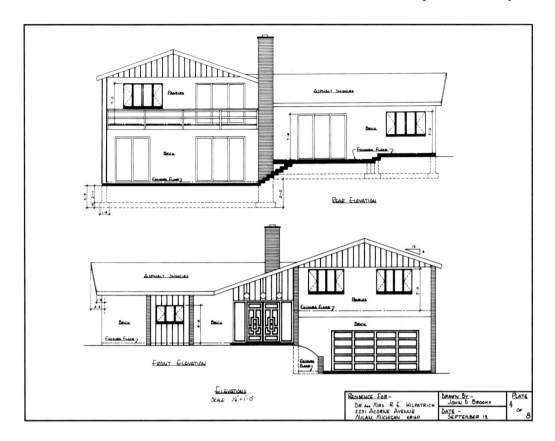

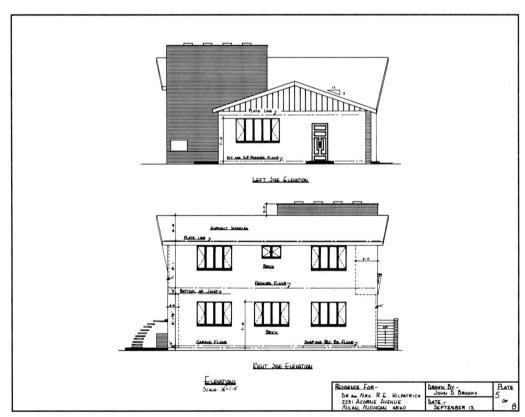

Figure 3-13. A front elevation shows the most impressive side of the structure. Elevations are also drawn of the sides and back of the house.

orthographic projections showing the exterior features of the building. They show placement of windows and doors, type of exterior materials used, steps, chimney, rooflines, and other exterior details.

The *electrical plan* is drawn from the floor plan, Figure 3-14. It locates switches, convenience outlets, ceiling outlet fixtures, television jacks, service entrance location, and the panel box. It also provides general information concerning circuits and special installations.

Construction details are usually drawn where more information is needed to fully describe how the construction is to be done. Typical drawings include details of kitchens, stairs, chimneys, fireplaces, windows and doors, and foundation walls, Figure 3-15. Construction details will also show items that require special construction, Figure 3-16.

A *pictorial presentation* is often included to show how the finished structure will appear, Figure 3-17. The pictorial method commonly drawn manually is the two-point perspective. Computer-generated pictorials are also created by some companies. Sometimes a physical model is used instead of, or in addition to, the pictorial to show the total structure.

A set of construction drawings is not complete without specification sheets. *Specifications* describe the quality of work and materials. They provide additional details that are not shown on the drawings. The drawings and the specifications form the basis of a legal contract between the owner and the builder.

Other Plans

There are other drawings that may be included in a set of residential construction drawings. These include a roof plan, roof framing plan, floor framing plan, heating and cooling plan, plumbing plan, landscaping plan, furniture plan, and expansion plan.

A *roof plan* should be included if the roof is complicated and not clearly shown by the other standard drawings. The roof plan may be incorporated into the plot plan. A *roof framing plan* should be included when the roof is complex and requires unique construction.

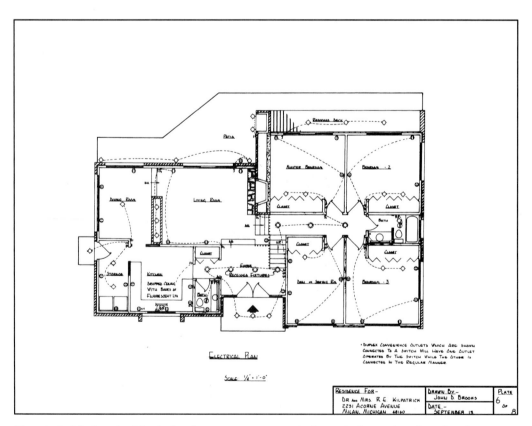

Figure 3-14. An electrical plan is a necessary part of a set of construction drawings.

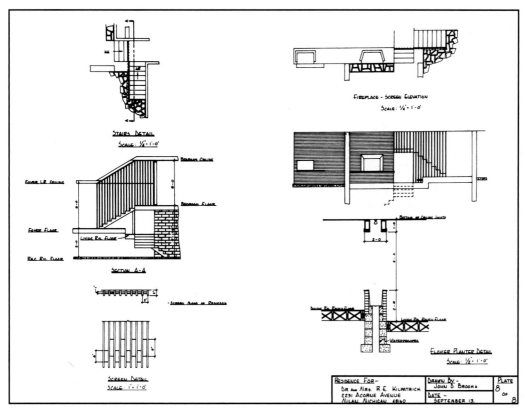

Figure 3-15. Construction details provide the contractor with exact specifications.

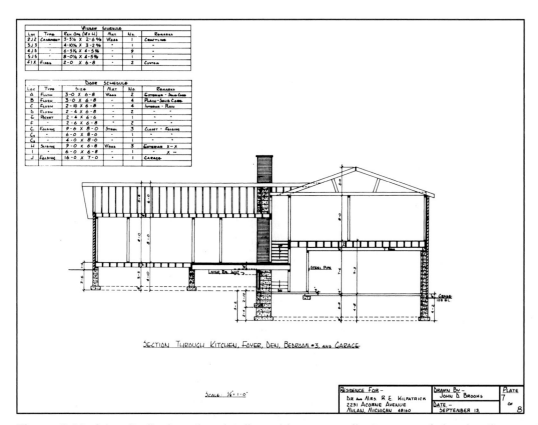

Figure 3-16. A longitudinal section detail provides an excellent means of showing the construction details for various levels in this house.

Figure 3-17. This expertly hand-rendered perspective shows the finished structure realistically and serves as an important communication device. (Sater Design Collection, Inc.)

A roof framing plan may be drawn to clarify construction aspects associated with the roof. The roof framing plan normally shows the rafters, ceiling joists, and supporting members.

A *floor framing plan* shows direction of joists and major supporting members. It does not show the layout of rooms and locations of walls. The floor plan shows these items.

The *heating and cooling plan* illustrates components of the climate control system of the house. These components include the furnace, air conditioner, heating and cooling ducts, and hot-water-heat pipes. The design of each system is usually performed by the contractor who installs the system.

A *plumbing plan* shows the location of pipes and plumbing fixtures. These features include the hot and cold water pipes, waste lines, vents, and the storage tank when needed. Also included is the location of plumbing fixtures and cleanouts.

The *landscaping plan* locates and identifies plants and other elements included in landscaping the site. This plan is sometimes combined with the plot plan.

A *furniture plan* identifies the furniture to be used and its placement in each area of the house. This plan can help determine the sizes of rooms. Even if a furniture plan is not included, care should be taken in the design process to allow ample space within rooms for standard size furniture.

An *expansion plan* shows how the structure has been designed to accommodate future expansion. While this information is often on a separate plan, it may be incorporated into one of the typical construction drawings.

Internet Resources

www.aia.org
   American Institute of Architects

www.archdigest.com
   Architectural Digest

www.bhg.com
   Better Homes and Gardens Magazine

www.builderonline.com
   Builder Magazine Online

www.certainteed.com
   CertainTeed Corporation

www.epa.gov
   US Environmental Protection Agency

www.homesalespro.com
   Media Lab, a web-based multimedia marketer for builders

www.iii.org
   Insurance Information Institute

Review Questions — Chapter 3

Write your answers on a separate sheet of paper. Do not write in this book.

1. List 12 factors, with respect to the design and location of a house, that should be considered when planning a residential structure.

2. The document that lists any legal claims against the property is called a _____.

3. The _____ is a legal document that transfers ownership of property.

4. List eight site features that may be found on a topographical drawing of the site.

5. If a home is to have its own septic system and water supply, the lot should be at least _____ in size. However, local codes may require a larger site or allow a smaller site.

6. What determines whether or not a house is functional?

7. List ten individual and family activities that space should be provided for in a house.

8. Why should one plan a house using standard (modular) sizes?

9. Exterior walls should be lengths divisible by _____ feet.

10. List the drawings which are ordinarily included in a set of residential house plans.

11. Why should a title search be made before purchasing a lot?

12. List four things that determine how much you can afford for housing.

13. Ownership of property is assigned through a legal document called a _____.

14. What is the difference between take-home pay and gross annual income?

15. A rule-of-thumb for determining how much you can spend on the purchase of a home is a sale price that is no greater than _____ times your gross annual income.

Suggested Activities

1. Obtain a map of your city or community and identify the approximate location of your house, condo, or apartment building on the map.

2. Determine the following characteristics for your house, condo, or apartment.

   a) How many square feet of living area does it have? Do not include the garage if you have one.

   b) What are the dimensions of the lot on which your house, condo, or apartment building sits?

   c) How far is it to the closest grocery store?

   d) How far is it to the school that you attend?

   e) Does your house have its own well and septic system?

   f) How many homes are under construction and for sale within a 1/2 mile radius of your house, condo, or apartment building?

3. Visit your local building inspector and ask to be shown copies of the codes that are used in your community. Ask how the cost of permits is calculated and what is required by the building department when applying for a permit.

4. Look around your neighborhood for a vacant lot or piece of property. Make a list of considerations that should be addressed if a house is to be constructed on this property. Include as many factors as necessary from this chapter that would apply to the property. Make a CADD drawing of the site.

5. Make a listing of the activity areas (spaces) that should be provided when planning a new home for your family's needs. Be sure to include all the needs of each member of your family and special group activity areas. Make a CADD drawing that shows the family activity areas.

6. Prepare a display for the bulletin board that illustrates the advantages of proper site consideration when planning a house. Use clippings from magazines and other publications to show how the architect made good use of all aspects of the property to enhance the beauty of the house.

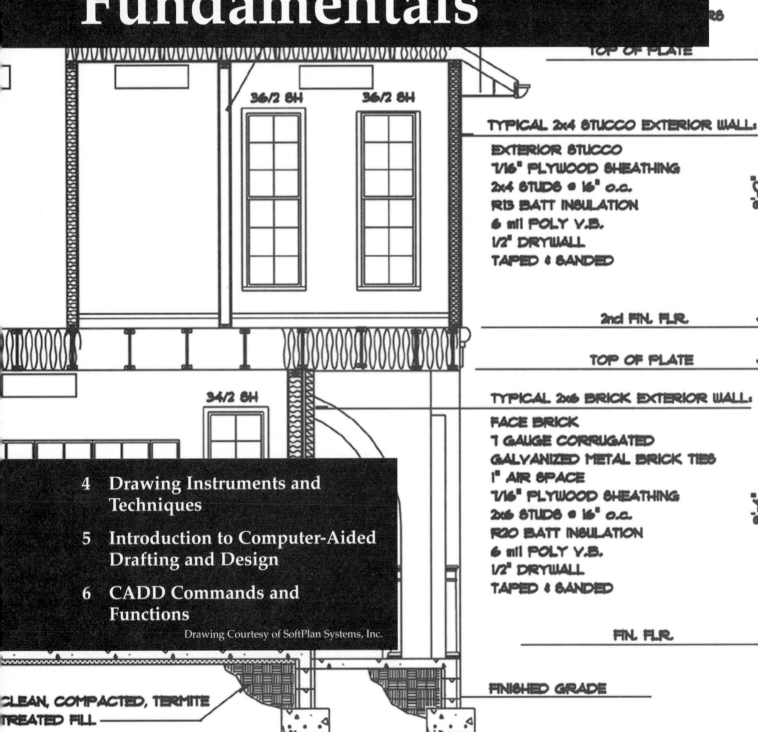

Section II
Architectural Drafting Fundamentals

TOP OF PLATE

36/2 SH   36/2 SH

TYPICAL 2x4 STUCCO EXTERIOR WALL:

EXTERIOR STUCCO
7/16" PLYWOOD SHEATHING
2x4 STUDS @ 16" O.C.
R13 BATT INSULATION
6 mil POLY V.B.
1/2" DRYWALL
TAPED & SANDED

2nd FIN. FLR.

TOP OF PLATE

34/2 SH

TYPICAL 2x6 BRICK EXTERIOR WALL:

FACE BRICK
7 GAUGE CORRUGATED
GALVANIZED METAL BRICK TIES
1" AIR SPACE
7/16" PLYWOOD SHEATHING
2x6 STUDS @ 16" O.C.
R20 BATT INSULATION
6 mil POLY V.B.
1/2" DRYWALL
TAPED & SANDED

FIN. FLR.

FINISHED GRADE

CLEAN, COMPACTED, TERMITE
TREATED FILL

20" WIDE x 8" DEEP
CONCRETE FOOTING c/w
3 - RUNS 15M REBAR

4   Drawing Instruments and Techniques

5   Introduction to Computer-Aided Drafting and Design

6   CADD Commands and Functions

Drawing Courtesy of SoftPlan Systems, Inc.

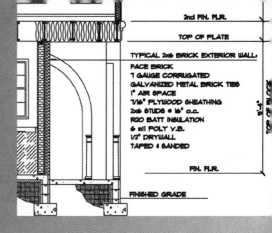

Drawing Instruments and Techniques

Objectives

After studying this chapter, you will be able to:

- Define the three principal views in orthographic projection.
- List and explain the use of architectural drafting equipment.
- Explain the difference between size and scale.
- Reproduce the standard alphabet of lines.
- Demonstrate an acceptable architectural lettering style.
- Freehand sketch.
- Identify the basic components of a CADD workstation.

Key Terms

Alphabet of Lines
Border Lines
Centerlines
Construction Lines
Crosshatch Lines
Cutting-Plane Lines
Dimension Lines
Extension Lines
Floor Plan
Freehand Sketching
Front Elevation
Grids
Guidelines
Hidden Lines

Left Side Elevation
Long Break Line
Object Lines
Orthographic
   Projection
Plan View
Proportion
Rear Elevation
Right Side Elevation
Section Lines
Short Break Lines
Symbols Library
Templates

An understanding of basic drafting practices and the use of equipment is a necessary introduction to architectural drawing and style. Most of the equipment and many of the principles are similar to those used in mechanical or technical drawing. A review of the basic drawing concepts will establish a foundation on which the techniques for architectural drawing can be developed.

Orthographic Projection

Orthographic projection is a fundamental drafting technique. It makes little difference whether you are drawing metal fasteners, electric motors, or houses, the principles remain the same. *Orthographic projection* is a means of representing the height, width, and depth of a three-dimensional object on two-dimensional paper. The point from which the object is viewed is infinity. For this reason, the projection lines are parallel to each other and no thickness can be seen in any of the orthographic views. Typically, three orthographic views are used in a multiview drawing to fully describe an object. However, additional views, such as an auxiliary view, may be required.

Three Principal Views

The three principal orthographic views in mechanical drafting are the top, front, and right side views. In architectural drafting, the views are basically the same with minor exceptions. The names are also slightly different.

The top view of a house is called the *plan view*. The plan view is used as the basis for most of the other views in a set of drawings for a house. There may be a roof plan, floor plan, foundation plan, and so on, developed from the basic plan view. The plan view of the floor plan is the most important view in architectural drafting. The *floor plan* is a section view taken about halfway up the wall. Figure 4-1 shows a small cottage drawn in orthographic projection using the normal arrangement. The cutting plane line in the front view shows how the plan view is derived for use in architectural drawings.

The front view of an object in mechanical drawing is the same as the *front elevation* in architectural drawing. Note that the word "view" is changed to "elevation." Architectural drafters ordinarily draw an elevation of all sides of the structure rather than just the front and right side, as is the practice in mechanical drafting. These elevations are called the front elevation, *right side elevation, left side elevation,* and *rear elevation.* Some complex structures require more than four elevations to provide a complete description.

Figure 4-2 illustrates how the plan view is used to project the elevations. In actual drawing, the elevations are *not* presented upside-down and on their side as shown in this illustration. The plan view is revolved so that each elevation is drawn in its natural position.

Architectural Drafting Equipment

An architectural drafter uses equipment that is designed for specific purposes. Using this specialized equipment requires skill and understanding. Traditional drafting equipment, such as triangles, scales, compasses, etc., can be used to manually produce architectural drawings, Figure 4-3. A computer-aided drafting and design (CADD) system can also be used to produce a drawing on a computer, which is then plotted on paper, Figure 4-4. The following sections briefly describe typical architectural drafting equipment.

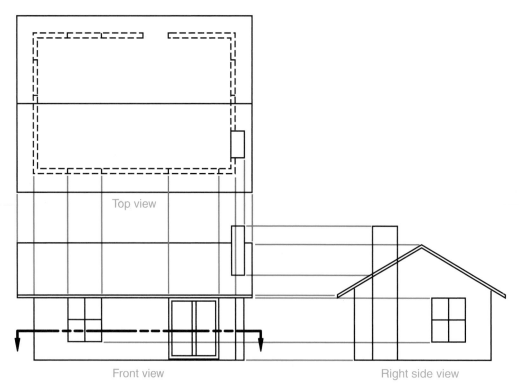

Top view

Front view   Right side view

Figure 4-1. This camp cottage shows the normal orthographic projection of views.

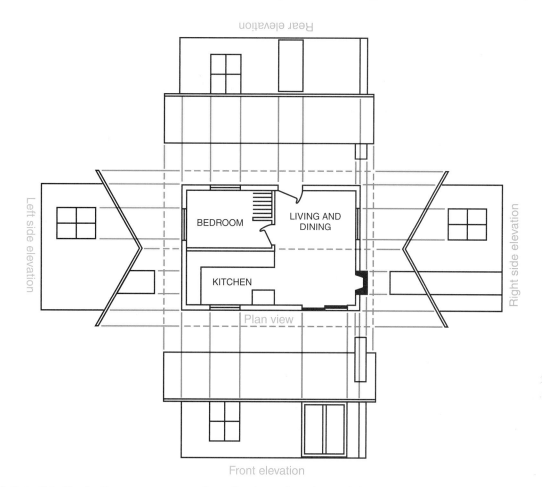

Rear elevation

Left side elevation

BEDROOM

LIVING AND DINING

KITCHEN

Plan view

Right side elevation

Front elevation

Figure 4-2. In this illustration, you can see how the four elevations of the camp cottage are projected from the plan view.

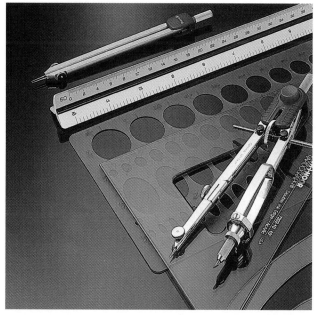

Figure 4-3. This drafting equipment is typical of the equipment used for traditional (manual) architectural drafting. (Koh-I-Noor Rapidograph, Inc.)

Figure 4-4. Modern CADD systems are powerful tools. This drafter is working on a cabinetry drawing.

Pencils

There are two principal types of pencils used in manual drafting—a common wood pencil and a mechanical pencil. Either type of pencil will give the desired results if kept sharp and used properly. Figure 4-5 illustrates the two types of pencils, lead for mechanical pencils, and a variety of pencil sharpening devices used to obtain a fine, conical point.

Wood pencils are still used by some manual drafters, but most are using the mechanical types. The mechanical pencil allows the drafter to change the hardness of lead at will. The hardness number is printed along the lead used in mechanical pencils. More important than easily changing lead hardness is that the lead is easier to sharpen and may be used close to the end.

The hardness number is printed on the side of the wooden pencil. Be sure to sharpen the proper end of a wooden pencil so as not to remove the hardness identification. In order to change hardness, the drafter needs to change pencils. Therefore, the drafter needs two or three different wooden pencils when working on a drawing.

Erasers

Most drafters prefer to use an eraser that is not attached to the pencil. Several common drafting erasers are shown in Figure 4-6. Select an eraser that will remove all traces of lead without destroying the surface of the paper or leaving colored marks. Some pink erasers will leave a pinkish color that detracts from the appearance of the finished drawing. Plastic erasers are preferred by many drafters for this reason. Electric erasers can be used to quickly erase large areas or multiple changes, Figure 4-7.

Figure 4-6. Two types of drawing erasers used by architects. Many drafters prefer plastic erasers.

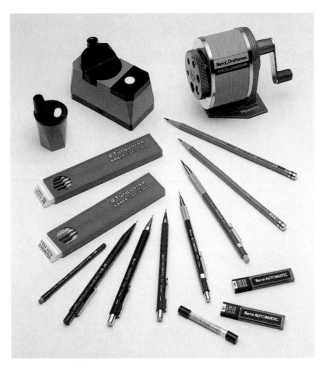

Figure 4-5. These are common pencils, leads, and pencil pointing (sharpening) devices used by a manual architectural drafter. (Berol USA)

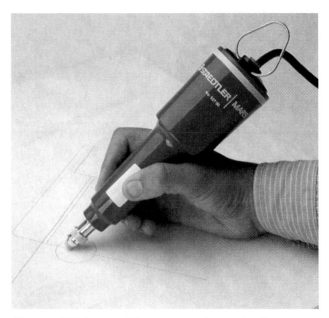

Figure 4-7. An electric eraser reduces the time required to erase large areas. (Staedtler Mars GmbH & Co.)

Erasing Shields

Erasing shields are made of metal or plastic and are usually thin to provide for accurate erasing, Figure 4-8. The shield allows lines to be erased without removing surrounding lines. Always use the erasing shield when there is a possibility of touching another line that you wish to save.

Paper

Most architectural drawings are finished on some type of tracing paper, vellum, or drafting film. This allows for easy duplication of the drawings using traditional diazo machines. Preliminary drawings are sometimes made on opaque drawing paper and then later traced for reproduction. Drafting paper, vellum, and film can be purchased in standard size sheets or rolls, Figure 4-9. The sheets are easier to use but are usually more costly.

The following chart shows two systems of standard drawing sheet sizes and the letter designation for each size. Both systems are approved by the American Standards Association and are commonly used.

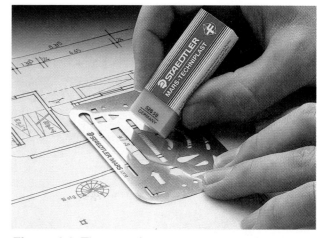

Figure 4-8. The use of an erasing shield will improve the quality of a drawing.
(Staedtler Mars GmbH & Co.)

Standard Drawing Sheet Sizes (Inches)

Multiples of 8-1/2″ × 11″ Size	Letter Designation	Multiples of 9″ × 12″ Size
8-1/2″ × 11″	A	9″ × 12″
11″ × 17″	B	12″ × 18″
17″ × 22″	C	18″ × 24″
22″ × 34″	D	24″ × 36″
34″ × 44″	E	36″ × 48″

Presentation plans are often completed on illustration board or some other special type medium designed for the particular artistic technique used in the presentation. As a general rule, the type of medium selected will depend on the intended use for which the drawing is being prepared and the presentation technique used.

Drawing Boards

Traditional drawing boards are made in standard sizes of 12″ × 18″, 18″ × 24″, 24″ × 36″,

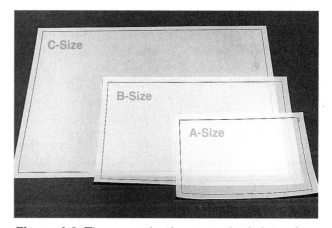

Figure 4-9. These are the three standard sizes of tracing paper commonly used in architectural drawing.

and 30″ × 42″. Most boards are white pine or basswood, or plywood with a vinyl cover. For those who still draft manually, drafting tables that have drawing-board tops are used most often. These tables are usually larger and have a drafting machine or straightedge permanently attached, Figure 4-10.

T-Square

The T-square is a traditional manual drafting instrument. It is manufactured from wood, metal, plastic, or a combination of these materials. The T-square slides along one edge of the drafting board and is used to draw horizontal lines. It also provides an edge against which triangles are placed to draw vertical

Figure 4-10. A drafting machine allows the drafter to easily draw straight lines and measure angles. (Vemco Corporation)

Figure 4-11. A vertical line is drawn along the edge of a triangle from the bottom toward the top.

and inclined lines. A T-square is used when a drafting machine is not available.

Triangles

Triangles are used for drawing lines that are not horizontal. The 45° and 30°-60° triangles are the common triangles used in drafting work. They are available in metal or plastic, but plastic is preferred because of its transparency. Draw vertical lines in an upward direction with the hand sliding along the triangle as shown in Figure 4-11. Adjustable triangles are also available that take the place of the 30°-60° and 45° triangles, Figure 4-12. When using the adjustable type, care should be taken to adjust it accurately.

Protractors

Protractors are used for measuring angles. They are produced in semicircular and circular styles. The semicircular type is extensively used by most architectural drafters. Measurements of less than half a degree is not possible with most common protractors. However, metal protractors with a vernier scale may be purchased that allow measurements accurately to one minute. Figure 4-13 illustrates the type of protractors commonly used by architectural drafters.

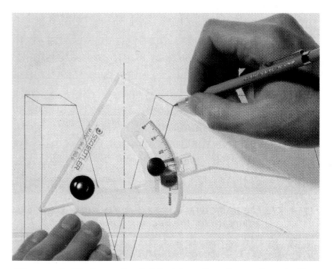

Figure 4-12. An adjustable triangle allows the drafter to draw lines at any angle. (Staedtler Mars GmbH & Co.)

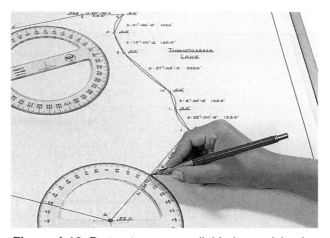

Figure 4-13. Protractors are available in semicircular and full circle styles.

Scales

Scales used in drawing are primarily the architect's scale, engineer's scale, and combination scale. Figure 4-14 shows a typical architect's and engineer's scale. Scales can be made of wood, plastics, metal, or a combination of these materials. Scales are designed in various configurations that include two-bevel, four-bevel, opposite bevel, and triangular shapes.

The architect's scale is usually divided into 3/32", 3/16", 1/8", 1/4", 1/2", 3/8", 3/4", 1", 1-1/2", and 3" to the foot. In addition, one edge is divided into 16 parts to the inch. The engineer's scale is divided into 10, 20, 30, 40, 50, and 60 parts to the inch. The combination scale is just what the name implies—a combination of the architect's and engineer's scales. It is divided into 1/8", 1/4", 1/2", 3/8", 3/4", and 1" to the foot and 50 and 16 parts to the inch. Decimal measurements can be made using the 50 scale.

The most significant difference in these scales is that the divisions on the architect's scale are based on twelve units to the foot while the divisions on the engineer's scale are based on ten units to the inch. The combination scale is designed to bridge the gap and provide both features. An architectural drafter usually needs both an architect's scale and an engineer's scale since certain drawings, such as topographical drawings and plot plans, require measurements in 10ths.

How to Use a Scale

The use of words "size" and "scale" should be clarified. In drafting terminology, one may say the drawing is "half size." This means exactly what it says. The drawing is one half as large as the real object. When the notation at the bottom of the drawing states Scale: 1/2" = 1'-0", then the drawing is 1/2 scale. One half scale in architectural drafting means that 1/2" on the drawing is equal to 1'-0" on the object (building). If you were to draw a 40' × 60' house at a scale of 1/2" = 1" (half size) you would need a piece of paper a little over 20' × 30'. Most residential floor plans are drawn at 1/4 scale, where 1/4" on the drawing equals 1'-0" on the house.

Study the 1/4 scale shown in Figure 4-15. Notice the last 1/4" of the scale on the right-hand side. It is divided into twelve parts that represent the 12 inches of one foot. Be careful not to confuse the 1/4 scale with the 1/8 scale that appears on the same face, but starts from the opposite end. The 1/4 scale has longer lines denoting each foot.

The scale shown in Figure 4-16 indicates a measurement of 16'-4" on the 1/4 scale. Always begin at zero on the scale and lay off the whole number of feet. Then, measure back from zero the number of inches. Use a sharp pencil and be very careful in pinpointing the exact length. Always draw as accurately as possible. This is a good habit to form.

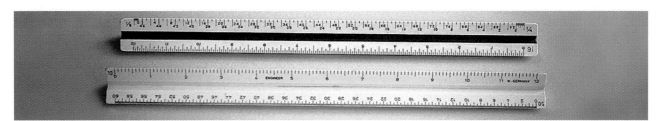

Figure 4-14. An architectural drafter uses both an engineer's and architect's scale.

Figure 4-15. The 1/8" = 1'-0" and 1/4" = 1'-0" scales are printed on the upper edge of this architect's scale. The 1/4" = 1'-0" scale is standard in architectural work.

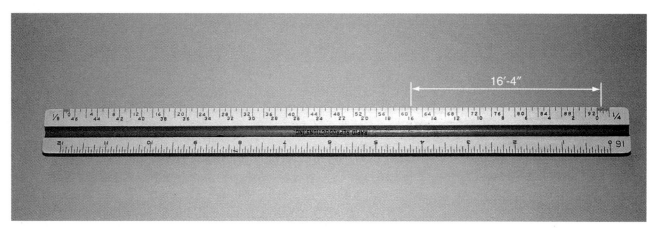

Figure 4-16. The proper method of measuring 16′-4″ using the 1/4″ = 1′-0″ scale.

Dividers

The dividers are used to divide a line into proportional parts, provide a quick way to measure a length that must be used a number of times, and other related operations. Divider points are shaped like needles. They must be kept sharp to be useful.

Architectural drafters use dividers in basically two sizes—large (about 6″) and small (about 4″). The small dividers usually have an adjustment wheel in the center or on the side. The large dividers often have a friction device instead of the wheel. Both types are useful and considered standard equipment, Figure 4-17.

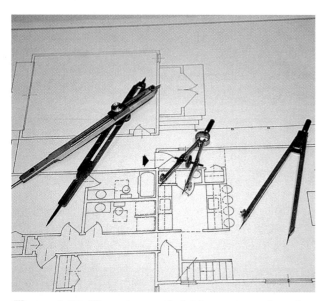

Figure 4-17. Three types of dividers—a small center wheel divider, a large friction type divider, and a proportional divider.

The Compass

The compass is used to draw circles, arcs, or radii. It is produced in different styles and sizes to match the dividers. Some have center adjusting wheels and others have side adjusting wheels. The most common varieties used by architectural drafters are the giant bow (about 6″ in length), medium-size friction compass, and the smaller center-wheel compass. Figure 4-18 shows a center-wheel compass with three types of drawing points. Large arcs may be drawn using a beam compass as illustrated in Figure 4-19.

The lead in the compass should be adjusted to the proper length, which is slightly shorter than the center point. A fine point should be placed on the lead. Use an F or H hardness lead. Some practice is required to draw sharp, smooth arcs. Hold the compass between your thumb and forefinger. Then, rotate the compass clockwise while leaning it slightly forward.

The center point of a compass is different from points on the divider. The compass center point may be cup shaped or have a

Figure 4-18. A large center-wheel compass.

Figure 4-19. A beam compass is used to draw a large arc.

point with a shoulder. This prevents the point from going too deep into the drawing board or vinyl cover.

Lettering Guides

Guidelines are used to help neatly letter a drawing. Lettering guides are used to draw these guidelines. A common lettering guide is the Ames Lettering Guide, Figure 4-20.

Irregular Curves

Irregular curves are used to draw curved lines that cannot be drawn with a compass. These lines usually have a series of centers and would be very difficult to construct with a compass. When using an irregular curve, line up at least four points and draw the line through three. Continue this process until the curve is completed. This procedure produces a smooth line. Figure 4-21 shows how a flexible curve could be used to draw a long curved line.

Case Instruments

The case instruments may include dividers, compass, lining pens, pencil pointers, spare parts, small screwdriver, and various other instruments. Some students may wish to purchase a set of case instruments rather than individual parts. Figure 4-22 shows a small set of case instruments.

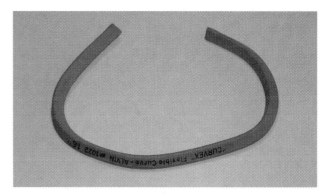

Figure 4-21. Flexible curves are used to draw curved lines that are not regular arcs.

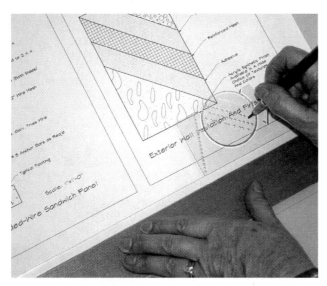

Figure 4-20. An Ames Lettering Guide can be used to draw guidelines for lettering.

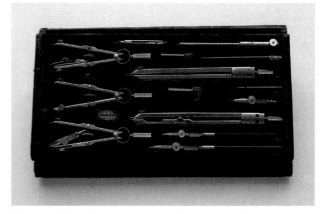

Figure 4-22. A beginner's set of case instruments.

Lettering Devices

Lettering devices are used when uniformity of letters is essential. Many styles and sizes of letters are available. One popular type is shown in Figure 4-23. Lettering in ink or pencil is possible with this type of lettering device.

Technical Pens

Technical pens are used to ink a drawing. Pen points are interchangeable and range in size from 000 (very fine) to 8 (about 1/16" wide), Figure 4-24.

Templates

Templates serve as a guide in drawing special lines or symbols. Most templates are made of plastic. Figure 4-25 shows a typical plastic template used in architectural drafting. The cutouts represent standard symbols and can be traced to form the symbol on the drawing. Some of the features on the templates are general in nature and may be used to form symbols not represented on the template. A wide variety of templates can be purchased in various scales to suit the requirements of most any drawing.

Grids

Grids are available in a wide variety of sizes and forms and have many uses in architectural drafting, Figure 4-26. Some grids are designed to be used under a sheet of tracing paper while others are designed to be drawn on directly.

Square grids are useful in sketching idea plans and in modular construction drawings. These grids are produced in standard-size sheets with 2, 4, 8, 16, and 32 squares per inch and include reproducible and nonreproducible grid lines.

Another type of grid used in architectural drawing is the perspective grid. These grids are quite useful and usually serve as underlays. Vanishing points are preselected on perspective grids. Numerous variations are available.

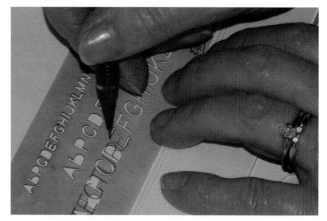

Figure 4-23. A stencil-type lettering device can be used to form precise letters.

Figure 4-24. A typical set of technical fountain pens. (Staedtler Mars GmbH & Co.)

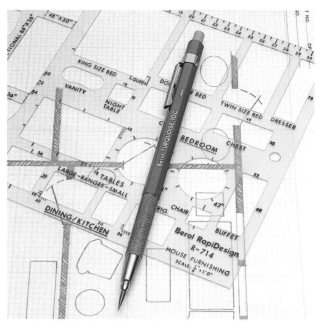

Figure 4-25. A typical template used in architectural drafting. (Berol USA)

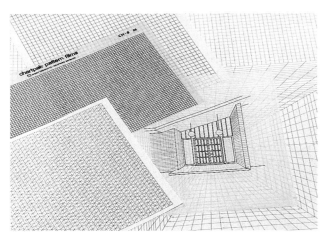

Figure 4-26. A variety of useful grids are available for architectural drafting.

Freehand Sketching

Freehand sketching is a method of making a drawing without the use of instruments. Most designers use sketches to "think through" an idea before an instrument or CADD drawing is made. It is also a useful technique for sharing ideas when an idea is still fluid and developing.

Freehand sketching requires only a pencil, preferably with a soft lead, and paper. You can use either plain paper or paper with a grid pattern, Figure 4-27. It is generally easier in the beginning to sketch on grid paper than on plain paper.

Once the techniques of sketching are mastered, you can represent your ideas to others or record them for future reference.

And, the beauty of this technique is that only a pencil and piece of paper are required.

Sketching Technique

When sketching, hold the pencil with a grip firm enough to control the strokes. Your arm and hand should have a free and easy movement. The point of the pencil should extend approximately 1-1/2" beyond your fingertips, Figure 4-28. Use your third and fourth fingers to steady your hand.

As you sketch, rotate the pencil slightly between strokes to retain the point longer. Initial lines should be sharp and light, not fuzzy. Avoid making grooves in the paper by applying a light pressure.

When sketching straight lines, your eye should be on the point where the line will end. Use a series of short strokes to reach that point. When all the lines are sketched, go back and darken the lines. When darkening lines, your eye should be on the tip of the lead.

Strive for neatness and good technique when sketching, but do not expect a freehand sketch to look like an instrument drawing. Good freehand sketches have a character all their own.

Sketching Horizontal Lines

Horizontal lines are sketched with a movement that keeps the forearm approximately perpendicular to the line being sketched. Four

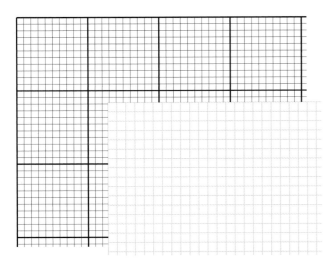

Figure 4-27. Cross-section paper can be used for freehand sketching.

Figure 4-28. When sketching, hold your pencil farther back than you would normally.

steps are essential in sketching horizontal lines, Figure 4-29. First, locate the end points of the line. Next, position your arm for a trial movement. Then, sketch a series of short, light lines. Finally, darken the line in one continuous motion.

Sketching Vertical Lines

Vertical lines are sketched from top to bottom using the same short strokes in series as for horizontal lines. When making the strokes, position your arm comfortably at about 15 degrees to the vertical line. You may find it easier to sketch vertical or horizontal lines if the paper is rotated at a slight angle. A finger and wrist movement or pulling arm movement are best for sketching vertical lines.

First, locate the end points of the line, Figure 4-30. Next, position your arm for a trial movement in drawing the line. Then, sketch several short, light lines. Focus on the end point of the line when sketching these lines. Finally, darken the lines. Focus your eye on the point of the lead when darkening the lines.

Sketching Inclined Lines and Angles

All straight lines that are not horizontal or vertical are called inclined lines. To sketch inclined lines, sketch between two points or at a designated angle. Use the same strokes and techniques as for sketching horizontal and vertical lines, Figure 4-31. If you prefer, rotate the paper to sketch these lines as if they are horizontal or vertical lines. Angles can be estimated accurately by first sketching a right angle (90 degrees), then subdividing it to get the desired angle. Refer to Figure 4-32 for an illustration of how to obtain an angle of 30 degrees.

Sketching Circles and Arcs

There are several methods of sketching circles and arcs—centerline method, enclosing square method, hand-pivot method, and free-circle method. All are sufficiently accurate, so

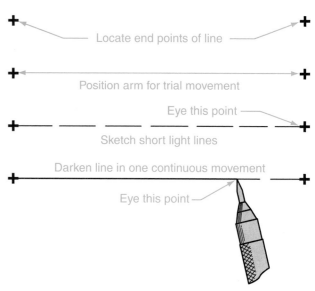

Figure 4-29. There are four basic steps to sketching a horizontal line.

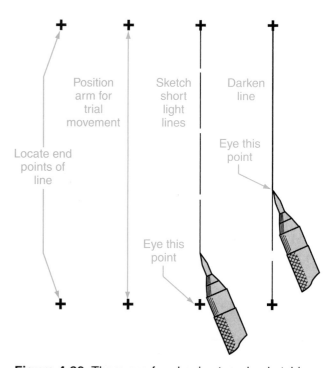

Figure 4-30. There are four basic steps in sketching a vertical line.

use the method best suited for the particular situation.

Six steps are used in the centerline method of freehand sketching circles. These steps are: locate centerlines, use a scrap piece of paper with radius marked to locate several points on the circle, position arm for trial movement,

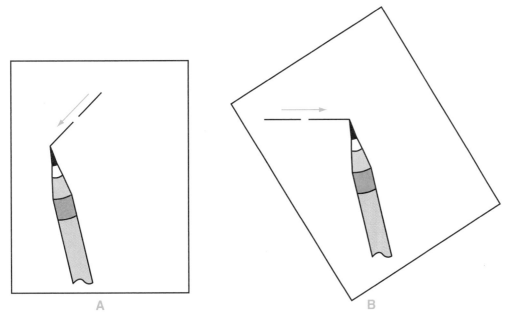

Figure 4-31. Use the same techniques to sketch inclined lines as for horizontal and vertical lines. A—Inclined lines can be drawn with the paper square to the drawing surface. B—Or, they can be drawn by rotating the paper so that they can be sketched as horizontal or vertical lines.

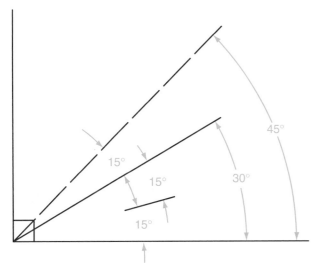

Figure 4-32. Estimating an angle by freehand sketching is done by first sketching a 90 degree angle. The 90 degree angle is then divided (estimation only, no instruments) into the appropriate angle.

sketch the circle in short sweeps, and darken the circle, Figure 4-33.

The following steps are necessary when sketching a circle by the enclosing square method. First, locate the centerlines of the circle. Second, sketch a box with the sides the same length as the diameter of the circle. Next,

sketch arcs where the centerlines meet the box. Finally, sketch the circle. See Figure 4-34.

The hand pivot method is a quick and easy method of sketching circles. First, locate the center of the circle. Next, using your small finger as a pivot and holding the pencil in the normal manner, rotate the paper 360 degrees. Your small finger should remain stationary on the center of the circle as you rotate the paper, Figure 4-35.

The free-circle method of freehand sketching circles involves more skill in performance, but can be developed with practice. With this method, you do not use any "guides" to help you sketch. You sketch the circle using only your hand-to-eye coordination.

Sketching Ellipses

Occasionally, it is necessary to sketch an ellipse. The rectangular method of sketching an ellipse is similar to sketching a circle with the enclosing square method. First, locate the centerlines of the ellipse. Then, draw a box with side lengths equal to the major (longest) and minor (shortest) diameters of the ellipse. Next, sketch arcs where the centerlines meet the box. Finally, sketch the ellipse, Figure 4-36.

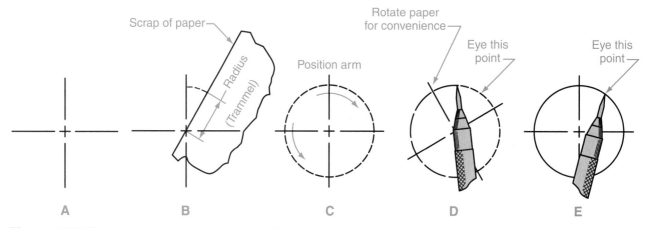

Figure 4-33. The centerline method is one method of sketching a circle.

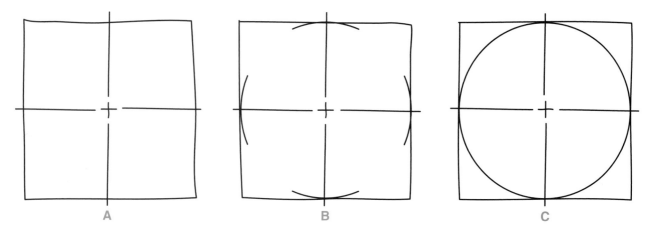

Figure 4-34. The enclosing square method is a method of sketching a circle.

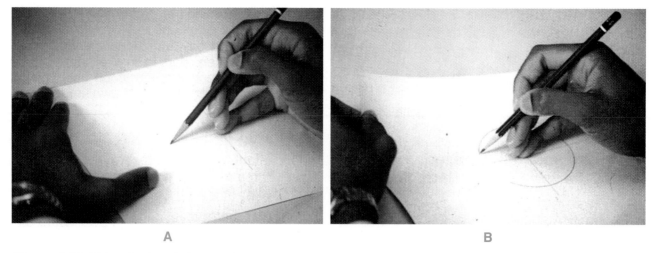

Figure 4-35. Using the hand-pivot method to sketch a circle. A—Position the pencil and your small finger. B—Rotate the paper.

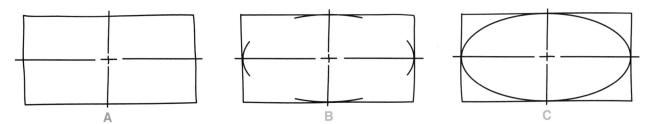

Figure 4-36. The rectangular method of sketching an ellipse is very similar to the "enclosing square method" of sketching a circle.

Sketching Irregular Curves

An irregular curve may be sketched free-hand by connecting a series of points at intervals of 1/4″ to 1/2″ along its path. Include at least three points in each stroke. "Lead out" of the previous curve into the next by overlapping strokes, Figure 4-37.

Proportion in Sketching

There is more to sketching than making straight or curved lines. Sketches must contain correct proportions. *Proportion* is the relation of one part to another, or to the whole object. You must keep the width, height, and depth of the object in your sketch in the same proportion to that of the object itself. If not, the sketch may convey an inaccurate description.

A most useful technique in estimating proportions is the unit method. This method involves establishing a relationship between distances on an object by breaking each distance into units. Compare the width to the height and select a unit that will fit each distance, Figure 4-38. Distances laid off on your sketch should be the same proportion, although the units may vary in size. This method is especially useful when making a sketch from a picture of the object.

Computer-Aided Drafting and Design

Computer-aided drafting and design (CADD) systems, like all computer systems, consist of hardware and software components.

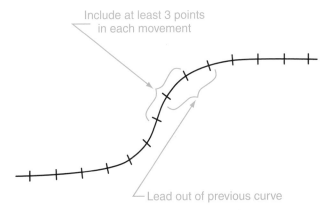

Figure 4-37. When sketching an irregular curve, include at least three points in each segment. Also, overlap each section as you sketch.

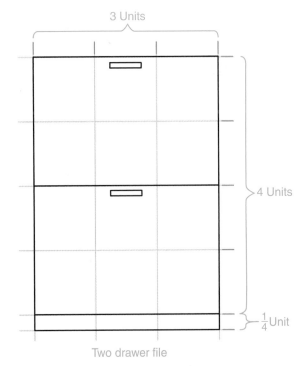

Figure 4-38. To use the unit method of gauging proportions, divide the object into equal-sized units. The proportion can be changed by either increasing or decreasing the size of the units on your sketch.

The hardware components of a computer system include the physical devices. The software programs are used by the drafter to create drawings or other documents. The computer hardware and software of a CADD system are tools for creating drawings, just like pencils and triangles are for manual drafting. CADD is introduced in the following sections and discussed in detail in Chapter 5.

CADD Hardware

The basic hardware in most CADD workstations includes the central processing unit (CPU), input devices, storage devices, and output devices, Figure 4-39. The CPU is the "brain" of the computer system. Input devices provide for data and information input to the computer. The keyboard is the standard input device, but a mouse and digitizing tablet are very useful in CADD work. Hard drives are generally the main storage devices on a computer. They hold the main operating system, the software, and electronic files created by the operator. The monitor is the most common output device. Some form of

hardcopy output device, usually a plotter, is needed to produce prints of drawings.

CADD Software

Computer software is the programming (commands) that tells the computer hardware which tasks to perform. CADD software directs the computer to perform drawing and design tasks selected by the drafter/designer to draw lines, shapes, or symbols, Figure 4-40. Hundreds of CADD software programs are currently available that range from very simple programs to extremely complex architectural engineering and construction (AEC) programs.

Output Devices

To make a hard copy of CADD drawings on paper or film, a plotter or printer output device is required. Pen plotters produce high-quality drawings using pens or pencils of various colors. Plotters are available in sizes to accommodate standard paper sizes up through

Figure 4-39. A typical CADD workstation used to produce architectural drawings.

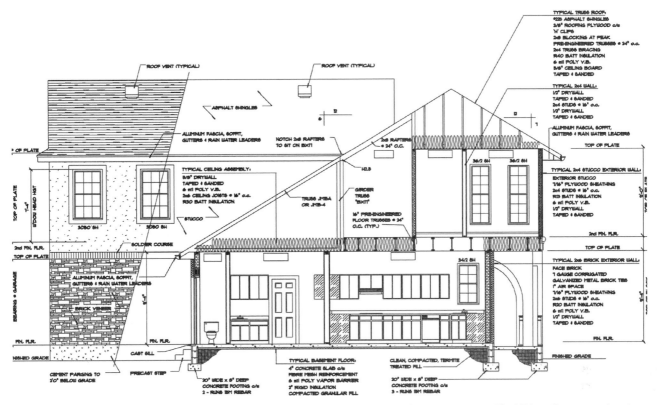

Figure 4-40. This section drawing was designed and drawn using a CADD system. (SoftPlan Systems, Inc.)

E-size (36″ × 48″). Laser and inkjet printers also produce good quality graphic reproductions. However, most laser printers are limited in size to 11″ × 14″, which is too small for architectural applications. Inkjet printers and plotters are available in all sizes and can produce drawings in color, Figure 4-41.

Figure 4-41. A plotter is a common way to produce a hard copy of a CADD drawing. This inkjet plotter is being used to produce a hardcopy of a rendering. (DesignJet Division, Hewlett-Packard)

Lines Used In Architectural Drawing

Architectural drafters use a number of different line types to help the reader clearly understand the drawing. Drawings are usually made for a customer or as a presentation. It is for the purpose of accurate communication that a specific line type is used in a given situation. Once a drafter learns these lines and uses them properly, communicating with others will be in a more precise manner. *The purpose of a drawing is to communicate ideas accurately and clearly.*

Drafters refer to the collection of line types used in drafting as the *Alphabet of Lines.* Many of the same line types used in mechanical or technical drafting are also used in architectural drawing. However, some line types may be slightly different in architectural work. Study Figure 4-42, which illustrates the major lines used in architectural drawing.

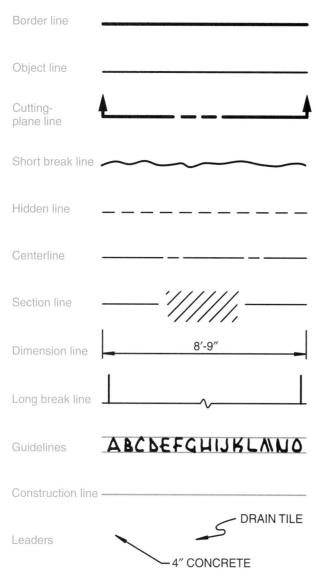

Border line	
Object line	
Cutting-plane line	
Short break line	
Hidden line	
Centerline	
Section line	
Dimension line	8'-9"
Long break line	
Guidelines	ABCDEFGHIJKLMNO
Construction line	
Leaders	DRAIN TILE / 4" CONCRETE

Figure 4-42. These are the general line types used in architectural drawing. Together, these line types are called the Alphabet of Lines.

Border Lines

Border lines are very heavy lines and are used to form a boundary for the drawing. They assure the reader that no part of the drawing is missing and provide a "finished" appearance to the drawing. A #4 (.047", 1.20 mm) technical or plotter pen should be used for the border line.

Object Lines

Object lines show the outline of the main features of the object. They are important lines and therefore should be easily seen. On an architectural drawing, such things as interior and exterior walls, steps, driveways, patios, fireplaces, doors, and windows are represented by object lines. The width of an object line should be between .024" (0.60 mm) and .028" (0.70 mm) wide. A #2 or 2-1/2 technical or plotter pen will produce these widths.

Hidden Lines

Hidden lines represent an edge that is behind a visible surface in a given view. In a floor plan, hidden lines are also used to indicate features above the cutting plane, such as an archway or wall cabinets in a kitchen. Hidden lines are usually not as thick as object lines. A #1 (.020", 0.50 mm) technical or plotter pen is recommended.

Centerlines

Centerlines indicate the center of holes and symmetrical objects such as windows and doors. Centerlines simplify dimensioning, but should not be used as extension lines. Centerlines may be drawn with a #0 (.014" or 0.35 mm) or #00 (.012" or 0.30 mm) technical or plotter pen.

Extension Lines

Extension lines are used to denote the termination point of a dimension line. They extend from a portion of the object to the dimension lines. Extension lines are thin lines, but are not construction lines. Therefore, draw them sharp and clear to about 1/16" past the dimension line. Use a #0 (.014" or 0.35 mm) or #00 (.012" or 0.30 mm) technical or plotter pen.

Dimension Lines

Dimension lines are used to show size and location. They are usually placed outside of the object. However, it is sometimes proper to place them within the object if the area is large and not too cluttered with other lines. All dimension lines have a dimension figure halfway between the ends with some form of symbol, such as an arrowhead, at the two terminal ends. Figure 4-43 shows accepted methods of terminating dimension lines and placing the dimension figures. Dimension lines are drawn with a #0 (.014" or 0.35 mm) or #00 (.012" or 0.30 mm) technical or plotter pen.

Long and Short Break Lines

Break lines are used to show that all of the part is not drawn. An example of where a break line might be found is across a paved driveway indicating that the drive is longer than shown on the plan.

When the break is two or three inches in length, a *long break line* is usually used. *Short break lines* are used where part of the object is shown broken away to reveal an underlying feature or part of the object removed for some other reason. Long break lines are thin and straight; short break lines are heavy and drawn freehand.

Long break lines may be drawn with a #0 (.014" or 0.35 mm) or #00 (.012" or 0.30 mm) technical or plotter pen. A #3 (.031" or 0.80 mm) technical or plotter pen is generally used for short break lines.

Cutting-Plane Lines

Cutting-plane lines are heavy lines used to show where the object is to be sectioned. Ordinarily, cutting-plane lines are labeled with a letter at each end or a flag at one end and a direction arrow at the other so that the section detail will be easily identified. A #3 (.031" or 0.80 mm) technical or plotter pen should be used for these lines.

Section Lines

Section lines or *crosshatch lines* are used to show that the feature has been sectioned. General section lines are usually drawn at a 45 degree angle. However, there are specific patterns to represent various types of material. A #00 (.012" or 0.30 mm) technical or plotter pen is generally used for section lines.

Guidelines

Guidelines are used for hand lettering. They are drawn very light and are for the drafter's use. Guidelines will help improve the quality of lettering and are, therefore, well worth the time and effort required to draw them. Guidelines are drawn in pencil only and are not needed on a CADD drawing.

Construction Lines

Construction lines are very light lines used in the process of constructing a drawing. They are to help the drafter and should not reproduce when a print is made. Draw your construction lines sharp and light. When placed on a CADD drawing, the lines should be on a separate layer and in a color different from other colors in the drawing.

Line Type Application

Figure 4-44 shows most of the general line types applied in a floor plan. Other line types are explained in this text in the areas pertaining to their specific use. A close examination of the lines shown in Figure 4-44 shows

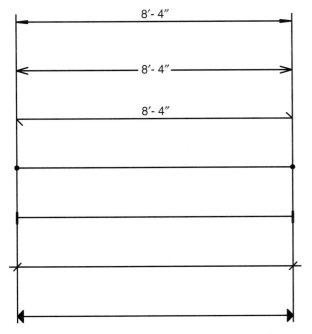

Figure 4-43. These are accepted terminators for dimension lines in architecture.

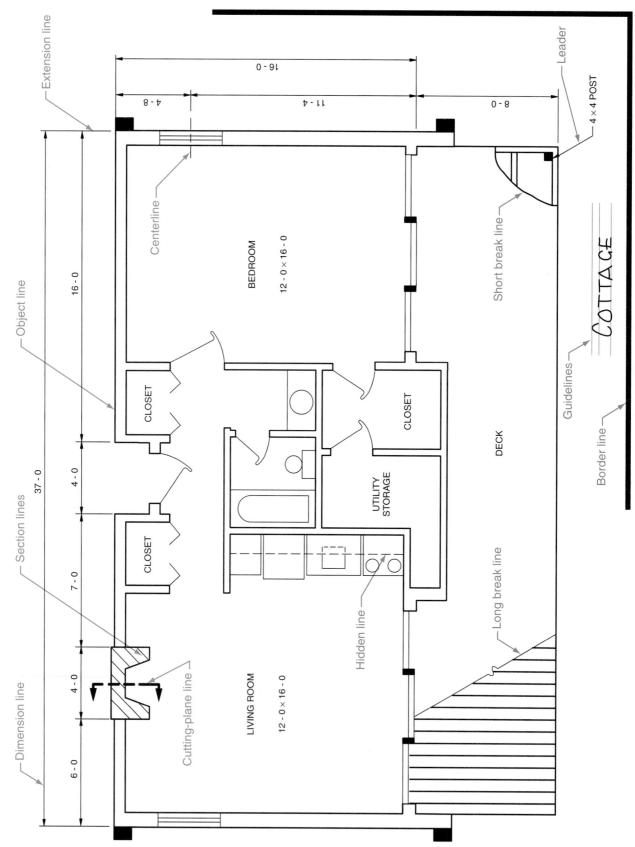

Figure 4-44. This floor plan illustrates most of the line types used by the architectural drafter.

that they vary in thickness (width) but not in shade. All lines on a manual drawing are black and vary only in width. A thin line may look like a lighter color than a thick line, but in reality, they are both black. On a CADD drawing, colors are often used to signify certain meanings.

In manual drafting, hard leads are used to draw thin lines. Soft leads are used to draw thick lines. Pencil lead grades range from 9H (very hard) to 9B (very soft). However, the leads from B to 9B are generally deemed too soft for use on architectural drawings.

Architectural Lettering

Architectural lettering is not the same as mechanical or technical lettering. An architectural drawing leans toward the artistic by nature. The "pure" letters used in mechanical drawing do not fit traditional architectural styles. Architectural lettering has more of an artistic flair.

There is no one correct architectural lettering style. Many acceptable styles present a certain artistic flair. Architects often like to develop their own personal style that is unique. Figure 4-45 shows three individual styles developed by architecture students. Each of the styles is different, but each is in keeping with the feeling of architecture.

Some Notes on Developing a Style of Lettering

1. Draw guidelines and use them. If you are developing a lettering style for CADD, you will not use guidelines.
2. Experiment with variations of uppercase (capital) letters to determine the ones you like best, Figure 4-46. Lowercase letters are seldom used for architectural lettering.
3. Select letter styles that produce artistic letters that are easily identified.
4. Apply the same style technique to all similar letters, Figure 4-47.
5. Letter the entire alphabet large enough so that the proportion of the letters is distinct.
6. Make a mental picture of each letter so that you may reproduce it the same each

Figure 4-46. A—Variations of standard letters may add interest to your style. B—These letters were generated from a custom CADD lettering style.

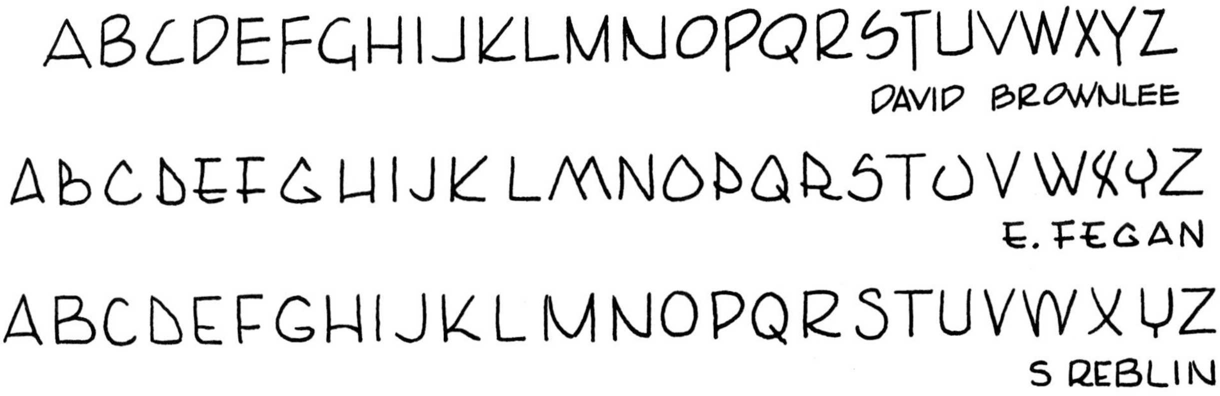

Figure 4-45. Architectural students should develop their own personal lettering style.

time. If you are developing a lettering style for CADD, save your style.

7. Practice your style until it becomes a part of you and flows easily. You will not need to practice if you are using CADD.

8. Use your style.

Architectural lettering should be vertical. If you learn to letter that way, you should never have to worry whether your method will be acceptable. Slanted letters usually indicate that the word is in italics. This is only used for emphasis applications.

Letter Spacing

The space between letters in a word is not constant. Figure 4-48 shows an example of spacing as a constant and a more pleasing arrangement with variable spacing. The ability to judge the space between letters must be carefully learned. Only practice will perfect this ability. Constant practice in lettering words helps develop the ability to space letters in a pleasing attractive manner. This is an area where CADD is a great advantage because letter and word spacing is automatic.

Word Spacing

Proper spacing between words is as important as the spacing between letters. Words must not appear to run together, nor should they be so far apart that part of the drawing area is wasted. A good rule to follow in spacing words is to allow approximately a letter-height distance between words. CADD automates this process and quickly produces proper spacing.

Letter Size

There are no absolute rules concerning lettering size. Generally, most information lettering in architectural drawing is 1/8″ or 3/32″ high. A technique that looks good and helps in the readability of lettering is to make the first letter of each word 1/8″ high and the remainder of the word 3/32″ high. This emphasizes the beginning of each word and tends to separate them, Figure 4-49. However, all letters are uppercase (capital) letters.

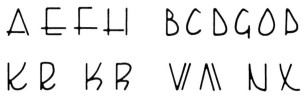

Figure 4-47. Treat similar letters the same way to increase unity of style.

Figure 4-48. Variable spacing of letters adds interest and is more pleasing to the eye.

Figure 4-49. Draw the first letter of each word larger than the succeeding letters for emphasis. However, uppercase letters are used for the entire word.

Titles and important words are usually lettered larger with bold underlines being used to direct attention to their importance. Underlining also helps to call attention to important information.

CADD Symbols Library

A significant architectural drafting time-saver and one of the chief reasons for using CADD is a symbols library. A *symbols library* is a collection of drafting symbols saved to a file that can be quickly inserted into a CADD drawing, Figure 4-50. In some ways, a symbols library is like a collection of symbol templates used in manual drafting. Most CADD AEC software packages include a series of standard symbols designed for use in architectural, engineering, and construction drawings. Most CADD programs also allow you to define your own symbols. A CADD drafter may have several symbols libraries for various applications, such as material sections, plan views of standard architectural symbols, or elevation views of structural elements.

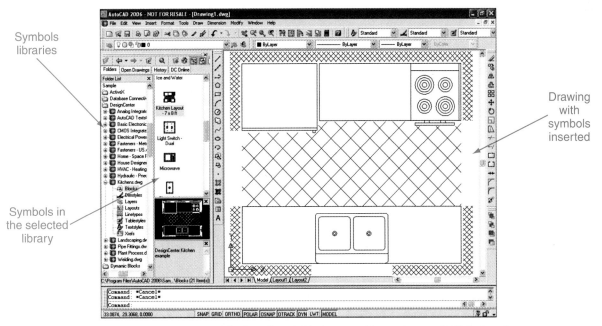

Symbols libraries

Drawing with symbols inserted

Symbols in the selected library

Figure 4-50. A symbols library allows the drafter to quickly insert objects into a CADD drawing.

Internet Resources

www.abbisoft.com
  AbbiSoft, a supplier of house plans

www.aia.org
  American Institute of Architects

www.ansi.org
  American National Standards Institute

www.autodesk.com
  Autodesk, Inc., publisher of AutoCAD and Autodesk VIZ

www.dell.com
  Dell Computers

www.iso.ch
  International Organization for Standardization

www.staedtler-usa.com
  US subsidiary of Staedtler Mars GmbH & Co., supplier of drafting products

www.thomasregister.com
  Thomas Register, a listing of manufacturers

www.vemcocorp.com
  Vemco Corporation, supplier of drafting products

Review Questions – Chapter 4

Write your answers on a separate sheet of paper. Do not write in this book.

1. The three principal orthographic views are _____, _____, and _____ views.

2. The plan view of the _____ is the most important view in a set of architectural drawings.

3. To erase accurately, use a(n) _____ _____.

4. Drafting paper is produced in standard sizes. The dimensions of B-size paper are _____ or _____.

5. The two triangles most commonly used in architectural drawing are the _____ and the _____ triangles.

6. The most accurate measurement possible with a common drafting protractor is _____.

7. A scale that is only divided into 10, 20, 30, 40, 50, and 60 parts to the inch is a(n) _____ scale.

8. If a drawing is half as large as the actual object, then the drawing is said to be _____.

9. If 1/4″ on the drawing equals 1′ on the object, then the scale is noted as _____.

10. Other than the scale, the instrument that is used to divide a length into proportional parts is the _____.

11. The instrument (not a template) used to draw circles and arcs is the _____.

12. Guidelines are used to _____.

13. The purpose of a drawing is to _____.

14. The _____ line is the widest line on a drawing and provides a "finished" look.

15. Visible lines are also called _____ lines.

16. Lines that are not visible are _____ lines.

17. Lines that are used to indicate the length of a line or edge are called _____ lines.

18. Architectural lettering is different from mechanical lettering. It is more _____.

19. Space between letters in a word is _____.

20. Letters on an architectural drawing are generally _____ or _____ high.

21. When sketching, hold the pencil so that approximately _____ inches extends beyond your fingertips.

22. When sketching _____ lines, you may want to rotate the paper and sketch them as horizontal and vertical lines.

23. List the typical hardware components of a CADD system.

24. Define computer software.

25. What is a symbols library?

Suggested Activities

1. Using an architectural style, letter the alphabet and numbers 0 through 1 on a sheet of grid paper. Make the lettering at least 1/4″ high so the proportions will be distinct.

2. Draw the Alphabet of Lines using proper line weights. Identify each line with its correct name. Design a title block that identifies the drawing. Place your name, the title of the drawing, the date, the class name, and the page number in the title block.

3. Visit a drafting supply store and make a list of the types of time-savers they carry in stock that are used in architectural drawing. Include the prices in the list.

4. Obtain a sketch pad with square grid lines. Measure your drafting lab and sketch a plan view showing the walls, doors, and windows. Dimension the plan as illustrated in this chapter. Use proper line symbols and line weights. Make the drawing at a scale of 1/4″ = 1′-0″.

5. Write letters to some of the major drafting equipment supply companies and ask for their specification literature. Prepare a bulletin board display by clipping and mounting illustrations of pieces of equipment and time-savers most used by the architectural drafter.

6. Visit a local computer store and ask for a demonstration of one of the popular CADD AEC software programs that they sell. Collect literature about the software program and the type of equipment required to run it. Make a report to your class on the program and equipment and share the literature.

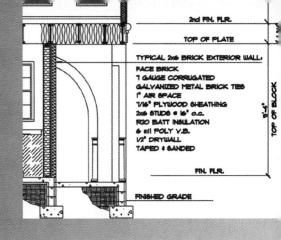

Introduction to Computer-Aided Drafting and Design

Objectives

After studying this chapter, you will be able to:

➤ Explain computer-aided drafting and design.

➤ Identify common applications for CADD in architecture.

➤ List the components of a typical CADD workstation.

➤ Identify features of CADD software and how they should be evaluated when selecting a program.

➤ Explain the advantages of AEC specific CADD software.

Key Terms

AEC Specific CADD Packages
Animation
CADD
CADD Workstation
Central Processing Unit (CPU)
Commands
Digitizer Puck
Display Controls
Drawing Aids
General Purpose CADD Packages
Inkjet Printers/Plotters
Input Device

Laser Printers/Plotters
Layers
Light Pens
Mainframe
Miniframe
Monitor
Network
Objects
Output Device
Pen Plotter
Rendering
Software
Storage Devices
Symbols Library
Video Card

What Is CADD?

CADD is an acronym for computer-aided drafting and design. Simply put, CADD is a tool that replaces pencil and paper for the drafter and designer. While CADD makes the process of designing a product or structure much easier, the fundamentals of design have not changed. This is very important to remember. *CADD is just a tool.* A drafter/designer using a computer system and the appropriate software can:

• Plan a part, structure, or other needed product.

• Modify the design without having to redraw the entire plan.

• Call up symbols or base drawings from computer storage.

• Automatically duplicate forms and shapes commonly used.

• Produce schedules or analyses.

• Produce hard copies of complete drawings or drawing elements in a matter of minutes.

The results produced using CADD can be quite complex, Figure 5-1. All types of architectural, engineering, and construction (AEC) drawings can be produced with CADD.

The computer used in CADD can be as simple as a home PC or as complex as a networked mainframe. The *software* is the instructions that makes the hardware perform the intended tasks. CADD software ranges from very basic programs that can be purchased for under $100 to programs that cost several thousands of dollars.

Initially, the letters CAD referred to computer-aided (or assisted) drafting, but now they can mean computer-aided drafting, computer-aided design, or both. However,

91

Figure 5-1. CADD has greatly improved the process of designing and creating complex projects. (Autodesk, Inc.)

CADD (with two Ds) is really larger in scope than CAD, integrating design, analysis, and often "premanufacturing" as well as drafting. To think of it in different terms, CADD includes CAD. However, do not get stuck on the terminology. It is more important for you to understand just for what CADD or CAD is used. This text uses the term CADD for all applications of computer-aided drafting, computer-aided design, and computer-aided drafting and design.

Why Use CADD?

There are many reasons to use CADD, but almost all of these reasons can be boiled down to one simple statement: *CADD saves time and money.* Once a design has been completed and stored in the computer, it can be called up whenever needed for copies or revisions. Revising CADD drawings is one of the greatest time- and money-saving benefits. Frequently, a revision that requires several hours to complete using traditional (manual) drafting methods can be done in a few minutes on a CADD system. In addition, some CADD packages automatically produce updated schedules

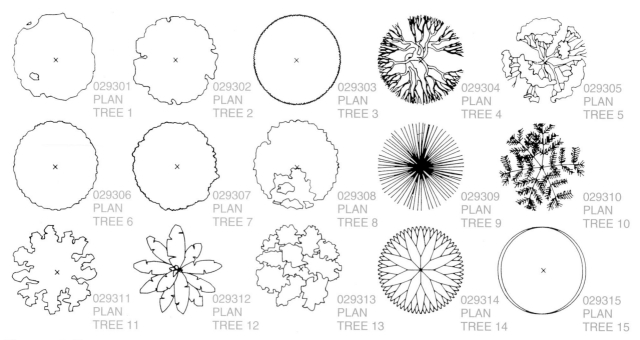

Figure 5-2. These tree symbols are stored in a symbols library. Any one of these symbols can be quickly inserted into a plot plan CADD drawing, repeatedly if needed. (Prime Computer, Inc.)

after you revise the original plan, thus eliminating the need to manually update the schedule.

Productivity

Modern CADD programs let the drafter/designer quickly develop and communicate ideas in a precise and professional manner. Once an operator learns how to use a given system, productivity is generally increased and work is typically of a higher quality. In addition, the drafter does not make an endless number of revised drawings for each small change. Instead, the change is made in the CADD system and a drawing (hard copy) is only generated as needed. In fact, editing drawings is often where CADD repays its cost to the company. Changes are easy to make and some software makes the corrections in every affected drawing or schedule. Even the most basic CADD packages speed the change process.

Another productivity benefit of CADD is the use of symbols libraries. A *symbols library* is a collection of standard shapes and symbols typically grouped by application, Figure 5-2.

These symbols can be inserted into drawings, thus eliminating the need to draw the symbols over and over. Inserting standard symbols and shapes is quick, easy, and accurate. Once a standard symbol has been drawn and stored in the library, it can be called up and placed as many times and in as many drawings as required. For example, symbols for trees, furniture, doors and windows, and common appliances are usually included in an architectural symbols library. Most companies also develop unique symbols for their own applications and store them in their symbols library.

The time saved by CADD in making drawings with many repetitive features is impressive. For example, the time required to hand draw bricks around a foundation wall is significant. Using a CADD software package, a symbol or hatch pattern can be applied to the area in a few seconds. Other examples of repetitive features include window details, typical wall sections, stair designs, cabinet details, paving and gutter sections, culverts, roof and floor truss details, and so on, Figure 5-3. It is easy to see that inserting standard details and making minor changes can save many hours in a single set of drawings.

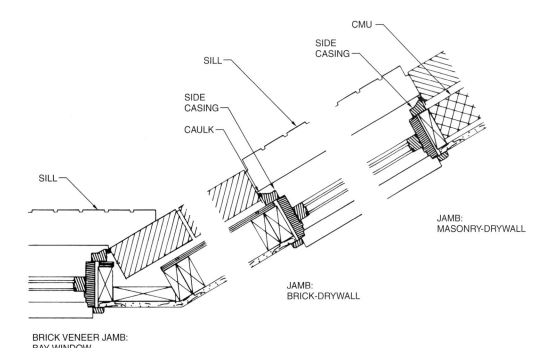

CMU

SIDE CASING

SILL

SIDE CASING

CAULK

SILL

JAMB: MASONRY-DRYWALL

JAMB: BRICK-DRYWALL

BRICK VENEER JAMB: BAY WINDOW

Figure 5-3. This complex window framing detail can be inserted into any drawing as required. It is quite obvious how much time can be saved by simply inserting the existing detail over redrawing the detail.

Flexibility

Flexibility is definitely one advantage of using a CADD system to generate drawings. Once a design is complete, printouts of all or portions of the design can be made in minutes. Depending on the equipment being used, a drawing may be:

- Plotted at any scale that will fit on the drafting medium.
- Plotted in several colors.
- Developed in sequential steps.
- Presented on different media depending on the intended use.

In addition, CADD offers the added flexibility of sharing drawing data with other CADD users. Generally, the other users do not even have to be using the same CADD software. Most CADD software programs have various options for sharing data, including import/export functions, e-mail options, and web posting capabilities.

Uniformity

Drawings produced on a CADD system will possess a high degree of uniformity regardless of who makes the drawings. Multiple skilled CADD drafters with strong drafting fundamentals can work on a single project and produce a result that is very uniform in appearance and adheres to standards. Each drafter must possess the technical knowledge to select the proper symbol, size, linetype, and so on. For example, every time a tree symbol is placed in a drawing, it is reproduced exactly the same as before. Every single-pole light switch drawn will be identical, Figure 5-4. Typically, the only variables are scale and rotation. Such uniformity greatly improves communication among those who use the final drawings. However, the CADD system cannot decide which symbols to place and where to place them, or determine good building practices. The drafter and designer must have strong architectural fundamentals to avoid creating beautiful, but meaningless, drawings.

Poor line quality is not an issue with a properly used CADD system. It is easy to

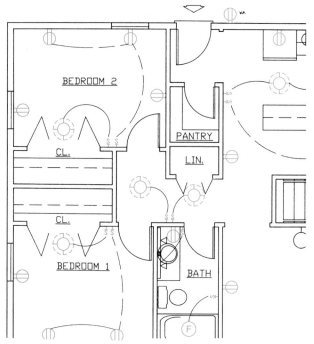

Figure 5-4. All symbols in this drawing are uniform. The only variable is the rotation of the symbols. In this case, all symbols use the same scale. Some of the symbols, but not all, are shown here in color to help identify them.

ensure consistency in line thickness and pattern scales, Figure 5-5. Smudged lines or sloppy lettering, both of which often lead to errors on the construction site, are not problems with CADD-generated drawings. In addition, since CADD drawings are typically duplicated by creating another printout, there is no degradation in quality from repeated duplication. Degradation can occur when a hand-created drawing is repeatedly duplicated on a diazo or blueprint machine.

Scale

One additional advantage of CADD for architecture is in scale. A set of architectural drawings will include many drawings, many with different scales. For example, a plot plan may be showing a site that is 100' × 200', the floor plan may be showing an overall size of 50' × 30', and the drawing showing wall sections may be showing an overall size of about 8' × 4'. To draw all of these manually requires the drafter to use several different drawing scales (instruments) and to keep

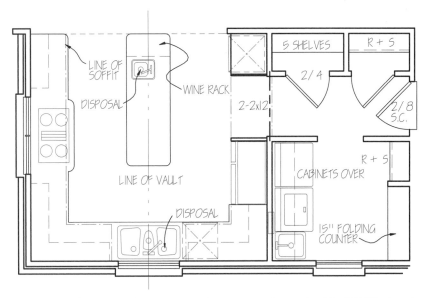

Figure 5-5. Line thickness and pattern scale are consistent in this CADD drawing. (Original drawing courtesy of Autodesk, Inc.)

them straight. This presents many opportunities for errors to be introduced. However, in CADD, objects are always drawn at their true size. Then, when the final drawings are plotted, the appropriate plot scale is calculated for each sheet. This is much faster than selecting and using the correct scale for each object or plan. Also, since the calculation is done only once, and often automatically, there is much less chance of errors.

Architectural CADD Applications

There are obvious applications for CADD in architecture. All drawings that would traditionally be done by hand are drawn on the computer. These include all of the construction drawings such as floor plans, elevations, plot plans, schedules, and so on. In addition to these obvious applications, there are several other applications for CADD in architecture, depending on the software you are using.

Schedule Automation

Some CADD packages have the ability to automatically generate window and door schedules, kitchen cabinet schedules, plumbing fixture schedules, lighting fixture schedules, and various reports, Figure 5-6. This may sound like a great time-saving feature, and it is when the drawing is properly created. If the drawing is not created with appropriate attributes, this feature is useless. Therefore, planning and proper drawing setup is very important.

In addition to automatically creating the schedules, some CADD programs have the ability to automatically update or correct the schedule when an item from the drawing is changed. The time required to redraw or update a schedule because of a simple change is significant using traditional drafting methods. Using CADD, such a change requires only a few seconds to complete.

Renderings

An important part of architectural design is the presentation drawings used to show a client the proposals. Presentation drawings are covered in detail in Chapter 33. A properly setup CADD drawing can be used to generate a computer *rendering*, or presentation drawing. This ability is typically found on mid-range and high-end CADD systems. However, this application is exceptionally suited for the right CADD program.

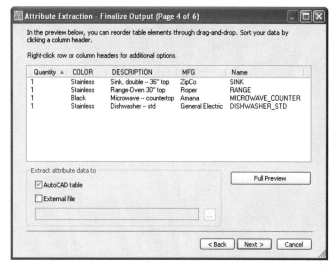

Figure 5-6. Some CADD programs have the ability to automatically generate schedules when the drawing is properly set up. Here, the manufacturer, product color, and a description are included in the schedule.

Animations

Related to presentation drawings are something called *animations* or rendered animations. These are basically just like Saturday morning cartoons, however, they represent a building, site, or other architectural feature. Animations can show features such as windows and doors opening, the changing effect of sunlight on a room, or present a room or building as a person would see it walking through. See Figure 5-7. With the right CADD

Figure 5-7. This interior room is being shown with animated sunlight. This can be used to determine if more or larger windows are needed, if a skylight should be added, or if additional interior light fixtures are required. (Eric K. Augspurger)

software and a skilled drafter, a client or review board can be shown a very accurate representation of what the final construction will look like. As with the ability to render, animation capabilities are typically found on mid-range and high-end CADD systems.

CADD Workstation

A *CADD workstation* generally consists of a computer or processor, monitor, graphics adapter, input and pointing device, and hard copy device, Figure 5-8. Most CADD programs, even high-end software, can be run on "up-to-date" home computer systems. These stand-alone systems are inexpensive, powerful, and can be purchased at most appliance and "super stores."

Often, several stand-alone systems are connected in a *network.* This allows each computer to share information through the network wiring. However, the "computing power" is contained in each individual machine. A network typically allows devices such as printers and plotters to be shared among the computers. Networks are generally found in larger offices and companies.

Some CADD programs are designed to run on a type of computer called a *mainframe.* This type of computer system consists of a

Figure 5-8. Most CADD software can be run on today's "off-the-shelf" PCs.

common processing unit centrally-located that is connected, or networked, to many remote terminals. Each terminal basically consists of a monitor, keyboard, and mouse or other input device, but a terminal does not have a central processing unit. In addition to having a common processing unit on the mainframe, the printer or plotter is also generally a common or central device and all terminals have access to it. A *miniframe* system functions like a mainframe but typically on a smaller scale.

Computer Components

Any computer basically consists of the central processing unit, an output device, an input device, and a storage device. The *central processing unit (CPU)* contains the processor, RAM, and input/output interfaces. This is the "box" found on most PCs.

The output device that all CADD systems have is the display or monitor. This "computer screen" provides visual feedback on what the computer is doing, and what you are doing with the computer. CADD systems also have a hard copy output device, such as a printer or plotter. However, this device may not be connected directly to the workstation.

All CADD systems also have a keyboard. This is an input device. CADD systems also have another input device generally in the form of a mouse or digitizer puck. These input devices allow the user to communicate with the CADD system.

Storage Devices

Storage devices are how data, such as drawings, are saved for later use. The storage device places the data on storage media. The computer hard drive in your home PC is a storage device with self-contained media. A CD-R drive, or CD-ROM recordable drive, is also a storage device. This device stores data on a recordable compact disc, or CD-R. Floppy drives, tape drives, Zip drives, and optical drives are other forms of storage devices. Each uses a different type of media on which data is stored.

Display Types and Sizes

The display device is typically referred to as the *monitor* or "screen." These are general terms that cover a wide range of display devices. There used to be several different types of display devices varying in display color, mechanical function, and size. Now, display devices are generally described in terms of size and screen properties.

Most monitors are cathode ray tubes (CRTs). These are just like a standard television set. Another common type of monitor is a liquid crystal display (LCD). These are found on laptop computers. The newer "flat" monitors are also generally LCDs.

When selecting a monitor for a CADD system, size is important. The size of a monitor is measured diagonally, just like a television. Generally, a 17" monitor is the smallest that can be effectively used with CADD. Many CADD systems have a 21" or larger monitor. The larger the monitor, the more actual drawing area can be displayed. With small monitors, most of the computer screen can be taken up by toolbars and menus.

Another important aspect of a CADD system's display device is the graphics adaptor or video card. The *video card* is the device that transmits data from the CPU to the monitor. Most video cards have their own RAM (memory). The more RAM on the card, the less of the CPU's RAM is consumed processing video information. There are also video cards specifically designed for CADD and high-end 3D graphics. Generally, one of these video cards is best suited for a CADD system. However, each card has advantages and disadvantages. When selecting a card, locate a hardware review in a computer or CADD magazine. There are several magazines aimed at the CADD market. These frequently conduct hardware reviews. Use this information to determine which card is best suited for your application.

Input Devices

An *input device* is a way to provide the computer with information. The most common input device is the keyboard. The second most common input device is the mouse. Both of these input devices can be found on nearly all computers.

A variation of the mouse is the trackball. This is like an upside-down mouse. Instead of moving the entire device to move the onscreen cursor, only the ball is moved. This can be more efficient than a mouse. However, many computer users find it difficult to switch from using a mouse to using a trackball.

A *digitizer puck* is another variation of a mouse. It is moved around like a mouse, but can have several buttons to activate a variety of functions. See Figure 5-9. However, digitizer pucks are specifically designed for use with CADD systems. The puck is moved on top of a tablet menu that displays tiles for commands. When over a command, it can be activated by pressing the appropriate button on the puck. The puck is also used to digitize a drawing that is placed on the digitizing pad.

Light pens are sometimes found on CADD systems. These devices work with a tablet menu, like a puck. When used with the proper display device, an appropriate light pen can also be used to select menu items directly on the monitor.

Output Devices

The monitor is the most common *output device*. However, as a drafter, you also need to create printouts of your drawings. There are several ways to produce a hard copy.

Figure 5-9. Digitizer pucks come in a variety of configurations. The light pens shown here are another type of input device. (Kurta)

The traditional method for creating hard copies of CADD drawings is the *pen plotter.* This is a device that moves paper around under a pen to trace the object lines in the drawing. The pen is typically a felt tip or ballpoint pen. However, the best pens have a ceramic or steel point similar to a technical pen. Pen plotters produce the hard copy as the drawing was drawn. This can be a disadvantage, especially if there are many colors in your drawing. The multiple pen changes can take a lot of time. Also, since the pen plotter moves the paper around, it takes more time to complete a plot. This is because a plotter plots vectors, or "complete" lines.

A common hard copy device is the *laser printer* or plotter. This device produces an output in much the same way as an office copy machine. They are fast, quiet, and easy to use. The drawing is produced as a raster image, which is a series of dots. The biggest disadvantage of laser printers is the lack of color in the hard copy. There are color laser printers and plotters, but these are generally expensive to purchase and operate. They also typically do not produce very good color. Another disadvantage for architectural drafting is that few inexpensive laser printers can produce D- and E-size prints.

Inkjet printers and *inkjet plotters* are becoming very popular. These are raster devices that are fast, quiet, and easy to use like a laser printer. They also produce very good color and are inexpensive to purchase. In the past, the ink has been a disadvantage of inkjet devices. It was not stable and could smudge or smear very easily. However, advances in this area have virtually eliminated this problem, *once the ink is dry.* An advantage of inkjet devices is that you can produce hard copies of renderings in full color. When printed on special "photo paper," it is often hard to tell a good rendering from a photograph. In the architectural field, this can be a great asset. Inkjet printers typically produce small-size prints, such as A- and B-size. Inkjet plotters can produce up to E-size prints.

All of these output devices have advantages and disadvantages. For example, pen plotters produce very high-quality line reproductions in color. However, they are slow and cannot be used to reproduce renderings. Laser printers are fast and inexpensive to operate, but most cannot produce color or large-size prints. Inkjet devices beautifully reproduce color renderings, but they can be slow and very expensive to operate. Be sure to determine exactly what your needs are before purchasing an output device.

Selecting a CADD Package

There is a wide variety of CADD programs on the market. These range from very basic programs that can only draw simple 2D objects to high-end programs that are fully 3D capable and have advanced features such as automated schedules. In order to get the best CADD system for your needs, you must first know *what* you want to accomplish with the software. If all you plan to do is produce 2D drawings, then you do not need all of the "bells and whistles" of a high-end system. But, if you are going to be producing 3D models and renderings, then you will probably need a high-end system. The answers to these basic questions may help you select the best package for you:

- How easy is the program to use? Does it provide help screens and clear instructions?

- What kind of support does the company provide after you purchase it? Do they provide updates either free or for a reasonable cost? Will they answer your questions over the phone? Is there training available at a local college or trade school? Remember, some CADD programs can be quite complex and you may need some help in using them.

- What are the hardware requirements of the package? If you need to upgrade your computer to run the software, perhaps another package with less requirements is better suited to your situation.

- Does the program require special hardware not common to other packages? If so, you might want to think twice before purchasing the package.

- How well does the package meet your needs? Is it useful to you?
- Check the warranty. What does it provide? What is the length of time covered?
- What are specific features of the software? Is it broad or narrow in application? Is it 2D or 3D? Is it compatible with other popular packages?
- How much does it cost? How does the cost compare with other similar packages? Consider a price-to-performance ratio.

You may be able to think of other questions to add to this list. These should be helpful in weeding out packages that do not fit your needs. If possible, use the program before you purchase it, or at least talk to someone who has used it.

For the purpose of this discussion, CADD programs are separated into two broad groups. These are general purpose and architectural, engineering, and construction (AEC) specific. *General purpose CADD packages* are usually designed for making typical mechanical drawings and other general drafting applications. *AEC specific CADD packages* typically have most, if not all, of the same functions as a general purpose program, but also have functions that would typically only be useful to an architect or construction technologist/engineer. Architectural/construction drawings can easily be created using general purpose CADD packages. However, an AEC specific program may be better suited to your particular architectural work.

General Purpose CADD Packages

General purpose CADD packages are available to meet a wide range of needs. Some are high-end programs and offer many advanced capabilities. Others provide only basic functions and are typically used for CADD education, home use, and basic applications. The next sections provide a brief description of the main features of popular general purpose CADD packages. This is not intended to be a comprehensive list. Remember, when selecting a software package, be sure to review your answers to the questions provided earlier.

Objects

Objects are the basic elements used to create drawings. They include items such as lines, points, circles, arcs, and boxes. Other objects such as polylines, fillets, chamfers, and freehand sketching add function to the program. These may not be available with basic CADD programs. The number and type of objects included in the program are very important for speed and ease of drawing.

Dimensions

Properly dimensioning a drawing is one of the fundamentals of drafting. Yet, dimensioning has always been time-consuming and a source of errors or omissions when done by hand. Most CADD packages provide the ability to automate dimensions. In fact, if the program does not provide this feature, you may want to think twice before purchasing it. An exception is software designed for rendering and animation as its main function, not typical drafting tasks.

Hatch Patterns

Hatching is an important feature of any drawing requiring a section view. Hatching is also used in architectural drafting to represent bricks, shingles, grass, siding, insulation, and many other features. Common CADD packages may include several standard hatch patterns, Figure 5-10. Some higher-end CADD programs also allow you to design your own patterns. This can be very time consuming. The more patterns that the software includes, the greater the savings in time.

If you are going to be modeling in 3D, hatching is not necessarily as important to you. Instead of hatch patterns, materials are defined and applied to objects. Then, the drawing is rendered to produce the final result.

Text

The ability to place text on a drawing is very important in most drafting situations. Therefore, it is important for the CADD software to have good text support. The number of typefaces, or fonts, available is not as important as how easy it is to place and edit text. However, you should also try to find a program that can use several different typefaces. Most Windows-based CADD software can use any font installed in Windows for text on a drawing.

Lettering style is *very* important in architectural drafting. An architect will not select a CADD package that forces them to use a "standard" font or text style. Therefore, it is important to select a CADD package that can use an appropriate architectural font. Some CADD packages also have the ability for the drafter to design and use their own font. Many architects prefer to use a personalized lettering style. For them, this "custom" feature is an important part of the CADD package.

Editing

The ability to edit a drawing is one of the most important aspects of CADD. Editing includes copying, erasing, moving, scaling, rotating, trimming, breaking, exploding, arraying, dividing, mirroring, extending, stretching, and a variety of other functions. A CADD program with several editing tools from which to choose is an advantage. Some of the basic CADD programs offer limited editing capabilities. You should stay clear of CADD software that does not offer an appropriate number of editing functions.

Layers, Colors, and Linetypes

Layers are similar to transparent drawing sheets on which you can draw. They allow various parts of a drawing to be placed on different "sheets" or layers. This feature is especially useful in creating several drawings that must relate to each other in some way. Layers also help when plotting a variety of outputs from a single complex drawing. Not all CADD programs support layers. However, the advantages of layers makes it worthwhile to invest in software that supports layers.

Object display color can be very useful when designing objects on a CADD system. For example, certain features can be assigned a certain color for easy viewing. In addition, color aids communication. Most CADD packages provide a number of colors, Figure 5-11.

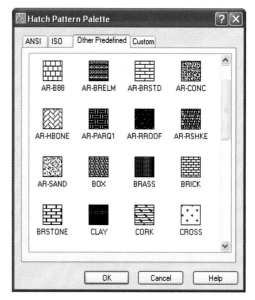

Figure 5-10. This CADD program allows you to choose from a variety of hatch patterns.

Figure 5-11. The ability to choose from an unlimited number of display colors is a big advantage of high-end CADD programs.

The Alphabet of Lines is an important part of drafting, whether the drawing is created by hand or on a CADD system. In order to correctly follow the Alphabet of Lines, a CADD system should have the ability to use different linetypes. In addition, the program should have the ability to set line thickness or width. Most general purpose CADD systems support several different linetypes. These linetypes may include continuous (solid), dashed, hidden, center, and phantom.

Coordinate Entry and Command Entry

A basic requirement to make drawings is the ability to tell the software where to place objects. There are generally several ways to do this in any given CADD program. For example, when drawing a line, you can generally type coordinates or pick points with the mouse or puck.

Just as there are different ways of providing locations, there are generally a variety of ways to give instructions to the software. These instructions are called *commands*. Generally, a command can be entered from a pull-down menu, screen menu, toolbar button, command line (keyboard), or digitizer tablet menu. The manner in which the command is entered does not change the function of the command. However, entering a command by different methods may change the steps needed to complete the command.

Drawing Units

Most CADD programs support different units of measure. Commonly supported units include architectural (fractional), engineering, scientific, and decimal. Decimal is used for both US Customary and Metric units.

Angular units of measure can also be in a variety of formats. Some common angular units of measure include decimal degrees, degrees/minutes/seconds, grads, radians, and surveyor's units. Several formats are useful for multiple applications.

Display Controls and Drawing Aids

Most drawings are much larger than the computer screen. Therefore, you need to change the magnification factor of the view and change the view itself. The functions that allow you to do this are called *display controls* and include zooming and panning commands, as well as other related commands. All CADD programs should have a variety of display controls. Higher-end CADD programs generally also provide a means to save views to be restored later. The ability to manipulate views is a very important part of CADD.

Drawing aids help you locate position on screen and on existing objects. They make the task of drawing easier, faster, and more accurate. All mid-range and high-end CADD programs offer a wide variety of drawing aids. Common drawing aids included display grid, grid snap, object snap, orthogonal mode, isometric mode, dynamic location, and construction planes. Without good drawing aids, CADD can be hard to manage.

Printing or Plotting

Nearly all CADD programs provide a printing or plotting function. This is how the drawing is transferred from the computer to a hard copy. Some rendering and animation programs do not provide printing functions. This is because the output is saved to a file that is then used in other software, which generally can print.

Program Customization

Program customization includes displaying and hiding toolbars, modifying menus or toolbars, creating new menus or toolbars, and writing macros or "programs" to help streamline the drawing process. The degree to which you can customize the software is especially important to an experienced CADD user. By customizing the program to suit their specific needs, the drafter can become highly efficient. In addition, program customization can help a CADD manager better standardize a departments drafting procedures.

3D Capability

Three-dimensional modeling is an advanced capability of some CADD programs. Much of the drafting done in CADD is in two dimensions, just like a manual drawing on paper. However, 3D modeling creates a "virtual" object in the computer that has width, length, and depth. The 3D object can be shaded or colored, rotated, and often animated, Figure 5-12.

There are two basic types of 3D models. Surface models are created by drawing a wireframe, much like a 2D drawing, and placing a skin over the wireframe. Solid models, on the other hand, have volume and mass. They are not empty on the inside like a surface model. Both types are used in architectural drafting. Unless there are specific requirements for one type or the other, which one is drawn depends

Figure 5-12. Three-dimensional modeling is used for a variety of applications. (Helmuth A. Geiser, Member AIBD)

on the software capabilities and drafter's preference. There is a general trend toward creating solid models because, in general, the final result can be used for analysis.

Mass property analysis provides important information. The information can be used for engineering calculations or for "premanufacturing" on the computer. Surface models are not generally suitable for mass property analysis. Solid models are almost exclusively used for mass property analysis.

Data Exchange

The ability for a CADD program to share data with other software is important for most applications. Even the most basic CADD programs support importing and exporting of a variety of file types. Before purchasing a CADD program that is not one of the more common programs, be sure to determine if it can import and export to common file types. One of the most common file types used to share data is the Drawing Interchange Format (DXF) format. This file format supports 2D and most 3D features. In addition, many CADD programs can also exchange data with database software, such as Microsoft Excel or Lotus 1-2-3.

AEC CADD Packages

Architectural, engineering, and construction (AEC) CADD packages are programs designed for a specific field. These packages generally include all of the functionality of general purpose CADD programs. However, they include tools and features for use in the AEC fields. The extra functions improve the workflow for AEC drafters. The sections cover some features often found in AEC CADD packages.

Schedule Generation

Most AEC CADD packages provide automatic schedule generation. The data is taken from the attributes of objects or symbols in the drawing. Also, once the original object or symbol is edited, the schedule is automatically updated. The ability to automatically generate schedules is a great time-saving function, especially on large projects.

Space Diagram Generation

Space diagrams are useful planning tools. They are simplified representations of floor plans and typically provide square footage or dimensions of the space. Some AEC programs will automatically convert a space diagram into a floor plan complete with wall thickness, Figure 5-13.

Stair Generation

Stair design requires a considerable effort, both to calculate and draw. Some AEC CADD programs include automated stair design features. The drafter enters basic data from the architect's sketches and the software automatically draws the stairs, Figure 5-14. Data that is typically entered may include the finished-floor-to-finished-floor height, stair width, and the run of the stairs. Some AEC CADD

programs also offer the ability to extract details from the drawn stairs. Generally, options are provided for wood, metal, and concrete/steel stairs. High-end AEC CADD programs also include elevators and escalators.

Hatch Patterns

AEC CADD programs offer hatch patterns that are specifically designed for the AEC field. A general purpose CADD program may not offer the patterns needed in the AEC field, such as shakes or shingles, various brick patterns, earth, sand, concrete, and foliage. These patterns can be difficult to create if they are not included in the program.

Walls

Architectural packages generally provide more than one method of generating walls, Figure 5-15. Often, walls can be drawn directly from space diagrams, as continuous walls, and from dimensions. Features such as intersection cleanup, wall thickness specification, and alignment are important time savers that can be found in most AEC CADD programs. If not available in the "standard" features, many CADD programs can be customized to add these features.

Symbols

AEC drawings typically contain many symbols. Symbols are used to represent various features, such as an electrical connection, tree, or plumbing fixture. Some types of symbols that may be found on an AEC drawing include:

- Standard door types.
- Standard window types
- Plumbing symbols.
- Electrical and lighting symbols.
- HVAC symbols.
- Furniture symbols.
- Tree and plant symbols.
- Appliance symbols.
- Vehicle symbols.
- Title symbols.
- Structural symbols.

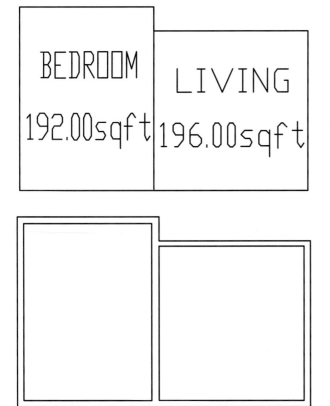

Figure 5-13. Some AEC CADD programs can take a space diagram (top) and create a floor plan from it (bottom).

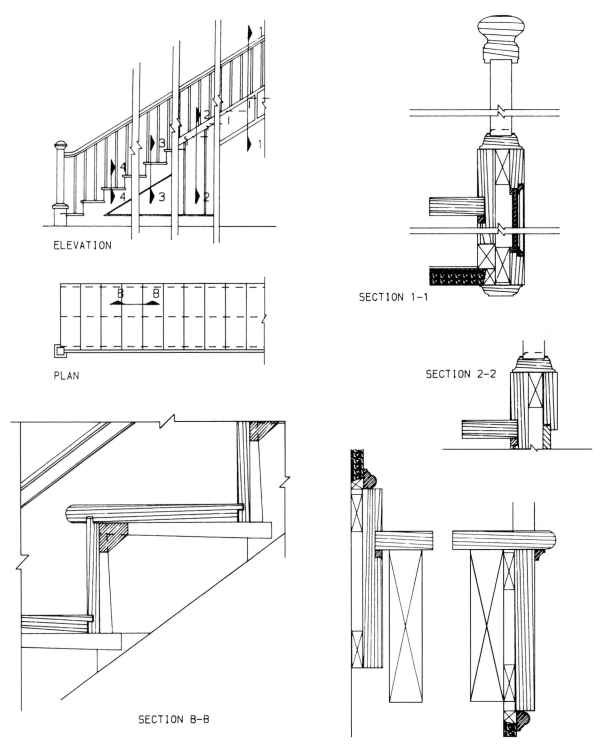

ELEVATION

PLAN

SECTION 1-1

SECTION 2-2

SECTION B-B

Figure 5-14. These standard wood stair construction details are generated from data supplied by the drafter. (Prime Computer, Inc.)

Standard Door and Window Types

Doors and windows require a considerable amount of time to draw from scratch. Therefore, it is important to have the appropriate symbols in a symbols library. A good AEC CADD package will include all of the standard door and window symbols, Figure 5-16. The symbols may be in a "general" library or may be in their own library. In addition, many window and door manufacturers provide symbols libraries of their products free of charge. Therefore, the ability to "add" these libraries to the CADD program is important for many architects and designers.

Structural Symbols

Structural symbols are a necessity for commercial work but also needed for residential design. Many AEC CADD programs include structural symbols in a library. Structural symbols can include I-beams, U-channel, and cast concrete members.

Plumbing Symbols

Most structures, whether residential or commercial, have some sort of piping or plumbing plan. AEC CADD programs include standard plumbing symbols in a library. Typical symbols include tub, lavatory, shower stall, toilet, bidet, plumbing lines, and valves. Some high-end AEC CADD programs that have 3D capabilities also provide 3D pipe symbols, or have the ability to add these symbols to the library.

Electrical and Lighting Symbols

Most residential and commercial structures require an electrical plan. Electrical symbols are simple to draw, but a single electrical plan may contain hundreds of symbols. Therefore, it is very important to have a good electrical symbols library that includes standard symbols. Most AEC CADD packages include several electrical and lighting symbols.

HVAC Symbols

Commercial structures include a heating, ventilating, and air conditioning (HVAC) plan.

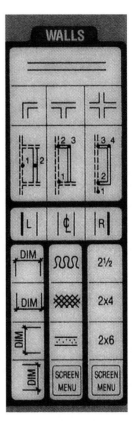

Figure 5-15. This digitizing tablet provides several options for drawing, manipulating, and hatching walls.

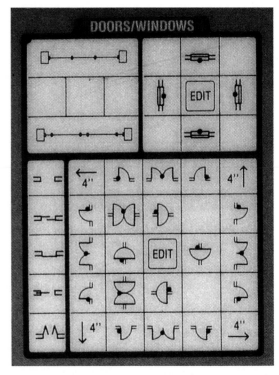

Figure 5-16. Standard window and door symbols should be included in a quality AEC CADD program.

Residential structures may also include an HVAC plan. HVAC symbols are often not included in lower-end AEC CADD packages or those designed just for residential applications.

Tree and Plant Symbols

Tree and plant symbols are used to show site details, landscaping details, or to "dress up" a drawing. Plant symbols are used on all plot plans and on many presentation drawings. Generally, these symbols are shown in a plan or elevation view. In addition, AEC CADD programs that have 3D capabilities often provide 3D views of plants and trees.

Furniture and Appliance Symbols

Symbols of typical furniture pieces are part of most AEC CADD packages. Some basic office furniture is typically offered with all AEC CADD programs, however, extended libraries are usually an additional purchase. AEC CADD programs that are 3D capable may provide one or two 3D symbols of furniture or appliances.

Title Symbols and Construction Details

Title symbols include meridian (north) arrows, revision triangle, drawing title, scale, and tags. These symbols are usually included in AEC CADD programs. Construction details are generally much larger and more complex than other symbols, Figure 5-17. Construction details are so specialized that most of these symbols are created by individual users or companies. They can save many hours of work in situations where a common detail is used over and over.

Vehicle Symbols

Vehicle symbols can range from basic block representations to fairly detailed plan and elevation views. Most AEC CADD programs only offer a few of these symbols, if any. However, they can generally be purchased separately. Perhaps the most commonly used vehicle symbols are 3D symbols. There are many different libraries available that contain 3D vehicle symbols.

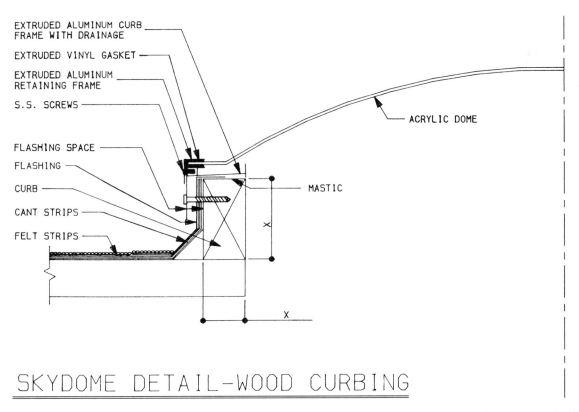

Figure 5-17. Construction details can be stored as symbols in a library. They are often created by individual users or companies. (Prime Computer, Inc.)

Internet Resources

www.autodesk.com
Autodesk, Inc., publisher of AutoCAD and Autodesk VIZ

www.bentley.com/products
MicroStation publisher

www.cadalyst.com
Cadalyst magazine

www.cadence.com
CADENCE magazine

www.compaq.com
Compaq computers

www.dell.com
Dell Computers

www.discreet.com
Discreet, publisher of 3ds max

www.hp.com
Hewlett-Packard

www.ptc.com
Parametric Technology Corporation, publisher of Pro/ENGINEER, Pro/MECHANICAL, Pro/DESKTOP

Review Questions – Chapter 5

1. What does CADD stand for?
2. What is the most basic reason for using CADD?
3. Explain what a symbols library is.
4. List three applications for CADD in architecture.
5. List the basic components of a CADD workstation.
6. What is a video card?
7. List three output devices.
8. What is a general purpose CADD package?
9. What does AEC stand for?
10. What is an AEC CADD package used for?

Suggested Activities

1. Using the Internet, search for various CADD software. Make a list with the software grouped by general purpose or AEC.

2. Identify the components of your CADD workstation.

3. Contact a local AEC firm that uses CADD. Identify the criteria they used to justify switch from manual drafting to CADD.

4. Obtain a plan for a municipal or residential project. Determine where CADD can be used in the project. Identify areas of the project in which CADD would provide a large benefit over traditional manual drafting.

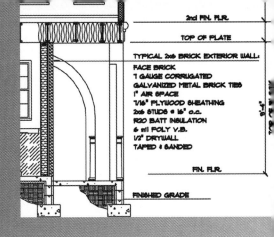

CADD Commands and Functions

6

Objectives

After studying this chapter, you will be able to:

➤ List several general categories of commands used in popular CADD programs.

➤ Sketch an example of linear, angular, and leader dimensioning.

➤ Explain drawing aids.

➤ Discuss the purposes of colors, linetypes, and layers in typical CADD programs.

➤ Explain layer naming conventions as related to architectural drawings.

➤ Describe 3D drawing.

➤ Explain rendering.

➤ Explain animation.

Key Terms

3D Modeling	Inquiry Commands
Animation	Layer
Attribute	Object Snap
Blocks	Parametric
Command Line	Pull-Down Menus
Commands	Regular Polygon
Display Control	Rendering
Commands	Round
Display Grid	Snap
Drawing Aids	Solid Modeling
Drawing Commands	Surface Modeling
Editing Commands	Symbols Library
Fillet	Toolbars
Grid Snap	Wireframe

Computer-aided drafting and design (CADD) is a powerful tool. However, just as with any tool, you have to know how to use it. *Commands* are the instructions you provide to CADD software to achieve the end result. There are several general groups of commands that are common to most CADD software. These groups are drawing commands, editing commands, display control commands, dimensioning commands, and drawing aid commands. Examples of these commands are discussed in this chapter. It is important to understand that each CADD package may have slightly different names for the commands discussed here. This may be confusing, but there are many similarities between various products.

Just as command names vary among CADD software, the method of command entry can vary as well. Even within a particular program there may be more than one way to enter a given command. For example, a command may be selected from a pull-down menu. *Pull-down menus* appear at the top of Windows-based software. The **File** menu found in a Windows application is a pull-down menu. In addition to pull-down menus, many CADD programs have *toolbars* that contain buttons. Picking a button activates a particular command. Also, some CADD programs have a *command line.* This is where a command can be typed to activate it. Finally, some CADD programs support the use of a tablet to enter commands with a puck. The method in which a command is activated does not change the basic function of the command.

Drawing Commands

Drawing commands form the foundation of any CADD program. These commands allow you to actually create objects on the computer screen. The most basic drawing command is the **LINE** command. After all, any object is made up of at least one line. In addition, many CADD programs have commands to automate the creation of certain objects, such as circles, rectangles, and polygons.

Line

The **LINE** command is the most frequently used command in a CADD program because it is the basic element of most drawings. Each straight line requires information as to the placement of the first point (one end) and the second point (other end). Generally, you can enter specific coordinates for the endpoints or pick the endpoints on screen, Figure 6-1.

AutoCAD Example:

Command: **LINE**↵
Specify first point: **3,5**↵ *(or pick a point on screen)*
Specify next point [or undo]: **6,4**↵ *(or pick a point on screen)*
Specify next point [or undo]:↵
Command:

Double Line

Some CADD packages provide a **DOUBLE LINE** command, although it may not have this name. This command is useful in creating walls on floor plans and similar applications where parallel lines are required, Figure 6-2. Most CADD programs allow you to set the distance between the double lines. In addition, some programs allow you to control how the corners and intersections are formed.

AutoCAD Example:

Command: **MLINE**↵
Current settings: Justification = Top, Scale = 1.00, Style = STANDARD
Specify start point or [Justification/Scale/STyle]: **0,0**↵ *(or pick a point on screen)*
Specify next point: **6,0**↵ *(or pick a point on screen)*
Specify next point or [Undo]: **6,4**↵ *(or pick a point on screen)*

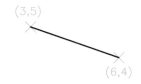

Figure 6-1. A line consists of two endpoints and a segment.

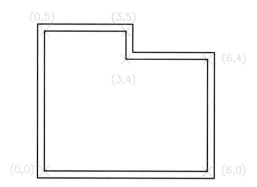

Figure 6-2. A double line can be used to quickly create walls.

Specify next point or [Close/Undo]: **3,4**↵ *(or pick a point on screen)*
Specify next point or [Close/Undo]: **3,5**↵ *(or pick a point on screen)*
Specify next point or [Close/Undo]: **0,5**↵ *(or pick a point on screen)*
Specify next point or [Close/Undo]: **CLOSE**↵ *(or pick a point on screen)*
Command:

Circle

The **CIRCLE** command automates the creation of a circle object. Instead of drawing several small straight-line segments to approximate a circle, this command draws an object based on the mathematical definition of a circle, Figure 6-3. Most CADD software allows you to select from several common methods of defining a circle. These methods include:

- Center and radius.
- Center and diameter.
- Three points on the circle.
- Two points on the circle.
- Radius and two lines or two circles to which the circle should be tangent.

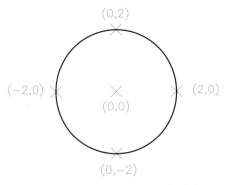

Figure 6-3. There are several ways to define a circle.

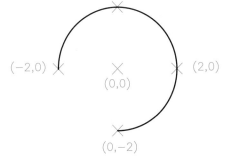

Figure 6-4. There are several ways to define an arc.

AutoCAD Example:

Command: **CIRCLE**↵
Specify center point for circle or [3P/2P/Ttr (tan tan radius)]: **0,0**↵ (*or pick a center point on screen*)
Specify radius of circle or [Diameter]: **DIAMETER**↵
Specify diameter of circle: **4**↵ (*or pick a point on the circle on screen*)
Command:

Arc

An arc is a portion of a circle. Just as the **CIRCLE** command automates the creation of a circle, the **ARC** command automates the creation of an arc, Figure 6-4. Most CADD software allows you to select from several methods of defining an arc. Examples include:

- Three points on the arc.
- Starting point, center, and endpoint.
- Starting point, center, and included angle.
- Starting point, center, and length of chord.
- Starting point, endpoint, and radius.
- Starting point, endpoint, and included angle.
- Starting point, endpoint, and a starting direction.

AutoCAD Example:

Command: **ARC**↵
Specify start point of arc or [Center]: **0,–2**↵ (*or pick a point on screen*)
Specify second point of arc or [Center/End]: **0,2**↵ (*or pick a point on screen*)
Specify end point of arc: **–2,0**↵ (*or pick a point on screen*)
Command:

Rectangle

A square or rectangle can be drawn using the **LINE** command. However, the **RECTANGLE** command automates the process of creating a square or rectangle, Figure 6-5. Most CADD software provides at least two methods for constructing a rectangle. These are specifying the width and height of the rectangle or specifying opposite corners of the rectangle.

AutoCAD Example:

Command: **RECTANGLE**↵
Specify first corner point or [Chamfer/Elevation/Fillet/Thickness/Width]: **1,5**↵ (*or pick a point on screen*)
Specify other corner point or [Dimensions]: **6,3**↵ (*or pick a point on screen*)
Command:

Polygon

The **POLYGON** command automates the construction of a regular polygon. A *regular polygon* is an object with sides of equal length and included angles. The **POLYGON** command can create an object with three or more sides. A common approach used by many CADD programs is to either inscribe the polygon

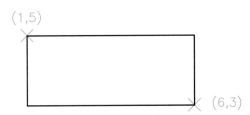

Figure 6-5. You can draw a rectangle by specifying opposite corners.

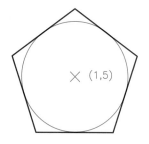

Circumscribed About a Circle   Inscribed Within a Circle

Figure 6-6. A polygon can be circumscribed (left) or inscribed (right).

within a circle or circumscribe it about a circle, Figure 6-6. The information required in these instances is radius of the circle, method desired, and number of sides for the polygon. Another method available in some CADD programs is to define the end points of one side of the polygon and the software generates the remaining sides to create a regular polygon.

AutoCAD Example:

Command: **POLYGON**⏎
Enter number of sides <4>: **5**⏎
Specify center of polygon or [Edge]: **1,5**⏎ *(or pick a point on screen)*
Enter an option [Inscribed in circle/Circumscribed about circle] <I>: **C**⏎
Specify radius of circle: **2**⏎
Command: ⏎
POLYGON Enter number of sides <5>: **5**⏎
Specify center of polygon or [Edge]: **6,5**⏎ *(or pick a point on screen)*
Enter an option [Inscribed in circle/Circumscribed about circle] <C>: **I**⏎
Specify radius of circle: **2**⏎
Command:

Text

You can add text to a drawing using the **TEXT** command. This is important for placing notes, specifications, and other information on a drawing, Figure 6-7. Most CADD packages provide several standard text fonts to choose from. Text generally can be stretched, compressed, obliqued, or mirrored. Placement can be justified left, right, or centered. Text can also be placed at angles.

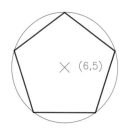

Figure 6-7. Text can be easily added to a drawing.

AutoCAD Example:

Command: **MTEXT**⏎
Current text style: "Standard" Text height: 0.2500
Specify first corner: **2,3**⏎ *(or pick a point on screen)*
Specify opposite corner or [Height/Justify/Line spacing/Rotation/Style/Width]: **9,5**⏎ *(or pick a point on screen)*
(enter the text in the **Multiline Text Editor** *dialog box and then pick the* **OK** *button)*
Command:

Hatch

Hatching is a fundamental part of drafting. In both mechanical and architectural drafting, hatching is used in section views to show cutaway parts and to represent specific materials. In architectural drafting, hatching is often used in pictorial drawings, such as for siding or bricks, Figure 6-8. Hatching is also used on plot plans to represent ground coverings, masonry features, water, and other features.

The **HATCH** command is used to hatch an area of a drawing. Areas to be hatched are selected with the pointing device and elements within the boundary can be excluded, if desired. Most CADD software includes several standard hatch patterns for use with the command. In addition, most CADD software allows you to add more patterns and define your own.

AutoCAD Example:

Command: **BHATCH**⏎

(In the **Boundary Hatch** *dialog box, select a pattern. Then, select the* **Pick Points** *or* **Select Objects** *button. When the dialog box is temporarily hidden, select internal points or pick objects to hatch. Then, press [Enter] to redisplay the dialog box. Pick the* **OK** *button to apply the hatch.)*
Command:

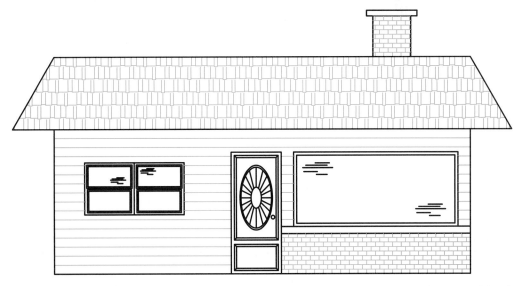

Figure 6-8. Hatch patterns can be used for many features. The hatch patterns on this elevation are shown in color.

Editing and Inquiry Commands

Editing commands allow you to modify drawings in several ways. *Inquiry commands* are designed to list the database records for selected objects; calculate distances, areas, and perimeters; and convert points on the screen to absolute coordinates (or the reverse). Common editing and inquiry commands described in this section include: **ERASE, UNDO, MOVE, COPY, MIRROR, ROTATE, FILLET, CHAMFER, EXTEND, ARRAY, SCALE, LIST, DISTANCE,** and **AREA.**

Erase

The **ERASE** command permanently removes selected objects from the drawing. Many CADD programs provide a "select" option in the command that allows you to select the objects to erase. Also, some programs provide a "last" option that erases the last object drawn.

AutoCAD Example:

Command: **ERASE**↵
Select objects: **LAST**↵
1 found
Select objects: ↵ *(or pick other objects on screen)*
Command:

Undo

The **UNDO** command reverses the last command. If the last command was **ERASE**, the objects that were deleted are restored. You can sequentially step back through previous commands, but you cannot "jump" a command in the sequence. Certain limits are usually applied to this command.

AutoCAD Example:

Command: **ERASE**↵
Select objects: **LAST**↵
1 found
Select objects: ↵
(the last object drawn is erased)
Command: **UNDO**↵
Enter the number of operations to undo or
    [Auto/Control/BEgin/End/Mark/Back] <1>: ↵
ERASE
(the erased object is restored)
Command:

Move

The **MOVE** command allows one or more objects to be moved from the present location to a new one without changing their orientation or size. Generally, you must pick a starting point and a destination point. Relative displacement is often used for this operation. With relative displacement, you pick any starting point. Then, you specify a displacement from that point in terms of units, or units and an angle.

AutoCAD Example:

Command: **MOVE**↵
Select objects: *(pick any number of objects using the cursor)*
Select objects: ↵
Specify base point or displacement: *(pick any point on screen)*
Specify second point of displacement or <use first point as displacement>: **@2,3**↵ *(the @ symbol specifies relative displacement; the object will be moved 2 units on the X axis and 3 units on the Y axis)*
Command:

Copy

The **COPY** command usually functions in much the same way as the **MOVE** command. However, it is used to place copies of the selected objects at the specified location without altering the original objects. Many CADD programs offer a "multiple" option to this command. This option allows multiple copies of the selected objects to be placed in sequence.

AutoCAD Example:

Command: **COPY**↵
Select objects: *(select the objects to copy)*
Select objects: ↵
Specify base point or displacement, or [Multiple]: **MULTIPLE**↵
Specify base point: *(enter coordinates or pick a point to use as the first point of displacement)*
Specify second point of displacement or <use first point as displacement>: *(enter coordinates or pick a second point of displacement for the first copy)*
Specify second point of displacement or <use first point as displacement>:*(enter coordinates or pick a second point of displacement for the second copy)*
Specify second point of displacement or <use first point as displacement>:*(enter coordinates or pick a second point of displacement for the third copy)*
Specify second point of displacement or <use first point as displacement>:↵
Command:

Mirror

The **MIRROR** command draws a mirror image of an existing object about a centerline. This command is especially useful when

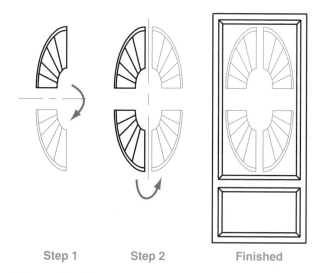

Step 1   Step 2   Finished

Figure 6-9. The scrollwork on this door was first mirrored vertically, then the original and the mirrored copy were mirrored horizontally. The mirrored copies and the final scrollwork on the door are shown here in color.

creating symmetrical objects. For example, if you draw one side of ornate scroll work on a door, you can use the **MIRROR** command to identically reflect the scroll work to the other side of the door, Figure 6-9. The **MIRROR** command in most CADD programs allows you to either keep or delete the original object during the operation. The mirror line can generally be designated.

AutoCAD Example:

Command: **MIRROR**↵
Select objects: *(select the objects to mirror)*
Select objects: ↵
Specify first point of mirror line: *(enter coordinates or pick an endpoint of the line about which to reflect the objects)*
Specify second point of mirror line: *(enter coordinates or pick the second endpoint of the line about which to reflect the objects)*
Delete source objects? [Yes/No] <N>: **NO**↵
Command:

Rotate

The **ROTATE** command is used to alter the orientation of objects on the drawing. Typically, you must specify a center for the rotation. This command is perhaps one of the most used editing commands.

AutoCAD Example:

Command: **ROTATE**↵
Current positive angle in UCS: ANGDIR=counter-clockwise ANGBASE=0
Select objects: *(pick the objects to rotate)*
Select objects: ↵
Specify base point: *(enter coordinates or pick a point about which to rotate the objects)*
Specify rotation angle or [Reference]: *(enter an angle or drag the cursor to the desired rotation)*
Command:

Scale

The size of existing objects can be changed using the **SCALE** command. When using the **SCALE** command, most CADD programs require you to specify a base point for the operation. This point is generally on the object, often the center of the object or a reference corner.

Some CADD programs are *parametric.* This means that you can change the base size parameter, or any other parameter, of the object without using the **SCALE** command. For example, in a parametric program you can scale a Ø5 circle up by 50% by simply changing its diameter to 7.5 without using the **SCALE** command.

AutoCAD Example:

Command: **SCALE**↵
Select objects: *(pick the objects to scale)*
Select objects:↵
Specify base point: *(enter coordinates or select a point about which the objects will be scaled)*
Specify scale factor or [Reference]: **1.5**↵
Command:

Fillet

A *fillet* is a smoothly fitted internal arc of a specified radius between two lines, arcs, or circles. A *round* is just like a fillet except it is an exterior arc, Figure 6-10. Most manufactured parts, including those for architectural applications, have some fillets or rounds. The **FILLET** command is used to place fillets and rounds onto the drawing. After drawing the curve, the command trims the original objects to perfectly meet the curve.

AutoCAD Example:

Command: **FILLET**↵
Current settings: Mode = TRIM, Radius = 0.2500
Select first object or [Polyline/Radius/Trim]: **RADIUS**↵
Specify fillet radius <0.2500>: **.50**↵
Select first object or [Polyline/Radius/Trim]: *(select one of the two objects between which the fillet or round is to be placed)*
Select second object: *(select the second of the two objects between which the fillet or round is to be placed)*
Command:

Chamfer

The **CHAMFER** command is very similar to the **FILLET** command. However, instead of a curve, a straight line is placed between the chamfered lines. Just as with the **FILLET** command, the original lines are trimmed to meet the straight line (chamfer). Depending on the CADD program, this command may require that the two objects to be chamfered are lines, not arc segments.

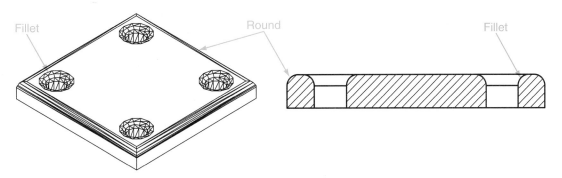

Figure 6-10. Fillets and rounds on a drawing.

AutoCAD Example:

Command: **CHAMFER**⏎
(TRIM mode) Current chamfer Dist1 = 0.5000, Dist2
    = 0.5000
Select first line or
    [Polyline/Distance/Angle/Trim/Method]:
    DISTANCE⏎
Specify first chamfer distance <0.5000>: **.25**⏎
Specify second chamfer distance <0.2500>:⏎
Select first line or
    [Polyline/Distance/Angle/Trim/Method]: *(pick the
    first line to chamfer)*
Select second line: *(pick the second line to chamfer)*
Command:

Extend

The **EXTEND** command is used to lengthen an object to end precisely at a boundary edge. The boundary edge is defined by one or more objects in the drawing. Most CADD programs place limitations on which types of objects can be extended. In addition, there are usually only certain types of objects that can be used as boundary edges.

AutoCAD Example:

Command: **EXTEND**⏎
Current settings: Projection=UCS Edge=None
Select boundary edges… *(pick the objects to use as
    a boundary)*
Select objects: 1 found
Select objects: ⏎
Select object to extend or shift-select to trim or
    [Project/Edge/Undo]: *(select the objects to extend
    to the boundary)*
Select object to extend or shift-select to trim or
    [Project/Edge/Undo]:⏎
Command:

Array

The **ARRAY** command is essentially a copy function. It makes multiple copies of selected objects in a rectangular or circular (polar) pattern. See Figure 6-11. CADD programs that have the capability of drawing in three dimensions typically have an option of the **ARRAY** command to create arrays in 3D.

AutoCAD Example:

Command: **-ARRAY**⏎ *(If you enter the command
    without the hyphen, the array settings are made in
    a dialog box.)*

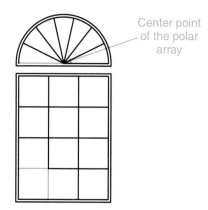

Center point of the polar array

Figure 6-11. The panels of glass in the semicircle were drawn as a polar array. The rectangular panes of glass were drawn as a rectangular array. The original objects are shown in color.

Select objects: *(pick the objects to array)*
Enter the type of array [Rectangular/Polar] <P>: **R**⏎
Enter the number of rows (---) <1>: **4**⏎
Enter the number of columns (¦¦¦) <1>: **3**⏎
Enter the distance between rows or specify unit cell
    (---): **5**⏎
Specify the distance between columns (¦¦¦): **5**⏎
Command: **-ARRAY**⏎
Select objects: *(pick the objects to array)*
Enter the type of array [Rectangular/Polar] <R>: **P**⏎
Specify center point of array: *(pick a point about
    which the objects will be arrayed)*
Enter the number of items in the array: **8**⏎
Specify the angle to fill (+=ccw, −=cw) <360>: **180**⏎
Rotate arrayed objects? [Yes/No] <Y>: **NO**⏎
Command:

List/Properties

The **LIST** and **PROPERTIES** commands show data related to an object. For example, the properties for a line may include the coordinates of the endpoints, length, angle from start point, and change in X and Y coordinates from the start point. These commands can be useful in determining the type of object, which layer it is drawn on, and its color and linetype settings.

AutoCAD Example:

Command: **LIST**⏎
Select objects: 1 found
Select objects:⏎
*(The text window is display listing the properties of
the selected object.)*
Command:

Distance

The **DISTANCE** command measures the distance and angle between two points. The result is displayed in drawing units. This command is very useful in determining lengths, angles, and distances on a drawing without actually placing dimensions.

AutoCAD Example:

Command: **DIST**↵
Specify first point: (*pick the first endpoint of the distance to measure*)
Specify second point: (*pick the second endpoint of the distance to measure*)
Distance = 9.1788, Angle in XY Plane = 29, Angle from XY Plane = 0
Delta X = 8.0000, Delta Y = 4.5000, Delta Z = 0.0000
Command:

Area

The **AREA** command is used to calculate the area of an enclosed space. Often, you can select a closed object or simply pick points on an imaginary boundary. Most CADD programs allow you to remove islands, or internal areas, Figure 6-12. The **AREA** command has many applications in architecture, from calculating the square footage of a house to determining the surface area of a garage floor, which is needed to determine the number of "yards" of concrete for the floor.

AutoCAD Example:

Command: **AREA**↵
Specify first corner point or [Object/Add/Subtract]: **ADD**↵
Specify first corner point or [Object/Subtract]: (*pick the first point of the area, as shown in Figure 6-12*)
Specify next corner point or press ENTER for total (ADD mode): (*pick the next point of the area, as shown in Figure 6-12*)
Specify next corner point or press ENTER for total (ADD mode): (*pick the next point of the area, as shown in Figure 6-12*)
Specify next corner point or press ENTER for total (ADD mode): (*pick the next point of the area, as shown in Figure 6-12*)
Specify next corner point or press ENTER for total (ADD mode): (*pick the next point of the area, as shown in Figure 6-12*)

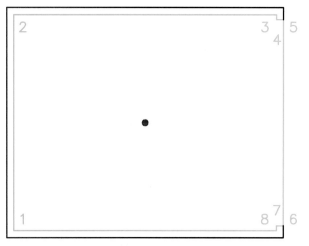

Figure 6-12. The **AREA** command can be used to quickly calculate how many square feet of tile are required for this garage floor. The surface to be covered in tile is outlined in color. Notice the drain that will be removed from the calculation.

Specify next corner point or press ENTER for total (ADD mode): (*pick the next point of the area, as shown in Figure 6-12*)
Specify next corner point or press ENTER for total (ADD mode): (*pick the next point of the area, as shown in Figure 6-12*)
Specify next corner point or press ENTER for total (ADD mode): (*pick the last point of the area, as shown in Figure 6-12*)
Specify next corner point or press ENTER for total (ADD mode):↵
Area = 657.3750, Perimeter = 103.5000
Total area = 657.3750
Specify first corner point or [Object/Subtract]: **SUBTRACT**↵
Specify first corner point or [Object/Add]: **OBJECT**↵
(SUBTRACT mode) Select objects: (*select the internal circle shown in Figure 6-12*)
Area = 1.7671, Circumference = 4.7124
Total area = 655.6079
 (SUBTRACT mode) Select objects:↵
Specify first corner point or [Object/Add]:↵
Command:

Display Control Commands

Display control commands are used to control how a drawing is displayed on the screen. These commands control the position and magnification of the screen window, save views for later use, and redraw or "clean up" the screen. Commands covered in this section that are common to CADD packages include **ZOOM**, **PAN**, **VIEW**, and **REDRAW/REGENERATE**.

Zoom

The **ZOOM** command increases or decreases the magnification factor, which results in a change in the apparent size of objects on the screen. However, the actual size of the objects does not change. You can think of this as using the zoom feature on a video camera or binoculars. **ZOOM** may be the most-used display control command. Generally, the **ZOOM** command has several options that may include zooming to the drawing limits or extents, dynamically zooming, and zooming by a magnification factor.

AutoCAD Example:

Command: **ZOOM**⏎
Specify corner of window, enter a scale factor (nX or nXP), or
    [All/Center/Dynamic/Extents/Previous/Scale/Window] <real time>: **.5**⏎
(the magnification factor is reduced by 50%)
Specify corner of window, enter a scale factor (nX or nXP), or
    [All/Center/Dynamic/Extents/Previous/Scale/Window] <real time>: **PREVIOUS**⏎
(the previous magnification factor is restored)
Command:

Pan

The **PAN** command moves the drawing in the display window from one location to another. It does not change the magnification factor. If you think of the drawing as being on a sheet of paper behind the screen, panning is moving the sheet so a different part of the drawing can be seen, Figure 6-13. The **PAN** command is useful when you have a magnification factor that you like, but there are objects that are "off" the screen.

AutoCAD Example:

Command: **PAN**⏎
Press ESC or ENTER to exit, or right-click to display shortcut menu.
(This is AutoCAD's "realtime" pan function; pick,

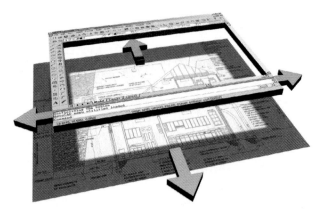

Figure 6-13. You can think of panning as moving a drawing sheet around underneath the CADD drawing screen. Only the portion of the drawing directly "below" the drawing area will be visible. (Eric K. Augspurger; print courtesy of SoftPlan Systems, Inc.)

hold, and drag to pan the drawing; then press [Enter] *or* [Esc] *to end the command.)*
Command:

View

When constant switching back and forth between views and magnification factors on a large drawing is required, the **VIEW** command can be used to speed the process. This command allows you to save a "snapshot" of the current drawing display. The "snapshot" includes the view and the magnification factor. You can then save the view and quickly recall it later. This can be much faster than zooming and panning to return to the desired view.

AutoCAD Example:

(Pan and zoom the drawing so the desired view is displayed.)
Command: **VIEW**⏎
*(The **View** dialog box is displayed; pick the **Named Views** tab and then the **New...** button; type a name in the **New View** dialog box that is displayed; then close both dialog boxes.)*
Command:

Redraw / Regenerate

The **REDRAW** command "cleans up" the display by removing marker blips, etc. Some commands automatically redraw the screen, as when a grid is removed or visible layers are changed. However, sometimes it is useful to request a redraw when other operations are being performed. The **REGENERATE** command forces the program to recalculate the objects in the entire drawing and redraw the screen. This operation takes longer than **REDRAW**, especially on large or complex drawings.

AutoCAD Example:

Command: **REGEN**↵
Regenerating model.
Command:

Dimensioning Commands

One of the advantages of using CADD is automated dimensioning. In almost all drafting applications, the drawing must be dimensioned to show lengths, distances, and angles between features on the objects (parts). The five basic types of dimensioning commands are **LINEAR**, **ANGULAR**, **DIAMETER**, **RADIUS**, and **LEADER**, Figure 6-14.

A linear dimension measures a straight line distance. The distance may be horizontal, vertical, or at an angle. Typically, you have several choices on how the dimension text is placed. The text may be aligned with the dimension lines, always horizontal on the drawing, or placed at a specified angle. In architectural drafting, dimension text for a linear dimension is *never* perpendicular to the dimension line.

An angular dimension measures the angle between two nonparallel lines. The lines can be actual objects or imaginary lines between an origin and two endpoints. Typically, you have the same text-placement options as with linear dimensions. In architectural drafting, dimension text for arcs and angles may be unidirectional (always horizontal).

The diameter and radius dimensions are very similar. A diameter dimension measures the distance across a circle through its center. A radius dimension measures the distance from the center of an arc to a point on that arc. A radius dimension can also be used for a circle, but is not typically used in that manner.

A leader is used to provide a specific or local note. A leader consists of an arrowhead (in some form), a leader line, and the note. Often, an optional shoulder is placed on the end of the leader before the note. In architectural drafting, a shoulder is always used.

AutoCAD Example:

Command: **DIM**↵
Dim: **HORIZONTAL**↵
Specify first extension line origin or <select object>: *(pick the first endpoint of the horizontal distance)*
Specify second extension line origin: *(pick the second endpoint of the horizontal distance)*
Specify dimension line location or [Mtext/Text/Angle]: *(drag the dimension to the correct location)*
Enter dimension text <15.500>: *(enter a value for the dimension text or press [Enter] to accept the default actual distance)*
Dim: **VERTICAL**↵
Specify first extension line origin or <select object>: *(pick the first endpoint of the vertical distance)*
Specify second extension line origin: *(pick the second endpoint of the vertical distance)*
Specify dimension line location or [Mtext/Text/Angle]: *(drag the dimension to the correct location)*
Enter dimension text <6.000>: *(enter the dimension value, the value provided is the actual on-screen dimension)*
Dim: *(press [Esc] to exit dimension mode)*
Command:

Drawing Aids

Drawing aids are designed to speed up the drawing process and, at the same time, maintain accuracy. Most CADD packages

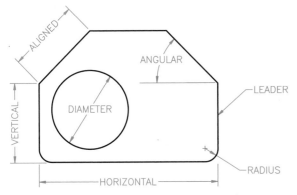

Figure 6-14. There are several types of dimensions that may appear on a drawing.

provide several different drawing aids. These can range from a display grid or viewport ruler to various forms of snap. The commands discussed in this section include **GRID**, **SNAP**, and **ORTHO**.

Grid

A *display grid* is a visual guideline in the viewport, much like the lines on graph paper. How the grid appears when displayed depends on which CADD program you are using. For example, AutoCAD uses dots to show the grid. See Figure 6-15. In most CADD programs with a grid function, you can change the density, or spacing, of the grid.

Some CADD programs also have rulers that can be displayed along the horizontal and vertical edge of the drawing screen. The display of these rulers is often controlled by a single command. However, the display may also be part of an **OPTIONS** or **SETTINGS** command, depending on the CADD program.

AutoCAD Example:

Command: **GRID**↵
Specify grid spacing(X) or [ON/OFF/Snap/Aspect]
    <0.5000>: **.25**↵
Command: **GRID**↵
Specify grid spacing(X) or [ON/OFF/Snap/Aspect]
    <0.2500>: **OFF**↵
Command:

Snap

Snap is a function that allows the cursor to "grab on to" certain locations on the screen. There are two basic types of snap. These are a grid snap and object snaps. A *grid snap* uses an invisible grid, much like the visible grid produced by the **GRID** command. When grid snap is turned on, the cursor "jumps" to the closest snap grid point. In most CADD programs, it is impossible to select a location that is not one of the snap grid points when grid snap is on. Just as with a grid, you can typically set the snap grid density or spacing.

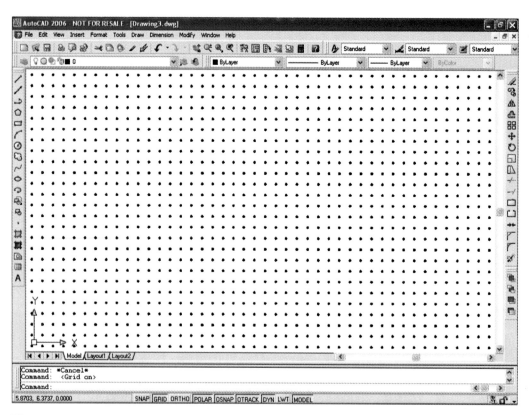

Figure 6-15. AutoCAD shows its grid as a matrix of dots.

An *object snap* allows the cursor to "jump" to certain locations on existing objects. Most CADD programs have several different object snaps. These can include endpoint, center, midpoint, perpendicular, tangent, and intersection, as well as many others. Depending on the CADD program you are using, there may be additional object snaps available. Generally, you can turn on the object snaps that you want to use while another command is active. For example, suppose you have a line already drawn and you want to draw another line from its exact midpoint. You can enter the **LINE** command, temporarily set the midpoint object snap, and pick the first endpoint of the second line at the midpoint of the first line.

Object snaps provide a very quick way of accurately connecting to existing objects. They are likely the most important feature of CADD software to ensure accuracy. Think twice before buying CADD software without object snaps.

AutoCAD Example:

Command: **LINE**↵
Specify first point: **MID**↵
of *(move the cursor close to the line from which to select the midpoint; when the snap cursor is displayed, pick to set the endpoint of the new line)*
Specify next point or [Undo]: *(move the cursor to the second endpoint of the new line and pick)*
Specify next point or [Undo]:↵
Command:

Ortho

The **ORTHO** command ensures that all lines and traces drawn using a pointing device are orthogonal (vertical or horizontal) with respect to the current drawing plane. The **ORTHO** command is useful in drawing "square" lines that will be later extended or trimmed to meet other objects. The command must be turned off to draw a line at an angle unless coordinates are manually entered.

AutoCAD Example:

Command: **ORTHO**↵
Enter mode [ON/OFF] <ON>: **ON**↵
(Lines can now only be drawn horizontal and vertical unless coordinates are entered.)
Command:

Layers

One of the fundamental tools in any good CADD program is the ability to draw on and manage layers. A *layer* is a virtual piece of paper on which CADD objects are placed. All objects on all layers, or sheets of paper, are visible on top of each other. If you are familiar with traditional (manual) drafting, you can think of layers as vellum overlays. Layers can be turned on and off, resulting in the display of only those objects needed. For example, in a floor plan, you may have a layer with the walls, one with the electrical plan, and one with the plumbing plan. Then, you can turn off the plumbing plan layer and only the walls and electrical plan are displayed.

Most CADD programs have a **LAYER** command that allows you to create and manage layers. Generally, you can assign a unique layer name and color to each layer. You can also use the **LAYER** command to control the visibility of layers. In addition, some CADD programs allow you advanced control over layers. For example, some CADD programs allow you to prevent certain layers from printing.

Proper layer management is very important to effective CADD drawing. This is especially true when the drawing is jointly worked on by several drafters, designers, or engineers. In an effort to standardize layer use in industry, several organizations have attempted to develop layer naming/usage standards. There is not one universally accepted standard. However, the American Institute of Architects (AIA) has developed *CAD Layer Guidelines*. These guidelines are used by many organizations, or used as a basis for an organization's own standards.

The AIA layer naming standards use a code based on a discipline, major group, minor group, and status. The discipline is a single letter used to indicate an industry, such as A for architectural or L for landscaping. The discipline code is followed by a hyphen and then a four letter major group, such as WALL for walls or FIXT for plumbing fixtures. The major group code is followed by a hyphen and then the minor group or status field. The minor group can itself be followed by the status field. The minor group is another four letter code that further defines the major group. The status field is a four character code that indicates if the features on that layer are new construction, remodeled features, or existing features that are to be retained. The minor group and status field are optional.

For example, following the AIA layer naming standard, a layer may be named A-WALL-FUTR. The objects drawn on this layer represent an architectural application (A). They are walls (WALL) or related to walls that are for future construction (FUTR).

It is important to follow whatever standards your company, department, or client require. While you should always attempt to follow accepted industry standards, such as the AIA guidelines, it is more important that every one working on a project follow the same convention no matter *what* that convention may be. For example, instead of following the AIA conventions, you and several coworkers may adopt a simple naming convention such as WALLS, FOUNDATION, and LANDSCAPE. If this layer naming scheme adequately meets your needs, then adopt it and make sure everyone follows the convention.

AutoCAD Example:

Command: **LAYER**⏎
(*In the* **Layer Properties Manager** *dialog box that is displayed, pick the* **New** *button to create a new layer, pick a color swatch to change a layer's display color, or make on-off and layer printing settings.*)
Command:

Colors and Linetypes

Another important "management" aspect of CADD programs is object display color. At a very simple level, object display colors help to visually catalog the objects in a drawing. For example, if all objects in a drawing are displayed in the same color, it can be hard to identify the individual features. On the other hand, if all walls are displayed in red, all doors are displayed in yellow, and all windows are displayed in green, at a glance anybody who is familiar with this color scheme can determine what is represented. Just as with layer names, it is important to adopt a color usage convention and make sure everybody sticks to it.

Often, object display colors are determined by the layer on which they are drawn. This is one reason that layer conventions are so important, as described in the previous section. However, most CADD programs allow you to "override" this setting and assign a specific display color to an object, regardless of which layer it is on. The command used to change an object display color can be **CHANGE**, **COLOR**, **PROPERTIES**, or another command. The exact command will be determined by the CADD program you are using.

Managing the types of lines used on a drawing is also important. Fortunately, there is an almost universally accepted practice called the Alphabet of Lines. This practice is covered in detail in Chapter 4. You should always follow the Alphabet of Lines. Just because you use CADD to create a drawing does not remove your responsibility to follow this practice. Most CADD programs provide several linetypes that conform to the Alphabet of Lines. You can typically adjust the scale of each line (or all lines) so your particular application better conforms. Do not let the ease at which lines can be drawn "slide" into bad drafting habits. *Always follow the Alphabet of Lines.*

As with colors, most CADD programs allow you to assign linetypes to individual objects. You can also generally assign a linetype based on which layer the object is currently "residing" on. While the Alphabet of Lines provides clear direction on which linetypes to use, be sure to develop a convention based on *how* the linetypes are assigned. Choose to assign linetypes "by layer" or "by object," or some combination of the two, and then be sure everybody follows that convention.

Blocks and Attributes

Blocks are special objects that can best be thought of as symbols inserted into a drawing. Most CADD systems support blocks. In addition, the block function of most CADD systems support a feature called attributes. An *attribute* is text information saved with the block when it is inserted into a drawing. For example, you may create a block that consists of all lines you would normally draw to represent a case-molded window. In addition to creating the block, you assign attributes to the block describing the window size, style, and manufacturer. See Figure 6-16A.

Attributes are often assigned to a block when it is created. However, another feature supported by many CADD programs is to prompt the user for attributes when the block is inserted, Figure 6-16B. This allows a single block, or symbol, to serve for many different sizes, styles, manufacturers, etc., for similar applications. Using the window example above, you may draw a generic window and prompt the user for a size, style, and manufacturer when the block is inserted.

One of the biggest advantages of using blocks and attributes is the ability to automatically generate schedules. For example, if you insert all windows as blocks with correctly defined attributes, some CADD systems can automatically generate a window schedule that can be used for design, estimating, and purchasing. With some CADD programs, this "generator" is within the program itself while other CADD programs link this function to database software, such as Excel or Lotus 1-2-3.

In addition to the advantage of automated schedules, blocks save time. Once you have spent the time to create the symbol, it is saved to a symbols library. A *symbols library* is a collection of blocks that are typically related, such as plumbing symbols, bathroom symbols, or electrical symbols. Then, the block can be inserted over and over. This saves the time of redrawing the symbol each time you need it. Blocks can save time even if attributes are not assigned to them.

AutoCAD Example:

Command: **ATTDEF**↵
*(In the **Attribute Definition** dialog box, enter a name to appear on screen in the **Tag:** text field, a prompt to appear on the command line in the **Prompt:** field, and a default value in the **Value:** field; then, select the **Pick Point<** button and specify where the attribute will be inserted; finally, pick **OK** in the dialog box to create the attribute.)*
Command: **WBLOCK**↵
*(In the **Write Block** dialog box, pick the **Select objects** button and pick the objects to include in the block on screen, including the attribute; then, complete the block definition in the **Write Block** dialog box and pick the **OK** button.)*
Command: **INSERT**↵
(Select the block you created; when prompted, enter information for the attributes.)
Command:

3D Drawing and Viewing Commands

When CADD programs were first developed, they were used to create two-dimensional (2D) drawings. This was the natural progression from traditional (manual) drafting,

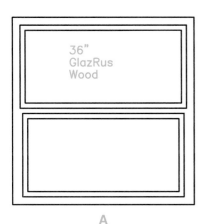

Command: **INSERT**↵
*(In the **INSERT** dialog box, pick the block)*
Specify insertion point or
   [Scale/X/Y/Z/Rotate/PScale/PX/PY/PZ/PRotate]:
   (specify an insertion point)
Enter attribute values
Enter window width: <36">:↵
Type manufacture name: <GlazRus>:↵
Enter wood or vinyl: <Wood>:↵
Command:

A   B

Figure 6-16. A—This window block contains attributes, which have values assigned. B—The AutoCAD command sequence for inserting the block and assigning attribute values.

which is strictly 2D on paper. As computers and CADD programs became more advanced, three-dimensional (3D) capabilities were added. At first, these capabilities made it easier to draw 3D representations, such as isometrics and perspectives, but these are really 2D drawings. Eventually, "true" 3D modeling capabilities were added to CADD programs. These features allow you to design, model, analyze, and in some cases "premachine" a part all within the computer.

Isometric Drawing

An isometric drawing is a traditional 2D pictorial drawing. It shows a 3D representation of an object, but it is really only two dimensional, Figure 6-17A. If you could rotate the "paper" computer screen, there would be no part of the object behind the current drawing plane, Figure 6-17B. Some CADD programs have drawing aids to help make isometric drawings. These drawing aids typically are a rotated grid, orthographic cursor, and snap representing the three isometric planes (top, left, right). The way in which these drawing aids are activated varies with the CADD program being used.

3D Modeling

Another type of 3D drawing is called *3D modeling.* This is "true" 3D where objects are created with a width, depth, and height. Unlike isometric drawing, if you rotate the screen "paper," you can see "behind" the object. See Figure 6-18. There are two general types of 3D models—surface and solid.

Surface modeling creates 3D objects by drawing a skin, often over a wireframe. A *wireframe* is a group of lines that represent the edges of a 3D model, but does not have a skin or "thickness." Surface modeling is used for rendering and animation. However, it is not often used for engineering applications because a surface model does not have volume or mass properties.

Solid modeling creates 3D objects by generating a volume. If you think of surface modeling as blowing up a balloon to obtain a

final shape, solid modeling is obtaining the final shape by filling it with water. A solid model can be analyzed for mass, volume, material properties, and many other data. Many CADD packages that can produce solid models also allow you to create cross sections, which is hard or impossible to do with a surface model. In addition, a solid model can be rendered and imported into many animation software packages.

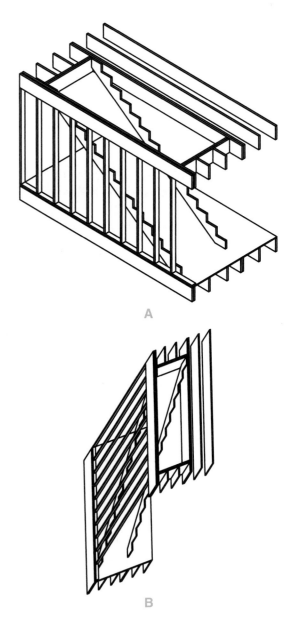

Figure 6-17. A—An isometric drawing of roughed-in stair stringers. This is a 2D isometric drawing. B—When the isometric drawing is viewed from a different viewpoint, you can see that it is two dimensional. Compare this to Figure 6-18B. (Eric K. Augspurger)

3D Views

CADD software that is 3D-capable typically has a **HIDE** command to remove lines that would normally be hidden in the current view. These are the lines that would be drawn as hidden lines in a 2D drawing. Hiding lines can help visualize the 3D model. The **HIDE** command is used in Figure 6-18.

In addition to hiding lines, you also need to be able to see the objects from different angles. It would be nearly impossible to create a 3D model of any complexity only being able to see a top view, for example. It may seem as if each CADD program has its own unique way of displaying different 3D views. Some CADD programs have preset isometric views. Others allow you to dynamically change the view. Yet other programs have both of these options and more. However, the basic goal of all of these functions is the same. You need to "rotate" the point from which you are viewing the model to better see another part or feature on the object. The object in Figure 6-18A is shown from a preset isometric viewing point. In Figure 6-18B, however, a dynamic viewing command was used to rotate the viewpoint.

AutoCAD Example:

Command: **3DORBIT**↵
Press ESC or ENTER to exit, or right-click to display shortcut-menu.
(*Using the cursor, pick and drag to change the view; press* [Esc] *to exit the command.*)
Command:

3D Animation and Rendering Commands

CADD programs that have 3D drawing capability generally have a command that allows you to create a hidden-line-removed display. This is discussed in the previous section. However, to create a more realistic representation of the 3D objects, most CADD systems have the ability to shade or color the model. This is called *rendering.* Rendering has

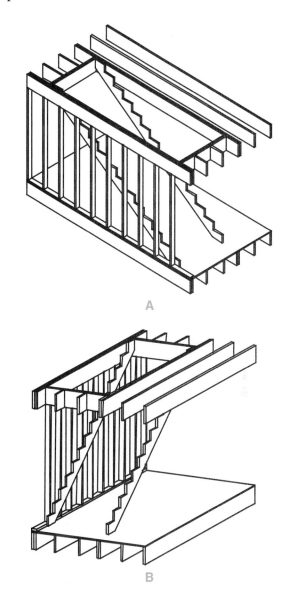

Figure 6-18. A—An isometric view of a 3D model. Compare this to Figure 6-16A. The two views are identical. B—When the 3D model is viewed from a different viewpoint, you can see that it is truly three dimensional. This viewpoint is the exact same viewpoint for the 2D isometric drawing in Figure 6-17B. (Eric K. Augspurger)

traditionally been done by hand with paint, charcoal, chalk, pencils, and ink. However, just as the process of creating a drawing has been automated with CADD, so too has the process of rendering the drawing. Generally, there is a **MATERIAL** command used to define and apply surface textures to objects. There is also typically a **RENDER** command used to "color" the drawing. Many high-end CADD programs can produce very realistic renderings, given enough "drafting" time to properly set up lights and materials, Figure 6-19.

Some CADD programs have the ability to add movement to objects in the drawing to create an animation. However, often the software used to create the drawing is not the software used to animate the model. For example, you may complete a 3D model using AutoCAD and then import the model into 3D Studio to add movement to the objects and render an animation. An *animation* is a series of still images played sequentially at a very fast rate, such as 30 frames per second, Figure 6-20. There are very small differences between each frame and, when each frame is viewed quickly, the brain "mistakes" these differences as movement. Generally, there is an **ANIMATE** command used to add movement to the objects and a **RENDER** command to render the animation.

Figure 6-19. This rendering shows a nice setup of lights and materials. Good planning and a lot of time were required to create this model.
(Helmuth A. Geiser, Member AIBD)

Figure 6-20. An animation is really a series of images played together at a fast rate. The slight differences between each image is interpreted by the brain as motion. There is not much difference between "neighboring" frames, however, over the length of the animation you can see that the window is opening and closing.
(Eric K. Augspurger)

Internet Resources

www.autodesk.com
Autodesk, Inc., publisher of AutoCAD and Autodesk VIZ

www.bentley.com/products
MicroStation publisher

www.cadalyst.com
Cadalyst magazine

www.cadence.com
CADENCE magazine

www.discreet.com
Discreet, publisher of 3ds max

www.ptc.com
Parametric Technology Corporation, publisher of Pro/ENGINEER, Pro/MECHANICAL, Pro/DESKTOP

Review Questions – Chapter 6

Write your answers on a separate sheet of paper. Do not write in this book.

1. Define *commands* as related to CADD.
2. List the five general groups of CADD commands.
3. Give three common methods for entering commands.
4. _____ commands allow you to create objects on the computer screen.
5. List three commands that belong to the general group in Question 4.
6. In general, what do editing commands allow you to do?
7. _____ commands are designed to list the selected database records for selected objects; calculate distances, areas, and perimeters; and convert points on the screen to absolute coordinates (or the reverse).
8. Describe the function of the **UNDO** command.
9. Give an example of where you might use the **MIRROR** command.
10. Define *fillet*.
11. Define *round*.
12. For what are display control commands used?
13. List three display control commands.

14. List the five basic types of dimensioning commands.
15. What is the purpose of drawing aids?
16. Explain layers.
17. List three "management" aspects of CADD drawings that should be addressed.
18. Define *block* and *attribute*.
19. An isometric drawing shows a 3D representation of an object in _____.
20. _____ create 3D objects by drawing a skin, often over a wireframe.
21. _____ create 3D objects by generating a volume.
22. For what is the **HIDE** command available in most CADD systems used?
23. Define *rendering*.
24. What does the **MATERIAL** command allow you to do?
25. How is movement created in an animation?

Suggested Activities

1. Using the reference section of this text for samples, create a basic symbols library. Create one symbols library that includes symbols from a variety of applications, such as plumbing, doors, windows, and electrical.

2. Identify the 3D commands in your school's CADD software. Create a list of the command name and what function it performs.

3. Obtain electronic examples of AEC renderings or animations. The Internet can be a great source for this, but be sure to download only those files labeled as "freeware" or "freely distribute." All others are copyrighted material.

4. Collect as many different examples of 3D computer-generated illustrations as you can. Search through books and magazines and bring them to class to share with your classmates. Classify each one as a wireframe, "true" 3D model, or possibly an animation.

Section III
Room and Space Planning

7 Room Planning—Sleeping Area and Bath Facilities

8 Room Planning—Living Area

9 Room Planning—Service Area

Room Planning—Sleeping Area and Bath Facilities

Objectives

After studying this chapter, you will be able to:

➤ Discuss factors that are important in the design of bedrooms.

➤ Plan the size and location of closets for a typical residence.

➤ Plan a furniture arrangement for a room.

➤ List requirements to make a bedroom accessible to the disabled.

➤ Implement important design considerations for bathrooms.

➤ Plan a bathroom that follows solid design principles.

➤ List the requirements to make a bathroom accessible to the disabled.

Key Terms

1/2 Bath	Living Area
3/4 Bath	Ribbon Windows
Full Bath	Service Area
Ground Fault Circuit	Sleeping Area
Interrupter (GFCI)	Split Bedroom Plan

Areas of a Residence

A residential structure can be divided into three basic areas: the sleeping area, living area, and service area, Figure 7-1. The *sleeping area* is where the family sleeps, rests, and bathes. The *living area* is where the family relaxes, entertains guests, dines, and meets together. The living area is discussed in detail in Chapter 8. The *service area* is the part of the house where food is prepared, clothes are laundered, goods are stored, the car is parked, and equipment for upkeep of the house is stored. The service area is discussed in Chapter 9.

These three basic areas are generally divided into rooms. Rooms provide privacy and help to separate and contain various activities. A house designer must understand the purpose for each room if a functional plan is to be developed.

In addition to the purpose of the room, the designer must know how the room will be used and by whom. According to the report *Americans with Disabilities, 1997 P70-73* issued in February 2001 by the US Census Bureau, 2.2 million people age 15 and older use a wheelchair and another 6.4 million use a cane, walker, crutches, or other aid. AARP, formerly called The American Association of Retired Persons, reports that there were 76 million Americans over the age of 50 in 2000; 35 million over the age of 65 according to the US Census. These numbers are projected to double in the next few years. Therefore, it is important to consider how all areas of the home can be made accessible to people with special needs, including the disabled and elderly.

Figure 7-1. A residence can be divided into three basic areas: the sleeping area, living area, and service area.

Designing with CADD

The design of bedroom and bathroom spaces may be developed easily and rapidly using modern CADD systems. Many of the elements used in the design of these rooms and furniture arrangements are commonly available as symbols. Often, manufacturers can supply CADD symbols of their specific products. Custom symbols can also be developed for use when needed. In addition, proposed designs can be rendered and shown to clients. Figure 7-2 shows a CADD-generated rendering of a large bathroom.

Figure 7-2. This CADD-generated presentation drawing demonstrates the usefulness of computer-generated images to describe a design idea. (SoftPlan Systems, Inc.)

Sleeping Area

Usually about one-third of the house is dedicated to the sleeping area. This area includes bedrooms, baths, dressing rooms, and nurseries. Normally, the sleeping area is in a quiet part of the house away from traffic and other noise. If possible, the sleeping area should have a south or southwest orientation so that it may take advantage of cool summer breezes, which usually prevail from this direction.

Bedrooms

Bedrooms are so important that houses are frequently categorized by the number they contain, such as "two-bedroom," "three-bedroom," or "four-bedroom." The size of the family usually determines the number of bedrooms needed. Ideally, each person would have their own bedroom. In the case of a couple with no children living at home, at least two bedrooms are desirable. The second bedroom could be used as a guest room and for other activities when there are no guests, Figure 7-3. A home with only one bedroom may be difficult to sell. Three-bedroom homes usually have the greatest sales potential. A three-bedroom home can provide enough space for a family of four. It may be wise to include an extra bedroom in the plan that can be used for other purposes until needed, Figure 7-4. It is usually more economical to add an extra room at the outset rather than expand later.

Grouping bedrooms together in a separate wing or level of the house affords solitude and privacy, Figure 7-5. A plan called the *split bedroom plan* separates the master bedroom from the remaining bedrooms to provide even greater privacy. Another plan might have a bedroom in another area of the home for an employee, live-in relative, or overnight guests. Each bedroom should have its own access to the hall. An attempt should be made to place each bedroom close to a bathroom. Some bedrooms may have their own private baths. A bedroom used by an older or handicapped person is more convenient if it contains its own bath.

Figure 7-3. This personalized bedroom provides mirrored doors so the young ballerina can practice. (Stanley Hardware)

Figure 7-4. An extra bedroom may be used as a den or for guests. (E. Uecker, Radiant Heat, Inc.)

Size and Furniture

One of the first problems in designing a bedroom is determining its size. How big is a "large" bedroom? How little is a "small" bedroom? The Federal Housing Administration (FHA) recommends 100 square feet as the minimum size. A small bedroom is shown in Figure 7-6. It has 99 square feet and the bare essentials in furniture. An average-size bedroom contains between 125 and 175 square feet, Figure 7-7. Such a room provides ample space for a double or twin bed, chest of drawers,

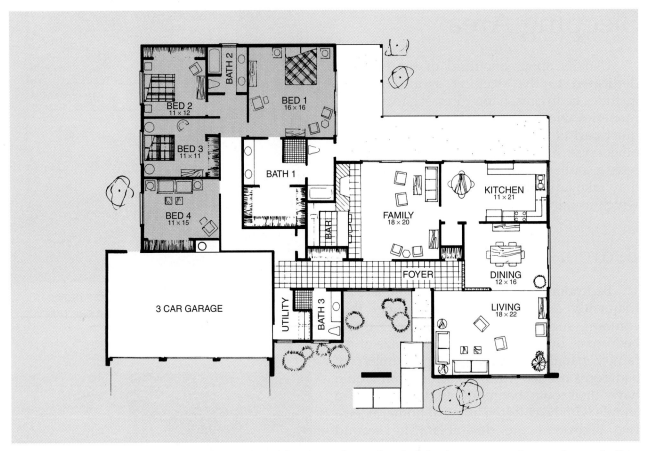

Figure 7-5. Bedrooms should be clustered together in a wing or level of the house away from noise and other activities.

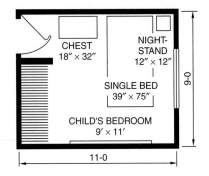

Figure 7-6. A small bedroom with the minimum: single bed, night stand, and chest of drawers.

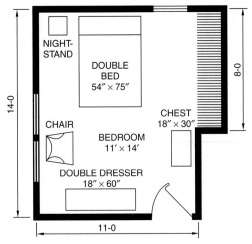

Figure 7-7. A medium-size bedroom contains room for a double bed, chest, chair, double dresser, and nightstand.

dresser, and other small pieces of furniture. A large bedroom has over 175 square feet of floor space, Figure 7-8. A room of this size provides space for additional furniture. A desk, chair, or television set may be included as bedroom furniture. The largest bedroom is usually considered to be the master bedroom. It may have its own private bath.

Bedroom design is directly related to furniture size and arrangement. First, determine common furniture sizes, Figure 7-9. Then, design the bedroom with a specific arrangement in mind. Figure 7-10 shows using CADD to plan a bedroom based on a specific furniture arrangement. The steps are simple: (1) Determine the size of furniture to be used; (2) Draw or insert an appropriate symbol to

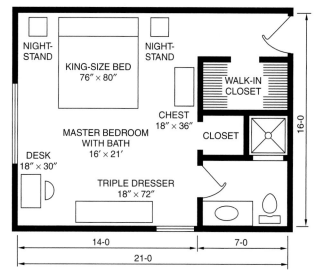

Figure 7-8. An arrangement for a large master bedroom with private bath.

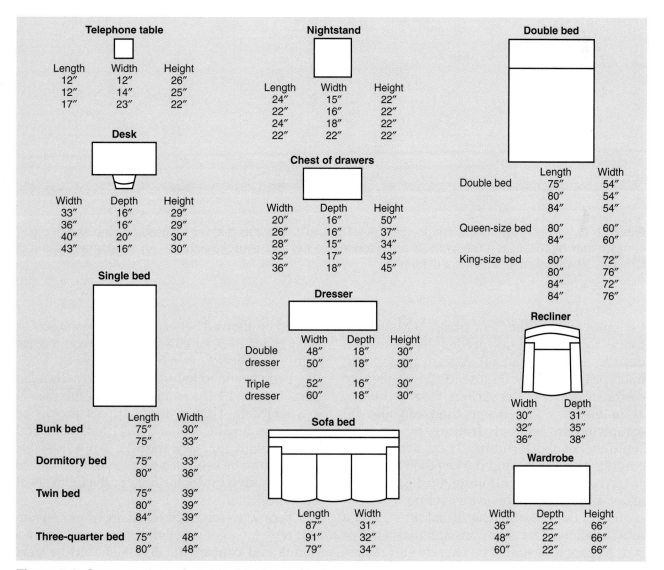

Figure 7-9. Common sizes of standard bedroom furniture.

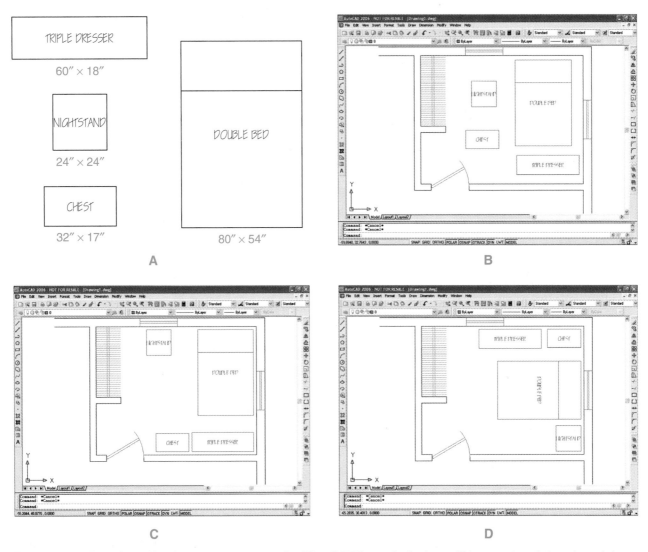

Figure 7-10. Planning a furniture arrangement. A—The CADD symbols that will be used and the size of the furniture they represent. B—The symbols are inserted into the floor plan drawing. C—An initial arrangement of furniture. D—The final arrangement of furniture.

the same scale as the floor plan; (3) Move and rotate the symbols as needed to create the desired arrangement; (4) Assign appropriate linetypes and colors. Be sure to allow adequate clearance between the various room elements, as in Figure 7-11. This method can also be completed in manual drafting by creating "cutouts" of the furniture. Then, arrange the cutouts, trace them, and darken the lines.

 When arranging furniture for the disabled, allow ample space for maneuvering a wheelchair without obstructions. In addition, space must be allowed for easy transfer into and out of bed. A space of 3' should be provided on at least one side of the bed for transfer. Four or more feet should be allowed between stationary objects. A clear space of 5' square usually is required for turning a wheelchair in front of a closet.

 Beds intended to be accessible to a disabled person must be the same height as the seat of a wheelchair. That is, the mattress should be the same height as the wheelchair seat and firm enough for easy transfer. An adjustable bed can also be used. A clearance space of 10" to 13" is required under the bed for the footrests of the wheelchair.

Bedrooms for the disabled are more convenient with an adjoining bathroom. In addition, a phone and controls for lights should be near the bed.

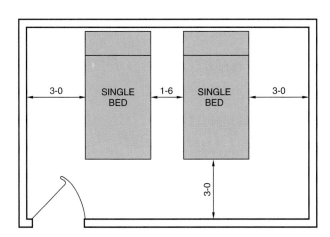
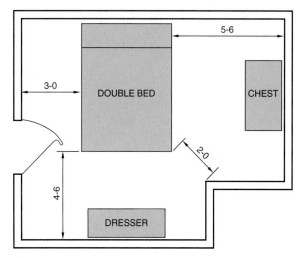

Figure 7-11. Examples of minimum space clearances for bedroom furniture.

Closets

Each bedroom must have a closet, Figure 7-12. The FHA recommends a minimum of four linear feet of rod space in a closet for a man and six feet for a woman. The minimum depth of a clothes closet is 24″. If space is available, a 30″ depth is desirable. When possible, closets should be located along interior walls. This provides noise insulation between rooms

Figure 7-12. A neat closet arrangement provides a place for each item as well as easy access. (Schulte Corporation)

and does not reduce exterior wall space. A bedroom normally has no more than two exterior walls. The use of one for closets will reduce the chance of cross ventilation through windows. In addition, closets should be located near the entrance of the room for easy access.

Access to the closet should receive serious consideration. Closets with full front openings are more accessible. A variety of doors may be selected: sliding, bifold, accordion, or flush. The usual height of a door is 6′-8″, but most doors are also available in 8′-0″ heights. Using doors that provide easy accessibility yet require little space is desirable. Good lighting is also a necessity. Fixtures may be placed inside the closet.

Bifold, accordion, or sliding doors generally allow for partial entry by wheelchair users. To be accessible to the disabled, clothing rods should be located 40″ to 48″ from the floor. Adjustable shelves provide greater accessibility and may be placed at various heights from 18″ to 45″ above the floor. The depth of shelves should not exceed 16″. Clothes hooks should not be more than 40″ from the floor.

Doors and Windows

Windows and doors are important bedroom features. An ideal bedroom will have windows on two walls. Window location and spacing is important. They should be located so that a draft will not blow across the bed. If the bedroom is on the first-floor level, wide, short windows may be desired to provide added privacy. These windows are called *ribbon windows.*

Each bedroom will have at least one entry door. The door should swing into the bedroom. Allow space along the wall for the door when it is open. Locating a door near a corner of the room usually results in less wasted space. To further conserve space, pocket or sliding doors may be used.

Interior doors are usually 1-3/8" thick and 6'-8" high. Standard widths range from 2'-0" to 3'-0" in increments of 2". The minimum recommended bedroom door width is 2'-6". A wider door, 2'-8" or 2'-10", provides for easier movement of furniture, especially adjacent to a hall. To accommodate a wheelchair, doorways should be at least 3'-0" wide.

Colors and Finishing

A well-planned bedroom is a cheerful, but restful, place. Carefully select colors that help to create a quiet and peaceful atmosphere.

Figure 7-13 shows an average size bedroom. This bedroom could function as a master bedroom, guest room, or regular bedroom. There is adequate ventilation through the large sliding windows. A private bath and large

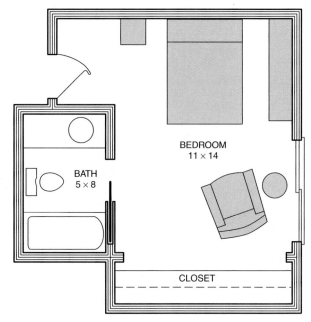

Figure 7-13. A quite versatile, average-size bedroom with a small private bath.

closet are assets. The lounge chair and small table provide a comfortable place to read or relax. Furniture is arranged in such a way that all pieces are easily accessible.

Figure 7-14 shows a bedroom with 156 square feet plus closet and bath. It is a functional arrangement. Adequate space is provided for traffic by the furniture arrangement. Ventilation

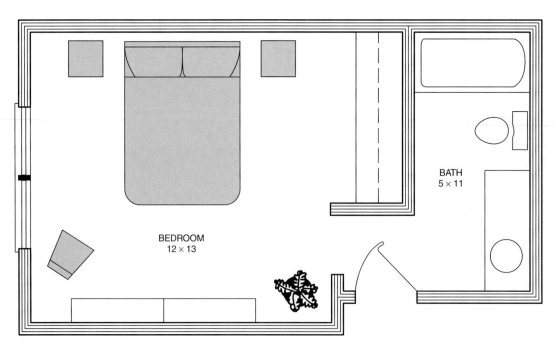

Figure 7-14. A bedroom with a private bath that can be shared with other rooms if needed.

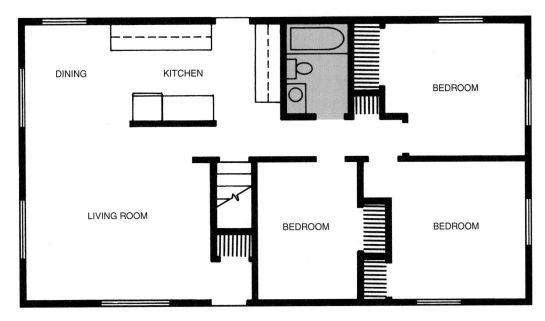

Figure 7-17. A well-planned, centrally located bath in a small house.

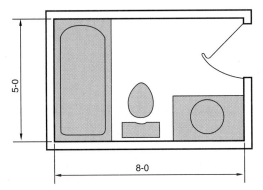

Figure 7-18. A planned layout for a minimum-size bathroom.

countertop and storage space than a guest bath. Most people prefer ample space for dressing, linen storage, and personal items. Larger bathrooms also allow for luxury or over-size tubs, Figure 7-19.

A large bathroom is most convenient for a wheelchair user. To be handicapped accessible, the bathroom must have a minimum of 5′ × 5′ clear space to allow turning of the wheelchair.

Accessibility

Accessibility to the bathroom is important, Figure 7-20. If there is only one bath for all the bedrooms, locate the door in a hall common to all the bedrooms. One should not be required to go through another room to reach the bath.

Figure 7-19. A large bathroom provides ample room for dressing, bathing, and grooming. It can also provide space for an oversize tub. (Summitville Tile)

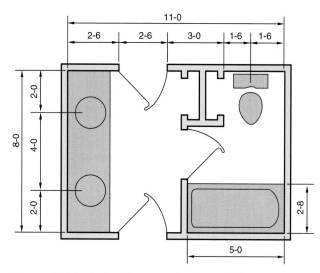

Figure 7-20. A double-entry bath provides maximum accessibility.

Bathroom doors are ordinarily not as wide as bedroom doors. A door width of 2'-6" or even 2'-4" is usually sufficient. If provisions are being made for wheelchair use, then the door should be a minimum of 2'-8" wide. Doors should swing into the bathroom and not interfere with any fixtures. In some instances, a pocket door is used to subdivide the bath into two or more areas, as in a two-compartment bath, Figure 7-21.

Primary Fixtures

The three primary fixtures found in most bathrooms are the lavatory, water closet (toilet), and tub or shower. The arrangement of the fixtures determines whether or not the bath is truly functional. For example, avoid locating the lavatory or water closet under a window. Provide ample space for each fixture in the

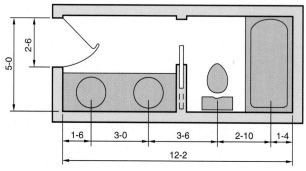

Figure 7-21. This two-compartment bath uses a pocket door as a divider.

room. Bathroom fixtures vary in size as shown in Figure 7-22. Check the manufacturer's specifications and code requirements for placement of each of the fixtures.

A mirror should be placed above the sink, Figure 7-23. Arrange the mirror so it will be well lighted and away from the tub to prevent fogging. The mirror should be tilted slightly downward for full viewing or be mounted low enough for a wheelchair user to see. Another

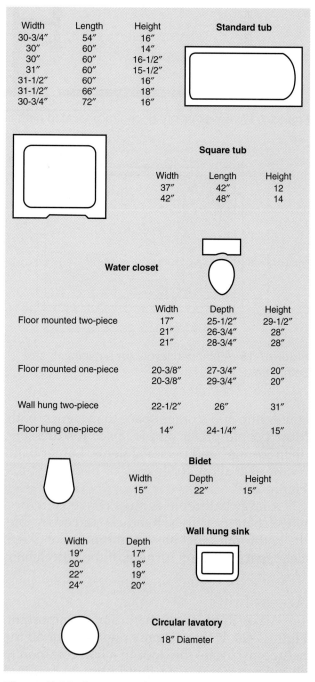

Figure 7-22. Common sizes of bathroom fixtures.

Figure 7-23. A lavatory should have a mirror above it. Avoid placing a lavatory or water closet under a window. (Photo courtesy of Kohler Co.)

option would be to install a full-length mirror on a bathroom wall or door. Medicine cabinets should be mounted so that the top shelf is not over 50-1/2″ from the floor; lower if mounted over a counter or sink.

Sink cabinets or vanities are popular and provide much-needed countertop and storage space. Lavatories can be circular or rectangular shape as well as other shapes. A typical base unit is shown in Figure 7-24. Twin lavatories are desirable when more than one person must share the bathroom. Wall-mounted and pedestal models are once again becoming popular, Figure 7-25. They usually provide sufficient knee space for wheelchair users. A variety of vanity base units is shown in Figure 7-26.

Figure 7-24. This lavatory-vanity combination illustrates how beauty and function enhance a bathroom.

Figure 7-25. This attractively designed bath is functional and easy to clean.

Allow 26″ to 30″ from the underside of the sink to the floor for wheelchair armrests. A space of 30″ to 34″ from the rim of the sink to the floor may be more preferable. If countertop sinks are used, insulate any exposed pipes to prevent burns. For easy reach, faucet handles should be a maximum of 18″ from the front of the sink. Lever-type handles provide greater usability.

Water closets are produced in a number of styles. The older style has a separate tank and stool. Many newer models are one-piece units, either floor- or wall-mounted, Figure 7-27. Wall-mounted water closets make cleaning easier. Most water closets require a space at least 30″ wide for installation, Figure 7-28. Allow 36″ for a handicapped person. Water closets should be placed so that they are not visible from another room when the bathroom door is open.

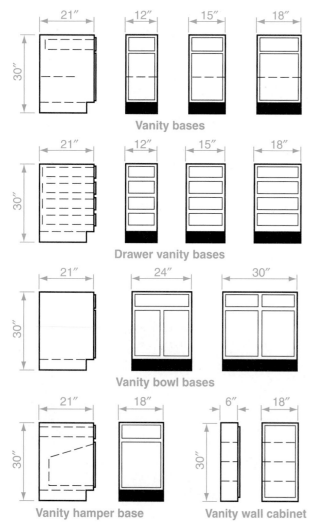

Figure 7-26. There are several standard vanity sizes and designs.

Figure 7-27. A contemporary one-piece water closet.

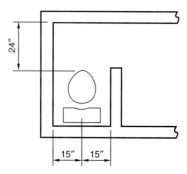

Figure 7-28. This is the minimum clearance for water closet installation. More space is required to be wheelchair accessible.

Wall-mounted water closets are more accessible for persons in wheelchairs. A water closet seat that is 20″ high is about the same height as most wheelchair seats and will provide for easy transfer. Elevated water closet seats are also available to provide access.

Regular bathtubs range in size from 54″ to 72″ long and 28″ to 32″ wide. The most common size is 30″ × 60″. Often, a shower is installed above the tub. This provides the convenience of both and does not require two separate facilities.

Bathtub rims should not be lower than 18″ from the floor to provide access from the wheelchair to the tub. Tubs may also have such safety features as nonskid bottoms and grab rails. In addition, various types of seats, stools, transfer seats, or lifts for use in bathtubs or showers are available. Bathtubs are available with built-in bath seat/platform on the opposite end of the tub from the drain.

Shower stalls are also popular. Many homes have a tub and separate shower stall. Prefabricated showers are available in metal, fiberglass, and plastic. More luxurious showers are usually made of ceramic tile, terrazzo, marble, or similar materials, Figure 7-29.

Hand-held shower heads may be more convenient and shower controls should be within reach of the user. Tub and shower floors should be flat and slip resistant. Common shower sizes range from 30″ × 30″ to 36″ × 48″.

Shower stalls are available for wheelchair users, Figure 7-30. Other stalls are available with a wall-mounted seat that will fold against the wall when not in use for persons who can transfer from a wheelchair to a seat. Placing a shower head over the center of the shower is more accessible for wheelchair users.

Additional Fixtures

Many modern homes include a bidet in bathrooms. Often, a bidet is only installed in the master bath. However, some home designs include a bidet in the main bath as well. A bidet is shown on the left in Figure 7-31.

Whirlpools, Jacuzzis™, and saunas can be installed in or near the bathroom. A whirlpool can be used as a bathtub, bubbling bath, or home spa, Figure 7-31. Powerful, pulsating jets of water are fully adjustable to provide a relaxing massage where it is needed the most. Some Jacuzzis™ may be used as a whirlpool or a bathtub as well. Saunas can be built as a part of the bath during construction or purchased in kits and added later. Some luxurious designs include a combination of a sauna, whirlpool, and steam bath.

Figure 7-29. This shower makes use of durable ceramic tile. (Photo courtesy of Kohler Co.)

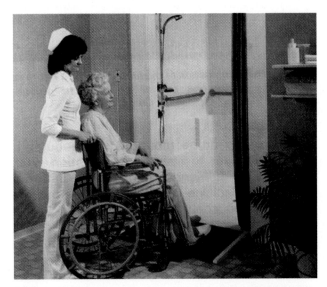

Figure 7-30. This one-piece, prefabricated shower is installed as a complete unit during construction. It is accessible for wheelchair users. (Aqua Glass)

Figure 7-31. The touch of a button will transform this whirlpool bath into a soothing water retreat. (Photo of courtesy of Kohler Co.)

Ventilation and Electricity

A bathroom *must* have ventilation. This may be provided by windows or an exhaust fan. If windows are used, care must be taken to locate them properly. Windows should be placed such that a draft is not produced over the tub and maximum privacy is secured.

If an exhaust fan is used, it should be located near the tub and water closet area. *Electrical switches should be placed so that they cannot be reached from the tub!* Plus, **ground fault circuit interrupter (GFCI)** receptacles should be used in the bathroom. These are fast-acting devices that detect short circuits and immediately shut off power to the receptacle.

Safety

Safety should be a prime consideration when planning the bath. Flooring materials that become slick when wet should not be used. Devices should be installed in tub and shower faucets to control water temperature thermostatically to eliminate scalding from hot water. Also, devices can be installed to control the water pressure so that when the cold water pressure is reduced, the hot water flow is automatically

reduced. Nonshatter or safety glass should be used in shower and tub enclosures.

Special provisions should be made for any handicapped persons who might use the bathroom. This may include installing a specially designed shower or tub, Figure 7-32. Grab bars

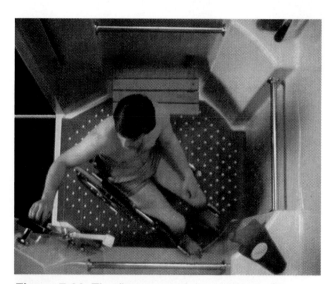

Figure 7-32. The floor area of the shower unit permits a 5′ turning radius for wheelchairs. Several grab bars are within easy reach. (Universal-Rundle Corporation)

should be provided, especially in the areas where the water closet, tub, and shower are located, Figure 7-33. Horizontal bars are designed for pushing up while vertical bars are designed for pulling up. Grab bars must be well anchored. They should be 1-1/4″ in diameter with a profile that can be easily grasped with no sharp edges. Grab bars should be no further than 1-1/2″ away from the wall.

Decor

The decor of a well-planned bath will provide for easy cleaning, resistance to moisture, and a pleasing atmosphere. Select fixtures that are appropriate for the desired color scheme of the room. Plants and art pieces may be added to enhance the beauty of the room. The bathroom need not be a dull room that is void of design and beauty, Figure 7-34.

Figure 7-35 shows a small bath that provides maximum convenience and practicality at a nominal cost. Economy is partially obtained by the supply and drains being placed on a single wall. Also, there is no wasted space in this functional bath. "Zones" may be created through the use of open-shelf cabinetry.

A large bath is shown in Figure 7-36. This 12′ × 15′ bath groups all the plumbing fixtures into an island unit at the center of the room. The square tub and twin vanities create a unique design. The entrance and closets may be rearranged to suit the particular needs of a given plan. A vent fan, heater, lighting, and shower curtain track are mounted in a ceiling unit.

Figure 7-37 shows a luxury bath. The 240 square feet area provides separate, private dressing and grooming areas for the husband and wife. "Her area" may be decorated in a completely feminine decor while "his area" may be distinctly masculine. The sanitary area, tub, and shower may be completely closed when desired. The shower and tub area are tiled and slightly sunken.

Figure 7-34. This contemporary bath combines beautiful materials and architectural detail to produce a focal point. (Pittsburgh Corning Corporation)

Figure 7-33. An example of a shower/tub combination that is accessible for the physically disabled. Notice the four grab bars and the sliding seat. (Photo courtesy of Kohler Co.)

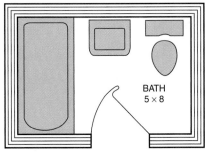

BATH
5 × 8

Figure 7-35. An economical bath with the supply and drains on a single wall.

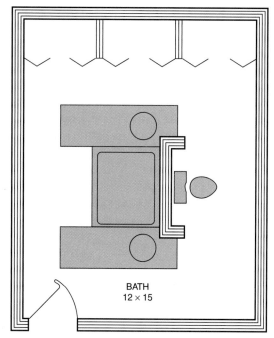

Figure 7-36. A large island bath with plumbing fixtures in a center cluster.

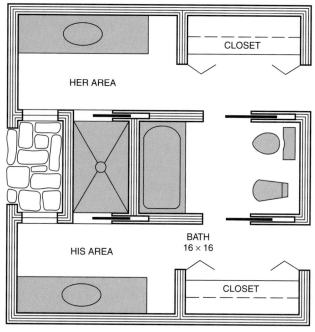

Figure 7-37. This "his" and "her" bath represents a luxury dressing and grooming area.

Internet Resources

www.gaf.com
GAF Materials Corporation, manufacturer of roofing materials

www.hotwater.com
A. O. Smith Water Products Company

www.jacuzzi.com
Jacuzzi, Inc.

www.kohler.com
Kohler Company

www.moen.com
Moen, Inc.

www.norcraftcompanies.com
Norcraft Companies L.L.C., supplier of kitchen and bath cabinets

www.owenscorning.com
Owens Corning

www.pricepfister.com
Price Pfister

www.velux.com
Velux, supplier of roof windows and skylights

www.wwpa.org
Western Wood Products Association

Review Questions – Chapter 7

Write your answers on a separate sheet of paper. Do not write in this book.

1. In bathroom design, which two electrical safety concerns must always be addressed?

2. List the three basic areas into which a residential structure may be divided.

3. In some design situations, a _____ is used to subdivide the bath into two compartments.

4. Which three materials are often used for bathroom showers in luxury homes?

5. Which three materials are commonly used for prefabricated bathroom showers in average homes?

6. Less space is wasted when the bedroom door is located near a _____ of the room.

7. FHA specifications recommend a minimum of _____ linear feet of closet rod space for a woman and _____ for a man.

8. FHA recommends that the minimum bedroom size be no smaller than:
   a) 100 square feet.
   b) 150 square feet.
   c) 200 square feet.
   d) 250 square feet.

9. A minimum size bathroom is _____.

10. Bathtubs range in size from 28″ × 54″ to 32″ × 72″. The most common size is _____.

11. List four types of doors generally used for closets.

12. A 3/4 bath contains only a _____, _____, and _____.

13. Allow _____ from the underside of the sink to the floor for wheelchair armrests.

14. Name two advantages of a wall-mounted water closet.

15. _____ must be well anchored, should be 1-1/4″ in diameter, have a profile that can be easily grasped with no sharp edges, and should be no further than 1-1/2″ away from the wall.

Suggested Activities

1. Select a floor plan of a house from a newspaper, magazine, or other literature. Using CADD, draw furniture symbols based on standard sizes. Refer to Figure 7-9. If CADD is not available, create paper cutouts. Then, plan furniture arrangements for each of the bedrooms. Prepare a short write-up of each room describing the furniture and arrangement. Include sizes of all pieces of furniture.

2. Design a small bathroom (5′ × 10′). Show the location and size of each fixture in a plan view.

3. Prepare a plan view for a clothes closet that is 3′ deep and 8′ in length. Show the maximum door access, clothes rod, and shelf storage area. Refer to the illustrations in this chapter for examples.

4. Design an average-size bedroom, as defined by the FHA. Make a plan view drawing of the room either manually or with CADD. Include the bed, dresser, chest of drawers, and other furniture to meet the needs of your own activities. You may want to include a study or reading area.

5. Look through a number of home design and planning magazines for closet arrangements. Prepare a display of clippings that illustrates maximum use of closet space for clothes, shoes, and other apparel.

6. Locate agencies and organizations that specify requirements for bath facilities to be handicapped-accessible. Enlist the help of your local librarian or the Internet to find at least two different sources. Then, obtain a list of these requirements from each source. Finally, design a bathroom for a disabled person that meets all of the requirements.

7. Using CADD, draw bedroom and bathroom symbols and add them to your symbols library for future use. Refer to Figure 7-9 and Figure 7-22.

Material Safety

As a drafter, you may not think about material safety. However, there are many types of materials that you come in contact with, and some may be considered hazardous. The Occupational Safety and Health Administration (OSHA) requires:

- A list be kept of all hazardous materials used on the premises.
- A file be maintained containing material safety data sheets (MSDS) on each hazardous material.
- Employees be trained in the proper use of hazardous materials.

Some materials that you may come in contact with include ammonia, cleaning fluids, inks, and toner. In addition to proper handling of these materials, they must be properly disposed of when you are done using them. For example, spent toner cartridges should not be placed in the garbage. They should be returned to a recycling facility for recharging and eventual reuse. When in doubt, check the facility's master list of hazardous materials. If the material is listed as hazardous, check the material's MSDS for hazards. Finally, check with the manufacturer or Environmental Protection Agency (EPA) for disposal procedures. A sample MSDS is shown below.

Material Safety Data Sheet

Preparation/Revision Date:

ACME Chemical Company

24 hour Emergency Phone: Chemtrec: 1-800-424-9300
Outside United States: 1-202-483-7616

Trade Name/Syn: **DICHLOROMETHANE * METHYLENE DICHLORIDE**
Chem Name/Syn: **METHYLENE CHLORIDE**
CAS Number: **75-09-2**
Formula: Ch_2Cl_2

NFPA Rating:

Health   4
Flammability   1
Reactivity   1

Statement of Hazard:
Possible cancer hazard. May cause cancer based on animal data. Harmful if swallowed or inhaled. Vapor irritating. May cause eye injury and/or skin irritation. May cause damage to liver, kidneys, blood, and central nervous system.

Effects of Overexposure-Toxicity-Route of Entry:
Toxic by ingestion and inhalation. Irritating on contact with skin, eyes, or mucous membranes. May cause eye injury. Inhalation of high vapor concentrations causes dizziness, nausea, headache, narcosis, irregular heartbeats, coma, and death. If vomiting occurs, methylene chloride can be aspirated into the lungs, which can cause chemical pneumonia and systemic effects. Medical conditions aggravated by exposure: heart, kidney, and liver conditions. Routes of entry: inhalation, ingestion.

Hazardous Decomposition Products:
HCL, phosgene, chlorine.

Will Hazardous Polymerization Occur?
Will not occur under normal conditions.

Is the Product Stable?
Product is normally stable.

Conditions to Avoid:
Contact with open flame, welding arcs, and hot surfaces.

Spill Procedures, Disposal Requirements/Methods:
Evacuate the area of all unnecessary personnel. Wear suitable protective equipment. Eliminate any ignition sources until the area is determined to be free from explosion or fire hazard. Contain the release with a suitable absorbent. Place in a suitable container for disposal. Dispose of in accordance with all applicable federal, state, and local regulations.

Ventilation:

Local exhaust: Recommended
Mechanical (Gen):   Recommended
Special: NA
Other: None

Respiratory Protection:
NIOSH/MSHA air supplied respirator.

Protective Gloves:
Viton, PVA, or equivalent to prevent skin contact.

Other Protective Equipment:
Safety glasses with side shields must be worn at all times; eyewash; fume hood.

Room Planning— Living Area

Objectives

After studying this chapter, you will be able to:

➤ Identify the rooms and areas that comprise the living area.

➤ Apply design principles to planning a living room.

➤ Integrate the furniture in a living room plan.

➤ Analyze a dining room using good design principles.

➤ Design a functional entry and foyer.

➤ Communicate the primary design considerations for a recreation room.

➤ Integrate patios, porches, and courts into the total floor plan of a dwelling.

Key Terms

Closed Plan
Courts
Decks
Foyer
Gazebo
Living Area
Main Entry
Open Plan

Patios
Porches
Service Entry
Special-Purpose Entries
Special-Purpose Rooms

The *living area* is the part of the house that most friends and guests see. This is the area that usually becomes the showplace. Comprising roughly one-third of the house, the living area serves a variety of functions. It is the location for family get-togethers and dining. It is also the area for recreation, entertaining, and just relaxing. The living area is not restricted to the interior of the structure. It includes patios, decks, and courts. The living area is designed for all activities that do not take place in the sleeping and service areas.

The living area is composed of a number of rooms. They include the living room, dining room, foyer, and recreation room. Special-purpose rooms, such as a sunroom or home office, are also included in the living area. Some of the "rooms" may not be rooms in the true sense; however, they serve the same purpose. The trend in design is to move away from many rooms toward a more open plan with fewer walls and doors. See Figure 8-1.

Figure 8-1. Note the openness of this bright, sunbathed living area. (The Oshkosh, WI private residence of Chancellor Richard H. Wells and family—formerly the Alberta Kimball Home)

149

Designing With CADD

The design of living spaces may be facilitated through the use of a CADD system. Time required to develop a suitable solution is greatly reduced through the manipulation of symbols to produce a variety of designs. In addition, computer-generated renderings can be used as presentation drawings to show clients how the space will look when complete.

Figure 8-2 shows the realism that can be presented with high-end CADD software.

Living Rooms

For many families, the living room is the center of activity. Depending on the specific occasion, it may be a play room for the children, a TV room, or a conversation place. Its size and arrangement will depend on the lifestyle of the members of the family who will ultimately use it. Figure 8-3 illustrates this point.

A

B

Figure 8-2. These computer-rendered illustrations present realistic representations of the final product. Notice the architectural details of the lanai and pool area. (Helmuth A. Geiser, member AIBD)

A

B

C

Figure 8-3. A—The feeling of warmth is expressed in the styling of this pleasant conversation area. B—Formality is emphasized in the design of this large living area. C—The modern lifestyle of the owners is expressed in the color and design of the living area. (Preway, Inc.)

The living room, like all other rooms in the house, should be used. It should not be planned just as a showplace. A properly designed living room can be a functional part of the house and, at the same time, a beautiful and charming area, Figure 8-4.

Size

Living rooms are of all sizes and shapes. A small living room may have as few as 150 square feet. An average-size living room may be around 250 square feet. A large living room may exceed 400 square feet. See Figure 8-5. The most important questions to ask regarding size and design of a living room are:

(1) What furniture is planned for this particular room? See Figure 8-6.

(2) How often will the room be used?

(3) How many people are expected to use the room at any one time?

(4) How many functions are combined in this one room? Is it a multipurpose room?

(5) Is the living room size in proportion to the remainder of the house?

Figure 8-4. This is an attractive living room that is designed for entertaining and relaxing. Clearly, this is a room that will be used.
(Manufactured Housing Institute)

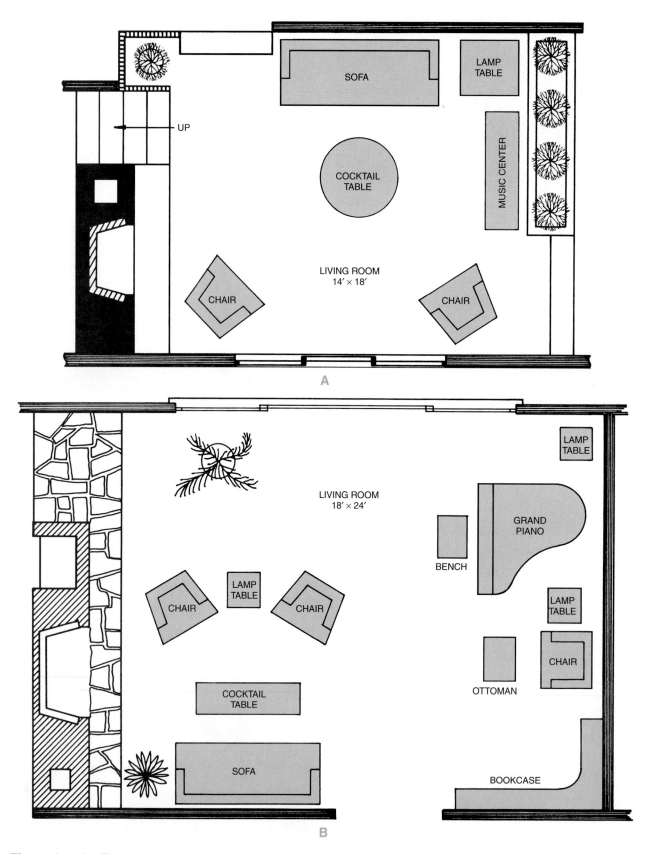

Figure 8-5. A—This sunken living room is an average size at about 250 square feet. B—A large living room with about 430 square feet.

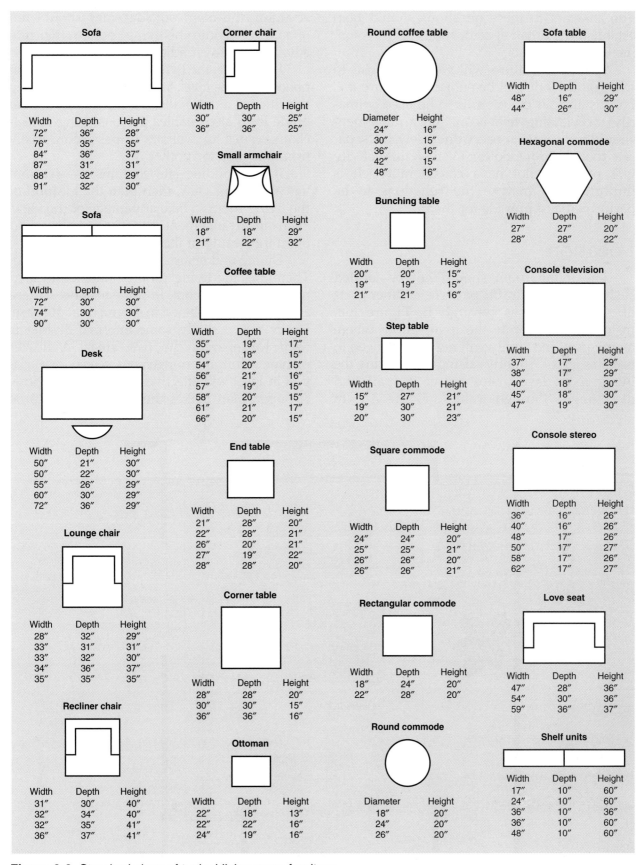

Figure 8-6. Standard sizes of typical living room furniture.

The answers to these questions should help establish the broad specifications of the room, including its size.

Specific furniture will reflect the use to which the room will be subjected, Figure 8-7. For instance, if the room is to be used primarily for viewing television, the arrangement should indicate that use. Conversely, if a separate room is provided for TV, then this activity will probably not be a consideration. It is important to analyze the functions to be performed and provide for them.

Location

The living room should not be located such that natural traffic patterns to other parts of the house pass through it, Figure 8-8. Instead, try to locate the living room where members of the family will not feel the need to use it as a hall. Slightly raising or lowering the living room level helps to set it apart and discourage "through traffic," Figure 8-9. In

addition, the main outside entry should not open directly into the living room, rather into a hallway or foyer adjoining the living room.

If possible, the living room should be positioned at grade level. This allows for expanding activities to a patio. Placing the living room at grade level also enables persons using wheelchairs, canes, or walkers to pass more easily from one area to another.

If the building site contains an area that has a pleasing view, then plan the location of the living room to take advantage of the view. Such an arrangement enhances the use and often the beauty of the living room.

Dining and entertaining are closely related. Therefore, the living room should be located near the dining room. In some instances, these areas may be combined to serve a dual purpose, Figure 8-10. Usually, some informal divider is used to separate the two areas. A flower planter, furniture arrangement, screen, or variation in level will effectively serve this purpose. An open plan makes the house appear to be

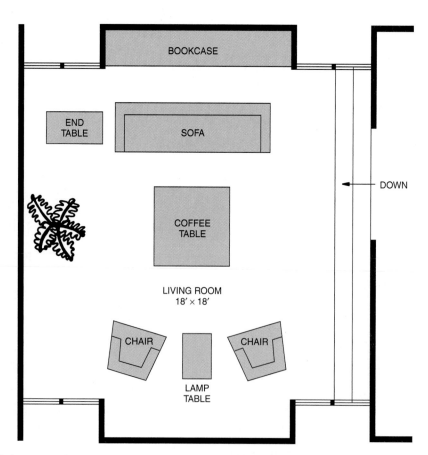

Figure 8-7. This living room is designed around a "conversation" concept.

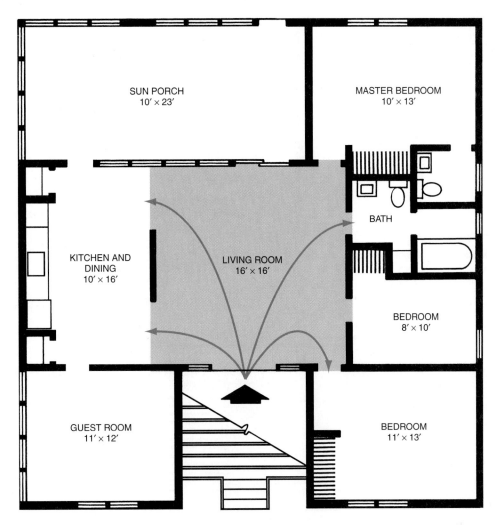

Figure 8-8. Notice how the traffic patterns from all of the surrounding rooms pass through this poorly located living room.

larger inside, while a closed plan tends to make the rooms look small.

Windows and Doors

Consider the orientation of the living room for maximum comfort and energy conservation. In warm climates, use a northern orientation to keep the living areas cool. The north side is usually shaded and cool, while the south side receives sun almost constantly. In cool climates, place the living room on the south side of the house to take advantage of winter sun.

Large windows or sliding doors further encourage the feeling of spaciousness and increases the enjoyment of the living room,

Figure 8-11. Exterior wall areas should not be broken with too many small windows and doors. Also, there needs to be adequate wall space for all of the required furniture.

Decor

Modern living rooms should be exciting, colorful, and inviting. Select bright, vivid colors that complement existing natural materials. Color, texture, and design may be used to emphasize the good points and minimize weak aspects of the room. See Figure 8-12.

The design of the living room should follow the exterior design. For example, the furnishings, wall and floor coverings, and window treatments of a Southern Colonial

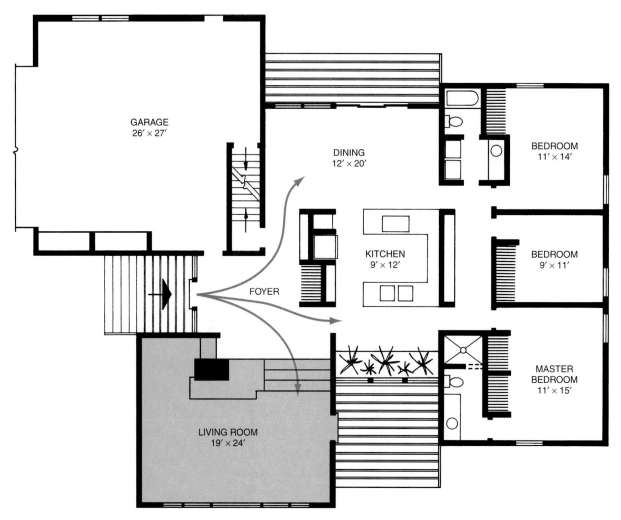

Figure 8-9. This living room is located near the kitchen and dining areas, yet no traffic patterns pass through it.

Figure 8-10. The living room and dining room are in close proximity to one another.

Figure 8-11. Large areas of glass add to the beauty and spaciousness of this living room.

Figure 8-12. Select bright colors that complement each other and the natural surroundings. The colors selected lend a mood or feel to the room. (Manufactured Housing Institute)

home should be traditional in design. On the other hand, contemporary furniture and decor are appropriate for a contemporary structure.

An average-size living room designed for conversation is shown in Figure 8-13. This layout lends itself to a corner location and restricts through traffic. Grade level placement permits access to a patio or porch. The fireplace is in an ideal spot for viewing from the conversation area.

Figure 8-14 shows a well-planned living room adjacent to the dining area. An area rug unifies the furniture arrangement and adds interest. The screen defines the living room boundary and at the same time makes it appear larger. Large windows provide an excellent viewing area.

Dining Rooms

Around the beginning of the 1900s, most new homes had a dining room. Then, shortly after World War II, fewer houses were being built with dining rooms. Now, the trend has changed again and dining rooms are popular. Most new homes today have a dining room. However, in each individual case, the determining factor of whether or not to include a dining room should be the lifestyle of those who will live in the house, rather than fad or fancy.

The main function of a dining room is to provide a special place for eating. In some instances, such as informal meals, this activity is performed in the kitchen rather than in a separate room or area. Many modern homes provide eating facilities in the kitchen for informal meals and separate dining room for more formal gatherings, Figure 8-15.

Plan

When planning the dining room, a decision should be made early as to whether an "open" or "closed" plan will be the most desirable. A *closed plan* places the dining room in a cubicle with little chance for overflow into other rooms, Figure 8-16. The house appears smaller and less dramatic than in an open plan.

The function and efficiency of the rooms will be enhanced by using an *open plan* where the dining and living rooms are not closed off from each other, Figure 8-17. Flower planters, screens, dividers, and partial walls may be used effectively to divide the dining area from the living room or kitchen and, at the same time, make the rooms appear larger, Figure 8-18. In some instances, it may be best if the dining

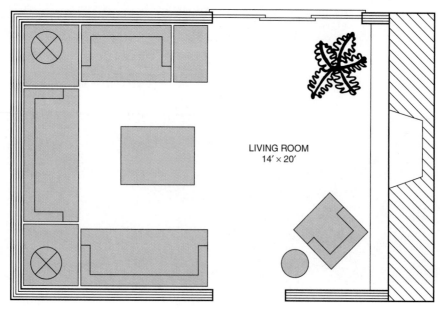

LIVING ROOM
14' × 20'

Figure 8-13. An average-size living room designed for conversation.

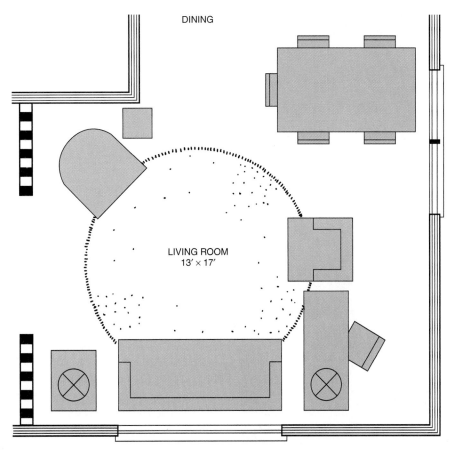

DINING

LIVING ROOM
13′ × 17′

Figure 8-14. An open-style living room adjacent to the dining room.

Figure 8-15. This large dining room is designed for formal gatherings. (NMC/Focal Point)

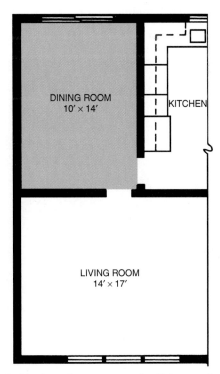

DINING ROOM
10′ × 14′

KITCHEN

LIVING ROOM
14′ × 17′

Figure 8-16. A wall separates the living and dining rooms. This is a closed plan because there is little chance for overflow between the two rooms.

Figure 8-17. A delightfully planned open dining area with cheerful colors and extensive lighting. (Armstrong World Industries, Inc.)

room is separated from the kitchen in order to reduce the sight and smell of food preparation. However, if you consider food preparation an integral part of entertaining, then the kitchen, living room, and dining area should all be close to each other.

Size

Dining rooms vary greatly in size. A small room, capable of seating four people around a table and providing space for a buffet, requires an area of approximately 120 square feet, Figure 8-19. A medium-size room, about 12' × 15', provides space for six to eight people with a buffet and china closet, Figure 8-20. Large dining rooms are about 14' × 18' or larger, Figure 8-21. In most cases, the dining room size depends on the number of people who will use the room at a given time, the furniture to be included in the room, and clearance allowed for traffic through the room.

Typical dining room furniture includes the table, chairs, buffet, china closet, and server or cart, Figure 8-22. Arrangement and spacing depends on the layout of the room, a pleasant outdoor vantage point, or orientation to other rooms, Figure 8-23. At least 2'-3" should be

Figure 8-18. A dwarf wall separates the dining room and living area in this open plan. (Manufactured Housing Institute)

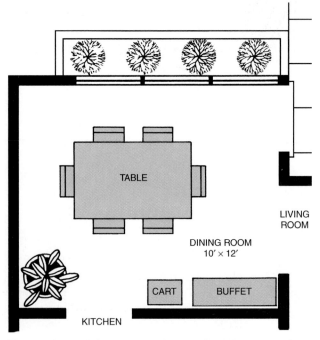

Figure 8-19. A floor plan of a small dining room that seats four to six people.

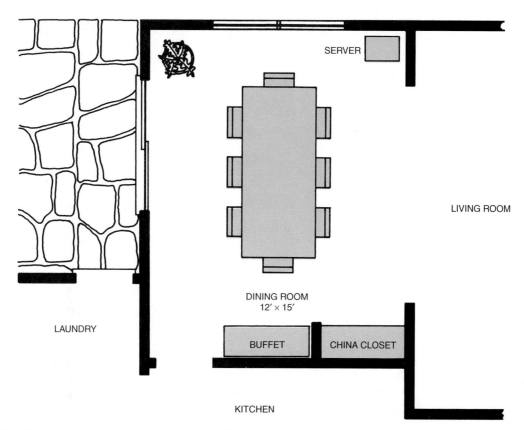

Figure 8-20. This is a medium-size dining room. It is arranged in respect to the other living areas.

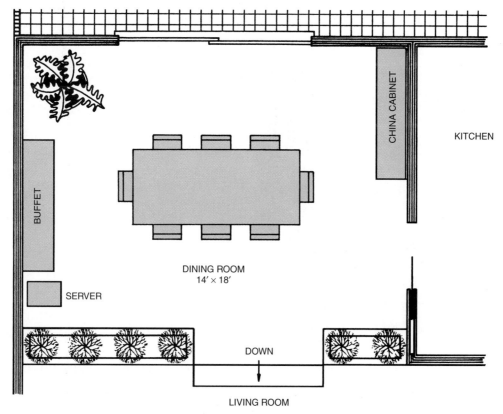

Figure 8-21. A large dining room seats eight or more people and is best suited for a large family or those who entertain frequently.

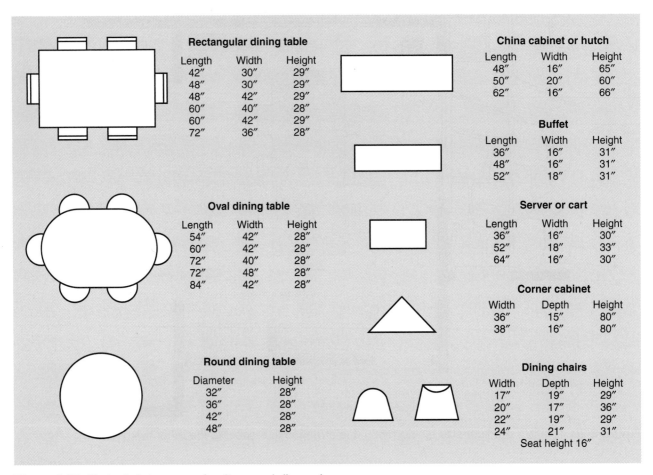

Rectangular dining table

Length	Width	Height
42″	30″	29″
48″	30″	29″
48″	42″	29″
60″	40″	28″
60″	42″	29″
72″	36″	28″

Oval dining table

Length	Width	Height
54″	42″	28″
60″	42″	28″
72″	40″	28″
72″	48″	28″
84″	42″	28″

Round dining table

Diameter	Height
32″	28″
36″	28″
42″	28″
48″	28″

China cabinet or hutch

Length	Width	Height
48″	16″	65″
50″	20″	60″
62″	16″	66″

Buffet

Length	Width	Height
36″	16″	31″
48″	16″	31″
52″	18″	31″

Server or cart

Length	Width	Height
36″	16″	30″
52″	18″	33″
64″	16″	30″

Corner cabinet

Width	Depth	Height
36″	15″	80″
38″	16″	80″

Dining chairs

Width	Depth	Height
17″	19″	29″
20″	17″	36″
22″	19″	29″
24″	21″	31″

Seat height 16″

Figure 8-22. Typical dining room furniture and dimensions.

Figure 8-23. This dining room is styled to reflect the decor of the adjacent rooms and take advantage of the outside view. (The Oshkosh, WI private residence of Chancellor Richard H. Wells and family—formerly the Alberta Kimball Home.)

allowed from center-to-center of chairs around the table. Also, be sure to provide ample space for serving. Usually, 2′-0″ is sufficient space between the back of the chairs and the wall.

To enable persons in wheelchairs to use the dining room, open leg space is needed for dining. Tables with legs that are far apart or that have pedestal legs provide space for wheelchair use. A minimum of 32″ is needed for passing between furniture pieces and/or walls.

Location

Location of the dining room is important. For efficient use, it should be adjacent to the kitchen and living room, Figure 8-24. In some instances, it may be desirable to locate it near the family recreation room as well. An ideal arrangement is one that places the dining room between the living room and kitchen. This provides for natural movement of guests

Figure 8-24. The kitchen and living room surround two sides of the dining room on the right.

from living room to dining with minimum confusion. Furthermore, added space is available in the living room if needed. This is especially true in an open plan, as in Figure 8-25.

Decor

Dining is generally a happy conversation time. Hence, the decor and lighting are important factors, Figure 8-26. Controlled lighting is desirable and makes possible a variety of moods. The color scheme used in the dining room is often the same as the living room, since it will most likely be an extension of that area. A bright, warm, and cheerful atmosphere is the desired result, Figure 8-27. In dining areas that are used frequently, flooring should be durable to withstand daily wear. Nonslip, hard-surface floors or low-pile carpeting are good choices for wheelchair users.

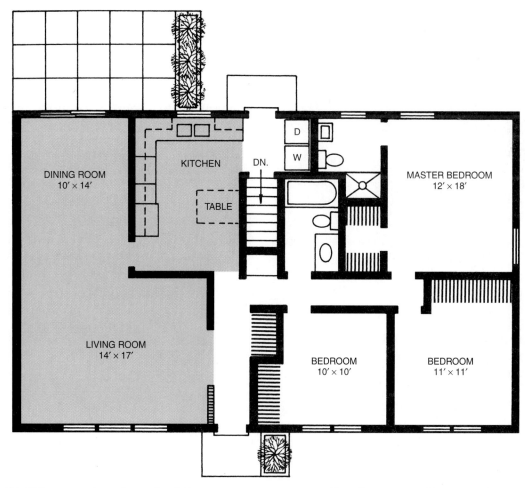

Figure 8-25. This open plan allows the living room to serve as overflow if an extra table or seating are required.

Figure 8-26. Graciousness is the theme of this dining room as evident in the lighting and decor. (Focal Point, Inc.)

Figure 8-27. A bright, cheery atmosphere is reflected in the open plan of this home. (Armstrong World Industries, Inc.)

Figure 8-28 shows a medium-size dining room. The relationship to the kitchen is ideal. However, the dining room cannot function as an overflow area for the living room. The living room is not adjacent. Boundaries of the dining room are defined by the area rug and the sofa. This is a good example of an open plan. Traffic is confined to the space along the edge of the room and does not interfere with activities in the kitchen or dining room. The

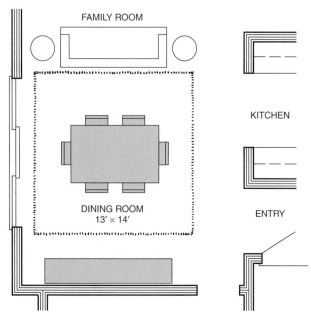

Figure 8-28. This is a good example of an open plan that is located close to the kitchen.

large sliding doors provide for a nice view of the patio or side yard.

The dining room in Figure 8-29 is ideally located between the kitchen and living room. This is a "semi-open" plan because the dining room is not enclosed with traditional doors, yet it is enclosed and defined by walls. The plan is functional and creates a desirable atmosphere for dining. This arrangement is well suited for a site with a nice view to the rear of the house. The room is large enough to allow for required traffic and to seat six to eight people.

Entryway and Foyer

Every house has at least one entryway. Most houses have two or three entryways. Many, but not all, houses also have a foyer. A well-planned house will have both an entryway and a foyer.

Entryway

There are three basic types of entryways—main entry, service entry, and special-purpose entry, Figure 8-30. The main entry should be designed to be impressive because it is the first part of the house that guests see when they

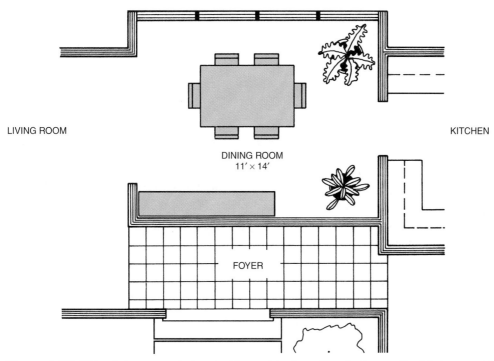

Figure 8-29. This dining room is located in an ideal position between the kitchen and living room.

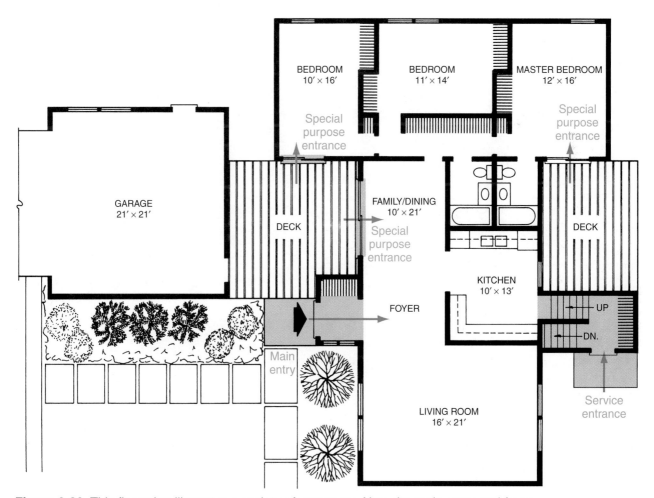

Figure 8-30. This floor plan illustrates a variety of entryways. Note the main entry and foyer.

arrive. An entry need not be large to be attractive. Creative use of materials and a functional arrangement will enhance beauty and design.

The *main entry* should be centrally located to provide easy access to various parts of the house, Figure 8-31. A main entry opening into a foyer is usually preferable to an entry leading directly into the living room. The entry should be designed in such a way that callers may be viewed without opening the door. Glass side panels provide visibility, natural light, and add to the design. In addition, protection from the weather is a major consideration in the design of an entryway. Either a large overhang may be provided or the entry may be recessed, Figure 8-32.

The main entry should not only be functional, but visually interesting. A recessed entry is impressive and helps to break up a long, plain front that might otherwise be uninteresting. An extended overhang may also add design and interest to a plain roof. An extra-tall door and ornate scrollwork can add visual

Figure 8-32. This open-air entry provides protection from the weather and adds interest to the overall design.

interest to the entryway, Figure 8-33. Well-styled doors are a key element in any entry. Doors should be carefully selected to conform to the overall design of the house and add that special touch of creative design. Added emphasis may be obtained by using two doors

Figure 8-31. This main entry is clearly defined and centrally located to ensure easy access to the different areas of the house. (Photo Courtesy of James Hardie® Siding Products)

Figure 8-33. Notice how this entry carries through the same theme of styling as the rest of the house. An extra tall door adds visual interest to the entry.

Figure 8-34. These double doors add a spacious appearance to the entry and increase its function.

instead of one. This technique places more emphasis on the entry and also increases its function, Figure 8-34. Regardless of the technique used, the style of the entry should be compatible with the remainder of the house. The use of totally different materials or a drastic change in proportion usually will not produce desirable results.

The size of the entry will depend somewhat on the size and design of the house. However, sufficient space should be provided to accommodate several people at any given time. To be handicapped accessible, the entry should be large enough to permit the door to open a full 90 degrees. There should also be 12″ to 18″ of space on the doorknob side of the entry and the foyer to allow for proper positioning of a wheelchair.

The typical size for an entry door is 3′-0″ wide, 6′-8″ high, and 1-3/4″ thick. In wheelchair-accessible homes, the entry door should have a 34″ clearing around it. This clearance provides space for the wheelchair plus room for the arms and hands to turn the wheels.

The *service entry* is usually connected to the kitchen. The overall design may be improved by placing a mudroom or utility room between the kitchen and service entry. *Special-purpose entries* are those providing access to patios, decks, and courts. Sliding doors are often used for this type of entry. Service and special-purpose entries are not intended to be as striking as the main entry, Figure 8-35.

Figure 8-35. This service door to the rear of the house is designed to match the house style. However, overall the entry is fairly "plain." (Therma-Tru, Division of LST Corporation.)

Foyer

The *foyer* functions as a place to greet guests and, in colder climates, remove overcoats and boots. Consequently, the floor covering material must be unaffected by water or dirt. It should also be easy to clean. Materials such as slate, terrazzo, ceramic or asphalt tile, or linoleum are generally used for foyer floors, Figure 8-36.

The foyer must have a coat closet. The minimum size required by FHA is 2′ × 3′ inside dimensions. A more desirable size would be 2′-6″ deep by 4′-0″ wide. The floor covering in the closet should also withstand mud and water.

Frequently, the foyer provides access to other rooms of the house through halls. Hall space should be kept to a minimum, since any area wasted in halls reduces the useful space available for other rooms of the house. The FHA recommends a minimum hall width of 3′-0″. A width of 3′-6″ or 4′-0″ is more desirable.

Figure 8-36. The flooring in a foyer must be able to withstand water and dirt. It should be easy to clean.

Decor

Decor of the foyer will most likely reflect the color scheme and materials used in the living room or other adjacent rooms. Yet, the foyer is an extension of the entry. If possible, the foyer should capitalize on the design aspects of the entry, Figure 8-37. For example, a two-story entry may be extended to include the foyer. This technique creates a unity between the inside and outside and can result in a very pleasing effect. Planters or potted plants may be used in the same way. They may also serve as informal dividers between the foyer and other rooms.

Foyers with an open feeling are more desirable than those that are small and closed, Figure 8-38. Using mirrors and windows helps create an open feeling. Lighting is an effective design tool that should not be overlooked. Plan the lighting for maximum effect both inside and outside the entry. The lighting of outside walks and entries should be carefully considered.

Size

The size of the foyer depends on several factors:

- The size of the house.
- Cost of the house.
- Location.
- Personal preference.

A minimum size for a foyer is about 6′ × 6′, Figure 8-39. An average size is 8′ × 10′. Anything larger than 8′ × 10′ is considered a large foyer, Figure 8-40.

Applications

The foyer shown in Figure 8-39 is well designed and functional. It is just slightly larger than a minimum-size foyer, but is well proportioned. The coat closet is easily accessible and the floor covering is durable tile or brick. This is a simple, functional design.

Figure 8-41 shows a split-entry with a main and a lower foyer. The main foyer is small, but adequate. The closet is convenient. The floor covering in both the main foyer and lower foyer is water- and soil-resistant slate. Even though the plan is complex with many walls and corners, this is a functional arrangement.

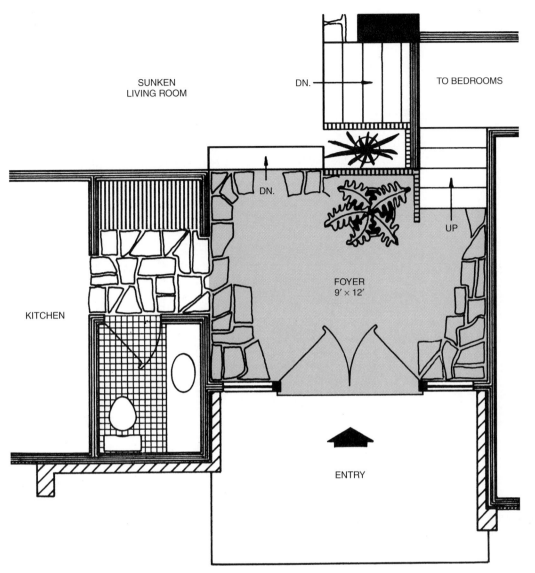

Figure 8-37. By having the foyer the same width as the entry, it becomes an extension of the entry.

Family Recreation Room

In new homes, there is a trend toward providing a specially designed room called a recreation room, family room, music room, hobby room, or rumpus room, Figure 8-42. These rooms can be generically called recreation rooms or "rec" rooms. The basic purpose of a recreation room is to provide a place where the family can play or pursue hobbies, Figure 8-43. A large house may have a number of recreation rooms, each planned for a specific activity. Design the room so that it is functional and easily maintained.

If located near the dining or living room, the recreation room can provide overflow space when needed. It may also be placed between the kitchen and garage since this provides an ideal location for pursuing hobbies, Figure 8-44. In some cases, it may be wise to locate the recreation room adjacent to a patio to take advantage of swimming pools, indoor-outdoor picnics, or sunbathing. Some designers favor placing the recreation room in the basement, Figure 8-45. This location takes advantage of a large area, separates noise from other living areas, contains the necessary structural details, and is easy to decorate and keep clean. Wherever the room is located it should be convenient to those who use it.

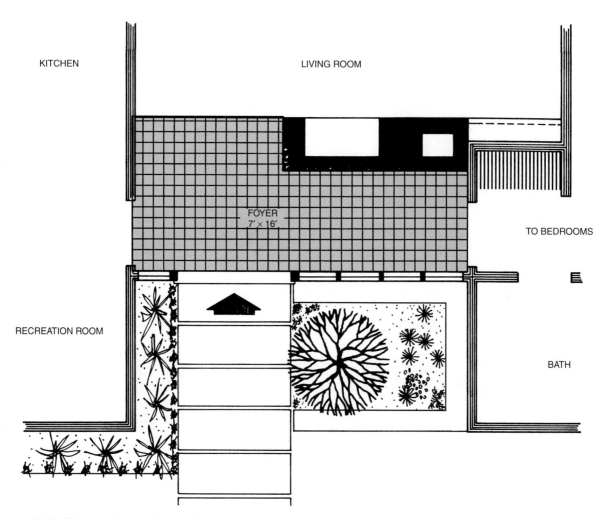

KITCHEN

LIVING ROOM

FOYER
7' × 16'

TO BEDROOMS

RECREATION ROOM

BATH

Figure 8-38. This is a large foyer with an open design that leads into three living areas. Also, notice the use of glass on the front of the foyer.

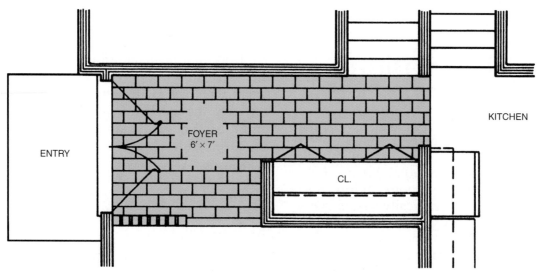

ENTRY

FOYER
6' × 7'

CL.

KITCHEN

Figure 8-39. A well-designed small foyer.

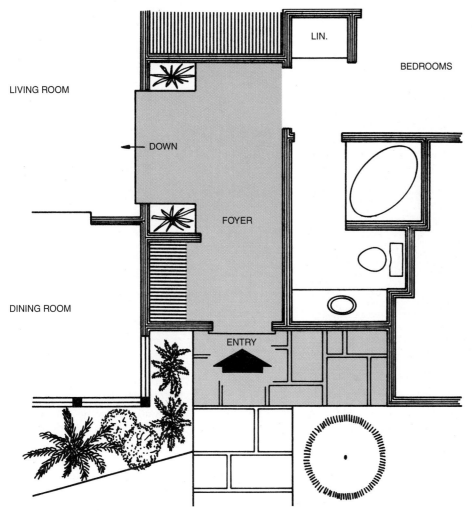

Figure 8-40. This is an attractive, nicely landscaped entry and complementary large foyer.

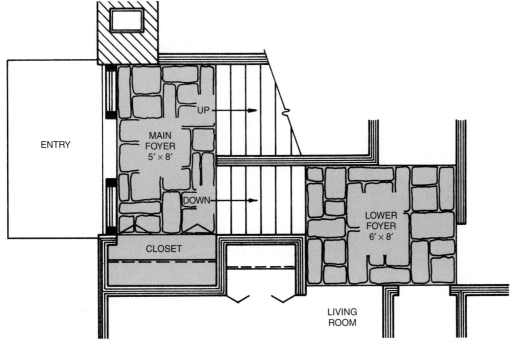

Figure 8-41. This split-entry is functional and convenient.

Figure 8-42. The activities in this simple recreation room are focused around the entertainment center.

Figure 8-43. A recreation room such as this appears warm and inviting for relaxing family activities. Notice that the floor surface is an easy-to-clean tile. (Photo Courtesy of Four Seasons Sunrooms)

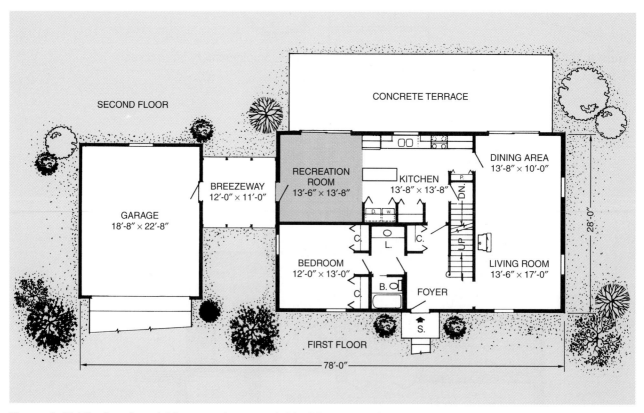

Figure 8-44. The location of this recreation room is ideal for games, family hobbies, and indoor-outdoor activities. (The Garlinghouse Company)

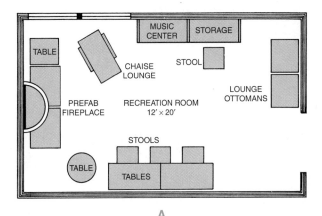

A

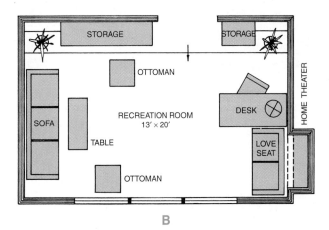

B

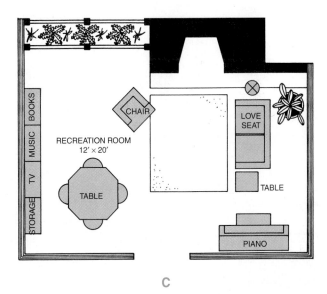

C

Figure 8-45. This basement recreation room is set up so it can function as a home office or be used for family activities. (Formica Corporation)

Size

Recreation rooms vary greatly in size. The number of people planning to use the room and the types of activities in which the family members will be engaged are important considerations in determining the size, Figure 8-46. A common size is 12′ × 20′ Furniture selection for the room is very important and depends on the anticipated activities, Figure 8-47. The recreation room typically receives a great deal of use. Therefore, choose furniture that is serviceable and resistant to wear.

To accommodate a person using a wheelchair, a space of 4′ to 5′ wide should be provided around furniture. To enable easy transfer to a sofa or chair, the seat should be the same height as the wheelchair seat and cushions should be firm. Power-operated elevating chairs are available that help a person get to a standing position.

The recreation room should include storage space for games and hobbies, Figure 8-48. Lighting must be good for those activities that require sensitive viewing, such as needlepoint or model building. Many recreation rooms are brightly lighted with fluorescent light to provide light for activities such as table tennis or other games.

Figure 8-46. A—This recreation room is designed primarily for relaxation, writing, and reading. Note the furniture arrangement and lack of TV. B—This recreation room illustrates an arrangement for hobbies or work and includes a home theater center.C—Styled for board games, singing, or a fireside chat, this design suggests further activity ideas.

A   B

Figure 8-47. The furniture in a recreation room should be selected for the anticipated use of the space. A—This restored attic is designed for entertaining guests. (Georgia-Pacific Corporation) B—The furniture helps emphasize the theme of this recreation room. (Wilsonart International)

Figure 8-48. Well-planned storage for toys, games, and other recreational equipment keeps the room tidy and easy to clean.

Decor

The recreation room is a good place to try out decorating ideas. Exercise your creative talents to develop individual and personal designs, Figure 8-49. The recreation room should feature floors that are easy to clean, suitable for a variety of activities, resistant to wear, and not slippery. Linoleum, ceramic tile, and vinyl tile are commonly used for recreation room floors. Deep pile carpeting should be avoided when persons in wheelchairs will be using the room. It is wise to select materials that are washable and mar resistant. Bright materials that are "alive with color" are desirable. Remember, this is a fun room!

Applications

Figure 8-50 shows a compact recreation room designed for conversation, reading, and relaxing. Large sliding glass doors opening onto the patio are an added attraction. This arrangement is quite functional for a "quiet" room. More vigorous activities may be performed on the patio, weather permitting.

The recreation room shown in Figure 8-51 is truly an "action" room. It is designed especially for young adults. The built-in conversation area is the focal point, but the raised dance area is a close second. This room would be popular in most any home with teenagers or young adults.

Special-Purpose Rooms

After the primary rooms of the living area have been planned, consider special-purpose rooms. *Special-purpose rooms* may include a dedicated home office, sunroom or atrium, greenhouse, ham radio room, and so on.

Some special-purpose areas may be placed in the corner of another room, like the home office shown in Figure 8-52. Other special-purpose rooms such as a music room or sunroom may be located to the side or rear of the house, Figure 8-53. Rooms that require a great deal of privacy, such as a dark room or

Figure 8-49. Creative decorating gives this recreation room life and excitement. You can try designs that you would not use in other, more formal areas of the house. (Formica Corporation)

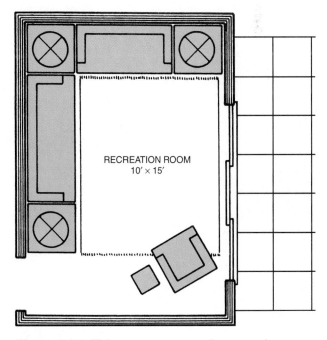

RECREATION ROOM
10′ × 15′

Figure 8-50. This compact recreation room is designed for reading, conversation, or relaxing.

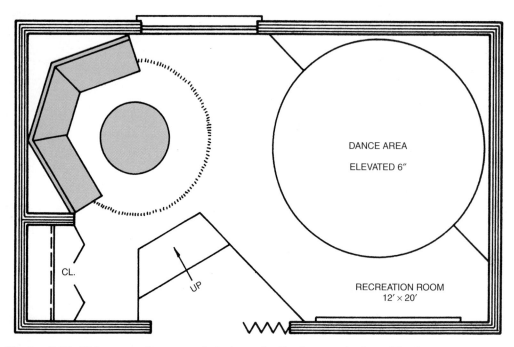

Figure 8-51. This recreation room is truly an "action" room designed for teenagers or young adults.

Figure 8-52. This home office is located in the corner of a larger room. (Sauder Woodworking Co.)

Jacuzzi™, should be placed in a remote area of the home.

In addition to location, many special-purpose rooms have unique requirements that should receive attention in the design process. These requirements may include storage, lighting, ventilation, plumbing, and electrical facilities, Figure 8-54.

Patios, Porches, Courts, and Gazebos

A well-designed house will extend its living facilities beyond its walls, as shown in Figure 8-55A. Patios, porches or decks, courts, and gazebos can effectively enlarge the area and function of a house. In addition, many people simply enjoy outdoor living. These activities should be planned for, Figure 8-55B.

Lighting is an important feature of any patio, porch, court, or gazebo. Without proper lighting, use after dark may be limited. In addition, much of the dramatic effect of the

Figure 8-54. Storage is a primary consideration in this special-purpose room. (Summitville Tile)

A

B

Figure 8-53. A—This formal music room can complement other functional areas of the home. (NMC/Focal Point) B—Located off the back of the house, this sunroom is an ideal place to enjoy a quiet activity such as reading. (Four Seasons Sunrooms)

A

B

Figure 8-55. A—This house has a deck that provides a large "living area" beyond the walls of the house. (Trex Co.)
B—An attractive and functional deck such as this complements the house and provides extended outdoor living.
(Thermal Industries, Inc.)

Figure 8-56. An extension of the dining room, this patio adds beauty and function to the house. Notice how it is at grade level.

feature will be lost. Lighting should be used as a design tool to assist in accomplishing an atmosphere and extend the usefulness of the structure. Lighting also adds safety and security.

Patios

Patios are usually near the house but not structurally connected to it. These are ordinarily located at ground level and are constructed for durability. Concrete, brick, stone, redwood, pressure-treated wood, and synthetic decking are commonly used construction materials. The floor of the patio shown in Figure 8-56 is textured concrete and an example of how a well-designed patio can add to the overall function of a house.

Patios are used for relaxing, playing, entertaining, and living, Figure 8-57. Each function

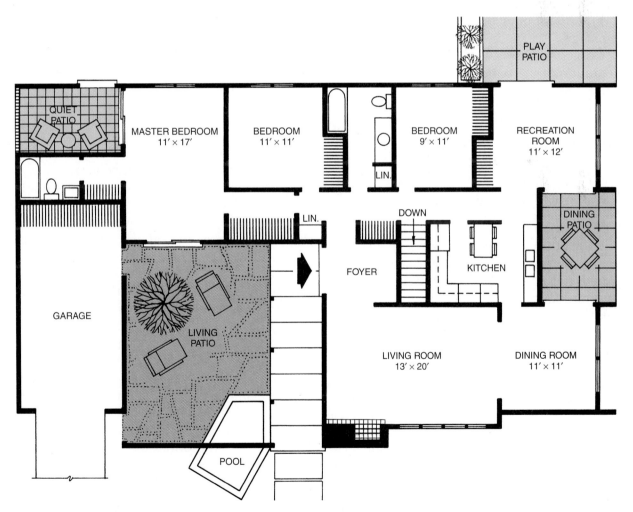

Figure 8-57. This floor plan has four patios designed for different types of activities. Notice their locations in relation to the rest of the house.

requires special consideration as to location, size, and design. Try to locate patios designed for relaxing on a quiet side of the house near the bedrooms where there is privacy, Figure 8-58. Privacy may be achieved through the use of screens, walls, or plants. A patio designed for entertaining and playing will most likely be large and located off of the living room, dining room, or recreation room. Play patios are usually less encumbered with furniture, planters, and screens. The play patio is usually designed for use by children and by adults for physical activities that require open space. The entry on a play patio sometimes doubles as a service entry.

A 10' × 14' patio is considered small, while a 20' × 30' patio is considered large. Design the patio to be proportional to the size of the house. A living or entertaining patio will most likely be located on the back side of the house where more space is available, Figure 8-59. Again, privacy must be considered in the planning stage.

Consideration should be given to the orientation of the patio in relation to sunlight, wind, and the view. In warm climates, providing shade may be a major factor. In the far north, ensuring ample sun may be a prime objective. A well-designed patio is a pleasant place, so if the surrounding area lacks natural beauty, more emphasis should be placed on design and styling. The use of flowers, pools, and screens helps to create a beautiful setting for dining, relaxing, or entertaining.

If the house has a swimming pool, the area around the pool can be designed as a patio. Figure 8-60 shows an example of a patio with a swimming pool as the main feature. This type of patio may be a living, entertaining, or play patio.

Porches

Porches and decks differ from patios in several ways. They are generally structurally connected to the house. Figure 8-61 shows a porch that is an integral part of a home with a spectacular view. Porches are also raised above grade level. They are usually covered while

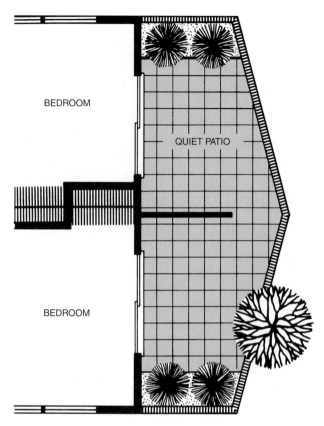

Figure 8-58. A quiet, secluded patio designed for privacy and comfort may be located off of bedrooms.

patios are not. Finally, porches are typically smaller than patios, but can be larger.

Porches that are not under a roof are called *decks*, Figure 8-62. Decks differ from patios in that they are typically above grade. Balconies and verandahs are other types of porches. Balconies are generally higher than the standard porch, Figure 8-63. They are sometimes located off of a second floor room. A verandah is typically larger than a porch and can accommodate furniture.

Porches may function as outdoor dining areas and entry extensions, Figure 8-64. If possible, the porch should be large enough to act as a small patio when needed. The usefulness of the porch in northern states may be increased by the addition of screens or glass. Glass allows the porch to be used during the winter months in northern climates.

Porches need not appear to be "tacked-on" to the structure. It is worth adding well-designed

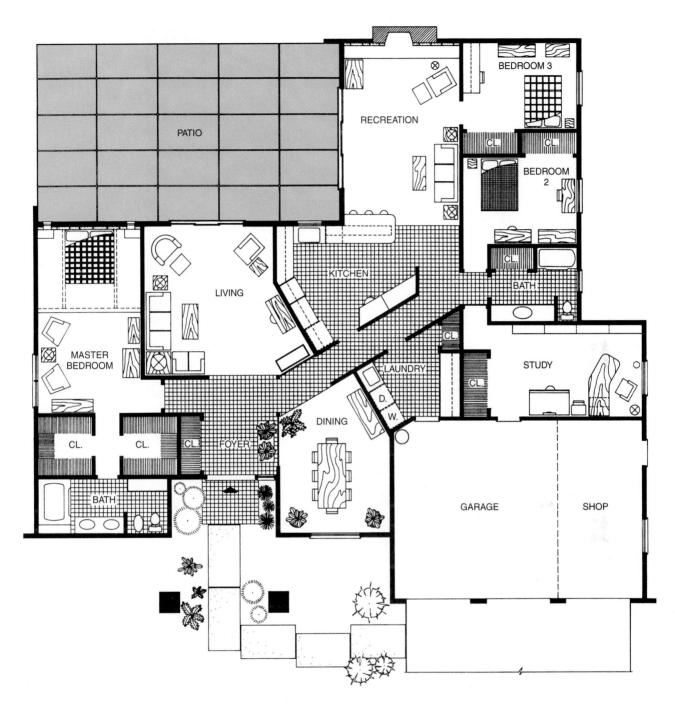

Figure 8-59. A living or entertaining patio is often located off the back of the house. Access to this patio is from the recreation room and living room.

Figure 8-60. The swimming pool surroundings can be used to form a beautiful and useful patio.

Figure 8-61. This enclosed porch is an excellent place to relax and enjoy a beautiful view. (Marvin Windows)

Figure 8-62. This multilevel deck enhances the architectural design of this home. (Trex Co.)

Figure 8-63. The second level verandah expands the living space of this home and enhances the architectural design. (Photo Courtesy of James Hardie® Siding Products)

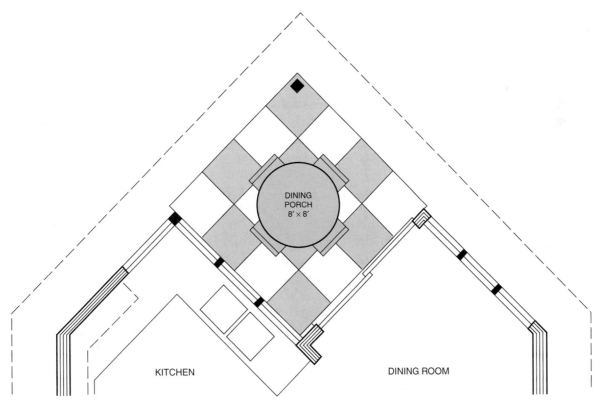

Figure 8-64. This small, covered dining porch is located adjacent to the dining room and kitchen.

Figure 8-65. This front porch is an integral part of the house. It does not appear "tacked-on" to the house. (Photo Courtesy of James Hardie® Siding Products)

porches to all house plans. If the porch is planned as an integral part of the house, the result will be pleasing, Figure 8-65.

Since porches and decks are above grade, a ramp is required for access by the disabled. A ramp with a slope between 1:12 and 1:20 should be planned. A steeper slope is hard to navigate with a wheelchair or walker.

Courts and Gazebos

Courts are similar to porches and patios and may have characteristics of both. They are totally or at least partially enclosed by walls or roof. Figure 8-66 shows a good example of an interior court. Courts may be used for dining, relaxing, talking, or entertaining. They may also serve as interior gardens to add a touch of spring throughout the year. Courts are sometimes used to break up floor plans, add interest, or provide natural light to an interior part of the house that has no exterior wall.

A beautiful gazebo or garden structure can provide an architectural focal point. A *gazebo* is a roofed structure, similar to a porch, that is detached from the house. It typically has open

sides. A gazebo can be a place from which to view the surrounding beauty of the lawn and gardens, Figure 8-67.

Applications

A large porch is shown in Figure 8-68. This porch would be a welcome addition to most any home. It is convenient to the living and dining rooms as well as the bedroom area. In a warm climate, this porch can provide a shaded area with a cross breeze. In a cold climate, the porch can be enclosed in glass to provide a simulated outdoor setting in the winter. In a moderate climate, windows that can be opened may be used to enclose the area. This provides a breeze in the summer, yet allows for an insulated enclosure in the winter.

Figure 8-69 shows an extensive porch and patio. The porch serves as a nice entry for the house. The patio extends the living area of the house to the outside and encourages outdoor living. It is partially enclosed with a fence to increase privacy and define its boundaries. The patio also provides a nice view from the living room.

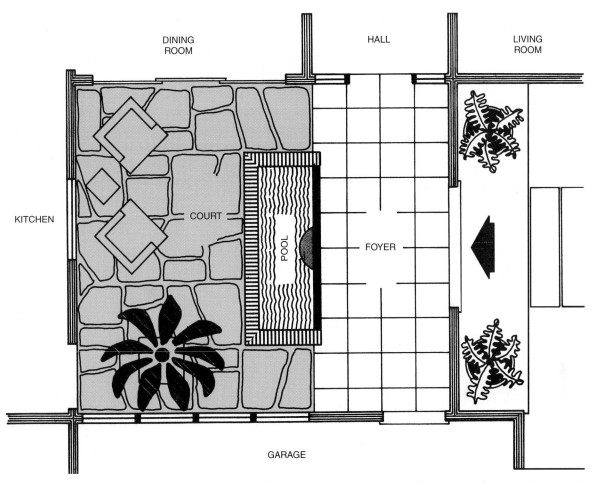

Figure 8-66. This approach to a romantic, Spanish-style courtyard is a good example of an interior court.

Figure 8-67. A gazebo is similar to a porch, but not attached to the house.

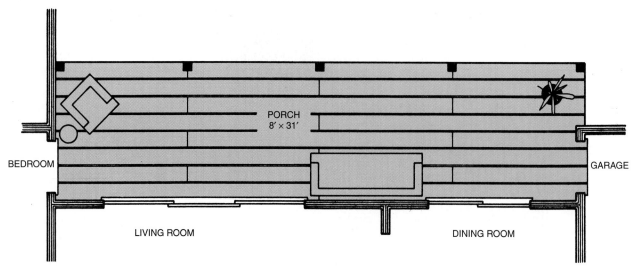

Figure 8-68. This porch is conveniently located near the garage, living room, dining room, and a bedroom.

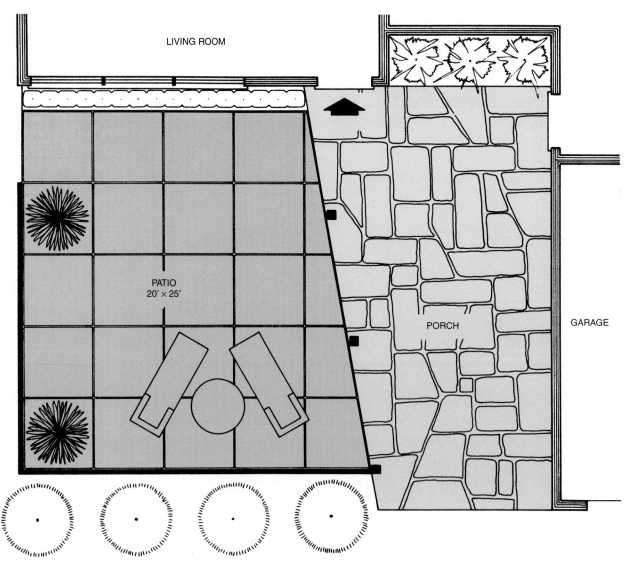

Figure 8-69. This house features a large porch that serves as an entry. In addition, a large patio off of the porch increases the living area of the house.

Internet Resources

www.archdigest.com
Architectural Digest

www.armstrong.com
Armstrong World Industries, Inc.

www.bhg.com
Better Homes and Gardens Magazine

www.congoleum.com
Congoleum Corporation, a supplier of flooring products

www.hartcoflooring.com
Hartco Flooring, An Armstrong Company

www.homecrestcab.com
HomeCrest Cabinetry

www.marvin.com
Marvin Windows and Doors

www.nationalgypsum.com
National Gypsum Company

www.schultestorage.com
Schulte Corporation, a manufacturer of storage solutions

www.sweets.com
Sweets Catalog File

Review Questions – Chapter 8

Write your answers on a separate sheet of paper.
Do not write in this book.

1. The normal width of an entry door is _____.

2. What is the purpose of the foyer?

3. A dining room measuring 16′ × 20′ would be considered a _____-size dining room.

4. List at least four ways in which the dining area may be separated from the living room without using a full-height wall.

5. List five questions that should be answered when determining the size and design of a living room.

6. The living area of a residential structure comprises about _____ of the total area of a house.

7. How does a porch differ from a patio?

8. List the three basic types of entryways.

9. Standard interior and exterior door height is _____.

10. List the rooms that typically comprise the living area.

11. Identify three special-purpose rooms that may be in the living area.

12. A porch without a roof is called a(n) _____.

Suggested Activities

1. Plan a medium-size living room with furniture. Present your plan in color for a bulletin board display. Prepare a short description of the intended use.

2. Draw the plans for a dining room that is designed to accommodate six people. Show the furniture. Use manual or CADD drafting.

3. Prepare a bulletin board display of different entryways. Use color copies of pictures, magazines, or color printouts from the Internet. Try to represent a broad range of designs.

4. Using CADD, design a recreation room for a specific hobby or activity. Describe the features of your design and how they relate to the activity.

5. Find a plan for a house that has no patio. Using CADD, plan a porch or patio. Print or plot the patio on vellum or film. Then, present the patio design as an overlay on the house plan.

6. Using CADD, plan a special-purpose room. Specify the equipment and furniture required. Explain the special requirements that must be met in the room.

7. Using CADD, draw symbols for furniture and other items that are found in the living area. Add these symbols to your symbols library for future use.

Handling, Storing, and Maintaining Tools, Equipment, and Drawings

Architectural drafting involves the use of many different tools and pieces of equipment. An architectural drafter using CADD may use:

- Computer workstation: Includes monitor, CPU, keyboard, mouse/puck, and printer/plotter.
- Removable storage media: Floppy disks and CD-ROMs.
- Printing supplies: Ink/toner and paper.
- Plotted drawings.

An architectural drafter using traditional (manual) methods may use:

- Pencils or lead holders.
- Pens and other inking devices.
- Paper and vellum.
- Erasers and brushes.
- Drafting tape.
- Diazo machines and supplies.
- Completed drawings.

Drafting equipment requires periodic inspection and regular maintenance to remain reliable and safe. The owner's manuals for all office and drafting equipment should be kept in an organized library where they can be easily located. These manuals provide detailed inspection, maintenance, and service information. Additional information may be found at the manufacturers' websites.

Plotters, printers, and other electronic equipment should be cleaned and serviced according to the instructions and schedules established by the manufacturers. Equipment should be repaired or replaced as needed. Electronic equipment should be powered through a surge protector. If a phone line is connected to the computer, such as to a modem, the line should also be run through a surge protector. An inventory of replacement toner and ink cartridges, plotter pens, paper, and other consumables should be kept on hand to prevent work stoppage when these items need to be replaced.

Manual drafting equipment such as triangles, T-squares, French curves, and protractors should be inspected periodically for warping, chips, or other physical defects. Damaged instruments should be replaced. Also, triangles, straightedges, and drafting machine blades (rules) can collect lead dust; they should be kept clean. An inventory of manual drafting equipment and consumables, such as paper, vellum, erasers, and pencils, should be maintained to prevent work stoppage.

In addition to proper maintenance, all equipment must be properly stored. For example, compasses and dividers have sharp points. These instruments must be stored in cases to prevent damage to the points. Also, magnetic computer disks are sensitive to dust and the magnetic fields produced by electrical cords, monitors, speakers, etc. If the disks are not properly stored, the data may be lost. Placing covers on plotters and printers when not in use can help keep dust out of the equipment.

Manual drawings and plotted CADD drawing must be properly stored. They should be identified by a properly drawn title block. All drawings must be identified by some sort of naming convention, which appears in the title block. Then, the sheets must be stored in a flat file or carefully rolled and stored in a tube.

CADD drawings are stored electronically and often plotted or printed only as needed. The electronic drawing files must be properly stored using a file naming convention that allows easy drawing retrieval. In addition, the electronic files (and all critical electronic data) must be archived on some form of backup system for safe keeping. As drawings are electronically revised, the backup of the drawing must also be replaced.

Room Planning— Service Area

Objectives

After studying this chapter, you will be able to:

➤ Plan the service area of a home by applying good design principles.

➤ Design a functional kitchen to meet a family's needs.

➤ Select kitchen appliances that are appropriate for a design.

➤ Plan an efficient clothes care center.

➤ Describe appropriate dimensions for garage space.

Key Terms

Clothes Care Center

Corridor Kitchen

Island Kitchen

L-Shaped Kitchen

Peninsula Kitchen

Service Area

Straight-Line Kitchen

U-Shaped Kitchen

Work Centers

Work Triangle

The *service area* supplements the living and sleeping areas of the house. It supplies equipment and space for maintenance, storage, and service. The service area includes the kitchen, clothes care center, garage or carport, utility, and storage, Figure 9-1. Due to its varied functions, design of the service area requires careful planning.

Designing with CADD

CADD systems can speed up the design process. For example, once a symbol is developed for the service area, it may be used as often as desired without having to draw it again. Placement and orientation of symbols is quick and easy. In addition, specialized CADD software is available for the design of kitchens, specifying windows, and pictorial representation. Figure 9-2 shows two very different types of CADD drawings.

Kitchen

A principal use for the kitchen is food preparation. Its use may, however, be extended to include dining, laundry, and storage, Figure 9-3. There are six basic kitchen styles:

- Straight Line
- L-Shaped
- Corridor
- Island
- U-Shaped
- Peninsula

Figure 9-1. The service area of this house includes the garage, kitchen, laundry, mud room, a bath, and some storage.

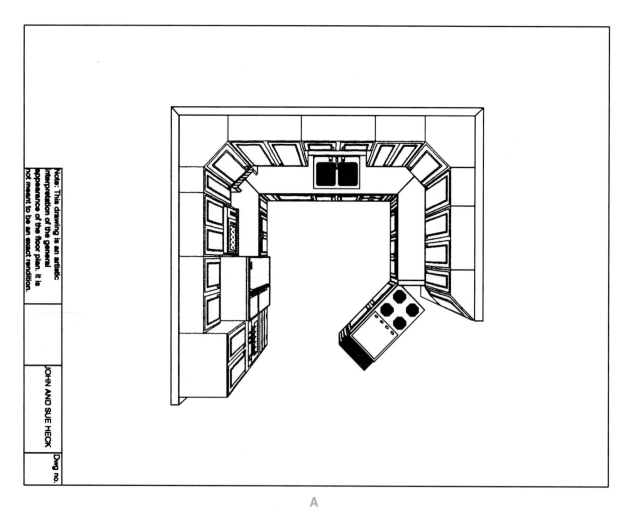

A

Figure 9-2. A—This one-point perspective drawing of a kitchen was drawn using CADD. (20-20 Computerized Design)

B

Figure 9-2. *Continued.* B—This CADD-rendered image of a kitchen shows enough detail to communicate even small design features. (SoftPlan Systems, Inc.)

Figure 9-3. This kitchen is designed for food preparation, dining, and storage.

Nearly every one of the kitchen styles can easily be adapted for a handicapped person. Toe space of 6″ deep and 8″ to 11″ high is needed under the cabinets for wheelchair footrests. Knee space of 28″ to 30″ wide, 27″ to 30″ high, and 21″ to 24″ deep can be provided by an overhang or extended counterspace.

Kitchen design presents unique problems. Inefficiency and added cost will result if the problems are not solved. From the standpoint of cost, the kitchen is usually the most expensive room in the house per square foot and receives the most use of any room.

Kitchen Planning

Planning of an efficient kitchen involves the placement of appliances, adequate storage cabinets, and food preparation facilities, Figure 9-4. This placement creates the *work centers*—food preparation center, cleanup center, and cooking center. In designing kitchens, give considerable thought to the general location of each of the kitchen work centers. The arrangement should be logical and minimize the amount of walking required by the homemaker, Figure 9-5.

The *work triangle* is one measure of kitchen efficiency. It is determined by drawing a line from the front-center of the range to the refrigerator to the sink and back to the range. The lengths of these three lines are added together to produce the length of the work triangle, Figure 9-6. For an efficient kitchen, this distance should not exceed 22′.

Figure 9-4. This contemporary kitchen has ample space for storage, food preparation facilities, and appliances. (Wilsonart International)

Figure 9-5. The arrangement of the work centers in this compact kitchen minimizes the amount of walking required when preparing food. (Lis King)

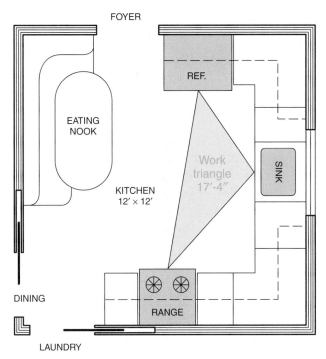

Figure 9-6. The work triangle is a good measure of kitchen efficiency. The combined length of the three sides should not exceed 22′.

Food and cooking utensil storage should be located near the areas where they are to be used, Figure 9-7. For example, pots and pans that are always used on the range should be stored near the cooking center. Do not store them near the food preparation center.

A kitchen that is handicapped accessible may follow the same layout as any other plan. However, the work surfaces should be lower, sinks should have clearance underneath, and cooking units should be accessible. In addition, ample space must be provided for wheelchairs.

Straight-Line Kitchen

The *straight-line kitchen* style is frequently used in small houses, cottages, and apartments. See Figure 9-8. Little space is required for this style and it usually provides for an efficient arrangement of kitchen facilities. Two disadvantages of the style are that it provides a limited amount of cabinet space and the result is usually not very interesting. The straight-line kitchen is seldom used unless space is very limited.

L-Shaped Kitchen

The *L-shaped kitchen* is located along two adjacent walls, Figure 9-9. This style results in an efficient workspace. Two work centers are

A

B

Figure 9-7. A—These food storage units are located near the food preparation center. (Wilsonart International) B—These pull-out drawers provide storage that is convenient and organized.

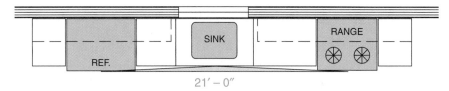

Figure 9-8. This is an example of a straight-line kitchen.

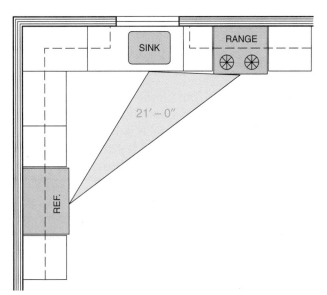

Figure 9-9. An L-shaped kitchen is located on two adjoining walls and provides a traffic-free work triangle.

attractive than a straight-line kitchen. Figure 9-10 shows two examples of L-shaped kitchens.

Corridor Kitchen

The *corridor kitchen,* as implied by the name, is located on two walls opposite each other, Figure 9-11. Corridor kitchens are usually small to medium in size and are ideal for long, narrow rooms, Figure 9-12. The open space between opposing cabinets should be at least four feet. A corridor kitchen tends to be an efficient workspace. However, the style is not recommended if traffic is to be heavy through the kitchen.

U-Shaped Kitchen

The *U-shaped kitchen* is probably the most popular and one of the most attractive of the six kitchen styles, Figure 9-13. It has a highly efficient workspace. The work triangle is compact and functional, Figure 9-14. In addition, there is no traffic through the kitchen

generally located along one wall and the third on the adjoining wall. This style is not intended for large kitchens because the efficiency of the plan is lost if the walls are too long. An L-shaped kitchen is usually more

A   B

Figure 9-10. A—This L-shaped kitchen has a contemporary decor. (Manufactured Housing Institute) B—An L-shaped kitchen with traditional decor.

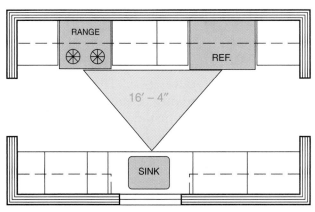

Figure 9-11. This typical corridor kitchen has plenty of cabinet space.

Figure 9-12. A compact corridor kitchen with convenient storage and an efficient workspace. Notice the meal planning center. (Manufactured Housing Institute)

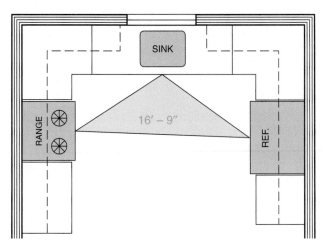

Figure 9-13. The U-shaped kitchen is perhaps the most popular style.

A

B

Figure 9-14. A—Efficiency and beauty are the key elements of this unique U-shaped kitchen.
B—This medium-size U-shaped kitchen is pleasant for preparing meals. The counter space on the left can be used for meal preparation or serving informal meals.

to other areas of the house. Most U-shaped kitchens are medium-size with the open space between the legs of the U being about 5' or 6'.

Peninsula Kitchen

The *peninsula kitchen* is a popular style because it provides plenty of workspace, Figure 9-15. It is attractive and can easily join with the dining area using the peninsula as a divider. The peninsula may be used as the cooking center, food preparation center, or eating area, Figure 9-16. As in a U-shaped kitchen, the amount of traffic is reduced and the work triangle is small.

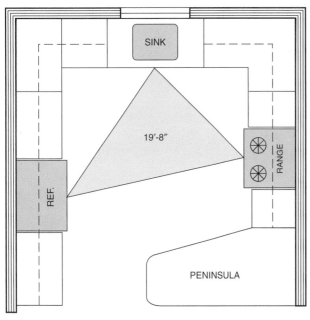

Figure 9-15. The peninsula kitchen is a popular style.

Island Kitchen

The *island kitchen* may be a modification of the straight-line, L-shaped, or U-shaped kitchen style, Figure 9-17. The island may house the sink, cooking center, or food preparation area. In some instances, it may serve as a countertop or snack bar, Figure 9-18. The island should be accessible from all sides. At least four feet clearance should be allowed on all sides of the island for easy access.

Cabinets and Appliances

Kitchen appliances include the stove/range, oven, refrigerator, dishwasher, microwave, garbage disposal, and so on. The appliances shown on a floor plan are those that are generally not movable. Appliances such as toasters

Figure 9-16. The peninsula in a peninsula kitchen can serve many functions. A—For cooking or serving. (Manufactured Housing Institute) B—As an eating area that can double as a hobby area. (Manufactured Housing Institute) C—As a food preparation center. (Wood-Mode Cabinetry)

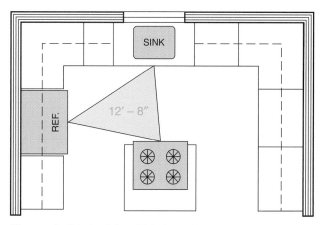

Figure 9-17. An island kitchen design.

and food processors are not typically shown on a floor plan, though they may be shown in a presentation drawing. Kitchen appliances are available in a variety of styles, colors, and sizes. Symbols and standard sizes of kitchen appliances and sinks are shown in Figure 9-19.

An electric stove or cooktop may provide more safety for the handicapped user than a gas appliance. A wall-type oven at eye level is more easily accessible than other types. An appropriate refrigerator must also be selected.

Kitchen cabinets provide the majority of storage space in most kitchens. They are produced in standard sizes, but may be made to custom sizes if required. Most standard base cabinets are 34-1/2″ high and 24″ deep with a width in 3″ increments, such as 15″, 18″, or 21″. Wall cabinets are either 12″ or 13″ deep. Cabinets 12″ to 30″ inches high (in 3″ increments) and 12″ to 36″ wide (in 3″ increments) are also available. Wall cabinets are also produced in taller dimensions, some as tall as 45″.

In base cabinets, compartmentalized drawers instead of shelves can bring the full depth of the base cabinets within reach of the handicapped user. Also roll-out bins, racks, baskets, and shelf trays can be used to make

A

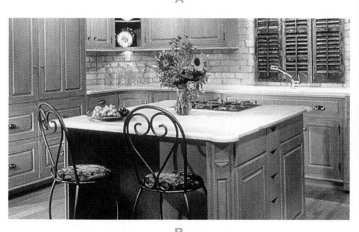

B

C

Figure 9-18. The island in an island kitchen design can serve many functions. A—The cleanup center. B—The cooking center. (Lis King) C—The food preparation center. (Lis King)

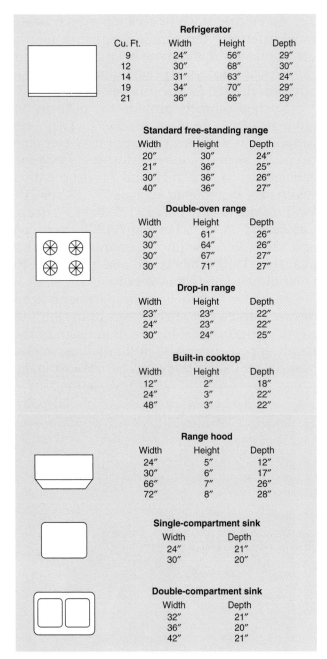

Refrigerator

Cu. Ft.	Width	Height	Depth
9	24″	56″	29″
12	30″	68″	30″
14	31″	63″	24″
19	34″	70″	29″
21	36″	66″	29″

Standard free-standing range

Width	Height	Depth
20″	30″	24″
21″	36″	25″
30″	36″	26″
40″	36″	27″

Double-oven range

Width	Height	Depth
30″	61″	26″
30″	64″	26″
30″	67″	27″
30″	71″	27″

Drop-in range

Width	Height	Depth
23″	23″	22″
24″	23″	22″
30″	24″	25″

Built-in cooktop

Width	Height	Depth
12″	2″	18″
24″	3″	22″
48″	3″	22″

Range hood

Width	Height	Depth
24″	5″	12″
30″	6″	17″
66″	7″	26″
72″	8″	28″

Single-compartment sink

Width	Depth
24″	21″
30″	20″

Double-compartment sink

Width	Depth
32″	21″
36″	20″
42″	21″

Figure 9-19. Appliance symbols and sizes.

base cabinets usable. A lazy Susan is convenient for wall or base cabinets in corners.

It is difficult for people in wheelchairs to reach shelves higher than 48″. The bottom of wall cabinets should be situated so the first shelf can be reached from a seated position, usually not more than 17″ above the counter. Cabinets over stoves and refrigerators are exceptions, however, mechanical assistance must be provided for these cabinets to be used by the handicapped. Shelves in wall cabinets should be adjustable.

A typical section through the base and wall cabinets is shown in Figure 9-20. Figure 9-21 shows the plan and elevation of a kitchen. Note how the wall and base cabinets are identified in the plan view. The numbers shown on the drawing are the manufacturer's stock numbers. The wall cabinets are illustrated with a hidden line while the base units are shown as object lines. A kitchen plan should also show the work triangle and specify its length.

Figure 9-22 illustrates the standard base and wall cabinets that most manufacturers produce as standard units. Be sure to check the specifications of the cabinets selected before drawing the kitchen plan. Careful consideration of all specifications and design requirements is an essential part of developing the kitchen plan.

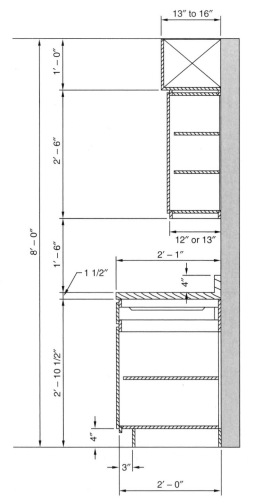

Figure 9-20. A typical section through the base and wall cabinets.

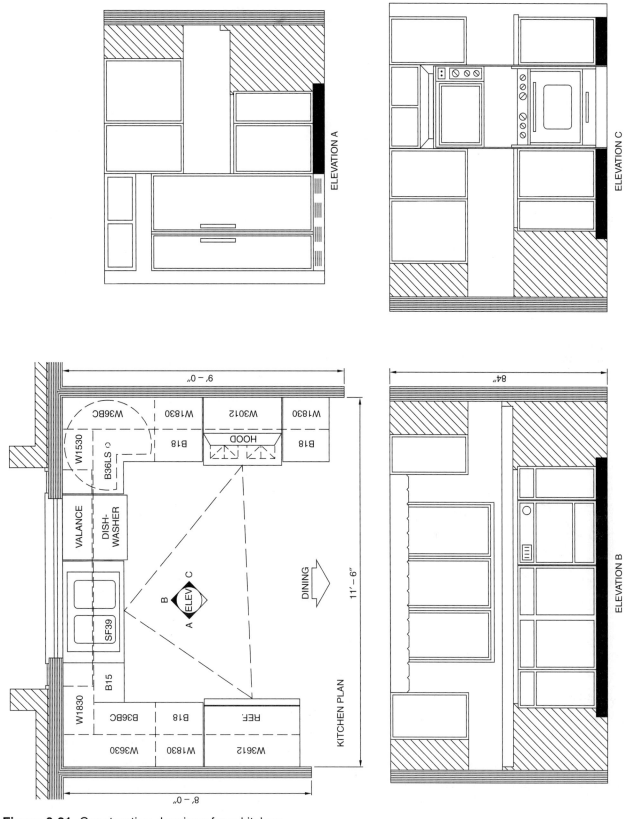

Figure 9-21. Construction drawings for a kitchen.

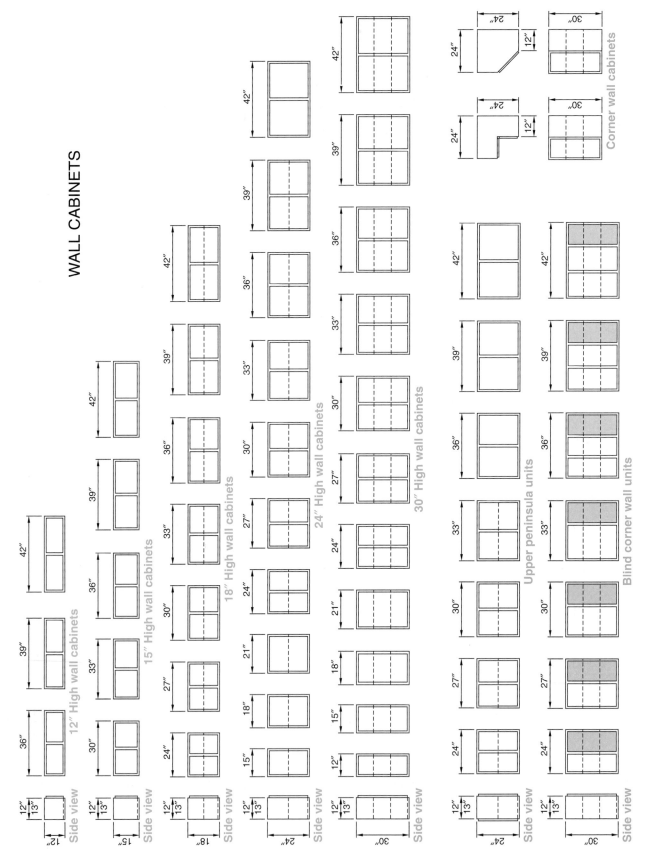

Figure 9-22. Standard wall cabinet sizes and designs.

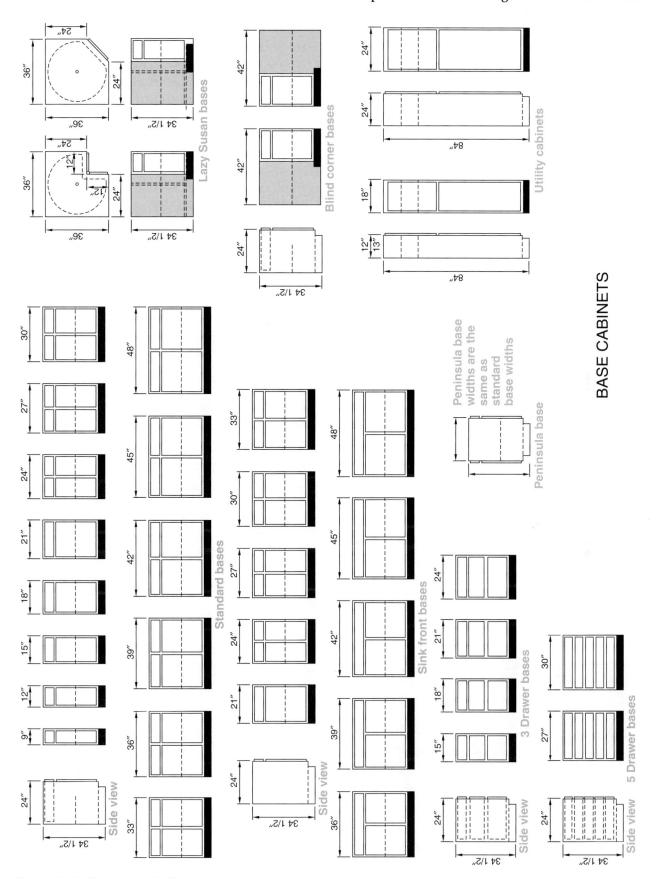

Figure 9-22 (Continued). Standard wall cabinet sizes and designs.

Location and Ventilation

Proper location of the kitchen is important. It is the prime element of the service area and its relation to other areas of the house requires careful evaluation.

Usually, the kitchen should be located near the service entrance. This is where groceries are brought into the house. Also, outside trash containers are usually located close to the service entrance. The kitchen should be located near the dining room. The laundry area and a bath should also be located close to the kitchen.

Try to locate kitchen windows so that children in their outside play area can be observed from the kitchen. Windows can also provide a way to exhaust heat from the kitchen in the summer months.

Good ventilation is a must in the kitchen. A wall fan is acceptable, but a range hood with a fan is better. A hood is more efficient at collecting fumes, Figure 9-23. The ventilation must exhaust either through an outside wall or the roof. The ventilation should not be exhausted into the attic or crawlspace.

Decor

The decor of the kitchen should be pleasant and well lighted. In addition to the main ceiling fixtures, lights over the sink, cooking center, and food preparation areas are needed. A dropped ceiling with banks of fluorescent lights is a popular way to supply an ample amount of light and at the same time add to the appearance of the kitchen. In addition, the lowered ceiling makes the room look larger. Lights mounted under the wall cabinets help illuminate the work centers.

Most appliances and fixtures are produced in many colors and styles, Figure 9-24. Select colors and styles that are consistent with the overall design of the kitchen. Choose materials that are durable and easy to maintain.

A

B

Figure 9-24. Appliances are available in many colors and materials. A—This beautiful kitchen sink will provide lasting quality, easy maintenance, and a hygienic area. Also, notice the stainless steel range and hood. (Photo Courtesy of Kohler Co.)
B—This kitchen refrigerator is designed to be energy efficient and match a certain decor.

Figure 9-23. This unique range hood has charcoal filters to reduce odor. It is large and efficient in removing odors.

Applications

Figure 9-25 shows an island kitchen. This efficient design has a desk for meal planning, ample storage, and easy access to the work centers. In addition, one side of the island serves as a breakfast area. The island serves as a room divider and is convenient to the adjoining living room.

The U-shaped kitchen shown in Figure 9-26 has many extras. There is a large desk that can be used for planning meals and storing many cookbooks. The design is efficient with lots of room provided for movement. The dining area is conveniently located next to the food preparation center. The utility closet can be used as additional storage for pots and pans or it can double as a small pantry. Another advantage of this plan is the service entry, which facilitates garbage removal and restocking supplies. This plan is designed for the person who enjoys planning and preparing large meals.

Kitchen Eating Areas

An eating area in the kitchen is convenient for serving informal meals and snacking. It should be located outside of the food preparation area, yet convenient to it. When planning a kitchen with an eating area, allow sufficient space. Thus, the overall size of the kitchen will be larger than one without an eating area. Good lighting is important for the eating area. The design should include ample lighting.

A kitchen eating area such as the one shown in Figure 9-27A is popular with many families. The arrangement of table and chairs is flexible to accommodate a varying number of people. Other households prefer an eating counter with chairs or stools, Figure 9-27B. A change in countertop height can separate the cooking area from the eating area. Allow for knee space under the counter. If chairs are to be used at the eating counter, the counter height should be 26".

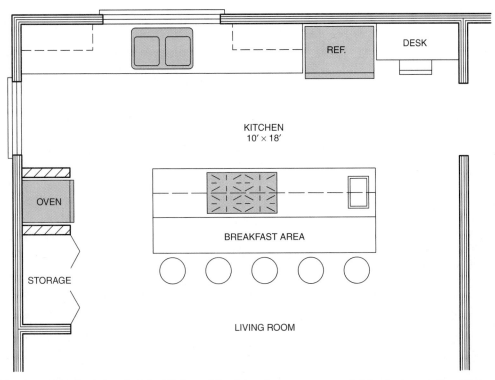

Figure 9-25. An island-style kitchen. The island serves as a divider between the kitchen and the living room. It also provides a breakfast area.

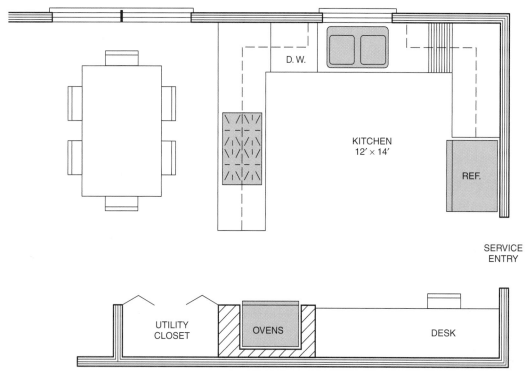

Figure 9-26. This stylish U-shaped kitchen is designed for planning and preparing large meals.

A

B

Figure 9-27. A—This attractive kitchen eating area allows for flexibility in serving people. B—Eating counters require less space than a table, but may not serve as many people.

Tables with pedestal legs or open leg space are more convenient for wheelchair users. Also, be sure to allow sufficient space around the table or counter for maneuvering the wheelchair.

Clothes Care Center

A *clothes care center* provides an area for washing, drying, pressing, folding, storing, and mending clothes. It is intended to be more than a "utility" room. Many traditional utility rooms are drab and are located away from other service areas of the house. If possible, locate the clothes care center near the kitchen. A large clothes care center can also serve as additional space for recreation activities, such as flower arranging, crafts, or other hobby.

The clothes care center is intended to be bright, cheerful, and convenient, Figure 9-28. It should be large enough to provide adequately for the activities to be performed there. The clothes care center must also provide ample storage for cleaners, soaps, sewing accessories, folded and pressed clothes, and so on, Figure 9-29.

The clothes care center must be well ventilated and lighted. The floor must be resistant to water and easy to clean. Ceramic tile or vinyl flooring are popular choices. However, durable hardwood floors are used as well.

Figure 9-28. This clothes care center is bright and cheerful. It provides ample workspace and convenient storage.

Countertops should be durable, soil resistant, and easy to clean, Figure 9-30.

Figure 9-31 shows the sizes and shapes of appliances and furnishings commonly used in a clothes care center. A well-designed clothes care center is illustrated in Figure 9-32. Note that this room includes all the functions associated with clothes care. The built-in ironing board saves space when not in use. The laundry tub/sink is near the washer for convenience. Cabinet storage space is provided above the washer, dryer, and sink.

A compact clothes care center is shown in Figure 9-33. This room is organized for

A

B

Figure 9-29. A—This clothes care center has ample storage, a built-in ironing board, and concealed waste container. (Wood-Mode Cabinetry) B—A washer, dryer, and ample storage space are the main features of this clothes care center.

maximum efficiency of space. The ironing board swings up into the wall so it is out of the way when not in use. Soiled clothes are collected in the bin below the clothes chute, which is convenient for wash day. A sewing and mending area is flanked by generous counter space. There is more than average storage available in this well-planned center.

The clothes care center shown in Figure 9-34 is designed for a basement location next to the recreation room. A series of storage shelves separates each area and adds many cubic feet of storage space. Wall cabinets line one wall and create a trim appearance, as well as adding storage space. Counter area is sufficient for folding clothes or mending. Organization is the key in this plan.

For greater wheelchair accessibility in the clothes care center, a front-loading washer can be

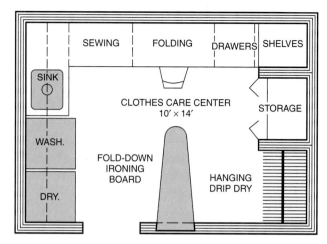

Figure 9-32. This well-designed clothes care center has all the facilities for washing, drying, pressing, folding, storing, and mending.

Figure 9-30. This clothes care center has a durable and easy-to-clean countertop. The floor is also durable and easy to clean.

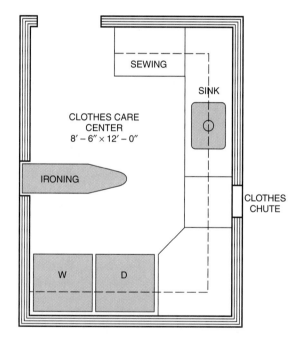

Figure 9-33. A clothes care center that is compact yet provides for washing, drying, sewing, storage, and ironing.

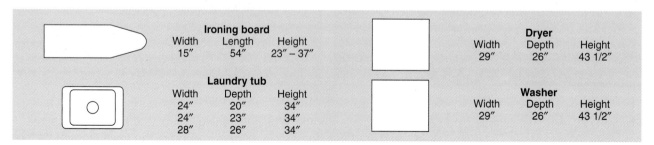

Ironing board		
Width	Length	Height
15″	54″	23″ – 37″

Laundry tub		
Width	Depth	Height
24″	20″	34″
24″	23″	34″
28″	26″	34″

Dryer		
Width	Depth	Height
29″	26″	43 1/2″

Washer		
Width	Depth	Height
29″	26″	43 1/2″

Figure 9-31. Furniture and appliance symbols used for a clothes care center.

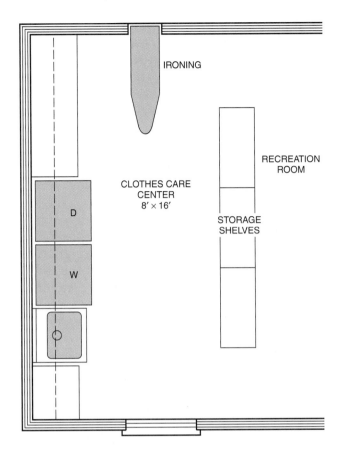

Figure 9-34. This clothes care center is designed for the basement.

used. Front-loading washers and dryers may be placed on a short platform for access to the units. However, all controls must be accessible. A stacked system (dryer above washer) minimize the number of steps required in the clothes care center and may be suitable for those who use canes, crutches, or walkers. Locating the clothes care center on the main floor eliminates having to climb stairs to get to it.

Garage or Carport

The primary purpose of a garage or carport is to provide shelter for the homeowner's cars. The garage or carport may be small and simple or large and complex. In addition, they can be attached to the house or detached (free standing).

Several factors should be considered when deciding between a garage or a carport. A carport is open on one or more sides, Figure 9-35. As such, it provides less protection and security for the car than a garage. In addition, certain house styles look better with a carport while other styles look better with a garage. In

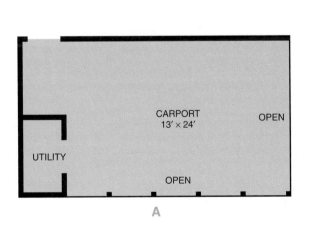

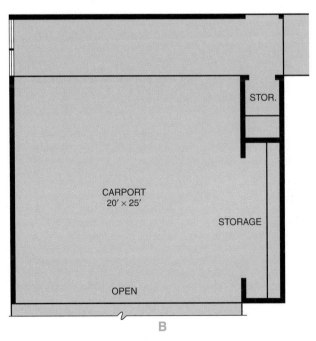

Figure 9-35. A—This single-stall carport is open on two sides and has a small utility area. B—This carport has space for two cars and lots of storage.

cold climates, a garage may be more desirable. Carports are less expensive to build than garages and may be satisfactory for warm, dry climates.

Size and Location

The size and location of the garage or carport will depend on the number of cars to be housed, the size and layout of the house, and the space available. A single-car facility may range in size from 11' × 19' to 16' × 25', Figure 9-36A. A space designed for two cars may be as small as 20' × 20' or as large as 25' × 25', Figure 9-36B. The overall space may be increased considerably if a work area or utility storage is planned into the facility, as in the right-hand illustration in Figure 9-36B.

To be handicapped accessible, a garage or carport should be a minimum of 24' long. This will provide space for passing in front or in back of the car. A minimum of 5' should be planned on the side of the car for a door to be fully opened and a wheelchair placed next to the car. A width of 12' to 14-1/2' is recommended for one car and a wheelchair.

Design

A garage or carport should be designed as an integral part of the style of the total structure, Figure 9-37. This does not mean that

Figure 9-36. The size of the garage or carport will depend on its intended use. A—The single-car garage on the left is small with no storage facilities. The single-car garage on the right has ample storage and a workbench. B—The two-car garage on the left has adequate storage. The two-car garage on the right is much larger because of the added workbench.

the facility must be attached. However, if care is not taken, an attached or detached garage or carport can detract from the appearance of the house.

If the garage is detached (free-standing), a walkway should be provided to the house. The walkway should lead to the service entrance and provide easy access to the kitchen. In some climates, a covered walkway may be desirable, Figure 9-38.

Plan the garage or carport with storage in mind, Figure 9-39. Provide space for outdoor recreation equipment and gardening tools, if no other specific facility is provided for that purpose. Many homes have a garage that is full of tools and other equipment and the car

Figure 9-37. The two-car garage on this house is well designed to be an integral part of the style of the house. (Photo Courtesy of James Hardie® Siding Products)

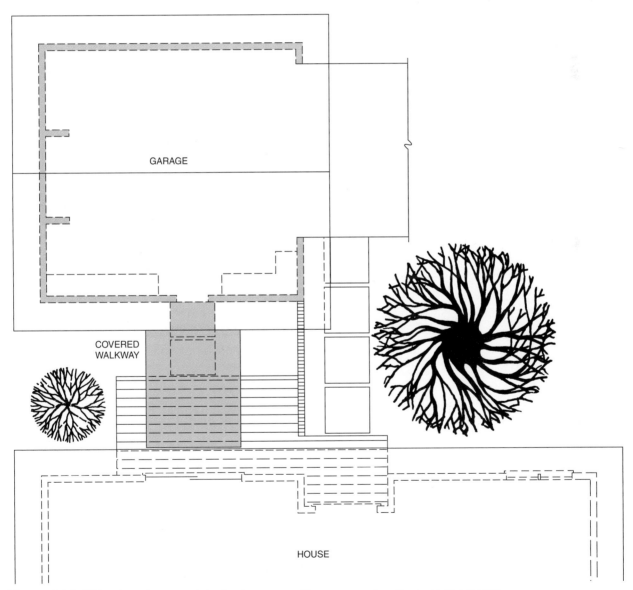

GARAGE

COVERED WALKWAY

HOUSE

Figure 9-38. This plan shows a detached garage with a covered walkway to the house.

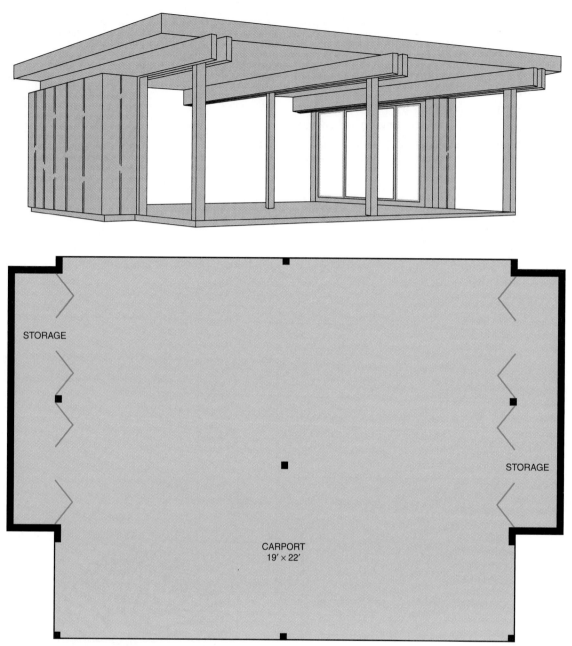

Figure 9-39. A perspective and plan view of a carport designed with storage in mind.

cannot be parked inside. This is often a result of poor planning. A few other design ideas may be worth mentioning:

- The floor of the garage or carport should be concrete at least 4″ thick and reinforced with steel or wire mesh.
- Good floor drainage is important. However, many cities prohibit a floor drain in the garage.
- Include an ample number of windows for ventilation and natural lighting.

- Supplement natural lighting with artificial lighting. Fluorescent lighting is popular in garages.
- If the garage is attached to the house, be sure to check the local building codes for special requirements regarding fire protection.
- Always plan the garage or carport for a standard-size car even though the prospective owner may have a compact car. If necessary, adjust the design for larger vehicles.

Doors

Garage doors are often called overhead doors. They are available in standard sizes and come in wood, fiberglass, plastic or vinyl, aluminum, and steel. Wood has been a traditional choice and is still preferred by many, but it requires frequent painting and is expensive. Metal doors are popular, require little maintenance, and are inexpensive. Fiberglass is very durable and allows some natural light to come through even with the door closed.

A single-car garage door is usually 8' or 9' wide and 7' or 8' high. A two-car garage door is usually 16' wide and 7' or 8' high. Recreational vehicles may require a higher garage door. Garage doors are also produced in widths of 18'. Figure 9-40 shows single- and two-car garage doors in different styles.

Driveway

The driveway should be planned concurrently with the garage. The minimum driveway width is 10' for a single-car garage. A two-car garage requires a wider driveway, at least at the garage.

If space is available, a turnaround is often recommended. This allows the driver to pull forward into the garage or carport and forward out onto the street. Backing directly onto the street should be avoided when possible. Figure 9-41 shows two turnarounds with dimensions.

Applications

The garage shown in Figure 9-42 is designed to be constructed from common building materials using common techniques. A slab foundation and stud walls constitute the basic structure. Standard trusses are used to form the gable roof. Bevel cedar siding is used on the exterior, however, vinyl siding can be used instead. The design is both economical and attractive.

The basic proportions of a garage or carport are relatively fixed, but several ideas may be applied to improve the appearance. For example, a Dutch hip, butterfly, or mansard roof may be used to give the structure a unique style. A different roof style will change the overall appearance considerably. The use of new siding materials, such as vinyl, may also improve an otherwise drab structure. Textured siding with rustic stain or weathered redwood boards add character and charm. Windows may be conventional types or fixed panels of colored glass or plastics. It is possible with the application of a few innovative ideas to transform a garage into an attractive structure that adds much to the total "home environment."

A

B

Figure 9-40. A—This three-car garage has a single-car garage door for each bay. B—This house has a two-car garage and a single-car garage.

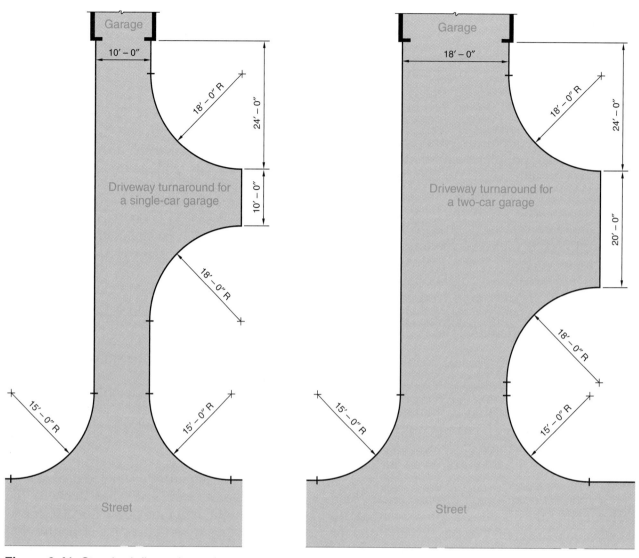

Figure 9-41. Standard dimensions of turnarounds for single- and two-car garages.

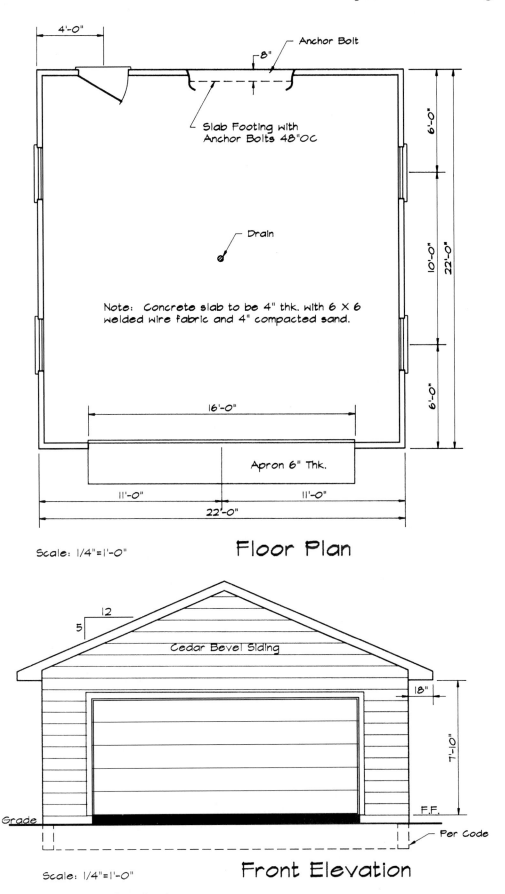

Figure 9-42. Plans for a basic two-car garage.

Internet Resources

www.anchorwall.com
Anchor Retaining Wall Systems

www.hurd.com
Hurd Windows and Patio Doors

www.jameshardie.com
James Hardie Building Products, Inc.

www.lpcorp.com
Louisiana-Pacific Corporation, a manufacturer of building materials

www.marvin.com
Marvin Windows and Doors

www.masonite.com
Masonite International Corporation, a door manufacturer

www.portcement.org
Portland Cement Association

www.raynor.com
Raynor Garage Doors

www.sterlingplumbing.com
Sterling Plumbing, A Kohler Company

www.whirlpool.com
Whirlpool Corporation

Review Questions – Chapter 9

Write your answers on a separate sheet of paper. Do not write in this book.

1. Kitchen cabinets are produced in standard widths, heights, and depths. The standard width increment is _____.

2. The dimensions of a single-car garage are approximately _____.

3. The minimum width of a driveway for a single-car garage is _____.

4. A clothes care center should provide for which activities? List at least four.

5. Identify the six basic kitchen designs.

6. The maximum acceptable length of the work triangle in a kitchen is _____.

7. The service area of a home generally includes which individual areas?

8. Kitchen base cabinets are normally _____ high.

9. Exhaust fumes from a kitchen hood fan should not be expelled into the _____.

10. List common materials in which overhead doors are available.

11. The standard width of a kitchen base cabinet is _____.

12. The counter height for a kitchen eating area that is designed for chairs should be _____.

Suggested Activities

1. Visit an appliance store and obtain literature on the newest kitchen appliance designs. Prepare a bulletin board display using pictures from the literature.

2. Secure specifications and price lists of kitchen cabinets from a manufacturer. Calculate the total cost for the cabinets shown in Figure 9-21.

3. Using CADD, plan a kitchen that includes the major elements of the work triangle. Draw the plan view and elevations. Identify the cabinets using the manufacturer's numbers and dimension the drawings.

4. Obtain three floor plans from magazines or other sources. Analyze the provisions for clothes care in each plan. Explain the strengths and weaknesses of each. Propose improvements where needed.

5. Measure the length and width of a standard-size car. Using CADD, design a plan (top) view symbol for a car. Develop symbols for at least three different styles of cars. Then, design a single-car garage that provides adequate space for the car and extra storage. Use the car symbols to help plan the garage.

6. Using CADD, draw kitchen symbols from this chapter. Add these to your symbols library for future use.

The Ergonomic Environment

Like other workers who spend long periods of time doing detailed work with a computer, drafters may be susceptible to eyestrain, back discomfort, and hand and wrist problems. *Ergonomics* is the science of adapting the workstation to fit the needs of the drafter. Applying ergonomic principles results in a comfortable and efficient environment. There are many types of ergonomic accessories that may improve a computer workstation, including wrist rests, specially designed chairs, and back supports. In addition, the following chart identifies a few things that can be done to create a comfortable environment and help prevent injury or strain to the operator's body. Finally, cleanliness is an important part of the drafting environment. Keep papers, computer disks, pens, rules, reference books, and other materials organized. The work area should not be cluttered with unneeded items. Properly store items not in use. Also, always read and understand safety manuals, follow safety instructions, and abide by safety requirements.

Eyes
- Position the monitor to minimize glare from overhead lights, windows, and other light sources. Reduce light intensity by turning off some lights or closing blinds and shades. You should be able to see images clearly without glare.
- Position the monitor so that it is 18″ to 30″ from your eyes. This is about an arm's length. To help reduce eyestrain, look away from the monitor every 15–20 minutes and focus on an object at least 20′ away for 1–2 minutes.

Wrists and Arms
- Forearms should be parallel to the floor.
- Periodically stretch your arms, wrists, and shoulders.
- Try using an ergonomic keyboard and mouse. The keyboard keeps the wrists in a normal body position and the mouse will fit your hand more comfortably.

Neck
- Adjust the monitor so that your head is level, not leaning forward or back. The top of the screen should be near your line of sight.

Back
- Use a chair that is comfortable and provides good back support. The chair should be adjustable and provide armrests.
- Sit up straight. This maintains good posture and reduces strain. Think about good posture until it becomes common practice.
- Try standing up, stretching, and walking every hour. This will also reduce strain.

Legs
- Keep your thighs parallel to the ground.
- Rest your feet flat on the floor or use a footrest.
- When taking a break, walk around. This will stretch the muscles and promote circulation through your body.

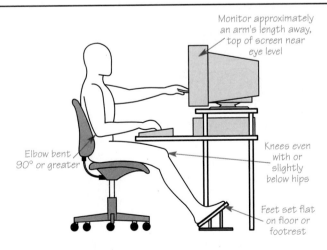

Monitor approximately an arm's length away, top of screen near eye level

Elbow bent 90° or greater

Knees even with or slightly below hips

Feet set flat on floor or footrest

Section IV
Plot Plans and Foundations

10 Plot Plans

11 Footings, Foundations, and Concrete

12 The Foundation Plan

Plot Plans

Objectives

After studying this chapter, you will be able to:

➤ Identify the various features shown on a typical plot plan.

➤ Visualize land elevations from contour lines.

➤ Recognize typical topographical symbols and apply them to site considerations.

➤ Properly locate a building on a site.

➤ Draw a plot plan using correct symbols and conventions.

➤ Draw a plot plan using CADD.

Key Terms

Benchmark	Plot Plan
Contour Interval	Property Lines
Contour Lines	Topographical
Landscape Plan	Features
Mean Sea Level	

A *plot plan* is a plan (top) view drawing that shows the site and location/orientation of the buildings on the property. The site plan presents information only about the property and utilities, Figure 10-1. It does not show proposed construction. The plot plan, however, shows both the property and proposed construction. A plot plan shows several specific features, such as:

- Length and bearing (direction) of each property line.
- Location, outline, and size of buildings on the site.
- Contour of the land.
- Elevation of property corners and contour lines.
- Meridian arrow. This symbol shows the direction of north.
- Trees, shrubs, streams, and gardens.
- Streets, driveways, sidewalks, and patios.
- Location of utilities.
- Easements for utilities and drainage (if any).
- Well, septic tank, and leach field.
- Fences and retaining walls.
- Lot number or address of the site.
- Scale of the drawing.

The plot plan is drawn using information provided by a surveyor and recorded on a site plan.

Property Lines

Property lines define the site boundaries. The length and bearing (direction) of each line must be identified on the plot plan. Property line lengths are measured with an engineer's scale to the nearest 1/100 foot. Figure 10-2 shows

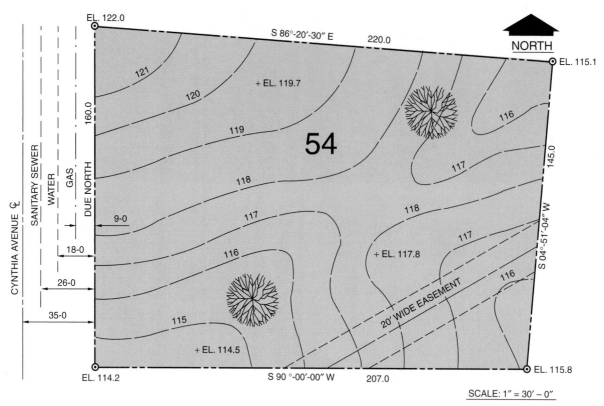

Figure 10-1. A site plan is prepared from information provided by a surveyor and does not include the location of buildings.

Figure 10-2. This property line is 175.25′ long and has a bearing of N 89° E.

a property line that is 175.25′ long and has a bearing of N 89° E (north eighty-nine degrees east).

Bearing angles are recorded in degrees from north or south and, if required, minutes and seconds are included. There are 360 degrees in a circle, 60 minutes in a degree, and 60 seconds in a minute. An example of a typical bearing might be S 63° W, while a more precise bearing would read S 63° 13′ 05″ W. Figure 10-3 shows a number of lines with bearings identified.

A *benchmark* is a permanent object used by surveyors to establish points of reference. If the property corner begins or ends on a benchmark, it is usually identified on the drawing with a special symbol. All other corners may be represented by drawing a small circle

centered on the exact property corner. See Figure 10-4.

It is customary when drawing the property lines of a site to begin at one corner and proceed in a clockwise manner until the beginning point is reached. Figure 10-5 shows the procedure for drawing the property lines of a site.

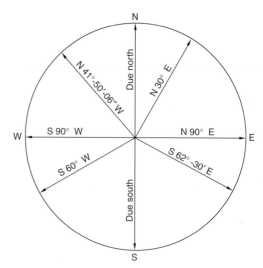

Figure 10-3. Bearings are measured from north or south and may include degrees, minutes, and seconds.

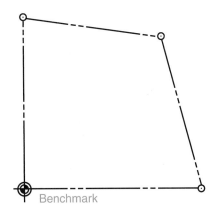

Figure 10-4. Property corners that are located at a benchmark are identified with a special symbol.

have the same elevation. The shoreline of a lake is a good example of a contour line. All points where the water meets the shore have the same elevation. Looking at several characteristics of contour should help to clarify the use of contour lines:

- The *contour interval* is the vertical distance between two adjacent contour lines. This interval may be any distance that is functional for the specific drawing. Figure 10-6 illustrates a contour interval of five feet. Be sure to identify the elevation of each contour line.

- Closely spaced contour lines indicated a steep slope, Figure 10-7.

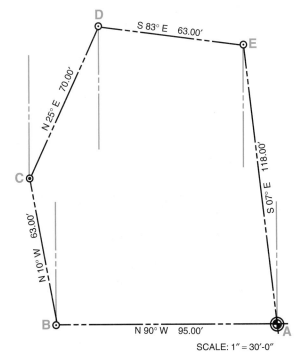

SCALE: 1″ = 30′-0″

Property line description

From point A	A line bears N 90° W	95.00′ to point B
From point B	A line bears N 10° W	63.00′ to point C
From point C	A line bears N 25° E	70.00′ to point D
From point D	A line bears S 83° E	63.00′ to point E
From point E	A line bears S 07° E	118.00′ to point A

Figure 10-5. These property lines are drawn to scale based on the property line descriptions provided.

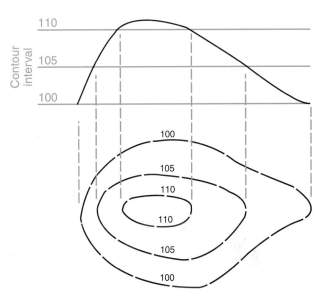

Figure 10-6. The contour lines on the bottom describe the contour shown in the elevation view based on a contour interval of 5 feet.

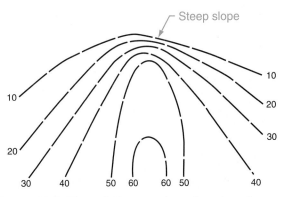

Figure 10-7. The relative spacing of contour lines represents the slope of the land. Contour lines that are close together indicate a steep slope.

Contour Lines

Contour lines help describe the topography of a site by depicting shape and elevation of the land. A contour line connects points that

- When contours are smooth and parallel, the ground surface is even. When contours are irregular, the ground surface is rough and uneven, Figure 10-8.

- Summits and depressions are represented by closed contour lines, as shown in Figure 10-9. The elevation in relation to the adjacent contour line indicates if the feature is a summit or depression.

- Contour lines of different elevations do not cross. The only instance where contour lines appear to touch is a vertical slope.

- Contour lines cross watersheds and ridge lines at right angles with the concave side of the curve facing the higher elevation. Proper symbols should be used to identify valleys and ridges, Figure 10-10.

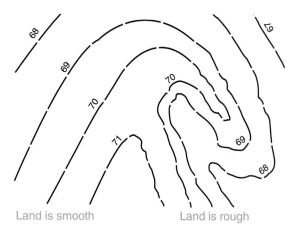

Figure 10-8. The smoothness of contour lines indicates the relative roughness of the land.

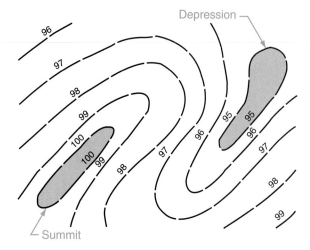

Figure 10-9. Summits and depressions are represented by closed contour lines.

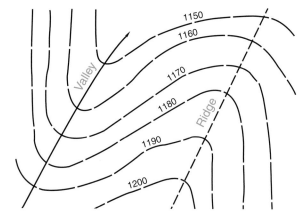

Figure 10-10. Ridges and valleys should be identified using the proper symbols.

The accepted reference elevation point for topographical surveys is ***mean sea level***. This is a standardized elevation. Many times, however, it is not important to know how far a point is from sea level, but what the relative difference is between two or more points. In residential home construction, relative elevations are usually sufficient.

Contour lines that are the result of a survey are usually represented by a series of thin free-hand lines about 1″ to 2″ in length. Estimated contours are represented by a line of short dashes similar to a hidden line, Figure 10-11.

Figure 10-12 shows the plotting of contours from a grid of elevations developed by a surveyor. The more measurements taken for a given area, the more accurately the contour lines represent the topography. When insufficient data are given, the resulting contour may be only moderately accurate or not accurate at all.

Topographical Features

Topographical features include trees, shrubs, streams, roads, utilities, fences, and similar features. These features are represented by symbols. Many symbols are standardized and readily recognizable. A few are not. When a nonstandard symbol is used, it should appear with an explanation in a legend on the drawing.

Figure 10-13 illustrates some of the more common topographical symbols. In some topo-

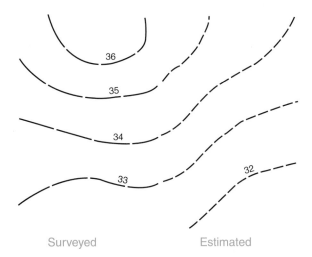

Figure 10-11. Surveyed contours are represented by thin lines about 1″ or 2″ long. Estimated contours are shown with a dash line.

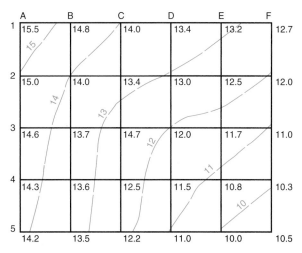

Figure 10-12. These contour lines shown in color were plotted from an elevation grid using data supplied by a surveyor.

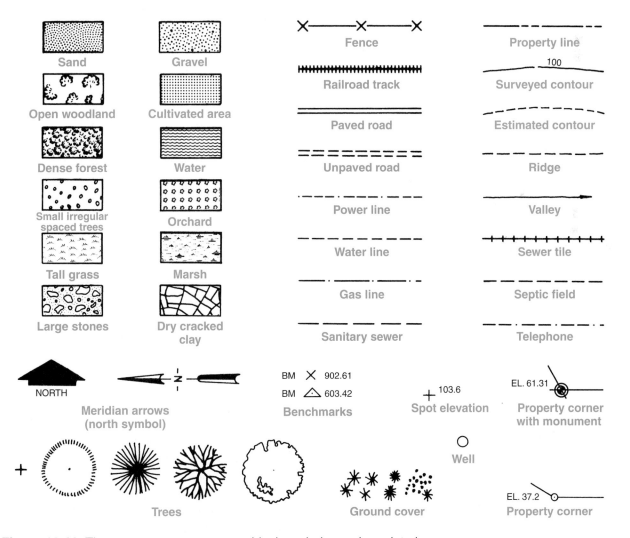

Figure 10-13. These are common topographical symbols used on plot plans.

graphical drawings, color plays an important role. When color is used, follow these guidelines.

- Black is used for lettering and human-built works, such as roads, houses, utilities, and other structures.
- Brown represents all land forms, such as contour lines.
- Blue is used for water features, such as streams, lakes, marsh, and ponds.
- Green is for vegetation.

Location of the Structure on the Site

A complete analysis should be made of the site to determine the ideal location for the structure. The analysis should include such things as natural contour, trees, view, surrounding houses, code restrictions, style of house to be built, solar orientation, winds, placement of well and septic system, and size and shape of the site. All of these factors will not apply in every situation, but they should be examined to determine their importance.

Once a specific location is decided on, the structure may be drawn on the plot plan. There are three commonly accepted methods of representing the house on the plot plan. The first method is to lay out the outside of the exterior walls omitting all interior walls and roof. Shade or crosshatch the space covered by the house, Figure 10-14A. The second method is to draw the exterior walls as hidden lines with the roof shown as solid lines (typical roof plan), Figure 10-14B. The third method shows exterior walls thickened with all interior walls, windows, and doors omitted, Figure 10-14C. When the distance between the house and property line is critical, it may be advisable to use the second method or add the overhang line to either of the other two methods. The distance from the roof overhang to the property line may then be shown.

The location of the house on the site must be dimensioned. The standard procedure is to dimension the distance of one corner of the house from adjacent lot lines, as shown in Figure 10-14. In some instances, this is not sufficient to clearly

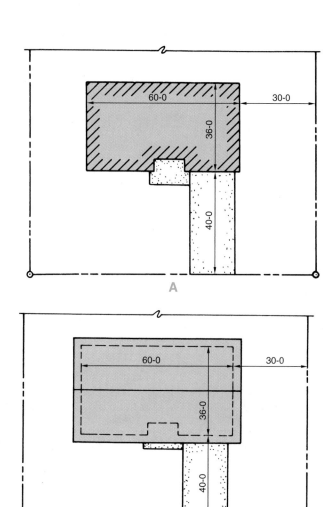

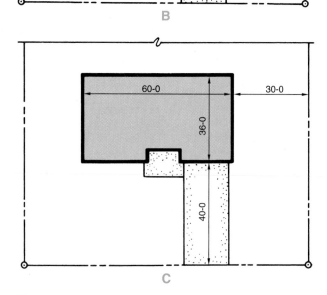

Figure 10-14. A house may be represented on a plot plan in one of three ways. A—By shading or cross-hatching the area covered by the house. The roof is not included. B—Using a roof plan to show the location and size of the house on a site. Exterior walls are represented as hidden lines. C—Using thickened exterior walls to show the location and size of a house on a site.

locate the structure. Figure 10-15 shows a more complex situation and its solution. In each instance, dimension the distance from the outside of the exterior wall, or roof extremities if this location is critical, to the property line. If required, show the overhang distance, too.

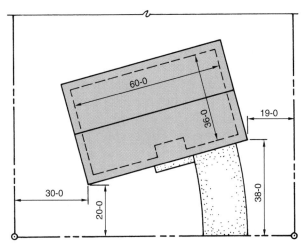

Figure 10-15. A house that is not positioned parallel to the property lines may require more than two dimensions to properly locate it on the site. A bearing line could also be used to show the position of the house.

Procedure for Drawing a Plot Plan— Manual Drafting

The following steps are recommended for drawing a plot plan. Omit any steps or items that do not apply to your situation.

1. Select a scale that provides the largest drawing on the paper size that you have chosen. All of the sheets in a set of drawings should be the same size for ease of handling. The property lines should be placed sufficiently inside the border to provide room for adding dimensions, notes, and a title block. Scales commonly used in drawing plot plans range from 1/8″ = 1′-0″ to 1″ = 30′-0″ and smaller.

2. Lay out the property lines using data supplied by the site plan or other source. Be extremely careful in this step to ensure an accurate drawing. Steps 2 through 6 are illustrated in Figure 10-16.

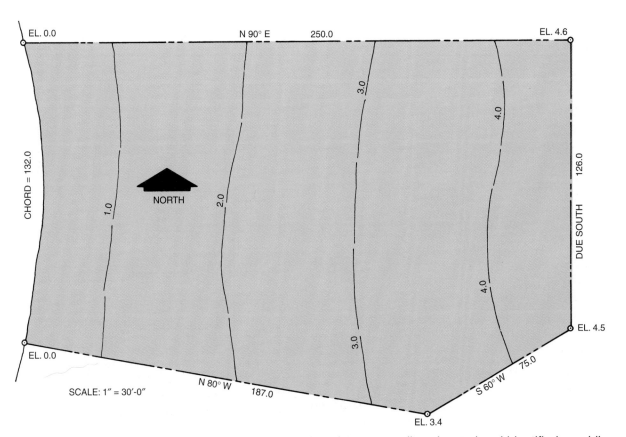

Figure 10-16. This is a partially complete plot plan that has the property lines located and identified, meridian arrow positioned, the scale shown, and the contour lines and corner elevations added.

3. Letter the bearing and length of each property line. Letter the scale near the bottom of the drawing.
4. Locate the meridian arrow (north symbol) in a place on the drawing where it will be easy to find, yet not interfere with the drawing.
5. Select a contour interval that is appropriate for your specific situation and plot the contour lines. If drawing manually, draw the lines lightly at this point. These are to be darkened in later.
6. Letter the elevation of each contour line and property corner.
7. Locate the house on the site. Dimension the overall length and width of the house. Steps 7 through 9 are shown in Figure 10-17.
8. Dimension the distance from the house to the two adjacent property lines. The elevation of a reference corner of the house is sometimes given.
9. Draw surrounding features such as the driveway, sidewalks, and patios. The size and elevation may be given for each if required.

10. Determine the centerline of the street and location of utilities. Draw these features using proper linetypes (symbols). Dimension their location. If a well and septic system are required, draw them at this point. Steps 10 through 12 are illustrated in Figure 10-18.
11. Draw other topographical features, such as trees and shrubs. If drawing manually, darken in all light contour lines at this point.
12. Check your drawing to be sure you have included all necessary elements.

Figure 10-19 shows a typical plot plan. This plot plan is for a large home site. The house has its own septic system and well.

Landscape Plans

The *landscape plan* is designed to show the type and placement of trees, shrubs, flowers, gardens, and pools on the site. This provides an excellent way to plan the total setting for the home. A landscape plan is not

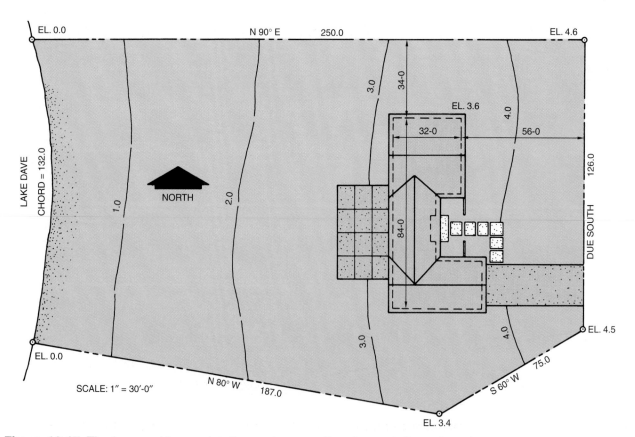

Figure 10-17. The house, drive, and patio are drawn on the plan and dimensioned.

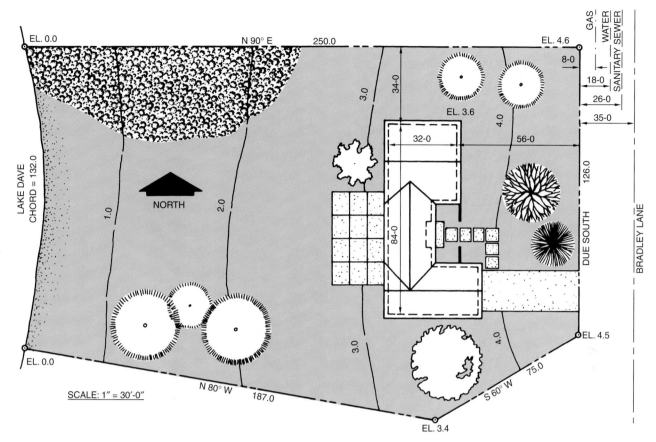

Figure 10-18. This is a completed plot plan showing the property lines, house location, north symbol, topographical features, centerline of the street, and utilities.

always required, but may be completed even when not required.

Much of the information presented on the plot plan is required on the landscape plan. Boundary lines, meridian arrow, outline of the house, driveway, walks, patios, and contour lines are needed to place the landscape elements into their proper perspective. Symbols are used to represent various types of plants. These symbols should be keyed to a chart to avoid confusion. There are more types of ornamental plants in the world than you can practically have symbols to use. Therefore, the same symbol can be used for different plants.

Figure 10-20 shows a typical landscape plan. When practical, the plant symbols should be drawn to proper scale. This produces a realistic idea of the components on the plan. Figure 10-21 shows the pleasing appearance that can result from using a landscape plan to arrange the landscape elements.

Procedure for Drawing a Plot Plan— CADD

Site plans, plot plans, and landscape plans can be drawn with most any CADD package. However, software designed specifically for these applications is available. These packages greatly facilitate drawing property lines and contour lines using standard data provided by surveyors. Compatibility is always a concern when two or more packages are to be used together. Be sure that your basic CADD package supports any specific-use software that you purchase.

The site characteristics are very important and play crucial roles in the final design plan. Figure 10-22 shows a computer-generated perspective of a house situated on an extremely

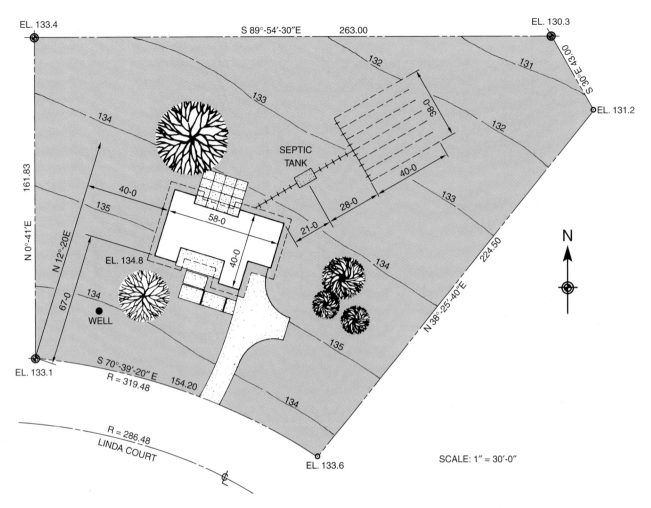

Figure 10-19. This plot plan is for a large site. The house has a septic system and well.

rugged site. This pictorial helps to visualize the intended integration of the site and structure.

The steps for drawing a plot plan using CADD are basically the same as described earlier. However, there are a couple differences. Use the following steps to draw a plot plan using CADD.

1. Draw all objects on the plot plan at full size. Also at this time, determine the final plot (print) scale. When setting up the drawing to plot, select a plot scale that will provide the largest drawing on the size of paper that you have chosen for the set of construction drawings. Scales commonly used in drawing plot plans range from 1/8″ = 1′-0″ to 1″ = 30′-0″ and smaller. The scale should be noted on the plot plan and used to determine the proper lettering height for notes and dimensions.

2. Lay out the property lines using proper linetypes and symbols. Draw the property lines on their own layer since the linetype is unique and very wide. If the plot plan is contained in the same file as the other drawings, place the plot plan on its own layer. Start at the reference corner, if there is one, and lay out each line in a clockwise manner until you reach the starting point.

3. Locate the building(s) on the site. Be careful to position the buildings according to code. Some communities require setbacks from the street and property lines. The driveway, patios, walks, and other flatwork may also be located at this time. Add property corner elevations, Figure 10-23. Place the building perimeter, drive, and walks on a single layer of their own. If the drawing file contains the entire set of drawings, the building perimeter should

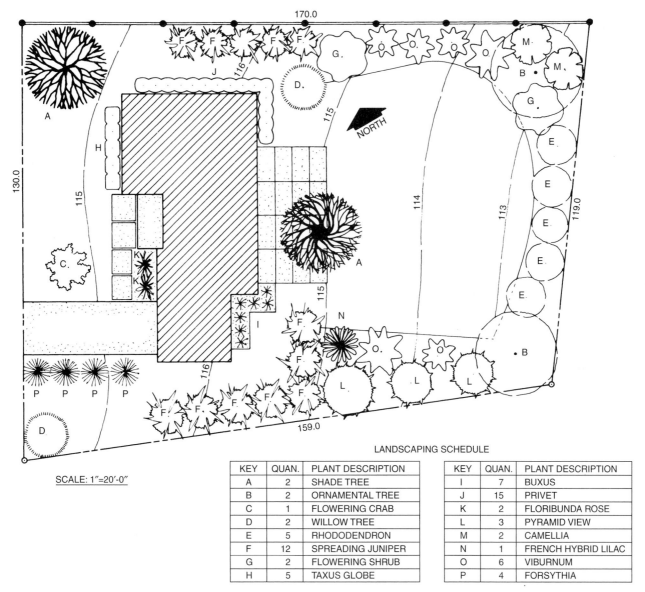

LANDSCAPING SCHEDULE

KEY	QUAN.	PLANT DESCRIPTION	KEY	QUAN.	PLANT DESCRIPTION
A	2	SHADE TREE	I	7	BUXUS
B	2	ORNAMENTAL TREE	J	15	PRIVET
C	1	FLOWERING CRAB	K	2	FLORIBUNDA ROSE
D	2	WILLOW TREE	L	3	PYRAMID VIEW
E	5	RHODODENDRON	M	2	CAMELLIA
F	12	SPREADING JUNIPER	N	1	FRENCH HYBRID LILAC
G	2	FLOWERING SHRUB	O	6	VIBURNUM
H	5	TAXUS GLOBE	P	4	FORSYTHIA

Figure 10-20. This is a typical landscape plan that shows the type and location of trees and shrubs on the property. Notice the key to the plant symbols.

Figure 10-21. A landscape plan was used to achieve this striking layout. (Elk Corporation)

Figure 10-22. This computer-generated rendering depicts the relationship between the structure and the site. (Helmuth A. Geiser, Member AIBD)

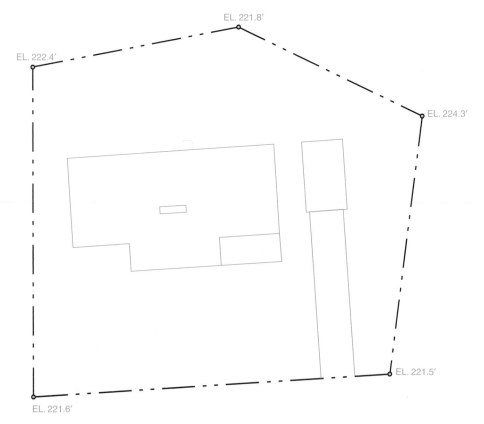

Figure 10-23. The property lines are drawn and the structures are located.

perfectly match the perimeter on the floor plan layer.

4. Draw the contour lines on their own layer. If your CADD software has a "freehand" function, use it to draw the contour lines. Choose an appropriate contour interval for the site. Label the elevation of each contour line. Steps 4 through 6 are shown in Figure 10-24.

5. Add house reference corner location dimensions. The reference corner of the house should be selected so the structure can be properly located on the site and placed correctly with respect to the grade. Locate the corner relative to a property corner or two property lines that form a right angle. Label the reference corner and provide its elevation. Dimensions should be placed on their own layer.

6. Additional features of the house, such as rooflines, may be added at this time. Long dashed lines are appropriate for the roofline. It will also need a separate layer.

The overall dimensions of the house should be shown on the plot plan to aid in staking out the house location on the site.

7. Other topographical features such as trees, streams, and right-of-ways can be added to the drawing now. Choose appropriate layers for these features. Use symbols from the symbols library or design your own. If you design your own, you may want to update your symbols library for future use.

8. Include property line data and north arrow. Property line data may be added to the drawing in the form of a chart or placed along each property line. The north symbol (meridian arrow) is very important and must be included on the plot plan.

9. Add the scale, title, utilities, septic tank and field, lot number, and well. All plot plans should include the scale and title. Add the other items as needed. Figure 10-25 shows a plot plan drawn with CADD.

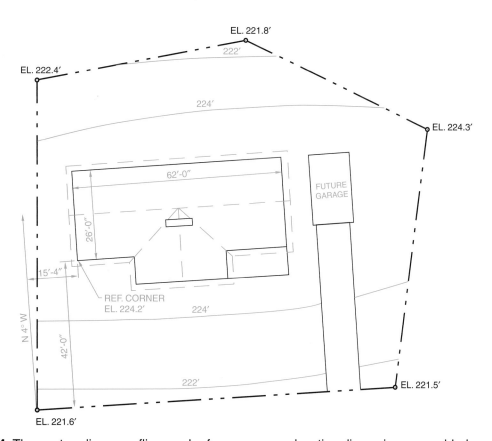

Figure 10-24. The contour lines, roofline, and reference corner location dimensions are added.

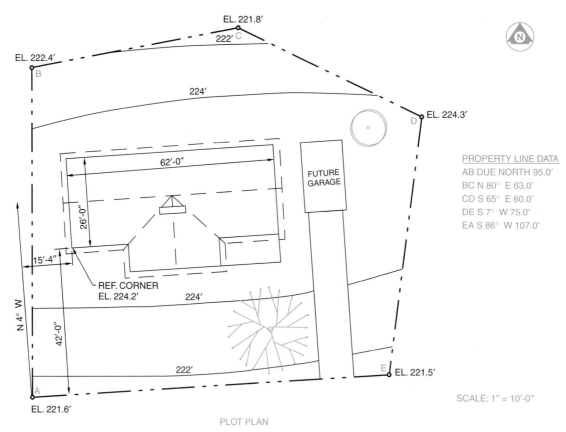

EL. 221.8'

222' C

EL. 222.4'

B

N

224'

EL. 224.3'
D

62'-0"

FUTURE
GARAGE

PROPERTY LINE DATA
AB DUE NORTH 95.0'
BC N 80° E 63.0'
CD S 65° E 60.0'
DE S 7° W 75.0'
EA S 86° W 107.0'

26'-0"

15'-4"

N 4° W

REF. CORNER
EL. 224.2'

224'

42'-0"

222'

E
EL. 221.5'

A

SCALE: 1" = 10'-0"

EL. 221.6'

PLOT PLAN

Figure 10-25. The plot plan is complete.

Internet Resources

www.autodesk.com
Autodesk, Inc., publisher of AutoCAD and Autodesk VIZ

www.bobcat.com
Melroe Co./Bobcat, a supplier of construction equipment

www.boralbricks.com
Boral Bricks

www.builderonline.com
Builder Magazine Online

www.concretehomes.com
Portland Cement Association

www.culturedstone.com
Cultured Stone, a producer of manufactured stone veneers

www.deere.com
Deere and Company, John Deere construction equipment

www.designbasics.com
Design Basics, Inc., a home design service

www.epa.gov
US Environmental Protection Agency

www.iii.org
Insurance Information Institute

Review Questions – Chapter 10

Write your answers on a separate sheet of paper. Do not write in this book.

1. A line on a plot plan that connects points of the same elevation is:
   a) A bearing line.
   b) A property line.
   c) A contour line.
   d) None of the above.

2. The plot plan contains information found on a site plan and also shows _____.

3. List at least five factors that help determine the ideal location and placement of a house on a site.

4. Symbols for plants on the landscape plan should be drawn to the proper _____ whenever possible.

5. What is the purpose of the meridian arrow?

6. Estimated contours are represented on the plot plan by using lines of _____.

7. List four topographical features represented on plot plans. Indicate the color for the symbol if color is to be used.

8. The standard procedure for locating a house on a plot plan is to dimension the distance from one corner of the house to adjacent _____ lines.

9. The two types of information needed about property lines are the length and _____ of each line.

10. The plan that shows the type and placement of trees, shrubs, flowers, gardens, and pools is the _____ plan.

11. When drawing a plot plan using CADD, all objects should be drawn at _____ scale.

12. When making a CADD plot plan, you can select topographical features from the _____ library to save time and improve consistency.

Suggested Activities

1. Select a vacant site in your community that is suitable for a home. Measure the site, determine north with a compass, and draw a site plan of the property using CADD. Show any trees that may be on the site and indicate approximate contour lines.

2. Select a floor plan of a house from a newspaper, magazine, or other source that is appropriate for the site plan you drew in Activity 1. Locate the house on the site. Using CADD, draw a plot plan showing the house and property.

3. Define these terms: property lines, meridian arrow, contour line, site plan, plot plan, landscape plan, bearing, benchmark, and depression.

4. Compile a list of fifteen ornamental trees and shrubs that grow in the area in which you live. Describe each one as to mature size and characteristics. Sketch a plan (top) view symbol for each one for use in a CADD system. Add them to your symbols library for future use.

5. Using a printout of the plot plan developed in Activity 2 and the sketches of tree and shrub symbols from Activity 4, draw a landscape plan. This can be a hand sketch.

6. Using CADD, draw the typical plot plan symbols in Figure 10-13. Add them to your symbols library.

Footings, Foundations, and Concrete
11

Objectives

After studying this chapter, you will be able to:

➤ Describe the procedure for staking out a house location.

➤ List the major considerations when designing a footing for a residential foundation.

➤ Analyze a typical floor plan to determine the appropriate foundation.

➤ Discuss the design considerations for wood, concrete, and masonry foundation walls.

➤ Calculate the load to be supported by a beam.

➤ Explain the purpose of a lintel.

Key Terms

9-12-15 Unit Method	Lintel
Batter Boards	Live Loads
Bearing Wall	Parge Coat
Cement	Pier Foundation
Concrete	Pilaster
Contraction Joints	Rigid Paving System
Creep	Post Foundation
Dead Loads	Screed
Flexible Paving	Slab Foundation
System	Stepped Footings
Float	T-Foundation
Footings	Trowel
Kip	Wood Foundations

It is very important to provide a good foundation for the residence that will be constructed. This requires careful planning and design on the part of the architect if the foundation is to support the structure as required. The architect can select from masonry, all-weather wood, or slab styles of foundation for the structure. See Figure 11-1.

Specialized CADD software packages are available to calculate spans permissible for various materials, generate details, and draw foundation plans. Many architects take advantage of these specialized CADD packages.

Staking Out House Location

Staking out the house is the process of placing stakes in the ground at the corners of the building. This is done to provide reference points as the foundation is built. The plot plan provides the necessary dimensions required for staking out the location of the house on the lot. The task is accomplished with a measuring tape and contractor's level. When angles other than 90° must be measured, a surveyor's transit is also required.

The first step in staking out the house is to locate each corner by laying off the distances indicated on the plot plan. A stake is driven into the ground at the location of each corner of the foundation to identify its position. Square corners may be laid out using the **9-12-15 unit method,** Figure 11-2. These proportions define a right triangle and establish a 90° angle corner. Measure 9 units along one leg of the corner and 12 units along the other leg. The distance between these two endpoints should

Figure 11-1. Three different types of residential foundations. A—Typical masonry foundation. B—All-weather wood foundation. (The Engineered Wood Association) C—Slab foundation.

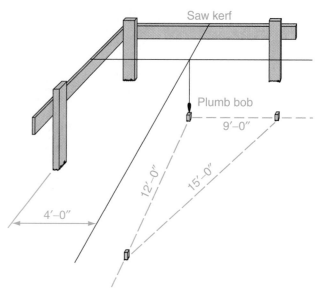

Figure 11-2. Squaring a corner using the 9-12-15 unit method.

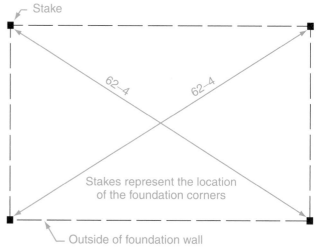

Figure 11-3. The accuracy of the layout may be checked by comparing diagonal measurements. Both measurements must be equal if all corners are 90°.

be 15 units. Adjust the angle between the legs until the distance is exactly 15 units. The position of all corners should then be checked for accuracy by diagonal measurement, Figure 11-3. Both diagonal measurements should be equal in a rectangle with perfect 90° corners.

Batter boards are used to retain the location of the foundation during excavation and construction. These are constructed of 2″ × 4″ stakes sharpened on one end and driven into the ground about 4′ outside of where the footing will be. A 1″ × 6″ board is nailed horizontally to the stakes so it is level. Each corner will have two batter boards. Each corner of the house should have batter boards. All horizontal batter boards should be in the same horizontal plane and have the same elevation.

A strong cord or string is stretched across the boards at opposite ends of the building and located directly above the corner stakes. A plumb bob is used for accurate placement of each stake. This is done for each side of the building. A saw kerf is usually made at the exact point on the horizontal batter board where the string is located. This prevents movement of the string along the board. After cuts are made in all batter boards, the lines of the house will be located, Figure 11-4.

A control point is needed to determine the depth of excavation and foundation wall height. The corner with the highest elevation is usually selected for this purpose. All depth or height measurements are made from this point. The finished floor should be at least 8" above the grade.

Excavation

In excavating for footings and foundation walls, the top soil is usually removed using a bulldozer or tractor with a blade. This soil is saved for final grading. A trencher or backhoe may be used to excavate for foundations when either slab construction or a crawl space is planned. In excavating for a basement, a backhoe or power shovel is generally used. Which piece of excavating equipment is used depends on the size of the excavation and type of soil.

Excavation for footings should be at least 6" below the average maximum frost penetration depth. See Figure 11-5 for the approximate frost depth in your area. In areas with a shallow frost depth, the footings should extend a minimum of 6" into undisturbed earth. Local codes usually specify the minimum footing depth for a given area.

Do not backfill under the proposed footings because uneven settling of the house may occur. In instances where part of the footings sit on rock, about 6" of the rock should be removed under the proposed footing and replaced with compacted sand to equalize settling.

On sites that have recently been filled and regraded, it is recommended that the footings extend down to the original undisturbed earth. The exception is when soil tests prove that the earth is sufficiently compacted to properly support the structure.

Excavation must be large enough to allow space to work when constructing the foundation wall and laying drain tile. A back slope is an outward taper of the excavation wall. The steepness of the back slope will depend on the type of soil encountered. Sandy soil is likely to cave-in and, therefore, requires a gentle back slope. On the other hand, an excavated wall in clay may be nearly vertical.

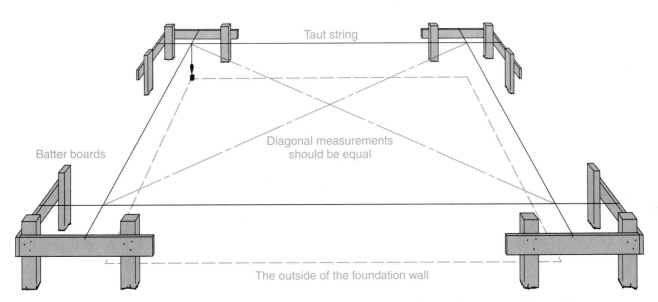

Figure 11-4. Batter boards are placed at each corner around the location of the proposed foundation.

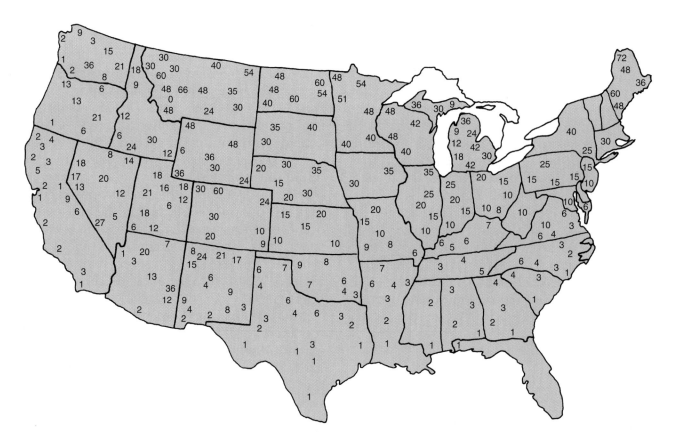

Figure 11-5. The average depth of frost penetration in inches for locations throughout the United States. (US Department of Commerce Weather Bureau)

Footing Shapes and Specifications

Footings increase the supporting capacity of the foundation wall by spreading the load over a larger area, Figure 11-6. If a foundation were to be built on rock, a footing would not be necessary. However, most houses are not built on such solid material and, therefore, need footings to support the heavy loads.

The size and type of footing should be suitable for the weight of the building and load-bearing capacity of the soil. Footings for most residential structures are made of poured concrete. The size of footing is typically based on the foundation wall thickness. The footing thickness is equal to the foundation wall thickness and the footing width is twice the wall thickness, Figure 11-7. Foundation walls should be centered on the footing. Therefore, the footing projects beyond each side of the foundation wall a distance equal to one-half the thickness of the foundation wall. This footing size is designed for most normal soil conditions ranging from sand to clay. If the soil load-bearing capacity is very poor, the size of footings should be increased and reinforced with steel.

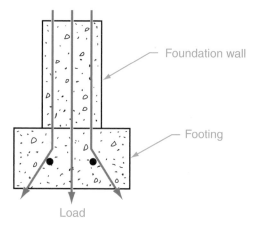

Figure 11-6. The footing distributes the building weight over a broad area.

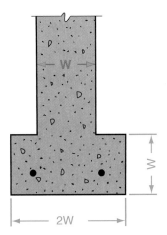

Figure 11-7. The proportions of the footing are typically based on the foundation wall thickness.

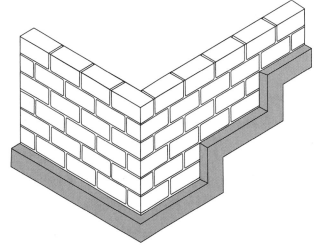

Figure 11-8. A stepped footing and foundation wall are required for a sloping or hilly site.

During construction, the load increases on the footing and compresses the average subgrade soil. This compression causes a slight settlement of the structure. Whenever there are two or more different subsoils under various parts of the house, a variation in settlement may occur due to the unequal compressibility of the soil. Also, the weight of most homes is greater on two of the four walls, which causes unequal loading. It is recommended that footings be large enough to minimize any of these differences in settlement to reduce cracking. Check your local code for recommended minimum footing size.

When footings must be located over soft or poorly drained soils, soils that are not uniform, or backfilled utility trenches, two Number 6 steel bars should be placed as reinforcement along the length of the footing 2″ from the bottom. Adding reinforcing bars to any footing will provide further stability to the structure.

Footings for fireplaces and chimneys are more massive than regular house footings. They must support greater weight. A solid footing reinforced with steel is usually required. The footing should be 12″ thick and extend 6″ beyond the perimeter of the chimney on all sides. The chimney footing should be cast integrally with the foundation wall footing if the chimney is located on an outside wall.

Stepped footings are frequently necessary when building on hilly terrain, Figure 11-8. If stepped footings are required, the steps should be placed horizontally and the height of the vertical step should not be more than three-fourths of the distance between the steps. Step height and length should be multiples of 8″ if the foundation is made of concrete block. Good building practice requires two 1/2″ steel bars in the horizontal and vertical footing where steps are located. If steel bars are not used, the footing will very likely crack at these points.

Foundation Walls

Foundation walls are the part of the house that extends from the first floor to the footing. A foundation wall may also be a basement wall. Materials used to build foundation walls include cast (poured) concrete, concrete block, pressure-treated wood, and stone or brick. Cast concrete and concrete block are widely used in residential structures. Pressure-treated wood foundations are gaining acceptance for residential structures. Brick is much more expensive than cast concrete, block, or wood, and is seldom used. Stone was once used extensively, but is now rarely used as a foundation material. Figure 11-9 illustrates these common foundation materials in section.

There are four basic types of foundation wall: T-foundation, slab foundation, pier or post foundation, and wood foundation, Figure 11-10. The type chosen for a particular situation will

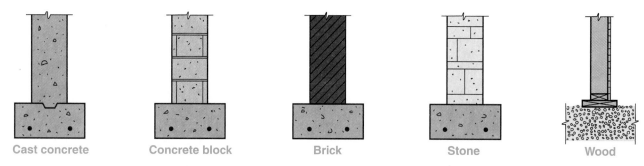

Figure 11-9. Cast concrete, concrete block, and wood are commonly used for foundation walls. Brick and stone were once popular but are now rare in new construction.

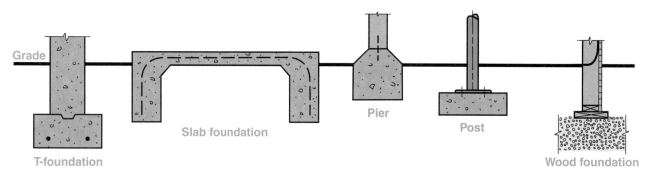

Figure 11-10. Common types of foundations used in residential construction.

depend upon the weight to be supported, load bearing capacity of the soil, location of the foundation in the building, climate, local codes, and preferred building practice. All of these factors should be considered when designing a foundation.

T-Foundations

The most common type of foundation is the *T-foundation*. The name is derived from the shape of the foundation and footing, which look like an inverted T. The foundation and footing are usually two separate parts, but may be cast as a single unit. Figure 11-11 shows several applications of the T-foundation that are commonly found in residential construction.

The concrete for footings of a T-foundation is usually placed in forms made from 2″ thick construction lumber, Figure 11-12A. The level form boards are nailed to stakes to prevent movement while the concrete is being cast. After the concrete is set, the forms are

removed. A new product that combines the form and drain tile is available, Figure 11-12B. This form remains as part of the structure to provide drainage around the foundation.

Slab Foundations

A *slab foundation* is an extension of a slab floor. It is placed at the same time as the floor is cast and is not a separate unit. It is sometimes called a thickened-edge slab. The foundation wall should extend down below the frost line, as in the case of the T-foundation. The addition of steel reinforcing bars or mesh is recommended for the slab foundation to prevent cracking due to settling. This type of foundation is also used for bearing wall partitions.

Some of the primary advantages of the slab foundation are that it requires less time, expense, and labor to construct. Since no separate footing is required, excavation is not as extensive as for the T-foundation. Less time is required since the entire foundation and floor is placed in one operation. Examples and

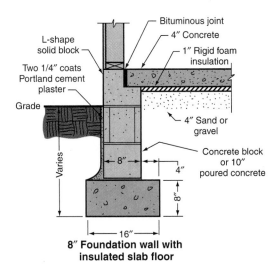

8″ Foundation wall with insulated slab floor

Labels: L-shape solid block; Two 1/4″ coats Portland cement plaster; Grade; Bituminous joint; 4″ Concrete; 1″ Rigid foam insulation; 4″ Sand or gravel; Concrete block or 10″ poured concrete; Varies; 8″; 4″; 8″; 16″

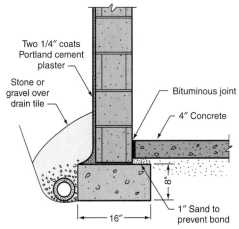

8″ Basement wall and footing

Labels: Two 1/4″ coats Portland cement plaster; Stone or gravel over drain tile; Bituminous joint; 4″ Concrete; 8″; 1″ Sand to prevent bond; 16″

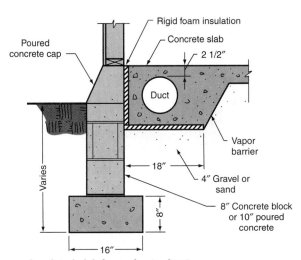

Insulated slab for perimeter heat with concrete block foundation

Labels: Rigid foam insulation; Concrete slab; 2 1/2″; Poured concrete cap; Duct; Vapor barrier; Varies; 18″; 4″ Gravel or sand; 8″ Concrete block or 10″ poured concrete; 8″; 16″

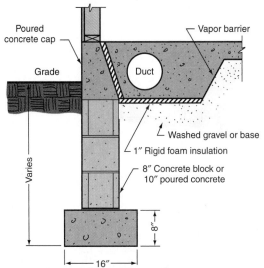

Insulated slab for perimeter heat with concrete block foundation

Labels: Poured concrete cap; Grade; Vapor barrier; Duct; Washed gravel or base; 1″ Rigid foam insulation; 8″ Concrete block or 10″ poured concrete; Varies; 8″; 16″

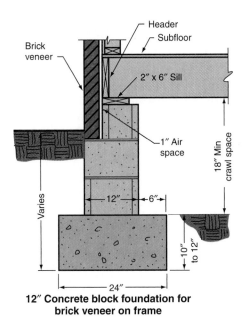

12″ Concrete block foundation for brick veneer on frame

Labels: Brick veneer; Header; Subfloor; 2″ x 6″ Sill; 1″ Air space; 18″ Min crawl space; Varies; 12″; 6″; 10″ to 12″; 24″

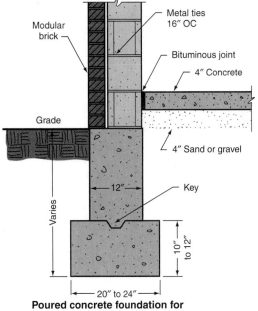

Poured concrete foundation for composite brick and block wall

Labels: Modular brick; Metal ties 16″ OC; Bituminous joint; 4″ Concrete; Grade; 4″ Sand or gravel; Key; Varies; 12″; 10″ to 12″; 20″ to 24″

Figure 11-11. Typical T-foundation details.

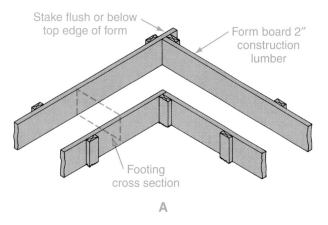

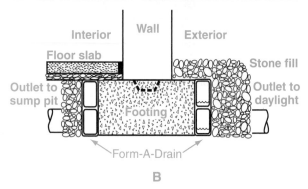

Figure 11-12. A—Footings are usually made by pouring concrete into form boards.
B—A new approach to footing forms uses plastic forms that remain in place to remove groundwater. (CertainTeed Corporation)

dimensions of typical slab foundations are illustrated in Figure 11-13.

Pier and Post Foundations

Many situations in residential construction lend themselves to the use of either a *pier foundation* or a *post (column) foundation.* The basic components of these foundation types include a footing and a pier or post (column). Frequently, it is cheaper and just as satisfactory to use piers rather than the T-foundation under parts of the building. For instance, when a crawl space is planned and the distance is too great for a single span, the pier foundation is a logical choice, Figure 11-14. Another common application that involves columns is in a basement or garage where the distance is too great to span with floor joists. Columns are used to support a beam that in turn supports the joists, rather than construct a bearing wall partition, Figure 11-15.

The basic difference between a pier and a column is their height. Piers are usually much shorter than posts (columns) and ordinarily located under, not within, the house. The terms "post" and "column" are often used interchangeably. Figure 11-16 illustrates a few of the common styles of piers used in residential construction. Figure 11-17 shows a column (jack post) application in a basement.

The footing for a post foundation is usually square or rectangular. The minimum thickness for one-story construction is 8″ with a minimum projection of 5″ beyond the face of the column or post. Two-story homes require a minimum thickness of 12″ and a minimum projection of 7″ beyond the face of the column or post. The column or post may be masonry, steel, or wood. If wood is used, it should be pressure-treated to resist decay.

Wood Foundations

Wood foundations are known by several names: permanent wood foundation (PWF), all-weather wood foundation (AWWF), and treated wood foundation. Basically, a wood foundation is a below-grade, plywood-sheathed, pressure-treated stud wall. The wood foundation is particularly attractive in

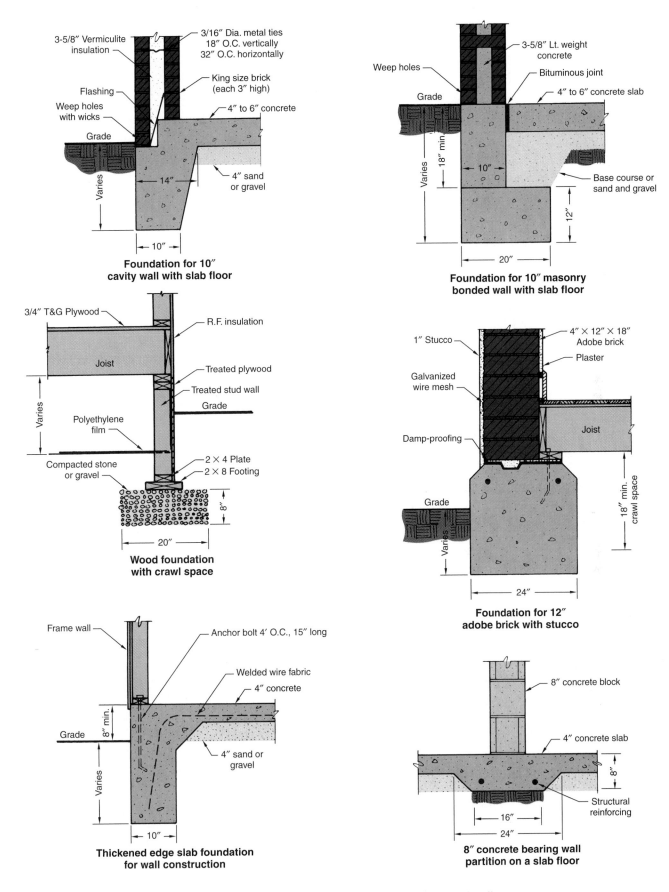

Figure 11-13. Typical thickened edge slab, slab floor, and wood foundation details.

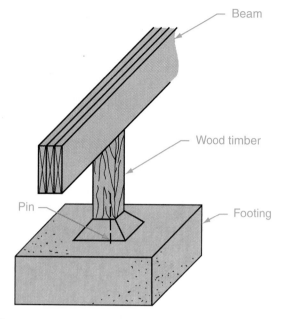

Figure 11-14. A typical pier foundation.

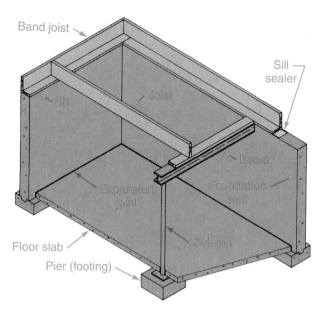

Figure 11-15. This column bears on a footing and supports a beam.

warmer climates where freezing of the ground is infrequent.

All wood used in the foundation is pressure-treated with chemical solutions that make the wood fibers useless as food for insects or fungus. The system is accepted by the Federal Housing Administration (FHA), the Department of Housing and Urban Development (HUD), Farmers Home Administration (FmHA), and by the major model building codes. It is rapidly gaining acceptance in state and local codes as well. The

system may be used in full basement or crawl space construction and is adaptable to most any site and light-frame building design, Figure 11-18.

For a structure with a crawl space, a trench is excavated to receive the footing and foundation wall. The depth of the excavation should be below the average maximum frost penetration depth. The trench should be at least 12" deep regardless of the frost depth. The excavation should allow for 2" of sand or 6" of crushed stone or gravel raked smooth in the

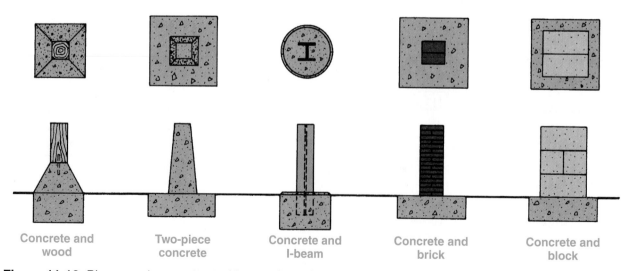

Figure 11-16. Piers may be constructed in a variety of styles.

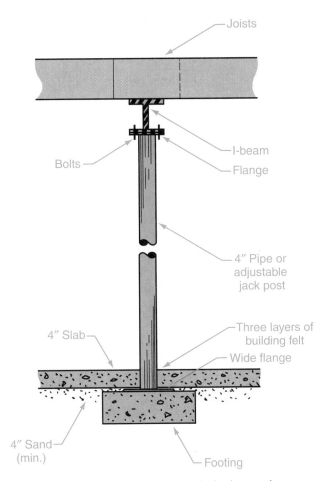

Figure 11-17. A pipe or adjustable jack post is frequently installed in a basement and used to support a steel beam on which floor joists rest.

bottom of the trench. This provides a level base for the footing. See Figure 11-19. It is essential that the base be perfectly level to ensure that the top plate of the foundation unit is level and accurately located. The actual footing, generally 10″ or 12″ wide, bearing (resting) on the ground must conform to the local code.

When a wood foundation is used for a house with a basement, the site is excavated to the depth as for other foundations. Plumbing lines are installed and provisions are made for foundation drainage according to local requirements. A basement sump should be installed in poorly drained soils or where ground water is a problem. The bottom of the excavation is then covered with 6″ to 8″ of porous gravel or crushed stone. This material is carefully leveled. Foundation footing plates made of 2″ × 8″, 2″ × 10″, or 2″ × 12″ pressure-treated material are placed directly on the gravel, Figure 11-20. The foundation walls are 2″ × 4″ or 2″ × 6″ stud frame. They are erected on the footing plates. Figure 11-21 shows a typical wood foundation system for a basement.

Nails and other fasteners used in a wood foundation should be made of silicon bronze,

Figure 11-18. This home has an all-weather wood foundation. (Osmose Wood Products)

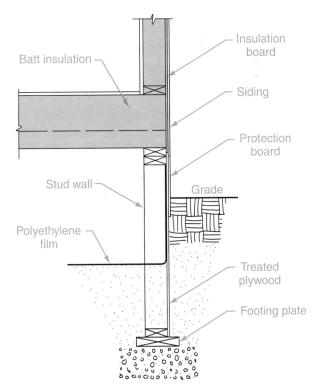

Figure 11-19. This is a section of a typical wood foundation for a crawl space.

Figure 11-20. The footing plate for a wood foundation basement wall bears directly on the stone. (Osmose Wood Products)

copper, or hot-dipped zinc-coated steel. Special caulking compounds are used to seal all joints in the plywood sheathing. Lumber and plywood that come in contact with the ground should be pressure-treated with waterborne preservative salts (ACA or CCA). All lumber and plywood in contact with the ground should be pressure-treated in accordance with the American Wood Preservers Bureau (FDN Standard), Figure 11-22.

After the basement wall is in place, the porous gravel or crushed stone base is covered with a polyethylene film 6 mil (.006 inch) thick. A screed board is attached to the inside of the foundation wall to serve as an elevation guide for the basement floor slab. The floor joists or trusses are then installed on the double top plate of the basement wall. Particular attention should be given to the attachment of the joists or trusses to ensure that inward forces will be transferred to the floor structure. On the sides of the structure where joists run parallel to the wall, blocking should be installed between the outside joists and first interior joists to resist lateral forces.

Before backfilling, a 6 mil polyethylene film should be applied to sections of the wall below grade to serve as a moisture barrier. All

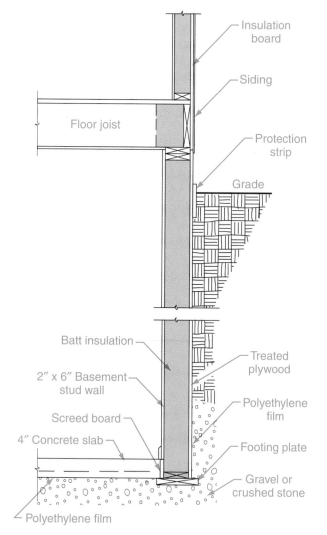

Figure 11-21. A typical wood foundation for a basement.

Figure 11-22. All wood in this basement wall has been pressure-treated to resist decay. (Osmose Wood Products)

joints should be lapped at least 6″ and sealed with adhesive. The top edge of the film should be bonded to the wall at grade level with adhesive. A treated wood strip is attached along this edge and caulked. This strip will later serve as a guide for backfilling. *Caution:* Backfilling should not begin until the basement floor has cured and the first floor is installed.

As with any foundation system, satisfactory performance requires full compliance with recommended standards covering design, fabrication, and installation. Standards for wood foundations are available from the American Forest and Paper Association (AF&PA) and The Engineered Wood Association (APA).

Concrete and Masonry Basement Walls

The thickness of concrete and masonry (block) basement walls depends on both the lateral earth pressure and the vertical load to be supported. The recommended minimum wall thickness at various depths below grade are shown in Figure 11-23. These dimensions are based on conventional residential construction and average soils. The height of the unbalanced fill is measured from the finished grade (exterior) to the basement floor.

Several factors influence the ability of a concrete or masonry basement wall to resist earth pressure. They include the height and thickness, bond of the mortar, vertical loading, support from crosswalls, pilasters or wall stiffeners, and support provided by the first floor framing. Lateral earth pressure may vary from almost zero to as great as the hydrostatic pressure of a liquid with the density of mud.

When local conditions indicate strong earth pressures (lateral force), pilasters can be used to strengthen the basement wall, Figure 11-24. A *pilaster* is a rectangular column that projects from a wall. Pilasters are also used for additional girder or beam support. Pilasters must be built at the same time that the basement wall is laid.

Blocks are frequently used to make pilasters. Pilaster blocks should have a minimum width of

16″ and project 4″ inside an 8″ thick basement wall; 6″ inside a 10″ thick wall. With 12″ masonry walls, pilasters are not usually required. In 8″ thick walls over 30′ long, the distance between pilasters should not be greater than 15′. In 10″ thick walls over 36′ long, this distance should not be greater than 18′. Pilasters may also be required to stiffen concrete foundation walls. Since concrete walls are generally 10″ thick, cast-in-place pilasters are spaced every 18′ along the perimeter of the wall.

Wall stiffeners provide another method of strengthening the walls. This is accomplished by placing a Number 4 bar in one core of the block from the top of the wall to the footing. The core of the block is the filled concrete.

A third procedure is to use continuous horizontal steel joint reinforcement at 16″ intervals vertically. This method will provide additional lateral support to the basement wall and help prevent cracking.

Basement walls should extend at least 8″ above the finished grade when using wood frame construction. Wood sills should be

Minimum thickness of basement walls*			
Type of unit	Minimum wall thickness, inches (Nominal)	Maximum height of unbalanced fill, feet**	
		Frame super-structure	Masonry and masonry veneer super-structure
Hollow load-bearing	8***	5	5
	10	6	7
	12	7	7
Solid load-bearing	8***	5	7
	10	7	7
	12	7	7

*Basement walls should be at least as thick as walls supported immediately above except as noted below.

**Heights shown may be increased to 7′ with approval of a building official if justified by soil conditions and local experience.

*** If the 8″ basement wall supports an 8′ wall, the combined height should not exceed 35′. If it supports brick veneer on wood frame or a 10″ cavity wall, it may be corbeled out a maximum of 2″ with solid units; but the total height of wall supported, including the gable, should not exceed 25′. Individual corbels should not project more than one-third of the height of the unit. If a concrete first floor is used, it helps provide adequate bearing for these walls and corbeling can be omitted.

Figure 11-23. This chart shows recommended minimum thicknesses for various wall loads. (Portland Cement Association)

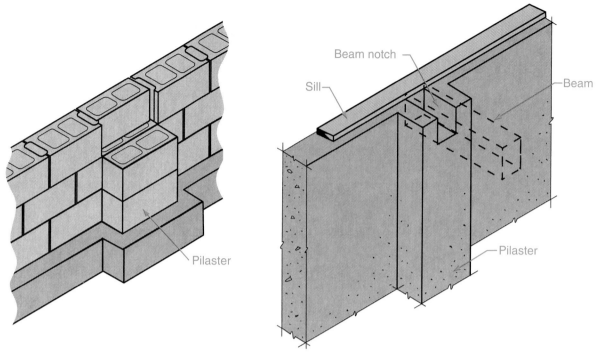

Figure 11-24. Pilasters add strength to a basement wall and may be used to support a beam.

anchored to the basement walls with 1/2" bolts 15" long and spaced approximately 4' apart. Anchor clips can also be used to attach the sill, Figure 11-25. Each sill piece should have at least two bolts. Anchor bolts are placed in the cores of the top two courses of masonry, which are then filled with mortar or concrete. Core filling may be supported by a piece of metal lath or similar material.

Basement walls may be slightly shorter than first and second floor walls. However, the distance from the top of the basement floor to

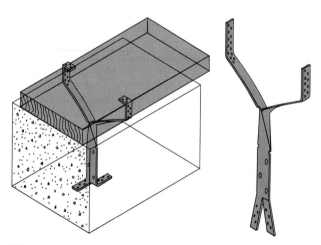

Figure 11-25. Anchor clips can be used to secure the sill plate to the foundation. (The Panel Clip Company)

the bottom of the floor joists above should be no less than 7'. A masonry basement wall that is 11 courses (rows) above the footing with a 4" solid cap provides a clear height of 7'-5" from the finished floor to the bottom of the floor joists, Figure 11-26. Some space will generally be required for heating ducts, pipes, and beams.

Load-bearing crosswalls in the basement should not be tied to the exterior walls in a masonry bond. Instead, they should be anchored with metal tie bars. The tie bars are usually 1/4" thick, 1-1/4" wide, and 28" long. Each end has a 2" right-angle bend that is embedded in block cores filled with mortar or concrete.

Floor loads are distributed more uniformly along the wall if the top course of block supporting the first floor is capped using one of:

- 4" solid block.
- Solid top block in which the hollow cores do not extend up into the top 4" of the block.
- Reinforced concrete masonry bond beam.
- Cores in the top course filled with concrete or mortar.

When the wood sill of the first floor bears on both the inner and outer face shells of the block, capping may be omitted.

Basement walls require damp-proofing on the outside to prevent groundwater from

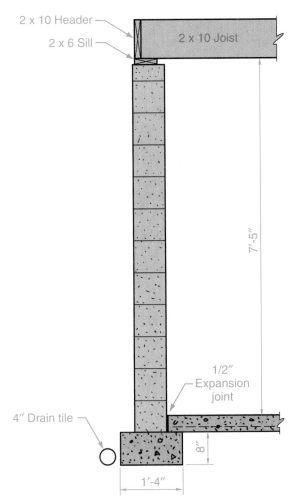

Figure 11-26. This basement wall provides an acceptable floor-to-ceiling height of 7'-5".

seeping through the wall. Cast concrete walls may be damp-proofed with a heavy coat of hot tar or two coats of cement-base paint. These paints are commercially prepared specifically for damp-proofing basements. Tar or paint is applied from the grade line to the footing.

Masonry (block) walls are damp-proofed by applying two 1/4" thick coats of cement-mortar or plaster to the wall. This is called a *parge coat*, which is a thin coat of plaster over the foundation wall. When the parge coat is dry, it is covered with hot tar or a similar material.

Both cast concrete and masonry walls require a 4" perforated drain tile or other water removal system around the perimeter of the footing. This tile removes excess groundwater and reduces the chance of water problems in the basement, Figure 11-27. The tile is covered with coarse stone or gravel to a depth of about 18" to allow water to seep into the tile.

In poorly drained and wet soils, added precautions may be advisable to ensure against water damage. A sump pump may be installed in the basement to remove any water that seeps in. The floor slab may be reinforced to resist uplift by groundwater pressure. A check valve in the floor drain will prevent water from flowing in through the drain from the storm sewer.

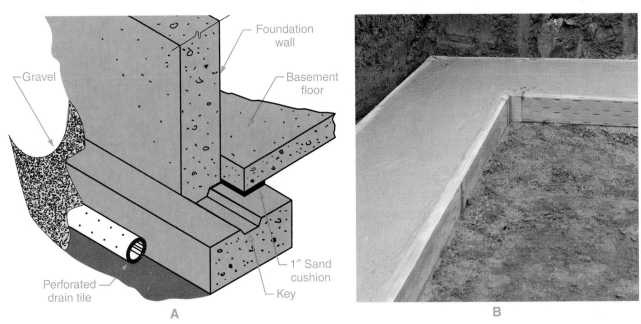

Figure 11-27. A—Drain tile placed along the footing helps prevent water problems in the basement. B—The product shown here is used as forms for the footings and serves as the drain tile. (CertainTeed Corporation)

Beams and Girders

Most houses have a span that is too great to have unsupported floor joists. Therefore, a beam or girder is required to support the joists and prevent excessive sagging. The beam is usually placed an equal distance from each outside wall or under a bearing wall. A *bearing wall* is designed to support part of the load of the structure. The beam runs perpendicular to the direction of the floor joists.

Beams may be either wood or metal. There are two types of traditional wood beams: built-up and solid. Built-up beams are used more frequently than solid ones because they are easier to handle, more readily available, and do not check (crack) to the extent of solid beams. However, solid beams are generally stronger and more fire-resistant. New wood beam options are covered in Chapter 13 under the heading *Engineered Wood Products*.

Two types of steel beams are commonly used. These are S-beams and wide-flange beams (W-beams), Figure 11-28. The S-beam used to be commonly called an I-beam. The wide-flange beam will support greater weight and is more stable than the standard S-beam. For these reasons it is more popular for residential construction.

The size of the beam needed is based on the weight of the structure, Figure 11-29. This weight must be known when calculating the beam size. Weights are designated either as live loads or dead loads. *Live loads* are those fixed or moving weights that are not a structural part of the house. Examples include furniture, occupants, snow on the roof, wind, etc. *Dead loads* are those static or fixed weights of the structure itself. Examples of dead loads are the weights of roofing, foundation walls, siding, joists, etc. To simplify matters, it will be assumed that loads found in a typical residence are as follows. Use these figures for load calculations in this text.

- **First Floor.** Live load plus dead load = 50 pounds per square foot.
- **Second Floor.** Live load plus dead load = 50 pounds per square foot.
- **Ceiling.** Live load plus dead load = 30 pounds per square foot.
- **Walls.** Dead load = 10 pounds per square foot.
- **Roof.** No load on the beam. Exterior walls generally support the roof.

Tables that give the greatest safe loads that beams will support usually record the weight in kips. One *kip* equals 1,000 pounds. Figure 11-30 shows span data for American Standard S-beams and W-beams. These loads are based on a fiber stress of 20,000 pounds, or the pressure they will withstand per square inch. This stress is usually sufficient for common residential construction situations.

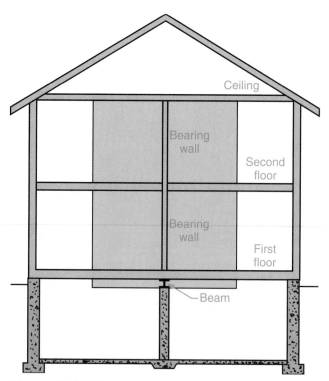

Figure 11-29. The shaded area represents the weight supported by the beam.

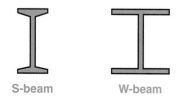

Figure 11-28. These are cross sections of two typical steel beams used in residential construction.

Maximum allowable uniform loads for American standard S-beams with lateral support
Span in feet

Size of beam	Weight of beam per foot	4	6	8	10	12	14	16	18	20	22	24	26	28	30	32	34	36	38	40
4 x 2-3/4	7.7	10	7	5																
	9.5	11	7	6																
5 x 3	10.0	16	11	8	6															
	11.3	20	13	10	8															
6 x 3-1/8	12.5	24	16	12	10	8														
	17.3	29	19	15	12	10														
7 x 3-3/4	15.3	35	23	17	14	12	10													
	20.0	40	27	20	16	15	13													
8 x 4	18.4	47	32	24	19	16	14	12												
	23.0	53	36	27	21	18	15	13												
10 x 4-3/4	25.4	80	54	41	33	27	23	20	18	16										
	35.0	97	65	49	39	32	28	24	22	20										
12 x 5	31.8	110	80	60	48	40	34	30	27	24	22	20								
	35.0	126	84	63	50	42	36	32	28	25	23	21								
12 x 5-1/4	40.8	144	100	75	60	50	43	37	33	30	27	25								
	50.0	168	112	84	67	56	48	42	37	34	31	28								
15 x 5-1/2	42.9	160	131	98	79	65	56	49	44	39	36	33	30	28	26	25				
	50.0	214	143	107	86	71	61	54	48	43	39	36	33	31	29	27				
18 x 6	54.7		196	147	118	98	84	74	66	59	54	49	45	42	39	37	35	33	31	
	70.0		226	170	136	113	97	85	76	68	62	57	52	49	45	43	40	38	36	
20 x 6-1/4	65.4		260	195	156	130	111	97	87	78	71	65	60	56	52	49	46	43	41	39
	75.0		281	211	169	140	120	105	94	84	77	70	65	60	56	53	50	47	44	42

Loads are in kips. 1 kip = 1,000 pounds

Maximum allowable uniform loads for wide flange W-beams with lateral support
Span in feet

Size of beam	Weight of beam per foot	4	6	8	9	10	12	14	18	20	22	24	26	28	30	32	34	36	38	40
8 x 5-1/4	17	47	31	24	19	16	13	12												
8 x 6-1/2	24		46	35	28	23	20	17												
8 x 8	31		60	46	37	30	26	23	20	18	16									
10 x 5-1/4	21	62	48	36	29	24	21	18	16	14										
10 x 8	33			74	58	47	39	33	29	26	23									
10 x 10	49				88	73	61	52	46	40	36	33	30	28	26					
12 x 6-1/2	27			74	57	45	38	32	28	25	23	21	19							
12 x 8	40				87	69	58	49	43	38	35	32	29							
12 x 10	53			108	94	79	67	59	52	47	43	39								
12 x 12	65				117	98	84	73	65	59	53	49	45	42	39					
14 x 6-3/4	30			93	70	56	46	40	35	31	28	25	23	21	20	19				
14 x 8	43				105	84	70	60	52	46	42	38	35	32	30	28				
14 x 10	61				123	102	88	77	68	62	56	51	47	44	41					
14 x 12	78				156	135	115	101	90	81	73	67	62	58	54					
14 x 14-1/2	87					152	132	115	102	92	84	77	71	66	61	57	54	51		
16 x 7	36			124	94	75	63	54	47	42	38	34	31	29	27	25	24	22		
16 x 8-1/2	58				157	126	105	90	78	70	63	57	52	48	45	42	39	37		
16 x 11-1/2	88					202	168	144	126	112	101	92	84	78	72	67	63	59		
18 x 7-1/2	50			148	119	99	85	74	66	59	54	49	46	42	40	37	35	33	31	
18 x 8-3/4	64				188	156	130	111	98	87	78	71	65	60	56	52	49	46	43	41
18 x 11-3/4	96				224	189	176	154	137	123	112	103	95	88	82	77	72	68	65	
21 x 8-1/4	62			211	169	141	120	105	94	84	77	70	65	60	56	53	50	47	44	42

Loads are in kips. 1 kip = 1,000 pounds

Figure 11-30. Span and load table for American Standard beams. (American Institute of Steel Construction)

Weight Calculations

The following example calculates the load for a two-story frame structure. The structure size is 28'-0" × 40'-0". Figure 11-31 shows the foundation walls and beam. This calculation assumes a bearing wall running the length of the house on both floors.

Width × length = Area of the house

28' × 40' = 1,120 square feet for each floor
8' × 40' = 320 square feet of wall area for each wall

Weight per square feet × number of square feet = total weight

Weight of first floor
1,120 square feet × 50 lbs./
square foot   = 56,000 lbs.
Weight of second floor
1,120 square feet × 50 lbs./
square foot   = 56,000 lbs.
Weight of ceiling
1,120 square feet × 30 lbs./
square foot   = 33,600 lbs.
Weight of roof on beam
(none in this example)   =   0 lbs.
Total   = 145,600 lbs.

One-half of the total weight bears on the center beam.
1/2 × 145,600 pounds   = 72,800 lbs.
Weight of first floor wall
320 square feet × 10 lbs./
square feet   =   3,200 lbs.
Weight of second floor wall
320 square feet × 10 lbs./
square feet   =   3,200 lbs.
Weight bearing on beam   = 79,200 lbs.

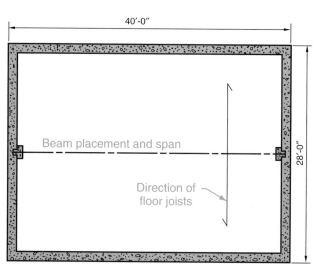

Figure 11-31. This is the foundation wall for the calculations in the text. Notice the direction of the joists and placement of the supporting beam.

Convert to kips by dividing by 1000. The weight in kips is 79.2 kips.

Beam Calculations

Since no posts are used, as shown in Figure 11-31, the span is 40'. The length of beam needed in this example is 40'. A beam large enough to support 79.2 kips over 40' is not practical. That is why no information for this condition appears in the charts in Figure 11-30. Therefore, the span must be decreased by adding one or more support posts. Study the chart in Figure 11-32 and the illustrations in Figure 11-33. Notice how the beam size and weight on the beam decreases with the addition of support posts. Any of the beams and post configurations shown in Figure 11-32

Effect of adding support posts				
	Span	Weight on beam	Size of beam and weight	Kips beam will support
One post S-beam W-beam	20' - 0" 20' - 0"	39.6 kips 39.6 kips	15" x 5-1/2" x 50.0 lbs./ft 14" x 8" x 43.0 lbs./ft	43 kips 42 kips
Two posts S-beam W-beam	13' - 4" 13' - 4"	26.4 kips 26.4 kips	10" x 4-3/4" x 35.0 lbs./ft 8" x 8" x 31.0 lbs./ft	28 kips 26 kips
Three posts S-beam W-beam	10' - 0" 10' - 0"	19.8 kips 19.8 kips	8" x 4" x 23.0 lbs./ft 8" x 6-1/2" x 24.0 lbs./ft	21 kips 23 kips

Figure 11-32. This chart shows the effect of adding support posts on the load capacity of the beam.

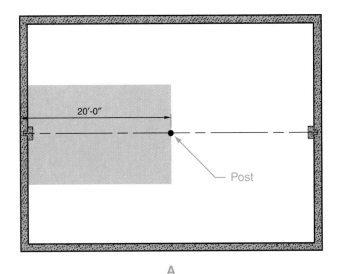

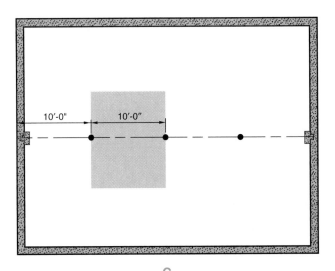

Figure 11-33. The shaded area represents the weight supported by the beam span. A—Effective beam span with one post. B—Effective beam span with two posts. C— Effective beam span with three posts.

would support the load of the structure. However, steel is sold by the pound so choose the smallest beam that will adequately do the job with a reasonable span.

Post Calculations

Once the size of beam and number of post supports have been determined, the size of each post must be calculated. This procedure is not as complex as the procedure for calculating beam sizes. If three posts are used for this example, each beam segment or 10'-0" span must support 19.8 kips (19,800 pounds). Each post must also support this weight because it must bear the weight on either side halfway to the next post. See Figure 11-34. Steel post design information is given in Figure 11-35. The required diameter of post is determined by finding the weight to be supported and length of the post on the chart.

The unbraced length in this example is 8' and the weight that must be supported by the post is 19.8 kips. The smallest column shown on the chart in Figure 11-35 is a nominal size of 3". This size is more than adequate since it will support 34 kips. Therefore, the support posts should be 3" in diameter; each weighs 7.58 pounds per foot or 60.64 pounds total.

Steel posts must have a flange welded on both ends and provision for attachment to the beam. The post may be bolted or attached with clips. The size of the top flange is determined

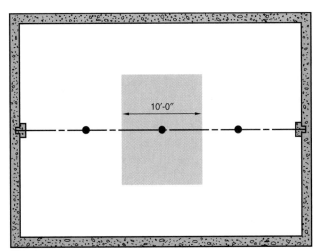

Figure 11-34. Each post must support the weight of the shaded area.

Maximum allowable concentric loads for standard steel pipe columns											
Nominal size in inches	Weight per foot in pounds	Unbraced length in feet									
		6	7	8	9	10	11	12	14	16	18
3	7.58	38	36	34	31	28	25	22	16	12	10
3-1/2	9.11	48	46	44	41	38	35	32	25	19	15
4	10.79	59	57	54	52	49	46	43	36	29	23
5	14.62	83	81	78	76	73	71	68	61	55	47
6	18.97	110	108	106	103	101	98	95	89	82	75

Loads are in kips. 1 kip = 1,000 pounds

Figure 11-35. Load table for standard steel pipe columns. (American Institute of Steel Construction)

by the width of the beam to be supported. The bottom flange (often 8″ × 8″) should be larger than the top flange to provide a larger bearing surface on the footing.

Lintels

A *lintel* is a horizontal structural member that supports the load over an opening such as a door or window. Lintels may be constructed of precast concrete, cast-in-place concrete, lintel blocks, or steel angle, Figure 11-36.

Openings in cast concrete walls do not require lintels. When lintels are used in a masonry wall, the ends must extend at least 4″ into the wall on either side of the opening. Figure 11-37 shows a precast lintel over a door in a concrete block wall. Common precast lintel sizes for residential construction are 4″ × 8″, 4″ × 6″, and 8″ × 8″ in a variety of lengths.

Lintels are also made of angle steel. They are available as equal angles (both legs the same size) or as unequal angles. The chart in Figure 11-38 identifies the size of angle steel required to support a 4″ masonry wall above an opening. Figure 11-39 shows an angle steel lintel supporting the load over a window opening in a brick wall.

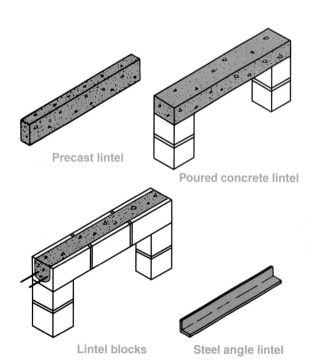

Precast lintel

Poured concrete lintel

Lintel blocks

Steel angle lintel

Figure 11-36. Four types of lintels frequently used in residential building construction.

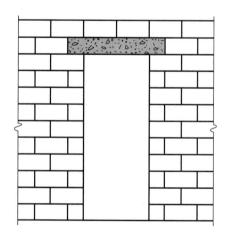

Figure 11-37. This masonry wall doorway has a precast lintel supporting the weight above the opening.

Steel angles to support 4″ masonry walls	
Span	Size of angle
0′ – 5′	3″ x 3″ x 1/4″
5′ – 9′	3-1/2″ x 3-1/2″ x 5/16″
9′ – 10′	4″ x 4″ x 5/16″
10′ – 11′	4″ x 4″ x 3/8″
11′ – 15′	6″ x 4″ x 3/8″
15′ – 16′	6″ x 4″ x 1/2″

Figure 11-38. This chart gives the size of angle steel for lintels.

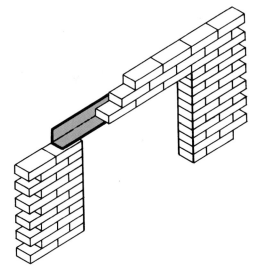

Figure 11-39. This angle steel lintel supports the load over the window opening in the brick wall.

Concrete and Masonry

Concrete is ordered by the cubic yard. The average home requires many "yards" of concrete. Fortunately, most contractors are near a ready-mix plant that produces concrete. The consistency of concrete is generally specified by how many bags of cement are contained in each yard of mix. A bag of cement is normally 94 pounds. A five-bag mix is considered the minimum for most jobs. A six-bag mix produces a stronger product and should be used when high strength or reinforcing is required.

A cubic yard is 27 cubic feet. However, when ordering concrete, figure that only 25 cubic feet of every yard will be useable. Some of the material will remain in the mixer, some will be spilled, and forms may sag. It is better to have a little more concrete than you need than to have too little.

Concrete is the result of combining cement, sand, aggregate (usually stone or gravel), and water. *Cement* is composed of a mixture of lime, silica, alumina, iron components, and gypsum. The proportions of the ingredients will vary with the requirements. However, sidewalks, driveways, footings, and basement floors usually contain one part cement, three parts sand, and five parts aggregate. Footings, as well as concrete floors, must have both a minimum compressive strength of 3,000 psi and minimum cement content of 5 bags (470 lbs.) per cubic yard. The amount of water used will most likely be 6 or 7 gallons for each bag of cement.

Concrete cures over a long period of time and should be kept moist for several days after it is placed. Failure to do this reduces strength and may harm the exposed surface. Temperature also affects the setting time of concrete. Cold weather slows down the curing process. Concrete should not be allowed to freeze before it has set. On the other hand, concrete should not get too hot as it cures.

When concrete is placed (poured), air pockets are commonly trapped within the mixture. It is necessary to work these air pockets out by vibrating or tamping. This action helps to form a more dense material and removes weak spots due to air pockets.

After the concrete has been placed, a screed is used to smooth the surface. The *screed* is a long straightedge, usually a board, that is worked back and forth across the surface. This action brings excess water to the surface and settles the aggregate. Power screeds are also available for large jobs.

When screeding is finished, the surface is then worked over with a float. A *float* is a short board, about a foot long, with a handle attached to one of the wide sides. The purpose of floating is to:

• Embed the large aggregate just beneath the surface.
• Remove any slight imperfections, lumps, and voids to produce a flat surface.
• Consolidate mortar at the surface in preparation for final steel-troweling.

As the mixture reaches the proper consistency, the troweling process is started. The *trowel* is rectangular and is used in a circular motion. This troweling action further hardens the surface and develops a very smooth finish. If a slightly rough surface is desired, it may be swept with a broom after the surface is troweled.

Large areas of concrete are likely to crack from expansion and contraction due to changes in temperature and moisture content. This cracking may be minimized or controlled by introducing *contraction joints.* These joints may be formed by cutting grooves in the freshly placed concrete with a jointing tool. They may also be cut into the slab with a power saw after the concrete has hardened. The depth of joints or grooves should be one-fourth of the thickness of the slab. Contraction joints should be placed in line with interior columns, at changes in the width of the slab, or at maximum spacing of about 20'.

A concrete slab is usually placed directly on firmly compacted sand 4" to 6" thick. The slab base (sand) should be thoroughly compacted to prevent settlement of the slab. Dry sand should be dampened to prevent absorption of too much mixing water from the fresh concrete. The slab base should also be sloped toward floor drains to ensure a uniform slab thickness. Floor slabs usually have a minimum thickness of 4".

Floor slabs should not be bonded to footings or interior columns. A sand cushion 1" thick may be used to separate the slab from the footing, Figure 11-40. A sleeve of three thicknesses of

building felt may be wrapped around columns to break the bond.

Concrete Blocks

Concrete blocks are used extensively in residential buildings. They are used to form exterior and, in some instances, interior walls. They may be purchased in a variety of sizes and shapes. In general terms, "concrete block" refers to a hollow concrete masonry unit usually 8" × 8" × 16". The actual size is 7-5/8" × 7-5/8" × 15-5/8". These dimensions allow for a 3/8" mortar joint. Therefore, the distance from the centerline of one mortar joint to the centerline of the next will be 8" or 16". Figure 11-41 shows a variety of concrete blocks that are frequently used in a residential structure.

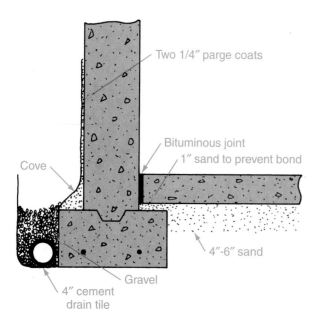

Figure 11-40. Floor slabs should not be bonded to the footing or foundation wall.

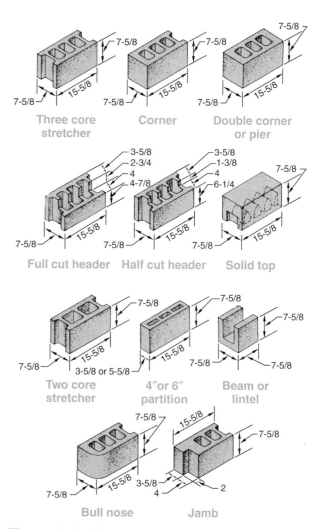

Figure 11-41. These are commonly used concrete blocks. The dimensions are actual sizes of the blocks.

A wide variety of decorative concrete blocks are available. They may be used to form a screen, fence, or wall, Figure 11-42. Use of decorative blocks should not be overlooked when searching for innovative materials. The applications for concrete blocks are limited only by a designer's imagination.

Paving

Brick or concrete pavers can be installed either as a rigid or flexible system. A rigid paving system is easily recognized by its mortar joints, Figure 11-43. A properly designed *rigid paving system* consists of a well-compacted subgrade, a properly prepared base, a reinforced concrete slab, a mortar setting bed, and brick paving with mortar joints between the pavers.

Flexible paving has a greater variety of design options than rigid paving. A *flexible paving system* consists of a well-compacted

Figure 11-43. This is a rigid paving system; it rests on a mortar setting bed.

subgrade beneath a layer of crushed stone, a sand setting bed, and fine sand between the pavers, Figure 11-44. A rigid edge restraint must be used to prevent horizontal movement called *creep*, Figure 11-45.

All brick paving units should conform to ASTM C902, *Standard for Pedestrian and Light*

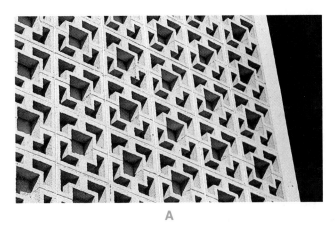

A

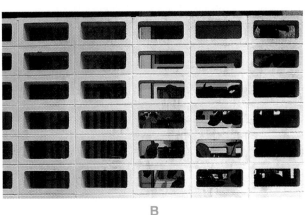

B

Figure 11-42. Decorative concrete blocks may be used to add a new design dimension.

A

B

Figure 11-44. A—Lime rock is spread and compacted to form the subgrade for a flexible paving system. B—A 1″ thick layer of compacted sand is added to the subgrade.

Figure 11-45. These pavers are being placed next to a wall that prevents creep

Figure 11-46. These pallets contain 2-1/4″ pavers that will be used for the driveway.

Traffic Paving Brick. For most exterior applications, a brick unit meeting or exceeding the requirements of Class SX should be used. If you use mortar, it should be Type M, conforming to ASTM C270. Portland-cement-lime mortars provide greater durability than other cement types.

Heavy traffic areas, such as driveways, should be constructed of 2-1/4″ pavers,

Figure 11-46. Patios and sidewalks may be constructed of 1-1/2″ pavers on a flexible base. Paving should be sloped at least 1/8″ to 1/4″ per foot to provide proper drainage. An expansion joint should be provided every 20′ for rigid paving and every 30′ for flexible paving. Solid curbs that prevent drainage should have weep holes every 16″ along the length.

Internet Resources

www.concretehomes.com
 Portland Cement Association

www.steel.org
 American Iron and Steel Institute

www.astm.org
 American Society for Testing and Materials

www.apawood.org
 The Engineered Wood Association

www.afandpa.org
 American Forest and Paper Association, formerly the National Forest Products Association

www.bcewp.com
 Boise Cascade Engineered Wood Products

www.anchorwall.com
 Anchor Retaining Wall Systems

www.builderonline.com
 Builder Magazine

www.sweets.com
 Sweets Catalog File

www.deere.com
 Deere and Company, John Deere construction equipment

www.energy.gov
 US Department of Energy

Review Questions – Chapter 11

Write your answers on a separate sheet of paper. Do not write in this book.

1. The dimensions necessary for staking out the house are found on the _____ plan.

2. What method may be used to check the accuracy of all corners of the house once it is staked out?

3. The purpose of batter boards is to _____.

4. The excavation for footings must extend at least _____ below the average maximum frost depth.

5. The size and type of footing should be suitable for the building _____ and soil bearing capacity.

6. The thickness of the footing is usually the same thickness as the _____.

7. Stepped footings are necessary for _____.

8. Concrete stepped footings may be reinforced using two _____ inch steel bars.

9. The most common foundation type is the _____.

10. List two advantages of the slab foundation.

11. The basic difference between a pier and column is the _____.

12. To which type of foundation do AWWF and PWF refer?

13. What prevents the wood in a wood foundation from rotting?

14. Why does the sand or gravel under the footing for a wood foundation need to be perfectly level?

15. Which three materials are used for nails and fasteners in a wood foundation?

16. The minimum clear height between a basement floor and bottom of the floor joists should be _____ feet. This height allows some space for heating ducts, pipes, and beams.

17. Long basement walls may need added lateral support. A _____ can be used to provide this support.

18. The materials commonly used to damp-proof basement walls are _____ and _____.

19. When the span is too great for unsupported floor joists, a _____ is used to provide support.

20. List two types of steel beams used in residential construction.

21. Weights are designated as live loads and dead loads. Snow on a roof is an example of a _____ load.

22. The load that a steel beam will safely support is usually given in _____.

23. A horizontal structural member that supports the load over an opening such as a door or window is known as a _____.

24. List the four ingredients in concrete.

25. Cold weather _____ the curing time of concrete.

26. A _____ is a long straightedge (board) that is worked back and forth across the surface of concrete to bring excess water to the surface and settle the aggregate.

27. Large areas of concrete are likely to crack from expansion and contraction due to temperature change. This cracking may be minimized or controlled through the use of _____.

28. The nominal size of a concrete block is 8″ × 8″ × 16″. The actual size of this block is _____.

Suggested Activities

1. Using CADD, draw a plan view of a 12′ × 20′ one-car garage. In a team of at least three students, stake out the garage using string, stakes, and a 50′ measuring tape. Use the 9-12-15 unit method of laying out a 90° corner. Refer to Figure 11-2. Check the accuracy by measuring the diagonals. Record the diagonal measurements.

2. Using a carpenter's level on a stool or other fixed surface, determine the difference in elevation at the four corners of the garage that you staked out in Activity 1. Procedure: Have one member of the team hold a pole or strip of wood vertically, with bottom end resting on the ground, over one of the corner stakes. Sight down the level and have your partner make a mark on the pole even with your line of sight. Be sure the level is not tilted. Duplicate this procedure for each corner. Measure difference between the marks on the rod. These distances represent the

variation in elevation. The same procedure can be done much more accurately with a contractor's level. Record your results.

3. Visit an excavation site for a residence in your community. Secure permission before entering the site. Measure the depth and size of excavation. Determine the size of footings and thickness of foundation walls. Prepare a sketch of the foundation layout with dimensions. Note the type of soil supporting the footings.

4. Select a foundation plan of a small structure with a slab floor, such as a garage or storage building. Calculate the amount of concrete required for the footings, foundation wall, and floor. Show your calculation and draw the foundation plan.

5. Calculate the size of a steel beam and columns required to support a frame house with foundation dimensions of 34'-0" × 48'-0". The spacing of your columns should not exceed 12'-0" for this activity.

6. Select a foundation detail from Figure 11-11 and draw it using CADD. Then, plot the drawing at a scale of 1" = 1'-0".

7. Select a foundation detail from Figure 11-13 and draw it using CADD. Then, plot the drawing at a scale of 1" = 1'-0".

The Foundation Plan

12

Objectives

After studying this chapter, you will be able to:

➤ Identify the primary features included in a foundation plan.

➤ Discuss the difference between a foundation plan and a basement plan.

➤ Design and draw a foundation plan for a typical residential structure using traditional or CADD methods.

Key Terms

Foundation Plan   Basement Plan
Brick Ledge

The *foundation plan* is a plan view drawing, in section, that provides all of the information necessary to construct the foundation. It is usually drawn after the floor plan and elevations have been roughed out. A foundation plan ordinarily includes:

- Footings for foundation walls, piers, and columns.
- Foundation walls.
- Piers and columns (posts).
- Dwarf walls. These are low walls built to retain an excavation or embankment.
- Partial walls, doors, and bath fixtures in the basement.
- Openings in the foundation wall, such as for windows, doors, and vents.
- Beams and pilasters.
- Direction, size, and spacing of floor joists or trusses.
- Drains and sump (if required).
- Details of foundation and footing construction.
- Complete dimensions and notes.
- Scale of the drawing.

The residential structure shown in Figure 12-1 has a rather complex foundation. It is critical to have an accurate foundation plan for this structure.

The foundation plan is prepared primarily for excavators, masons, carpenters, and cement workers who build the foundation. Be sure to present the information that they need to build the foundation. Also, hatch patterns are typically used on a foundation plan to show various materials. Common patterns are shown in Figure 12-2.

Figure 12-1. This house has a complex foundation. An accurate foundation plan is important to ensure that the house is properly constructed. (Sater Design Collection, Inc.)

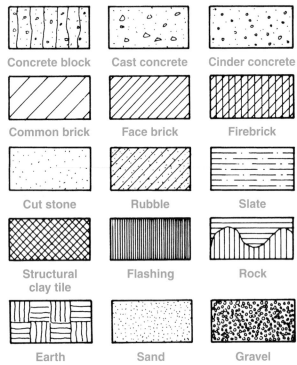

Figure 12-2. Hatch patterns representing different materials are commonly used on a foundation plan.

Preliminary Steps to Drawing a Foundation Plan

The foundation plan is drawn from information presented on the floor plan, plot plan, and elevations. It is important that dimensions on the foundation plan and floor plan are accurate and consistent. The preliminary floor plan may be used as an underlay for drawing the foundation plan. These procedures reduce the time required to make the drawing and help to keep errors to a minimum.

Before drawing the foundation plan, determine the type of exterior walls specified on the floor plan. This step is important because the dimensions of the foundation may not be the same for different types of exterior walls. For example, the foundation size will be larger for a brick veneer house than a house with a stud wall frame. The reason for the difference is that the basic house size is measured to the outside of the stud wall for both types of construction. However, a 4″ *brick ledge* on which the brick veneer rests is required for the brick veneer house. This adds 8″ to the total length and width of the foundation over a stud wall structure. See Figure 12-3. The plot plan and elevation should also be examined to anticipate the need for stepped footings, retaining walls, and problems related to the grade, Figure 12-4.

Determine the required size of footings and foundation walls from the available information. Check the maximum frost penetration depth for the area. Refer to the building code to be sure that all requirements are met before proceeding. If the soil bearing capacity is questionable, conduct a soil bearing test. See Figure 12-5.

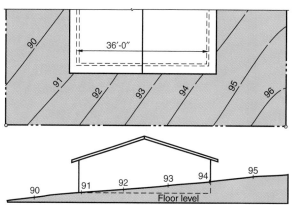

Figure 12-4. In this example, no consideration has been given to the existing grade. As a result, the finished floor level is below grade. This is most likely in conflict with the building code.

Figure 12-5. A soil bearing test is being made to determine the load-bearing capacity of the soil. (K & S Testing and Engineering, Inc.)

Drawing a Foundation Plan

Drawing a foundation plan using manual drafting techniques includes the following steps. All items will not apply to every situation.

1. Select the scale. Residential structures are usually drawn to 1/4″ = 1′-0″ scale. Be sure to use the same size tracing sheets for all drawings in the set. Steps 1 through 4 are shown in Figure 12-6.

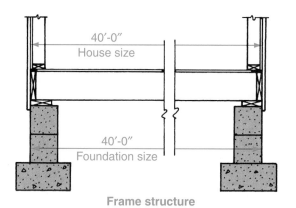

Frame structure

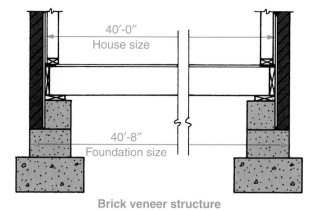

Brick veneer structure

Figure 12-3. A brick veneer house requires a foundation wall 8″ longer and wider than if the same house is a stud wall structure.

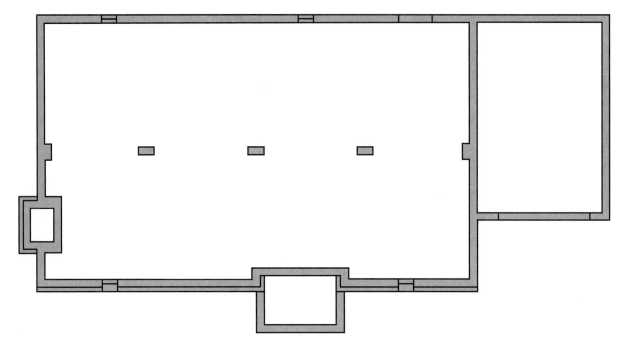

Figure 12-6. A partially completed foundation plan that shows the foundation walls, piers, pilasters, and vent openings.

2. Locate the outline of the foundation walls on the paper allowing ample space for dimensions, notes, and a title block. Use the floor plan as an underlay or draw the foundation plan from dimensions obtained from the floor plan.

3. Draw the foundation walls, piers, pilasters, and the foundation for a fireplace and chimney.

4. Indicate breaks in the foundation wall for windows, doors, access holes, and vents.

5. Lay out and draw the footings for the foundation walls. Use a hidden line. Steps 5 through 10 are shown in Figure 12-7.

6. Draw the footings for the piers and columns (posts).

7. Draw the footings for the fireplace and chimney.

8. Locate the supporting beam if one is required. Draw the beam using a single, thick centerline.

9. Show the size, spacing, and direction of floor joists or trusses using the standard notation.

10. Identify the location of sections needed to provide additional information.

11. Draw and dimension the necessary sections, Figure 12-8.

12. Determine the location of the dimensions needed to show the size of all aspects of the foundation. The length and thickness of all foundation wall segments must be dimensioned. Pier locations are dimensioned to the center rather than to the edge. Steps 12 through 17 are shown in Figure 12-9.

13. Draw the dimension lines and add the required dimensions.

14. Letter any necessary notes.

15. Shade the drawing with proper material symbols (hatch patterns).

16. Add the title block, scale, and name of drawing in the proper location.

17. Check the drawing to be sure you have included all necessary information.

The Basement/Foundation Plan

In climates where the frost penetration depth is several feet, basements are usually included in the plans. Since the footings must be below the frost depth, it is comparatively inexpensive to excavate the soil under the

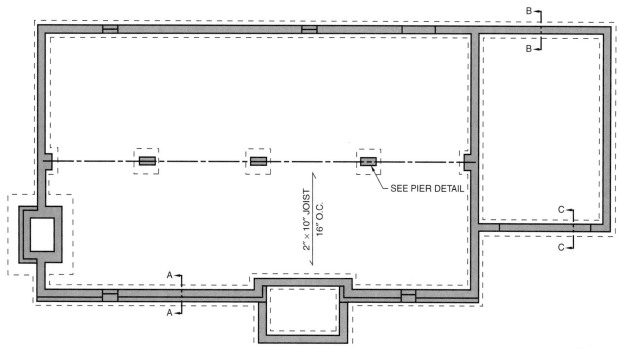

Figure 12-7. Footings for the foundation walls and the piers, the supporting beam, all section symbols, and the floor joist data have been added to the foundation plan.

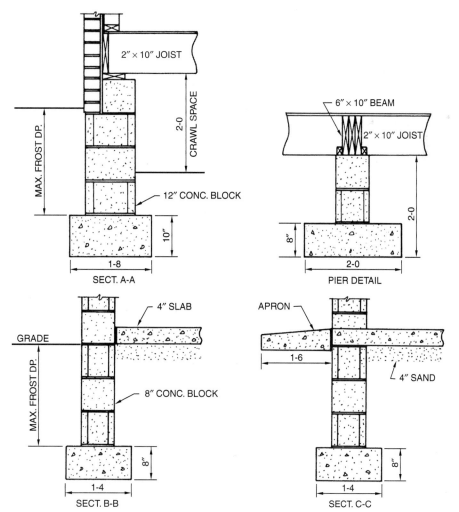

Figure 12-8. These foundation details are required to further describe the foundation construction.

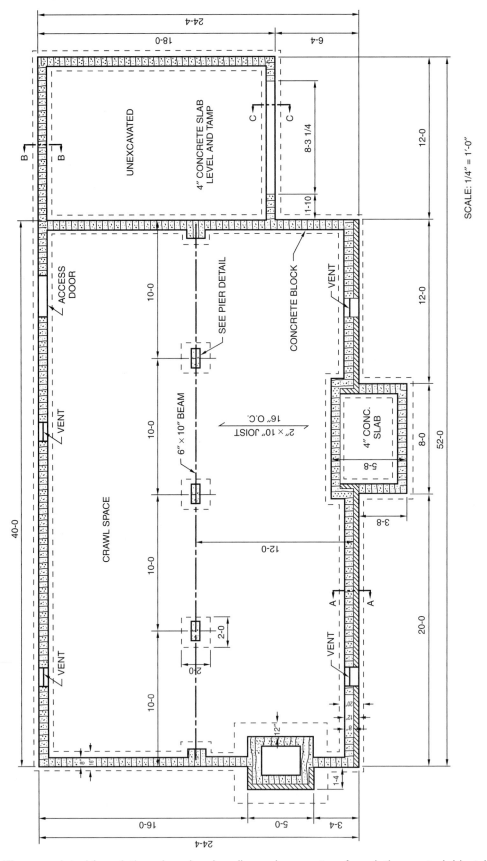

Figure 12-9. The completed foundation plan showing dimensions, notes, foundation material hatch pattern, and drawing scale. This house has a stud wall frame with a brick veneer along the front.

house and extend the foundation down a few more feet. This additional excavation provides usable space at much less cost per square foot than the first floor level. Basements are also popular in crowded areas where building sites are small.

The *basement plan* is a combination foundation and floor plan. It includes the information commonly shown on the foundation plan and, at the same time, shows interior walls, stairs, windows, and doors in the basement. The split-level house is a good example of where a foundation plan is required for one section of the house and a basement plan for the other. Figure 12-10 illustrates the use of a basement and a foundation plan to show construction for a split-level house.

Procedure for Drawing a Basement Plan

The procedure for drawing a basement plan is much the same as for a foundation plan. However, there are several additional features on a basement plan. The following steps should help to clarify the procedure using manual drafting techniques.

1. Select the proper scale to be used. Again, most residential plans are drawn at 1/4" = 1'-0" scale. Steps 1 through 4 are shown in Figure 12-11.

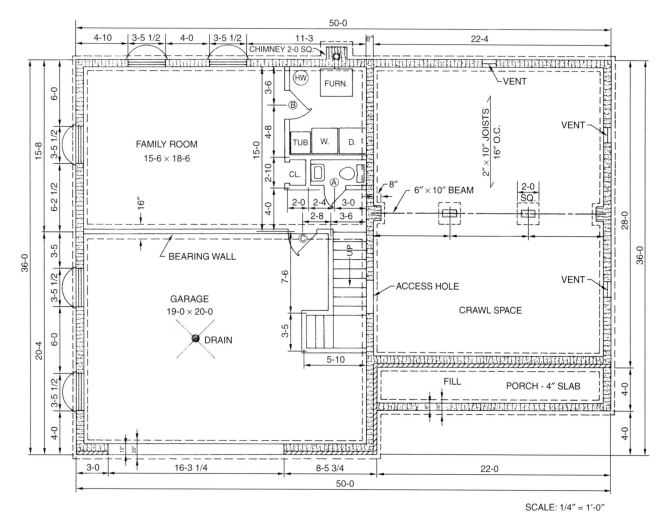

SCALE: 1/4" = 1'-0"

Figure 12-10. A finished basement/foundation plan for a split-level house. The house is a stud wall structure with some brick veneer.

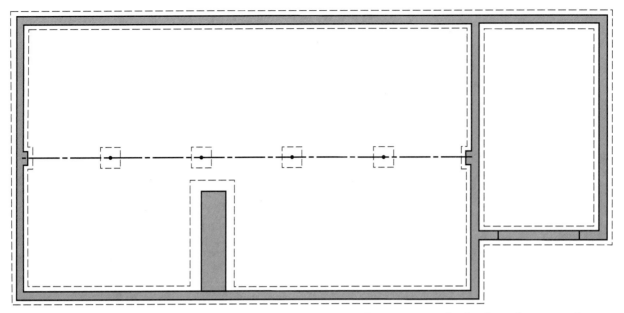

Figure 12-11. A partially completed basement plan showing the foundation walls, footings, beam, and posts/columns.

2. Draw the exterior foundation walls using the floor plan as an underlay or from information taken from the floor plan. Be sure the foundation walls are correctly positioned with respect to the first floor walls.

3. Draw the footings for the foundation walls, chimney, and fireplace. Also draw the piers and columns (posts).

4. Locate and draw the beam and supports or bearing wall partition(s).

5. Design the room layout in the basement area and darken in the lines. Steps 5 through 9 are shown in Figure 12-12.

6. Indicate breaks in the basement walls for windows or doors.

7. Locate and draw the stairs leading to the basement.

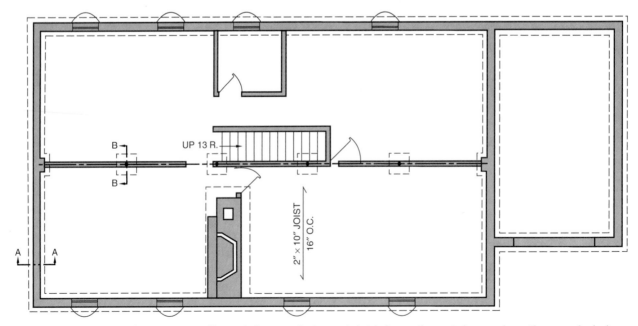

Figure 12-12. Interior basement walls and doors, windows, joint information, stairs, and section symbols have been added to the partially completed plan.

8. Show the size, spacing, and directions of floor joists or trusses using the standard notation.

9. Identify the location of sections required to provide additional information about the basement construction.

10. Draw and dimension the necessary sections, Figure 12-13.

11. Locate and draw permanent bath fixtures such as water closet, tub, and lavatory. Also, locate the furnace, hot water heater, water storage tank, water softener, sump, and floor drains. Not all of these items are necessary on every plan. Steps 11 through 18 are shown in Figure 12-14.

12. Determine the location of dimensions needed to show all features. Dimension interior frame walls to the center of the walls. Do not dimension to the center of foundation walls.

13. Draw the dimension lines and add the required dimensions.

14. Letter any necessary notes.

15. Show electrical switches, outlets, and fixtures. This step is required if a separate basement electrical plan is not going to be included in the set of drawings.

16. Shade the foundation walls with the proper material symbols (hatch pattern).

17. Add the title block, scale, and name of drawing in the proper location.

18. Check the drawing to be sure you have included all necessary information.

Using CADD to Draw a Foundation and Basement Plan

The procedure for drawing a foundation or basement plan with CADD is basically the same as when using manual drafting techniques. However, there are a couple of differences. For example, the drawing is created at full scale. Then, an appropriate scale is selected when the drawing is plotted. The following steps outline drawing a foundation or basement plan using CADD.

1. Make a copy of the floor plan on a new foundation plan layer.

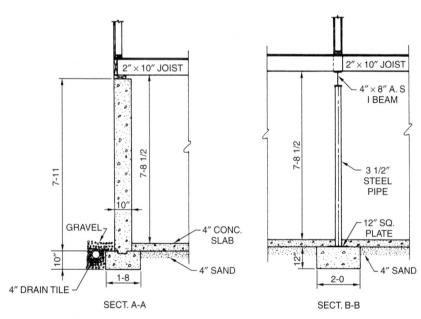

Figure 12-13. These are foundation details required to further describe the foundation construction.

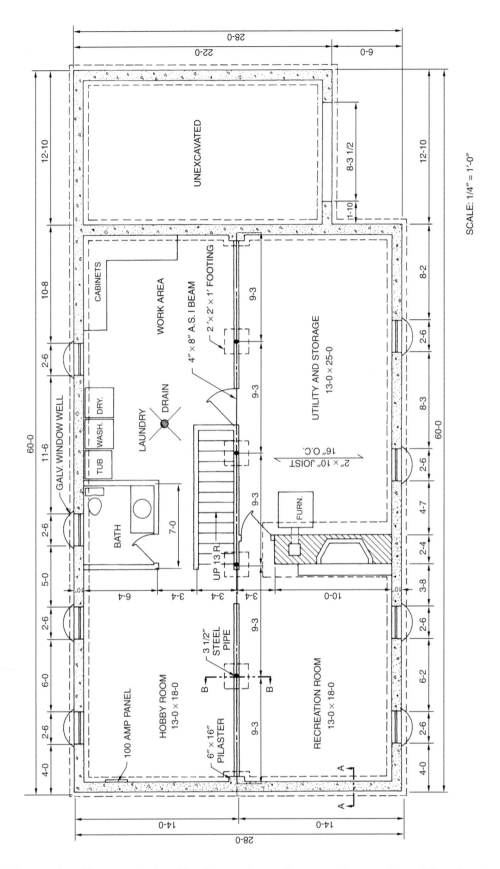

Figure 12-14. A completed basement plan. The foundation walls are cast concrete and the structure has a stud wall frame.

2. Draw the outside line of the foundation walls and delete the outside line of the floor plan wall, if they do not coincide. Generally, the outside of the foundation walls are identical to the outside of the rough stud walls on the floor plan in a frame structure with siding. Brick or other veneer is added to the outside of this point. The foundation wall is wider than a frame wall; therefore, the inside line will fall inside the floor plan. Generally, the foundation wall will be 8", 10", or 12" thick, but there are exceptions. A 12" thick wall will be used in this example. The footings and foundation walls should be drawn on separate layers since the line widths and linetypes are different. Piers and their footings may be added to these layers since they use similar linetypes and are part of the foundation. Draw all footings. Figure 12-15 shows the foundation wall, footings, and chimney located and drawn.

3. For a basement plan, draw the stairs, interior walls, windows, and doors. Place the stairs on their own layer for easy use with other layers/plans. This is an appropriate time to turn off the floor plan layer since it is no longer needed for the foundation/basement plan.

4. Draw all interior walls and insert door and window symbols into the plan. These items should be on a basement floor plan layer; symbols should be on their own layer. Take advantage of an existing symbols library or begin one of your own. Also at this point, add other features such as joist direction arrow and window wells, Figure 12-16.

5. Dimension the plan in the same manner as for manual drafting.

6. Insert symbols for appliances, fixtures, and the furnace. These should be placed on a symbols layer.

7. Add cutting plane symbols where required and label room names and sizes.

8. Add the scale and title to the foundation plan layer.

9. Look over the plan to be sure it is complete. Figure 12-17 shows the completed basement plan.

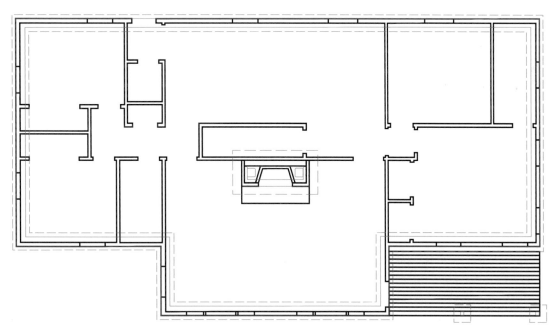

Figure 12-15. The floor plan for the first floor is copied to the foundation/basement plan layer. Footings and piers are then added. Notice how the floor plan layer is visible on top of the foundation/basement plan layer.

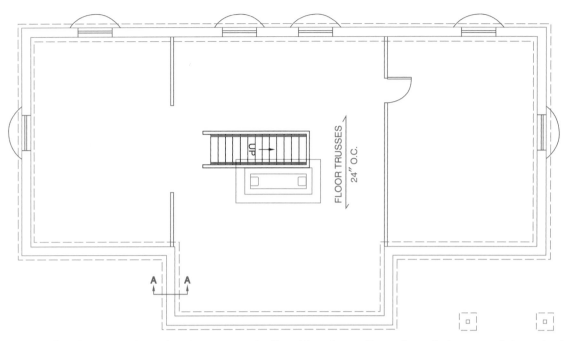

Figure 12-16. The floor plan layer has been turned off and interior walls, stairs, windows, and doors in the basement are added.

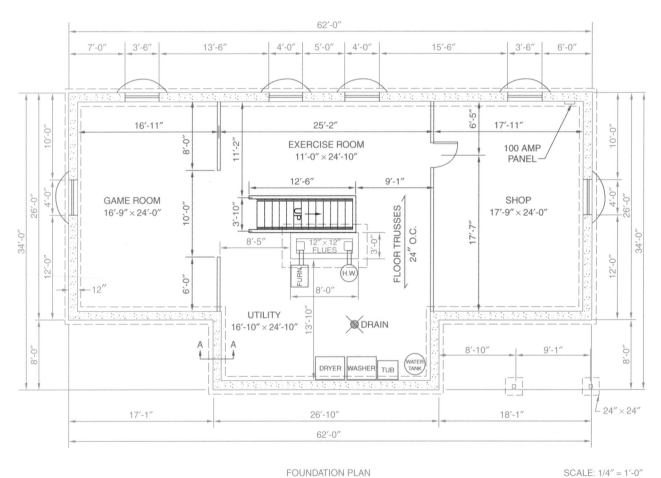

FOUNDATION PLAN   SCALE: 1/4″ = 1′-0″

Figure 12-17. A completed foundation/basement plan drawn with CADD.

Internet Resources

www.wwpa.org
Western Wood Products Association

www.hebel.com
Babb International Inc., suppliers of auto-claved aerated concrete

www.culturedstone.com
Cultured Stone

www.gp.com/build/index.html
Georgia Pacific Corporation, supplier of building products

www.lpcorp.com
Louisiana-Pacific Corporation, manufacturer of building materials

www.architectural-ornament.com
Architectural Ornament, Inc., manufacturer of polyurethane architectural molding

www.concretehomes.com
Portland Cement Association

www.anchorwall.com
Anchor Retaining Wall Systems

www.sweets.com
Sweets Catalog File

www.thomasregister.com
Thomas Register

Review Questions – Chapter 12

Write your answers on a separate sheet of paper. Do not write in this book.

1. Explain the foundation plan and its purpose.

2. Residential foundation plans are usually drawn or plotted at _____ scale.

3. List eight features that are usually shown on a foundation plan.

4. For whom is the foundation plan primarily prepared?

5. The foundation plan is drawn from information presented on the _____ plan, _____ plan, and _____.

6. A brick ledge is _____ wide.

7. List three considerations that should be checked to help determine the height of foundation walls and size of footings.

8. The _____ linetype is drawn thick to indicate a supporting beam on the foundation plan.

9. Hatch patterns are used on the foundation plan to show _____.

10. How is a basement plan different from a foundation plan?

11. Why is a basement a logical choice for cold climates?

12. When drawing a foundation plan in CADD, how is the floor plan initially used?

13. How are doors, windows, and appliances typically drawn on the foundation plan when using CADD?

14. When the foundation plan is drawn in CADD, at what scale is the plan drawn?

Suggested Activities

1. Select a floor plan for a garden or storage shed. Develop a foundation plan for the structure with a slab foundation. Add necessary dimensions, symbols, and notes. Provide sufficient information so that the foundation can be constructed from your drawings without additional resources.

2. Locate a floor plan for a cottage or vacation home. Then, design and draw the foundation for this house using CADD. Completely dimension the drawing and indicate details needed to explain the construction.

3. Using CADD, draw the foundation plan for a two-car garage that has a slab foundation. Assume the garage is stud wall construction and is 20'-0" × 20'-0". Show anchor bolts or sill anchor clips every 4'-0" along the perimeter. Check the required footing depth for your area and make the design meet the requirement.

4. Select a house floor plan from a magazine or other source. Draw a foundation plan for the house. Calculate the size of beam required, number and size of posts or columns needed, and the size and spacing of floor joists. Include dimensions and notes.

Section V
Construction Systems

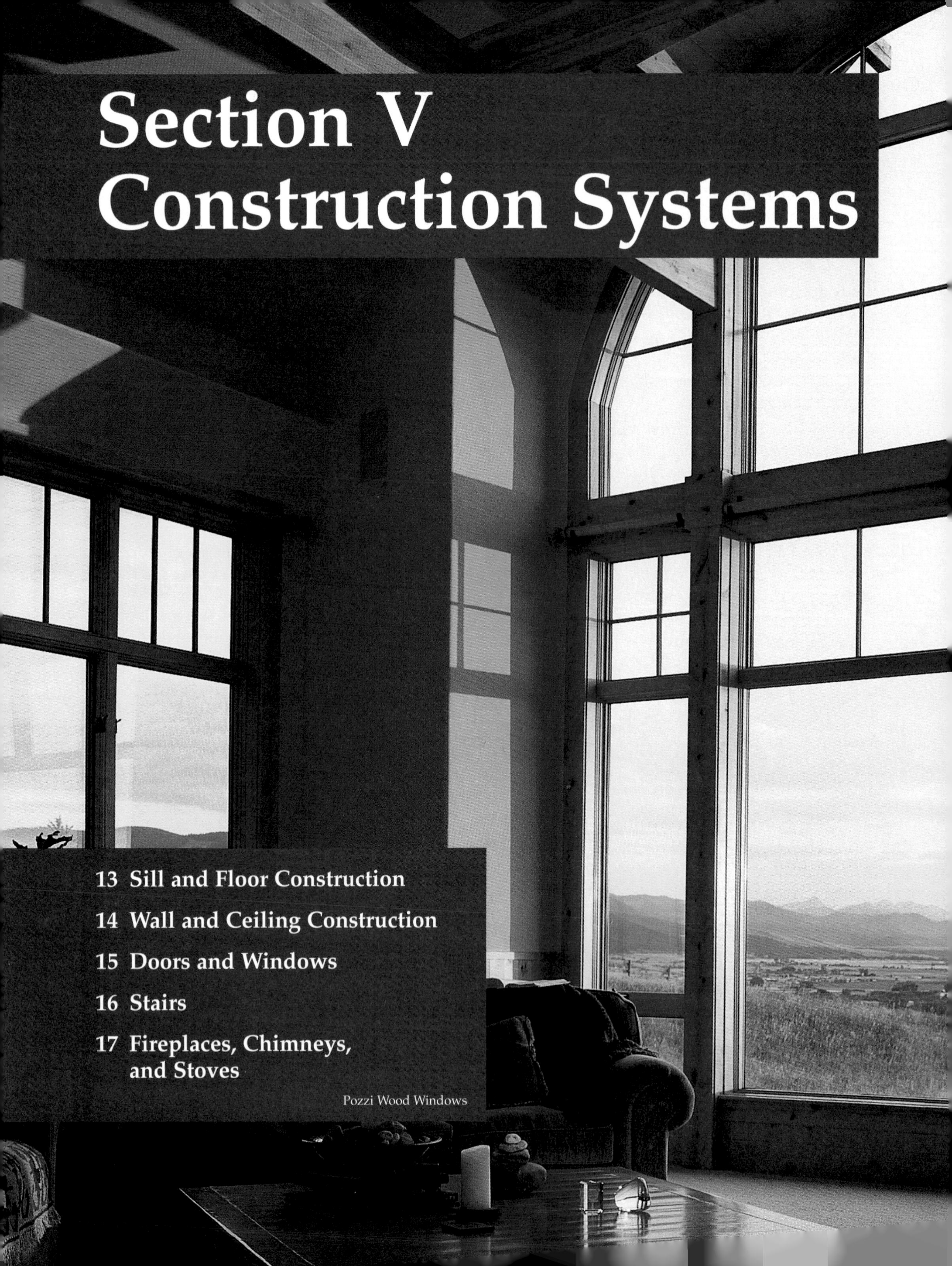

13 Sill and Floor Construction

14 Wall and Ceiling Construction

15 Doors and Windows

16 Stairs

17 Fireplaces, Chimneys, and Stoves

Pozzi Wood Windows

Sill and Floor Construction

13

Objectives

After studying this chapter, you will be able to:

- Explain the difference between platform and balloon framing.
- Plan the appropriate floor support using joists or trusses for a structure.
- Determine proper joist sizes using a typical span data chart.
- Describe the components of a floor system.
- Explain the principles of post and beam construction.
- Select the appropriate engineered wood products for specific applications in residential construction.

Key Terms

Balloon Framing
Beam
Box Sill
Cantilevered Joists
Cement Mortar Mix
Chords
Cross Bridging
Curtain Walls
Engineered Wood
    Products (EWPs)
Floor Trusses
Glulam Beams
Joists
Laminated Veneer
    Lumber (LVL)
Longitudinal
    Method
Mudsill
Oriented Strand
    Board (OSB)
Parallel Strand
    Lumber (PSL)
Platform Framing
Post and Beam
    Construction
Sill
Subfloor
Transverse Method
Web
Wood I-Beams

The commonly used method of floor framing varies from one section of the country to another. Even within a given area, builders may use different methods based on personal preference and experience. However, there are two basic types of floor framing. These are platform and balloon framing. Both types of framing have structural components called plates, joists, and studs. Another type of construction is called post and beam. This construction can be used for framing walls and floors.

Platform Framing

Platform framing is called as such because the floor joists form a platform on which the walls rest. Another platform, which is either the ceiling joists or floor joists of the upper floor, rests on the walls. Platform framing is used more extensively than balloon framing and popular for several reasons. It is satisfactory for both one- and two-story structures and is easy and fast to construct. Shrinkage is uniform throughout the structure. Also, the platform automatically provides a fire-stop between floors. Construction is safe because the work is performed on solid surfaces.

In platform framing, the sill is the starting point in constructing a floor. A *sill* is the lowest member of the frame of a structure. It rests on the foundation and supports the floor joists or the uprights (studs) of the wall. The sill in most residential construction is 2″ × 6″ dimensional lumber (actual dimensions are 1-1/2″ × 5-1/2″). Platform framing uses a method of sill construction known as *box sill* construction. The box sill consists of a 2″ × 6″ plate called a sill or *mudsill* and a header that is the same size as the floor joists, Figure 13-1. Figure 13-2 shows a detail of the first and second floor of a structure constructed with platform framing and box sill construction.

Generally, a seal is required between the foundation and sill plate. This seal prevents outside air from entering the house. Figure 13-3 shows one method of sealing the space between the foundation and sill plate.

Balloon Framing

Balloon framing was once used extensively, but in recent years has diminished in importance. The distinguishing features of *balloon framing* are that the wall studs rest directly on the sill plate and each floor "hangs" from the studs.

Two advantages of balloon framing are small potential shrinkage and good vertical stability. The vertical shrinkage in a two-story house built with platform framing is sometimes great enough to cause cracking. This is usually not the case with balloon framing. The disadvantages of balloon framing include a less than desirable surface on which to work during construction and the need to add fire-stops.

In balloon framing, one of two types of sill construction are used—solid (standard) sill or T-sill, Figure 13-4. In solid sill construction, the

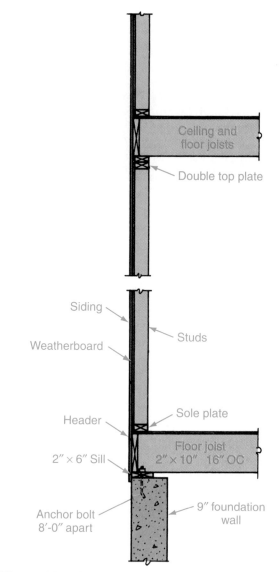

Figure 13-2. This section shows the details of a first and second floor constructed using platform framing and box sill construction.

Figure 13-3. One-inch thick fiberglass insulation is frequently used as a sill sealer.

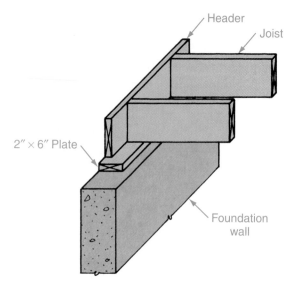

Figure 13-1. Box sill construction consists of a sill on which a header and joists rest.

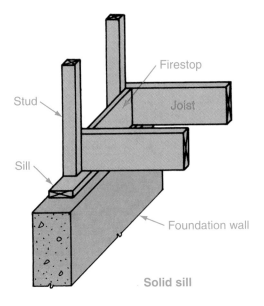

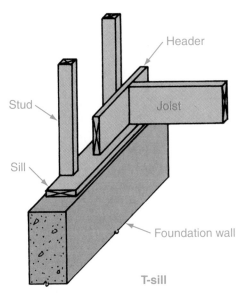

Figure 13-4. In balloon framing, either solid sill or T-sill construction is used.

studs are nailed directly to the sill and joists. No header is used. Joists are supported by a ribbon and nailed to the studs on the second floor level, Figure 13-5. A fire-stop must be provided between the studs using pieces cut to the proper length. Solid sill construction is used more extensively than T-sill construction in two-story homes.

In T-sill construction, a header rests on the sill and serves as a fire-stop. The studs rest on the sill and are nailed to the header as well as the sill plate. The sill in T-sill construction may be 8″ or 10″ wide to provide a broader supporting base on which the joists rest.

Joists and Beams

Joists provide support for the floor. They are usually made from a common softwood, such as southern yellow pine, fir, larch, hemlock, or spruce. However, engineered wood joists and metal joists are also available.

The size of floor joists ranges from a nominal size of 2″ × 6″ to 2″ × 12″. Figure 13-6 provides the actual dimensions of dimensional construction lumber. The size of joist required for a given situation depends on the length of the span, load to be supported, species and grade of wood, and distance the joists are

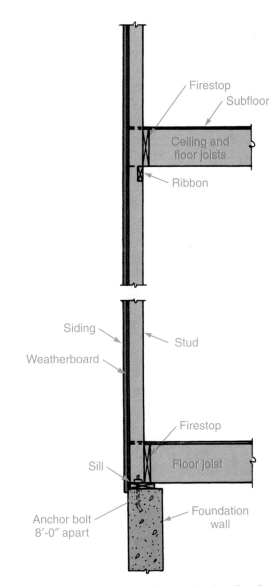

Figure 13-5. This section shows the details of a first and second floor constructed balloon framing and solid sill construction.

Standard lumber sizes		
Dimension lumber		
Product classification (nominal size)	**Actual sizes**	
	Unseasoned*	Dry*
2" × 2"	1-9/16" × 1-9/16"	1-1/2" × 1-1/2"
2" × 3"	1-9/16" × 2-9/16"	1-1/2" × 2-1/2"
2" × 4"	1-9/16" × 3-9/16"	1-1/2" × 3-1/2"
2" × 6"	1-9/16" × 5-5/8"	1-1/2" × 5-1/2"
2" × 8"	1-9/16" × 7-1/2"	1-1/2" × 7-1/4"
2" × 10"	1-9/16" × 9-1/2"	1-1/2" × 9-1/4"
2" × 12"	1-9/16" × 11-1/2"	1-1/2" × 11-1/4"
Board lumber		
Product classification (nominal size)	**Actual sizes**	
	Unseasoned*	Dry*
1" × 2"	25/32" × 1-9/16"	3/4" × 1-1/2"
1" × 3"	25/32" × 2-9/16"	3/4" × 2-1/2"
1" × 4"	25/32" × 3-9/16"	3/4" × 3-1/2"
1" × 6"	25/32" × 5-5/8"	3/4" × 5-1/2"
1" × 8"	25/32" × 7-1/2"	3/4" × 7-1/4"
1" × 10"	25/32" × 9-1/2"	3/4" × 9-1/4"
1" × 12"	25/32" × 11-1/2"	3/4" × 11-1/4"

*Dry lumber is defined as being 19% or less in moisture content. Unseasoned lumber is over 19% moisture content. The size of lumber changes approximately 1% for each 4% change in moisture content. Lumber stabilizes at approximately 15% moisture content under normal use conditions.

Figure 13-6. The actual size of common dimensional and board lumber is smaller than the nominal size. (National Forest Products Association)

spaced apart. In the case of metal joists, the gauge of metal should be considered instead of the species and grade of lumber.

Floor joists may be spaced 12", 16", or 24" on center (OC). A spacing of 16"OC is most common. Floor joist span data for the three most common species of wood joists are given in Figure 13-7. The chart assumes a maximum deflection of 1/360th of the span with a normal live load, which is the amount that most codes require. The normal live load is 30 or 40 pounds per square foot. The procedure for using the span data chart is:

1) Determine the species of wood to be used.

2) Select the appropriate live load capacity required for the structure.

3) Determine the lumber grade to be used. Number 2 dense is the usual choice for fir, larch, and southern yellow pine.

4) Scan the lumber grade row and note the maximum spans.

5) Select the joist size and spacing that will adequately support the desired live load. A spacing of 16"OC is typical.

Example: The span is 14'-0" and Number 1 dense southern pine is to be used for the joists. The live load is 30 pounds per square foot. The chart shows that the following choices would meet these conditions: 2" × 8" joists 12"OC or 16"OC; 2" × 10" joists 12"OC, 16"OC, or 24"OC; and 2" × 12" joists 12"OC, 16"OC, or 24"OC. The most reasonable selection would be 2" × 8" joists placed 16"OC. This will span a maximum of 14'-5", is the smallest dimensional lumber, and allows the greatest spacing at that size.

Steel floor joists are beginning to be accepted for residential construction. Builders generally select joist depths ranging from 6" to 12" with steel thicknesses from 0.034" to 0.101". Continuous span joists are preferred over lapped joists on multiple span conditions. Steel joists are usually spaced 24"OC, but spacing of 12"OC or 16"OC is also used, Figure 13-8.

A floor system may also be constructed using girders or trusses in the place of floor joists, as discussed in the next section. These are usually 4" × 6", 4" × 8", or 4" × 10" depending on the span. The purpose of this approach is to use fewer support members (joists). The typical spacing of girders or trusses in this system is 48"OC with 1-1/8" thick tongue-and-groove plywood as the floor decking.

In most house designs, the total distance that joists must span is too great for unsupported joists. A *beam* or load-bearing wall is needed to support the joists and effectively reduce the span. The beam may be a solid timber, built-up from dimensional lumber, or a metal S- or W-beam. Load-bearing walls may be concrete block, cast concrete, or frame construction. Several methods of supporting floor joists with a beam are commonly used. Figure 13-9 shows some of these methods.

Partition walls that run parallel to the floor joists require added support, Figure 13-10. It is good practice to double the joists under these partition walls. If the space between the joists is used as a cold air return duct, solid blocking

FLOOR JOIST SPAN DATA

30 PSF LIVE LOAD, 10 PSF DEAD LOAD, DEF. <360

Species or Group	Grade	2" x 8"			2" x 10"			2" x 12"		
		12"OC	16"OC	24"OC	12"OC	16"OC	24"OC	12"OC	16"OC	24"OC
Douglas Fir and Larch	Sel. Struc.	16'-6"	15'-0"	13'-1"	21'-0"	19'-1"	16'-8"	25'-7"	23'-3"	20'-3"
	No.1 & Btr	16'-2"	14'-8"	12'-10"	20'-8"	18'-9"	16'-1"	25'-1"	22'-10"	18'-8"
	No.1	15'-10"	14'-5"	12'-4"	20'-3"	18'-5"	15'-0"	24'-8"	21'-4"	17'-5"
	No.2	15'-7"	14'-1"	11'-6"	19'-10"	17'-2"	14'-1"	23'-0"	19'-11"	16'-3"
	No.3	12'-4"	10'-8"	8'-8"	15'-0"	13'-0"	10'-7"	17'-5"	15'-1"	12'-4"

40 PSF LIVE LOAD, 10 PSF DEAD LOAD, DEF. <360

Species or Group	Grade	2" x 8"			2" x 10"			2" x 12"		
		12"OC	16"OC	24"OC	12"OC	16"OC	24"OC	12"OC	16"OC	24"OC
Douglas Fir and Larch	Sel. Struc.	15'-0"	13'-7"	11'-11"	19'-1"	17'-4"	15'-2"	23'-3"	21'-1"	18'-5"
	No.1 & Btr	14'-8"	13'-4"	11'-8"	18'-9"	17'-0"	14'-5"	22'-10"	20'-5"	16'-8"
	No.1	14'-5"	13'-1"	11'-0"	18'-5"	16'-5"	13'-5"	22'-0"	19'-1"	15'-7"
	No.2	14'-2"	12'-7"	10'-3"	17'-9"	15'-5"	12'-7"	20'-7"	17'-10"	14'-7"
	No.3	11'-0"	9'-6"	7'-9"	13'-5"	11'-8"	9'-6"	15'-7"	13'-6"	11'-0"

30 PSF LIVE LOAD, 10 PSF DEAD LOAD, DEF. <360

Species or Group	Grade	2" x 8"			2" x 10"			2" x 12"		
		12"OC	16"OC	24"OC	12"OC	16"OC	24"OC	12"OC	16"OC	24"OC
Southern Pine	Sel. Struc.	16'-2"	14'-8"	12'-10"	20'-8"	18'-9"	16'-5"	25'-1"	22'-10"	19'-11"
	No.1	15'-10"	14'-5"	12'-7"	20'-3"	18'-5"	16'-1"	24'-8"	22'-5"	19'-6"
	No.2	15'-7"	14'-2"	12'-4"	19'-10"	18'-0"	14'-8"	24'-2"	21'-1"	17'-2"
	No.3	13'-3"	11'-6"	9'-5"	15'-8"	13'-7"	11'-1"	18'-8"	16'-2"	13'-2"

40 PSF LIVE LOAD, 10 PSF DEAD LOAD, DEF. <360

Species or Group	Grade	2" x 8"			2" x 10"			2" x 12"		
		12"OC	16"OC	24"OC	12"OC	16"OC	24"OC	12"OC	16"OC	24"OC
Southern Pine	Sel. Struc.	14'-8"	13'-4"	11'-8"	18'-9"	17'-0"	14'-11"	22'-10"	20'-9"	18'-1"
	No.1	14'-5"	13'-1"	11'-5"	18'-5"	16'-9"	14'-7"	22'-5"	20'-4"	17'-5"
	No.2	14'-2"	12'-10"	11'-0"	18'-0"	16'-1"	13'-2"	21'-9"	18'-10"	15'-4"
	No.3	11'-11"	10'-3"	8'-5"	14'-0"	12'-2"	9'-11"	16'-8"	14'-5"	11'-10"

40 PSF LIVE LOAD, 10 PSF DEAD LOAD, DEF. <240

Species or Group	Grade	2" x 6"			2" x 8"			2" x 10"		
		12"OC	16"OC	24"OC	12"OC	16"OC	24"OC	12"OC	16"OC	24"OC
Redwood	Cl. All Heart	--	7'-3"	6'-0"	--	10'-9"	8'-9"	--	13'-6"	11'-0"
	Const. Heart	--	7'-3"	6'-0"	--	10'-9"	8'-9"	--	13'-6"	11'-0"
	Const. Common	--	7'-3"	6'-0"	--	10'-9"	8'-9"	--	13'-6"	11'-0"

These spans are based on the 1993 AFTA (formerly NFPA) span tables for joists and rafters. These grades are the most commonly available. Source: Western Wood Products Association, Southern Pine Association, and California Redwood Association.

Figure 13-7. Spans are calculated on the basis of dry sizes with a moisture content equal to or less than 19%. Floor joist spans are for a single span with calculations performed based on the modulus of elasticity (E) and maximum fiber bending stress (F_b) allowed.

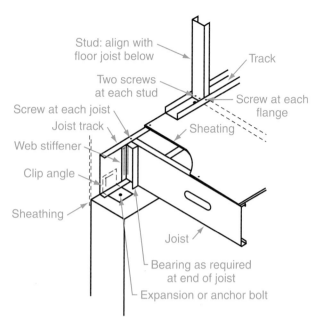

Figure 13-8. This is typical steel framing where the floor joists rest directly on the foundation.

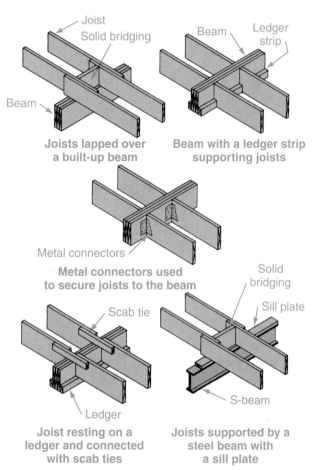

Joist
Solid bridging

Beam

Joists lapped over a built-up beam

Beam   Ledger strip

Beam with a ledger strip supporting joists

Metal connectors

Metal connectors used to secure joists to the beam

Scab tie

Ledger

Joist resting on a ledger and connected with scab ties

Solid bridging

Sill plate

S-beam

Joists supported by a steel beam with a sill plate

Figure 13-9. These are common methods of supporting floor joists with beams.

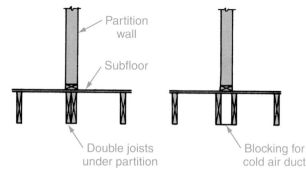

Partition wall

Subfloor

Double joists under partition

Blocking for cold air duct

Figure 13-10. Joists should be doubled under partition walls that run parallel to the joists.

is used between the joists. Openings in the floor for stairs and chimneys also require double joist framing. Figure 13-11 shows how such an opening is framed and identifies the various parts.

Cross bridging is used to stiffen the floor and spread the load over a broader area, Figure 13-12. Bridging boards are ordinarily $1'' \times 3''$ in size with the ends cut at an angle so they fit snugly against the joist. They are nailed securely in place midway between the beam and wall. Metal bridging is also available, Figure 13-13.

Floor Trusses

A truss is a rigid framework designed to support a load over a span. Engineered wood *floor trusses,* designed for light-frame

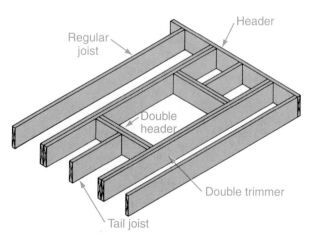

Regular joist

Header

Double header

Double trimmer

Tail joist

Figure 13-11. Framing around openings for fireplaces and stairs require double joists.

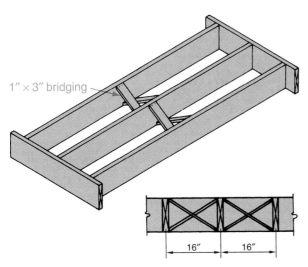

Figure 13-12. Bridging is used to stiffen the floor and required by many codes.

construction, are often used in place of floor joists in residential structures. These trusses consist of a top chord, bottom chord, and web.

The top and bottom *chords* are the horizontal flanges at the top and bottom of the truss. The *web* is the framework between the chords.

Trusses provide clear spans with a minimum of depth in a lightweight assembly that is easy to handle, Figure 13-14. In addition, the open web construction reduces sound transmission through the floor/ceiling assemblies and makes the installation of plumbing, heating, and electrical systems easy.

Engineered floor trusses are designed with the aid of computers to ensure accurate load capacities. They are usually fabricated from 2″ × 4″ or 2″ × 6″ lumber and generally spaced 24″OC. Figure 13-15 shows typical specifications for engineered wood floor trusses. Each truss has a built-in camber (upward curve) so that the floor/ceiling will be level once the load of the house is applied. Stress-graded lumber is used in their construction so that a minimum amount of material is required. Some trusses have wood webs.

Figure 13-13. Metal bridging can be quickly installed.

Figure 13-14. Engineered wood floor trusses are lightweight, easy to handle, and easy to install. (Trus Joist)

Other trusses are fabricated with wood chords and galvanized steel webs, Figure 13-16. The metal webs have teeth that are pressed into the sides of the chords. A reinforcing rib in the metal web withstands both tension and compression forces.

Subfloor

The *subfloor* is affixed to the floor joists and provides the surface on which the underlayment for the final finished floor will rest. Plywood, tongue-and-groove boards, common boards, and other panel products are used for subfloors. The large size (4' × 8') of plywood and other panel sheets and the comparatively short time required to nail the sheets in place makes these products very popular as subfloors. One-half inch thick plywood, composite board, waferboard, oriented strand board, and structural particleboard may be used when joists are spaced 16"OC, Figure 13-17. However, some builders prefer 5/8" stock over 1/2" stock. When these products are used, it is important that the joist spacing is very accurate. All edges of the panels must be supported, Figure 13-18.

In some areas, there is a trend to combine the subfloor and underlayment (usually 5/8" particleboard) into a single thickness that is generally 1-1/8" thick. These sheets have tongue-and-groove edges and require no blocking between the joists. A single thickness sheet of 3/4" tongue-and-groove plywood may also be used for some applications.

Plywood should be installed so that the grain direction of the outer plies is at right angles to the joists. The floor will be stronger when the plywood is positioned in this manner. Panel products should also be staggered so that end joints in adjacent panels are on different joists. A slight space must be allowed between sheets for expansion.

Subfloor panels may also be glued, as well as nailed, to the joists. Structural tests have shown that stiffness is increased by 25% with 2" × 8" joists and 5/8" plywood. Another advantage to gluing is that the system produces a squeak-free structure, eliminates nail-popping, and reduces labor costs.

MANUFACTURED 2″ × 4″ WOOD FLOOR TRUSSES

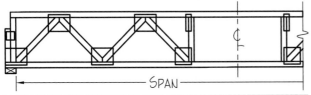 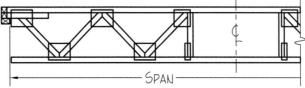

Bottom chord bearing type			
Depth	Clear spans	#Diagonal webs	Camber
12″	7′-2″	4	.063″
	9′-8″	6	.063″
	12′-2″	8	.063″
	14′-8″	10	.134″
	17′-2″	12	.237″
	19′-8″	14	.365″
	21′-4″	16	.507″
14″	9′-8″	6	.063″
	12′-2″	8	.063″
	14′-8″	10	.095″
	17′-2″	12	.178″
	19′-8″	14	.288″
	22′-7″	16	.449″
	24′-0″	18	.569″
16″	12′-2″	8	.065″
	14′-8″	10	.070″
	17′-2″	12	.132″
	19′-8″	14	.228″
	22′-2″	16	.346″
	25′-1″	18	.505″
	26′-1″	20	.596″
18″	14′-8″	10	.065″
	17′-2″	12	.120″
	19′-8″	14	.176″
	22′-2″	16	.268″
	24′-8″	18	.367″
	27′-6″	20	.600″
	27′-10″	22	.630″
20″	14′-8″	10	.063″
	17′-2″	12	.081″
	19′-8″	14	.140″
	22′-2″	16	.226″
	24′-8″	18	.327″
	27′-6″	20	.451″
	29′-6″	22	.630″
22″	17′-2″	10	.066″
	19′-8″	12	.114″
	22′-2″	14	.184″
	24′-8″	16	.266″
	27′-6″	18	.367″
	30′-0″	20	.520″
	31′-1″	22	.630″
24″	17′-2″	12	.063″
	19′-8″	14	.095″
	22′-2″	16	.153″
	24′-8″	18	.235″
	27′-2″	20	.325″
	30′-0″	22	.431″
	32′-6″	24	.630″

Top chord bearing type			
Depth	Clear spans	#Diagonal webs	Camber
12″	6′-10″	4	.063″
	9′-4″	6	.063″
	11′-10″	8	.063″
	14′-4″	10	.122″
	16′-10″	12	.233″
	19′-10″	14	.376″
	21′-4″	16	.507″
14″	9′-5″	6	.063″
	11′-11″	8	.063″
	14′-5″	10	.088″
	16′-11″	12	.167″
	19′-5″	14	.273″
	21′-4″	16	.429″
	24′-0″	18	.569″
16″	12′-0″	8	.063″
	14′-6″	10	.067″
	17′-0″	12	.126″
	19′-6″	14	.219″
	22′-4″	16	.337″
	24′-10″	18	.489″
	26′-1″	20	.596″
18″	14′-6″	10	.063″
	17′-0″	12	.098″
	19′-6″	14	.170″
	22′-0″	16	.260″
	24′-10″	18	.378″
	27′-8″	20	.617″
	27′-10″	22	.630″
20″	14′-6″	10	.063″
	17′-0″	12	.079″
	19′-6″	14	.136″
	22′-0″	16	.221″
	24′-10″	18	.337″
	27′-4″	20	.442″
	29′-6″	22	.630″
22″	17′-1″	12	.065″
	19′-7″	14	.112″
	22′-1″	16	.181″
	24′-10″	18	.275″
	27′-4″	20	.381″
	30′-2″	22	.534″
	31′-1″	24	.630″
24″	17′-1″	12	.063″
	19′-7″	14	.093″
	22′-1″	16	.150″
	24′-7″	18	.231″
	27′-5″	20	.335″
	30′-2″	22	.443″
	32′-6″	24	.630″

Wood floor trusses are typically manufactured from #3 southern yellow pine. Pieces are joined together with 18 and 20 gauge galvanized steel plates applied to both faces of the truss at each joint. Where no sheathing is applied directly to top chords, they should be braced at intervals not to exceed 3′-0″. Where no rigid ceiling is applied directly to bottom chords, they should be braced at intervals not to exceed 10′-0″.

Manufactured wood floor trusses are generally spaced 24″OC and are designed to support various loads. Typical trusses shown here were designed to support 55 psf (live load - 40 psf, dead load - 10 psf, ceiling dead load - 5 psf). A slight bow (camber) is built into each joist to that it will produce a level floor when loaded. Allowable deflection is 1/360 of the span.

Some of the longer trusses require one or more double diagonal webs at both ends. Wood floor trusses are a manufactured product which must be engineered and produced with a high degree of accuracy to attain the desired performance. See your local manufacturer or lumber company for trusses available in your area.

Figure 13-15. Design specifications for typical engineered wood floor trusses.

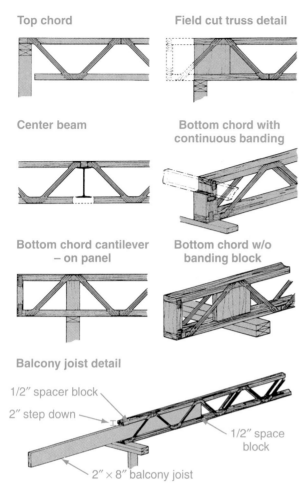

Figure 13-16. These trusses have wood chords, but the webs are galvanized steel. (TrusWal Systems, Inc.)

Figure 13-17. Many structural wood panels are manufactured for construction uses. The products shown here are (from top to bottom): waferboard, structural particleboard, composite plywood, oriented strand board, and plywood. (Georgia-Pacific Corporation)

Cantilevered Joists

Some home designs include a section of the floor that projects beyond a lower level. This design element is called a cantilever. When the floor joists run perpendicular to the cantilevered section, joists with extra length form the cantilever. However, when the joists are parallel to the overhanging area, *cantilevered joists* are required. Figure 13-19 illustrates a typical framing technique for a cantilevered floor section.

A rule of thumb to follow in determining the necessary length of the cantilevered joists is to extend the joists inside the structure a distance at least twice the distance that they overhang outside the structure. If the inside distance is too short, the floor along the outside wall may sag over time. If a ledger

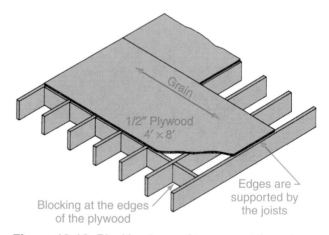

Figure 13-18. Blocking is used to support the edges of 1/2″ plywood used for the subfoor. All edges of the panel must be supported.

strip is used, it should be located along the top of the inside double header joist. This is because the force will be up rather than down as in a normal situation.

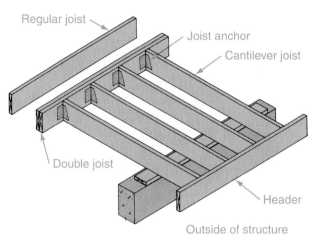

Figure 13-19. Cantilevered joists should extend at least twice as far inside the house as they extend outside of it.

Framing Under Slate or Tile

Certain areas of the home frequently have ceramic tile, slate, or stone floors. These materials require a substantial base. If a concrete base is provided, the floor framing must be lowered to provide for the concrete. The dead weight may be as much as 50 pounds per square foot in a bathroom with a tile floor and heavy fixtures. Several techniques are used to provide the needed support. A smaller size joist may be used and the space between joists reduced to provide adequate support, Figure 13-20. This is

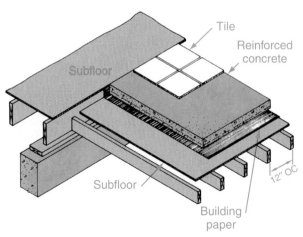

Figure 13-20. Using smaller size joists placed closer together than normal can provide the additional support needed for areas of slate and ceramic tile.

a common solution to the problem. Another technique is to use one or more beams under the section to support the added weight.

The concrete base for the tile or stone should be reinforced with wire mesh and cast on a plywood subfloor covered with building paper. A special type of concrete, known as a *cement mortar mix,* is generally used. It is a mixture of one part Portland cement and six parts sand.

Engineered Wood Products

Engineered wood products (EWPs) are in a new class of structural wood members that has been evolving for over twenty years. These products are being used more and more in new construction. EWPs combine wood veneers and fibers with adhesives to form beams, headers, joists, and panels that have uniformly high quality and strength, Figure 13-21. In addition, EWPs address the lumber industry's most pressing problem—supply—by making more efficient use of material that was generally thought to be unusable. Wood from smaller trees and inferior species are now being used in engineered wood products to make high-quality products.

Industry analysts predict that the use of engineered wood products will continue to grow. In 1999, engineered wood I-beam production in North America increased by 27%. In that same year, laminated veneer lumber (LVL) production in North America grew by 21%. Total EWP production in 1999 represented more than 5% of the dimensional lumber supply in North America.

Advances in adhesive technology over the past 50 years have made EWPs possible. Phenol-formaldehyde and urea-formaldehyde resins are the most common adhesives for EWPs. The resins of choice for structural-use products are the waterproof phenolics, but they are much more expensive than the urea resins. Some manufacturers are beginning to use methylene diphenylisocynate (MIDI) and polymeric MIDI (PMDI) adhesives because they have a shorter press time. Some claim that

A   B

Figure 13-21. A—Band boards are available in 9-1/4″, 11-1/4″, 12″, 14″, and 16″ depths. They eliminate the need for ripped plywood bands and provide solid backing for deck and siding attachments. (Alpine Structures) B—Engineered headers are available in 1-1/4″ depth and 3-1/2″ width, which matches other framing members for one-piece installation. (Alpine Structures)

they also have increased dimensional stability and release less gas during production than the formaldehydes.

Engineered wood products as a whole have certain advantages and disadvantages that should be considered. These products have increased quality and consistency. Weaknesses, such as knots, are not found in EWPs as they are in solid lumber. In addition, the uniform drying of EWP components to 8% to 12% moisture content before they are compressed into the final stage produces a more predictable, consistent product from piece to piece. Traditional kiln-dried lumber is usually dried to a 15% to 19% moisture content that is more prone to shrinking and warping. EWPs provide superior design flexibility through greater widths, depths, and beam lengths that are not possible with solid lumber, Figure 13-22. Appearance is also a consideration in some applications. Certain EWPs have a distinctive grain-like pattern that some people prefer over the appearance of framing lumber and can be left exposed for painting or staining.

The greatest disadvantage for EWPs as a group is the lack of industry standards. Products within the same general category can vary greatly because of different proprietary production methods. Each product has its own characteristics making it difficult to make comparisons.

Oriented Strand Board (OSB)

Oriented strand board (OSB) is a product in which long strands of wood are mixed with resin, placed in layers, and pressed and cured, Figure 13-23. It has been commercially available for many years, first appearing on the market in 1978. However, OSB was not readily accepted at the time due to the poor reputation of earlier, low-quality particleboard panels. OSB has since established itself as a quality product and is widely used for roof and wall sheathing, subflooring, siding, and webs for wood I-beams.

Figure 13-22. This roof system has long spans that would require support if built with traditional dimensional lumber. However, these parallel strand beams can span the distance with no inner support.

Figure 13-23. Oriented strand board is a high-quality, engineered wood panel product that is replacing plywood in many applications. (The Engineered Wood Association)

Aspen is the preferred wood for making OSB. It is a low-density wood that is easily cut into long strands parallel to the grain. Longer strands produce stronger boards. The strands are mixed with a resin and then mechanically oriented in layers. The outer layers are oriented parallel to the long dimension while the inner layers (core) are parallel to the short dimension. Once the strands are laid, the panel is compressed to its final thickness and the resin cures.

Additional information about oriented strand board can be obtained from:
American Forest & Paper Association
1111 19th St., NW, Suite 800
Washington, DC 20036
info@afandpa.org

The Engineered Wood Association (APA)
PO Box 11700
Tacoma, WA 98411
help@apawood.org

Advantages of OSB

- OSB is less expensive to manufacture than plywood because it is made from abundant, fast-growing trees.

- OSB has an unique appearance that is appealing as a design element for certain applications.

Disadvantages of OSB

- OSB is subject to swelling because it is manufactured to a 2% to 5% moisture content. Plywood is generally about 6%.

- OSB is not designed for applications subject to permanent exposure to the elements. Therefore, it is not an acceptable replacement for exterior grade plywood in all instances.

Installation/application

Oriented strand board is made in panel sizes similar to plywood, typically 4' × 8', but it is generally available in sizes up to 8' × 24'. Manufacturers recommend leaving a space of 1/8" along all edges to prevent buckling problems when used in roof and wall applications. Installation of OSB near plumbing is not recommended because of potential water drips or leaks. The same nailing schedules that apply to plywood apply to OSB, but it can be nailed to within 1/4" from the edge of the panel without breaking out.

Parallel Strand Lumber (PSL)

Parallel strand lumber (PSL) is a product in which thin strands of wood are glued together under pressure, Figure 13-24. This is a fairly new category of engineered wood products. PSL products have been commercially available in the United States since about 1990. It was developed in 1969, but endured 19 years of research and development before being commercialized in Canada in 1988.

PSL is used for beams, columns, and headers. The products provide high strength and span capacity. Low-moisture content virtually eliminates shrinking and checking. According to the manufacturer, pressure-treated PSL is also available for exterior applications. Use of PSL products has increased dramatically in the past few years.

The manufacturing process for PSL begins with debarking logs and peeling them into

Figure 13-24. Both post and beams are available as parallel strand lumber. (Alpine Structures)

thin veneers. The veneers are then clipped into 1/2″ wide strands, which are then combined with adhesives and cured under pressure using microwave-generated heat. Large billets 12″ wide by 17″ deep are formed and then sawed to specified sizes.

Advantages of PSL

- PSL is very strong.
- PSL allows long spans and more design flexibility.

Disadvantages of PSL

- Engineered connections are required for side-loading or hanging joists on only one side of a multiple-ply PSL beam.
- PSL should not be drilled or notched and should be stored on site according to manufacturer's recommendations to avoid swelling.

Installation/application

Parallel strand lumber is available in widths ranging from 1-3/4″ to 7″. Two plies of the 2-11/16″ thick members will match a typical 5-1/2″ thick wall. Lengths up to 66′ are available.

PSL beams can support higher loads than solid beams, so a greater bearing area may be required. Contact the manufacturer for tables outlining the required bearing lengths. PSL beams eliminate the need for on-site construction of built-up beams since they are available in large widths and lengths. The proper connectors must always be used, Figure 13-25.

Additional information about parallel strand lumber can be obtained by contacting:
Trus Joist Headquarters
200 East Mallard Drive
Boise, ID 83706
www.tjm.com

Laminated Veneer Lumber (LVL)

Laminated veneer lumber (LVL) is a product in which veneers of wood are stacked in parallel and glued under pressure. LVL was

Figure 13-25. Large parallel strand beams should be connected using standard steel beam connectors. (Alpine Structures)

first used for high strength aircraft parts in the 1940s. However, commercial production of LVL for high-grade structural members did not begin until 1971. Only recently has LVL received much attention from the building industry. LVL has gained code approval from the Council of American Building Officials (CABO). Laminated veneer lumber is used for headers, beams, columns, joists, and as flanges for wood I-beams, Figure 13-26.

The manufacturing process for LVL is similar to the process used to make plywood. The primary difference between plywood and LVL is that the plies are parallel in LVL, rather than perpendicular, to maximize strength. Southern yellow pine and Douglas fir are generally the woods of choice. Stressed-graded veneer panels are peeled on a veneer lathe in thicknesses of 1/10" or 1/8" thick. A waterproof adhesive is applied to the plies before bonding with heat and pressure. The end joints are staggered, which results in a continuous billet of lumber up to 1-3/4" thick and 4' wide. Two or more billets can be glued together to form thicker members. The billet is then cut to the desired widths.

Advantages of LVL

- The high strength of LVL allows long spans, thereby increasing design flexibility.
- LVL can be built-up on site to form larger members.

Figure 13-26. Laminated veneer lumber has excellent strength and span capacity. It is used as a header in this wall. (Trus Joist)

Disadvantages of LVL

- LVL is more expensive than solid lumber.
- LVL is manufactured to a lower moisture content than solid lumber and, therefore, reaches equilibrium on the job site at a different rate than solid lumber.
- LVL must be sized for specific load conditions and cannot be used as a standard material.

Installation/application

The 1-3/4" thick billet is the most common LVL material. It can be used individually for joists or combined with other billets to form headers or beams. It is available in depths from 5-1/2" to 14" and in lengths up to 66'. LVL is also produced in a horizontal orientation. It is available in widths of 8-1/2" and 5-1/2" and in depths from 5-1/2" to 24". Lengths are produced up to 66'.

LVL generally should not be mixed with solid lumber in the same floor assembly due to different moisture content of the products. Like any other girder, header, or beam, LVL beams should not be drilled or notched for electrical or plumbing pass-throughs.

Additional information about laminated veneer lumber can be obtained by contacting: Boise Cascade Engineered Wood Products Corporate Headquarters:
PO Box 50
Boise, ID 83728-0001
info@bcewp.com

Louisiana-Pacific Corporation (LP)
Headquarters/Corporate Office
805 SW Broadway
Portland, OR 97205
customer.support@lpcorp.com

Glue-Laminated Lumber

Glue-laminated beams, columns, and arches were the first engineered wood products. They were first produced in the 1950s. Glue-laminated members, also called *glulam beams*, consist of 1× or 2× lumber that is glued in stacks to the desired shape and size, Figure 13-27. The individual laminations may

Figure 13-27. This home makes extensive use of glue-laminated members. (The Engineered Wood Association)

be end-joined with adhesives to provide continuous lengths. Therefore, virtually any length and depth can be produced. This product relies on solid sawed lumber produced with traditional milling techniques, which recovers only about 50% of the log.

Glue-laminated beams are manufactured to a national standard (ANSI, AITE A190.1-1983) that has been accepted by all three United States model building codes. Three appearance grades are available: industrial, architectural, and premium. The industrial grade is the least attractive with visible glue stains, press marks, and knotholes. The architectural grade is sanded on four sides with large knotholes filled with putty. The premium grade beam has all checks and holes filled.

Advantages of glue-laminated lumber

- High Strength. The high strength of glue-laminated lumber is probably the greatest advantage.
- Glue-laminated beams are available either straight or with a camber to offset dead-load deflection.
- Glue-laminated beams are dimensionally stable and are very attractive.

Disadvantages of glue-laminated lumber

- The cost of glue-laminated lumber is high.

- Glue-laminated lumber requires special handling and storage to prevent damage.
- The large beams are very heavy and require special equipment to handle them.

Installation/application

Technical support from the manufacturer is required for most glue-laminated lumber products. Manufacturers provide span charts, installation details, and technical assistance. Special connectors are needed for these large members and heavy loads. Generally, for beams that remain exposed, the connection can be custom made. Manufacturers offer these suggestions to reduce checking and preserve the finished surface.

- Keep the beams covered, but allow the wood to breathe.
- Keep the beam off the ground, even if the wrapper is still on.
- Keep the beams out of the direct sunlight to prevent tanning.
- Keep the beams from rapid or extreme drying.
- Avoid sudden humidity changes.
- Seal the beams as soon as possible after unwrapping.
- Seal any new cuts immediately.
- If possible, condition the beams by allowing them to slowly acclimate to the interior of the building.

Additional information about glue-laminated lumber can be obtained by contacting:
American Institute of Timber Construction
7012 S. Revere Parkway Suite 140
Englewood, CO 80112
info@aitc-glulam.org

Engineered Wood Systems
PO Box 11700
Tacoma, WA 98411
www.glulambeams.org
help@apawood.org

Wood I-Beams or Joists

Wood I-beams or joists are typically made from 2″ × 4″ machine-stressed lumber or LVL flanges grooved to receive a 3/8″ OSB or plywood web that is glued in place, Figure 13-28. They are high-strength, low-weight, and produced by a variety of manufacturers. Wood I-beams are available in flange widths of 1-3/4″ and 2-5/16″ and depths from 9-1/2″ to 20″. Lengths up to 66′ are produced.

The American Society for Testing and Materials standard ASTM D5055-90 lists common criteria for I-beams and was approved and published in July 1990. This standard includes accepted measures for the industry-wide development of design values and quality control, but presently each manufacturer uses their own proprietary process. These processes include variations related to production techniques, joints for the flange-web connection, types of adhesives, and the grade and types of flange and web material. Further, each manufacturer formulates their own design and materials to meet the performance specifications, which include criteria for vertical loads, lateral bracing, joist depth and spacing, and deflection.

Advantages of wood I-beams

- Speed of construction is most likely the chief advantage of wood I-beams. Beams are light for their length and may span the entire width of a house, thereby reducing by half the number of joists that need to be handled.

Figure 13-28. Wood I-beams are used primarily for long span applications in floor and roof systems. (Boise Cascade Corporation)

- Some wood I-beams have knockout holes to speed the installation of plumbing and electrical cable.
- Wood I-beams are dimensionally stable. They are also very straight.

Disadvantages of wood I-beams

- Wood I-beams require more effort to cut than solid lumber because of the uneven surface.
- Some building departments do not allow the use of wood I-beams.
- Wood I-beams are more expensive than solid lumber or roof trusses.

Installation/application

Wood I-beams are used in a similar manner as traditional floor joists or rafters, Figure 13-29. They can be worked with using

Figure 13-29. This house has I-beams as floor joists, parallel strand lumber beams, and band boards used in the construction of the floor system. (Boise Cascade Corporation)

conventional nails, tools, and readily available metal connectors. Wood I-beams, like other engineered wood products, are manufactured to a lower moisture content than solid lumber and therefore reach equilibrium at the job site at a different rate than solid lumber. As a result, wood I-beams and solid lumber should not be used together in the same floor or roof assembly.

Web stiffeners or blocks are normally used at bearing points to help reduce the load on the flange-web connection. This is very important in the case of deeper joists. Manufacturers also have recommendations for nail size and the size and location of holes through the web. The flange material should not be cut.

Additional information about wood I-beams can be obtained by contacting:
Boise Cascade Engineered Wood Products Corporate Headquarters:
PO Box 50
Boise, ID 83728-0001
info@bcewp.com

Georgia-Pacific Corporation
133 Peachtree Street, NE
Atlanta, GA 30303
www.gp.com

Louisiana-Pacific Corporation (LP)
Headquarters/Corporate Office
805 SW Broadway
Portland, OR 97205
customer.support@lpcorp.com

Weyerhaeuser Company
PO Box 9777
Federal Way, WA 98063-9777
bldgmaterials@weyerhaeuser.com

Post and Beam Construction

Post and beam construction uses posts, beams, and planks as framing members that are larger and spaced farther apart than conventional framing members, Figure 13-30. Post and beam construction provides a greater

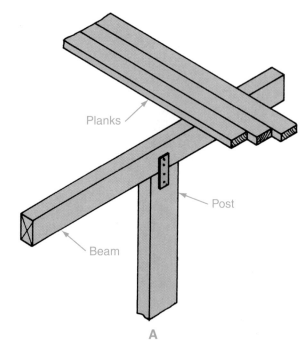

Figure 13-30. A—The three components of post and beam construction. B—An example of post and beam construction. (The Engineered Wood Association)

freedom of design than conventional framing techniques. The system is basically simple, but presents problems related to larger structural sizes, framing connectors, and joining methods.

Most of the weight of a post and beam building is carried by the posts. The walls do not support much weight and are called *curtain walls.* Curtain walls provide for wide expanses of glass without the need for headers, Figure 13-31. Wide overhangs are also possible by extending the large beams to the desired length. Spacing of the posts is determined by the design of the building and the load to be supported.

The foundation for a post and beam structure may be a continuous wall or a series of piers on which each post is located. The size of the wall footings or piers is determined by the weight to be supported, soil bearing capacity, and local building codes.

The posts should be at least 4″ × 4″. The posts should be at least 6″ × 6″ if they are supporting the floor. The vertical height of the posts is also a factor in determining the post size. Check local codes for requirements.

Beams may be solid, laminated, reinforced with steel, or plywood box beams. Figure 13-32 shows a variety of beam types. The spacing and span of the beams will be determined by the size and kind of materials and load to be supported. In most normal situations, a span of 7′-0″ may be used when 2″ thick tongue-and-groove subfloor or roof decking is applied to the beams. Thicker beams must be used if a span greater

Figure 13-31. Post and beam construction permits broad expanses of glass and provides the warm glow of natural wood. (Pozzi Wood Windows)

 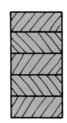  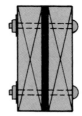 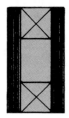

Solid beam   Horizontal-laminated beam   Vertical-laminated beam   Steel-reinforced beam   Box beam

Figure 13-32. A variety of beams are used in post and beam construction.

than 7'-0" is required. See the span tables shown in Figure 13-33.

Two systems of roof beam placement are possible with post and beam construction.

See Figure 13-34. The first system is the *longitudinal method.* Here, the beams are placed at right angles to the roof slope. Therefore, roof decking is laid from the ridge pole to the eaves

Span data for glued laminated roof beams* Maximum deflection 1/240th of the span														
Beam size (actual)	Wgt. of beam per lin. ft. in pounds	Span in feet												
		10	12	14	16	18	20	22	24	26	28	30	32
		Pounds per lin. ft. load bearing capacity												
3" × 5-1/4"	3.7	151	85										
3" × 7-1/4"	4.9	362	206	128	84								
3" × 9-1/4"	6.7	566	448	300	199	137	99						
3" × 11-1/4"	8.0	680	566	483	363	252	182	135	102				
4-1/2" × 9-1/4"	9.8	850	673	451	299	207	148	109					
4-1/2" × 11-1/4"	12.0	1,036	860	731	544	378	273	202	153				
3-1/4" × 13-1/2"	10.4	1,100	916	784	685	479	347	258	197	152	120		
3-1/4" × 15"	11.5	1,145	1,015	870	759	650	473	352	267	206	163	128	104
5-1/4" × 13-1/2"	16.7	1,778	1,478	1,266	1,105	773	559	415	316	245	193	154	124
5-1/4" × 15"	18.6	1,976	1,647	1,406	1,229	1,064	771	574	438	342	269	215	174
5-1/4" × 16-1/2"	20.5	2,180	1,810	1,550	1,352	1,155	933	768	586	457	362	290	236
5-1/4" × 18"	22.3	2,378	1,978	1,688	1,478	1,308	1,113	918	766	598	478	382	311

Example: Clear span   = 20'-0"
Beam spacing = 10'-0"
Dead load   = 8 lbs./sq. ft. (roofing and decking)
Live load   = 20 lbs./sq. ft. (snow)
Total load   = Live load + dead load × beam spacing
              = (20 + 8) × 10 = 280 lbs./lin. ft.
The beam size required is 3-1/4" × 13-1/2", which supports 347 lbs./lin. ft. over a span of 20'-0".
*Beams may be Douglas fir, larch or southern yellow pine.

Span data for glued laminated floor beams* Maximum deflection 1/360th of the span														
Beam size (actual)	Wgt. of beam per lin. ft. in pounds	Span in feet												
		10	12	14	16	18	20	22	24	26	28	30	32
		Pounds per lin. ft. load bearing capacity												
3" × 5-1/4"	3.7	114	64										
3" × 7-1/4"	4.9	275	156	84	55								
3" × 9-1/4"	6.7	492	319	198	130	89							
3" × 11-1/4"	8.0	590	491	361	239	165	119						
4-1/2" × 9-1/4"	9.8	738	479	298	196	134	96						
4-1/2" × 11-1/4"	12.0	900	748	541	359	248	178	131	92				
3-1/4" × 13-1/2"	10.4	956	795	683	454	316	228	169	128	98			
3-1/4" × 15"	11.5	997	884	756	626	436	315	234	178	137	108		
5-1/4" × 13-1/2"	16.7	1,541	1,283	1,095	732	509	367	271	205	158	123	96	
5-1/4" × 15"	18.6	1,713	1,423	1,219	1,009	703	508	376	286	221	173	137	109
5-1/4" × 16-1/2"	20.5	1,885	1,568	1,340	1,170	939	678	505	384	298	235	187	151
5-1/4" × 18"	22.3	2,058	1,710	1,464	1,278	1,133	886	660	503	391	309	247	200

Example: Clear span   = 20'-0"
Beam spacing = 10'-0"
Dead load   = 7 lbs./sq. ft. (decking and carpet)
Live load   = 40 lbs./sq. ft. (furniture and occupants)
Total load   = Live load + dead load × beam spacing
              = (40 + 7) × 10 = 470 lbs./lin. ft.
The beam size required is 5-1/4" × 15", which supports 508 lbs./lin. ft. over a span of 20'-0".
*Beams may be Douglas fir, larch or southern yellow pine.

Figure 13-33. Span data for glued laminated floor and roof beams. Local building codes should be checked for specific requirements. (Potlatch Forests, Inc.)

line. The second system is called the *transverse method.* The beams follow the roof slope and decking runs parallel to the roof ridge.

The conventional method of fastening small members by nailing does not provide a satisfactory connection in post and beam construction. Therefore, metal plates or connectors are used. These are fastened to the post and beam with lag screws or bolts. Figure 13-35 shows a number of metal fasteners used to connect various beam segments.

Decking planks for the roof and floor range in thickness from 2″ to 4″. The planks are usually tongue-and-grooved along the long edges and they may be tongue-and-grooved on the ends as well. Figure 13-36 illustrates several plank designs which are available. Roof decking span information is given in Figure 13-37.

The underside of the planked roof is usually left exposed. If insulation is required, it may be placed above the decking and under the roofing material. Rigid type insulation should be used.

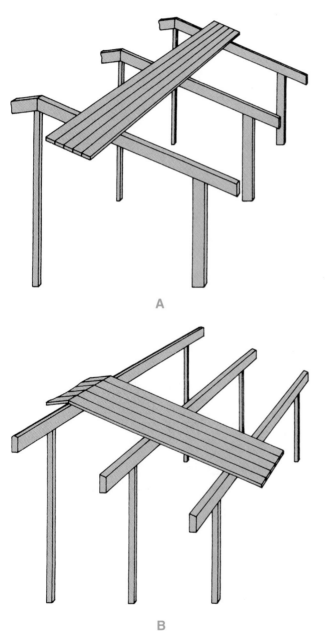

Figure 13-34. A—The longitudinal method of placing roof beams. B—The transverse method of placing roof beams.

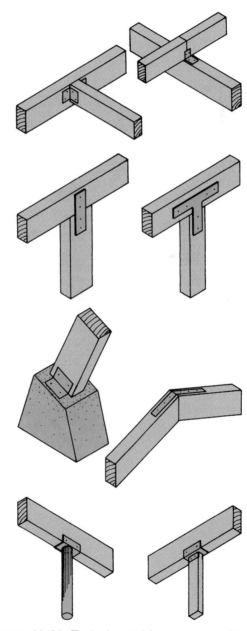

Figure 13-35. Typical metal fasteners used to connect large beam segments.

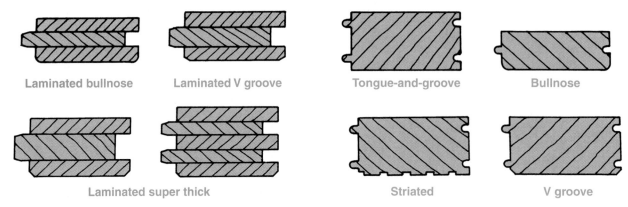

Laminated bullnose   Laminated V groove   Tongue-and-groove   Bullnose

Laminated super thick   Striated   V groove

Figure 13-36. Planks are available in several designs for use in post and beam construction.

Span data for roof decking with a maximum deflection of 1/240th of the span Live load = 20 lbs./sq. ft.			
		Simple spans	
		Douglas fir, larch, southern yellow pine	Western red cedar
Thickness (nominal)	**Lumber grade**	Span	Span
2″	Construction	9′-5″	8′-1″
2″	Standard	9′-5″	6′-9″
3″	Select dex.	15′-3″	13′-0″
3″	Compl. dex.	15′-3″	13′-0″
4″	Select dex.	20′-3″	17′-3″
4″	Compl. dex.	20′-3″	17′-3″

		Random lengths	
		Douglas fir, larch, southern yellow pine	Western red cedar
Thickness (nominal)	**Lumber grade**	Span	Span
2″	Construction	10′-3″	8′-10″
2″	Standard	10′-3″	6′-9″
3″	Select dex.	16′-9″	14′-3″
3″	Compl. dex.	16′-9″	13′-6″
4″	Select dex.	22′-0″	19′-0″
4″	Compl. dex.	22′-0″	18′-0″

		Comb. simple and two-span continuous	
		Douglas fir, larch, southern yellow pine	Western red cedar
Thickness (nominal)	**Lumber grade**	Span	Span
2″	Construction	10′-7″	8′-9″
2″	Standard	10′-7″	6′-9″
3″	Select dex.	17′-3″	14′-9″
3″	Compl. dex.	17′-3″	13′-6″
4″	Select dex.	22′-9″	19′-6″
4″	Compl. dex.	22′-9″	18′-0″

Figure 13-37. Span data for Douglas fir, larch, southern yellow pine, and western red cedar planking.

Internet Resources

www.fpl.fs.fed.us
Forest Products Laboratory

www.apawood.org
The Engineered Wood Association

www.southernpine.com
Southern Pine Council

www.wwpa.org
Western Wood Products Association

www.gaf.com
GAF Materials Corporation, manufacturer of roofing materials

www.bcewp.com
Boise Cascade Engineered Wood Products

www.rewardwallsystems.com
Reward Wall Systems, supplier of insulated concrete form wall systems

www.builderonline.com
Builder Magazine

www.reemay.com
Reemay, Inc., manufacturer of nonwoven spunbonded products (like house wrap)

www.alcoahomes.com
Aluminum Company of America (ALCOA) Building Products, Inc

Review Questions – Chapter 13

Write your answers on a separate sheet of paper. Do not write in this book.

1. The two basic types of floor framing being used today are _____ and _____ framing.

2. The lowest member of the frame of a structure, which rests on the foundation and supports the floor joists and wall studs, is the _____.

3. The actual dimensions of a 2″ × 6″ framing member are _____.

4. Platform framing utilizes a method of sill construction known as _____ sill construction.

5. Two types of sill construction used with balloon framing are _____ and _____ construction.

6. List two advantages of balloon framing.

7. The floor of a house is supported by _____ or trusses.

8. Name three softwoods that are commonly used for joists.

9. The most common spacing for floor joists is _____ OC.

10. Traditional kiln-dried lumber has a _____ percent moisture content.

11. What size floor joist should be used if the span is 14′-0″, Number 1 southern pine is to be used, the live load is 30 pounds per square foot, and the joist spacing is 16″OC? Use the span data chart.

12. The purpose of cross bridging is to stiffen the floor and _____.

13. The thickness of plywood commonly used for subfloors is _____.

14. Identify five types of panel products that may be used for subflooring.

15. Name four advantages of engineered wood floor trusses.

16. Why do floor trusses have a built-in camber?

17. A _____ is a part of the house that extends out over a lower section.

18. List the three elements of post and beam construction.

19. Identify four types of beams used in post and beam construction.

20. Two systems of roof beam placement are used in post and beam construction. They are the _____ method and the _____ method.

21. List three common thicknesses in which roof decking is manufactured.

22. What type of insulation is used with a planked roof?

23. What is the greatest single disadvantage of EWPs as a group?

24. One of the disadvantages of OSB is that it is subject to _____ because it is manufactured to a 2% to 5% moisture content.

25. What are the three common uses for parallel strand lumber (PSL)?

26. PSL is available in lengths up to _____ feet.

27. What is the main difference between plywood and LVL?

28. Name the three appearance grades of glue-laminated lumber.

29. Wood I-beams are available in lengths up to _____ feet.

Suggested Activities

1. Obtain a set of house plans and identify:
   a) Size of floor joists or trusses required.
   b) Spacing of floor joists or trusses.
   c) Type of sill construction specified.
   d) Thickness and type of subfloor material to be used.
   e) Size of sill plate.
   f) Type and size of bridging.
   g) Specie and grade of lumber specified for joists or trusses.
   h) Method of framing used (such as balloon or platform).
   i) Type of construction details shown relating to sill and floor.

2. In small groups, write out definitions for the following terms. Then, provide examples of each using the plans from Activity 1. If no examples appear on the plans, provide an example of where the item/term may be used.
   a) span
   b) live load
   c) dead load
   d) cantilevered
   e) beam
   f) partition
   g) post
   h) reinforced concrete
   i) construction grade
   j) nominal dimension
   k) fire-stop
   l) dimension lumber
   m) header
   n) sill
   o) laminated
   p) slope
   q) tongue-and-groove
   r) striated

3. Select a floor plan of a house and prepare a list of materials for the first floor, such as the sill, header, joists, and subfloor materials.

4. Using your CADD system, design and draw the floor framing for a house of your design. Show the spacing, size, specie, and grade of joists used. Draw the necessary construction details.

5. Using your CADD system, draw a typical foundation section for a house with a crawlspace in your area of the country. Assume the foundation to be 8" concrete blocks and the footing 8" × 16" concrete. Show proper material hatch patterns.

Wall and Ceiling Construction

14

Objectives

After studying this chapter, you will be able to:

➤ List the members of a typical frame wall.

➤ Explain methods of frame wall construction.

➤ Explain information shown on a ceiling joist span data chart.

➤ Sketch the various types of exterior walls used in residential construction.

➤ Explain the applications, advantages, and disadvantages of steel framing in residential construction.

➤ Identify the basic processes used to produce a quality, three-coat stucco finish.

Key Terms

Access Hole
Ashlar Stonework
Brick
Brown Coat
Cavity Walls
Common Brick
Coursed Rubble
Cripples
Face Brick
Finish Coat
Firecut
Furring Strips
Lath

Masonry Wall
Moisture Barrier
Rubble Stonework
Scratch Coat
Sole Plate
Solid Blocking
Structural C
Stucco
Three-Coat Stucco
   System
Trimmers
Uncoursed Cobweb

Residential wall construction is usually one of three types: frame, masonry, or combination frame and masonry. The wall panels may be constructed on site or prefabricated at another location and transported to the site for final construction. The trend is toward more prefabrication and less onsite construction.

Frame Wall Construction

Frame wall construction involves the proper arrangement of the wall framing members, which are typically construction lumber, Figure 14-1. Figure 14-2 shows the various framing members used in conventional wood construction. These include the sole plate, top plates, studs, and bracing. Not shown in the figure are headers over wall openings. Plates and studs are usually nominal 2″ × 4″ lumber. Headers or lintels are

Figure 14-1. This computer-generated rendering is of a typical frame structure. Standard construction practices are incorporated in the design. (ART, Inc.)

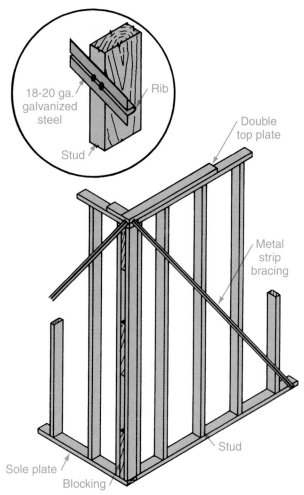

Figure 14-2. This frame wall corner shows various framing members and their relationship to each other.

typically constructed from larger stock. Bracing may be 1″ × 4″ stock, metal strap, or plywood sheathing.

Wall framing lumber must have good stiffness and nail-holding properties, be free from warp, and be easy to work. Species that meet these criteria include Douglas fir, southern yellow pine, hemlock, spruce, and larch. The most common lumber grade used is Number 2 or its equivalent. The moisture content of the lumber should be between 15% and 19%.

The wall is usually constructed flat on the subfloor since it provides a large, flat work surface. The frame is then lifted vertical into the correct position. A wall panel may extend along an entire side of the building if sufficient help is available to raise the wall. Otherwise, the wall may be built in smaller sections. Exterior frame walls are flush with the outside of the foundation wall or moved 1/2″ to 3/4″ inside to allow for the thickness of sheathing, weatherboard, or rigid foam insulation, Figure 14-3.

Specialized CADD software is available to aid in the design of frame walls. Automatic framing plans and material lists are features associated with some of the more sophisticated software packages. However, a thorough understanding of frame wall construction is a prerequisite whether using traditional drafting methods or a CADD system.

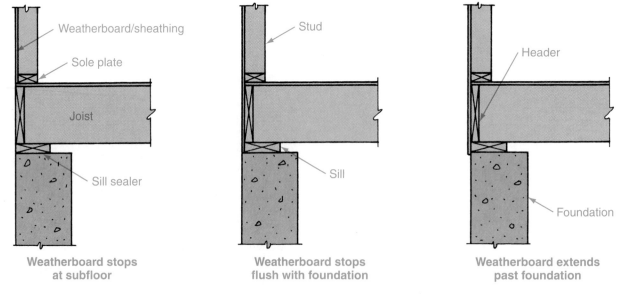

Weatherboard stops at subfloor

Weatherboard stops flush with foundation

Weatherboard extends past foundation

Figure 14-3. The sheathing, weatherboard, or rigid insulation may end at the subfloor, the top of the foundation, or extend below the top of the foundation.

Plates

Frame wall construction usually begins with the *sole plate,* which is the bottom horizontal member of the wall on which studs rest. First, the stud spacing is marked off on the sole plate, Figure 14-4. The sole plate acts as an anchor for the wall panels and a nailer for interior and exterior wall sheathing.

Wall studs are cut to length (usually 7'-9" when 1-1/2" material is used) and nailed to the sole plate. A top plate is then placed on and nailed to the top of the studs. A second top plate is added after the wall is in place on which the ceiling joists rest. The distance from the top of the subfloor to the bottom of the ceiling joists is usually 8'-1 1/2". This distance provides a finished wall height of 8'-0", which is typical.

Headers

Openings for doors and windows are framed before the wall is moved to the vertical position. Each wall opening requires a header or lintel to support the weight above the opening. Two basic approaches used in constructing headers are solid blocking and cripple construction.

In *solid blocking,* the header size is increased to completely fill the space from the top of the rough opening to the top plate. See Figure 14-5. Two 2" × 12" pieces of dimension lumber are nailed together with a piece of 1/2" plywood between them to form a 3-1/2" thick header. Trimmers are placed inside the opening. *Trimmers* are studs that support the header over an opening in the wall. This method reduces construction time, but increases shrinkage.

Figure 14-5 also illustrates cripple construction for headers. This method uses cripple studs and trimmers firmly nailed to the sole and top plates. *Cripples* are studs that are not full length due to a wall opening. Trimmers are also placed inside the opening.

The length of the header is equal to the width of the rough opening plus the thickness of two trimmers, Figure 14-6. Header sizes vary with the span and load requirements. The chart shown in Figure 14-7 provides sizes for various situations. *Check the local code to be sure these specifications are permitted in your area.* Trussed headers are required for openings wider than 8'-0" or in situations involving extremely heavy loads. Figure 14-8 illustrates two types of trussed headers.

Rough openings for windows and doors are dimensioned on the floor plan to the center of the opening when located in a frame wall. Specific dimensions are usually provided by the window and door schedule. The width is listed first and the height second. The rough opening height of most doors is 6'-10". The top of all windows is usually the same distance above the floor.

Exterior Corners and Bracing

Typical methods of framing used to form exterior wall corners are shown in Figure 14-9. The corner must provide a nailing edge for the interior wall material and adequate support for the structure.

Corner bracing is required by most codes. Two methods of bracing are commonly used to provide added support. In one method, diagonal corner braces of 1" × 4" lumber or metal straps are used from the top corner of the wall down to the sole plate. This method is shown in Figure 14-2. The second method, which seems to be gaining in popularity, makes use of

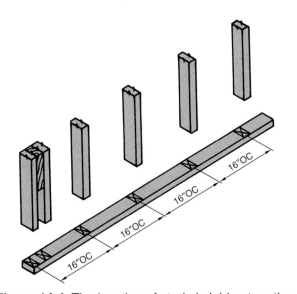

Figure 14-4. The location of studs is laid out on the sole plate.

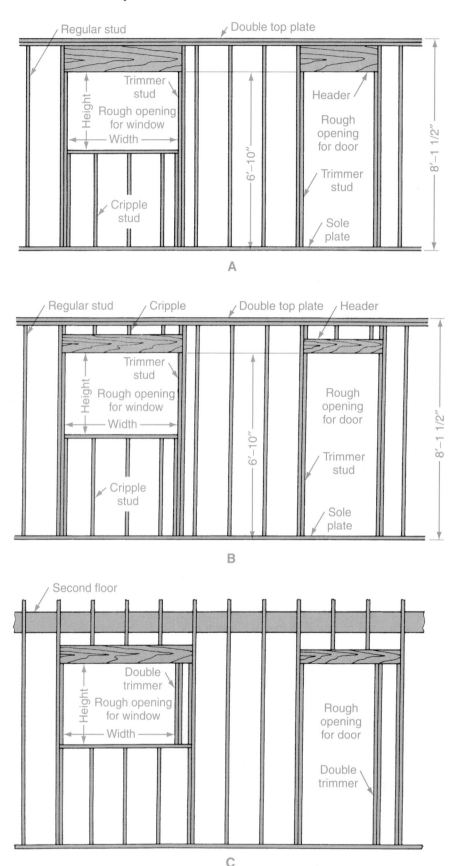

Figure 14-5. A—Solid blocking is used to form the header over a window and door opening in this platform framing example. Studs are 16″OC. B—Cripples used above the header in platform framing with 16″OC studs. C—Cripples used above the header in balloon framing with 16″OC studs.

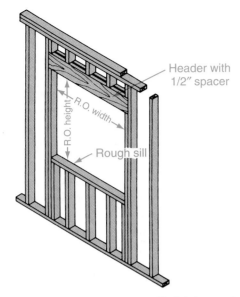

Figure 14-6. The rough opening (R.O.) for a window is the area between the trimmers and the rough sill and header. The header length is the rough opening width plus two trimmer widths.

a sheet of 1/2" plywood or other similar panel nailed to the studs at each corner, Figure 14-10.

Interior Walls

Interior frame walls are constructed in the same way as exterior walls. They have sole plates, studs, and double top plates. Interior walls must be securely fastened to the exterior

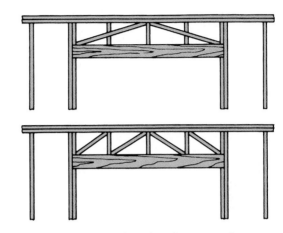

Header size	Maximum span
2" × 6"	3'-6"
2" × 8"	5'-0"
2" × 10"	6'-6"
2" × 12"	8'-0"

Note: Header size refers to size of material used and not the overall size of the header. Each header is constructed of two pieces, on edge, with plywood spacer between.

Figure 14-7. Typical header sizes for given spans.

Figure 14-8. Trussed headers increase the supporting strength and possible span.

walls that they intersect. A nailing edge must be provided for the plaster base, drywall, or paneling. This may be accomplished by using a 2" × 6" secured to cross blocking or by doubling the exterior wall studs at the intersection of the

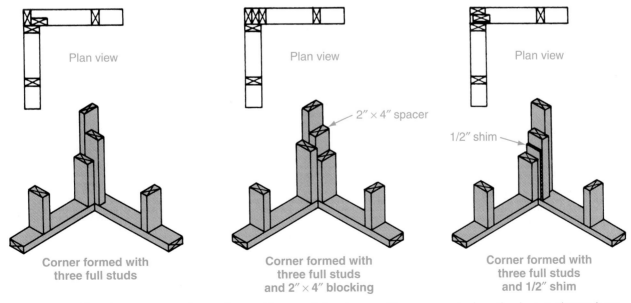

Figure 14-9. Exterior corner posts are framed in a variety of ways. Three accepted methods are shown here.

partition. Figure 14-11 illustrates both methods. The same arrangement is used at the intersection of all interior walls.

Figure 14-10. One-half inch plywood sheathing may be used as bracing for the exterior wall corners.

Steel Framing

Steel as a residential building material was explored shortly after World War II. However, those early steel houses experienced problems and were generally not accepted by the public. Also, once the surplus war steel ran out, steel homes were more expensive than wood homes. Then, in the early 1970s, companies like US Steel again began to market steel framed houses due to technological advances in production and materials. However, the public was still not ready to accept the all-steel house.

Today, many things have changed. Wood is becoming scarce and more expensive. The quality of new growth lumber is not as good as when timber was cut from older, larger, and stronger trees. Designers and builders are looking for alternatives to wood to improve quality and reduce cost. Vast destruction from hurricanes, fire, earthquakes, and floods has focused new evaluation on building materials, codes, construction methods, and quality of work. Steel framing has performed well and has captured the interest of insurance companies, builders, and prospective home buyers.

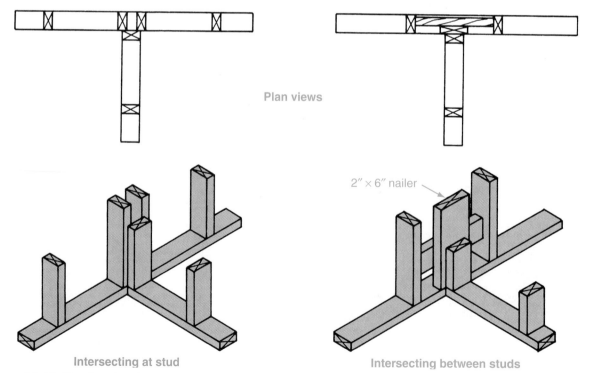

Figure 14-11. The framing for the intersection of partitions and exterior walls is accomplished by using extra studs or blocking and a nailer.

Environmental and economic concerns have also forced the building industry to pursue alternative materials and methods. Steel framing is made from a recyclable material and has a proven record in commercial construction. Many builders are adapting residential steel framing because of steel's price and supply stability. While the price of lumber has been erratic, the price of steel has been relatively constant since the 1980s. The price of steel framing is now competitive with wood.

Advantages of Steel Framing

Several advantages of steel framing are evident for builders, homeowners, and the environment. The benefits to builders include:

- Steel framing can be used with all common types of finishing materials.
- Fewer members are generally required due to the inherent strength of steel.
- Steel will not rot, shrink, swell, split, or warp and is noncombustible.
- Steel is consistent in quality and competitively priced.
- Steel members are available in a variety of precut, standard shapes and sizes, as well as custom shapes and sizes, Figure 14-12. This minimizes construction waste. Lengths up to 40′ are possible.
- Steel members weigh as little as 40% of wood members; therefore, foundation and seismic loads can be reduced.

Figure 14-12. Steel framing is available in custom shapes and sizes.

- Framing members are manufactured with prepunched holes for piping and electrical wiring.

Benefits to the homeowner include:

- Steel framing does not require treatment for termites. It is free of resin adhesives and other chemicals needed to treat wood framing products.
- Because of its strength, steel can span greater distances providing larger open spaces and increased design flexibility.
- Steel framed structures resist fires, earthquakes, and hurricanes because of steel's inherent strength and noncombustible qualities.
- Insurance premiums can be lower for a steel framed house.
- Remodeling can be easily accomplished because nonbearing walls can be easily removed, altered, and relocated.

In addition to benefits for builders and homeowners, there are significant environmental benefits. These environmental benefits include:

- All steel products are recyclable. Presently, the recycling rate of steel products in the US is about 66%—the highest rate of any material. During the last decade about one trillion pounds of steel scrap have been recycled, reducing waste going to landfills.
- Steel products can be recycled repeatedly without degradation or loss of properties.
- The steel industry is the single largest recycler in North America because recycled steel is an integral ingredient in steel production.
- Magnetic separation makes steel the easiest and most economical material to remove from the solid waste stream.
- The amount of energy required to produce a ton of steel has been reduced by 34% since 1972. (Source: American Iron and Steel Institute)

Disadvantages of Steel Framing

Steel framing does have some disadvantages that hinder its acceptance. For example, there is a lack of familiarity with the product. Building officials, designers, and tradespeople need to be educated about steel framing systems' methods and capabilities relative to residential construction.

Another disadvantage is that structures using steel framing require engineering analysis. Even though manufacturers of steel framing systems provide engineering analysis as part of the package, designers and builders need to develop greater familiarity with the capabilities of these systems.

Questions regarding the thermal performance of steel framed structures remain unanswered. CABO's 1989 Model Energy Code shows that the conductivity of a wall framed with steel is up to 110% higher than a comparable wall framed with wood. Further, the June 1992 draft of the ASHRAE Proposed Standard 90.2 includes parallel path correction factors ranging from 0.45 to 0.60 for wall frames that contain metal stud assemblies.

Simply stated, a steel framing member does not insulate against heat transfer as well as a wood framing member.

The workability of steel is also a disadvantage. The standard 25-gauge nonbearing studs are flimsy and hard to work with. For those not accustomed to working with steel, it can have sharp edges that will slice your skin if not handled properly. "Hemmed" track is safer than "unhemmed." Steel is hard to cut and most of a carpenter's tools will not work on steel. In addition, eye protection is a must, although proper eye protection should be used when working with wood, too.

Steel Framing Components

The steel component known as the *structural C* or C-section is the predominant shape used for floor joists, wall studs, roof rafters, and ceiling joists, Figure 14-13.

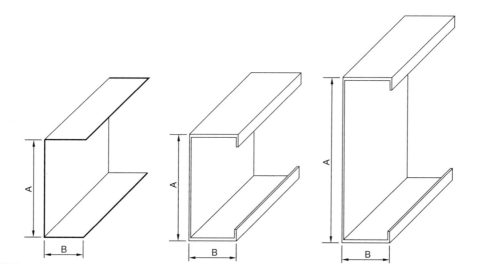

Channel studs		C Studs		C Joists	
2-1/2"	1"	2-1/2"	1-1/4"	5-1/2"	1-7/8"
3-1/4"	1-3/8"	3"	1-3/8"	6"	1-5/8"
3-5/8"		3-5/8"	1-1/2"	7-1/4"	1-3/4"
4"		3-1/4"	1-5/8"	8"	2"
6"		4"		9-1/4"	2-1/2"
		5-1/2"		10"	
		6"		12"	
		7-1/2"			
		8"			

Figure 14-13. Common sizes of the three predominately-used steel framing members.

Standard dimensions are nearly identical to those of dimensional lumber. Flange widths are generally 1-1/2″ and web depths range from 2″ to 12″. Steel thicknesses from 12 to 22 gauge are available. Studs used in typical load-bearing applications are 16 to 20 gauge. The C-section is available unpunched or pre-punched in lengths from 8′ to 16′. Prepunched studs have holes at strategic locations that allow wiring and plumbing to be routed through the stud. A grommet must be placed in every hole through which wires pass to prevent cutting of the wire insulation, unless conduit is used.

A track or channel member is used for rim joists, top and bottom plates, and blocking. It is generally the same gauge as the framing material. The track is also available in unpunched or prepunched in lengths up to 10′ with flange lengths of 1″ or 1-1/4″.

Angle steel can be used as a ledger or a connection bracket. It can also be used for stiffening, bracing, or blocking.

Cold- and hot-rolled channel are similar in shape and gauge to the track member. Smaller-size channel is used for stiffening, bracing, and blocking. Hot-rolled channel is used for furring. Cold-rolled Z members may be used in structural applications. These applications include roof purlins or in lighter gauges for furring.

All members are fastened with screws, Figure 14-14. These are typically 1/2″ long, low profile, zinc coated, pan head screws. Plastic grommets are required at all penetrations of the steel framing to protect electrical wiring. Steel framing is zinc galvanized to protect it from corrosion and rust.

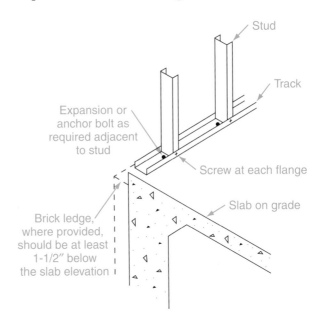

Figure 14-14. This is a typical attachment of steel frame wall on slab construction. All steel framing members are screwed together.

Wall and Roof Systems

The construction elements of a framed house include three main assemblies: floors, walls, and roofs. Steel framing is often consistent with wood framed construction, but there are some differences. These are covered in the next sections.

Walls

Two types of steel studs are used for walls. Structural C studs are used for interior and exterior load-bearing walls. Drywall studs are used for nonbearing interior partitions. The structural C studs used in wall construction range in size from 2-1/2″ to 8″ and in thickness from .034″ to .071″. The drywall metal studs are available in sizes from 1-5/8″ to 6″ with thicknesses from .018″ to .034″. Spacing is usually 24″ on center (OC).

Roofs

The broad range of available sizes and thicknesses of steel framing members allow this system to be used in virtually any roof system, Figure 14-15. The rafter and ceiling joist systems used for traditional lumber-built houses are possible as well as on-site and off-site trusses. Spacing is usually 24″OC.

More information on this product is available from the American Iron and Steel Institute. Literature and videos are available.
American Iron and Steel Institute
1101 17th Street, NW
Suite 1300
Washington, DC 20036
www.steel.org

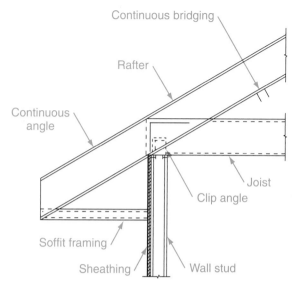

Figure 14-15. Steel framing can be applied to roof construction.

Ceiling Construction

After the exterior and interior walls are erected, plumbed, braced, and the second top plates added, ceiling joists may be put in place. These are usually positioned across the width of the house and in the same direction as the rafters. The required size of ceiling joists will depend on the load to be supported, span, wood species, spacing of joists, and grade of lumber used. Span data for ceiling joists in three common species of wood is given in Figure 14-16. Check the local code to be sure that your selection is acceptable.

Basic construction of the ceiling is similar to floor construction. The main differences are that a header is not required around the perimeter and smaller size of lumber is used. Long spans may require support from a bearing wall partition or beam. If a beam is used, it may be located below the joists or placed flush with them using ledger strips. Both methods are illustrated in Figure 14-17.

The upper corner of the ceiling joists often interferes with the roof slope. To prevent this interference, the corner is usually cut to match the slope. This is shown in Figure 14-18.

Roof trusses are now being used in residential construction to a much greater extent than before. This approach eliminates the traditional ceiling joist and rafter. See Chapter 19

Roof Designs for design and construction procedures.

General Framing Considerations

An *access hole* must be provided in the ceiling to allow entry into the attic. This opening is usually in a closet and may be as small as two feet square. Framing around the opening is the same as for openings in the floor. Double headers are used for large holes, such as for a disappearing stairway. However, double headers are not usually required for small openings.

There are a number of areas in the house that require special framing. Openings for heating ducts, wall backing for various fixtures, and extra support for the bathtub are examples of situations that require attention. Figure 14-19 illustrates some of these special framing details.

Framing for a bay window presents special problems. Figure 14-20 shows one accepted method for framing a bay window. Note that the floor joists extend beyond the wall to provide support for the unit. If the unit is at right angles to the floor joists, then cantilevered joists should be used to support the unit.

Masonry Wall Construction

A *masonry wall* is constructed entirely of brick, concrete block, stone, clay tile, terra cotta, or a combination of these materials. Solid masonry walls for residential construction are usually 8″ thick. Concrete block walls are popular in many sections of the country. These walls are also called *cavity walls.* Block walls are relatively inexpensive to construct and a variety of textures and designs are possible. Walls that require more than one thickness of masonry must have all thicknesses bonded together. They may be bonded

CEILING JOIST SPAN DATA

SPECIES OR GROUP	GRADE	2" x 4"			2" x 6"			2" x 8"			2" x 10"		
20 PSF LIVE LOAD, 10 PSF DEAD LOAD, DEF. <240 — Drywall ceiling; No future room development; Limited attic storage available.		12"OC	16"OC	24"OC	12"OC	16"OC	24"OC	12"OC	16"OC	24"OC	12"OC	16"OC	24"OC
Douglas Fir and Larch	Sel. Struc.	10'-5"	9'-6"	8'-3"	16'-4"	14'-11"	13'-0"	21'-7"	19'-7"	17'-1"	27'-6"	25'-0"	20'-11"
	No.1 & Btr	10'-3"	9'-4"	8'-1"	16'-1"	14'-7"	12'-0"	21'-2"	18'-8"	15'-3"	26'-4"	22'-9"	18'-7"
	No.1	10'-0"	9'-1"	7'-8"	15'-9"	13'-9"	11'-2"	20'-1"	17'-5"	14'-2"	24'-6"	21'-3"	17'-4"
	No.2	9'-10"	8'-9"	7'-2"	14'-10"	12'-10"	10'-6"	18'-9"	16'-3"	13'-3"	22'-11"	19'-10"	16'-3"
	No.3	7'-8"	6'-8"	5'-5"	11'-2"	9'-8"	7'-11"	14'-2"	12'-4"	10'-0"	17'-4"	15'-0"	12'-3"

SPECIES OR GROUP	GRADE	2" x 4"			2" x 6"			2" x 8"			2" x 10"		
20 PSF LIVE LOAD, 10 PSF DEAD LOAD, DEF. <240 — Drywall ceiling; No future room development; Limited attic storage available.		12"OC	16"OC	24"OC	12"OC	16"OC	24"OC	12"OC	16"OC	24"OC	12"OC	16"OC	24"OC
Southern Pine	Sel. Struc.	10'-3"	9'-4"	8'-1"	16'-1"	14'-7"	12'-9"	21'-2"	19'-3"	16'-10"	26'-0"	24'-7"	21'-6"
	No.1	10'-0"	9'-1"	8'-0"	15'-9"	14'-4"	12'-6"	20'-10"	18'-11"	15'-11"	26'-0"	23'-2"	18'-11"
	No.2	9'-10"	8'-11"	7'-8"	15'-6"	13'-6"	11'-0"	20'-1"	17'-5"	14'-2"	24'-0"	20'-9"	17'-0"
	No.3	8'-2"	7'-1"	5'-9"	12'-1"	10'-5"	8'-6"	15'-4"	13'-3"	10'-10"	18'-1"	15'-8"	12'-10"

ROOF RAFTER SPAN DATA

SPECIES OR GROUP	GRADE	2" x 6"			2" x 8"			2" x 10"			2" x 12"		
20 PSF LIVE LOAD, 10 PSF DEAD LOAD, DEF. <240 — Roof slope 3:12 or less; Light roof covering; No ceiling finish.		12"OC	16"OC	24"OC	12"OC	16"OC	24"OC	12"OC	16"OC	24"OC	12"OC	16"OC	24"OC
Douglas Fir and Larch	Sel. Struc.	16'-4"	14'-11"	13'-0"	21'-7"	19'-7"	17'-2"	27'-6"	25'-0"	21'-10"	33'-6"	30'-5"	26'-7"
	No.1 & Btr	16'-1"	14'-7"	12'-9"	21'-2"	19'-3"	16'-10"	27'-1"	24'-7"	20'-9"	32'-11"	29'-6"	24'-1"
	No.1	15'-9"	14'-4"	12'-6"	20'-10"	18'-11"	15'-10"	26'-6"	23'-9"	19'-5"	31'-10"	27'-6"	22'-6"
	No.2	15'-6"	14'-1"	11'-9"	20'-5"	18'-2"	14'-10"	25'-8"	22'-3"	18'-2"	29'-9"	25'-9"	21'-0"
	No.3	12'-6"	10'-10"	8'-10"	15'-10"	13'-9"	11'-3"	19'-5"	16'-9"	13'-8"	22'-6"	19'-6"	15'-11"

SPECIES OR GROUP	GRADE	2" x 6"			2" x 8"			2" x 10"			2" x 12"		
20 PSF LIVE LOAD, 15 PSF DEAD LOAD, DEF. <240 — Roof slope greater than 3:12; Light roof covering; Drywall ceiling; No snow load.		12"OC	16"OC	24"OC	12"OC	16"OC	24"OC	12"OC	16"OC	24"OC	12"OC	16"OC	24"OC
Douglas Fir and Larch	Sel. Struc.	16'-4"	14'-11"	13'-0"	21'-7"	19'-7"	17'-2"	27'-6"	25'-0"	21'-7"	33'-6"	30'-5"	25'-1"
	No.1 & Btr	16'-1"	14'-7"	12'-5"	21'-2"	19'-3"	15'-9"	27'-1"	23'-7"	19'-3"	31'-7"	27'-4"	22'-4"
	No.1	15'-9"	14'-3"	11'-7"	20'-9"	18'-0"	14'-8"	25'-5"	22'-0"	17'-11"	29'-5"	25'-6"	20'-10"
	No.2	15'-4"	13'-3"	10'-10"	19'-5"	16'-10"	13'-9"	23'-9"	20'-7"	16'-9"	27'-6"	23'-10"	19'-6"
	No.3	11'-7"	10'-1"	8'-2"	14'-8"	12'-9"	10'-5"	17'-11"	15'-7"	12'-8"	20'-10"	18'-0"	14'-9"

SPECIES OR GROUP	GRADE	2" x 6"			2" x 8"			2" x 10"			2" x 12"		
20 PSF LIVE LOAD, 10 PSF DEAD LOAD, DEF. <240 — Drywall ceiling; Light roofing; Snow load.		12"OC	16"OC	24"OC	12"OC	16"OC	24"OC	12"OC	16"OC	24"OC	12"OC	16"OC	24"OC
Southern Pine	Sel. Struc.	16'-1"	14'-7"	12'-9"	21'-2"	19'-3"	16'-10"	26'-0"	24'-7"	21'-6"	26'-0"	26'-0"	26'-0"
	No.1	15'-9"	14'-4"	12'-6"	20'-10"	18'-11"	16'-6"	26'-0"	24'-1"	20'-3"	26'-0"	26'-0"	24'-1"
	No.2	15'-6"	14'-1"	11'-9"	20'-5"	18'-6"	15'-3"	25'-8"	22'-3"	18'-2"	26'-0"	26'-0"	21'-4"
	No.3	12'-11"	11'-2"	9'-1"	16'-5"	14'-3"	11'-7"	19'-5"	16'-10"	13'-9"	23'-1"	20'-0"	16'-4"

SPECIES OR GROUP	GRADE	2" x 6"			2" x 8"			2" x 10"			2" x 12"		
30 PSF LIVE LOAD, 15 PSF DEAD LOAD, DEF. <240 — Drywall ceiling; Medium roofing; Snow load.		12"OC	16"OC	24"OC	12"OC	16"OC	24"OC	12"OC	16"OC	24"OC	12"OC	16"OC	24"OC
Southern Pine	Sel. Struc.	14'-1"	12'-9"	11'-2"	18'-6"	16'-10"	14'-8"	23'-8"	21'-6"	18'-9"	26'-0"	26'-0"	22'-10"
	No.1	13'-9"	12'-6"	10'-11"	18'-2"	16'-6"	13'-11"	23'-2"	20'-3"	16'-6"	26'-0"	24'-1"	19'-8"
	No.2	13'-9"	11'-9"	9'-7"	17'-7"	15'-3"	12'-5"	21'-0"	18'-2"	14'-10"	24'-7"	21'-4"	17'-5"
	No.3	10'-6"	9'-1"	7'-5"	13'-5"	11'-7"	9'-6"	15'-10"	13'-9"	11'-3"	18'-10"	16'-4"	13'-4"

THESE SPANS ARE BASED ON THE 1993 AFTA (FORMERLY NFPA) SPAN TABLES FOR JOISTS AND RAFTERS. THESE GRADES ARE THE MOST COMMONLY AVAILABLE.

Figure 14-16. Ceiling joist and rafter span data are in feet and inches for Douglas fir/larch and southern yellow pine. Spans are based on dry lumber size with a moisture content equal to or less than 19%. Calculations were based on the modulus of elasticity (E) and maximum fiber bending stress (F_b) allowed for ceiling joists. Rafter spans were based on the fiber bending stress (F_b) and allowable modulus of elasticity (E). Rafter spans are horizontal distances.

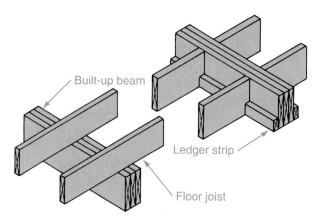

Figure 14-17. Two methods of supporting ceiling joists with a built-up beam.

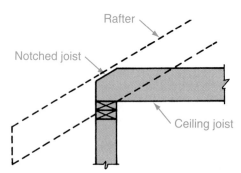

Figure 14-18. Ceiling joists are usually notched to match the roof slope to prevent interference with the roof sheathing.

by using a header course every 16″ vertically or corrugated metal wall ties may be placed in the mortar joints, Figure 14-21. Metal wall ties should be placed no farther apart than 16″ vertically and 32″ horizontally.

One disadvantage of a solid masonry wall is that furring strips are required on the inside of the wall if drywall, plaster, or paneling is used. *Furring strips* are usually 2″ × 2″ or 1″ × 3″ lumber affixed to the wall to provide a nailing surface. Insulation can be added on the inside of a solid masonry wall as shown in Figure 14-22.

Floor joists are placed directly into openings in solid brick and stone walls. Each joist end is cut at an angle to prevent toppling the wall if the house should catch fire, Figure 14-23. This cut is known as a *firecut*.

Flashing and termite shields should be used at the base of solid masonry or brick veneer walls, Figure 14-24. Flashing prevents moisture from entering the structure. Termites are a threat in a large part of the country and

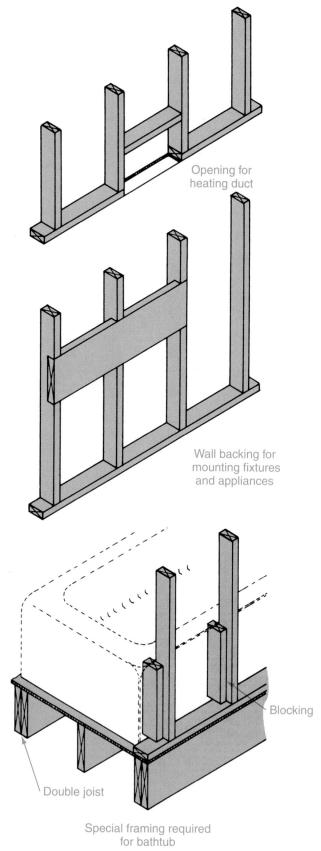

Figure 14-19. These are examples of areas that usually require special framing.

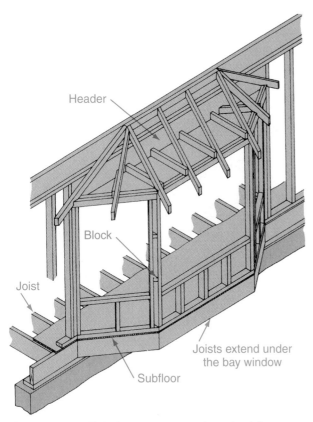

Header

Block

Joist

Subfloor

Joists extend under the bay window

Figure 14-20. This is one accepted method for framing a bay window.

Figure 14-22. Insulation can be applied between furring strips on the inside of a solid masonry wall to reduce heat loss. Notice the furring strips in place under the window.

cause millions of dollars in damage each year. Termite shields help prevent infestation.

The top plate for the roof must be anchored securely to the solid masonry wall, Figure 14-25. The usual procedure in a brick wall is to place anchor bolts between the bricks. Nuts are threaded onto the bolts to hold the plate in place. A lintel block is used in concrete block construction and anchor bolts are cast in place. The plate is then secured by nuts threaded onto the bolts.

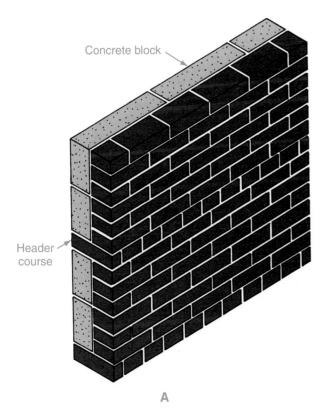

Concrete block

Header course

A

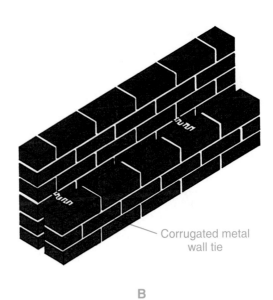

Corrugated metal wall tie

B

Figure 14-21. A solid masonry wall of more than one thickness must be bonded. A—Using a header course. B—Using corrugated metal wall ties.

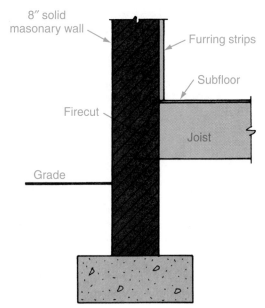

Figure 14-23. Floor joists in a solid masonry wall require a firecut to prevent excessive wall damage in the event of a fire.

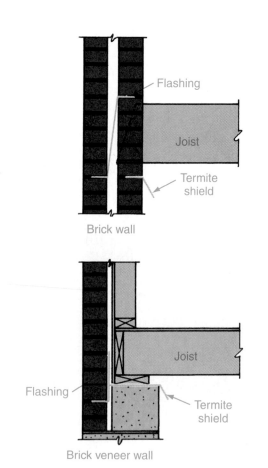

Figure 14-24. Flashing is used to control moisture. Termite shields are required where termites are a threat.

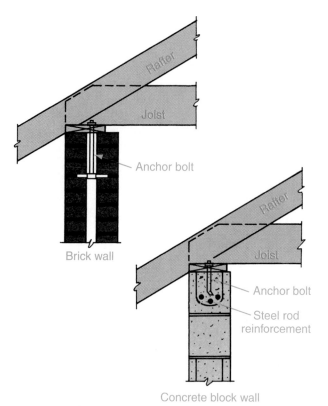

Figure 14-25. The top plate is securely attached to masonry walls with anchor bolts embedded in the wall.

Stonework

Often, stonework is used with a masonry wall to provide a decorative look. The stonework mason must apply a certain amount of artistry to the work due to the various size and texture of the material. Stonework is commonly classified as ashlar or rubble.

Ashlar stonework uses dressed, cut, or squared stones. Each stone is generally rectangular in shape, a specific size, and fits in an exact place in the pattern, Figure 14-26. This type of stonework may have a more regular pattern or finished appearance.

Rubble stonework is made up of undressed stones of irregular shapes. If the stones are generally flat and rectangular, the result may look like courses (rows) of stone. This is called *coursed rubble*, Figure 14-27A. Rubble stonework can also have a random pattern, Figure 14-27B. Another type of rubble stonework is called *uncoursed cobweb* or *polygonal rubble.* The stones in this stonework

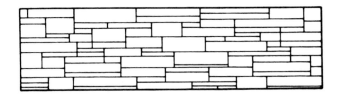

Figure 14-26. Ashlar stonework has more or less rectangular stones in a fairly regular pattern.

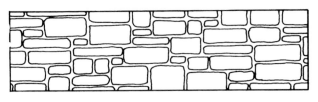

A

B

Figure 14-27. A—Coursed rubble stonework. B—Random rubble stonework.

are dressed with relatively straight edges to fit a particular place in the pattern, Figure 14-28. However, the finished stonework has a rubble, not ashlar, appearance.

Masonry Veneer

Solid brick and stone walls have been used extensively in years past. However, because of their construction cost, they are diminishing in importance for residential purposes. The same exterior effect may be obtained with a brick or stone veneer on frame construction. The term "veneer" is commonly used to indicate that a less expensive or desirable material has been covered up with some type of facing material. The veneer does not help support the weight of the building. This type of wall will be better insulated, less expensive to construct, and present fewer construction problems than a solid wall. Figure 14-29 shows how a brick veneer wall is typically insulated on the frame wall side.

Masonry veneer is usually placed 1″ away from the frame wall to provide a dead air space for insulation and a means of escape for moisture that condenses on the inside of the masonry. The facing (veneer) is usually 4″ thick, but may range from approximately 1″ to 6″. Figure 14-30 shows a construction detail of brick veneer over frame construction.

Figure 14-28. Uncoursed cobweb or polygonal rubble stonework.

Figure 14-29. Insulation with a reflective-type vapor barrier is being applied to the frame side of a structure with a masonry veneer. (CertainTeed Corporation)

Brick Names and Sizes

Brick is a fired clay product. The final color is ordinarily determined by the natural color of the clay, which is the primary ingredient. However, earth colors are sometimes added to produce a wider variety of colors. Brick may be purchased in single colors or in a mixture to produce a blend.

There are two basic types of brick used for wall construction—face brick and common brick. *Face brick* is usually uniform in size and has sharp corners and lines. *Common brick* is not as uniform in size and color and may have a lip on one or more edges. In recent years, common brick has been used more widely as a facing material and has a character that is quite different from the face brick. It produces a rustic appearance and the texture is much more distinct. It looks especially good with a deep rake joint to accent the individual character of each brick.

The names of brick shapes are well established. However, brick sizes are not standardized. Sizes of brick frequently used in residential construction are shown in the chart in Figure 14-31.

Specific terms apply to the position or way in which the brick is laid. Figure 14-32 illustrates accepted terminology. Note that these terms apply to the position of the brick in the wall and not the type or size of the brick.

Numerous types of mortar joints are used in brickwork. Figure 14-33 shows some joints used in residential construction. Masons have tools designed specifically for making these joints.

A discussion of brickwork would not be complete without mentioning some of the brick bonds that are recognized standards. Figure 14-34 illustrates a few of the many bonds. The running bond is used extensively in brick veneer construction. The common bond is the most popular for solid masonry walls.

Traditional Three-Coat Stucco

Stucco is a coating applied to the outside of a structure. Generally, the term "stucco" refers to exterior applications, while "plaster" refers to interior spaces. There are three stucco systems in general use today: traditional three-coat stucco, synthetic stucco (one-coat), and the exterior insulation finish system (EIFS). Each system produces acceptable results when application procedures are carefully followed.

The traditional *three-coat stucco system* has been in use for many years and has performed well over time. Successful applications are possible in all sections of the US. See Figure 14-35. The stucco material consists of Portland cement, lime, sand, and water. The material is applied in three coats, hence the name.

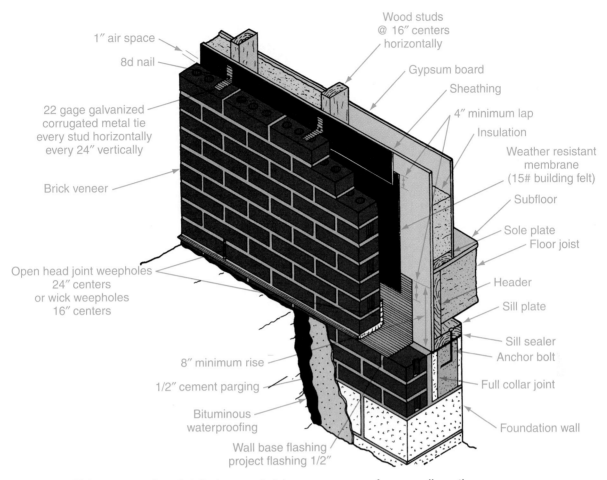

Figure 14-30. This construction detail shows a brick veneer over a frame wall section.

Brick names and sizes		
Name	**Nominal size**	**Actual size**
Roman	4 × 2 × 12″	1-5/8 × 3-5/8 × 11-5/8″
Modular	2-2/3 × 4 × 8″	2-1/4 × 3-5/8 × 7-5/8″
SCR Brick	2-2/3 × 6 × 12″	2-1/8 × 5-1/2 × 11-1/2″
Standard	2-2/3 × 4 × 8″	2-1/4 × 3-3/4 × 8″
Norman	2-2/3 × 4 × 12″	2-1/4 × 3-5/8 × 11-5/8″
Firebrick*	2-2/3 × 4 × 9″	2-1/2 × 3-5/8 × 9″

*Firebrick is not used for exterior wall construction, but is included because it is used in fireplaces.

Figure 14-31. This chart shows the dimensions of common bricks.

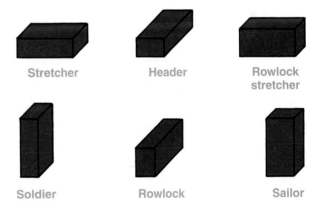

Figure 14-32. Bricks are laid in six basic positions. Each position has a specific name.

Traditional three-coat stucco produces a protective shell around the structure that requires little maintenance. But, it can be repaired if necessary. Since Portland cement stucco resists insects, weather, and rotting, it can have an effective life span of 100 years or more if the underlying structure remains sound.

Problems with stucco applications are generally the results of poor workmanship or improper installation, rather than with the material itself. This is true of any of the three systems. Many builders prefer traditional stucco and continue to use it either in addition to, or instead of, the newer, one-coat, fiber-reinforced

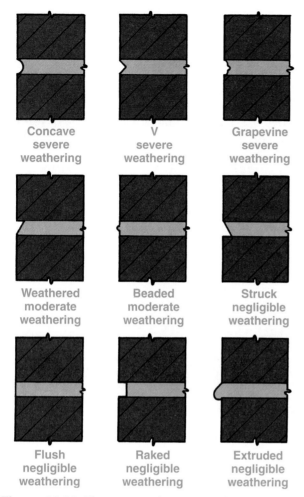

Concave severe weathering

V severe weathering

Grapevine severe weathering

Weathered moderate weathering

Beaded moderate weathering

Struck negligible weathering

Flush negligible weathering

Raked negligible weathering

Extruded negligible weathering

Figure 14-33. There are various types of mortar joints.

Figure 14-35. Stucco will protect the exterior of this home for many years.

stucco products made with acrylic polymers. EIFSs have had their problems, but are still being used for certain applications.

Preparing for Stucco

The proper preparation for stucco cannot be over emphasized. But, most important, a rigid structure is essential. Three-coat stucco can be applied to most any type of wall system—concrete blocks, poured concrete, brick, metal or wood frame, and so on. See Figure 14-36.

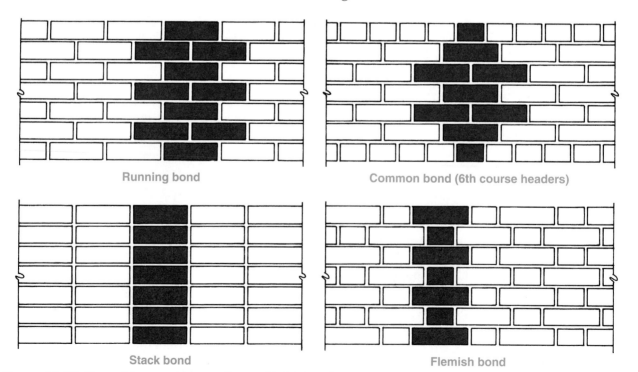

Running bond

Common bond (6th course headers)

Stack bond

Flemish bond

Figure 14-34. Four of the most frequently used brick bonds are shown here.

Figure 14-36. Stucco can be applied to just about any type of wall system. A—Wood frame ready to receive moisture-resistant barrier prior to stucco. B—Stucco applied directly to concrete block walls.

Stucco is not structural and adds no strength to the building structure. It is a protective shell around the structure. It can resist normal expansion and contraction due to the changes in temperature and moisture, but it cannot resist severe stresses resulting from uneven settling or movement in the structure itself.

Cracks in masonry walls will "telescope" through the stucco. Bowed studs can cause thin spots of less than 7/8" thickness in the stucco that will result in cracking. Movement in plywood that is not properly spaced and nailed will also cause stucco to crack. Mixing engineered lumber and standard lumber framing materials can create uneven expansion and contraction that may result in cracking the stucco shell.

Moisture Barrier and Flashing

In order for a stucco application to be successful, moisture must be prevented from entering behind the stucco shell. Even though stucco allows moisture vapor to readily pass through and is relatively unaffected by moisture, high concentrations will have a devastating effect on the framing members and sheathing that support the stucco in a wood frame structure. Wood frame structures are naturally more susceptible to moisture damage than masonry or concrete buildings.

Moisture barriers and flashing are used to prevent moisture from entering the space behind the stucco, Figure 14-37. These elements should be viewed as an integral part of the total wall system, with special attention given to joints, openings, and penetrations in the wall.

Moisture barriers are membranes that protect most of the wall area. The Uniform Building Code specifies at least a Grade D (10 minute) paper for the exterior membrane, but this is minimal and will not resist severe rain for extended periods. Heavier paper (28-pound, 30 minute paper) is available that increases the protection and is recommended for a high-quality job.

Kraft paper is used as flashing around wall openings and other areas of wall penetration. The type of kraft paper used has a layer of asphalt between two sheets of traditional kraft paper. However, this paper tears easily, does not resist punctures, and will wrinkle, making it difficult to keep the paper flat. Even though this is the industry standard, it leaves much to be desired as a flashing material.

Figure 14-37. Metal lath and PVC corner bead have been attached with rust-proof fasteners just prior to the scratch coat. The weather-resistant barrier can also be seen under the lath.

Doubling the thickness increases protection, but is still not very satisfactory. Another product that may be a better choice is a 20-mil rubberized asphalt membrane sandwiched between a face of 4-mil polyethylene sheet and a back of polyester. This product is very water resistant, will stretch, and resists tearing.

When a hole or tear does occur in the flashing paper, caulk may be used to repair the spot. However, care should be taken to reduce damage and, therefore, the number of repairs. Caulk is also used to seal the flashing at wall openings and penetrations. It is important to select a caulk that adheres to the construction materials under the conditions of use.

Lath (Reinforcement)

The purpose of *lath* is to provide support and attachment for the layers of stucco and to connect the stucco to the structure. It is available as self-furring wire lath or rib lath. A moisture-proof membrane is generally attached to the lath at the factory for faster installation. See Figure 14-38. Lath is attached to the sheathing with furring nails or staples that resist corrosion from contact with the mortar. Lath should be installed in the proper orientation to increase adherence of the mortar during application.

Scratch or Foundation Coat

The *scratch coat*, also called the foundation coat, is the first stucco layer in the three-

Figure 14-38. The base coat is being applied with a trowel.

coat process. The purpose of the scratch coat is to embed the reinforcement in stucco and provide support for the next coat. The scratch coat is a rich mixture of about one part cement to two to four parts sand. It can be applied by hand with a trowel or pumped. Hand troweled surfaces are believed to be more dense and harder than pumped surfaces, but there are advocates of both methods. The scratch coat is generally 3/8″ thick.

When the scratch coat has begun to set, the surface should be roughened with a scarifier rake or scratching trowel to secure a better bond for the next coat. Since the scratch coat is relatively thin, it will dry rapidly and should be misted lightly with water to ensure proper curing. Misting is particularly important if the weather is hot and dry.

The scratch coat is ready for the next coat (brown coat) when the surface is hard enough to resist scoring from a nail dragged across the surface. Be sure that at least 95% of the lath is embedded by this coat before proceeding to the next coat.

Brown Coat

The second stucco layer in the three-coat process is called the *brown coat*. The function of the brown coat is to cover any visible lath, add strength to the shell, true up the surface, and provide an appropriate surface for the final decorative finish coat. The brown coat is applied with a trowel and leveled with a straightedge to a thickness of about 3/8″. Together, the scratch and brown coats should be at least 7/8″ thick. This layer should be flush with the corner bead and ready to receive the final finish coat. Misting may be required if the coat dries too quickly and surface cracks begin to appear.

Finish Coat

The third stucco layer in the three-coat process is called the *finish coat*. See Figure 14-39. This is the decorative layer and is where texture or design patterns are applied to the surface. Only about 1/8″ of thickness is added by the finish coat. The finish coat may be

Figure 14-39. The finish coat has been applied to this structure.

Figure 14-40. This stucco surface has received a primer and finish coat of paint.

applied by machine or hand, depending on the desired texture or personal preference. Color may be applied as part of the mortar finish or the surface may be painted later.

The finish coat should be maintained at the proper temperature for at least 48 hours following application. Stucco should cure for 28 days before painting. Spraying regularly with water, unless prohibited by coloring agents, will aid in curing and removing scum from the textured surface. Figure 14-40 shows a painted stucco surface. Figure 14-41 shows a close-up of the texture.

Figure 14-41. This close-up shows the detailed texture of a stucco surface.

Internet Resources

www.architectural-ornament.com
Architectural Ornament, Inc., manufacturer of polyurethane architectural molding

www.astm.org
ASTM International, formerly the American Society for Test Materials

www.concretehomes.com
Portland Cement Association

www.gp.com/build/index.html
Georgia-Pacific Corporation, supplier of building products

www.iza.com
International Zinc Association

www.jameshardie.com
James Hardie Building Products, Inc.

www.knauffiberglass.com
Knauf Fiber Glass, manufacturer of thermal and acoustical fiberglass insulations

www.modplas.com
Modern Plastics

www.reynoldsbp.com
Reynolds Building Products

www.steel.org
American Iron and Steel Institute

Review Questions – Chapter 14

Write your answers on a separate sheet of paper. Do not write in this book.

1. List five factors that affect the size of ceiling joists.

2. Name the five standard parts of a frame wall.

3. Which properties must lumber used for wood framing have?

4. Name three softwoods commonly used as framing lumber.

5. The acceptable range of moisture content for framing lumber is _____ percent.

6. Finished wall height in most residential structures is _____.

7. The framing member used to span the distance over an opening in the wall, such as a door or window, is called a _____ or _____.

8. Identify an advantage of using a large solid header instead of a smaller header with cripples.

9. Studs that are not full length and used above or below openings in a wall are called _____.

10. The rough opening height for most doors is _____.

11. If a window has a rough opening width of 5'-2", the chart in Figure 14-7 indicates that the header size should be _____.

12. Name three areas of the house that require special framing consideration.

13. The purpose of a header course of brick in a masonry wall is to _____.

14. The spacing of metal wall ties should be no farther apart than _____ vertically and _____ horizontally.

15. Solid masonry walls for residential construction are usually _____ thick.

16. Concrete block walls are sometimes called _____ walls.

17. The angle cut on the end of floor joists to be used with a solid masonry wall is called a _____.

18. The two types of stonework are _____ and _____.

19. In a masonry veneer wall, the air space between the veneer and stud wall is usually about _____ wide.

20. The top plate is secured to a solid masonry wall by the use of _____.

21. Brick is made primarily of _____.

22. There are basically two types of bricks. These are _____ and _____.

23. The most popular brick bond for solid masonry walls is the _____ bond.

24. Name four factors that seem to be driving the move toward accepting steel framing in residential construction.

25. How does the use of steel framing provide an environmental benefit?

26. How are "drywall studs" used in steel frame structures?

27. What is stucco?

28. The expected life of properly-installed three-coat stucco can exceed _____ years.

29. Stucco can be applied to most any surface so long as the structure is _____.

30. Care must be taken to prevent _____ from entering behind the stucco.

31. For stucco, _____ is used to repair pinholes, tears in the paper, and to seal flashing at penetrations and openings.

Suggested Activities

1. Build a scale model at 1" = 1'-0" of a wall section that has at least one door, one window, and an intersecting partition. Identify the parts.

2. Select a simple floor plan for a frame house. Lay out the wall framing indicating trimmers, cripples, spacing blocks, and full studs.

3. Collect samples of building materials to be displayed in class. Identify each of the materials and explain where each might be used in the construction of a house.

4. Build scale models at 1/4 size of framing for corners, wall intersections, and openings for doors and windows. Prepare plan view drawings for display with the models.

5. Visit a building site where a house is being constructed using conventional methods. Obtain permission before entering the site. Determine the species and grade of the framing lumber. Identify if the type of framing is balloon or platform.

6. Photograph as many different brick bonds as you can find in the area surrounding your home. Have the photos processed and prepare a display that identifies each bond.

7. Using CADD, draw the brick bonds shown in Figure 14-34.

8. Using CADD, draw the framing illustrations shown in Figure 14-5.

Doors and Windows 15

Objectives

After studying this chapter, you will be able to:

➤ List the functions that doors and windows perform.

➤ Compare the types of doors used in a residential dwelling.

➤ Draw proper door and window symbols on a typical floor plan.

➤ Explain the information shown in a window or door detail.

➤ Prepare window and door schedules.

Key Terms

Accordion Door	Hopper Window
Awning Window	Horizontal Sliding
Basic Unit Size	Window
Bay Window	Jalousie Window
Bi-Fold Door	Mullions
Bow Window	Muntins
Box Bay	Overhead Sectional
Brick Mold	Door
Casement Window	Panel Door
Casing	Picture Window
Circle Top Window	Pocket Door
Clerestory Window	Prehung Units
Combination	Rails
Window	Rough Opening
Door Jamb	Sash Opening
Door Schedule	Sash
Double-Action Door	Sill
Double-Hung	Skylight
Window	Sliding Doors
Drip Cap	Special-Shape
Dutch Door	Window
Flush Door	Stiles
French Doors	Transom Bar
Glass Size	Window Schedule

Doors and windows perform several functions in a residential structure. They shield an opening from the elements, add decoration, emphasize the overall design, provide light and ventilation, and expand visibility. Windows and doors are necessary features of all residential structures and should be planned carefully to ensure maximum contribution to the overall design and function of the structure.

Designing with CADD

Most of the larger window manufacturers—Andersen, Weather Shield, Pella/Rolscreen, Caradco, and Marvin—provide CADD packages that facilitate the drawing and specifying of their windows and doors, Figure 15-1. Be sure the package is compatible with your CADD software before you purchase it. Most manufacturers also provide window and door symbols for standard CADD packages. These symbols can be manipulated during the design process and then used to create a schedule of the windows and doors. In addition, several manufacturers have 3D symbols. These can be very useful when 3D illustrations are to be created, Figure 15-2.

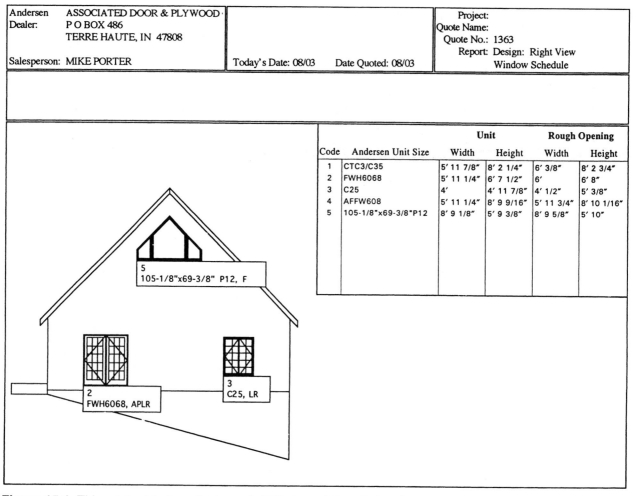

Andersen Dealer:	ASSOCIATED DOOR & PLYWOOD P O BOX 486 TERRE HAUTE, IN 47808		Project: Quote Name: Quote No.: 1363 Report: Design: Right View Window Schedule
Salesperson: MIKE PORTER		Today's Date: 08/03 Date Quoted: 08/03	

Code	Andersen Unit Size	Unit		Rough Opening	
		Width	Height	Width	Height
1	CTC3/C35	5' 11 7/8"	8' 2 1/4"	6' 3/8"	8' 2 3/4"
2	FWH6068	5' 11 1/4"	6' 7 1/2"	6'	6' 8"
3	C25	4'	4' 11 7/8"	4' 1/2"	5' 3/8"
4	AFFW608	5' 11 1/4"	8' 9 9/16"	5' 11 3/4"	8' 10 1/16"
5	105-1/8"x69-3/8"P12	8' 9 1/8"	5' 9 3/8"	8' 9 5/8"	5' 10"

Figure 15-1. This printout is from Andersen's "Window of Knowledge System." Other reports include: quote, energy, performance, and graphics reports. (Andersen Corporation)

Interior and Exterior Doors

A number of classification systems may be used to identify the various styles and types of doors in residential construction. Two broad classes are interior and exterior doors. Doors may also be grouped according to the method of construction, uses, function, or location. Interior and exterior doors are typically 6'-8" high and available in various widths.

Interior Doors

There are several common types of interior doors. These types include flush, panel, bifold, sliding, pocket, double-action, accordion, Dutch, and French. The next sections describe these types.

Interior doors should be a minimum of 32" wide to permit comfortable passage of a wheelchair. Lever-type or vertical pull-handles may be easier for a handicapped person to operate. Automatic door openers may be required in some cases.

Flush doors

Flush doors are smooth on both sides and usually made of wood, Figure 15-3. Standard interior wood flush doors are 1-3/8" thick. They are hollow-core doors that have a wood frame around the perimeter. Wood braces or a composition material is placed in the cavity to support the faces of the door. Interior flush doors are produced in a wide range of widths,

Figure 15-2. This beautiful CADD rendering shows all of the intricate details of the windows that add greatly to the realistic appearance of the drawing. (Helmuth A. Geiser, member AIBD)

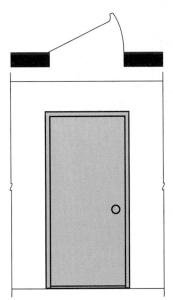

Figure 15-3. A flush door shown with its plan view symbol.

from 2'-0" to 3'-0". The standard width increment is 2". Both surfaces of the door are usually covered with 1/8" Masonite or plywood of mahogany or birch.

Panel doors

A *panel door* has a heavy frame around the outside and generally at least one cross member. The frame and cross members form small panels, Figure 15-4A. The vertical members are called *stiles* and the horizontal members are *rails.* Panels that are thinner than the frame are placed in grooves on the inside edges of the stiles and rails to enclose the space. The panels may be wood, glass, metal, or some other material. Panel doors are usually produced in white pine, but may be constructed of other woods or plastic. Figure 15-4B shows the plan view symbol and elevation view of a panel door.

Bi-fold doors

A *bi-fold door* is made of two parts that together form the door. They may be attached to the side jambs with conventional hinges or secured to the head jamb and floor using a pivot hinge. Bi-fold doors may be flush, paneled, or louvered, Figure 15-5. They are popular as closet doors, but are seldom used

A

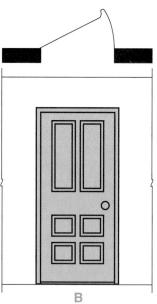

B

Figure 15-4. A—This is a typical panel door used in residential construction. (Morgan Products, Ltd.) B—A panel door shown with its plan view symbol.

A

B

Figure 15-5. Bi-fold doors come in many styles. A—With panels. (Morgan Products, Ltd.) B—Louvered.

for other applications. Bi-fold doors are installed in pairs with each door being the same width. Usual widths are 1'-0" to 2'-0". Wood, plastic, and metal bi-fold doors are produced in the standard 6'-8" height, as well as 8'-0". The usual thickness is 1-1/8" for wood or plastic and 1" for metal. See Figure 15-6 for the symbol and elevation view.

Sliding doors

Sliding doors, or bypass doors, are popular where there are large openings, Figure 15-7. They are frequently used as closet doors. Any number of doors may be used for a

given opening. The width is not critical because the doors are hung from a track mounted on the head jamb. Door pulls are recessed to allow the doors to pass without interference. Glides are installed on the floor to prevent the bottoms from swinging in or out.

Sliding doors may be flush, paneled, or louvered. They are usually constructed from wood, but other materials may be used. The major problem with wood sliding doors is warping since they are not restrained by hinges.

Pocket doors

Pocket doors are a variation of the sliding door and usually the flush style. A pocket door is hung from a track mounted on the head jamb. Ordinarily, only one door is used to close an opening. The door rests in a wall pocket when open, Figure 15-8.

Pocket doors are frequently used between rooms such as the kitchen and dining room. The chief advantage is that they require no space along the wall when open. However, they are difficult to operate and present problems if outlets or cabinets are to be located on the wall outside of the pocket cavity. Pocket door frames of metal and wood are usually purchased already assembled.

Double-action doors

Double-action doors are hinged in such a way that they can swing through an arc of

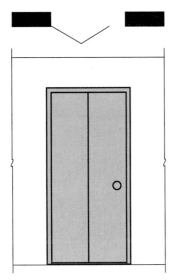

Figure 15-6. A bi-fold door shown with its plan view symbol.

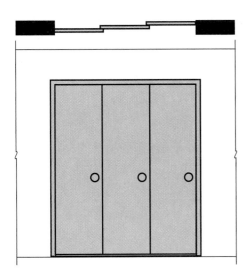

Figure 15-7. Three sliding doors shown with their plan view symbols.

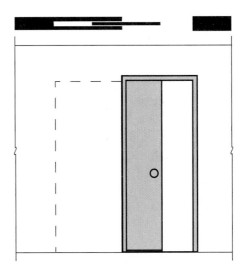

Figure 15-8. A pocket door shown with its plan view symbol.

180°, Figure 15-9. A special double-action, spring-loaded hinge is used and mounted in the center of the side jamb. This door is generally used between rooms that experience a great deal of traffic, yet require the door to be closed most of the time. Double-action doors may be single or double doors. A flush, panel, or louvered style can be used.

Accordion doors

Accordion doors are frequently used to close large openings where bi-fold or sliding doors are not acceptable, Figure 15-10A. They require little space and are produced in a large variety of materials and designs. They may be constructed from wood, plastics, or fabric. Individual hinged panels are sometimes used, as well as a large folded piece of fabric or other material. The door is supported on a track mounted on the head jamb, Figure 15-10B.

Dutch doors

A *Dutch door* is composed of two parts—an upper and lower section. The upper section may be opened independently of the lower section. This allows for light and ventilation, Figure 15-11. A Dutch door may be used between the kitchen and dining room or as an exterior door.

A

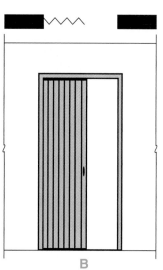

B

Figure 15-10. A—These beautiful, paneled accordion doors are an effective way to close off a large opening. (Pella/Rolscreen Company) B—An accordion door shown with its plan view symbol.

French doors

French doors are panel doors with the panels made from glass, Figure 15-12. They are popular where the door leads to a patio or terrace. They may also be used between rooms.

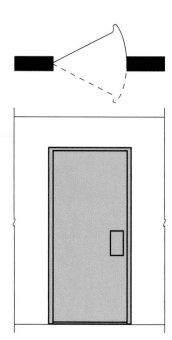

Figure 15-9. A double-action door shown with its plan view symbol.

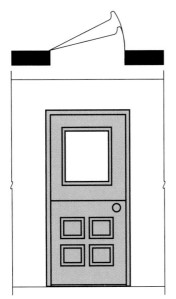

Figure 15-11. A Dutch door shown with its plan view symbol.

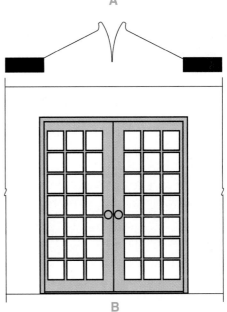

A

B

Figure 15-12. A—French doors are functional as well as decorative. When closed, they provide privacy for this sitting room. (Morgan Products, Ltd.) B—French doors shown with their plan view symbol.

Exterior Doors

Residential exterior doors are similar to some of the interior types, but also have decided differences. Exterior wood doors are usually not hollow core as are many interior doors. They are also thicker than interior doors and may have one or more glass panels to provide visibility.

Common exterior door styles include flush, panel, and swinging or sliding glass. Garage doors are also exterior doors. Exterior doors, other than garage doors, are ordinarily 3'-0" wide. However, other widths are often available.

Figure 15-13 shows plan view symbols for various types of exterior doors. Compare these symbols to the interior door symbols shown earlier in this chapter.

Flush doors

The flush door is one of the most popular exterior doors. Standard exterior flush wood doors are usually 1-3/4" thick. These doors are produced from birch, mahogany, oak, and several other woods, as well as metal. Moldings or other decorative millwork may be added to the flush door to enhance its appearance, Figure 15-14.

Panel doors

Exterior panel doors are available in a great variety of styles. They are constructed from white pine, oak, fir, and various other woods, as well as metal and plastics. These doors are produced in the same sizes as flush doors. Figure 15-15 shows a traditional panel door that is still popular today.

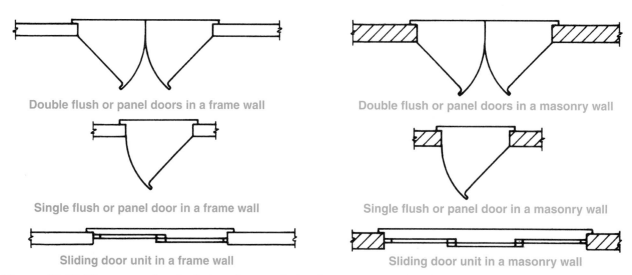

Figure 15-13. These are standard plan view symbols of common exterior doors.

Figure 15-14. This exterior door is a flush type door. It has decorative molding to provide the look of a panel door and includes an attractive leaded-glass light. (Peachtree Doors, Inc.)

Sliding and swinging glass doors

In recent years, sliding and swinging glass doors have gained popularity, Figure 15-16. Sliding doors are usually made of wood and follow typical sliding glass door sizes. Metal units are also available. Figure 15-17 shows some of the standard sizes of exterior sliding glass doors that are available.

Garage Doors

The most popular type of garage doors is the *overhead sectional door,* Figure 15-18. Garage doors are available in wood, metal,

Figure 15-15. This traditional panel door is made of metal. This style of door is also available in wood.

and plastics. Each material has its advantages and personal choice is usually the determining factor in selection. The chart in Figure 15-19 shows standard garage door sizes.

If an automatic garage door opener is to be installed, proper space and wiring must be

A

B

Figure 15-16. A—These sliding glass doors provide a panoramic view and easy access to the deck. (Pella/Rolscreen Company) B—These swinging glass doors allow access to the deck and natural light into the dining room. (The Atrium Door and Window Corporation)

provided. Additional headroom is required above the open door to mount the motor drive on the ceiling. An electrical outlet is required to operate the opener. Check the manufacturer's installation requirements for the specific door.

Specifying Doors

Each door identified on the foundation/ basement plan and floor plan should appear in a *door schedule* with its specifications. Information included on the door schedule should be obtained from manufacturers' literature. Specifications vary and it is important to have exact information for the schedule. A typical door schedule is shown in Figure 15-20. The door schedule should be placed on the sheet with the floor plan or elevations, if space permits. Otherwise, it should be located in the details section of the set of drawings.

Door Details

An interior or exterior door is placed inside a *door jamb,* which is the frame that fits inside the rough opening, Figure 15-21. Jambs may be constructed from wood or metal. Wood jambs are more common in residential construction. A jamb consists of three parts— two side jambs and a head jamb across the top. Jambs for exterior doors are ordinarily 1-1/8" thick while interior jambs are 3/4". The door stop is a rabbet joint in the thicker exterior jambs, but is applied to the face of interior jambs, Figure 15-22.

Jambs are available already assembled with the door hung and ready for installation. These are called *prehung units.* Prehung units are adjustable for slight variations in wall thickness. Consult the manufacturer's literature to determine the preferred rough opening size.

Rough openings for interior doors are usually framed 3" more than the door height

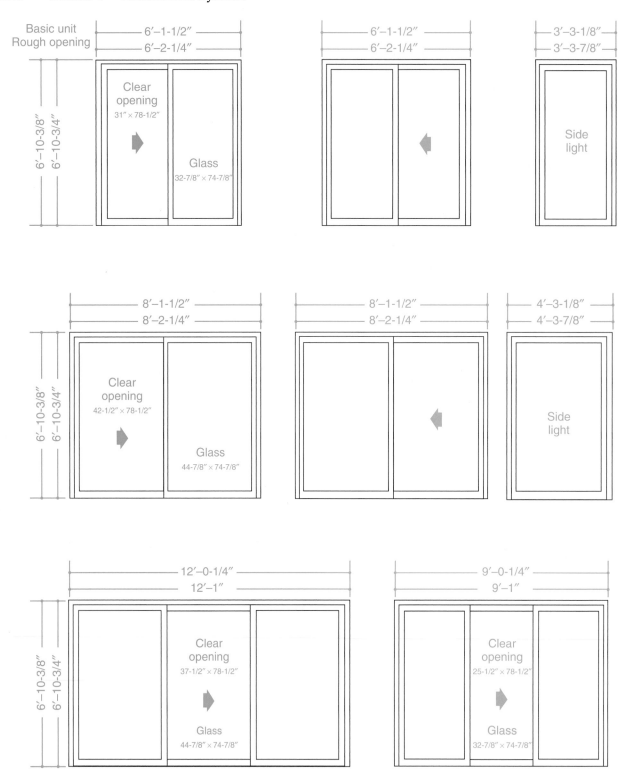

Figure 15-17. Standard sizes of glass sliding doors.

and 2-1/2″ more than the door width. This provides ample space for the jambs and the necessary leveling and squaring. The space between the jamb and rough framing is covered with trim called *casing*. Exterior casing is usually thicker than interior casing. When installed in a masonry wall, casing is called *brick mold*. In frame construction, a *drip cap* is used over the top piece of trim to shed water. Such a strip is not necessary in masonry construction.

Figure 15-18. This overhead sectional garage door is made of steel.

Garage door sizes		
Height	**Single door width**	**Double door width**
6'-6"	8'-0"	15'-0"
6'-6"	9'-0"	16'-0"
6'-6"	10'-0"	18'-0"
7'-0"	8'-0"*	15'-0"
7'-0"	9'-0"	16'-0"*
7'-0"	10'-0"	18'-0"
8'-0"	8'-0"	—

*These sizes are the most frequently used.

Figure 15-19. This chart shows common garage door sizes.

Exterior doors require a sill at the bottom of the door opening between the two side jambs. A *sill* is designed to drain water away from the door and provide support for the side jambs. Sills are constructed from wood, metal, concrete, and stone. Figure 15-23 shows a typical exterior flush door detail in frame and

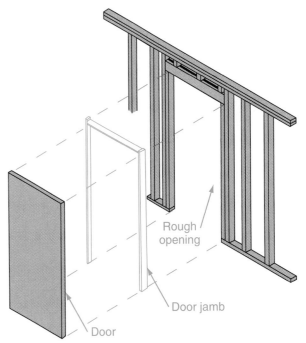

Figure 15-21. The door jamb fits inside the rough opening and supports the door.

brick veneer construction. Door and window construction details are usually drawn in section through the head jamb, the side jamb, and the sill. The head jamb is the jamb across the top of the opening.

Construction details for exterior sliding door units are slightly more complicated than other doors, Figure 15-24. Exterior sliding door jambs vary from one manufacturer to another. The number of door units may also affect the size and shape of the jambs. When specifying exterior sliding doors, it is advisable to secure specifications from the manufacturers to ensure accuracy.

Door schedule						
Sym.	**Quan.**	**Type**	**Rough opening**	**Door size**	**Manufacturer's number**	**Remarks**
A	2	Flush	3'-2-1/2" × 6'-9-1/4"	3'-0" × 6'-8"	EF 36 B	1-3/4" Solid core, birch
B	6	Flush	2'-10-1/2" × 6'-9-1/4"	2'-8" × 6'-8"	IF 32 M	1-3/8" Hollow core, mahogany
C	2	Flush	2'-8-1/2" × 6'-9-1/4"	2'-6" × 6'-8"	IF 30 M	1-3/8" Hollow core, mahogany
D	8	Bi-fold	See manufacturer's specs.	6'-0" × 6'-8"	BF 36 AL	Two units each 36" wide, aluminum
E	2	Sliding	4'-2-1/2" × 6'-9-1/4"	4'-0" × 6'-8"	IF 24 M	1-1/8" Hollow core, mahogany
F	1	Garage	See manufacturer's specs.	16'-0" × 7'-0"	G 16 S	Two light overhead sectional, alum.

Figure 15-20. A typical door schedule for a set of residential house plans.

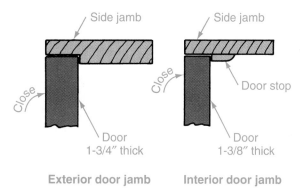

Figure 15-22. Details of interior and exterior wood door jambs.

Ordinarily, it is not necessary to draw detailed window and door section drawings in conventional construction. However, if special framing or uncommon construction is involved, then these drawings are a necessary part of a set of construction drawings.

Windows

When selecting windows for a dwelling, it is important to remember the functions that windows perform. They admit light from the outside; provide fresh air and ventilation to the various rooms; help to create an atmosphere inside by framing an exterior view; and add detail, balance, and design to the exterior of the house.

A uniform amount of light across a room is desirable. Proper design and placement of windows will help to eliminate dark corners and extremely bright areas. The following guidelines will help achieve a more evenly lighted room.

- Glass area should be at least 20% of the floor area of the room. This amount of glass will provide suitable natural light even on cloudy days. When the light outside is very bright, the intensity may be controlled with shades or draperies.

- For increased light, face the principle windows toward the south.

- One large window opening will produce less contrast in brightness than several smaller openings.

- Better distribution of light will be accomplished if windows are placed on more than one wall.

- Windows placed high on a wall will provide a greater degree of light penetration into the room than windows placed low.

- Select the window shape that gives the type of light distribution desired in the room. Tall, narrow windows tend to give a thin and deep penetration. Short, wide windows produce a shallow penetration over a broad area.

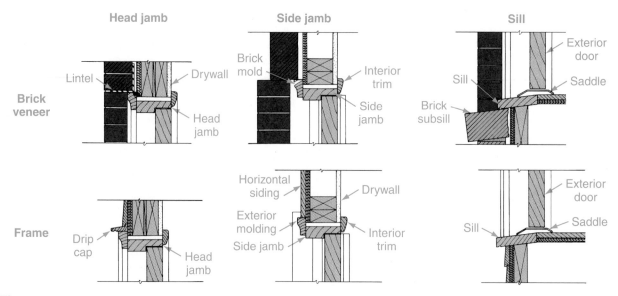

Figure 15-23. Exterior door details for frame and brick veneer construction.

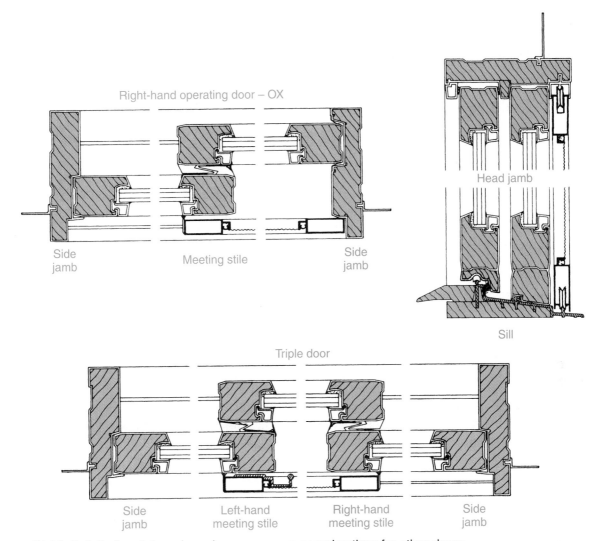

Figure 15-24. Details for sliding glass doors are more complex than for other doors.

Natural ventilation in a home is necessary all year long, but is especially important during the summer months. If windows are located with adequate ventilation in mind, comfort will be increased considerably. Apply these guidelines for efficient ventilation.

- Openings for ventilation should be at least 10% of the floor area.
- Placement of openings for ventilation should take advantage of prevailing breezes.
- Locate windows in such a way to achieve the best movement of air across the room. Furniture should be placed so it will not interfere with the flow of air through the room.

Windows may often be used to enhance an existing view or provide a selective one. Large areas of glass tend to make a room look larger.

The size and shape of the windows will frame the view, so it is important to select a window of the proper proportions… one that does not have obstructions to the view. The following points will aid the designer in specifying the proper window for a particular view.

- A large area of fixed glass provides clear viewing without obstructions.
- Horizontal and vertical divisions in the window or between windows should be thin to minimize obstruction.
- The sill height of windows should be determined on the basis of furniture, room arrangement, and view.

Designing a home to be functional, efficient, and pleasing to the eye on the exterior is no small task. Some of the guidelines provided may conflict. A home that has been designed for light, view, and ventilation may not have a pleasing exterior appearance. The challenge is to meet all design requirements in a creative manner.

The placement and number of windows affect the overall design appearance of the home. Even though windows should be selected to fulfill interior needs, the size, placement, and type may be varied slightly to improve the outside appearance of the home. Windows can add to the continuity of the design. They should relate to the solid wall areas rather than appear to be just a variety of openings in a wall, Figure 15-25.

Window Types

Many types of windows are available for residential construction, Figure 15-26. Most types have unique proportions and may be constructed differently, depending on if they are made of wood, metal, or plastic. In addition, windows of the same general type purchased from different manufacturers will

seldom be exactly the same. For these reasons, it is very important to obtain window specifications from the manufacturer.

Three basic types of windows are typically used in residential construction: sliding, swinging, and fixed. A fourth type—combination—is possible using two or more types of windows to form a unit. Windows placed in a location other than a typical wall account for a fifth type or category. The windows in this category include skylights and clerestory windows. The specific window selected for a given application will depend on:

- The function(s) to be performed.
- Architectural style of the structure.
- Construction considerations.
- Building codes.
- Personal taste.

Sliding windows

There are two types of sliding windows most commonly used in residential construction. These types are double-hung and horizontal sliding.

Figure 15-25. The windows of this attractive home complement the basic wall areas and add to the overall design balance. (Sater Design Collection, Inc.)

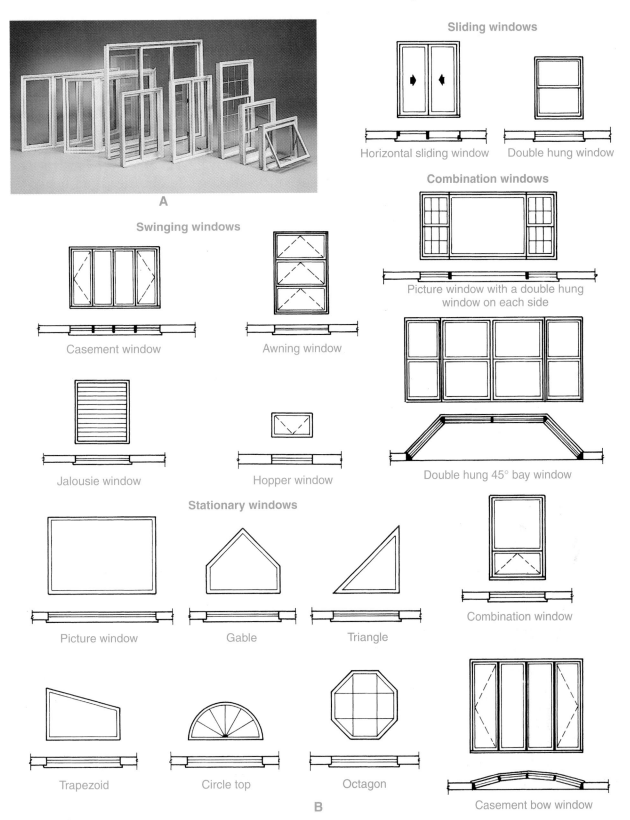

Figure 15-26. A—Typical windows used in residential construction. (Caradco) B—Exterior and plan views of residential windows.

Double-hung windows. *Double-hung windows* have two sashes, Figure 15-27. The *sashes* slide up and down in grooves formed in the window frames. The weight of each sash is usually counterbalanced or friction devices can be used to hold the sashes in the desired positions.

Muntins are small vertical and horizontal bars that separate the total glass area into smaller units. *Mullions*, not to be confused with muntins, are larger horizontal or vertical members that are placed between window units.

Figure 15-28 gives the sizes of double-hung windows produced by one manufacturer. Note that four different sizes are given for each window. The *basic unit size* represents the overall dimensions of the window unit. The *rough opening* size is the rough framed space in a wall required to install the window. *Sash opening* refers to the size of the opening inside the frame or the outside dimensions of the sash. *Glass size* is the unobstructed glass size. This would be the same as the inside dimensions of the sash.

Double-hung window details are presented in Figure 15-29. Sections are traditionally drawn at the head jamb, side jamb, and sill, in a similar fashion as drawing doors. When a number of windows are placed together to form a unit it is often necessary to draw a section of the support mullion also.

Horizontal sliding or glider windows. *Horizontal sliding windows* ordinarily have two sashes, Figure 15-30. In some models both sashes are movable; in others, one sash is fixed. A track attached to the head jamb and sill provides for movement. Rollers are usually not required for windows unless they are quite large. Figure 15-31 gives the standard sizes of one brand of horizontal sliding windows. Construction details are shown in Figure 15-32.

Swinging windows

There are four types of swinging windows most commonly used in residential construction. These are casement, awning, hopper, and jalousie windows.

Casement windows. A *casement window* has sashes hinged at the side that swing outward. A single window unit may have several sashes separated by vertical mullions or a single sash. See Figure 15-33. A casement window may be opened or closed by using a crank, a push-bar on the frame, or a handle on the sash.

Casement windows are produced in a wide variety of sizes, Figure 15-34. Single units may be placed together to form a larger section. Figure 15-35 shows the construction details for one type of casement window.

The hinge position on a hinged window may be shown in the exterior elevation view by using a dashed line, as shown in Figure 15-36. It is usually advisable to indicate the direction of swing in this manner.

Awning windows. An *awning window* has sashes that are hinged at the top and swing out at an angle and resembles an awning when open, Figure 15-37. An awning window may have several sashes or only a single sash.

Crank-operated awning windows are manufactured in a wide variety of sizes. Figure 15-38 shows some of the standard sizes offered by one company. The head jamb, side jambs, sill, and transom bar details for a crank-type awning window are shown in Figure 15-39. The *transom bar* is a horizontal divider.

Figure 15-27. This is a double-hung window styled to be reminiscent of the Victorian era. (Weather Shield Mfg., Inc.)

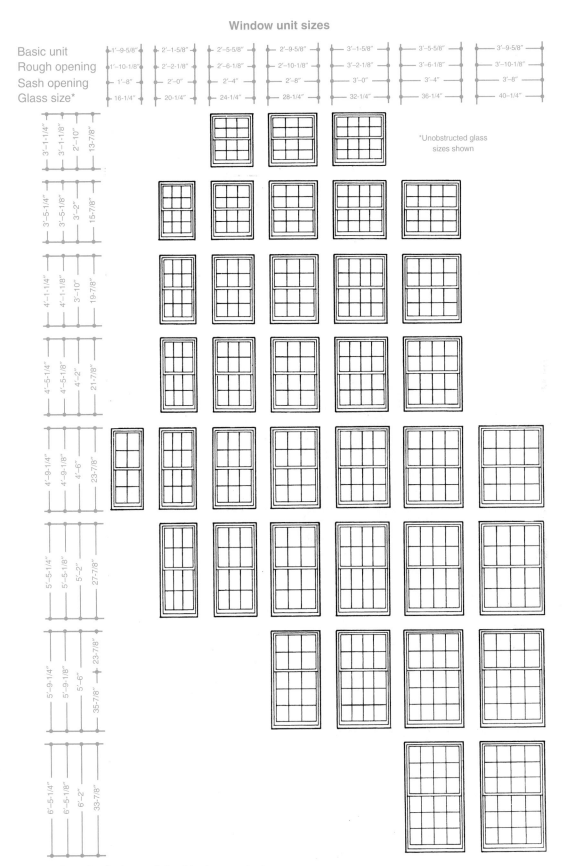

Figure 15-28. Standard sizes of double-hung windows.

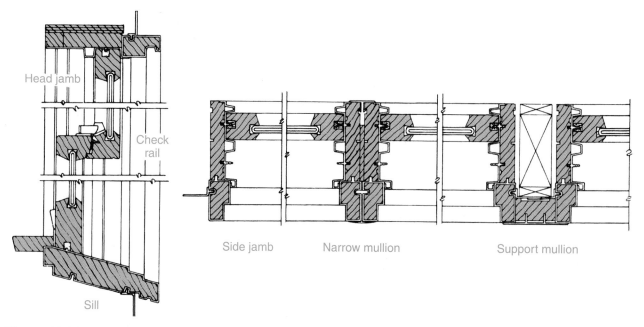

Head jamb

Check rail

Sill

Side jamb   Narrow mullion   Support mullion

Figure 15-29. Double-hung window details for a vinyl-clad wood window.

Figure 15-30. This cutaway of a vinyl-clad sliding window with insulated glass shows the details of its construction. (Caradco)

Hopper windows. The *hopper window* is usually a window that is hinged at the bottom and swings to the inside of the house. It is hinged at the bottom and is opened by a lock-handle at the top of the sash. It is usually manufactured as a single unit only, Figure 15-40. Hopper windows are popular for use as basement windows.

Hopper windows direct air upward and should be placed low on the wall, when not used in a basement, for best ventilation. They are easy to open and wash from the inside. The major disadvantage of a hopper window is the inward swing. This interferes with the use of space in front of the window.

Hopper windows are produced in a relatively small number of sizes. Figure 15-41 shows some available sizes. Section details are shown in Figure 15-42A for frame wall construction. Figure 15-42B shows a section detail through a hopper window in a concrete block wall, which is typical for a basement installation.

Jalousie windows. A *jalousie window* has a series of narrow, horizontal glass slats that are held in metal clips, which in turn are fastened to an aluminum frame. In residential applications, the slats are usually 3″ wide. The slats operate in unison similar to Venetian or miniblinds.

Jalousie windows are produced in a variety of sizes. Widths range from 18″ to 48″ in increments of 2″. Lengths are available from 17″ to 99-1/2″ in increments of 2-1/2″. Louver

Sizes and layouts

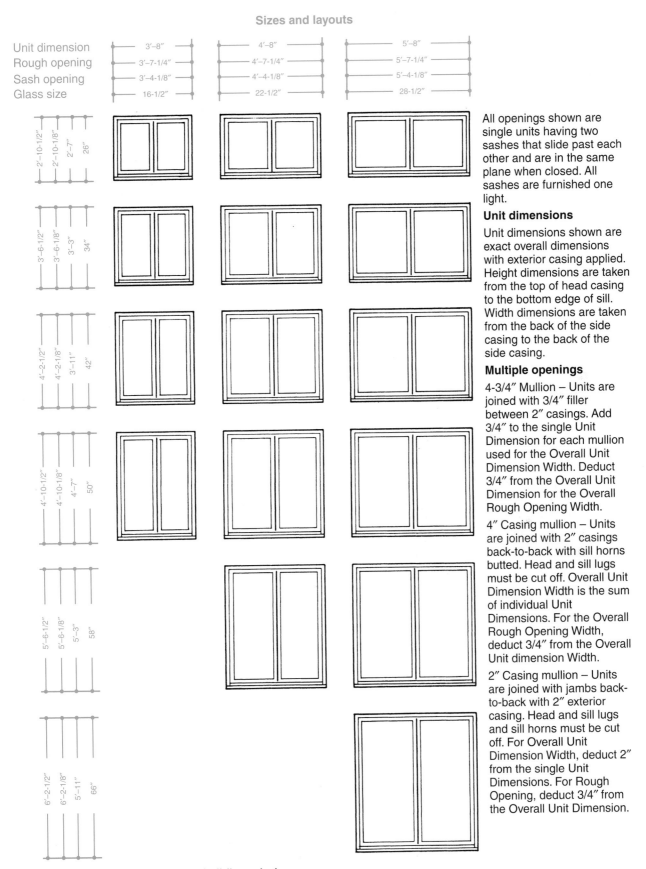

All openings shown are single units having two sashes that slide past each other and are in the same plane when closed. All sashes are furnished one light.

Unit dimensions

Unit dimensions shown are exact overall dimensions with exterior casing applied. Height dimensions are taken from the top of head casing to the bottom edge of sill. Width dimensions are taken from the back of the side casing to the back of the side casing.

Multiple openings

4-3/4″ Mullion – Units are joined with 3/4″ filler between 2″ casings. Add 3/4″ to the single Unit Dimension for each mullion used for the Overall Unit Dimension Width. Deduct 3/4″ from the Overall Unit Dimension for the Overall Rough Opening Width.

4″ Casing mullion – Units are joined with 2″ casings back-to-back with sill horns butted. Head and sill lugs must be cut off. Overall Unit Dimension Width is the sum of individual Unit Dimensions. For the Overall Rough Opening Width, deduct 3/4″ from the Overall Unit dimension Width.

2″ Casing mullion – Units are joined with jambs back-to-back with 2″ exterior casing. Head and sill lugs and sill horns must be cut off. For Overall Unit Dimension Width, deduct 2″ from the single Unit Dimensions. For Rough Opening, deduct 3/4″ from the Overall Unit Dimension.

Figure 15-31. Sizes of horizontal sliding windows.

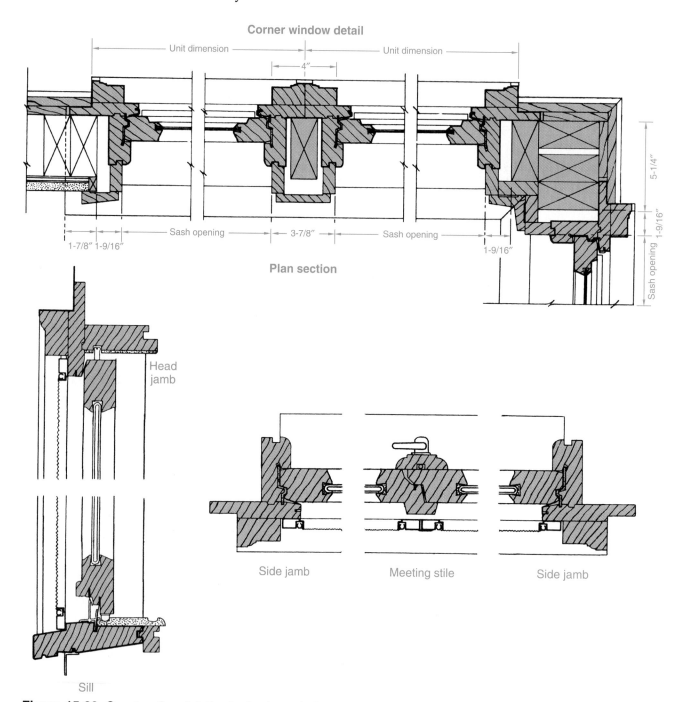

Figure 15-32. Construction details of a horizontal sliding window.

Figure 15-33. Casement windows are hinged on their side and can be operated with a hand crank. (Marvin Windows)

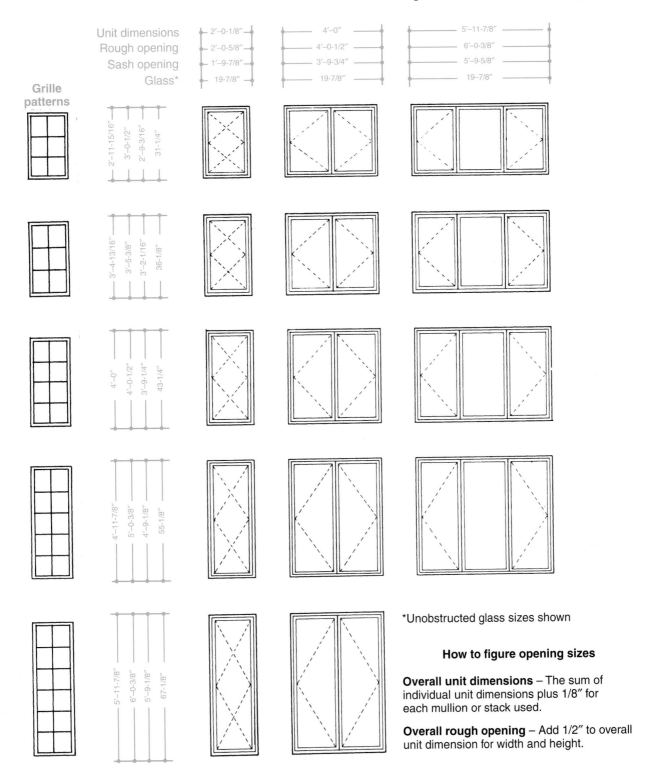

Figure 15-34. Standard casement window sizes.

*Unobstructed glass sizes shown

How to figure opening sizes

Overall unit dimensions – The sum of individual unit dimensions plus 1/8″ for each mullion or stack used.

Overall rough opening – Add 1/2″ to overall unit dimension for width and height.

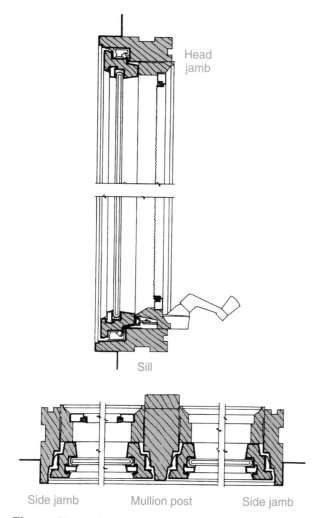

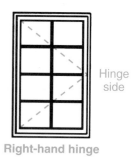

Left-hand hinge   Right-hand hinge

Figure 15-36. A dashed line may be used to indicate the hinged side of windows.

Figure 15-35. Construction details of a casement window.

Figure 15-37. An awning window swings out and resembles an awning when open. (Caradco)

(slat) lengths are usually 2″ shorter than the window width (called the buck size). Head jamb, side jamb, sill, and mullion details for an aluminum jalousie window are shown in Figure 15-43.

Fixed windows

The purpose of fixed windows is to provide a view and/or admit light. They do not permit ventilation. Fixed windows are more likely to be custom made and, therefore, may be sized for a specific application. Since they do not open, weather stripping, hardware, and screens are not required. Examples of fixed windows include picture windows, circle top windows, and special shapes.

Picture windows. *Picture windows* are fixed-glass units and are usually rather large. The term "picture window" is used because the view is framed, like a picture. These windows are often the center unit of a group of regular windows. See Figure 15-44.

Picture windows may be purchased in standard sizes or custom-made on the job. Figure 15-45A gives the standard sizes of picture window units produced by one manufacturer. Figure 15-45B illustrates the construction details of a manufactured picture window.

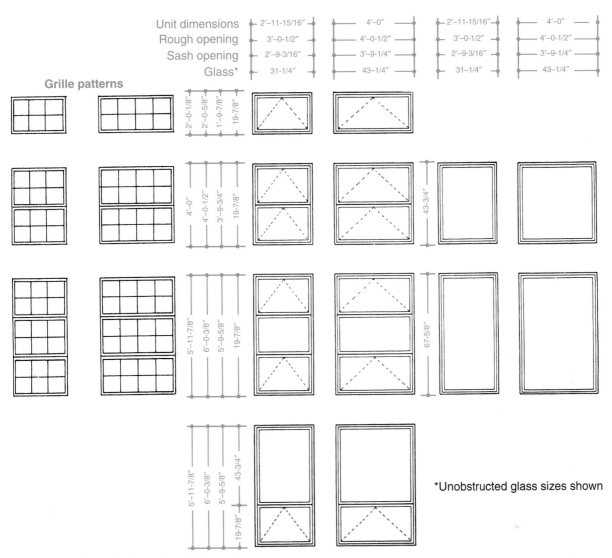

Figure 15-38. Standard awning window sizes.

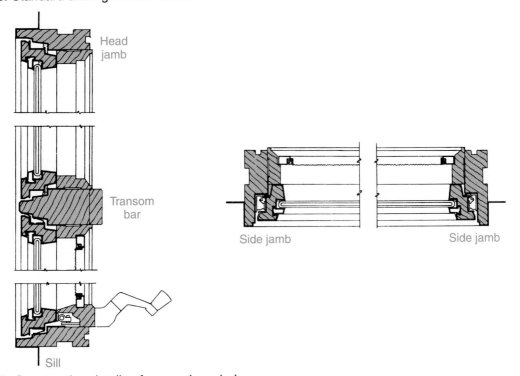

Figure 15-39. Construction details of an awning window.

Figure 15-40. Hopper windows are popular for basement applications. (Andersen Corporation)

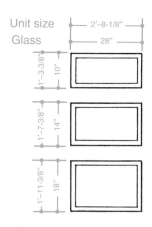

Figure 15-41. Common hopper window sizes.

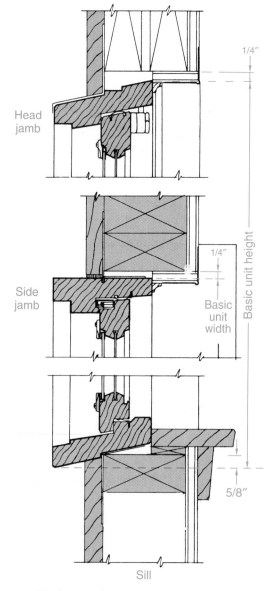

Single frame wall construction with drywall interior returned into jambs. Note position of unit in wall.

A

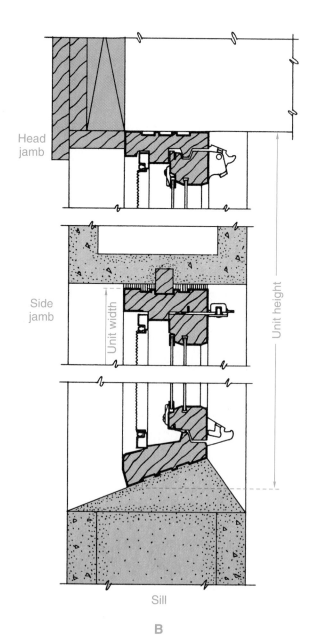

Sill

B

Figure 15-42. Construction details of hopper windows. A—In frame wall construction. B—In concrete block wall construction.

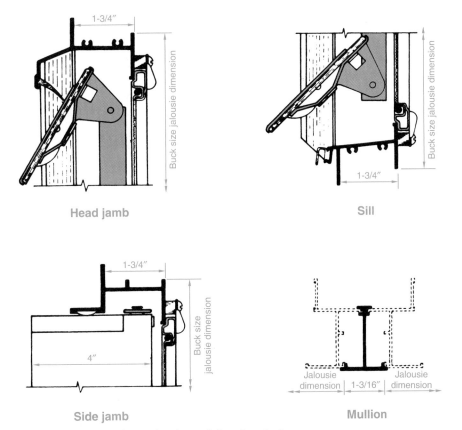

Figure 15-43. Construction details of an aluminum jalousie window.

Figure 15-44. The center window is a picture window and consists of a large, fixed glass section. The design element of dividers in the adjacent double-hung windows is carried over to the picture window. Note: The three windows as a unit may be considered a bay window. (Pella/Rolscreen Company)

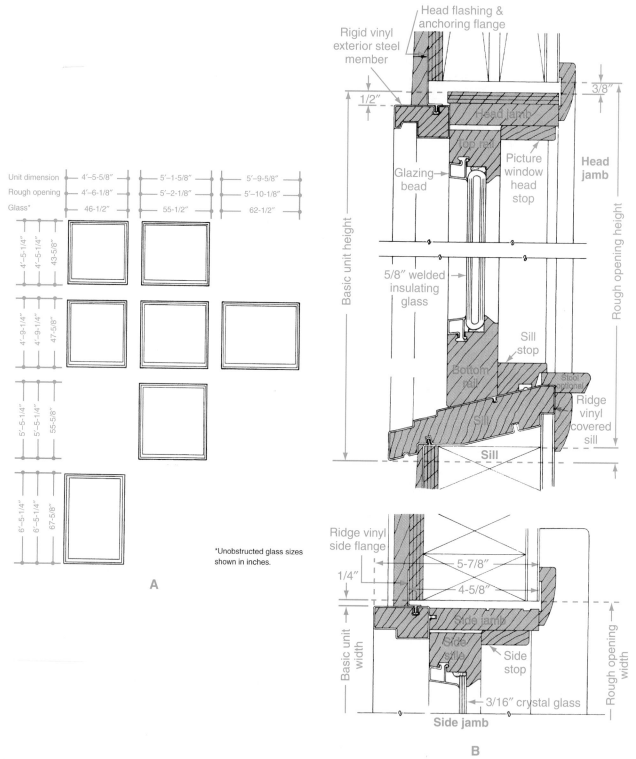

Figure 15-45. A—Standard picture window sizes in sash units. B—Construction details of a picture window.

Circle top windows. *Circle top windows* are circular windows typically installed above another window. They are available in quarter circles, half circles, ellipses, or full circles. Circle tops can be installed as single units or joined to other types of windows, Figure 15-46. Figure 15-47A shows the standard sizes produced by one manufacturer. A typical construction detail of a manufactured circle top window is shown in Figure 15-47B.

Figure 15-46. Circle top windows. A—With a casement window in a single unit. (Shouldice) B—In combination with a door and double-hung windows. (Peachtree Doors, Inc.)

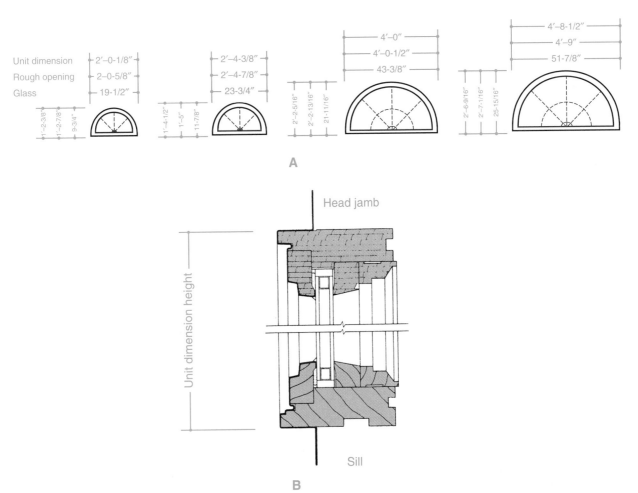

Figure 15-47. A—Typical standard sizes of circle top windows. B—Construction details of a circle top window.

Special-shape windows. *Special-shape windows* provide a wide range of interesting design options that can be used to individualize residential structures, Figure 15-48. These units are fixed windows in made-to-order shapes and sizes. If produced by the same manufacturer as other windows in the house, they may be combined with most any standard window to create a dramatic effect. Figure 15-49 shows some of the most popular special-shape windows.

Combination windows

Combination windows are a mixture of two or more types of windows. The three most popular types include bay windows, bow windows, and picture windows combined with swinging or sliding windows.

Bay and bow windows are combination windows that project out from the structure, Figure 15-50. They may be constructed using most any kind of windows including double-hung, casement, and fixed panels.

Bay windows. *Bay windows* generally have a double-hung window on either side of a fixed center window. The side windows are normally placed at 45° to the exterior wall. A typical 45° bay window detail is shown in Figure 15-51. A variation on the bay window design is called the *box bay*, Figure 15-52. It combines a picture window parallel to the wall with two casement windows placed at 90° to the wall. Box bay windows are also called garden windows.

Bow windows. *Bow windows* are a combination of windows that form an arc extending outside the wall. Combinations of four to seven units are common, Figure 15-53. Bow windows are usually constructed with casement windows. Figure 15-54 shows typical plan views for several bow windows using casements.

Skylights and clerestory windows

Skylights and clerestory windows are generally used to admit light into areas of the structure that receive little or no natural light. *Skylights* are located on the roof. *Clerestory windows* are placed high on a wall. See Figure 15-55. The use of these windows, especially

A

B

C

Figure 15-48. A—This contemporary home features custom windows that enhance the overall design of the structure. (The Oshkosh, WI private residence of Chancellor Richard H. Wells and family—formerly the Alberta Kimball Home) B—This full circle window adds visual interest to the house. C—This unique custom window adds an individual touch. (Weather Shield Mfg., Inc.)

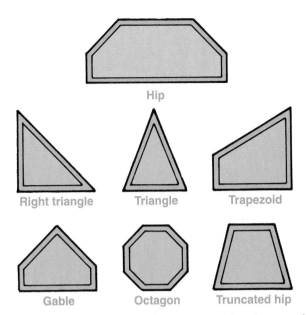

Figure 15-49. These are the most popular shapes of special-shape windows.

Figure 15-50. A unique bay window especially suited for this location. (Marvin Windows)

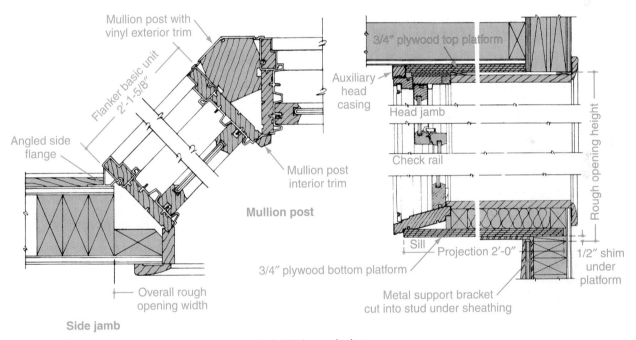

Figure 15-51. Construction details of a typical 45° bay window.

clerestory windows, can produce pleasing architectural effects. Some skylights and clerestory windows may be opened for ventilation.

Skylights are available in several basic sizes and shapes. The most common shape is rectangular and designed to fit between the roof trusses, Figure 15-56. Custom-made skylights are possible to meet most any design situation, Figure 15-57. Clerestory windows may be custom-made fixed windows or a series of standard windows, Figure 15-58.

Figure 15-52. A typical box bay window provides an excellent location for plants. (Andersen Corporation)

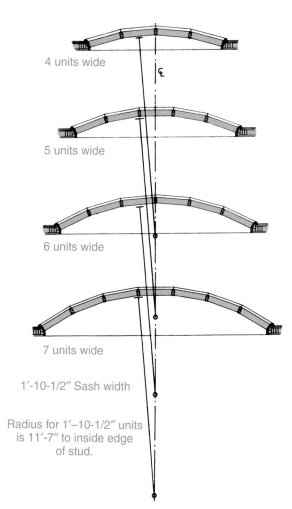

4 units wide

5 units wide

6 units wide

7 units wide

1′-10-1/2″ Sash width

Radius for 1′–10-1/2″ units is 11′-7″ to inside edge of stud.

Figure 15-54. The plan view layout for several casement bow windows.

Figure 15-53. This large bow window provides a panoramic view. (Pozzi Wood Windows)

Figure 15-55. A unique application of both clerestory windows and skylights. (KraftMaid Cabinetry)

Figure 15-56. This rectangular skylight is designed to fit between the roof trusses. (Pella/Rolscreen Company)

Figure 15-58. The clerestory windows shown here are a series of standard windows. (Manufactured Housing Institute)

Figure 15-57. These custom skylights provide a contemporary accent to the ceiling of this "retro-styled" kitchen. (Lis King)

Window Schedules

A *window schedule* provides information about all windows in a structure such as type of window, size, identifying symbol, manufacturer's number, and installation. The window schedule may be placed on the same sheet as the floor plan or elevation, if space permits. Otherwise, it may be located on one of the other drawings. Care must be taken to ensure that all windows are listed on the schedule and are properly identified. A sample window schedule is shown in Figure 15-59.

Window schedule						
Sym.	Quan.	Type	Rough opening	Sash size	Manufacturer's number	Remarks
A	6	Casement	3′–6-1/8″ × 5′-1″	3′–2-1/4″ × 4′–9-1/4″	3N3	Primed, screens, insluating glass
B	1	Casement	3′–6-1/8″ × 3′–3-1/4″	3′–2-1/4″ × 3′–1-1/2″	2N3	Primed, screens, insluating glass
C	1	Casement	5′–6-1/2″ × 8′–4-1/2″	5′–2-5/8″ × 8′–1″	5N5	Primed, screens, insluating glass
D	1	Casement	2′–5-7/8″ × 3′–5-1/4″	2′–2″ × 3′–1-3/4″	2N2	Primed, screens, insluating glass
E	5	Hopper	1′–8″ × 5′–5″	1′–4″ × 5′–2″	314	Exterior casing or subsill not included
F	2	Fixed	2′–4″ × 6′–9-1/4″	See remarks	Custom	Glass size – 2′–0″ × 6′–8″ insul.

Figure 15-59. This typical window schedule layout includes the necessary information.

Internet Resources

www.alcoahomes.com
   Aluminum Company of America (ALCOA) Building Products, Inc

www.caradco.com
   Caradco, a manufacturer of wood windows and patio doors

www.hurd.com
   Hurd Windows and Patio Doors

www.marvin.com
   Marvin Windows and Doors

www.mihomeproducts.com
   MI Home Products, a manufacturer of windows and doors

www.pella.com
   Pella Corporation, a manufacturer of windows and doors

www.pinecrestinc.com
   Pinecrest, Inc., a manufacturer of fine custom wood products

www.pozzi.com
   Pozzi Wood Windows

www.velux.com
   Velux, supplier of roof windows and skylights

www.windsorwindows.com
   Windsor Windows and Doors

Review Questions – Chapter 15

Write your answers on a separate sheet of paper. Do not write in this book.

1. List five functions of doors and windows.

2. Name eight types of interior doors.

3. Interior flush doors are usually _____ thick.

4. The horizontal members in panel doors are called _____ and vertical members are called _____.

5. The main use of bi-fold doors in residential construction is for _____.

6. Standard height for most interior and exterior doors is _____.

7. A door that hangs from a track mounted on the head jamb and slides into the wall when opened is a _____ door.

8. A door that swings through a 180° arc is called a _____ door.

9. Name two ways in which exterior doors are different from interior doors.

10. Exterior doors are usually _____ wide.

11. The most common type of garage door is the _____ type.

12. Door and window construction details are usually section drawings cut through the _____, _____, and _____.

13. What is the function of a drip cap?

14. The glass area should be at least _____ percent of the floor area of any room.

15. Name one type of window that does not provide ventilation.

16. Name four different types of windows.

17. The small vertical and horizontal bars that separate the total glass area into smaller units are called _____.

18. What does the rough opening size of a window represent?

19. Which window is hinged at the side and swings out?

20. A window that is commonly used in basements is the _____ window.

21. Information about all windows shown in the architectural drawings is recorded on a _____.

Suggested Activities

1. Make a list of the types and sizes of doors and windows in your home. Obtain sales literature from various manufacturers for the doors and windows on your list.

2. Build a scale model of an exterior or interior door, jambs, and rough framing. Use CADD to make plan, elevation, and section drawings. Present the model and drawings to the class explaining the features.

3. Select a floor plan for a small- to medium-size house. Using CADD, draw the floor plan. Then, plan the windows for the house following the guidelines presented in this chapter for ventilation, light, and view. Insert window symbols into the walls. Design and draw new symbols as needed. Finally, create a window schedule for the house.

4. Visit a local lumber company and examine the cutaway models of the windows they carry. Measure the various parts of one model and prepare a sketch. Identify the type of window and the manufacturer. Collect any specification data about the windows that you can and bring the material to class for reference purposes.

5. Using CADD, draw various window and door symbols. Add these to your symbols library for future use.

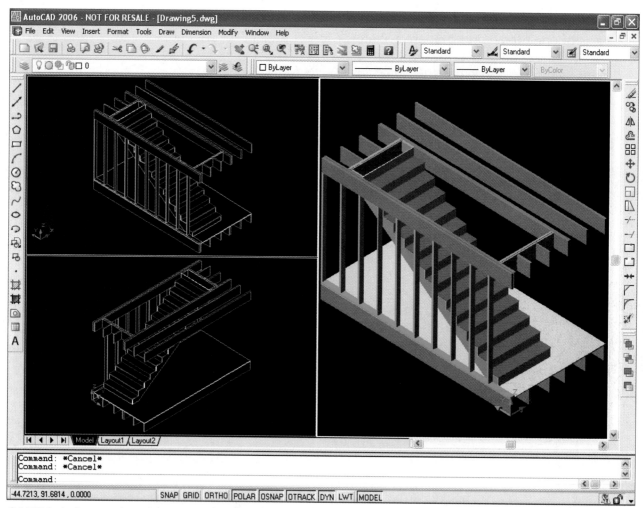

CADD is being used to plan a set of stairs. This particular project is being developed as a solid model.

Stairs 16

Objectives

After studying this chapter, you will be able to:

➤ Define common stair terminology.

➤ Explain the appropriate use of the various stair designs.

➤ Design a stairway for a residential structure.

➤ Draw structural details for main stairs.

➤ Perform stair calculations for a residential stairway.

➤ Identify model code requirements for handrails and guardrails.

Key Terms

Balusters
Circular Stairs
Double-L Stairs
Enclosed Stairs
Guardrails
Handrails
Headroom
Housed Stringer
L Stairs
Landing
Main Stairs
Narrow U Stairs
Newel
Nosing
Open Stairs
Plain Stringer

Rise
Riser
Run
Service Stairs
Spiral Stairs
Stairway
Straight Run Stairs
Stringer
Total Rise
Total Run
Tread
U Stairs
Well Hole
Wide U Stairs
Winder Stairs

A *stairway* or "stairs" is a series of steps that is installed between two or more floors of a building. A stairway may or may not have landings or platforms within the flight of stairs. Stairways provide easy access to various levels of the home. All styles of homes have stairs, except a ranch with no basement. The prime considerations in stair design should be easy ascent/descent and safety.

A house may have a *main stairs* from the first floor to the second floor or from a split foyer to the first floor. The main stairs are usually assembled with prefabricated parts of good quality, Figure 16-1. The treads are generally made of hardwoods such as oak, maple, or birch. Some houses may also have *service stairs* intended for frequent, heavy use. These are typically constructed on location and made of Douglas fir or pine construction lumber. Service stairs are generally of a lesser quality than main stairs.

For a home where a handicapped person will live or spend time, a stairlift or elevator may be necessary to allow access to other levels of the house. Stairlifts are available for a person to sit on or that will accommodate a person in a wheelchair.

Types of Stairs

Six general types of stairs are commonly used in residential construction. These types are straight run, L, double-L, U, winder, and spiral. Another stair type—circular—is sometimes used in very large, expensive homes.

Straight run stairs, as the name implies, have no turns, Figure 16-2. These are the stairs used most in home construction. They are not as expensive to construct as other types of

Figure 16-1. This beautiful main stairway is visible from the entrance and constructed with quality materials. (Arcways, Incorporated)

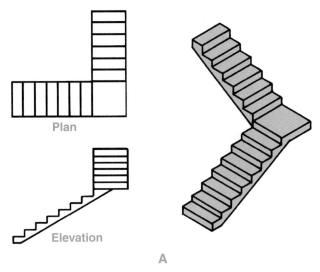

Figure 16-3. A—L stairs. B—These are long L stairs. Notice that the landing and turn are toward the top of the stairs.
(Manufactured Housing Institute)

stairs. However, straight run stairs require a long, open space that may be difficult to accommodate in the floor plan.

L stairs have one landing and turn at some point along the flight of stairs, Figure 16-3. If the landing is near the top or bottom of the stairs, the term "long L" is used to describe the stairs. L stairs are used when the space required for a straight run stairs is not available.

Double-L stairs have two 90° turns and two landings along the flight, but are not U shaped, Figure 16-4. They may be used when space is not available for either straight or L

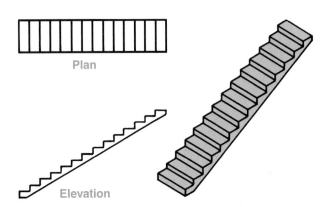

Figure 16-2. Straight run stairs.

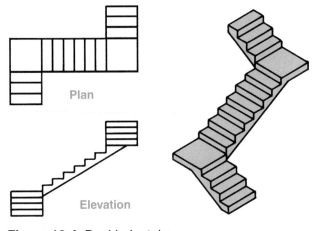

Figure 16-4. Double-L stairs.

stairs. Double-L stairs are not frequently used in residential construction. They are expensive to build and break up the floor plan.

U stairs have two flights of steps parallel to each other with a landing between, Figure 16-5. This type of stairs may be constructed as either wide U stairs or narrow U stairs. The difference between the two is the horizontal space between the flights. *Narrow U stairs* have little or no space between the flights, as shown in Figure 16-5. *Wide U stairs* have a space between each flight. This space is called a *well hole*.

Winder stairs have pie-shaped steps that are substituted for a landing, Figure 16-6. This type of stairs is used when the space is not sufficient for the L, double-L, or U stairs. The midpoint width of the triangular steps in winder stairs should be equal to the tread width of the regular steps. For instance, if the regular tread width is 10″, then each triangular step should also be 10″ at the midpoint. Winder stairs are not as safe as other types and should be avoided whenever possible.

Spiral stairs are steps that rise in a circle about a center point, Figure 16-7. These stairs are gaining in popularity and can be very decorative. Spiral stairs may be used where little space is available. Most spiral stairs are made from welded steel. However, they can be constructed from modular wood components. Several manufacturers supply components and finished stairs. Spiral stairs are not very safe since they generally have triangular steps similar to winder stairs.

Circular stairs are trapezoidal steps that rise along an irregular curve or arc. These stairs are custom made. Many fine, large homes utilize these stairs, Figure 16-8. Circular stairs require a lot of space and are expensive to build.

Stair Terminology

Several terms are associated with stairs. The following list defines the terms you must understand before beginning the design of stairs. Refer to Figure 16-9, Figure 16-10,

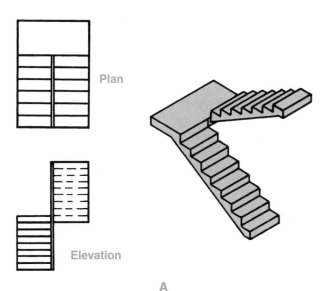

A

B

Figure 16-5. A—U stairs. B—These stairs are narrow U stairs. Notice the lack of a well hole. (California Redwood Association)

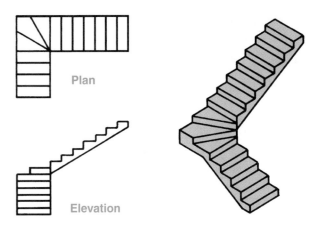

Figure 16-6. Winder stairs.

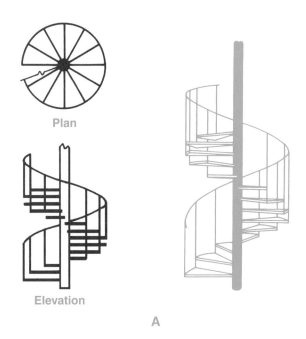

Plan

Elevation

A

B

Figure 16-7. A—Spiral stairs. B— These decorative spiral stairs are made from prefabricated parts. (Arcways, Incorporated)

Figure 16-11, Figure 16-12, and Figure 16-13 as you study this list.

- *Balusters:* Vertical members that support the handrail on open stairs.
- *Enclosed stairs:* Stairs that have a wall on both sides; also known as closed, housed, or box stairs.
- *Headroom:* The shortest clear vertical distance measured between the nosing of the treads and the ceiling. The minimum headroom is 6'-6". However, some organizations may recommend a different minimum. For example, FHA recommends a minimum of 6'-8".
- *Housed stringer:* A stringer that has been routed or grooved to receive the treads and risers.
- *Landing:* The floor area at either end of the stairs and possibly at some point between, as in the case of an L stairs.
- *Newel:* The main posts of the handrail at the top, bottom, and points where the stairs change direction.
- *Nosing:* The rounded projection of the tread that extends past the face of the riser.
- *Open stairs:* Stairs that have no wall on one or both sides.
- *Plain stringer:* A stringer that has been cut or notched to fit the profile of the stairs.
- *Rise:* The distance from the top surface of one tread to the same position on the next tread.
- *Riser:* The vertical face of a step.
- *Run:* The distance from the face of one riser to the face of the next.
- *Stringer:* A structural member that supports the treads and risers; also called the carriage.
- *Total rise:* The total floor-to-floor height of the stairs.
- *Total run:* The total horizontal length of the stairs.
- *Tread:* The horizontal member of each step on which a person steps.

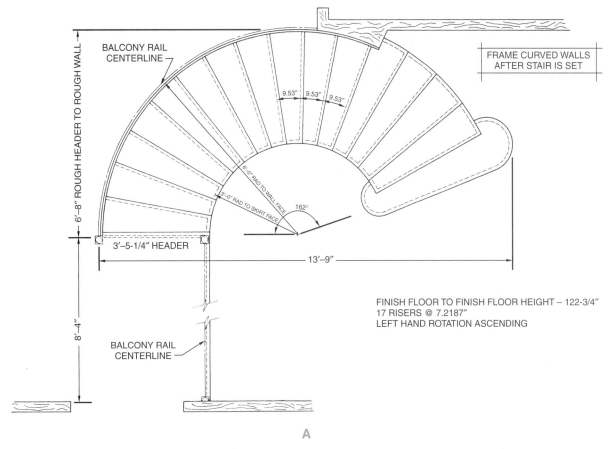

BALCONY RAIL CENTERLINE

6'-8" ROUGH HEADER TO ROUGH WALL

FRAME CURVED WALLS AFTER STAIR IS SET

9.53" 9.53" 9.53"

6'-0" RAD TO WALL FACE

3'-0" RAD TO SKIRT FACE

162°

3'-5-1/4" HEADER

13'-9"

8'-4"

BALCONY RAIL CENTERLINE

FINISH FLOOR TO FINISH FLOOR HEIGHT – 122-3/4"
17 RISERS @ 7.2187"
LEFT HAND ROTATION ASCENDING

A

B

Figure 16-8. A—Plan view of typical circular stairs. (Arcways, Incorporated) B—Ample space is available in this gracious home for a circular stairway. (Pittsburgh Corning Corporation)

Figure 16-9. The newel, handrail, and balusters are identified on this stairway. These are open stairs.

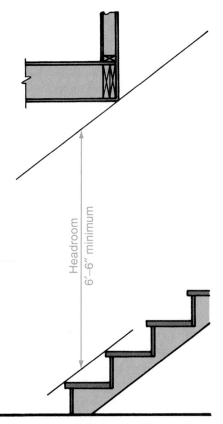

Figure 16-10. Sufficient headroom is an important consideration in the design of stairs. The minimum is 6'-6", but some organizations may have other recommendations. FHA, for example, recommends a minimum of 6'-8".

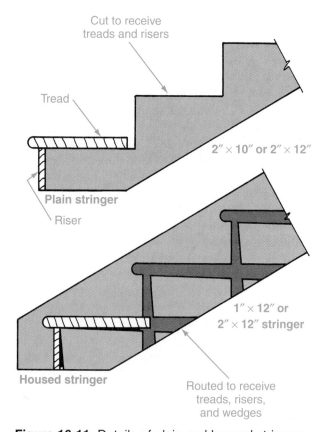

Figure 16-11. Details of plain and housed stringers.

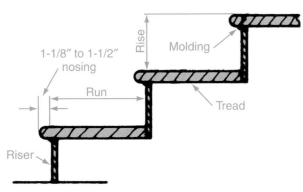

Figure 16-12. Tread and riser terms.

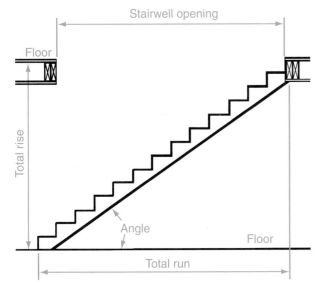

Figure 16-13. Critical stair dimensions.

Designing with CADD

Many AEC CADD programs have features to aid the drafter in creating stairs that are safe and of a structurally sound design. These features may come with the software or may need to be purchased as a special add on. In addition, some large manufacturers provide software to aid in specifying their product. Figure 16-14 shows a residential design incorporating exterior stairs that were designed using CADD.

Stair Design

Properly designed and constructed stairs must support the weight required by the application. They will also be wide enough to provide easy passage of people and furniture. The proper slope for stairs is between 30° and 35°, Figure 16-15.

Figure 16-16 illustrates a stair design that is simple and appropriate for some types of construction. This type of stairs is called open riser stairs. Notice that the stairway is open, has large treads, and does not have risers.

Figure 16-14. The stairs on this home were drawn using CADD software. (Helmuth A. Geiser, member AIBD)

Figure 16-15. These exterior stairs are constructed at the proper angle to afford safe travel to the upper level of the condo.

Figure 16-16. This is an open riser stairway. Notice the large treads and lack of risers. (Western Wood Products Association)

Stringers

The main supporting members of the stairs are the stringers. Several types of stringers are used, but plain stringers and housed stringers are the most common. Figure 16-11 shows these two types of stringers. Usually two stringers are sufficient. However, a main stairway should not be less than 3'-0" wide. Therefore, if the width of the stairs exceeds 3'-0", a third stringer is required. The extra stringer is placed midway between the outside stringers and under the treads and risers.

Plain stringers are generally cut from 2" × 12" straight-grain fir. The treads are usually 2" fir or other softwood and the risers 1" white pine. The treads and risers are nailed directly to the stringers. This type of construction is used for service stairs and occasionally for main stairs if they are to be carpeted. Stairs with plain stringers are sturdy, but they tend to squeak and do not have a finished appearance.

Housed stringers are made from finished lumber and are generally purchased precut or preassembled. However, the stringers may be cut from 1" × 12" or 2" × 12" lumber. Grooves 1/2" deep are usually routed in the stringers to hold the treads and risers. The bottom and back sides of the grooves are wider than the thickness of the treads and risers so that wedges may be driven in to hold them in place. Figure 16-17 illustrates how the wedges are inserted in the grooves. The treads, risers, and wedges are glued and nailed in place.

Treads and Risers

The two other primary parts of a set of stairs are the treads and risers. Standard treads are available in 1-1/4" oak in 10-1/2" and 11-1/2" widths. Both widths are 1-1/16" thick actual size. The rounded nose is not included in calculations. A tread width of 10-1/2" is the most popular choice. Risers are 3/4" thick actual size and vary in width depending on the slope of the stairs. The ideal riser height is between 7" and 7-5/8". Clear white pine is the customary riser material.

The slope of stairs may be specified in degrees or as a ratio of the rise to run or riser to tread. Several rules have been devised for

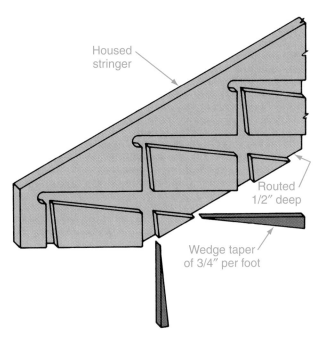

Figure 16-17. Wedges are used in a housed stringer to help hold the treads and risers in place. Treads, risers, and wedges are glued and nailed to the stringer.

Figure 16-18. These stairs in an older home violate Rule 1 of good stair design because they slope at close to 45°, rather than the appropriate 30° to 35°. (Brad L. Kicklighter)

calculating the slope of stairs. Four of these rules are:

- **Rule 1.** The slope of the stairs should be between 30° and 35°. Many older stairs are too steep and, therefore, not safe. Figure 16-18 shows an example of such a case.
- **Rule 2.** The sum of two risers and one tread should equal 25″.
- **Rule 3.** The product of the riser height multiplied by the tread width should equal approximately 75″.
- **Rule 4.** The sum of one riser and one tread should equal 17″ to 18″.

If a 10″ tread is used in an example for each of the rules, the following riser heights will be required.

	Tread Width	Riser Height	Approximate Slope
Rule 1	10″	7″	35°
Rule 2	10″	7-1/2″	37°
Rule 3	10″	7-1/2″	37°
Rule 4	10″	7″ to 8″	35° to 38°

In these examples, a riser height of 7″ is the only one that creates stairs that fall within the

proper slope angle. However, the slope angle can be reduced by increasing the tread width. For example, if the tread width is 10-1/2″ then the riser height would be 7-1/4″. Using Rule 2, this combination would result in an angle slightly less than 35°. A ratio of 7-1/4″ to 10-1/2″ is considered ideal.

The first rule generally will not be applied to service stairs since they are normally steeper than main stairs. However, if the treads are 10″ wide, the riser should be between 5-3/4″ and 7″ to produce a 30° to 35° slope. A riser height of less than 7″ is considered too short; therefore, a 7:10 ratio and 35° slope are acceptable for service stairs.

A stairway must provide a handrail for support while ascending or descending the stairs. Unless the stairs are very wide, one rail is sufficient. The recommended height of the handrail is shown in Figure 16-19. Note that the height is greater at a landing than along the incline. Also, refer to the section *Code Requirements For Handrails and Guardrails* later in this chapter.

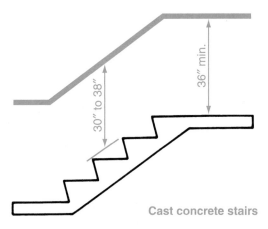

Figure 16-19. Recommended handrail heights for all stairs.

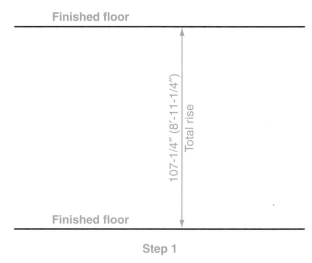

Figure 16-20. The first step in drawing stairs is to determine the total rise and lay out the finished floor lines.

Stair Calculations and Drawing Procedure

The following procedure may be used to determine the number and size of treads and risers for a set of stairs. This procedure can be used with manual drafting or CADD.

1. Determine the total rise of the stairs. The total rise is calculated by adding the distance from finished lower floor to finished ceiling, the thickness of the ceiling material, the width of the floor joists, the thickness of the subfloor, and the thickness of the finished floor, as shown below.

Finished lower floor to finished ceiling	8'-0"
Thickness of ceiling material (drywall)	1/2"
Width of the floor joists (2" × 10" lumber)	9-1/4"
Thickness of the subfloor (1/2" plywood)	1/2"
Thickness of the finished floor and underlayment	1"
Total rise =	8'-11 1/4"

Since the size of each step is in inches, the total rise is converted to inches (total rise = 107-1/4"). Figure 16-20 shows the first step in drawing stairs.

2. Determine how many risers will be required by first dividing the total rise by

seven. Seven inches is an ideal riser height and, therefore, a logical place to start. When 107-1/4" is divided by seven, the result is 15.32 risers. The number of risers must be a whole number, so either 15 or 16 risers will be required. When 107-1/4" is divided by 15, a riser height of 7.15" is produced. This figure seems to be acceptable so further calculations will be based on 15 risers each 7.15" high. Figure 16-21

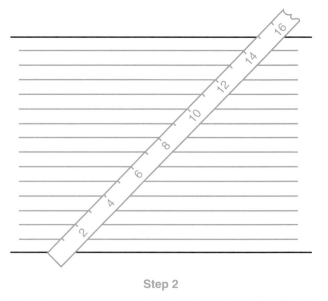

Figure 16-21. Divide the total rise into the specified number of risers. The number of risers in this example is 15.

shows how the total rise is divided into 15 equal parts. In CADD, the "divide" function can be used or you can place points every 7.15" vertically. *Each riser must be exactly the same height.*

3. Determine the tread size and total run that will yield a stair slope between 30° and 35°. A 10-1/2" tread width is common and will be used for a trial calculation. *There is always one less tread than the number of risers.* This is because the second floor serves as the top tread. The sum of two risers (7.15" + 7.15") and one tread (10-1/2") equals 24.80". This is very close to the sum of 25 required by Rule 2 and indicates that the combination will be acceptable.

   For comparison, Rule 3 and Rule 4 will be applied. Rule 3 says that the product of the riser height and tread width should be approximately 75". Therefore, if 7.15" is multiplied by 10.5" the product is 75.1". This is acceptable. Rule 4 indicates that the sum of one riser and one tread should equal 17" to 18". If 7.15" is added to 10-1/2" the result is 17.65". This is within the required range. After all examinations, the tread width will be 10-1/2".

   The total run, which is 147", is determined by multiplying the tread width (10-1/2") by the number of treads (14). Figure 16-22 shows how the total run and tread widths are drawn. In CADD, use the divide command to determine the locations of the 14 risers.

4. Darken the tread and riser lines, draw the bottom edge of the stringer, and locate stairwell rough opening size. This dimension is a function of the headroom dimension. Minimum headroom is 6'-6". Step 4 is shown in Figure 16-23.

5. Remove all construction lines. Add dimensions and notes, Figure 16-24.

Structural Details

Procedures for building stairs vary widely from one part of the country to another. Local codes often specify restrictions. Also, carpenters have their own preferences that add to the variations. Regardless of the procedure

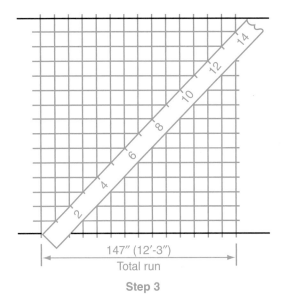

Figure 16-22. Lay out the total run and divide it into the required number of treads. The number of treads in this example is 14.

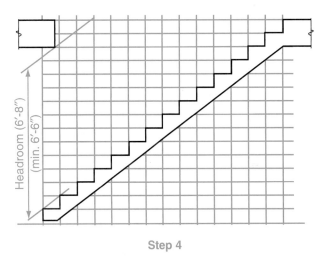

Figure 16-23. Darken the tread and riser object lines. If using CADD, trim the construction lines to create the final object lines. Also, draw the stairwell rough opening.

followed, the construction techniques must produce stairs that are sound. Figure 16-25 shows the rough framing for open, straight run stairs with plain stringers. Ordinarily, this rough framing is not shown on a set of construction drawings. However, a plan view and elevation with various section details are shown. Figure 16-26 illustrates a typical stair detail drawing found in a set of residential plans.

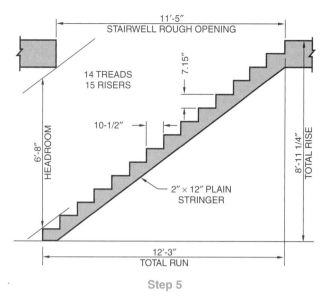

Step 5

Figure 16-24. Erase all construction lines. In CADD, you can erase the lines or turn off their layer. Also, add dimensions and notes.

Code Requirements for Handrails and Guardrails

Stairs have recently received special attention by model codes. Most state and local codes are based on national or regional model codes. Therefore, local codes generally adopt changes in the model codes. The organizations that write model codes are the Building Officials and Code Administrators International (BOCA), International Conference of Building Officials (ICBO), and Southern Building Code Congress International (SBCCI). The Council of American Building Officials (CABO) is an umbrella organization to which these groups belong and acts as a model for the other codes.

All codes require railings on stairs and ramps. Railings come in two varieties: handrails

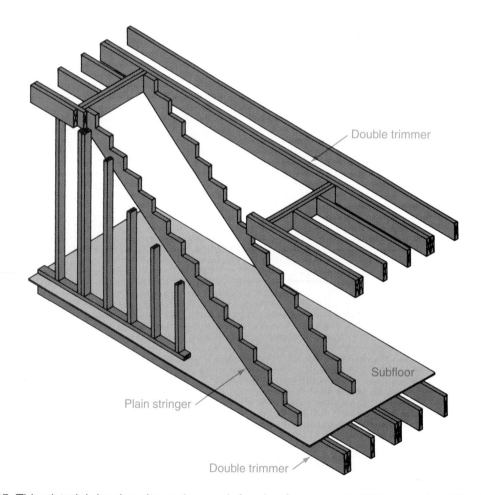

Figure 16-25. This pictorial drawing shows the rough framing for open, straight run stairs with plain stringers.

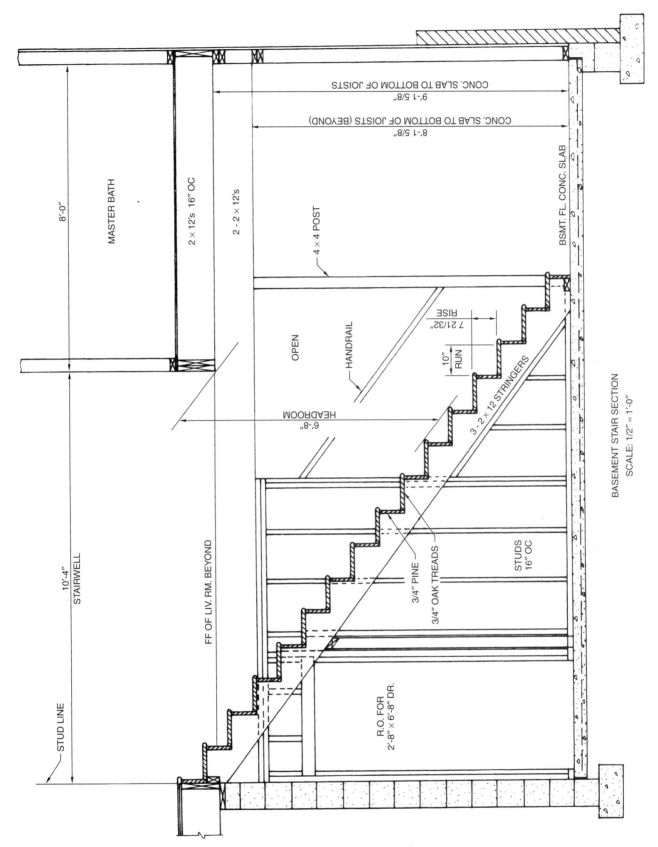

Figure 16-26. This is a typical stair detail that might be found on a set of residential drawings.

and guardrails. *Handrails* help people steady themselves as they traverse areas like stairs and ramps where they might slip, trip, or fall. Handrails usually consist of a single rail installed at a specified height. *Guardrails* keep people from falling over the edge of a balcony or off the side of a staircase. Guardrails must extend from the code-mandated height down to a specified distance above the floor. The guardrail is formed by the vertical baluster beneath the handrail. The BOCA National Building Code requires the following for dwellings.

- Handrail Height: 30" to 38" above the tread nosing.
- Handrail Finger Space: Between 1-1/2" and 3-1/2".
- Maximum Handrail Size: 1-1/4" to 2" circular; 2-1/4" maximum cross section for other shapes.
- Handrail Strength: Able to resist a 200 lb. concentrated load applied at any point.
- Guardrail Height: 36" minimum on stairs and landings that are 30" above grade.
- Baluster Spacing: Spaced so that a 4" sphere cannot pass through any opening.
- Space Below Lower Stair Rail: Spaced so that a 6" sphere cannot pass through.

The railing as a system must meet several minimum code requirements for loading and impact. For example, the top railing in a guardrail system must be able to resist a concentrated load of 200 pounds applied in any direction at any point along its length. In another test, the railing must resist a uniform load of 50 pounds per linear foot applied horizontally concurrently with a uniform load of 100 pounds per linear foot applied vertically downward. Concentrated and uniform loads are not applied simultaneously. BOCA additionally requires that the entire railing system resist an overall force of 25 psi applied laterally to the surface. This test includes the spaces between railings.

In response to these requirements, manufacturers limit the length of their railing assemblies according to the particular material's capacity for loading. Therefore, lengths generally range from 3' to 12'. As a general rule, PVC has less than 18% of the longitudinal tensile strength of a similar aluminum or fiber reinforced plastic (FRP) section. Tensile strength in the transverse direction (across the railing) presents a different picture. FRP has one-third the tensile strength of aluminum, but more than 1.6 times that of PVC. Be sure to consult the code that applies in your area when specifying handrails and guardrails.

Adaptations for Special Needs

Stairs can be a significant obstacle for a disabled person. If a person has difficulty walking but can still use stairs, the stairway may be adapted by simply installing sturdy handrails on both sides of the stairway. In addition, the treads should be covered with a nonskid surface and risers should be closed, not open. Ideally, risers should be lower and the treads wider than normal, which would require rebuilding an existing stairway. These features can easily be incorporated into stairs in new construction.

Some disabilities prevent a person from using stairs at all. In these cases, other adaptations must be implemented. For example, an existing stairway may need to be retrofitted with a stairlift. The installation of an elevator or ramp may also be required.

Stairlifts/Elevators

Installing a stairlift is a consideration for people who cannot climb stairs. A stairlift carries a person up and down on a special seat built into a fixture installed on the wall. Some stairlifts are constructed to lift a person seated in a wheelchair.

Installing an elevator is another alternative. In an existing home, a large closet may be converted into an elevator. In new construction, this feature can easily be incorporated into the design in the most efficient location.

Ramps

Ramps may be installed at entries to enable disabled persons to enter a structure. Ramps are required for those persons in wheelchairs. Ramps should have nonslip surfaces and, if possible, protection from rain, snow, and ice.

The recommended slope for a ramp is 1' rise for every 12' of distance, or a ratio of 1:12. In other words, to access a height of 3', the minimum ramp length is 36'. If a more gradual slope is required, a longer ramp should be planned.

The maximum length of a ramp section is 30'. Ramps longer than 30' should be built in two or more sections. Each section must be separated by a landing at least 5' square. Landings are necessary rest stops for individuals who have difficulty moving uphill. An entry platform should extend 18" beyond the handle side of the door to allow a wheelchair user to open the door easily.

The recommended width of a ramp is 48". However, the minimum width is 32"; 36" for wheelchair use.

Handrails should be placed on both sides of the ramp for safety. A handrail height of 3' is commonly used. Wheelchair users, however, can pull themselves up the ramp more easily when handrails are 30" high. If curbs are used, they should be placed on both sides of the ramp at least 2" high.

Internet Resources

www.acornstairlifts.com
   Acorn Stairlifts

www.arcways.com
   Arcways, Inc., a manufacturer of custom stairways

www.ibhs.org
   Institute for Business and Home Safety

www.iii.org
   Insurance Information Institute

www.lpcorp.com
   Louisiana-Pacific Corporation, a manufacturer of building materials

www.natlhardwood.org
   National Hardwood Lumber Association

www.archdigest.com
   Architectural Digest

www.sweets.com
   Sweets Catalog File

Review Questions – Chapter 16

Write your answers on a separate sheet of paper. Do not write in this book.

1. Stairs connecting the first and second floor or from a split foyer to the first floor are known as _____ stairs.

2. Identify the six general types of stairs.

3. Which type of stairs always has two landings along the flight of steps?

4. The type of stairs that has two parallel flights of steps is the _____ stairs.

5. Pie-shaped steps are generally associated with _____ stairs.

6. Vertical members that support the handrail on open stairs are known as _____.

7. Stairs with walls on both sides are known as _____ stairs.

8. Minimum headroom for stairs is _____.

9. The two main types of stringers used in home stair construction are _____ and _____ stringers.

10. The rounded part of the tread that extends past the face of the riser is the _____.

11. A stair without a wall on one or both sides is a(n) _____ stair.

12. A stringer that has been cut or notched to match the profile of the stairs is a(n) _____ stringer.

13. Define rise.

14. Define run.

15. The total floor-to-floor vertical height of the stairs is known as the _____.

16. The total horizontal length of the stairs is the _____.

17. The proper slope angle for a set of main stairs should be between _____ and _____ degrees.

18. The minimum recommended width for main stairs is _____.

19. Treads on service stairs are frequently made from softwood, but main stair treads are usually _____.

20. The ideal tread-to-riser ratio is _____ to _____.

Suggested Activities

1. Locate as many different stair designs as you can. Measure the tread width and riser height. Identify the materials used for construction. Using CADD, draw a profile of the tread and riser. Measure the slope using the appropriate CADD function. Rate the stairs as to ease of travel and safety.

2. Locate a house in your community that is under construction. Obtain permission before entering the construction site and then examine the stair framing. Measure the floor-to-floor distance and width of the stairs. If possible, interview the head carpenter and ask how a set of stairs is laid out. Report your findings to the class.

3. Using CADD, design an enclosed, straight run stairs with housed stringers. The distance from the finished floor to the finished floor is 9'-1 1/4". The distance between the finished walls is 3'-4". Provide the necessary drawings, dimensions, and notes.

4. Visit a local lumber company that sells precut stairs. Collect information and literature about these stairs. Bring this literature to class to help build a catalog file on stairs.

5. Select a basic type of stairs. Using CADD, create the necessary construction drawings. Then, build a scale model as accurately as possible. Display this model along with the construction drawings.

Fireplaces, Chimneys, and Stoves

Objectives

After studying this chapter, you will be able to:

➤ Compare various types of fireplaces that are appropriate for a residence.

➤ Identify the parts of a standard masonry fireplace and chimney.

➤ Apply the appropriate principles to design a typical fireplace.

➤ Use a fireplace design data chart.

➤ Explain the difference between a radiant and circulating stove.

Key Terms

Ash Dump
Circulating Stove
Cleanout
Cricket
Damper
Fire Chamber
Fireclay
Flue
Hearth
Inner Hearth
Prefabricated Metal
  Fireplace
Projecting Corner
  Fireplace

Radiant Heat
Radiant Stove
Saddle
Single-Face Fireplace
Smoke Chamber
Smoke Shelf
Three-Face Fireplace
Three-Way Fireplace
Two-Face Adjacent
  Fireplace
Two-Face Opposite
  Fireplace

Most everyone enjoys the sound and warmth of a blazing fire. The fireplace is often a focal point in the living room or family room. Including a fireplace in a home plan is an important design consideration, Figure 17-1. However, many homes have fireplaces that are pleasing to the eye, yet fail to operate properly. Care must be taken in the design and construction of a fireplace and chimney to make sure the fireplace will safely perform as desired.

Fireplace Design Considerations

Several types of fireplaces are being constructed in modern residences. Some are traditional in design while others are contemporary, Figure 17-2. Increasingly, metal fireplaces are finding their way into the home. Some of these are wood burning, but many are

Figure 17-1. An attractive fireplace may be the focal point of a living room. (Superior Fireplace Company)

Figure 17-2. Fireplaces come in many styles. A—Traditional. (Stone Products Corporation) B—Contemporary. (Heatilater, Inc.)

gas-fired and designed to look like a wood fire. Often, the design of the fireplace draws on the building materials for its charm, Figure 17-3.

Generally, fireplaces may be identified as single face, two-face opposite, two-face adjacent, three face, or prefabricated metal, Figure 17-4. Each type has specific design requirements that must be met if the fireplace is to perform safely and properly. These design specifications are discussed later in this chapter.

Figure 17-3. The colors in the stones used in the design of this fireplace accent the wallcovering materials in the room.

Fireplace/Chimney Terms

Several terms are associated with fireplaces and chimneys. The following list defines some of the terms that should be understood before designing a fireplace.

- *Ash dump:* The cavity below the fireplace where ashes can collect and be removed.
- *Cleanout:* A door to allow access for removal of ashes from the ash dump.
- *Damper:* Regulates airflow and prevents downdraft.
- *Fireclay:* A fire-resistant, mortar-like refractory material used as a bonding agent between the firebrick.
- *Flue:* The path for smoke to pass up the chimney.
- *Hearth:* Protects the floor from sparks.
- *Inner hearth:* The floor of the fireplace.
- *Smoke chamber:* The area just above the smoke shelf and damper.
- *Smoke shelf:* Causes downdrafts to be deflected upward.

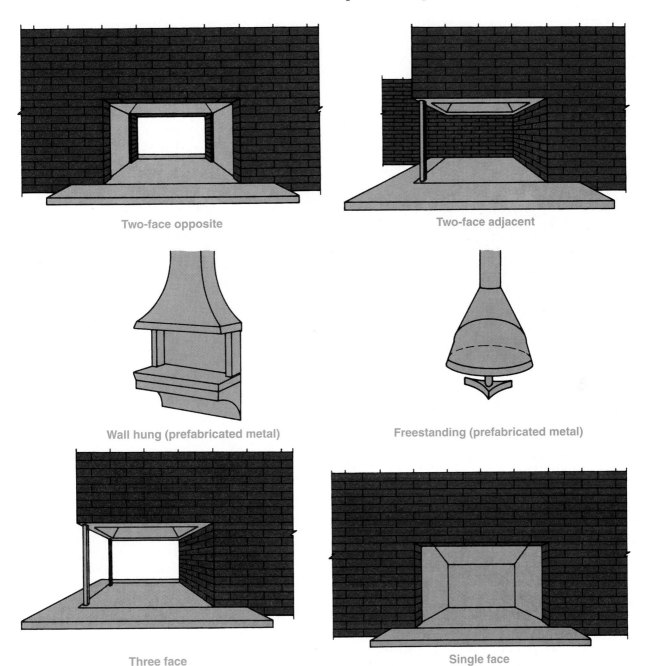

Two-face opposite

Two-face adjacent

Wall hung (prefabricated metal)

Freestanding (prefabricated metal)

Three face

Single face

Figure 17-4. There are several general types of fireplaces.

Designing with CADD

Some CADD packages include an option or function for automating the design process of fireplaces. Generally, all the drafter has to specify is the width of the opening and the desired style of fireplace. The plan view, elevations, and details are automatically generated.

Figure 17-5 shows a computer-generated rendering of a room with a fireplace.

Hearth and Fire Chamber

The hearth should extend at least 16″ in front of the fireplace to protect the floor from

Figure 17-5. The fireplace is a focal point in this computer-rendered living room/kitchen combination. (SoftPlan Systems, Inc.)

sparks, Figure 17-6. In addition, it should be constructed from a noncombustible material. In conventional construction, the hearth extends beneath the fireplace to form an inner hearth. It is usually covered with firebrick inside the fireplace and stone, slate, or ceramic tile in front of the fireplace. The hearth may be flush with the floor or raised to a desirable height.

The *fire chamber* is where the fire is contained. It is usually lined with firebrick set in fireclay. The shape of the fire chamber is critical and must be designed to direct hot gases and smoke into the throat for passage up the chimney. In addition, if the chamber is too deep, little heat will be reflected out into the room. On the other hand, if it is too shallow, the fireplace is likely to smoke into the room. The wall thickness on the back and sides of the fire chamber should be a minimum of 8″, as noted in Figure 17-6.

When space is available below the fireplace and finished floor, an ash dump is desirable. A metal trap door is located in the middle of the fireplace floor and connected to the ash chamber below. A cleanout is provided in the ash chamber for the removal of ashes.

In newer residential construction, extensive use is made of prefabricated steel, heat-circulating fireplaces. The units include not only the inner hearth and fire chamber, but also the throat, damper, smoke shelf, and smoke chamber, Figure 17-7. These units are very efficient because the sides and back consist of a double-wall passageway where the air is heated. Cool air is drawn into the passageway, heated, and returned to the room through registers located at a higher level. Installation is generally easy. Figure 17-8 shows the step-by-step procedure for installing a prefabricated, heat-circulating fireplace in frame construction.

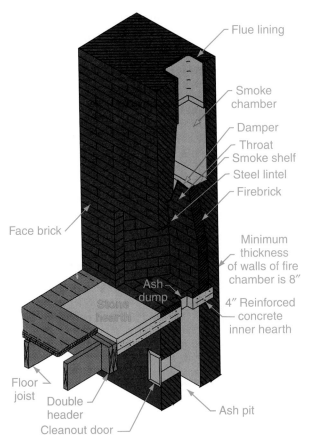

Flue lining

Smoke chamber

Damper

Throat

Smoke shelf

Steel lintel

Firebrick

Minimum thickness of walls of fire chamber is 8″

4″ Reinforced concrete inner hearth

Face brick

Ash dump

Stone hearth

Floor joist

Double header

Cleanout door

Ash pit

Figure 17-6. This three-dimensional section drawing of a fireplace shows various details of the construction.

Figure 17-7. This is a cutaway view of a prefabricated steel, heat-circulating fireplace. (Heatilator, Inc.)

Figure 17-8. Installation of a prefabricated steel, heat-circulating fireplace in frame construction. (Heatilator, Inc.)

Damper and Smoke Shelf

Every fireplace should have a damper to regulate the flow of air and stop downdrafts of cold air when the fireplace is not in operation. The damper is located in the throat of the fireplace and opens toward the back of the throat. The damper opening should be larger than the area of the flue lining and as long as the width dimension of the fireplace. It should be placed 6″ or 8″ above the top of the fireplace opening. Standard damper sizes are shown in Figure 17-9. Dampers are produced in both steel and cast iron.

The smoke shelf causes cold air flowing down the chimney to be deflected upward into the rising warm air. This action prevents down rushing cold air from forcing smoke into the room. The smoke shelf height is determined by the location of the damper. An example of a smoke shelf is shown in Figure 17-6.

The smoke chamber is the area just above the smoke shelf and damper. This is basically pyramidal in shape with the backside usually vertical. The chamber is normally constructed from brick or other masonry.

Flue

The flue begins at the top of the smoke chamber and extends to the top of the chimney. The flue usually has a clay lining. This is illustrated in Figure 17-6. Each flue

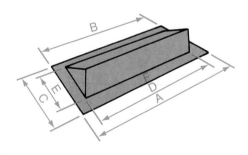

Damper specifications

Steel dampers					
	Damper dimension				
Width of fireplace	A	B	C	D	E
24″ to 26″	28-1/4″	26-3/4″	13″	24″	9-1/2″
27″ to 30″	32-1/4″	30-3/4″	13″	28″	9-1/2″
31″ to 34″	36-1/4″	34-3/4″	13″	32″	9-1/2″
35″ to 38″	40-1/4″	38-3/4″	13″	36″	9-1/2″
39″ to 42″	44-1/4″	42-3/4″	13″	40″	9-1/2″
43″ to 46″	48-1/4″	46-3/4″	13″	44″	9-1/2″
47″ to 50″	52-1/4″	50-3/4″	13″	48″	9-1/2″
51″ to 54″	56-1/4″	54-3/4″	13″	52″	9-1/2″
57″ to 60″	62-1/2″	60-3/4″	13″	58″	9-1/2″
Cast iron dampers					
	Damper dimension				
Width of fireplace	A	B	C	D	E
24″ to 26″	28″	21″	13-1/2″	24″	10″
27″ to 31″	34″	26-3/4″	13-1/2″	30″	10″
31″ to 34″	37″	29-3/4″	13-1/2″	33″	10″
35″ to 38″	40″	32-3/4″	13-1/2″	36″	10″
39″ to 42″	46″	38-3/4″	13-1/2″	48″	10″
43″ to 46″	52″	44-3/4″	13-1/2″	48″	10″
47″ to 50″	57-1/2″	50-1/2″	13-1/2″	54″	10″
51″ to 54″	64″	56-1/2″	14-1/2″	60″	11-1/2″
57″ to 60″	76″	58″	14-1/2″	72″	11-1/2″

Figure 17-9. These damper design specifications are typical of products on the market. (Donley Brothers Company)

requires at least 4″ of masonry on all sides. If a liner is not used, the wall thickness must be a minimum of 8″. Each fireplace in a structure must have its own flue. Ideally, the flue will be centered directly above the fireplace and installed in a straight vertical line. A small amount of offset is permissible; however, efficiency is reduced when the flue is not straight.

The flue must be large enough to provide the necessary updraft. A rule of thumb to follow in selecting the proper flue size is the cross-sectional area of the flue should be at least 1/10th of the fireplace opening. For example, if the fireplace opening is 32″ × 48″, the area is 1536 square inches. One-tenth of 1536 square inches is 153.6 square inches. A standard flue size that has at least this area is a 12″ × 16″ flue, which has 192 square inches. Standard flue sizes are shown in Figure 17-10. It is better to have a flue that is slightly too large than one that is too small; however, a flue that is significantly oversize will not function properly.

Proper flue size is also related to several other factors. If the height of the flue is less than 14′, the size should be increased to provide the necessary updraft. The updraft is increased by making the flue higher. Prevailing winds and surrounding trees and buildings also affect the draft. If the flue is sheltered, the size should be increased. Most codes require that the flue extend at least 2′ above the highest point of the roof, Figure 17-11.

This is a safety factor, since sparks may fly out of the top and cause a roof fire.

A single chimney may have several flues. A flue is required for a gas furnace, a gas water heater, an incinerator, and each fireplace. The efficiency of a chimney may be increased if it is placed within the house, rather than on an outside wall. The warmer the chimney, the better the performance.

Framing around Fireplace and Chimney

The chimney is a free-standing structure. It does not support any part of the house. In fact, fire codes prohibit direct contact of framing with surfaces of the fireplace or chimney. A minimum of 2″ of clearance is required between the chimney and framing. This space should be filled with a noncombustible material. The openings in the floor, ceiling, and roof through which the chimney passes must have double headers and trimmers to give the necessary support, Figure 17-12.

Clay flue liner sizes		
New sizes	**Round (dia.)**	**Old sizes**
8″ × 12″	8″	8-1/2″ × 8-1/2″
12″ × 12″	10″	8-1/2″ × 13″
12″ × 16″	12″	13″ × 13″
16″ × 16″	15″	13″ × 18″
16″ × 20″	18″	18″ × 18″
20″ × 20″	20″	20″ × 20″
20″ × 24″	22″	24″ × 24″

New flue sizes conform to the new modular dimension system. Sizes shown are nominal. Actual size is 1/2″ less each dimension. All flue liners listed above are 2′-0″ long.

Figure 17-10. Flue liners are available in round and rectangular shapes. Most are made of clay.

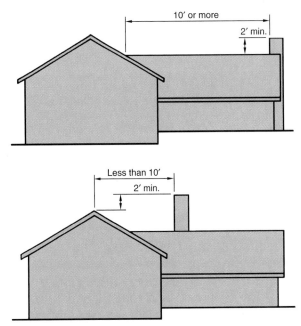

Figure 17-11. Recommended chimney heights above the roof.

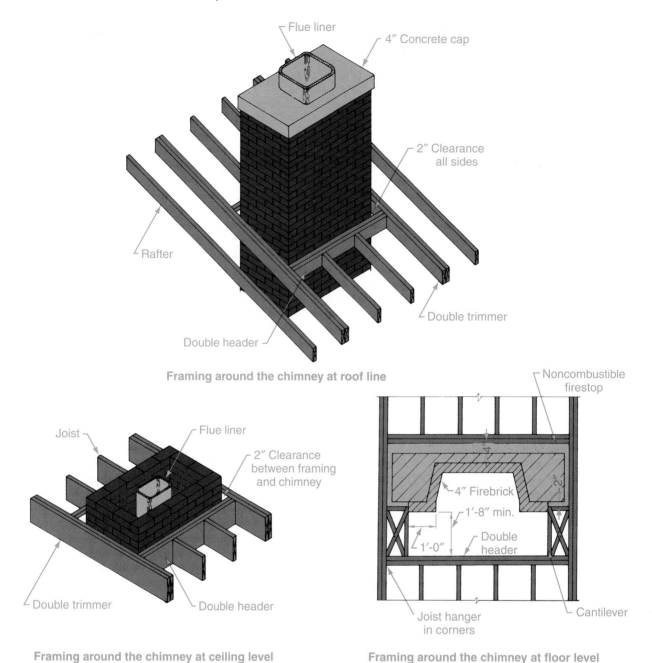

Figure 17-12. Typical framing for chimneys and fireplaces.

If a chimney is located along the ridge line (the peak or highest point) of a roof, the chance of water problems is minimized. However, if the chimney must be located along a single slope of the roof, special precautions must be taken to prevent leaking. Water can back up along the chimney and roof intersections and seep under the shingles. To prevent this, a *saddle* or *cricket* is built on the high side of the chimney to shed water. A saddle is especially necessary if the roof slope is low or the chimney is wide. Figure 17-13 shows the framing for a saddle.

The masonry above the fireplace opening must be supported by a lintel, just as over a door or window. An angle steel lintel is the most common type. This is shown in Figure 17-6. The required size of angle will vary with the width of the fireplace opening. A 3″ × 3″ × 1/4″ angle will be sufficient for an opening of 60″ wide.

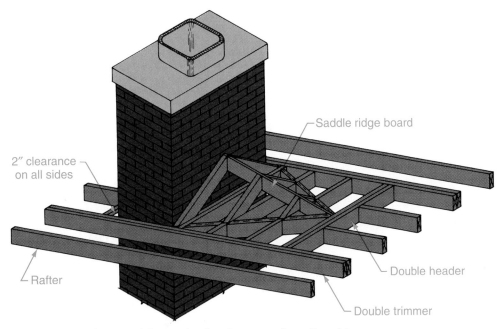

Figure 17-13. The framing for a saddle to shed water away from the chimney.

Fireplace Specifications

Generally, fireplaces may be identified as single face, two-face opposite, two-face adjacent, three face, or prefabricated metal. The type of fireplace and size of opening is the beginning point in designing a fireplace. Each type has specific design requirements that must be met if the fireplace is to be safe and perform properly. The specifications for each type are covered in the next sections.

Single-Face Fireplace

The *single-face fireplace* has a single opening on one face and is the most popular type, Figure 17-14. It is the least complicated to construct and usually functions better than the other types. Figure 17-15 provides specifications for several single-face fireplaces. The proper damper size can be determined from the chart in Figure 17-9.

Two-Face Opposite Fireplace

A *two-face opposite* fireplace is open on both the front and back sides, Figure 17-16. Its primary advantage is that two rooms can view the fireplace. Care must be taken to prevent a draft from one side to the other that may result in smoke being blown into a room. Figure 17-16 shows specifications pertaining to this type fireplace.

Figure 17-14. This is a single-face fireplace that adds to the basic architectural style of the room. (Heatilator, Inc.)

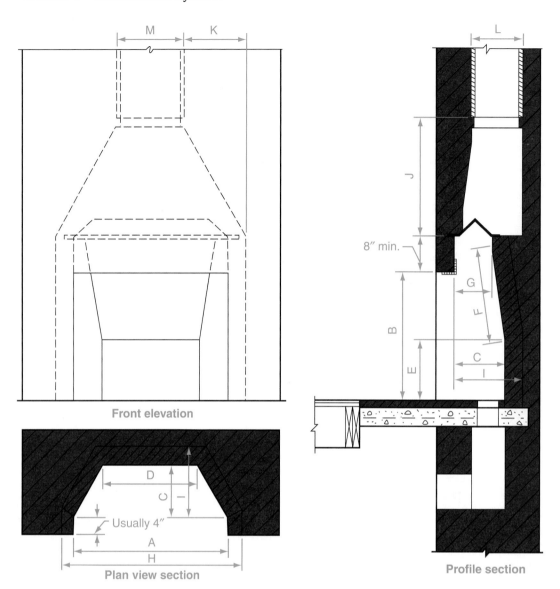

Front elevation

Plan view section

Profile section

8″ min.

Usually 4″

Design data for single-face fireplaces

Width	Height	Depth	Back	Verti-back	Slope back	Throat	Width	Depth	Smoke chamb	Flue lining sizes				
										Rectangular		Round	Modular	
A	B	C	D	E	F	G	H	I	J	K	L × M		K	L × M
24	24	16	11	14	15	8-3/4	32	20	19	11-3/4	8-1/2 × 8-1/2	8	10	8 × 12
26	24	16	13	14	15	8-3/4	34	20	21	12-3/4	8-1/2 × 8-1/2	8	11	8 × 12
28	24	16	15	14	15	8-3/4	36	20	21	11-1/2	8-1/2 × 13	10	12	8 × 12
30	29	16	17	14	18	8-3/4	38	20	24	12-1/2	8-1/2 × 13	10	13	12 × 12
32	29	16	19	14	21	8-3/4	40	20	24	13-1/2	8-1/2 × 13	10	14	12 × 12
36	29	16	23	14	21	8-3/4	44	20	27	15-1/2	13 × 13	12	16	12 × 12
40	29	16	27	14	21	8-3/4	48	20	29	17-1/2	13 × 13	12	16	12 × 12
42	32	16	29	14	23	8-3/4	50	20	32	18-1/2	13 × 13	12	17	16 × 16
48	32	18	33	14	23	8-3/4	56	22	37	21-1/2	13 × 13	15	20	16 × 16
54	37	20	37	16	27	13	68	24	45	25	13 × 18	15	26	16 × 20
60	37	22	42	16	27	13	72	27	45	27	13 × 18	15	26	16 × 20
60	40	22	42	16	29	13	72	27	45	27	18 × 18	18	26	16 × 20
72	40	22	54	16	29	13	84	27	56	33	18 × 18	18	32	20 × 20
84	40	24	64	20	26	13	96	29	67	36	20 × 20	20	36	20 × 20
96	40	24	76	20	26	13	108	29	75	42	24 × 24	22	42	20 × 20

Dimensions are in inches. Flue sizes are for a chimney height of at least 14′–0″.

Figure 17-15. Design specifications for single-face fireplaces.

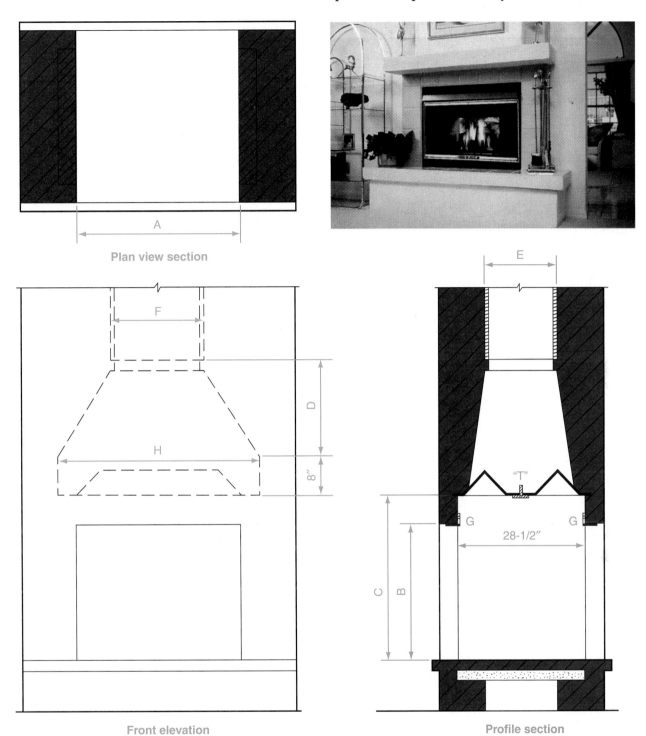

Plan view section

Front elevation

Profile section

Design data for two-face opposite fireplaces

A	B	C	D	Old flue size		Round	New mod. size		Angle G 2 req'd.	H	Tee length
				E	F		E	F			
28	24	35	19	13	13	12	12	16	36	36	35
32	29	35	21	13	18	15	16	16	40	40	39
36	29	35	21	13	18	15	16	20	42	44	43
40	29	35	27	18	18	18	16	20	48	48	47
48	32	37	32	18	18	18	20	20	54	56	55

Dimensions are in inches.
Flue sizes are for a chimney height of at least 14'-0".
Angle G is 3" × 3" × 1/4"

Figure 17-16. Design specifications for two-face opposite fireplaces. Two rooms may benefit from a two-face opposite fireplace, as shown in the photo. (Superior Fireplace Company)

Two-Face Adjacent Fireplace

A *two-face adjacent* fireplace is open on the front and one side, Figure 17-17. It may be open on the right or left side. This type is also known as a *projecting corner fireplace*. Design specifications are shown in Figure 17-17.

Three-Face Fireplace

A *three-face fireplace* is open on three sides, Figure 17-18. Ordinarily, two long sides and one short side are open. This is also known as a *three-way fireplace*. This type is somewhat of a novelty; however, it can add interest and design if the interior room layout is properly arranged. Figure 17-18 gives design specifications for the three-face type.

Prefabricated Metal Fireplaces and Stoves

Prefabricated metal fireplaces and stoves are becoming more popular as a greater number of styles are produced. These are constructed of metal and come with the firebox and internal components assembled. Some metal fireplaces are wall-mounted, some are enclosed in masonry, and others are free-standing models, Figure 17-19. These units may be purchased complete with all the necessary parts required to install them. No masonry work is needed for the wall-mounted types. The local code should be consulted prior to installation. Figure 17-20 shows installation details of a typical prefabricated metal fireplace.

Prefabricated steel, heat-circulating fireplaces are designed to draw air in from the room, heat it, and return warmed air to the room. They are manufactured in several designs, Figure 17-21. These units require framing or masonry enclosures. See Figure 17-19A. Vents are visible at the top and bottom of the unit.

Fireplace inserts are also efficient in circulating warmed air. These units are designed for existing masonry fireplaces. Figure 17-22 shows a masonry fireplace that has a metal insert with glass doors and vents.

Stoves

Wood- or coal-burning stoves generally produce more usable heat than fireplaces. They are frequently located in such a manner that heat is radiated from all sides. They are typically used as local sources of heat, rather than a total heating system, Figure 17-23. The heating efficiency of stoves varies greatly among manufacturers and models.

There are two main types of stoves: radiant stoves and circulating stoves. Both types produce *radiant heat*, which is heat that passes through the air with no assistance from air flow. A *radiant stove* warms a room only through radiant heat. However, a *circulating stove* uses air flow, as well as radiant heat, to distribute warmth throughout a room.

A circulating stove has an outer jacket to facilitate air movement. The jacket is designed to draw cold air in, warm it, and return warmed air to the room. Some stoves have a small blower to assist the air movement, others produce air flow without mechanical assistance. Circulated air flow provides more even heat than is possible with a radiant stove. Circulating stoves are safer and may be placed closer to combustible material than radiant stoves because of their lower surface temperature, Figure 17-24.

Stoves are frequently classified according to their heating efficiency. Low-efficiency stoves range from 20% to 30% efficient. Examples of low-efficiency stoves include simple box stoves, Franklin stoves, pot belly stoves, and some parlor stoves. Medium-efficiency stoves range from 35% to 50% efficient. They provide better combustion and have less air leakage into the stove. Most

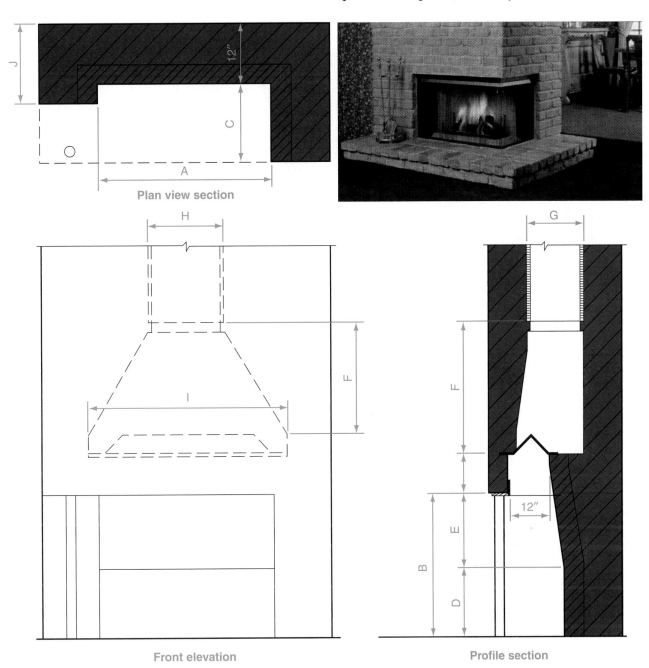

Design data for two-face adjacent fireplaces

A	B	C	D	E	F	Old flue		Round	Mod. flue		I	J	Corner post height
						G	H		G	H			
28	26-1/2	16	14	20	29-1/4	13	13	12	12	12	36	16	26-1/2
32	26-1/2	16	14	20	32	13	13	12	12	16	40	16	26-1/2
36	26-1/2	16	14	20	35	13	13	12	12	16	44	16	26-1/2
40	29	16	14	20	35	13	18	15	16	16	48	16	29
48	29	20	14	24	43	13	18	15	16	16	56	20	29
54	29	20	14	23	45	13	18	15	16	16	62	20	29
60	29	20	14	23	51	13	18	15	16	20	68	20	29

Dimensions are in inches.
Flue sizes are for a chimney height of at least 14'–0".

Figure 17-17. Design specifications for two-face adjacent fireplaces. (Superior Fireplace Company)

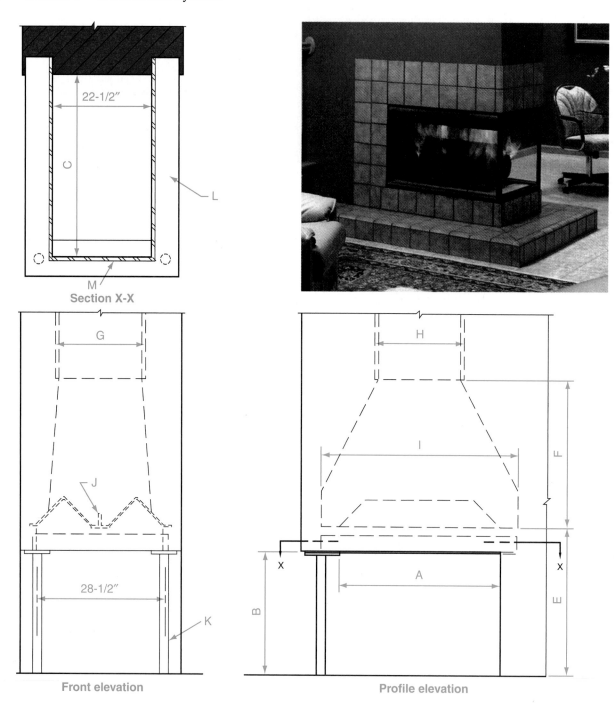

Section X-X

Front elevation

Profile elevation

Design data for three-face fireplaces

A	B	C	E	F	Old flue size		Round	New modular flue size		I	Steel tee	Post height	Angle 2 req'd.	Special welding tee
					G	H		G	H		J	K	L	M
28	26-1/2	32	32	24	18	18	18	16	20	36	35	26-1/2	36	34
32	26-1/2	36	32	27	18	18	18	20	20	40	39	26-1/2	40	34
36	26-1/2	40	32	32	18	18	18	20	20	44	43	26-1/2	44	34
40	26-1/2	44	32	35	18	18	18	20	20	48	47	26-1/2	48	34
48	26-1/2	52	32	35	20	20	20	20	24	56	55	26-1/2	56	34

Dimensions are in inches.
Flue sizes are for a chimney height of at least 14'–0".

Figure 17-18. Design specifications for three-face fireplaces. (Superior Fireplace Company)

Figure 17-19. Prefabricated metal fireplaces can be wall mounted, enclosed in masonry, or freestanding. A—Enclosed in masonry. (Superior Fireplace Company) B—Freestanding. (Stone Products Corporation)

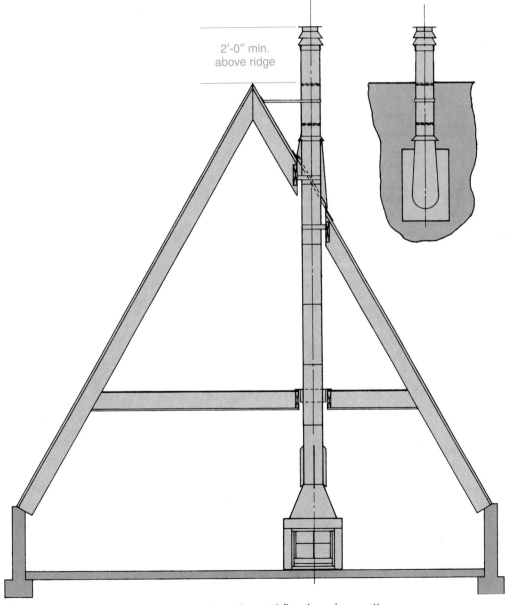

2'-0" min. above ridge

Figure 17-20. A typical installation of a prefabricated metal fireplace in a cottage.

Figure 17-21. Three common designs of prefabricated steel, heat-circulating fireplaces. From left to right: single-face, two-face adjacent, and two-face opposite. (Superior Fireplace Company)

Figure 17-22. A masonry fireplace with a metal insert is an efficient way to circulate warm air. This model provides efficiency and is visually appealing. (Eneco Corporation)

Figure 17-23. A wood-burning stove suitable as a local heating source for this large family room. Heat radiates from all sides of the stove. (Vermont Castings)

include a device to ensure a constant burning rate. High-efficiency stoves are over 50% efficient. They include all of the features of the medium-efficiency stoves, but also use baffles, long smoke paths, and heat exchange devices to increase heat output, Figure 17-25.

A stove may be located in front or inside of an existing fireplace, Figure 17-26. When the stove is positioned in front of the fireplace, the opening should be covered with sheet metal to reflect the heat back into the room. It is very important to follow the manufacturer's installation instructions as well as the local code requirements when installing a stove.

Figure 17-24. Circulating stoves may be placed closer to combustible materials than radiant stoves. This wood-burning stove combines function with beauty. (Heatilator, Inc.)

Figure 17-25. This is a high-efficiency stove that is made of cast iron and has large glass doors to view the fire. Note the fire-resistant materials behind and beneath the stove. (Vermont Castings)

Figure 17-26. This stove, which sits inside an existing masonry fireplace, is classically styled and blends nicely with the atmosphere of the room. (Vermont Castings)

Internet Resources

www.ansi.org
   American National Standards Institute

www.architectural-ornament.com
   Architectural Ornament, Inc., manufacturer of polyurethane architectural molding

www.boralbricks.com
   Boral Bricks

www.concretehomes.com
   Portland Cement Association

www.epa.gov
   US Environmental Protection Agency

www.ibhs.org
   Institute for Business and Home Safety

www.martinindustries.com
   Martin Industries, Inc., manufacturer of Martin fireplaces

www.meltonclassics.com
   Melton Classics, Inc., a producer of millwork

www.napoleon.on.ca
   Napoleon, a manufacturer of fireplaces, stoves, and inserts

www.sweets.com
   Sweets Catalog File

Review Questions – Chapter 17

Write your answers on a separate sheet of paper. Do not write in this book.

1. List the five general types of fireplaces.
2. The part of the fireplace designed to protect the floor from sparks is the _____.
3. If the fire chamber is too shallow, what may happen?
4. The _____ deflects cold air flowing down the chimney into the rising warm air.
5. The area in the fireplace just above the smoke shelf and damper is called the _____.
6. A rule of thumb to follow in selecting the proper flue size is to choose a flue that has at least _____ the sectional area of the fireplace opening.
7. Increasing the flue height will _____ the draft.
8. Most codes require that the flue extend at least _____ above the highest point of the roof.
9. Why will a chimney placed within the house function better than one on an outside wall?
10. Allow a minimum clearance of _____ between the chimney and framing.
11. The purpose of a saddle or cricket is to _____.
12. The most common type of lintel used above the openings of fireplaces is _____.
13. A fireplace that has only one front opening is known as a _____.
14. A fireplace that is open on the front and one side (not the back) is a _____.
15. A type of fireplace (not stove) that requires no masonry is the _____.
16. Wood- or coal-burning stoves are ordinarily used as _____ sources of heat.
17. Name the two main types of stoves.
18. Name three features that are unique to a high efficiency stove.

Suggested Activities

1. Select a residential plan that has a fireplace. Draw the fireplace details and dimension the drawings.
2. Using CADD, design a fireplace following the principles outlined in this chapter. Draw the plan view and front elevation of the fireplace. Build a scale model of a fireplace. Describe the materials to be used in the actual fireplace.
3. Collect literature and materials commonly used in fireplaces and bring to class. Display the literature and materials and describe them in class.
4. Locate a residence under construction that has a fireplace. Obtain permission to enter the construction site. Measure the opening and depth of the fireplace. Sketch the fireplace. Bring the sketch to class and be prepared to discuss the construction techniques used.
5. Visit your local building department and secure local code restrictions about the installation of wood burning stoves. Summarize the main points in class.
6. Using CADD, draw the plan view and profile in section of a single-face fireplace that has a opening width of 28".

18 The Floor Plan

19 Roof Designs

20 Elevations

James Hardie® Siding Products

The Floor Plan

18

Objectives

After studying this chapter, you will be able to:

➤ List the information required on a typical floor plan.

➤ Represent typical materials using standard architectural hatch patterns (symbols).

➤ Design and draw a residential floor plan using accepted techniques.

➤ Dimension a floor plan in a clear and precise manner.

➤ Identify well drawn floor plans.

➤ Identify poorly drawn floor plans.

➤ Draw a floor plan using CADD.

Key Terms

Floor Plan
Material Hatch
   Patterns

Material Symbols
Overall Dimensions

The *floor plan* is the heart of a set of construction drawings. It identifies the location and dimensions of exterior and interior walls, windows, doors, major appliances, cabinets, fireplaces, and other fixed features of the house. The floor plan is the one plan to which all tradeworkers refer. When designing a residence, the floor plan is usually the first drawing on which work is completed. It is the basis for many other plans. The floor plan may be finished, however, near the end of the design process since modifications are frequently required during the development of the other plans.

The floor plan is not a typical top view; it is actually a section drawing. An imaginary cutting plane passes through the structure about four feet above, and parallel to, the floor. The cutting plane may be higher or lower as necessary to cut through the required details. In some instances, an offset plane is required to change levels, as in the case of a split-level house.

Figure 18-1 shows a presentation drawing for a three-bedroom house. Figure 18-2 shows the floor plan of the house. Many common features found on a floor plan are identified in the figure. Sometimes when the structure is not complex, the floor plan may include information that would ordinarily be found on other drawings. For example, the electrical plan, heating/cooling plan, or plumbing plan might be combined with the floor plan. Be careful not to include too much information on a single drawing or the drawing will become cluttered and confusing.

Figure 18-1. Study this pictorial of a three-bedroom house. Then, examine its floor plan shown in Figure 18-2. (Sater Design Collection, Inc.)

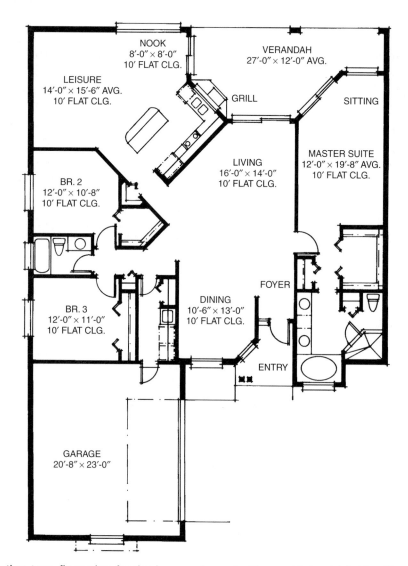

Figure 18-2. A presentation-type floor plan for the house shown in Figure 18-1, which identifies many of the common features found on a floor plan. (Sater Design Collection, Inc.)

Required Information

Information about the following features should be included on the floor plan.
- Exterior and Interior Walls
- Size and Location of Windows and Doors
- Built-In Cabinets and Appliances
- Permanent Fixtures
- Stairs
- Fireplaces
- Walks, Patios, and Decks
- Room Names
- Material Symbols
- Location and Size Dimensions
- Drawing Scale

Frequently, related structures, such as a detached garage or swimming pool, are also shown on the floor plan.

Location and Size of Walls

Walls should be drawn accurately. Use the chart shown in Figure 18-3 as a guide to nominal wall thicknesses. Any variations in wall thicknesses on a drawing will be readily evident and detract from the neatness of the drawing.

When drawing manually, set your dividers to the proper wall thickness dimension. Then,

use the dividers to measure wall thickness rather than try to measure each time with your scale. When drawing using CADD, use the **OFFSET**, **DOUBLE LINE**, or similar command to draw the wall at the proper thickness.

Since the floor plan is a section drawing, hatch patterns (symbols) should be used to indicate materials. See Figure 18-4 for examples of hatch patterns common for walls.

Location and Size of Windows and Doors

When locating windows and doors on the drawing, place a centerline through the middle of the opening for frame walls. In masonry construction, the centerline is not needed because dimensions are to the opening. The opening shown in the wall for windows is the sash width. The actual door width is shown as the opening in the wall for doors. Sills are drawn for windows and exterior doors. The door swing must be indicated on the floor plan. Refer to Chapter 15 for appropriate window and door symbols. Figure 18-5 shows how a window and exterior door are represented on the floor plan.

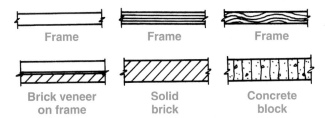

Figure 18-4. These are several common hatch patterns (symbols) used to indicate wall materials on a floor plan.

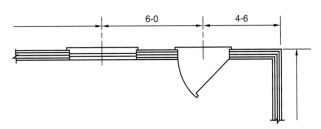

Figure 18-5. Windows and doors are located with a centerline in frame construction. The type of window and door swing direction should be shown.

Wall thickness chart	
Wood frame walls	
Exterior walls (with sheathing and siding)	6″
Interior walls (with drywall both sides)	5″
Concrete block walls	
Exterior walls	8″, 10″, or 12″
Interior walls	4″ or 8″
Brick veneer exterior	
Veneer on frame	10″
Veneer on concrete block	12″
Brick exterior walls	
Two courses of brick	8″
Two courses of 2″ air space	10″
Three courses of brick	12″

Figure 18-3. This chart shows nominal wall thicknesses.

Occasionally, a plain opening or archway may be desired rather than a door. In this case, hidden (dashed) lines are used to show that the opening does not extend to the ceiling, Figure 18-6. Hidden lines are used on the floor plan to indicate that a feature is above the cutting plane or hidden by some other detail.

Cabinets, Appliances, and Permanent Fixtures

The location and size of kitchen cabinets, bathroom vanities, fixtures, and appliances must be indicated on the floor plan. These features are drawn using standard symbols that represent specific sizes. Never guess at the size of an appliance or fixture. Obtain information related to each item, record the necessary dimensions and specifications, and include that information in the plans.

Refer to symbols and location procedures covered in Chapter 7 and Chapter 9. Also, examine local codes related to clearances and installation procedures acceptable in your area.

Stairs and Fireplaces

If a stairway or fireplace is to be included, only information about the basic size and location needs to be recorded on the floor plan. Detail drawings will be included in the set of drawings for these two features.

For stairs, the direction of flight, number of risers, and width of the stairs are given on the floor plan. See Figure 18-7. For a fireplace, the basic width, length, location, and shape of the opening are shown on the floor plan. Either a simplified or detailed symbol may be used to identify the fireplace, Figure 18-8. The detailed symbol is usually preferred. Additional flues that may be housed in the chimney are frequently included on the floor plan.

Walks, Patios, and Decks

Several outside features of the house are commonly included on the floor plan. Walks,

Figure 18-6. These are two methods of representing interior wall openings other than windows and doors.

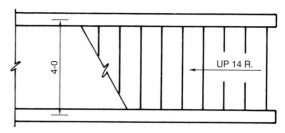

Figure 18-7. Certain information about a set of stairs is usually included on the floor plan,

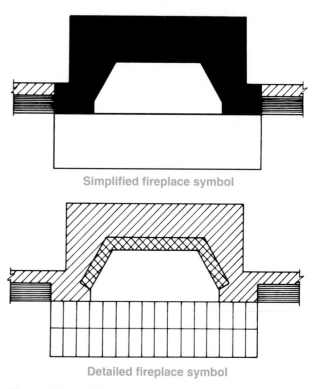

Figure 18-8. A fireplace may be represented using a simplified or detailed symbol.

patios, and decks are examples. Sizes and materials should be indicated on the plan, as well as locations. These features help to present the total plan and are important elements.

Room Names and Material Symbols

Room names add information that is important in communicating the plan to others. The room name should be lettered slightly larger (3/16″) than the surrounding lettering. Ideally, the room name should be in the center of the room. This may be shifted to one side or lowered if needed. The approximate size of the room may be added immediately below the name. This can be helpful for those who are not too familiar with construction drawings.

Material symbols or *material hatch patterns* are a type of shorthand for the drafter. Symbols (hatch patterns) are used rather than trying to describe each material with words. Use a material symbol whenever the material should be identified. If the symbol is not a standard one, identify it. Several common building material symbols are shown in Figure 18-9.

Dimensioning

Dimensions on a floor plan may show the size or location of a feature. *The importance of proper and careful dimensioning cannot be overemphasized.* Proper placement of dimensions requires good judgment. Locate dimensions where one would logically look for them.

Dimension lines in architectural drafting are generally continuous lines with the dimension figure placed above the line. Dimension figures are always parallel (never perpendicular) to the dimension line. Any accepted termination symbol may be used as long as you are consistent throughout the set of drawings. Review Chapter 4 for additional information.

When drawings are so crowded with dimensions that it is difficult to see the objects, move dimension lines out from the drawing far enough (at least 3/4″) so the dimension, as well as the object lines, may be clearly seen. Spacing between the dimension lines may be 1/4″ or 3/8″ as desired. Dimension lines may be located within the house area if that seems to be the logical place for them. Refrain from using long leaders. The maximum length of a leader should be two inches.

Dimensions in architectural drawing are recorded in feet and inches. In drawing plans, feet and inch marks may be omitted as a general rule. A dimension such as 12-6 could not mean anything other than the dimension 12 feet 6 inches. When the dimension is less than one foot, one of two procedures may be used. Either place a zero in the foot location followed by the number of inches (0′-6″ or 0-6) or record the length as so many inches and show the inch mark (6″).

Interior walls are commonly dimensioned to their center. A short line is drawn down the middle of the wall at the termination point of the dimension to show that the center is indicated. See Figure 18-10A.

Exterior frame walls are dimensioned to the outside of the stud wall. This usually includes the weatherboard or sheathing but not the siding, Figure 18-10A. Brick veneer walls are dimensioned to the outside of the stud wall, Figure 18-10A. Solid masonry walls are dimensioned to the outside of the wall, Figure 18-10B. Windows and doors in masonry walls are dimensioned to the opening, rather than a centerline.

Overall dimensions are necessary to provide the total length and width of the structure. Always add all the dimensions that together equal the overall dimension to verify proper dimensions. One of the most frequent errors in dimensioning is that partial dimensions do not add up to equal the total distance.

The overall length and width of major wall segments should be lengths that are multiples of 4′. Building material sizes are keyed to this dimension and much unnecessary waste will result if this rule is not applied.

Frequently, notes are required to present information that cannot be represented by a conventional dimension or symbol. These notes should be brief and located where they are easy to see. Include only required information. Notes may be lettered 1/8″ high or slightly smaller. They should be read from the bottom of the sheet; not from the edge.

Scale and Sheet Identification

Residential floor plans are usually drawn to a scale of 1/4″ = 1′-0″. A detail may be a larger scale and the plot plan smaller, but the other drawings should be 1/4″ = 1′-0″. The size of paper selected for the plans will be

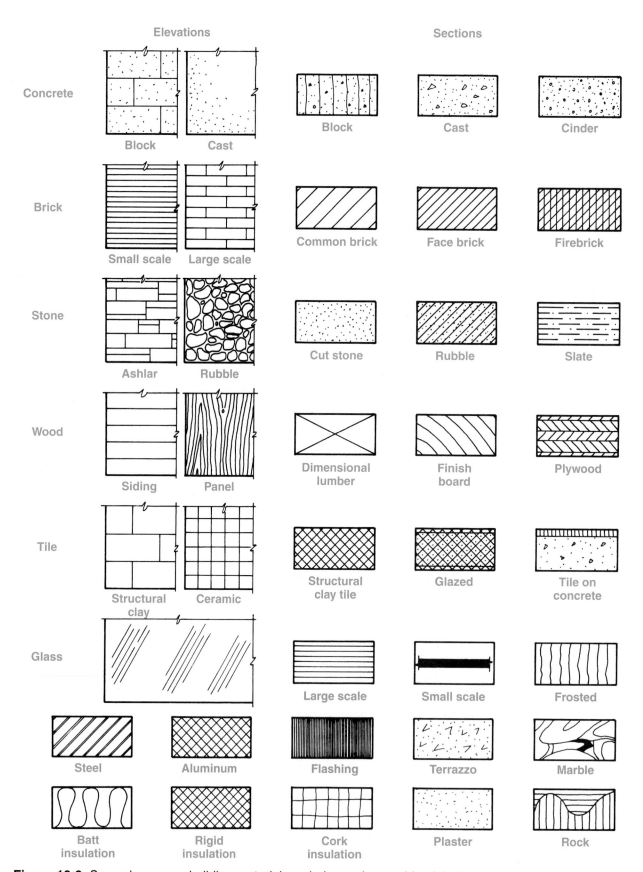

Figure 18-9. Several common building material symbols used on residential plans.

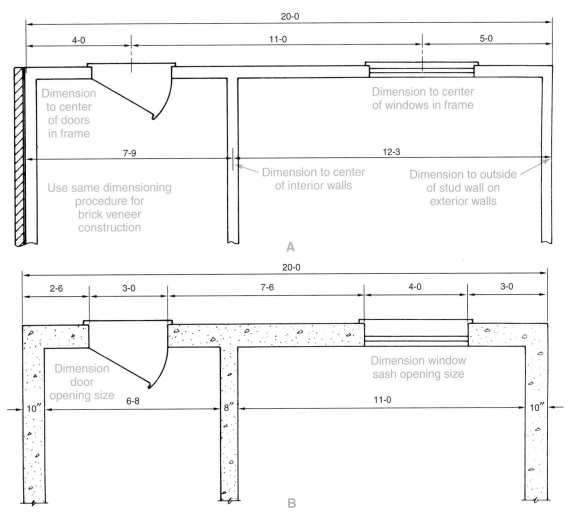

Figure 18-10. A—Recommended method of dimensioning frame wall and brick veneer construction. B— Solid masonry walls (cast concrete, block, brick, or stone) are usually dimensioned as shown.

determined by the size of the structure. A sheet of 18″ × 24″ paper is large enough for most plans. The scale must appear at the bottom of each drawing, except on the pictorial representation of the total house.

Number the sheets in a set of construction drawings so the reader may determine if the set is complete. This is important. A method that works well is to number each sheet like: Sheet 1 of 6, Sheet 2 of 6, etc. The sheet number should appear in the lower right-hand corner of each sheet.

Metric System of Dimensioning

The metric system of measurement is standard in most countries outside the US. Many US companies, especially those who have international business, use the metric system or dual dimensioning, which shows both metric and inch dimensions. However, in the US residential construction industry, the US Customary (inch) system is standard. Before the metric system can be accepted by the US building industry, new lumber sizes and standards must be decided on and accepted.

Even though the metric system is not standard in the US, a simple floor plan is shown in Figure 18-11 to illustrate metric dimensioning. The basic units for linear measurement in the construction industry should be restricted to the meter (m) and the millimeter (mm). Thus, on drawings, whole number dimensions always indicate millimeters and decimal numbers (to three decimal places) always indicate meters.

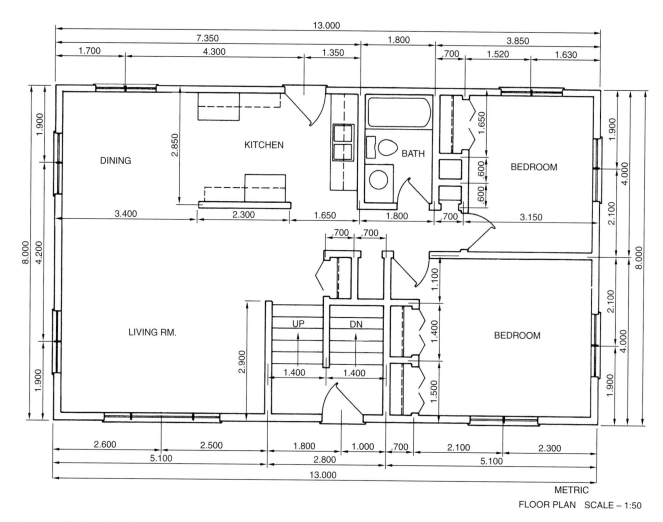

Figure 18-11. This floor plan is dimensioned in metric units.

Drawing a Floor Plan

The first step in designing a house is to determine the requirements of the structure and record them as preliminary sketches. These rough sketches will provide direction for drawing the plan to scale. The steps in the following sections should aid you in drawing a floor plan once the basic requirements are determined and some preliminary sketches are developed.

The floor plan for a split-level house is shown in Figure 18-12. This illustration shows the typical floor plan presentation for a split-level house. First and second level floor plans of a common two-story house are shown in Figure 18-13.

Expansion plans have much to offer. When additions are planned in the initial design stage,

the expanded house does not appear "added on to." Also, fewer basic changes are required when additions are ultimately made. The plan shown in Figure 18-14 is designed for expansion. The basic house, 28' × 52', contains the necessary space for a small family. As the family grows, the house can be enlarged to meet the family's needs. A bedroom and bath could be added first and the breezeway, bath, and mudroom added later. Finally, the garage, storage, and porch may be built to complete the expanded plan, which measures approximately 34' × 74'.

Procedure—Manual Drafting

1. Lay out the exterior walls. Draw the walls as light construction lines. Be sure that the overall length and width of the house are measured to the proper place on the walls

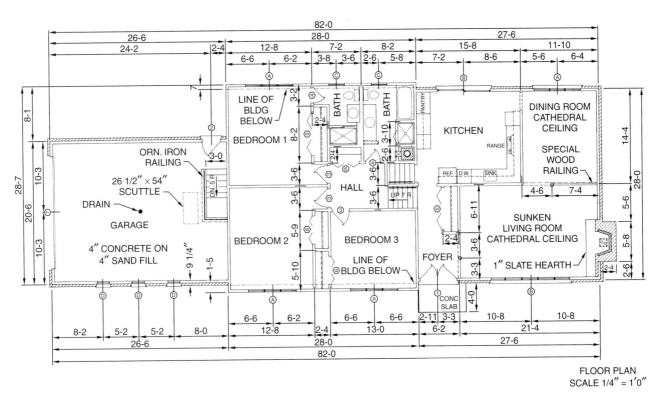

Figure 18-12. This is the upper level floor plan for a split-level house. The basement/foundation plan of this house would present the lower level layout. (Donald F. Sowa, A.R.A.)

and that walls are the correct thickness. Steps 1 and 2 are shown in Figure 18-15.

2. Locate the interior walls as light construction lines. Set your dividers to the desired wall thickness and use them to transfer the dimension. Use the center of the wall for locating its position.

3. Determine the location of the windows and doors. Both of these features will be dimensioned to the centerline of the opening in frame wall construction, so locate the centerline first. Indicate the swing of doors and type of window. Darken lines used for windows and doors. Include sills if appropriate. Steps 3, 4, and 5 are shown in Figure 18-16.

4. Draw the stairs. If the house has no stairs, go to the next step. Measure the width of the stairs and lay out the treads. The height between finished floors must be determined and the tread and riser height calculated before this step may be completed accurately. See Chapter 16 for an explanation of stair design and construction. Draw equally spaced lines to represent the stair treads. Show the direction of travel and the number of risers.

5. If the house is to have a fireplace, locate and draw the fireplace. Review Chapter 17. Since the dimensions of a fireplace must be exact to ensure proper operation, some preliminary work must be done before the fireplace can be drawn on the floor plan. Identify the type and size of fireplace that is desired and record these dimensions for further use. Darken the fireplace outline and fire chamber size. You may now darken all exterior and interior walls.

6. Locate and draw walks, patios, and decks. These elements of the plan should be well thought out. Materials and designs should be selected that will complement the total structure. Lay out and draw these elements. Steps 6, 7, and 8 are shown in Figure 18-17.

7. Draw the kitchen cabinets, appliances, and bathroom fixtures. Kitchen base cabinets are usually 24″ deep; wall cabinets 12″ deep. The base units are shown as solid lines while the wall cabinets are indicated

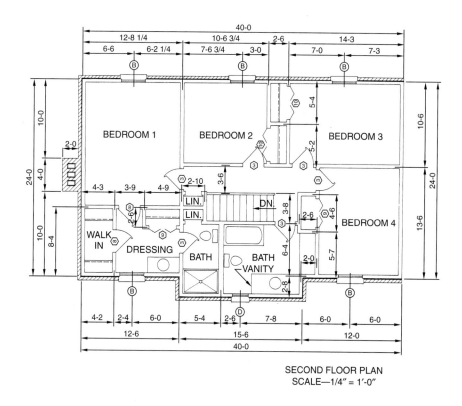

SECOND FLOOR PLAN
SCALE—1/4″ = 1′-0″

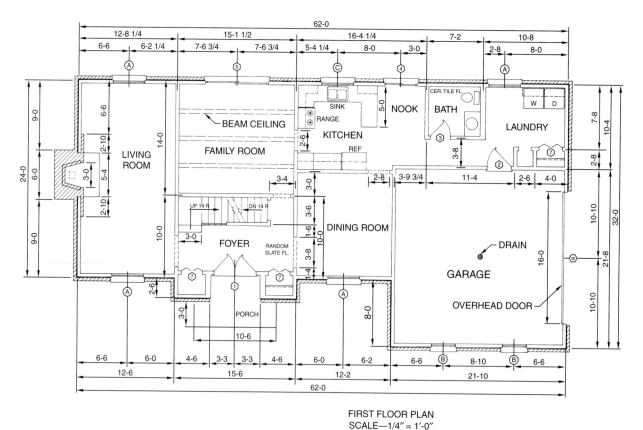

FIRST FLOOR PLAN
SCALE—1/4″ = 1′-0″

Figure 18-13. The first floor and second floor plans for a brick veneer, two-story house.

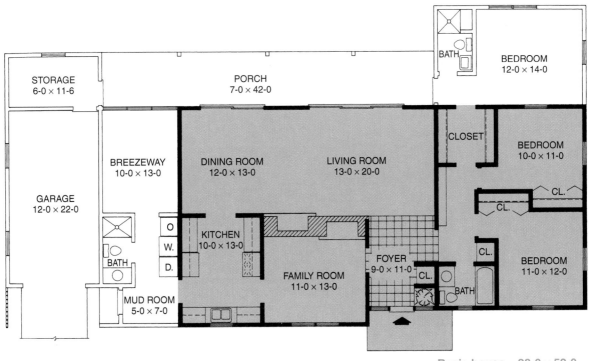

Figure 18-14. This basic house may be expanded from 1456 to 2516 square feet. The preplanned additions include a bedroom, breezeway, mudroom, storage, garage, porch, and two baths.

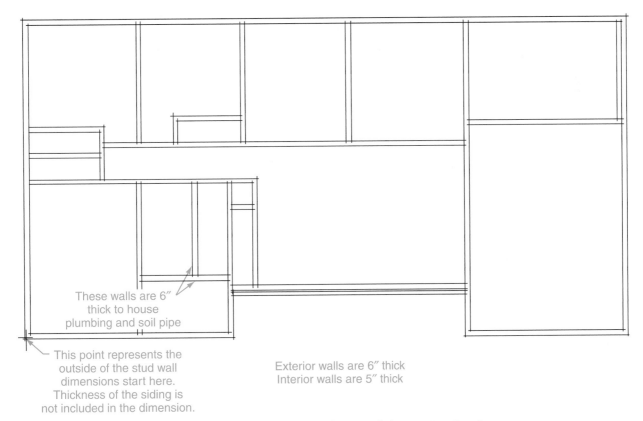

Figure 18-15. Lay out the interior and exterior wall locations as light construction lines.

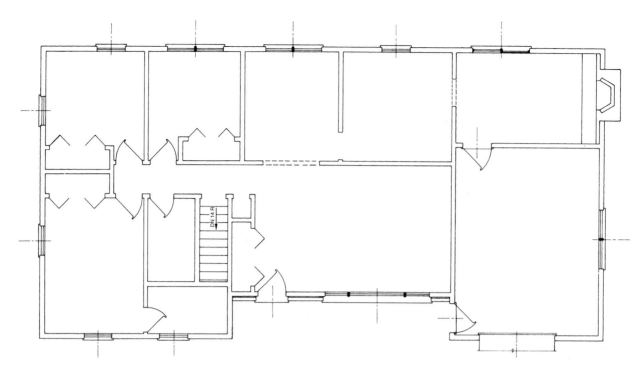

Figure 18-16. Windows, doors, a fireplace, and stairs have been added to the layout. Lines showing walls and symbols have been darkened.

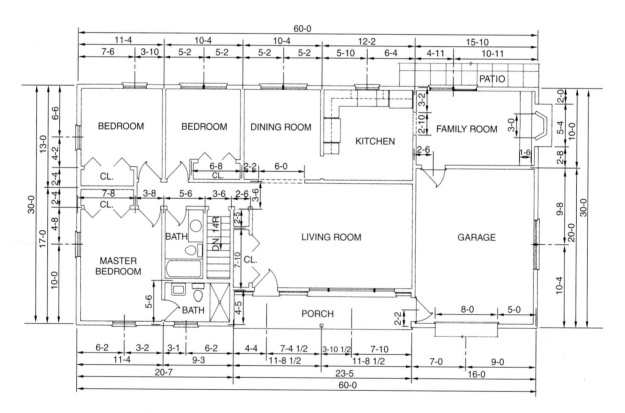

Figure 18-17. A patio and porch, kitchen cabinets, bathroom fixtures, room names, and dimensions have been added to the plan.

using a hidden linetype (symbol). The refrigerator and range are usually deeper than 24" and should be represented as such. Bathroom vanities and fixtures should be located and drawn in the same way as kitchen cabinets and appliances. Be sure to check the code for required fixture clearances. Refer to Chapters 7 and 9 for information on bathrooms and kitchens.

8. Add dimensions, notes, and room names. Keep in mind the dimensioning guidelines that are presented earlier in this chapter. Make sure the dimensions are accurate and complete. Letter the room name in the center of each room and show the approximate room size below the name if desired. Look over the drawing and add any general or specific notes that seem warranted. Note: It is important to show dimensions for all exterior wall features on the wall where they are located.

9. Add material and identification symbols. It is better to wait until the drawing is nearly finished to add material symbols so they do not interfere with dimensions or notes. Add the necessary symbols and darken remaining light lines. *All object lines, hidden lines, centerlines, etc., on a drawing should be black and only vary in width.* Exceptions are guidelines and construction lines. You may wish to remove the construction lines, but do not remove the guidelines. Steps 9 and 10 are shown in Figure 18-18.

10. Draw the title block and add the scale. The scale is important and should be placed in a prominent location near the bottom of the drawing. It may be located in the title block if all drawings on the sheet are the same scale. The title block should include the sheet number, name of drawing, scale, date, who the drawing is for, who made the drawing, and any other necessary information.

11. Check the entire drawing. Examine all aspects of the drawing for accuracy and completeness.

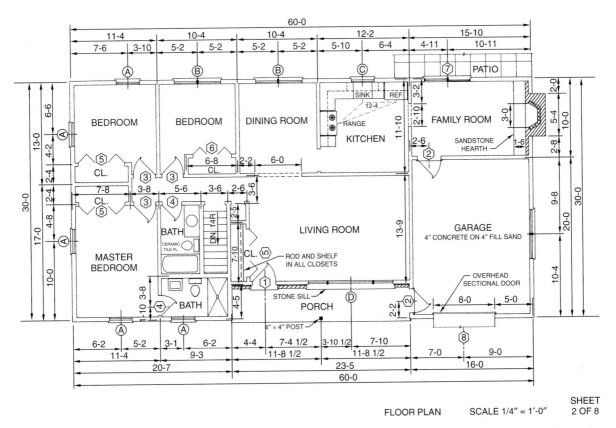

FLOOR PLAN   SCALE 1/4" = 1'-0"   SHEET 2 OF 8

Figure 18-18. The floor plan is completed by adding material and identification symbols, notes, scale, and name of the drawing.

Procedure—CADD

A CADD system greatly speeds the process of drawing and designing a floor plan. Automatic wall generation, repetitive use of symbols, dimensioning features, and elimination of hand lettering cut the design and drafting time to a fraction of that required by a traditional (manual) drafter. You must still know the basics of design, but the actual representation of your design is fast and accurate. See Figure 18-19.

Most generic CADD packages can be used to draw floor plans, but a package designed especially for architectural work is much preferred. Most have an extensive symbols library and dimension styles that are generally used by architects. Some software also includes an architectural font for lettering that can give the drawing a hand-drawn appearance. The decision on which CADD package to purchase is dependent on cost, expected use, and package features.

The following steps can be used with most CADD systems. The specific commands may vary, but the basic procedure should still apply.

1. Prepare a space diagram. A space diagram is an effective tool for determining how the various rooms and areas fit together. The diagram should be drawn to scale with each room or area identified and the number of square feet noted for each. A space diagram should be placed on its own layer. Figure 18-20 shows a completed space diagram. The total area of the floor plan is 1778.91 square feet.

2. Draw the exterior and interior walls. Two approaches are commonly used to draw the walls on the floor plan. First, the **DOUBLE LINE**, **OFFSET**, or similar command can be used to draw the walls, Figure 18-21A. Second, some CADD programs can convert a space diagram into a floor plan, Figure 18-21B. The key advantages to using this procedure are speed and cleanup of wall corners and intersections.

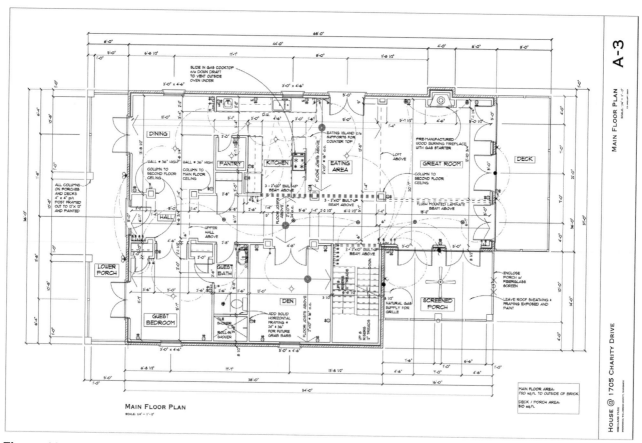

Figure 18-19. The use of standard symbols from a symbols library and automated dimensioning significantly reduced the time required to draw this floor plan in CADD. (SoftPlan Systems, Inc.)

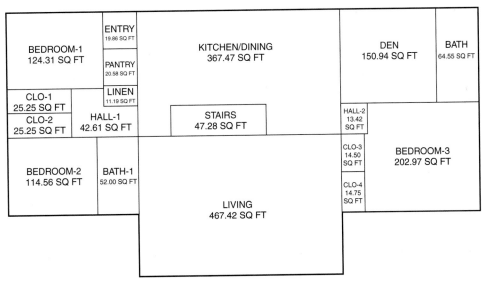

Figure 18-20. This computer-generated space diagram shows the designated room name and area.

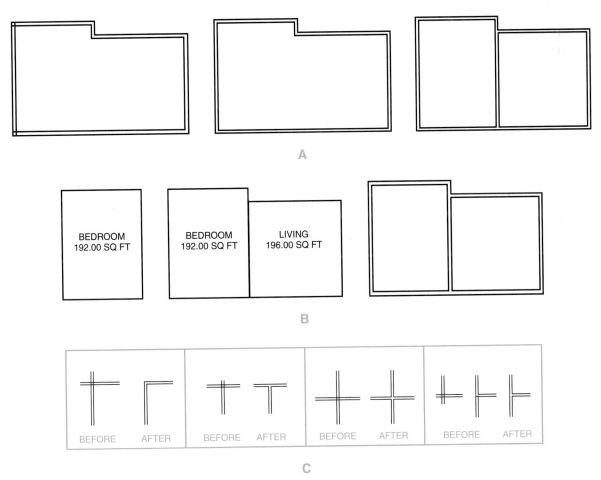

Figure 18-21. A—Developing a floor plan using the **DOUBLE LINE** command. B—Converting a space diagram into a floor plan. C—Four typical wall areas that require cleanup.

Figure 18-21C illustrates four typical wall areas that require cleanup.

Two important things to remember when locating and drawing exterior and interior walls on a floor plan is their proper thickness and measurement location. The thickness of all walls should be drawn as accurately as possible. Interior walls are generally 4-1/2" thick, which allows for drywall on both sides of a 3-1/2" (actual size) stud. Exterior walls vary considerably depending on type and construction technique. A typical exterior frame wall might be 5-3/32" in actual thickness. This thickness is the result of 1/2" drywall, 3-1/2" stud, 3/4" rigid foam insulation, and 11/32" P.W. siding. In CADD, it is just as easy to draw a wall 5-3/32" thick as it is one 6" thick. Draw the wall to the exact dimension instead of a nominal thickness.

The measurement location is to where the wall is dimensioned. Interior walls are generally dimensioned to the center of the wall. Therefore, an automatic dimension to the center of an interior wall should produce a reasonable figure like 6'-2" or 12'-3", but not 10'-1 7/16". Exterior frame walls are usually dimensioned to the outside of the rough frame wall, which includes the weatherboard or rigid foam insulation on the outside of the studs, but not the siding or veneer. These lengths should also be reasonable. Try to plan a structure so that the overall length and width are multiples of 4', if possible.

Figure 18-22 shows the floor plan for the space diagram in Figure 18-20 after this step is completed. Note the difference in thickness of the exterior and interior walls. Also see how the intersections are handled where an interior wall becomes an exterior wall in the large center area. Remember to place the floor plan on its own layer.

3. Locate the windows and doors. When windows and doors are located in a frame wall structure, they are dimensioned to the center of the unit. This is true even if the unit has more than one door or window. Plan the location of these elements so that they complement the overall design, but also use location dimensions that are at least multiples of 1". Window sills may or may not be included, depending on the desires of the designer. Figure 18-23 shows the plan with windows and doors added. These elements should be plotted with thinner lines than the walls. Therefore, place them on a separate layer or assign a different object color.

4. Draw the stairs. Put the stairs on a layer by itself for easy modification of the floor plan. Also, consider the final plotted line thickness and assign a pen width and object color as appropriate.

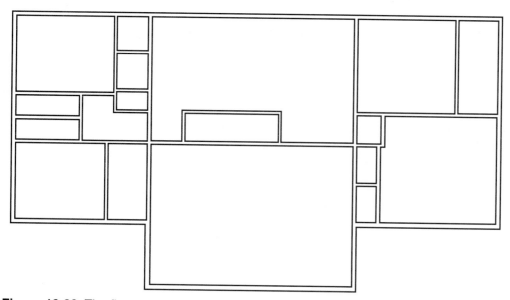

Figure 18-22. The floor plan developed from the space diagram in Figure 18-20. All wall intersections have been cleaned up.

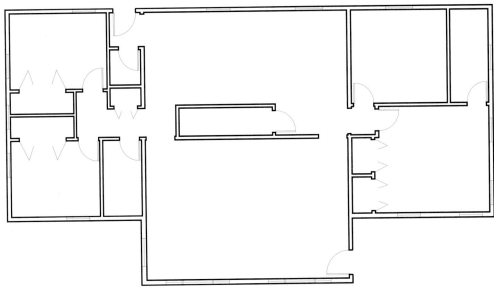

Figure 18-23. Windows and doors have been added by inserting symbols from the symbols library.

The one-story house in this example has a basement. Therefore, the total distance from the finished basement floor to the finished first floor must be determined before the stairs can be designed. The total rise for this house is 10′-2″. This is greater than usual because rather large wood floor trusses will be used.

Some CADD programs can calculate the tread width and riser height for each step and automatically draw the stairs. Whether or not you have this option, the stairs should conform to good design principles. See Chapter 16 for complete details on

stair design. The stair treads, handrails, and direction of travel should be shown on the floor plan. Figure 18-24 shows steps 4 through 7.

5. Locate and draw the fireplace in its proper location using appropriate hatch patterns. The fireplace should have its own layer. Also, consider the final plotted line thickness and assign a pen width and object color as appropriate.

Study Chapter 17 before drawing the fireplace. Proper design is essential to satisfactory operation. Identify the type and size of fireplace. Find the necessary dimensions in

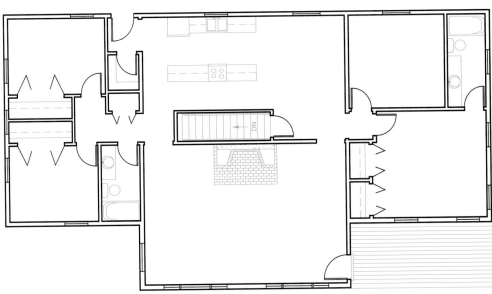

Figure 18-24. Cabinets, fixtures, appliances, and stairs have been added to the floor plan.

the Reference Section or Chapter 17 and record them for use in this drawing.

6. Locate and draw walks, patios, and porches. These elements should be considered extensions of the floor plan. Careful thought should go into their design and placement. Draw these elements on the floor plan. You may want to use a separate layer for these elements. Consider the final plotted line thickness when selecting a layer and object color.

7. Draw the kitchen cabinets, appliances, and bathroom fixtures. Review the sections in the text dealing with the layout and design of kitchens and baths before adding these elements. Good planning in these areas is essential. Add the kitchen cabinets, appliances, and bathroom fixtures to the floor plan using standard symbols from the symbols library and the appropriate linetypes. Assign an appropriate object color and layer to the symbols.

8. Add dimensions to the plan. All construction features on the floor plan should be dimensioned unless the location or size is very obvious. For example, a door placed

at a standard 4″ offset or a set of bi-fold doors that fills the space in front of the closet need not be dimensioned. However, if there is any doubt, dimension the feature. Remember, the extension lines begin at the outside of the rough stud wall and do not include the thickness of the siding or veneer.

Every window, door, intersecting wall, or offset in the exterior wall must be dimensioned. Each exterior segment should have partial dimensions, as well as an overall length dimension. Study the arrangement of dimensions in Figure 18-25 to see how dimensions should be arranged on a drawing. Be sure your dimensions are accurate and add up properly. Use the dimensioning capabilities of your CADD program to accomplish this task. Be sure to assign the correct layer and color to dimensions.

9. Add room names, notes, material symbols, scale, and title. Use the **TEXT** command to enter room names and sizes, scale, notes, and title. Assign an appropriate layer and object color to these items based on the

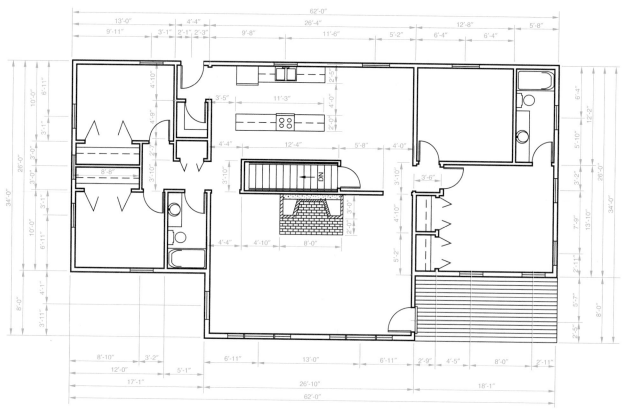

Figure 18-25. The dimensions have been added to the floor plan following proper guidelines.

final plotted line thickness. Add any material symbols that are appropriate for this drawing, but do not overdo it. Construct a title block, if you desire. Steps 9 and 10 are shown in Figure 18-26.

10. Check over the entire drawing. Examine all aspects of the drawing for accuracy, good design, and missing items. When you are sure it is complete, save and plot the drawing.

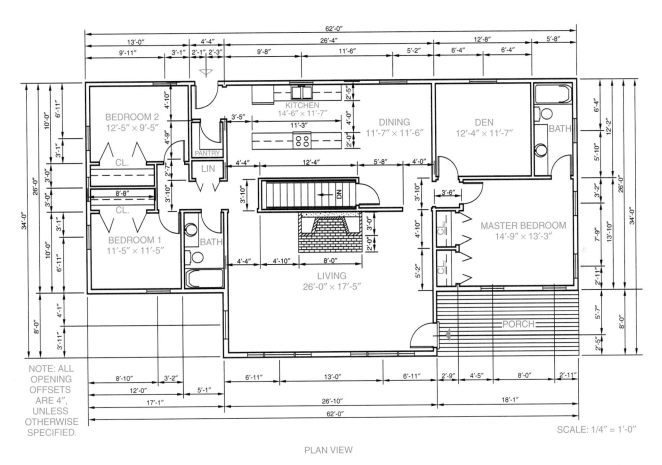

Figure 18-26. Labels and room sizes have been added to the floor plan.

Internet Resources

www.abbisoft.com
AbbiSoft, a supplier of house plans

www.aia.org
American Institute of Architects

www.alumag.com
Alumax, An Alcoa Company, manufacturer of bath enclosures and shower doors

www.anchorwall.com
Anchor Retaining Wall Systems

www.autodesk.com
Autodesk, Inc., publisher of AutoCAD and Autodesk VIZ

www.bhg.com
Better Homes and Gardens Magazine

www.hbgcolumns.com
HB&G Building Products, a manufacturer of columns and molding

www.archdigest.com
Architectural Digest

www.saterdesign.com
The Sater Design Collection, Inc.

Review Questions – Chapter 18

Write your answers on a separate sheet of paper. Do not write in this book.

1. A floor plan is not a typical top view, but a _____ drawing.

2. What is the purpose of a floor plan?

3. The scale of most residential floor plans is _____.

4. The actual thickness of an exterior frame wall with 1/2″ insulation board, 1/2″ dry wall, and 5/8″ siding on a 1-1/2″ × 3-1/2″ framing member (stud) is 5-1/8″. However, an exterior frame wall may be represented as a nominal thickness of _____ on the floor plan.

5. In frame wall construction, windows and doors are dimensioned to their _____.

6. In a solid masonry wall, windows and doors are dimensioned to the _____.

7. How is an archway commonly indicated on floor plan?

8. List the three items generally given on the floor plan about a set of stairs.

9. Identify the material indicated by the following hatch patterns (symbols) in a section view.

   a)

   b)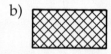

   c)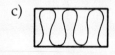

   d)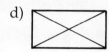

   e)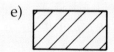

   f)

10. Show the two ways of representing a dimension of 4 inches on a floor plan.

11. A(n) _____ is an effective tool for determining how the various rooms and areas fit together.

12. Interior walls are usually dimensioned to the _____ of the wall.

13. In CADD, windows and doors can be inserted from the _____.

14. List four advantages of CADD that reduce the design and drafting time over traditional (manual) drafting.

Suggested Activities

1. Find a floor plan for a small house or cottage from a magazine, newspaper, or other source. Draw it to 1/4″ = 1′-0″ scale. Show all necessary dimensions, notes, and symbols. Prepare a window and door schedule. Present your drawing along with a copy of the original. Use traditional (manual) drafting.

2. Design a ranch-style house that:
   • Is on a flat lot.
   • Has three bedrooms.
   • Has two bathrooms.
   • Includes a living room, kitchen, and dining room.
   • Has a patio and a fireplace.
   • Has a two-car attached garage.
   • Does not have a basement (slab floor).
   • Is frame construction.

3. Using CADD, draw a floor plan for a one-bedroom apartment with a living room, combined kitchen and dining area, bath, and a small storage area. Interior walls are frame and exterior walls are brick veneer on 8″ concrete block. Show the calculated living space on the floor plan.

4. Secure the floor plan for a house or apartment that you feel has a poor arrangement and use of space. Redesign this plan using CADD to achieve proper use of space and room arrangement. Present both for comparison.

5. Add any new symbols that you developed in this chapter to your CADD symbols library.

Roof Designs
19

Objectives

After studying this chapter, you will be able to:

➤ Name and sketch ten different types of basic roof designs.

➤ Describe the construction of a typical frame roof.

➤ Draw a roof that has a typical roof slope (pitch).

➤ Interpret information found on a rafter span chart.

➤ Explain the importance of proper attic ventilation and roof flashing.

➤ Compile the appropriate information to order roof trusses for a house.

Key Terms

Box Cornice	Rafter
Clear Span	Rake
Close Cornice	Rise
Cornice	Roof Sheathing
Downspout	Roof Slope
Flashing	Roof Truss
Free-Form Roof	Run
Gable End	Warped Roof
Gussets	Wide Box Cornice
Gutters	with Lookouts
Narrow Box Cornice	Wide Box Cornice
Open Cornice	without Lookouts
Parasol Roof	

Types of Roofs

The overall appearance of a home is greatly affected by the roof lines and materials used for roof construction, Figure 19-1. The designer has many standard styles from which to choose. One of these styles should complement the basic design of the home being constructed. Figure 19-2 shows several roof types used in residential construction. These types are discussed in the following sections.

Gable Roof

The gable roof is a very popular type of roof. It is easy to build, sheds water well, provides for ventilation, and can be applied to a variety of house shapes and designs. The gable roof is a triangular roof with a gable at each end.

Winged Gable

The winged gable roof is essentially a gable roof extended at the peak. Lookout rafters are necessary to provide support for the increased overhang. This style of roof provides an attractive design feature on the roof.

Hip Roof

The hip roof is slightly more difficult to build than a gable roof, but is still a popular choice. It does not provide for ventilation as well as some other designs and increases the chance for leakage due to the hips and valleys. A hip roof does not have gables at the ends, rather a sloped roof section (hip).

Figure 19-1. An architect's design of the roof and selection of roofing materials has a significant impact on the finished appearance of the residence. (Photo Courtesy of James Hardie® Siding Products)

Dutch Hip

The Dutch hip roof is basically a hip roof with a small gable at each end. These gables can provide ventilation if vents are installed. However, the gables also increase the chance of leakage.

Flat Roof

A flat roof is the most economical roof to construct, but does not add much to the design of most houses. It requires a "built-up" or membrane roof covering rather than conventional shingles. A built-up roof consists of layers of roofing felt and tar or some other material, such as rubber topped with gravel. Actually, most so-called flat roofs are pitched at about 1/8" to 1/2" per foot to aid in drainage. The flat roof is popular in warmer areas of the country where wide overhangs are desirable for shade and where little or no snow falls.

Shed Roof

A shed roof is similar to a flat roof, but has more pitch. It is frequently used for additions to existing structures or in combination with other roof styles. A built-up roof is generally required unless the roof has a pitch of over 3:12, or three feet of rise for each 12 feet of run.

Mansard Roof

The popularity of the mansard roof varies. For several years, it was used infrequently. Then, it became popular for several years. Now, its popularity is again fading. It is a French design and more difficult to construct than the hip or gable roof. However, a mansard roof does have interesting lines.

Gambrel Roof

The gambrel roof is sometimes called a barn roof because it has been used extensively on barns. This type of roof provides additional headroom in the attic or second story.

Butterfly Roof

The butterfly roof is not widely used. From the 1950s through the early 1970s, some

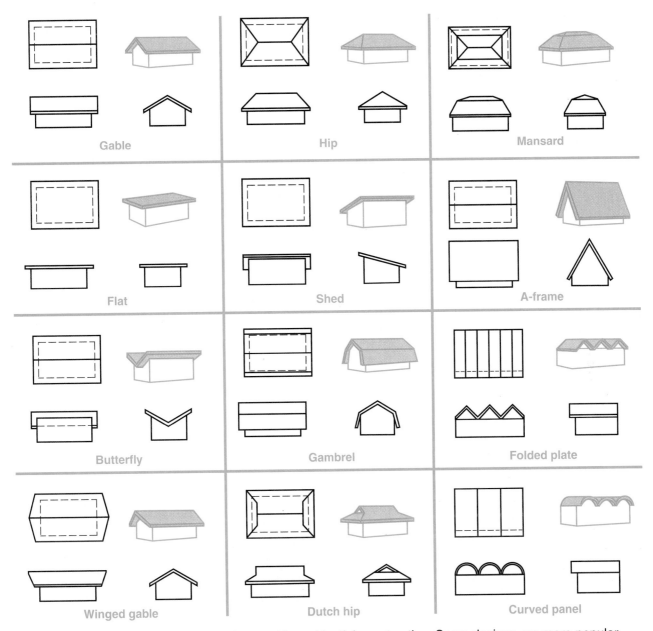

Figure 19-2. These roof designs may be used in residential construction. Some designs are more popular than others.

contemporary homes were built with this type of roof. However, this type of roof is now rare in new construction. A butterfly roof has the advantage of providing plenty of light and ventilation. However, drainage is a problem. Flashing should extend far up each slope along the valley to prevent leaking.

A-Frame Roof

The A-frame roof provides not only a roof, but the walls of the structure. Originally, it was used for cottages. However, it has also been applied to homes, churches, and other structures.

Folded Plate Roof

The folded plate roof has limited use in single-family houses. However, it is quite popular for small condominiums, motels, and small commercial buildings. Modular, prefabricated roof units are available. As the cost of the modular units decreases, the popularity of this design may increase. However, this roof has the same drainage problems as the butterfly roof.

Curved Panel Roof

The curved panel roof is similar to the folded plate roof in style and application. It has only limited use in home construction. This roof is available in prefabricated modules. It also has the same drainage problems as the butterfly and folded plate roofs.

Contemporary Roof Types

Several roof types that do not belong to the other categories are being experimented with. These can be classified as contemporary and should be identified. The *parasol roof* looks like an upturned parasol (umbrella). It is usually constructed from concrete.

Warped roofs are limitless in design. The most common shape for a warped roof is a hyperbolic paraboloid, which gives the roof an appearance similar to a kite in flight. Warped roofs may be constructed from concrete, molded plywood, or plastics.

Complete freedom is possible with the *free-form roof.* It may include planar, curved, and warped surfaces. This type of roof can be produced in any shape that can be achieved by stretching fabric over a support frame. The final roofing material is applied to the fabric. Urethane foam is a popular choice of material for this roof. It is sprayed over a network of pipes and net material. It is strong and weather resistant.

In addition to the above three roof types, there are many variations of the standard types. Figure 19-3 shows several residential structures with roof styles that are variations of basic hip and gable roofs.

A

B

C

D

Figure 19-3. Some contemporary roofs are variations of basic roof types. A—Gable roof with dormers. (Photo Courtesy of James Hardie® Siding Products) B—Hip roof with a gable extension. C—Roof with multiple hip sections. D—Roof with multiple gables. (Photo Courtesy of James Hardie® Siding Products)

Traditional Frame Roof Construction

There are several features of traditional frame roof construction. These are covered in the next sections. It is important to understand these features and their impact on the roof before designing a roof.

Rafters

The roof framing is designed to support the roof covering materials. The framing must be strong and rigid. Roof framing consists of several distinct structural elements. The first and most basic of these elements is the *rafter.* Common rafters are perpendicular to the top wall plate. They extend from the ridge of the roof to the plate or beyond. Figure 19-4 shows a plan view of the roof framing for a simple structure. Note that several types of rafters other than common rafters are identified.

Rafters are cut to the proper dimensions by locating the ridge cut, seat cut, plumb cut, and tail cut, Figure 19-5. The precise layout of these cuts is determined by the slope of the roof and the clear span of the building. Terms that must be understood before calculating rafter dimensions and roof pitch are rise, run, and clear span. The *rise* of a roof is the vertical

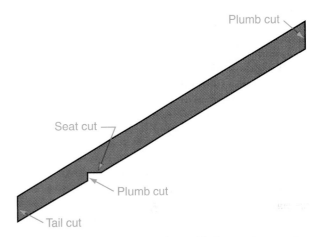

Figure 19-5. A common rafter with the various cuts labeled.

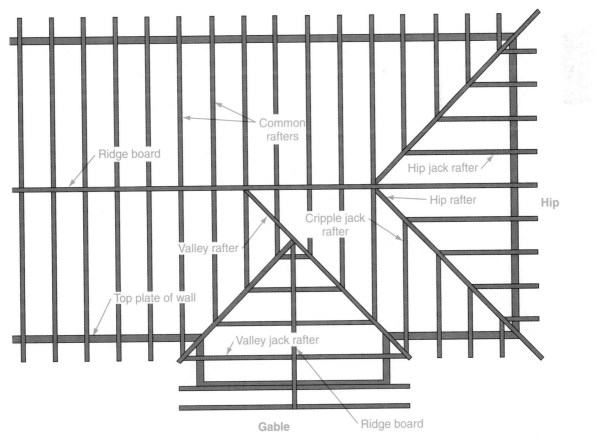

Figure 19-4. The structural members of typical roof framing are identified here.

distance measured from the top of the wall plate to the underside of the rafters. The *run* of a roof is one-half the distance of the clear span. The *clear span* is the horizontal distance from the inside of one exterior stud wall to the inside of the opposite exterior stud wall. See Figure 19-6.

Roof slope is the slant of the roof and may be given on a drawing by showing a slope ratio diagram or a fractional pitch indication, as shown in Figure 19-6. The slope diagram represents the ratio between the rise and run of the roof. The run is always expressed in this ratio as 12 units. The fractional pitch is calculated using the formula:

Pitch = Rise / Clear Span

Figure 19-7 shows several common roof pitches used in residential construction. When designing a roof, try to use one of the standard roof pitches (slopes).

Roof slope may also be shown using an angular dimension. For example, a roof with a 45° slope has a 12:12 or 1/2 pitch. However, this method is seldom used because it is difficult to measure as accurately as the other methods.

Rafter sizes will depend on the distance to be spanned, spacing of the rafters, and weight to be supported. Rafter span data is given in Figure 19-8. Rafters for roofs with low slopes may also serve as a base for the finished ceiling. In this instance, they are acting as

rafters and ceiling joists, Figure 19-9. A light roofing material is one that weighs less than four pounds per square foot, Figure 19-10. Anything heavier is considered heavy roofing. Slate and clay tile are examples of heavy roofing materials.

Cornice

The *cornice* is the overhang of the roof at the eave line that forms a connection between the roof and side walls. In a gable roof, it is formed on two sides of the building. The cornice continues around all four sides on a hip or flat roof.

The three types of cornices frequently used in residential buildings are the open cornice, box cornice, and close cornice. The *open cornice* may be used with exposed-beam construction, contemporary, or rustic designs, Figure 19-11. Rafter ends are exposed and are usually tapered or curved to prevent a bulky appearance.

A *box cornice* has the space between the end of a projecting rafter and the wall enclosed with a soffit board. There are three basic types of box cornices: the narrow box, wide box with lookouts, and wide box without lookouts. A *narrow box cornice* is usually between 6″ and 12″ wide. The soffit board is nailed directly to the bottom side of the rafters, Figure 19-12. A *wide box cornice with lookouts* normally

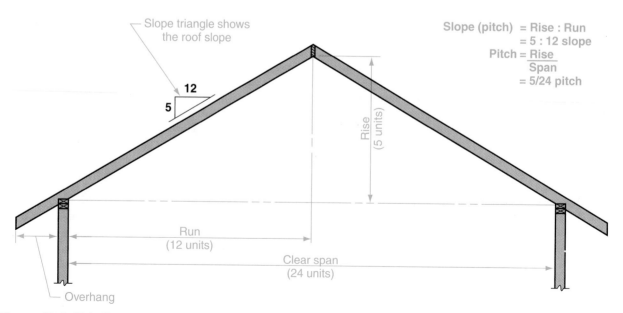

Figure 19-6. This illustration shows the roof rise, run, and span, and two methods of calculating slope (pitch).

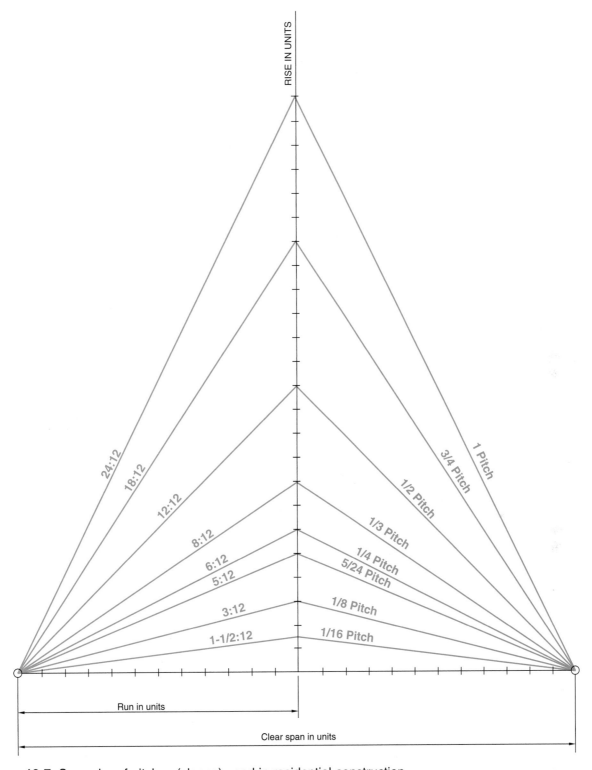

Figure 19-7. Several roof pitches (slopes) used in residential construction.

Maximum Span Comparisons for Rafters

Roof Slope of 3:12						
20 psf Live Load, 10 psi Dead Load, Def. <240, C_D = 1.25						
Species and Grade	2" x 6"		2" x 8"		2" x 10"	
	16"OC	24"OC	16"OC	24"OC	16"OC	24"OC
SP No. 1	14'-4"	12'-6"	18'-11"	16'-6"	24'-1"	21'-1"
DFL No. 1	14'-4"	12'-6"	18'-11"	15'-10"	23'-9"	19'-5"
SP No. 2	14'-1"	12'-3"	18'-6"	15'-10"	23'-2"	18'-11"
HF No. 1	13-9"	12'-0"	18'-1"	15'-6"	23'-1"	18'-11"
DFL No. 2	14'-1"	11'-9"	18'-2"	14'-10"	22'-3"	18'-2"
SPF No. 1 and No. 2	13'-5"	11'-9"	17'-9"	14'-10"	22'-3"	18'-2"
HF No. 2	13'-1"	11'-5"	17'-3"	14'-8"	21'-11"	17'-11"
SP No. 3	11'-8"	9'-6"	14'-10"	12'-2"	17'-7"	14'-4"
DFL No. 3	10'-10"	8'-10"	13'-9"	11'-3"	16'-9"	13'-8"
HF No. 3	10'-10"	8'-10"	13'-9"	11'-3"	16'-9"	13'-8"
SPF No. 3	10'-10"	8'-10"	13'-9"	11'-3"	16'-9"	13'-8"
Roof Slope of 6:12						
30 psf Live Load, 15 psf Dead Load, Def. <180, C_D = 1.15						
Species and Grade	2" x 6"		2" x 8"		2" x 10"	
	16"OC	24"OC	16"OC	24"OC	16"OC	24"OC
SP No. 1	13'-6"	11'-1"	17'-0"	13'-11"	20'-3"	16'-6"
DFL No. 1	12'-0"	9'-10"	15'-3"	12'-5"	18'-7"	15'-2"
SP No. 2	11'-9"	9'-7"	15'-3"	12'-5"	18'-2"	14'-10"
HF No. 1	11'-9"	9'-7"	14'-10"	12'-1"	18'-1"	14'-9"
DFL No. 2	11'-3"	9'-2"	14'-3"	11'-8"	17'-5"	14'-3"
SPF No. 1 and No. 2	11'-3"	9'-2"	14'-3"	11'-8"	17'-5"	14'-3"
HF No. 2	11'-1"	9'-1"	14'-0"	11'-6"	17'-2"	14'-0"
SP No. 3	9'-1"	7'-5"	11'-7"	9'-6"	13'-9"	11'-3"
DFL No. 3	8'-6"	6'-11"	10'-9"	8'-10"	13'-2"	10'-9"
HF No. 3	8'-6"	6'-11"	10'-9"	8'-10"	13'-2"	10'-9"
SPF No. 3	8'-6"	6'-11"	10'-9"	8'-10"	13'-2"	10'-9"

NOTE: These spans were calculated using published design values for comparison purposes only. They included the repetitive factor, C_R = 1.15, but do not include composite action of adhesive and sheathing. Spans may be slightly different than other published spans due to rounding.

C_D = Load Duration Factor, SP = Southern Pine, DFL = Douglas Fir-Larch, HF = Hem-Fir, SPF = Spruce-Pine-Fir

Figure 19-8. The maximum allowable rafter span may be determined by referring to these charts. The rafter span is the horizontal distance between supports. This is not to be confused with rafter length, which must be calculated using the rise and run of the roof.

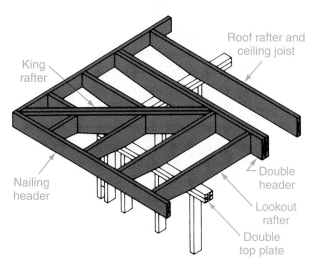

Figure 19-9. The rafters in this low-pitched roof also serve as ceiling joists.

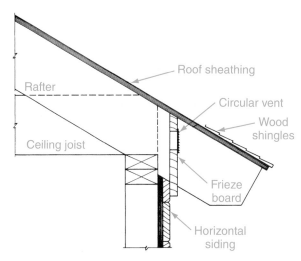

Figure 19-11. This section view shows an open cornice.

Figure 19-10. A—These shingles are a light roofing material. (Marvin Windows) B—These two-piece mission tiles are a heavy roofing material. (Craycroft Brick Company) C—These flat clay shingles are a heavy roofing material. (Craycroft Brick Company)

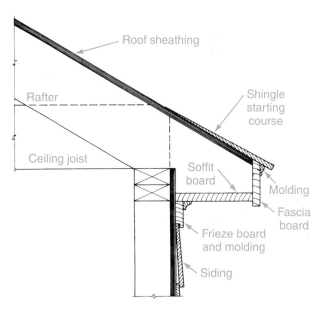

Figure 19-12. This section view shows a narrow box cornice.

requires additional support members, called lookouts, for fastening the soffit. Figure 19-13 shows a wide box cornice with lookouts. A *wide box cornice without lookouts* has a sloped soffit. The soffit material is nailed to the underside of the rafters. This type of cornice is frequently used when the overhangs are very wide, Figure 19-14.

A *close cornice* is one in which the rafter does not project beyond the wall. The roof is terminated by a frieze board and molding, Figure 19-15.

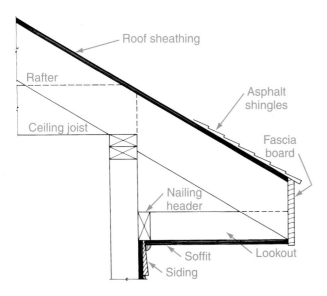

Figure 19-13. This section view shows a wide box cornice with lookouts.

Rake or Gable End

The *rake* or *gable end* is the extension of a gable roof beyond the end wall of the house. The amount of overhang and treatment at the gable should be about the same as the cornice. The style of house must be considered when designing the gable end. A narrow box cornice is normally used for Cape Cod or colonial homes. The same proportions should be extended to the gable end. For example, if a close cornice is used, then a close rake should also be used. Figure 19-16 shows the framing for a gable end

with a wide overhang. A close rake is less expensive to build, but wide overhangs provide for side wall protection and less frequent painting.

Roof Trusses

The *roof truss* is an assembly of members that form a rigid framework of triangular shapes. This arrangement permits wide, unsupported spans with a minimum amount of material. Figure 19-17 shows several roof truss designs.

The information needed to purchase the proper truss for a house includes the span, roof pitch, spacing of the trusses, and anticipated roof load. A roof that can support a load of 40 pounds per square foot is adequate for most applications.

Most roof truss manufacturers provide design services, but others have developed CADD software that produces a truss design that will support the required load for the span specified. Similar software is also available to individuals.

Lightweight wood roof trusses are designed to span distances of 20′ to 32′, and in some instances even more. Most lightweight trusses are made from 2″ × 4″ lumber; however, 2″ × 6″ lumber may be used for wider spans and heavier loads. Prefabricated trusses are readily available for standard widths and pitches. Many times they are less expensive than conventional framing. Time and expense is saved in the framing. Trusses for nonstandard dimensions may be built on the site or factory produced.

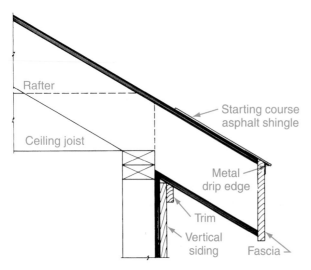

Figure 19-14. This section view shows a wide box cornice without lookouts.

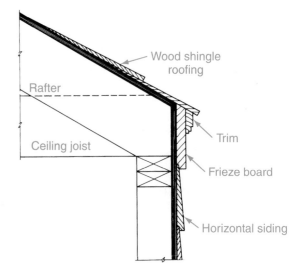

Figure 19-15. This section view shows a typical close cornice.

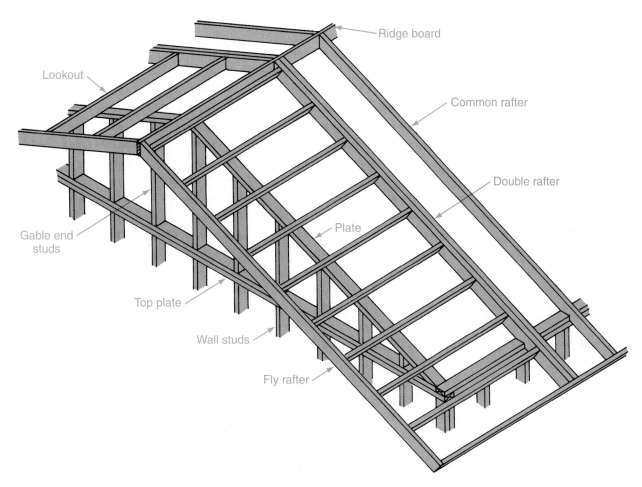

Figure 19-16. This framing is for a gable end with a wide overhang.

Wood trusses that are commonly used in residential construction are the W-type truss, king-post or K-post truss, and scissors truss, Figure 19-18. Most trusses are designed to be placed 24"OC. Ceiling materials are nailed to the bottom of the trusses. *Gussets* are frequently used to fastened the members of a wood truss together, Figure 19-19. Gussets are made from metal or 3/8" or 1/2" plywood.

Roof trusses that extend the bottom chord beyond the exterior wall provide additional space for ceiling insulation, Figure 19-20. This construction allows 12" of batt insulation to be extended to the outside of the exterior wall without interfering with attic ventilation. This amount of insulation is generally not possible with traditional roof framing methods. The increased airflow reduces moisture condensation on the underside of the roof sheathing and prevents damage to the structure.

Ventilation

Providing for adequate ventilation in the attic space is a necessity. If sufficient ventilation is not provided, moisture will probably form on the underside of the roof sheathing and, in time, damage will result. Also, a well-ventilated attic will help to cool the interior of the house during the summer.

Ventilation in the attic space is usually accomplished through the use of louvered openings in the gable ends and along the underside of the overhang. Ridge ventilators are also available that provide an efficient means of expelling hot air when coupled with soffit openings, Figure 19-21. The difference between the temperature of air in the attic and the outside causes air movement and thus reduces the temperature inside.

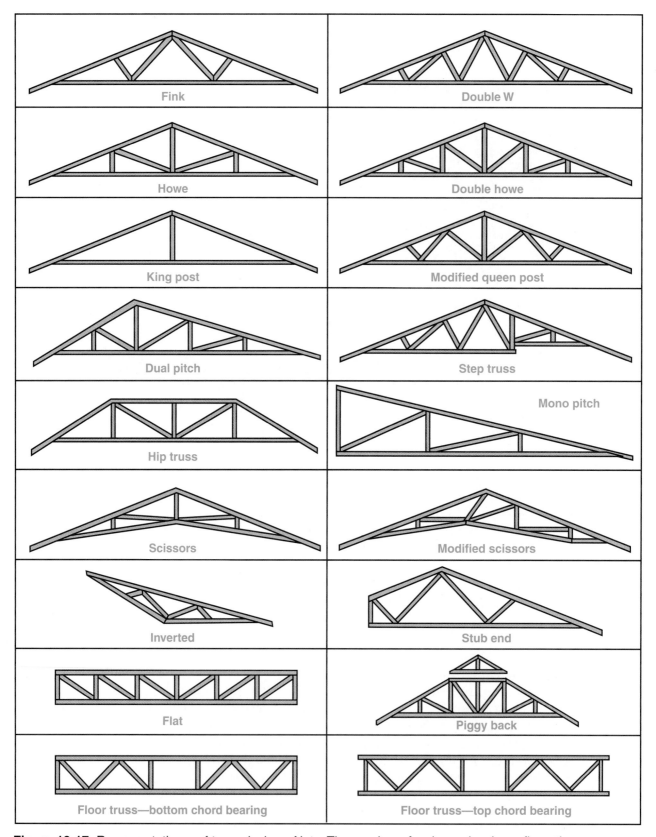

Figure 19-17. Representative roof truss designs. Note: The number of webs and web configurations can vary from those shown here.

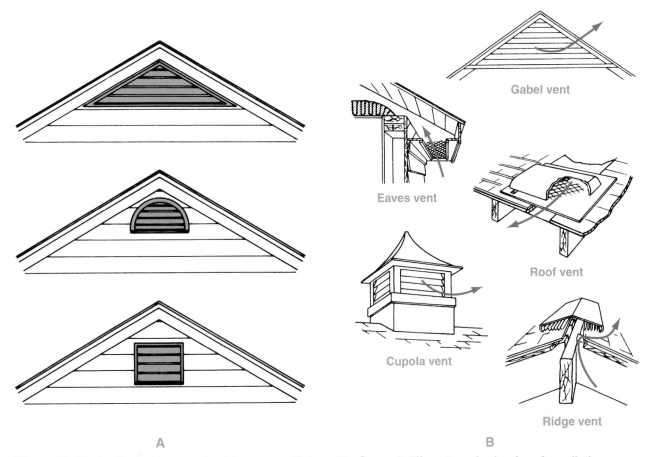

Figure 19-22. A—Typical louvered gable-type ventilators. B—Several different methods of roof ventilation are possible.

placed beneath the surface material at a distance sufficient to prevent the penetration of water. Figure 19-23 shows flashing around a chimney.

Roof valleys may be flashed with metal or two thicknesses of 90# roll-type roofing. The width of valley flashing should be no less than specified below.

Roof Slope	Flashing Width
Less than 4:12	24″
4:12 to 7:12	18″
Over 7:12	12″

Figure 19-24 shows valley flashing under an asphalt shingle roof. Frequently a ribbon of asphalt-roofing mastic is used under the shingles adjacent to the valley flashing to aid in waterproofing the roof.

A small metal edging is normally used at the gable and eaves line to act as a drip edge. This flashing prevents water from entering

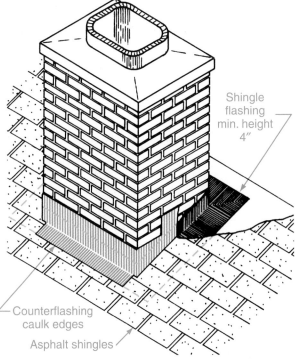

Figure 19-23. Flashing around a chimney is composed of shingle flashing and counterflashing.

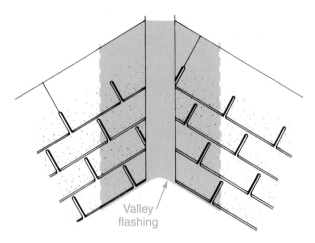

Figure 19-24. The width of valley flashing is dependent on the roof slope, but should be a minimum of 12″.

behind the shingles and protects the fascia and rake boards, Figure 19-25.

Gutters and Downspouts

Gutters collect the water from the roof and direct it to an outlet. A *downspout* is a vertical pipe that receives the water from the gutter outlet. An extension at the bottom of the downspout directs water out away from the house. This prevents water from running directly off the eaves and splattering the house and running down the foundation wall.

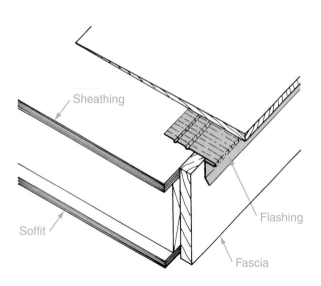

Figure 19-25. Drip edge flashing prevents water from entering behind the shingles and protects the fascia.

Gutters are usually pitched 1″ to 1-1/2″ per 20′. This slope permits even flow and prevents water from standing in the gutter.

Several styles of gutters and downspouts are available in copper, vinyl, aluminum, and galvanized sheet metal. Several common shapes and sizes of gutters are shown in Figure 19-26. The ogee style gutter is a popular type. Wood gutters are attractive on some home styles, but they are diminishing in importance due to high installation and maintenance costs.

The standard length for a gutter segment is 10′. However, several installers offer seamless gutters. Seamless gutters are manufactured to length either on site or in the shop. Flat roll stock is placed in the machine and the formed gutter is produced to any needed length. Downspouts and elbows can also be manufactured on site using similar machines.

Roof Sheathing and Roofing

Roof sheathing is placed over the rafters to support the roofing material. Sheathing may be planks, individual boards, plywood, or other approved panel product. Plywood is a popular choice, except when wood shingles are used as the roofing material. Usually 1″ × 3″ strips spaced several inches apart are used for wood shingle roofs, Figure 19-27.

The thickness of sheathing will vary with the spacing of the rafters or supporting beams. For rafters spaced 16″OC or 24″OC, 1/2″ standard sheathing-grade plywood is used. The plywood must be laid with the face grain perpendicular to the rafters, as in floor sheathing. The sheets should be staggered so that two sheets side-by-side do not end on the same rafter.

When individual boards are used as sheathing, they are usually no wider than 6″ or 8″. For rafters 16″OC or 24″OC, the minimum board thickness is 3/4″. Each board should be long enough to span a minimum of two rafters. Longer boards are desired for gable ends.

The roofing material used on a house should have a long life and provide a waterproof surface. Materials that have stood the test of time and proven to be satisfactory

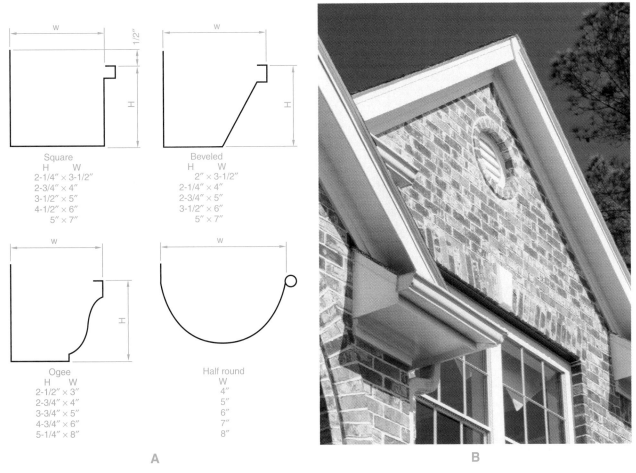

Figure 19-26. A—Typical gutter designs and sizes. B—Ogee style gutter made from aluminum. (Photo Courtesy of James Hardie® Siding Products)

Figure 19-27. This roof has wood shingles. You can see the strips of wood used to support the shingles.

include asphalt shingles, wood shingles, tile, slate, roll roofing, copper, aluminum, galvanized steel, layers of felt and tar, and rubber membrane roofing. An example of a house with wood shingles is shown in Figure 19-28. Factors that influence the selection of the roofing material are cost, local codes, roof pitch, design, and individual preference.

More homes have asphalt shingle roofs than any other type of roofing material. The usual recommended minimum weight of asphalt shingles is 235 pounds per square for square-butt strip shingles. A "square" of shingles will cover 100 square feet. Therefore, if the roof area is 200 square feet, two squares of shingles are needed for the roof. The square-butt strip shingle is 12″ × 36″ and is laid on 5″ intervals. A layer of 15-pound, saturated-felt building paper is ordinarily placed on the sheathing before laying the shingles. This acts as a moisture barrier.

Figure 19-28. The wood roof shingles on this house are visually appealing and blend nicely with the other building materials.

New Roofing Materials

New roofing materials are always being designed. These materials are stronger to reduce damage from severe storms. Also, an effort is being made to make them attractive and, in some cases, simulate the look of traditional roofing materials. Two new options for roofing materials are asphalt laminate shingles and metal roofing.

Asphalt Laminate Shingles

Traditional asphalt shingles are slowly being replaced by asphalt laminate shingles, Figure 19-29. Laminates are thicker and heavier than traditional asphalt shingles. This makes them more wind resistant and, therefore, less likely to be blown off the roof during high winds.

Advantages of laminates
• Resists high winds better than traditional asphalt shingles.
• Can add a raised, three-dimensional appearance to the roof.
• Provides the appearance of greater depth to lower-pitched roofs.

Disadvantages of laminates
• More expensive than traditional asphalt shingles.
• Increased thickness makes installation more difficult.
• Heavier to handle.
• Harder to cut.

Metal Roofing

Metal roofing is gaining wider acceptance for residential construction across all regions of the US. It is compatible with most roof designs because of the wide range of styles available.

One of the big advantages of metal roofing is its ability to resist high winds. Some products claim a wind resistance of up to 230 miles per hour. In addition, many metal roofing styles simulate the appearance of clay tile, cedar shingles, slate, or copper, Figure 19-30.

Figure 19-29. The laminate shingles on this roof add considerable depth and eye appeal to this structure. Notice how they simulate the appearance of traditional wood shingles. (Photo Courtesy of James Hardie® Siding Products)

Figure 19-30. The raised seam metal roof on this contemporary home is resistant to high wind, as well as visually pleasing. (Photo Courtesy of James Hardie® Siding Products)

Advantages of metal roofing
- Broad range of styles available.
- Can be used with most roof assemblies.
- Very high wind resistance.
- Can simulate the appearance of other roofing materials.
- Has a long life and requires little maintenance.

Disadvantages of metal roofing
- Costs more than a comparable asphalt shingle roof.
- Installation demands more precision during application.
- Fading is a problem with some metal finishes.

Internet Resources

www.alside.com
Alside, Inc., a manufacturer of low-maintenance siding

www.atas.com
ATAS International, Inc., a manufacturer of metal roofing

www.bcewp.com
Boise Cascade Engineered Wood Products

www.calredwood.org
California Redwood Association

www.certainteed.com
CertainTeed Corporation

www.cor-a-vent.com
Cor-A-Vent, Inc., a manufacturer of roof vents

www.elkcorp.com
Elk Corporation of America, a manufacturer of premium roofing materials

www.gaf.com
GAF Materials Corporation, manufacturer of roofing materials

www.met-tile.com
Met-Tile, a manufacturer of metal roofing

www.stone-slate.com
Slate/Select, Inc., a supplier of simulated slate roofing

Review Questions – Chapter 19

Write your answers on a separate sheet of paper. Do not write in this book.

1. Give the names of ten distinct roof types.
2. The purpose of roof framing is _____.
3. The roof framing member that extends from the ridge to the top plate or beyond is called a(n) _____.
4. If a roof has a pitch of 3:12 and the rise is 6′, the span is _____.
5. The roof span is measured from _____ to _____.
6. The _____ of a roof is one-half the span.
7. The formula for calculating the fractional pitch of a roof is _____.
8. The pitch of a roof that has a slope of 45° is _____.
9. List three things that determine rafter size.
10. A lightweight roofing material is one that weighs less than _____ pounds per square foot.
11. The _____ is the overhang of the roof at the eaves line that forms a connection between the roof and sidewalls.
12. List the three types of cornices that are frequently constructed on homes.
13. List two purposes of attic ventilation.
14. The total area of ventilator openings should be a minimum of _____ of the ceiling area.
15. Name two materials commonly used for roof flashing.
16. Roof sheathing on most homes is _____ thick plywood.
17. Identify five roofing materials that are used on residential structures.
18. The recommended minimum weight of asphalt shingles is _____ pounds per square.
19. List two advantages of the roof truss over conventional framing techniques.
20. Identify three types of trusses that are commonly used in residential construction.
21. List information required to purchase roof trusses for a home.
22. What is a gusset?
23. Name two newer roofing materials that have greater wind resistance than traditional asphalt shingles.

Suggested Activities

1. Look through magazines and cut out or copy pictures of houses that represent various roof styles. Mount the pictures on illustration board for display.
2. Write to several manufacturers of roof covering materials and ask for specifications and descriptive literature about their products. Display the literature and then add it to the classroom collection.
3. Build a scale model of an open cornice, a box cornice, or close cornice. Use a scale of 1″ = 1′-0″ and label the various parts. Using CADD, make a section drawing of the model. Display your model and the section drawing.

4. Using CADD, design a roof for a 24′ × 36′ cottage or a small house of your choice. Try to be innovative in the design. Draw a plan view, elevations, and a section of the roof. Dimension the drawings and describe the materials used.

5. Design three different types of trusses. Compare their strength by building a scale model of each and applying weight until each breaks. Write a description of your testing procedure and report your results. Present your drawings, models, and data to the class.

6. Using CADD, draw each of the cornice sections shown in Figure 19-11, Figure 19-12, Figure 19-13, Figure 19-14, and Figure 19-15.

Elevations

20

Objectives

After studying this chapter, you will be able to:

➤ List features that should be included on an exterior elevation.

➤ Identify the dimensions commonly shown on elevations.

➤ Explain symbols that are often found on elevations.

➤ Draw a typical exterior elevation that demonstrates proper techniques.

Key Terms

Elevation
Grade Line

Typical Wall Section

An *elevation* is an orthographic projection drawing that shows one side of the building. When the term "elevation" is used in connection with a set of construction drawings, it ordinarily refers to an exterior elevation. Various interior elevations may be drawn, but they are usually considered to be "details."

The purpose of an elevation is to show the finished appearance of a given side of the building and furnish vertical height dimensions. Four elevations are customarily drawn—one for each side of the house. In some instances, however, more than four elevations may be required to describe the structure.

Elevations provide height information about basic features of the house that cannot be shown very well on other drawings. They also indicate the exterior materials, such as siding and roof covering. Figure 20-1 shows a photograph of a typical residence and its floor plan. Figure 20-2 shows the front elevation of the house. Compare the features shown on the floor plan and elevation.

Required Information

Several features should be included on elevations. These include the identification of the specific side of the house that the elevation represents, grade lines, finished floor and ceiling levels, location of exterior wall corners, windows and doors, roof features, vertical dimensions of important features, porches, decks and patios, and material symbols.

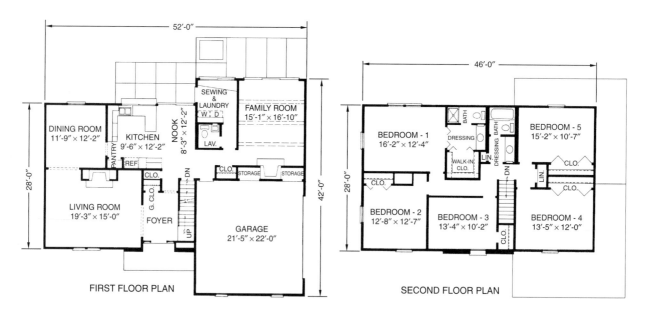

FIRST FLOOR PLAN

SECOND FLOOR PLAN

Figure 20-1. This photo shows a typical residence. The floor plans for the house are also shown. The front elevation for the house is shown in Figure 20-2.

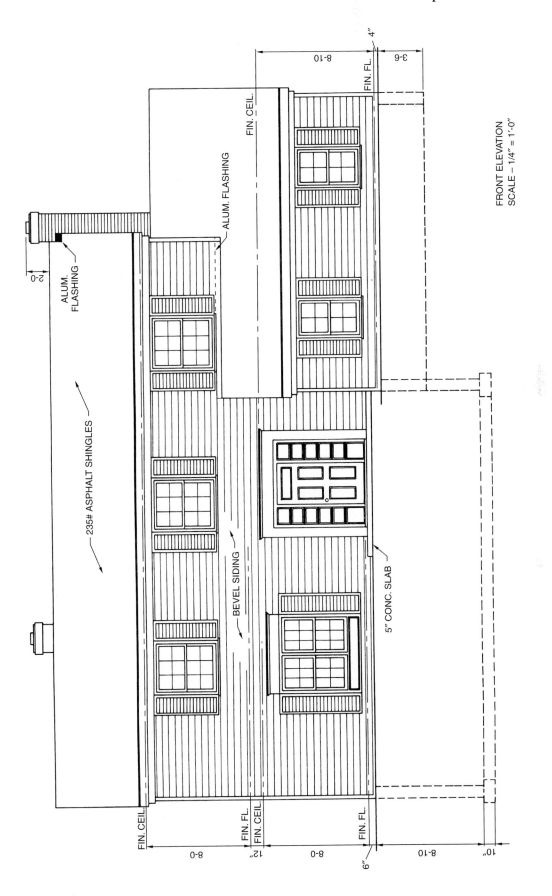

Figure 20-2. This front elevation is for the house shown in Figure 20-1.

Elevation Identification

Each elevation must identify which wall is represented. The two methods commonly used to identify the elevation are by structure side (front, rear, right side, and left side) and by compass points (north, south, east, and west). The first method of designation is preferred by most designers as there is a possibility of confusion when specifying compass points. The right and left side of the structure are determined by facing the front of the building. The right side elevation is then on the right side. Identify each elevation immediately below the drawing to avoid confusion.

Grade Line, Floors, and Ceilings

The reference point for most elevations is the *grade line*. Study the plot or site plan to determine the existing grade along each exterior wall of the house. If the existing grade is not satisfactory, a final grade line should also be indicated on each elevation that requires grading. It is frequently helpful to indicate the desired elevation height of the grade at each corner of the house. This information is recorded on the plot plan, as well as the elevation drawing, if the site is not relatively level.

All features that are below grade should be drawn as hidden lines. Examples of below-grade features include foundation walls, footings, and window wells (areaways).

The floor-to-ceiling height is an important feature shown on the elevation. Two methods of representing this height are commonly used. The first is to indicate the distance from the finished floor to the finished ceiling. The floor and ceiling are represented using a centerline. The usual distance from the finished floor to the finished ceiling is 8'-0" for the first floor and 7'-6" or 8'-0" for the second floor. The second method is to show the construction dimension. This is measured from the top of the subfloor to the top of the wall plate. In this instance, the construction dimension for the first floor is 8'-1 1/2"; the second floor dimension is 7'-7 1/2" or 8'-1 1/2". Carpenters usually prefer the later method

because it does not require them to do any calculation.

The minimum recommended height for garage ceilings is 8'-0". Basements must have a clear headroom space of at least 6'-2" with all beams and heating ducts above this height. A full-height basement ceiling is more desirable and should be specified where practical.

Most codes require that the top of the foundation wall be at least 8" above the grade to protect the framing members from moisture. This requirement should be kept in mind when drawing elevations. The garage floor may be slightly higher than the grade, but should be at least 4" lower than an interior floor when the garage is attached to the house.

Walls, Windows, and Doors

All visible wall corners are shown on the elevation using object lines. In rare instances, it may be desirable to show hidden walls. The exact wall height should be determined by drawing a wall section through the wall and locating the grade, sill, floor joists, and top plate, Figure 20-3. The section is helpful since the overhang will extend below the top of the wall in most instances. In other words, the exact wall height will be located above the line of the overhang in an elevation.

Windows and doors that are located on an exterior wall must be included on the elevation. Placement along the wall may be projected from the floor plan, but the vertical height is shown only on the elevation drawing. It is customary to place tops of windows the same height as the tops of doors. The lower face of the head jamb is considered the height of the opening. This dimension is usually 6'-10" from the top of the subfloor.

Show sufficient detail on windows and doors to accurately indicate the window. If windows are hinged, show the swing using the proper symbol. See Chapter 15. If the windows or doors have brick mold or other trim, then show this on the elevation. The glass material symbol (hatch pattern) for an elevation may be used if desired. Sometimes it is desirable to show the window and door identification symbols on the elevation, as well as the floor plan.

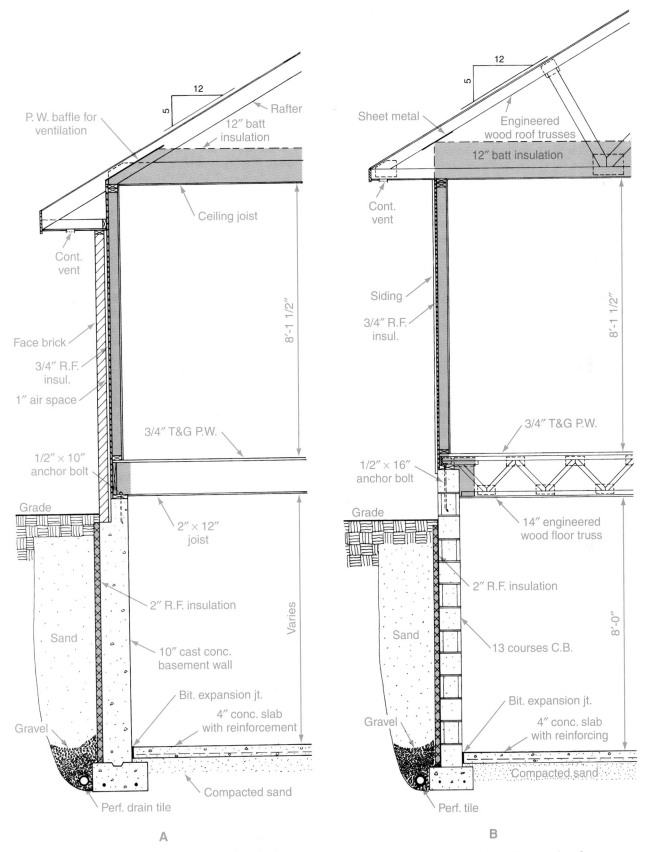

P. W. baffle for ventilation

Rafter

12

5

12" batt insulation

Ceiling joist

Cont. vent

Face brick

3/4" R.F. insul.

1" air space

1/2" × 10" anchor bolt

Grade

3/4" T&G P.W.

8'-1 1/2"

2" × 12" joist

Sand

2" R.F. insulation

10" cast conc. basement wall

Varies

Bit. expansion jt.

4" conc. slab with reinforcement

Gravel

Perf. drain tile

Compacted sand

A

Sheet metal

12

5

Engineered wood roof trusses

12" batt insulation

Cont. vent

Siding

3/4" R.F. insul.

3/4" T&G P.W.

8'-1 1/2"

1/2" × 16" anchor bolt

Grade

14" engineered wood floor truss

Sand

2" R.F. insulation

13 courses C.B.

8'-0"

Bit. expansion jt.

Gravel

4" conc. slab with reinforcing

Perf. tile

Compacted sand

B

Figure 20-3. A—Wall section for a typical brick veneer structure with a basement. B—Wall section for a typical frame structure with a basement.

Roof Features

Showing roof features on an elevation drawing is important. It is here that the roof style and pitch are shown, as well as the chimney height and size. The roof pitch may be indicated using the fractional pitch or slope triangle. The slope triangle is usually preferred and it is placed on an elevation that shows the angle of the roof.

Gable ends must be drawn first to determine roof height. If more than one roof height is anticipated, the highest section should be drawn first. When a roof is complex, an elevation drawing may not be completed without first constructing several details to determine various heights and termination points. The procedure for drawing a gable end is:

1. Locate the top of the upper wall plate and the centerline of the proposed ridge location. The ridge is usually in the center between the exterior walls.
2. Lay out the desired slope starting from the top-inside corner of the wall plate. A line from this point to the ridge will determine the underside. Note: A variation of this procedure will be necessary for certain roof trusses.
3. Measure the width of the rafter perpendicular to the bottom edge and draw the top edge parallel to the bottom edge of the rafter.
4. Measure the amount of desired overhang. Do not forget to add the thickness of roof sheathing.
5. Repeat the procedure for the other side of the roof.

Chimneys that intersect the roof usually require more than one view to determine the points where they pass through the roof. First draw the view where the roof slope is shown. This view will indicate where the chimney passes through the roof. These points may then be projected to other views.

The chimney height above the highest roof point must be dimensioned. A minimum height above the highest roof point is usually 2'-0".

Chimney flashing, roof covering material, and gable ventilators are also shown on the elevation. Use proper symbols and adequate dimensions and notes on the drawings to describe these features. Other details, such as roof ventilators, vent pipes, and gutters, may be shown if desired.

Dimensions, Notes, and Symbols

The dimensions that are placed on the elevation are mainly height dimensions. Features that must be dimensioned include the thickness of the footing, distance from the footing to the grade, distances from finished floors to finished ceilings, overhang width, height of the top of windows and doors, and height of chimney above the roof. Other dimensions may be required for details such as deck railing, retaining walls, and planters.

Notes should be included where additional information is needed or would be helpful to the builder. Some of the typical notes found on an elevation drawing provide grade information, exterior wall material notation, roof covering material identification, fascia material, and flashing material. Other notes may be required for specific situations.

Several symbols are commonly used on elevations. The roof pitch symbol is always shown and the exterior wall covering is usually a material symbol (hatch pattern). Many designers show material symbols extensively on the front elevation, but sparingly on the remaining views. Window swing symbols and cutting-plane lines are also drawn if needed.

Drawing a Typical Wall Section

The *typical wall section* is very important in constructing accurate elevations. It is also an integral part of a set of construction drawings. Care should be taken when drawing typical wall sections to be sure that all height measurements are correct. Many questions will need answers before an accurate typical wall section can be drawn:

- Will the house have a basement, crawl space, or slab foundation?

- How will the house relate to the present grade?
- Must the grade be modified to accommodate the structure?
- What are the heights from the finished floors to the finished ceilings?
- How thick is the floor(s)?
- What type of roof construction is planned?
- Will standard rough opening heights be used for windows and doors?
- What kind of exterior materials will be used?
- What type of soffit will be used?

Once these questions are answered, an accurate typical wall section can be drawn to provide the height measurements needed to draw an elevation. The following sequential steps may be used to draw a typical wall section with manual drafting or CADD.

1. Gather the necessary information and choose a scale. The first step in drawing any detail is to determine the necessary information. A guess is not good enough. You must know the specific dimensions, construction procedure, etc., to draw a detail. Once you have the information, you can begin to communicate it to others. Plan to use a scale that will show the elements of the detail. Common scales used include: 1/2″ = 1′-0″, 3/4″ = 1′-0″, and 1′ = 1′-0″.

2. Layout the footing, foundation wall, and floor slab. If you have not studied Chapter 11 *Footings, Foundations, and Concrete*, this would be an ideal place to begin. If drawing in CADD, select an appropriate layer for the footing and foundation wall. Draw these elements. Locate the basement slab and show a portion of it. Figure 20-4 shows a foundation wall, footing, and floor slab for a typical house.

3. Draw the first floor, wall, and roof structure. Once the foundation wall is properly constructed, the floor joists or trusses may be located and drawn. If using CADD, be sure to consider the layers, linetypes, and colors you wish to use. Figure 20-5 shows a photo of a CADD screen during this construction. The use of different colors helps to define the different parts of the

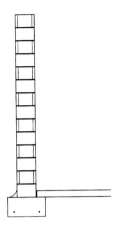

Figure 20-4. A typical wall section detail in process. Here, the footing, basement floor, and basement wall have been constructed.

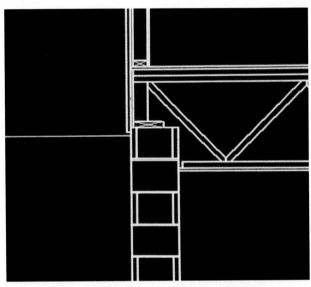

Figure 20-5. This photo of a CADD screen shows the construction of a wall section in progress.

drawing. Also, each color represents a different layer and pen size.

Continue drawing the first floor exterior wall and roof trusses. In CADD, use actual sizes rather than nominal sizes. Zoom in on small parts so that they may be more easily seen and manipulated.

Once the wall is completely roughed in, it is wise to sit back and look it over carefully to be sure it represents good building practice. Figure 20-6 shows the wall section to this point.

4. Add details and material symbols (hatch patterns). Position and draw the grade line.

Figure 20-6. The first floor joists, wall, and roof details are added to the wall section.

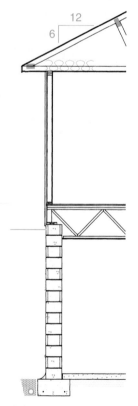

Figure 20-7. The grade line, drain tile, and material symbols (hatch patterns) are added to the wall section.

Place it on the appropriate layer if drawing in CADD. Add details such as gusset plates, drain tile, and a roof slope triangle. Include material symbols (hatch patterns) for insulation, concrete, sand, and gravel. Earth can also be included, if you desire. See Figure 20-7.

5. Add dimensions and notes. A typical wall section should include all of the required dimensions—height from the finished floor to the ceiling, thickness of the floor system, thickness and width of footing, height of foundation wall, overhang length, and so on. Be thorough. Use local notes to identify materials. Identify the grade elevation. Add other information that is pertinent for your drawing.

6. Add the scale and title. In CADD, place these on the appropriate layers. Then, look over your work to be sure that you are finished. Figure 20-8 shows the completed wall section.

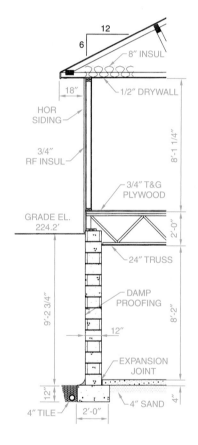

Scale: 1/2″ = 1-′0″

Wall section

Figure 20-8. Notes and dimensions are added to complete the wall section.

Procedure for Drawing an Elevation—Manual Drafting

There are numerous accepted procedures for drawing elevations. The procedure presented here is a logical approach that yields fast and accurate results, if followed carefully.

1. Draw a section through the wall to be represented by the elevation. This section should be the same scale (1/4″ = 1′-0″) as the floor plan and proposed elevation. The wall section drawing must be very accurate since it will be used to project the height of wall and roof elements to the elevation. If all the exterior walls of the house are the same type construction and height, then only one section will be required. However, if each wall is different, a section for each wall will be needed. These section drawings may be discarded after the elevations are complete. Similar drawings will be made at a larger scale later. Steps 1 and 2 are shown in Figure 20-9.

2. Place the floor plan directly above the space where the elevation is to be drawn. The exterior walls to be represented by the elevation should be facing down toward the elevation. Some drafters prefer to draw the elevation on top of the floor plan rather than below it. Either method is acceptable.

3. Project the heights of the grade line, depth and thickness of footings, window and door heights, eaves line, and roof height

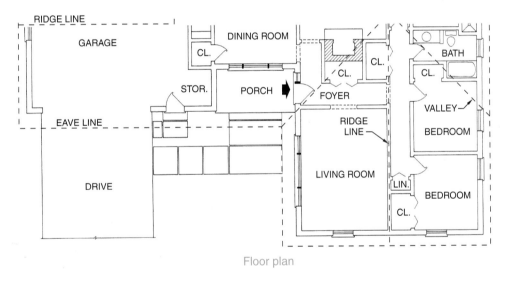

Floor plan

Elevation will be drawn here

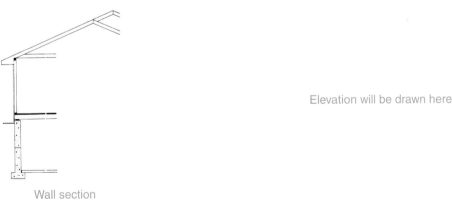

Wall section

Figure 20-9. The floor plan and a wall section are drawn around the area in which the elevation is to be drawn.

across from the section drawing to the space reserved for the elevation. These horizontal lines should be very light construction lines. Steps 3 and 4 are shown in Figure 20-10.

4. Project the horizontal length of exterior walls, windows, doors, and other elements down from the floor plan. These vertical lines may be drawn dark since their proper length will already have been determined.

5. Darken each feature and remove the construction lines. At this point, the elevation is complete enough to determine if changes are desired in the overall design. Make any changes now before proceeding on. Steps 5 and 6 are shown in Figure 20-11.

6. Add details such as railings, window muntins, trim, window wells, and gable

ventilators. Information on many of these features must be secured from reference sources such as Sweets Catalog File.

7. Add dimensions, notes, and symbols. It is good practice to draw material symbols last since they may interfere with other information if drawn earlier.

8. Check the drawing to be sure that all features are shown as desired. Add the title and scale. See Figure 20-12, which shows the finished elevation.

Repeat these steps for each elevation that needs to be drawn. It is customary to draw two elevations on a single sheet if space permits. For example, you may draw the front and rear elevations on the same sheet. See Figure 20-13. Note that material symbols are more brief on the rear elevation than appear on the front elevation.

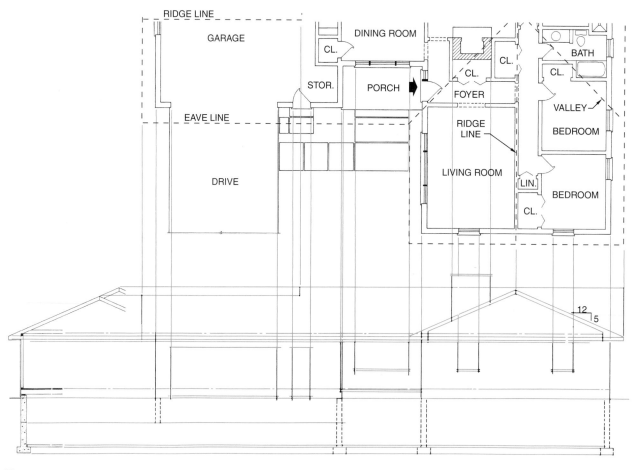

Figure 20-10. Basic features of the house have been projected from the floor plan and wall section with light construction lines to the location where the elevation is to be drawn. Vertical lines can be darkened at this point.

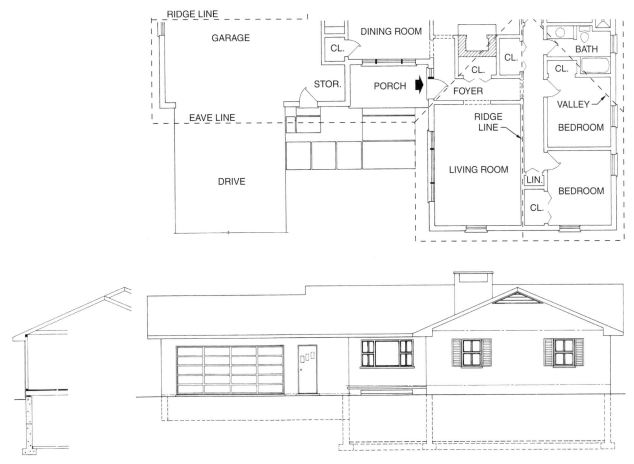

Figure 20-11. Each feature has been darkened and construction lines removed. Note that some of the required dimensions could not be projected from the floor plan or the section. These must be secured from other sources.

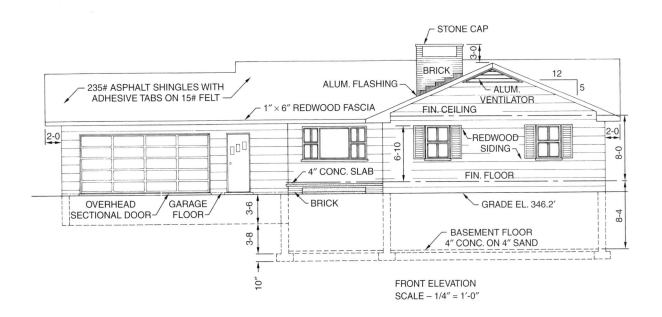

Figure 20-12. Dimensions, notes, and symbols are added to complete the elevation.

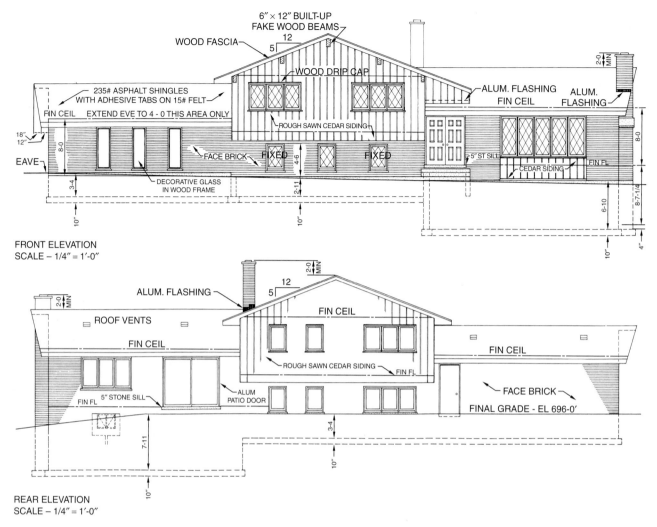

Figure 20-13. It is customary to show two elevations on a single sheet when possible. Also, note how material symbols (hatch patterns) are used less extensively on the rear elevation.

Procedure for Drawing an Elevation—CADD

The procedure for drawing an elevation using CADD is essentially the same as for traditional drafting, but there are some unique considerations. The following sequential steps can be used to draw an elevation using CADD.

1. Draw a typical wall section to provide height measurements. Figure 20-14 shows a typical wall section with sufficient information to construct a front elevation. The scale of this drawing should be 1/4″ = 1'-0″ if the drawing is to be used to project the various heights. If the wall section will be used to measure distances instead of projecting lines, the scale is normally larger. The 1/4″ scale section drawing will be discarded after the elevations are completed, but the larger scale detail may be used in the detail section. The **SCALE** command is typically used to change the size of the wall section as needed. The rest of this procedure is based on projecting lines.

2. Place a copy of the floor plan above the space where the elevation is to be drawn. The arrangement of the floor plan should be such that the side to be drawn faces down toward the elevation. Figure 20-15 shows the floor plan properly positioned to draw the front elevation. Note: Only the information needed to draw the elevation

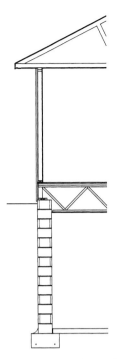

Figure 20-14. This typical wall section was drawn with CADD and will be used to construct the front elevation.

is included on the floor plan copy. This is easily done by turning off those layers that contain unwanted material.

3. Project features to be drawn on the elevation from the floor plan, as shown in Figure 20-15. This can be done as each projection line is needed or all elements can be projected at one time. Projection lines should be placed on a separate layer to facilitate removal when you are finished with them.

4. Locate the foundation wall, footings, and grade line heights on the elevation. All of these lines will be dashed (hidden) lines except the grade line. Make separate layers for these two linetypes since both will be different plotted widths than the projection lines. Figure 20-16 shows the foundation completed up to the grade line.

5. Locate the wall height and roof lines on the elevation. The exterior walls above the grade can now be drawn, as well as the roof. Notice in Figure 20-17 that the finished floor and finished ceiling on the first floor are

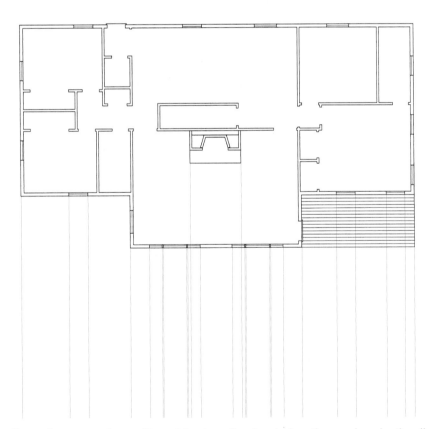

Figure 20-15. The floor plan properly positioned to draw the front elevation and projection lines are drawn. Note: The typical wall section is off the screen at this point because of the zoom factor used to show details of the floor plan more clearly.

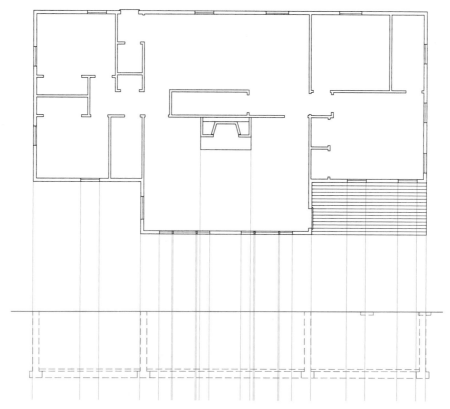

Figure 20-16. The footings, basement floor, and basement walls have been added to the elevation.

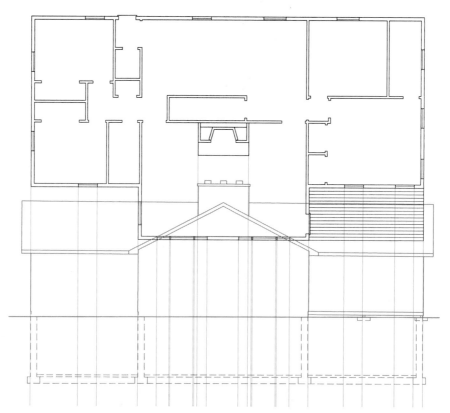

Figure 20-17. The above-grade walls are added. Notice how the floor plan overlaps the elevation. This is not a problem because the layer on which the floor plan copy resides will be turned off for plotting.

represented using a centerline. These lines will be used for dimensioning, so they may be located on the dimension layer. The exterior wall lines should have a layer of their own since they will be a different width than any of the previous lines. The chimney has also been added; it is 3'-0" above the highest point of the roof.

This is a good place to sit back and look at the overall proportions of the house. Changes can be made easily at this point.

6. Locate the height of windows, doors, and any other features. Windows are time consuming to draw one at a time, so they should be developed and stored in the symbols library for use when needed. Placing window symbols on a separate layer would make it easy to call up different window styles for compatibility with the house style. Figure 20-18 shows the windows completed. Now, all of the exterior features have been added.

7. Add dimensions, material symbols, notes, scale, and title. Notes and dimensions are best added first so they will not interfere with material hatch patterns. The scale and title can be added last. Separate layers may be used for the siding, dimensions, notes, scale, and title. Figure 20-19 shows the completed front elevation with sufficient detail to accurately communicate the intended design.

Elevations for the remaining sides of the house should be drawn using the same procedure for each one. Generally, material hatch patterns are used less on the other elevations, especially if the same material is used on all sides.

The steps above can be used to create elevations with any CADD program. However, some advanced CADD software can automatically construct elevations using data identified while developing the floor plan. When drawing in three-dimensional (3D) space, X, Y, and Z coordinates are required for each object. Therefore, when drawing the floor plan in 3D, you are not only drawing the "top view" of the walls, you are also providing the height of the walls. However, depending on your current view, you may not be able to see the wall height. This 3D information is then used by the computer to generate any view desired. See Figure 20-20.

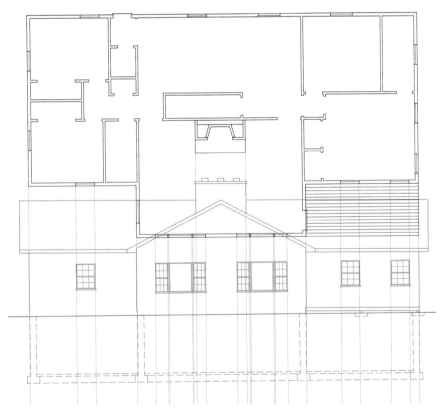

Figure 20-18. All of the exterior features have been added.

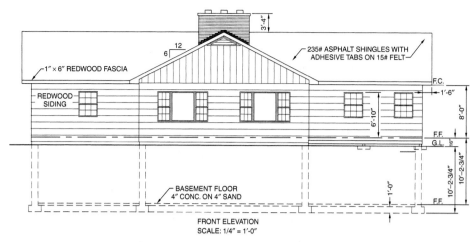

Figure 20-19. The front elevation is now complete.

Figure 20-20. This front elevation was generated from data supplied when the floor plan was developed. (Helmuth A. Geiser, member AIBD)

Internet Resources

www.atas.com
   ATAS International, Inc., a manufacturer of metal roofing

www.caradco.com
   Caradco, a manufacturer of wood windows and patio doors

www.cemplank.com
   Cemplank, a manufacturer of fiber-cement building products

www.culturedstone.com
   Cultured Stone, a producer of manufactured stone veneers

www.gp.com/build/index.html
   Georgia Pacific Corporation, supplier of building products

www.marvin.com
   Marvin Windows and Doors

www.peasedoors.com
   Pease Entry Systems

www.pozzi.com
   Pozzi Wood Windows

www.raynor.com
   Raynor Garage Doors

www.windsordoor.com
   Windsor Door, a manufacturer of garage doors

Review Questions – Chapter 20

Write your answers on a separate sheet of paper. Do not write in this book.

1. What is the primary purpose of an elevation drawing?

2. How many exterior elevations are usually required for a home? Name them.

3. The reference point for most elevations is the _____.

4. Features on the elevation drawing that are below grade are represented with a _____ line.

5. On most houses, the distance from the finished floor to the finished ceiling is _____ for the first floor.

6. The distance from the finished floor to the finished ceiling on the second floor may be _____ or _____.

7. The minimum recommended clear ceiling height of a basement (after ductwork and beams are installed) is _____.

8. The foundation wall should be at least _____ above the grade.

9. How is a typical wall section helpful for constructing the elevation?

10. The lower face of the head jamb is considered to be the height of the opening for a window or door. The distance from the subfloor to this point is usually _____.

11. Where is the slope triangle located on an elevation drawing?

12. The minimum height that a chimney must extend above the highest point of the roof is _____.

13. How are height dimensions usually obtained for exterior elevations?

14. How are width dimensions usually obtained for exterior elevations?

15. Which CADD command would typically be used to change the size of a detail from 1″ = 1′-0″ to 1/4″ = 1′-0″?

Suggested Activities

1. Select a floor plan of a house and, using CADD, draw a section through the front wall. Draw the section at a scale of 1/2″ = 1′-0″. Add dimensions and notes. Present the floor plan with the section.

2. Draw the four elevations for one of the floor plans that you developed in Chapter 18. Follow the procedure presented in this chapter. Add all necessary dimensions and notes. Submit the elevations with the floor plan.

3. Select a home from the newspaper or a magazine that shows a photo and the floor plan. Using CADD, draw a front elevation of the home using a different style roof and exterior materials. Do not change the floor plan. Present your revision along with the originals.

4. Select an older home in your community and sketch a front elevation. Obtain permission and then measure the house to determine the required dimensions. Redesign the front using good design and unique application of materials. Draw an elevation of your new design.

5. Using CADD, draw a front elevation of the house shown in the photo below. The width of the house is 26′-0″. The windows and door are 3′-0″ wide. The ceiling height on the first floor is 12′-0″ and 8′-0″ on the second floor. Dimension the appropriate features.

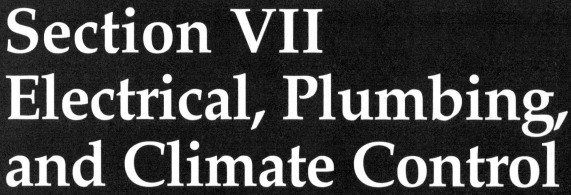

Section VII
Electrical, Plumbing, and Climate Control

21 Residential Electrical

22 Information, Communication, and Security Wiring

23 The Electrical Plan

24 Residential Plumbing

25 The Plumbing Plan

26 Residential Climate Control

27 Climate Control Plan

Photo Courtesy of Kohler Co.

Residential Electrical 21

Objectives

After studying this chapter, you will be able to:

➤ Define typical residential electrical terms.

➤ Plan for the electrical needs of a modern home.

➤ Identify and explain the three types of electrical circuits used in a residential structure.

➤ Calculate circuit requirements for a residence.

➤ Explain the advantages and disadvantages of low voltage exterior lighting.

Key Terms

Ampere (amp)
Branch Circuit
Circuit Breaker
Circuit
Conductor
Convenience Outlet
Dimmer Switch
Distribution Panel
Fuse
Ground-Fault
  Circuit Interrupter
  (GFCI)
Individual
  Appliance Circuits

Lighting Circuits
Lighting Outlet
Ohm
Receptacle
Service Drop
Service Entrance
Service Panel
Single-Pole Switch
Special Appliance
  Circuits
Three-Way Switch
Voltage
Watt

Planning for the electrical needs of a home requires a basic understanding of several factors. These factors include an understanding of related terms, electrical requirements for lighting and appliances, code restrictions, and safety considerations. This chapter provides an overview of the electrical needs of a home.

Electrical Terms

There are several terms associated with the electrical system of a house. In order to properly design a system and communicate with others, an understanding of these terms is required. The following list provides definitions for some common electrical terms.

- *Ampere (amp):* The unit of current used to measure the amount of electricity flowing through a conductor per unit of time.
- *Circuit:* A path through which electricity flows from a source to one or more devices and then returns to the source.
- *Circuit Breaker:* A safety device designed to open and close a circuit by nonautomatic means, and to open the circuit automatically on a predetermined overload of current.
- *Conductor:* A material, such as copper, that permits the flow of electricity; usually refers to a wire.
- *Convenience Outlet:* A contact device attached to a circuit to allow electricity to be drawn off for appliances or lighting.
- *Fuse:* A safety device that breaks (opens) the circuit when it is overloaded by melting a fusible link.
- *Lighting Outlet:* An outlet intended for a lighting fixture.

- *Ohm:* The unit of measure of electrical resistance in a circuit.

- *Receptacle:* A contact attached to a circuit to allow electricity to be drawn off for appliances or lighting; the same as a convenience outlet.

- *Service Drop:* The overhead service conductors between the last utility pole and the first point of attachment to the house; may be overhead or underground.

- *Service Entrance:* The fittings and conductors that bring electricity into the building.

- *Service Panel:* The main distribution box that receives the electricity and distributes it to various points in the house through branch circuits. The service panel contains the main disconnect switch fuse or breaker that supplies the total electrical system of the house.

- *Voltage:* Pressure that forces current through a wire. One volt is the force that causes one ampere of current to flow through a wire that has one ohm of resistance.

- *Watt:* A unit of measure of work in a circuit; one watt is equal to one ampere under one volt of pressure (amp × volts = watts). Most appliances are rated in watts.

Service Entrance and Distribution Panel

The foundation of a residential electrical system is the service entrance and service panel, also called a distribution panel. Residential service entrance equipment may be one of two types. These are the circuit breaker type or switch and fuse type, Figure 21-1. Either method provides overcurrent protection by opening the circuit if the current draw (load) is too high.

A residence may have 120 or 240 volt service. Only two conductors are required for 120 volt service, but three are necessary for 240 volt service. Even if no 240 volt appliances are to be installed when the home is built, 240 volt service entrance equipment is recommended. This is becoming standard procedure and it is less expensive to install initially than at a later date. Figure 21-2 illustrates how 120 volts is derived from 240 volt service.

A

B

Figure 21-1. Residential service entrance equipment. A—Distribution panel. B—Circuit breakers. (Square D Company)

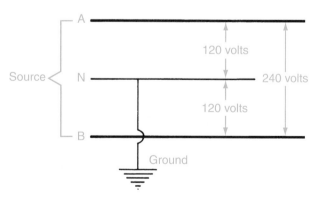

Figure 21-2. Two voltages are available from this 240 volt, three-wire service drop. Half of the 120 volt circuits are connected to A and N; the other half to B and N. All 240 volt circuits are connected to A and B.

The most common arrangement of electrical service to a house is with the service conductors first terminating at the meter. The incoming service may be overhead or underground. Figure 21-3A shows an underground service layout. Figure 21-3B shows a common method of anchoring the service drop to the house for overhead service. Several service entrance designs are possible. However, a service head must be used if the service entrance is located along the eaves line of a single-story home. In addition, the service drop must be at least 10′ above the ground at all points and 12′ above driveways. No conductor may be closer than 3′ to windows, doors, porches, or similar structures where they may be touched.

Copper or aluminum electrical conductor (cable) is used to bring the current from the service head or underground cable to the meter and then the distribution panel. The size of this conductor will depend on the size of service entrance equipment to be used in the home and the amount of amperage supplied by the electric company. The table in Figure 21-4

Service entrance conductor sizes (when demand factor is 80 percent or less)				
Number of wires	Open air installation		Installed in conduit	
	Size	Amperage	Size	Amperage
3	4	70	4	110
3	2	100	2	140
3	1/0	150	1/0	200
3	2/0	175	2/0	225
3	3/0	200	3/0	260

These sizes are for copper wire. If aluminum wire is used, at least two sizes larger will be required to handle the amperage indicated.

Figure 21-4. This chart shows the amperage rating for various conductor sizes.

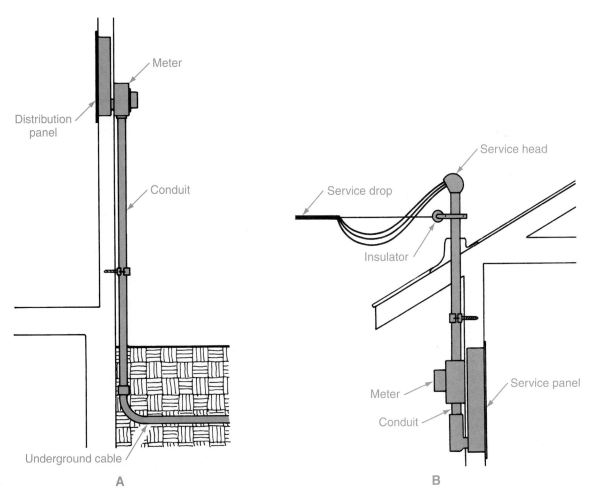

Figure 21-3. Electrical service to a house can be overhead or underground. A—Underground service is common in most new construction. B—Overhead service.

shows the size wire usually recommended for various amperage ratings.

Figure 21-5 shows typical conductor sizes and designations. Notice how the conductor diameter increases as the designation number decreases. Number 12 conductor is generally recommended for branch lighting circuits of most residential installations. The smallest circuit conductor permitted by the National Electrical Code is Number 14.

Conductor size is important in a residential electrical system because current flowing through the wires produces heat. If the wire is too small for the amount of current, it may cause a fire. Even if a fire does not result, the heat increases resistance in the wire and electricity is wasted.

From the meter, the conductors are terminated at the service panel or *distribution panel*, Figure 21-6. This is where the electricity is received from the meter and is distributed to various points in the house through branch circuits. The main disconnect switch or breaker is usually located in the distribution panel. This switch disconnects all current to the house and should be located as close to the incoming service as possible.

The capacity of the service entrance equipment should be sufficient to supply both present and future demands. The National Electrical Code recommends that a minimum of 100 amp service be provided for all residences. However, many homes will require 150 amp, 200 amp, or higher service.

The most common overcurrent protection device used in the distribution panel in new construction is the circuit breaker. The heart of the system is the individual branch circuit breaker, Figure 21-7. Breakers are safe, reliable, and easy to use, which accounts for their popularity. Figure 21-8 shows a distribution panel designed for circuit breakers.

Branch Circuits

Any home will have several branch circuits. A *branch circuit* is one of several individual circuits from the distribution panel that is routed to similar devices. Appliances and outlets are grouped together so that smaller breakers or fuses and smaller conductors (wires)

Figure 21-5. Relative wire sizes and gauge number designations.

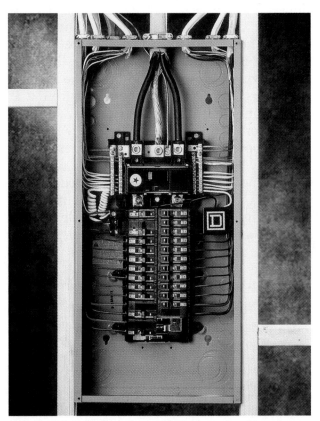

Figure 21-6. This typical distribution panel box has the cover removed to show service entrance conductors, main disconnect switch, and wiring. (Square D Company)

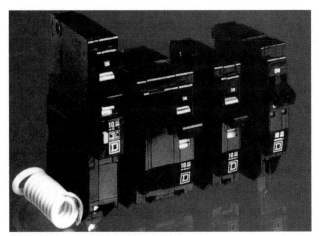

Figure 21-7. Circuit breakers come in a variety of sizes and capacities. (Square D Company)

Figure 21-8. This distribution panel contains the main breaker (top, with yellow star), 240 volt circuits (large breakers, second from the top), and 120 volt circuits (small breakers on the bottom). (Square D Company)

may be used. Switches and outlets are not designed for large conductors. If a house had only one giant circuit to supply 100 amps of current, the wire would be very large, costly, and impossible to handle. Also, if the fuse were to blow or breaker were to trip, the total structure would be without power. Just as important, it would not be possible to install the proper fuse protection for various appliances that require far smaller amounts of current. These are just some of the reasons branch circuits are needed.

The National Electrical Code (NEC) specifies three types of branch circuits that should be used in a residential structure—lighting circuits, special appliance circuits, and individual appliance circuits. These circuits are introduced below and explained in the next sections.

- *Lighting Circuits:* These are primarily for lighting. They serve permanently installed lighting fixtures, as well as receptacle outlets into which lamps, radios, television, clocks, and similar 120 volt devices, other than kitchen appliances, are plugged.

- *Special Appliance Circuits:* Special appliance circuits are located in the kitchen, usually above the countertop. These are designed for

electric fry pans, mixers, blenders, toasters, and similar appliances that require large amounts of current. A different special appliance circuit may also be used along a workbench in the home shop.

- *Individual Appliance Circuits:* These are circuits that serve single, permanently installed appliances such as a range, water heater, washer, dryer, water pump, and table saw. Each appliance will have its own circuit.

Lighting Circuits

Lighting circuits are frequently Number 12 copper wire conductor with 20 amp overcurrent protection. This combination provides 2400 watts of lighting capacity ($120 \times 20 = 2400$). The code requires a minimum of three watts of lighting power for each square foot of floor space. One lighting circuit would be sufficient for 800 square feet of floor space if this minimum were applied. Again, this is a minimum and probably not satisfactory for most homeowners. One lighting circuit for each 400 square feet would be more advisable.

Calculation of the number of lighting circuits recommended for a typical 48′ × 60′ residence is performed as follows.

1. Figure the total area included in the house. (48′ × 60′ = 2880 square feet)

2. Divide the total area in the house by 400. (2880 / 400 = 7.2 lighting circuits)

The number of lighting circuits required for a house with 2880 square feet is seven. The following table shows the minimum and recommended number of lighting circuits for various size houses.

RESIDENTIAL LIGHTING CIRCUITS		
Number of Square Feet	Number of Lighting Circuits	
	Code Minimum	Recommended
1000	2	3
1200	2	3
1600	3	4
2000	3	5
2400	4	6
2800	5	7

Special Appliance Circuits

Special appliance circuits generally require Number 12 copper wire conductor with a 20 amp overcurrent protection. Each of these circuits is capable of supplying 2400 watts (20 × 120 = 2400). However, no lighting outlets may be operated from these circuits. The National Electrical Code specifies a minimum of two special appliance circuits in the kitchen and each similar room. Special appliance circuits may be appropriate in other areas of the house such as a sewing room, garage, or shop. However, two special appliance circuits may not be sufficient for today's large kitchens and expanded work areas.

Individual Appliance Circuits

Some appliances require such a large amount of electricity that they must have their own circuit. Such circuits are called individual appliance circuits. The following appliances are usually operated on individual appliance circuits.

- Air Conditioner
- Attic Fan
- Clothes Dryer
- Clothes Washer
- Countertop Oven
- Dishwasher
- Furnace
- Garbage Disposal
- Range
- Table Saw
- Water Heater
- Water Pump

In addition to these, any 120 volt, permanently-connected appliance that is rated at over 1400 watts or has an automatically starting electric motor should have its own circuit.

Individual appliance circuits may be 120 or 240 volts, depending on the requirements of the appliance on the circuit. Always check the rating of the appliance. The chart in Figure 21-9 shows the approximate requirements of several appliances.

Circuit Requirement Calculations

The size of service entrance equipment and number and type of branch circuits are dependent on a number of factors. These include the size of the house, size and number of appliances, and lighting to be installed. The increased load from planned future expansions should also be considered. The following shows how circuit requirement calculations are performed in one example.

Size of Residence = 1500 square feet

Lighting Circuits:
1500 square feet @ 3 watts per square feet = 4500 watts

Special Appliance Circuits:
2 circuits for kitchen = 4800 watts
(120 volts × 20 amp × 2 = 4800 watts)

Individual Appliance Circuits:
1 circuit (240 volts) for self-contained range = 12,000 watts
1 circuit (240 volts) for dryer   =   5,000 watts
1 circuit for water heater   =   2,000 watts
1 circuit for clothes washer   =   700 watts
1 circuit for garbage disposal =   300 watts
1 circuit for dishwasher   =   1,200 watts
1 circuit for furnace   =   800 watts
                        Total = 31,300 watts

For 120/240 volt 3-wire system feeders:
31,300 watts / 240 volts = 130.4 amps

This house will require 150 amp service. Main circuit breakers are produced in ratings of 30, 40, 50, 60, 70, 100, 125, 150, 175, and 200 amps. Since 130.4 is between 125 and 150, the logical choice is 150 amp service. This would also provide a spare circuit for future use.

Outlets and Switches

All convenience outlets, switches, and joints where conductors are spliced must be housed in an electrical box. Also, all lighting fixtures must be mounted on a box. There are several types of boxes for various uses. Two common types of boxes are shown in Figure 21-10. Boxes are made from metal with a galvanized coating or from other insulating materials.

Outlets

Figure 21-11 shows various convenience outlets. Each has a distinct design or purpose. Placement of convenience outlets, switches, and lighting fixtures require some thought.

Typical Appliance Requirements				
Appliance or equipment	Typical watts	Usual voltage	Wire size	Recommended fuse size
20,000 Btu Air Conditioner	1,200	120/240	12	20 amp
Band Saw	300	120	12	20 amp
Bathroom Heater	2,000	120/240	12	20 amp
Blender	300	120	12	20 amp
Coffee Maker	900	120	12	20 amp
Dehumidifier	350	120	12	20 amp
Dishwasher	1,200	120/240	12	20 amp
Dryer (electric)	5,000	120/240	10	30 amp
Electric Fry Pan	1,200	120	12	20 amp
Electric Range with Oven	12,000	240	6	50–60 amp
Furnace	800	120	12	20 amp
Garage Door Opener	750	120	12	20 amp
Garbage Disposal	300	120	12	20 amp
Hand Iron	1,100	120	12	20 amp
Home Computer	145	120	12	20 amp
Home Freezer	350	120	12	20 amp
Ironer	1,500	120	12	20 amp
Microwave Oven	1,450	120	12	20 amp
Range Oven (separate)	5,000	120/240	10	30 amp
Range Top (separate)	5,000	120/240	10	30 amp
Refrigerator	300	120	12	20 amp
Roaster	1,400	120	12	20 amp
Rotisserie	1,400	120	12	20 amp
Table Saw	1,000	120/240	12	20 amp
Television	300	120	12	20 amp
Toaster	1,000	120	12	20 amp
Trash Compactor	400	120	12	20 amp
VCR/DVD Player	24	120	12	20 amp
Waffle Iron	1,000	120	12	20 amp
Washer	700	120	12	20 amp
Water Heater	2,000–5,000	120	10	20 amp

Figure 21-9. This chart shows the approximate requirements for several appliances. Refer to the manufacturer's specifications for actual usage.

Figure 21-10. Typical metal and plastic electrical boxes used in residential construction.

Code requirements, furniture arrangements, and personal preference all play a role in the location. The code states that in living areas no point along a wall should be more than 6′ from a convenience outlet and each room should have a minimum of three outlets. Placement of outlets about 8′ apart is more satisfactory and recommended. This results in no point along a wall being more than 4′ from a convenience outlet. The height of most convenience outlets is 12″ or 18″ above the floor. The kitchen is an exception where the special appliance outlets are usually placed above the countertop. It is common practice to switch one or more outlets in each room where lamps are to be located. This saves wear on the lamp and is more convenient.

Frequently, home designers forget to include weatherproof outlets and ample exterior lighting, Figure 21-12. These outlets

Figure 21-12. This is a typical weatherproof outlet, which is required for damp locations.

Figure 21-11. Several types of outlets are used in residential electrical systems. (Leviton Manufacturing Co., Inc.)

provide a source of power for outside work or play. Placing at least one outlet on each side of the exterior is recommended. Exterior lighting, on the other hand, enhances the appearance of the house and improves safety. Lighting fixtures and convenience outlets should also be located in the attic and crawl spaces of the house.

There are several types of outlets that may be classified as "special outlets." These include telephone jacks, television antenna outlets (cable, satellite, or aerial), built-in outlets for home entertainment or theater speakers, entrance signals, burglar alarm systems, and automatic fire-alarm systems, Figure 21-13.

 Entrance signals, such as doorbells and chimes, can be wired to signaling devices for disabled persons. For example, a doorbell can be wired to lights or fans in a number of rooms. When the doorbell is activated, the light or fan comes on to alert deaf or deaf-blind occupants that somebody is at the door. These are specialized installations. Information is usually supplied by the manufacturer or the systems are professionally installed.

Switches

Figure 21-14 shows a variety of switch types. Switches should be located in a logical place 48″ above the floor. For persons seated in wheelchairs, a height of 30″ to 40″ may be more convenient. Care must be taken not to mount them behind doors or other hard-to-get-to places.

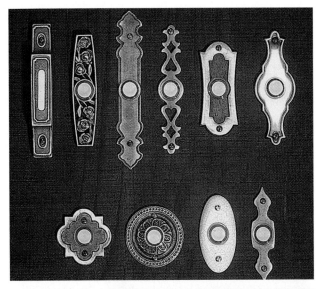

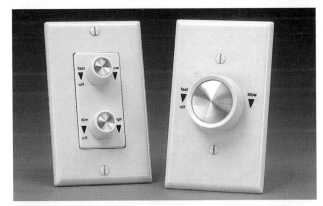

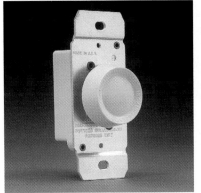

Figure 21-13. An assortment of special residential telephone outlets. (Leviton Manufacturing Co., Inc.)

Figure 21-14. Various styles of residential switches. (Leviton Manufacturing Co., Inc.; Broan-NuTone, A Nortek Company)

Switches in a bathroom should not be located within reach of the bathtub or shower. This is a very unsafe situation. The primary objective when designing the placement of switches in the bathroom is to avoid this situation.

Most switches in a house operate one fixture and are the single-pole type. A *single-pole switch* simply opens and closes the circuit. In some instances three-way switches may be used for extra convenience. A *three-way switch* allows a fixture to be turned on and off from two locations, Figure 21-15. Common locations for three-way switches are entrances, garages, stairs, and rooms that have more than one entrance. Fixtures may also be switched from three locations using two three-way switches and one four-way switch, Figure 21-16.

A *dimmer switch* is a special switch that allows the light to be adjusted to the desired brightness, Figure 21-17. It is commonly used for a main dining room ceiling fixture. The dimmer switch will fit into a regular electrical box.

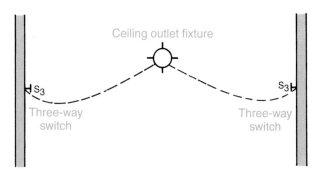

Figure 21-15. A fixture or outlet may be switched from two locations using two three-way switches.

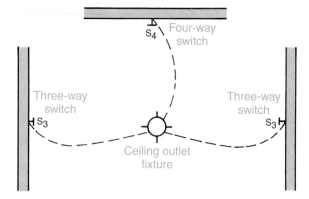

Figure 21-16. One or more fixtures or outlets may be operated from three locations using two three-way switches and one four-way switch.

Figure 21-17. A dimmer switch is used to vary the intensity of an incandescent light. (Leviton Manufacturing Co., Inc.)

Ground-Fault Circuit Interrupter (GFCI)

A *ground-fault circuit interrupter (GFCI)* is a safety device that continually monitors the amount of current going to the load and compares it to that coming back, Figure 21-18. So long as the two are equal, the electricity continues to flow. However, if the amount of

Figure 21-18. A duplex GFCI outlet.

current returning is less than it should be, the GFCI will trip (open) the circuit. The logic of GFCI design is that if the current is not coming back via the wire, it must be going somewhere else. Often, this is through a person to the earth.

A GFCI could save your life. If you are ever unlucky enough to receive an electrical shock, but fortunate enough to have a GFCI in the circuit, it will feel like you are being stuck with a needle. Then, the GFCI will trip and open the circuit, thus stopping the current.

The time it takes for a GFCI to open a circuit is no more than 1/30 of a second to comply with UL standards. The amount of current imbalance that the GFCI must detect before it trips is four to six milliamps (thousandths of an amp). Most people can tolerate this much current for 1/30 of a second before their heart goes into fibrillation, which means that the heart goes out of synchronization and can result in death.

GFCIs can be placed as any receptacle. A type of GFCI can also be placed as a breaker in the distribution panel to protect an entire branch circuit. The preferred location is generally at the receptacle for convenience and less cost. The National Electrical Code (NEC) defines when and how GFCIs should be used. Some of the more common regulations are:

- **Kitchen.** All countertop receptacles within a 6′ straight-line distance from the sink must have GFCI protection.
- **Bathroom.** All receptacles installed in bathrooms must have GFCI protection.
- **Garage.** Every receptacle in a garage must have GFCI protection unless it is not readily accessible, such as a receptacle located on the ceiling for a garage door opener or one servicing a plug-in appliance occupying dedicated space, such as a freezer.
- **Outdoors.** All receptacles installed outdoors that are readily accessible and within 6′-6″ of grade level must have GFCI protection.
- **Unfinished basements and crawlspaces at or below grade level.** All receptacles installed in these locations must have GFCI protection except for a dedicated branch circuit for a plug-in appliance, a laundry circuit, or a single receptacle supplying a permanently installed sump pump.

Low Voltage Exterior Lighting

Good outdoor lighting is both functional and aesthetic. It is functional because it will provide light when and where you need it for outdoor activities such as entertaining, cooking out, yard games, or safety and security. Outdoor lighting is aesthetic because it will increase the beauty of your yard, garden, and exterior of the home at night.

Low voltage (12 volt) lighting systems are a popular way to add lighting to the exterior of a house. The system consists of the lights, wire, one or more controllers, and transformers. These systems are generally more expensive to install than standard 120 volt lighting, but they are considered safer for outdoor use, easier to install, and use less energy. Installation of 120 volt wiring is best left to the professionals. As always, check with your local building department to secure permits and determine specific code requirements in your area before installing a low voltage lighting system.

Planning Low Voltage Exterior Lighting

Planning is necessary for effective outdoor lighting. First, begin by deciding where you will need light at night for safety, activities, and security. Then you can plan for the decorative lighting. But, no matter what your specific purpose, there are some basic considerations to think about. Following are some things to keep in mind when planning for low voltage exterior lighting.

- **Try to avoid glare.** Glare is the reason for discomfort we feel when looking at a light that is too bright or aimed directly at us. Good lighting design avoids glare.
- **Outdoor light fixtures are either decorative or hidden.** Decorative fixtures, such as carriage lamps, are meant to be seen, Figure 21-19. Only the effect of a hidden lamp, not the fixture itself, is meant to be seen.
- **Use shielded fixtures to hide the light source.** Shielded fixtures let you see a lighted object,

Figure 21-19. A decorative low voltage lighting fixture that is meant to be seen.

rather than the light itself. Shielding can be a diffusing panel or frosted globe.

- **Hide fixtures where they cannot be seen.** By locating fixtures at ground level or up in a tree, glare can be reduced. Obviously, decorative fixtures should not be hidden.
- **Use more, smaller lights.** Several smaller sources of light are better than a few bright lights. For example, several low voltage light sources along a drive or sidewalk is pleasing to look at and does not produce glare, Figure 21-20.

- **Remember safety when planning lighting.** Consider adding lights to improve safety along the driveway, front walk, and steps; around the front and back entries; on the deck or patio; around the swimming pool; and in planted areas. Figure 21-21 shows a house with lighting added for security and beauty.

Figure 21-20. A lantern-type fixture designed to be placed along a sidewalk or other walkway with many other lights, usually the same type.

Figure 21-21. This front lamppost will provide safe lighting for the sidewalk entrance to this house. Also, notice the uplighting that details the taller plants in front of the house. (Photo Courtesy of James Hardie® Siding Products)

- **Use light to shape an outdoor space.** For example, uplighting sharpens shapes. Notice the trees in the foreground of Figure 21-21. Backlighting shows the form of an object more clearly. Shadowing can make a plant seem larger and more prominent. Grazing will emphasize the texture of textured surfaces. Downlighting provides general lighting or focused lighting. Moonlighting is used to cast shadows to provide a more realistic appearance to the yard.

Low Voltage Wiring Considerations

Low voltage lighting systems are generally easy for most homeowners to install. Many types and sizes of prepackaged sets are readily available from home centers. Also, individual components—lights, wire, controllers, and transformers—can be purchased separately for a custom layout. The following points should be considered when planning and/or installing low voltage exterior lighting.

- Generally, when lights are a great distance from the transformer, they provide less light due to a voltage drop. To avoid this condition, use a tee design with half the lights on each side of the tee. You might use Number 10 wire for the main lines and Number 12 wire between the lights to further reduce the voltage drop.

- A good rule of thumb is to put no more than 100 watts of lighting on one line or leg of the tee. For example, if you were to put ten lights each of 20 watts on a circuit, half of them would be attached to each leg of the tee. Thus, each leg of the tee has 100 watts of lighting (5 lights × 20 watts = 100 watts), Figure 21-22.

- Choose the proper size transformer for your planned layout. Purchase a transformer with a built-in photocell and timer. You may need more than one transformer for a large layout with several circuits. Also, the gauge of the low voltage wire is related to the length of the run and the number and size of lights used.

- Use a ground fault circuit interrupter (GFCI) as a power source. Remember, the transformer in a low voltage system will be connected to a 120 volt power source. The transformer should be housed in a watertight box, if located outside.

- Consider an indoor switch and timer combination. This will enable you to bypass the automatic controller so the lights can be turned on and off as desired.

- Try to prevent corrosion before it starts. Corrosion in lines and connectors reduces the brightness of lights in a low voltage system. Where a light fixture connects to the branch line is one major point of corrosion. Many manufacturers provide clip-on connectors that generally corrode. A better idea is to splice the wires together and use

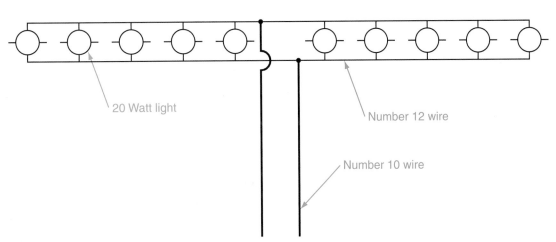

20 Watt light

Number 12 wire

Number 10 wire

Figure 21-22. Recommended wiring layout for low voltage lights on one circuit. Each leg of the tee has 100 watts of lighting.

waterproof wire nuts. Adding silicone gel inside the nut will add more protection.

- Call the utility company before you dig and ask them to locate underground wires and pipes. The service is generally free and it might save you lots of time and money.

- As a practical matter, leave a little extra wire as you hook up the lights in the event you decide to move a light after you test the effect.

- After checking out the entire setup, then you can bury the wires at least 6″ deep. Note: Each fixture should receive between 10.5 and 12 volts of power for a uniform appearance.

Internet Resources

www.eagle-electric.com
Cooper Wiring Devices

www.flexiduct.com
Geist Manufacturing, Inc., manufacturer of Flexiduct cord covers

www.ge.com/product/home/lighting.htm
General Electric, home lighting products

www.homecabling.com
The Siemon Company, a manufacturer of home cabling systems

www.homecontrols.com
Home Controls, Inc., a supplier of home automation equipment

www.ittnss.com
ITT Industries, network systems and services

www.leviton.com
Leviton, a manufacturer of electrical and electronic products

www.lutron.com
Lutron, a manufacturer of lighting control products

www.seagulllighting.com
Sea Gull Lighting Products, Inc.

www.westpenn-cdt.com
West Penn Wire/CDT, a manufacturer of electronic cable

Review Questions – Chapter 21

Write your answers on a separate sheet of paper. Do not write in this book.

1. The term given to the pressure that forces current through a conductor is _____.

2. Two types of overcurrent protection devices found in residential service entrance equipment are _____ and _____.

3. Material, such as copper wire, that carries the flow of electricity is called a(n) _____.

4. The result of multiplying amps by volts is _____.

5. How many service entrance conductors are required for 240 volt service?

6. The service drop must be at least _____ feet above the ground at all points and _____ feet above driveways.

7. Most wires used in residential wiring are made from what material?

8. Which conductor is larger in diameter: Number 12 or Number 14?

9. If the wiring in a circuit is too small for the load, what is likely to happen?

10. The smallest conductor that may be used in a residential lighting circuit is Number _____ wire.

11. The purpose of the main disconnect switch is to _____.

12. The National Electrical Code recommends a minimum of _____ amp service for all residences.

13. The type of overcurrent protection used in most homes today is the _____.

14. List three types of branch circuits found in a home.

15. The minimum number of special appliance circuits required for a kitchen is _____.

16. A lighting circuit has _____ amp overcurrent protection if Number 12 conductors are used.

17. The code requires a minimum of _____ watts of lighting power for each square foot of floor space in the home.

18. One lighting circuit should provide lighting for _____ square feet if the code were followed.

19. A 1500 square feet house would require _____ lighting circuits using the code minimum watts per square foot.

20. A special appliance circuit is usually wired with Number _____ copper conductors with a _____ amp fuse.

21. How many watts can be supplied if the voltage is 120 volts and the current is 20 amps?

22. Identify five appliances that would require an individual appliance circuit.

23. The most common overcurrent protection device used in the distribution panel in new construction is the _____.

24. The minimum number of convenience outlets permitted in a single room is _____.

25. No point along a wall should be more than _____ feet from a convenience outlet.

26. To switch a lighting fixture from two locations, you would need a _____ switch.

27. In a _____ light fixture, the light source is hidden from the eye allowing you see a lighted object, rather than the light itself.

28. Name three major components of a low voltage lighting system.

29. In a low voltage lighting system, a light a great distance from the transformer will provide less light due to the _____.

30. Name three advantages of outdoor low voltage lighting over the standard 120 volt system.

Suggested Activities

1. Determine the service entrance rating for your home or apartment. Count the number of 120 volt and 240 volt circuits. Calculate the amperage required for all the appliances, equipment, and lighting. Determine if the incoming service is sufficient to operate all requirements. Show all your work.

2. Visit a home under construction that has the rough electrical wiring in place. Secure permission to enter the construction site. Count the number of convenience outlets, switches, and lighting fixtures in the house. Determine the number of circuits and size of the main breaker. Is the house adequately wired? Organize your findings and report to the class.

3. Write to manufacturers that produce residential electrical supplies. Ask for literature and specifications for electrical boxes, wire, service entrance equipment, switches, and fixtures. Display the material and add it to the class collection for future use.

4. Prepare a bulletin board illustrating the circuits in a house and the equipment, appliances, and lighting they serve.

5. Open the CADD drawing of the site plan that you drew in Activity 2 in Chapter 10. Plan an exterior low voltage lighting plan that applies the principles discussed in this chapter.

6. Using your CADD system, create several commonly used electrical symbols. Use the Reference Section of this text for examples. Add the symbols to your symbols library.

Information, communication, and security wiring requires special cables, enclosures, and equipment. (Leviton Manufacturing Co., Inc.)

Information, Communication, and Security Wiring

22

Objectives

After studying this chapter, you will be able to:

➤ Identify the features related to information, communication, and security that should be considered when designing a new home.

➤ List the types of lines or cables used in residential telephone systems.

➤ Define common terms associated with information, communication, and security wiring.

➤ List the components of a security system designed to protect residential property.

➤ Discuss the components of a home automation system.

➤ Describe the elements of a low-voltage switching system.

Key Terms

Alarm Functions
Analog Data
Bundled Cable
Cable Pair
Combination
   Systems
Communication/
   Recording
   Functions
Digital Data
Hard-Wired Systems
Monitoring Functions
Motion Detectors
Network
Panic Button
Perimeter System
Power Line
   Technology

Programming
   Functions
Radio Grade 6
   (RG-6) Cable
Relays
Signaling Circuits
Structured Wiring
   Systems
Structured Wiring
Switching Functions
Twisted-Pair Wire
Unshielded Twisted-
   Pair (UTP) Cable
Wiring Cabinet
Wiring Closet

Introduction

Many new technologies have emerged in the past few years that provide for security systems, home automation, and information and communication via voice and data lines. Some of these technologies, such as sound systems, cable television, and telephone wiring, are familiar to most builders. However, the cabling and devices that make home automation and security systems work are emerging technologies and not as familiar to most builders.

The best time to consider these system options is when planning and designing a new home. The cost is less and system integration is more efficient when these systems are installed as the home is constructed. However, an existing house can be retrofitted with these systems in some cases.

Modern technology features that might be considered when designing a new home can be divided into five general areas. These areas are based on the function of the feature. The five areas are monitoring functions, switching (activating) functions, programming functions, communication/recording functions, and alarm functions.

Monitoring Functions

Devices that perform *monitoring functions* examine certain aspects of the house to determine their status. The device then reports the status either to the homeowner or to another device that can act on the status. Some examples of conditions that may be monitored include movement within the house; sound within the house; window and door status, such as open or closed; intruder actions and movements;

heating, cooling, and humidity levels; and smoke and carbon monoxide gas levels.

Switching (Activating) Functions

Devices that perform *switching functions* initiate an action based on an input. For example, when the temperature drops below a certain level, the furnace is switched on based on a signal from the thermostat. Some actions that switching devices may initiate include turning lights on or off; turning appliances on or off; activating an audio system; activating various functions of an entertainment center; opening or closing draperies, shades, and skylights; and locking or unlocking doors, windows, and vents.

Programming Functions

Devices that perform *programming functions* can control a sequence of events. For example, a timer on a lamp is a simple device that performs a programming function. At a certain programmed time, the timer turns the light on. At another programmed time, the timer turns the light off. Devices that perform programming functions can be used to create a timed sequence for lighting, an entertainment system, or climate control system, Figure 22-1.

Communication/Recording Functions

Devices that perform *communication/ recording functions* allow voice, video, or data communication; record voice, video, or data communication; or both. Examples of these devices include intercoms, voice or video phones, and closed-circuit video cameras. A device that allows commands to another device to be remotely entered by phone or Internet would also be a communication device.

Alarm Functions

Devices that perform *alarm functions* alert the home owner or a home security

agency to potential dangers based on a signal from a monitoring device. For example, a motion detector may provide a signal to an intruder alert, which in turn alerts the homeowner and home security agency, Figure 22-2. Other alarm devices may alert the home owner to unsafe conditions from gas and smoke or warn of a malfunctioning appliance.

Figure 22-1. This programmable lighting controller can set ten separate lighting scenes from multiple locations. (Lutron Electronics, Inc.)

Figure 22-2. This motion sensor detects movement inside the house, which may be an intruder, and will alert the occupants and/or the security command center.

Information and Communication Wiring

A new home in today's society should have a minimum of two standard telephone lines. These lines provide the wiring for information transfer and communication. One line is generally dedicated to voice communication. This is the traditional phone line. The other telephone line is used for data transmission, such as for Internet access.

The telephone lines are two wires called a *cable pair.* The wires are powered at the telephone company with a direct current to operate the telephone equipment. The cable pair from the telephone company terminates in a cable termination box on the outside of the house. From there, the cable pair enters the building and usually connects to a terminal block (42A block) or network interface device inside the building. The terminal block is the point of connection for all the telephones in the home. Single telephone service on a single circuit can be used by one or more telephones or modems as each device is connected in parallel.

Telephone cable is designed for both indoor and outdoor use. There are three kinds of indoor wiring: solid wire, stranded wire, and spiral ribbon wire. Solid wire is generally used inside the wall where flexibility is not required. Stranded wire is generally used between the device and the wall jack where a flexible cable is needed. Solid and stranded wire can be attached to terminal screws with a screwdriver, Figure 22-3. Spiral ribbon wire is generally used inside a wiring cabinet. Spiral ribbon wire requires a special tool for installation.

Telephone cable pairs are color coded. Black, green, red, and yellow are the colors used in four-wire telephone cable, Figure 22-4. Terminal screws are also color coded to match the cable. Standard electrical boxes or terminal blocks may be used for termination points. Be sure to check your local code for specific requirements. Do not mix four-wire cable and the more preferred band-striped twisted-pair wire (Category 3 or 5). *Twisted-pair wire* is a

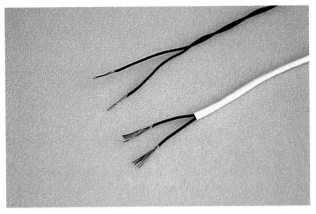

Figure 22-3. Solid (top) and stranded telephone wire.

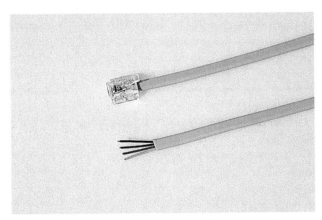

Figure 22-4. Common four-wire telephone cable colors are black, green, red, and yellow. An RJ-11 standard telephone jack is shown installed on the line (top).

product in which each pair of wires is twisted together to preserve signal quality. The wires have a stripe on the insulation to make identification easy.

Signaling Circuits

Signaling circuits supply the electrical power to buzzers, doorbells, chimes, signal lights, or warning devices. Remote-control, low-voltage circuits are also included in this category. The National Electrical Code (Article 725) specifies three classes of signaling circuits:

- **Class 1 Circuits:** Those circuits where power is limited to no more than 30V (volts) and not over 1000VA (volt-amps). These circuits are used for remote motor-switching systems.

- **Class 2 Circuits and Class 3 Circuits:** Those circuits whose power is not to exceed 30V and 100VA. These circuits are used for chimes, doorbells, humidistats, and thermostats.

The conductors used for buzzers, bells, and chimes range in size from Number 16 to 20, Figure 22-5. These devices normally require between 6 and 20 volts. This type of wire is often called "bell wire."

Doorbell circuits may be battery operated or powered by a transformer connected to a 120V power source. The transformer is usually located on an outlet box connected to the 120V supply. The connection must be made within the box and then connected to the bell or buzzer. Conductors serving buzzers, bells, or chimes must never be run with regular full-power circuits that operate on 120V or 240V.

Data and Video Conductors

Most computer and data networks are connected using *unshielded twisted-pair (UTP)* cable, also known as "Category 5" or "Cat 5." The Electronic Industries Association (EIA) and the Telecommunications Industry Association (TIA) have established two cable/wiring standards. These standards are T568A and T568B. The standards describe the parameters of use and installation for voice and data communication using UTP cable.

UTP cable is designed to reject interference from other cable current as well as maximize the speed of data transmission. This

Figure 22-6. Category 5 cable is the most popular cable for computer and data networks. Notice the twisted pairs.

cable has eight conductors of Number 24 wire bundled inside a PVC jacket, Figure 22-6. The conductors are twisted together into pairs to reduce electrical interference. Each wire is color-coded for uniformity and ease of use. The wire colors are white, green, orange, blue, and brown. In fact, the wire color is very important as each one has a definite location in a standard RJ-45 jack that is used with Category 5 cable. Figure 22-7 shows an RJ-45 jack and the more familiar RJ-11 telephone jack. Notice the size difference.

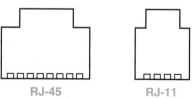

Figure 22-7. RJ-45 jacks are used with Category 5 cable. RJ-11 jacks are used with typical telephone cable. Notice the size difference.

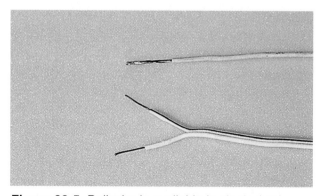

Figure 22-5. Bell wire is available in single (top), double (bottom), or multiple conductor configurations.

The standard pin colors in an RJ-45 jack may be compatible with either the T568A or T568B standard. Usually, however, T568B is the choice for new construction, while T568A was most likely used in older installations. In any case, the two systems should not be mixed in an installation. The standard pin colors for T568B are:

Pin Number	Wire Color
1	White/Orange
2	Orange
3	White/Green
4	Blue
5	White/Blue
6	Green
7	White/Brown
8	Brown

The pin colors are the same for T568A, except that the colors on pins 2 and 6 are reversed.

The color of the PVC jacket is also significant. It can be used to identify several types of applications during the installation process and, thereby, reduce errors. For example, a standard color scheme is:

- Blue: Use for standard telephone lines.
- Red: Use for key-type commercial telephone lines.
- Yellow: Use for maintenance and security alarms.
- Green: Use for auxiliary circuits and network connections.
- Orange: Use for incoming phone cable and for setting circuits apart.
- White or Silver: Use for horizontal data cables, computers, and PBX equipment.

Structured Wiring

Structured wiring is an organized arrangement of high-quality cables and connections that distribute services throughout the home. Older homes most likely have a minimal wiring structure with one line for a telephone and one line for cable TV, although many older homes are not wired for cable TV. This arrangement does not permit optimal high speed lines for computers or fax machines. The lines were designed for voice only, not data or device communication.

Newer homes that are wired for the latest technology have Category 5 cable, which is capable of carrying information at high speeds, such as for high-speed Internet access. Also, high-quality video cable (RG-6 quad shield) provides access to digital video services, such as digital satellite and digital cable, for greater channel selection and picture quality. Further, structured wiring efficiently distributes incoming services to the rooms where they are desired.

The central hub of a structured wiring installation is the *wiring closet*. All devices are connected to the wiring closet with Category 5 cable or Radio Grade 6 cable, depending on the requirements of the device. Wiring closets may be mounted between the studs or mounted on the wall. The wiring closet should be located where it will be most efficient. For example, it should not be located close to the house electrical service panel as this will cause electrical interference. Also, it should be located so cable lengths can be less than 285 feet. Runs over this length can reduce signal integrity.

Radio Grade 6 Cable

Radio Grade 6 (RG-6) cable is a type of coaxial cable that is capable of high speed digital data transmission in high bandwidths between the 50 MHz and 500 MHz. RG-6 quad shield cabling (75 ohm) is composed of a core of solid copper wire surrounded by insulation and copper braiding, Figure 22-8. It is used for cable TV, digital cable, digital satellite, cable modems, and in-home security cameras (video applications). The predecessor to RG-6, RG-59, is not designed to handle high bandwidth digital transmission effectively and is being replaced by RG-6.

Digital data refers to information that is converted to only a few specific values, commonly described as "1s and 0s." Because the values are specific, digital data can be transmitted, received, and recreated with no loss of content. In contrast to digital data, *analog data* is always received with noise added into the content. Because of this signal

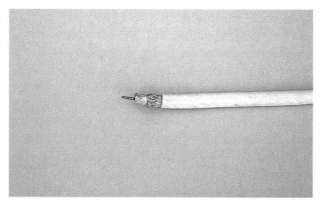

Figure 22-8. Radio Grade 6 (RG-6) cable is used for cable TV, digital cable, digital satellite, cable modems, and other video applications.

distortion, digital content (CDs, DVDs, HDTV) is usually preferred over analog content (cassette tape, VHS, aerial TV).

Security Wiring

Home security has become a greater concern as the traditional community has disappeared. We are bombarded daily with reports of break-ins, assaults, and burglaries. Agencies, such as the FBI, keep track of crime report statistics that make it clear everyone is vulnerable. For example, it is reported that 38% of all assaults occur during a home invasion, 60% of all reported rapes occur during a home invasion, 2 out of 3 burglaries are residential, and 67% of all burglaries involve forcible entry (52% during the daylight hours).

Fire detection is a safety and security concern that should be included in the overall security strategy. Residential property is involved in 60% of the structural fires started by arsonists, according to the FBI. Eighty percent of all fire deaths occur in the home and someone is killed by a fire somewhere in the U.S. every two hours. Fire safety, therefore, should be a part of every home security system.

Systems to Protect Property

If you only need protection for your property while your home is unoccupied, a minimal system may be all that is required. Since the earliest warning is not necessary for personal protection, it will probably be acceptable to detect an intruder after they are already inside the home.

For property protection, frequently, only the doors are protected and then motion detectors are relied on for cost effectiveness. For example, if you wish to protect a one-story house and your only concern is for burglar and fire protection when you are away, the following system might be adequate:

• Control Panel: This is the brains of the system.
• Touch Pad: This provides a method of telling the system what to do.
• Siren: This provides a warning and/or frightens intruders.
• Door Sensors: Doors are the locations of frequent entry; these sensors detect entry.
• Passive Infrared (PIR) or Motion Sensor: These devices sense movement or body heat of an intruder in the house.
• Smoke Detectors: These devices sense the presence of smoke and should be on every level of the home.

This system may be adequate for some homeowners. However, a system such as this provides limited protection. It would not be effective if there are items of special value, such as artwork, jewelry, or firearms.

Systems to Protect Occupants and Property

The first line of defense of a security system designed to protect the occupants as well as the property is a *perimeter system*. In a perimeter system, all doors and windows are wired with magnetic switches inside the frame. An alarm is activated when a switch is disturbed by opening a door or window. Every point of entry—main entry doors, service doors, basement doors, sliding glass doors, and all windows—must be included for the perimeter to be secure. These security systems are controlled through a keypad, Figure 22-9.

A perimeter system should also include glassbreak detection. The magnetic switches

Figure 22-9. The security system keypad, located inside this enclosure, enables the control of all system functions. This keypad also features a built-in audio alarm that will sound during alarms and trouble.

Figure 22-10. A motion detector such as this one will detect an intruder that has gotten inside the home by bypassing the perimeter system.

located in the frames of doors and windows will only detect an intruder if the window or door is opened. They will not detect entry through a broken window. High-tech glass-break detectors contain a small microphone connected to a sound processor. The microphone is tuned to the frequency of breaking glass, and the processor measures the sound against a preset characteristic pattern. In addition, a shock sensor detects the tiny shock wave that passes through the home when the glass is broken. So, only when there is the sound of breaking glass and a resulting shock wave will the alarm be activated.

Interior protection is still necessary even though all entry points and glass areas have been protected. An intruder might gain entry in some other way, such as cutting a hole in the roof or removing an attic vent. *Motion detectors* provide the final line of defense for home security systems, Figure 22-10. They detect an intruder that is inside the home after bypassing the perimeter system.

An added level of interior protection is necessary because the intruder may have the technical knowledge to disarm the system or, like any device, a perimeter switch may fail. In this event, a method to manually sound an alarm is needed. Most security system consoles have a *panic button* that permits a silent alarm to be sent to a monitoring station or to set off an audible alarm siren.

Finally, fire protection should be a part of every home security system. Smoke detectors provide the earliest warning of fire, Figure 22-11. Most deaths from nighttime fire are the result of smoke inhalation, not fire, because the victim does not wake up. The fire system remains active even when the burglar alarm is turned off. Check with your local building department to determine the location and number of smoke detectors you need. But, generally, they should be placed in every bedroom, hall, and level of the house.

When a fire or intruder is detected, the residents must then be alerted to the emergency. This is usually accomplished with

Figure 22-11. This smoke detector is wired to the home security system and remains active even when the burglar alarm is turned off.

sounders located where they can be heard by everyone in the home. In addition, a loud (120 decibels at 10′) electronic siren should be located outside the home. Exterior lighting should be controlled by the security system, too. This will alert neighbors and help frighten away an intruder.

Even though these alarms, sirens, and detectors will greatly increase the chances of surviving a fire or intruder, central station monitoring is a sure way to call others for help. Central station monitoring is provided by a private home security agency. There are several national chains, as well as many local agencies. Consult your local yellow pages or police or fire departments for recommendations.

Wiring for Security

The cable of choice by most everyone in the security system field is Category 5. It is required for data networks and is equally satisfactory for telephones, equipment control, or security sensors. However, high-grade video equipment and speakers should not be wired with Category 5 cable. RG-6 quad shield cable is required for video equipment. Dedicated speaker wire, generally specified by the manufacturers, should be used for speakers.

Knowing which kind of cable to use for each device is very important. However, sometimes the most difficult decision is where to put the device. Some devices, such as smoke detectors, motion sensors, magnetic door and window switches, etc., are easy to locate because of their function. But, other elements in the system, like nodes for data communication and jacks for video or home automation, are more difficult to locate. Naturally, a good set of construction drawings will help, but the lifestyle of the occupants will also dictate some choices.

All cables from the speakers, computers, security sensors, video cameras—all the elements of a high-tech security system—must be routed to a single location. This location is the *wiring cabinet.* It should be somewhat centrally located, not too close to the electrical distribution panel, and readily accessible. Figure 22-12 shows a typical whole-house

Figure 22-12. A typical home-security wiring cabinet.

security system wiring cabinet. It is located in a closet away from the electrical distribution panel.

Home Automation

Home automation is a reality today. Structured wiring is now in 20% of new construction and expected to grow to 70% by 2005, as reported by the US building industry. Thirty million homes will have DSL or cable modem service by 2004. Today, 52% percent of US households have at least one personal computer and 36% have Internet access.

Consider the following scenario, which is possible now with "smart" products. Before returning home from vacation, you call your home and tell it to warm up. The furnace is activated by a central controller and the inside temperature is comfortable when you arrive. Then, before going to bed, you use your phone to tell the house "good night." The one command sets the thermostat to a lower temperature, sets the house lighting to "nighttime," arms the security system, and checks the home's electronic locks. Then at 6:00 AM, a "good morning" sequence turns up the thermostat, turns on a light in the master bath, turns off the outside lighting at dawn, and wakes you up at 7:00 AM with your favorite radio station. If you get up during the night for a cold drink of juice from the refrigerator, the house gently brightens the lights in front of you and then dims them after you pass. The security system keeps track of you so it knows not to call the police as you pass the sensors. Any new presence, such as a potential burglar, would trigger an alarm and tell you which room had been entered. Further, your washing machine, loaded with clothes the night before, will begin its work midmorning after the solar water heater indicates that there is enough warm water to wash clothes.

The key to the scenario described above is the ability of products to "talk" and "listen" to one another—to *network.* A network can be as small as two appliances that can talk to each other or as comprehensive as all the electronic products in a home talking to one another. In complex systems, a central controller is needed to manage communication and actions between all systems based on the homeowner's instructions, Figure 22-13.

Efforts to develop a network standard have been underway for several years. In the US, there are a number of different home network efforts: Consumer Electronic Bus (CEBus), Smart House®, Echelon®, and Integrated Networks. Each approach is quite different in scope, business structure, and intended market. The CEBus is being supported by consumer electronics manufacturers such as Home Controls, Incorporated. Other companies, like Carrier and Eaton, are original supporters of Smart House® for new construction and retrofit. Still other companies are supporting Echelon or Integrated Networks.

The Electronic Industries Association's CEBus is the only North American effort that meets the definition of an open standard. This is a committee effort with volunteer participation and is open to all companies. Manufacturers can send their messages on any media found in the home—electric wire, telephone wire, radio frequency, infrared (line of sight), coaxial cable, and optical fiber.

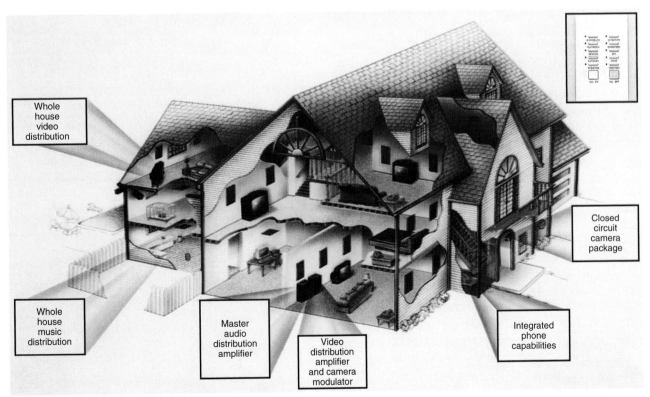

Whole house video distribution

Whole house music distribution

Master audio distribution amplifier

Video distribution amplifier and camera modulator

Closed circuit camera package

Integrated phone capabilities

Figure 22-13. This home automation system networks the TV, VCR, phone, and stereo so they can work together based on the homeowner's instructions. (Square D Company)

The Smart House Limited Partnership (SHLP) is a for-profit consortium funded by the National Association of Home Builders and private home builder investors. Smart House® has a totally new system of wiring throughout the home. It uses three types of multiconductor cable as well as gas plumbing. Cable must be installed at the time of construction. A central controller manages the system.

Echelon Corporation offers a third philosophy of creating a network. Unlike CEBus and Smart House®, Echelon's network is intended for any environment in which electronic products need to communicate. Echelon has created LONWorks® (local operating networks) that includes all the pieces necessary to build a network. Manufacturers will use Echelon technology to achieve communications in their own products. Echelon is licensing its technology to chipmakers and will receive royalties.

The Leviton Integrated Networks™ (LIN) is a product of Leviton Manufacturing Company. It is a structured wiring system that is gaining popularity. Leviton offers a simple solution for today's technology-wired home. It supports high-speed Internet and computer networking, whole-house audio, multiroom video, and home and family video security monitoring capabilities.

It is too early to know which, if any, home automation approach will ultimately win the marketplace. However, the potential for this market is very large. The indications are that the home automation market will expand over the next several years. As the market expands, new players will inevitably join the marketplace with new products.

Types of Home Automation Systems

For discussion purposes, home automation systems may be grouped into four basic approaches. These approaches are generally centered around the hardware and, in some cases, the software. These approaches or groups include hard-wired systems, power line technology, structured wiring systems, and combination systems. There are advocates for each type of system and a need for each. However, factors such as cost, convenience, complexity, or features provided will likely drive the decision to choose a particular system.

Hard-Wired Systems

Hard-wired systems are dedicated (stand-alone) systems that are self-contained and part of the infrastructure of the building. These are the least used in residential automation systems. They are much more likely to be found in commercial or industrial applications. The primary reasons for their lack of popularity in residential situations is level of complexity, cost, and need for highly skilled professionals to design, install, and maintain the system.

Hard-wired systems are used in security and surveillance applications because of their high level of reliability. They are also used in heating, ventilation, and air conditioning applications in large buildings where constant monitoring is necessary. Other common applications include sophisticated lighting control that might be found in a theater, teaching facility, or a high-end home, Figure 22-14. Hard-wired systems are seldom used for computer networks or video applications. Even though hard-wired systems are not used for computer networks, devices such as control panels for sound or

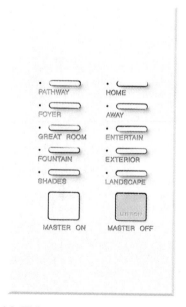

Figure 22-14. This programmable lighting controller can set ten separate lighting scenes for multiple locations. (Lutron Electronics, Inc.)

lighting can be programmed using a computer connected through its USB or serial port.

Hard-wired systems, in some instances, can be controlled remotely through hand-held controllers or through the Internet. In addition, progress is being made to combine hard-wired systems with structured wiring systems. For example, Figure 22-15 shows Home Automation Incorporated's Omni Pro II security module. This module works with Leviton's structured wiring enclosure, Figure 22-16.

Power Line Technology

More than 20 years ago, a protocol called X10 was developed to automate the home. This protocol is used in *power line technology* to send signals over existing electrical wiring to control almost any electrical device—lamps, appliances, or other equipment.

A basic power line technology system, or X10 system, generally includes three components. See Figure 22-17.

* Hardware modules to switch on/off appliances, lamps, or other electrical equipment. Most anything plugged into a regular convenience outlet can be switched on and off with a module.

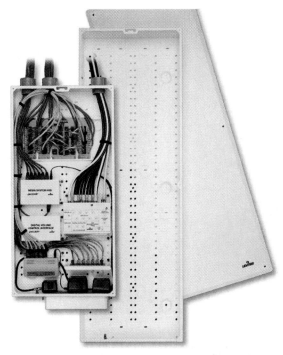

Figure 22-16. A typical wiring enclosure used in hard-wired systems. (Leviton Manufacturing Co., Inc.)

* Computer interface to send commands to the modules. This is often an interface with a personal computer via the serial port, the Internet, or home network connection.

Figure 22-15. This security and automation package accepts standard sensors for fire, lighting, HVAC, appliances, and intrusion. (Home Automation, Inc.)

Figure 22-17. This system package provides everything needed for both programmed and manual control of lighting and appliances using a home's existing wiring. (Leviton Manufacturing Co., Inc.)

- Software program to control the interfaced hardware.

Power line technology has been popular in the remodel market, because no new cabling is needed. X10 systems are inexpensive when compared to other options. However, they do not provide as many features as other systems. Also, the fact that existing wire is used severely limits what can be part of the home security or automation system.

Structured Wiring

Structured wiring systems provide for complete home security and home automation in one package. Functions may include a telephone network; computer network; satellite, cable, or antenna TV service; telecommunication service; broadband technology; video distribution; in-home cameras; links to a security system; and provision for future technology. All of these separate systems are joined in one network connection center wiring closet or cabinet, Figure 22-18.

The wiring in a structured wiring system generally consists of Category 5 cable from the

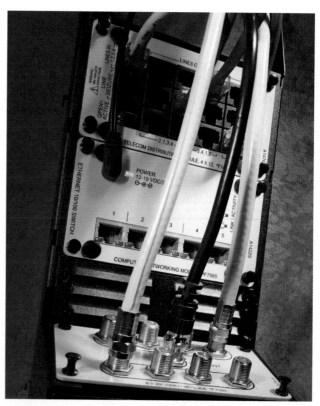

Figure 22-18. This wiring enclosure is for a structured wiring system. Notice the patch cables used to connect the devices. (Greyfox Systems)

wiring closet to all locations within the home for security, entertainment, phone, computer and Internet devices. Radio Grade 6 quad shield cable is also installed for cable TV, digital cable, digital satellite, cable modems, and in-home cameras. Manufacturers of speakers, motor controls, or other unique applications that are a part of the structured wiring system will specify the proper cable for their devices. As with other systems, a computer interface is possible with most systems for programming and control functions.

You have the option of using individual cables to each location to save several feet of cable in a typical installation or you can use bundled cable. *Bundled cable* has several conductors inside one PVC jacket, Figure 22-19. Most any combination of cables is available to meet the needs of each location in the home.

In structured wiring, it is very important that all hardware—cable, plugs, jacks, and faceplates—be compatible and have the same rating. There are numerous products on the market, such as those shown in Figure 22-20,

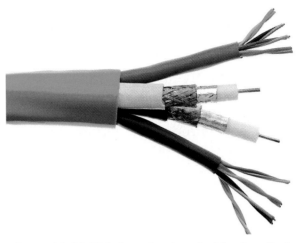

Figure 22-19. This is a structured wiring bundled cable that contains two Category 5E cables and two quad-shield coax. (Belden Electronics Division)

that work together to build the structured wiring system.

Finally, structured wiring seems to be the system of choice for new construction. However, it is very difficult to install such a system in an existing home. If a remodeling is

Figure 22-20. A modular jack and faceplate system provides for custom configured terminations. (OnQ Technologies, Inc.)

in progress where the walls are stripped to the studs, structured wiring may be an option.

Combination Systems

Combination systems pick and choose from hard-wired systems, power line technology, and structured wiring systems. Therefore, the opportunity exists to design a very high tech, custom system. A combination system might be just the approach where cost is not a limiting factor and the owner wants a totally custom installation to meet special needs or desires. See Figure 22-21.

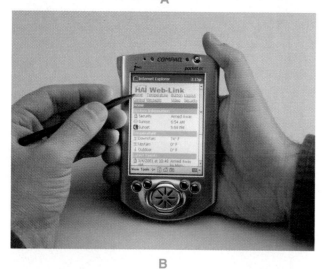

Figure 22-21. A—This totally custom combination system allows the homeowner to access and control the system over the Internet. (Home Automation, Inc.) B—A hand-held PDA enables a homeowner to monitor their system from a remote location via the Internet. (Home Automation, Inc.)

Several companies are turning their attention to the combination system market in anticipation of an expanding market. A few include Home Director System, Honeywell's Your Home Expert, Lutron's RF devices, BeAtHome System, and FutureSmart's Super Pro 16. When looking ahead, what is now very complicated with numerous types of cabling, wiring closets, plugs and jacks, etc., might just move toward a simpler solution. Consider a single type of cable for everything. One group, DiLan (Domestic Integrated Local Area Network), uses Category 5E (or Cat 5 enhanced) for everything.

Home Automation Summary Questions

The following list of questions may be helpful if you are planning a home automation/security system. The answers may eliminate or lead you toward a certain system.

- What do you want to accomplish with the system?
- Do you plan to install the system yourself or hire professionals?
- Is this new construction or an existing home?
- Which basic approach best fits your needs, cost, and housing structure?
- Is there a packaged product that meets your needs?
- Which devices do you wish to monitor or control?
- Do you have a proposed location for a wiring cabinet?
- Have you planned the location of devices that are a part of the system?
- Have you decided on the style of jacks, plugs, and faceplates? See Figure 22-22.
- Will an intercom/music system be part of your system? See Figure 22-23.
- Will your system provide for future developments and new technology?
- Do you have enough information to proceed?

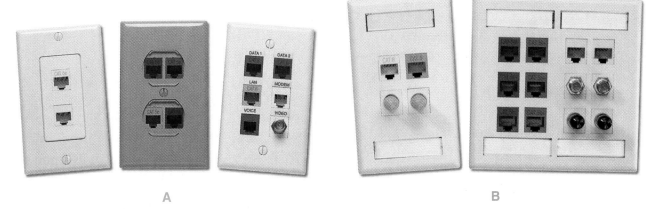

Figure 22-22. There are a variety of wall plates that are used with home automation systems. (Leviton Manufacturing Co., Inc.)

Figure 22-23. This voice/music intercom master control station facilitates communication and monitoring at numerous locations. (Broan-NuTone, A Nortek Company)

Low-Voltage Switching

In using low-voltage switching, convenience outlets are wired in the conventional way with Number 12 or 14 conductors. Switches, on the other hand, are wired to relays using conductors similar to those used for wiring doorbells and chimes. These conductors carry only 24 volts provided by a transformer that supplies current for the relays. *Relays* are electrically operated switches. The switches do not require boxes.

Low-voltage switching, or remote control wiring as it is sometimes called, has possibilities for unique installations. Remote control systems (low-voltage switching) provide a simplified way of controlling lights in all parts of the home from one or more locations. For example, it is possible to operate fixtures located at various points in the house from the master bedroom. This is one of the advantages of low-voltage switching.

Internet Resources

www.archtek.com
Archtek Telecom Corp, manufacturer of SmartLink® broadband access equipment

www.echelon.com
Echelon Corporation, publisher of the BeAtHome system

www.elanhomesystems.com
ELAN Home Systems, supplier of whole-house entertainment, communication, and control systems

www.elkproducts.com
ELK Products, Inc., supplier of home security and automation products

www.hanaonline.org
Consumer Electronics Association TechHome Division

www.leviton.com
Leviton, a manufacturer of electrical and electronic products

www.lolcontrols.com
Lightolier® Controls, a manufacturer of lighting controls

www.mssystems.com
M & S Systems, a manufacturer of music and communication systems

www.smarthome.com
Smarthome®, Inc., a supplier of home automation equipment

www.x10.com
X10 Home Solutions, a supplier of home automation products

Review Questions - Chapter 22

Write your answers on a separate sheet of paper. Do not write in this book.

1. Telephone lines are two wires called a _____.

2. Which of the following types of telephone wire requires a special tool to install it?
   a. solid wire
   b. stranded wire
   c. ribbon stranded wire

3. In four-wire telephone cable, the colors are generally:
   a. yellow, black, green, orange
   b. orange, green, yellow, red
   c. green, brown, white, blue
   d. black, green, red, yellow

4. The National Electrical Code specifies _____ different classes of signaling circuits.

5. Bells, buzzers, and chimes usually operate between _____ and _____ volts and use bell wire.

6. The cabling used to connect most computer and data networks is known as _____.

7. The most common cable/wiring standard for new construction is _____.

8. What is the maximum length of cable for a Category 5 cable for reliable performance?
   a. 285 feet
   b. 150 feet
   c. 1,000 feet
   d. 750 feet

9. _____ is a type of coaxial cable composed of a core of solid copper wire surrounded by insulation and a copper braid.

10. For property protection, frequently, only the _____ are protected and then motion detectors are relied on for cost effectiveness.

11. The first line of defense of a security system designed to protect the occupants as well as the property is a _____ system.

12. _____ detectors provide the earliest warning of fire.

13. The key to a functional home automation system is a:
    a. network
    b. digital telephone
    c. solar panel
    d. home robot

14. Name three of the four basic systems or approaches to home automation.

15. The type of jacks and plugs used with Category 5 cable is _____.

16. In low voltage switching, switch conductors carry _____ volts provided by a transformer.

Suggested Activities

1. Search the Internet to find information about data and video conductors. Prepare a report on your findings. Identify your sources.

2. Go to your local home center. Make a list of the hardware and software items they carry for a home automation system. Identify the functions that each performs.

3. Draw new CADD symbols related to home automation, security wiring, video, data, signaling circuits, information and communication wiring. Add these symbols to your symbols library.

4. Select a floor plan that you like that does not include home automation features. Using CADD, design a home automation system. Include a security system as part of the home automation system. Place symbols for the home automation system on a separate layer.

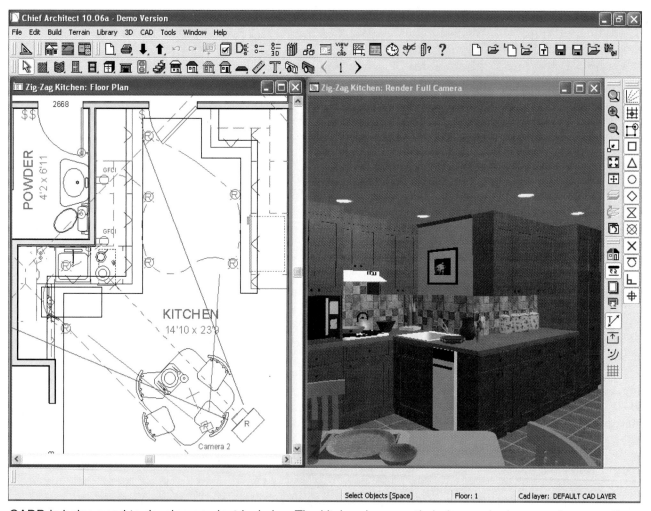

CADD is being used to develop an electrical plan. The kitchen is currently being worked on, as shown on the left. A rendered view of the kitchen appears on the right

The Electrical Plan

Objectives

After studying this chapter, you will be able to:

➤ Describe an electrical plan and identify its features.

➤ Identify typical electrical symbols found on a residential electrical plan.

➤ Draw an electrical plan for a residential structure using manual drafting techniques.

➤ Draw an electrical plan for a residential structure using CADD.

Key Terms

Electrical Plan
Fluorescent Light
Incandescent Light

Lighting Fixture
  Schedule

The purpose of the *electrical plan* is to show the location and type of electrical equipment to be used. It is a plan view section drawing, similar to the floor and foundation plans, and usually traced from the floor plan. The electrical plan shows the meter, distribution panel box, electric outlets, switches, and special electrical features. It identifies the number and types of circuits in the home. A schedule that specifies the lighting fixtures may be included. Convenience and trouble-free operation is dependent on a well-planned and properly installed electrical system.

Required Information

There are several items that need to be included on the electrical plan. Information that should be on the plan includes the service entrance capacity, meter and distribution panel location, placement and type of switches, location and type of lighting fixtures, special electrical equipment, number and types of circuits, and electrical fixture schedule.

Symbols and a legend and notes that help to describe the system must also be included. Electrical symbols commonly used on an electrical plan are shown in Figure 23-1. Amperage rating of the service required should be designated beside the symbol representing the distribution panel.

Service Entrance

The National Electrical Code (NEC) requires that the service entrance equipment be located as close as practical to the point

Information, Communication, and Security Wiring Symbols

Figure 23-1. These are electrical symbols commonly found on an electrical plan.

where the wires attach to the house. For example, the service conductors should not run for 15' or 20' inside the house before they reach the main disconnect switch. The closer the main breaker is to the meter the better.

Another factor to be considered in locating the service entrance is where the largest amounts of electricity will be used. In most houses, this is the kitchen. Try to locate the meter and distribution panel close to the area of highest usage. Larger loads require larger conductors. Therefore, it is less expensive to have the distribution panel close to the large loads. Also, voltage drops are reduced with shorter runs, thereby creating a more efficient system.

Electric meters are weatherproof and are designed for exterior installation. An outside location is usually preferred to allow for easier meter readings. However, the meter may be located inside or outside the house.

Switches

The number and placement of switches throughout the house will be related to the number of lighting fixtures, switched convenience outlets, and other equipment, such as whole-house fans. Take into consideration the traffic patterns and try to select the most logical location for each switch. The electrical plan must show whether the switches are single-pole, three-way, four-way, or another type. Use proper symbols to show the type.

A home may require several types of switches. The least expensive type of switch is a simple on-off toggle switch. A little more expensive, but preferred by many people, are the low-noise quiet switch or the completely silent mercury switch. Other types include push button, dimmer, and delayed action switches.

Switches are shown on the electrical plan connected to the fixtures, appliances, and outlets that they operate. A thin hidden line or centerline is generally used to show the connection. These lines *do not* represent the actual wiring, but merely indicate which switch operates a given outlet or fixture. Draw the lines using an irregular curve, rather than a straightedge or freehand. In CADD, the **SPLINE** or **POLYLINE** command and **SPLINE** option can be used. Straight lines tend to be confused with other lines on the drawing and freehand lines are sloppy.

Convenience Outlets

Convenience outlets should be placed about 6′ or 8′ apart along the wall of all rooms. Most outlets are the 120 volt, duplex type that have two receptacles. However, some may be split-wired to provide two different circuits at one convenience outlet or one half is switched. Special purpose outlets may have only one or several receptacles, depending on their use. They may be 120 volt or 240 volt. All convenience outlets should be grounded or GFCI to prevent severe shock.

Convenience outlets may be switched or always "hot." Most rooms will require at least one switched outlet for a lamp. It is wise to think about the furniture arrangement before drawing the electrical plan so that outlets and switches may be more conveniently located.

Several kinds of special outlets may be installed. Each of these should have a unique symbol and be identified in a legend. Use the proper symbol. If you are not sure if the symbol is standard, identify it in the legend on the electrical plan.

Lighting

The level of lighting, or brightness, is measured in foot-candles. It is difficult to determine how many foot-candles of light will be desirable for everyone. Some people prefer more light than others. Sufficient light should

Figure 23-2. This reading niche requires special lighting. (Georgia-Pacific Corporation)

be provided for the activity to be pursued in a given area, Figure 23-2.

Basically, two types of lights are used in residences—incandescent and fluorescent. An *incandescent light* is the traditional screw-in "lightbulb." A *fluorescent light* has a tube, not a bulb, and is often in schools and businesses. Fluorescent lights are popular in kitchens and workshops because of the bright illumination they provide. Fluorescent lights are also available that replace screw-in incandescent lightbulbs. All lightbulbs and tubes should be shielded in a way that minimizes glare. Allowable exceptions are in closets and storage areas. Diffusing bowls and shades are commonly used to reduce glare.

Lighting fixtures may be permanently attached to the ceiling or wall. They can also be freestanding lamps that are plugged into convenience outlets, either switched or unswitched. The trend seems to be using more freestanding lamps and fewer ceiling-mounted fixtures. However, a ceiling fixture should be planned in the dining room centered over the table.

Recessed lighting fixtures are suitable for certain areas of the home such as hallways, foyers, and special emphasis areas. Many varieties of recessed fixtures are available. Each should be evaluated carefully before making a selection. Another type of lighting fixture that is popular in special areas is track lighting. This is a system where several fixtures are mounted on a track and can be adjusted to different locations.

Lighting fixtures that are to be located outside the house must be rated for exterior applications. Plan adequate lighting for walks, drives, porches, patios, and other outside areas. Exterior lighting should be used to enhance the appearance of the home as well as make it more functional. Refer to Chapter 21 for information on low voltage exterior lighting.

Each lighting fixture should be represented on the electrical plan with the proper symbol. The symbol should be placed in the actual location where the fixture is to be installed. If the placement must be exact, dimension the location. Frequently, a *lighting fixture schedule* is included in the electrical plan. This schedule identifies the fixtures to be used, Figure 23-3.

Other Devices

Several other electrical devices should be shown on the electrical plan. The location of a permanent telephone and all telephone jacks should be indicated. Be sure to differentiate between the permanent unit and jacks. Items such as an intercom system, home security devices, TV antenna jack, cable or satellite TV jack, door chimes, and audio outlets should also be included and identified.

LIGHTING FIXTURE SCHEDULE						
TYPE	MANUFACTURE	CATALOG NO.	NO. REQ'D.	MOUNTING HEIGHT	WATTS	REMARKS
A	SEARS	34K3546	2	7' - 10"	100	BRUSHED ALUMINUM
B	LIGHTOLIER	4107	1	CEILING	150	
C	LIGHTOLIER	4233	2	CEILING	75	
D	SEARS	34K3113C	8	CEILING	80	RAPID START 48"
E	MOLDCAST	MP 232	4	GABLE PEAK	150	TWIN FLOODS
F	PROGRESS	P–180	7	CEILING	100	RECESSED 10" SQUARE
G	SEARS	34K1899C	1	CEILING	240	POLISHED CHROME CHAND.
H	LIGHTOLIER	6349	2	6" ABOVE MIRROR	60	
I	ALKCO	330–RS	1	UNDER CABINET	40	
J	EMERSON	220	2	CEILING	60	FAN AND LIGHT COMBINATION
K	PROGRESS	P–318	2	18" BELOW CEILING	100	EXTERIOR – HANGING

Figure 23-3. This is a typical lighting fixture schedule that includes the necessary information about each fixture.

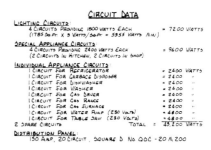

TYPE	MANUF.	CAT. NO.	No REQ.	MOUNTING HGT.	WATTS	REMARKS
A	PROGRESS	P4014	1	CEILING	240	CHANDELIER
B	SEARS	34 K 3165	2	CEILING	100	CERAMIC HOLDERS
C	SEARS	34 K 3113	4	CEILING	80	SUSPENDED CEILING
D	PROGRESS	P7163	2	ABOVE MIRROR	80	RAPID START
E	SEARS	34 K 2734	2	CEILING	100	
F	PROGRESS	P6406	6	CEILING	100	RECESSED 10" SQ.
G	PROGRESS	P6676	7	CEILING	100	RECESSED 8" RND.
H	PROGRESS	P4449	2	12" BELOW CEIL.	100	EXT. HANGING
I	SEARS	34 K 3546	4	7'-0"	100	BRUSHED ALUM.
J	PROGRESS	P5228	3	1'-6"	60	
K	SEARS	34 K 3622	3	GABLE PEAK	150	TWIN FLOODS
L	PROGRESS	P7002	1	UNDER CAB.	40	

LIGHTING FIXTURE SCHEDULE

CIRCUIT DATA

LIGHTING CIRCUITS:
4 CIRCUITS PROVIDING 1800 WATTS EACH = 7200 WATTS
(1785 SQ. FT. X 3 WATTS/SQ.FT. = 5355 WATTS MIN.)

SPECIAL APPLIANCE CIRCUITS:
4 CIRCUITS PROVIDING 2400 WATTS EACH = 9600 WATTS
(2 CIRCUITS IN KITCHEN, 2 CIRCUITS IN SHOP)

INDIVIDUAL APPLIANCE CIRCUITS:
1 CIRCUIT FOR REFRIGERATOR = 2400 WATTS
1 CIRCUIT FOR GARBAGE DISPOSER = 2400 "
1 CIRCUIT FOR DISHWASHER = 2400 "
1 CIRCUIT FOR WASHER = 2400 "
1 CIRCUIT FOR GAS DRYER = 2400 "
1 CIRCUIT FOR GAS RANGE = 2400 "
1 CIRCUIT FOR GAS FURNACE = 2400 "
1 CIRCUIT FOR WATER PUMP (230 VOLTS) = 4800 "
1 CIRCUIT FOR TABLE SAW (230 VOLTS) = 4800 "
2 SPARE CIRCUITS   TOTAL = 43,200 WATTS

DISTRIBUTION PANEL:
150 AMP, 20 CIRCUIT, SQUARE D No. QOC - 20 M 200

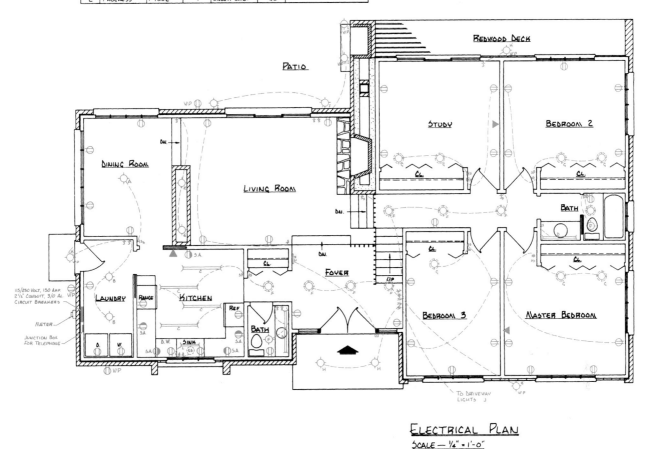

ELECTRICAL PLAN
SCALE — 1/4" = 1'-0"

Figure 23-4. This residential electrical plan shows the necessary electrical features for the first floor.

Branch Circuits

A well-designed electrical plan will indicate the number and type of branch circuits required for the house. These are usually specified in note or diagram form on the same sheet as the electrical plan. It is not necessary to specify the exact circuit for each outlet, but the number of lighting, special appliance, and individual appliance circuits should be listed. This information must be determined before the size of the service equipment can be specified. Follow the guidelines discussed in Chapter 21.

Procedure for Drawing an Electrical Plan—Manual Drafting

Figure 23-4 shows an electrical plan for a split-level house. The following procedure was used to develop this plan using manual drafting techniques.

1. Trace all exterior walls, interior walls, and major appliances from the floor plan.

2. Locate the meter and distribution panel. Indicate the voltage and amperage rating. Check local code requirements. Also, locate the telephone junction box and home security or automation wiring enclosure.
3. Show all convenience outlets using the proper symbols. Be sure to indicate those that are 240 volt, split-wired; weatherproof; or other special purpose outlet.
4. Locate all ceiling and wall lighting outlets. Carefully check the use of symbols.
5. Show all special outlets and fixtures, such as telephone, chimes, intercom, home security sensors, smoke alarms, data jacks, and so on.
6. Locate the switches and connect them to the outlets and lighting fixtures that they operate.
7. Add the lighting fixture schedule and symbol legend if necessary.
8. Note the number and type of circuits required.
9. Letter all other notes and the title, scale, and sheet number.
10. Check the drawing carefully to be sure that all information is accurate and complete.

Procedure for Drawing an Electrical Plan—CADD

An electrical plan can be drawn with a CADD system using the same basic steps explained for manual drafting. In addition, application-specific software is available that automates the design of the electrical plans. The primary elements of these programs include a symbols library and the automatic generation of connecting lines.

Figure 23-5 shows an electrical plan that was drawn using CADD and the step-by-step sequence described below. This procedure is basically the same as the one explained for manual drafting.

1. Copy all exterior walls, interior walls, and major appliances from the floor plan layer to the electrical plan layer.
2. Locate the meter and distribution panel. Indicate the voltage and amperage rating. Check local code requirements. Also, locate the telephone junction box and home security or automation wiring enclosure.
3. Insert the proper symbols for all convenience outlets. These should be placed on the electrical symbols layer. Be sure to indicate those that are 240 volt, split-wired; weatherproof; or other special purpose outlet.
4. Insert the proper symbols for all ceiling and wall lighting outlets. These should also be placed on the electrical symbols layer.
5. Insert symbols for all special outlets and fixtures, such as telephone, chimes, intercom, home security sensors, smoke alarms, data jacks, and so on. These should be placed on the electrical symbols layer.
6. Insert the proper symbols for all switches. These should be placed on the electrical symbols layer.
7. Connect switches to the outlets and lighting fixtures that they operate. Use the **SPLINE** command or **POLYLINE** command and **SPLINE** option to draw the lines. Use a hidden or centerline linetype. These lines should be placed on a separate layer to achieve proper line width when plotting.
8. Add the lighting fixture schedule and symbol legend, if necessary.
9. Add a note indicating the number and type of circuits required. Create all other notes and add the title, scale, and sheet number. Specific notes should be placed on their own layer for ease of manipulation.
10. Check the drawing carefully to be sure that all information is accurate and complete.

Figure 23-6 shows a portion of another electrical plan drawn with CADD. A rendered view of the building it represents is shown on the screen as well. The style used by this company is slightly different than described in this chapter, but the result is highly functional. Notice the proper use of symbols.

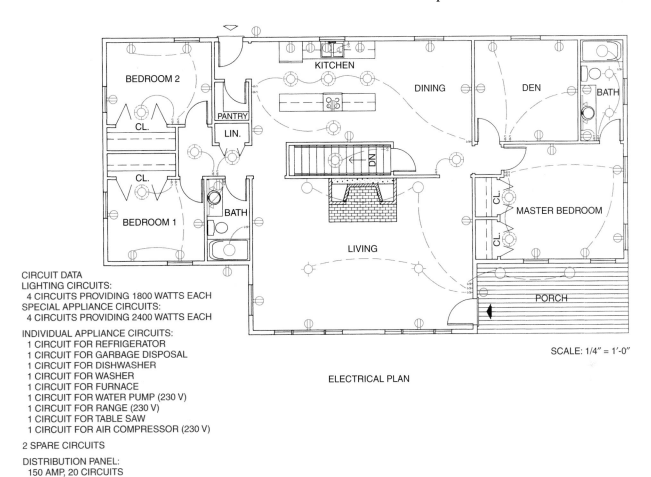

CIRCUIT DATA
LIGHTING CIRCUITS:
  4 CIRCUITS PROVIDING 1800 WATTS EACH
SPECIAL APPLIANCE CIRCUITS:
  4 CIRCUITS PROVIDING 2400 WATTS EACH

INDIVIDUAL APPLIANCE CIRCUITS:
  1 CIRCUIT FOR REFRIGERATOR
  1 CIRCUIT FOR GARBAGE DISPOSAL
  1 CIRCUIT FOR DISHWASHER
  1 CIRCUIT FOR WASHER
  1 CIRCUIT FOR FURNACE
  1 CIRCUIT FOR WATER PUMP (230 V)
  1 CIRCUIT FOR RANGE (230 V)
  1 CIRCUIT FOR TABLE SAW
  1 CIRCUIT FOR AIR COMPRESSOR (230 V)

2 SPARE CIRCUITS

DISTRIBUTION PANEL:
  150 AMP, 20 CIRCUITS

SCALE: 1/4″ = 1′-0″

ELECTRICAL PLAN

Figure 23-5. This residential electrical plan was drawn using CADD.

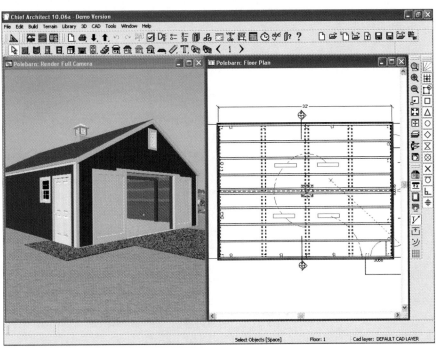

Figure 23-6. The CADD software used to generate the electrical plan as well as the rendered view of the building enabled the drafter/designer to communicate ideas in a very effective fashion. A prospective client can easily visualize what the designer intends. (ART, Inc.)

Internet Resources

www.brasslight.com
Brass Light Gallery

www.cooperlighting.com
Cooper Lighting

www.eagle-electric.com
Cooper Wiring Devices

www.flexiduct.com
Geist Manufacturing, Inc., manufacturer of Flexiduct cord covers

www.ge.com/product/home/lighting.htm
General Electric, home lighting products

www.homecontrols.com
Home Controls, Inc., a supplier of home automation equipment

www.hunterfan.com
Hunter Fan Company

www.leviton.com
Leviton, a manufacturer of electrical and electronic products

www.lutron.com
Lutron, a manufacturer of lighting control products

www.progresslighting.com
Progress Lighting

Review Questions – Chapter 23

Write your answers on a separate sheet of paper. Do not write in this book.

1. List the information required in an electrical plan.

2. Identify a major factor to consider when locating the service entrance equipment.

3. The preferred location for the electric meter is _____ the house.

4. Identify the following electrical symbols.

   a.

   b. S_3

   c. ▫

   d. ▼

   e. ⊖

5. Name three types of switches that may be used in the home.

6. Convenience outlets are grounded to prevent _____.

7. The purpose of a lighting fixture schedule is to _____.

8. The two types of lights used in a house are _____ and _____.

9. Why would you need to use more than one layer to show the switches, outlets, and connections on an electrical plan?

Suggested Activities

1. Select a floor plan of a small house or cottage and draw an electrical plan using CADD techniques. Show all outlets, switches, distribution panel, meter, and other required electrical features. Identify the number of lighting, special appliance, and individual appliance circuits. Follow the procedure presented in this chapter and use appropriate layers.

2. Using the same plan as in Activity 1 or some other plan, develop a schematic of the circuits in the house and the appliances, fixtures, and outlets that each circuit serves. Indicate the size of conductors and overcurrent protection required.

3. Visit your local utility company, building inspector, and electrical materials distributor. Collect materials relative to house wiring, code requirements, and materials used in residential electrical systems. Bring this information to class and share it with your classmates.

4. Collect several different examples of track lighting from magazines and manufacturers' literature. Prepare a bulletin board from the material collected.

5. Using CADD, draw the electrical plan shown in Figure 23-4. Be sure to use proper layers and linetypes in your construction.

6. Develop electrical symbols and add them to your CADD symbols library. Refer to Figure 23-1 for examples.

Residential Plumbing
24

Objectives

After studying this chapter, you will be able to:

➤ Discuss the purpose of a residential plumbing system.

➤ Identify the elements contained in a residential water supply system.

➤ Identify the elements of a residential water and waste removal system.

➤ Explain the operation of various in-house water treatment systems.

➤ Explain the layout of a private sewage disposal system.

Key Terms

Activated Carbon System
Branch Main
Building Main
Cleanout
Cold Water Branch Lines
Cold Water Main
Disposal Field
Distillation System
Hot Water Branch Lines
Hot Water Main
House Drain
House Sewer

Ion Exchange
Main Stack
Percolation Test
Plumbing Fixture
Reverse Osmosis System
Secondary Stacks
Septic Systems
Septic Tank
Soil Stack
Stack Wall
Trap
Vent Stack
Water Softener

The residential plumbing system is taken for granted and is seldom a concern of homeowners. However, it is a very important part of the house. A residential plumbing system provides an adequate supply of water for household use in desired locations and removes the waste through a sanitary sewer or private septic system. There are three principal parts to a residential plumbing installation: the water supply, water and waste removal, and plumbing fixtures that facilitate the use of water. A well-designed and efficient system is functional and will remain relatively trouble free.

Water Supply System

A residential water supply system begins at the city water main or a private source, such as a well, lake, or stream. The supply pipe that enters the house is known as the *building main*, Figure 24-1. It may be necessary to include in the system a water softener, filter, or some other treatment device in the building main. The building main branches after any treating device into two lines—the cold water and the hot water mains. Since the water supply system is under pressure, pipes may follow any path that is convenient and cost effective. Note: It is customary to provide a branch line to hose bibs upstream of any water treating device. Hose bibs, which are exterior faucets, do not generally supply soft or filtered water.

The *cold water main* extends to various parts of the house to provide unheated water to the fixtures. *Cold water branch lines* are run from the cold water main to each of the fixtures. Branch lines are smaller than mains. If a branch line is to supply more than one fixture, the diameter of the pipe must be increased to provide an ample amount of water.

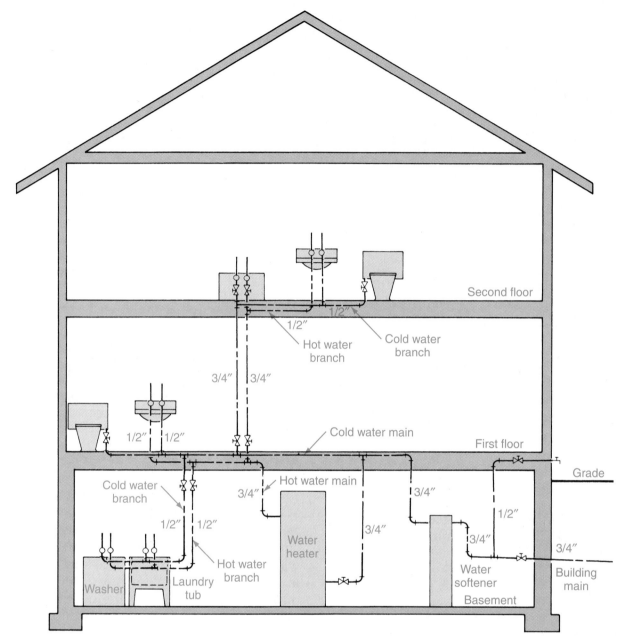

Figure 24-1. This illustration shows the different components of a residential water supply system.

The *hot water main* supplies heated water to the fixtures that require it. The hot water main comes from the branch in the building main to the water heater, Figure 24-2. From the water heater, it usually travels parallel to the cold water main to where both hot and cold water are required, such as sinks. *Hot water branch lines* run from the hot water main to each fixture.

The location of the pipes may depend on several factors. In cold climates, care should be taken to locate pipes along interior walls to keep them from freezing. Otherwise, the pipes should be insulated. Frost-free hose bibs are also available. Large, heavy pipes present a problem when they must pass through a joist. The customary solution is to place the pipe near the top of the joist and block the space above. See Figure 24-3.

Pipes used in the water supply system may be threaded galvanized steel pipe, plastic, or copper tubing with soldered joints when used inside the house, Figure 24-4. Water supply pipes underground or in concrete are

Shutoff valves should be supplied for each main line, branch line, and fixture. This is done so it is possible to isolate a single fixture from the system without shutting off the entire water supply.

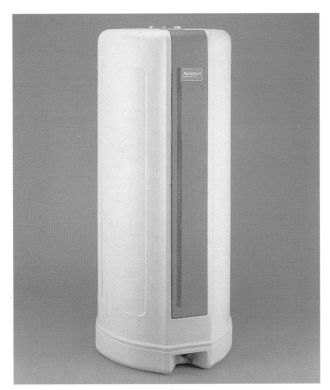

Figure 24-2. The hot water main connects to the top of this electric water heater. (Marathon Water Heater Company)

usually special heavy-duty copper tubing with soldered or flare-type joints. Some codes permit the use of plastic pipe for cold water or drain lines, as shown in Figure 24-5. Check the local code requirements before planning the system.

Today, copper tubing is used extensively for water supply systems. Rigid copper tubing (type L), copper fittings, and copper valves are typically used for all interior installations. Copper pipe is available in 1/2″, 3/4″, 1″, and larger diameters. Main lines are usually at least 3/4″ in diameter and branch lines are a minimum of 1/2″ in diameter.

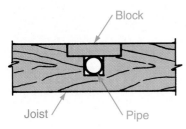

Figure 24-3. When a large pipe, such as a drain, must pass through a joist, the joist should be blocked to prevent severe weakening of the member.

Figure 24-4. Galvanized steel (top), copper (middle), and plastic (bottom) pipe and fittings are used in residential plumbing systems.

Figure 24-5. This plumbing installation has copper pipe and fittings for the water supply system and plastic pipe for the drain system.

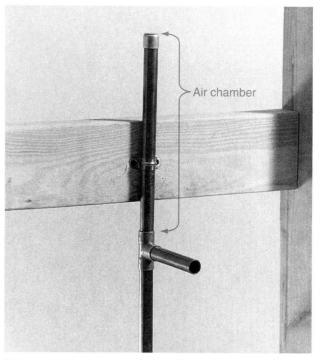

Figure 24-6. An air chamber should be used at each faucet to reduce noise by cushioning the water flow. The chamber can simply be a length of pipe that is capped.

Many codes require that an air compression chamber be located at each faucet. Even if not required by code, this is good plumbing practice. The chamber cushions the water flow and reduces pipe noise during use. Most air chambers are simply short risers constructed from pipe with the end closed, Figure 24-6.

As stated earlier, cold and hot water branch lines usually run parallel to each other. Generally, they are placed about 6″ apart. If they must be placed closer than this, some type of insulating material should be used to prevent the transfer of heat from one pipe to the other. Efficiency may be improved in any system if the hot water lines are insulated. In high-humidity areas, the cold water lines may need to be insulated as well to prevent excess condensation.

Fixtures that use small amounts of hot water, such as lavatories, may have a small, "on-demand" water heater located near the fixture, Figure 24-7. These units produce

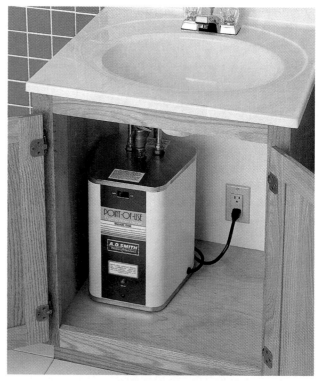

Figure 24-7. An "on-demand" water heater located under the sink provides instant hot water. A cold water line is all the plumbing needed. (A. O. Smith Water Products Company)

instant hot water and require that only a cold water line be piped to the unit. An electric heating element provides the heat.

In-House Water Treatment Devices

There are several reasons a homeowner may want an in-house water treatment device. Some water sources, such as a lake, may provide safe drinking water, but may also have an odor that is less than pleasant. Some water sources, such as from a well, may have high iron content or be too "hard" for household use. Water treatment devices can help reduce these unwanted conditions.

There are four main types of in-house water treatment devices. These types are reverse osmosis, distillation, water softeners, and activated carbon. The proper system for a given situation will depend on several factors, such as the impurities to be removed, amount of water needed, and cost. Local area professionals can help in the decision of which system to purchase.

In a *reverse osmosis system*, the line pressure forces water through a thin semipermeable membrane. The purified water is slowly collected in a small storage tank, while the contaminants that were unable to pass through the membrane are drained away. This process can remove from 90% to 99% of the impurities in water, including lead and other toxic metals, arsenic, nitrates, and organic contaminants. However, it is not effective against high levels of minerals. This process wastes three to five gallons of water for each gallon produced.

A *distillation system* works by heating water to make steam, which is then condensed in a coil to produce distilled water. This process removes most dissolved solids, including salts and heavy metals, but is not effective against volatile organic compounds. Distillation is slow, requiring up to two hours to produce one quart of distilled water. The heat produced by the process is a negative factor in the summer.

A *water softener* uses the line pressure to push hard water through a canister filled with a synthetic resin where a process called ion exchange is performed. *Ion exchange* causes the hard calcium and magnesium ions to be dissolved and exchanged for soft ions in the resin. Water produced by sodium-based water softeners has a small amount of sodium added and, therefore, may not be suitable for people on low sodium diets. Nonsodium-based water softeners are also available.

In an *activated carbon system*, the line pressure forces water through one or more canisters filled with activated carbon granules. These granules trap contaminates such as chlorine, organic chemicals, and pesticides. These contaminates can produce bad odors and tastes. Some activated carbon systems also effectively remove lead. High-volume models can deliver from 1/3 gallon to three gallons of pure water per minute. Filters must be replaced regularly to prevent bacteria build-up.

Water and Waste Removal

Used water and other waste is carried to the sanitary sewer or septic system through the waste removal or drainage system, Figure 24-8. These pipes are isolated from the water supply system and must be sized for sufficient capacity, have the proper slope and venting, and have provisions for cleanout.

In planning a residential plumbing system careful consideration should be given to the drainage network. It is practical to drain as many of the fixtures as possible into a single main drain. Unlike the water supply system, the drainage system is not under pressure. It depends on gravity to carry the waste to the sewer. All drainpipes must be pitched and large enough (usually 4") to prevent solids from accumulating at any point within the system. Drainpipes are generally smooth inside with a minimum of projections and sharp turns.

Several types of pipe may be used for waste removal. Cast iron pipe is used extensively. Copper and brass alloy pipes, which will not rust and are easy to install, are also frequently used. Other materials used include fiber and plastic. Many local codes specify the type of pipe to use, so check the code.

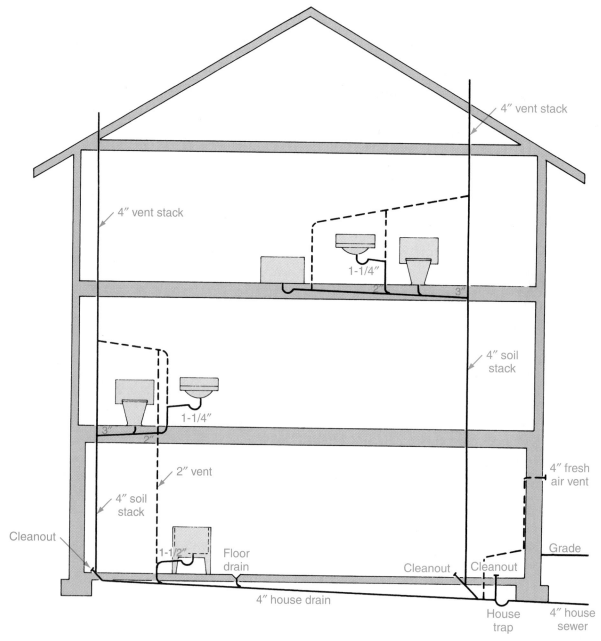

Figure 24-8. This illustration shows the components of a residential drainage system.

A vertical drainpipe that collects waste from one or more fixtures is called a *soil stack*. Stacks that have water closets draining into them are called *main stacks*. Every house must have at least one main stack. There may be several main stacks if the house has more than one bathroom. Main stacks are generally about 3" in diameter if copper or PVC is used; 4" if cast iron is used.

Stacks that do not drain water closets are called *secondary stacks*. These stacks may be smaller in diameter than main stacks; usually 1-1/2". Each fixture is connected to the stack using a *branch main*. These pipes must slope toward the stack to facilitate drainage.

All stacks (main stacks and secondary stacks) extend down into or below the basement or crawl space and empty into the house drain. The *house drain* is basically horizontal with a slight slope and must be large enough to handle the anticipated load. All houses will have at least one house drain, but may have several. Once the house drain passes to the outside of the house it is called a *house sewer*.

The house sewer empties into the city sanitary sewer or a private septic system.

Waste in the drainage system creates gases that have an unpleasant odor and may be harmful. These gasses are dissipated into the air through the soil stack that protrudes about 12″ above the roof. This portion of the soil stack is called the *vent stack.* In addition to providing an escape for gases, the soil stack/vent stack provides an air inlet to the drainage system. Drains must be exposed to atmospheric pressure to operate properly.

A *trap* is installed below each fixture to prevent gases from escaping through the fixture drain into the house. The trap is always filled with water to block the reverse flow of gases, Figure 24-9. Water closets do not require a trap because they are manufactured with an internal trap.

Each stack requires a cleanout located at the base of the stack. The *cleanout* permits the use of a cable to free waste from the house drain or sewer. A stack cleanout is shown in Figure 24-10. Cleanouts should also be installed anywhere the drainage system plumbing makes a sharp bend.

Where 4″ cast iron pipe is used for the soil and vent stack, a 2″ × 4″ stud wall will not provide sufficient space to house the pipe. In this case a 2″ × 6″ stud should be specified. This wall is commonly referred to as a *stack wall.*

House sewers are frequently not as deep as basement floors. Since a drain in the basement floor is desirable, and water will not flow uphill, a pump must be used. A concrete or tile pit, or sump, is located in an inconspicuous place in the basement and the floor is usually sloped toward a drain that flows into the sump, Figure 24-11. An automatic sump pump is installed in the sump and connected to the house drain or storm drain, depending on local code requirements. When water reaches a

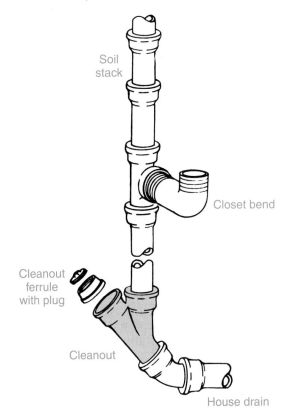

Figure 24-10. Cleanouts are required at the base of all stacks. This drawing illustrates a typical cleanout.

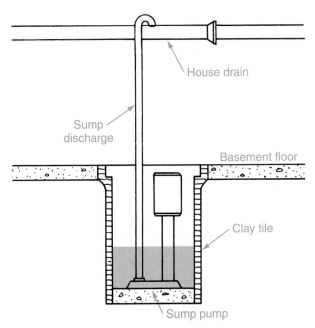

Figure 24-11. A sump pump removes water from the basement and discharges it into the house drain or outside.

Figure 24-9. A trap is always filled with water to block the escape of gases from the drainage system into the house.

predetermined level in the sump, the pump operates and removes the water.

Plumbing Fixtures

The third part of the residential plumbing system is the fixtures. A *plumbing fixture* is any device, such as a bathtub, shower, water closet, sink, dishwasher, etc., that requires water, Figure 24-12. Fixtures are the most obvious part of the plumbing system because they are visible. The choice of fixtures is important. They are expensive to install and replace. Choose them wisely.

The National Code specifies minimum clearance and location dimensions that must be used when installing various fixtures. Be sure ample space is allowed for the fixture.

Manufacturers specify roughing-in measurements for each of their fixtures. Figure 24-13 illustrates the type of information supplied by one manufacturer.

Water Conservation

In the past, almost all residential water closets (toilets) used gravity and five to six gallons of water to rinse the bowl clean and wash the waste down the drain. Then, in 1975 pressurized toilet tanks were introduced, which helped reduce the amount of water required. But, during the 1980s, the limitations of our water supply became a concern. Demand for fresh water increased significantly and, in some areas of the country, water conservation laws were passed.

Figure 24-12. There are several plumbing fixtures that can be seen in this illustration. Counterclockwise from the right, they are: sink, bathtub, shower, and water closet. (Photo Courtesy of Kohler Co.)

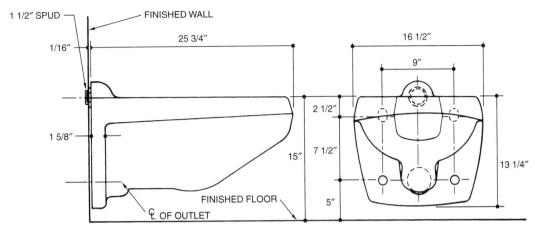

Figure 24-13. This is an example of rough-in specifications for a wall-mounted residential bathroom fixture. These specifications must be given consideration in the planning stages of the dwelling. (Courtesy of Kohler Co.)

Toilet manufacturers responded by developing low-flow, water-saving models. The new models used 3.5 gallons per flush (gpf) instead of the old five or six gallons. However, even by the end of the 1980s, only a few manufacturers offered low-flow models. Then, severe water shortages in California prompted that state's legislature to make 1.6 gpf toilets mandatory in all new residential construction. Other states soon followed California's lead.

Finally, the US Congress passed a national standard that addressed water conservation—the National Energy Policy Act. This Act stipulates that all new toilets manufactured in, or imported into, the United States after January 1, 1994 for residential use must consume no more than 1.6 gpf, Figure 24-14. Although the National

Energy Policy Act permits manufacturers to continue making 3.5 gpf toilets for commercial installations, some states, including California, New York, Massachusetts, and Texas, require 1.6 gpf designs for commercial use as well. Also, since January 1, 1994, the flow rate on shower heads, kitchen faucets, and lavatory faucets is set at 2.5 gallons per minute at 80 psi of line pressure.

Private Sewage Disposal System

Private sewage disposal systems, called **septic systems,** are used for rural and isolated homesites that cannot be connected to public sewers. A septic system has two basic components—the septic tank and the disposal field. Proper construction and maintenance of a private septic system are vitally important. The improper disposal of sewage may be a serious threat to the health and well-being of those in the surrounding area. A large number of disease producing organisms thrive in sewage.

Usually before a building permit may be issued for construction of a septic system, the site is examined by a health department sanitarian to determine if the site is suitable for a private sewage disposal system. The site must have an adequate area and the proper soil. The

Figure 24-14. This water closet (right) uses a maximum of 1.6 gpf with the option of a light flush of 1.1 gpf. (Photo Courtesy of Kohler Co.)

suggested minimum dimensions for placement of the well, septic tank, and disposal field on a one acre site are shown in Figure 24-15. Generally, the minimum lot size is one acre. A large land area and suitable soil conditions are necessary to isolate the disposal system from all wells, lakes, and streams to prevent contamination. Septic systems should also be isolated from property lines and buildings. Check with your local health department for minimum distances required.

Septic Tank

In a septic system, sewage from the house sewer first enters the septic tank. The *septic tank* performs two basic functions. It removes about 75% of the solids from the sewage by bacterial action before discharging the sewage into the disposal field. It also provides storage space for the settled solids while they undergo digestive action.

A septic tank should be watertight. It is usually constructed of reinforced concrete or concrete blocks with mortared joints and interior surface coated with cement and sand

plaster. Figure 24-16 shows the construction of a typical septic tank.

The liquid capacity of the septic tank should be about 1-1/2 times the sewage flow from the house over a 24-hour period. In no case should the capacity be less than 750 gallons. Frequently, the number of bedrooms in a home is used as an indication of the size septic tank required. The size should take into consideration clothes washers, dishwashers,

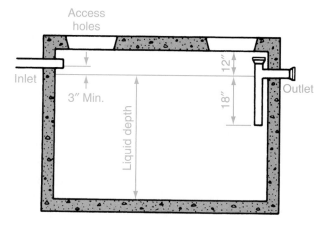

Figure 24-16. Construction of a typical cast concrete septic tank.

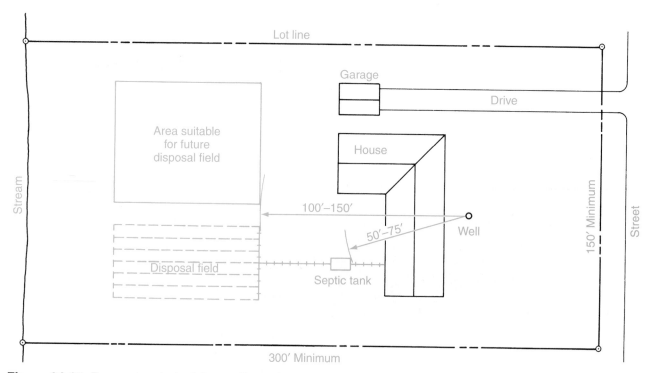

Figure 24-15. Recommended minimum dimensions for placement of private septic system and water well with respect to the house and property lines.

garbage disposals, and other devices that discharge into the sewer. It is customary to double the liquid capacity when a garbage disposal is used.

Disposal Field

The function of the *disposal field* is to receive sewage in liquid form from the septic tank and allow it to seep into the soil. The disposal field is also called the drain field or the leach field. Dry and porous soil containing sand or gravel is ideal for a disposal field.

The disposal field may be constructed using clay tile, perforated fiber pipe, or perforated plastic pipe. The drain field lines are laid nearly level about two feet below the surface of the ground or below the frost line. A slope of 1" in 50' is typical. The drain lines are positioned in a bed of pebbles usually covered with straw. Figure 24-17 shows some of the

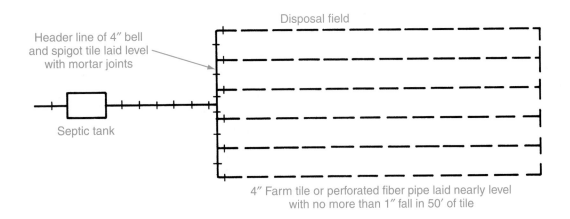

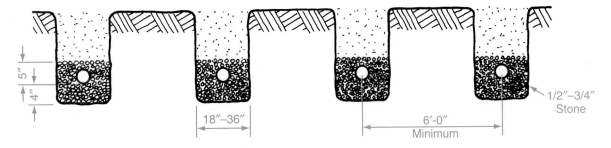

Tile in Individual Trenches

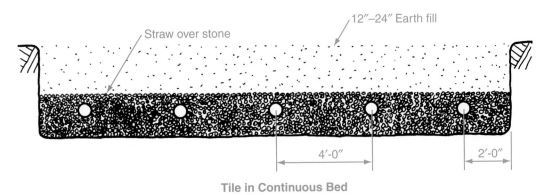

Tile in Continuous Bed

Figure 24-17. A disposal field may be constructed using either tile in individual trenches or in a continuous bed. A continuous bed requires less space than the individual trench bed.

important construction features of a disposal field.

The disposal field should be located in such a manner that surface water drainage is diverted away from it. If the disposal field becomes flooded, it will cease to function. The disposal field should also be located downhill from any water well. It should never be placed under a driveway, parking lot, paved area, or in a place where heavy vehicles may drive over it.

Disposal Field Soil Tests

The suitability of the soil for a disposal field must be determined by soil tests. These tests are known as *percolation tests.* They determine how readily the soil will absorb water and provide a guide for the required design and size of the disposal field.

The percolation rate is determined by filling a test hole with water to completely saturate the immediate area. After complete saturation, water is added to provide 4″ to 8″ of water in the test hole. The drop in water level is measured at 30 minute intervals until the hole is dry. The drop in level that occurs during the final 30 minute period is used to calculate the percolation rate for that test hole.

The standard percolation rate must be no greater than 45 minutes per inch. One test hole five feet deep or deeper is generally required to determine groundwater level and consistency of subsoil. The chart in Figure 24-18 shows the recommended seepage area required for various percolation rates.

Calculation of Disposal Field Size

The following example shows how to calculate the correct size of a disposal field. The example is for a three bedroom home with a percolation rate of 25 minutes per inch.

1. If the tile is placed in individual trenches, the seepage area required would be 3 × 375 square feet or 1125 square feet. See the chart in Figure 24-18. Using 2′ wide trenches, 562 linear feet of trench would be required (1125 square feet/ 2 square feet per linear foot = 562 linear feet). Therefore, 8 trenches each 70′ long will provide the required field.

2. If the tile is placed in a continuous bed, the seepage area required would be 3 × 375 square feet or 1125 square feet. See the chart in Figure 24-18. A 28.5′ × 40′ bed will provide the required field (28.5′ × 40′ = 1140 square feet).

3. The minimum necessary gross area available to install the disposal field and provide space for future expansion and replacement is:

2-1/2 × 1125 square feet = 2812 square feet

DISPOSAL FIELD DESIGN		
Standard Percolation Rate (Minutes Per Inch)	Soil Drainage	Required Seepage Area (Square Feet Per Bedroom)
15 or less	Good	275
16–30	Fair	375
31–45	Poor	500
Over 45	Not Suitable	—

Figure 24-18. Recommended seepage area required for various percolation rates.

Internet Resources

www.alumag.com
Alumax, An Alcoa Company, manufacturer of bath enclosures and shower doors

www.aquaglass.com
Aqua Glass, a manufacturer of acrylic and gelcoat fiberglass products

www.flowguardgold.com
B. F. Goodrich's FlowGuard Gold home page

www.hotwater.com
A. O. Smith Water Products Company

www.jacuzzi.com
Jacuzzi, Inc.

www.kohler.com
Kohler Company

www.moen.com
Moen, Inc.

www.pricepfister.com
Price Pfister

www.sterlingplumbing.com
Sterling Plumbing, A Kohler Company

www.vanguardpipe.com
Vanguard Piping Systems, Inc.

Review Questions – Chapter 24

Write your answers on a separate sheet of paper. Do not write in this book.

1. Identify the three parts of any residential plumbing system.
2. The pipe that enters the house from the city water main or private well is called the _____.
3. A faucet on the outside of the house is usually called a _____.
4. The cold water line that connects to a fixture is known as a _____.
5. List two types of pipe commonly used in the water supply system.
6. Main waterlines are usually at least _____ in diameter.
7. The purpose of an air compression chamber located at each faucet is to _____.
8. List three places where a shutoff valve is required.
9. The force that causes water to flow in the waste removal system is _____.
10. The usual size of most main drainpipes is _____.
11. A vertical drainpipe that collects waste from one or more fixtures is called a _____.
12. Stacks which do not drain a water closet are known as _____ stacks.
13. All individual drains in the house empty into the _____ drain.
14. Gases are prevented from entering the house through fixture drains by a _____.
15. Each stack requires a _____ at the base of the stack.
16. A wall that houses a soil and vent stack is called a _____.
17. A _____ removes water from a basement when the house drain is higher than the basement floor.
18. A _____ is any device that requires water.
19. List the two main parts of a private sewage disposal system.
20. Identify two requirements that must be met before a private sewage disposal system may be installed.
21. The percentage of solids removed from sewage in the septic tank is _____ percent.
22. The minimum size septic tank is _____ gallons.
23. The addition of one appliance may double the required size of the septic tank. That appliance is a(n) _____.
24. The purpose of the disposal field is to _____.
25. The type of soil best suited for a disposal field is _____.
26. Recommended slope for drain lines in the septic field is _____.
27. Suitability of soil for a disposal field may be determined using a _____ test.

Suggested Activities

1. Visit a house under construction that has the rough plumbing installed. Secure permission to enter the site. Identify the hot and cold water supply systems and the drainage system. Make notes as to the size and type of pipes used. Check to see where shutoff valves are located and determine if the house sewer is to be connected to a public sanitary sewer or private system. Make a sketch of the supply and drainage systems.

2. Visit your local building or plumbing inspector. Ask for specifications and requirements for residential plumbing in your area. Invite the inspector to speak to the class.

3. Write to several manufacturers of plumbing supplies and ask for catalogs showing their products. Examine the material and add it to the class collection.

4. Using a sandbox, build a scale model of a private sewage disposal system for a three bedroom house with a soil percolation rate of 25 minutes per inch. Display the model.

5. Visit a local plumbing supply store and examine materials used in residential plumbing. Report the relative costs of plastic, steel, and copper pipe and fittings.

6. Using CADD, draw the standard plumbing symbols located in the reference section. Add these to your symbols library.

The Plumbing Plan

25

Objectives

After studying this chapter, you will be able to:

➤ Explain the purpose of a residential plumbing plan.

➤ Identify the components of a residential plumbing plan.

➤ Draw plumbing symbols and fixtures on a plumbing plan using proper techniques.

➤ Develop a residential plumbing plan.

➤ Compile a plumbing fixture schedule.

Key Terms

Plumbing Fixture Schedule

Plumbing Plan

Water Supply

The *plumbing plan* shows the location, size, and type of all plumbing equipment to be used. It is a plan view drawing that shows the complete plumbing system. The plumbing plan is generally traced from the floor plan and shows water supply lines, waste disposal lines, and plumbing fixtures. Gas lines and built-in vacuum systems (if required) are also included on the plumbing plan.

The plumbing system should be coordinated with the electrical and climate control systems. Convenience, as well as health and safety, depends to a considerable extent on a well-planned plumbing system that operates efficiently.

Required Information

The plumbing plan should include the waste lines and vent stacks, water supply lines, drain and plumbing fixture locations, and size and type of pipe to be used. Proper plumbing symbols should be used and identified in a legend. A plumbing fixture schedule is also required, as well as any notes needed to fully describe the plumbing system.

Draw the outline of all plumbing fixtures that require plumbing. Check the local code to determine clearance dimensions and minimum space requirements for plumbing fixtures. Locate plumbing for fixtures where access may be provided for servicing. This is a requirement of the National Plumbing Code.

Usually, a single plumbing plan will be adequate for a ranch-type house with or without a basement. A split-level or two-story house may require two or more plans. Piping that serves a given level of the house is then shown on that plan view.

Waste Lines and Vent Stacks

Proper location and sufficient size are the major considerations in planning the waste lines. The waste line network is usually designed first and then the whole system planned around it.

Each water closet must have a main stack. A sufficient number of secondary stacks must also be included to properly vent the other plumbing fixtures. Waste lines and vent stacks are larger in size than water supply lines. The chart in Figure 25-1 shows the minimum sizes for residential waste and vent lines.

Since waste lines and vent stacks are larger than supply lines, they are usually drawn using a wider line than that used for supply lines, Figure 25-2. Try to maintain a proper size relationship between all elements of the drawing.

As stated in the previous chapter, waste lines are not under pressure and depend on gravity to move the waste. The lines must be sloped slightly, usually 1/4" per foot, to facilitate even flow. The required slope should be shown on the plumbing plan in either a general or specific note.

Care should be taken in locating the house drain and sewer so they are the desired height to properly connect with the public sewer or private septic system. The house drain should be no longer than necessary. Study all facets of the layout before deciding on the final location of the house drain and sewer.

Water Supply Lines

The *water supply* begins at the city water main or private water source. Show the building main on the plumbing plan with the proper shutoff valves, meter, and size of pipe. Use the proper symbols. Also, show any required water softener, filter, water storage tank, or other treatment devices positioned along the building main, Figure 25-3. Show the location of the water heater and identify it. Hose bibs and other plumbing fixtures that do not require softened or filtered water should be connected to the building main before it reaches the softener. Shutoff valves must be

Minimum Waste, Vent, and Supply Pipe Sizes				
Plumbing Fixture	**Waste**	**Vent**	**Supply—Cold**	**Supply—Hot**
Bathtub	1-1/2"	1-1/4"	1/2"	1/2"
Bidet	1-1/2"	1-1/2"	1/2"	1/2"
Water Closet	3"	2"	3/8"	—
Lavatory	1-1/2"	1-1/4"	3/8"	3/8"
Service Sink	2"	1-1/4"	1/2"	1/2"
Shower	2"	1-1/4"	1/2"	1/2"
Laundry Tub	1-1/2"	1-1/4"	1/2"	1/2"
Floor Drain	2"	1-1/4"	—	—
Building Main	4" (House Drain)	—	3/4"	—
Cold Water Main	—	—	—	3/4"
Hot Water Main	—	—	—	3/4"
Cold Water Branch	—	—	1/2"	—
Hot Water Branch	—	—	—	1/2"

Figure 25-1. This chart shows the minimum sizes for waste, vent, and supply pipes.

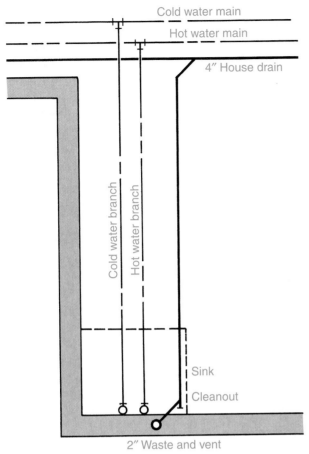

Figure 25-2. Draw the lines for water supply and waste in different widths. Also, notice how different linetypes (symbols) are used.

provided for each plumbing fixture in the water supply system.

Identify the plumbing fixtures that require a water supply and determine the size of pipe needed for each. Each hot and cold water branch line should be sized so it will have the proper water-carrying capacity. Indicate the size of each line in the water supply system and specify the type of pipe to be installed.

Drain Locations

Floor drains are usually located in basements and attached garages. They are usually connected to the storm sewer or a dry well, not to the sanitary sewer system. Indicate drains with the proper symbol and show the location of the pipe leading to the storm sewer or dry well.

Size and Type of Pipe

The proper pipe size for a given installation will depend on the average amount of water used, peak loads, water pressure on the line, and length of the pipe run. Friction reduces the flow of water; therefore, larger pipe should be used for long runs. Rather than try to calculate the pipe size for each plumbing fixture and branch line in the house, refer to the minimum pipe sizes recommended by the Federal Housing Administration. These minimum sizes are shown in the chart in Figure 25-1.

The plumbing plan should specify the type of pipe to be used throughout the system. Several types are available. It is advisable to check the local code to be sure that the type you wish to use is acceptable.

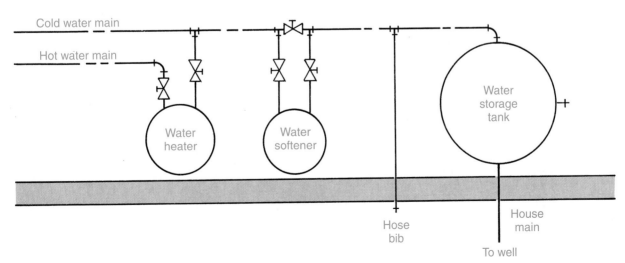

Figure 25-3. This is typical supply piping where a water storage tank, water softener, and water heater are required.

Copper pipe is a frequent choice for the water supply system. The pipe size is a nominal diameter that refers to the approximate inside diameter of the pipe. For example, a 1″ copper pipe, Type L, has a 1.025″ inside diameter (ID) and 1.125″ outside diameter (OD). Type L is a medium weight copper pipe; Type K is heavier and Type M lighter. Type L is usually used for inside hot and cold water lines. Copper tubing with a designation of DWV is also available. It is thinner than Type M and used in the sewage disposal system. DWV refers to "drain, waste, and vent."

Plumbing Fixture Schedule

A *plumbing fixture schedule* is useful in planning the plumbing system, ordering the plumbing fixtures, and installing the system. Information that is customarily shown on a plumbing fixture schedule includes identifying symbols, names of plumbing fixtures, number required, pipe connection sizes, and a space for remarks. A typical residential plumbing fixture schedule is shown in Figure 25-4.

Symbols and Legend

Use standard symbols whenever possible. Standard symbols are recognized and accepted by drafters, designers, contractors, and trade-workers. If there is a chance that a symbol may not be standard or commonly used, then the symbol should be explained in a legend. The legend should appear on the plan where the symbols are used. Figure 25-5 shows some standard plumbing symbols. It is important to note that symbols are not usually drawn to the exact size of the feature that they represent. For this reason, care must be taken in choosing the appropriate symbol size.

Notes

Frequently, information other than that represented by symbols, dimensions, and specifications is needed to describe the plumbing installation. This information is recorded in general notes on the plumbing plan. They are usually located above the title block or in some other prominent place. Notes

| IDENT. SYMBOL | TYPE OF FIXTURE | NO. REG'D. | MANUFACTURER AND CATALOG NO. | PIPE CONNECTION SIZES | | | | | | REMARKS |
				C W	H W	S & W	VENT	TRAP	GAS	
(W/C)	WATER CLOSET	1	ELJER "SILETTE" NO. E 5000 ONE-PIECE	3/8″	–	3″	2″	–	–	VITREOUS CHINA TWILIGHT BLUE
(W/C)	WATER CLOSET	1	ELJER "SILETTE" NO. E 5000 ONE-PIECE	3/8″	–	3″	2″	–	–	VITREOUS CHINA TUSCAN TAN
(T)	BATHTUB	1	ELJER "RIVIERA" NO. E 1120	1/2″	1/2″	2″	1-1/2″	2″	–	ENAMELED CAST IRON TUSCAN TAN
(L)	LAVATORY	2	ELJER "BRENDA" NO. E 3328	1/2″	1/2″	2″	1-1/2″	1-1/2″	–	VITREOUS CHINA TUSCAN TAN
(L)	LAVATORY	1	ELJER "BARROW" NO. E 3471	1/2″	1/2″	2″	1-1/2″	1-1/2″	–	VITREOUS CHINA TWILIGHT BLUE
(S)	SINK	1	ELJER "KENTON" NO. E 2325	1/2″	1/2″	2″	1-1/2″	1-1/2″	–	ENAMELED CAST IRON WHITE 32″ × 20″
(W/S)	WATER SOFTNER	1	SEARS "SERIES 60" NO. W 42 K 3482N	3/4″	–	–	–	–	–	17-1/2″ DIA. × 42″ HIGH DRAIN REQUIRED
(W/H)	WATER HEATER	1	SEARS "MODEL 75" NO. 42 K 33741N	3/4″	3/4″	–	4″	–	1/2″	40 GAL. CAPACITY NATURAL GAS
(C/W)	CLOTHES WASHER	1	WHIRLPOOL "SUPREME 80"	1/2″	1/2″	2″	1-1/2″	1-1/2″	–	AVOCADO GREEN
(D/W)	DISH WASHER	1	WHIRLPOOL SSU 80	1/2″	1/2″	2″	1-1/2″	1-1/2″	–	AVOCADO GREEN
(H B)	HOSE BIB	3	CRANE B-106	3/4″	–	–	–	–	–	

Figure 25-4. A typical residential plumbing fixture schedule.

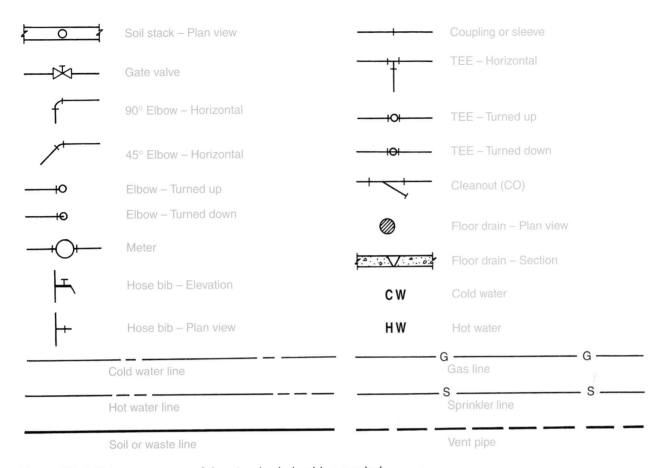

Figure 25-5. These are some of the standard plumbing symbols.

may refer to materials, installation procedures, or any other facet of the plumbing system. When more than one drawing is needed for the plumbing plan, notes must appear on the drawing to which they refer.

Procedure for Drawing Plumbing Plan—Manual Drafting

Several decisions and calculations must be made before the plumbing plan can be drawn. The exact plumbing fixtures to be used should be determined. Manufacturer catalogs are good sources of this information. The exact placement of each plumbing fixture must be decided. The location of utilities, such as sewer, water, storm drains, and gas, must be established. The plot

plan usually provides this information. After initial information has been gathered, the drawing may proceed. The following steps are suggested.

1. Trace the floor plan showing only the exterior and interior walls, doors and windows, and features that relate to the plumbing plan. Steps 1 and 2 are shown in Figure 25-6.
2. Draw the symbols for all plumbing fixtures that are to be connected to the house plumbing system. Plumbing fixtures may be drawn using a hidden line to draw attention to them.
3. Locate and draw the house drain, soil stacks, and vent stacks. Be sure to include cleanouts. Steps 3 and 4 are shown in Figure 25-7.
4. Connect all plumbing fixtures and floor drains to the house drain. Show all fittings and secondary vents that are used.
5. Locate and draw the building main for the water supply system. Connect the water

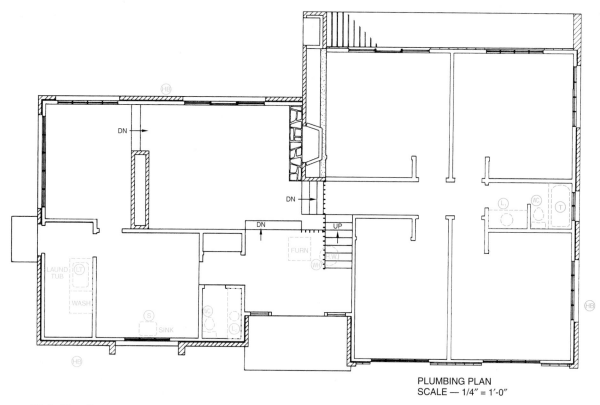

PLUMBING PLAN
SCALE — 1/4″ = 1′-0″

Figure 25-6. The floor plan has been traced and the plumbing fixtures that are to be connected to the plumbing system are drawn as hidden lines.

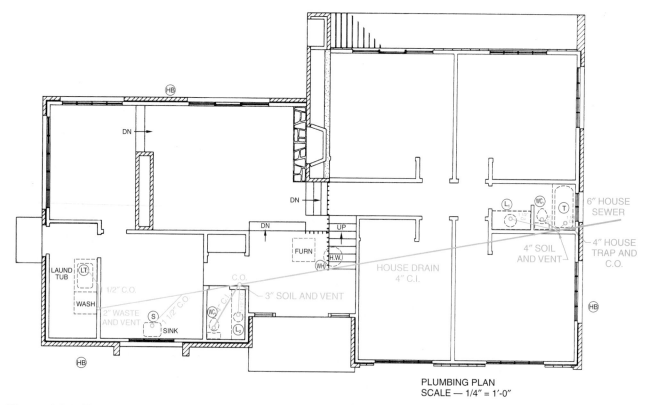

PLUMBING PLAN
SCALE — 1/4″ = 1′-0″

Figure 25-7. The waste piping, including drains, soil stacks, vent stacks, and cleanouts, is added to the drawing. Notice how the pipe material, such as copper (Cu) and cast iron (CI), is indicated.

supply piping to the water heater, water softener, and hose bibs. Steps 5 through 8 are shown in Figure 25-8.

6. Draw the cold and hot water mains. Include shutoff valves where they are required. Draw the cold and hot water lines parallel where possible.

7. Locate and draw all cold water and hot water branch lines. Include shutoff valves. Use the proper symbols.

8. Identify each element of the plumbing system and show pipe sizes.

9. Include a plumbing fixture schedule, symbol legend, and any required general notes.

10. Add the scale and title block to the drawing. Check the entire drawing for accuracy and omissions. Figure 25-9 shows the completed plumbing plan.

This procedure may be repeated for each floor level of the house that requires a plumbing plan.

Be sure to include any other appropriate piping on the plumbing plan. This may vary from one house to the next. For example, piping

for a built-in vacuum cleaning system should be shown on the plumbing plan. Figure 25-10 shows the power unit for such a system and a pictorial view of the inlets around a house.

Procedure for Drawing Plumbing Plan—CADD

Standard CADD software can be used to develop the plumbing plan. Specialized CADD programs for piping drafting are available that can also be used for the design of residential plumbing systems. The main advantage of specialized software is the inclusion of a piping symbols library, which eliminates the need to design your own symbols, Figure 25-11. The procedure for drawing a plumbing plan using standard CADD software is basically the same as for manual drafting.

1. On the plumbing plan layer, trace the floor plan showing only the exterior and interior

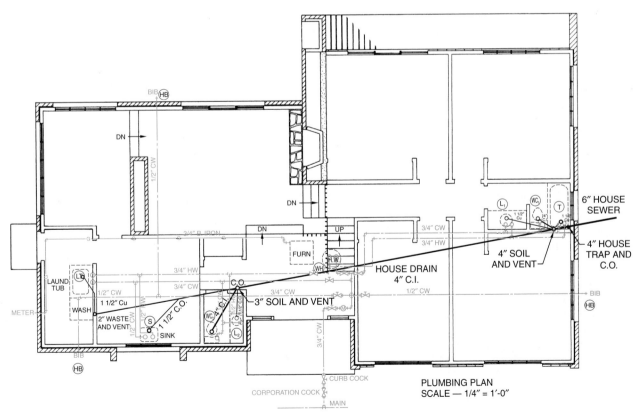

Figure 25-8. The water supply system is added to the drawing. Shutoff valves are included.

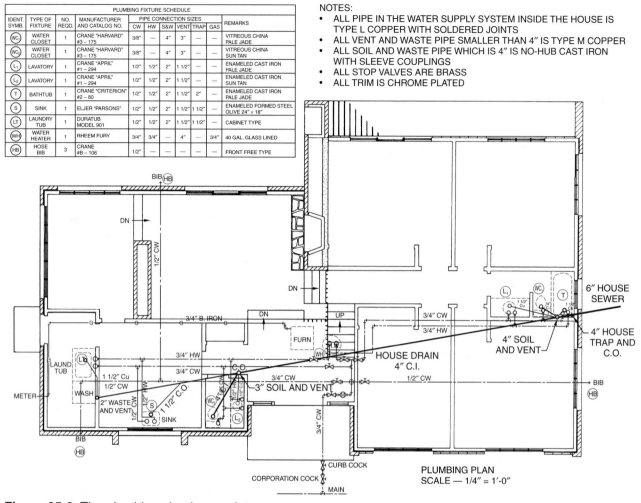

PLUMBING FIXTURE SCHEDULE

IDENT. SYMB.	TYPE OF FIXTURE	NO. REQD.	MANUFACTURER AND CATALOG NO.	CW	HW	S&W	VENT	TRAP	GAS	REMARKS
WC₁	WATER CLOSET	1	CRANE "HARVARD" #3 – 175	3/8"	—	4"	3"	—	—	VITREOUS CHINA PALE JADE
WC₂	WATER CLOSET	1	CRANE "HARVARD" #3 – 175	3/8"	—	4"	3"	—	—	VITREOUS CHINA PALE JADE
L₁	LAVATORY	1	CRANE "APRIL" #1 – 294	1/2"	1/2"	2"	1 1/2"	—	—	ENAMELED CAST IRON PALE JADE
L₂	LAVATORY	1	CRANE "APRIL" #1 – 294	1/2"	1/2"	2"	1 1/2"	—	—	ENAMELED CAST IRON SUN TAN
T	BATHTUB	1	CRANE "CRITERION" #2 – 80	1/2"	1/2"	2"	1 1/2"	2"	—	ENAMELED CAST IRON PALE JADE
S	SINK	1	ELJER "PARSONS"	1/2"	1/2"	2"	1 1/2"	1 1/2"	—	ENAMELED FORMED STEEL OLIVE 24" × 18"
LT	LAUNDRY TUB	1	DURATUB MODEL 901	1/2"	1/2"	2"	1 1/2"	1 1/2"	—	CABINET TYPE
WH	WATER HEATER	1	RHEEM FURY	3/4"	3/4"	—	4"	—	3/4"	40 GAL. GLASS LINED
HB	HOSE BIB	3	CRANE #B – 106	1/2"	—	—	—	—	—	FRONT FREE TYPE

NOTES:
- ALL PIPE IN THE WATER SUPPLY SYSTEM INSIDE THE HOUSE IS TYPE L COPPER WITH SOLDERED JOINTS
- ALL VENT AND WASTE PIPE SMALLER THAN 4" IS TYPE M COPPER
- ALL SOIL AND WASTE PIPE WHICH IS 4" IS NO-HUB CAST IRON WITH SLEEVE COUPLINGS
- ALL STOP VALVES ARE BRASS
- ALL TRIM IS CHROME PLATED

PLUMBING PLAN
SCALE — 1/4" = 1'-0"

Figure 25-9. The plumbing plan is complete.

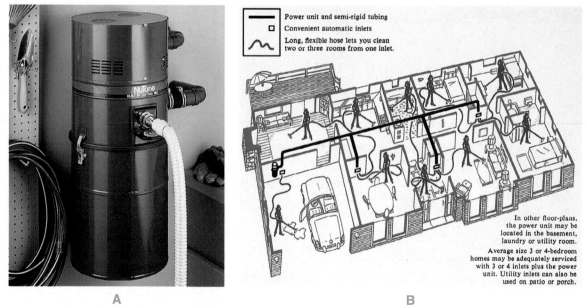

A   B

Figure 25-10. A—The power unit for an in-house vacuum system. B—This pictorial shows the typical locations for inlets. The piping for this system should be shown on the plumbing plan. (Broan-NuTone, A Nortek Company)

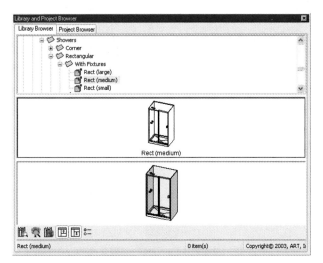

Figure 25-11. Some CADD programs include plumbing symbols in a symbols library. This particular program includes 3D symbols.

walls, doors and windows, and features that relate to the plumbing plan.

2. Insert symbols for all plumbing fixtures that are to be connected to the house plumbing system. Symbols should be placed on their own layer. Plumbing fixtures may be drawn using a hidden line to draw attention to them.

3. Locate and draw the house drain, soil stacks, and vent stacks. Be sure to include cleanouts. Waste lines are wide lines (0.7 mm) and should be placed on a separate layer to facilitate correct plotting.

4. Connect all plumbing fixtures and floor drains to the house drain. Show all fittings and secondary vents that are used.

5. Locate and draw the building main for the water supply system. Connect the water supply piping to the water heater, water softener, and hose bibs. Water supply lines are thin lines (0.35 mm) and should be placed on a separate layer to facilitate correct plotting.

6. Draw the cold and hot water mains. Include shutoff valves where they are required. Draw the cold and hot water lines parallel where possible.

7. Locate and draw all cold water and hot water branch lines. Include shutoff valves. Use the proper symbols and place symbols on their own layer.

8. Identify each element of the plumbing system and show pipe sizes.

9. Include a plumbing fixture schedule, symbol legend, and any required general notes.

10. Add the scale and title block to the drawing. Check the entire drawing for accuracy and omissions.

Repeat this procedure for each floor level of the house that requires a plumbing plan.

Internet Resources

www.alumag.com
 Alumax, An Alcoa Company, manufacturer of bath enclosures and shower doors

www.ansi.org
 American National Standards Institute

www.aquaglass.com
 Aqua Glass, a manufacturer of acrylic and gelcoat fiberglass products

www.flowguardgold.com
 B. F. Goodrich's FlowGuard Gold home page

www.jacuzzi.com
 Jacuzzi, Inc.

www.kohler.com
 Kohler Company

www.moen.com
 Moen, Inc.

www.pricepfister.com
 Price Pfister

www.sterlingplumbing.com
 Sterling Plumbing, A Kohler Company

www.vanguardpipe.com
 Vanguard Piping Systems, Inc.

Review Questions – Chapter 25

Write your answers on a separate sheet of paper. Do not write in this book.

1. Explain the purpose of a plumbing plan.

2. Name two major considerations in planning the waste lines.

3. The part of the plumbing system usually designed first is _____.

4. The plumbing fixture that requires a main stack is a(n) _____.

5. A water closet requires a waste line that is a minimum of _____ in diameter.

6. The force that carries waste and water down the waste lines is _____.

7. Most house mains for the water supply system are _____ in diameter.

8. Floor drains are usually connected to a dry well or _____.

9. Identify four factors that affect the size of pipe required for a given situation.

10. The nominal diameter of copper pipe refers to the _____ dimension.

11. The type of copper pipe usually used for drains, vents, and waste lines is _____.

12. The feature on the plumbing plan that shows the name of plumbing fixtures, manufacturer's catalog number, pipe connection sizes, remarks, and identification symbols for plumbing fixtures is called the _____.

13. To what does DWV refer?

14. What is the main advantage of specialized CADD software for piping drafting?

15. List two features that may be found on a plumbing plan that are not the waste system, supply system, or plumbing fixtures.

Suggested Activities

1. Study Figure 25-6 and list the plumbing fixtures and/or appliances that are connected to the plumbing system. Using manufacturer catalogs, select appliances and fixtures for the house. Then, create a plumbing fixture schedule.

2. Select a floor plan from a magazine or newspaper. Draw the floor plan using CADD. Then, design the water and waste removal system. Determine the size pipe required for each drain and plumbing fixture. Specify the type of material to be used. Draw the plan to 1/4" = 1'-0" scale. Use the proper linetype and weight. Add necessary notes.

3. Using the same floor plan as above, design the water supply system. Determine the pipe size for each branch and main line. Draw the plan in CADD using the proper symbols, linetype, and line weight.

4. Sometimes an isometric drawing is made of the entire plumbing system to further illustrate the layout. If your CADD system has isometric capabilities, create an isometric drawing of the plumbing system you designed in Activity 1 and Activity 2. Do not include the walls and floors of the house, but identify the important features of the system.

5. Visit a local plumbing shop or home improvement center and obtain samples of typical plumbing materials used in residential construction. Identify each item and explain where it might be used in the plumbing system.

6. Using CADD, draw standard plumbing symbols. Examples can be found in the reference section of this book. Add these to your symbols library.

Residential Climate Control 26

Objectives

After studying this chapter, you will be able to:

- Discuss the components of a complete climate control system.
- List the advantages and disadvantages of various types of residential heating systems.
- Perform heat loss calculations for a typical residential structure.
- Select building materials that will provide the best insulation properties.

Key Terms

British Thermal Unit (Btu)
Counterflow Furnace
Dehumidifier
Design Temperature Difference
Electric Radiant System
Forced-Air System
Heat Loss
Heat Pump
Horizontal Furnace
Humidifier
Hydronic System
Infiltration
Inside Design Temperature
Insulation
One-Pipe System
Outside Design Temperature
Plenum
Radiant System
Relative Humidity
Resistivity
Solar Orientation
Thermostat
U Factor
Upflow Furnace
Ventilation
Weatherstripping

The ability to control the temperature inside our house is often taken for granted. However, keeping the house warm in the winter and cool in the summer is an important aspect of life in our technologically advanced society. Increasingly, new homes are being built with complete climate control systems. A complete climate control system involves not only temperature control, but humidity control, air circulation, and air cleaning. This provides a healthful atmosphere in which to live.

Temperature Control

Temperature control includes both heating and cooling. The efficiency with which the control is accomplished is dependent on several conditions. Adequate insulation that is properly installed is of prime importance, Figure 26-1.

Figure 26-1. Proper installation of adequate insulation is an important aspect of efficient temperature control. (CertainTeed Corporation)

Insulation serves to prevent the transfer of heat from one location to another. It helps to keep the house warm in winter and cool in summer. Without insulation, a much larger unit and more energy are required to maintain the desired temperature. This is one reason that older homes are very expensive to heat or cool.

Insulation should be placed in the ceiling, in the exterior walls, and under the floor when the house has a crawl space, Figure 26-2. Houses that are built on slab foundations should have rigid foam insulation along the inside of the foundation wall and horizontally along the perimeter of the floor, Figure 26-3.

Ventilation is another important factor in an efficient temperature control system, Figure 26-4. *Ventilation* reduces the temperature and moisture content in the house, crawl space, and attic by replacing the air in a space with fresh outside air. If the attic and crawl space do not have the proper amount of ventilation, moisture is likely to condense and cause damage. If the attic is hot

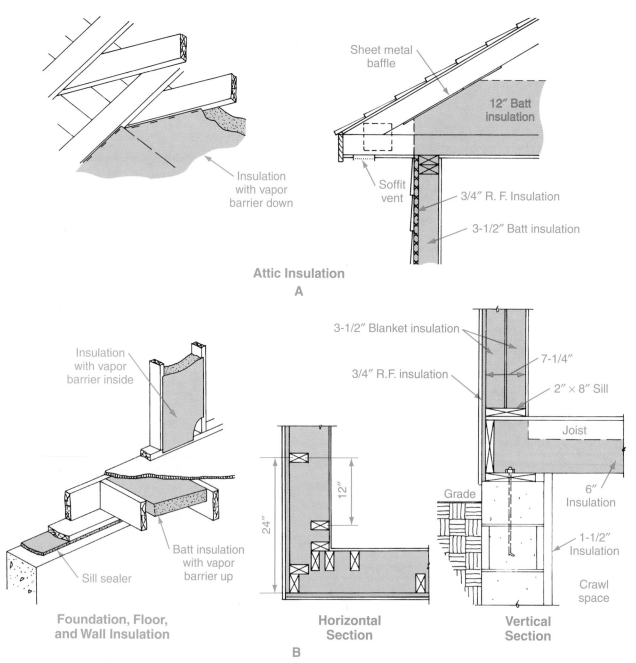

Figure 26-2. Adequate insulation must be installed in several locations. A—In the ceiling and soffit area. B—In foundations, floors, and walls.

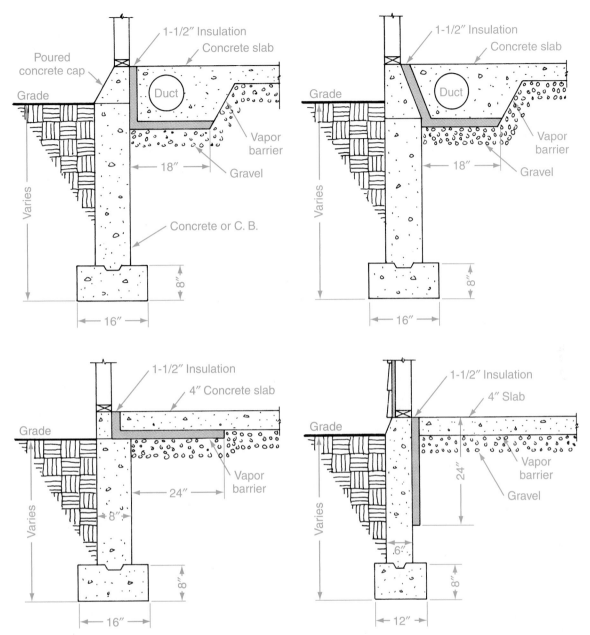

Figure 26-3. Slab foundations should be insulated and have vapor barriers to reduce heat loss and moisture condensation.

and moist, the house will be more difficult to cool. Figure 26-5 shows an attic fan and how it can be used to ventilate the attic space.

A third factor that affects the efficiency of the heating or cooling system is the *solar orientation* of the house. This is how the house is located on the lot in relation to the sun. The west walls of the house should be protected from the sun in the summer. In some cases this may be accomplished with trees or a garage that shade the west wall. In cold climates, an attempt should be made to place all large areas

of glass on the south side of the house away from the cold winter north winds and in position to take advantage of the winter sun.

There are other factors that have a bearing on the efficiency of the temperature control system. *Weatherstripping* seals small cracks around doors and windows to reduce heat loss. Light-colored roofing materials absorb less heat from the sun than dark-colored materials. If a house located in a warm climate does not have shade trees, then a light-colored roof will most likely be preferred. Overhangs shade

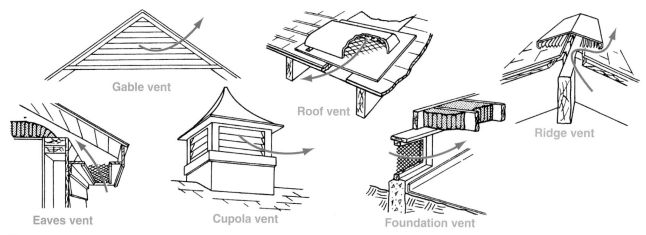

Figure 26-4. The attic and crawl space should be ventilated for more efficient heating and cooling. Insufficient ventilation may cause damage to sheathing and other structural members due to excess moisture.

Figure 26-5. Proper attic ventilation is needed to reduce moisture and aid cooling in warm weather. An attic fan can improve attic ventilation. (Broan-NuTone, A Nortek Company)

exterior walls and reduce the amount of heat entering the house, Figure 26-6A. Landscaping not only serves to improve the appearance of a home, but may be used to block cold winds and provide shade, Figure 26-6B. Insulated glass reduces heat loss and lowers the cost of heating and cooling, Figure 26-7A. In extremely warm climates, windows with bronze glass and built-in shades reduce heat gain in the house, Figure 26-7B.

Humidity Control

Air in our homes contains a certain amount of water (moisture). The amount of moisture in the air related to the temperature level is called humidity. More specifically, humidity is the ratio (percentage) of water vapor in the atmosphere to the amount required to saturate it at a given temperature. This is properly called *relative humidity.* A comfortable humidity level is around 50% when the temperature is about 75°F.

Air will hold more water when the temperature is high than when it is low. During the winter months, the amount of moisture in the indoor air drops to a low level because of expanding the air during heating and the low relative humidity outside the house. If water is not added to the air to increase the humidity, throat and skin irritations are likely. Also, furniture may crack and separate at the glue joints. For these reasons, a *humidifier* is

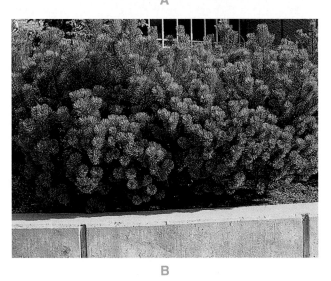

Figure 26-6. A—Overhangs shade the sides of the house and can reduce heat gain in the summer. (California Redwood Association) B—Landscaping is an effective method of blocking cold winds from hitting the house. In northern climates, plants are most effective when placed on the north side of the dwelling.

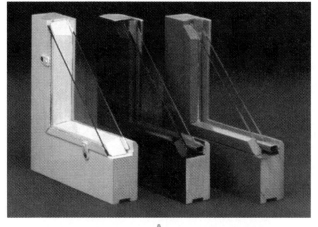

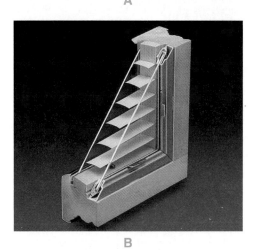

Figure 26-7. A—Three different types of insulated glass windows. (Marvin Windows) B—Cutaway view of window with double glazing and built-in shade. The exterior glass is bronze. (Pella/Rolscreen Company)

Figure 26-8. This power humidifier may be mounted on the plenum or a supply duct of a forced-air heating system. (Copyright Carrier Corporation)

commonly used to increase the moisture level. Humidifiers may be attached directly to the plenum or heating ducts of a forced warm air system or a free-standing model may be used, Figure 26-8.

In the summer, the problem is too much moisture in the air. When the humidity is high, the air feels "sticky" and people are uncomfortable. Wood doors, windows, and drawers can swell and not operate smoothly. When the moisture content is too high, water is likely to condense on windows. This condition, if allowed to persist, may cause damage to the woodwork. A *dehumidifier* may be installed to remove water from the air. This device condenses water on cold coils and thus removes it from the air. This process reduces the relative humidity. Humidity control is important for total comfort and should be considered when planning a climate control system.

Air Circulation and Cleaning

Continued recirculation of the air in a house will result in stale and unhealthy air. Therefore, some provision should be made to add fresh air into the house. In addition, circulation helps reduce localized areas of high or low humidity. High concentrations of moist air in the kitchen, laundry room, and bath are distributed throughout the house when the air is circulated.

The air in most homes contains dust and other particles. Therefore, consideration should be given to adding some type of air cleaning device. Most furnaces have built-in filters, while others include electronic air cleaning grids, Figure 26-9. Electronic grids are effective and will remove up to about 95% of the dust particles in the air as it passes through the grid.

Programmable Thermostats

A furnace or air conditioner is controlled by a thermostat. A *thermostat* is an automatic sensing device that sends a signal to the furnace or air conditioner at a temperature set by the homeowner. The thermostat is usually located on an inside wall of the house. If located on an exterior wall, the outside temperature may influence the thermostat function. The thermostat should also be located where it will be free from cold air drafts and heat from lamps.

The old dial-style thermostat has mostly been replaced by newer digital models, Figure 26-10. But, neither of these thermostats is "intelligent." Manufacturers say that an "intelligent" programmable thermostat can reduce your heating and cooling costs up to 33%. Programmable thermostats have a microprocessor and can automatically control your home's heating and cooling systems, Figure 26-11. These devices have a liquid crystal display and a small keypad for programming.

A typical heating/cooling program for the thermostat may partition the day into several periods, each set for a specific temperature. For example, during a northern winter heating season, the thermostat might be programmed as follows.

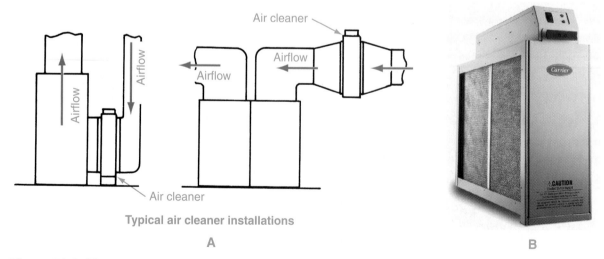

Typical air cleaner installations

A

B

Figure 26-9. Electronic air cleaners can be installed with most forced-air heating, cooling, or ventilation systems. (Photo Copyright Carrier Corporation)

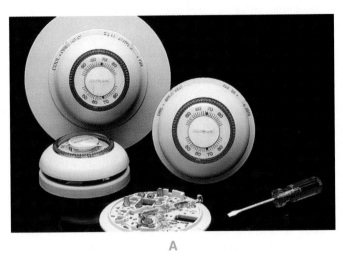

Figure 26-10. A—This is the older dial-style thermostat used in residential heating and cooling systems. (Honeywell, Inc.) B—This is a newer digital-style thermostat used in residential heating and cooling systems.

Figure 26-11. Programmable digital thermostats can be used to maximize energy savings. (Copyright Carrier Corporation)

- At 11:00 pm, the temperature is set to 60°F for the nighttime hours. This will save considerable energy.
- At 6:00 am, the temperature is set to 75°F so the house is warm when you get up.
- When you leave for work or school, the temperature is set to a lower temperature, such as 65°F, to save energy during the day.
- A half an hour before you return in the evening, the temperature is set to 75°F so the house is warm when you return.

At any time during the program, you can manually adjust the temperature setting if you need to for any reason. The program can be returned to normal function by simply touching a button. Most programmable digital thermostats also include a "vacation" mode that will maintain a set temperature for almost any period of time.

The programmable thermostat can control air conditioning during the cooling season in a fashion similar to the heating season. Or, you may choose to have a single cooling cycle per day to reduce the temperature in the house only when it is the warmest outside. Some thermostats automatically adjust for seasonal changes using an internal calendar programmed into the thermostat. Most models contain battery backup so reprogramming is not required if the power fails. Batteries should be changed every year to prevent system failure as a result of a dead battery and a power failure.

In many areas of the country, utility companies are working with homeowners to reduce power consumption during peak times to lower costs. Some new programmable digital thermostats allow electricity consumption by the home air conditioner or furnace to be remotely controlled by the power company through the thermostat. Communication to and from the thermostat is achieved via the wireless two-way paging network, Internet, wireless radio frequency, or telephone lines, depending on the specific product. But, homeowners retain ultimate control and can override the temperature changes if desired.

Some "smart" thermostats even have the ability to perform self-diagnostic tests and communicate with a service technician over the Internet. This technology will eventually allow users to control their heating, ventilation, and air conditioning systems from virtually anywhere in the world, which will help lower their energy consumption and energy costs.

Cooling Systems

Cooling systems remove heat from a building and provide cool, clean, dehumidified air. This allows a home to be comfortable in warm, humid weather. Also, since windows are closed while the cooling system is on, infiltration of dirt, pollen, and dust is reduced. A central air conditioner is the most efficient type of residential cooling system. Heat pumps are frequently used to cool homes as well. The operation of heat pumps is discussed in the heating section of this chapter. Room (window) air conditioners are not cooling systems, but they are used in some homes and many apartments for local cooling.

As room air is cooled, moisture in the air condenses on the fins of the condenser. The water is then drained away. This process dehumidifies the air and increases the comfort level inside the house.

The cooled and dried air is moved to various parts of the living space through a system of ducts. If a forced-air furnace is present, the ducts of the heating system may be used. The furnace blower is then used to move the air through the ducts. Otherwise, an independent blower and ductwork are required.

The most common residential cooling system is the compressor-cycle system. This system uses the heating and cooling of a compressed chemical refrigerant to cool air. See Figure 26-12. High-temperature refrigerant vapor passes through the compressor where it is pressurized. The high-pressure, high-temperature gas then travels through the condenser where it cools to a liquid state. The high-pressure, low-temperature liquid then travels through an orifice. This changes the refrigerant to a low-pressure, low-temperature liquid. The refrigerant then passes through the evaporator coil where it removes heat from the air in the home as it changes into a gas again. This low-pressure, high-temperature gas returns to the compressor and the cycle begins again.

Compressor-cycle units normally have two separate components. The compressor and condenser are in a separate unit that is located outside the home, Figure 26-13. These are the "hot" parts of the unit and, therefore, placed outside the house. The cooling coils are mounted in the ductwork of the house.

Room air conditioning units contain a compressor, condenser, evaporator coil, and fan all in one unit, Figure 26-14. They are usually installed in a window or wall opening designed for the unit. The condenser and compressor are located in the unit in a way such that they are outside the living space. Room air conditioners should be well covered during cool weather because cold air will enter the room through the unit.

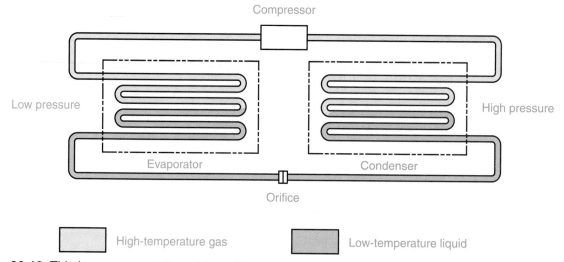

Figure 26-12. This is a representation of the refrigerant and pressure states inside a compressor-cycle air conditioning system.

Types of Heating Systems

Heating systems are usually one of four basic types. These types are forced-air, hydronic, electric radiant, and heat pumps. The next sections cover each type in detail. Choosing the "right" system for a particular home will depend on the availability of fuels, temperature variations, cost of installation and maintenance, type of house, and personal preference of the owner.

Forced-Air Systems

A *forced-air system* heats air in a furnace and forces it through pipes or ducts to all parts of the house, Figure 26-15. A fan or blower is used to push the warm air. Cool air is drawn through cold air return ducts to the furnace. Before the cool air enters the heating chamber, it passes through a filter that removes dust and other particles. Some forced-air systems have built-in humidifiers, dehumidifiers, and air cleaners.

The forced-air system is popular because it is relatively inexpensive to purchase and install, quickly provides adequate amounts of heat, humidification is simple, and the ductwork may be used for central air conditioning. Furnaces may be located in the attic, crawl space, or main level, Figure 26-16. There are

Figure 26-13. This is a compressor-condenser unit for a central air conditioning system, which is located outside the house. (Copyright Carrier Corporation)

Figure 26-14. Room air conditioners contain the compressor-condenser unit, evaporator coil, and fan. They are placed in windows or openings cut into the wall. (General Electric Company)

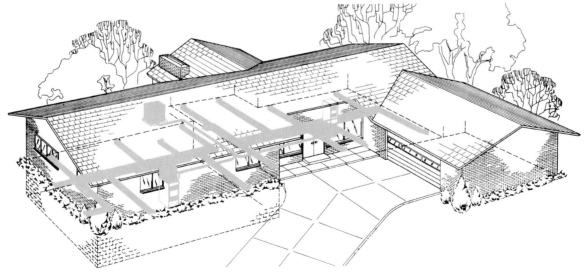

Figure 26-15. A forced-air system uses ductwork and a blower to deliver air to various parts of the home. This forced-air system is used for both heating and cooling.

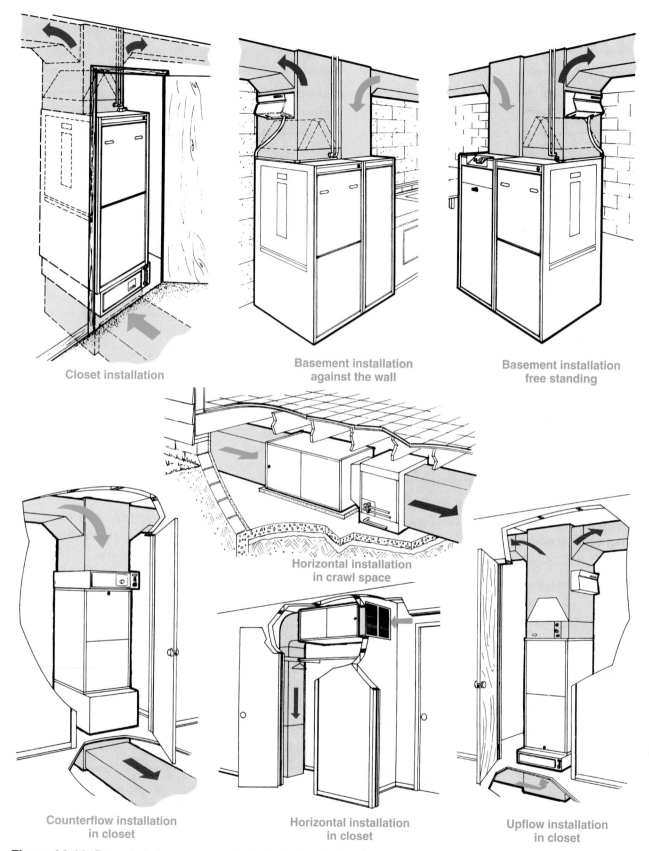

Closet installation

Basement installation
against the wall

Basement installation
free standing

Horizontal installation
in crawl space

Counterflow installation
in closet

Horizontal installation
in closet

Upflow installation
in closet

Figure 26-16. Forced-air furnaces can be installed in the basement, crawl space, or a first-floor closet. (Lennox Industries, Inc.)

three basic types of forced-air furnaces available for residential installations. These are standard upflow, counterflow, and horizontal.

The *upflow furnace* is designed for basement installation because the plenum is on top of the furnace, Figure 26-17A. The **plenum** is the chamber where warmed air is collected for distribution. When the furnace is to be located on the main floor with ducts below the floor, a *counterflow furnace* is required, Figure 26-17B. On this type of furnace, the plenum is on the bottom and the warm air is forced downward. If the furnace is to be installed in the attic or crawl space, a *horizontal furnace* is a logical choice, Figure 26-17C. They require minimum clearance and can be suspended from ceilings and floor joists or installed on a concrete slab.

A typical forced-air system for a small home uses one thermostat that controls the temperature for the entire home. Large homes frequently require zones, which are areas that each have a thermostat to control temperature in that area. Systems that have zones usually require a separate furnace for each zone.

Forced-air systems do have some disadvantages. They produce rapid movement of air that can cause drafts, which is objectionable to some people. Also, noise is often transmitted through the ducts. The noise level is generally higher than with other systems due to the blower. In addition, ductwork is designed to fit between the joists and wall studs, Figure 26-18. However, the ducts are large and sometimes difficult to route to all parts of the dwelling. Furniture can also interfere with air movement, thus reducing the effectiveness of a forced-air system.

Hydronic Systems

A *hydronic system,* or hot water system, consists of a boiler, water pipes, and radiators or radiant panels, Figure 26-19. The boiler heats the water in the system. The hot water is then pumped to the radiators, which are located throughout the house. Heat is transferred from the water to the air at the radiator. The cooled water is then returned from the radiator to the boiler for reheating.

The type of hydronic system used in most homes is known as the *one-pipe system.* The

A

B

C

Figure 26-17. There are three basic types of forced-air furnaces. A—Upflow. (Copyright Carrier Corporation) B—Counterflow. (Copyright Carrier Corporation) C—Horizontal. (United Technologies Carrier)

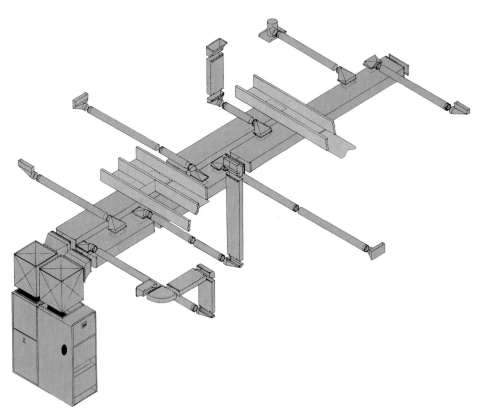

Figure 26-18. The plenum and other ductwork of a forced-air system is designed to fit within the joists and studs of a frame structure. (The Williamson Company)

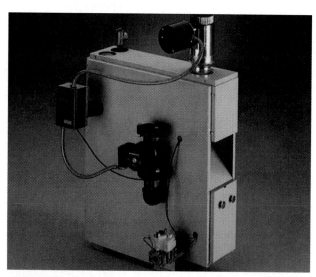

Figure 26-19. This is the boiler unit for a gas-fired hydronic heating system. The circulating pump can be seen on the side of the unit. (Copyright Carrier Corporation)

one-pipe system uses radiators, or convectors as they are sometimes called, connected in series. Heated water carried in the main pipe is diverted to the radiators and is then returned

to the furnace, Figure 26-20. Special connectors allow small amounts of hot water to enter the radiators and equalize heat in radiators throughout the home.

Old-style radiators are seldom used in new homes. Baseboard convectors are now the most common radiator, Figure 26-21. These are produced in several styles and efficiently transmit heat to the surrounding air.

Another type of hydronic heating system utilizes copper pipes or other type of tubing embedded in a concrete floor or plastered ceiling. This system is often referred to as a *radiant system,* Figure 26-22. It is popular in mild climates and locations where the temperature is not likely to drop rapidly in a short period of time. A radiant heating system is silent and is completely hidden from sight.

One of the major advantages of a hydronic heating system is that each room may be controlled individually. Frequently the home is zoned into two or three areas that require about the same temperature. Each zone is then controlled by a separate thermostat. This adds to the heating comfort.

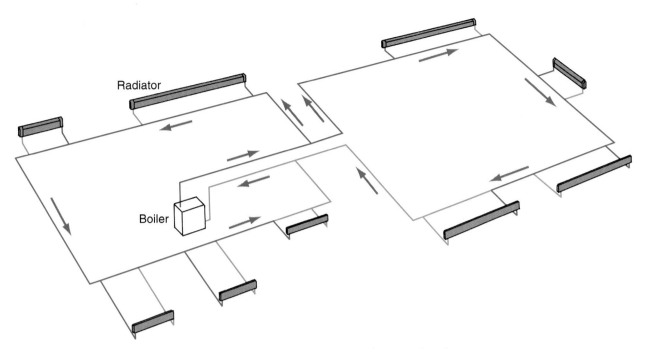

Figure 26-20. This is a one-pipe hydronic system. This system has two heating zones.

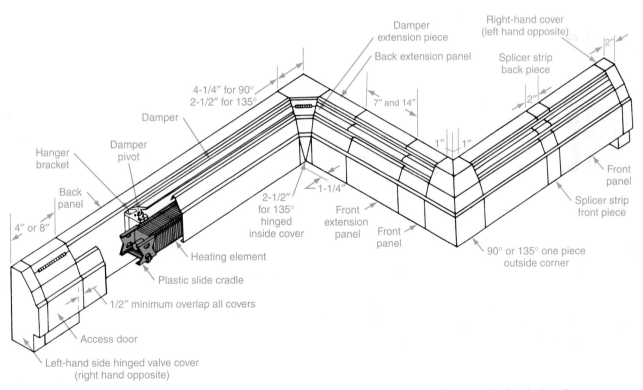

Figure 26-21. Baseboard convectors are the most common type of radiator for new hydronic heating systems. (Crane Co.)

Other advantages of a hydronic heating system include the absence of noise transmitted from room to room, no registers to occupy wall space, and no drafts. Hydronic heat is clean, quiet, and efficient. However, it has no provision for cooling, air filtration, or humidification. Also, the reaction time is slow when compared to other systems. These may

Figure 26-22. A—These are the main controls of a radiant system. B—These pipes for a radiant system will be embedded in a concrete floor. (Vanguard Plastics Inc.)

be considered serious deficiencies in some sections of the country.

Electric Radiant Systems

An *electric radiant system* uses resistance wiring to produce heat. The wire is embedded in the ceiling, floor, or baseboards, Figure 26-23.

This system is clean, quiet, and produces a constant level of heat. The entire system is hidden if the wires are in the ceiling or floor. Heat control for each room or area is practical. No chimney is required, as is with most gas- or oil-fired systems. The electric radiant system is dependable and free from maintenance problems. Figure 26-24 shows a typical installation.

Figure 26-23. A—This bathroom has a baseboard radiant electric heating unit. (Radiant Electric Heat, Inc.) B—A cove radiant electric heating unit can be seen above the window in this kitchen. (Radiant Electric Heat, Inc.)

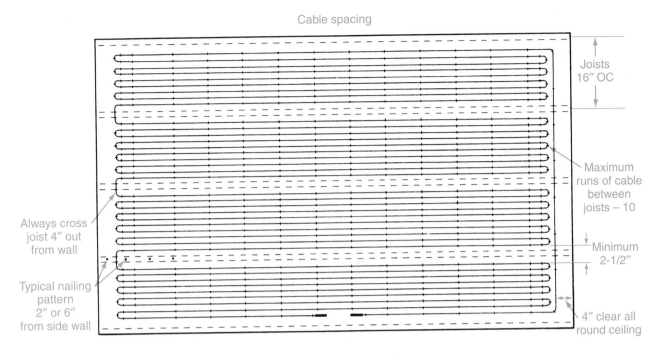

Cable spacing

Joists 16" OC

Maximum runs of cable between joists – 10

Minimum 2-1/2"

Always cross joist 4" out from wall

4" clear all round ceiling

Typical nailing pattern 2" or 6" from side wall

Typical ceiling layout pattern

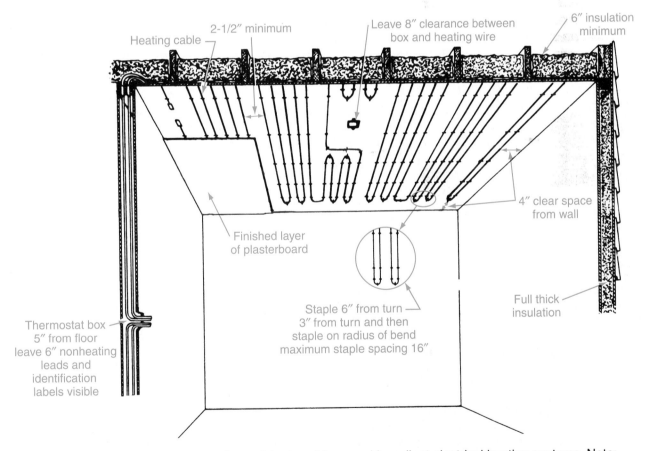

2-1/2" minimum

Leave 8" clearance between box and heating wire

6" insulation minimum

Heating cable

4" clear space from wall

Finished layer of plasterboard

Full thick insulation

Staple 6" from turn 3" from turn and then staple on radius of bend maximum staple spacing 16"

Thermostat box 5" from floor leave 6" nonheating leads and identification labels visible

Figure 26-24. This is a typical layout for resistance wiring used in radiant electrical heating systems. Note: One watt of electricity will provide 3.415 Btus of heat.

Disadvantages of electric radiant systems include no provision for humidification, air filtration, or cooling. Also, as with a hydronic system, the system is slow to recover if the temperature drops suddenly. Finally, in some areas of the country electric radiant systems are expensive to operate due to the cost of electricity.

Heat Pumps

A *heat pump* serves the dual purpose of heating and cooling, Figure 26-25. It is essentially a refrigeration unit that "pumps" or transfers natural heat from air or water to heat or cool the house. Heat pumps operate on the principle that there is some heat in all air and water, and that this heat can be removed. Heat that has been removed is pumped into the house to heat it or pumped from the house to cool it.

A heat pump requires electricity to operate a compressor. Therefore, it is clean and needs no chimney. Since the main unit is located outside the house, limited interior space is required. Heat pumps are highly efficient in mild climates. In addition, air cleaning and humidification are easy.

A disadvantage of heat pumps is that efficiency drops considerably when the temperature is below 30°F. For this reason, air-to-air heat pumps are not practical for cold climates. An air-to-air system also requires a duct system and blower to move air around in the house. Therefore, installation costs generally are higher than for other systems.

Figure 26-25. This is a heat pump compressor/condenser unit designed for outside installation. (Copyright Carrier Corporation)

Ground-Source Heat Pumps

Typical air-to-air heat pumps are very popular in mild climates for both heating and cooling, but their efficiency suffers when the temperature reaches extremes. However, newer ground-source "geothermal" heat pumps improve the overall efficiency by using the earth as an inexpensive source of heat and a place to deposit heat.

A ground-source heat pump uses an antifreeze solution, instead of air, for the heat source and heat sink. The antifreeze is circulated through a long loop of plastic pipe buried in the ground in a deep trench. Wells are also used for this purpose.

The temperature of the subsoil is between 40°F and 50°F year-round. This temperature is much warmer than cold air in the winter and much cooler than hot air in the summer. Tests by the Environmental Protection Agency (EPA) have shown that ground-source heat pumps produce from three to five times as much energy (in heat) as is required from the consumer (in electricity) to run the system. But, the initial installation cost of the system is high.

Carbon Monoxide Detectors

Any dwelling that has a combustion appliance, such as a gas stove or furnace, should have a carbon monoxide (CO) detector. A CO detector is inexpensive insurance against health risks. A properly functioning detector can provide an early warning to occupants before carbon monoxide concentrations reach a dangerous level. CO is an odorless, colorless gas and high levels of CO can cause death.

Like smoke detectors, CO detectors should be mounted on hallway ceilings outside the bedrooms. For added safety, place additional detectors near any combustion equipment. Be sure to select a device that meets the Underwriters Laboratories Standard 2034. To meet this standard, a detector must sound the alarm when CO concentrations reach 100 ppm for 90 minutes, 200 ppm for 35 minutes, or 400 ppm for 15 minutes. For more information on CO and CO detectors, refer to Chapter 38 of this text.

Heat Loss Calculations

Before the proper size of heating or cooling unit may be determined, heat loss calculations are required for exposed surfaces of the home. There are several terms with which you should become familiar. These are:

- *British thermal unit (Btu).* One Btu is the quantity of heat required to increase the temperature of 1 pound of water 1°F. Furnaces and air conditioners are rated in Btus. Final heat loss calculations will be in Btus.

- *Design temperature difference.* The difference between the outside design temperature and the inside design temperature is the design temperature difference.

- *Heat loss.* This is the amount of heat that passes through the exposed surfaces of the house for average temperatures.

- *Infiltration.* Heat lost through spaces around windows and doors is known as infiltration. For calculation purposes, it has been estimated that infiltration is equal to one air exchange per hour. For example, if a room is 10′ × 18′ and has an 8′ ceiling the total volume is 1440 cubic feet. This figure, 1440 cubic feet, is the amount of air infiltration.

- *Inside design temperature.* The desired room temperature level is called the inside design temperature. The inside design temperature used in calculations is typically 70°F.

- *Outside design temperature.* The outside design temperature is the average outdoor temperature for the winter months. An average of the coldest temperatures for the months of October through March is used to determine the outdoor design temperature.

- *Resistivity.* The ability of a material to resist the transfer of heat or cold is its resistivity; commonly known as the R factor. Materials that transmit heat readily are known as conductors while those that do not are called insulators.

- *U factor.* The U factor, or U as it is commonly called, is the number of Btus transmitted in one hour through one square foot of a building material for each degree of temperature difference. U factors for common building materials may be determined by taking the reciprocal of the resistivity of the material. This is done by dividing 1.00 by the resistance factor. See Figure 26-26.

Figure 26-27 shows several energy-conserving exterior wall assemblies with R factors identified for each material. The total R and U factors are also shown for each assembly.

Calculation Procedure

First, determine the heat loss for walls, ceiling, and floor of each room. Once these calculations are complete, the total house heat loss can be calculated. These figures are important in determining the proper size of heating or cooling units for the house.

The following sections show calculations for determining a heating unit size. The procedure for calculating the size of cooling unit is the same, except that the design temperature difference must reflect summer temperatures rather than winter. Also, an allowance should be made for very humid locations. A larger unit will be required.

Walls

1. Find the total exterior wall area by multiplying the length by the height. This is the gross wall area.
2. Subtract the area filled by windows and doors in the exterior walls. The resulting area is called the net wall area.
3. Add the resistivity for each of the materials used in the construction of each wall. Each wall that is constructed differently must be calculated separately. Take the reciprocal of the sum. This figure is the U factor for the net wall area.
4. Determine the U factor for each door and window in the exterior wall by taking the reciprocal of the resistivity.

	Resistivity to Heat Loss of Common Building Materials					
	Material	**Resistivity**			**Material**	**Resistivity**
4"	Concrete or stone	.32		1/2"	Plywood	.65
6"	Concrete or stone	.48		5/8"	Plywood	.80
8"	Concrete or stone	.64		3/4"	Plywood	.95
12"	Concrete or stone	.96		3/4"	Softwood sheathing or siding	.85
4"	Concrete block	.70			Composition floor covering	.08
8"	Concrete block	1.10		1"	Mineral batt insulation	3.50
12"	Concrete block	1.25		2"	Mineral batt insulation	7.00
4"	Common brick	.82		4"	Mineral batt insulation	14.00
4"	Face brick	.45		2"	Glass fiber insulation	7.00
4"	Structural clay tile	1.10		4"	Glass fiber insulation	14.00
8"	Structural clay tile	1.90		1"	Loose fill insulation	3.00
12"	Structural clay tile	3.00		1/2"	Gypsum wallboard	.45
1"	Stucco	.20		1"	Expanding polystyrene, extruded	4.00
15lb	Building paper	.06		1"	Expanding polystyrene, molded beads	3.85
3/8"	Sheet rock or plasterboard	.33			Single thickness glass	.88
1/2"	Sand plaster	.15			Glassweld insulating glass	1.89
1/2"	Insulation plaster	.75			Single glass with storm window	1.66
1/2"	Fiberboard ceiling tile	1.20			Metal edge glass	1.85
1/2"	Fiberboard sheathing	1.45		4"	Glass block	2.13
3/4"	Fiberboard sheathing	2.18		1-3/8"	Wood door	1.82
	Roll roofing	.15			Same with storm door	2.94
	Asphalt shingles	.16		1-3/4"	Wood door	1.82
	Wood shingles	.86			Same with storm door	3.12
	Tile or slate	.08				

Figure 26-26. This chart shows resistivity of common building materials. The U factor can be calculated by taking the reciprocal of the resistivity.

5. Calculate the design temperature difference by subtracting the outside design temperature from the inside design temperature. Example: IDT = 70°F, ODT = –10°F, therefore 70°F minus –10°F = 80°F. The design temperature difference for this example is 80°F.

6. Determine the Btu loss per hour (Btu/H) for the net wall area by multiplying the net wall area by the net wall U factor by the design temperature difference. Record this figure.

7. Determine the Btu/H for the windows by multiplying the window area by the glass U factor by the design temperature difference. Record this figure.

8. Determine the Btu/H for the doors by multiplying the door area by the door U factor by the design temperature difference. Record this figure.

Ceiling

1. Find the total ceiling area by multiplying the length by the width.

2. Determine the U factor for the ceiling by adding the resistivity for each material used and taking the reciprocal.

3. Calculate the Btu/H by multiplying the ceiling area by the total ceiling U factor by the design temperature difference. Record the figure.

Floor

1. Find the total floor area of the floor by multiplying the length by the width. Heat loss is only calculated for floors over unheated areas, such as a crawl space or slab-type floors.

2. Determine the U factor for the floor by adding the resistivity for each material used and taking the reciprocal.

3. Calculate the Btu/H by multiplying the floor area by the total floor U factor by the design temperature difference. Note that the design temperature difference may not be the same here as for walls and ceiling with heating ducts and hot water pipes that are not insulated. If the area is properly

303 Siding Direct to Studs – U = 0.08

- 1/2" Gypsum wallboard
- Vapor barrier
- R11 Batt insulation
- 2" × 4" Studs
- APA 303 Plywood siding (11/32" or thicker)

	R
Outside air film	0.17
11/32" plywood siding	0.43
R11 batt insulation	11.00
1/2" gypsum wallboard	0.45
Inside air film	0.68
	$R_T = 12.73$
	$U = 1/R_T = 0.08$

303 Siding Over Fiberboard Sheathing – U = 0.07

- 1/2" Gypsum wallboard
- Vapor barrier
- R11 Batt insulation
- 1/2" Fiberboard sheathing
- 2" × 4" Studs
- APA 303 Plywood siding (11/32" or thicker)

	R
Outside air film	0.17
11/32" plywood siding	0.43
1/2" fiberboard sheathing	1.32
R11 insulation	11.00
1/2" gypsum wallboard	0.45
Inside air film	0.68
	$R_T = 14.05$
	$U = 1/R_T = 0.07$

303 Siding Direct to Studs – U = 0.07

- 1/2" Gypsum wallboard
- Vapor barrier
- R13 Batt insulation
- 2" × 4" Studs
- APA 303 Plywood siding (11/32" or thicker)

	R
Outside air film	0.17
11/32" plywood siding	0.43
R13 batt insulation	13.00
1/2" gypsum wallboard	0.45
Inside air film	0.68
	$R_T = 14.73$
	$U = 1/R_T = 0.07$

303 Siding Over Rigid Insulation – U = 0.05

- 1/2" Gypsum wallboard
- Vapor barrier
- R13 Batt insulation
- 2" × 4" Studs
- R4 Rigid foam insulation
- APA 303 Plywood siding (11/32" or thicker)

	R
Outside air film	0.17
11/32" plywood siding	0.43
R4 rigid foam insulation	4.00
R13 batt insulation	13.00
1/2" gypsum wallboard	0.45
Inside air film	0.68
	$R_T = 18.73$
	$U = 1/R_T = 0.05$

303 Siding Direct to Studs – U = 0.05

- 1/2" Gypsum wallboard
- Vapor barrier
- R19 Batt insulation
- 2" × 6" Studs
- APA 303 Plywood siding (15/32" or thicker for studs 24" OC)

	R
Outside air film	0.17
15/32" plywood siding	0.59
R19 batt insulation	19.00
1/2" gypsum wallboard	0.45
Inside air film	0.68
	$R_T = 20.89$
	$U = 1/R_T = 0.05$

Figure 26-27. Exterior wall assemblies showing R factors for each material and total R and U factors for each assembly. (The Engineered Wood Association)

vented and pipes and ducts are insulated, then some design temperature difference may be used. Record this figure.

Infiltration

1. Determine the volume of air in the room or home under consideration by multiplying the length by the width by the height. This volume is equal to the air infiltration.
2. Calculate the air infiltration Btu/H heat loss by multiplying the volume of air infiltration by the U factor (.018) by the design temperature difference. Note that .018 Btu/H is required to warm one cubic foot of air 1°F. This is a constant and may be used in each calculation. Record this figure.

Final Calculations

1. List the Btu/H for the walls, windows, doors, ceiling, floor, and air infiltration.
2. The sum of these values is the total heat loss in Btu/H. This figure represents the size of units required for the room or house being calculated.

Example of Heat Loss Calculation

The following example applies the above procedure to the room shown in Figure 26-28. This is a "real-life" calculation of heat loss. The necessary construction details and R factors are also shown in Figure 26-28.

Calculations for Walls

1. Total exterior area.

$$12'\text{-}0'' \times 8'\text{-}0'' = 96 \text{ square feet}$$
$$18'\text{-}0'' \times 8'\text{-}0'' = \underline{144 \text{ square feet}}$$

Gross exterior wall area = 240 square feet

2. Window area.

$$6'\text{-}0'' \times 5'\text{-}0'' = 30 \text{ square feet}$$
$$6'\text{-}0'' \times 5'\text{-}0'' = \underline{30 \text{ square feet}}$$

Total window area = 60 square feet

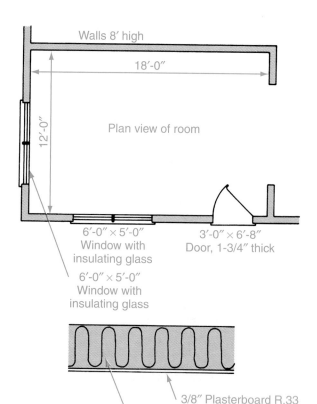

Walls 8' high

18'-0"

Plan view of room

12'-0"

6'-0" × 5'-0"
Window with
insulating glass

3'-0" × 6'-8"
Door, 1-3/4" thick

6'-0" × 5'-0"
Window with
insulating glass

3/8" Plasterboard R.33
4" Glass fiber insulation

Ceiling section

3/4" Wood siding R.85
1/2" Fiberboard sheathing R1.45
4" Glass fiber insulation R14.00
3/8" Plasterboard R.33

Wall section

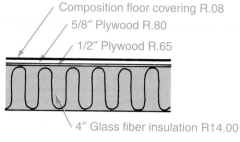

Composition floor covering R.08
5/8" Plywood R.80
1/2" Plywood R.65

4" Glass fiber insulation R14.00

Floor section

Figure 26-28. This room is used for the heat loss calculations in the text.

Door area.

3'-0" × 6'-8" = 21 square feet (approximate, includes the rough opening space)

Net wall area.

Net wall area = Gross wall area – doors and window area
= 240 square feet – 81 square feet
= 159 square feet

3. Resistivity of wall materials.

3/4" softwood siding R factor	= .85
1/2" fiberboard sheathing R factor	= 1.45
4" glass fiber insulation R factor	= 14.00
3/8" plasterboard R factor	= .33
Total resistivity	= 16.63

U factor for net wall = 1.00 ÷ 16.63 = .060

4. U factor for doors and windows.

1-3/4" wood door = .55
Insulating glass window = .54 for each

5. Design temperature difference.

Inside design temperature	=	70°F
Outside design temperature	=	–5°F
Design temperature difference	=	75°F

6. Btu/H for net wall.

Net wall area × U factor × temperature difference

159 square feet × .060 × 75°F = 715.50
Btu/H for the net walls = 715.50

7. Btu/H for the windows.

Window area × U factor × temperature difference

60 square feet × .54 × 75°F = 2430.00
Btu/H for the windows = 2430.00

8. Btu/H for the door.

Door area × U factor × temperature difference

21 square feet × .55 × 75°F = 866.25
Btu/H for the door = 866.25

Calculation for Ceiling

1. Total ceiling area.

12'-0" × 18'-0" = 216 square feet

2. U factor for ceiling.

3/8" plasterboard R factor	=	.33
4" glass fiber insulation R factor	=	14.00
Total resistivity	=	14.33

U factor for ceiling = 1.00 ÷ 14.33 = .070

3. Btu/H for the ceiling.

Ceiling area × U factor × temperature difference

216 square feet × .070 × 75°F = 1134.00
Btu/H for the ceiling = 1134.00

Calculation for Floor

1. Total floor area.

12'-0" × 18'-0" = 216 square feet

2. U factor for floor.

Composition floor covering R factor	=	.08
5/8" plywood R factor	=	.80
1/2" plywood R factor	=	.65
4" glass fiber insulation R factor	=	14.00
Total resistivity	=	15.53

U factor for floor 1.00 / 15.53 = .064

3. Btu/H for the floor.

Floor area × U factor × temperature difference

216 square feet × .064 × 75°F = 1036.80
Btu/H for the floor = 1036.80

Calculation for Air Infiltration

1. Volume of air.

Length × width × height
18'-0" × 12'-0" × 8'-0" = 1728 cubic feet
Volume of air = air infiltration

2. Btu/H for air infiltration.

Volume of air × .018 × temperature difference

1728 cubic feet × .018 × 75°F	= 2332.80
Btu/H for air infiltration	= 2332.80

Summary Calculations

Btu/H for net walls	=	715.50
Btu/H for the windows	=	2430.00
Btu/H for the door	=	866.25
Btu/H for the ceiling	=	1134.00
Btu/H for the floor	=	1036.80
Btu/H for air infiltration	=	2332.80
Total Btu/H	=	8515.35

The total room heat loss is 8,515 Btu/H. Therefore, a heating unit capable of producing this amount of heat is required to effectively heat the room.

True Window R-Value

Comparing window performance has never been easy because manufacturers have always used a center-of-glass R value to rate the efficiency of windows. But, the true R value of the total window is affected by the materials used in the frame and the way in which the glass is sealed at the edges. The process of comparison has become easier through the work of a nonprofit group in Silver Spring, Maryland. The National Fenestration Ratings Council (NFRC) rates overall R values instead of center-of-glass R values to provide a more realistic measure. The chart in Figure 26-29 shows a comparison using the two methods. Many states now require the NFRC label on all new windows.

CADD Heat Loss Calculations

The calculation of heat loss or gain in a structure is time consuming and confusing for many. However, CADD software is available to help with this chore. In many cases, however, the specific data must still be entered into the program for calculation. Frequently, a report is generated that can be used as needed.

R-Values: Old vs. New		
Window type	Center-of-glass	Whole window
Anderson Perma-Shield Casement	R 4.2	R 3.1
Marvin Clad Casemaster, low-e/argon	R 4.0	R 3.1
Hurd Insol-8	R 8.1	R 5.5

Source: NFRCs Certified Product Directory

Figure 26-29. This chart shows a comparison of center-of-glass and whole window R values for selected windows.

Internet Resources

www.bvc.com
*Ventamatic, Ltd. supplier of Cool Attic
ventilators*

www.carrier.com
Carrier Corporation

www.honeywell.com/yourhome
Honeywell Home and Building Controls

www.lennox.com
Lennox Indoor Comfort Systems

www.trane.com
The Trane Company

Review Questions – Chapter 26

Write your answers on a separate sheet of paper.
Do not write in this book.

1. Identify the four features of a climate control system.
2. Name five factors that help increase the efficiency of temperature control.
3. The amount of water in the air relative to the temperature is called _____.
4. A comfortable humidity level is about _____ percent at 75°F.
5. Identify two possible outcomes from having too little moisture in the air.
6. Name two effects of too much moisture in the house.
7. The device that removes moisture from the air in a house is called a _____.
8. List the four basic types of heating systems.
9. How does a forced-air system operate?
10. Identify three types of furnaces that are used in forced-air systems.
11. What is a thermostat?
12. List the three main parts in a hydronic system.
13. Name three advantages of the hydronic system.
14. A(n) _____ uses resistance wiring to produce heat.
15. A heat pump is essentially a _____ unit.
16. Which part of the equipment in a central air conditioning system is placed outside?

Suggested Activities

1. Select a plan of a medium-size home and get an estimate from your local gas and electricity company as to the cost of heating this home. Also ask for their recommendations for insulation and ventilation. Report your findings.
2. Using a plan supplied by your instructor, calculate the total heat loss and specify the size heating unit required. Show your calculations.
3. Contact people in your community who have forced-air, hydronic, and electric radiant heating systems and ask their opinion regarding dependability, advantages, disadvantages, economy, and serviceability of the systems. Report their reactions.
4. Visit a local heating and air conditioning equipment supplier. Ask for catalogs and other literature showing heating and cooling equipment, or search the Web for manufacturers' literature. Add this material to the classroom collection.
5. Prepare a chart for each heating system discussed in the text showing advantages and disadvantages of each system. Display your chart.
6. Using CADD, draw standard climate control symbols. Use the reference section of this book for examples. Add the symbols to your symbols library.

The heat in this indoor pool room is provided by electric radiant heat. The units are located near the ceiling. All heating and cooling units must be indicated on the climate control plan. (Radiant Heat.; Uecker, E.)

Climate Control Plan 27

Objectives

After studying this chapter, you will be able to:

➤ List features included on a residential climate control plan.

➤ Plan the ductwork for a typical forced-air system.

➤ Select an appropriate heating or cooling unit for a given structure.

➤ Draw a climate control plan using proper symbols and conventions.

Key Terms

Climate Control
 Equipment
 Schedule
Climate Control Plan
Ducts
Extended Plenum
 System

Inlets
Pipes
Radial System
Register
Wall Stack

A *climate control plan* shows the location, size, and type of heating, cooling, ventilating, humidification, and air cleaning equipment and the required piping or ducts. This system should be closely coordinated with the structural, plumbing, and electrical aspects of the house. The climate control plan is a plan view section drawing of the home traced from the floor plan.

Required Information

The climate control plan should include information on size and location of the distribution system. It should also include the location of thermostats and registers or baseboard convectors, climate control equipment location and type, and an equipment schedule. Heat loss calculations and any general or specific notes needed to fully describe the system must also be included on the plan.

Distribution System

The distribution system usually consists of ducts or pipes. *Ducts*, or ductwork, can be round or rectangular and are used in a forced-air system to move large quantities of air for heating or cooling. *Pipes* are used in hydronic systems to distribute hot water or steam from the boiler to radiators, baseboard units, or radiant panels. The distribution system must be represented on the climate control plan using the proper symbols, Figure 27-1. The ducts should be drawn as close to scale as possible. The climate control plan is generally 1/4″ = 1′-0″. Sizes should be shown on the plan. Pipes are indicated by single lines and are not drawn to scale.

Planning Outlet and Inlet Locations

A perimeter system of outlets is generally specified. This provides uniform heating or cooling by concentrating the conditioned air where it is needed most—along the outside walls, Figure 27-2. The outlet in a forced-air system is called a *register*. In a hydronic or electric radiant heat system, the outlet is typically a baseboard unit. There should be at least one outlet in each large area to be conditioned. This includes rooms, halls, stairwells, etc., that are to be heated or cooled. An average room has up to 180 square feet of floor space. Larger rooms or areas usually should be counted as two or more rooms. If a room has more than 15' of exterior wall, then two or more outlets should be used.

Inlets, or cold air returns, are required for forced-air systems. They receive air to be returned to the furnace or air conditioning coil. However, they are not needed for hydronic or electric radiant systems. If the house is a compact, one-story structure, one inlet is usually sufficient. However, if the house is L- or U-shaped or has several levels, then two or more inlets should be planned. Remember that closed doors and dead-end corridors block air circulation. Registers and inlets are available in several sizes, Figure 27-3.

Planning Ductwork

The two basic types of ductwork for forced-air systems are the radial system and the extended plenum system, Figure 27-4. In the *radial system*, round ducts radiate out in all directions from the furnace. The *extended plenum system* has a large rectangular duct (plenum) for the main supply. Round ducts extend from the main supply to each register, Figure 27-5. The extended plenum system is usually preferred.

The round duct used to supply registers in the extended plenum system may be 6" or 8" in diameter. An 8" duct is generally recommended when the system is to be used for cooling as well as heating. The larger size is necessary when the same blower is used because cool air moves slower than warm air. A vertical duct designed to fit between the studs is called a *wall stack* and is usually 12" × 3-1/4".

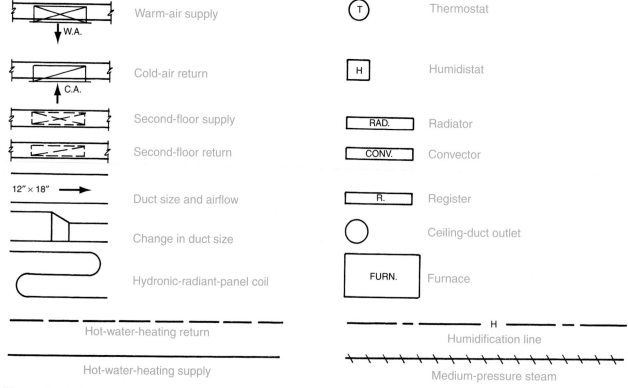

Figure 27-1. Typical symbols used in a climate control system.

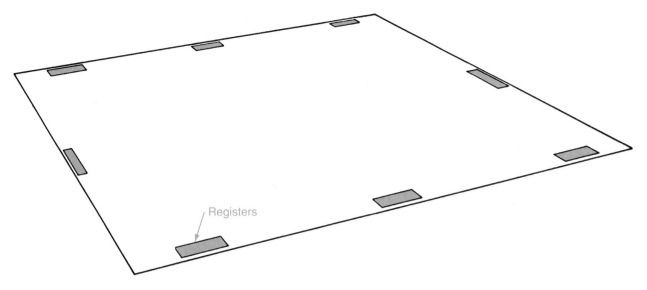

Figure 27-2. A perimeter system of outlets provides uniform heat or cooling.

The size of the rectangular extended plenum is based on the number and size of round ducts it serves. All rectangular ducts are 8″ deep and vary in width from 10″ to 28″. The sectional area of the supply duct should equal the total area of all round register ducts. The extended plenum may remain the same size throughout its entire length or may be reduced in size as fewer registers remain to be supplied. As a rule of thumb, the rectangular extended plenum

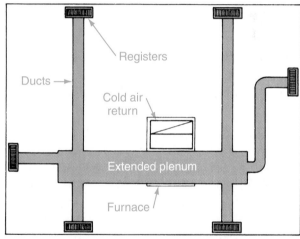

Extended plenum system

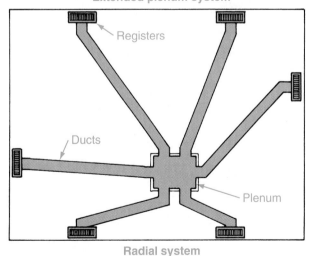

Radial system

Figure 27-4. The extended plenum and radial systems are common ductwork systems used for residential climate control.

Register sizes		
Type	**Size**	**Supply**
Floor Diffuser	6″ × 12″	8″ Duct
Floor Diffuser	4″ × 12″	6″ Duct
Floor Diffuser	2-1/4″ × 12″	6″ Duct
Baseboard Diffuser	2-1/4″ × 15″	6″ Duct
Baseboard Diffuser	2-1/4″ × 24″	6″ Duct
Inlet sizes		
Type	**Size**	**Furnace Size**
Baseboard Grille	6″ × 14″	—
Baseboard Grille	6″ × 30″	40,000 BTU
Ceiling or Wall Grille	16″ × 20″	75,000 BTU
High Side-Wall Grille	6″ × 14″	—
Floor Grille	8″ × 30″	60,000 BTU
Floor Grille	12″ × 30″	80,000 BTU
Floor Grille	18″ × 24″	90,000 BTU

Figure 27-3. This chart shows common register (outlet) and inlet (cold air return) sizes.

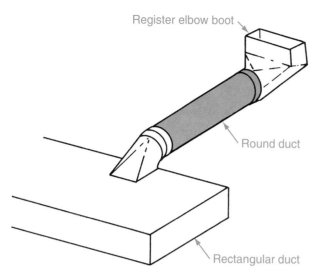

Figure 27-5. Round duct, either 6" or 8" in diameter, is frequently used to connect the register to the main supply duct.

size may be determined by using the following procedure. Remember, it is 8" deep.

- For 6" ducts, multiply the number of round ducts by 2 and add 2 to the product. The result is the required width of the plenum duct. Example: A rectangular plenum is to serve six 6" round ducts. Therefore, $6 \times 2 = 12 + 2 = 14"$; the plenum duct will be $8" \times 14"$.

- For 8" ducts, multiply the number of round ducts by 3 and add 2 to the product. The result is the required width of the plenum duct. Example: A rectangular plenum is to serve six 8" round ducts. Therefore, $6 \times 3 = 18 + 2 = 20"$; the plenum duct will be $8" \times 20"$.

Planning Piping for a Hydronic System

The main hot water supply from the boiler must be large enough to provide for adequate heating. The size of copper pipe usually considered to be adequate for most installations is:

- 1" main for up to 71,000 Btu
- 1-1/2" main for 72,000 to 160,000 Btu
- 2" main for 161,000 to 240,000 Btu

The required size of baseboard unit or convector cabinet will depend on the heat loss for a given area. It is best to calculate the heat loss for each room and then plan the number

and size outlets to match this value. The chart in Figure 27-6 shows the output rating for several common convector cabinets and fin-tube baseboard units. Locate outlets below windows for most efficient heating. Any room that is over 15' long should have at least two outlets.

Thermostats and Climate Control Equipment

Every automatic climate control system requires at least one thermostat. A forced-air system will need only one thermostat if one furnace is used. Sometimes two furnaces are installed if the house is large or if more than one zone is required. Each zone needs a thermostat to provide accurate control. As many zones as desired may be used with electric radiant or hydronic systems, each with its own thermostat.

Location of the thermostat is important because it measures the temperature and

Convector Cabinets		
Length	**Thickness**	**Btu/H output**
24"	6-3/8"	3,400
32"	6-3/8"	4,800
36"	8-3/8"	6,900
40"	8-3/8"	7,800
48"	8-3/8"	9,600
56"	8-3/8"	11,400
60"	10-3/8"	19,400
Fin-Tube Baseboard Units		
Btu/H output		
Length	**Single**	**Double**
2'	—	2,280
4'	2,870	4,560
6'	4,260	6,840
8'	5,680	—

Figure 27-6. This chart shows several common convector cabinet and fin-tube baseboard unit sizes.

activates the furnace. If it is placed where the sun may shine on it, in a draft, or near a lamp, the performance may not be satisfactory. Locate the thermostat on an inside partition in a place where the temperature will be representative of the room(s) as a whole. Show the location on the climate control plan using the proper symbol. Other equipment should be indicated on the plan using symbols or notes.

Schedules, Calculations, and Notes

Various schedules may be useful on the climate control plan. A *climate control equipment schedule* provides an orderly means of specifying equipment to be used in the system. Including a register schedule may be desirable because it can reduce the amount of information placed on the drawing. Placing too much information on the drawing will cause it to be crowded.

A complete climate control plan will show a summary of the heat loss calculations. These calculations are important and form the basis for equipment selection. If space permits, the summary should be located on the climate control plan.

Add any other information on the plan that you feel will be helpful or desirable to the builder or subcontractors. Notes should be short and to the point.

Procedure for Drawing Climate Control Plan— Manual Drafting

Just as in the plumbing and electrical plans, many decisions and calculations must be made before completing the climate control plan. The type of heating and cooling system(s)

must be determined and heat loss calculated for each room. Other drawings of the structure should be studied to determine the most practical layout before starting to draw. After all these preliminary details are addressed, then you may proceed with the drawing of the plan. The following procedure is suggested.

1. Trace the floor plan showing exterior and interior walls, doors and windows, and other features that relate to the climate control system. Steps 1, 2, and 3 are shown in Figure 27-7.
2. Locate the equipment to be used for heating, cooling, humidification, and air cleaning.
3. Locate registers, coils, baseboard units, or other means of temperature exchange on the plan. Use the proper symbols.
4. Draw the air return ducts using a hidden line. Also, draw the cold air return inlets. This step is for forced-air systems only. Steps 4, 5, 6, and 7 are shown in Figure 27-8.
5. Draw the supply duct or hot water main and connect it to the registers, convectors, etc.
6. Locate thermostats and any other required controls.
7. Identify the size of ducts or pipe and other equipment.
8. Create schedules as required. Steps 8, 9, and 10 are shown in Figure 27-9.
9. Add the title block, scale, necessary notes, and dimensions.
10. Check the drawing for accuracy and to be sure that it is complete.

Drawing Climate Control Plans Using CADD

The step-by-step procedure for drawing a climate control plan with CADD is similar to that described above for manual drafting. One significant difference, however, is the use of layers. Layers are useful in specifying pen widths, linetypes, colors, and other relationships. For example, the cold air return in a forced-air system is shown as a hidden line. This line is usually drawn as a medium width line (0.35 mm). Only those features that use this particular linetype should be drawn on that layer.

If this approach is followed consistently, modifications and additions can easily be made to the drawing and a specific layer can be "turned off" to see other details more clearly. Layers are, therefore, very important design tools that the drafter/designer can use to produce drawings more efficiently.

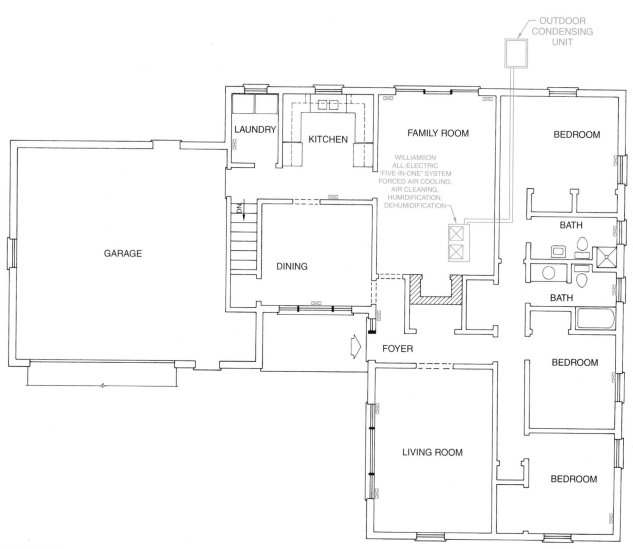

Figure 27-7. The location of the furnace, outdoor condensing unit, and registers are added to the climate control plan. The furnace is in the basement below the main floor level.

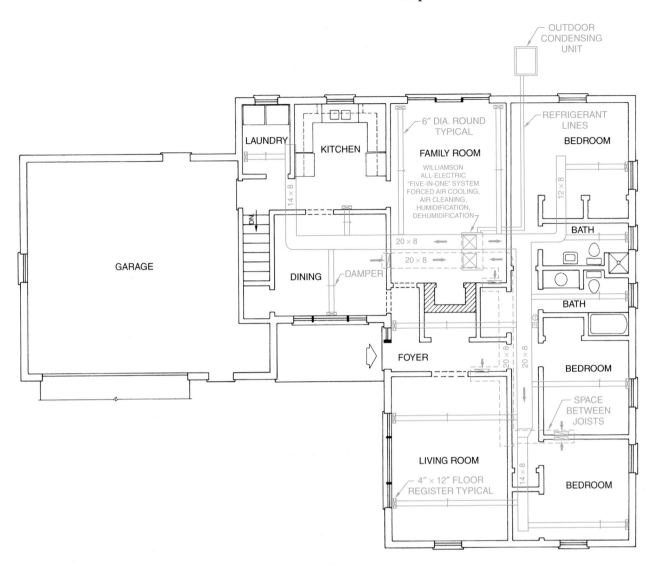

Figure 27-8. The location of supply and cold air return ducts and return registers are added to the climate control plan.

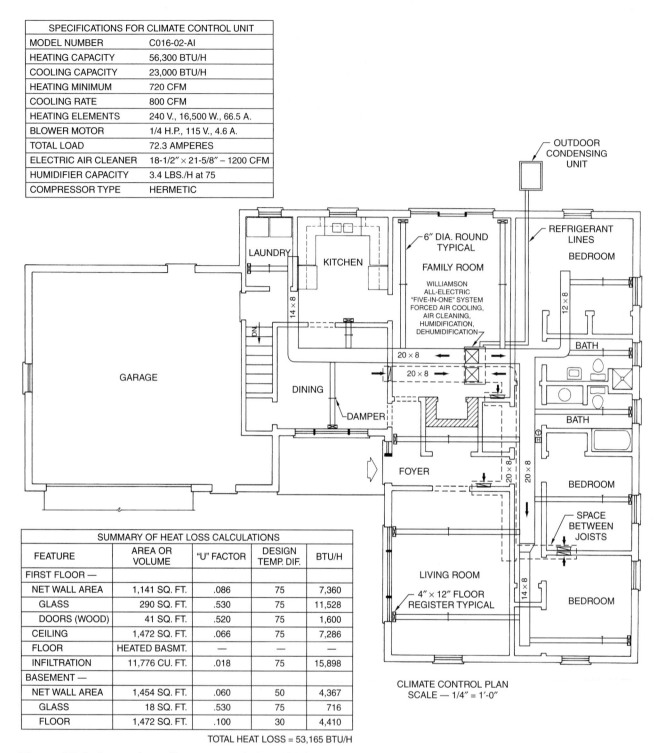

SPECIFICATIONS FOR CLIMATE CONTROL UNIT	
MODEL NUMBER	C016-02-AI
HEATING CAPACITY	56,300 BTU/H
COOLING CAPACITY	23,000 BTU/H
HEATING MINIMUM	720 CFM
COOLING RATE	800 CFM
HEATING ELEMENTS	240 V., 16,500 W., 66.5 A.
BLOWER MOTOR	1/4 H.P., 115 V., 4.6 A.
TOTAL LOAD	72.3 AMPERES
ELECTRIC AIR CLEANER	18-1/2″ × 21-5/8″ – 1200 CFM
HUMIDIFIER CAPACITY	3.4 LBS./H at 75
COMPRESSOR TYPE	HERMETIC

SUMMARY OF HEAT LOSS CALCULATIONS				
FEATURE	AREA OR VOLUME	"U" FACTOR	DESIGN TEMP. DIF.	BTU/H
FIRST FLOOR —				
NET WALL AREA	1,141 SQ. FT.	.086	75	7,360
GLASS	290 SQ. FT.	.530	75	11,528
DOORS (WOOD)	41 SQ. FT.	.520	75	1,600
CEILING	1,472 SQ. FT.	.066	75	7,286
FLOOR	HEATED BASMT.	—	—	—
INFILTRATION	11,776 CU. FT.	.018	75	15,898
BASEMENT —				
NET WALL AREA	1,454 SQ. FT.	.060	50	4,367
GLASS	18 SQ. FT.	.530	75	716
FLOOR	1,472 SQ. FT.	.100	30	4,410

TOTAL HEAT LOSS = 53,165 BTU/H

CLIMATE CONTROL PLAN
SCALE — 1/4″ = 1'-0″

Figure 27-9. A complete climate control plan with basement and first floor installations shown. The furnace and ductwork may be drawn on the foundation basement plan and the registers shown on the floor plan, if desired.

Internet Resources

www.bvc.com
Ventamatic, Ltd, supplier of Cool Attic ventilators

www.carrier.com
Carrier Corporation

www.honeywell.com/yourhome
Honeywell Home and Building Controls

www.invensysclimate.com
Invensys Climate Controls

www.lennox.com
Lennox Indoor Comfort Systems

www.trane.com/residential
The Trane Company

Review Questions – Chapter 27

Write your answers on a separate sheet of paper. Do not write in this book.

1. What is the purpose of the climate control plan?

2. Identify four features that should be included on a climate control plan.

3. _____ are used to distribute heat throughout a house in a forced-air system, while _____ are used to distribute heat in a hydronic system.

4. The scale of a residential climate control plan will most likely be _____.

5. Why is a perimeter heat system generally specified?

6. When should a room have more than one register?

7. Name the two basic types of ductwork systems.

8. The round ducts used to connect registers to the extended plenum are either _____ or _____ in diameter.

9. A rectangular plenum duct that will supply four 6″ pipes should be what size?

10. A vertical duct designed to fit between the studs is called a _____.

11. If a house has three heating zones, it will normally require _____ thermostats.

12. Name two types of schedules that may be found on a climate control plan.

Suggested Activities

1. Locate a house under construction that has the heating equipment in place. Secure permission to enter the structure. Examine the installation carefully and report on the following points.

   a) Type and size of house.

   b) Type of heating system and any other comfort provisions.

   c) Number of registers or convectors.

   d) Number of cold air returns, if any.

   e) Size of heating and/or cooling unit.

2. Using a simple plan provided by your instructor or designed yourself, plan an appropriate climate control system. The system should provide for heating, cooling, humidification, and air cleaning. If any of these items are not necessary in your section of the country, omit them from the plan.

3. Create an isometric drawing that represents the essential elements of a heating system. You may choose a forced-air, hydronic, electric radiant, or heat pump system. Label the parts and prepare a display.

4. Using CADD, design a climate control plan for the house shown in Figure 18-14. Place features of the climate control plan on separate layers as appropriate. Assign linetypes and colors as appropriate.

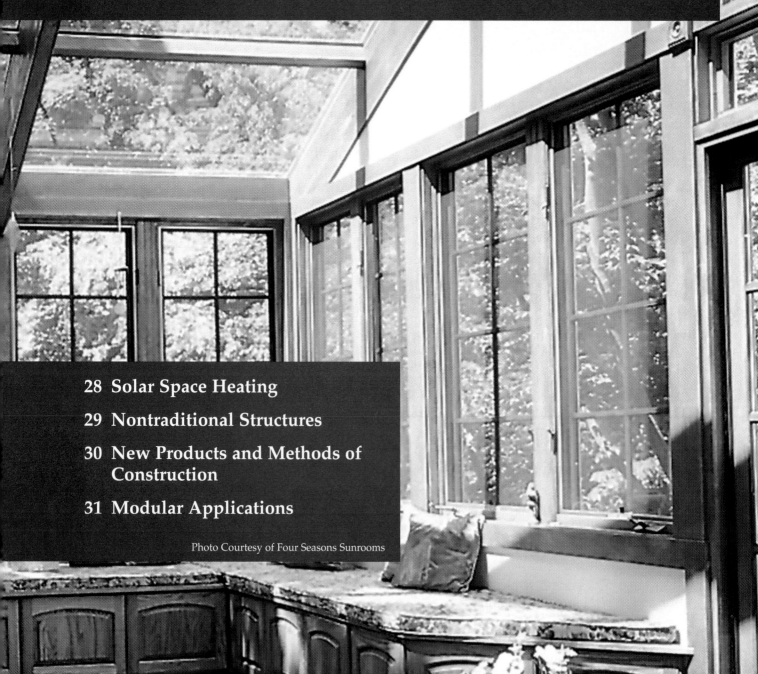

Section VIII
Alternative Construction, Products, and Methods

28 Solar Space Heating

29 Nontraditional Structures

30 New Products and Methods of Construction

31 Modular Applications

Photo Courtesy of Four Seasons Sunrooms

Solar Space Heating

Objectives

After studying this chapter, you will be able to:

➤ Describe the two basic types of solar space heating.

➤ Explain how a passive solar space-heating system works.

➤ Compare direct, indirect, and isolated passive solar-gain systems.

➤ Identify the two most frequently used active solar systems.

➤ List the advantages and disadvantages of solar space heating.

Key Terms

Absorber Plate
Active Solar Space
  Heating
Attached
  Greenhouse
Conduction
Convection
Direct Gain Systems
Indirect Gain
  Systems
Isolated Gain
  Systems
Passive Solar Space
  Heating

Radiation
Solar Radiation
Sun Space
Thermal Mass
Thermosiphoning
Trombe Wall
Warm Air Solar
  System
Warm Water Solar
  System
Water Storage Wall

Solar space heating is an important consideration for the architect because of increased heating costs and apparent dwindling fuel supplies. Using free, natural heat from the sun is prudent if it can be trapped and utilized in an efficient and practical manner. Energy from the sun is called *solar radiation.* Solar heating involves extracting heat from solar radiation, distributing the heat throughout the living and working space in the dwelling, and storing excess heat for future use. Two basic methods or systems have evolved to capture solar energy for space heating. These are passive solar systems and active solar systems.

Insulation

With all solar systems, adequate insulation is necessary to prevent the loss of trapped interior heat. If possible, insulation should be placed on the outside of masonry walls. This allows their mass to be used for heat storage in the interior. In most nonsolar designs, insulation is generally located on the interior surface of masonry walls. However, this allows stored heat to be released to the exterior, rather than the interior. Frame walls have little mass and, therefore, store small amounts of heat. The location of insulation in a frame wall is not as important as it is with masonry walls.

Passive Solar Systems

Passive solar space heating involves capturing, storing, and using solar radiation to heat a dwelling without the use of fans or pumps to circulate the heat. Heat from the sun is collected by, and stored in, the building itself. Purely passive systems use only convection, conduction, and radiation as a means of distributing heat.

Convection refers to the transfer of heat by a moving fluid. Fluids include liquids and gases. *Conduction* is the flow of heat through an object by transferring heat from one molecule to another. *Radiation* is the flow of heat from a warm source through space in waves of infrared or visible light energy. This energy travels in straight lines from the source.

The most common types of passive solar systems may be classified as direct gain, indirect gain, and isolated gain or sun space systems. The word "gain" refers to the way heat is extracted from solar radiation. The basis of these groupings is the way in which each system works.

Direct Gain Systems

Direct gain systems are the most popular type of passive solar space heating system. *Direct gain systems* incorporate large areas of south-facing glazing (glass or other material) that permit large amounts of sunlight to enter the interior space of the dwelling to directly heat the air inside, Figure 28-1. The heat generated by the sunlight is stored in massive

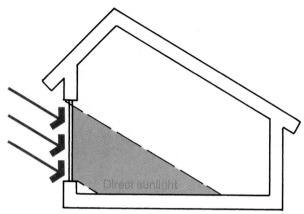

Figure 28-1. Direct gain systems use solar radiation entering directly through glazing into the space to be heated.

masonry structures within the house. During the night and periods of cloudiness, the heat stored in thick, interior, masonry walls, floors, and furnishings is released to the interior space.

The two keys to a successful direct gain passive system are large amounts of sunlight entering the living space and sufficient thermal mass to store the excess heat, Figure 28-2. A *thermal mass* is a material that can store large amounts of heat, such as stone, masonry, and concrete. If the thermal mass structures are positioned in direct sunlight within the living space, they become solar collectors as well as heat storage devices.

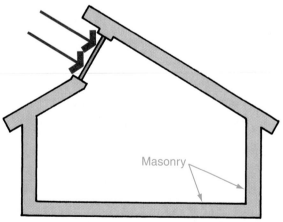

Direct Gain Clerestory

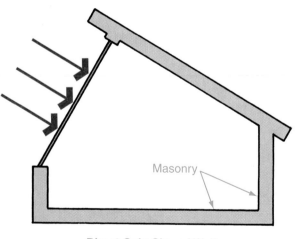

Direct Gain Sloped Wall

Figure 28-2. These two designs illustrate some possible applications of the direct gain system with additional thermal mass to store excess heat entering the interior dwelling space. Notice they are positioned to act as solar collectors as well as provide thermal mass.

A large thermal mass inside the living space is necessary to help modulate temperature extremes within the structure. If insufficient mass is present, the temperature will likely rise to uncomfortable levels during the day and fall to uncomfortable levels during the night. Therefore, large amounts of stone, thick concrete walls and floors, drums filled with water, or other massive structures form an integral part of a direct gain passive system, Figure 28-3.

A large thermal mass also helps to even out indoor temperatures during the warm summer months. The large thermal mass is cooler than the interior air during the day and thus absorbs heat from the air. This, in turn, reduces the temperature of the living space. The stored heat is released during the night when temperatures drop and provides a more uniform temperature in the dwelling.

Different materials are able to store different amounts of heat. For example, the same volume of water will store more than twice as much heat (quantity) at a given temperature as concrete, stone, or adobe, all of which are common thermal mass materials. See Figure 28-4 for a comparison of the thermal properties of typical building materials.

Indirect Gain Systems

Indirect gain systems heat the interior space by storing heat in a thermal mass, then releasing the heat into the interior space. In these systems, a large thermal mass is placed between the sun and the living space. Frequently, a thick masonry or concrete wall is positioned directly behind a large area of south-facing glazing to receive the solar radiation. Air is allowed to circulate around the wall to carry heat to the dwelling interior.

One popular indirect gain system utilizes a *Trombe wall*, Figure 28-5. This is a massive

Thermal Properties of Materials			
Material	Heat capacity by weight Btu/lb/°F	Heat capacity by volume Btu/ft³/°F	Density lbs/ft³
Adobe	0.24	25	106
Aluminum	0.214	36.2	169
Brick	0.20	24	120
Concrete	0.22	31	140
Rock	0.21	21	100
Steel	0.11	54	490
Water	1.00	62.4	62.4
Wood	0.60	19	32

Figure 28-4. Thermal properties of common building materials.

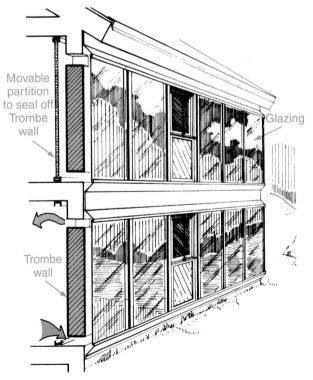

Figure 28-5. A Trombe wall is an example of an indirect gain solar system. (National Solar Heating and Cooling Information Center)

Figure 28-3. The massive stone materials in the interior of this passive solar home store heat.

wall that is dark colored on the exterior-facing side to absorb more heat and located inside the structure immediately behind a large glazed area. Vents at the top and bottom of the wall permit cool air to enter the space between the wall and glazing at the bottom, become heated, rise by convection to the top of the wall, and return to the dwelling interior. Heat is also transmitted by conduction through the wall to the inside surface. Radiation and convection then distribute the heat throughout the interior space.

At night in the heating season, the vents in a Trombe wall must be closed to prevent reverse thermosiphoning. *Thermosiphoning* is the result of a fluid expanding and rising. Reverse thermosiphoning will cool the room by allowing the warm room air to enter the space between the Trombe wall and glazing. The air is cooled as it comes in contact with the cold glass. Cold air will sink to the bottom of the wall and enter the dwelling, thus cooling the room. This is not desired during the heating season.

The *water storage wall* is another type of indirect gain system. Water is inexpensive and capable of storing large amounts of heat. Therefore, it is frequently used as a thermal mass. Drums, fiberglass tubes, and large pipes are typical storage containers. They are located just behind a south-facing glazed area, similar to the Trombe wall. The containers are generally painted black and act as collectors and storage. A typical drum wall will store approximately twice as much heat as a Trombe wall of the same volume, Figure 28-6. The drum wall, however, may not appeal to some because of its appearance and possible noise created by expansion and contraction due to heating and cooling. Further, the potential problems of evaporation, corrosion, and leaking are considerations.

A phase-change material, such as glauber's salt, has some possible advantages as a thermal storage material. Phase-change materials change from a solid to liquid state as they heat up. These materials are generally capable of storing more heat per unit of volume and are slow to store and release heat—a desirable trait for maintaining comfort over an extended period. The cost of these materials, however, is

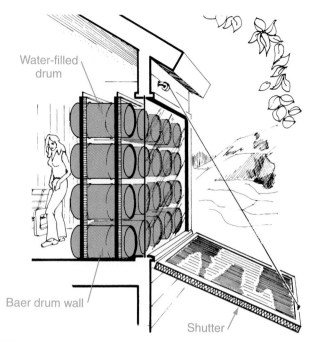

Figure 28-6. This Baer Drum Wall, developed by Steve Baer of Zomeworks, is an example of an indirect gain system. (National Solar Heating and Cooling Information Center)

a negative factor, as is their reduced effectiveness over a period of time.

Isolated Gain Systems

Isolated gain systems collect and store solar energy in an area outside of the living space. A typical example of this type of system is shown in Figure 28-7. The solar radiation is extracted using a solar collector outside the home. The storage is a rock bed located beneath the structure. Thermosiphoning moves warm air up into the dwelling while cool air returns to the rock storage and collector to be warmed again. Figure 28-8 shows another example of an isolated gain system where the rock storage is outside the dwelling.

Advantages of the isolated gain system include less interior space dedicated to heat collection devices, large areas of interior space are not exposed to the sun, and the collected heat is easier to control. Disadvantages include the generally greater expense to construct this type of isolated gain system and the difficulty of retrofitting an existing structure.

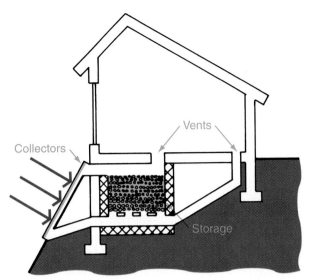

Figure 28-7. This is an example of an isolated gain system. It utilizes a series of collectors outside the dwelling and rock storage beneath the floor.

Another type of isolated gain system that is increasing greatly in popularity is the *attached greenhouse* or *sun space,* Figure 28-9. A solar greenhouse must have proper orientation (south-facing) if it is to provide any solar heat to the dwelling. An attached greenhouse will reduce heat loss in the dwelling even when it is not producing usable heat by shielding the wall from winter winds. Frequently, the attached greenhouse is combined

Figure 28-9. This large, attached greenhouse is an example of an isolated gain solar system. It extends the space of the dwelling and provides some heat. Notice how trees have been placed to shade the greenhouse during the summer. (Photo Courtesy of Four Seasons Sunrooms)

with other techniques, such as a Trombe wall, water-filled drums, or collectors, to provide additional solar heat, Figure 28-10.

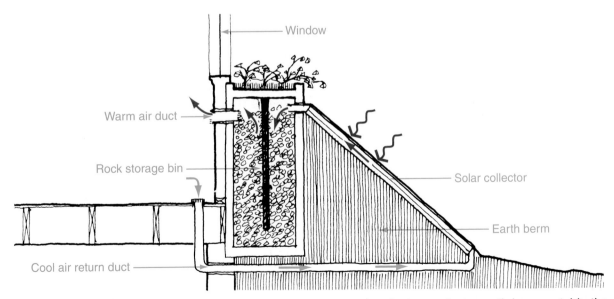

Figure 28-8. An isolated gain system with the solar collector and rock storage in an earth berm outside the dwelling. (National Solar Heating and Cooling Information Center)

In colder climates, solar greenhouses should have a double glazing of glass, plastic, or fiberglass to reduce heat loss. Additionally, air infiltration should be reduced to the minimum to reduce further heat loss. Thick concrete floors that are insulated below and around the edges will add much heat storage, but will not be effective if not isolated from the foundation and soil below. As with other systems, a large thermal mass is required for maximum performance.

Summary of Principles

The principles utilized in the design of passive solar applications can be applied to dwellings with active solar or conventional heating systems. Architectural considerations include:

- Proper sun orientation for large glass areas, Figure 28-11.
- Roof overhang lengths, Figure 28-12.
- Adequate insulation.
- Adequate thermal mass.
- Concern for airflow inside a structure.

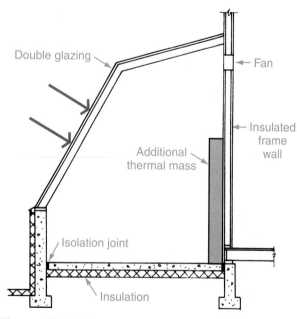

Figure 28-10. This section detail of an attached greenhouse shows how an additional thermal mass is included to provide heat for a longer period of time.

These factors should always be considered in the design process of any structure, regardless of whether or not solar heating is incorporated in the design.

Active Solar Systems

Active solar space heating involves collecting heat from solar radiation and then using pumps, fans, or other devices to distribute the heat to desired locations. Two basic types of active solar systems are commonly used for residential space heating. They are warm air systems and warm water systems. Warm air systems are more popular for home heating. Warm water systems have more commercial applications.

Warm Air Solar Systems

A typical *warm air solar system* contains an array or group of collectors, called a bank; a heat storage box filled with stones or other thermal mass; and one or more blowers with controls for operating the system, Figure 28-13. Solar collectors for warm air systems are readily available in a wide range of sizes, qualities, and prices. They range in efficiency from around 15% to about 65%. Some have built-in insulation while others do not. Collectors are also made with single, double, and triple glazing. The amount of insulation and the type of glazing greatly affect the performance in cold climates. A quality collector should form an airtight box and have a highly transparent glazing and sufficient insulation to retain its heat during cold weather, Figure 28-14.

Every solar collector has some type of *absorber plate* that is designed to absorb heat from solar radiation. There are many designs and styles, Figure 28-15. However, most are flat plate collectors. Design characteristics that an efficient warm air absorber plate should include are:

- It should present as much surface area to the sun as possible to receive maximum heating. Refer to the Sun Angle Chart in Figure 28-11 to select the best collector angle for your location.

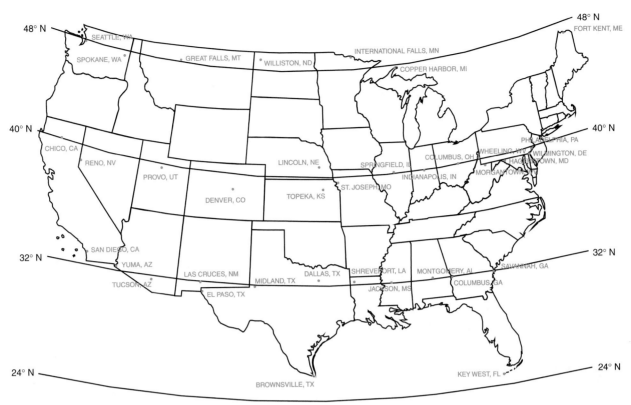

US Cities Near Selected Latitudes

Sun Angle Chart

	Sun angle per latitude at solar noon			
Date	**24°N**	**32°N**	**40°N**	**48°N**
January 21	46.0	38.0	30.0	22.0
February 21	56.0	48.0	40.0	32.0
March 21	66.0	58.0	50.0	42.0
April 21	77.6	69.6	61.6	51.5
May 21	86.0	78.0	70.0	62.0
June 21	89.0	81.5	73.5	65.5
July 21	86.6	78.6	70.6	62.6
August 21	78.3	70.3	62.3	54.3
September 21	66.0	58.0	50.0	42.0
October 21	55.5	47.5	39.5	31.5
November 21	46.2	38.2	30.2	22.2
December 21	42.6	34.6	26.6	18.6
	US cities near these latitudes			
	Key West, FL Brownsville, TX Kauai, HI	Savannah, GA Columbus, GA Montgomery, AL Jackson, MS Shreveport, LA Dallas, TX Midland, TX El Paso, TX Las Cruces, NM Tucson, AZ Yuma, AZ San Diego, CA	Philadelphia, PA Wilmington, DE Hagerstown, MD Morgantown, WV Wheeling, WV Columbus, OH Indianapolis, IN Springfield, IL St. Joseph, MO Topeka, KS Lincoln, NE Denver, CO Provo, UT Reno, NV Chico, CA	Ft. Kent, ME Copper Harbor, MI International Falls, MN Williston, ND Great Falls, MT Spokane, WA Seattle, WA

Figure 28-11. A Sun Angle Chart is useful when planning south-facing windows or areas of glass for maximum light penetration during the winter months and shading during summer. The sun angle is also of prime importance in selecting the tilt angle for solar collectors. Note: The lowest sun angle is achieved on December 21st and the highest sun angle occurs on June 21st. The angles shown are with respect to a horizontal surface.

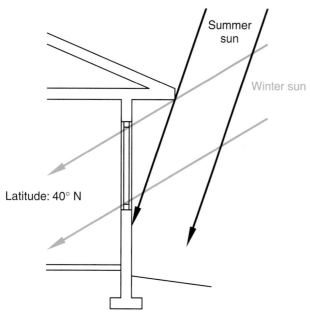

Figure 28-12. The length of roof overhangs and placement of windows needs to receive careful consideration when designing a structure to receive winter sun inside the structure and to shade the exterior wall during the summer.

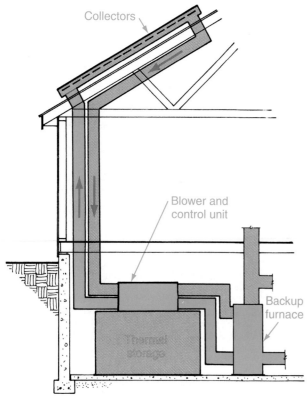

Figure 28-13. This example shows a roof-mounted, warm air active solar system. This system is connected to a backup heating system for extended cloudy periods.

Figure 28-14. This combination warm air and domestic hot water collector has ample insulation. The absorber plate is isolated from the collector box frame to reduce heat lost by conduction.

- It should allow air to flow over a large surface area as it passes through the collector for efficient heat release.

- Excessive turbulence should not be created in the collector by the absorber plate. This will reduce airflow and increase heat loss through the glazing.

- Increased efficiency is generally accomplished by maintaining airflow behind the absorber plate and having a dead air space between it and the glazing.

- The most efficient absorber plate material is generally metal.

Copper is the most efficient, and expensive, common material used for warm air absorber plates. Aluminum is the most used material for absorber plates. Steel plates are used in some collectors, but they are not as efficient as aluminum and copper. Absorber plate coatings are usually flat black, but some other colors such as dark green or purple are capable of collecting nearly as much energy.

The tilt and orientation of a solar collector is important for maximum collection of heat. Generally, a south-facing collector will perform best, Figure 28-16. However, a variation of up to 15° will have little effect on the performance. The proper tilt angle of the collector is generally agreed to be between 50° and 60° from the horizon for best results during the entire heating season. The objective

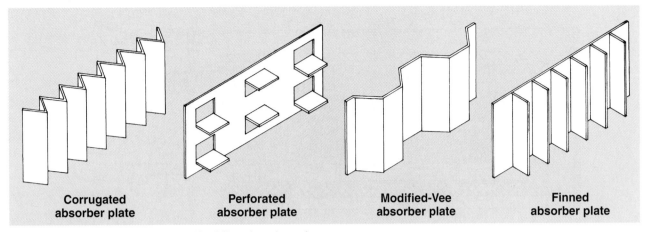

Corrugated absorber plate   **Perforated absorber plate**   **Modified-Vee absorber plate**   **Finned absorber plate**

Figure 28-15. Examples of modified flat absorber plates.

is to position the collector so the sun's rays will strike the absorber plate at a perpendicular angle for as long as possible.

Heat storage for a warm air system is a major concern. Warm air systems generally use a large box or crawl space area filled with stone, Figure 28-17. The thermal mass must be well insulated to reduce heat loss. The size of stone most frequently used in the storage box is 2" to 3" in diameter.

The size of storage needed is related to the amount of solar radiation available, area of collector surface, efficiency of storage media, heat loss in the storage area, and household needs. However, the storage should generally be large enough to store heat for three days of cloudy weather. A storage area that is too large

can present as big a problem as one that is too small. If the storage is too large, a "useful" level of heat may not be attained by the system. If the storage is too small, not enough heat will be available during cloudy weather. Also, efficiency will drop in the collectors because the return air to the collectors will be too warm to efficiently remove heat from the collector. The average storage size for warm air systems usually ranges from 1/2 to 2 cubic feet of stone for each square foot of collector area.

Distribution of heat from the collectors and storage area to the living space is accomplished with a blower. The blower is similar to one used in a typical forced-air heating system. Some warm air solar systems use two

Figure 28-16. Collectors have been attached to the south gable areas of this home. This position will capture significant heat during winter months.

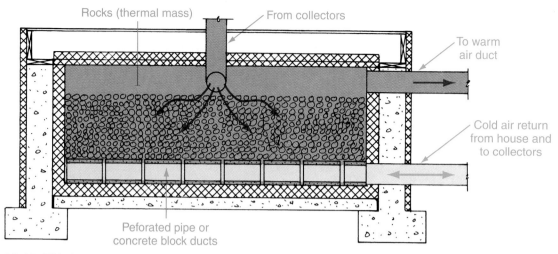

Figure 28-17. This is a typical warm air storage configuration that uses rock as the thermal mass.

blowers to manage airflow more efficiently and to provide additional control. The blower system is activated by a complex set of controls that respond to temperature sensors located in the collectors, storage area, and living space. The need for a high-quality control system cannot be overemphasized.

Warm Water Solar Systems

A typical *warm water solar system* is composed of a bank of collectors, a warm water storage tank, a pump to circulate the water, some form of heat exchange device in the living space, and controls for operating the system, Figure 28-18. Solar collectors used with water systems are similar to flat plate warm air collectors except that tubes are attached to the absorber plate or cavities within the absorber plate. This allows water to circulate over or through the heated plate, Figure 28-19. Great care must be taken in the design and construction of water collectors because of the corrosive action of water and higher pressure than is present in an air-type system.

Another concern for a water system that is not present in an air system is the threat of freezing. If water in the collectors freezes, damage will likely result. This will cost money to fix and result in the loss of operation for a period of time. Methods for preventing freezing include using a mixture of water and antifreeze, providing a draindown procedure when the temperature drops below a certain point in the collectors, and using some fluid other than water in the system.

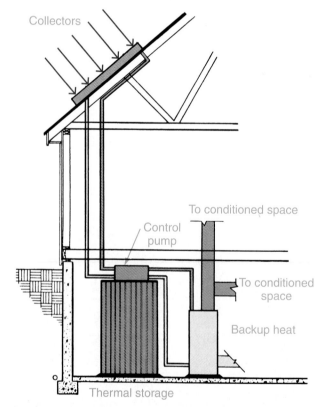

Figure 28-18. This example shows a roof-mounted, warm water active solar system. This system is connected to a backup heating system for extended cloudy periods.

Figure 28-19. A typical warm water solar collector with single glazing and insulation behind the absorber plate. (Lennox Industries, Inc.)

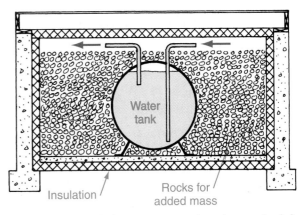

Water tank

Insulation

Rocks for added mass

Figure 28-20. This large warm water storage tank is encased in thick insulation to prevent heat loss. It is located in a crawl space. The stone provides additional thermal mass.

Each of the solutions to the freezing problem has drawbacks. Antifreeze tends to break down under high temperatures and forms glycolic acid, which is rather corrosive. A draindown system is effective if it works every time. However, some systems will not drain down if the power is off. Nonaqueous (nonwater) fluids, such as Dow's QZ-1132 silicone-based heat-transfer fluid, can be used. However, these fluids are expensive; more viscous, which requires a larger pump; and have a lower specific heat than water, which means they hold less heat. A system that uses plain water and has an automatic gravity draindown system is probably the most trouble-free system.

Other considerations of water collectors are similar to warm air collectors. These considerations include glazing, insulation, efficiency, and quality of construction. The cost of water collectors is generally somewhat higher than their warm air counterparts.

Warm water solar systems generally use a large insulated tank to store the heated water. A common location is in the basement or crawl space, Figure 28-20. The size of the water storage tank, like the size of a rock storage area, is related to the amount of solar radiation available, area of the collector surface, efficiency of the storage media, heat loss in the storage area, and household needs. A tank large enough to store heat for three days, assuming the proper amount of collector area has been determined, would require roughly 1-1/4 to 2 gallons of water per square foot of collector area.

Distribution of heat from the collectors and storage tank to the living space is accomplished using a pump similar to one used in a typical hydronic heating system. The pump is activated by a series of controls that respond to temperature sensors located in the collectors, storage tank, and living space. Several liquid-to-air heat exchangers are needed to heat the air inside the dwelling. This type of heat exchanger is typically a copper tube with aluminum fins surrounding the tube. Baseboard convectors that are used for hydronic heating systems are examples of liquid-to-air heat exchangers.

Advantages of Solar Heating

Passive and active solar heating systems have some advantages over conventional heating systems. Some of these include:

- Solar systems are clean, nonpolluting, and environmentally attractive.
- Solar systems use convection, conduction, and radiation where possible to move heat to desired areas.
- Solar systems are safe and inexpensive to operate.
- Solar systems utilize free energy that is available for the taking.

Disadvantages of Solar Heating

Some disadvantages associated with passive and active solar heating systems include:

- Solar heating systems are not as dependable as conventional heating systems. They are affected by the weather.
- Some areas of the country have little sunshine during the coldest months and, therefore, are poor prospects for solar heating.
- Some solar systems, especially active systems, are expensive to install and generally require a conventional backup heating system.
- Larger temperature variations are more frequent with solar heating systems than with conventional systems.

Calculation of Btus Possible for Any Given Location

Several factors affect the total Btus that may be produced by a typical solar collector in a specific geographical location. Some of these include:

- Mean solar radiation.
- Total hours of sunshine.
- Efficiency of the collector.

Efficiency is discussed earlier in this chapter. If the efficiency of a collector is assumed to be 35%, then the possible Btus per square foot produced can be calculated for the collector for any given geographical location.

The following example is for Ypsilanti, Michigan, which is located at 42 degrees 15 minutes North Latitude. Mean solar radiation and hours of sunshine for the Ypsilanti area have been measured and recorded by the local weather bureau. Averages are available in the *ASHRAE Handbook of Fundamentals*. Possible hours of sunshine are available from the US Naval Observatory web site at http://aa.usno.navy.mil/data. Only the months of October through April will be considered as these constitute the heating season.

The chart in Figure 28-21A shows the amount of sunshine recorded for Ypsilanti during each month of the heating season. The chart in Figure 28-21B shows the intensity of solar radiation for the months covered in the chart in Figure 28-21A. It is reasonable to conclude from these data that a 28 square foot collector that is 35% efficient could produce 762,009 Btus during the heating season in Ypsilanti, Michigan (77,756 $\times$ .35 $\times$ 28 = 762,009).

Calculation Procedure for Hours of Sunshine

1. Record the possible hours of sunshine for the month in the first column of the chart. Get this information from the US Weather Service or http://aa.usno.navy.mil/data.
2. Record the actual hours of sunshine for the month in the second column of the chart. Get this information from the your local weather service, newspaper, or other source.
3. Determine the average hours of sunshine per day by dividing the total hours of sun for the month (343 hours for October) by the number of days in the months (31). This will equal the average hours of sunshine/day (11.1 hours) for October. Record the value on the chart in the third column.
4. Determine the percent of sun possible by dividing the hours of sun received for the month (189 hours) by the possible hours of sun (343 hours). This will equal the percent of sun possible (55.1%). Record the value in the last column.
5. Determine the equated full days of sunshine per month by multiplying the number of days in the month (31) by the percent of sun possible for the month. This will equal the equated full days of sun for the month (17.08). Record this value in the fourth column.

Hours of Sunshine					
Month	Possible hours of sunshine	Hours of sunshine in Ypsilanti	Average hours of sunshine per day	Equated full day per month	Percent sun possible
October	343	189	11.1	17.08	55.1
November	294	98	9.8	9.99	33.3
December	288	89	9.3	9.58	30.9
January	295	90	9.5	9.46	30.5
February	296	128	10.6	12.10	43.2
March	371	180	12.0	15.04	48.5
April	402	212	13.4	15.81	52.7

A

Solar Radiation Available				
Month	Mean solar radiation	Constant*	Btus per ft^2 per day	Btus per ft^2 per month
October	260	3.687	958.62	16,373
November	140	3.687	516.18	5,157
December	108	3.687	398.20	3,815
January	125	3.687	460.88	4,360
February	208	3.687	766.90	9,279
March	305	3.687	1124.54	16,913
April	375	3.687	1382.63	21,859
			Heating season total =	77,756

*Solar radiation is measured in Langleys.
One Langley is equal to 3.687 Btus per square foot per day.

B

Figure 28-21. A—Amount of sunshine recorded for Ypsilanti, MI. B—Intensity of solar radiation for Ypsilanti, MI.

6. Repeat the procedure for each month of the heating season to fill in the total chart.

Calculation Procedure for Total Solar Radiation Available in Btus

1. Record the mean solar radiation for October in the first column of the chart. Get this information from the US Weather Service or ASHRAE. This value is reported in Langleys and will need to be converted to Btus.
2. One Langley is equal to 3.687 Btus/ft^2/day. This is a constant. Record it in the second column of the chart.
3. Determine the number of Btus/ft^2/day by multiplying the mean solar radiation by the constant 3.687. This product for October in the example is 958.62 Btus/ft^2/day. Record the value in the third column on the chart.
4. Determine the Btus/ft^2/month by multiplying the number of Btus/ft^2/day by the number of equated full days per month in the first chart (958.62 × 17.08). The product is the Btus/ft^2/month (16,373). Record this value in the last column of the chart.
5. Repeat this procedure for each month of the heating season to complete the chart.
6. Add up the values in the last column to equal the yearly total Btus/ft^2/month (77,756).

In this example, one could expect one square foot of collector to collect 77,756 Btus over the heating season. But since the collector is assumed to be only 35% efficient, the effective value is 27,215 Btus/ft^2. Hence, a 28 square foot collector could be expected to produce 762,009 Btus during the seven month heating season (27,215 x 28 = 762,009).

Internet Resources

aa.usno.navy.mil/data
  US Naval Observatory

www.ari.org
  Air Conditioning and Refrigeration Institute

www.ases.org
  American Solar Energy Society

www.crest.org
  Renewable Energy Policy Project

www.earthship.org
  Earthship Global Website

www.eren.doe.gov
  Department of Energy, Office of Energy Efficiency and Renewable Energy

www.glowcoreac.com
  GlowCore A.C., Inc., a manufacturer of boilers

www.harterindustries.com
  Harter Industries, a manufacturer of solar pool-heating products

www.heliodyne.com
  Heliodyne, Inc., a manufacturer of solar heating products

www.nrel.gov
  National Renewable Energy Laboratory

www.pfgindustries.com
  Modular Radiant Technologies, Inc., a manufacturer of radiant heating products

www.seia.org
  Solar Energy Industries Association

Review Questions – Chapter 28

Write your answers on a separate sheet of paper. Do not write in this book.

1. What are the two basic types of solar energy heating systems?
2. Purely passive solar energy systems use three means of distributing heat. List them.
3. Name the three basic categories that include most types of passive solar energy systems.
4. Describe how a direct gain system works.
5. What is the purpose of a large thermal mass?
6. List three building materials that are frequently used as a thermal mass.
7. Which can store more heat, a cubic foot of stone or a cubic foot of water?
8. How do indirect and direct solar gain systems differ?
9. Describe how water can be used as a large thermal mass.
10. A popular example of an indirect solar gain system utilizes a _____ wall to collect heat.
11. What is thermosiphoning?
12. A water storage wall is an example of a(n) _____ solar gain system.
13. List two disadvantages of phase-change materials, such as glauber's salt, used for thermal storage.

14. Describe an isolated gain system.

15. Name two advantages of the isolated gain system.

16. An attached greenhouse or sun space is an example of an _____ gain system.

17. How is an active solar heating system different from a passive solar heating system?

18. What are the two main types of active solar systems?

19. What is the efficiency range of most solar collectors used with active systems?

20. Every solar collector has some type of _____ plate.

21. The most common design or style of collector is the _____ plate collector.

22. What is the most popular material used for absorber plates?

23. What color are most absorber plates painted?

24. What type of thermal mass is generally used for warm air systems?

25. A solar collector facing _____ will collect the most heat.

26. A _____ is used to distribute heat in a warm air system.

27. List five architectural considerations for any solar system.

28. List two threats to a warm water solar system.

29. Generally, in cold climates, collectors should have _____ glazing.

30. In a warm water system, _____ heat exchangers are needed to heat the air inside the dwelling.

Suggested Activities

1. Contact a local meteorologist to secure weather data from the past heating season (October-April) for your area. Specifically, request the hours of sunshine per month and solar radiation available during the same months. From this data, calculate the amount of Btus falling on each square foot of a properly positioned collector for each month of the heating season.

2. Using the data generated in Activity 1, calculate the number of Btus that might be delivered to a dwelling if the total efficiency of the system is 50% efficient. Assume 800 square feet of collector area.

3. Write to or e-mail several companies that produce active solar systems for residential application and request technical literature related to their systems. Study this literature and report your findings to the class.

4. Plan a cottage that utilizes one of the passive solar gain systems discussed in this chapter. Explain how the system works.

5. Using CADD, design a cottage that uses an attached greenhouse on the south side to collect and store energy. Show a section through the building similar to Figure 28-10.

This home has an array of photovoltaic panels installed on the roof. Solar power and heating also appeals to the same homeowners who are interested in nontraditional structures. (Lindal Cedar Homes, Inc., Seattle, WA)

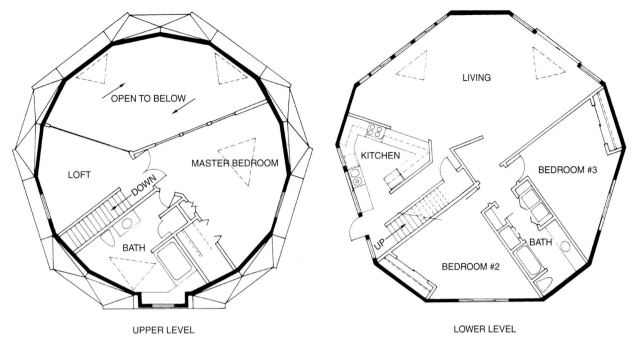

UPPER LEVEL   LOWER LEVEL

Figure 29-13. This is a typical first and second floor layout for a 45′ diameter dome home. (Cathedralite Domes)

Figure 29-14. This 39′ diameter dome provides 1500 square feet of floor space on two levels. (Domes and Homes, Inc.)

to one another or combined with a conventional structure. Typical roofing materials, such as asphalt shingles and cedar shakes, may be used to weatherproof the exterior.

Dome Variations

Most manufactured dome homes are not true geodesic domes, rather variations that use the central idea of a geodesic dome. The true

geodesic dome described by Fuller is produced by dividing the surface of a sphere into a series of small triangles. These are joined together to enclose a space resulting in a dome. Most true geodesic domes have from 60 to 120 triangles.

The large number of components may present problems for home application. Difficulty may also be encountered due to the degree of accuracy required to join a large number of triangles. Also, the small triangles do not lend themselves to large openings for windows and doors.

There are variations of the original geodesic dome that reduce the number of units and incorporate other shapes in addition to triangles. These designs have made the dome concept more feasible to the housing market. One design variation, called the Hexadome, combines 24 triangles and three trapezoids to form a dome up to 32′ in diameter. Each panel unit is constructed from standard construction lumber and plywood. Each unit is also large enough to accept standard windows and doors. Construction of the dome is accomplished by bolting six triangular panels together to form a raised hexagon. Four of these hexagons are required with three trapezoids to complete the dome. Figure 29-15

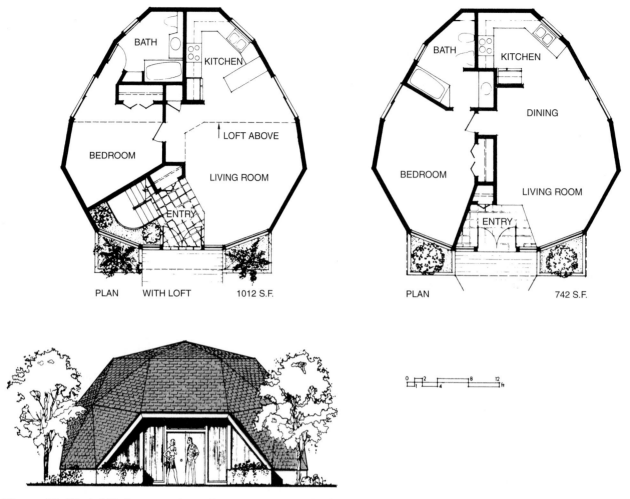

Figure 29-15. A 32′ diameter dome forms a cozy one-bedroom home. A loft can be added to the plan, which could be used as another bedroom. (Hexadome of America)

shows a 32′ diameter Hexadome plan that has 742 square feet of floor space, which can be expanded to 1012 square feet by adding a loft.

Another variation of the geodesic dome uses basic triangular units, but mixes different size triangles to form hexagons and pentagons, which in turn enclose the sphere. The appearance of this dome variation is very similar to the Hexadome. Figure 29-16 clearly illustrates the use of raised hexagons and pentagons in a 39′ diameter dome.

Typical Dome Construction

Most residential dome applications use typical construction techniques and materials to form the basic triangular panels. The panels can be purchased complete and ready to bolt together, precut at the factory and

Figure 29-16. Triangular panels are combined to form raised hexagons and pentagons in this 39′ diameter dome. (Domes and Homes, Inc.)

shipped as individual pieces, or built completely on site from standard lumber and plywood. Figure 29-17 shows typical panel designs for a 32′ Hexadome. The frames for the triangles in this example are cut from 4″ × 4″ lumber and a 4″ × 8″ board is used for the base of the trapezoid. Studs are 2″ × 4″ construction with 1/2″ construction-grade exterior plywood sheathing. The sheathing is nailed and glued to the studs.

Once the dome panels are constructed and bolted together, the entire shell of the dome is ready to be placed on the foundation. A crane will be required for this operation. Another procedure is to erect the panels of the dome directly on the foundation. However, a crane will still be required to place the top hexagon in place.

The foundation for a dome structure may be any one of the standard types used for conventional construction. A basement, crawl space, or slab foundation is compatible with dome construction. Once the type of foundation, basic size of dome, and dome style are selected, the foundation shape may be located on the site. Figure 29-18 shows the basic foundation shape for a 32′ diameter Hexadome with openings and walls indicated.

Riser walls support the entire structure while providing additional headroom on the second floor. Remember, however, that the dome itself is self supporting. The Hexadome in Figure 29-15 requires three riser walls to support the dome. Each is 9′-3″ long and made from 2″ × 6″ construction lumber with plywood sheathing, concrete blocks, or cast concrete. The riser walls must be strong and solidly attached to the foundation, Figure 29-19. Wooden riser walls must be solidly braced during placement of the dome to prevent movement of the structure and accidents. *Wing walls* on either side of the riser walls will completely enclose the structure. Wing walls are shown in Figure 29-15 on both sides of the entry door.

The construction of most dome structures is similar to the example discussed here. Completion of the home is the same as for any frame structure.

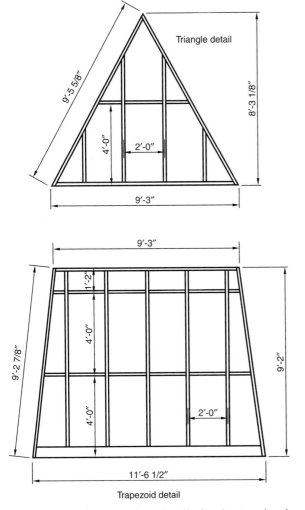

Figure 29-17. Construction details for the two basic panel shapes used in a 32′ diameter Hexadome.

Figure 29-18. This is a basic foundation shape. Walls and openings are located.

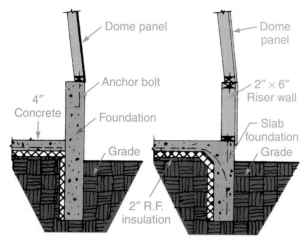

Figure 29-19. Typical foundation details. Left—Raised concrete foundation wall with slab floor. Right—Thickened edge slab with a wood riser wall.

Advantages of Domes

Dome structures have some advantages when compared with typical residential construction. Following are some of the most obvious advantages of domes.

- Domes are a very efficient system that is strong and versatile.
- Domes provide an open, obstruction-free floor space that lends itself to a wide variety of floor plans, Figure 29-20.
- Factory production makes it possible to erect a dome from standard panels in just a few hours.
- The basic dome shape requires less energy for heating and air conditioning than conventional rectangular shapes that cover the same floor space.
- Domes are economical to build since less materials are required.
- The interior of a dome home is exciting and fun to decorate due to the varied shapes and surfaces.

Disadvantages of Domes

Although there are many advantages to domes, there are some disadvantages of dome homes. Disadvantages of dome homes include the following.

Figure 29-20. The interior space of a dome may be used in any manner since no interior structural support is needed for the shell. (Monterey Domes)

- Walls that are not vertical or form square corners may present some problems with typical furniture and appliances.
- More custom built-ins may be required due to the unique design of the structure. Custom work adds cost.
- The dome design may not be compatible with surrounding homes and, therefore, not a good choice in some communities.
- Banks, insurance companies, and building departments are generally not familiar with this type of construction. They may be reluctant to lend money, insure, or approve the design for construction.
- Resale may be more difficult than a conventional home because the dome structure is different.

Internet Resources

www.anchorwall.com
Anchor Retaining Wall Systems

www.bfi.org
The Buckminster Fuller Institute

www.eldoradostone.com
Eldorado Stone, a manufacturer of stone veneers

www.epsmolders.org
EPS Molders Association, an association for the expanded polystyrene industry

www.fibermesh.com
Synthetic Industries Concrete Systems

www.forms.org
Insulating Concrete Form Association

www.increte.com
Increte Systems, a manufacturer of decorative concrete systems

www.keystonewalls.com
Keystone Retaining Wall Systems

www.owenscorning.com
Owens Corning

www.portcement.org
Portland Cement Association

www.recousa.com
The Reinforced Earth Company

Review Questions – Chapter 29

Write your answers on a separate sheet of paper. Do not write in this book.

1. Name several considerations that are important for earth-sheltered dwellings, but may not be for conventional above-grade structures.

2. In a northern location, an earth-sheltered dwelling should face _____.

3. What may be used to shield large glass areas in the summer?

4. Why is wind an important consideration for the orientation of an earth-sheltered dwelling?

5. From which direction do winter winds come in the northern hemisphere?

6. What does the topography of a site include?

7. What is the primary reason for designing and building an earth-sheltered dwelling?

8. Which types of soil are generally unsuitable for building an earth-sheltered dwelling?

9. How much pressure does water-saturated soil exert?

10. Heat loss in a building is a function of the amount of _____ through which heat can escape.

11. Explain why earth placed against walls and on the roof reduces heat loss.

12. Which two basic roof systems are used to support the roof loads in earth-sheltered structures?

13. Name the three design variations used in most earth-sheltered dwellings.

14. Which earth-sheltered design may have openings facing several directions?

15. The _____ design of an earth-sheltered house has the living spaces located around a central courtyard, and all windows open to the court.

16. Who developed the geodesic dome concept?

17. The basic geodesic dome is an engineered system of _____ spaceframes based on mathematically precise divisions of a sphere.

18. List at least four advantages of the dome structure.

19. Why do domes have less heat loss per square foot of floor space over conventional construction?

20. Most manufactured dome homes usually range in size from about _____ to _____.

21. The basic modular shape used in most domes is the _____.

22. The Hexadome variation of the geodesic dome combines 24 triangles and three trapezoids to form a dome up to 32' in diameter. Another variation mixes different size triangles to form _____ and _____ to enclose the sphere.

23. One piece of heavy equipment may be required on site to assemble a dome home. Name it and explain why it is needed.

24. A dome structure can be built on most any conventional type foundation. Give two examples.

25. Give the two purposes of a riser wall.

Suggested Activities

1. Using CADD, plan and draw an earth-sheltered dwelling using one of the three basic types presented in this chapter as a guide. Build a model of the proposed plan and get a rough estimate of the cost to build the structure from a local builder. Report your results.

2. Visit your local building department or a well-drilling firm to determine the types of soil in your area. Collect samples for display and report on the acceptability of each soil type for earth-sheltered dwellings.

3. Interview a local bank loan officer and a building contractor concerning earth-sheltered dwellings. Obtain the bank and building company policies for these homes. List major reasons for acceptance or rejection for financing, insuring, and/or constructing earth-sheltered dwellings.

4. Go to your local library, bookstore, or magazine stand and secure several books or magazines that list manufacturers of dome homes. The Internet may also be a source. Write to or e-mail three manufacturers and request information about their products. Study the literature and share it with your classmates.

5. Using CADD, plan and draw a simple dome structure. Then, build a scale model of the structure. Explain the advantages and disadvantages of this type of structure.

6. Using a plan supplied by your instructor, obtain information from your local gas and electric company on the cost of heating and cooling a dome home. If needed, modify the plan to increase its energy efficiency. Report your findings to the class.

New Products and Methods of Construction

Objectives

After studying this chapter, you will be able to:

➤ Describe the proper application of exterior insulation finish systems.

➤ Explain the advantages and disadvantages of foam core structural sandwich panels in residential construction.

➤ Select an appropriate alternative to traditional formed concrete wall systems.

➤ Describe alternative concrete block construction products.

➤ Describe the key elements in a frost-protected shallow foundation.

➤ Identify deck materials that are weather-resistant.

➤ Discuss the advantages and disadvantages of the Hebel Wall System.

Key Terms

Autoclave

Exterior Insulation
  Finish Systems
  (EIFS)

Hard-Coat EIFS

Insulated Concrete
  Wall System

Insulated Wall
  Forms

Slab-on-Grade
  Construction

Soft-Coat EIFS

Structural Foam
  Sandwich Panels

Superinsulation

Thermal Lag

Welded-Wire
  Sandwich Panels

Introduction to Products and Methods

These are exciting times in residential design and construction. Many new materials and methods of construction are being introduced each year. Some will stand the test of time and become the standard of the future. Products like plywood, roof trusses, floor trusses, plastic pipe, rigid foam insulation, cement roof tiles, fiberglass tub and shower units, and insulated windows were all innovations in their time. But now they have been accepted by designers, builders, code groups, and home buyers as standard materials and constructions.

Some innovative products and techniques, however, have not stood the test of time. Exterior porcelain steel modular panels were once thought to be the wave of the future, but ended up being short lived. Aluminum framing came on the scene a few years ago, only to disappear after a short time. Asbestos cement products and formaldehyde-based foam insulation were driven from use because of health concerns. Factory-built homes have been around since World War II, but have never been very important in residential construction.

This chapter aims to describe some of the newer products and methods of construction that may become broadly accepted in residential design and construction in the future, Figure 30-1. Most are beyond the experimental stage, but may not be accepted by all of the model building codes. Be sure to check your

Figure 30-1. Several innovative products and building techniques are being utilized in the construction of this large home. (The Engineered Wood Association)

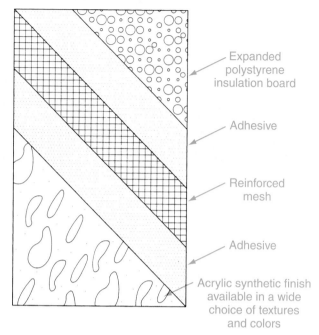

Expanded polystyrene insulation board

Adhesive

Reinforced mesh

Adhesive

Acrylic synthetic finish available in a wide choice of textures and colors

Figure 30-2. A typical exterior wall insulation and finish system generally consists of four major components that provide permanent insulation, shape, and texture to form a unique exterior wall.

local building code before specifying or using any of these "new" materials or techniques.

Exterior Insulation Finish Systems (EIFS)

The use of *exterior insulation finish systems (EIFS)* for commercial and residential applications has grown dramatically in the last few years. The systems are sometimes called "synthetic stucco." They provide lots of flexibility with colors and architectural detail, as well as good insulation without thermal gaps, Figure 30-2.

There are two generic types of EIFS: polymer-based (PB) and polymer-modified (PM). Polymer-based systems are the most widely used. PB systems are often called *soft-coat EIFS* and are typically thin (about 1/8"), adhesively attached, and flexible. The flexibility reduces the need for numerous control joints. However, they cannot tolerate prolonged wetting. Therefore, this material should not be used as a coat for swimming pools or walls that stand in water.

Polymer-modified (PM) systems, often called *hard-coat EIFS,* are usually greater than 1/4" thick and mechanically attached. They are not sensitive to moisture. However, PM systems require frequent control joints, similar to cement stucco.

Additional information about exterior insulation finish systems (EIFS) can be obtained by contacting:
Dryvit Systems, Inc.
One Energy Way
PO Box 1014
West Warwick, RI 02893
www.dryvit.com

Advantages of EIFS

There are many advantages of EIFS. Some of these advantages include:

- Construction time is reduced using EIFS compared to traditional stucco.
- Design freedom is increased to develop complex architectural details.
- Thermal performance of the wall is improved and air infiltration is reduced.

- The finished result of a quality installation and workmanship is very attractive and popular, Figure 30-3.

Disadvantages of EIFS

There are also some disadvantages of EIFS. Some of these disadvantages include:

- *Installation details from the manufacturer must be followed to the letter!* Poor quality of work has been responsible, according to HUD, for most product failures. Applications with exposed mesh and inadequately thick coats account for most of the claims of poor quality of work.
- Many applications experience cracking at V-grooves, openings, and board joints; sealant failure; and water damage due to improper application.
- Standards for materials and application need to be revised to provide a reasonable service life without extensive maintenance and early repair.
- EIFS should not be adhesively applied to gypsum sheathing. This material is vulnerable to water penetration.
- There are too few people knowledgeable about EIFS in the industry at present.

Installation/Application

A high quality of work is critical if EIFS installations are to last. The major concerns during application are:

- **Board application.** Good adhesion must be provided between the insulation board and substrate. Joints should be offset between the sheathing and window or door openings and decorative V-grooves.
- **Base coat.** Be sure the base coat is at least 3/32″ thick. Apply it in two layers. Use primer on all cementitious base coat surfaces.
- **Mesh.** Always offset laps in the mesh from edges of openings, grooves, and corners. Use diagonal mesh to reinforce the corners at openings. Use double-layer mesh, lapped at least 4″, at all outside and inside corners. Fully embed the mesh. Use high-impact mesh at all surfaces near grade or walkways where additional wear and tear is expected.
- **Sealant joints.** Provide a smooth, straight, solid surface to receive sealants. Use a primer on all surfaces that will receive a sealant. Apply the sealant to the base coat only. Tool all sealant joints.

Structural Foam Sandwich Panels

Structural foam sandwich panels are structural members made of two strong, stiff skins adhered to a foam core that is 3-1/2″ to 11-1/4″ thick, Figure 30-4. This forms a single structure that resists twisting, warping, and cracking. The skins are typically 7/16″ oriented strand board (OSB) or plywood. The foam core is a lightweight, but relatively thick, low-density expanded polystyrene, extruded polystyrene, or rigid polyurethane. The thick rigid foam core produces a high R-value. Sometimes the inside is faced with wallboard, either above or over the OSB.

The very first structural panels were built by the US Forest Products Laboratory in the 1930s. Those panels consisted mostly of plywood skins glued to a core of wood-framing

Figure 30-3. Exterior insulation finish systems (EIFS) are very popular for homes across America. (United States Gypsum Company)

Figure 30-4. Structural foam sandwich panels are structural members made of two skins adhered to a thick core of rigid expanded polystyrene insulation. (AFM Corporation)

members or paper honeycomb. Today, we call these "stressed-skin panels." Not all stressed-skin panels are insulated and not all foam panels with facings are stressed-skinned. This discussion focuses on structural foam core panels and does not include stressed-skinned panels.

In the 1950s the use of structural sandwich panels began to expand because of the superior energy performance of these panels. Today the use of structural foam sandwich panels continues to increase. These structural panels have gained acceptance as a viable alternative to traditional wall framing systems.

Additional information about structural foam sandwich panels can be obtained by contacting:
Building Systems Councils of National Association of Home Builders
1201 15th Street, NW
Washington, DC 20005
www.buildingsystems.org

Advantages of Structural Foam Sandwich Panels

- Speed is cited by builders as the greatest advantage of using structural foam sandwich panels. Sandwich panels replace three stages in standard construction: framing, sheathing, and insulation. If all of the exterior dimensions are increments of 4', the speed at which panels can be erected is greatly increased. Precut panels also speed the building process, but add to the cost. The largest panels may require a crane, Figure 30-5.

- Superior energy performance is cited by manufacturers as a distinct advantage of structural foam sandwich panels. A well-built, superinsulated, stick-built home will compare favorably with sandwich panel construction. However, most production built homes do not match the energy performance of sandwich panel construction. Further, foams used in panels provide between 25% and 100% higher R-value per inch than fiberglass. And, there is less conductive heat loss through framing members since most panel systems use very little dimension lumber.

- Strength is cited by manufacturers and builders as an advantage of structural foam sandwich panels. Testing showed that panels outperformed typical frame walls by factors of between two and six depending, on the

Figure 30-5. A prefabricated structural foam sandwich panel is being installed. Larger panels may require a crane to place. (AFM Corporation)

test. The strength of these panels is especially important when a natural disaster, such as a hurricane or earthquake, strikes.

- Less moisture migration is an important advantage of foam core sandwich panels. This property is provided by the inherent vapor-retarding characteristics of the foam itself. Depending on the thickness and density of the core, most urethanes and some polystyrenes have a permeability rating of less than one. This technically qualifies the panel as a vapor barrier.

Disadvantages of Structural Foam Sandwich Panels

- Durability is a lingering question. Sandwich panels have been tested using accelerated aging techniques and the results were very promising, but panel homes just have not been around long enough to know how they compare with typical stick-built homes. It is advisable to check the manufacturer's warranty against delamination. They generally range from 15 years to "the life of the structure."

- Questions about the performance of sandwich panels in fire persist. Unsheathed foams burn readily, but tests show that panel assemblies perform well when drywall was applied over OSB. However, a frequent criticism of urethane foam is that it releases deadly hydrogen cyanide when burned. This is also the case with many household materials. Again, the protective surface of the panel (drywall and OSB) is the key to a safer product.

- The use of chlorofluorocarbons in the production of extruded polystyrene, polyurethane, and poly-isocyanurate foams is a definite disadvantage because CFCs and HCFCs have been associated with ozone depletion. Expanded polystyrene (EPS) foams are not produced with CFCs. Ozone-safe substitutes will replace CFCs and HCFCs in the very near future.

- Ants and termites do not receive nourishment from foam, but they will tunnel in it, which will reduce the insulation value and

irritate the homeowner with chewing sounds at night. Extensive tunneling can reduce the structural integrity. Some panels are being treated with insect repellents to prevent the problem.

- When sandwich panels are used to form a roof, the temperature of the roof can be 20°F hotter than it would be over a vented attic. This additional heat will shorten the life of asphalt shingles placed over the panels.

- Small ridge lines may be visible on a roof where the panels join. Manufacturers recommend leaving a 1/4" gap between panels to reduce the bulge. The gap should be sealed with an expanding foam sealant.

- A disadvantage of any new product or process is the time it takes for tradespeople to become familiar with it. Since the use of foam core structural sandwich panels is a total building system, the problem of familiarity cuts across many trades and increases the problem.

Installation/Application

Structural foam sandwich panels present a new way to build structures. Therefore, the decision to use this approach should be decided on at the beginning of the design process, not after the home has been designed. Using modular lengths for all exterior walls and placing window and door openings in optimum locations will improve the construction process as well as the final product, Figure 30-6.

Typical wall panels are 3-1/2", 5-1/2", or 7-1/4" thick while roof panels are either 9-1/4" or 11-1/4" thick. These dimensions are similar to traditional construction, but not all panel systems are manufactured or installed in the same way. Some manufacturers provide installation training for builders while others offer their own erection crews.

Erecting panel structures requires some special tools. Large roof and wall panels require a small crane to lift the panels in place. Some type of winch-and-strap system is also useful to help ensure that panel edges are butted tightly together. Special cutting tools may be needed to cut openings in the panels.

Figure 30-6. This residential structure was designed to be constructed with factory-built structural foam sandwich panels. (AFM Corporation)

Extra-large circular saws are needed to cut through panels at roof ridges and eaves. The foam must be removed to a depth of 1-1/2" around door and window openings, which is best done using a hot wire tool. Chases for electrical wiring and plumbing present special problems if not planned for early in the design process.

Concrete Wall Systems

The use of concrete in above-grade applications in residential construction has been mainly in moderate climates because of concrete's low-insulative properties. New

opportunities now exist as a result of the development of insulated systems. Even though the concept of combining insulating and structural materials is not new, it has only been in the last few years that the use of combined systems has gained acceptance in the building industry. Several systems are being produced and many will most likely not survive, but the purpose here is to describe three systems that seem the most promising. These three include insulated wall forms, insulated concrete wall systems, and welded-wire sandwich panels.

The driving force behind the development of new concrete wall systems is to improve the thermal performance of concrete walls. When looking at options for insulating concrete walls, it is important to consider the concept of superinsulation and thermal lag. *Superinsulation* aims to reduce heat transmission through the building envelope by increasing R-values to achieve better thermal performance. However, R-values do not necessarily provide a true measure of a building's thermal performance because they fail to account for variations in temperature and the thermal storage capacity of materials. Structures with a large thermal mass, such as concrete structures, are able to delay the transfer of heat due to the heat storage capacity of the building mass. This principle is *thermal lag* and the basis for passive solar systems.

Materials that have large thermal masses, such as concrete, can store large amounts of thermal energy (heat) during the day when energy is needed the least and then release it later when it is needed the most. This is a decided advantage if the outside temperature varies in a suitable range. At best, the mass is generally not great or reliable enough to be depended on in most typical residential structures across the country.

New developments for insulating concrete walls can reduce conductive heat loss by using insulation and improving heat retention capacity by using the mass. The result is an insulated concrete wall with an R-value of 20 or more.

Insulated Concrete Wall Forms

Insulated wall forms can be used to create foundation and exterior walls in residential construction. These can be classified into two main categories:

• Concrete cast between two rigid polystyrene foam panels. Products in this category are Lite-Form™ and Plasti-Fab Enermizer Building Systems™.

• Interlocking blocks of plastic foam insulation that are stackable and whose hollow cores are filled with concrete. Products in this category include SmartBlock™, Reddi-Form™, EcoBloc™, Keeva Wall™, Greenblock™, and Polysteel Forms™.

Lite-Form™

Lite-Form™ is an insulated wall system that uses panels of plastic foam insulation as forms for concrete, Figure 30-7. The panels are separated with plastic ties so that the space between the panels can be filled with concrete. The insulation panels remain in place and become part of the wall. This results in a concrete wall that is insulated on both sides. Additional information about Lite-Form™ can be obtained by contacting:

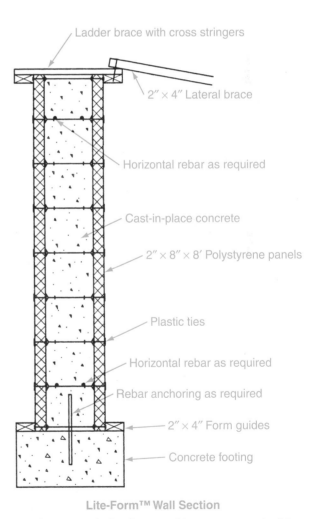

Ladder brace with cross stringers

2″ × 4″ Lateral brace

Horizontal rebar as required

Cast-in-place concrete

2″ × 8″ × 8′ Polystyrene panels

Plastic ties

Horizontal rebar as required

Rebar anchoring as required

2″ × 4″ Form guides

Concrete footing

Lite-Form™ Wall Section

Figure 30-7. This building technique allows the insulation panels to remain in place and become a part of the wall, which results in an insulated concrete wall. (Lite-Form, Inc.)

Lite-Form Incorporated
1950 West 29th Street
South Sioux City, NE 68776
www.liteform.com

Advantages. The following are advantages of Lite-Form™.

- Thermal performance of the wall is increased. The fully insulated wall reduces thermal breaks and achieves an R-value of about 20.

- Durability of the wall is increased because expansion and contraction of the wall is reduced, hence cracking is reduced.

- Construction of the concrete wall requires less time. The lightweight forms permit factory or on-site assembly and skilled labor is not required for installation. Costly stripping is not required since the forms remain in place. Furring strips are not required as drywall or paneling can be attached directly to the form boards.

- The construction season can be extended in cold climates. The insulation permits the concrete to be cast in cold weather.

Disadvantages. The following are disadvantages of Lite-Form™.

- Extra care must be taken during the casting process. If the concrete is cast too rapidly, the forms can blow out causing damage and waste.

- A pump truck with a hydraulic boom is suggested to place the concrete properly in the forms.

- Foundations built with foam forms cost more.

Installation/Application. Form sections are built from 8″ high by 8′ long strips of polystyrene. Special form ties and corner ties are required. The wall form is built course by course until the desired height is reached. A typical footing is generally used. The completed form is braced and reinforced before filling with concrete.

Exterior siding or interior paneling can be screwed into the plastic ties. Any polystyrene that is above the grade and exposed should be covered with a trowel-applied protective coating. Electrical and plumbing lines can be installed in the 2″ thick insulation. Conduit may be required by some codes.

SmartBlock™

SmartBlock™ is manufactured by American ConForm Industries. It is representative of the second category of insulated concrete wall forms—interlocking blocks of plastic foam insulation that are stackable and whose hollow cores are filled with concrete, Figure 30-8. SmartBlock™ is molded of a flame-retardant expanded polystyrene (EPS) that possesses both thermal and acoustical properties. Additional information about SmartBlock™ can be obtained by contacting:

American ConForm Industries
1820 South Santa Fe Street
Santa Ana, CA 92705
www.smartblock.com

Advantages. The following are advantages of SmartBlock™.

- Thermal performance of the wall is increased. The fully insulated wall reduces thermal breaks and achieves an increased R-value.

- Durability of the wall is increased because expansion and contraction of the wall is reduced, hence cracking is reduced.

- Construction of the concrete wall requires less time.

Figure 30-8. SmartBlock™ is one type of insulated concrete wall form. The interlocking blocks of plastic foam insulation are stackable and provide the form for concrete. (American ConForm Industries, Inc.)

- The construction season can be extended in cold climates.
- The system can be finished with most external building finishes.

Disadvantages. The following are disadvantages of SmartBlock™.

- Extra care must be taken during the casting process to prevent blowout.
- A pump truck with a hydraulic boom is necessary to place the concrete properly.
- Foundations built with foam blocks cost more.

Installation/Application. SmartBlocks™ are 10" × 10" × 40" and weigh two pounds each. They are stacked course by course and joined with an interlocking tongue and groove, Figure 30-9. Unskilled labor can be used to stack the blocks so that the hollow cores are over vertical reinforcing rods placed according to the local code requirements. Bracing is required as specified by the manufacturer. Electrical and plumbing lines can be installed within the thickness of the block shell.

Insulated Concrete Wall Systems

Composite Technologies manufactures an *insulated concrete wall system* under the brand name Thermomass™. This system places a panel of plastic foam insulation between two conventional metal or wood forms. Proprietary connectors hold the foam panel in place while the concrete is cast, Figure 30-10. Additional information about Thermomass™ can be obtained by contacting:
National Concrete Masonry Association
13750 Sunrise Valley Drive
Herndon, VA 20171
www.ncma.org
Composite Technologies Corporation
1000 Technology Drive
PO Box 950
Boone, IA 50036
www.thermomass.com

Advantages of Thermomass™

- The proprietary connectors enable the panel of insulation to be located in the middle of the concrete wall, thus reducing fire hazard or outgasing.
- Eliminates the need to provide special protection for the insulation or fastening techniques.

Disadvantages of Thermomass™

- The amount of labor is increased installing the special connectors.
- Concrete must be placed on both sides of the insulation evenly to prevent breakage.
- Conventional concrete forms are used, which require removal, cleaning, and storage.

Figure 30-9. The SmartBlock™ system can be used to cost-effectively create almost any shape of wall. (American ConForm Industries, Inc.)

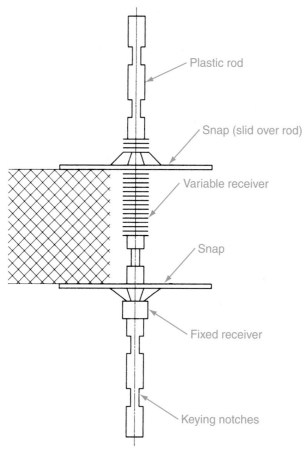

Figure 30-10. The key ingredient in the Thermomass™ insulated concrete wall system is the proprietary connectors that hold the panel of insulation in the middle of the concrete wall during the casting process.

Installation/Application

The central feature of the Thermomass™ System is its proprietary connectors. The connectors are 10″ or 12″ long and made from pultruded fiber-reinforced vinyl with molded plastic collars. A 2″ or 4″ thick rigid insulation panel is held in place by the connectors during concrete placement. Holes must be drilled through the insulation panel for each connector.

Welded-Wire Sandwich Panels

Welded-wire sandwich panels provide the framework and structural reinforcement for a panel construction system. Each sandwich panel consists of a three-dimensional, welded-

wire spaceframe that is integrated with a foam plastic insulation core, Figure 30-11. Different thicknesses of core are used depending on the required specifications. Panels can be completed at the site with a layer of shotcrete or the exterior layer may be precast. Welded-wire sandwich panels may be used as floors, load-bearing walls, partition walls, or roofs. Additional information about welded-wire sandwich panels can be obtained by contacting:

National Concrete Masonry Association
13750 Sunrise Valley Drive
Herndon, VA 20171
www.ncma.org
National Precast Concrete Association
10333 North Meridian Street, Suite 272
Indianapolis, IN 46290
www.precast.org

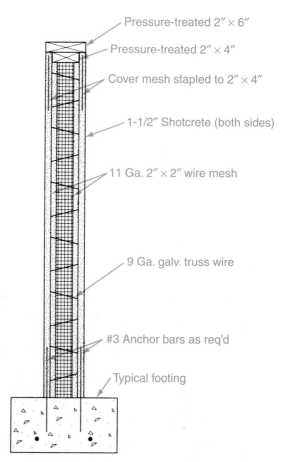

Figure 30-11. In a welded-wire sandwich panel, concrete must be placed on both sides of the foam insulation panel simultaneously to prevent breakage.

Advantages of welded-wire sandwich panels

- Use of welded-wire sandwich panels can reduce overall construction time.
- The panels are lightweight, typically 1.2 pounds per square foot, and easy to handle.
- Panels have a high fire rating because the finished surface is concrete.
- The structure produced by this process is durable and resistant to high winds, moisture, and termites.

Disadvantages of welded-wire sandwich panels

- Most local codes require structural calculations by a registered professional.
- The system requires skills and tools that are somewhat uncommon to the residential construction industry.

Installation/Application

The standard size panel is 4' long by 8' wide by 5-1/2" thick. This thickness includes the first coat of shotcrete. Panels can be obtained in lengths up to 24'. Panels may be fastened together using lap mesh, rebar, and tie wire. Openings for windows and doors can be cut on site or at the factory. Electrical and plumbing lines are placed between the wire and the foam panel. The final finish on the panel is accomplished by hand troweling the 1" to 1-1/2" layer of shotcrete to the desired surface finish.

Insulated Concrete Block Systems

Concrete masonry units (CMU) have enjoyed great popularity as an alternative to concrete and wood frame walls, especially in the more moderate climates. The industry is very familiar with the product and all model building codes recognize concrete block construction. Further, concrete masonry has proven to be a durable material. It is only logical, therefore, that an effort would be made to improve the thermal performance of this basic building material. Several new types of block that incorporate insulating techniques are being developed in the industry. The most common approach to producing an insulated block is to place a fill material in the block as the wall is built. Plastic inserts can also be placed into the cores of conventional block. Also, blocks with specially designed, insulating cores can be used.

Integra™

Integra™, developed by Superlite Builders Supply, Inc., involves laying a block wall and filling the core with foam. The foam is poured into the cores as a liquid and as it expands, it fills the voids, Figure 30-12. Additional information about Integra™ can be obtained by contacting:

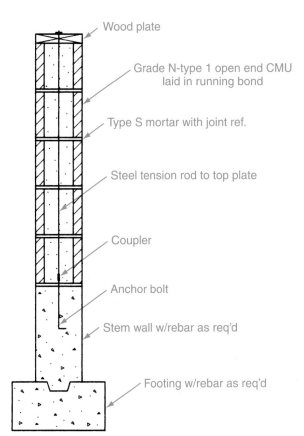

Figure 30-12. The Integra™ wall system must be post tensioned by the manufacturer, who also installs the polyurethane insulation.

Labels in figure:
- Wood plate
- Grade N-type 1 open end CMU laid in running bond
- Type S mortar with joint ref.
- Steel tension rod to top plate
- Coupler
- Anchor bolt
- Stem wall w/rebar as req'd
- Footing w/rebar as req'd

National Concrete Masonry Association
13750 Sunrise Valley Drive
Herndon, VA 20171
www.ncma.org

Advantages of Integra™

- The product is effective and relatively inexpensive.
- The foam fills all spaces within the blocks to reduce infiltration and condensation.

Disadvantages of Integra™

- The walls must be post tensioned by the manufacturer or its appointed licensee.
- The manufacturer must install the polyurethane insulation.

Installation/Application

The Integra™ system requires the use of grade N-type I open end concrete masonry units in running bond with type S mortar. The wall must be laid with horizontal joint reinforcing and vertical steel tension rods that are used for post tensioning to strengthen the wall. The proprietary blended polyurethane is poured into the block cavities and then the wall is capped with a wood plate that becomes part of the post tensioning system.

Therma-Lock™

Therma-Lock™ is a type of insulating block that has plastic inserts, which are usually installed during the manufacturing process, Figure 30-13. The Therma-Lock™ system was developed by Therma-Lock Products, Inc. Additional information about Therma-Lock™ blocks can be obtained by contacting:
Therma-Lock Products, Inc.
162 Sweeney Street
North Tonawanda, NY 14120

Advantages of Therma-Lock™

- Construction time is reduced because the blocks arrive at the building site insulated and ready for use, Figure 30-14.

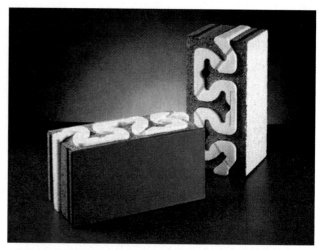

Figure 30-13. Therma-Lock™ blocks have high thermal performance because no concrete webs extend through the block to conduct heat. (Therma-Lock Products, Inc.)

- Thermal performance is greatly improved because no concrete webs extend through the block to act as a thermal bridge.
- Therma-Lock™ blocks are made to standard dimensions.
- Therma-Lock™ blocks can be made in any architectural finish.

Figure 30-14. Therma-Lock™ blocks arrive at the job site with the insulation installed. (Therma-Lock Products Inc.)

Disadvantage of Therma-Lock™

• None are apparent.

Installation/Application

Therma-Lock™ blocks are laid in the conventional manner with typical mortar. No special tools are required. The blocks are available in 8", 10", and 12" widths. R-values of 15, 19, and 24 respectively are claimed by the manufacturer for Therma-Lock™ blocks.

Frost-Protected Shallow Foundation

Slab-on-grade construction, which has a slab foundation, has become the norm in the South because it is a simple, efficient way to build houses. However, builders in cold climates have generally not used this type of construction because of the added cost involved in frost protection. Now, research has led to the development of a new, frost-protected shallow foundation design that is practical for most all areas of the US.

The design shown in Figure 30-15 is one shallow foundation design that works, according to the National Association of Home Builders (NAHB) Research Center. In this design, borate-treated expanded polystyrene

(EPS) insulation is installed along the stem wall and horizontally away from the bottom of the foundation wall. A footing may be necessary in some types of soils. The horizontal insulation essentially moves the frost line away from the house, essentially eliminating concern about the frost depth. This design also includes thicker insulation at the slab edge corners, Figure 30-16.

The amount of insulation needed at each corner depends on the severity of the climate. In climates having fewer than 2,500 heating degree days no horizontal insulation is required. However, thicker insulation is still required at the slab edge corners. Recommended insulation R-values also vary by climate from R-4.5 to R-10.1 for stem walls and from R-1.7 to R-13.1 for the horizontal insulation. The Air Freezing Index, which is a measure of winter severity, is the basis for the recommended R-value of insulation.

A word of caution: Be sure to check your local code to see if it permits burying rigid foam insulation around the perimeter of the structure. Termites and other wood-boring insects frequently nest in rigid foam in below-grade applications. The International Code Council (ICC) included a provision in their

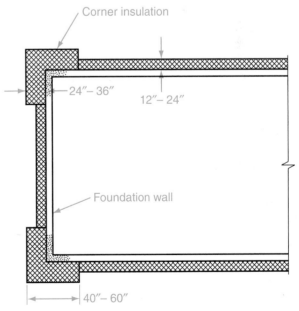

Figure 30-16. This plan view of a frost-protected shallow foundation shows the placement of insulation around the foundation wall.

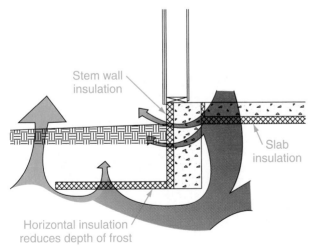

Figure 30-15. This is a typical section of a frost-protected shallow foundation.

code for one- and two-family dwellings that restricts the use of rigid foam insulation below grade in areas with a high probability of termite infestation. These areas include Florida, Georgia, South Carolina, Alabama, Mississippi, Louisiana, the eastern half of Texas, and California. In response to this problem, some manufacturers of EPS rigid insulation have added a borate treatment that effectively repels these insects from nesting in the insulation. However, insects can still circumvent the foam board and enter the structure through a seam or joint.

Housing and Urban Development (HUD) comparison studies show that, even though the additional insulation increased the construction costs, the savings in excavation and concrete work more than offset the expense. Additional information about frost-protected shallow foundations can be obtained by contacting the National Association of Home Builders Research Center.

NAHB Research Center
400 Prince George's Boulevard
Upper Marlboro, MD 20774
www.nahbrc.org

Weather-Resistant Deck Materials

In the past, most builders of docks, decks, and other exterior wood walkways have used pressure-treated lumber, redwood, or cypress. But, in time, these materials deteriorate from exposure to the weather and insects. In an effort to find longer lasting and better looking substitutes, a variety of safe and durable alternatives have come to the market place. There are basically two groups of alternative products: naturally rot-resistant hardwoods (mostly tropical) and synthetic materials made from recycled plastic.

Weather-Resistant Tropical Hardwoods

Pressure-treated softwoods, namely southern yellow pine, are the most used decking material today. But, in recent years, naturally weather-resistant tropical hardwoods are being used more and more. There are many species available and choosing the "right" one can be perplexing. For example, several species that used to be grouped under the single name "Philippine mahogany" are now separately identified as meranti, cambara, bater, and pelawon. In addition, some of these species, such as meranti, have several subspecies. Meranti is available as dark red meranti, light red meranti, white meranti, and yellow meranti. The situation is further complicated by the addition of trade names. One example is Pau Lope®, which is a trade name for ipe. It is also known as African pencil cedar, juniper, and red juniper.

Before choosing one of these woods, do your homework to increase your chances of making the "right" decision. Using tropical hardwood as a decking material is definitely an expensive alternative to pressure-treated lumber. But, the characteristics that make these woods desirable are their natural resistance to decay, interesting colors, and unique grain patterns, Figure 30-17. Some tropical hardwoods require regular coating with a water-repellent material to prevent color change, checking, or splitting. They do, however, eliminate the health and disposal issues that concern people with respect to pressure-treated lumber.

Environmentalists worry about depleting the tropical forests. However, conscientious and respected growers harvest tropical hardwoods from well-managed forests or on

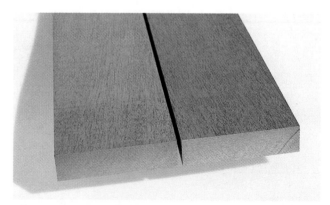

Figure 30-17. Weather-resistant tropical hardwoods, such as this red meranti, can be used as decking material.

plantations. The lumber from these sources are independently certified as "well-managed." Lumber from these sources does not threaten the species or harm the environment.

Synthetic Decking

The environmental, health, and maintenance issues associated with pressure-treated lumber and some domestic and tropical hardwoods has created interest in synthetic decking materials as acceptable substitutes. Residential builders and remodelers are beginning to select decking and accessories made from recycled plastic or wood-plastic composites instead of pressure-treated lumber. These materials simulate real wood. These materials can be worked with common woodworking tools and do not require special framing systems. However, the cost of synthetic decking is high, even if they do resist weather and insects.

Solid plastic decking is UV resistant to reduce fading and is available in several colors. Solid plastic decking is, however, weaker than wood-plastic products. Wood-plastic components can be painted or stained just like real wood or left to weather to gray. Complete decking systems are available from numerous manufacturers made from solid plastic or wood-plastic materials. The next sections discuss a representative sample of some of the products on the market today.

Perma-Poly™

Perma-Poly™, made by Renew Plastic, is a solid plastic deck board made from recycled high-density polyethylene (HDPE). This product is available in the form of 5-1/2" wide deck boards with square or tongue-and-groove edges. Thicknesses of 3/4", 1", and 1-1/2" in lengths up to 16' are available. This material can be cut, routed, and installed with conventional fasteners.

Dream® Deck

Dream® Deck is the product name for plastic deck boards made by Thermal Industries, Inc. The boards are 100% PVC and hollow in cross section. They are held in place by metal rails that are attached to the framing below. The boards are UV resistant and available in white, earth tone, and gray colors. Railing parts and post covers are also available to match the deck boards. See Figure 30-18.

Trex®

Trex® is a well-known wood-plastic composite made with waste wood fiber and recycled polyethylene, Figure 30-19. It is impervious to moisture, resistant to insects and chemicals, and dimensionally stable. Trex® is available in several colors. Some fading is evident if left unfinished. This product is available in one size: 5/4" × 6" decking boards. It can be used for decking boards, railings or trim, but not for posts or structural framing as it is too flexible.

TimberTech®

TimberTech®, a product of Crane Plastics, is a composite made from recycled wood fibers and plastic resin. It is produced as hollow extrusions with tongue-and-groove joints, Figure 30-20. The extrusions are light-weight and fit together with hand pressure. Fasteners are hidden and cover caps are available to cover the exposed ends to achieve a sharp-looking finished product. TimberTech®

Figure 30-18. In the installation of Dream® Deck boards, metal rails attach the decking boards to the supporting frame. (Thermal Industries, Inc.)

Figure 30-19. Trex® deck boards are made of waste wood fiber and recycled polyethylene. (Trex Co.)

Figure 30-20. TimberTech® is a composite decking material made from recycled wood fiber and plastic resin. (TimberTech Limited)

is naturally brown in color, but can be painted or stained with oil-based stains, if desired. If left natural, it will fade to light gray over time.

EON™

EON™ is the product name for a complete thermoplastic decking system made by CPI Plastics Group Ltd. The deck boards are 1-1/2″ × 5-1/2″ and in lengths of 12′, 16′, and 20′. The boards have a wood grain finish in several colors. See Figure 30-21. They can also be painted with latex or acrylic paint. The decking is attached with T-clips and 2-1/2″ screws. Accessories such as railings, posts, post caps, and fascia claddings are also available.

Advantages of weather-resistant deck materials

- More durable than traditional materials.
- Safer than pressure-treated lumber.
- Synthetics will not warp, check, or split.
- Environmentally friendly.

Disadvantages of weather-resistant deck materials

- Cost is much higher than pressure-treated lumber.
- Some products, namely tropical hardwoods, require special installation procedures.
- Confusing array of products.

Additional information

Additional information about weather-resistant deck materials can be obtained from the manufacturers. Contact them at:

TimberTech Limited
894 Prairie Road
Wilmington, OH 45177
www.timbertech.com

Trex Company (Trex®)
160 Exeter Drive
Winchester, VA 22603
www.trex.com

Renew Plastics (Perma-Poly™)
PO Box 480
Luxemburg, WI 54217
www.renewplastics.com

Figure 30-21. EON™ is a thermoplastic decking system. The deck boards are 1-1/2″ × 5-1/2″. (CPI Plastics Group Ltd.)

Thermal Industries, Inc. (Dream® Deck)
301 Bruston Avenue
Pittsburgh, PA 15221
www.thermalindustries.com

CPI Plastics Group Ltd. (EON™)
979 Gana Court
Mississauga, Ontario
L5S 1N9
Canada
www.eonoutdoor.com

The Hebel Wall System

The Hebel wall system is composed of aerated concrete blocks that are produced in an autoclave. An *autoclave* is a device that can treat a product in a vessel under high temperature and pressure. The ingredients in the product include cement, lime, quartz sand, water, and an expansion agent. The agent causes the mixture to rise like bread dough forming tiny individual air cells in the concrete while the mixture is being heated under pressure in the autoclave. The product is about 70% to 80% air, thus making it one-fifth of the weight of ordinary concrete. It is considered to be an ultra-lightweight concrete. See Figure 30-22.

Hebel blocks are 8″ × 8″ × 24″ and weigh from 30 to 34 pounds each. They are solid and precisely cut to fit together with thin-bed mortar. Hebel walls are inorganic, which makes them resistant to insects, rot, corrosion, and rust. The solid blocks produce a quiet interior and are fire resistant. The UL fire rating is eight hours compared to about one hour for frame wall construction. Another advantage of the Hebel wall system is the high insulation value of the blocks, making it an excellent choice for home construction. Without any additional insulation, a Hebel wall usually exceeds the R-factor of traditional construction, thus reducing heating and cooling costs. Additional information can be obtained from:
Babb International
Hebel PAAC Division
6600 Highlands Parkway
Smyrna, GA 30082
www.hebel.com

Figure 30-22. This is a sample of Hebel's autoclaved concrete product.

Internet Resources

www.buildingsystems.org
Building Systems Councils of National Association of Home Builders

www.dryvit.com
Dryvit Systems, Inc.

www.forms.org
Insulating Concrete Form Association

www.eonoutdoor.com
CPI Plastics Group Ltd.

www.hebel.com
Hebel Building Systems

www.liteform.com
Lite-Form Incorporated

www.nahbrc.org
NAHB Research Center

www.ncma.org
National Concrete Masonry Association

www.oikos.com/keeva
Keeva International, Inc.

www.plastifab.com
Plasti-Fab, a Division of PFB Corporation, manufacturer of Enermizer

www.precast.org
National Precast Concrete Association

www.reddi-form.com
Reddi-Form, Inc., a manufacturer of insulating concrete forms

www.renewplastics.com
Renew Plastics

www.smartblock.com
American ConForm Industries

www.thermalindustries.com
Thermal Industries, Inc.

www.thermomass.com
Composite Technologies Corporation

www.timbertech.com
TimberTech Limited

www.trex.com
Trex Company

Review Questions – Chapter 30

Write your answers on a separate sheet of paper. Do not write in this book.

1. What is another name for exterior insulation finish systems (EIFS)?

2. Name three advantages of EIFS over traditional stucco.

3. Describe the construction of a structural foam sandwich panel.

4. Which of the following is an area of concern about structural foam sandwich panels?
   a) Durability over time.
   b) Performance during a fire.
   c) Insect infestation.
   d) Reduced life of asphalt shingles over sandwich panels.
   e) All of the above are concerns.

5. What are the typical wall thicknesses of structural foam sandwich panels?

6. What is the driving force behind the development of new concrete wall systems?

7. What is the approximate R-value of an insulated concrete wall system?

8. What is the standard size of a welded-wire sandwich panel?

9. What is the most common approach to producing an insulated block?

10. Where is the rigid foam insulation placed in a frost-protected shallow foundation?

11. Name two categories of alternatives to pressure-treated deck material.

12. What size are Hebel blocks? How much do they weigh?

Suggested Activities

1. Select one of the new materials discussed in this chapter. Collect literature about it and prepare a presentation for your class.

2. Invite a local builder to class to discuss the use of new materials and methods in residential construction.

3. Collect examples of the new products presented in this chapter (where possible) and display them for examination by the class.

4. Contact your local building department to determine which of the new materials described in this chapter are approved for use in your area.

5. Do an Internet search of the materials covered in this chapter to locate material symbols/hatch patterns from the suppliers. Be sure to locate material marked "freely distribute." With permission from your instructor, download the hatch patterns and add them to your symbol library.

Modular Applications

Objectives
After studying this chapter, you will be able to:

➤ List the advantages of modular applications in the construction industry.

➤ Apply modular concepts to the design of a simple residence.

➤ Describe panelized construction.

➤ Explain industrialized housing.

Key Terms

Industrialized Housing
Major Module
Minor Module

Modular Components
Standard Module
Stick-Built

Traditionally, residential structures have been built by fastening together thousands of small pieces, such as boards, bricks, etc., on the job site. This type of construction is generally known as *stick-built.* It requires a great deal of time and labor and is costly. In recent years, much experimentation has been underway in an effort to speed up the process of building a house and reduce the cost. Experiments have involved precut lumber, factory-built wall assemblies, modular components, and industrialized housing. Each of these has helped to further the technology of efficient home construction, but a big payoff is still to be realized. Industries are just beginning to be truly successful in applying mass production techniques to house construction. Also, home designers are now using more modular sizes in their plans.

In the past, people associated factory-built houses with cheap, poorly designed and constructed "boxes." However, this is no longer an accurate picture. The modular concept can be applied to any style or house design, Figure 31-1.

Standardization

Successful application of the modular concept to on-site construction or factory-built homes requires standardization. Manufacturers are moving toward standard-size building materials that lend themselves to modular construction. Some of the common material sizes that are considered modular include:

A

B

Figure 31-1. A—This beautiful home is a factory-built, modular construction house. (Photo courtesy of Lindal Cedar Homes, Inc., Seattle, Washington) B—This striking chalet-style home was constructed using factory-precut components. (Photo courtesy of Lindal Cedar Homes, Inc., Seattle, Washington)

4″ × 8″	16″ × 96″
4″ × 12″	48″ × 32″
8″ × 16″	48″ × 48″
16″ × 16″	48″ × 96″
16″ × 32″	48″ × 120″
16″ × 48″	48″ × 144″

Plywood sheets, interior paneling, floor tiles, etc., are all designed to be integrated into modular systems. Other materials will most likely join the ranks in the future.

The modular concept plans for length, width, and height using the *standard module*, which is a 4″ cube. These standard modules are combined to produce larger units or modules. For example, the *major module* is a 4′-0″ cube or 12 standard modules on each side. Cubes that are 16″ or 24″ are *minor modules*, Figure 31-2. It is evident, then, that a modular length must be a multiple of 4″. Minor modules of 16″ and 24″ are important because studs and joists are spaced those distances.

Modular panel components are usually produced in widths ranging from 16″ to 196″ in multiples of 16″, Figure 31-3. These panels

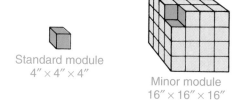

Standard module
4″ × 4″ × 4″

Minor module
16″ × 16″ × 16″

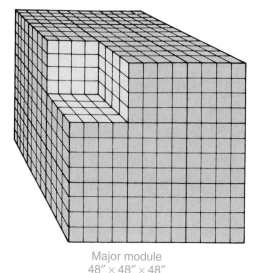

Major module
48″ × 48″ × 48″

Figure 31-2. All modules have side lengths that are multiples of 4″ and each module is a cube.

are then fastened together to form a wall. In the modular system, exterior walls are generally multiples of 4'-0", if feasible. This saves materials and reduces cutting time. Windows are located in the panels with their tops at a constant height.

A structure that incorporates modular principles must be designed with definite modules in mind. Lengths, widths, and heights must be planned to coincide with modular-size materials with specifications given for materials to be used. The drafter should use a modular grid as a guide in designing and dimensioning the structure. A typical modular grid for use in manual drafting is shown in Figure 31-4. A CADD drafter should set up a display grid that follows the modular dimensions. A few simple rules have been devised for modular planning and dimensioning:

- Lengths must be multiples of 4".

- House corners and other details of the structure should begin and terminate on grid lines, Figure 31-5.

- Grid dimensions are shown on the plan.

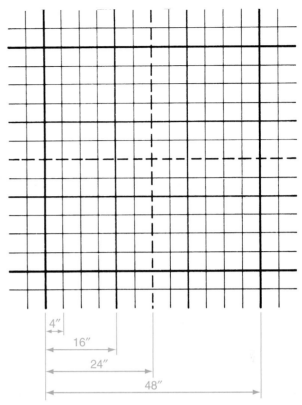

Figure 31-4. A typical modular grid for use in manual drafting. Three different weight lines represent 4", 16", and 48" modules.

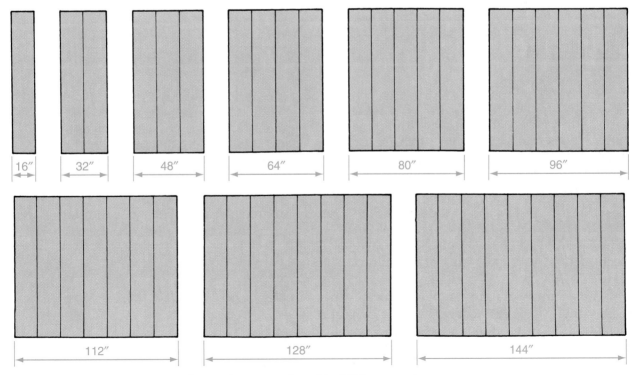

Figure 31-3. Modular factory-built panels are produced in 16" increments.

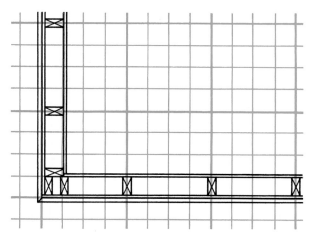

Figure 31-5. House corners and other details should coordinate with the grid lines. Grid lines are shown on the plan.

- Floor levels are located on grid lines. The top of the subfloor and top of a finished concrete slab are located on the grid line, Figure 31-6.

- Dimensions that end on a grid line have an arrowhead terminator. Dimensions that end off the grid have a dot terminator, Figure 31-7.

- Partitions are usually centered on grid lines, Figure 31-8. However, modular-length interior walls are not nearly as important as outside walls.

Modular Components

Modular components are building parts that have been preassembled either in a plant or on-site. These assemblies include floor panels, roof panels, wall sections, or roof trusses, Figure 31-9. They may be constructed from wood, concrete, plywood, plastics, fiberglass, steel, aluminum, paper, or most any other building material. Panels may also be made from layers of different materials, Figure 31-10.

There are several advantages to prefabricated panels (panelized construction). Some of these are design freedom and aesthetic appeal, high strength-to-weight ratios, uniform quality, more efficient use of materials, lower cost, and reduced time required for installation. Several

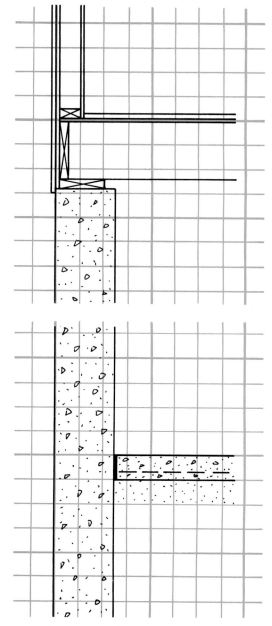

Figure 31-6. The top of a subfloor or slab floor should coincide with a grid line.

companies are producing modular components in this growing field.

Industrialized Housing

The term *industrialized housing* refers to houses built in a factory. Many types of houses

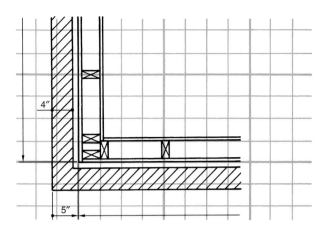

Figure 31-7. When dimensioning a modular drawing, a dimension that terminates on a grid line is shown with an arrow. Dimensions that terminate off a grid line are shown with a dot.

Figure 31-10. A thick core of rigid expanded polystyrene insulation is adhesively welded between two faces to form a single structure that resists twisting, warping, and racking. (Associated Foam Manufacturers, Inc.)

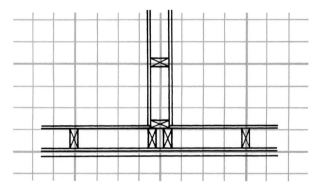

Figure 31-8. Partitions are usually centered on a grid line.

are being built in plants today, all of which are composed of modules, Figure 31-11. Modules range in size from 12′ × 20′ to 14′ × 40′ and larger. A width of 14′ seems to be ideal because it is large enough for a fair size room and 14′ is the maximum width that most states will allow on the highway. The larger modules are generally built on a production line much the same as an automobile, Figure 31-12.

Figure 31-9. The frame of this home will be covered with factory-built, insulated, modular panels, which are stacked in the foreground. (Northern Energy Homes)

Figure 31-11. This luxury home is a factory-built, ranch-style house erected on a regular foundation. (Manufactured Housing Institute)

Figure 31-12. These wall panels under construction on a production line will be used in a manufactured home. (Manufactured Housing Institute)

Some facilities are so advanced that computer-directed systems are being used. The computer calculates placement of studs for each wall panel and automatic nailers fasten the materials together. The trend toward more automatic equipment will continue as factory-built houses receive public acceptance and production increases. Figure 31-13 shows some of the operations involved in producing a factory-built home.

The quality of many factory-built homes is better than traditional construction. Jigs and fixtures are used to cut and fit parts, thus accuracy is improved. Better-quality lumber is usually used because a warped board will not fit the jig properly.

Factory-built house modules are more than just a shell. Most have the plumbing,

A

B

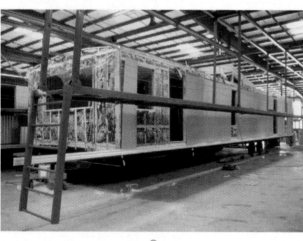

C

D

Figure 31-13. Producing a factory-built home. A—The roof is being assembled. B—The frame is being welded. Each home is built on a heavy steel frame for easy handling and transportation. C—The exterior walls are assembled on the frame. D—Vinyl siding is applied to finish the home. (Manufactured Housing Institute)

wiring, finished floors, and doors installed. They can be shipped to the site and lifted into place by a large crane on one day and the homeowners can move in within the next few days, Figure 31-14. Most are set on a regular foundation and ready to be connected to the water, sewer, gas, and electricity as soon as they are located.

The versatility of these modules is evidenced by the fact that they may be set side-by-side, end-to-end, directly on top of each other, or cantilevered to form interesting and functional shapes.

Modules within modules are also popular, Figure 31-15. For example, a kitchen module that is complete with cabinets, range, refrigerator, and floor covering may be "plugged into" a larger, half-house-size module. Bathroom modules can also be produced in the same manner. As the selection becomes greater, one will be able to select separate kitchen, bath, and living room modules to make up the total house. A house may then be ordered just as you can a new car.

Factory-built houses of the future will not necessarily look like they do today. As materials new to the housing industry are used for various house components and new processes are developed, more complex shapes

Figure 31-15. This living room module is nearing completion and will have the electrical wiring, plumbing for the gas fireplace, and built-in units installed when it leaves the factory. (Manufactured Housing Institute)

and rounded corners will be commonplace, Figure 31-16. The factory-built house of tomorrow should be more functional and afford a wider variety of configurations to choose from. If predictions are realized, the relative cost of housing will decline as factories move into full swing of home production.

Figure 31-14. This modular house section is being set into place beside another section. Once these sections are connected, the house will be ready for occupancy. (Manufactured Housing Institute)

Figure 31-16. The final shape of this factory-built home will not be a "box" like so many earlier modular homes. More design options will be available in the future. (Manufactured Housing Institute)

Internet Resources

www.avisamerica.com
Avis America, a manufacturer of modular homes

www.cardinalhomes.com
Cardinal Homes, Inc., a manufacturer of modular homes

www.custruct.com
Customized Structures, Inc., a manufacturer of modular homes

www.deltechomes.com
Deltec Homes, a supplier of modular construction components

www.insulspan.com
Insulspan, Inc., a manufacturer of insulated structural panels

www.lindal.com
Lindal Cedar Homes, a manufacturer of modular homes

www.logcabinhomes.com
Log Cabin Homes

www.logcabins.com
Jim Barna Log Systems

www.northamericanhousing.com
North American Housing Corporation, a manufacturer of modular homes

www.wausauhomes.com
Wausau Homes, a manufacturer of modular homes

Review Questions–Chapter 31

Write your answers on a separate sheet of paper. Do not write in this book.

1. Name four techniques that have been tried in an effort to reduce the cost and time required to build a residential structure.

2. In designing a structure that incorporates modular principles, the lengths, widths, and heights must be planned to coincide with _____ materials.

3. Building parts that have been preassembled in a plant are called _____.

4. Identify four advantages of using prefabricated panels.

5. Identify the standard size of:
   a) Standard Module.
   b) Major Module.
   c) Minor Module.

6. All modules should be a multiple of _____ inches.

7. Modular panels are usually produced in multiples of _____ inches.

8. When drawing a modular plan, dimensions terminating on a grid line are represented with a(n) _____ terminator while dimensions terminating off a grid line terminate with a(n) _____.

9. With respect to a frame floor, the grid line is located _____.

10. The term industrialized housing refers to _____.

11. List two reasons why a 14'-0" width appears ideal for industrialized housing modules.

12. List two reasons why the quality of industrialized housing is likely to be better than a stick-built home.

Suggested Activities

1. Choose a nonmodular floor plan and redesign it following the principles of modular construction. Dimension the plan and present both drawings for a comparison.

2. Invite a local builder to class to discuss methods that may be used in the design process to conserve materials when building a house.

3. Using CADD, design a residence that follows the principles of modular construction and makes use of standard roof and wall panels. Information about these panels may be secured from The Engineered Wood Association, National Lumber Manufacturing Association, Weyerhaeuser Company, and others.

4. Using CADD, design a two-car garage that makes use of formed roof modules. The modules may be plywood, curved or flat stressed skin panels, or precast concrete modules. Use your imagination and try for a unique, but functional, design. Be sure to follow modular design principles.

5. Design a modular unit boat dock that may be expanded by simply adding more modules. Choose your own materials.

Section IX
Presentation Methods

32 Perspective Drawings

33 Presentation Drawings

34 Architectural Models

Sater Design Collections, Inc.

Perspective Drawings
32

Objectives

After studying this chapter, you will be able to:

➤ Explain the purpose of a perspective drawing.

➤ Explain the difference between one-, two-, and three-point perspectives.

➤ Prepare a one- or two-point perspective drawing using the office method.

➤ Explain how changing the viewing position, angle, and height alters the perspective.

➤ Describe how to create a perspective using CADD.

Key Terms

Common Method
Cone of Vision
Ground Line
Horizon Line
Office Method

Perspective
Picture Plane
Station Point
True Length Line
Vanishing Points

A type of pictorial drawing commonly used for communication purposes is the *perspective.* This type of drawing provides a realistic image of the object, Figure 32-1. Objects appear smaller when they are farther away from the viewer. A perspective drawing applies this and other principles to achieve an accurate representation of the object. The result gives a three-dimensional representation showing more than one side of the object.

Two other types of pictorial drawings are also used as presentation (communication) drawings. These are isometric and oblique drawings. Figure 32-2 shows isometric, oblique, and perspective drawings of the same object to illustrate the difference between the three methods. Isometric and oblique drawings do not show a building as realistically as a perspective. However, both are useful for some types of presentations and are generally much easier to draw than a perspective.

Drawing perspectives using traditional construction methods is very time-consuming. However, CADD programs that have 3D capabilities can create perspectives in seconds, once the model is complete. As 3D models are constructed, the computer stores X, Y, and Z coordinate data for each object. This allows the model to be viewed at any angle, from which perspective drawings can be generated. Figure 32-3 shows a very realistic, CADD-generated, two-point perspective of a house with landscaping. This perspective closely approaches the accuracy that could be gained by taking a photograph of the real object.

Figure 32-1. This is a perspective that has been hand-rendered. It is a true representation of the actual home. (Sater Design Collection, Inc.)

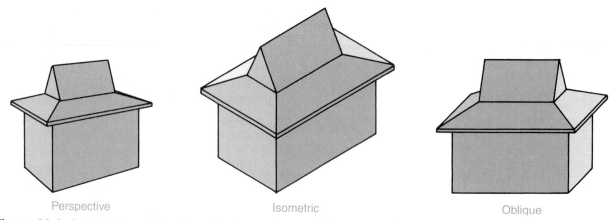

Perspective   Isometric   Oblique

Figure 32-2. Any of these pictorial methods may be used for presentation drawings. However, a perspective is the most realistic representation.

Figure 32-3. This rendered perspective was produced with CADD software designed for architectural drafting. (Helmuth A. Geiser, member AIBD)

Perspectives

There are three basic types of perspectives. See Figure 32-4.
- One-point or parallel perspective.
- Two-point or angular perspective.
- Three-point or oblique perspective.

One- and two-point perspectives are commonly used for residential structures. Three-point perspectives are generally used for tall, commercial buildings. Therefore, they are of little interest to the residential architect.

A perspective drawing differs from an orthographic drawing in the position of the station point. The station point is the location of the observer's eye and is explained later. In orthographic projection, the station point is infinitely far away from the picture plane. Therefore, all visual rays or projection lines are parallel to one another. In a perspective, however, the station point is a measurable distance from the object or picture plane,

Figure 32-5. Therefore, the object lines converge at a vanishing point. The picture plane and vanishing points are explained later.

Terminology

There are three parts or areas to a layout used to create a perspective. These are the elevation drawing, plan drawing, and perspective drawing. See Figure 32-6. The perspective drawing is the final result. In addition, there are several terms related to perspective drawings. These should be understood before planning and drawing a perspective.

Ground line (GL)

The *ground line* represents the horizontal ground plane, the plane on which the object rests. In the least complex situation, the object to be drawn is positioned so that the foremost corner touches the picture plane that is

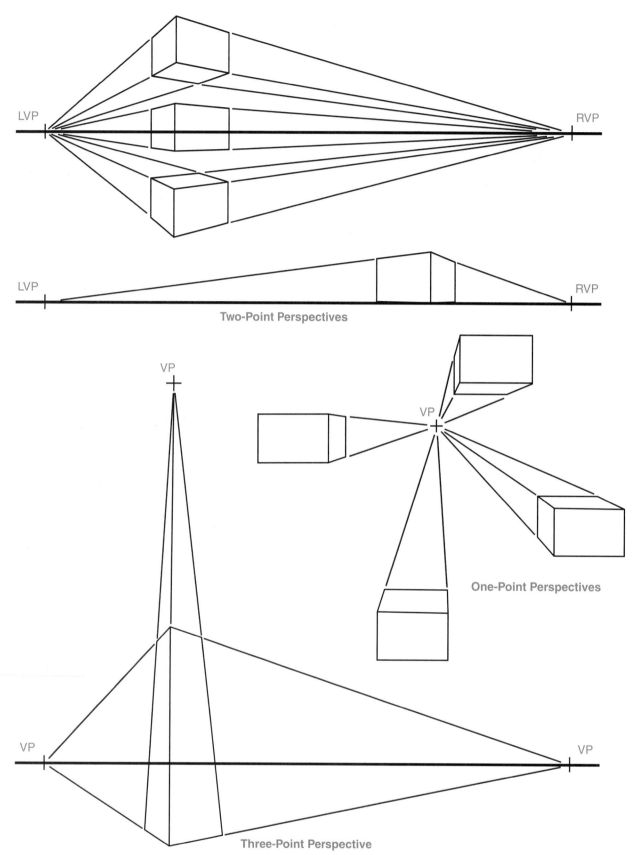

Two-Point Perspectives

One-Point Perspectives

Three-Point Perspective

Figure 32-4. The three basic types of perspectives are named for the number of vanishing points used to create the drawing. Notice how the object lines converge at the vanishing points.

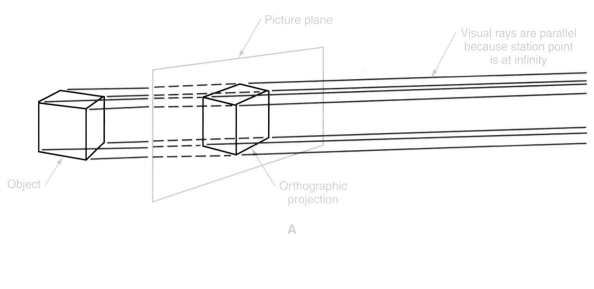

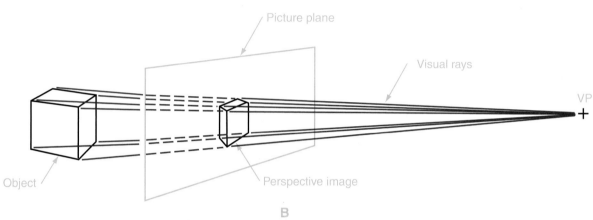

Figure 32-5. A—In an orthographic projection drawing, the station point is infinitely far from the drawing plane. B—In a perspective drawing, the station point is a measurable distance from the drawing plane.

perpendicular to the ground plane. The ground line is drawn in the elevation part of the perspective layout. When the object touches the picture plane in the plan view, it must also touch the ground line in the perspective drawing. If the object is placed behind the picture plane, then the object will appear to be above the ground line. Objects that pass through the picture plane will extend below the ground line.

Horizon line (HL)

The *horizon line* represents the place where the ground and sky meet. It is, therefore, drawn in the elevation part of the layout. The distance between the ground line and horizon line represents the height of the observer's eye above the ground. This may be

measured at the same scale as the plan view and elevation.

Picture plane (PP)

In all types of drawing, objects are shown as they would appear on an imaginary, transparent *picture plane*. The picture plane may be in front of, behind, or pass through the object. It is a vertical plane and, therefore, perpendicular to the ground plane. It is represented as a line, called the picture plane line, on the plan part of the layout and normally located between the object and the station point (observer's eye).

Any portion of the object that touches the picture plane is true size in the perspective drawing. Any portion of the object that is behind the picture plane appears smaller than

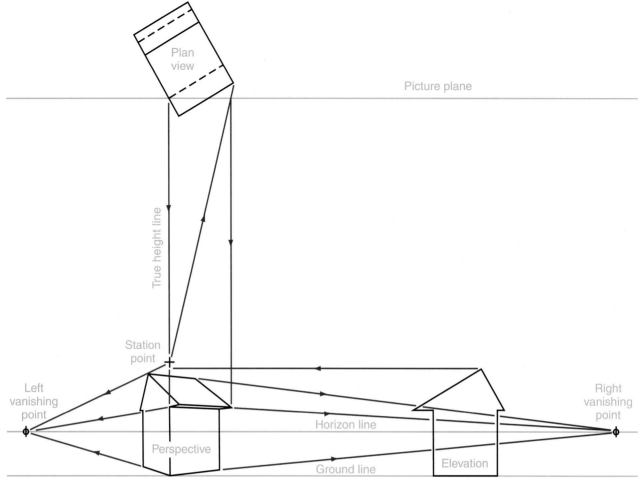

Figure 32-6. A typical two-point perspective with the components identified.

scale on the perspective drawing. Parts of the object that are in front of the picture plane (between the plane and the station point) appear larger than scale in the perspective drawing.

Station point (SP)

The *station point* is the location of the observer's eye and, therefore, the beginning point of the visual rays or sight lines. The rays radiate out from the station point to the object that is represented in the plan view. They pass through the picture plane and locate the various points of the object on the picture plane.

In a two-point perspective, the station point is located only in the plan view. In a one-point perspective it is located in the elevation view as well. In both instances, the distance that the station point is positioned from the

picture plane may be measured using the same scale as the plan and elevation drawings.

True length line (TL)

A *true length line,* or true height line as it is frequently called, is established where the object touches the picture plane. This true length line is used to project heights to the perspective drawing. It is always necessary to find at least one true length line in the perspective drawing so that height measurements may be made. If the object does not touch the picture plane, then a side may be extended until it touches the picture plane, thus establishing a true length corner.

Vanishing points

Vanishing points are the points at which all lines on the object will converge if extended. One-, two-, or three-point perspectives are named for the number of vanishing points used to create the drawing. Vanishing points are always located on the horizon line in one- and two-point perspectives. The sides of the object recede toward the vanishing points. The sides also become smaller as they approach the point.

A two-point perspective has a right vanishing point (RVP) and left vanishing point (LVP). The procedure for locating these is discussed later in this chapter. The one-point perspective has one vanishing point and it need not be formally identified, using popular construction techniques, unless desired.

Two-Point Perspectives

An architectural drafter should be able to draw objects so that they appear similar to the way they do in real life. Two-point perspectives are especially appropriate for exterior views. They produce a photo-like result that is quite accurate in detail, Figure 32-7. This provides an effective way to communicate with prospective clients and other interested parties.

Before beginning to draw a perspective, you should be aware that several relationships affect the final perspective drawing. These relationships must be understood and controlled if the resulting drawing is to be satisfactory.

- **The distance the station point is from the picture plane.** Figure 32-8 shows how the perspective on the picture plane increases in size as the station point is moved farther away from the picture plane. Proper location of the station point is critical to the final perspective. If it is too close, the drawing will be distorted and unrealistic.

The *cone of vision* is the angle between opposite sides of the object with its vertex at the station point. In most instances, position the station point so that it forms a cone of vision of between 30° and 45°. To locate the station point with a proper cone of vision, draw a vertical line down from the corner of the object that touches the picture plane. Then, place a 30° or 45° triangle over the line

Figure 32-7. This two-point perspective was carefully crafted to show the proposed residence in the best light. The result is strikingly realistic. (Helmuth A. Geiser, member AIBD)

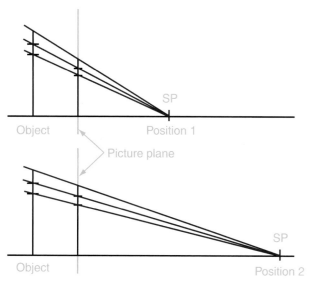

Figure 32-8. The image on the picture plane is larger when the station point is moved from Position 1 to Position 2, which is farther away.

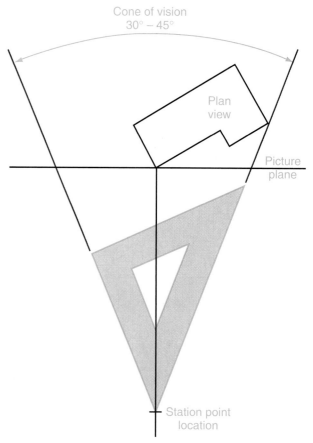

Figure 32-9. Using a triangle to locate the station point at the minimum distance from the picture plane. The entire object must be within the cone of vision.

so that half of the angle falls on either side of the line. In CADD, two intersecting lines that form a 30° or 45° angle can be used in place of the triangle. Next, move the triangle or intersecting lines along the vertical line. When the entire object is within the cone of vision represented by the triangle, the minimum distance has been established for the station point. Figure 32-9 illustrates the procedure.

Moving the station point in relation to the picture plane also affects the position of the vanishing points. As the station point moves closer to the picture plane, the vanishing points come closer together. As the station point moves away, the vanishing points move farther apart.

The station point may also be moved from side to side to improve the viewing position. However, it should not be moved too far either way because distortion will result. The same effect may be accomplished by changing the angle of the plan view with respect to the picture plane, rather than moving the station point.

- **The position of the object with respect to the picture plane.** Two factors are at work in this relationship. First, the angle that the object forms with the picture plane will affect which portions of the object are emphasized

in the final drawing, Figure 32-10. The most common position is with an angle of 30° on one side and 60° on the other. This may be varied to suit the particular object.

The second factor relating to the position of the object with respect to the picture plane is whether the object is behind, in front of, or passing through the picture plane, Figure 32-11. When the object is behind the picture plane, it appears smaller than one in front of the picture plane. Therefore, size is dependent on this placement. Also, if the station point is not sufficiently far away when the object is in front of the picture plane, distortion is greatly increased and will likely spoil the drawing.

- **The vertical height of the station point or horizon line.** The appearance of the final perspective will vary greatly depending on the height of the station point. In a two-point

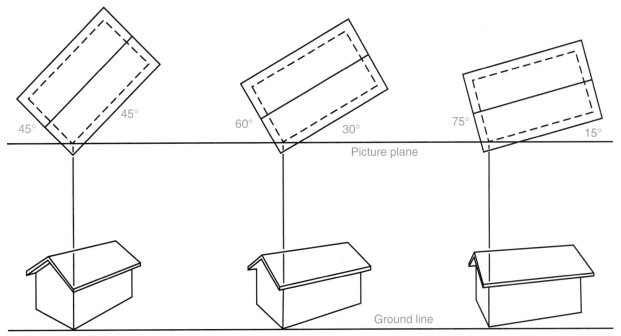

Figure 32-10. The angle that the object makes with the picture plane may be varied to place emphasis on a certain part of the object.

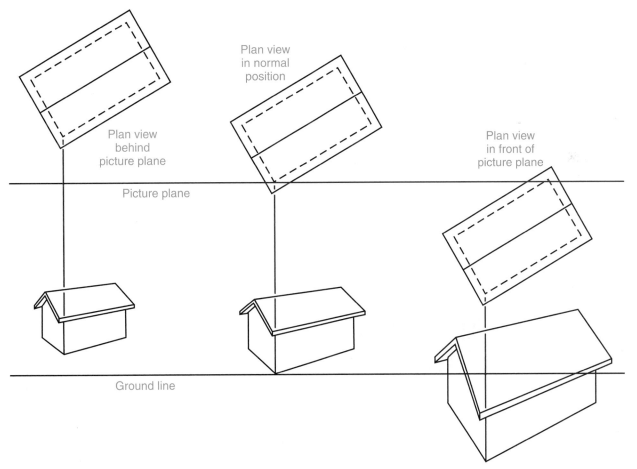

Figure 32-11. As an object is moved from behind to in front of the picture plane, it increases in size. Also, notice the distortion in the right-hand perspective.

perspective, this height is the distance from the ground line to the horizon line. The horizon line may be located well above the ground line (20′ to 30′), a conventional height of 5′ or 6′, on the ground line, or below the ground line, Figure 32-12. Names have been attached to some of these relative positions such as "bird's eye view" and "worm's eye view." The proper height will depend on the particular object and which features are to be emphasized. In residential perspectives, the station point is commonly located at ground level, a person's height, or about 30′ high.

These relationships must be kept in mind when laying out a perspective. In starting out, only one factor should be varied at a time to see the effect on the final outcome. If several things are changed at once, the effect of a single factor may never be known.

Two-Point Perspective Drawing Sequence

Several methods for drawing two-point perspectives are in use, but the method most frequently used is the *common method* or *office method.* The following procedure is used for drawing this type of two-point perspective.

1. Draw the plan view or roof plan of the object on a sheet of drawing paper. Draw an elevation view on a separate sheet of paper. Both need to be the same scale. See Figure 32-13. In CADD, you may want to draw each of these as blocks to be inserted later.

2. Secure a large sheet of paper to the drawing table. In CADD, you may need to set the drawing limits or extents to an appropriately large size and/or select a large paper size. Draw the picture plane line near the top of the sheet, the ground line near the bottom of the sheet, and the horizon line the desired distance above the ground line. These lines must be parallel, Figure 32-14.

3. Place the plan view or roof plan at a 30° angle with the picture plane so that the front corner touches the picture plane, Figure 32-15. Locate the elevation on the ground line to the extreme right or left side of the paper.

4. Draw a vertical line down from the point where the object touches the picture plane. Locate the station point using the cone of vision procedure described earlier, Figure 32-16.

5. Determine the location of the right and left vanishing points by drawing two construction lines from the station point to the

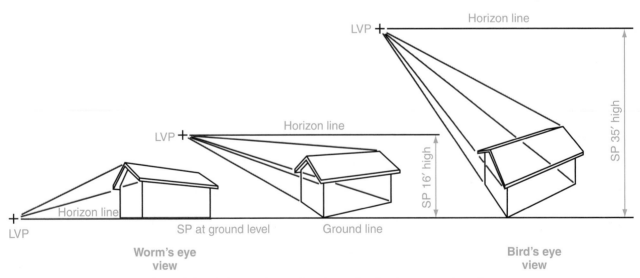

Figure 32-12. Changing the height of the station point alters the final perspective view.

Plan view

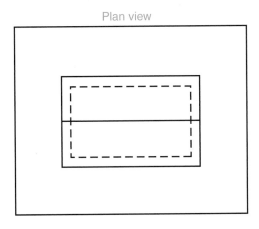

Elevation

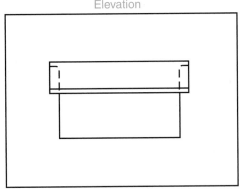

Figure 32-13. Procedure for drawing a two-point perspective—Step 1.

picture plane line. These construction lines must be parallel to the sides of the object in the plan view. See Figure 32-17. Draw a vertical line from the point where each of these lines intersects the picture plane down to the horizon line. This is the location of the right and left vanishing points.

6. Draw a true height (true length) line from the corner of the object that touches the picture plane down to the ground line. Project the object height of that corner from the elevation view to the TL line. The distance from the ground line to this point is the true height and the location of the object corner in the perspective drawing, Figure 32-18.

7. Determine the location of the other corners of the object by drawing sight lines from the station point to each corner in the plan view. The point where the sight line crosses the picture plane is projected down to the perspective. Each corner of the object will be on one of these lines, Figure 32-19.

8. The length and vertical location of these corners may be found by projecting the vertical true length from the true height corner to the vanishing points, Figure 32-20. Sides of the object that extend away to the right are projected to the right vanishing point; sides that extend to the left are projected to the left vanishing point. Inclined or oblique lines cannot be projected to either vanishing point. Their end points must be located and simply connected.

9. The back two sides of the object may be completed by projecting the corners to the vanishing points. The location where the projection lines cross is the fourth corner. Check the accuracy of your work by drawing a vertical line down from the point where the sight line for the remaining corner crosses the picture plane. It should pass through the point where the two projection lines cross, Figure 32-21. This corner will not be visible in the finished drawing.

10. To draw the ridge of the object, first extend the ridge line in the plan view until it touches the picture plane. Then, draw a vertical line from the point at which the ridge intersects the picture plane down to the ground line. This establishes a new TL line, Figure 32-22. Project the height of the ridge over to the TL line and project this point to the right vanishing point. The right vanishing point is used because the ridge extends away to the right.

11. Find the length of the ridge in the perspective by extending sight lines from the station point to the ends of the ridge on the plan view. The point where each sight line crosses the picture plane determines the length of the ridge, Figure 32-23. Project a vertical line down from each of these points to the ridge line in the perspective.

12. The roof overhang height may be determined by drawing a new TL line down from the point where the overhang crosses the picture plane in the plan view. Project the fascia board width on the elevation over to this TL line. The top and bottom edge of the fascia passes through these two points. Project these points to the right vanishing point. The length of the

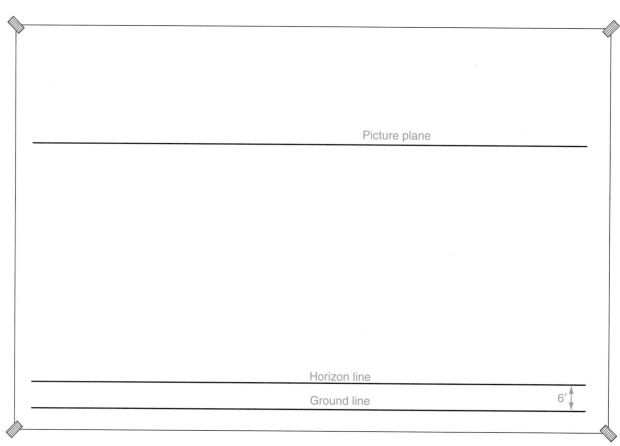

Figure 32-14. Procedure for drawing a two-point perspective—Step 2.

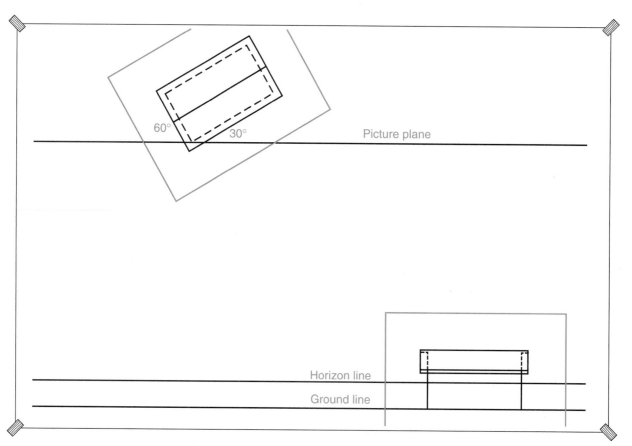

Figure 32-15. Procedure for drawing a two-point perspective—Step 3.

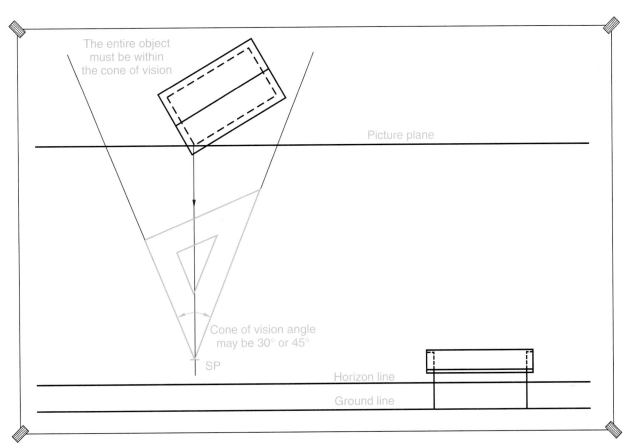

Figure 32-16. Procedure for drawing a two-point perspective—Step 4.

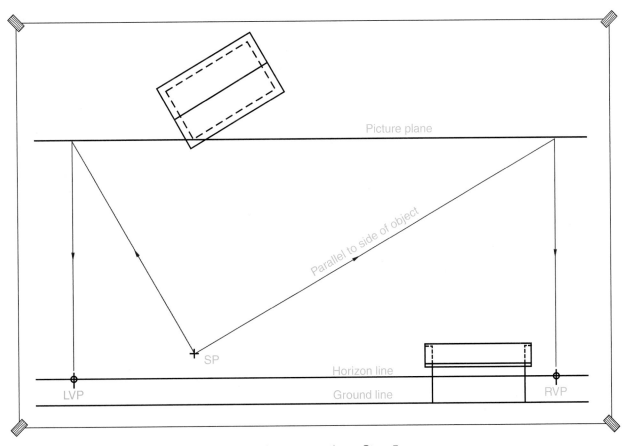

Figure 32-17. Procedure for drawing a two-point perspective—Step 5.

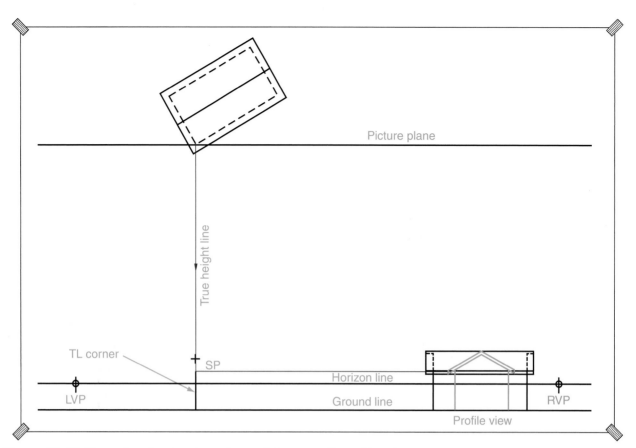

Figure 32-18. Procedure for drawing a two-point perspective—Step 6.

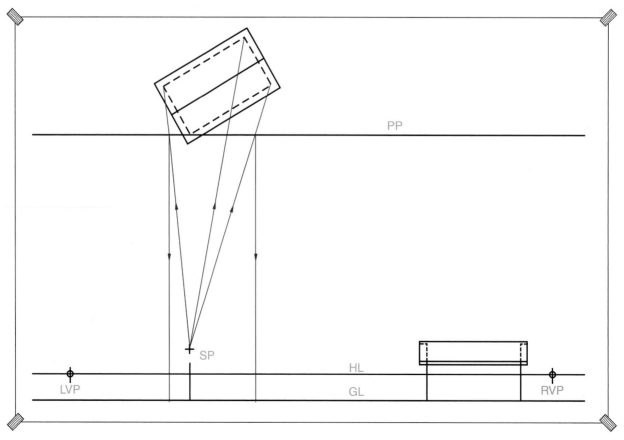

Figure 32-19. Procedure for drawing a two-point perspective—Step 7.

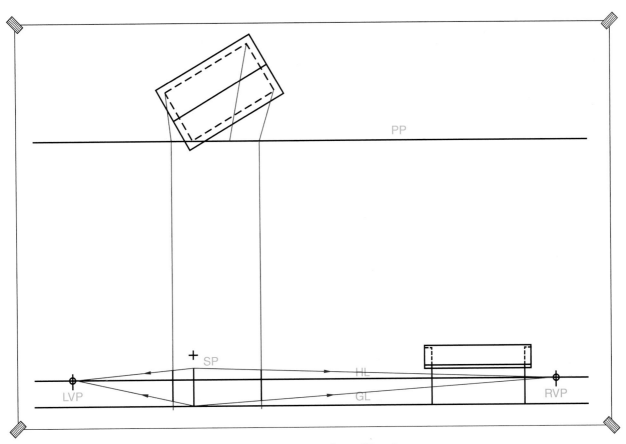

Figure 32-20. Procedure for drawing a two-point perspective—Step 8.

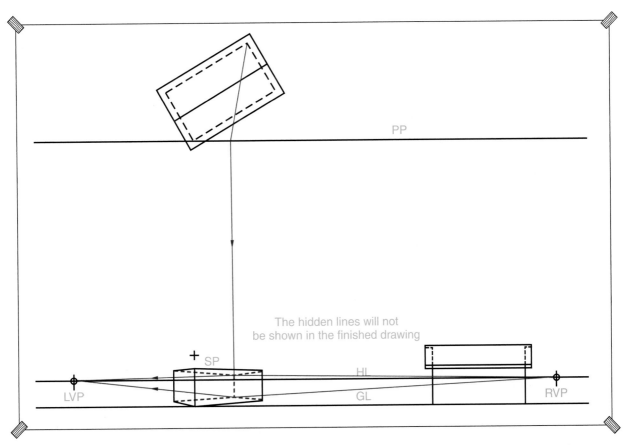

Figure 32-21. Procedure for drawing a two-point perspective—Step 9.

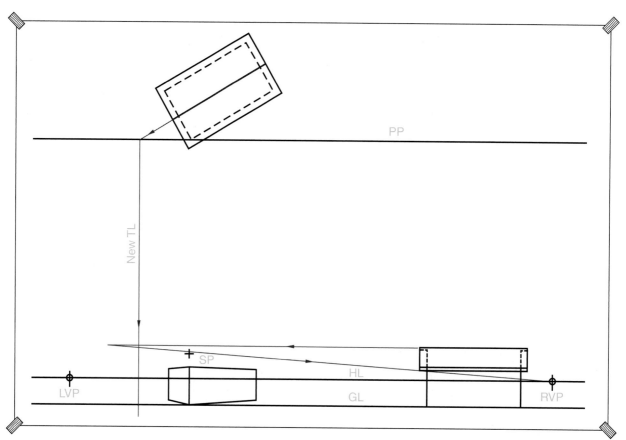

Figure 32-22. Procedure for drawing a two-point perspective—Step 10.

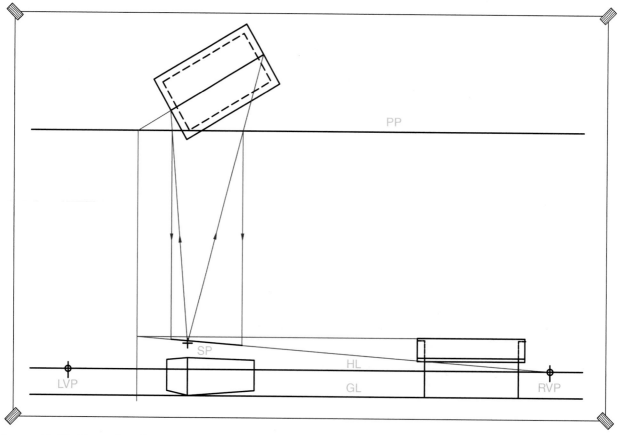

Figure 32-23. Procedure for drawing a two-point perspective—Step 11.

fascia may be determined by extending sight lines from the station point to the corners on the plan view. The points where the sight lines cross the picture plane give the horizontal location for each corner, Figure 32-24.

13. The perspective may be completed by locating the remaining roof corner and connecting the ridge to the three visible corners. The extreme-left-corner height is drawn by projecting the top and bottom of the fascia board at the front corner to the left vanishing point and dropping the sight line location from the plan view. Where they cross is the roof corner. Connect the roof corner to the roof ridge. Draw the gable trim boards as shown in Step 6 of this procedure. The peak point of the gable under the roof may be located by finding the point on the plan view and dropping a line down to the perspective. Connect the top of the left corner to this peak point, Figure 32-25.

Establishing a new TL line is useful in rapidly determining the height of features that are not located on the principal sides of the object. Examples of these features are roof ridges, overhangs, and chimneys.

A perspective of a more complex house is shown in Figure 32-26. Note that the same procedures have been followed in drawing this perspective as the previous example.

One-Point Perspectives

One-point perspectives are not used as frequently as two-point perspectives, but they are well suited for interior drawings. Room and furniture layouts, kitchen cabinet pictorial details, and interior space studies are all candidates for one-point perspective techniques, Figure 32-27. One-point perspectives may also be used in some situations for exterior views, Figure 32-28. Entries, courts, porches, and exterior architectural details

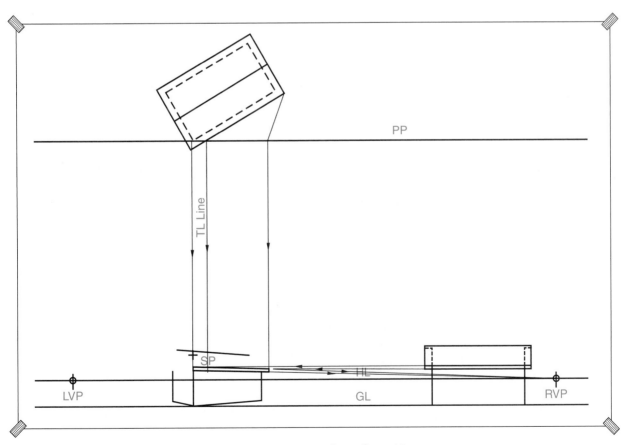

Figure 32-24. Procedure for drawing a two-point perspective—Step 12.

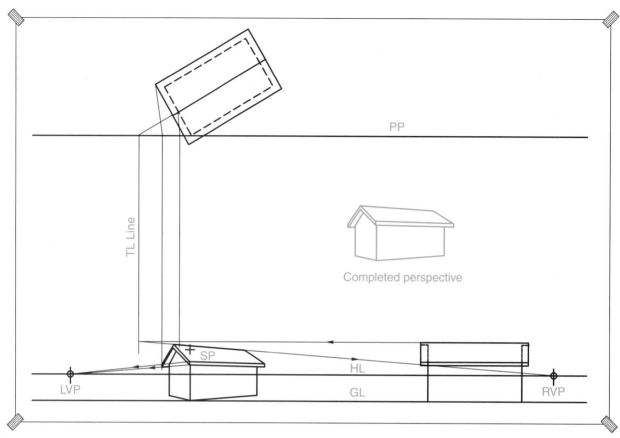

Figure 32-25. Procedure for drawing a two-point perspective—Step 13.

Figure 32-26. A typical two-point perspective of a residence. This drawing was made by following the steps outlined in the text. (Sater Design Collection, Inc.)

may sometimes be best shown in one-point perspective, Figure 32-29.

The procedure for drawing a one-point perspective using the office (common) method is similar in some respects to that for a two-point perspective. However, there are several differences. One of the most important differences is the selection of an elevation from which to project height measurements. Sight lines must be projected from the station point in the elevation to the object to determine the height in the perspective. Any elevation is acceptable for the two-point perspective, but a specific elevation is necessary for the one-point perspective. Another difference in drawing the one-point perspective is that the vanishing point does not have to be located unless desired. However, the main difference is the most frequent position of the plan view. In one-point perspective, the plan view is

usually placed parallel to the picture plane so that the horizontal and profile planes project to the vanishing point.

One-Point Perspective Drawing Sequence

Figure 32-30 shows a typical one-point perspective of a kitchen. This perspective was developed using the following step-by-step drawing sequence. These steps can be used to draw any common one-point perspective.

1. Select a sheet of drawing paper about the size of a large drawing board. In CADD, you may need to set the drawing limits or extents to an appropriately large size and/or select a large paper size. Draw the plan view near the top-left side. Draw the right-side elevation in the same orientation in the lower-right

Figure 32-27. This living room layout is drawn as a one-point (parallel) perspective. (Helmuth A. Geiser, member AIBD)

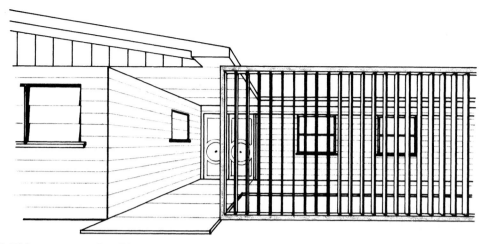

Figure 32-28. This entrance detail is a one-point perspective and captures the major design elements as well, or better, than a two-point perspective could.

Figure 32-29. This is an example of a one-point perspective exterior layout.

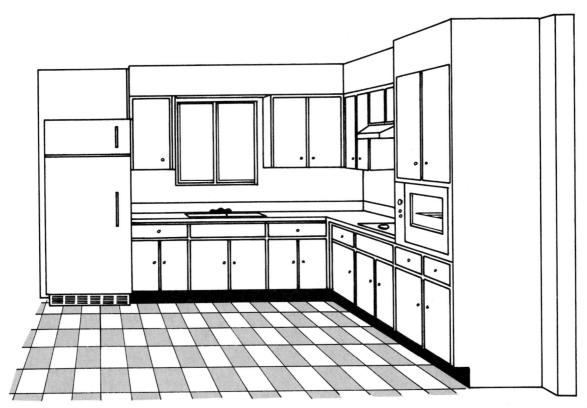

Figure 32-30. This is a one-point perspective of a kitchen that was drawn using the procedure presented in the text. (David Brownlee)

corner. The picture plane should be drawn so that it touches the front of the plan view and the left side of the elevation. Draw the picture plane line in both the plan and elevation views. Study Figure 32-31 carefully to be sure that you understand which elevation is to be drawn. The space between these drawings in the lower-left corner is where the perspective will be drawn.

2. Determine the location from where you wish to view the object. If one side should be emphasized more than the other, the station point should be slightly on the opposite side of the object. Locate the station point in relation to the plan view first. Label it SP^P. The station point in the plan view indicates from how far away and how much to the right or left you are viewing the object. Next, locate the station point in relation to the elevation view. This view shows the height of the viewing position. The height is measured from the ground line or floor line vertically. Label this station point SP^E, Figure 32-32. *The station point must be the same distance from the picture plane in both views.*

3. Any feature that touches the picture plane is true size. You may project these points down from the plan view and across from the elevation. Where the lines cross is the location of each feature, Figure 32-33.

4. Features that are behind the picture plane appear smaller than scale in the perspective. They may be drawn by projecting sight lines from the SP^P to each point of the detail in the plan view. Where a sight line crosses the picture plane is the horizontal location of the feature, Figure 32-34. The vertical location is determined by projecting sight lines from the SP^E to the elevation drawing. Where a sight line crosses the profile view of the picture plane is the height of the feature. Connect the points in the perspective to outline each detail.

5. The floor in this example has a tile floor that forms a grid. The grid may be located by first projecting those points that touch

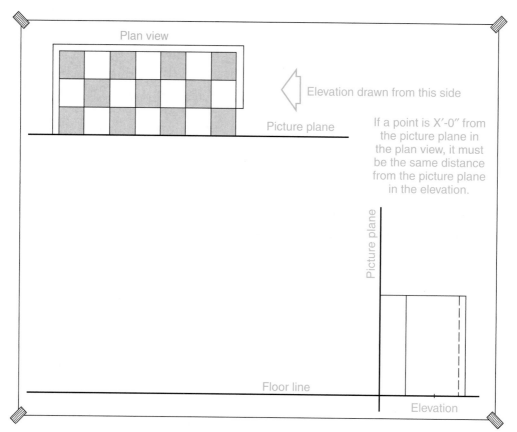

Figure 32-31. Procedure for drawing a one-point perspective—Step 1.

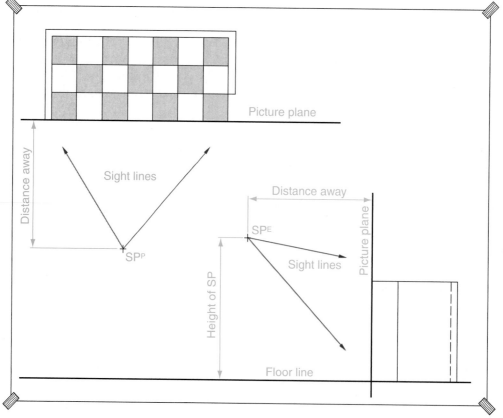

Figure 32-32. Procedure for drawing a one-point perspective—Step 2.

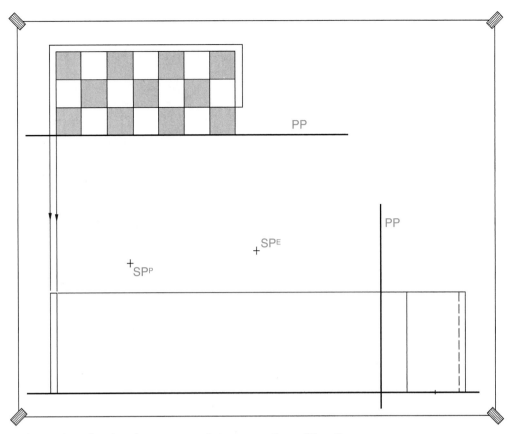

Figure 32-33. Procedure for drawing a one-point perspective—Step 3.

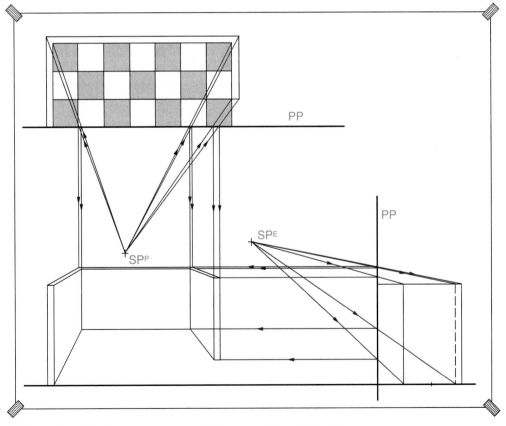

Figure 32-34. Procedure for drawing a one-point perspective—Step 4.

the picture plane in the plan view down to the floor line. The grid line ends that touch the back wall must be located in the perspective by drawing a sight line from the SP^P to each end, Figure 32-35. The place where the sight line crosses the picture plane is the horizontal location of the point. The same procedure is followed in the elevation using SP^E to determine the vertical location of each point. Connect the points to complete the grid.

6. Figure 32-36 shows the completed perspective.

Computer-Generated Perspectives

The procedures outlined earlier for drawing one- and two-point perspectives can be used with any CADD software to create perspectives. However, the final result is a 2D drawing, just as it would be if the perspective is drawn by hand. Many CADD programs today have the capability of drawing in 3D. Generally, these programs record the X, Y, and Z coordinate data for all points or features on a 3D object or "model." One of the biggest advantages of a 3D model is that the object can be viewed from any angle. This means that the object can be rotated "inside" the computer to show a different side or feature.

The point from which the object is viewed is called the viewpoint. Most CADD programs can generate isometric, oblique, and perspective drawings from any defined viewpoint. However, depending on the software, you may not be able to select the type of perspective. Once the perspective is generated from a viewpoint, the drawing can be plotted as a wireframe or a hidden-line-removed plot.

Creating a perspective from a 3D model is quick and efficient. Often, the perspective is generated in a few seconds. Compare this to

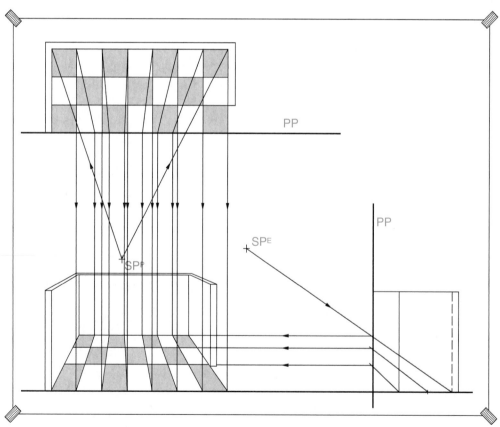

Figure 32-35. Procedure for drawing a one-point perspective—Step 5.

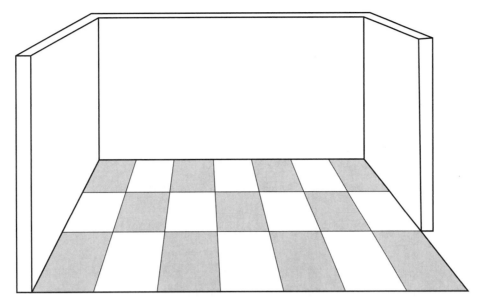

Figure 32-36. The completed one-point perspective.

the several hours it may take to draw a perspective in 2D using traditional means. However, in order for the perspective to be correctly generated, the original 3D model must be properly created. Any errors in the model are often magnified in the computer-generated perspective.

In addition to generating perspectives, most CADD software with 3D capabilities can also render the model. To render the model is to color or shade the objects, giving them "mass" and "depth." Renderings are often used as presentation drawings. See Figure 32-37. Models that are rendered for presentation purposes generally have materials or textures applied to the objects, lighting added to the scene, and details such as trees or people added. Presentation drawings are covered in Chapter 33.

Figure 32-37. This rendering will be used as a presentation drawing. The perspective was generated from a 3D model. Materials, lights, and details were added to the scene before it was rendered. (SoftPlan Systems, Inc.)

Perspective Grids

One of the problems in constructing a two-point perspective using manual drafting techniques is the large size of the layout. It is not uncommon for the vanishing points for a residential perspective to be five feet apart or more. The use of a perspective grid reduces the size of work space needed and time required to draw a large perspective, Figure 32-38. The

chief disadvantage is the limited freedom in choosing the position of the station point and placement of the picture plane. Many grid variations are available, but each is for a specific layout. A supply of several variations from which to choose would be required if the best position is be achieved in each drawing.

A thorough understanding of perspectives is necessary before grids may be used effectively. A grid will not ensure a successful drawing if the person using it is not skillful in drawing perspectives beforehand.

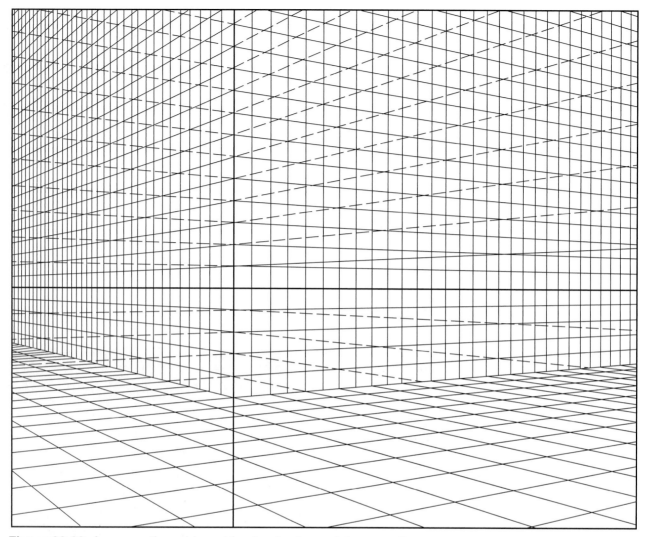

Figure 32-38. A perspective grid used for drawing two-point perspectives.

Complex Features in Perspective

Frequently, objects to be drawn in perspective contain elements that are circular, curved, or not parallel to any of the principal reference planes. Such features may appear to be difficult to draw. However, the following paragraphs describe simple techniques that should be helpful when drawing complex features in perspective.

Circular objects, such as a round top table or oval area rug, can be easily drawn if a series of points or a grid is superimposed over the surface, Figure 32-39. Locate several points on the curve that define the details of the surface. Then, draw the curve by connecting the points with a French or irregular curve.

Other objects that have a series of soft curves, such as a sofa or chair, can be drawn as though they have hard, sharp edges. Then, the lines can be softened freehand, Figure 32-40. Other objects that involve a great deal of free

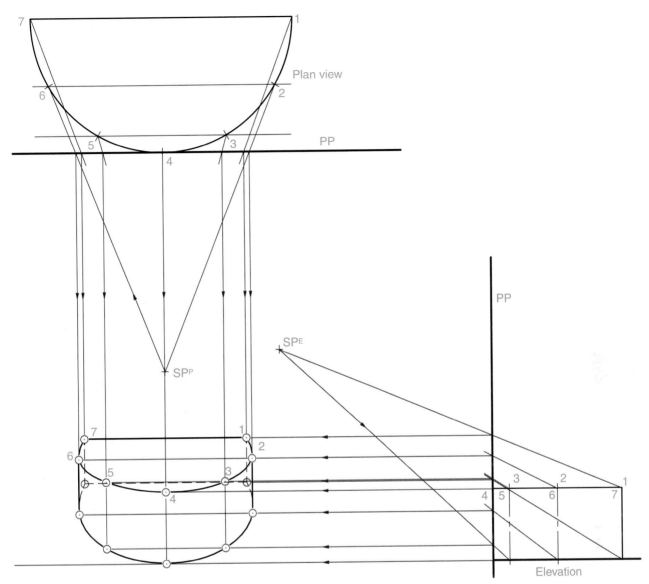

Figure 32-39. This illustrates one method of drawing curved or circular objects in a one-point perspective.

form must be boxed in and then drawn freehand within the space designated, Figure 32-41.

Remember, to draw any object you are only connecting a series of points. If a sufficient number of points are located and connected accurately, the result will be true to form. Reduce complex objects to simple parts and construct them one at a time, rather than try to locate all points and then connect them. Once you understand the procedure used in drawing perspectives you will be able to draw complex objects by applying the procedure over and over.

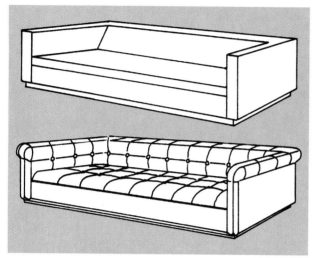

Figure 32-40. An object with soft curves, such as this sofa, may be "blocked in" first (top) and then softened freehand (bottom).

Figure 32-41. The details of this sofa and chair were drawn freehand after the basic shapes were boxed in perspective. (Darlana Fowler)

Internet Resources

www.chiefarch.com
> *ART Incorporated, publisher of Chief Architect software*

www.designbasics.com
> *Design Basics, Inc., a home design service*

www.designgroupstudio.com
> *Eric Brown Design Group, designers of The Palladian Design Collection*

www.homesofelegance.com
> *Homes of Elegance*

www.meltonclassics.com
> *Melton Classics, Inc., a producer of millwork*

www.nemetschek.net
> *Nemetschek North America, formerly Diehl Graphsoft, publisher of VectorWorks*

www.saterdesign.com
> *The Sater Design Collection, Inc.*

www.softplan.com
> *SoftPlan Architectural Design Software*

www.studerdesigns.com
> *Studer Residential Designs*

Review Questions – Chapter 32

Write your answers on a separate sheet of paper. Do not write in this book.

1. Name three types of pictorial drawings that are used as presentation drawings.

2. Identify the three basic types of perspectives.

3. The type of perspective commonly used for exterior views is the _____.

4. The ground line is drawn in the _____ part of the perspective layout.

5. The distance between the ground line and the horizon line represents the _____.

6. An edge in the perspective view is true height when it _____.

7. Parts of the object that are in front of the picture plane appear _____ than scale.

8. The location of the observer's eye is called the _____.

9. In a perspective layout, what indicates the distance that an observer is standing away from the picture plane?

10. All heights on a perspective must be measured on the _____.

11. Vanishing points are always located on the _____ line.

12. A two-point perspective has _____ vanishing points.

13. If a station point is moved from 20' to 30' away from the picture plane, what is the effect on the size of the perspective on the picture plane?

14. The standard angle at which objects are usually placed with respect to the picture plane is _____.

15. To determine the minimum distance between the station point and the picture plane, the entire object must fit within a _____ of between 30° and 45°.

16. If the station point is too close to the picture plane, the perspective may be _____.

17. Identify three common station point heights used in drawing two-point perspectives.

18. If the station point is moved closer to the picture plane, how will this affect the distance between the vanishing points in a two-point perspective?

19. One-point perspectives are well suited for _____ views, entries, courts, and porches.

20. How are heights determined in a one-point perspective?

21. The main disadvantage of using a perspective grid is _____.

22. What construction technique can be used to draw a circular object in perspective?

Suggested Activities

1. Using a simple, straight-line object supplied by your instructor, draw several two-point perspectives from different distances and positions. Identify how far away and how high the station point is in each drawing. Draw these representations using traditional methods.

2. Select a floor plan and elevation view from a newspaper or magazine. Using CADD, draw a two-point perspective of the residence. Use the procedure described in this chapter to create a 2D perspective. Display your work in class.

3. Look through old issues of Better Homes and Gardens, House and Home, House Beautiful, Home Modernizing Guide, or similar magazines. Make photocopies or cut out perspective drawings of homes. Mount these pictures for display.

4. Select a large photograph (not a drawing) of a home or building from a magazine. Mount the photo on a piece of illustration board or stiff paper. Locate the horizon line and vanishing points and label each.

5. If your CADD system has 3D capabilities, draw a house of your own design using 3D techniques. Do not draw any interior features. Create a perspective display of the house and plot a hidden-line-removed hardcopy.

This presentation floor plan is used in sales literature for luxury condominiums. (WCI Communities, Inc.)

Presentation Drawings

33

Objectives

After studying this chapter, you will be able to:

➤ Explain the purpose of a presentation drawing.

➤ List methods commonly used to increase the degree of realism in a presentation plan.

➤ Render presentation drawings using a variety of methods.

➤ Explain entourage.

➤ Describe lighting for a CADD 3D model to be rendered.

➤ Explain walkthrough animation.

Key Terms

Animation Key	Rendering
Entourage	Tweens
Keyframe	Walkthrough
Presentation	Animation
Drawing	

The purpose of a *presentation drawing* is to show the finished structure. It can also present various parts of the building in a form that is more meaningful than construction drawings. Presentation drawings are shown to those people who are interested in the structure, such as the owner, and are generally rendered to enhance their appearance.

Rendering

Presentation drawings require a degree of realism that may be accomplished through rendering. *Rendering* is the process of representing or depicting an object or scene in an artistic form by adding colors and shading, Figure 33-1. Shades, shadows, and textures provide much more realism that just clear sharp lines. There are several popular methods of rendering presentation drawings. They include:

Figure 33-1. This beautiful rendering of the front elevation captures the essence of this magnificent home. This rendering was completed using CADD. (Helmuth A. Geiser, member AIBD)

637

Airbrush
Appliqué
CADD
Colored Pencils
Felt-Tipped Pen
Ink
Pencil
Scratchboard
Tempera
Watercolor

Each of these methods has advantages that should be considered before beginning the project. Various materials and techniques are often combined in a single rendering. The techniques described in the next sections represent the majority used for rendering presentation plans. Each requires a certain amount of artistic ability and skill to produce a satisfactory rendering. The ability to prepare renderings is well worth developing.

Pencil Rendering

Pencil rendering is popular and probably the easiest. No special materials are needed and the product is highly acceptable if well done. Several common exterior materials are shown rendered in pencil in Figure 33-2. A perspective drawing inked on vellum and rendered in pencil by a student is shown in Figure 33-3.

The pencils used for rendering are generally softer than those used for construction-type drawings. One of the problems encountered in pencil rendering is the difficulty in keeping the drawing clean. A good procedure is to cover the surrounding area to prevent smudges and smears.

Ink Rendering

Renderings to be used for reproduction are best done in ink, when completed by hand.

Brick   River rock   Cedar shake siding   Wood grain

Random rubble   Stone   Cement block screen   Cut stone

Figure 33-2. Common exterior materials rendered in pencil.

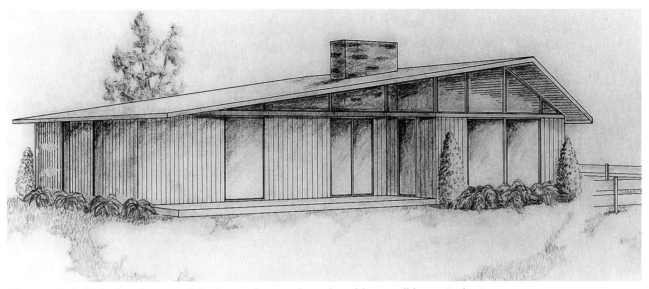

Figure 33-3. This drawing was inked on velum and rendered in pencil by a student.

Lines are sharper and fine detail is possible with ink, Figure 33-4. Ink can also be used to shade areas. This is accomplished with a series of parallel lines, a dot pattern, or solid shading. Drawing inks are produced in a broad spectrum of colors that are quite useful in rendering, Figure 33-5.

Watercolor Rendering

Watercolor rendering is one of the most effective forms of rendering, Figure 33-6. Vivid colors or broad expanses of light wash are

possible with watercolor. A light wash is achieved by using very little paint with lots of water. While a watercolor rendering is one of the most effective types, it is also one of the most difficult to execute. Practice and patience are necessary to develop this technique. A watercolor rendering is shown in Figure 33-7.

Tempera Rendering

Tempera paint is a type of water-soluble paint. It differs from watercolor, which is

Figure 33-4. This inked rendering has tremendous detail and depth. (The Garlinghouse Company)

Figure 33-5. Colored inks were used to add realism to this rendering. (The Garlinghouse Company)

transparent, in that it is opaque. Tempera is frequently used for monotone renderings, such as the one shown in Figure 33-8. Advantages of this technique include a broad selection of colors that can be obtained by mixing and the ease of mending mistakes if the brush slips or the color is not satisfactory.

Colored Pencil Rendering

Colored pencils may be used to obtain satisfactory rendering. Light shades or strong strokes are easily accomplished. Even the beginning student can achieve success with this technique, Figure 33-9. Either regular

Figure 33-6. A faithful reproduction of a house in watercolors. (Ken Hawk)

Figure 33-7. Watercolor rendering produces a very realistic effect. (Sater Design Collection, Inc.)

Figure 33-8. A monotone type rendering in tempera. (The Aladdin Co.)

Figure 33-9. The basic technique used in this rendering is colored pencil. It has been combined with ink and watercolors. (Ed Fegan)

colored pencils or watercolor pencils may be used. Drawings rendered in watercolor pencil can be transformed into a watercolor rendering by applying water to the drawing with a brush.

Felt-Tipped Pen Rendering

Certain types of presentation drawings may be effectively rendered using felt-tipped pens (Magic Markers™). Presentation plot plans are frequently rendered using these types of pens. The result is distinct and differs greatly from other techniques. Fine detail may be accomplished by mixing other techniques with the marker. Figure 33-10 shows a perspective loosely rendered in felt-tipped pen by a beginning student.

Scratchboard Rendering

Scratchboard rendering produces a drawing with a great deal of character. A scratchboard is a special white illustration

board with a black coating. Lines are scratched through the black coating to reveal the white background. The result is a drawing of white lines on a black background. Such a rendering commands attention from the viewer. Figure 33-11 shows an example of a scratchboard rendering.

Figure 33-10. Felt-tipped pens were used to create this loose, but effective, rendering.

Figure 33-11. This is a scratchboard rendering.

Appliqué Rendering

Appliqué rendering is accomplished by attaching a pressure-sensitive transparent film on top of the drawing sheet. The film may be a series of dots, lines, symbols, or color. Several manufacturers are producing these films and it is possible to achieve striking results with them.

Airbrush Rendering

Airbrush renderings are frequently produced by professional illustrators. A great deal of practice is required to produce a high-quality rendering using this technique. An airbrush is simply an air nozzle that sprays paint or colored ink. If examined closely, you will find the surface of the rendering is covered with many small dots of color that form subtle shades and shadows, Figure 33-12. Areas not being sprayed should be blocked out with paper or rubber cement to prevent the accidental spraying of these areas.

Computer-Generated Renderings

Computer-generated renderings have developed to the point where they are being used in product literature, sales promotions, and client reports. These renderings are both professional and photorealistic. Full-color, three-dimensional representations complete with materials, lighting, and shadows are typical.

Many CADD packages are available that can produce sophisticated renderings. See Figure 33-13. However, these programs are generally expensive, require large amounts of memory, and must be run on a high-speed computer. Some lower-cost CADD software can produce adequate renderings. In general, however, the best renderings are produced with high-end software on high-end machines.

Some CADD programs include a large library of materials (textures) and entourage. Materials and entourage are important in presenting a realistic result. Most CADD programs that support materials include a feature or option that allows you to develop your own and save them for future use. This is an important feature because you do not need to recreate materials over and over.

CADD programs with advanced rendering functions typically allow you to place and adjust light sources, Figure 33-14. The most basic lighting is a light source behind and to one side of the observer. However, the best method for lighting a scene is triangle lighting used in traditional photography. This method of lighting uses a key light in front of the scene, a fill light to one side of the scene, and a backlight toward the rear of the scene. The key light provides most of the illumination. The fill light is used to remove shadows. The backlight is used to bring the object out of the background.

Figure 33-12. These airbrush renderings illustrate the realism possible using the technique. (Progress Lighting)

Figure 33-13. This computer-generated rendering shows how realistic these presentation drawings can be. (Helmuth A. Geiser, member AIBD)

Figure 33-14. Lighting in this computer-generated scene is key to its effectiveness. (Helmuth A. Geiser, member AIBD)

The observer's position with respect to each surface will determine the amount of lighting needed on a given surface. Lights can be moved and their properties adjusted to produce the most pleasing effect. When the scene is rendered, shadows are automatically generated. A high-end CADD program with a full range of rendering and lighting capabilities can be used to realistically render any scene, Figure 33-15.

Shading and Shadows

Shading and shadows are used on presentation drawings to create realism. Exposing the object to a light source produces areas on the object that are lighter than those areas that are not exposed to the light. The areas on the object that are not exposed to the light should

be shaded or darkened. In CADD, this task is usually automatic once the proper lighting is set up. However, in traditional renderings, you must determine which areas of which objects should be shaded.

To determine the areas of an object that should be shaded, the angle of the sun (light source) must first be determined. Once the angle of the sun is established, then all shading is drawn from that angle. In a traditional rendering, 30°, 45°, or 60° is used as the angle of light. As the angle is increased, more shadow is cast on the object. See Figure 33-16. A light source location should be selected that will produce the most pleasing and realistic appearance. Also, select a shadow depth that does not cover important information.

The shape of an object influences how the shading appears on the surface of the object. For example, when an object has sharp edges, there is a sharp transition from light (no shading) to dark (shaded). But, objects that are curved have a gradual transition from light to

Figure 33-15. The ceiling fixture in this computer-generated rendering provides a realistic light source for this kitchen drawing. (ART, Inc.)

dark as the surface moves from no shade to full shade. See Figure 33-17.

Shading can be drawn using several patterns. Figure 33-18 shows three common patterns that can be rendered with pencil or ink. Experiment with different methods before selecting the one to be used on a specific project. Begin by laying out the areas to be shaded. Then, draw the shadows created by changes in the object surface. Do not make the shading too dark. Doing so will produce an un-realistic rendering. Be sure to keep all shading consistent as to angle and shading technique. Practice will improve your technique.

Entourage

Entourage (pronounced "an-tur-azh") refers to surroundings such as trees, shrubs, cars, people, and terrain. These features add to

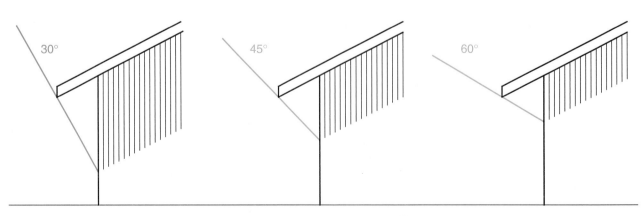

Figure 33-16. The angle of the sun makes a significant amount of difference in the shading on a structure.

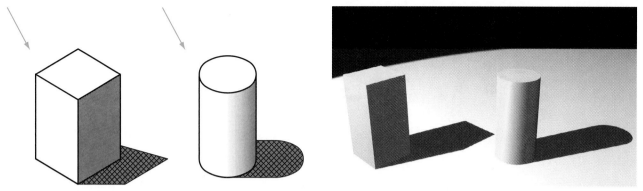

Figure 33-17. Shadows should accurately represent the shape of the object casting them.

the realism of a drawing and show an architectural structure in its proper setting. Entourage usually represents objects in simplified form, rather than trying to make them look exactly as they would appear. Always draw entourage to the proper scale. Information regarding appropriate sizes of surroundings may be obtained from the Architectural Graphic Standards.

Architects usually develop a personal style of drawing entourage. For those who do not feel comfortable in drawing these features, appliqués, rub-on symbols, and rubber stamps are available that can be used to add a professional appearance to their drawings. Figure 33-19 shows some entourage symbols that are representative of those commonly used by architects.

There are several suppliers of entourage for CADD drawings. Symbols or blocks are available for traditional 2D layouts in elevation, plan, and pictorial views. In addition, entourage is available for use with 3D models. Many suppliers offer various trees, cars, trucks, people, and animals. In addition, some suppliers offer animated entourage for use with 3D animations. Entourage for 3D models is generally available in several resolutions,

from low to high. High-resolution 3D entourage can be very realistic.

In addition to commercial products, you can produce your own entourage and save it in a library for future use. Also, digital images, such as scanned photographs, can be incorporated into CADD drawings as backgrounds and material textures. This can be useful in showing a proposed building as it would appear on a site. See Figure 33-20.

Types of Presentation Plans

Several types of presentation drawings or plans are used to represent a structure. Exterior and interior perspectives, rendered elevations, presentation plot plans, floor plans, and sections are commonly prepared to help "sell" the plan to a prospective client. These drawings are designed to present the structure to the layperson, who may not understand a set of construction drawings, in an accurate and honest manner. They may also be used for advertising and other purposes, Figure 33-21.

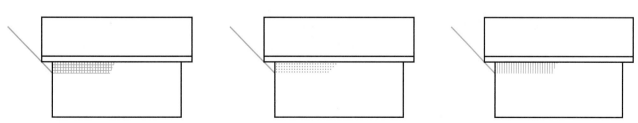

Figure 33-18. These are three different techniques that can be used to shade areas.

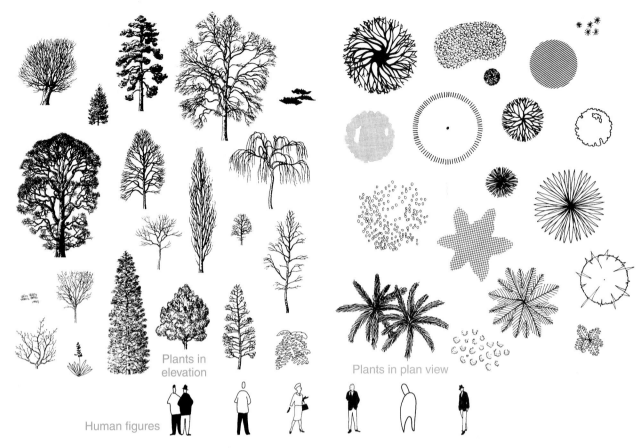

Figure 33-19. Typical entourage symbols.

Figure 33-20. A digital image of the site was used as background for this computer-generated rendering. (Helmuth A. Geiser, member AIBD)

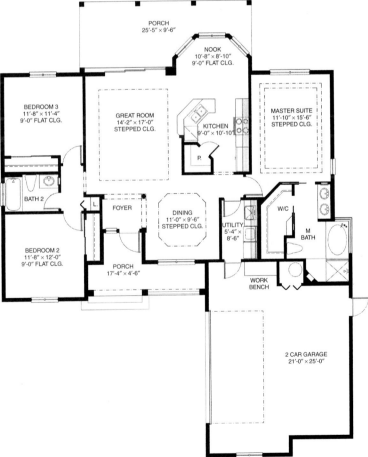

Figure 33-21. This presentation floor plan and perspective are used in marketing literature to sell the construction plans for this house. (Sater Design Collection, Inc.)

Presentation plans are being used more and more to communicate ideas. People understand architectural ideas better if they are presented in a manner in which they are accustomed. Presentation plans do just that and are, therefore, very useful, Figure 33-22. However, creating presentation plans requires talents and skills that are not required to create technical drawings. Still, presentation plans are definitely an integral part of architectural drafting and should be mastered.

Exterior Perspectives

The exterior perspective should present the structure as accurately as possible. Any distortion present in the drawing may misrepresent the appearance and create a false impression. Figure 33-23A shows a home that is faithfully represented. Figure 33-23B shows an elaborate home rendered in such a manner that the exquisite design is emphasized. Both examples are accurate representations of the actual homes.

Rendered Elevations

An elevation is an orthographic drawing and does not show depth. However, the addition of material symbols, trees, and other entourage can transform an elevation into an effective presentation drawing, Figure 33-24A. Even though no depth is shown in the structure, the feeling of depth is accomplished through shades, shadows, textures, and surroundings. Presentation elevations are frequently used instead of exterior perspectives because they are faster to draw and, if presented well, usually quite satisfactory, Figure 33-24B.

Presentation Plot Plans

Presentation plot plans are used to show the relationship between the site and structure. This is essentially a plan view of the site showing important topographical features, the house location, and property boundaries. The presentation plot plan gives a bird's eye view of the layout and provides an opportunity to show off the type of living afforded by the surroundings. Several styles of presentation plot plans are possible. Figure 33-25 shows two different treatments.

Presentation Floor Plans

Presentation floor plans may be used to emphasize features such as furniture arrangement, space utilization, and conveniences, Figure 33-26. Color may be used to call attention to similar features or to separate areas. The color should be functional, if possible, rather than used just to "color" the drawings. The specific use intended for the drawing should be evident by the presentation technique used. Figure 33-27 shows contrasting styles of presentation floor plans.

Rendered Sections

Frequently, a complex structure requires a rendered longitudinal section to emphasize the various levels, Figure 33-28. Such a plan is effective in communicating the internal layout of the house. The realistic way in which information is presented helps clarify the plan.

Walkthrough Animation

A type of computer animation called a walkthrough animation can be considered a type of presentation plan or drawing. The purpose of a walkthrough animation is to show a client, inspector, or review board a realistic representation of a building before construction begins, just as a traditional presentation drawing does. The design can be altered, different materials selected, and lighting added or adjusted based on client feedback. Then, a new walkthrough animation can be created and presented for approval. This "virtual construction," while sometimes expensive itself, can save a tremendous amount of money if alterations are eliminated from later in the building process.

A

B

Figure 33-22. A—This computer-generated one-point perspective accurately depicts the details of the design. (Helmuth A. Geiser, member AIBD) B—This drawing is an effective communication device because it is easily understood. Notice the effective use of entourage. (ART, Inc.)

Figure 33-23. A—This two-point exterior perspective is an accurate representation of the earth-sheltered home. (The Garlinghouse Company) B—This color rendering emphasizes the luxury of the home. (Larry Campbell)

As you learned in Chapter 6, an animation is a series of images played back-to-back so quickly that the brain sees small differences between each image as motion. A *walkthrough animation* shows an animated view of how a building would appear to a person actually walking through it. A flyby animation is essentially the same type of animation, except it shows what the exterior of a building would look like to a person flying by in a plane or driving by in a car.

The process by which a walkthrough animation is created varies greatly from one program to the next. The following example is based on a popular 3D modeling, rendering, and animation program called 3ds max. Look at the simple floor plan in Figure 33-29. Once the model is created, the first step in making a walkthrough animation is to determine the path that the viewer will take when "walking" through the house. The path replicates where a person would walk. For example, you do not

NORTH

A

B

Figure 33-24. A—Presentation elevations are sometimes used to represent a residential structure rather than a perspective, as this example of the home in Figure 33-23B shows. (Larry Campbell) B—This simple presentation elevation rendered in colored pencil by a student is quite effective. (A. Sewell)

normally walk right next to a wall, rather travel near the middle of the room. In addition, you should determine where the viewer will look while moving along the path. For example, the viewer can always look straight ahead. On the other hand, the viewer may turn their head to one side to focus on a feature in the room.

Next, you need to determine how long the animation will be. This is dependant on several factors. For example, a computer plays animations at 30 frames per second. That means that a one-minute-long animation needs to be 1800 frames. However, an animation of this length may require several megabytes of storage and take several hours to render. Therefore, you may need to shorten the animation. Do not make the animation too short, though, or it will look as if you are running through the building instead of walking.

Now, you need to determine at what time, or on which frame, certain important actions must occur, Figure 33-30. For example, the viewer may need to open a door before exiting the room. A frame on which an important action takes place is called a *keyframe.* The frames in between keyframes are called *tweens.* In computer animation, you define the keyframes and the computer calculates the tweens.

Once you determine which frames are keyframes, you need to define the motion on the keyframe. Most software with an animation feature has an animation mode that must be on in order to animate movement. When an object is moved while animation mode is on, the computer records the movement as data for the keyframe. These data are stored in an *animation key* that is created or "set" on each keyframe. See Figure 33-31.

After all animation keys are set on the appropriate keyframes, the animation needs to be rendered. You should have already set the total number of frames in the animation. Now, you need to determine the width and height of

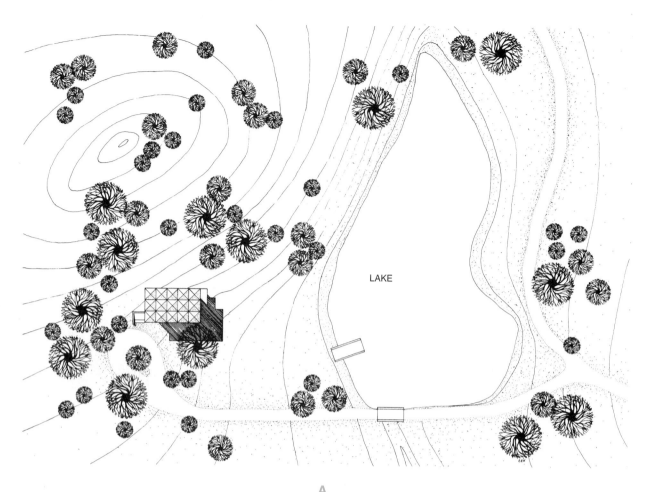

A

B

Figure 33-25. A—This is an ink rendering of a site plan. B—This presentation plot plan is drawn over an elevation of the site. (Larry Campbell)

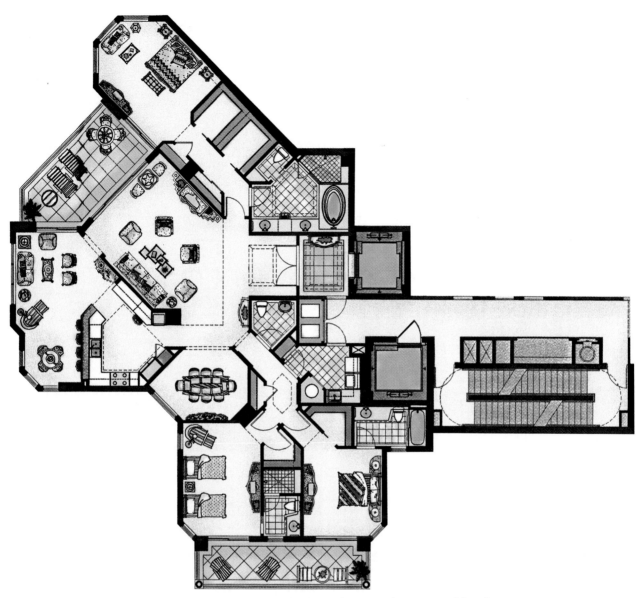

Figure 33-26. A presentation floor plan that emphasizes the use of space and furniture. (WCI Communities, Inc.)

the animation, the file type, and the file location. Common animation file types are AVI and MOV. Most computers, both PC and Macintosh platforms, have default programs to view these file types. Once everything is set, the walkthrough animation can be rendered.

A word of warning. The larger the size and the longer the length of the animation, the longer it will take to render. An animation that is 640 × 480 pixels—a common computer display resolution—and two minutes (3600 frames) in length may take several hours, if not days, to render. In fact, if you have a processor speed in the lower hundred megahertz range (under 500MHz), do not even attempt to render such an animation. Special effects, complex materials, and including numerous shadow-casting lights in the scene also increase the rendering time.

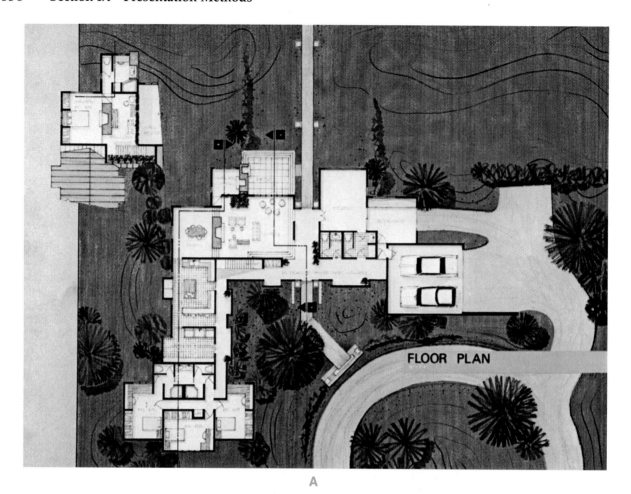

A

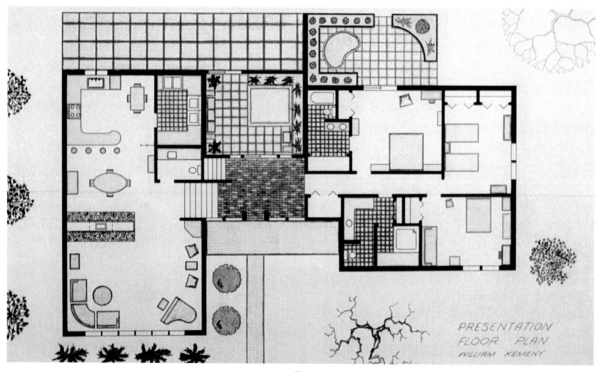

B

Figure 33-27. A—This presentation floor plan is rendered in ink and colored chalk. (Larry Campbell) B—The color in this presentation floor plan is very functional and calls attention to various elements of the plan. (William Kemeny)

SECTION

SECTION

Figure 33-28. These rendered sections of the residence shown in Figure 33-23B provide an effective means of illustrating the complex structure. (Larry Campbell)

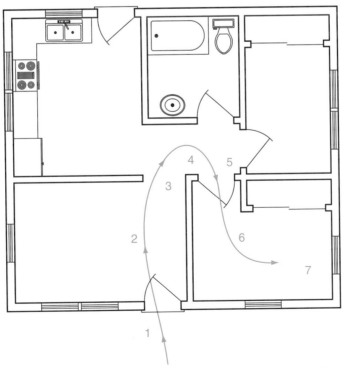

Figure 33-29. A walkthrough animation will be created for this simple floor plan. The path that the viewer will "walk along" is shown here in color. The numbers refer to action numbers identified in Figure 33-30.

Action Number	Keyframe	Action
1	90	Pause at front door and open door.
2	330	Turn and look at living room.
3	420	Turn and move to doorway to hall.
4	510	Move to center of hall.
5	600	Pause at doorway and open door.
6	690	Enter bedroom.
7	840	Pause in front of window and view exterior.
Note: There are 900 total frames in the animation resulting in 30 seconds of playback.		

Figure 33-30. The keyframes for the walkthrough animation are shown here with the action identified. The action numbers are illustrated in Figure 33-29.

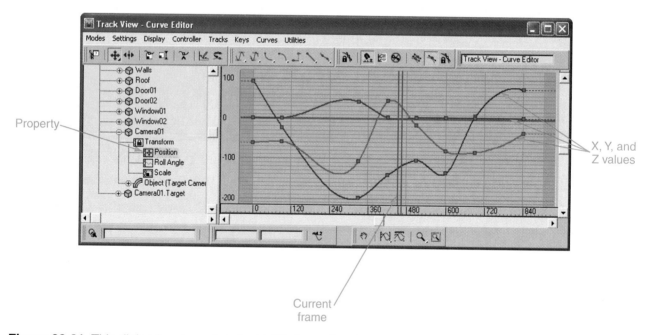

Figure 33-31. This dialog box from Autodesk VIZ shows the data recorded for an animation key. The red, green, and blue curves at the right of the dialog box represent the camera's movement on the X, Y, and Z coordinate axes.

Internet Resources

www.abbisoft.com
AbbiSoft, a supplier of house plans

www.abracadata.com
Abracadata, publisher of Premier Architect™

www.autodesk.com
Autodesk, Inc., publisher of AutoCAD and Autodesk VIZ

www.cadsoft.com
CADSOFT Corporation, publisher of software for AEC

www.chiefarch.com
ART Incorporated, publisher of Chief Architect software

www.datacad.com
DATACAD, LLC, publisher of DATACAD software

www.details-details.com
Architectural Details, Inc., a supplier of predrawn architectural details

www.discreet.com
Discreet, publisher of 3ds max

www.saterdesign.com
The Sater Design Collection, Inc.

www.softplan.com
SoftPlan Architectural Design Software

Review Questions – Chapter 33

Write your answers on a separate sheet of paper. Do not write in this book.

1. _____ is the process of representing or depicting an object or scene in an artistic form by adding colors and shading.
2. Identify six common methods of rendering.
3. _____ is popular and perhaps the easiest rendering technique.
4. Renderings to be used for reproduction are best done in _____.
5. A rendering method in which pressure-sensitive transparent films are placed over the drawing is called _____ rendering.
6. Briefly explain how an airbrush works.
7. What is the function of entourage on a presentation drawing?
8. What are the three types of lights used in triangle lighting?
9. Identify five types of presentation plans that may be used to "sell" a residential structure.
10. An elevation is a(n) _____ drawing and shows no depth.
11. Name three features that may be emphasized on a presentation floor plan.
12. What is a walkthrough animation?
13. How does a walkthrough animation differ from a flyby animation?
14. Give two factors that affect the length of time required to render a walkthrough animation.
15. Define the following terms.
    a) Keyframe.
    b) Tween.
    c) Animation Key.

Suggested Activities

1. Place a piece of tracing paper over the photograph used in Activity 4 in Chapter 32 and make a rendering in pencil. Do the drawing freehand. Compare your drawing with the photograph.
2. Collect renderings of architectural structures from magazines or brochures. Display these for style and inspiration in the drawing room.
3. Select a simple construction floor plan. Develop a presentation floor plan that emphasizes the furniture layout.
4. Render the two-point perspective that you drew for Activity 2 in Chapter 32. Use a technique specified by your instructor or one of your choice.
5. Draw a one-point perspective of one of the rooms in the house used for the presentation floor plan in Activity 3 above or one of your own design. Illustrate the furniture in your perspective.
6. Render the interior perspective created in Activity 5 above in color. Mount it on illustration board if drawn on paper. Display your drawing on the bulletin board.

7. Develop a presentation plot plan showing property boundaries, house location, drive, walks, and topographical features. Present the plan in color.

8. Using 3D modeling techniques, develop a simple house model. Generate a rendering of the house in perspective.

9. Using the house model from Activity 8 above, design a walkthrough (flyby) animation where the viewer walks around the entire house exterior. Determine a path and keyframes. If you have software with animation capabilities, animate and render the scene.

Architectural Models 34

Objectives

After studying this chapter, you will be able to:

➤ Explain the various types of architectural models used to represent residential structures.

➤ List the features commonly included in a presentation model.

➤ Summarize the steps for constructing a balsa wood model.

Key Terms

Architectural Model
Balsa
Presentation Model
Small Scale Solid Model
Structural Model

An *architectural model* is a physical, scaled model of the actual house and a portion of the site (lot). It provides the ultimate means of showing how the finished home will look in all three dimensions. The model may be viewed from any position and greatly increases the amount of information communicated. Models are useful in checking the finished appearance of an architectural design and "selling" a design to a client. Advanced CADD programs can also produce "virtual" architectural models that serve a similar purpose, Figure 34-1.

Types of Models

Several types of models are used to represent architectural structures. One type is the *small scale solid model*, which shows only the exterior shape of the building and is not hollow, Figure 34-2. This is frequently used to show how a building will relate to surrounding buildings. Scales used range from 1/32″ = 1′-0″ to 1/8″ = 1′-0″. Very little detail is shown on solid models.

Structural models are frequently used to show construction features of a residence. All structural materials used should be cut to scale and proper building methods represented, Figure 34-3. Structural models are usually 1/2″ = 1′-0″ or 1″ = 1′-0″ scale. If the scale is too small, the materials will be difficult to work with. Since the purpose of a structural model is to show the basic construction, most siding and roofing materials are left off to expose the structural aspects, Figure 34-4. This type of model is useful when unique construction procedures are to be used.

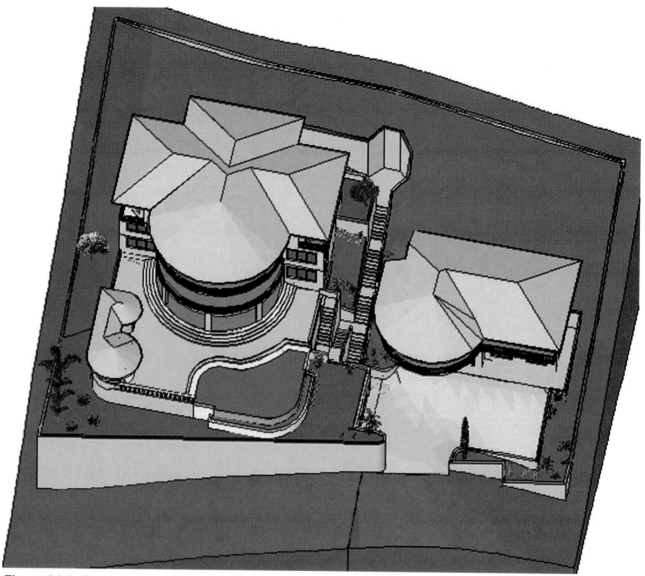

Figure 34-1. An architectural model such as this one provides a clear picture to a prospective client of the structure on the site. (Helmuth A. Geiser, member AIBD)

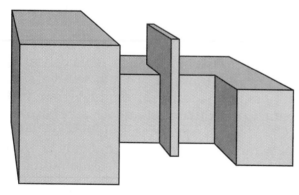

Figure 34-2. A small scale solid model is frequently used to study the mass of a building or show its relation to surrounding buildings.

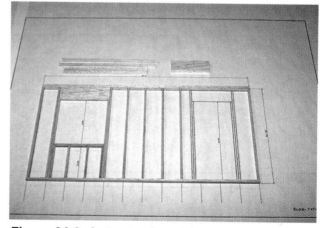

Figure 34-3. A structural model under construction using materials cut to the proper scale. (Brad L. Kicklighter)

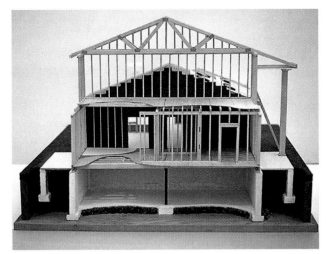

Figure 34-4. This structural model shows the framing of the building.

Figure 34-5. This presentation model is 1/2″ = 1′-0″ scale and accurately represents the materials to be used on the house. (Brad L. Kicklighter)

Most architectural models for residential use are *presentation models.* The purpose of a presentation model is to show the appearance of the finished building as realistically as possible, Figure 34-5. A primary concern is to select materials that will closely resemble materials used in construction. Presentation models are usually 1/4″ = 1′-0″ scale. They may be larger or smaller, depending on the amount of detail desired, size of the structure, and funds for model construction, Figure 34-6.

Materials Used in Model Construction

There are several basic materials that are commonly used for architectural model construction. Some model builders prefer sheets of Styrofoam® called foam board. This

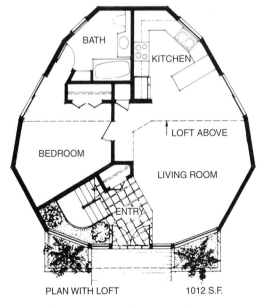

Figure 34-6. New and unique types of homes are frequently modeled before actual construction.

material is easy to cut and can be made to resemble various exterior building materials. It is easy to glue and can be painted with various kinds of paint. However, Styrofoam® is soft and may be scratched or easily broken.

Another popular material for architectural models is cardboard or illustration board. Figure 34-7 shows a residential model made from foam board and illustration board. Cardboard is easy to obtain, glues well, and may be painted with almost any type of paint. Two disadvantages are that cardboard warps easily and it must be cut with a knife or razor-type blade, rather than by sawing. Pin holes are also more visible than with other materials.

Balsa wood is another popular material for building models of homes. *Balsa* is a soft-wood available in a wide variety of sizes. It is easy to cut with a sharp knife, can be sawed, is easy to finish, and can be sanded and scored to represent exterior materials. In addition, a balsa wood model does not warp as much as cardboard and is stronger.

Constructing a Balsa Model

The following procedure is presented as an aid to building a presentation-type model from balsa. This is a typical procedure that can be applied to many different models. The model in this example has a removable roof.

1. Obtain a set of plans for the home that is drawn at a scale of $1/4'' = 1'-0''$. In some instances, it may be desirable to build a model to another scale, but the majority of residential models are $1/4'' = 1'-0''$ scale. Typically, only the floor plan and elevations are needed to build the model, Figure 34-8. The procedure presented here relates to a house on a flat site. However, if the building site is not flat, a plot plan should be drawn using the same scale as the other plans. It is usually not necessary to draw the entire site at $1/4'' = 1'-0''$ scale, but only the portion represented by the model. If the roof is complex, it may be desirable to develop a second floor or roof plan to aid in building the upper portion of the model, Figure 34-9.

2. A decision must be made concerning the size of the base for the model. A prime consideration to be remembered is storage and handling. If the base is large, it may be hard to store and transport. A good-size base for an average residence is $30'' \times 30''$ or $30'' \times 36''$. The base should be $3/4''$ plywood if the site is relatively flat. If the site is rolling, it must be accurately represented by building up the high spots with plaster of Paris, Styrofoam® or cardboard, Figure 34-10. A lighter base should be used to reduce weight. It should be noted that if the site is flat, the model may be completed on a workbench and placed on the base. If the site is rolling, it may be easier to build the model on the base.

Figure 34-7. The roof and interior walls of this model are made from illustration board. The exterior walls are made from Styrofoam® sheets.

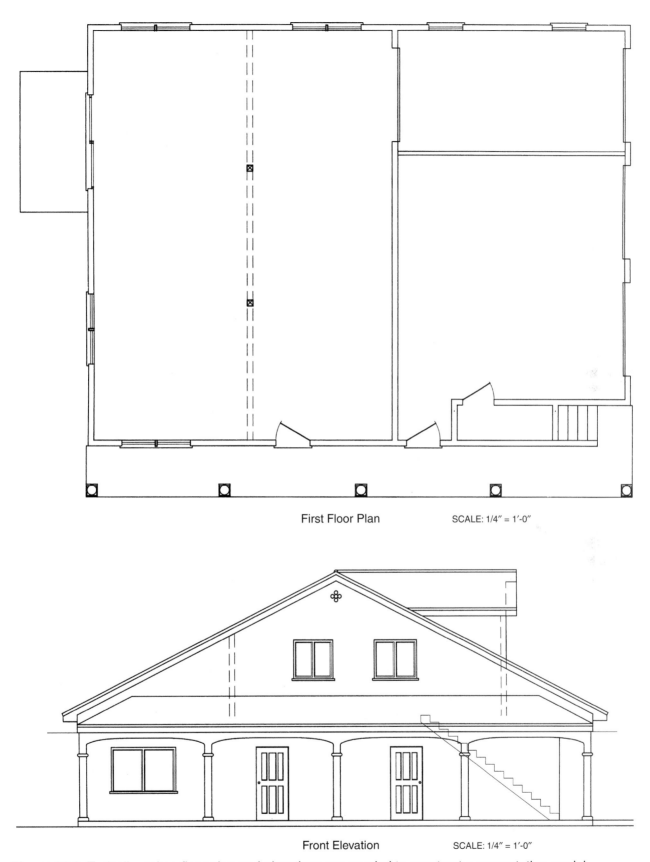

First Floor Plan   SCALE: 1/4″ = 1′-0″

Front Elevation   SCALE: 1/4″ = 1′-0″

Figure 34-8. Typically, only a floor plan and elevations are needed to construct a presentation model.

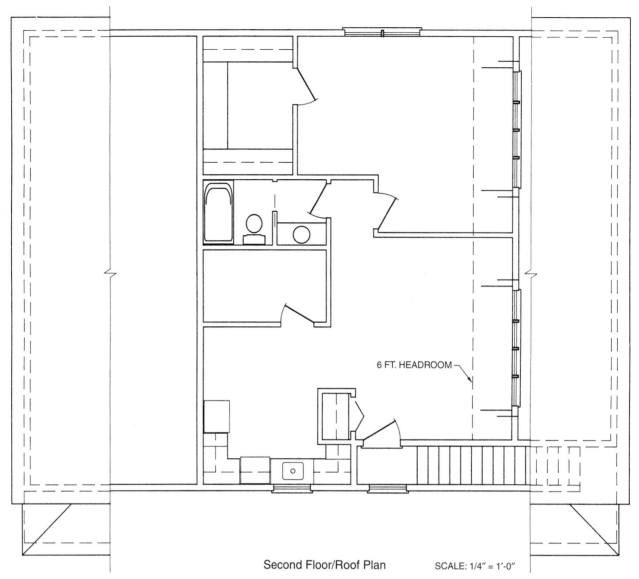

6 FT. HEADROOM

Second Floor/Roof Plan   SCALE: 1/4″ = 1′-0″

Figure 34-9. If the house has a complex roof, a second floor plan or roof plan may be needed to construct the model.

3. After studying the floor plan and elevations, select a piece of balsa that approximates the thickness for the exterior walls of the model. Usually 3/16″ or 1/4″ thick material is used. Lay out the length of one exterior wall and any openings in the wall, such as windows and doors. Cut this piece accurately, paying close attention to details. The corners may be mitered or butt jointed. A mitered corner is usually neater.

Proceed with the next exterior wall by cutting it to length and locating the windows and doors. Construct all the exterior walls in the same manner. Then, glue the walls together. Place them on the floor plan to ensure accuracy. See Figure 34-11.

4. Lay out each section of interior wall on a piece of 1/8″ thick balsa. This thickness closely approximates the thickness of an interior wall drawn to scale. Cut out each interior wall segment and glue the pieces together in their proper locations on the plan.

5. Apply the trim around windows and doors and insert exterior doors. This is usually 1/8″ thick material. The window

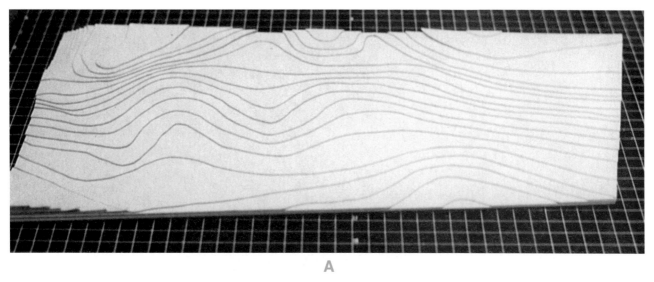

A

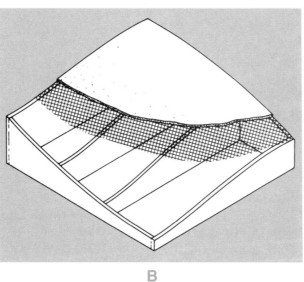

B

Figure 34-10. A—This model of a site is made from foam core. B—A rolling site may be modeled by building a support frame cut to the proper contour covered with screen and plaster of Paris.

glass may also be installed now or after the interior is painted. For best results, 1/16″ thick Plexiglas® may be used for window glass.

Exterior siding, brick, or other material may be applied to the walls. You may wish to make your own siding or represent other materials by scoring the board or gluing on thin strips. If you cut your own strips of siding be sure to make them to scale. Commercial materials are available at hobby and model train shops. Again, choose materials that are to scale. If materials in sheet form are to be used, rubber cement will work fine for applying them to the walls. If individual strips are to be used, model cement or other fast drying cement is recommended.

6. Paint the interior walls with tempera paint. The walls may be painted in soft pastels or white. Dark colors usually do not look realistic and should be avoided. Any wood siding or three-dimensional brick, stone, or shingles should also be painted or stained. Exterior materials are available on plastic sheets that are embossed to provide a three-dimensional effect. These should be finished with enamel. The mortar joints should be painted with a water-based paint and wiped. This

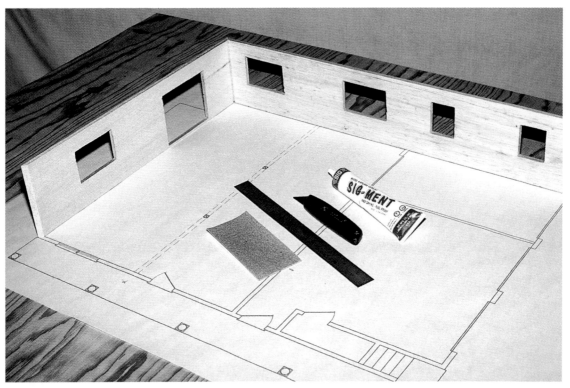

Figure 34-11. Two exterior walls have been completed and glued together. The floor plan is used as a template to ensure accuracy.

technique produces a realistic appearance. Figure 34-12 shows the completed first and second floor.

7. Roof construction comes next. The roof may be assembled on the roof plan or on the model. Experience has shown that the most satisfactory results are usually obtained by assembling the roof on the model. Since the roof framing will not be seen in a presentation model it is not necessary to cut each rafter and ceiling joist. Lay out the gables on 1/4″ thick balsa and cut them out. Cut ridge boards from similar stock and glue them in place at the peaks of the gables. Use straight pins to hold the pieces in place until the glue dries. The roof sheathing may be 1/4″ balsa glued to the gables and ridge board. This thickness approximates the scaled thickness of the rafters and sheathing on the house. Use a strip of 1/16″ thick balsa to represent a fascia board. If the home has a chimney, build a chimney to scale and accurately locate it on the roof. Finish the roof by gluing strips of sandpaper or other realistic roofing material to the sheathing. Be sure to represent flashing. This may be aluminum or copper foil. Figure 34-13 shows the completed roof.

8. After the floor area has been painted or covered with an appropriate material, locate the model on the base and glue it in place. Next, paint the area surrounding the house bright green. For best results apply two coats and sprinkle grass flock before the second coat dries. Add trees, shrubs, drive, and walk. The plants may be purchased or fabricated from a sponge and/or twigs. Use your imagination to develop a landscape that looks realistic. Do not add so many plants that the landscape appears cluttered. The walk and drive may be painted balsa or sandpaper glued in place.

9. Check the model to be sure all details are complete.

Figure 34-14 shows another model completed using the above procedure. Notice the landscaping details. Furniture and major fixtures can be carved out of soap or wood and glued into place for added attraction. Again, the main consideration is scale. There is no limit to the amount of realism that may be

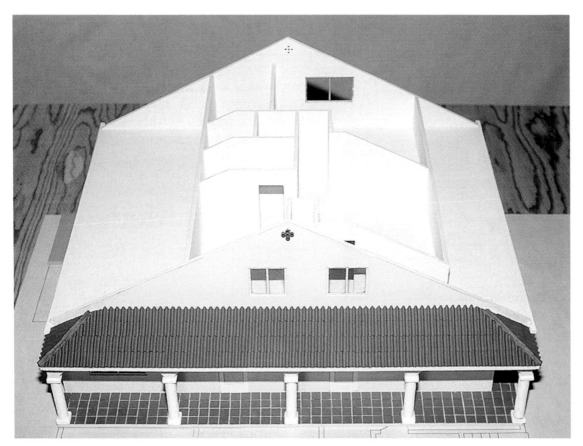

Figure 34-12. The first and second floor are complete. The second floor can be removed to show first floor layout. Tempera colors were used to paint the walls and floor. The paving was made from individual squares of 1/32″ balsa. Columns were made from 1/2″ diameter dowel rods. (Brad L. Kicklighter)

Figure 34-13. The roof has been completed and placed on the model. The terra cotta tile was made from corrugated cardboard. Small pegs are attached to the underside of the roof to ensure proper placement. (Brad L. Kicklighter)

Figure 34-14. A completed model with landscaping, drive, and walk. The model was mounted on a piece of 3/4″ × 30″ × 36″ plywood. The trees and plants were made from dried flowers. The grass is bright green flock made especially for models. Paving was made from balsa strips. (Brad L. Kicklighter)

incorporated in a model. Use your imagination. Be creative and develop a truly realistic presentation model. Figure 34-15 shows a residential model made from plaster of Paris. The shrubbery is lichen.

Laser-Cut Model Parts

Hand-cut model parts can be eliminated through the use of a laser cutting machine. Equipment is now available that uses CADD drawing data to guide the cutter. The principle of the machine is similar to that of a plotter, but instead of putting lines on paper, these machines cut or score the material where the lines would have been. Materials such as Plexiglas®, plastics, wood, cardboard, paper, fabrics, rubber, and composites can be cut or scored with a range of beam widths. Cutting speeds are about three inches per second.

Figure 34-15. This residential presentation model was constructed from 12 identical plaster castings. Two castings form each room module, which are the same shape. Two slightly modified modules form the decks. Each module is supported by a foundation pedestal.

Internet Resources

www.aia.org
American Institute of Architects

www.archdigest.com
Architectural Digest

www.bhg.com
Betters Homes and Gardens Magazine

www.kernlasers.com
Kern Electrics and Lasers, Inc., a supplier of laser cutting equipment

www.mcfeelys.com
McFeely's Square Drive Screws, a supplier of model building supplies

www.modernplastics.com
Modern Plastics, a supplier of plastic materials

www.rockler.com
Rockler Woodworking and Hardware

www.woodcraft.com
Woodcraft, a supplier of wood and woodworking materials

www.woodshopnews.com
Woodshop News Magazine

www.woodworker.com
Woodworker's Supply, Inc.

Review Questions – Chapter 34

Write your answers on a separate sheet of paper. Do not write in this book.

1. Name three types of architectural models that may be used for homes.

2. The scale of most residential models is _____.

3. Identify the three types of materials that are commonly used in the construction of a model house (not finishing materials).

4. What is the first step in building an architectural model?

5. A plot plan is needed when building a model for a house on a site that is not _____.

6. The size of base for an average-size residence usually is about _____.

7. Because the model base must be strong, _____ thick plywood is commonly used.

8. Exterior walls are usually thicker than interior walls. What is the material thickness of most exterior walls on house models that are constructed at 1/4″ = 1′-0″ scale?

9. The material used for interior walls is usually _____ thick on a 1/4″ = 1′-0″ scale model.

10. _____ colors of paint should be avoided because they do not look realistic.

11. How can soap be used in a house model?

Suggested Activities

1. Using the Internet, find a web site that sells hobby materials that you would need to construct an architectural model. If you do not have access to the Internet, visit a local hobby shop. Make a list of the materials you think you may need and record prices. Also, write down the address of the shop. Compare your findings with other members of the class.

2. Secure a floor plan of a free-standing (detached) three-car garage. Construct a balsa model to scale. A scale of 1/4″ = 1′-0″ is suggested. Mount the model on a base 12″ square. Record the time required to build the model and total cost. Display the model and your data for the class.

3. Obtain the plans for an attractive one-story home. Build a presentation model of the home. Mount it on a suitable base and landscape the site. Display the model along with the plans.

4. Carve a permanent fixture, such a bathtub or water closet, from soap. Check dimensions of the carving for accuracy.

5. Design a storage or garden house using CADD. Plot the floor plan and elevations. Build a structural model of your design. Present your design and model for analysis.

6. Using CADD, design a small cottage. Plot the floor plan and elevations. Build a 1/4″ = 1′-0″ presentation model of your design.

This is an excellent example of a finely-detailed architectural presentation model. (Brad L. Kicklighter)

Section X
Specifications and
Estimating

35 Material and Tradework Specifications

36 Estimating Building Cost

Photo courtesy of James Hardie® Siding Products

Material and Tradework Specifications

Objectives

After studying this chapter, you will be able to:

➤ Explain the purpose of material and tradework specifications.

➤ List the sources of specification guides.

➤ Identify the format followed by typical contract specification sheets.

➤ Use a *Description of Materials* form.

Key Terms

Contract
  Specification Sheet
Material
  Specifications
Tradework
  Specifications

The architect is generally responsible for the preparation of material specifications and tradework specifications for residential structures. *Material specifications* involve the types of materials, fixtures, and other physical items. *Tradework specifications* involve the work to be completed and its quality. These specifications provide written information on details and products that supplements the drawings. The specifications become part of the complete set of building plans. When the house is to be constructed for sale, the architect supplies the needed, complete specifications. When the home is being designed and constructed for a specific client, the architect and customer usually develop a "specifications outline" together.

Purpose of Specifications

Working drawings and specification sheets (specs) become part of the total contract between the builder and owner. They are legal and binding on both parties. This illustrates the necessity of carefully preparing specifications for materials, fixtures, and tradework that leaves little or no chance for misunderstandings between the contractor and owner, Figure 35-1. Various forms for developing specifications are available. Some of these are short, while others are long and highly detailed. In some instances, the architect simply prepares specifications to the agreement of both parties.

Construction details are found on the working drawings. These details do not need to be repeated. Therefore, many of the details of the actual building construction do not show up on the specification sheets.

Figure 35-1. The architect is reviewing the working drawings and specification sheets for the new residence under construction with the clients. (Marvin Windows)

The owner should carefully discuss the details of construction with the architect and, in most cases, rely on the architect's judgment and suggestions for structural materials. On the other hand, the architect should carefully listen to the client's desires in such details as floor coverings, paint colors, type and style of hardware, plumbing fixtures, wallpaper, and other items involving individual taste. These items allow the clients to express their own personal tastes and preferences.

While material specifications are quite factual, the question of tradework and quality of construction is more difficult to define. What may appear to be a quality job of cabinet construction to one person may appear sloppy to another. It is the purpose of the specifications to include what both the contractor and owner agree on as an acceptable degree of tradework quality. The contractor should employ or subcontract only to qualified, skilled tradeworkers.

Specification Formats

There are many types and styles of standard specifications in both long and short form. Specification guides or outlines may be purchased locally or supplied by the architect.

Standard forms are also available from such organizations as the American Institute of Architects (AIA) and the Department of Veterans Affairs (VA). The VA form *Description of Materials* has become one of the leading guides for writing specifications. Information provided by specification forms should include:

- A description of the materials to be used. This includes sizes, quality, brand names, style, and specification numbers.
- List of required building operations. These are usually described under major headings such as excavation, masonry, carpentry, millwork, plumbing, electrical, insulation, etc.
- Notes relative to cash allowances for such items as lighting fixtures and hardware that are to be selected by the owner. Expenditures over the cash allowance must be paid by the owner.
- An indication that all of the specifications refer to the detailed plans of the working drawings.
- A statement or agreement on the quality of tradeworker's skill. This statement or agreement is often drawn up as a separate part of the contract. This is important to provide a definition of quality.
- Liability covered by the contractor during construction.

Examples of Specifications

Figure 35-2 shows a typical *contract specification sheet* prepared by an architect. This is a document that contains details of the responsibilities of the parties involved in a construction project. To create this document, the architect and owner review the working drawings together and come to an agreement on details of construction, design, and appliances.

A standard form, as shown in Figure 35-3, provides the necessary major headings for specifications. Each section may be filled in or left blank, as agreed to by the architect and client. Each topic on this standard specification form should be carefully discussed with the architect, and in some cases the builder, so that all understand and agree to its content.

CONTRACT SPECIFICATIONS

Mr. and Mrs. Frank E. Smith Residence
1103 Douglas Street
Glendale, GA

Date_____

EXCAVATION: House to be excavated to depths shown on drawings, backfilled and graded with existing soil. Excavation overcut in garage and lower level to be filled with sand. Twelve inches of sand to be furnished under garage floor. Tree removal is included only within building or drive area.

CONCRETE: All concrete to be 5 bag mix. Included is all foundation work, front sidewalk, garage floor, lower level floor, basement floor, and front stoop. Garage floor to have 6/6 wire mesh. All tie rods in lower level and basement are to be broken off on the inside and outside of foundation and inside of walls to have brushed cement finished coat. Furnish and install Andersen basement windows complete with area wells and grates.

WATERPROOFING: Exterior of lower level and basement to receive two coats of Portland cement plaster and one spray coat of bituminous waterproofing.

STEEL: All steel beams, angles, plates, columns, and lintels are a part of this contract.

LUMBER: All floor joists are to be 2 × 10 kiln-dried southern yellow pine. All studs to be 2 × 4 white fir precuts. Ceiling joists and roof rafters to be 2 × 6 white fir. Roof sheathing and subfloor to be 4 × 8 × 1/2 C-D plywood. Exterior siding to be channel type prestained rough sawn cedar. Fascia and soffit to be 1 × 8 prestained rough sawn cedar. Basement and lower level stairs to have 2 × 10 oak treads, pine risers, and stringers. Two rows of 1 × 3 cross bridging to be installed.

MASONRY: Residence to have face brick four sides with an allowance of $500/3000. Fireplace to be face brick at $500/3000 allowance with slate hearth, colonial damper, cast iron ash drop and cleanout, 13/13 tile flue. Color mortar or raked joints will be extra.

CARPENTRY: All carpentry labor is included for all rough and trim work, including installation of all cabinets, tops, appliances, and hardware. Front door, garage service door, and door from garage to lower level to be weather stripped and to have aluminum thresholds.

STAIRWAY: Stairway from first to second floor to be mill-made with oak treads and pine or white wood risers and stringers. Furnish railings for foyer and dining room.

MILLWORK: All trim to be Colonial white pine; all interior doors to be Colonial pine panel (first and second floor) 1-3/8" flush white birch on lower level; front and garage service doors to be 1-3/4" pine panel; door from garage to lower level to be 1-3/4" solid core pine panel; door from garage to lower level to be 1-3/4" solid core birch. All windows to be Andersen casements in insulating glass with screens on operating windows and muntin bars where indicated on drawings. All windows to have birch stools.

CABINETS: All kitchen and vanity cabinets to be birch or oak, prefinished, with ranch or provincial grooves and lap type doors with flush surface. Purchaser to select from standard finishes.

COUNTERTOPS: Kitchen and vanity countertops to be post formed one piece Formica and scribed to the wall. Maple cutting block to be included over dishwasher.

FLOORING: Floors for living room, dining room, upper hall, and bedrooms to be 5/8" plywood. Floors under ceramic tile in second floor baths and foyer to be 1/2" plywood. Floors in kitchen to be 5/8" underlayment plywood screwed in place. All floors to be laid directly on top of subfloors.

CERAMIC TILE: Foyer, lower hall, and closet to have ceramic floor with an allowance of $10 per square foot in place. Baths No. 1 and No. 2 to have ceramic floors and base with an allowance of $10 per square foot in place. Ceramic tile walls and ceiling of two showers and walls only at one tub with an in-place allowance of $10 per square foot All ceramic to be laid in mastic.

RESILIENT FLOORS: Kitchen floor to be vinyl inlaid with an installed allowance of $20 per square yard. Stairway from kitchen to lower hall, lower hall, laundry room, and future powder room to have vinyl tile floor with an allowance of $1.50 per square foot installed. Rubber base to be installed in workshop, lower hall, laundry room, future powder room, and den. Five chrome fixtures to be supplied and installed in second floor hall bath, four chrome fixtures in master bath, and two chrome fixtures in lower powder room.

DRYWALL: All drywall to be 1/2" adhesive applied before nailing (three coat finish) garage ceiling and firewall to be 5/8" fire code with three exterior walls to be 1/2" regular drywall.

INSULATION: Ceiling of house to have 12" fiberglass insulation except cathedral ceiling in living and dining room to have 4" fiberglass batt insulation. Walls of house to have 3-1/2" fiberglass batts and 3/4" rigid foam weatherboard. Garage ceiling and garage exterior walls are insulated similar to house.

GLAZING: Obscure DS glass to be installed in basement sash. A 54" × 48" plate glass mirror to be installed in upper hall bath. Decorative glass panels to be installed in garage.

SHINGLES: All shingles to be 235 lb. asphalt with adhesive tabs laid over 15 lb. roofing felt.

HEATING AND SHEET METAL: A Carrier or Bryant gas forced-air furnace and electric air conditioner to be installed with deluxe high wall returns on the second floor. A power humidifier, copper gutters and downspouts and flashing, exhaust ducts for fans are part of this contract.

WROUGHT IRON: A wrought iron railing is to be supplied and installed at stairway in garage.

PLUMBING: All plumbing fixtures to be Kohler in almond except blue in bath No. 2. Two water closets to be Willworth model. Two lavatories to be Castelle, one tub to be Caribbean, two prefab shower bases, one 32" × 21" stainless steel kitchen sink, one single compartment standard laundry tub. Water heater to be Rheem Fury 40 gal. glass lined. All faucets to be Moen mixing valve type. Shutoff valves are included at all sinks, lavatories, and water closets. Three hose bibs to be installed (front free type). Floor drain to be installed in basement, laundry room, and garage. Drawing tile to be installed around lower level and deep basement leading into a submersible sump pump for grade discharge. Gas lines to be run to furnace and water heater. Install dishwasher and disposal. All water lines to be copper and all sewer lines to be PVC. Install bypass for future softener by owner. Rough in only for powder room lavatory and water closet.

ELECTRICAL: 200 amp underground electrical service with circuit breakers, one recessed chime with front and rear button. Install 240 volt outlet for range and oven. Provide electrical installation of furnace, power humidifier, dishwasher, and disposal. Light fixture allowance is $1250.00.

HARDWARE: Interior and exterior door locks to be Schlage A Series. Kitchen cabinet and vanity hardware to be America. Allowance for all finish hardware is $800.00 which includes closet rods, hinges, locks, latches, pulls, door bumpers, etc.

PAINTING: First floor and lower level trim to be stained, sealed, an varnished. Walls and ceilings of house to receive a prime and finish coat. Exterior trim on windows and doors to receive two coats. Walltex is included at $16.00 per roll for baths No. 1 and 2. Second floor trim and doors to be painted (bedroom level).

APPLIANCES: Kitchenaid dishwasher No. KUDS215, Kitchenaid Disposal No. KBDS200, Kitchenaid Range top No. KECG260 with Grille, Kitchenaid Double Oven No. KEMS376. All are part of contract.

DRIVEWAY: A blacktop drive is to be installed over blacktop base

MEDICINE CABINETS: None in contract.

GARAGE DOOR: A 16'-0" × 7'-0" × 1-3/8" flush Masonite overhead garage door to be installed as manufactured by the Overhead Door Co.

SHOWER DOORS: Two shower doors are to be provided.

PATIO DOOR: An Arcadia aluminum framed patio door 8'-0" wide with insulating glass and screen to be installed in kitchen.

GAS LIGHT: A standard gas post light is to be installed at front of driveway.

PERMIT: All permits and inspection fees are included in this contract.

SURVEY: Topography, survey, and building site are a part of this contract.

INSURANCE: Contractor to carry builders risk, covering fire theft, liability, and property damage. Purchaser to insure building upon final closing.

QUALITY: Contractor to provide all material necessary to build on real estate in a good, substantial, and quality tradeworker manner.

Figure 35-2. A set of contract specifications for a home designed specifically for the owner. Details of the specifications are planned by hours of discussions between the architect and client.

Description of Materials

U.S. DEPARTMENT OF HOUSING AND URBAN DEVELOPMENT
DEPARTMENT OF VETERANS AFFAIRS
FARMERS HOME ADMINISTRATION

HUD's OMB APPROVAL NO. 2502-0192 (exp. 1/31/2001)
and 2502-0313 (exp. 8/31/2001)

Public reporting burden for this collection of information is estimated to average 30 minutes per response, including the time for reviewing instructions, searching existing data sources, gathering and maintaining the data needed, and completing and reviewing the collection of information. This agency may not collect this information, and you are not required to complete this form, unless it displays a currently valid OMB control number.
The National Housing Act (12 USC 1703) authorizes insuring financial institutions against default losses on single family mortgages. HUD must evaluate the acceptability and value of properties to be insured. The information collected here will be used to determine if

[ ] Proposed Construction   [ ] Under Construction   No. .... (To be inserted by HUD, VA

Name and address of Mortgagor or Sponsor	Name and address of Contractor or Builder

Instructions

1. For additional information on how this form is to be submitted, number of copies, etc., see the instructions applicable to the HUD Application for Mortgage Insurance, VA Request for Determination of Reasonable Value, or FmHA Property Information and Appraisal Report , as the case may be.
2. Describe all materials and equipment to be used, whether or not shown on the drawings, by marking an X in each appropriate check-box and entering the information called for each space. If

3. Work not specifically described or shown will not be considered unless required, then the minimum acceptable will be assumed. Work exceeding minimum requirements cannot be considered unless specifically described.
4. Include no alternates, "or equal" phrases, or contradictory items. (Consideration of a request for acceptance of substitute materiels or equipment is thereby precluded.)
5. Include signatures required at the end of this form.
6. The construction shall be completed in compliance with the related drawings and specifications, as amended during processing. The specifications include this Description of

1. Excavation
Bearing soil, type ....

2. Foundations
Footings concrete mix .... strength psi .... Reinforcing ....
Foundation wall material .... Reinforcing ....
Interior foundation wall material .... Party foundation wall ....
Columns material and sizes .... Piers material and reinforcing ....
Girders material and sizes .... Sills material ....
Basement entrance areaway .... Windows areaways ....
Waterproofing .... Footing drains ....
Termite protection ....
Basementless space ground cover .... insulation .... foundation vents ....
Special foundations ....
Additional information ....

3. Chimneys
Material .... Prefabricated (make and size) ....
Flue lining material .... Heater flue size .... Fireplace flue size ....
Vents (material and size) gas or oil heater .... water heater ....
Additional information ....

4. Fireplaces
Type [ ] solid fuel [ ] gas burning [ ] circulator (make and size) .... Ash dump and clean-out ....
Fireplace facing .... lining .... hearth .... mantel ....
Additional information ....

Figure 35-3. This standard Department of Veterans Affairs form lends itself well to all types of specifications for residential construction. *Continued.* (Department of Veterans Affairs)

5. Exterior Walls

Wood frame wood grade, and species .... ☐ Corner bracing Building paper or felt ....

Sheathing ....thickness........................width............ ☐ solid ☐ spaced ....o.c. ☐ diagonal ....

Siding .... grade ....type .... size...........exposure ....fastening ....

Shingles .... grade ....type .... size...........exposure ....fastening ....

Stucco .... thickness ....Lath ....weight .... lb.

Masonry veneer..Sills ....Lintels ....Base flashing ....

Masonry ☐ solid ☐ faced ☐ stuccoed total wall thickness ....facing thickness ....facing material ....

Backup material ....thickness .... bonding ....

Door sills ....Window sills ....Lintels ....Base flashing ....

Interior surfaces dampproofing,..................coats of...furring ....

Additional information

Exterior painting material

Gable wall construction ☐ same as main walls ☐ other construction ....

6. Floor Framing

Joists wood, grade, and species..other.............................bridging ....anchors ....

Concrete slab ☐ basement floor ☐ first floor ☐ ground supported ☐ self-supporting mix ....thickness ....

reinforcing ....insulation ....membrane ....

Fill under slab material ....thickness ....

Additional information

7. Subflooring (Describe underflooring for special floors under Item 21)

Material grade and species...size ....type ....

Laid ☐ first floor ☐ second floor ☐ attic .... sq. ft. ☐ diagonal ☐ right angles

Additional information

8. Finish Flooring (Wood only. Describe underflooring for special floors under Item 21)

Location	Rooms	Grade	Species	Thickness	Width	Bldg. Paper	Finish
First floor							
Second floor							
Attic floor	sq. ft.						

Additional information

9. Partition Framing

Studs wood, grade, and species...size and spacing ....Other.....................................

Additional information

10. Ceiling Framing

Joists wood, grade, and species ....Other..................................Bridging ....

11. Roof Framing

Rafters wood, grade, and species ....Roof trusses (see detail) grade and species ....

Additional information ....

12. Roofing

Sheathing wood, grade, and species .... ☐ solid ☐ spaced.............. o.c.

Roofing......................................grade ....size.............type...

Underlay.. weight or thickness.........................size..................fastening.....................

Built-up roofing... number of plies...................surfacing material..

Flashing material... gage or weight.........................☐ gravel stops ☐ snow guards

Additional information

ref. HUD Handbook 4145.1 &4950.1 form HUD-92005 (10/84)
VA Form 26-1852 and form FmHA 424-2

Figure 35-3. *Continued.* (Department of Veterans Affairs)

13. Gutters and Downspouts

Gutters material .... gage or weight .... size .... shape ....

Downspouts material .... gage or weight .... size .... shape .... number ....

Downspouts connected to ☐ Storm sewer ☐ sanitary sewer ☐ dry-well ☐ Splash blocks material and size ....

Additional information

14. Lath and Plaster

Lath ☐ walls ☐ ceilings material .... weight or thickness .... Plaster coats .... finish ....

Dry-wall ☐ walls ☐ ceilings material .... thickness .... finish ....

Joint treatment

15. Decorating (Paint, wallpaper, etc

Rooms	Wall Finish Material and Application	Ceiling Finish Material and Application
Kitchen		
Bath		
Other		

Additional information

16. Interior Doors and Trim

Doors type .... material .... thickness ....

Door trim type .... material .... Base type .... material .... size ....

Finish doors .... trim ....

Other trim (item, type and location) ....

Additional information

17. Windows

Windows type .... make .... material .... sash thickness ....

Glass grade .... ☐ sash weights ☐ balances, type .... head flashing ....

Trim type .... material .... Paint .... number coats ....

Weather-stripping type .... material .... Storm sash, number ....

Screens ☐ full ☐ half   type .... number .... screen cloth material ....

Basement windows type .... material .... screens, number .... Storm sash, number ....

Special windows ....

Additional information

18. Entrances and Exterior Detail

Main entrance door   material .... width .... thickness .... Frame material .... thickness ....

Other entrance doors   material .... width .... thickness .... Frame material .... thickness ....

Head flashing .... Weatherstripping type .... saddles ....

Screen doors   thickness .... number .... screen cloth material .... Storm doors thickness .... number ....

Combination storm and screen doors thickness .... number .... screen cloth material ....

Shutters ☐ hinged ☐ fixed   Railings .... Attic louvers ....

Exterior millwork grade and species .... Paint .... number coats ....

Additional information

19. Cabinets and Interior Detail

Kitchen cabinets, wall units material .... lineal feet of shelves .... shelf width ....

Base units material .... counter top .... edging ....

Back and end splash .... Finish of cabinets .... number coats ....

Medicine cabinets make .... model ....

Other cabinets and built-in furniture

Additional information

Retain this record for three years   Page 3 of 6   ref. HUD Handbook 4145.1 &4950.1 form HUD-92005 (10/84)
                                                                             VA Form 26-1852 and form FmHA 424-2

Figure 35-3. *Continued.* (Department of Veterans Affairs)

20. Stairs

Stair	Treads		Risers		Strings		Handrail		Balusters	
	Material	Thickness	Material	Thickness	Material	Size	Material	Size	Material	Size
Basement										
Main										
Attic										

Disappearing make and model number ....

Additional information

21. Special Floors and Wainscot (Describe Carpet as listed in Certified Products Directory)

	Location	Material, Color, Border, Sizes, Gage, Etc.	Threshold Material	Wall Base Material	Underfloor Material
Floors	Kitchen				
	Bath				

	Location	Material, Color, Border, Sizes, Gage, Etc.	Height	Height Over Tub	Height in Showers (From Floor)
Wainscot	Bath				

Additional information

22. Plumbing

Fixture	Number	Location	Make	MFR's Fixture Identification No.	Size	Color
Sink						
Lavatory						
Water closet						
Bathtub						
Shower over tub						
Stall shower						
Laundry trays						

Bathroom accessories ☐ Recessed material .... number .... ☐ Attached material .... number ....

Additional information

☐ Curtain rod   ☐ Door   ☐ Shower pan material................................... *(Show and describe individual system in complete detail in separate
Water supply ☐ public ☐ community system ☐ individual (private) system*   drawings and specifications according to requirements.)
Sewage disposal ☐ public ☐ community system ☐ individual (private) system*
House drain (inside) ☐ cast iron ☐ tile ☐ other.........................House sewer (outside) ☐ cast iron ☐ tile ☐ other ....
Water piping ☐ galvanized steel ☐ copper tubing ☐ other .... Sill cocks, number...
Domestic water heater type.............................. make and model ....heating capacity.................................... gph. 100°rise.
Storage tank material.. capacity......................... gallons
Gas service ☐ utility company ☐ liq. pet. gas ☐ other..................................... ☐ Gas piping   ☐ cooking   ☐ house heating
Footing drains connected to ☐ storm sewer ☐ sanitary sewer ☐ dry well ☐ Sump pump make and model
capacity.. discharges into ....

Additional information

Figure 35-3. *Continued.* (Department of Veterans Affairs)

23. Heating

☐ Hot Water   ☐ Steam ☐ Vapor   ☐ One-pipe system   ☐ Two-pipe system

☐ Radiators   ☐ Convectors   ☐ Baseboard radiation   Make and model ....

☐ Radiant panel ☐ floor ☐ wall ☐ ceiling   Panel coil material...

☐ Circulator   ☐ Return pump make and model ....capacity.................................gpm.

Boiler make and model .... Output.............. Btuh. net rating ....Btuh.

Additional information

Warm air ☐ Gravity ☐ Forced   Type of system ....

Duct material supply .... return .... Insulation ....thickness .... ☐ Outside air intake

Furnace: make and model .... Input .... Btuh. output .... Btuh.

Additional information

☐ Space heater   ☐ floor furnace ☐ wall heaterinput ....Btuh. output ....Btuh. number units ....

Make, model

Additional information

Controls make and types

Additional information

Fuel: ☐ Coal ☐ oil   ☐ gas ☐ liq. pet. gas ☐ electric   other .... storage capacity ....

Additional information

Firing equipment furnished separately ☐ Gas burner, conversion type☐ Stoker hopper feed ☐ bin feed

Oil burner ☐ pressure atomizing ☐ vaporizing   ....

Make and model ....

Control ....

Additional information

Electric heating system type .... Input ....watts @ .... volts output ....Btuh.

Additional information

Ventilating equipment ☐ attic fan, make and model .... capacity ....cfm.

☐ kitchen exhaust fan, make and model ....

Other heating, ventilating, or cooling equipment ....

Additional information

24. Electric Wiring

Service ☐ overhead ☐ underground Panel ☐ fuse box ☐ circuit-breaker   make .... AMP's .... No. circuits ....

Wiring ☐ conduit   ☐ armored cable ☐ nonmetallic cable ☐ knob and tube ☐ other ....

Special outlets ☐ range ☐ water heater ☐ other ....

Doorbell ☐ Chimes ☐ Push-button locations ....

Additional information

25. Lighting Fixtures

Total number of fixtures.. Total allowance for fixtures, typical installation, $...

Nontypical installation...

Additional information

Figure 35-3. *Continued.* (Department of Veterans Affairs)

26. Insulation

Location	Thickness	Material, Type, and Method of Installation	Vapor Barrier
Roof			
Ceiling			
Wall			
Floor			

27. Miscellaneous: (Describe any main dwelling materials, equipment, or construction items not shown elsewhere; or use to provide additional information where the space provided was inadequate. Always reference by item number to correspond to numbering used on this form.)

Hardware (make, material, and finish)

Special Equipment (State material or make, model and quantity. Include only equipment and appliances which are acceptable by local law, custom and applicable FHA standards. Do not include items which, by established custom, are supplied by occupant and removed when he vacates premises or chattels prohibited by law from becoming realty.)

Porches

Terraces

Garages

Walks and Driveways

Driveway width················· base material ·························thickness ·················surfacing material ·······························thickness ·······························

Front walk width················ material··························· thickness ·············Service walk width ·················material ··········thickness ·······························

Steps material ·· treads ················· risers ················Cheek walls ···

Other Onsite Improvements

(Specify all exterior onsite improvements not described elsewhere, including items such as unusual grading, drainage structures, retaining walls, fence, railings, and accessory structures.)

Landscaping, Planting, and Finish Grading

Topsoil········ thick ☐ front yard ☐ side yards ☐ rear yard to ································feet behind main building

Lawns (seeded, sodded, or sprigged) ☐ front yard ······························☐side yards ························· ☐ rear yard ·······························

Planting ☐ as specified and shown on drawings ☐ as follows:

··············· Shade trees deciduous················ caliper ············Evergreen trees ························ to ···················B&B ·····························

··············· Low flowering trees deciduous ···················· to ···················· ············Evergreen shrubs························ to ···················B&B·····························

··············· High-growing shrubs deciduous ··················· to ··················· ············Vines, 2-year ···

··············· Medium-growing shrubs deciduous ············· to ··················· Other

··············· Low-growing shrubs deciduous ···················· to ···················

Identification - This exhibit shall be identified by the signature of the builder, or sponsor, and/or the proposed mortgagor if the latter is known at the time of application.

Date (mm/dd/yyyy)·· Signature

Signature

Figure 35-3. *Continued.* (Department of Veterans Affairs)

Internet Resources

www.aia.org
   American Institute of Architects

www.amercon.com
   The American Contractor, a publisher of software for construction and service contractors

www.a-systems.net
   A-Systems Corporation, publisher of accounting software for the construction industry

www.buildertools.com
   Builder Software Tools, Inc.

www.cdci.com
   Construction Data Control, Inc. (CDCI), a publisher of software for construction professionals

www.cpsenet.com
   Computer Presentation Systems, Inc., a provider of software for homebuilders

www.dealbuilder.com
   DealBuilder, a publisher of residential project planning software

www.ecs-inc.com
   Enterprise Computer Systems, Inc., a provider of technology solutions for the building materials industry

www.va.gov
   Department of Veterans Affairs

Review Questions – Chapter 35

Write your answers on a separate sheet of paper. Do not write in this book.

1. Briefly list the six major types of information that should be included in any set of specifications for a residential structure.

2. Why is it important that the architect listen carefully to the desires of the client when writing specifications?

3. The architect often writes the complete specifications for a house when the house is constructed for _____.

4. Specification sheets and working drawings become part of the _____ between the builder and the owner.

5. A cash allowance is often provided for which items?

6. Why is an agreement on tradeworker quality an important item on a specification sheet?

7. Explain why many of the details of the actual building construction do not show up on the specification sheets.

Suggested Activities

1. Prepare a specification sheet, as illustrated in Figure 35-2, for one of the homes you have designed during this course. Or, use a set of working drawings supplied by your instructor. Have another student be the client. Use this person's suggestions for appliances, floor coverings, and other items.

2. Write to manufacturers of appliances and plumbing fixtures or visit their web sites. Prepare a bulletin board display of the latest fixtures that a client can select from when planning a new home.

3. Visit a brick supplier and obtain information on the types of face brick available for residential construction and present prices. Write a short report on how you would present the selection of face brick and cost allowance to a client when planning specifications.

4. Secure a set of working drawings for a residence. Using the Department of Veterans Affairs form *Description of Materials,* fill in all necessary information. Note: This form can be downloaded from their web site. Plan the specifications as if you were to be the owner. Using the material obtained in Activity 2, make selections based on your preferences.

5. If your CADD system has schedule-generation functions, create an automated schedule for use in specifying materials or workmanship quality.

Estimating Building Cost

36

Objectives

After studying this chapter, you will be able to:

➤ Explain the process of estimating the building cost.

➤ Generate a typical materials list for a simple structure.

➤ Estimate the cost of a residential structure using the square foot or cubic foot method.

Key Terms

Cubic Foot Method
Estimating
Material Takeoff
Square Foot Method

Preliminary Estimates

After the house has been designed, construction drawings completed, and material and tradework specifications prepared, an estimate should be made of the cost to build the house. *Estimating* is an organized effort to determine the total cost of materials, labor, and other services required to build a house. Two methods of estimating the cost of building a home are the square foot method and the cubic foot method. A rough estimate of the building cost may be determined by using either method.

Square Foot Method

The *square foot method* produces an estimate of the building cost based on the total area in the house. The first step is to compute the number of square feet in the house. Then, this number is multiplied by a constant that is determined by local conditions. Garages, porches, and basements are figured separately since they are not as expensive to construct as the living part of the house. These are usually figured at one half of the cost per square foot of the living area.

The number of square feet is determined by multiplying the length of the house by the width. All wall thicknesses are included in the total. For example, a 24' × 60' house with a 20' × 20' garage has 1440 square feet of living space plus 400 square feet of garage space. If the building cost per square foot is $100, then building cost of the living area is 1,440 × $100 = $144,000. The building cost of the garage is 400 × $50 = $20,000. The estimated building cost of the complete home then is $164,000. This price does not include the land.

The constant of $100 per square foot is used for comparative purposes. This figure is reasonable for some areas, but may vary substantially in different locations, for different styles of homes, and by materials specified. For example, a ranch-style home is more expensive to build than a two-story home that provides the same area of living space. Most builders use a different constant for each house style and adjust it for special features, such as an extra bath or fireplace. Before trying to calculate the cost of a home, check with local builders to determine the constant for your area.

Cubic Foot Method

The *cubic foot method* produces an estimate of the building cost based on the volume of the house, rather than area. The volume of a house is determined by finding the area and then multiplying this by the height. The height is figured from the floor to the ceiling for each level of the house, including the basement. The attic volume is also included, which is calculated by finding the area (length by the width) and multiplying this figure by 1/2 of the rise. The rise of the roof is the distance from the ceiling to the ridge. This procedure takes into account the volume lost due to the sloping roof.

If the 24′ × 60′ house is used for the cubic foot method, the area is 1,440 square feet and the height is 8′. Therefore, 1,440 × 8 = 11,520 cubic feet for the living space, not including the attic. The area of the attic is 1,440 square feet and the rise is 4′. Therefore, 1,440 × 2 = 2,800 cubic feet for the attic. The total cubic feet for the house is 11,520 + 2,880 = 14,400 cubic feet. If the cost for a cubic foot is $10, the estimated building cost for the living space is 14,400 × $10 = $144,000.

The volume of the garage must also be computed and added to this figure. The volume is 400 × 8 = 3,200 cubic feet. The garage attic with a rise of 3′ is 400 × 1-1/2 = 600 cubic feet. The total volume of the garage is 3,200 + 600 = 3,800 cubic feet. The cost per cubic foot of garage space is figured at 1/2 of the cost per cubic foot of the living space. Therefore, the estimated building cost of the garage is 3,800 × $5 = $19,000. Total estimated building cost of the house using the cubic foot method is $144,000 + $19,000 = $163,000, not including land cost.

Compare the estimates calculated by the square foot method and the cubic foot method. The difference in estimated building cost is $1000 in this case. Remember, in order to achieve an accurate estimate with either method, you must use an accurate constant.

More Accurate Estimates

There are so many variables involved in the cost of a home that estimates obtained by the square foot or cubic foot method may vary considerably from the actual cost. A cost estimate that is more accurate may be obtained by determining the quantity, quality, and cost of materials to be used and the cost of labor required for installation. This method is called *material takeoff.* You must also include an allowance for material waste, supervision, and overhead.

The first step in compiling an accurate estimate is to study the construction drawings very carefully to become fully acquainted with the various elements of the structure. The specifications must also be examined carefully to determine the quality of materials and tradework specified. Both of these factors affect the final cost, Figure 36-1.

After one is intimately familiar with the plans, a list may be compiled of the materials required to construct the house. Most estimates follow the headings as listed on a good set of specifications. The order of the headings usually coincides with the construction sequence. When all the materials have been listed and priced, a total cost for materials can be calculated. Prices should be secured from sources where the materials will be purchased to get an accurate figure. A typical materials list is shown in Figure 36-2.

Now that the cost of materials has been determined, the labor cost must be calculated.

Figure 36-1. The nonstandard sizes and unique styles found on this house considerably increased the building cost. (Photo Courtesy of James Hardie® Siding Products)

In the past, labor cost was less than half of the total building cost for a house. Today, in most sections of the country the labor cost ranges from 60% to 80% of the total building cost. The labor cost for building a house has steadily increased year after year. It would be wise to research this area carefully before trying to estimate labor cost. Publications are available, such as the Building Construction Cost Data Book, that give detailed information on labor cost for various areas of the country. General contractors and subcontractors can also provide help in arriving at the projected cost. Their experience will enable them to make an accurate estimate of labor cost for a given job.

Other costs that must be included in the total building cost are the fees for permits. Most areas require a building permit, plumbing permit, electrical permit, and health permit. Also, there may be impact fees and

fees for hookup of electrical, gas, sewer, telephone, and water services. The cost of these permits and fees may be as small as a few dollars or as much as several hundred dollars. In addition, many builders add the cost of insurance to protect materials and workers in the event of an accident or damage. This cost should also be added to the cost of construction. Investigate these areas to determine their exact costs.

Once all of these elements are evaluated, the total building cost of the house can be calculated. This estimate will most likely be more accurate than the approximate methods presented earlier, but it may still be a few hundred dollars off. It is impossible to exactly calculate the building cost of a house, Figure 36-3. The final building cost may vary from the estimate for several reasons, such as material price fluctuations and labor overruns.

Article and Description	Price	Amount	Article and Description	Price	Amount
General Information			**Carpenter's Lumber List (continued)**		
Area of Basement, 1240 Square Feet _____			Deck Beams		
Area of First Floor, 2250 Square Feet _____			2 Pcs., 2 × 10 × 14'-0" _____		
Height of Basement Floor to First Floor,			2 Pcs., 2 × 10 × 12'-0" _____		
9'-1 5/8" and 10'-1 5/8" _____			4 Pcs., 2 × 10 × 8'-0" _____		
First Floor Ceiling Height, 8'-0", 7'-0" and Slopes _____			2 Pcs., 2 × 8 × 18'-0" _____		
Ceiling to Roof, 4'-6" and 3'-1" _____			12 Pcs., 2 × 8 × 14'-0" _____		
Size of Garage and/or Carport, 24'-1" × 22'-10" _____			10 Pcs., 2 × 8 × 10'-0" _____		
			4 Pcs., 2 × 8 × 6'-0" _____		
Excavating and Grading (will vary with local site conditions)			Deck Flooring		
Rough Excavating, depends on site_____			21 Pcs., 2 × 6 (redwood) × 14'-0" _____		
Trench Excavating (wall footings), 19 Cubic Yards _____			18 Pcs., 2 × 6 (redwood) × 12'-0" _____		
Backfill, depends on site and soil _____			18 Pcs., 2 × 6 (redwood) × 10'-0" _____		
Finished Grading, depends on site _____			18 Pcs., 2 × 6 (redwood) × 8'-0" _____		
Hand Excavating (column footings), 1/2 Cubic Yard_____			Lintels		
Material Sub Total_____			2 Pcs., 2 × 12 × 15'-0" (Flitch beams) _____		
Labor Sub Total _____			8 Pcs., 2 × 12 × 18'-0" (Flitch beams) _____		
			6 Pcs., 2 × 12 × 3'-4" _____		
Masonry			2 Pcs., 2 × 12 × 3'-8" _____		
Concrete Footings, 19.5 Cubic Yards _____			2 Pcs., 2 × 12 × 5'-0" _____		
Concrete Walls			2 Pcs., 2 × 12 × 7'-0" _____		
4" Block, 40 Square Feet _____			8 Pcs., 2 × 12 × 9'-0" _____		
8" Block, 1600 Square Feet _____			2 Pcs., 2 × 12 × 10'-0" _____		
10" Block, 40 Square Feet _____			Stair Stringers		
12" Block, 420 Square Feet _____			3 Pcs., 2 × 12 × 16'-0" _____		
Exposed Concrete above Grade (block), 60 Square Feet _____			Exterior Wall Plates, 2 × 4 × 1260' _____		
Reinforcing Rods			Exterior Wall Plates, 2 × 6 × 150' _____		
2 - #4×4'-0" _____			Exterior Studs		
18 - #3×30'-0" _____			180 Pcs., 2 × 4 × 8'-0" _____		
Wire Mesh Reinforcing, 2100 Square Feet _____			93 Pcs., 2 × 4 × 9'-0" _____		
Concrete Basement Floor 4" Thick ×1200 Square Feet _____			7 Pcs., 2 × 4 × 10'-0" _____		
Patio Floor 4" Thick × 225 Square Feet_____			9 Pcs., 2 × 4 × 11'-0" _____		
Concrete Platforms on Ground (@ garbage cans),			6 Pcs., 2 × 4 × 12'-0" _____		
4" Thick × 15 Square Feet _____			Interior Plates		
Concrete Sidewalks (under flagstone walk),			2 × 4, 800' _____		
4" Thick × 15 Square Feet _____			2 × 6, 30' _____		
Garage Floor, 4" Thick × 600 Square Feet _____			2 × 8, 105' _____		
Concrete Steps (under flagstone), 7 Square Feet _____			Interior Studs		
Concrete Hearth setting bed for flagstone for fireplace,			55 Pcs., 2 × 4 × 9'-0" _____		
3" Thick × 6 Square Feet _____			7 Pcs., 2 × 6 × 9'-0" _____		
Flue Lining			10 Pcs., 2 × 8 × 9'-0" _____		
12" × 16" T.C., 21' _____			210 Pcs., 2 × 4 × 8'-0" _____		
8" × 8" T.C., 19' _____			11 Pcs., 2 × 6 × 8'-0" _____		
220 Firebrick_____			25 Pcs., 2 × 8 × 8'-0" _____		
2400 Common Brick and Chimney_____			Headers		
Mortar, 8.2 Cubic Yards _____			2 Pcs., 2 × 12 × 4'-0" _____		
Drain Tile (depends on site), as required _____			18 Pcs., 2 × 4 × 3'-0" _____		
Chimney Cap, 15 Square Feet_____			16 Pcs., 2 × 4 × 2'-8" _____		
Supported Concrete Slabs,			6 Pcs., 2 × 6 × 4'-4" _____		
1" setting bed × 185 Square Feet _____			4 Pcs., 2 × 8 × 6'-4" _____		
Supported Concrete Slabs, 4" Thick × 175 Square Feet_____			Roof Sheathing 1/2" Plywood, 3850 Board Feet _____		
Stone Veneer, 8" Thick × 34'-0"×10'-0" _____			Ridge Boards, 2 × 10, 110' _____		
Pea Gravel Patio and Walk, 3 Cubic Yards_____			Rafters		
19,000 Exterior Face Brick _____			60 Pcs., 2 × 8 × 22'-0" _____		
Flagstones, 250 Square Feet _____			97 Pcs., 2 × 8 × 16'-0" _____		
6 Vents in Foundation Walls _____			14 Pcs., 2 × 8 × 12'-0" _____		
Cement Block Quoins			4 Pcs., 2 × 8 × 10'-0" _____		
160, 8" Blocks_____			Fascia Cornice 1 × 10, 340' _____		
15, 10" Blocks_____			Porch Steps		
45, 12" Blocks_____			2 Pcs., 2 × 12 × 10'-0" _____		
Water Proofing Foundation Walls, 850 Square Feet _____			Waterproof Roofing Paper, 38-1/2 Squares _____		
Material Sub Total _____			Building Paper under Wood Floor, 21-1/2 Squares _____		
Labor Sub Total _____			Posts		
			1 Pc., 4 × 4 × 8'-0" _____		
Carpenter's Lumber List			Girders Laminated Beams		
Joists			1 Pc., 5-1/4" × 14-1/2" × 24'-0" _____		
42 Pcs., 2 × 12 × 20'-0" _____			Porch Posts		
38 Pcs., 2 × 12 × 18'-0" _____			8 Pcs., 4 × 4 × 8'-0" _____		
23 Pcs., 2 × 12 × 16'-0" _____			Porch Railing 2 × 4, 128 Linear Feet _____		
3 Pcs., 2 × 12 × 8'-0" _____			Porch Cap 2 × 6, 64 Linear Feet _____		
Bridging 1 × 4, 340 Square Feet _____			Exterior Sheathing 1/2" Insulating Board,		
Sub Flooring, 2010 Square Feet _____			2400 Square Feet _____		
Ceiling Joists _____			Siding, 1250 Square Feet_____		
13 Pcs., 2 × 8 × 20'-0" _____			Basement Stair Posts		
27 Pcs., 2 × 16 × 18'-0" _____			1 Pc., 4 × 4 × 8'-0" _____		
8 Pcs., 2 × 6 × 16'-0" _____			Basement Stair Railings		
50 Pcs., 2 × 6 × 12'-0" _____			1 Pc., 2 × 4 × 6'-0" _____		
23 Pcs., 2 × 6 × 8'-0" _____					
8 Pcs., 2 × 6 × 14'-0" _____			(Continued on next page)		

Figure 36-2. Typical list for materials, fixtures, and finishes. (Continued)

Article and Description	Price	Amount	Article and Description	Price	Amount
Soffits or Roof Overhang			**Cabinets and Miscellaneous Millwork (continued)**		
1/2″ Plywood, 3′-4″ × 205′			**Kitchen Cupboards**		
1/2″ Plywood, 2′-0″ × 145′			Doors and Exposed Faces, 180 Square Feet		
Scaffolding and Extra Joists (approx.), as required			Sides and Partitions, 100 Square Feet		
Plastic Ceiling at Kitchen and Master Bath			Shelves, 115 Square Feet		
3 Pcs., 1 × 12 × 14′-0″			Backs, Sides, and Bottom, 90 Square Feet		
Valance			Tops (Plastic Laminated), 65 Square Feet		
1 × 6, 126′			1 × 2 Framing, 220′		
1 × 10, 132′			Wood Legs at Island, 7		
Furring Strips, as required			Drawer Track, 20 Ft.		
Wind Stops at Eaves, 300′			**Basement Stairs**		
Battens 1 × 2, 1100′			16 Pine Risers 7-1/2″ × 3/4″ × 3′4″		
Shelving			15 Oak Treads 10-1/2″ × 1-1/4″ × 3′4″		
10 Pcs., 1 × 10 × 10′-0″			Decorative Screen-In Foyer, 7′-0 × 11′-0″		
8 Pcs., 1 × 10 × 8′-0″			Clothes Chute Door 3/4″ Plywood, 1′-0″ × 2′-6″		
Rafter Ties			**Bathroom Cabinets (1st Floor)**		
2 × 4, 70′			1 × 2 Frame, 53′		
24 Pcs., 2 × 4 × 10′-0″			1 × 4 Kickboard, 12′-4″		
Material Sub Total			Doors, etc., 31 Square Feet		
Labor Sub Total			Shelves, etc., 67 Square Feet		
			Special Beams (false)		
MILLWORK			2 Pcs., 2 × 4 × 18′-0″		
Windows and Screens (as selected)			5 Pcs., 4 × 4 × 18′-0″		
Window Frames			**Window Valances**		
4 4′-0″ × 6′-0″ Vertical Sliding Steel Windows			1 × 10, 130′.		
3 Double 4′-0″ × 6′-0″ Vertical Sliding Steel Windows			1 × 6, 130′.		
4 4′-0″ × 5′-0″ Vertical Sliding Steel Windows			**China Closets**		
1 3′-0″ × 3′-0″ Horizontal Sliding Steel Windows			3 16″ × 28″ × 1/4″ Plate Glass Shelves		
Fixed Plastic Screen (weather resistant)			2 54″ Adjustable Shelf Standards		
			6 16″ Adjustable Shelf Brackets		
Note: Provide frames for above plastic screens.			3″ × 1-1/8″ × 2′-4″ Plate Glass Shelves		
Storm Sash and Window screens or Rolling Metal Screens,			2-1/4″ × 1-1/8″ × 4′-8″ Plate Glass Shelve		
as required			3/4″ × 3/4″ × 9′-0″ Plate Glass Shelves		
			15″ × 24″ × 1/4″ Frosted Plastic Top		
Doors and Trim			3/4″ Plywood, 40 Square Feet		
Exterior Door Frames			2 × 6 – 4′-8″		
4 Frames for 2′-8″ × 6′-8″ × 1-3/4″ Solid Core Wood Doors			1 × 3 – 5′-0″		
1 Frame for 2-2′-8″ × 6′8″×1-3/4″ Solid Core Wood Doors			2 × 3 – 2′-4″		
1 Frame for 2′-8″ × 6′-8″ × 1-3/8″ Hollow Core Wood Doors			**Breakfast Room Cabinets**		
1 Frame for 16′-0″ × 8′-0″ Sliding Glass Door			Kickboard 1 × 4, 8′.		
3 Frames for 8′-0″ × 6′-8″ Sliding Glass Door			Doors and Sides, 56 Square Feet		
Interior Door Frames			Shelves, 53 Square Feet		
8 Frames 2′-8″ × 6′-8″ × 1-3/8″ Hollow Core Wood Doors			Frame 1 × 2, 53′		
7 Frames 2′-4″ × 6′-8″ × 1-3/8″ Hollow Core Wood Doors			**Full Length Mirror**		
3 Frames 4′-0″ × 6′-8″ × 1-3/8″ Hollow Core Wood Doors			**Baths**		
(folding)			1 80 × 50		
2 Frames for 6′-0″ × 6′-8″ × 1-3/8″ Hollow Core			1 68 × 50		
Wood Doors (folding)			**Basement**		
Special Door Frames			1 68 × 50		
1 Frame for 2′-0″ × 6′-8″ Shower Door (master bath)			Material Sub Total		
Exterior Doors			Labor Sub Total		
6 2′-8″ × 6′-8″ × 1-3/4″ Solid Core Doors					
1 2′-8″ × 6′-8″ × 1-3/8″ Hollow Core Door			**Insulation**		
1 16′-0″ × 8′-0″ Sliding Glass Door			Batt Type Ceilings, 2230 Square Feet		
3 8′-0″ × 6′-8″ Sliding Glass Doors			Batt Type Walls, 1650 Square Feet		
Interior Doors			Material Sub Total		
8 2′-8″ × 6′-8″ × 1-3/8″ Hollow Core Doors			Labor Sub Total		
7 2′-4″ × 6′-8″ × 1-3/8″ Hollow Core Doors					
6 2′-0″ × 6′-8″ × 1-3/8″ Hollow Core Folding Doors (louvered)			**Weatherstripping and Caulking**		
4 3′-0″ × 6′-8″ × 1-3/8″ Hollow Core Folding Doors (louvered)			Windows, 275′		
Interior Door Trim, 330 Linear Feet			Exterior Doors, 205′		
Screen Doors, as required			Material Sub Total		
			Labor Sub Total		
Cabinets and Miscellaneous Millwork					
Room Base, 375′			**Plastering or Drywall**		
Clothes Closet Hook Strips, 75′			Living Room Walls, 340 Square Feet		
(Including Storage Closet but not Kitchen)			Living Room Ceiling, 530 Square Feet		
At other shelving, 125′			Dining Room Walls, 290 Square Feet		
Closet Shelving, 1′-6″ × 115′			Dining Room Ceiling, 215 Square Feet		
Closet Shelving, 1′-8″ × 12′-6″			Foyer Walls, 31 Square Feet		
Closet Poles, 50′			Foyer Ceiling, 102 Square Feet		
Outside Door Thresholds, Entry – Bronze Thresholds, × 5′-4″			Hall Walls, 250 Square Feet		
Ceiling Mold around Chimney, 30′-0″			Hall Ceiling, 80 Square Feet		
Kitchen Broom Closet and Pantry			Basement Stairway Walls, 300 Square Feet		
5 Shelves 1′-8″ × 3/4″ × 2′-6″			Basement Stairway Ceiling, 35 Square Feet		
2 Sides 1′-8″ × 3/4″ × 8′-0″			Kitchen Walls, 490 Square Feet		
10 Cleats, 1′-2″ × 1′-8″			Kitchen Ceiling, 290 Square Feet		
			(Continued on next page)		

Figure 36-2. Typical list for materials, fixtures, and finishes. (Continued)

Article and Description	Price	Amount	Article and Description	Price	Amount
Plastering or Drywall (continued)			**Painting and Finishing (continued)**		
Bathroom Walls			Living Room Floor		
Basement, 65 Square Feet_____			Flagstone, 38 Square Feet_____		
1st Floor, 230 Square Feet_____			Carpeted, 408 Square Feet_____		
Bathroom Ceiling			Dining Room Walls, 290 Square Feet_____		
Basement, 50 Square Feet_____			Dining Room Ceiling, 215 Square Feet_____		
1st Floor, 85 Square Feet_____			Dining Room Floor		
Bedroom Walls			Flagstone Passage, 14 Square Feet_____		
Basement, 410 Square Feet_____			Carpeted, 201 Square Feet_____		
1st Floor, 780 Square Feet_____			Foyer Walls, 31 Square Feet_____		
Bedroom Ceilings			Foyer Ceiling, 102 Square Feet_____		
Basement, 245 Square Feet_____			Foyer Floor Flagstone, 102 Square Feet_____		
1st Floor, 480 Square Feet_____			Hall Walls, 250 Square Feet_____		
Closet Walls			Hall Ceiling, 80 Square Feet_____		
Basement, 120 Square Feet_____			Hall Floor, 80 Square Feet_____		
1st Floor, 610 Square Feet_____			Basement Stairway Walls, 300 Square Feet_____		
Closet Ceilings			Basement Stairway Ceiling, 35 Square Feet_____		
Basement, 16 Square Feet_____			Kitchen Walls, 325 Square Feet_____		
1st Floor, 105 Square Feet_____			Kitchen Plastic Ceiling, 48 Square Feet_____		
Garage Walls, 600 Square Feet_____			Kitchen Ceiling, 240 Square Feet_____		
Garage Ceiling, 515 Square Feet_____			Kitchen Floor, 290 Square Feet_____		
Laundry Walls Basement, 195 Square Feet_____			Bathroom Walls		
Laundry Ceiling Basement, 65 Square Feet_____			Basement, 60 Square Feet_____		
Storage Room Walls, 120 Square Feet_____			1st Floor, 230 Square Feet_____		
Storage Room Ceiling, 21 Square Feet_____			Bathroom Ceilings		
Study Walls, 350 Square Feet_____			Plastic Ceiling, 51 Square Feet_____		
Study Ceiling, 170 Square Feet_____			Basement, 50 Square Feet_____		
Material Sub Total_____			1st Floor, 105 Square Feet_____		
Labor Sub Total_____			Bathroom Floors		
			Basement, 20 Square Feet_____		
Finish Flooring			1st Floor, 115 Square Feet_____		
Living Room, 408 Square Feet_____			Bedroom Walls		
Dining Room, 201 Square Feet_____			Basement, 410 Square Feet_____		
Foyer, 102 Square Feet_____			1st Floor, 780 Square Feet_____		
Halls, 80 Square Feet_____			Bedroom Ceilings (including valances)		
Basement Stairway, 50 Square Feet_____			Basement, 245 Square Feet_____		
Kitchen, 290 Square Feet_____			1st Floor, 480 Square Feet_____		
Bathrooms, 115 Square Feet_____			Bedroom Floors		
Bedrooms, 450 Square Feet_____			Basement, 245 Square Feet_____		
Closets, 100 Square Feet_____			1st Floor, 450 Square Feet_____		
Storage Room, 22 Square Feet_____			Closet Walls		
Study, 155 Square Feet			Basement, 120 Square Feet_____		
Material Sub Total_____			1st Floor, 520 Square Feet_____		
Labor Sub Total_____			Closet Ceilings		
			Basement, 16 Square Feet_____		
Painting and Finishing			1st Floor, 90 Square Feet_____		
Exterior Siding, 1250 Square Feet_____			Closet Floors		
Exterior Cornice, 360'_____			Basement, 18 Square Feet_____		
Exterior Doors (both sides), 230 Square Feet_____			1st Floor, 90 Square Feet_____		
Basement Doors (both sides), 270 Square Feet_____			Garage Walls, 600 Square Feet_____		
Basement Stairs (top sides), 94 Square Feet_____			Garage Ceiling, 515 Square Feet_____		
Interior Doors (both sides), 720 Square Feet_____			Laundry Walls		
Interior Door Trims, 330'._____			Concrete Block, 80 Square Feet_____		
Sheet Metal Items			Other, 195 Square Feet_____		
Chimney Flashing, 16'_____			Laundry Ceiling, 65 Square Feet_____		
Wall Flashing @ Decks, 41'_____			Laundry Floor, 65 Square Feet_____		
Ridge Vent, 116'_____			Breakfast Room Walls, see Kitchen_____		
Kitchen Cupboards (including Shelves and Interior),			Breakfast Room Ceiling, see Kitchen_____		
650 Square Feet_____			Breakfast Room Floor, see Kitchen_____		
Linen Closets (including Shelves), 145 Square Feet_____			Storage Room Walls, 120 Square Feet_____		
Broom Closet and Pantry (including Shelves), 200 Square Feet			Storage Room Ceiling, 21 Square Feet_____		
Closet Shelving (both sides), 150 Square Feet_____			Storage Room Floor, 21 Square Feet_____		
Closet Poles, 50'_____			Study Walls, 350 Square Feet_____		
Closet Hook Strip (clothes closets), 75'_____			Study Ceiling (including Valance), 170 Square Feet_____		
Wood Base, 375'_____			Study Floor, 155 Square Feet_____		
Porch Posts (pipe columns), 35'_____			Special Mold Quarter Round, 500'_____		
Garage Doors (both sides), 225 Square Feet_____			Bathroom Cabinets (including shelves and interior)		
Exposed Bricks			Basement, 105 Square Feet_____		
Interior, 200 Square Feet_____			1st Floor, 210 Square Feet_____		
Exterior, 1250 Square Feet_____			China Cabinet (including shelves and interior), 35 Square Feet		
Interior Beams			Deck Steps (one side), 20 Square Feet_____		
4 × 4 False Beams, 112'_____			Full Length Mirrors		
5-1/4 × 14-1/2 Laminated Beams, 48'_____			Baths		
Exterior Cinder Block Walls, 60 Square Feet_____			1 80×50_____		
Living Room Walls, 340 Square Feet_____			1 68×50_____		
Living Room Ceiling (including top side of Valance),			Basement		
615 Square Feet_____			1 68×50_____		
			(Continued on next page)		

Figure 36-2. Typical list for materials, fixtures, and finishes. (Continued)

Article and Description	Price	Amount	Article and Description	Price	Amount

Painting and Finishing (continued)
Square Edge Trim 3/4 × 3/4, 10' _____
Battens 1 × 2, 1100' _____
Wood Decks
    2 × 6 Flat 3/16" Spacers, 365 Square Feet _____
  2 2 × 10 Beams, 42' _____
  2 2 × 8 Beams, 132' _____
  1 2 × 8 Beams, 14' _____
Guard Rail, 190' _____
        Material Sub Total _____
        Labor Sub Total _____
			Finish Hardware (continued)
			  20 Pr. 3-1/2 × 3-1/2 Butts _____
			  10 Pulls _____
			  10 Catches _____
			Miscellaneous Cabinets - Dining Room
			    2 Pr. Cabinet Hinges _____
			    2 Pulls _____
			    2 Catches _____
			1 Mail Box Unit _____
			5 Floor Door Stops _____
			16 Regular Door Stops _____
			1 Doz. Coat and Hat Hooks _____
			Miscellaneous Small Hardware, as required _____
			1 Overhead Garage Door Unit 16'-0" × 7'-0" _____
			Shower Door (Master Bath)
			    1 Pr. Metal Hinges _____
			    1 Knob Set Unit _____
			    1 Friction Catch _____
			        Material Sub Total _____
			        Labor Sub Total _____		

Miscellaneous Hardware
40 Foundation Anchor Bolts 1/2" Diam. ABs to Sill _____
1 Clean out Door Frame Unit _____
1 Ash Dump Unit _____
1 Fireplace Damper Unit _____
2 Angle Iron Fireplace Lintels 3-1/2" × 3-1/2" × 1/2" × 5'-4" _____
1 Angle Iron Fireplace Lintel 3-1/2" × 3-1/2" × 1/2" × 6'-0" _____
Nails approximately 400 Lbs. _____
1 Dowel for Wood Post Anchors and Footings _____
Lally Columns 3" Diam. Pipe Columns
    1 2'-0" _____
    1 7'-0" _____
    3 8'-6" _____
Miscellaneous Builders Hardware, as required _____
250 Wall Ties _____
Roof Beams Flitch Plates
    4 11" × 3/8" × 18'-0" _____
    1 11" × 3/8" × 15'-0" _____
    1 Angle 3-1/2" × 3-1/2" × 3/8" × 3'-0" _____
    1 Angle 3-1/2" × 3-1/2" × 1/2" × 4'-4" _____
5 Column Caps for 3" Diam. Pipe Column Units _____
5 Column Bases for 3" Diam. Pipe Column Units _____
Wire Mesh Reinforcement, (see Masonry Section) _____
Steps down to Living Room Floor
    4 Angles 1-1/2" × 1-1/2" × 3'-0" _____
    2 Junior Channels 12" × 1-1/2" × 5'-0" _____
Miscellaneous Bolts at Deck Rail 32 Machine Bolts 3/4" Diam. × 6" _____
Extra Heavy Corrugated Sheets Metal Forming, 180 Square Feet _____
Reinforcement Bars, see Masonry Section _____
        Material Sub Total _____
        Labor Sub Total _____
			Sheet Metal Work
			Flashing around Chimney, 16 Linear Feet _____
			Flashing at Vertical Walls at Exterior Decks, 41' _____
			Exhaust Fan Grills
			    3 Bathroom required _____
			    1 Kitchen required _____
			4 – 8" Diam. Ducts to Roof Vents _____
			Valleys, 40' _____
			Ridge Vent, 116' _____
			1 Metal Clothes Chute Unit 12" × 16" _____
			Metal Lined Bread Drawer, 12 Square Feet _____
			        Material Sub Total _____
			        Labor Sub Total _____		

			Floor Finishing Material
			Resilient _____
			Tile _____
			Wood _____
			Carpet _____
			Tile Fireplace Hearth _____
			Cove Base _____
			Miscellaneous _____
			        Material Sub Total _____
			        Labor Sub Total _____		

Finish Hardware
2 Basement Doors
    2 Pr. 3-1/2 × 3-1/2 Butts _____
    2 Latch Sets _____
1 Pr. Front Entrance Doors
    3 Pr. 4 × 4 Butts _____
    1 Lockset _____
1 Rear Entrance Door
    1-1/2 Pr. 4 × 4 Butts _____
    1 Lockset _____
4 Side Doors (including Doors from Garage)
    6 Pr. 4 × 4 Butts _____
    4 Locksets _____
Screen Doors (as required) _____
4 Bathroom Doors
    4 Pr. 3-1/2 × 3-1/2 Butts _____
    4 Locksets (Bath) _____
    3 - 8'-0" × 6'-8" Glass Sliding Door Unit _____
    1 - 16'-0" × 8'-0" Glass Sliding Door Unit _____
Double Acting Doors
    1 2'-8" × 6'-8" _____
    1 Pr. 3-1/2 × 3-1/2 Double Acting _____
    1 Push Plate each Side _____
9 Interior Doors
    9 Pr. 3-1/2 × 3-1/2 Butts _____
    9 Latch Sets _____
Storm Sashes, as required _____
Kitchen Cabinets (Storage and Bathroom included)
    41 Pr. Cabinet Hinges _____
    95 Knobs or Pulls _____
    42 Friction Catches _____
Closets Folding Wood (4 panel)
    3 4'-0" × 6'-8" _____
    2 6'-0" × 6'-8" _____
			Wall Finishing Material
			Work Tabletops and Backs Plastic Laminated, 90 Square Feet _____
			Tile Base in Bathroom, 80' _____
			Tile or Chrome inserts in Bathroom
			    3 Toilet Paper Holders _____
			    3 Soap Dishes and Grab Bars _____
			  10 Towel Bars _____
			    3 Robe Hooks _____
			Bathroom Tile Wainscot, 270 Square Feet _____
			        Material Sub Total _____
			        Labor Sub Total _____		

			Roofing
			38-1/2 Sqs. Owner's Choice _____
			        Material Sub Total _____
			        Labor Sub Total _____		

			Plumbing Note: This survey does not list the quantities of each item required for the mechanical equipment, as there is a variation in any system chosen. However, the form given will be of assistance to your dealer in arriving at an accurate estimate. 1 Double Kitchen Sink _____ 3 Water Closet Units _____ 2 Bath Tubs _____ 3 Shower Head Units _____ 3 Floor Drain Units _____ 4 Top Mounted Lavatories _____ Automatic Washer Outlet _____ 4 Hose Bib Units _____ (Continued on next page)		

Figure 36-2. Typical list for materials, fixtures, and finishes. (Continued)

Article and Description	Price	Amount	Article and Description	Price	Amount
Plumbing (continued)			**Electric Wiring (continued)**		
Hot Water Heater 40 Gallons Gas fired Unit (50 Gallons Electric)			2 23'-0" Single Tube Units (Living Room)_____		
1 Garbage Disposer Unit _____			1 14'-0" Single Tube Unit (Bedroom) _____		
Miscellaneous			1 13'-0" Single Tube Unit (Bedroom) _____		
Gas Range, Grill with Cover and Rotisserie, Hood with 2 Dual			1 12'-6" Single Tube Unit (Bedroom) _____		
Blowers (1200 CFM), Built-In Refr.-Freezer _____			Material Sub Total _____		
Material Sub Total _____			Labor Sub Total _____		
Labor Sub Total _____					
			Telephone Wiring		
Electric Wiring			Note: Call the nearest telephone company business office for		
21 Ceiling Outlets (6 Spots) _____			assistance in planning adequate built-in telephone		
4 Bracket Outlets, Outside Fixtures _____			facilities. These will include:		
57 Duplex Receptacles_____			1. Entrance pipe or underground entrance conduit _____		
10 Waterproof Receptacles _____			2. Galvanized iron protector cabinet _____		
32 Wall Switches _____			3. Interior thin-wall conduit to all outlets _____		
1 Dimmer Switch Dining Room Spots _____			4. Standard outlet boxes with telephone cover_____		
10 Three-way Switches _____			5. Telephone or jack locations_____		
1 Set Entrance Chime _____			6. Miscellaneous or special items_____		
1 Ceiling Outlet (vapor-proof) over Master Bath Shower _____			Material Sub Total _____		
2 Push Buttons_____			Labor Sub Total _____		
7 Porch Lights Twin Floods @ each Unit _____					
7 Hall and Entrance Lights 150 W Ceiling Flush Mounted Units			**Heating**		
1 Kitchen Fan – Hood-Fan Combination Unit_____			A heating unit will be required of sufficient size for a house with		
1 Bathroom Exhaust Fan _____			3490 square feet and/or 30,250 cubic feet.		
1 Bathroom Combination Heater and Ventilator_____			Material Sub Total _____		
1 Bathroom Combination Heater, Ventilator and Light_____			Labor Sub Total _____		
2 – 240V Receptacles (Dryer and Range)_____					
Special Tubular Light Installations					
2 2'-0" Single Tube Units (20W) _____					
11 4'-0" Single Tube Units (40W) _____					

Figure 36-2. Typical list for materials, fixtures, and finishes. (Continued)

Figure 36-3. Careful attention must be given to details when estimating the building cost. Even with this attention to detail, the final building cost may vary from the estimate for several reasons. (CertainTeed Corporation)

Even builders who have been in the business for years sometimes fail to accurately estimate the cost of a job. Therefore, it is extremely important that you learn to prepare drawings and specifications accurately to help eliminate unexpected costs. Be sure all specifications are complete and easy to understand.

Internet Resources

www.bidrite.net
Progressive Programming Corporation, distributor of construction estimating software

www.builders-software.com
Builders Software Enterprises, a provider of estimating and job cost accounting software

www.buildsoft.com
Buildsoft Construction Scheduling and Estimating Software

www.cdci.com
Construction Data Control, Inc. (CDCI), a publisher of software for construction professionals

www.ecs-inc.com
Enterprise Computer Systems, Inc., a provider of technology solutions for the building materials industry

www.rsmeans.com
RS Means, publisher of the Building Construction Cost Data Book

Review Questions–Chapter 36

Write your answers on a separate sheet of paper. Do not write in this book.

1. List two methods commonly used to calculate preliminary building cost estimates.

2. If the building cost of a house with 1,500 square feet is estimated, using the square foot method, to be $100,000, what is the cost per square foot constant?

3. Explain how a more accurate estimate of the building cost can be computed.

4. List the permits usually required for building a new home.

5. The cost of labor to construct a house may be determined accurately by consulting _____.

6. The cost of materials required to build a house should be secured from _____.

Suggested Activities

1. Using a house plan that you have designed using CADD, calculate the building cost using the square foot method. Use the appropriate CADD commands to calculate the area. Your instructor will help you determine the price per square foot in your area.

2. Using the same plan in Activity 1 above, calculate a more accurate estimate for materials only by listing the materials to be used and pricing them in detail. Use prices from a local lumber company and other material suppliers.

3. Establish current rate for carpenters, plumbers, electricians, masons, and all other skilled tradeworkers who work together to build a house. Record rates and sources used. Prepare a report and present it to your class.

Section XI
Remodeling, Health, Safety, and Careers

37 Architectural Remodeling, Renovation, and Preservation

38 Designing for Health and Safety

39 Career Opportunities

Reference Section

Acknowledgments

Glossary

Index

FEMA News Photo

Architectural Remodeling, Renovation, and Preservation

Objectives

After studying this chapter, you will be able to:

➤ List the reasons that people remodel and the factors they should consider before beginning a remodeling project.

➤ Compare the five main types of remodeling according to cost, complexity, and time required.

➤ Evaluate the needs of a family and select an appropriate type of remodeling.

➤ Explain renovation.

➤ Identify three types of historical preservation.

➤ Explain the role of the family, interior designer, architect, and contractor in a remodeling, renovation, or preservation project.

Key Terms

Adaptive Reuse
Addition
Attic
Dehumidifying
  System
Dormers

Historic Preservation
Moisture Barrier
Remodeling
Renovation
Restoration

Remodeling is changing an existing space into a new form. It can be a wise investment that will increase the value of a home. It may also be a way to change part or all of a home's appearance. The least complex type of remodeling involves making changes to a room that is already used or changing an unused space so it can be used as a living area. Adding on to homes generally require more complex changes.

Renovation is returning a home to its original condition. However, current styles, new materials, and state of the art appliances may be used in the renovation. Many older houses have suffered from neglect for various reasons. For example, a house that has been rental property may be slightly damaged by each tenant over a number of years. Instead of making proper repairs, the landlord performs only the bare minimum of repairs. Over the span of several years, the value of this house drops as it becomes less desirable to live in. However, through renovation the house can be returned to its original condition and once again be a desirable place to live. Often, renovation is called "rehab." Many metropolitan areas have several building rehab programs to encourage renovation of deteriorating homes in declining areas. Renovation is not restoration or preservation.

Historic preservation involves returning a building to its original condition while maintaining traditional styles, materials, and in some cases furnishings. There are different types of historical preservation, which are discussed later in this chapter.

No matter which type of project is planned, all family members can be involved. Family members may plan and gather information on their own or they may consult architects, contractors, and interior designers. The decisions made will affect the family for many years, so they should be made carefully.

Choosing to Remodel

A family may decide to remodel for several reasons. As a family grows, its living patterns and needs may change.

- New family members may need their own bedrooms.
- Entertaining may become more common, requiring more adequate kitchen and living spaces, Figure 37-1.
- Increases in income may result in more disposable income and spur the desire for updated styles and appliances.
- As the work schedules of family members become busier, a more efficient home may be needed.
- Older homes may need newer equipment or better insulation to keep up with higher fuel prices, Figure 37-2.

The present home may not be capable of meeting these new needs.

When housing changes are needed, moving may not be a desirable alternative. Families may have close ties with neighbors, schools, and community organizations. The

Figure 37-2. This older house is a prime candidate for remodeling to improve the HVAC, plumbing, and electrical systems.

home may also hold sentimental value. In addition, if much time and money have been spent on landscaping, moving may not be worthwhile, Figure 37-3. These factors and the high cost of building or buying a new home may make remodeling a more practical alternative.

A desire or need for change is only one factor to consider when deciding whether or not to remodel. Other factors may affect the type of remodeling chosen or persuade a family not to remodel at all. For instance, if a family plans to move within a year or two, remodeling is probably not a worthwhile investment. However, some homeowners

Figure 37-1. As families grow and change, their housing needs change. This remodeled kitchen is up-to-date and efficient, making activities quicker and more pleasant. (Lis King)

Figure 37-3. This family has spent a lot of time, effort, and money in the landscaping around their house. Yet, the house cannot meet the family's expanding needs. This house is a good candidate for remodeling. (Manufactured Housing Institute)

remodel in anticipation of the desires of prospective home buyers. Although remodeling can increase property value, most home buyers prefer to make their own changes to a home. This makes remodeling for the sole purpose of increasing the sale value a waste of time and money for the homeowner.

Local building ordinances and property taxes are also considerations when making remodeling choices. Remodeling may require several building permits and all changes must comply with local codes. If remodeling increases the value of a home, it may also increase the property taxes on the home. Usually, adding on to the structure and exterior remodeling are more likely to require building permits and increase taxes. Remodeling of unused spaces within the home may be a better choice if building ordinances and higher taxes are concerns.

The cost, time, and effort required to remodel must also be considered before starting a project. All three factors are affected by the size and complexity of the remodeling project. An accurate estimate of all costs of remodeling, including all building materials, utility additions, and labor, should be obtained before starting any project. Larger projects can be very expensive and may require financing. However, the costs can be spread out over months or even years by remodeling in stages. Stretching the inconvenience of a remodeling project over a long period, however, may not be desirable.

A remodeling project can vary in cost depending on the amount of time and effort spent by family members. If all work is contracted to professionals, the job will be finished quickly with little effort from family members. However, contracted work is usually expensive and good communication and supervision by a family member is needed to ensure that work is done as desired.

At the other extreme, all work may be done by family members. This method can save a great deal of money in labor costs. The finished work may also be more personalized than would have been possible with contractors. However, the project will probably require much more time and, unless the homeowner is very familiar with the type of work

involved, serious errors in remodeling may occur.

Many families choose to do some remodeling on their own and contract professionals for the most difficult jobs, Figure 37-4. For instance, paneling and painting may be done by family members but complex wiring changes should be handled by an electrician. This method allows good results at a low cost. It also ensures safe construction and eliminates frustration with jobs that are too difficult for the amateur.

Remodeling is not just an option used by homeowners that do not want to move. It also offers choices to home buyers who cannot afford custom-built housing. Many buy less expensive housing and remodel to meet their own needs. They may also choose to renovate an old home.

Types of Remodeling

Remodeling can meet a family's needs in several ways. Each type of remodeling should be considered so that needs can be met in the simplest, most satisfactory way possible. Remodeling may be divided into five main types: changing lived-in areas, making unused space livable, adding on, buying to remodel, and preserving an historic home. Each category varies in the level of change, complexity,

Figure 37-4. Professional subcontractors may be hired to do complex jobs like building walls or a roof structure.

cost, and time required for remodeling. Many remodeling projects may include more than one type of remodeling.

Changing Lived-In Areas

Changes within a used or "lived-in" room are generally remodeled to update equipment, improve traffic patterns, or give a room a new appearance, Figure 37-5. Kitchens are most commonly changed and, generally, the most expensive room to remodel. Bathrooms, bedrooms, and other rooms may be changed as well.

Remodeling a lived-in room usually does not require major changes, such as tearing down a bearing wall or rewiring. Occasionally, a window or door may be enlarged or moved. Kitchen or bathroom remodeling may require relocation of some plumbing and wiring receptacles. However, changes are usually less complex than the changes required in other types of remodeling.

Kitchens

Kitchens are usually remodeled when the homeowner wants to update or add appliances. While updating appliances, the homeowner may also want to improve the use of space, traffic patterns, availability of storage, and the efficiency of the work triangle. Information on kitchen planning in Chapter 9 *Room Planning—Service Area* can help in evaluating the present kitchen and planning the new one.

Many changes can be made to increase the efficiency of a kitchen. The traffic circulation path can be improved by moving doors so that traffic patterns do not interfere with the work triangle. An appliance may be moved to make a more efficient work triangle. General and local lighting may be enhanced.

Counter space may be added to make room for food preparation or to allow space for countertop appliances. Many new appliances can be mounted under wall cabinets to provide easy access and clear the counter space below. Storage space may be added or present storage space may be improved for more efficient use of space. For instance, a

A

B

C

Figure 37-5. An old ceramic tile floor is being replaced with new tile in an up-to-date design. A—Removing the old tile. B—Planning the placement and design of the new tile. C—The finished tile floor.

corner cabinet with space that is difficult to reach may be replaced with a lazy Susan. Pull-out storage may also be used to improve access to items in cabinets.

If several new appliances are added or major appliances are moved, rewiring will be necessary. Additional circuits may also be needed. Changes in plumbing lines will be needed if the sink is moved, if a refrigerator with an automatic ice maker is added, or if a built-in dishwasher is moved or added. New ventilation must be installed when the range is moved or a gas grill is added.

Bathrooms

Like kitchens, bathrooms are often remodeled to update old fixtures. They can be costly to remodel if changes in plumbing lines are needed. Water and waste lines must be checked to make sure that they are the correct size for new plumbing installations. Locating new fixtures in the same positions as old ones can reduce remodeling costs.

Other improvements may be made in bathrooms as well. Bathrooms may be enlarged by moving a wall. They may be improved by adding storage space. Skylights may be added for natural lighting and ventilation. New floor and wall treatments, such as ceramic tile, may be installed for easier maintenance.

Other Rooms

The appearances of bedrooms, living rooms, dining rooms, and other rooms that do not house major appliances can be changed dramatically with relatively minor remodeling projects. Most often, floor, wall, and ceiling treatments are updated, Figure 37-6. New lighting fixtures may also be added. Partial walls or built-in storage may be added to a room. Many times, these projects are simple enough for family members to do on their own.

More complicated changes may include moving or widening a doorway to improve traffic circulation. Windows may also be added or enlarged to improve the view and increase ventilation. A wall may be removed so that two rooms are made into one. These changes are more complicated and should be done by someone with experience. The changes may affect the structural support of the house. In addition, wiring and insulation may have to be altered.

Figure 37-6. This dining area has been remodeled by adding a new ceramic tile floor, new window treatments, and a large mirror. Also, the dining chairs have been reupholstered.

Making Unused Space Livable

Many homes have areas that are not used as living space. These areas include garages, porches, attics, and unfinished basements. Although these areas need changes to make them suitable for living, they have sound roofs, walls, and floors. It may be less expensive to remodel these areas than to add on to a home. Also, remodeling unused space is often quicker and more convenient than adding on space.

Garages and Porches

Garages and porches are often converted into bedrooms, baths, dining rooms, family rooms, sunrooms, or studies, Figure 37-7. These areas are often remodeled because they are conveniently located in relation to other rooms in the house. For instance, a porch adjoining a kitchen would make a convenient breakfast room.

The foundations under these areas should be checked to see if they are deep enough to comply with local building codes. Foundation requirements for garages and porches may be different than for living areas. A *moisture barrier* should be placed between the foundation and flooring materials. This is

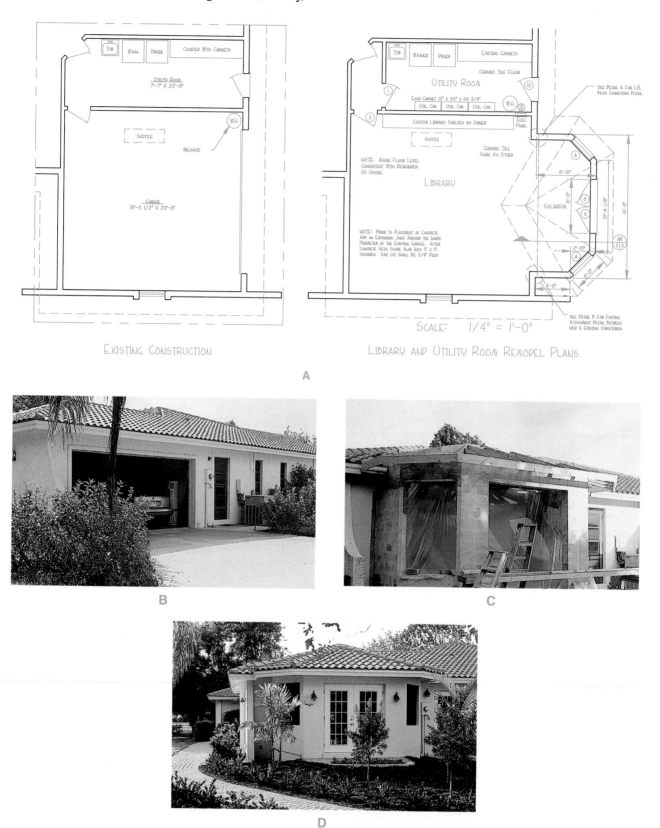

Figure 37-7. The conversion of a two-car garage into a library/solarium. A—The working drawings. B—The garage before remodeling. C—Remodeling in progress. D—The completed project.

a membrane that retards the flow of moisture vapor and reduces condensation. Insulation should be added to meet the R-value recommended for living spaces. Additional wiring for lighting and outlets usually is needed.

Windows and doors are often changed or added when remodeling garages and porches. Insulated glass windows or storm windows may replace the original windows, Figure 37-8. The garage door may be replaced with a sliding glass door or with a window. Doors that adjoin a garage or porch to the house may be relocated for more logical access. Sliding glass doors, panel doors, or open doorways may be used to connect the remodeled area to the home.

Some type of heating supply is needed in remodeled porches and garages. If the room is open to an original room in the house, heating from the original room may be enough for both areas. However, if the room is separate, it will need its own heat supply. Heating ducts and vents may be extended into the room from the home heating system. A fireplace, stove, electric heating unit, or small furnace may also be used to heat the room. To ensure proper heating and cooling of the remodeled area, it may be wise to consult an HVAC professional for this aspect of the project.

Unfinished Basements

Unfinished basements are often remodeled to be used as family rooms, recreation areas, hobby areas, and workshops, Figure 37-9. Bedrooms may also be placed in basements if sufficient lighting and an outside entrance is provided. Bathrooms and a small kitchen area may be desired if the basement will be used for entertaining.

Basement areas are often damp, so vapor barriers and a dehumidifying system should be added for comfort. A *dehumidifying system* removes moisture vapor from the air to reduce the relative humidity in the space. If flooding or seepage is common, a sump pump should be added. Also, any leaks in the walls or floors should be properly repaired before installing wall and floor materials. If the foundation is sound, flooring materials can be applied directly to the surface. Paneling and drywall should be applied to furring strips to allow space for wiring and insulation.

Basements can be gloomy if sufficient light is not provided. Window wells and windows may be enlarged to increase natural light. Illuminated ceilings and recessed lighting are popular artificial lighting for basements. Additional wiring for light fixtures and outlets will be needed.

A   B

Figure 37-8. The original windows have been replaced with insulated glass in this extensively-remodeled home. A—Before. B—After. (Norandex/Reynolds Building Products)

Figure 37-9. Dreary, unfinished basements are often converted into cheerful, usable family rooms. (Georgia Pacific Corporation)

Additional plumbing lines will be needed if a bath or kitchen area is added to the basement. New fixtures should be placed as close as possible to existing plumbing lines to reduce cost.

Stairways and entrances may be moved or added when remodeling a basement. The original stairway may interfere with the desired floor plan for the basement. It can be moved to allow more efficient use of the space. Basement entrances are usually placed in a service area. However, if the remodeled basement is a living area, an entrance from an upstairs living area may be more appropriate. A second stairway may be added for this purpose, Figure 37-10. If a basement is converted into a living area, a direct exit to the outdoors may be required. Check local fire protection codes and laws to be sure the remodeling project meets regulations.

Attics

An *attic* is the space between the ceiling and roof of a structure. In some house styles, such as a Cape Cod, the attic is frequently converted to a bedroom, hobby room, or conversation area, Figure 37-11. If a bedroom is placed in this area, a bathroom should also be added.

Before converting an attic, ceiling joists, now to be floor joists, should be checked to determine if they are strong enough to support the appropriate live load. Adequate headroom and usable floor space should also be available. At least 7' of height should be allowed between the floor and the finished ceiling. The ceiling may slope from 7' to 5' high. However, the areas that have a low ceiling will be limited in use. If the floor is not strong enough or if adequate space is not available, remodeling may become complex and expensive.

Figure 37-10. This new spiral stairway connects the remodeled basement with the living room. (Logan Company)

Windows and skylights can be added to an attic for natural lighting. *Dormers* allow in natural light and increase the amount of usable space in an attic by adding headroom. However, they are more costly to add than skylights and regular windows because they require modifications in the roof structure.

Adequate insulation for a living area should be placed in the attic ceiling and walls. Proper ventilation is especially important since warm air tends to get trapped in attics. Ceiling fans and vents may be helpful. Additional wiring may also be required. If a bathroom is added, plumbing lines will be needed.

Adding On

Converting existing unused spaces may not be possible or practical. In these situations, the family may choose to build additional space onto a home. This new space is called an *addition.* Any type of space, such as a bedroom, bathroom, den, or garage, may be

A

B

Figure 37-11. A—This unfinished attic will be remodeled. (Georgia Pacific Corporation) B—The remodeling is complete. (Georgia Pacific Corporation)

added to a home, Figure 37-12. Additions may also be used to enlarge an existing room, such as a living room or kitchen.

When a room is built onto a home, the floor plan can be designed to meet the specific needs of the family. The new addition should harmonize with other rooms in the house.

Before

After

Figure 37-12. This ground-level addition of a garage required a new foundation and framework.

Guidelines for planning rooms are covered in Chapter 7 through Chapter 9.

Building permits and inspections are almost always necessary with additions. Timing is important because weather conditions can hamper much of the work involved in building an addition. Also, local zoning laws may restrict the types of additions allowed on a home. Usually, the exterior walls of a home must be kept a minimum distance from lot lines.

Ground-level additions

Adding on is usually more complex than changing areas within the original structure. It involves changing a home's basic structure. A new area is created from the foundation to the roof, which alters the exterior appearance of the home. A ground-level addition may have a crawlspace or basement below and a second floor and/or attic space above.

Adding on to a home usually involves the removal of part or all of an existing exterior wall. Most exterior walls are bearing walls, except for end walls of a one-story house with a gable roof. Temporary supports must be used when such a wall is removed and some type of permanent load-bearing support must be in place before the remodeling is finished, Figure 37-13.

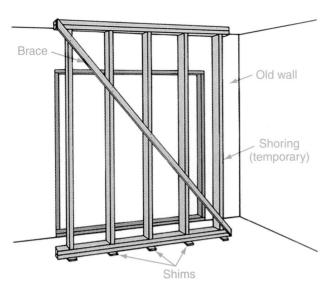

Figure 37-13. Temporary support, or shoring, must be used during construction when a load-bearing wall is removed.

Walls that are to be removed likely contain wiring and plumbing. Rerouting of these lines may be necessary. Also, you must check for underground plumbing mains and cables before digging for an addition's foundation. In most states, this is required by law.

Any planned addition should blend well with the architectural style of the existing home. The size, shape, and placement of the addition should not be obtrusive or overpowering. The exterior design should be in the same style as the original house, Figure 37-14. The placement, size, and style of windows and doors in the addition should blend with the original structure. Landscaping elements can be used to blend the new addition into the original house.

The type of space to be added, location of rooms in the original home, and availability of space should be considered when deciding where to place the addition. For instance, a game room or party room should not be located adjacent to the sleeping area. However, this would be a good location for another bedroom. Also, lot boundaries may eliminate one or two sides of the home as a location for the addition.

Second-story additions

Some homes may not have enough yard space for a ground-level addition. For example,

Figure 37-14. The raised entry module added to the existing entry blends seamlessly with the existing structure. A—Entry before remodeling. B—Remodeling in progress. C—Completed project.

in some areas, especially metropolitan areas, the original house was built on a very small lot. Often, these homes are already at the permitted boundary limit. In addition, many areas have "green space" requirements that dictate a certain ratio of yard area to house area. For these homes, the addition of a second story may be considered, Figure 37-15. These additions are usually much more expensive and complex than ground-level additions. The roof must be removed and replaced to make room for the second story. In addition, the foundation and first floor walls must be strong enough to support the weight of a second story. Stairways connecting the first and second floors must also be built.

In addition to green space requirements, some areas also have height restrictions. In these cases, if the house does not have a basement, one can be added. Adding a basement is very expensive and requires professional planning and construction. Generally, adding a basement should only be considered when all other options have been eliminated.

Buying to Remodel

Many home buyers would like a custom-built home, but cannot afford one. Often, these people buy less-expensive housing and remodel to meet their own needs and tastes. For example, most subdivisions contain a limited number of house styles. Yet, with additions, exterior changes, and interior changes, these houses can be remodeled to fit the lifestyle of the family. Therefore, when looking for a house to buy, also visualize what can be done with the structure and land.

Before

After

Figure 37-15. Second-story additions are complex and expensive, but may be an option to consider.

Renovation

Another option for home buyers that is gaining popularity is renovation of an old home, Figure 37-16. Many old homes can be purchased at a reasonable cost because they are not suitable for living. However, their basic structure is sound. See Figure 37-17. These homes may be renovated so that the finished home is much more valuable than the cost of the renovation. This is also an alternative to building from scratch.

Renovation is a major project requiring much time, money, and careful planning. Preliminary planning is especially important. Building codes must be strictly followed. It may require many lengthy and expensive projects to reach the "finished" home. See Figure 37-18. Many of these projects will require contracted work.

Some home buyers include the cost of remodeling in the amount of their house mortgage. Others obtain a mortgage for the cost of the house only and pay for the remodeling without financing. Another option is to refinance the house after all work is completed and use the equity from the increase in value to pay off the renovation expenses.

Careful inspection of a home is important when buying to renovate. Some homes may be very inexpensive, but renovating them would cost more than building a new home. A sound foundation and floor substructure are essential. All wood should be checked for insects and dry rot. If support beams are unsound, renovation will probably be too expensive to be worthwhile. Other areas to check are wiring, heating, roofing, walls, and insulation. Renovation can be expensive if major changes in these areas are needed.

The types of changes that will be needed and their estimated costs should be considered before purchasing a house for renovation. Often, it may be better to purchase a home that is a few thousand dollars more, but has sound wiring, plumbing, and structural members. The lower-priced house may ultimately cost more to renovate than the more expensive but structurally sound house.

Historic Preservation

In recent years, there has been a renewed interest in historic preservation. Motivation for preservation has come from several areas:

- Special groups who wish to preserve buildings of historical significance.
- Preservationists who believe old buildings should be saved for future generations.
- Architects, designers, and historians who wish to preserve our architectural heritage.

A   B

Figure 37-16. A—This old home is in very poor condition. B—Renovation has made the home a nice place to live. (Norandex/Reynolds Building Products)

Figure 37-17. Many cities have old houses that may be purchased inexpensively and renovated. This renovated home is attractive, has much character, and is now a nice place to live.

- Environmentalists who believe that preservation is one method of slowing the depletion of the earth's natural resources.

- Governmental agencies that wish to improve the quality of life in a community by creating uses for abandoned or neglected buildings.

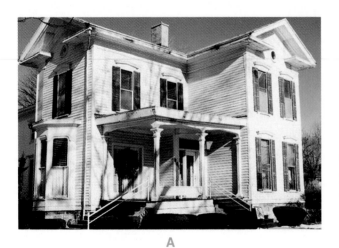

A   B

Figure 37-18. Remodeling an old house requires much work on the interior and exterior. A—Before. B—After. (Norandex/Reynolds Building Products)

- Developers and landlords who see an opportunity to make profits from seemingly worthless old buildings.
- Individuals who see opportunities in developing desirable living spaces in structures that presently are uninhabitable or were designed for other purposes.

Terms such as restoration, remodeling, and adaptive reuse are used to describe various types of historic preservation.

Restoration

Restoration involves returning a structure to its original condition. See Figure 37-19. Many historic homes of an earlier period are painstakingly restored in every detail. Authentic materials, designs, and colors are researched to ensure accuracy. Furnishings of the period are collected for use in the structure, Figure 37-20. In short, an intense effort is exerted to return its appearance to a previous era.

Preservation through Remodeling

Remodeling, by definition, involves changing the structure to meet new needs, use new technology, or comply with new code requirements. However, altering the structure may often be counter to its preservation. Generally, remodeling of residential structures undergoing historical preservation only modifies slightly the intended use of the dwellings. The most common remodeling projects for historical preservation include changing room layouts, adding space, or upgrading plumbing or wiring systems. It is possible to maintain the original restored exterior appearance while remodeling the interior to meet new needs. Without remodeling, the building would be unable to meet the needs and may be demolished.

Figure 37-19. This Victorian home in Newnan, Georgia, has been restored to its original splendor.

Figure 37-20. These authentic furnishings are in the upstairs sitting room of the restored home of President Benjamin Harrison in Indianapolis, Indiana. (President Benjamin Harrison Memorial Home)

Adaptive Reuse

Adaptive reuse is the process of changing the function of a building. One example is changing an old factory building or warehouse into housing units. Sometimes buildings sit idle because they need extensive repairs or are no longer needed for their original purpose. They become eyesores and locations for crime and mischief. As a result, there is significant pressure from community groups and individuals to reclaim these buildings as useful structures. Through adaptive reuse, they can once again be functional assets to the community, Figure 37-21.

Preparing Remodeling, Renovation, and Preservation Plans

A good remodeling, renovation, or preservation job is carefully planned before any work begins. Planning involves appraising the original house, determining the desired and needed changes, and drawing plans. An interior designer, an architect, or a contractor may be consulted in the planning stages.

The first step of planning involves determining the weak and strong points of the present home. Limited space and storage, inefficient appliances, and poor natural lighting are examples of items that may need changing. However, walls, molding, and flooring materials may be worth saving.

The second step is to evaluate the existing plumbing, heating/cooling, wiring, and insulation. If updating or repairs will be needed within a few years, it may be less expensive and more convenient to make changes during the current project. Replacing windows, doors, and appliances to increase a home's energy efficiency may also be considered.

After the area to be worked on has been evaluated, the next step in the project is to create a rough sketch of the original space. The sketch should include any architectural details such as windows, doors, steps, and fireplaces. Desired changes can be drawn, evaluated, and altered until a finished plan results, which is the final step in planning the project. The final

Figure 37-21. These old warehouses have been converted into restaurants, shops, and condominiums. This is an example of adaptive reuse. (Photo Courtesy of James Hardie® Siding Products)

plan should follow the guidelines presented earlier in Chapter 7 through Chapter 9.

The finished plan should be used when consulting contractors, ordering materials, and applying for building permits. Professionally drawn floor plans and elevations or rough plans with specified dimensions may be used. However, if contractors or subcontractors will do any work, professional symbols are essential, Figure 37-22.

Interior Designer

An interior designer may be consulted in the planning stages of remodeling. Some decorating, department, and home improvement stores offer the free services of a decorator if products are purchased from their store. A freelance designer or a design firm may also be consulted.

A designer can also help to put the needs and desires of a family into concrete plans. They can help select materials that will be both functional and tasteful. Fabric samples, paint chips, and samples of other materials to be used in a room can be coordinated by the designer. They can make suggestions to improve the design or the function of any material within a room. The designer can also help the family choose materials that fit within a budget.

Interior designers can also help in evaluating the overall floor plan of a room. They can make suggestions for improving the efficiency of circulation and the overall use of space. The interior designer can be consulted separately or with an architect.

Architect

When major projects are planned, an architect will probably be consulted. An architect can also make suggestions to improve a remodeling plan. They can make sure that the

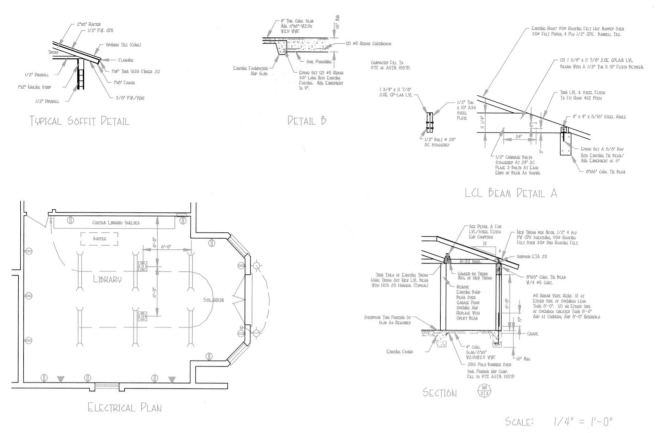

Figure 37-22. Use of proper drawings and symbols is important. These are detail drawings for the remodeling project shown in Figure 37-7.

overall style of the home's exterior will remain well designed. An architect can also help determine whether remodeling plans comply with building, plumbing, and electrical codes.

An architect can make final drawings of the proposed plan and write specifications for materials. The family may consult an architect only to evaluate and draw plans, or they may use the architect to contact a contractor and supervise the remodeling work to completion.

Contractor

After planning is finished, a contractor may be hired to do the remodeling work. Many contractors specialize in remodeling. The contractor will obtain any necessary building permits and schedule the work of any subcontractors needed for the project. Subcontractors may include carpenters, plumbers, electricians, masons, and painters.

When a contractor is hired for a project, they will usually charge one fee for both materials and labor. This helps to eliminate the chance of unexpected expenses. If some work will be done by family members, then a contractor may not be needed. A family member may choose to serve as the contractor and hire any specific subcontractors needed. When a contractor is not used, an interior designer or architect can help to estimate costs or the family can make their own estimates. However, some unpredicted expenses will probably occur.

Internet Resources

www.amerrock.com
American Rockwool Association, resources for rockwool insulation

www.calclosets.com
California Closets, customized storage solutions

www.hartcoflooring.com
Hartco Flooring, An Armstrong Company

www.hoovercompany.com
Hoover, manufacturer of central vacuum systems and vacuum cleaners

www.kitchenaid.com
KitchenAid, a manufacture of home appliances

www.lennox.com
Lennox Indoor Comfort Systems

www.met-tile.com
Met-Tile, a manufacturer of metal roofing

www.pozzi.com
Pozzi Wood Windows

www.sweets.com
Sweets Catalog File

www.whirlpool.com
Whirlpool Corporation

Review Questions

Write your answers on a separate sheet of paper. Do not write in this book.

1. List five reasons a family may choose to remodel.

2. Why would a family choose remodeling over buying a new house?

3. List three factors to be considered when making remodeling decisions.

4. What are the five main types of remodeling?

5. If an attic is to be converted into usable space, what is the minimum height between the floor and finished ceiling?

6. What precautions should be taken when tearing down an exterior wall?

7. If a family is looking to purchase a house to remodel or renovate, what are some possible factors that would make them select a slightly more expensive house over a cheaper one?

8. What are the steps in planning a remodeling, renovation, or preservation project?

9. _____ is the process of changing the function of a building.

10. List the three types of historical preservation.

Suggested Activities

1. Write a short essay discussing the planning involved when remodeling an attic into a studio workplace.

2. Plan a family room addition to the house shown in Figure 33-26. Include plans for any other features that will add to the overall design of the house. Use either traditional or CADD methods to draw your remodeling plan.

3. Find a residence in your community that is a candidate for historical preservation. Take a series of photographs of the building. Research the history of the building and the area in which it resides. Determine if restoration, preservation through remodeling, or adaptive reuse is best for this building. Present your analysis to the class.

Fire prevention in the home is important to avoid disasters such as this one.

38 Designing for Health and Safety

Objectives

After studying this chapter, you will be able to:

➤ Identify fire hazards around the home and explain preventative measures.

➤ Explain the hazards associated with carbon monoxide and discuss preventative measures.

➤ Explain the hazards associated with radon in residential housing and describe preventative measures.

➤ Discuss problems in residential structures associated with excess moisture.

➤ Describe the dangers associated with weather- and nature-related events such as earthquakes, floods, tornadoes, and hurricanes.

➤ List steps that can be taken to mitigate the damage and destruction of weather- and nature-related events.

Key Terms

Carbon Monoxide (CO)
Condensation
Earthquake Zone
Flash Floods
Floodplains
Hurricane Codes
Hurricane
Mold

Radon
Safe Room
Smoke Detector
Stachybotrys atra
Storm Surge
Tornado
Ventilation
Water Vapor

Introduction

Contrary to what you may think, the home is generally not a safe place. Experts say that more injuries occur in the home than anywhere else. Therefore, an intensive effort should be made to design structures that are safe for the occupants. Granted, the model building codes are most concerned with creating a safe structure. However, this chapter focuses on certain areas that deserve special consideration beyond structural integrity. The areas discussed in this chapter include smoke and fire detection, carbon monoxide (CO) detection, radon detection and mitigation, moisture and mold problems, weather- and nature-related safety, and general home safety.

Smoke and Fire Detection

Structural fires are a significant danger to every home. According to recent national statistics, residential property was involved in 60% of the structural fires started by arsonists. Every 15 seconds, somewhere in the US a fire department is responding to a fire. Someone is killed by a fire somewhere in the US every two hours. More than $250 in property is lost to a fire per second. Eighty percent of all fire deaths occur in the home. Home fires are one of the most serious hazards, most often affecting small children and the elderly. The leading causes of deadly fires include:

- Falling asleep while smoking.

- Improperly using flammable materials to start a fire.

- Operating unsafe electrical or heating equipment.
- Placing materials that will burn too close to a potential source of ignition.

Fire Prevention

A few common sense rules can help prevent a fire in your home. Here are a few of the most obvious ones.

- Keep an operable fire extinguisher in an obvious location. This will not prevent a fire, but may allow you to extinguish a small fire before it gets out of control.
- Do not overload electrical circuits, Figure 38-1. Overloaded circuits generate excess heat that may ignite nearby materials.
- Have your heating system inspected yearly. A dirty or improperly operating heating system can ignite a fire.
- Keep matches and lighters out of the hands of children.
- Store flammable liquids in approved containers.
- Dispose of trash on a regular schedule. An accumulation of trash can be fuel for a fire.
- Select upholstered furniture that is resistant to smoldering cigarettes.
- Use seasoned wood in wood-burning stoves and fireplaces. Green wood creates creosote buildup. This can lead to a chimney fire.
- Have fireplaces and wood-burning stoves cleaned on a regular basis. This removes any creosote buildup.

Smoke Detectors

A *smoke detector* is a small appliance that gives a loud warning signal when it detects smoke in the house, Figure 38-2. Detectors for the hearing impaired set off an ultrabright strobe light. There are two basic types of smoke detectors—ionization and photoelectric. The ionization type responds more rapidly to fires where flames are visible, but the photoelectric detector is faster in detecting a smoldering or slow-burning fire. Both types provide early warning of a fire.

Make sure your home has an adequate number of detection devices to provide real protection. Less than one-third of all homes have sufficient smoke alarms. For best coverage, according to the US Consumer Product Safety Commission, you need at least one smoke detector on each floor of the house, including the basement and finished attic.

On the first floor, the living room or family room is often a good central location for a smoke detector. Another central spot is the top of the stairwell between the first and second floors. In this location, a detector will "sniff out" the first signs of a fire on either floor and sound an early warning. If bedrooms are far apart—on different floors or down a long hall from one another—consider installing a detector outside each bedroom. For detailed instructions on where to install detectors be sure to refer to the model's "use-and-care" guide.

Figure 38-1. This electrical outlet is overloaded, which is a definite fire hazard.

Figure 38-2. This is a typical residential smoke alarm. This model is battery powered.

Some smoke alarms are powered by batteries or household current with a battery backup. A chirping detector alerts you to replace the battery. New lithium batteries last about ten years making once-a-year battery replacement a thing of the past. But, you must still check each device at least once a year to see that it is working properly. Your life may depend on it.

Figure 38-3. This bathroom door lock set may be opened from the outside with any slender probe or "key."

Fire Safety Code Requirements

The model building codes specify minimum requirements for fire safety. The following list identifies the requirements often cited by codes that may be readily enforced by law.

- Every occupied room in a residence must have at least two exits. One of these exits must be a doorway. Also, bedrooms that are below grade (basement) must be directly accessible to the outside.
- The only access to an occupied room may not be a folding stairs, ladder, or trapdoor.
- Every bedroom must have a window that can be easily opened by hand from the inside, unless the room has two interior exits or a direct exterior exit. The window must have a clear opening of at least five square feet, no less than 22" in any dimension and be no more than 48" from the floor to the bottom of the window.
- Exit paths from bedrooms to exits must be at least 3' wide.
- Exit paths from any room must not pass through a room controlled by another family nor through a space subject to locking.
- All exit doors must be at least 24" wide.
- All stairs must be at least 36" wide with risers not over 8" and treads over 9".
- Quick-opening devices must be used on all storm windows, screens, and burglar guards.
- Inside quick-release catches must be used as door-locking devices for easy exit.
- Bathroom door locks must provide for opening from the outside without a special key. See Figure 38-3.

- Children must be able to easily open closet doors from the inside.
- Smoke detectors should be installed outside each sleeping area and on every level of the house used for occupancy.
- Escape must not be blocked in the event of a malfunction of a combustion heater or stove.

More information is available in the National Fire Codes. Also, check your local code for additional requirements. Many areas, such as large metropolitan areas, may have codes that exceed these requirements.

Fire Extinguishers

Every residence should have a functioning fire extinguisher, Figure 38-4. Locate the fire extinguisher where it is easily found when needed. Fire extinguishers are classified according to the type of burning material on which they are to be used. The Class A extinguisher should be used for fires involving paper, wood, fabric, and other ordinary combustible materials. Class B extinguishers are to be used for burning liquids, such as a grease fire. Class C extinguishers are for use on electrical fires. Many fire extinguishers are labeled ABC and can be used on all types of fires.

Carbon Monoxide (CO) Detection

Carbon monoxide (CO) is an odorless, tasteless, invisible gas that is potentially

Figure 38-4. A typical home or office dry chemical "ABC" fire extinguisher that may be used on fires involving oil, gasoline, grease, flammable liquids, wood, paper, and cloth and on electrical fires.

deadly. It is produced wherever there is incomplete combustion. Dangerous CO concentrations may be produced by wood stoves, gas or oil furnaces, fireplaces, gas ranges, clothes dryers, water heaters, space heaters, charcoal grills, or even cars in an attached garage.

The risk posed by properly installed and functioning appliances is minimal. However, sloppy installation, damaged equipment, or improper construction practices can allow CO to enter the living space in harmful concentrations. Today's more energy-efficient, airtight home designs can compound the problem by trapping CO-polluted air in the home.

Carbon Monoxide Poisoning

Carbon monoxide is absorbed into the body through the lungs and binds to the hemoglobin in red blood cells. This reduces the blood's ability to transport oxygen. Eventually, CO displaces enough oxygen to result in suffocation. The result of this suffocation is brain damage or death. One-third of all

survivors of CO poisoning have lasting memory disorders or personality changes. In addition, heart attacks have been associated with high CO levels.

Air-borne CO concentrations are measured in parts per million (ppm). The percentage of CO in the blood is called COHb. It is a function of the CO concentration in the air and the length of time a person is exposed to the CO. Even though CO concentrations of 15,000 ppm can kill you in minutes, longer exposures to small concentrations are also dangerous. The longer exposure allows CO to build up in the bloodstream, resulting in a lethal COHb.

Symptoms of low-level carbon monoxide poisoning are similar to those of the flu. Symptoms include headaches, drowsiness, fatigue, nausea, and vomiting. These symptoms could result from the exposure to concentrations of 350 ppm for one hour. Exposure to 350 ppm for a period of four hours can cause brain damage or death.

Since the symptoms of CO poisoning are easily mistaken for the flu, some health experts believe that it has been underreported. Medical experts estimate that one-third of all cases of CO poisoning go undetected. According to the Mayo Clinic, accidental exposure to CO in the home contributes to approximately 1500 deaths annually. In addition, an estimated 10,000 persons in the US seek medical attention or lose at least one day of normal activities because of CO inhalation.

CO Detectors

When combustion appliances are used in the home, a CO detector is inexpensive insurance against unnecessary health risks, Figure 38-5. A properly working detector can provide an early warning to occupants before gas concentrations reach a dangerous level. If a home has even one combustion appliance, it should have a CO detector.

An appropriate CO detector should have a label that says it meets or exceeds Underwriters Laboratories Standard 2034. To meet this standard, a detector must sound the alarm when CO concentrations reach 100 ppm for 90 minutes, 200 ppm for 35 minutes, and

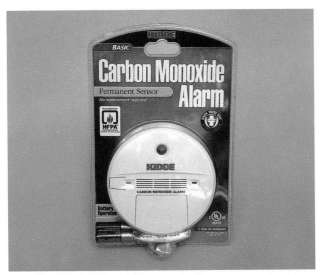

Figure 38-5. This residential carbon monoxide detector is battery operated.

any combustion equipment. Models currently on the market are powered either by 115-volt household current or batteries. Figure 38-6 shows possible sources of CO gas and the recommended location of CO detectors.

Radon Detection

Radon is an invisible, odorless, tasteless, radioactive gas. It comes from the natural decay of uranium found in soil, rock, and water. Radon moves through the ground to the air above and into the home. It is found all over the United States and in any type of building. However, you are likely to get the greatest exposure at home because you spend most of your time at home. Radon can be dangerous in high concentrations.

The Environmental Protection Agency (EPA) has estimated that 1 out of 15 homes in the United States has elevated radon levels. According to the surgeon general, radon is the second leading cause of lung cancer in the United States. In the past few years, the

400 ppm for 15 minutes. Detectors are available that will detect CO concentrations as low as 5 ppm.

Like smoke alarms, CO detectors should be mounted on the hallway ceiling outside the bedrooms. For additional safety, a CO detector should be placed in the furnace room and near

Potential Carbon Monoxide Sources in the Home

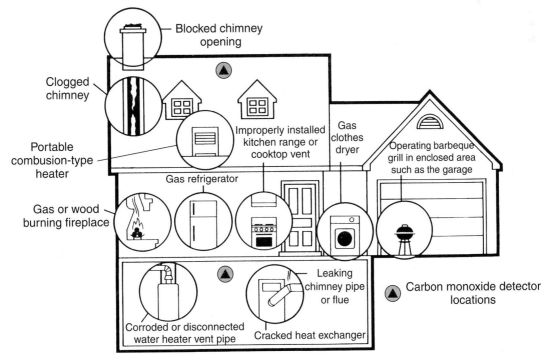

Figure 38-6. This drawing identifies potential carbon monoxide sources in the home and where carbon monoxide detectors should be located. (Provided by First Alert®)

detection of radon in homes has become a concern. In October of 1988, Congress passed the *Indoor Radon Abatement Act* setting the goal for the EPA of reducing indoor radon levels to those of outdoor air—0.2 to 0.5 picocuries per liter of air (pCi/L). Radon level is sometimes expressed in working levels (WL) instead of picocuries per liter.

Radon in the Home

Any home can be subject to high levels of radon whether it is old or new. Radon enters the home through cracks in solid floors, construction joints, cracks in walls, gaps in suspended floors, gaps around service pipes, cavities inside walls, and the water supply. Typically, radon levels from water are not as great as from soil. The rate at which radon enters a home depends on the amount of radon in the soil, number of cracks and openings between the home and soil, and ventilation in the home.

Fresh air dilutes radon. When homes are closed up for winter heating or summer air conditioning, the radon levels start to build. Unoccupied homes trap and build up higher levels than homes that are occupied. Natural air movement tends to draw a greater concentration of the soil gas inside the house.

Radon Testing

The EPA recommends that radon levels be checked in any structure having one or two floors. The test is very simple and requires only a few minutes to administer. There are several kinds of testing devices available, Figure 38-7. The two general types of testing devices are short-term and long-term. When selecting a test kit, look for the statement "Meets EPA Requirements" on the package.

Short-term testing requires 2 to 90 days, depending on the device. Passive devices include charcoal canisters, alpha track detectors, electret ion chambers, continuous monitors, and charcoal liquid scintillation devices. An advantage of using a short-term device is that the results of the test are available within a short period of time. A disadvantage of this

Figure 38-7. This radon gas test kit provides two calibrated short-term radon gas detectors. This allows you to conduct two tests at the same time and in the same location in order to get the most accurate results.

type of testing device is that it does not provide year-round average radon levels. Radon levels vary from day to day and season to season.

Long-term testing devices take more than 90 days. Passive devices include alpha track and electret detectors. Active devices require power to function and include continuous radon monitors and continuous working level monitors. Active devices continuously measure and record the amount of radon or its decay products in the air of the home. The advantage of using a long-term device is that it provides a year-round average of radon levels. A disadvantage is that it requires a longer period of time to obtain the test results.

Radon testing should be carried out when the house is occupied. Doors and windows should be kept closed as much as possible. The detector should be placed in the lowest level, such as the basement or first floor. Place the detector 20″ above the floor and away from drafts, high heat, high humidity, and exterior walls.

At the completion of the test, the testing device is sent to a laboratory for analysis. If the reading on a short-term test is 4pCi/L (0.02 WL) or higher, a second test is recommended. If the results on a long-term or second short-term test are 4pCi/L (0.02 WL) or higher, take steps to remove the radon from the house. For readings between 4 and 20pCi/L, take action within a few years. If the readings are above 20pCi/L, take action within a few months. Readings below 4pCi/L may provide some risk and future testing is suggested. The EPA recommends testing for radon every few years to determine if larger amounts of radon are seeping into the house.

Radon Mitigation

Reducing radon is called "radon mitigation." There are several methods of radon mitigation for homes and there are several factors to consider when selecting a method. The radon level, costs of installation and system operation, house size, and foundation types are all factors that should be taken into consideration when selecting the method to use. When selecting a contractor to mitigate the radon from your house, use one that is state certified or one who has completed EPA's Radon Contractor Proficiency Program. If you plan to do the repairs yourself, help is available from your state or the EPA. Basements and slab-on-grade construction require the following three-step process:

1. Soil-gas entry should be minimized by sealing joints, cracks, and other openings in slabs, below-grade walls, and floors, including openings for the sump pump. In addition, gas-retarding barriers—polyethylene membranes under floors and parging on outside walls—should be installed.

2. Install an active, fan-driven radon-removal vent-pipe system, Figure 38-8. A passive system may also be installed that can be activated later by adding a fan, usually in the attic.

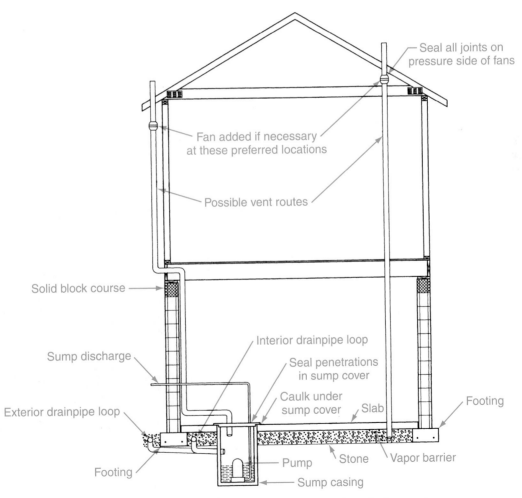

Figure 38-8. This diagram shows an active, fan-driven radon-removal vent-pipe system.

3. Reduce the "stack" or "chimney" effect in basements, which can draw soil gas into the home. This can be done by closing air passages between floors and providing make-up air from outside for combustion devices and exhaust fans.

Crawl spaces require the diversion of radon before it reaches the living space. The crawl space should be adequately vented to outside air. To prevent radon gas from seeping into the structure, the soil should be covered with a polyethylene membrane or concrete and the tops of block foundation walls should be sealed. Seal openings in floors and ductwork with caulks, foams, and tapes. More information on radon mitigation is available from:

Environmental Protection Agency
Ariel Rios Bldg
1200 Pennsylvania Ave NW
Washington, DC 20460
www.epa.gov

National Safety Council
1121 Spring Lake Drive
Itasca, IL 60143-3201
www.nsc.org

National Radon Safety Board
PO Box 426
Putnam Valley, NY 10579
www.nrsb.org

Moisture and Mold Problems

The occurrence of moisture and mold problems in residential structures has increased significantly in recent years. One of the reasons for this is because new buildings are constructed to have less air infiltration and heat loss/gain. In fact, some studies by the EPA have shown that many new homes have poorer air quality inside the home than outdoor levels. This condition has resulted in the term "sick house syndrome."

In many instances, the root problem is excessive moisture within the structure. This is frequently due to unwanted moisture entering the building from a variety of locations. When this moisture remains over time, the growth of unhealthy mold sets in, Figure 38-9. Gradual deterioration of the building materials accompanies mold growth. Once this cycle begins, the space inside the dwelling may rapidly reach a point where it is not healthy for occupants.

The purpose of this section is to examine the potential problem, explore the process of water vapor migration and condensation, and identify possible preventative measures. In addition, several health hazards associated with excessive mold buildup in the home are identified and discussed.

Migration of Water Vapor

All air contains some invisible moisture called *water vapor*. Relative humidity is a measure of water vapor in the air. When air is warm, it can hold more moisture than when it is cold. When water vapor comes in contact with a cold surface, it condenses to form water or frost, if the surface is 32°F or lower. The temperature at which water vapor condenses varies in relation to the surface temperature and the amount of water vapor in the air. The most common visual example of *condensation* in the home is the formation of water or frost on the glass in a window during cold weather.

Figure 38-9. Moisture was unnoticed in this closet, leading to the obvious mold growth. (FEMA News Photo)

Condensation becomes a serious problem in the home when it occurs on or within the walls, floors, and ceilings. Evidence of condensation may be seen as:

- Damp spots on ceilings and the room side of exterior walls.
- Water and frost on inside surfaces of windows.
- Moisture on basement sidewalls and floors.
- Water-filled blisters on outside paint surfaces.
- Marbles of ice on attic floors resulting from condensation of water on points of nails through roof sheathing.

The amount of vapor pressure depends on the amount of vapor in the air. This pressure forces moisture to dryer, lower-pressure areas. Thus, excessive moisture in a warm house is forced to the outside in cold weather and condensation on the inner surfaces or within the walls may occur. By controlling the amount of water vapor, condensation can be prevented.

Since water vapor is not visible or easily detected until it condenses, occupants are generally not aware of a problem. As a result, little thought is generally given to control of water vapor until condensation problems arise.

Sources of Water Vapor

Everyday household activities produce considerable moisture inside the dwelling. Some of the most obvious sources of water vapor inside the home include people, bathing facilities, cooking processes, laundry, and open gas flames. Sources of water vapor in the structure itself may include wet plaster, seepage in basements, unexcavated basements, and foundation leaks. Water vapor will always be present inside the home from routine activities, but with proper ventilation the moisture is not excessive or harmful, Figure 38-10. However, moisture from leaks, wet basements, etc., should be prevented.

Water condensation is not only a cold-weather problem, but a summertime problem as well. For example, what happens if warm, moist air from the outside on muggy days

Figure 38-10. A typical bathroom ventilation fan removes water vapor from inside the house and thus reduces the chance of mold growing. (Broan-NuTone, A Nortek Company)

enters the cool basement air? Condensation occurs when the warm air comes in contact with cool basement walls, floors, and cold-water pipes. This is just like the condensation on a cold glass of ice water. Also, houses whose first floor is concrete laid on the ground exhibit condensation problems in the summertime.

Preventative Measures

The control of excessive moisture vapor or humidity, and thus condensation, varies with the type of structure and the parts of a house. There are three principal cures that may reduce condensation problems. These can be used individually or in combination.

- Reduce interior humidity by controlling water vapor at the source, ventilating, and eliminating deliberately added moisture.
- Use vapor barriers to stop the flow of moisture through building materials—membranes and paints.
- Raise inner surface temperatures by insulating.

To avoid condensation in a house built over a crawl space, the crawl space must be kept dry. The following points should be considered.

- Grade the lot correctly for good drainage.
- Use gutters and downspouts and/or wide overhangs to eliminate rain seepage.

- Lay a moistureproof cover on the ground of the crawl space to prevent the rise of moisture. Generally, a polyethylene film 4 mil or 6 mil thick will serve this purpose.
- Provide foundation vents to allow escape of moisture from the crawl space.
- Where floor insulation is used, install a vapor barrier either directly above it or between the subfloor and the finish flooring.

To avoid condensation in a slab floor construction, follow these recommendations:

- Insulate by using gravel, cinders, crushed rock, or other insulating material underneath the floor.
- Good drainage is essential.
- Install insulation at the edges of the slab and install a vapor barrier under the slab to prevent ground moisture from entering the building, Figure 38-11.

Ventilation

Ventilation in the home can be used to reduce excessive humidity that cannot be controlled at its source, Figure 38-12. The model building codes generally specify the number and size of vents to use in a given structure. But, there are so many variables that the minimum recommendation may not be sufficient in every case. It is more satisfactory

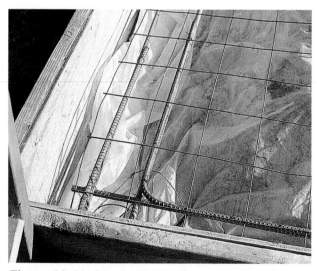

Figure 38-11. A polyethylene film placed under a concrete slab will reduce moisture penetration through the slab.

Figure 38-12. A popular fan-powered roof vent that is capable of cooling an attic of up to 1800 square feet. (Broan-NuTone, A Nortek Company)

to provide controlled (powered) ventilation than to depend on uncontrolled vents and cracks around windows and doors, etc. If a home is heated by a combustion-type furnace, an outside air intake can be added to the system. The same is true for a combustion-type water heater and fireplace. Proper ventilation may be the solution to most moisture vapor problems in the home.

Health Hazards Associated with Mold

Molds can be found almost anywhere moisture is present. Therefore, the moisture control within a house is an important part of mold prevention. Certain molds present health hazards. To help reduce these hazards, it is important to reduce the chances of mold growth.

Molds are a type of fungus and reproduce through the production of spores. These spores are always present in the air inside and outside our homes. When mold spores settle on organic materials in the presence of moisture, they may begin to grow. For example, molds live in the soil and break down plant materials by digestion. In this instance, molds play a positive role by helping to reduce dead plant materials.

There are molds that can grow on wood, paper, carpet, and foods, Figure 38-13. Mold

Figure 38-13. This wood has mold growing on it. During the construction process, lumber should be protected from excessive moisture to reduce the chance of mold growth.

Figure 38-14. Black mold (Stachybotrys atra) can grow on wood, fiberboard, gypsum board, paper, ceiling tiles, and cardboard. The carpet and padding shown here have been infested. (Floor Seal Technology, Inc.)

growth will generally occur indoors when excessive moisture accumulates over a period of time. It is virtually impossible to eliminate mold spores inside the home. But, the best way to reduce mold growth in the home is to control moisture.

Types of molds

According to the EPA, there are about 50 to 100 common types of mold in the home that may cause health problems. Molds that are commonly found in indoor air include Cladosporium, Pencillum, and Alternaria species. More serious molds, however, are the pathogenic species of fungi that are sometimes present in indoor air. These may include Aspergillus flavus, Aspergillus fumigatus, Aspergillus niger, and Stachybotrys atra.

Stachybotrys atra is commonly called "black mold." It is a greenish-black mold that can grow on material with a high cellulose and low nitrogen content. Materials of this type include wood, fiberboard, gypsum board, paper, ceiling tiles, and cardboard, Figure 38-14. Stachybotrys atra is associated with a number of deaths, particularly infant deaths. Not all black mold is Stachybotrys atra, but moldy homes are not healthy.

Health problems

Exposure to mold has been identified as a potential cause of many health problems, such as asthma, sinusitis, nosebleeds, chest congestion, allergic responses, and infection type diseases. Allergic responses include allergic rhinitis (hay fever), skin and upper respiratory tract irritation, and hypersensitivity Pneumonitis. Infection-type diseases include athlete's foot, yeast infections, histoplasmosis, and aspergillosis.

Health officials report that the most common health problems caused by indoor molds produce allergy-type symptoms. However, other more serious health problems can occur. In general, exposure to mold results in the following types of ailments.

- Upper respiratory infections.
- Breathing difficulties.
- Coughing.
- Sore throat.
- Nasal and sinus congestion.
- Skin and eye irritation.

Mold Prevention and Removal

If you discover a mold problem in your home, you should remove the mold and take steps to reduce or eliminate excessive moisture indoors. Follow these principles:

- Remove any visible mold from hard surfaces and allow to dry. Soft materials, such as carpet and ceiling tiles, that contain mold should be replaced.

- Eliminate unwanted water from leaky faucets or other sources.
- Clean and dry drip pans in your appliances on a regular basis.
- Vent clothes dryers to the outside.
- When bathing, cooking, or using the washer, use an exhaust fan or open a window.
- Take steps to reduce indoor humidity to between 30% and 50% relative humidity.

Surfaces with mold should be cleaned with a household bleach and water mixture. Be sure the area is ventilated and apply the bleach-water mixture with a sponge. Allow the mixture to work for 15 minutes, then dry the surface. Be sure to wear an approved mask and rubber gloves. When in doubt, consult a professional.

Weather- and Nature-Related Safety

Every area of the country is faced with one or more destructive force of nature, such as flooding, hurricanes, tornadoes, and earthquakes. However, some areas are more prone to certain types of natural destructive forces. Each year, flooding is responsible for more property damage and deaths than hurricanes, tornadoes, and earthquakes combined. Any residential structure should be designed and built to reasonably resist the destructive forces of nature. This section will examine the major weather- and nature-related hazards that have a particular impact on how and where dwellings are constructed.

Earthquakes

An *earthquake zone* is an area that is prone to earthquakes. Most people think of California when earthquakes are mentioned. But, anywhere west or just east of the Rocky Mountains is an earthquake zone. In addition, the area along the Mississippi River from Arkansas through Tennessee to Illinois is in the New Madrid earthquake zone. The most severe earthquake on record in the United States was along the New Madrid fault. Other earthquake zones include the southern Appalachians, New England, and Alaska.

As indicated on the seismic zone map in Figure 38-15, there is some chance of earthquake damage in all regions of the country. Areas that have a very low chance of damage include the southern halves of Florida and Texas, a portion of the Gulf Coast, and the islands of Hawaii.

Reducing earthquake damage to dwellings

Five basic areas need to be addressed to reduce the hazards of earthquakes—siting considerations, soil and foundation types, building shapes and mass, structural details, and drainage. A thorough analysis of any existing or proposed structure should take all of these factors into account. An excellent source of design information is *Earthquake Safe: A Hazard Reduction Manual for Homes* published by:
Builders Booksource
1817 Fourth Street
Berkeley, CA 94710
www.buildersbooksite.com

The notion that a structure can be "earthquake proof" is misleading. It is impossible for

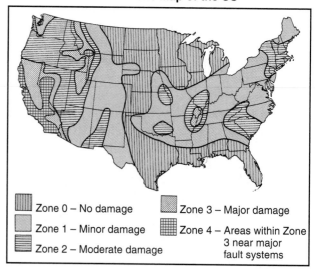

Seismic Zone Map of the US

Zone 0 – No damage
Zone 1 – Minor damage
Zone 2 – Moderate damage
Zone 3 – Major damage
Zone 4 – Areas within Zone 3 near major fault systems

Figure 38-15. This seismic zone map shows areas most likely to experience earthquakes. (Provided by the International Conference of Building Officials)

a structure to be earthquake proof. However, the need to reduce the risk of serious structural failure is valid. Four kinds of structural elements need careful consideration to determine what kinds of strengthening strategies are practical. They include:

- The foundation that supports the building.
- The horizontal members, such as floors.
- The columns, posts, and other vertical members that transfer the weight of the structure to the foundation.
- All points of connection.

These elements are covered in Chapter 23 of the *1988 Uniform Building Code*. Also, check with your local building department for specific recommendations.

Interior space

You can reduce damage inside your home by doing the following things before an earthquake strikes.

- Securely attach pictures and mirrors to the wall.
- Anchor bookcases, shelving units, and filing cabinets to the wall.
- Cover windows and glass doors with safety film.
- Add a ledge to shelves to prevent spilling. Place heavier items on the bottom shelves.
- Install latches on drawers and cabinets to prevent their contents from spilling.
- Secure hanging items to the permanent structure of your house.
- Connect computers, TVs, and other small appliances to their support base.
- Use straps or cables to secure large appliances and water heaters to the wall.
- Fit all gas appliances with flexible connections and/or breakaway gas shut-off devices. Check your local code to see what is approved.

House structure

The following summary is illustrative of the types of things that can be done to reduce structural damage due to an earthquake.

- Bolt the sill plate to the foundation with anchor bolts spaced no farther than 4' apart, Figure 38-16.
- Reinforce cripple walls (short walls) with a plywood shear wall that connects the sill plate, cripple studs, and wall plates. Generally, 1/2" CDX plywood is used for one-story homes, 5/8" plywood for two-story houses, and 3/4" plywood for three-story structures.
- Install blocking at the midspan and ends of floor joists. Long spans may require additional blocking. Use angle steel or metal angle clips to attach the joists ends to the rim joists and between the rim joist and sill plate.
- Add metal clips, T-straps, or steel brackets at all connections between posts and beams, Figure 38-17. Beams should be securely attached to piers with heavy metal straps and anchor bolts.
- Hurricane ties should be installed between the top plates or bond beams and the rafters and ceiling joists, Figure 38-18.
- Chimneys are particularly vulnerable to earthquake damage. A large, reinforced footing; structural steel bracing; ties to framing; and reduced weight above the roof line can reduce the potential for damage.

Figure 38-19 shows the destructive forces of earthquakes on residential structures.

Figure 38-16. The sill plate should be bolted to the foundation with anchor bolts spaced no farther than 4' apart.

Figure 38-17. Thick metal straps have been added to the connections between the posts and beam in this structure to resist lateral forces.

Figure 38-18. Hurricane ties should be placed between the concrete bond beam and each roof truss to resist uplift forces.

Floods

Every state in the US experiences flooding at some point. Those communities located in low-lying areas, near a body of water, or downstream from a dam have the highest risk. *Flash floods* are especially dangerous because they represent a high volume of fast-moving water that can appear suddenly. Consider these facts:

- The force of 6″ of swiftly moving water can cause you to lose your footing.

Figure 38-19. These homes were damaged by the Janurary 2004 San Simeon earthquake in California. This was a 6.5 magnitude earthquake. (FEMA News Photo)

- Flash flood waters move at very fast speeds, can move boulders, uproot trees, demolish buildings, and wash out bridges.
- It takes only 2′ of moving water to sweep an automobile away.

Floods are at or near the top of the list of the most common and devastating of all natural disasters, Figure 38-20. Flooding is possible or even likely in most communities in the US following heavy thunderstorms, spring rains, or winter snow thaws. Some of the worst floods have been caused by dam failures that release very large amounts of water in a very short time, thus causing a flash flood.

Floodplain risk

Historically, people have built their homes next to bodies of water—rivers, lakes, ocean—for obvious reasons. Water was the main mode of transportation. Building next to a body of water has benefits, but there are drawbacks as well. Authorities say that floods have caused a greater loss of life and property and have disrupted more families and communities in the US than all other natural hazards combined.

Natural *floodplains* have been identified throughout the US according to the average number of years between flooding, such as a 100-year floodplain or a 500-year floodplain. These areas are referred to by local building departments when issuing building permits. Generally, new buildings are prohibited in floodplains that flood frequently or permitted only if the elevation of the structure is located significantly above the floodplain, Figure 38-21. In any case, new rules and requirements have

Figure 38-21. The finished floor of this house is 14' above the existing grade to be above the highest point of a 100-year flood.

resulted from the experience of building in a floodplain and flood mitigation has become very important to everyone.

Flood mitigation

Examples of flood mitigation include relocating homes out of the floodplain, elevating homes above the base floodplain (usually the 100-year floodplain), and minimizing the vulnerability to flood damage through both structural and nonstructural means, Figure 38-22. Check your local model building code for information regarding building in flood-prone areas before selecting a site for a new home or purchasing an existing home.

Tornadoes

"Tornado Alley" covers the part of the US that runs north from Texas, through eastern Nebraska, and northeast to Indiana. It is known for the number and severity of tornadoes. But, you are still vulnerable to tornadoes even if you live outside of this area. Texas, Oklahoma, and Kansas may have more tornadoes than other states, but the rest of the US also has tornadoes on a regular basis.

Homes that are built strictly to current model building codes for high-wind regions have a much better chance of surviving violent

Figure 38-20. This aerial photograph shows flooded homes in LeClaire, IA, along the Mississippi River in 2001. (FEMA News Photo)

Figure 38-22. When elevating a structure to mitigate flood damage, be sure all exterior appliances are elevated as well. (FEMA News Photo)

Figure 38-23. This home was severely damaged by an F4 tornado in December 2005. Tornados can happen at any time of the year. (FEMA News Photo)

windstorms than homes that do not meet these requirements. In spite of what you might think, wind speeds in most tornadoes are at or below the design speeds planned for in most typical building codes. Records show that about 85% of all reported tornadoes have wind speeds of 112 mph or less. In other words, a house built to code will resist the majority of tornadoes.

What is a tornado?

A *tornado* is a swirling column of air extending from a thunderstorm cloud down to the ground. Most tornadoes generally form when warm, humid air along the ground is pushed up rapidly by cooler air. This movement of air then develops into a spinning vortex or funnel and can become a tornado. A tornado may also be a byproduct of a hurricane. The average tornado is about 200 yards wide and several miles long. Winds typically swirl in a cyclonic direction (counterclockwise in the northern hemisphere).

Tornado season

Tornadoes can form at most any time of the year. The peak season varies by location. In general, tornadoes in the US are most prevalent in the months of April, May, and June, Figure 38-23. This is the time of year when warm, humid air from the Gulf of Mexico is

pushed up from the south and collides with cold northern winds over the Great Plains. This fits the model required for tornado formation.

Tornadoes can occur at any time of day or night. However, approximately 80% form between noon and midnight. An average year will produce between 800 and 1,000 tornadoes in the US.

Building to resist tornadoes

No above-ground structure is completely tornado-proof. However, there are steps that can be taken to give a house a better chance of surviving a tornado. The following recommendations are intended to aid the design and building processes.

Windows. Install impact-resistant windows. These windows are specially designed to resist high winds and are commonly available in hurricane-prone areas.

Entry doors. Exterior doors should have at least three hinges and a one-inch long dead bolt security lock. Anchoring the door frames securely to the wall framing is very important.

Sliding glass doors. These doors are more vulnerable to wind damage than most other doors because of their large exposure. Install impact-resistant door systems made of laminated glass, plastic glazing, or a combination.

Garage doors. Garage doors are highly susceptible to wind damage because of their size and construction. Have a qualified inspector determine if both the door and frame will resist high winds. If purchasing a new door, check the wind rating and select a door that will withstand at least 110 mph winds.

Roofs. Be sure the roof covering and sheathing will resist high winds. All roofing materials are not equal in this respect. If you are replacing an existing roof, a qualified roofing contractor can take the following steps to increase the stability of the roof.

1. Remove the existing roofing materials down to the sheathing.
2. Inspect the rafters or trusses to be sure they are securely connected to the walls.
3. Cut out and replace any damaged sheathing. Be sure it is nailed according to the recommended schedule required by the local code.
4. Install a roof covering that is designed for high wind areas. Attachment must follow manufacturer's specifications.

Gables. Gable end walls must be braced properly to resist high winds. Check the current model building code for "high-wind regions" for guidance or consult your local building department.

Connections. Connections between the foundation and walls, floor and walls, and roof structure and walls are critical points, Figure 38-24. Appropriate connectors must be used and attached properly if the total structure is to resist high winds.

Figure 38-24. Joists hangers were used in this structure to increase the strength of the structure and resist damaging winds.

Anchors. The exterior walls must be properly anchored to the foundation. Approved anchor bolts and/or straps and fasteners can be used for this purpose.

Upper stories. If the house has more than one story, be sure the wall framing of the upper stories is properly connected to the lower wall framing. Use approved straps and fasteners.

Roof framing. Anchor the roof framing to the exterior walls with approved straps, clips, and fasteners. Consult the model building code for specifications or get help from your local building department.

Tornado warnings

No dwelling is tornado-proof, so you should take steps to protect yourself and your family when a tornado threatens. A tornado watch is issued when conditions are favorable for tornado formation. A tornado warning is issued when a tornado has been sighted or detected on radar.

Most communities have a severe weather warning system. Be familiar with it. Make sure every member of your family knows what to do when a "watch" or "warning" is sounded. During the "watch" phase of the storm, remove anything in your yard that can become flying debris before the storm strikes. Do *not* attempt this after the warning is sounded.

When a tornado warning is sounded, seek shelter immediately. Decide ahead of time where you will seek shelter. It could be a local community shelter or your own underground storm cellar. Some newer homes have a *safe room* within the house that has been constructed to withstand tornado-force winds. Stay away from windows and preferably under something sturdy like a workbench or staircase. Seek the center and lowest section of the structure.

Develop a family plan for protection, escape, and a meeting place to reunite if members become separated. Assemble an emergency kit that includes:

- Three-day supply of drinking water and food.
- First aid supplies.
- Portable NOAA weather radio.

- Basic tools.
- Flashlight.
- Work gloves.
- Emergency cooking equipment.
- Portable lantern.
- Fresh batteries.
- Clothing.
- Blankets.
- Prescription medications.
- Extra keys.
- Eyeglasses.
- Credit cards and cash.
- Important documents, including insurance policies.

Contrary to what you may have heard, do not open your windows. This only increases water and wind damage to the inside of the house. Do not stay in a trailer, mobile home, or manufactured home during a tornado. These units are too light to resist tornadoes even if they have tie-downs. Do not attempt to ride out the storm in an automobile. A strong tornado can pick up a vehicle and destroy it.

Hurricanes

A *hurricane* is a tropical storm (cyclone) with winds that have reached a constant speed of 74 miles per hour (64 knots) or more. Hurricane winds blow in a large spiral around a relatively calm center called the eye. The eye is usually 20 to 30 miles across, but the storm may extend out to 400 miles or more. Areas in the United States that are the most vulnerable to hurricanes include the Atlantic and Gulf coasts from Texas to Maine; the Caribbean territories; and tropical areas of the western Pacific that include Hawaii, Guam, American Samoa, and Saipan. August and September are the peak months of the hurricane season, but the season lasts from June 1st through November 30th.

When a hurricane approaches land, it usually brings torrential rains, high winds, and storm surges. Of these three events, the storm surge is generally the most dangerous. A *storm surge* is a dome of ocean water fueled by the hurricane that can be 20' at its highest

point and up to 100 miles wide. The power of the surge can demolish communities along the coast as it sweeps ashore. Statistics show that 9 out of 10 hurricane fatalities can be attributed to the storm surge.

The greatest damage from hurricanes occurs as they make landfall. Damage is caused by strong winds, storm surge, flooding, tornadoes, and rip tides. Together, these forces can demolish most any structure in their path.

Storms like hurricanes are called by different names in the different parts of the world. For example, systems that develop over the Atlantic or the eastern Pacific Oceans are called hurricanes. But, in the western North Pacific and Philippines, these systems are referred to as typhoons. Storms of this magnitude in the Indian and South Pacific Oceans are called tropical cyclones.

US hurricanes

On average, ten tropical storms develop each year in the North Atlantic. Of these, six usually reach hurricane strength and two may strike the coast of the United States. The most deaths in US history resulting from a single hurricane was the Galveston, Texas hurricane in 1900. This hurricane took 6,000 lives.

In 2005, there were 27 named tropical storms, 13 of which became hurricanes. Seven of the hurricanes were considered major and three were category five (the strongest). On average, there are 10 named storms, six of which become hurricanes. There are only two major hurricanes in a typical year. Hurricane Katrina hit the Gulf Coast in 2005 and became the second deadliest hurricane in US history, Figure 38-25. Nearly 1300 people lost their lives in Hurricane Katrina. In addition, reconstruction costs were estimated at over $200 billion. Another major storm, Hurricane Wilma, also hit the US in 2005 causing several billion dollars in damage.

Hurricane mitigation through codes

Many states and local governments in coastal areas of the US have enacted *hurricane codes* and/or restrictions. These codes are designed to reduce damage to property during a hurricane. For example, Florida has instituted

A   B

Figure 38-25. A—Hurricane Katrina devastated the Gulf Coast. Weeks after the hurricane, flooding, fires, and other problems continued. B—With so much destruction, air, soil, and water quality became a major concern. This technician is collecting soil samples for testing. (FEMA News Photo)

the Coastal Construction Control Line (CCCL). This defines the extent of a zone from the coastline inland that is subject to flooding, erosion, and other impacts during a 100-year storm. Properties located between the ocean and the CCCL are subject to state-enforced elevation and construction requirements. The CCCL foundation and elevation requirements in this area are even more stringent than National Flood Insurance Program (NFIP) coastal (V-Zone) requirements. Likewise, the CCCL wind load requirements for properties between the ocean and the CCCL are more stringent than the wind load requirements of the model building codes.

There is emerging proof that more stringent codes and enforcement works. Take for example the experience gained from Hurricane Opal. On October 4, 1995, it struck a portion of the Florida coastline as a Category 3 hurricane with 110–115 mile per hour winds. According to the Florida Department of Environmental Protection, none of the 576 major habitable structures located seaward of the CCCL and permitted by the state under then current codes sustained substantial damage, Figure 38-26. Most of the damage was caused by coastal flooding that included storm surge, wind-generated waves, flood-induced

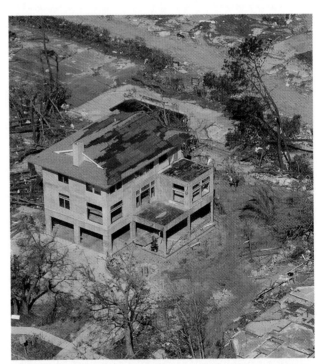

Figure 38-26. This home survived Hurricane Katrina because of its design while the neighboring structures were reduced to rubble. (FEMA News Photo)

erosion. Floodborne debris also contributed to damage. By contrast, 768 of the 1366 major habitable structures located seaward of the CCCL either not permitted by the state or constructed prior to state permitting requirements sustained substantial structural damage during the storm. It is very clear that increased structural requirements and stricter enforcement are worth the efforts.

Building to resist hurricanes

The following recommendations are intended to provide broad guidance in the design and building of a dwelling that will more likely resist the forces of a hurricane. However, local and state codes should always be consulted.

Landscaping. Use shredded bark as a landscaping material instead of gravel or rock. Remove weak branches and trees that could fall on the house during a storm.

Windows. Install impact-resistant window systems. Or, install impact-resistant shutters or panels that cover window openings to glass being broken by flying debris, Figure 38-27.

Entry doors. Install at least three hinges on exterior doors that are 6'-8" high. Four hinges should be installed on exterior doors that are 8'-0" high. Install a dead bolt security lock with a bolt at least one inch long. Be sure door frames and hinges are securely anchored to the wall framing. Doors should be solid-core or steel doors.

Sliding glass doors. Reduce the vulnerability of sliding glass doors to wind damage by installing an impact-resistant door system made from laminated glass, plastic glazing, or a combination of plastic and glass. Or, install hurricane panels that completely cover the entire door.

Garage doors. Garage doors are highly susceptible to wind damage because of their large area. Purchase a door that is certified to withstand at least 110 mph winds. Be sure the track system has the same rating and is solidly anchored to the wall with bolts or screws. Doors wider than 8' must have metal stiffeners to resist hurricane-level winds, Figure 38-28.

Roofs. The roof structure and covering are areas of significant concern during very high winds. Select a roofing material that is designed to resist high winds, Figure 38-29. Be sure to follow recommended installation procedures. Roof sheathing should be fastened as prescribed by the code in your area. This may include the use of construction adhesive, as well as nails. Every truss or rafter must be secured to the exterior wall with clips and/or straps. Proper nailing is very important to the quality of the installation. In addition, the roof structure must be braced inside to produce a rigid structure able to resist hurricane winds.

Gables. The end walls of a gable roof are particularly vulnerable to high wind damage. Make certain they are braced properly. Check

Figure 38-27. Hurricane storm panels have been custom made to fit each exterior opening in this building. They will resist damage from 120 mph winds.

Figure 38-28. The strength of garage doors can greatly be increased by adding metal stiffeners to each panel of the door. This door will resist 120 mph winds.

Figure 38-29. The roofing material being applied to this home is colored concrete tile. When attached properly, it will resist typical hurricane-strength winds.

with your local building department or truss manufacturer.

Connections. Reinforce the points where the roof and the foundation meet the exterior walls of the structure. This is generally accomplished through the use of anchors, straps, or clips. Walls are usually anchored to the foundation using anchor bolts or straps placed around the perimeter of the foundation at about 4′ intervals, Figure 38-30. Second story framing must be securely fastened to the lower level through the use of straps that bridge the floor joist area.

Hurricane warnings

Prepare an escape plan for when a hurricane threatens. Most communities have a

Figure 38-30. Anchor bolts are used in this slab-type foundation to connect the exterior walls to the foundation.

disaster preparedness plan and you should be familiar with it. Create a family plan as well. Identify escape routes and select an emergency meeting place for your family to gather if you become separated. Contact relatives to relieve their concern.

Also, prepare your home for the storm before it arrives. Hurricanes usually take several days to develop and that provides time to get ready. Develop an emergency kit that includes:

- Three-day supply of drinking water and food that does not require refrigeration or cooking.
- Do not forget the pets and food for them.
- First aid supplies.
- Portable NOAA weather radio.
- Toolbox with basic tools.
- Flashlight and extra batteries.
- Work gloves.
- Personal hygiene items.
- Emergency cooking equipment.
- Portable lanterns.
- Clothing and blankets.
- Prescription drugs.
- Extra house and car keys.
- Eyeglasses.
- Credit cards and cash.
- Important documents, including insurance policies.

Prepare a complete description of your personal belongings. Videotaping your home and its contents is a good idea. Store this list or tape in a safe place.

Remove items from outside the home that might be blown about during the storm. Follow news reports about the weather so you know what to expect. Shut off the water and gas supply. Disconnect all electrical appliances except food storage. Wrap outside electric motors with plastic to prevent water damage. Be sure to fill the fuel tanks in your vehicles because fuel may not be available for evacuation or for several days following the storm. Finally, obey evacuation orders from local authorities.

General Home Safety

The majority of us believe that our homes are safe. Survey evidence shows, however, that most are not. So, what can be done to improve the safety of a home? First, take a look at some of the statistics related to home safety.

- According to the National Safety Council, about one-third of the 28,400 accidental deaths that occur in homes each year in the US are from falls.

- Each year about 200,000 people older than 65 end up in the hospital with a broken hip suffered in a fall. Many of these happened in the home.

- Nearly half of all home fires and three of every five fire-related deaths in the US occur in residences without smoke detectors.

- About 3,300 people died and 17,700 were injured in US house fires in 1997. (Most recent statistics)

- Most electrical shocks in the home resulted from the misuse of household appliances.

- The major causes of accidents in the home are falls, burns, electrical shock, and poisonings.

The first step in preventing accidents and injuries in the home is to be sure that your home meets the model building code in your area. The major purpose of the code is to improve safety. Newly constructed homes are inspected and must pass or an occupancy permit is not issued. However, older homes or homes that are not well maintained most often would not pass such an inspection.

Secondly, many common sense actions that relate to every day living can improve home safety. For example:

- Keep stairs free of toys and other items.
- Remove trip-hazards from traffic circulation patterns.
- Keep the area around a fireplace or heater free of combustible materials.
- Secure flammable and toxic liquids.
- Limit the use of extension cords.
- Keep electrical and mechanical appliances and devices in good repair.
- Choose rugs with nonskid backing
- Provide adequate lighting in hazard-prone areas, Figure 38-31.
- Childproof your home if you have young children.
- Follow good housekeeping practices.

These are just some of the common-sense things you can do to improve safety in your home.

Figure 38-31. The exterior lighting at the main entry of this home will reduce the chance of tripping accidents on the entry steps. (Manufactured Housing Institute)

Internet Resources

www.buildingsystems.org
Building Systems Councils of National Association of Home Builders

www.cdc.gov
Centers for Disease Control and Prevention

www.concretehomes.com
Portland Cement Association

www.epa.gov
US Environmental Protection Agency

www.fema.gov
Federal Emergency Management Agency

www.ibhs.org
Institute for Business and Home Safety

www.iii.org
Insurance Information Institute

www.noaa.gov
National Oceanic and Atmospheric Administration

www.sweets.com
Sweets Catalog File

www.weather.com
The Weather Channel

Review Questions—Chapter 38

Write your answers on a separate sheet of paper. Do not write in this book.

1. Which of the following may help prevent a fire in your home?
   a) Have your heating system inspected yearly.
   b) Store flammable liquids in approved containers.
   c) Do not overload electrical circuits.
   d) All of the above are correct.

2. Identify two locations in the home where a smoke detector should be installed.

3. When considering fire safety, every occupied room must have at least _____ means of exit.

4. Which type of fire extinguisher should be used on a grease fire?
   a) Class A.
   b) Class B.
   c) Class C.
   d) Class X.

5. _____ is an odorless, tasteless, invisible, potentially deadly gas that is produced wherever there is incomplete combustion.

6. _____ is a gas produced by the natural decay of uranium found in the soil, rock, and water.

7. List three steps that can reduce radon accumulation in basements and slab-on-grade construction.

8. List four conditions that indicate excessive moisture in the home.

9. Which of the following is *not* generally a source of water vapor in the structure?
   a) Wet plaster.
   b) Wet basements.
   c) Leaks
   d) Drippy outside hose bib.

10. _____ break down plant materials by digesting them.

11. The way to control indoor mold growth is to control _____.

12. The most common health problems caused by indoor _____ produce allergy-type symptoms.

13. Which of the following molds is a greenish black mold commonly called black mold and can cause serious health problems?
   a) Stachybotrys atra.
   b) Pencillum.
   c) Cladosporium.
   d) Aspergillus flavus.

14. Each year _____ is responsible for more property damage and deaths than any destructive force of nature.

15. The area along the Mississippi River from Arkansas through Tennessee to Illinois is in the _____ earthquake zone.

16. In which months do tornadoes most frequently occur in the US?
    a) January, February, and March.
    b) April, May, and June.
    c) July, August, and September.
    d) October, November, and December.

17. At what sustained wind speed does a tropical storm become classified as a hurricane?
    a) 34 mph.
    b) 64 mph.
    c) 74 mph.
    d) 94 mph.

18. What are the peak months of the hurricane season?
    a) June and July.
    b) August and September.
    c) September and October.
    d) May and June.

19. Which of the following generally accounts for the most (about 1/3 of the total) accidental deaths in the home in the US?
    a) Drownings.
    b) Falls.
    c) Fires.
    d) Electrocution.

Suggested Activities

1. Examine your home and prepare a list of fire hazards. Then, prepare a plan to eliminate the hazards.

2. Go to your local home building center or hardware store. Identify the carbon monoxide detectors that are available. Make a list of the features of the products, price, and general information given on the packaging. Prepare a written report.

3. Research the topic of radon gas. Determine those sections of the country where the radon hazard is most prevalent. Identify common methods of radon mitigation in those areas. Prepare a report on your findings.

4. Prepare a report on one of the major weather- or nature-related hazards. This may be on earthquakes, floods, tornadoes, or hurricanes, but select a hazard common to your area. Be sure to include such things as areas of the country most vulnerable, frequency, cost in lives and dollars, and preventative measures. Record your sources.

Career Opportunities

Objectives

After studying this chapter, you will be able to:

➤ List various career options in architecture and residential construction.

➤ Compare the duties and educational requirements of various occupations in architecture and construction.

➤ Describe the type of objectives found in a model ethics code.

➤ Explain why job site safety is important.

➤ List leadership traits.

➤ Explain the advantages and disadvantages of entrepreneurship.

Key Terms

Architect
Architectural Drafter
Architectural
  Illustrator
Bachelor's Degree
Construction
  Technologist

Entrepreneur
Estimator
Land Surveyor
Residential Designer
Specifications Writer
Work Ethic

Careers in Architecture and Construction

The fascinating world of architecture and residential construction has been illustrated throughout this text by many related career and job opportunities. Home construction requires the knowledge and skills of a variety of tradeworkers and professionals. Certain occupations will be more interesting and exciting to some people than others. It is important to look at each career and what it offers in order to determine which job peaks your interest. This chapter outlines a number of career opportunities and should provide an overall picture of the role people play in residential architecture, designing, and construction. Take a close look at the duties, functions, responsibilities, and educational requirements of each career.

Architect

The architect's duties include a great deal of creativity and sensitivity to form and materials, Figure 39-1. An *architect* designs structures by working closely with the client in making preliminary drawings, sketches, and suggestions for materials to be used. When the architect and client mutually agree on a final design for the structure, working drawings are prepared as described throughout the previous chapters.

An architect may also have the responsibility of assisting the client in selecting a building contractor and may represent the

Figure 39-1. An architect checks on the work in progress.

owner in dealing with the contractor during construction. It is usually the architect's duty to periodically check construction as it proceeds to see that the plan is being followed and the specified materials are being used.

Education requirements for an architect may vary according to the background of the individual. However, the general practice requires a baccalaureate or *bachelor's degree* from an accredited college or university. This degree generally requires four years of full-time study. In many cases, a master's degree for advanced study is obtained. In some instances, a two-year program along with a number of years of practical experience will meet the necessary requirements. All states require an examination to obtain a license. The license indicates that the person is a registered architect. This also ensures that the person is qualified to design structures that meet the standards for safety, health, and property. Job opportunities for an architect appear to be very favorable. However, relatively few architects are employed full time in residential home design. Most architects work for large firms that design commercial buildings.

Architectural Drafter

Architectural drafters generally draw the details of working drawings and make tracings from original drawings that the architect or designer has prepared, Figure 39-2. They often begin as junior drafters and are given more difficult assignments as they gain experience in the architectural firm. Many architectural drafters are satisfied with their position and retain this job as a career. Others may take the licensing examinations with the goal of becoming architects or beginning new firms on their own.

Educational requirements for the architectural drafter usually include graduation from high school with some courses in architectural drawing. Proficiency with a CADD system is also desirable. Extensive study at a technical institute, vocational school, or community college is desirable for further experience and better job placement.

Architectural Illustrator

An *architectural illustrator* prepares drawings, sketches, renderings, and illustrations to present ideas to potential clients and as advertisements for commercial catalogs and publications. They have completed a high level of study and have a high degree of artistic skill. They usually begin their study in architectural drafting or art and branch off into this specialized field, Figure 39-3. Chapter 33 *Presentation Drawings* provides an overview of the various techniques used by architects and illustrators in preparing presentations and renderings.

Figure 39-2. CADD workstations and software are common tools for the architectural drafter.

Figure 39-3. Architectural illustrators use many techniques to communicate the plan to others.

Figure 39-4. A specifications writer checks the exacting details of all requirements to go into the contract of an architectural project.

Photographs, models, and computer-generated renderings are replacing some of the traditional work of the architectural illustrator. However, there is still great need for people who are highly skilled in this area and have computer expertise. Just as architectural drafting is moving toward CADD, architectural illustration is moving toward computer-generated illustrations.

As you study architectural design, you may find you have a flair for preparing illustrations. This career may be well suited for you. Educational requirements are similar to those of the architectural drafter or commercial artist. Job opportunities are normally found in larger architectural firms.

Specifications Writer

The job of the *specifications writer* is to prepare all the written information needed to describe materials, methods, and fixtures to be used in the structure, Figure 39-4. Chapter 35 *Material and Tradework Specifications* provides a broad overview of the types of information a specifications writer will prepare.

Just as for architects, the specifications writer must be knowledgeable in all phases of construction, building materials, hardware, tradework, and fixtures. A college degree is normally required with emphasis on drawings, industrial materials, and building construction. In some cases, a specifications writer may advance to this position from experience in the construction industry and related

study. There are many job opportunities for people with skill in specifications writing.

Estimator

The person who calculates the costs of materials and labor for a building is the *estimator*, Figure 39-5. An estimator's responsibilities are extremely important since any error in judgment or material estimates could prove very costly to the company. They must prepare all the paperwork necessary to inform

Figure 39-5. An estimator reviews the set of plans to prepare the cost of materials.

the architect or builder of what the total cost of the structure will be. Selling prices and profits are then determined from this information.

An architectural estimator for a large company or corporation will normally have a college degree with emphasis on mathematics. Computer experience is normally required and familiarity with a computer-based estimating package is advisable. A good background in economics and structural materials is also valuable. In smaller companies, an estimator is often promoted from drafting work or the building trades and given additional training to master the necessary job skills.

Surveyor

In architectural work, a *land surveyor* is primarily concerned with establishing areas and boundaries of real estate property. A surveying team usually includes a rod worker, chain worker, instrument worker, and party chief. They are involved with the planning and subdivision of land and the preparation of property descriptions, Figure 39-6. It is also their responsibility to prepare maps and plats that show defined areas and natural or artificially created features above and below the ground level. Surveyors must prepare drawings and written specifications. The American Society of Civil Engineers identifies four major categories in the field of surveying: land surveying, engineering surveying, geodetic surveying, and cartographic surveying.

The surveyor should be skilled in the use of surveying equipment, Figure 39-7. They should also be exacting in collecting data and knowledgeable about mapping. An understanding of the principles of real estate property law is also valuable. Many features of a residential structure will be dependent on the surveyor's skill in measuring grade level and property lines. Many building code requirements are based on these data.

Educational requirements for a surveyor normally include a bachelor's degree in surveying or civil engineering. However, many technical institutes and community colleges offer two year programs that allow a person with practical experience to become a surveying technician. Education in CADD and surveying software is also desirable, Figure 39-8.

Figure 39-7. This surveying technician is collecting information about a building site that will be measured more accurately with typical surveying instruments. (Rolatape Corporation)

Figure 39-6. A surveying team is involved in the planning and subdivision of land and the preparation of property descriptions.

Figure 39-8. Education in CADD is valuable to a surveyor.

Teaching Architectural Drafting

A teaching career in architectural drafting is a very interesting and rewarding experience for many people. There are considerable opportunities to teach architecture in high schools, trade or vocational schools, community colleges, and universities, Figure 39-9.

The educational requirements for teaching architecture vary according to the type of school and program. However, one should possess a bachelor's degree in architecture or industrial technology. Teaching architectural technology or graduate programs in architectural drafting will normally require an advanced degree, either a master's or doctorate, and practical experience.

Construction Technologist

Construction technologists are qualified for both supervisory and technical roles in the construction industry. Areas of specialization of the construction technologist include managing construction, purchasing, expediting, specifications writing, estimating and bidding, quality control, and site supervision.

A construction technologist typically has a bachelor's degree in construction technology. This major requires a strong background in science and knowledge of construction

methodology. Experience in construction, although not essential, is extremely helpful.

Residential Designer

A **residential designer** is a specialist familiar with the complex process of planning and designing a residential structure, codes, ordinances, design options, and product choices. They may or may not hold a degree in architecture, but must have at least six years of higher education and professional design experience to receive National Council of Building Designer Certification (NCBDC) credentials. For those who have chosen the building design profession, there is no greater evidence of competency than achieving the status of Certified Professional Building Designer (CPBD). All professional members must maintain their education through a continuing education program. The organization that represents this group of professionals is the American Institute of Building Design (ABID). It has members in 47 states, Canada, Europe, Asia, and Australia.

Keeping a Job and Advancing a Career

There are many items that affect your job performance and how your employer views

Figure 39-9. Teaching architectural drafting is a very interesting and rewarding career.

you. These items can determine how you advance in a job and even if you keep the job. These items include following a model ethics code, your work ethic, job site safety, and leadership traits. Special care must be taken to address these items so your job is not in jeopardy and you maintain the potential for advancement.

Model Ethics Code

Ethical practice has always been a concern of individuals and businesses who wish to be successful over the long term. Many organizations have developed goals aimed at encouraging ethical practices. One such organization, the National Association of Home Builders (NAHB), has adopted a model ethics code. The twelve objectives of the NAHB code of ethics are:

I.   To conduct business affairs with professionalism and skill.

II.   To provide the best housing value possible.

III.   To protect the consumer through the use of quality materials and construction practices backed by integrity and service.

IV.   To provide housing with high standards of safety, sanitation, and livability.

V.   To meet all financial obligations in a responsible manner.

VI.   To comply with the spirit and letter of business contracts and manage employees, subcontractors, and suppliers with fairness and honor.

VII.   To keep informed regarding public policies and other essential information that affect your business interests and those of the building industry as a whole.

VIII. To comply with the rules and regulations prescribed by law and government agencies for the health, safety, and welfare of the community.

IX.   To keep honesty as our guiding business policy.

X.   To provide timely response to items covered under warranty.

XI.   To seek to resolve controversies through a nonlitigation dispute resolution mechanism.

XII.   To support and abide by the decisions of the association in promoting and enforcing this code of ethics.

Work Ethic

Your *work ethic* includes your enthusiasm for the work, willingness to work late to meet deadlines, and whether you are on site and prepared to work at starting time. It will be a very important consideration in keeping a job or receiving a promotion. Employers are very concerned about the attitude you bring to the workplace. Other factors that have a bearing on your work ethic center around how you relate to fellow workers:

* Do you talk to others so they cannot get their work done?
* Do you treat others with respect?
* Are you a gossip or critic of everyone else's work?
* Do you run to the boss with every little thing?
* Are you a constant complainer?
* Do you always have an excuse for poor work or unfinished work?
* Do you admit to mistakes and learn from them?

These and many other related characteristics are part of your work ethic. If you expect to be happy in the workplace and progress to positions of more responsibility, then you will pay attention to your work ethic and personal behavior.

Job Site Safety

Construction is a dangerous business. In fact, construction is consistently cited by the Occupational Safety and Health Administration (OSHA) as one of the most dangerous occupations in the US. When all occupations are considered, an employee sustains an on-the-job injury every 18 seconds and a worker is killed every 47 minutes in this country. Job safety must be a primary concern for every employer and employee.

Statistics show that 5% of all accidents are caused by unsafe conditions; the other 95% are caused by unsafe actions. Unsafe workers will find a way to injure themselves regardless of warning signs, safety nets, guards, etc. The solution is to train workers to work safely. Working safely involves a thorough understanding of the tools, equipment, and materials being used. It also involves thinking safety. Some of the techniques that can be employed to sharpen concern for safety on the job site include:

- Testing the knowledge of workers to be sure they understand the proper use of their tools and machines.
- Discussing safety procedures every few weeks.
- Demonstrating safe work practices.
- Developing a set of company safety rules.
- Enforcing safe work practices.

A safety program is not something you can just write up and distribute; it is an ongoing effort between the contractor, crew leaders, and workers on the site. When an accident occurs, everyone should participate in a discussion about the particulars—how it happened and what could have prevented it from happening.

Leadership on the Job

As you progress to a job or position that involves managing others, you will be expected to exert leadership. Consider the following points that successful leaders possess.

- Speak simply and directly.
- Share the credit.
- Have a vision.
- Be positive.
- Be optimistic and enthusiastic.
- Avoid sarcasm.
- Meet problems head on.
- Check the small things.
- Do not take yourself too seriously.
- Be friendly, not a friend.
- Control your emotions.
- Always be truthful.
- Treat everyone fairly.
- Be constructive, do not criticize.
- Always be a role model.
- Have fun.

Entrepreneurship

Some day you may want to own or manage your own business. A person who starts, manages, and assumes the risks of a new business is called an *entrepreneur.* If owning your own business is a goal, you may want to consider the following.

There are positive and negative aspects of owning your own business. Every year many new businesses are started, but most fail. The reasons generally cited for failure include lack of adequate financing, poor management of the enterprise, and lack of knowledge required. However, some advantages of owning a business include being your own boss, the chance to make more money, and the satisfaction of building a successful enterprise. On the other hand, disadvantages include the enormous responsibility of making decisions, long hours, risk of failure, and responsibility for the livelihood of others.

Some "business opportunities" are not really opportunities at all. If it is too good to be true, it probably is. Ask questions such as:

- Is the location good?
- How much overhead, such as utilities, taxes, payroll, and insurance, will the business have?
- What about the competition?
- How will you hire good employees?
- Can you manage a work force?
- What business skills and knowledge do you have?
- Can you get financing?
- What government regulations apply to your business?
- What type of business organization should you choose?
- What are your goals?

- How will you advertise your product or service?
- Where can you get good advice?
- What governmental agencies offer help?

Every business should have definite, well-defined goals. Goals provide direction and help in making decisions concerning your product or service to be offered for sale. Consider these questions:

- Will the product or service be conventional or unique?
- How will you gain the support and respect of your employees?
- What kind of image do you wish your company to convey to others?
- Who will purchase your product or service?
- How much should you charge?
- How will you reward productive workers?

- How will you protect your workers against injury on the job?
- What activities will help you meet your goals?
- How will you organize your business to maintain high efficiency and quality?
- Do you have the strength and determination to own and manage a business?
- What are the long term consequences to you and your family? Are you prepared to risk failure?

Just having a good idea or quality product or service is not enough to have a successful business. It needs constant attention to detail and solid planning. Risk of failure is always present and may be brought about by forces beyond your control. However, the rewards of running a successful business generally outweigh the liabilities, Figure 39-10.

Figure 39-10. The reward for an entrepreneur is the satisfaction of seeing their ideas and hard work completed. (Pittsburgh Corning Corporation)

Internet Resources

www.aia.org
American Institute of Architects

www.aibd.org
American Institute of Building Design

www.archdigest.com
Architectural Digest

www.asla.org
American Society of Landscape Architects

www.bls.gov/oco/
US Department of Labor's Occupational Outlook Handbook

www.builderonline.com
Builder Magazine Online

www.fema.gov
Federal Emergency Management Agency

www.ibhs.org
Institute for Business and Home Safety

www.msel.nist.gov
National Institute for Standards and Technology—Material Science and Engineering Laboratory

www.nait.org
National Association of Industrial Technology

www.nibs.org
National Institute of Building Sciences

Review Questions – Chapter 39

Write your answers on a separate sheet of paper. Do not write in this book.

1. The architect's duties include a great deal of creativity and sensitivity to _____ and _____.

2. Why do state laws require an architect to be registered (licensed)?

3. List three institutions where a person may teach architecture.

4. A person who calculates the costs of materials and labor for a residential structure is known as a(n) _____.

5. In architectural work, a(n) _____ is primarily concerned with establishing areas and boundaries of real estate property.

6. The architectural drafter usually performs which two duties?

7. Many architects have the responsibility of assisting the client in selecting a(n) _____.

8. A person who prepares all the written information needed to describe the materials, methods, and fixtures to be used for a house is known as _____.

9. What is the practical reason for establishing and adhering to a model ethics code?

10. The three reasons cited why new businesses generally fail are _____, _____, and _____.

Suggested Activities

1. Using library references such as the Occupational Outlook Handbook, select a career related to architecture. Write a report covering such topics as job opportunities, educational requirements, job responsibilities, and predicted factors for success.

2. Prepare a bulletin board display that depicts the many jobs involved in architecture. Make use of pictures, magazine clippings, industrial literature, and actual drawings to illustrate the ways in which the architect influences the construction of a residential structure.

3. Make a visit to a local architect's office or an architectural firm to ask questions and observe their operation. Prepare a list of the various responsibilities and skills required by those involved with residential architecture and construction. Make note of the use of any new techniques or equipment in architectural designing.

4. To become better acquainted with educational offerings in architecture, obtain catalogs from community colleges, technical schools, and universities or use the Internet to review offerings. Write down the names of courses available and prerequisites. Discuss with your class the many directions a person may take in making architecture a career.

5. Interview a builder or tradesperson to determine factors they believe are important in progressing on the job. Report your findings to the class.

6. Invite an entrepreneur to class to discuss the pros and cons of owning your own business.

Project Planning and Management

Now that you have completed this text, you should have the broad base of knowledge needed to successfully plan and carry out an architectural project. As you have seen, this text progresses sequentially through the steps of an architectural project. The first two sections, Chapter 1 through Chapter 6, provide basic background information. Building on this information, your architectural project starts with Chapter 7:

- Room and Space Planning: Sleeping area and bath facilities (Chapter 7), living area (Chapter 8), and service area (Chapter 9).
- Plot Plans and Foundations: Plot plans (Chapter 10); footings, foundations and concrete (Chapter 11); and the foundation plan (Chapter 12).
- Construction Systems: Sill and floor construction (Chapter 13); wall and ceiling construction (Chapter 14); doors and windows (Chapter 15); stairs (Chapter 16); and fireplaces, chimneys, and stoves (Chapter 17).
- Formulating a Design: The floor plan (Chapter 18), roof designs (Chapter 19), and elevations (Chapter 20).
- Electrical, Plumbing, and Climate Control: Residential electrical (Chapter 21); information, communication, and security wiring (Chapter 22); the electrical plan (Chapter 23); residential plumbing (Chapter 24); the plumbing plan (Chapter 25); residential climate control (Chapter 26); and climate control plan (Chapter 27).
- Presentation Methods: Perspective drawings (Chapter 32), presentation drawings (Chapter 33), and architectural models (Chapter 24).

This is basically a step-by-step procedure for creating your architectural project. The other chapters and the appendix material in this text provide valuable information on alternative methods/systems, estimating, health/safety concerns, and renovation.

Reference Section

Building Material Symbols

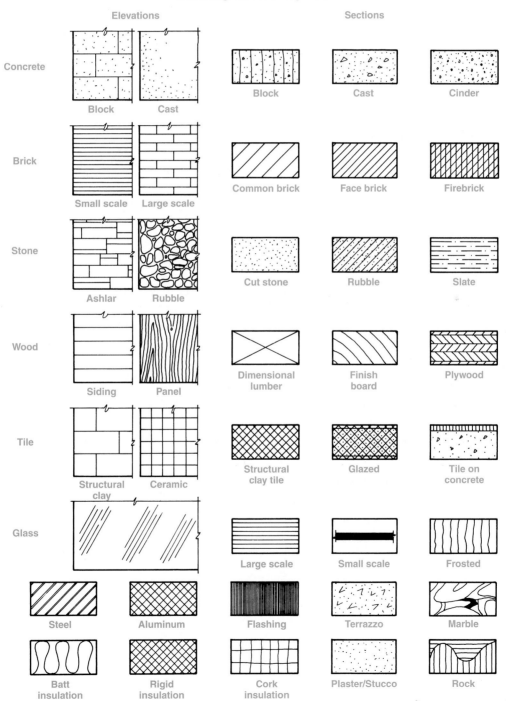

Elevations

Sections

Concrete
- Block
- Cast
- Block
- Cast
- Cinder

Brick
- Small scale
- Large scale
- Common brick
- Face brick
- Firebrick

Stone
- Ashlar
- Rubble
- Cut stone
- Rubble
- Slate

Wood
- Siding
- Panel
- Dimensional lumber
- Finish board
- Plywood

Tile
- Structural clay
- Ceramic
- Structural clay tile
- Glazed
- Tile on concrete

Glass
- Large scale
- Small scale
- Frosted

- Steel
- Aluminum
- Flashing
- Terrazzo
- Marble

- Batt insulation
- Rigid insulation
- Cork insulation
- Plaster/Stucco
- Rock

Topographical Symbols

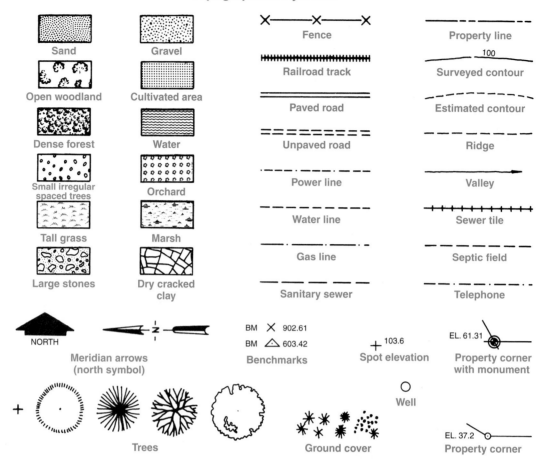

Plumbing Symbols

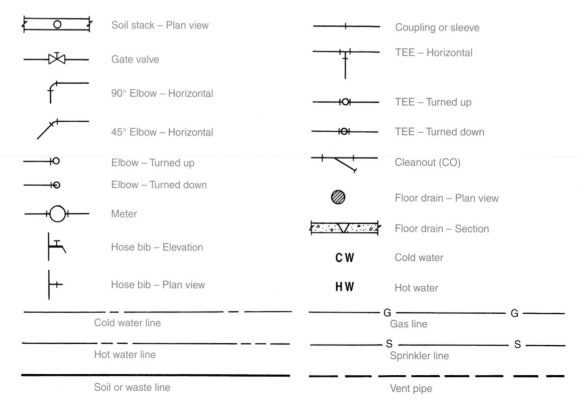

Climate Control Symbols

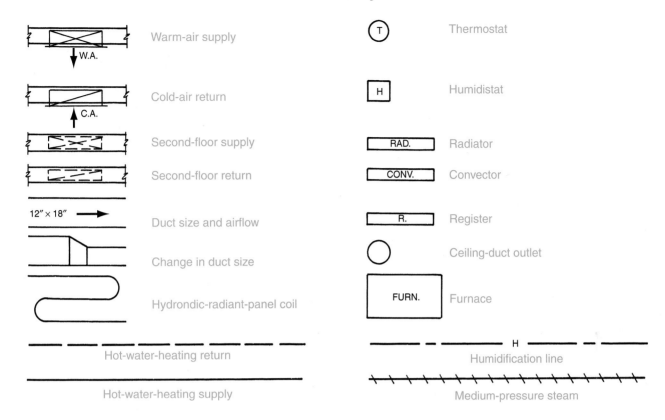

Warm-air supply	Thermostat
Cold-air return	Humidistat
Second-floor supply	Radiator
Second-floor return	Convector
Duct size and airflow	Register
Change in duct size	Ceiling-duct outlet
Hydrondic-radiant-panel coil	Furnace
Hot-water-heating return	Humidification line
Hot-water-heating supply	Medium-pressure steam

Electrical Symbols

Ceiling outlet fixture		Single receptacle outlet		S	Single-pole switch
Recessed outlet fixture		Duplex receptacle outlet		S_2	Double-pole switch
Drop cord fixture		Triplex receptacle outlet		S_3	Three-way switch
Fan hanger outlet		Quadruplex receptacle outlet		S_4	Four-way switch
Junction box		Split-wired duplex receptacle outlet		S_{WP}	Weatherproof switch
Fluorescent fixture		Special purpose single receptacle outlet		S_L	Low-voltage switch
Telephone		240 volt outlet			Push button
Intercom		Weatherproof duplex outlet			Chimes
Ceiling fixture with pull switch		Duplex receptacle with switch			Television antenna outlet
Thermostat		Flush mounted panel box		S_D	Dimmer switch
Special fixture outlet A, B, C, Etc.		Special duplex outlet A, B, C, Etc.		$S_{A, B, C, Etc.}$	Special switch

ANSI Architectural Symbols

LIGHTING OUTLETS

Ceiling	Wall	
○	─○	Surface or Pendant Incandescent, Mercury-Vapor, or Similar Lamp Fixture
Ⓡ	─Ⓡ	Recessed Incandescent, Mercury-Vapor, or Similar Lamp Fixture
▭○▭	▭○▭	Surface or Pendant Individual Fluorescent Fixture
▭○Ⓡ	▭○Ⓡ	Recessed Individual Fluorescent Fixture
▭○▭▭		Surface or Pendant Continuous Row Fluorescent Fixture
▭○Ⓡ▭		Recessed Continuous Row Fluorescent Fixture
├──┼──┤		Bare-Lamp Fluorescent Strip
Ⓧ	─Ⓧ	Surface or Pendant Exit Light
ⓇⓍ	─ⓇⓍ	Recessed Exit Light
Ⓑ	─Ⓑ	Blanket Outlet
Ⓙ	─Ⓙ	Junction Box
Ⓛ	─Ⓛ	Outlet Controlled by Low-Voltage Switching when Relay is Installed in Outlet Box

RECEPTACLE OUTLETS

Grounded	Ungrounded	
⊖	⊖UNG	Single Receptacle Outlet
⊖	⊖UNG	Duplex Receptacle Outlet
⊕	⊕UNG	Triplex Receptacle Outlet
⊕	⊕UNG	Quadruplex Receptacle Outlet
⊜	⊜UNG	Duplex Receptacle Outlet—Split Wired
⊕	⊕UNG	Triplex Receptacle Outlet—Split Wired
⊿	⊿UNG	Single Special-Purpose Receptacle Outlet
⊿	⊿UNG	Duplex Special-Purpose Receptacle Outlet
⊖R	⊖UNG R	Range Outlet (typical)

Grounded / Ungrounded (Special)

Grounded	Ungrounded	
▲DW	▲UNG DW	Special Purpose Connection or Provision Connection
⊖X in	⊖UNG X in	Multi-Outlet Assembly
─Ⓒ	─ⒸUNG	Clock Hanger Receptacle
─Ⓕ	─ⒻUNG	Fan Hanger Receptacle
▣	▣UNG	Floor Single Receptacle Outlet
▣	▣UNG	Floor Duplex Receptacle Outlet
▣	▣UNG	Floor Special-Purpose Outlet

SWITCH OUTLETS

S	Single-Pole Switch
S₂	Double-Pole Switch
S₃	Three-Way Switch
S₄	Four-Way Switch
Sₖ	Key-Operated Switch
Sₚ	Switch and Pilot Lamp
Sₗ	Switch for Low-Voltage Switching System
Sₗₘ	Maser Switch for Low-Voltage Switching System
S─⊖	Switch and Single Receptacle
S─⊖	Switch and Double Receptacle
S_D	Door Switch
S_T	Time Switch
S_CB	Circuit Breaker Switch
S_MC	Momentary Contact Switch or Pushbutton for other than Signaling System
Ⓢ	Ceiling Pull Switch

RESIDENTIAL OCCUPANCIES

▣	Pushbutton
◹	Buzzer
○▢	Bell
○▢	Combination Bell-Buzzer
[CH]	Chime
◇	Annunciator

Courtesy of Leviton Manufacturing Co., Inc.

Standard Vanity Sizes and Designs

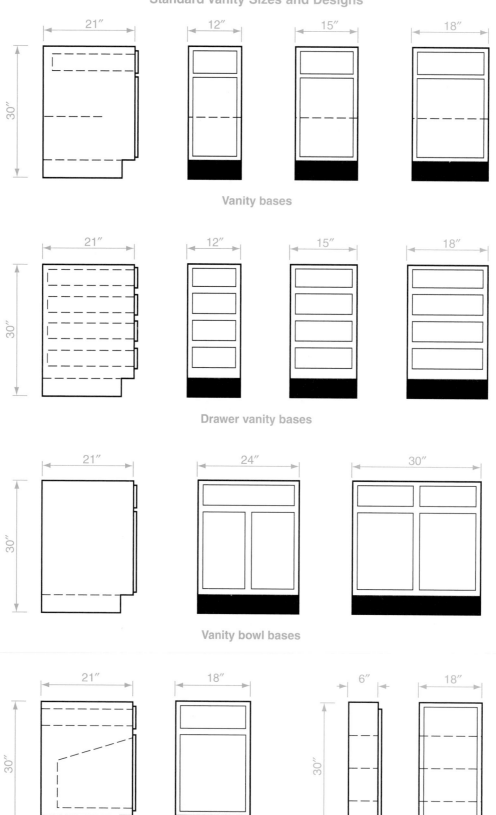

Vanity bases

Drawer vanity bases

Vanity bowl bases

Vanity hamper base

Vanity wall cabinet

Standard Wall Cabinet Sizes and Designs

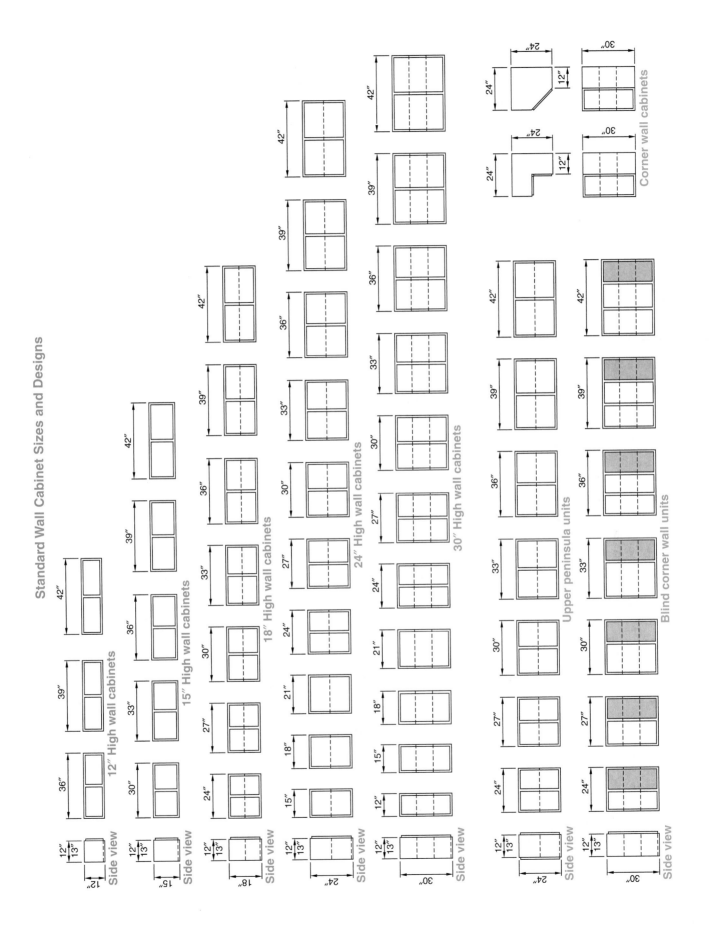

12" High wall cabinets

15" High wall cabinets

18" High wall cabinets

24" High wall cabinets

30" High wall cabinets

Upper peninsula units

Corner wall cabinets

Blind corner wall units

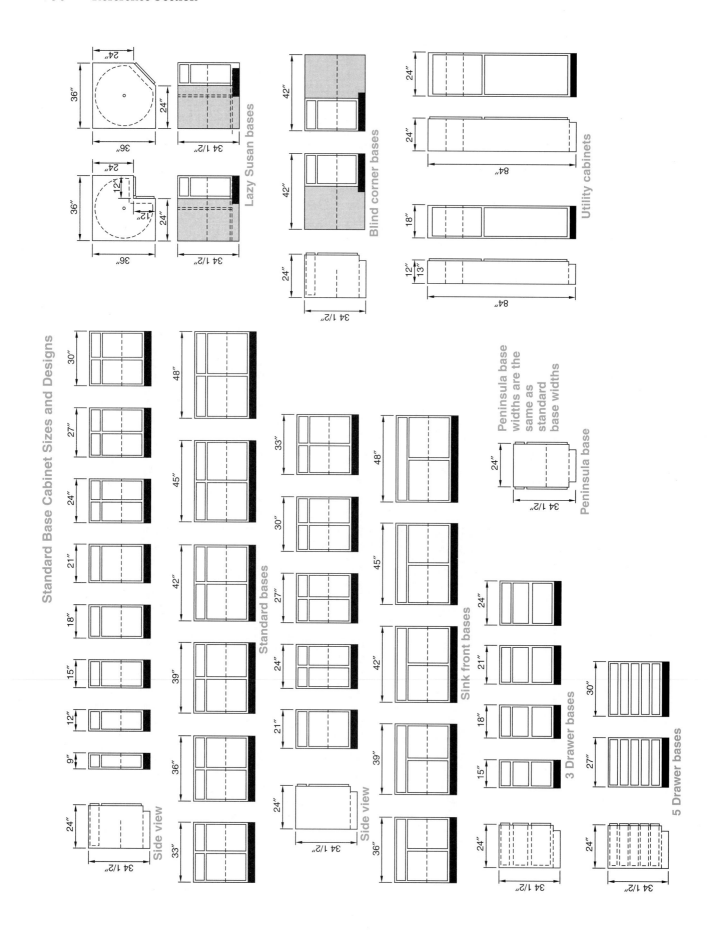

Double-Hung Windows—Standard Sizes

Basic unit	1'–9-5/8"	2'–1-5/8"	2'–5-5/8"	2'–9-5/8"	3'–1-5/8"	3'–5-5/8"	3'–9-5/8"
Rough opening	1'–10-1/8"	2'–2-1/8"	2'–6-1/8"	2'–10-1/8"	3'–2-1/8"	3'–6-1/8"	3'–10-1/8"
Sash opening	1'–8"	2'–0"	2'–4"	2'–8"	3'–0"	3'–4"	3'–8"
Glass size*	16-1/4"	20-1/4"	24-1/4"	28-1/4"	32-1/4"	36-1/4"	40-1/4"

*Unobstructed glass sizes shown

Row heights (Basic unit / Rough opening / Sash opening / Glass size*):

- 3'–1-1/4" / 3'–1-1/8" / 2'–10" / 13-7/8"
- 3'–5-1/4" / 3'–5-1/8" / 3'–2" / 15-7/8"
- 4'–1-1/4" / 4'–1-1/8" / 3'–10" / 19-7/8"
- 4'–5-1/4" / 4'–5-1/8" / 4'–2" / 21-7/8"
- 4'–9-1/4" / 4'–9-1/8" / 4'–6" / 23-7/8"
- 5'–5-1/4" / 5'–5-1/8" / 5'–2" / 27-7/8"
- 5'–9-1/4" / 5'–9-1/8" / 5'–6" / 35-7/8" / 23-7/8"
- 6'–5-1/4" / 6'–5-1/8" / 6'–2" / 33-7/8"

Horizontal Sliding Windows—Standard Sizes

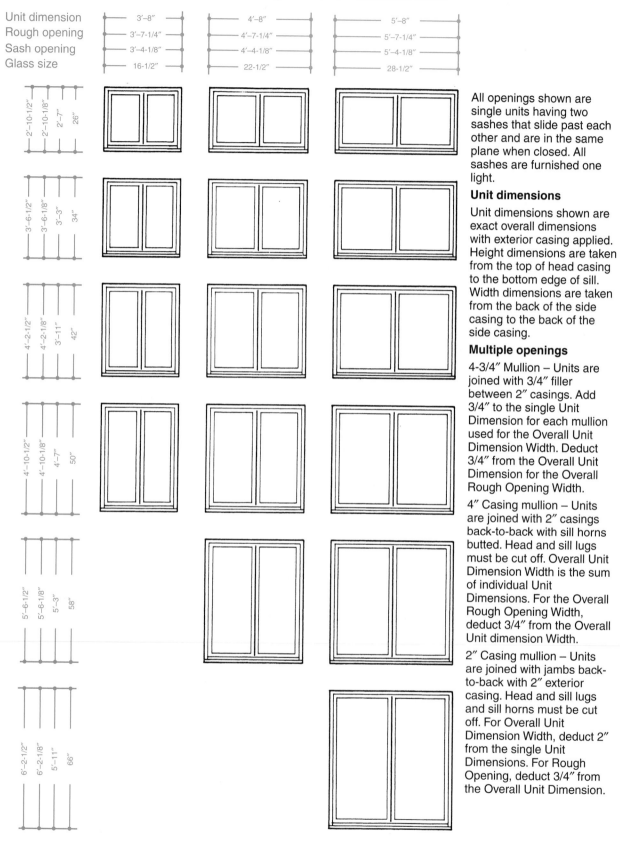

All openings shown are single units having two sashes that slide past each other and are in the same plane when closed. All sashes are furnished one light.

Unit dimensions

Unit dimensions shown are exact overall dimensions with exterior casing applied. Height dimensions are taken from the top of head casing to the bottom edge of sill. Width dimensions are taken from the back of the side casing to the back of the side casing.

Multiple openings

4-3/4″ Mullion – Units are joined with 3/4″ filler between 2″ casings. Add 3/4″ to the single Unit Dimension for each mullion used for the Overall Unit Dimension Width. Deduct 3/4″ from the Overall Unit Dimension for the Overall Rough Opening Width.

4″ Casing mullion – Units are joined with 2″ casings back-to-back with sill horns butted. Head and sill lugs must be cut off. Overall Unit Dimension Width is the sum of individual Unit Dimensions. For the Overall Rough Opening Width, deduct 3/4″ from the Overall Unit dimension Width.

2″ Casing mullion – Units are joined with jambs back-to-back with 2″ exterior casing. Head and sill lugs and sill horns must be cut off. For Overall Unit Dimension Width, deduct 2″ from the single Unit Dimensions. For Rough Opening, deduct 3/4″ from the Overall Unit Dimension.

Casement Windows—Standard Sizes

Unit dimensions
Rough opening
Sash opening
Glass*

Grille patterns

*Unobstructed glass sizes shown

How to figure opening sizes

Overall unit dimensions – The sum of individual unit dimensions plus 1/8″ for each mullion or stack used.

Overall rough opening – Add 1/2″ to overall unit dimension for width and height.

Awning Windows—Standard Sizes

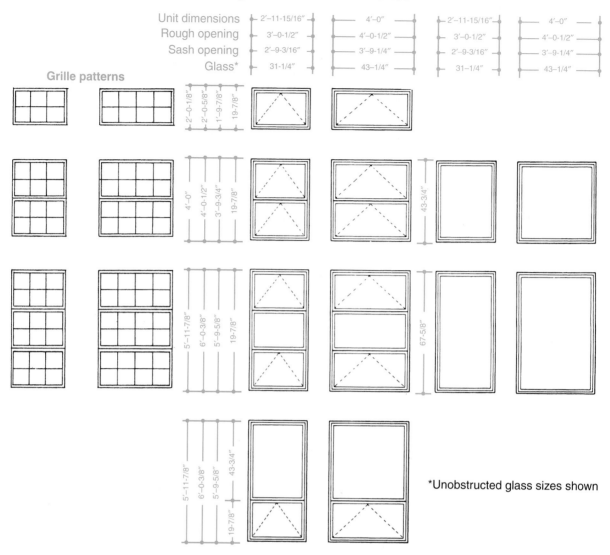

*Unobstructed glass sizes shown

Hopper Window Sizes

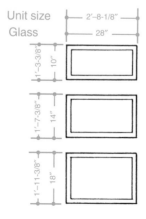

Picture Windows—Standard Sizes

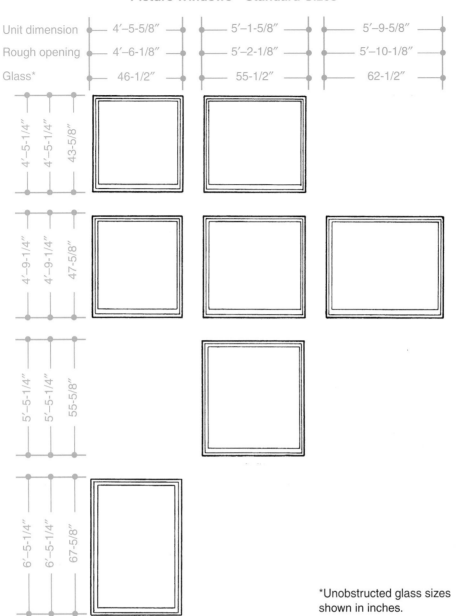

Unit dimension   4'–5-5/8"   5'–1-5/8"   5'–9-5/8"
Rough opening   4'–6-1/8"   5'–2-1/8"   5'–10-1/8"
Glass*   46-1/2"   55-1/2"   62-1/2"

4'–5-1/4"   4'–5-1/4"   43-5/8"

4'–9-1/4"   4'–9-1/4"   47-5/8"

5'–5-1/4"   5'–5-1/4"   55-5/8"

6'–5-1/4"   6'–5-1/4"   67-5/8"

*Unobstructed glass sizes
shown in inches.

Glass Sliding Doors—Standard Sizes

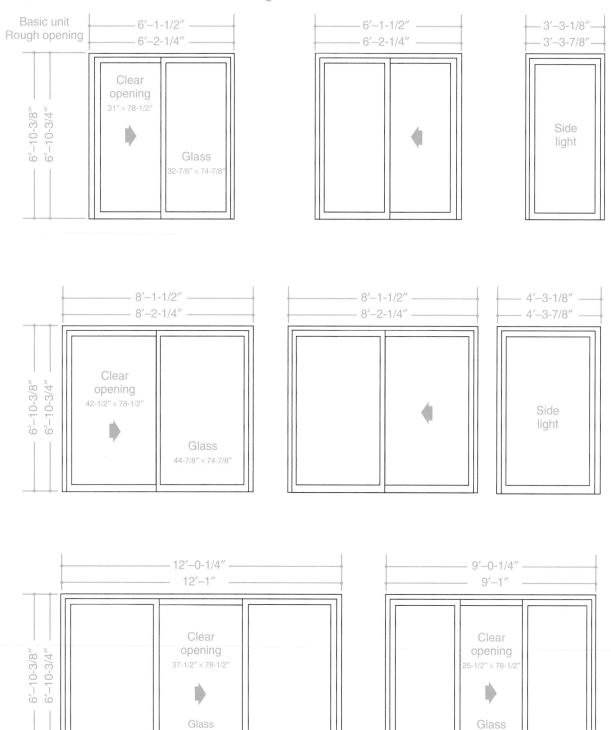

Design Data For W-Type, K-Post, and Scissors Trusses

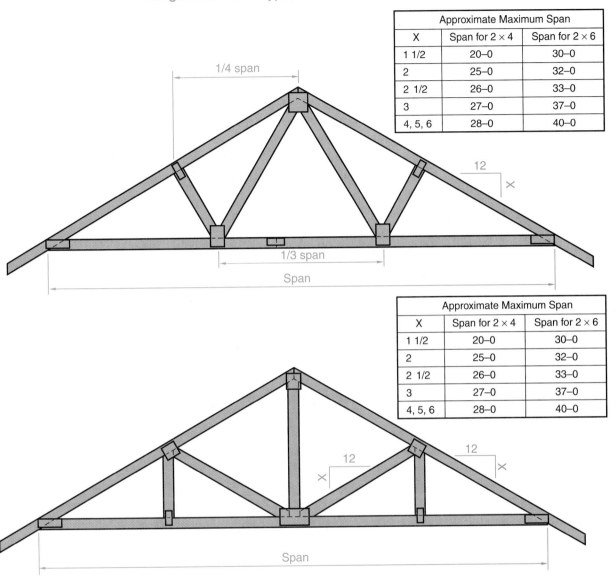

Approximate Maximum Span		
X	Span for 2 × 4	Span for 2 × 6
1 1/2	20–0	30–0
2	25–0	32–0
2 1/2	26–0	33–0
3	27–0	37–0
4, 5, 6	28–0	40–0

Approximate Maximum Span		
X	Span for 2 × 4	Span for 2 × 6
1 1/2	20–0	30–0
2	25–0	32–0
2 1/2	26–0	33–0
3	27–0	37–0
4, 5, 6	28–0	40–0

Approximate Maximum Span		
X	Span for 2 × 4	Span for 2 × 6
4, 5, 6	28–0	40–0

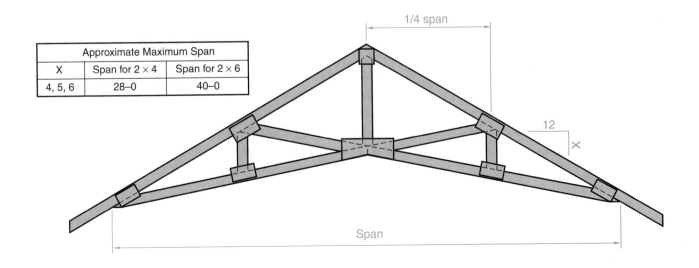

Floor Joist Span Data

30 PSF LIVE LOAD, 10 PSF DEAD LOAD, DEF. <360

Species or Group	Grade	2" x 8"			2" x 10"			2" x 12"		
		12"OC	16"OC	24"OC	12"OC	16"OC	24"OC	12"OC	16"OC	24"OC
Douglas Fir and Larch	Sel. Struc.	16'-6"	15'-0"	13'-1"	21'-0"	19'-1"	16'-8"	25'-7"	23'-3"	20'-3"
	No.1 & Btr	16'-2"	14'-8"	12'-10"	20'-8"	18'-9"	16'-1"	25'-1"	22'-10"	18'-8"
	No.1	15'-10"	14'-5"	12'-4"	20'-3"	18'-5"	15'-0"	24'-8"	21'-4"	17'-5"
	No.2	15'-7"	14'-1"	11'-6"	19'-10"	17'-2"	14'-1"	23'-0"	19'-11"	16'-3"
	No.3	12'-4"	10'-8"	8'-8"	15'-0"	13'-0"	10'-7"	17'-5"	15'-1"	12'-4"

40 PSF LIVE LOAD, 10 PSF DEAD LOAD, DEF. <360

Species or Group	Grade	2" x 8"			2" x 10"			2" x 12"		
		12"OC	16"OC	24"OC	12"OC	16"OC	24"OC	12"OC	16"OC	24"OC
Douglas Fir and Larch	Sel. Struc.	15'-0"	13'-7"	11'-11"	19'-1"	17'-4"	15'-2"	23'-3"	21'-1"	18'-5"
	No.1 & Btr	14'-8"	13'-4"	11'-8"	18'-9"	17'-0"	14'-5"	22'-10"	20'-5"	16'-8"
	No.1	14'-5"	13'-1"	11'-0"	18'-5"	16'-5"	13'-5"	22'-0"	19'-1"	15'-7"
	No.2	14'-2"	12'-7"	10'-3"	17'-9"	15'-5"	12'-7"	20'-7"	17'-10"	14'-7"
	No.3	11'-0"	9'-6"	7'-9"	13'-5"	11'-8"	9'-6"	15'-7"	13'-6"	11'-0"

30 PSF LIVE LOAD, 10 PSF DEAD LOAD, DEF. <360

Species or Group	Grade	2" x 8"			2" x 10"			2" x 12"		
		12"OC	16"OC	24"OC	12"OC	16"OC	24"OC	12"OC	16"OC	24"OC
Southern Pine	Sel. Struc.	16'-2"	14'-8"	12'-10"	20'-8"	18'-9"	16'-5"	25'-1"	22'-10"	19'-11"
	No.1	15'-10"	14'-5"	12'-7"	20'-3"	18'-5"	16'-1"	24'-8"	22'-5"	19'-6"
	No.2	15'-7"	14'-2"	12'-4"	19'-10"	18'-0"	14'-8"	24'-2"	21'-1"	17'-2"
	No.3	13'-3"	11'-6"	9'-5"	15'-8"	13'-7"	11'-1"	18'-8"	16'-2"	13'-2"

40 PSF LIVE LOAD, 10 PSF DEAD LOAD, DEF. <360

Species or Group	Grade	2" x 8"			2" x 10"			2" x 12"		
		12"OC	16"OC	24"OC	12"OC	16"OC	24"OC	12"OC	16"OC	24"OC
Southern Pine	Sel. Struc.	14'-8"	13'-4"	11'-8"	18'-9"	17'-0"	14'-11"	22'-10"	20'-9"	18'-1"
	No.1	14'-5"	13'-1"	11'-5"	18'-5"	16'-9"	14'-7"	22'-5"	20'-4"	17'-5"
	No.2	14'-2"	12'-10"	11'-0"	18'-0"	16'-1"	13'-2"	21'-9"	18'-10"	15'-4"
	No.3	11'-11"	10'-3"	8'-5"	14'-0"	12'-2"	9'-11"	16'-8"	14'-5"	11'-10"

40 PSF LIVE LOAD, 10 PSF DEAD LOAD, DEF. <240

Species or Group	Grade	2" x 6"			2" x 8"			2" x 10"		
		12"OC	16"OC	24"OC	12"OC	16"OC	24"OC	12"OC	16"OC	24"OC
Redwood	Cl. All Heart	--	7'-3"	6'-0"	--	10'-9"	8'-9"	--	13'-6"	11'-0"
	Const. Heart	--	7'-3"	6'-0"	--	10'-9"	8'-9"	--	13'-6"	11'-0"
	Const. Common	--	7'-3"	6'-0"	--	10'-9"	8'-9"	--	13'-6"	11'-0"

These spans are based on the 1993 AFTA (formerly NFPA) span tables for joists and rafters. These grades are the most commonly available. Source: Western Wood Products Association, Southern Pine Association, and California Redwood Association.

Spans are calculated on the basis of dry sizes with a moisture content equal to or less than 19%. Floor joist spans are for a single span with calculations performed based on the modulus of elasticity (E) and maximum fiber bending stress (F_b) allowed.

Ceiling Joist and Rafter Span Data

CEILING JOIST SPAN DATA

20 PSF Live Load, 10 PSF Dead Load, Def. <240											
Drywall ceiling; No future room development; Limited attic storage available.											
Species or Group / Grade	2" x 4"			2" x 6"			2" x 8"			2" x 10"		
	12"OC	16"OC	24"OC	12"OC	16"OC	24"OC	12"OC	16"OC	24"OC	12"OC	16"OC	24"OC

Douglas Fir and Larch

Grade	12"OC	16"OC	24"OC	12"OC	16"OC	24"OC	12"OC	16"OC	24"OC	12"OC	16"OC	24"OC
Sel. Struc.	10'-5"	9'-6"	8'-3"	16'-4"	14'-11"	13'-0"	21'-7"	19'-7"	17'-1"	27'-6"	25'-0"	20'-11"
No.1 & Btr	10'-3"	9'-4"	8'-1"	16'-1"	14'-7"	12'-0"	21'-2"	18'-8"	15'-3"	26'-4"	22'-9"	18'-7"
No.1	10'-0"	9'-1"	7'-8"	15'-9"	13'-9"	11'-2"	20'-1"	17'-5"	14'-2"	24'-6"	21'-3"	17'-4"
No.2	9'-10"	8'-9"	7'-2"	14'-10"	12'-10"	10'-6"	18'-9"	16'-3"	13'-3"	22'-11"	19'-10"	16'-3"
No.3	7'-8"	6'-8"	5'-5"	11'-2"	9'-8"	7'-11"	14'-2"	12'-4"	10'-0"	17'-4"	15'-0"	12'-3"

20 PSF Live Load, 10 PSF Dead Load, Def. <240											
Drywall ceiling; No future room development; Limited attic storage available.											

Southern Pine

Grade	12"OC	16"OC	24"OC	12"OC	16"OC	24"OC	12"OC	16"OC	24"OC	12"OC	16"OC	24"OC
Sel. Struc.	10'-3"	9'-4"	8'-1"	16'-1"	14'-7"	12'-9"	21'-2"	19'-3"	16'-10"	26'-0"	24'-7"	21'-6"
No.1	10'-0"	9'-1"	8'-0"	15'-9"	14'-4"	12'-6"	20'-10"	18'-11"	15'-11"	26'-0"	23'-2"	18'-11"
No.2	9'-10"	8'-11"	7'-8"	15'-6"	13'-6"	11'-0"	20'-1"	17'-5"	14'-2"	24'-0"	20'-9"	17'-0"
No.3	8'-2"	7'-1"	5'-9"	12'-1"	10'-5"	8'-6"	15'-4"	13'-3"	10'-10"	18'-1"	15'-8"	12'-2"

ROOF RAFTER SPAN DATA

20 PSF Live Load, 10 PSF Dead Load, Def. <240											
Roof slope 3:12 or less; Light roof covering; No ceiling finish.											
Species or Group / Grade	2" x 6"			2" x 8"			2" x 10"			2" x 12"		
	12"OC	16"OC	24"OC	12"OC	16"OC	24"OC	12"OC	16"OC	24"OC	12"OC	16"OC	24"OC

Douglas Fir and Larch

Grade	12"OC	16"OC	24"OC	12"OC	16"OC	24"OC	12"OC	16"OC	24"OC	12"OC	16"OC	24"OC
Sel. Struc.	16'-4"	14'-11"	13'-0"	21'-7"	19'-7"	17'-2"	27'-6"	25'-0"	21'-10"	33'-6"	30'-5"	26'-7"
No.1 & Btr	16'-1"	14'-7"	12'-9"	21'-2"	19'-3"	16'-10"	27'-1"	24'-7"	20'-9"	32'-11"	29'-6"	24'-1"
No.1	15'-9"	14'-4"	12'-6"	20'-10"	18'-11"	15'-10"	26'-6"	23'-9"	19'-5"	31'-10"	27'-6"	22'-6"
No.2	15'-6"	14'-1"	11'-9"	20'-5"	18'-2"	14'-10"	25'-8"	22'-3"	18'-2"	29'-9"	25'-9"	21'-0"
No.3	12'-6"	10'-10"	8'-10"	15'-10"	13'-9"	11'-3"	19'-5"	16'-9"	13'-8"	22'-6"	19'-6"	15'-11"

20 PSF Live Load, 15 PSF Dead Load, Def. <240											
Roof slope greater than 3:12; Light roof covering; Drywall ceiling; No snow load.											

Douglas Fir and Larch

Grade	12"OC	16"OC	24"OC	12"OC	16"OC	24"OC	12"OC	16"OC	24"OC	12"OC	16"OC	24"OC
Sel. Struc.	16'-4"	14'-11"	13'-0"	21'-7"	19'-7"	17'-2"	27'-6"	25'-0"	21'-7"	33'-6"	30'-5"	25'-1"
No.1 & Btr	16'-1"	14'-7"	12'-5"	21'-2"	19'-3"	15'-9"	27'-1"	23'-7"	19'-3"	31'-7"	27'-4"	22'-4"
No.1	15'-9"	14'-3"	11'-7"	20'-9"	18'-0"	14'-8"	25'-5"	22'-0"	17'-11"	29'-5"	25'-6"	20'-10"
No.2	15'-4"	13'-3"	10'-10"	19'-5"	16'-10"	13'-9"	23'-9"	20'-7"	16'-9"	27'-6"	23'-10"	19'-6"
No.3	11'-7"	10'-1"	8'-2"	14'-8"	12'-9"	10'-5"	17'-11"	15'-7"	12'-8"	20'-10"	18'-0"	14'-9"

20 PSF Live Load, 10 PSF Dead Load, Def. <240											
Drywall ceiling; Light roofing; Snow load.											
Species or Group / Grade	2" x 6"			2" x 8"			2" x 10"			2" x 12"		
	12"OC	16"OC	24"OC	12"OC	16"OC	24"OC	12"OC	16"OC	24"OC	12"OC	16"OC	24"OC

Southern Pine

Grade	12"OC	16"OC	24"OC	12"OC	16"OC	24"OC	12"OC	16"OC	24"OC	12"OC	16"OC	24"OC
Sel. Struc.	16'-1"	14'-7"	12'-9"	21'-2"	19'-3"	16'-10"	26'-0"	24'-7"	21'-6"	26'-0"	26'-0"	26'-0"
No.1	15'-9"	14'-4"	12'-6"	20'-10"	18'-11"	16'-6"	26'-0"	24'-1"	20'-3"	26'-0"	26'-0"	24'-1"
No.2	15'-6"	14'-1"	11'-9"	20'-5"	18'-6"	15'-3"	25'-8"	22'-3"	18'-2"	26'-0"	26'-0"	21'-4"
No.3	12'-11"	11'-2"	9'-1"	16'-5"	14'-3"	11'-7"	19'-5"	16'-10"	13'-9"	23'-1"	20'-0"	16'-4"

30 PSF Live Load, 15 PSF Dead Load, Def. <240											
Drywall ceiling; Medium roofing; Snow load.											

Southern Pine

Grade	12"OC	16"OC	24"OC	12"OC	16"OC	24"OC	12"OC	16"OC	24"OC	12"OC	16"OC	24"OC
Sel. Struc.	14'-1"	12'-9"	11'-2"	18'-6"	16'-10"	14'-8"	23'-8"	21'-6"	18'-9"	26'-0"	26'-0"	22'-10"
No.1	13'-9"	12'-6"	10'-11"	18'-2"	16'-6"	13'-11"	23'-2"	20'-3"	16'-6"	26'-0"	24'-1"	19'-8"
No.2	13'-6"	11'-9"	9'-7"	17'-7"	15'-3"	12'-5"	21'-0"	18'-2"	14'-10"	24'-7"	21'-4"	17'-5"
No.3	10'-6"	9'-1"	7'-5"	13'-5"	11'-7"	9'-6"	15'-10"	13'-9"	11'-3"	18'-10"	16'-4"	13'-4"

THESE SPANS ARE BASED ON THE 1993 AFTA (FORMERLY NFPA) SPAN TABLES FOR JOISTS AND RAFTERS. THESE GRADES ARE THE MOST COMMONLY AVAILABLE.

Ceiling joist and rafter span data are in feet and inches for Douglas fir/larch and southern yellow pine. Spans are based on dry lumber size with a moisture content equal to or less than 19%. Calculations were based on the modulus of elasticity (E) and maximum fiber bending stress (F_b) allowed for ceiling joists. Rafter spans were based on the fiber bending stress (F_b) and allowable modulus of elasticity (E). Rafter spans are horizontal distances.

Glued Laminated Floor and Roof Beams—Span Data

Span data for glued laminated roof beams* Maximum deflection 1/240th of the span														
Beam size (actual)	Wgt. of beam per lin. ft. in pounds	Span in feet												
		10	12	14	16	18	20	22	24	26	28	30	32
		Pounds per lin. ft. load bearing capacity												
3″ × 5-1/4″	3.7	151	85										
3″ × 7-1/4″	4.9	362	206	128	84								
3″ × 9-1/4″	6.7	566	448	300	199	137	99						
3″ × 11-1/4″	8.0	680	566	483	363	252	182	135	102				
4-1/2″ × 9-1/4″	9.8	850	673	451	299	207	148	109					
4-1/2″ × 11-1/4″	12.0	1,036	860	731	544	378	273	202	153				
3-1/4″ × 13-1/2″	10.4	1,100	916	784	685	479	347	258	197	152	120		
3-1/4″ × 15″	11.5	1,145	1,015	870	759	650	473	352	267	206	163	128	104
5-1/4″ × 13-1/2″	16.7	1,778	1,478	1,266	1,105	773	559	415	316	245	193	154	124
5-1/4″ × 15″	18.6	1,976	1,647	1,406	1,229	1,064	771	574	438	342	269	215	174
5-1/4″ × 16-1/2″	20.5	2,180	1,810	1,550	1,352	1,155	933	768	586	457	362	290	236
5-1/4″ × 18″	22.3	2,378	1,978	1,688	1,478	1,308	1,113	918	766	598	478	382	311

Example: Clear span   = 20′-0″
Beam spacing = 10′-0″
Dead load   = 8 lbs./sq. ft. (roofing and decking)
Live load   = 20 lbs./sq. ft. (snow)
Total load   = Live load + dead load × beam spacing
                      = (20 + 8) × 10 = 280 lbs./lin. ft.
The beam size required is 3-1/4″ × 13-1/2″, which supports 347 lbs./lin. ft. over a span of 20′-0″.
*Beams may be Douglas fir, larch, or southern yellow pine.

Span data for glued laminated floor beams* Maximum deflection 1/360th of the span														
Beam size (actual)	Wgt. of beam per lin. ft. in pounds	Span in feet												
		10	12	14	16	18	20	22	24	26	28	30	32
		Pounds per lin. ft. load bearing capacity												
3″ × 5-1/4″	3.7	114	64										
3″ × 7-1/4″	4.9	275	156	84	55								
3″ × 9-1/4″	6.7	492	319	198	130	89							
3″ × 11-1/4″	8.0	590	491	361	239	165	119						
4-1/2″ × 9-1/4″	9.8	738	479	298	196	134	96						
4-1/2″ × 11-1/4″	12.0	900	748	541	359	248	178	131	92				
3-1/4″ × 13-1/2″	10.4	956	795	683	454	316	228	169	128	98			
3-1/4″ × 15″	11.5	997	884	756	626	436	315	234	178	137	108		
5-1/4″ × 13-1/2″	16.7	1,541	1,283	1,095	732	509	367	271	205	158	123	96	
5-1/4″ × 15″	18.6	1,713	1,423	1,219	1,009	703	508	376	286	221	173	137	109
5-1/4″ × 16-1/2″	20.5	1,885	1,568	1,340	1,170	939	678	505	384	298	235	187	151
5-1/4″ × 18″	22.3	2,058	1,710	1,464	1,278	1,133	886	660	503	391	309	247	200

Example: Clear span   = 20′-0″
Beam spacing = 10′-0″
Dead load   = 7 lbs./sq. ft. (decking and carpet)
Live load   = 40 lbs./sq. ft. (furniture and occupants)
Total load   = Live load + dead load × beam spacing
                      = (40 + 7) × 10 = 470 lbs./lin. ft.
The beam size required is 5-1/4″ × 15″, which supports 508 lbs./lin. ft. over a span of 20′-0″.
*Beams may be Douglas fir, larch, or southern yellow pine.

Courtesy of Potlatch Forests, Inc.

Manufactured 2″ × 4″ Wood Floor Trusses

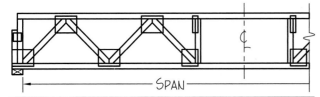

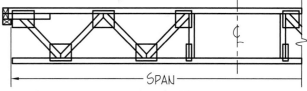

Bottom chord bearing type			
Depth	Clear spans	#Diagonal webs	Camber
12″	7′-2″	4	.063″
	9′-8″	6	.063″
	12′-2″	8	.063″
	14′-8″	10	.134″
	17′-2″	12	.237″
	19′-8″	14	.365″
	21′-4″	16	.507″
14″	9′-8″	6	.063″
	12′-2″	8	.063″
	14′-8″	10	.095″
	17′-2″	12	.178″
	19′-8″	14	.288″
	22′-7″	16	.449″
	24′-0″	18	.569″
16″	12′-2″	8	.065″
	14′-8″	10	.070″
	17′-2″	12	.132″
	19′-8″	14	.228″
	22′-2″	16	.346″
	25′-1″	18	.505″
	26′-1″	20	.596″
18″	14′-8″	10	.065″
	17′-2″	12	.120″
	19′-8″	14	.176″
	22′-2″	16	.268″
	24′-8″	18	.367″
	27′-6″	20	.600″
	27′-10″	22	.630″
20″	14′-8″	10	.063″
	17′-2″	12	.081″
	19′-8″	14	.140″
	22′-2″	16	.226″
	24′-8″	18	.327″
	27′-6″	20	.451″
	29′-6″	22	.630″
22″	17′-2″	10	.066″
	19′-8″	12	.114″
	22′-2″	14	.184″
	24′-8″	16	.266″
	27′-6″	18	.367″
	30′-0″	20	.520″
	31′-1″	22	.630″
24″	17′-2″	12	.063″
	19′-8″	14	.095″
	22′-2″	16	.153″
	24′-8″	18	.235″
	27′-2″	20	.325″
	30′-0″	22	.431″
	32′-6″	24	.630″

Top chord bearing type			
Depth	Clear spans	#Diagonal webs	Camber
12″	6′-10″	4	.063″
	9′-4″	6	.063″
	11′-10″	8	.063″
	14′-4″	10	.122″
	16′-10″	12	.233″
	19′-10″	14	.376″
	21′-4″	16	.507″
14″	9′-5″	6	.063″
	11′-11″	8	.063″
	14′-5″	10	.088″
	16′-11″	12	.167″
	19′-5″	14	.273″
	21′-4″	16	.429″
	24′-0″	18	.569″
16″	12′-0″	8	.063″
	14′-6″	10	.067″
	17′-0″	12	.126″
	19′-6″	14	.219″
	22′-4″	16	.337″
	24′-10″	18	.489″
	26′-1″	20	.596″
18″	14′-6″	10	.063″
	17′-0″	12	.098″
	19′-6″	14	.170″
	22′-0″	16	.260″
	24′-10″	18	.378″
	27′-8″	20	.617″
	27′-10″	22	.630″
20″	14′-6″	10	.063″
	17′-0″	12	.079″
	19′-6″	14	.136″
	22′-0″	16	.221″
	24′-10″	18	.337″
	27′-4″	20	.442″
	29′-6″	22	.630″
22″	17′-1″	12	.065″
	19′-7″	14	.112″
	22′-1″	16	.181″
	24′-10″	18	.275″
	27′-4″	20	.381″
	30′-2″	22	.534″
	31′-1″	24	.630″
24″	17′-1″	12	.063″
	19′-7″	14	.093″
	22′-1″	16	.150″
	24′-7″	18	.231″
	27′-5″	20	.335″
	30′-2″	22	.443″
	32′-6″	24	.630″

Wood floor trusses are typically manufactured from #3 southern yellow pine. Pieces are joined together with 18 and 20 gauge galvanized steel plates applied to both faces of the truss at each joint. Where no sheathing is applied directly to top chords, they should be braced at intervals not to exceed 3′-0″. Where no rigid ceiling is applied directly to bottom chords, they should be braced at intervals not to exceed 10′-0″.

Manufactured wood floor trusses are generally spaced 24″OC and are designed to support various loads. Typical trusses shown here were designed to support 55 psf (live load - 40 psf, dead load - 10 psf, ceiling dead load - 5 psf). A slight bow (camber) is built into each joist to that it will produce a level floor when loaded. Allowable deflection is 1/360 of the span.

Some of the longer trusses require one or more double diagonal webs at both ends. Wood floor trusses are a manufactured product which must be engineered and produced with a high degree of accuracy to attain the desired performance. See your local manufacturer or lumber company for trusses available in your area.

Courtesy of Trus Joist.

Beam Data

Maximum allowable uniform loads for American standard S-beams with lateral support
Span in feet

Size of beam	Weight of beam per foot	4	6	8	10	12	14	16	18	20	22	24	26	28	30	32	34	36	38	40
4" x 2-3/4"	7.7	10	7	5																
	9.5	11	7	6																
5" x 3"	10.0	16	11	8	6															
	11.3	20	13	10	8															
6" x 3-1/8"	12.5	24	16	12	10	8														
	17.3	29	19	15	12	10														
7" x 3-3/4"	15.3	35	23	17	14	12	10													
	20.0	40	27	20	16	15	13													
8" x 4"	18.4	47	32	24	19	16	14	12												
	23.0	53	36	27	21	18	15	13												
10" x 4-3/4"	25.4	80	54	41	33	27	23	20	18	16										
	35.0	97	65	49	39	32	28	24	22	20										
12" x 5"	31.8	110	80	60	48	40	34	30	27	24	22	20								
	35.0	126	84	63	50	42	36	32	28	25	23	21								
12" x 5-1/4"	40.8	144	100	75	60	50	43	37	33	30	27	25								
	50.0	168	112	84	67	56	48	42	37	34	31	28								
15" x 5-1/2"	42.9	160	131	98	79	65	56	49	44	39	36	33	30	28	26	25				
	50.0	214	143	107	86	71	61	54	48	43	39	36	33	31	29	27				
18" x 6"	54.7		196	147	118	98	84	74	66	59	54	49	45	42	39	37	35	33	31	
	70.0		226	170	136	113	97	85	76	68	62	57	52	49	45	43	40	38	36	
20" x 6-1/4"	65.4		260	195	156	130	111	97	87	78	71	65	60	56	52	49	46	43	41	39
	75.0		281	211	169	140	120	105	94	84	77	70	65	60	56	53	50	47	44	42

Loads are in kips. 1 kip = 1,000 pounds

Maximum allowable uniform loads for wide flange W-beams with lateral support
Span in feet

Size of beam	Weight of beam per foot	4	6	8	9	10	12	14	18	20	22	24	26	28	30	32	34	36	38	40
8" x 5-1/4"	17	47	31	24	19	16	13	12												
8" x 6-1/2"	24		46	35	28	23	20	17												
8" x 8"	31		60	46	37	30	26	23	20	18	16									
10" x 5-1/4"	21	62	48	36	29	24	21	18	16	14										
10" x 8"	33		74	58	47	39	33	29	26	23										
10" x 10"	49			88	73	61	52	46	40	36	33	30	28	26						
12" x 6-1/2"	27		74	57	45	38	32	28	25	23	21	19								
12" x 8"	40		87	69	58	49	43	38	35	32	29									
12" x 10"	53			108	94	79	67	59	52	47	43	39								
12" x 12"	65				117	98	84	73	65	59	53	49	45	42	39					
14" x 6-3/4"	30		93	70	56	46	40	35	31	28	25	23	21	20	19					
14" x 8"	43			105	84	70	60	52	46	42	38	35	32	30	28					
14" x 10"	61				123	102	88	77	68	62	56	51	47	44	41					
14" x 12"	78				156	135	115	101	90	81	73	67	62	58	54					
14" x 14-1/2"	87					152	132	115	102	92	84	77	71	66	61	57	54	51		
16" x 7"	36		124	94	75	63	54	47	42	38	34	31	29	27	25	24	22			
16" x 8-1/2"	58			157	126	105	90	78	70	63	57	52	48	45	42	39	37			
16" x 11-1/2"	88				202	168	144	126	112	101	92	84	78	72	67	63	59			
18" x 7-1/2"	50			148	119	99	85	74	66	59	54	49	46	42	40	37	35	33	31	
18" x 8-3/4"	64			188	156	130	111	98	87	78	71	65	60	56	52	49	46	43	41	
18" x 11-3/4"	96				224	189	176	154	137	123	112	103	95	88	82	77	72	68	65	
21" x 8-1/4"	62			211	169	141	120	105	94	84	77	70	65	60	56	53	50	47	44	42

Loads are in kips. 1 kip = 1,000 pounds

Planking Span Data

Thickness (nominal)	Lumber grade	Span data for roof decking with a maximum deflection of 1/240th of the span Live load = 20 lbs./sq. ft.	
		Simple spans	
		Douglas fir, larch, southern yellow pine Span	Western red cedar Span
2″	Construction	9′-5″	8′-1″
2″	Standard	9′-5″	6′-9″
3″	Select dex.	15′-3″	13′-0″
3″	Compl. dex.	15′-3″	13′-0″
4″	Select dex.	20′-3″	17′-3″
4″	Compl. dex.	20′-3″	17′-3″

Thickness (nominal)	Lumber grade	**Random lengths**	
		Douglas fir, larch, southern yellow pine Span	Western red cedar Span
2″	Construction	10′-3″	8′-10″
2″	Standard	10′-3″	6′-9″
3″	Select dex.	16′-9″	14′-3″
3″	Compl. dex.	16′-9″	13′-6″
4″	Select dex.	22′-0″	19′-0″
4″	Compl. dex.	22′-0″	18′-0″

Thickness (nominal)	Lumber grade	**Comb. simple and two-span continuous**	
		Douglas fir, larch, southern yellow pine Span	Western red cedar Span
2″	Construction	10′-7″	8′-9″
2″	Standard	10′-7″	6′-9″
3″	Select dex.	17′-3″	14′-9″
3″	Compl. dex.	17′-3″	13′-6″
4″	Select dex.	22′-9″	19′-6″
4″	Compl. dex.	22′-9″	18′-0″

Resistivity to Heat Loss of Common Building Materials

	Material	Resistivity			Material	Resistivity
4″	Concrete or stone	.32		1/2″	Plywood	.65
6″	Concrete or stone	.48		5/8″	Plywood	.80
8″	Concrete or stone	.64		3/4″	Plywood	.95
12″	Concrete or stone	.96		3/4″	Softwood sheathing or siding	.85
4″	Concrete block	.70			Composition floor covering	.08
8″	Concrete block	1.10		1″	Mineral batt insulation	3.50
12″	Concrete block	1.25		2″	Mineral batt insulation	7.00
4″	Common brick	.82		4″	Mineral batt insulation	14.00
4″	Face brick	.45		2″	Glass fiber insulation	7.00
4″	Structural clay tile	1.10		4″	Glass fiber insulation	14.00
8″	Structural clay tile	1.90		1″	Loose fill insulation	3.00
12″	Structural clay tile	3.00		1/2″	Gypsum wallboard	.45
1″	Stucco	.20		1″	Expanding polystyrene, extruded	4.00
15lb	Building paper	.06		1″	Expanding polystyrene, molded beads	3.85
3/8″	Sheet rock or plasterboard	.33			Single thickness glass	.88
1/2″	Sand plaster	.15			Glassweld insulating glass	1.89
1/2″	Insulation plaster	.75			Single glass with storm window	1.66
1/2″	Fiberboard ceiling tile	1.20			Metal edge glass	1.85
1/2″	Fiberboard sheathing	1.45		4″	Glass block	2.13
3/4″	Fiberboard sheathing	2.18		1-3/8″	Wood door	1.82
	Roll roofing	.15			Same with storm door	2.94
	Asphalt shingles	.16		1-3/4″	Wood door	1.82
	Wood shingles	.86			Same with storm door	3.12
	Tile or slate	.08				

The Metric System

Linear Measure

10 millimeters	=	1 centimeter
10 centimeters	=	1 decimeter
10 decimeters	=	1 meter
10 meters	=	1 decameter
10 decameters	=	1 hectometer
10 hectometers	=	1 kilometer

Square Measure

100 square millimeters	=	1 square centimeter
100 square centimeters	=	1 square decimeter
100 square decimeters	=	1 square meter
100 square meters	=	1 square decameter
100 square decameters	=	1 square hectometer
100 square hectometers	=	1 square kilometer

Cubic Measure

1000 cubic millimeters	=	1 cubic centimeter
1000 cubic centimeters	=	1 cubic decimeter
1000 cubic decimeters	=	1 cubic meter

Liquid Measure

10 milliliters	=	1 centiliter
10 centiliters	=	1 deciliter
10 deciliters	=	1 liter
10 liters	=	1 decaliter
10 decaliters	=	1 hectoliter
10 hectoliters	=	1 kiloliter

Weights

10 milligrams	=	1 centigram
10 centigrams	=	1 decigram
10 decigrams	=	1 gram
10 grams	=	1 decagram
10 decagrams	=	1 hectogram
10 hectograms	=	1 kilogram
100 kilograms	=	1 quintal
10 quintals	=	1 metric ton

Weights and Measures Conversion Table

Linear Measure

1 inch	=		=	2.54 centimeters
1 foot	=	12 inches	=	0.3048 meters
1 yard	=	3 feet	=	0.9144 meters
1 rod	=	5-1/2 yards	=	5.029 meters
1 rod	=	16-1/2 feet	=	5.029 meters
1 furlong	=	40 rods	=	201.17 meters
1 mile (statute)	=	5280 feet	=	1609.3 meters
1 mile (statute)	=	1760 yards	=	1609.3 meters
1 league (land)	=	3 miles	=	4.83 kilometers

Square Measure

1 square inch	=		=	6.452 square centimeters
1 square foot	=	144 square inches	=	929 square centimeters
1 square yard	=	9 square feet	=	0.8361 square meters
1 square rod	=	30-1/4 square yards	=	25.29 square meters
1 acre	=	43,560 square feet	=	0.4047 hectare
1 acre	=	160 square yards	=	0.4047 hectare
1 square mile	=	640 acres	=	259 hectares
1 square mile	=	640 acres	=	2.59 square kilometers

Cubic Measure

1 cubic inch	=		=	16.387 cubic centimeters
1 cubic foot	=	1728 cubic inches	=	0.0283 cubic meters
1 cubic yard	=	27 cubic feet	=	0.7646 cubic meters

Chain Linear Measure (For Surveyor's Chain)

1 link	=	7.92 inches	=	20.12 centimeters
1 chain	=	100 links	=	20.12 meters
1 chain	=	66 feet	=	20.12 meters
1 furlong	=	10 chains	=	201.17 meters
1 mile	=	80 chains	=	1609.3 meters

Chain Square Measure

1 square pole	=	625 square links	=	25.29 square meters
1 square chain	=	16 square poles	=	404.7 square meters
1 acre	=	10 square chains	=	0.4047 hectare
1 square mile	=	640 acres	=	259 hectares
1 section	=	640 acres	=	259 hectares
1 township	=	36 square miles	=	9324.0 hectares

Angular and Circular Measure

1 minute	=	60 seconds
1 degree	=	60 minutes
1 right angle	=	90 degrees
1 straight angle	=	180 degrees
1 circle	=	360 degrees

Weights of Building Materials

In pounds per cubic foot (pcf) or pounds per square foot (psf).				
Material	**Weight**		**Material**	**Weight**
Concrete			**Wood Construction (continued)**	
With stone, reinforced	150 pcf		Ceiling, joist and plaster	10 psf
With stone, plain	144 pcf		Ceiling, joist and 1/2″ gypsum board	7 psf
With cinders, reinforced	110 pcf		Ceiling, joists and acoustic tile	5 psf
Light concrete			Wood shingles	3 psf
(Aerocrete)	65 pcf		Spanish tile	15 psf
(Perlite)	45 pcf		Copper sheet	2 psf
(Vermiculite)	40 pcf		Tar and gravel	6 psf
Metal and Plaster			**Stone**	
Masonry mortar	116 pcf		Sandstone	147 pcf
Gypsum and sand plaster	112 pcf		Slate	175 pcf
Brick and Block Masonry (includes mortar)			Limestone	165 pcf
4″ brick wall	35 psf		Granite	175 pcf
8″ brick wall	74 psf		Marble	165 pcf
8″ concrete block wall	100 psf		**Glass**	
12″ concrete block wall	150 psf		1/4″ plate glass	3.28 psf
4″ brick veneer over 4″ concrete block	65 psf		1/8″ double strength	1.63 psf
Wood Construction			1/8″ insulating glass with air space	3.25 psf
Frame wall, lath and plaster	20 psf		4″ glass block	20.00 psf
Frame wall, 1/2″ gypsum board	12 psf		**Insulation**	
Floor, 1/2″ subfloor + 3/4″ finished	6 psf		Cork board, 1″ thick	.58 psf
Floor, 1/2″ subfloor and ceramic tile	16 psf		Rigid foam, 2″ thick	.3 psf
Roof, joist and 1/2″ sheathing	3 psf		Blanket or batt, 1″ thick	.1 psf
Roof, 2″ plank and beam	5 psf			
Roof, built-up	7 psf			

Brick and Block Courses

Number of Courses — Block	Number of Courses — Brick*	Height of Courses	Number of Courses — Block	Number of Courses — Brick*	Height of Courses
	1	0′-2 5/8″	13	39	8′-8″
	2	0′-5 3/8″		40	8′-10 5/8″
1	3	0′-8″		41	9′-1 3/8″
	4	0′-10 5/8″	14	42	9′-4″
	5	1′-1 3/8″		43	9′-6 5/8″
2	6	1′-4″		44	9′-9 3/8″
	7	1′-6 5/8″	15	45	10′-0″
	8	1′-9 3/8″		46	10′-2 5/8″
3	9	2″-0″		47	10′-5 3/8″
	10	2′-2 5/8″	16	48	10′-8″
	11	2′-5 3/8″		49	10′-10 3/8″
4	12	2′-8″		50	11′-1 3/8″
	13	2′-10 5/8″	17	51	11′-4″
	14	3′-1 3/8″		52	11′-6 5/8″
5	15	3′-4″		53	11′-9 3/8″
	16	3′-6 5/8″	18	54	12′-0″
	17	3′-9 3/8″		55	12′-2 5/8″
6	18	4′-0″		56	12′-5 3/8″
	19	4′-2 5/8″	19	57	12′-8″
	20	4′- 5 3/8″		58	12′-10 5/8″
7	21	4′-8″		59	13′-1 3/8″
	22	4′-10 5/8″	20	60	13′-4″
	23	5′-1 3/8″		61	13′-6 5/8″
8	24	5′-4″		62	13′-9 3/8″
	25	5′-6 5/8″	21	63	14′-0″
	26	5′-9 3/8″		64	14′-2 5/8″
9	27	6′-0″		65	14′-5 3/8″
	28	6′-2 5/8″	22	66	14′-8″
	29	6′-5 3/8″		67	14′-10 5/8″
10	30	6′-8″		68	15′-1 3/8″
	31	6′-10 5/8″	23	69	15′-4″
	32	7′-1 3/8″		70	15′-6 5/8″
11	33	7′-4″		71	15′-9 3/8″
	34	7′-6 5/8″	24	72	16′-0″
	35	7′-9 3/8″			
12	36	8′-0″			
	37	8′-2 5/8″			
	38	8′-5 3/8″			

*Individual course heights are only approximations. They will not add up mathematically since mortar joints may vary in thickness. It is only important that courses average 2-2/3″ over heights such as 4′, 6′, and 8′. Mortar joints are 3/8″.

Maximum Span Comparisons for Rafters

Roof Slope of 3:12						
20 psf Live Load, 10 psf Dead Load, Def. <240, C_D = 1.25						
Species and Grade	2" x 6"		2" x 8"		2" x 10"	
	16"OC	24"OC	16"OC	24"OC	16"OC	24"OC
SP No. 1	14'-4"	12'-6"	18'-11"	16'-6"	24'-1"	21'-1"
DFL No. 1	14'-4"	12'-6"	18'-11"	15'-10"	23'-9"	19'-5"
SP No. 2	14'-1"	12'-3"	18'-6"	15'-10"	23'-2"	18'-11"
HF No. 1	13'-9"	12'-0"	18'-1"	15'-6"	23'-1"	18'-11"
DFL No. 2	14'-1"	11'-9"	18'-2"	14'-10"	22'-3"	18'-2"
SPF No. 1 and No. 2	13'-5"	11'-9"	17'-9"	14'-10"	22'-3"	18'-2"
HF No. 2	13'-1"	11'-5"	17'-3"	14'-8"	21'-11"	17'-11"
SP No. 3	11'-8"	9'-6"	14'-10"	12'-2"	17'-7"	14'-4"
DFL No. 3	10'-10"	8'-10"	13'-9"	11'-3"	16'-9"	13'-8"
HF No. 3	10'-10"	8'-10"	13'-9"	11'-3"	16'-9"	13'-8"
SPF No. 3	10'-10"	8'-10"	13'-9"	11'-3"	16'-9"	13'-8"
Roof Slope of 6:12						
30 psf Live Load, 15 psf Dead Load, Def. <180, C_D = 1.15						
Species and Grade	2" x 6"		2" x 8"		2" x 10"	
	16"OC	24"OC	16"OC	24"OC	16"OC	24"OC
SP No. 1	13'-6"	11'-1"	17'-0"	13'-11"	20'-3"	16'-6"
DFL No. 1	12'-0"	9'-10"	15'-3"	12'-5"	18'-7"	15'-2"
SP No. 2	11'-9"	9'-7"	15'-3"	12'-5"	18'-2"	14'-10"
HF No. 1	11'-9"	9'-7"	14'-10"	12'-1"	18'-1"	14'-9"
DFL No. 2	11'-3"	9'-2"	14'-3"	11'-8"	17'-5"	14'-3"
SPF No. 1 and No. 2	11'-3"	9'-2"	14'-3"	11'-8"	17'-5"	14'-3"
HF No. 2	11'-1"	9'-1"	14'-0"	11'-6"	17'-2"	14'-0"
SP No. 3	9'-1"	7'-5"	11'-7"	9'-6"	13'-9"	11'-3"
DFL No. 3	8'-6"	6'-11"	10'-9"	8'-10"	13'-2"	10'-9"
HF No. 3	8'-6"	6'-11"	10'-9"	8'-10"	13'-2"	10'-9"
SPF No. 3	8'-6"	6'-11"	10'-9"	8'-10"	13'-2"	10'-9"

NOTE: These spans were calculated using published design values for comparison purposes only. They included the repetitive factor, C_R = 1.15, but do not include composite action of adhesive and sheathing. Spans may be slightly different than other published spans due to rounding.

C_D = Load Duration Factor, SP = Southern Pine, DFL = Douglas Fir-Larch, HF = Hem-Fir, SPF = Spruce-Pine-Fir

The maximum allowable rafter span may be determined by referring to these charts. The rafter span is the horizontal distance between supports. This is not to be confused with rafter length, which must be calculated using the rise and run of the roof.

Conversion Diagram for Rafters

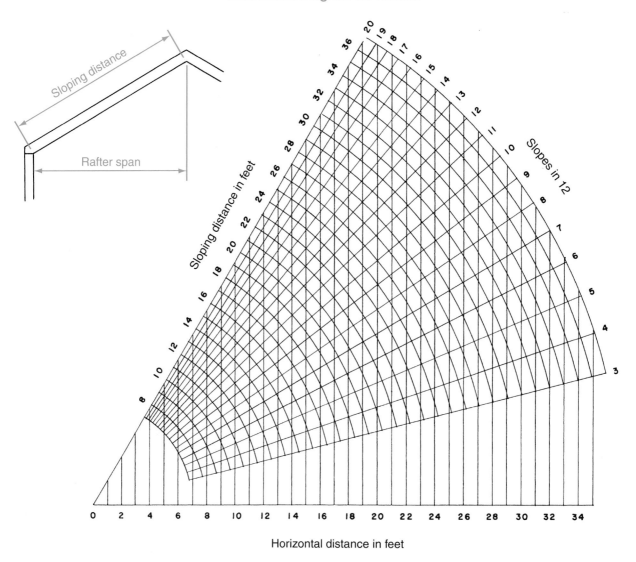

Horizontal distance in feet

To use the diagram, select the known horizontal distance and follow the vertical line to its intersection with the radial line of the specified slope. Then, proceed along the arc to read the sloping distance. In some cases, it may be desirable to interpolate between the one foot separations. The diagram may also be used to find the horizontal distance corresponding to a given sloping distance or to find the slope when the horizontal and sloping distances are known.

Example: With a roof slope of 8/12 and a horizontal distance of 20′, the sloping distance is 24′.

Plywood Grades and Specifications

The material in this Appendix is provided by The Engineered Wood Association (APA) and is from its Product Guide, Grades, and Specifications *material.*

Classification of Species				
Group 1	**Group 2**	**Group 3**	**Group 4**	**Group 5**
Apitong	Cedar, Port	Alder, Red	Aspen	Basswood
Beech, American	Orford	Birch, Paper	Bigtooth	Poplar, Balsam
Beech, Sweet Yellow	Cypress	Cedar, Alaska	Quaking	
Douglas fir 1[a]	Douglas fir 2[a]	Fir, Subalpine	Cativo	
Kapur	Fir	Hemlock, Eastern	Cedar	
Keruing	Balsam	Maple Bigleaf	Incense	
Larch, Western	California Red	Pine	Western Red	
Maple, Sugar	Grand	Jack	Cottonwood	
Pine	Noble	Lodgepole	Eastern	
Caribbean	Pacific Silver	Ponderosa	Black (Western Poplar)	
Ocote	White	Spruce	Pine	
Pine, Southern	Hemlock, Western	Redwood	Eastern White	
Loblolly	Lauan	Spruce	Sugar	
Longleaf	Almon	Engelmann		
Shortleaf	Bagtikan	White		
Slash	Mayapis			
Tanoak	Red			
	Tangile			
	White			
	Maple, Black			
	Mengkulang			
	Meranti, Red[b]			
	Mersawa			
	Pine			
	Pond			
	Red			
	Virginia			
	Western White			
	Spruce			
	Black			
	Red			
	Sitka			
	Sweetgum			
	Tamarack			
	Yellow Poplar			

(a) Douglas fir from trees grown in the states of Washington, Oregon, California, Idaho, Montana, Wyoming, and the Canadian provinces of Alberta and British Columbia shall be classed as Douglas fir Number 1. Douglas fir from trees grown in the states of Nevada, Utah, Colorado, Arizona, and New Mexico shall be classed as Douglas fir Number 2.

(b) Red meranti shall be limited to species having a specific gravity of 0.41 or more based on green volume and oven dry weight.

Plywood Grades and Specifications

Typical APA Trademarks

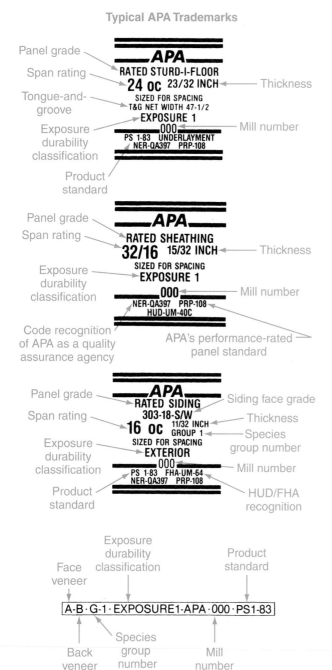

Veneer Grades

A	Smooth, paintable. Not more than 18 neatly made repairs, boat, sled, or router type, and parallel to grain, permitted. May be used for natural finish in less demanding applications.
B	Solid surface. Shims, sled or router repairs, and tight knots to 1" across grain permitted. Wood or synthetic repairs permitted. Some minor splits permitted.
C Plugged	Tight knots to 1-1/2". Knotholes to 1" across grain and some to 1-1/2" if total width of knots and knotholes is within specified limits. Synthetic or wood repairs. Discoloration and sanding defects that do not impair strength permitted. Limited splits allowed. Stitching permitted.
C	Improved C veneer with splits limited to 1/8" width and knotholes or other open defects limited to 1/4" × 1/2". Admits some broken grain. Wood or synthetic repairs permitted.
D	Knots and knotholes to 2-1/2" width across grain and 1/2" larger within specified limits. Limited splits allowed. Stitching permitted. Limited to Interior, Exposure 1, and Exposure 2 panels.

Grade

The term "grade" may refer to *panel grade* or to *veneer grade*. Panel grades are generally identified in terms of the veneer grade used on the face and back of the panel (e.g., A-B, B-C, etc.) or by a name suggesting the panel's intended end use (e.g., APA Rated Sheathing, Underlayment, etc.).

Veneer grades define veneer appearance in terms of natural, unrepaired-growth characteristics and allowable number and size of repairs that may be made during manufacture. The highest quality veneer is "A[1]," the lowest "D." The minimum grade of veneer permitted in Exterior plywood is "C." "D" veneer is used only in panels intended for interior use or for

---

(1) *Some manufacturers also produce a premium "N" grade (natural finish) veneer, available only on special order.*

applications protected from permanent exposure to the weather.

Exposure Durability

APA trademarked panels may be produced in four exposure durability classifications—Exterior, Exposure 1, Exposure 2, and Interior. The exposure durability classification relates to glue bond, and thus to structural integrity. Since aesthetic (nonstructural) attributes of panels may be compromised to some degree by exposure to weather[2], installation recommendations in this APA publication are designed to provide optimum overall performance.

Exterior panels have a fully waterproof bond and are designed for applications subject to permanent exposure to the weather or to moisture.

```
════════════════
═══APA═══
RATED SHEATHING
48/24 23/32 INCH
SIZED FOR SPACING
EXTERIOR
═════000═════
PS 1-83   C-C
NER-QA397  PRP-108
════════════════
```

```
════════════════
═══APA═══
A-C    GROUP 1

EXTERIOR
═════000═════
PS 1-83
════════════════
```

Exposure 1 panels have a fully waterproof bond and are designed for applications where long construction delays may be expected prior to providing protection, or where high moisture conditions may be encountered in service. Exposure 1 panels are made with the same exterior adhesives used in Exterior panels. However, because other compositional factors may affect bond performance, only Exterior panels should be used for permanent exposure to the weather.[3]

```
════════════════
═══APA═══
RATED SHEATHING
32/16 15/32 INCH
SIZED FOR SPACING
EXPOSURE 1
═════000═════
NER-QA397  PRP-108
HUD-UM-40C
════════════════
```

```
════════════════
═══APA═══
A-D    GROUP 1

EXPOSURE 1
═════000═════
PS 1-83
════════════════
```

NOTE. All-veneer APA Rated Sheathing Exposure 1, commonly called "CDX" in the trade, is frequently mistaken as an Exterior panel and erroneously used in applications for which it does not possess the required resistance to weather. "CDX" should only be used for applications as outlined under Exposure 1 above. For sheathing grade panels that will be exposed permanently to the weather, specify APA Rated Sheathing Exterior (C-C Exterior under PS 1.)

Exposure 2 panels (identified as Interior type with intermediate glue under PS 1) are intended for protected construction applications where only moderate delays in providing protection from moisture may be expected.

```
════════════════
═══APA═══
RATED SHEATHING
40/20 19/32 INCH
SIZED FOR SPACING
EXPOSURE 2
═════000═════
NER-QA397  PRP-108
HUD-UM-40C
════════════════
```

```
════════════════
═══APA═══
RATED STURD-I-FLOOR
20 OC 19/32 INCH
SIZED FOR SPACING
T&G NET WIDTH 47-1/2
EXPOSURE 2
═════000═════
NER-QA397  PRP-108
HUD-UM-40C
════════════════
```

Interior panels that lack further glueline information in their trademarks are manufactured with interior glue and are intended for interior applications only.

```
┌────────────────────────────────────┐
│ A-B · G-1 · INT-APA · 000 · PS1-83 │
└────────────────────────────────────┘
```

```
════════════════
═══APA═══
A-B    GROUP 2

INTERIOR
═════000═════
PS 1-83
════════════════
```

(2) *Although glue bond durability is described by exposure durability classification, panel surface may become uneven and irregular under prolonged moisture exposure. Panels should be allowed to dry, and panel joints and surfaces may need to be sanded before applying some finish materials.*
(3) *Exposure 1 panels may also be used when exposure to the outdoors is on the underside only, such as at roof overhangs.*

Species Group Number

Plywood manufactured under US Product Standard PS 1-83 may be made from over 70 species of wood. These species are divided according to strength and stiffness properties into five groups. Group 1 species are the strongest and stiffest, Group 2 the next strongest and stiffest, and so on. The group number appearing in an APA trademark is based on the species used for face and back veneers.[1] Some species are used widely in plywood manufacture; others rarely. Check local availability if a particular species is desired.

Span Ratings

Some APA trademarked panels—APA Rated Sheathing, APA Rated Sturd-I-Floor and APA Rated Siding—carry numbers in their trademarks called Span Ratings. These denote the maximum recommended center-to-center spacing in inches of supports over which the panel should be placed in construction applications.

APA rated sheathing

Span ratings appear as two numbers separated by a slash, such as 32/16, 48/24, etc.[2] The left-hand number denotes the maximum recommended spacing of supports when the panel is used for roof sheathing with the long dimension or strength axis of the panel across three or more supports. The right-hand number indicates the maximum recommended spacing of supports when the panel is used for subflooring with the long dimension or strength axis of the panel across three or more supports. A panel marked 32/16, for example, may be used for roof sheathing over supports 32" on center or for subflooring over supports 16" on center.

APA rated Sturd-I-Floor panels

APA rated Sturd-I-Floor panels are designed specifically for single-floor (combined subfloor-underlayment) applications under carpet and pad, and are manufactured with span ratings of 16", 20", 24", 32", and 48". These, like those for APA rated sheathing, are based on application of the panel with the long dimension or strength axis across three or more supports.

APA rated siding

APA rated siding is produced with span ratings of 16" and 24". Panels and lap siding may be used direct to studs or over nonstructural wall sheathing (Sturd-I-Wall construction), or over nailable panel or lumber sheathing (double-wall construction). Panels and lap siding with a span rating of 16" may be applied direct to studs spaced 16" on center. Panels and lap siding bearing a span rating of 24" may be used direct to studs 24" on center. When used over nailable structural sheathing, the span rating of rated siding panels refers to the maximum recommended spacing of vertical rows of nails, rather than to stud spacing.

(1) *Where face and back veneers are not from the same species group, the higher group number used, except for sanded panels 3/8" thick or less and decorative (including APA Rated Siding 303) panels of any thickness. These are identified by face species because they are chosen primarily for appearance and used in applications where structural integrity is not critical. Sanded panels greater than 3/8" thick are identified by face species if C or D grade backs are at least 1/8" thick and are not more than one species group number larger.*
(2) *An exception is APA rated sheathing intended for use as wall sheathing only. The trademarks for these panels contain a single number similar to the span rated for APA rated sidings.*

Guide to APA Performance Rated Panels
Trademarks Shown are Typical Facsimiles

APA rated sheathing

Specially designed for subflooring, wall sheathing and roof sheathing, but also used for broad range of other construction, industrial and do-it-yourself applications. Can be manufactured as conventional plywood, as a composite, or as oriented strand board. Span Ratings: 12/0, 16/0, 20/0, 24/0, 24/16, 32/16, 40/20, 48/24
Wall: 16"OC
Wall: 24"OC
Exposure Durability Classifications: Exterior, Exposure 1, Exposure 2
Common Thicknesses: 5/16, 3/8, 7/16, 15/32, 1/2, 19/32, 5/8, 23/32, 3/4

be manufactured as conventional plywood, composite, or oriented strand board. All plies in Structural I plywood panels are special improved grades and panels marked PS 1 are limited to Group 1 species. (Structural II plywood panels are also provided for, but rarely manufactured. Application recommendations for Structural II plywood are identical to those for APA rated sheathing plywood.)
Span Ratings: 20/0, 24/0, 24/16, 32/16, 40/20, 48/24
Exposure Durability Classifications: Exterior, Exposure 1
Common Thicknesses: 5/16, 3/8, 7/16, 15/32, 1/2, 19/32, 5/8, 23/32, 3/4.

APA rated Sturd-I-Floor

Specially designed as combination subfloor-underlayment. Provides smooth surface for application of carpet and pad, and possesses high-concentrated and impact load resistance. Can be manufactured as conventional plywood, a composite, or oriented strand board. Available square edge or tongue-and-groove.
Span Ratings: 16, 20, 24, 32
Exposure Durability Classifications: Exterior, Exposure 1, Exposure 2
Common Thicknesses: 19/32, 5/8, 23/32, 3/4, 1, 1-1/8

APA rated siding

For exterior siding, fencing, etc. Can be manufactured as conventional veneered plywood, a composite, or an overlaid oriented strand board siding. Both panel and lap siding are available. Special surface treatment such as V-groove, shallow channel groove, deep groove (such as APA Texture 1-11), kerfed groove, brushed, rough sawed and texture-embossed (MDO). Span rating (stud spacing for siding qualified for APA Sturd-I-Wall applications) and face grade classification (for veneer-faced siding) indicated in trademark. Exposure Durability Classification: Exterior.

APA structural I rated sheathing

Unsanded grade for use where cross-panel strength and stiffness or shear properties are of maximum importance, such as panelized roofs, diaphragms and shear walls. Can

Note: Specify performance-rated panels by thickness and span rating. Span ratings are based on panel strength and stiffness. Since these properties are a function of panel composition and configuration as well as thickness, the same span rating may appear on panels of different thicknesses. Similarly, panels for the same thickness may be marked with different span ratings.

Typical Asphalt Prepared Roofing Products

Product	3 Tab self sealing strip shingle	2 and 3 tab hex strip	Individual lock down	Individual staple down	Giant individual American	Giant individual Dutch lap
Approx. Shipping Weight per Square	235 lb. / 300 lb.	195 lb.	145 lb.	145 lb.	330 lb.	165 lb.
Packages per Square	3 or 4	3	2	2	4	2
Length	36" / 36"	36"	16"	16"	16"	16"
Width	12" / 12"	11-1/3"	16"	16"	12"	12"
Shingles per Square	80 / 80	86	80	80	226	113
Side or End Lap			2-1/2"	2-1/2"		3"
Top Lap	7" / 7"	2"			11"	2"
Head Lap	2" / 2"	2"			6"	
Exposure	5" / 5"	5"			5"	10"

Product	Saturated felt	Smooth roll	Mineral surfaced roll	Pattern edge roll	19" Selvage double coverage
Approx. Shipping Weight per Square	15 lb. / 30 lb.	65 lb. / 50 lb.	90 lb. / 90 lb. / 90 lb.	105 lb. / 105 lb.	110 lb. to 120 lb.
Packages per Square	1/4 / 1/2	1 / 1	1	1 / 1	2
Length	144' / 72'	36' / 36'	36'	42' / 48'	36'
Width	36" / 36"	36" / 36"	36"	36" / 32"	36"
Units per Square			1.0 / 1.075 / 1.15		
Side or End Lap	4" to 6" / 4" to 6"	6" / 6"	6" / 6" / 6"		
Top Lap	2" / 2"	2" / 2"	2" / 3" / 4"	2" / 2"	19"
Head Lap					2"
Exposure	34" / 34"	34" / 34"	34" / 33" / 32"	16" / 14"	17"

Recommended Styles of Welded Wire Fabric Reinforcement for Concrete

Type of Construction	Recommended Style	Remarks
Barbeque Foundation Slab	6×6-W2.0×W2.0 to 4×4-W2.9×W2.9	Use heavier style fabric for heavy, massive fireplaces or barbeque pits.
Basement Floors	6×6-W1.4×W1.4, 6×6-W2.0×W2.0, or 6×6-W2.9×W2.9	For small areas (15' maximum side dimension) use 6×6-W1.4×W1.4. As a rule of thumb, the larger the area or the poorer the subsoil, the heavier the gauge.
Driveways	6×6-W2.9×W2.9	Continuous reinforcement between 25' to 30' contraction joints.
Residential Foundation Slabs	6×6-W1.4×W1.4	Use heavier gauge over poorly drained subsoil or when maximum dimension is greater than 15'.
Garage Floors	6×6-W2.9×W2.9	Position at midpoint of 5" or 6" thick slab.
Patios and Terraces	6×6-W1.4×W1.4	Use 6×6-W2.0×W2.0 if subsoil is poorly drained.
Porch Floor A) 6" thick slab up to 6' span B) 6" thick slab up to 8' span	6×6-W2.9×W2.9 4×4-W4.0×W4.0	Position 1" from bottom form to resist tensile stresses.
Sidewalks	6×6-W1.4×W1.4 or 6×6-W2.0×W2.0	Use heavier gauge over poorly drained subsoil. Construct 25' to 30' slabs as for driveways.
Steps (free span)	6×6-W2.9×W2.9	Use heavier style if more than five risers. Position fabric 1" from bottom form.
Steps (on ground)	6×6-W2.0×W2.0	Use 6×6-W2.9×W2.9 for unstable subsoil.

Gypsum Wallboard Application Data

Thickness	Approx. Weight lbs/ft^2	Size	Location	Application Method	Max. Spacing of Framing Members
1/4"	1.1	4' × 8' to 12'	Over existing walls & ceilings	Horizontal or vertical	
3/8"	1.5	4' × 8' to 14'	Ceilings	Horizontal	16"
3/8"	1.5	4' × 8' to 14'	Sidewalls	Horizontal or vertical	16"
1/2"	2.0	4' × 8' to 14'	Ceilings	Vertical Horizontal	16" 24"
1/2"	2.0	4' × 8' to 14'	Sidewalls	Horizontal or vertical	24"
5/8"	2.5	4' × 8' to 14'	Ceilings	Vertical Horizontal	16" 24"
5/8"	2.5	4' × 8' to 14'	Sidewalls	Horizontal or vertical	24"
1"	4.0	2' × 8' to 12'		For laminated partitions	

Sizes and Dimensions for Reinforcing Bars

Weight	Nominal Dia	Size	Number	Nominal Cross Section Area	Nominal Perimeter
.376 lb/ft	.375"	3/8	3	.11 in^2	1.178
.668 lb/ft	.500"	1/2	4	.20 in^2	1.571
1.043 lb/ft	.625"	5/8	5	.31 in^2	1.963
1.502 lb/ft	.750"	3/4	6	.44 in^2	2.356
2.044 lb/ft	.875"	7/8	7	.60 in^2	2.749
2.670 lb/ft	1.000"	1	8	.79 in^2	3.142
3.400 lb/ft	1.128"	1*	9	1.00 in^2	3.544
4.303 lb/ft	1.270"	1-1/8*	10	1.27 in^2	3.990
5.313 lb/ft	1.410"	1-1/4*	11	1.56 in^2	4.430
7.650 lb/ft	1.693"	1-1/2*	14	2.25 in^2	5.320
13.600 lb/ft	2.257"	2*	18	4.00 in^2	7.090

These sizes rolled in rounds equivalent to square cross section area.

Recommended Foot Candle Levels

Area	Level
TV Viewing	5 FC
Storage	10 FC
Stairway	20 FC
Dining	20 FC
Bedroom	20 FC
Bath	30 FC
Living	30 FC
Den	30 FC
Reading	50 FC
Sewing	50 FC
Kitchen	50 FC
Shop	70 FC
Drawing	100 FC

Design Temperatures and Degree Days (Heating Season)

State	City	Outside Design Temperature (°F)	Degree Days (°F-Days)
Alabama	Birmingham	19	2,600
Alaska	Anchorage	−25	10,800
Arizona	Phoenix	31	1,800
Arkansas	Little Rock	19	3,200
California	Los Angeles	41	2,000
California	San Francisco	35	3,000
Colorado	Denver	−2	6,200
Connecticut	Hartford	1	6,200
Florida	Tampa	36	600
Georgia	Atlanta	18	3,000
Idaho	Boise	4	5,800
Illinois	Chicago	−3	6,600
Indiana	Indianapolis	0	5,600
Iowa	Des Moines	−7	6,600
Kansas	Wichita	5	4,600
Kentucky	Louisville	8	4,600
Louisiana	New Orleans	32	1,400
Maryland	Baltimore	12	4,600
Massachusetts	Boston	6	5,600
Michigan	Detroit	4	6,200
Minnesota	Minneapolis	−14	8,400
Mississippi	Jackson	21	2,200
Missouri	St. Louis	4	5,000
Montana	Helena	−17	8,200
Nebraska	Lincoln	−4	5,800
Nevada	Reno	2	6,400
New Hampshire	Concord	−11	7,400
New Mexico	Albuquerque	14	4,400
New York	Buffalo	3	7,000
New York	New York City	12	5,000
North Carolina	Raleigh	16	3,400
North Dakota	Bismarck	−24	8,800
Ohio	Columbus	2	5,600
Oklahoma	Tulsa	12	3,800
Oregon	Portland	21	4,600
Pennsylvania	Philadelphia	11	4,400
Pennsylvania	Pittsburgh	5	6,000
Rhode Island	Providence	6	6,000
South Carolina	Charleston	23	2,000
South Dakota	Sioux Falls	−14	7,800
Tennessee	Chattanooga	15	3,200
Texas	Dallas	19	2,400
Texas	San Antonio	25	1,600
Utah	Salt Lake City	5	6,000
Vermont	Burlington	−12	8,200
Virginia	Richmond	14	3,800
Washington	Seattle	28	5,200
West Virginia	Charleston	9	4,400
Wisconsin	Madison	−9	7,800
Wyoming	Cheyenne	−6	7,400

A more complete listing of monthly and yearly degree days and outside design temperatures can be found in the ASHRAE *Guide and Data Book.*

Wood Foundations

Typical Wood Foundation

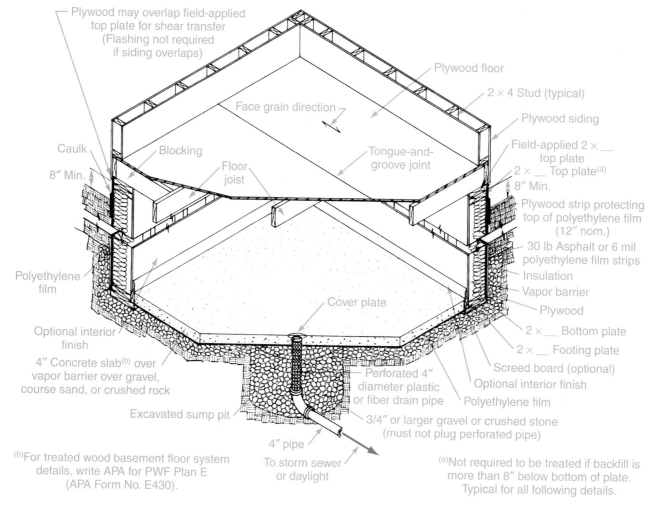

Plywood may overlap field-applied
top plate for shear transfer
(Flashing not required
if siding overlaps)

Plywood floor

2 × 4 Stud (typical)

Plywood siding

Field-applied 2 × __
top plate

2 × __ Top plate(a)

Caulk

Blocking

Face grain direction

Tongue-and-
groove joint

8″ Min.

Floor
joist

8″ Min.

Plywood strip protecting
top of polyethylene film
(12″ nom.)

30 lb Asphalt or 6 mil
polyethylene film strips

Insulation

Vapor barrier

Plywood

2 × __ Bottom plate

2 × __ Footing plate

Screed board (optional)

Optional interior finish

Polyethylene film

Polyethylene
film

Cover plate

Optional interior
finish

4″ Concrete slab(b) over
vapor barrier over gravel,
course sand, or crushed rock

Excavated sump pit

Perforated 4″
diameter plastic
or fiber drain pipe

3/4″ or larger gravel or crushed stone
(must not plug perforated pipe)

4″ pipe

To storm sewer
or daylight

(b)For treated wood basement floor system
details, write APA for PWF Plan E
(APA Form No. E430).

(a)Not required to be treated if backfill is
more than 8″ below bottom of plate.
Typical for all following details.

Courtesy of The Engineered Wood Association.

Wood Foundations

Crawl Space

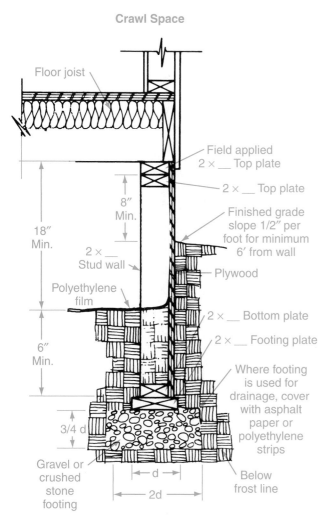

Floor joist

Field applied
2 × __ Top plate

2 × __ Top plate

8" Min.

18" Min.

Finished grade
slope 1/2" per
foot for minimum
6' from wall

2 × __
Stud wall

Plywood

Polyethylene
film

2 × __ Bottom plate

2 × __ Footing plate

6" Min.

Where footing
is used for
drainage, cover
with asphalt
paper or
polyethylene
strips

3/4 d

d

2d

Gravel or
crushed
stone
footing

Below
frost line

Courtesy of The Engineered Wood Association.

Crawl Space PWF on Concrete Footing

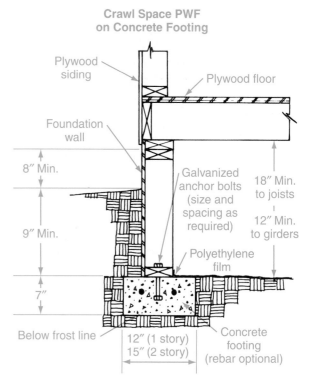

Plywood
siding

Plywood floor

Foundation
wall

8" Min.

9" Min.

Galvanized
anchor bolts
(size and
spacing as
required)

18" Min.
to joists

12" Min.
to girders

Polyethylene
film

7"

Below frost line

12" (1 story)
15" (2 story)

Concrete
footing
(rebar optional)

Courtesy of The Engineered Wood Association.

Wood Foundations

Basement Wall

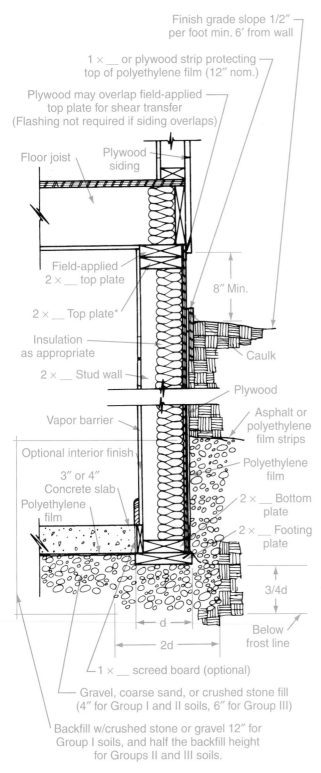

Finish grade slope 1/2" per foot min. 6' from wall

1 × __ or plywood strip protecting top of polyethylene film (12" nom.)

Plywood may overlap field-applied top plate for shear transfer (Flashing not required if siding overlaps)

Floor joist

Plywood siding

Field-applied 2 × __ top plate

8" Min.

2 × __ Top plate*

Insulation as appropriate

2 × __ Stud wall

Caulk

Vapor barrier

Plywood

Optional interior finish

Asphalt or polyethylene film strips

3" or 4" Concrete slab

Polyethylene film

Polyethylene film

2 × __ Bottom plate

2 × __ Footing plate

d

2d

3/4d

Below frost line

1 × __ screed board (optional)

Gravel, coarse sand, or crushed stone fill (4" for Group I and II soils, 6" for Group III)

Backfill w/crushed stone or gravel 12" for Group I soils, and half the backfill height for Groups II and III soils.

*Not required to be treated if backfill is more than 8" below bottom of plate. Typical for all following details.

Knee Wall with Brick Veneer

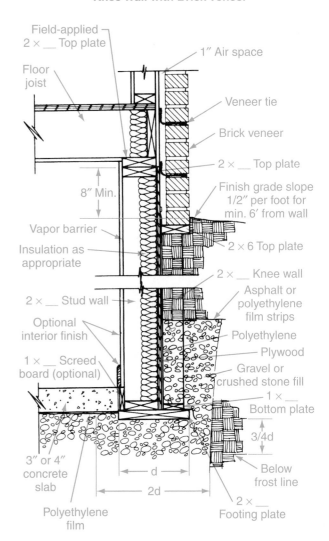

Field-applied 2 × __ Top plate

Floor joist

1" Air space

Veneer tie

Brick veneer

2 × __ Top plate

8" Min.

Finish grade slope 1/2" per foot for min. 6' from wall

Vapor barrier

2 × 6 Top plate

Insulation as appropriate

2 × __ Knee wall

2 × __ Stud wall

Asphalt or polyethylene film strips

Optional interior finish

Polyethylene

1 × __ Screed board (optional)

Plywood

Gravel or crushed stone fill

3" or 4" concrete slab

1 × __ Bottom plate

3/4d

Polyethylene film

d

2d

Below frost line

2 × __ Footing plate

Wood Foundations

Garage PWF Details—Exterior Walls

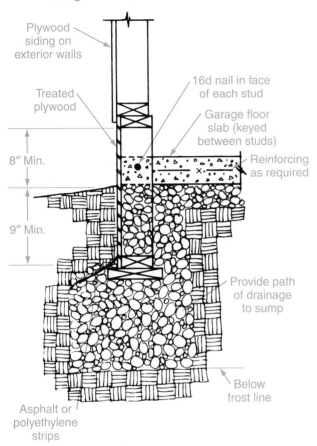

Plywood siding on exterior walls

Treated plywood

16d nail in face of each stud

Garage floor slab (keyed between studs)

Reinforcing as required

8" Min.

9" Min.

Provide path of drainage to sump

Below frost line

Asphalt or polyethylene strips

Courtesy of The Engineered Wood Association.

Garage PWF Details—Interior Walls (Between House and Garage)

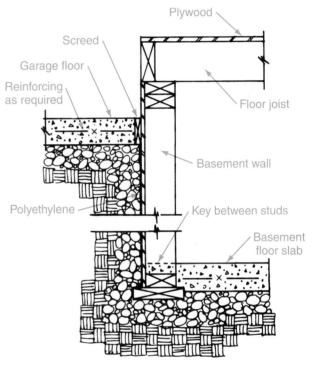

Plywood

Screed

Garage floor

Reinforcing as required

Floor joist

Basement wall

Polyethylene

Key between studs

Basement floor slab

Courtesy of The Engineered Wood Association.

Garage PWF Details—Garage Door

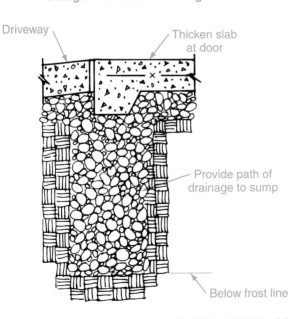

Driveway

Thicken slab at door

Provide path of drainage to sump

Below frost line

Courtesy of The Engineered Wood Association.

Fire and Sound Rating for Typical Insulated Construction Assemblies

2″ × 4″ Wood Stud Partition

2″ × 4″ wood studs 16″OC
CertainTeed 3-1/2″ (R-11) sound control batts or Insul-Safe III fiberglass insulation
1/2″ regular gypsum wallboard

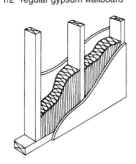

STC 37

2″ × 4″ Wood Stud Resilient Channel Partition

2″ × 4″ wood studs 16″OC
CertainTeed 3-1/2″ (R-11) sound control batts
Resilient channels 24″OC one side
5/8″ type "X" gypsum wallboard

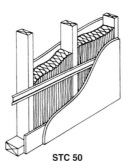

STC 50
Fire Rating 1 hour

2″ × 4″ Wood Stud Partition

2″ × 4″ wood studs 24″OC
CertainTeed 3-1/2″ (R-11) sound control batts
2 layers 5/8″ type "X" gypsum wallboard each side

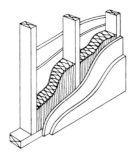

STC 46
Fire Rating 2 hours

Staggered Wood Stud Partition

2″ × 4″ wood studs staggered 16″OC
2″ × 6″ wood plates
CertainTeed 2-1/2″ (R-8) sound control batts all stud spaces
1/2″ regular gypsum wallboard

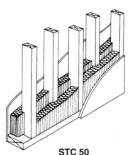

STC 50
Fire Rating 1 hour

Double Wood Stud Partition

2″ × 4″ wood studs 16″OC (double row)
Separate 2″ × 4″ wood plates
CertainTeed 3-1/2″ (R-11) sound control batts all stud spaces
1/2″ regular gypsum wallboard

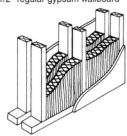

STC 55
Fire Rating 1 hour

Exterior Wood Stud Wall

2″ × 4″ wood studs 16″OC
CertainTeed 3-1/2″ (R-11) sound control batts
Interior: 1/2″ regular gypsum wallboard
Exterior: 1/2″ gypsum sheathing and 3/8″ exterior plywood

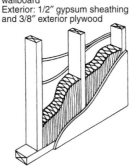

STC 37
Fire Rating 1 hour

Exterior Wood Stud Wall

2″ × 4″ wood studs 16″OC
CertainTeed 3-1/2″ (R-11) sound control batts
Interior: resilient channel and 5/8″ type "X" gypsum wallboard
Exterior: 1/2″ gypsum sheathing and 3/8″ exterior plywood

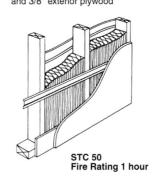

STC 50
Fire Rating 1 hour

2-1/2″ and 3-5/8″ Steel Stud Partitions

2-1/2″ or 3-5/8″ steel studs 24″OC
CertainTeed 2-1/2″ (R-8) or 3-1/2″ (R-11) sound control batts
1/2″ regular gypsum wallboard

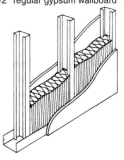

STC 45 w/ 2-1/2″ studs
STC 46 w/ 3-5/8″ studs

Steel Stud Partition
2-1/2″ steel studs 24″OC
CertainTeed 2-1/2″ (R-8) sound control batts
5/8″ type "X" gypsum wallboard

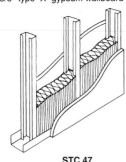

STC 47
Fire Rating 1 hour

Steel Stud Partition

2-1/2″ steel studs 24″OC
CertainTeed 2-1/2″ (R-8) sound control batts
2 layers 1/2″ type "X" gypsum wallboard each side

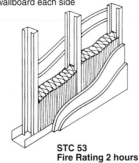

STC 53
Fire Rating 2 hours

Floor/Ceiling Construction

Wood joists 16″OC
CertainTeed 3-1/2″ (R-11) sound control batts
Resilient channel
1/2″ type "X" gypsum wallboard
5/8″ plywood subfloor
3/8″ particle board underlayment
carpet and pad

STC 53
IIC 73
Fire Rating 1 hour

Floor/Ceiling Construction

Wood joists 16″OC
CertainTeed 3-1/2″ (R-11) sound control batts
Resilient channel
1/2″ type "X" gypsum wallboard
5/8″ plywood subfloor
1-1/2″ cellular or lightweight concrete
carpet and pad

STC 60
IIC 73
Fire Rating 1 hour

Wall System Selection Chart for Wood Stud Walls

Fire Rating	Test Number	STC	Construction Description
1 hour*	W01480	64	Double wood studs 16"OC; double layer 1/2" type "X" gypsum wallboard each side, one thickness R-11 fiberglass insulation
1 hour*	W01080	60	Double wood studs 16"OC; double layer 1/2" type "X" gypsum wallboard one side, single layer other side; two thicknesses R-11 fiberglass insulation
1 hour	W2869	59	Double wood studs 16"OC; single layer 1/2" type "X" gypsum wallboard each side; two thicknesses R-11 fiberglass insulation
2 hour	W4269	58	Double wood studs 16"OC; double layer 5/8" type "X" gypsum wallboard one side; no insulation
1 hour*	W01180	57	Double wood studs 16"OC; double layer 1/2" type "X" gypsum wallboard one side; single layer other side; one thickness R-11 fiberglass insulation
N/A	W2969	56	Double wood studs 16"OC; single layer 1/2" type "X" gypsum wallboard each side; one thickness R-11 fiberglass insulation
1 hour*	OCF448	56	Double wood studs 16"OC; single layer 5/8" type "X" gypsum wallboard each side; one thickness R-11 fiberglass insulation
1 hour	W01580	54	Double wood studs 16"OC; double layer 1/2" type "X" gypsum wallboard each side; no insulation
N/A	W00980	48	Double wood studs 16"OC; double layer 1/2" type "X" gypsum wallboard one side; single layer other side; no insulation
1 hour*	W4169	52	Double wood studs 16"OC; double layer 5/8" type "X" gypsum wallboard one side; single layer other side; no insulation
N/A	W3469	47	Double wood studs 16"OC; single layer 1/2" type "X" gypsum wallboard each side; no insulation
1 hour*	W06282	46	Double wood studs 16"OC; single layer 5/8" type "X" gypsum wallboard each side; no insulation
1 hour*	W4869	55	Staggered wood studs 24"OC; double layer 1/2" type "X" gypsum wallboard each side; one thickness R-11 fiberglass insulation
N/A	W4769	53	Staggered wood studs 24"OC; double layer 1/2" type "X" gypsum wallboard one side; single layer other side; one thickness R-11 fiberglass insulation
1 hour*	W4669	52	Staggered wood studs 24"OC; double layer 1/2" type "X" gypsum wallboard each side; no insulation
1 hour	OC5FC	51	Staggered wood studs 16"OC; single layer 1/2" gypsum wallboard each side; two thicknesses R-11 fiberglass insulation
N/A	OC4FC	49	Staggered wood studs 16"OC; single layer 1/2" type "X" gypsum wallboard each side; one thickness R-11 fiberglass insulation
N/A	W4569	47	Staggered wood studs 24"OC; double layer 1/2" type "X" gypsum wallboard one side; single layer other side; no insulation
1 hour*	W5769	46	Staggered wood studs 16"OC; single layer 5/8" type "X" gypsum wallboard one side; one thickness R-11 fiberglass insulation
1 hour*	W5869	43	Staggered wood studs 16"OC; single layer 5/8" type "X" gypsum wallboard each side; no insulation
N/A	OC3FC	39	Staggered wood studs 16"OC; single layer 1/2" type "X" gypsum wallboard each side; no insulation
1 hour*	W2569	45	Single wood studs 16"OC; double layer 1/2" type "X" gypsum wallboard each side; one thickness R-11 fiberglass insulation
N/A	W2469	40	Single wood studs 16"OC; double layer 1/2" gypsum wallboard one side; single layer 1/2" gypsum wallboard other side; one thickness R-11 fiberglass insulation
N/A	W2069	39	Single wood studs 16"OC; single layer 1/2" type "X" gypsum wallboard one side; one thickness R-11 fiberglass insulation
N/A	W2269	38	Single wood studs 16"OC; double layer 1/2" type "X" gypsum wallboard one side; single layer other side; no insulation
N/A	W2169	35	Single wood studs 16"OC; single layer 1/2" type "X" gypsum wallboard each side; no insulation
1 hour	OCF424	34	Single wood studs 16"OC; single layer 5/8" type "X" gypsum wallboard each side; no insulation

Double Wood Studs

Staggered Wood Studs

Single Wood Studs

*Some of the above test results are estimated.

Clearance Requirements

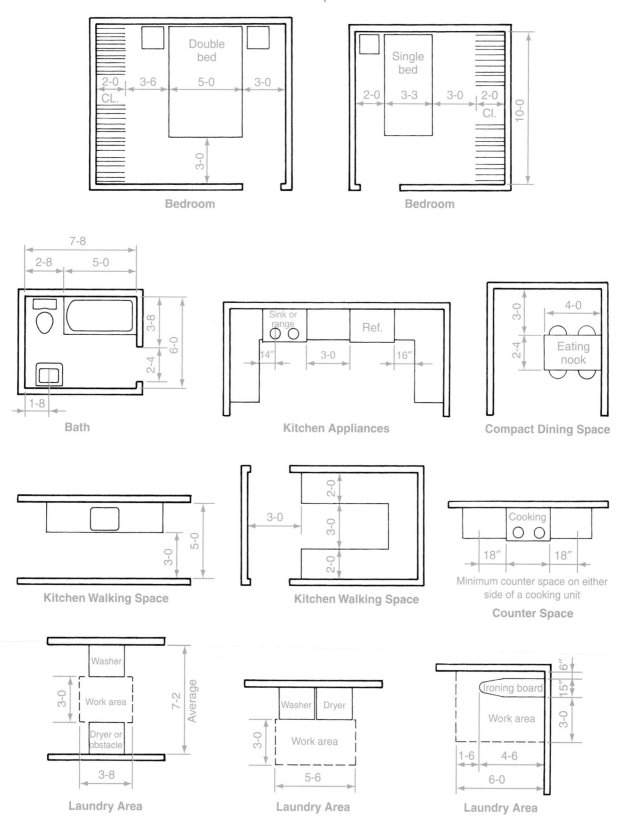

Building Requirements

303 Siding Direct to Studs – U = 0.08

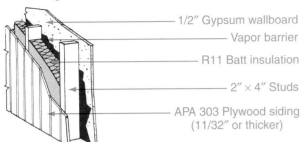

- 1/2″ Gypsum wallboard
- Vapor barrier
- R11 Batt insulation
- 2″ × 4″ Studs
- APA 303 Plywood siding (11/32″ or thicker)

	R
Outside air film	0.17
11/32″ plywood siding	0.43
R11 batt insulation	11.00
1/2″ gypsum wallboard	0.45
Inside air film	0.68
R_T =	12.73
U = $1/R_T$ =	0.08

303 Siding Over Fiberboard Sheathing – U = 0.07

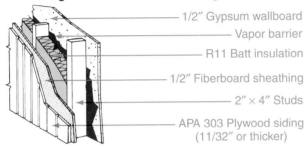

- 1/2″ Gypsum wallboard
- Vapor barrier
- R11 Batt insulation
- 1/2″ Fiberboard sheathing
- 2″ × 4″ Studs
- APA 303 Plywood siding (11/32″ or thicker)

	R
Outside air film	0.17
11/32″ plywood siding	0.43
1/2″ fiberboard sheathing	1.32
R11 insulation	11.00
1/2″ gypsum wallboard	0.45
Inside air film	0.68
R_T =	14.05
U = $1/R_T$ =	0.07

303 Siding Direct to Studs – U = 0.07

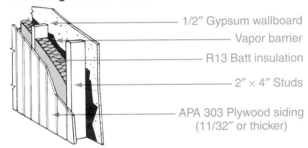

- 1/2″ Gypsum wallboard
- Vapor barrier
- R13 Batt insulation
- 2″ × 4″ Studs
- APA 303 Plywood siding (11/32″ or thicker)

	R
Outside air film	0.17
11/32″ plywood siding	0.43
R13 batt insulation	13.00
1/2″ gypsum wallboard	0.45
Inside air film	0.68
R_T =	14.73
U = $1/R_T$ =	0.07

303 Siding Over Rigid Insulation – U = 0.05

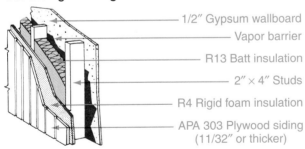

- 1/2″ Gypsum wallboard
- Vapor barrier
- R13 Batt insulation
- 2″ × 4″ Studs
- R4 Rigid foam insulation
- APA 303 Plywood siding (11/32″ or thicker)

	R
Outside air film	0.17
11/32″ plywood siding	0.43
R4 rigid foam insulation	4.00
R13 batt insulation	13.00
1/2″ gypsum wallboard	0.45
Inside air film	0.68
R_T =	18.73
U = $1/R_T$ =	0.05

303 Siding Direct to Studs – U = 0.05

- 1/2″ Gypsum wallboard
- Vapor barrier
- R19 Batt insulation
- 2″ × 6″ Studs
- APA 303 Plywood siding (15/32″ or thicker for studs 24″ OC)

	R
Outside air film	0.17
15/32″ plywood siding	0.59
R19 batt insulation	19.00
1/2″ gypsum wallboard	0.45
Inside air film	0.68
R_T =	20.89
U = $1/R_T$ =	0.05

Abbreviations

Acoustic	ACST	Dishwasher	DW	Platform	PLATF
Acrylonitrile butadiene styrene	ABS	Door	DR	Plumbing	PLMB
Actual	ACT	Double hung	DH	Plywood	PLY
Addition	ADD	Down	DN	Polyvinyl chloride	PVC
Adhesive	ADH	Downspout	DS	Prefabricated	PREFAB
Aggregate	AGGR	Drain	D or DR	Property	PROP
Air conditioning	AIR COND	Drawing	DWG	Push button	PB
Alternate	ALT	Drywall	DW	Radiator	RAD
Aluminum	AL	Elbow	ELL	Random length	RL & W
American Association of		Electric	ELEC	Range	R
Registered Architects	ARA	Elevation	EL or ELEV	Receptacle	RECP
American Institute of		Entrance	ENT	Recessed	REC
Architects	AIA	Estimate	EST	Reference	REF
American Society for Testing		Excavate	EXC	Refrigerator	REF
and Materials	ASTM	Exterior	EXT	Register	REG
American wire gage	AWG	Fabricate	FAB	Reinforce	REINF
Amount	AMT	Family room	FAM R	Return	RET
Ampere	AMP	Federal Housing Authority	FHA	Riser	R
Anchor bolt	AB	Finish	FIN	Roof	RF
Approximate	APPROX	Firebrick	FBRK	Roofing	RFG
Architectural	ARCH	Fireproof	FP	Rough	RGH
Area	A	Fitting	FTG	Round	RD
Asbestos	ASB	Fixture	FIX	Schedule	SCH
Asphalt	ASPH	Flange	FLG	Section	SECT
Assembly	ASSY	Flashing	FLSHG	Self-closing	SC
Automatic	AUTO	Floor	FL	Service	SERV
Average	AVG	Floor drain	FD	Sewer	SEW
Balcony	BALC	Flooring	FLG	Sheet metal	SM
Basement	BSMT	Footing	FTG	Shelves	SHVL's
Bathroom	B	Foundation	FDN	Shower	SH
Beam	BM or BMS	Frame	FR	Siding	SDG
Bedroom	BR	Full size	FS	Sill cock	SC
Benchmark	B M	Gallon	GAL	Socket	SOC
Between	BET	Galvanized	GALV	Soil pipe	SP
Bits per inch	bpi	Glass	GL	Specification	SPEC
Blocking	BLKG	Grade	GR	Square	SQ
Board feet	BD FT	Gypsum	GYP	Stairs	ST
Bottom	BOT	Hall	H	Standpipe	ST P
Bracket	BRKT	Hardware	HDW	Station point	SP
British thermal unit	Btu	Header	HDR	Steel	STL
Broom closet	BC	Heater	HTR	Structural	STR
Building	BLDG	Horizontal	HORIZ	Surface	SUR
Buzzer	BUZ	Hose bibb	HB	Surface four sides	S4S
Cabinet	CAB	Inside diameter	ID	Surface two sides	S2S
Casing	CSG	Insulation	INS	Suspended ceiling	SUSP CLG
Cast iron	CI	Interior	INT	Switch	S or SW
Cathode ray tube	CRT	International Standards		Symbol	SYM
Caulking	CLKG	Organization	ISO	Tee	T
Ceiling	CL	Joint	JT	Telephone	TEL
Cement	CEM	Joist	JST	Television	TV
Centerline	CL or ℄	Kiln dried	KD	Temperature	TEMP
Center to center	C to C	Kitchen	K	Terra cotta	TC
Central processing unit	CPU	Kitchen cabinets	KC	Thermostat	THERMO
Ceramic	CER	Kitchen sink	KS	Thickness	THK
Circuit	CKT	Laminated	LAM	Tongue and groove	T & G
Circuit breaker	CIR BKR	Landing	LOG	Tread	TR
Cleanout	CL or CO	Laundry	LAU	Unfinished	UNFIN
Closet	CLOS or CL	Lavatory	LAV	Vanishing point	VP
Clothes dryer	CLD	Leader	LDR	Vanity	VAN
Column	COL	Level	LEV	Ventilation	VENT
Composition	COMP	Light	LT	Ventilator	V
Concrete	CONC	Linen closet	LCL	Vertical	VERT
Concrete block	CONC B	Linoleum	LINO	Wall cabinet	W CAB
Construction	CONST	Living room	LR	Wall vent	WV
Copper	COP or CU	Lumber	LBR	Water	W
Counter	CTR	Manufacturer	MFR	Water closet	WC
Courses	C	Material	MATL	Water heater	WH
Cross section	X-SECT	Maximum	MAX	Waterproof	WP
Cubic feet	CU FT	Medicine cabinet	MC	Weep hole	WH
Cubic yard	CU YD	Metal	MET	Wide flange	WF
Damper	DMPR	Minimum	MIN	Window	WDW
Decorative	DEC	Modular	MOD	With	W/
Detail	DET	Molding	MLDG	Wood	WD
Diagram	DIA	National Electric Code	NEC	Wrought iron	WI
Dimension	DIM	Plate glass	PL GL	Zinc	Z or ZN
Dining room	DR	Plates	PLTS		

The Residential TJI® Joist

TJI® joists are the essential ingredient to constructing today's highest-quality floors and roofs with the greatest of ease. Lightweight, long lengths, and the unique I-configuration make for fast, efficient construction. Precision-engineered design is the key to stiff, silent floors.

Joists in lengths to 60′ speed installation by eliminating laps over beams or walls and since a TJI® joist is only about half the weight of an ordinary joist, a typical floor or roof can be put in place in a fraction of the time. The I-shape makes nailing to the plate much easier, too.

TJI® joists are available from Trus Joist stocking lumber dealers throughout the United States and Canada in four depths: 9-1/2″, 11-7/8″, 14″, and 16″.

9-1/2″ TJI®/25 Joist   11-7/8″ TJI®/25 Joist   14″ TJI®/35 Joist   16″ TJI®/35 Joist

Code Evaluations: FHA 689, NER 119.   **Note:** NER evaluation includes BOCA, ICBO, and SBCCI.

Microllam® LVL Headers & Beams

High strength, consistent dimensions, and exceptional workability make Microllam® laminated veneer lumber (LVL) the perfect material for almost every header and beam application in residential construction.

Microllam® LVL is 1-3/4″ thick and available in seven depths from 5-1/2″ to 18″ and in lengths to 60′ from Trus Joist stocking dealers throughout the United States and Canada. Two or more pieces can be nailed or bolted together right on the job site to form a header or beam for almost any load condition found in residential construction. Two 1-3/4″ thick pieces match conventional 2″ × 4″ wall framing to eliminate shimming.

Microllam® LVL's unique manufacturing process eliminates many of the problems caused by twisting, shrinking, splitting, and checking, thus reducing material waste.

18″   16″   14″   11-7/8″   9-1/2″   7-1/4″   5-1/2″

Code Evaluations: NER 119, NER 126, FHA 925.   **Note:** NER evaluation includes BOCA, ICBO, and SBCCI.

TJI® Joist Floor Details and Span Charts

Typical Floor Framing

For installation stability:
Temporary strut lines
(1″ × 4″ min.) 8′ on center max.
Fasten at each joist
with 2-8d nails min.

Microllam® LVL header
or TJI® joist header

**NOTE: Bridging is
not required.**

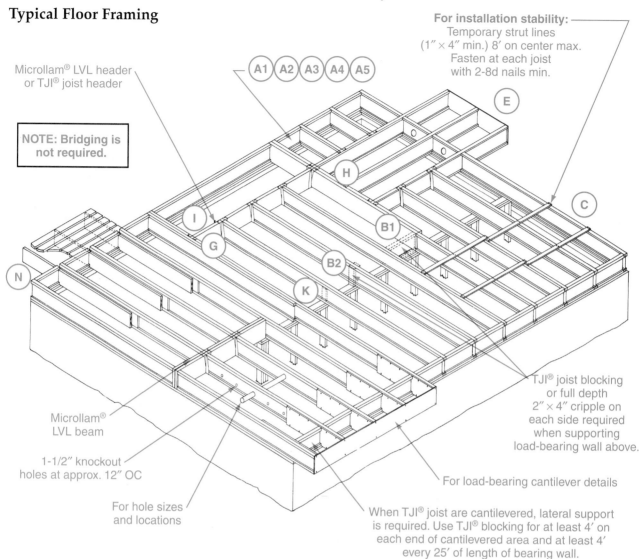

A1 A2 A3 A4 A5

E

H

I

G

B1

B2

N

K

C

TJI® joist blocking
or full depth
2″ × 4″ cripple on
each side required
when supporting
load-bearing wall above.

Microllam®
LVL beam

1-1/2″ knockout
holes at approx. 12″ OC

For hole sizes
and locations

For load-bearing cantilever details

When TJI® joist are cantilevered, lateral support
is required. Use TJI® blocking for at least 4′ on
each end of cantilevered area and at least 4′
every 25′ of length of bearing wall.

TJI® Floor Joist Details

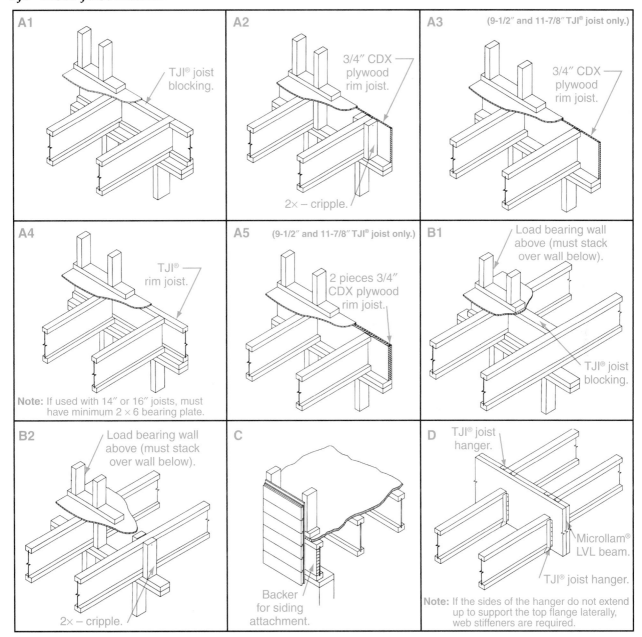

A1 — TJI® joist blocking.

A2 — 3/4″ CDX plywood rim joist. 2× – cripple.

A3 (9-1/2″ and 11-7/8″ TJI® joist only.) — 3/4″ CDX plywood rim joist.

A4 — TJI® rim joist. **Note:** If used with 14″ or 16″ joists, must have minimum 2 × 6 bearing plate.

A5 (9-1/2″ and 11-7/8″ TJI® joist only.) — 2 pieces 3/4″ CDX plywood rim joist.

B1 — Load bearing wall above (must stack over wall below). TJI® joist blocking.

B2 — Load bearing wall above (must stack over wall below). 2× – cripple.

C — Backer for siding attachment.

D — TJI® joist hanger. Microllam® LVL beam. TJI® joist hanger. **Note:** If the sides of the hanger do not extend up to support the top flange laterally, web stiffeners are required.

General Notes

Minimum Bearing Length

1-3/4″ minimum bearing required at joist ends; 3-1/2″ minimum bearing at intermediate supports.

Rim Joists or Blocking

1. For single-story applications and second floors of two-story applications, use detail A1, A2, A3, A4, or A5.
2. For main floor rim of two-story applications, use detail A1, A2, A4, or A5.
3. Assumes 1000 PLF vertical load transfer for each layer of 3/4″ CDX plywood rim joist.
4. Assumes 2000 PLF vertical load transfer for each TJI® joist blocking panel or rim joist.
5. When plywood rim is used, bracing complying with code shall be carried to the foundation or TJI® joist solid blocking used for a minimum of 4′ at each end and at least 4′ every 25′ of length of bearing wall.
6. 2″ × ___ cripples for details A2 and B2 must be 1/16″ longer than depth of joist. Web stiffeners may also be required.
7. Other 3/4″ APA 48/24 rated sheathing may be used for rim joist in lieu of 3/4″ CDX plywood.

Nailing Requirements

1. Nail joists at bearings with two 8d nails (one each side), 1-1/2″ minimum from end to avoid splitting.
2. Nail TJI® joist blocking or rim to bearing plate with 8d nails at 6″ on center. When used for shear transfer, nail to bearing plate with same nailing as the plywood shear schedule.
3. Nail TJI® rim joist, 3/4″ CDX plywood rim, or plywood closure to TJI® joist with two 8d nails, one each at top and bottom flange. With 14″ and 16″ TJI® rim joists, use 16d nails.

Filler and Backer Blocks

9-1/2″ and 11-7/8″ TJI® joist:
    Filler block: 2″ × 6″
    Backer block: 3/4″ plywood
14″ and 16″ TJI® joist:
    Filler block: 2″ × 8″ + 1/2″ plywood
    Backer block: two pieces 1/2″ plywood

TJI® Floor Joist Details (Continued)

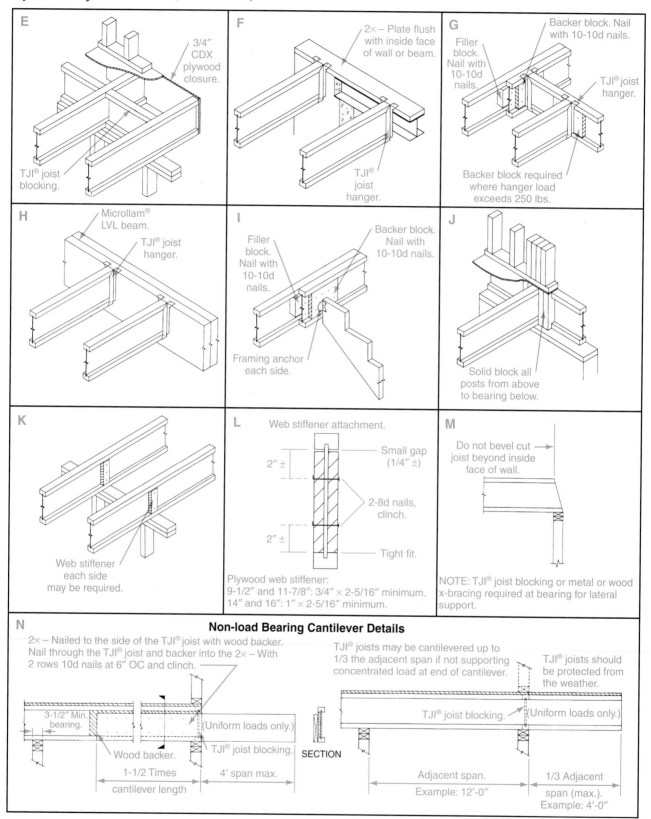

E

3/4" CDX plywood closure.

TJI® joist blocking.

F

2× – Plate flush with inside face of wall or beam.

TJI® joist hanger.

G

Backer block. Nail with 10-10d nails.

Filler block. Nail with 10-10d nails.

TJI® joist hanger.

Backer block required where hanger load exceeds 250 lbs.

H

Microllam® LVL beam.

TJI® joist hanger.

I

Filler block. Nail with 10-10d nails.

Backer block. Nail with 10-10d nails.

Framing anchor each side.

J

Solid block all posts from above to bearing below.

K

Web stiffener each side may be required.

L

Web stiffener attachment.

Small gap (1/4" ±)

2" ±

2-8d nails, clinch.

2" ±

Tight fit.

Plywood web stiffener:
9-1/2" and 11-7/8": 3/4" × 2-5/16" minimum.
14" and 16": 1" × 2-5/16" minimum.

M

Do not bevel cut joist beyond inside face of wall.

NOTE: TJI® joist blocking or metal or wood x-bracing required at bearing for lateral support.

N   **Non-load Bearing Cantilever Details**

2× – Nailed to the side of the TJI® joist with wood backer. Nail through the TJI® joist and backer into the 2× – With 2 rows 10d nails at 6" OC and clinch.

3-1/2" Min. bearing.

(Uniform loads only.)

Wood backer.

TJI® joist blocking.

1-1/2 Times cantilever length

4' span max.

TJI® joists may be cantilevered up to 1/3 the adjacent span if not supporting concentrated load at end of cantilever.

TJI® joists should be protected from the weather.

TJI® joist blocking.

(Uniform loads only.)

SECTION

Adjacent span.
Example: 12'-0"

1/3 Adjacent span (max.).
Example: 4'-0"

TJI® Roof Joist Details

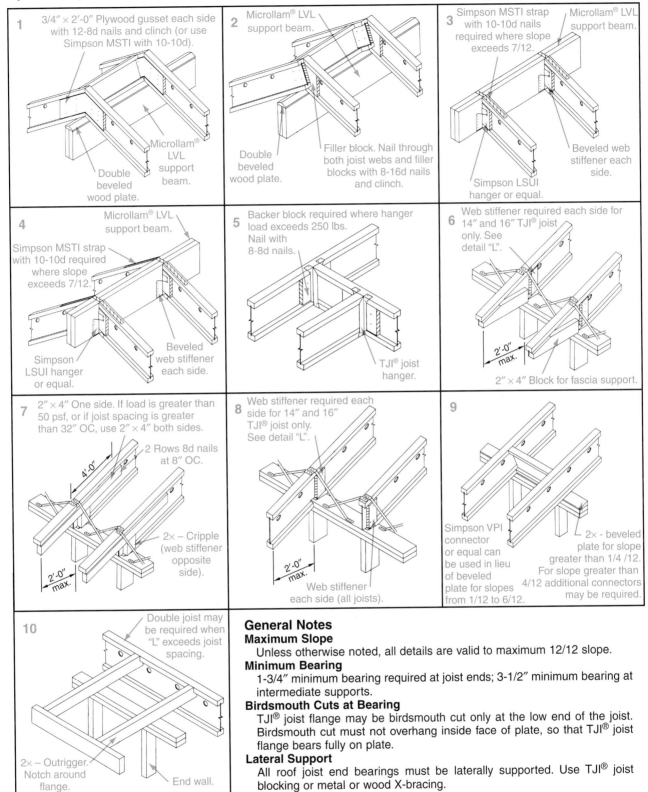

1 3/4″ × 2′-0″ Plywood gusset each side with 12-8d nails and clinch (or use Simpson MSTI with 10-10d). Double beveled wood plate. Microllam® LVL support beam.

2 Microllam® LVL support beam. Double beveled wood plate. Filler block. Nail through both joist webs and filler blocks with 8-16d nails and clinch.

3 Simpson MSTI strap with 10-10d nails required where slope exceeds 7/12. Microllam® LVL support beam. Beveled web stiffener each side. Simpson LSUI hanger or equal.

4 Microllam® LVL support beam. Simpson MSTI strap with 10-10d required where slope exceeds 7/12. Simpson LSUI hanger or equal. Beveled web stiffener each side.

5 Backer block required where hanger load exceeds 250 lbs. Nail with 8-8d nails. TJI® joist hanger.

6 Web stiffener required each side for 14″ and 16″ TJI® joist only. See detail "L". 2′-0″ max. 2″ × 4″ Block for fascia support.

7 2″ × 4″ One side. If load is greater than 50 psf, or if joist spacing is greater than 32″ OC, use 2″ × 4″ both sides. 4′-0″. 2 Rows 8d nails at 8″ OC. 2× – Cripple (web stiffener opposite side). 2′-0″ max.

8 Web stiffener required each side for 14″ and 16″ TJI® joist only. See detail "L". 2′-0″ max. Web stiffener each side (all joists).

9 Simpson VPI connector or equal can be used in lieu of beveled plate for slopes from 1/12 to 6/12. 2× - beveled plate for slope greater than 1/4 /12. For slope greater than 4/12 additional connectors may be required.

10 Double joist may be required when "L" exceeds joist spacing. 2× – Outrigger. Notch around flange. End wall.

General Notes

Maximum Slope
Unless otherwise noted, all details are valid to maximum 12/12 slope.

Minimum Bearing
1-3/4″ minimum bearing required at joist ends; 3-1/2″ minimum bearing at intermediate supports.

Birdsmouth Cuts at Bearing
TJI® joist flange may be birdsmouth cut only at the low end of the joist. Birdsmouth cut must not overhang inside face of plate, so that TJI® joist flange bears fully on plate.

Lateral Support
All roof joist end bearings must be laterally supported. Use TJI® joist blocking or metal or wood X-bracing.

Ventilation
1-1/2″ knockout holes at 12″OC may be used for cross-ventilation of joist space. Consult an expert on ventilation for specific requirements.

TJI® Joist Roof Span Chart

Low Slope (6/12 or less) and High Slope (6/12 through 12/12)
Maximum clear span in feet and inches (based on horizontal spans)

Joist Spacing		Live / Dead Load PSF	9-1/2" TJI®/25		11-7/8" TJI®/25		14" TJI®/35		16" TJI®/35	
			Low Slope	High Slope	Low Slope	High Slope	Low Slope	High Slope	Low Slope	High Slope
12"OC	Non-Snow (125%)	20/10	23'-10"	21'-5"	28'-4"	25'-6"	35'-3"	31'-9"	39'-1"	35'-2"
		20/15	22'-6"	20'-1"	26'-9"	23'-11"	33'-4"	29'-9"	36'-11"	33'-0"
		20/20	21'-5"	19'-0"	25'-6"	22'-7"	31'-9"	28'-2"	35'-2"	31'-3"
	Snow (115%)	25/10	22'-7"	20'-5"	26'-11"	24'-4"	33'-6"	30'-4"	37'-1"	33'-7"
		25/15	21'-6"	19'-3"	25'-7"	23'-0"	31'-11"	28'-7"	35'-4"	31'-8"
		30/10	21'-7"	19'-7"	25'-9"	23'-4"	32'-0"	29'-1"	35'-6"	32'-2"
		30/15	20'-8"	18'-7"	24'-7"	22'-2"	30'-8"	27'-7"	33'-11"	30'-7"
		40/10	19'-9"	18'-3"	23'-6"	21'-9"	29'-3"	27'-1"	32'-5"	30'-0"
		40/15	19'-4"	17'-6"	23'-0"	20'-10"	28'-8"	25'-11"	31'-9"	28'-9"
		50/10	18'-3"	17'-0"	21'-9"	20'-3"	27'-1"	25'-2"	30'-0"	27'-11"
		50/15	18'-3"	16'-7"	21'-9"	19'-9"	27'-1"	24'-7"	30'-0"	27'-3"
16"OC	Non-Snow (125%)	20/10	21'-6"	19'-5"	25'-8"	23'-1"	31'-11"	28'-9"	35'-4"	31'-10"
		20/15	20'-4"	18'-2"	24'-3"	21'-8"	30'-2"	26'-11"	33'-5"	29'-10"
		20/20	19'-4"	17'-2"	23'-0"	20'-6"	28'-8"	25'-6"	31'-9"	28'-3"
	Snow (115%)	25/10	20'-5"	18'-6"	24'-4"	22'-0"	30'-4"	27'-5"	33'-7"	30'-5"
		25/15	19'-5"	17'-5"	23'-2"	20'-9"	28'-10"	25'-11"	31'-11"	28'-8"
		30/10	19'-6"	17'-9"	23'-3"	21'-1"	29'-0"	26'-4"	32'-1"	29'-2"
		30/15	18'-8"	16'-10"	22'-3"	20'-1"	27'-8"	25'-0"	30'-8"	27'-8"
		40/10	17'-10"	16'-6"	21'-3"	19'-8"	26'-5"	24'-6"	29'-4"	27'-2"
		40/15	17'-5"	15'-10"	20'-9"	18'-10"	25'-10"	23'-6"	28'-8"	26'-0"
		50/10	16'-6"	15'-4"	19'-7"	18'-3"	24'-5"	22'-9"	26'-9"	25'-3"
		50/15	16'-5"	15'-0"	19'-6"	17'-10"	24'-5"	22'-3"	24'-8"	23'-3"
19.2"OC	Non-Snow (125%)	20/10	20'-2"	18'-2"	24'-1"	21'-8"	30'-0"	27'-0"	33'-2"	29'-11"
		20/15	19'-1"	17'-1"	22'-9"	20'-4"	28'-3"	25'-3"	31'-4"	28'-0"
		20/20	18'-2"	16'-2"	21'-7"	19'-3"	26'-11"	23'-11"	29'-10"	26'-6"
	Snow (115%)	25/10	19'-2"	17'-4"	22'-10"	20'-8"	28'-5"	25'-9"	31'-6"	28'-6"
		25/15	18'-3"	16'-5"	21'-9"	19'-6"	27'-0"	24'-4"	29'-11"	26'-11"
		30/10	18'-4"	16'-8"	21'-10"	19'-10"	27'-2"	24'-8"	30'-1"	27'-4"
		30/15	17'-6"	15'-10"	20'-10"	18'-10"	26'-0"	23'-5"	28'-9"	26'-0"
		40/10	16'-8"	15'-6"	19'-11"	18'-5"	24'-9"	23'-0"	26'-8"	25'-4"
		40/15	16'-4"	14'-10"	19'-2"	17'-8"	24'-0"	22'-0"	24'-3"	22'-8"
		50/10	15'-5"	14'-5"	17'-10"	17'-1"	22'-5"	21'-4"	22'-8"	21'-8"
		50/15	15'-0"	14'-1"	16'-6"	15'-7"	20'-8"	19'-6"	20'-11"	19'-9"
24"OC	Non-Snow (125%)	20/10	18'-8"	16'-10"	22'-3"	20'-1"	27'-8"	25'-0"	30'-8"	27'-8"
		20/15	17'-7"	15'-9"	21'-0"	18'-9"	26'-2"	23'-5"	29'-0"	25'-11"
		20/20	16'-9"	14'-11"	20'-0"	17'-9"	24'-10"	22'-1"	27'-6"	24'-6"
	Snow (115%)	25/10	17'-9"	16'-1"	21'-1"	19'-1"	26'-3"	23'-10"	29'-2"	26'-5"
		25/15	16'-10"	15'-2"	20'-1"	18'-0"	25'-0"	22'-6"	26'-2"	23'-10"
		30/10	16'-11"	15'-5"	20'-2"	18'-4"	25'-1"	22'-10"	26'-6"	24'-11"
		30/15	16'-2"	14'-7"	18'-8"	17'-2"	23'-4"	21'-6"	23'-7"	21'-9"
		40/10	15'-5"	14'-4"	17'-2"	16'-3"	21'-6"	20'-5"	21'-9"	20'-8"
		40/15	14'-2"	13'-2"	15'-7"	14'-7"	19'-6"	18'-3"	19'-10"	18'-6"
		50/10	13'-2"	12'-8"	14'-7"	14'-0"	18'-3"	17'-6"	18'-6"	17'-9"
		50/15	12'-2"	11'-6"	13'-6"	12'-9"	16'-10"	15'-11"	17'-1"	16'-2"

1. Roof joists to be sloped 1/4" in 12" minimum. No camber provided.
2. Maximum deflection is limited to L/180 at total load, L/240 at live load.

3. Tables are based on a support beam or wall at the high end. Applications utilizing ridge boards are not covered by these tables.

TJI® Design Properties and Span Charts

Design Properties

Depth (Inches)	Weight (PLF)[1]	EI* 10⁶In²lbs	Maximum Veritical Shear (lbs)			Maximum Resistive Moment (ft-lbs)		
			100%	115%	125%	100%	115%	125%
9-1/2" TJI/25 Joist	1.9	170	805	925	1006	2940	3380	3675
11-7/8" TJI/25 Joist	2.2	285	875	1006	1094	3935	4525	4920
14" TJI/35 Joist	2.8	550	1100	1265	1375	6450	7420	8060
16" TJI/35 Joist	3	745	1100	1265	1375	7570	8705	9460

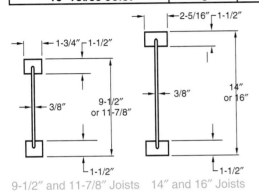

9-1/2" and 11-7/8" Joists   14" and 16" Joists

*The following formula approximates the uniform load deflection of Δ (inches)

$$\Delta = \frac{5w\ell^4}{384\,EI} + \frac{w\ell^2}{2.7dx\times10^5}$$

w = uniform load in pounds per lineal inch
ℓ = clear span in inches
d = out to out depth of the joist
EI = value from table

NOTE: The shear values above are based on an assumed minimum bearing length of 1-3/4".

[1] Weight shown are for Douglas Fir Microllam® LVL flanges. For southern yellow pine Microllam® LVL flanges, increase weight approximately 20%.

Residential Floor Span Charts

Minimum Criteria per Code

OC Spacing	Joist Depth			
	9-1/2"	11-7/8"		16"
12"	18'-7"		27'-3"	30'-1"
16"		20'-2"	24'-8"	27'-4"
19.2"	15'-11"	18'-11"	23'-2"	25'-8"
24"	14'-9"	17'-6"	20'-3"	21'-10"

NOTE: Based on minimum code deflection criteria of L/360 at live load. For stiffer floors, please see "Trus Joist Recommended Span" table. See "A Word About Floor Performance" below.

Trus Joist Recommended Spans

OC Spacing	Joist Depth			
	9-1/2"	11-7/8"	14"	16"
12"	16'-10"	20'-0"	24'-6"	27'-1"
16"	15'-4"	18'-2"	22'-3"	24'-8"
19.2"	14'-5"	17'-1"	20'-11"	23'-2"
24"	13'-4"	15'-10"	19'-4"	21'-5"

NOTE: Based on L/480 live load deflection.

General Notes

1. Based on residential floor load of 40 psf live load and 10 psf dead load.
2. Assumes composite action with single layer of glue-nailed plywood decking for deflection only. *Spans shall be reduced 5" where sheathing panels are nailed only.*
3. Spans are based on clear distance between supports.
4. Web stiffeners (see detail "K") are required at intermediate supports where joists are continuous span, bearing width is less than 5-1/4", and either span is greater than:
   13'-8" (for 9-1/2" and 11-7/8" TJI® joists @ 24"OC)
   17'-2" (for 11-7/8" TJI® joists @19.2"OC)
   19'-2" (for 14" and 16" TJI® joists @ 24"OC)
   24'-0" (for 16" TJI® joists @ 19.2"OC)

A Word About Floor Performance

The spans indicated in the "Minimum Criteria Per Code" chart above meet or exceed all code requirements and may provide acceptable performance to the user. But, in addition to safely supporting the loads to be imposed on it, a floor system must perform to the satisfaction of the end user. Since expectancy levels may vary from one user to another, designing a floor system becomes a subjective issue requiring judgment as to the sensitivity of the occupant.

The second span chart above entitled "Trus Joist Recommended Spans" has been developed as a guide to help builders construct higher-quality floors. Spans in the "Trus Joist Recommended Spans" chart were developed using stricter deflection limits (see note under chart) to limit deflection over longer spans.

In addition to joist deflection, several other factors may affect the performance of the floor system. A glue-nailed floor system will perform better than a nailed floor. Deflection of the sheathing material between the joists can be reduced by increasing the thickness of sheathing or decreasing the spacing of the joist. Proper installation, including adequate and level support for the joists, and care in fastening of the joists and sheathing are essential to the system performance.

In some cases where the system is stiff and very little dead load exists (i.e. partition walls, ceilings, furniture, etc.) vibrations may occur. Vibrations are generally sufficiently dampened when a ceiling is directly attached to the bottom flange of the joists. When the joists occur in a crawlspace or over an unfinished basement, the vibration can be minimized by nailing a continuous 2" × 4" (flat) perpendicular to the joists' bottom flanges at midspan and tying off to the end walls.

Microllam® LVL Details

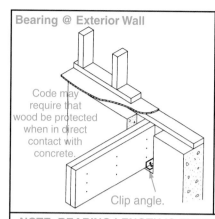

Bearing @ Exterior Wall

Code may require that wood be protected when in direct contact with concrete.

Clip angle.

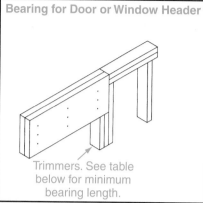

Bearing for Door or Window Header

Trimmers. See table below for minimum bearing length.

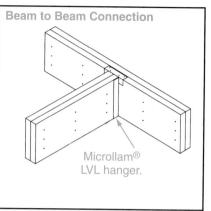

Beam to Beam Connection

Microllam® LVL hanger.

NOTE: BEARING LENGTH IS EXTREMELY CRITICAL AND MUST BE CONSIDERED FOR EACH APPLICATION.

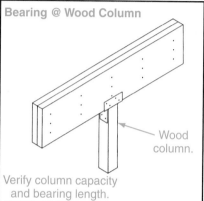

Bearing @ Wood Column

Wood column.

Verify column capacity and bearing length.

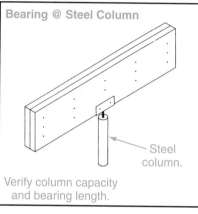

Bearing @ Steel Column

Steel column.

Verify column capacity and bearing length.

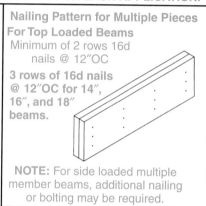

Nailing Pattern for Multiple Pieces For Top Loaded Beams

Minimum of 2 rows 16d nails @ 12"OC

3 rows of 16d nails @ 12"OC for 14", 16", and 18" beams.

NOTE: For side loaded multiple member beams, additional nailing or bolting may be required.

Bearing Length Requirements

	Minimum Bearing Length								
	One-Piece Beam			Two-Piece Beam			Three-Piece Beam		
Reaction (Pounds × 1,000)	100%	115%	125%	100%	115%	125%	100%	115%	125%
1	1.5"	1.5"	1.5"	1.5"	1.5"	1.5"	1.5"	1.5"	1.5"
2	3"	2.5"	2.5"	1.5"	1.5"	1.5"	1.5"	1.5"	1.5"
3	4"	3.5"	3"	2"	1.5"	1.5"	1.5"	1.5"	1.5"
4	5"	4.5"	4"	3"	2.5"	2.5"	2"	1.5"	1.5"
5	6"	5.5"	5"	3.5"	3"	3"	2.5"	2"	2"
6	7.5"	6.5"	6"	4"	3.5"	3"	3"	2.5"	2.5"
7	8.5"	7.5"	7"	4.5"	4"	3.5"	3"	3"	2.5"
8	9.5"	8.5"	8"	5"	4.5"	4"	3.5"	3"	3"
9	—	—	—	5.5"	5"	4.5"	4"	3.5"	3"
10	—	—	—	6"	5.5"	5"	4.5"	4"	3.5"
11	—	—	—	6.5"	6"	5.5"	4.5"	4"	4"
12	—	—	—	7.5"	6.5"	6"	5"	4.5"	4"
13	—	—	—	8"	7"	6.5"	5.5"	5"	4.5"
14	—	—	—	8.5"	7.5"	7"	6"	5"	5"
15	—	—	—	9"	8"	7.5"	6"	5.5"	5"
16	—	—	—	9.5"	8.5"	8"	6.5"	6"	5.5"
17	—	—	—	—	—	—	7"	6"	5.5"
18	—	—	—	—	—	—	7.5"	6.5"	6"
19	—	—	—	—	—	—	7.5"	7"	6.5"
20	—	—	—	—	—	—	8"	7"	6.5"
21	—	—	—	—	—	—	8.5"	7.5"	7"
22	—	—	—	—	—	—	9"	8"	7"

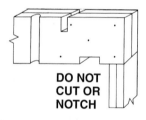

DO NOT CUT OR NOTCH

Notes

1. A minimum of 1.5" of bearing length is required.
2. Bearing across full width of beam is assumed.
3. Assumes structural adequacy of supporting member.
4. Assumes 500 psi bearing stress on beam. May be further limited by bearing stress on supported member.
5. *16" and 18" deep beams are to be used in multiple-member units only.*
6. Lateral support required at bearing points.
7. Nails installed on the narrow face (top edge) shall not be spaced any closer than 4" for 10d common and 3" for 8d common.

Allowable Load in Pounds per Linear Foot (PLF)

Total load column limits deflection to L/180. For stiffer criteria, check L/240 column.
Check local code for deflection criteria.

Span (ft)	One-1-3/4″ × 5-1/2″ Total Load Snow (115%)	Non-Snow (125%)	Defl. L/240	One-1-3/4″ × 7-1/4″ Total Load Snow (115%)	Non-Snow (125%)	Defl. L/240	One-1-3/4″ × 9-1/2″ Total Load Snow (115%)	Non-Snow (125%)	Defl. L/240	One-1-3/4″ × 11-7/8″ Total Load Snow (115%)	Non-Snow (125%)	Defl. L/240
4	1348	1465	1402	1986	2159	—	3006	3268	—	4494	4885	—
5	863	938	764	1432	1556	—	2126	2311	—	3006	3268	—
6	599	611	458	994	1081	989	1632	1774	—	2259	2455	—
7	393	393	295	730	794	646	1199	1303	—	1805	1962	—
8	267	267	201	559	591	444	918	998	943	1392	1502	—
9	190	190	142	423	423	317	725	788	681	1092	1187	—
10	139	139	104	312	312	234	587	639	507	884	961	943
11	105	105	79	236	236	177	486	516	387	731	795	725
12	81	81	61	183	183	138	402	402	301	614	668	569
13	64	64	48	145	145	109	319	319	239	523	569	454
14	52	52	39	117	117	88	257	257	193	451	490	367
15	42	42	31	95	95	71	211	211	158	393	402	301
16	—	—	—	79	79	59	174	174	131	334	334	250
17	—	—	—	66	66	49	146	146	109	280	280	210
18	—	—	—	56	56	42	123	123	93	237	237	178
19	—	—	—	47	47	35	105	105	79	203	203	152
20	—	—	—	41	41	30	90	90	68	174	174	131
21	—	—	—	—	—	—	78	78	59	151	151	113
22	—	—	—	—	—	—	68	68	51	132	132	99
23	—	—	—	—	—	—	60	60	45	116	116	87
24	—	—	—	—	—	—	53	53	40	102	102	77
25	—	—	—	—	—	—	47	47	35	90	90	68
26	—	—	—	—	—	—	42	42	31	81	81	60
27	—	—	—	—	—	—	—	—	—	72	72	54
28	—	—	—	—	—	—	—	—	—	65	65	49
29	—	—	—	—	—	—	—	—	—	58	58	44
30	—	—	—	—	—	—	—	—	—	53	53	40

Microllam® LVL Design Properties

Size	Maximum Vertical Sheer (lbs) 100%	115%	125%	Maximum Resistive Moment (ft-lbs) 100%	115%	125%	Moment of Inertia (in⁴)	Weight (lbs/ft)[1]
1-3/4″ × 5-1/2″	1830	2105	2285	2345	2695	2930	25	2.50
1-3/4″ × 7-1/4″	2410	2770	3010	3890	4475	4860	55	3.25
1-3/4″ × 9-1/2″	3160	3630	3950	6385	7345	7980	125	4.25
1-3/4″ × 11-7/8″	3950	4540	4940	9615	11055	12015	245	5.30
1-3/4″ × 14″	4655	5355	5820	13000	14950	16250	400	6.25
1-3/4″ × 16″	5320	6120	6650	16605	19100	20760	595	7.15
1-3/4″ × 18″	5985	6880	7480	20610	23700	25760	850	8.00

Allowable Design Stresses

Modulus of elasticity	E	$= 2.0 \times 10^6$ spi	*For 12-inch depth. For other depths, multiply by $\left[\dfrac{12}{d}\right]^{\frac{1}{6}}$
Flexural stress	$F_b{}^*$	$= 2800$ psi	*See NER 126 for additional design information.
Tension parallel to grain	F_t	$= 1850$ psi	
Compression perpendicular to grain parallelt to glue line	F_c	$= 500$ psi	*Assumes continuous lateral support of top of beam (simple span applications).
Compression parallel to grain	$F_c\text{II}$	$= 2700$ psi	
Horizontal shear perpendicular to glue line	F_v	$= 285$ psi	[1]Weights shown are for Douglas Fir Microllam® LVL. For southern yellow pine Microllam® LVL, increase weight approximately 10%.

Microllam® LVL Allowable Load (Roof)

One–1-3/4" × 14"			One–1-3/4" × 16"*			One–1-3/4" × 18"*			
Total Load		Defl.	Total Load		Defl.	Total Load		Defl.	
Snow (115%)	Non-Snow (125%)	L/240	Snow (115%)	Non-Snow (125%)	L/240	Snow (115%)	Non-Snow (125%)	L/240	Span (ft)
6424	6983	—	9177	9975	—	—	—	—	4
4015	4364	—	5244	5700	—	6883	7481	—	5
2920	3174	—	3671	3990	—	4588	4988	—	6
2294	2494	—	2824	3069	—	3441	3741	—	7
1869	2031	—	2294	2494	—	2753	2993	—	8
1477	1605	—	1886	2050	—	2294	2494	—	9
1196	1300	—	1528	1661	—	1896	2061	—	10
988	1074	—	1263	1372	—	1567	1703	—	11
831	903	899	1061	1153	—	1317	1431	—	12
708	769	720	904	983	—	1122	1219	—	13
610	663	586	779	847	—	967	1051	—	14
532	578	482	679	738	701	843	916	—	15
467	508	401	597	649	586	741	805	—	16
414	450	338	529	575	494	656	713	687	17
369	382	286	472	513	420	585	636	586	18
327	327	245	423	460	360	525	571	503	19
282	282	211	382	414	311	474	515	435	20
244	244	183	346	360	270	430	467	379	21
213	213	160	315	315	236	392	426	331	22
187	187	141	277	277	207	358	389	292	23
166	166	124	244	244	183	329	344	258	24
147	147	110	217	217	163	303	306	229	25
131	131	98	194	194	145	273	273	205	26
117	117	88	173	173	130	244	244	183	27
105	105	79	156	156	117	220	220	165	28
95	95	71	141	141	105	198	198	149	29
86	86	64	127	127	95	180	180	135	30

Notes

- This table is based on uniform loads and simple spans.
- Table is for one beam. When properly fastened together, double the values for two beams; triple for three. When top loaded, fasten together with a minimum of two rows of 16d nails at 12"OC. *Use three rows of 16d nails at 12"OC for 14", 16", and 18" beams.*
- Microllam® lumber beams are made without camber; therefore, in addition to complying with the deflection limits of the applicable building code, other deflection considerations should be evaluated, such as ponding (positive drainage is essential) and aesthetics.
- Roof members should either be sloped for drainage or designed to account for load and deflection as specified in the applicable building code.
- Assumes continuous lateral support of the top edge of beam.
- Lateral support required at bearing points.
- Bearing area to be calculated for specific application.
- * *16" and 18" deep beams are to be used in multiple-member units only.*

Microllam® LVL Allowable Load (Floor)

Allowable Load in Pounds per Linear Foot (PLF)

Span (ft.)	One-1-3/4" × 5-1/2" Live Load	One-1-3/4" × 5-1/2" Total Load	One-1-3/4" × 7-1/4" Live Load	One-1-3/4" × 7-1/4" Total Load	One-1-3/4" × 9-1/2" Live Load	One-1-3/4" × 9-1/2" Total Load	One-1-3/4" × 11-7/8" Live Load	One-1-3/4" × 11-7/8" Total Load	One-1-3/4" × 14" Live Load	One-1-3/4" × 14" Total Load	One-1-3/4" × 16"* Live Load	One-1-3/4" × 16"* Total Load	One-1-3/4" × 18"* Live Load	One-1-3/4" × 18"* Total Load
6	305	458	660	865	1353	1419	—	1964	—	2539	—	3192	—	3990
7	197	295	431	635	903	1043	—	1570	—	1995	—	2455	—	2993
8	134	201	296	444	926	798	1144	1202	—	1625	—	1995	—	2394
9	95	142	211	317	454	631	837	949	—	1284	—	1640	—	1995
10	70	104	156	234	338	507	629	769	981	1040	—	1329	—	1649
11	53	79	118	177	258	387	484	636	760	860	1085	1098	—	1363
12	41	61	92	138	201	301	379	534	599	722	861	923	—	1145
13	—	—	73	109	160	239	302	454	480	615	694	786	952	976
14	—	—	58	88	129	193	245	367	390	531	566	678	781	841
15	—	—	48	71	105	158	201	301	321	462	468	590	647	733
16	—	—	39	59	87	131	167	250	268	401	390	519	542	644
17	—	—	—	—	73	109	140	210	225	338	329	460	458	570
18	—	—	—	—	62	93	119	178	191	286	280	410	390	509
19	—	—	—	—	53	79	101	152	163	245	240	360	335	457
20	—	—	—	—	45	68	87	131	141	211	207	311	290	412
21	—	—	—	—	39	59	76	113	122	183	180	270	252	374
22	—	—	—	—	—	—	—	—	107	160	157	236	221	331
23	—	—	—	—	—	—	—	—	94	141	138	207	194	292
24	—	—	—	—	—	—	—	—	83	124	122	183	172	258
25	—	—	—	—	—	—	—	—	—	—	109	163	153	229
26	—	—	—	—	—	—	—	—	—	—	97	145	136	205

1. To size a beam for use in a floor, it is necessary to check both live load and total load. Make sure the selected beam will work in both columns.
2. Live load column is based on deflection of L/360. Check local code for other deflection criteria.
3. Total load column limits deflection to L/240.
4. For deflection limits of L/240 and L/480 multiply loads shown in L/360 by 1.5 and 0.75 respectively.

Notes
- This table is based on uniform loads and simple spans.
- Table is for one beam. When properly fastened together, double the values for two beams; triple for three. When top loaded, fasten together with a minimum of two rows of 16d nails at 12"OC. *Use three rows of 16d nails at 12"OC for 14", 16", and 18" beams.*
- Microllam® LVL beams are made without camber and will deflect under load.
- Assumes continuous lateral support of the top edge of beam
- Lateral support required at bearing points.
- Bearing area to be calculated for specific application.

16" and 18" deep beams are to be used in multiple-member units only.

Side-Loaded Microllam® LVL Connection for Multiple-Member Units

No. of pieces	Nailed Connection[1] — 2 rows 16d common wire at 12"OC	Nailed Connection[1] — 3 rows 16d common wire at 12"OC	Through-Bolted Connection[2] — 2 rows 1/2" bolts at 24"OC staggered	Through-Bolted Connection[2] — 2 rows 1/2" bolts at 12"OC	Through-Bolted Connection[2] — 2 rows 1/2" bolts at 6"OC
2	420	630	580	1160	2320
3	320	480	440	880	1760
4	Not Recommended		Should only be used when loads are applied to **both** sides of the members. 390	780	1560

Maximum Uniform Load Applied to Outside Member (PLF)

Notes
- Verify adequacy of beam in Table 6 or Table 8.
- Values listed are for 100% stress level. Increase 15% for snow-loaded roof conditions; increase 25% for non-snow roof conditions.
- Other connections are possible with specific design by the design professional.
  (1) For a three-piece member, the nailing specified is from each side for a total of six nails per foot (three from each side).
  (2) Bolt holes are to be the same diameter as the bolt and located 2" from the top and bottom of the member.

International Residential Code

A single model code for residential construction suitable for use throughout the US is now a reality. It is the International Residential Code (IRC) and incorporates input from BOCA, ICBO, and SBCCI. It was approved in September 1999 and published January 2000. State adoptions of the IRC are expected in 2003.

The IRC covers one- and two-family detached dwellings and apartment buildings up to three stories. The new IRC is the result of pressure from manufacturers of building materials and architects. Both groups cited inconsistencies in the existing model codes:

- BOCA's National Building Code. Used mainly in the Northeast and Midwest.
- ICBO's Uniform Building Code. Used in the West.
- SBCCI's Standard Building Code. Used in the Southeast.
- CABO's One and Two Family Dwelling Code.

The IRC is a complete, stand-alone code. It includes chapters on foundations, framing, plumbing, electrical, mechanical, fuel gas, and energy. An entire residential dwelling can be built from this code. It includes identical requirements for electrical and gas that are presented in the NFPA National Electrical Code and the American Gas Association's Fuel Gas Code.

The IRC also includes detailed requirements for some newer construction methods, such as steel stud construction, frost-protected shallow foundations, and insulated concrete forms. The new code provides for regional differences in factors such as frost depths, snow loads, and the level of termite threat. Criteria for building in areas subject to flooding, high winds, and seismic activity are also included.

Rigid Foam Comparison

	Expanded Polystyrene (EPS)	Extruded Polystyrene (XPS)	Polyisocyanurate (PIR)
Insulating Value	R-4 per inch	R-5 per inch	R-74 per inch
Density	0.9 pcf to 1.8 pcf	2 pcf	Varies
Compressive Strength	10 psi to 25 psi	30 psi	16 psi to 25 psi
Perm-Rating	5.0 per inch	1.2 per inch	0.4 to 1.6 per inch
Foil Face	Yes	Yes	Yes
Polyethylene Face	Yes	Yes	Yes
Kraft Paper Face	Yes	Yes	Yes
Fiberglass Mat Face	No	No	Yes
Fire Resistance	Softens at 165°F Melts at 200°F	Softens at 165°F Melts at 200°F	Maximum service temperature is 250°F
Common Applications	Exterior Stucco Below Grade Under Slab Wall Frames	Exterior Stucco Below Grade Under Slab Wall Frames	Exterior Stucco Roof Applications Under Slab Wall Frames
Gases Produced when Burned	Carbon Monoxide Carbon Dioxide	Carbon Monoxide Carbon Dioxide	Hydrogen Cyanide* Nitrogen Oxide*

*Chemical asphyxiants

CSI Specification

Construction Specifications Institute, Inc., publishes a coding system that identifies construction activity areas that should be considered when planning a structure. Major divisions of the system are listed here to acquaint you with the classifications.

Introductory Information
00001 Project Title Page
00005 Certifications Page
00007 Seals Page
00010 Table of Contents
00015 List of Drawings
00020 List of Schedules

Bidding Requirements
00100 Bid Solicitation
00200 Instructions to Bidders
00300 Information Available to Bidders
00400 Bid Forms and Supplements
00490 Bidding Addenda

Contracting Requirements
00500 Agreement
00600 Bonds and Certificates
00700 General Conditions
00800 Supplementary Conditions
00900 Addenda and Modifications

Division 1—General Requirements
01100 Summary
01200 Price and Payment Procedures
01300 Administrative Requirements
01400 Quality Requirements
01500 Temporary Facilities and Controls
01600 Product Requirements
01700 Execution Requirements
01800 Facility Operation
01900 Facility Decommissioning

Division 2—Site Construction
02050 Basic Site Materials and Methods
02100 Site Remediation
02200 Site Preparation
02300 Earthwork
02400 Tunneling, Boring, and Jacking
02450 Foundation and Load-Bearing Elements
02500 Utility Services
02600 Drainage and Containment
02700 Bases, Ballasts, Pavements, and Appurtenances
02800 Site Improvements and Amenities
02900 Planting
02950 Site Restoration and Rehabilitation

Division 3—Concrete
03050 Basic Concrete Materials and Methods
03100 Concrete Forms and Accessories
03200 Concrete Reinforcement
03300 Cast-in-Place Concrete
03400 Precast Concrete
03500 Cementitious Decks and Underlayment
03600 Grouts
03700 Mass Concrete
03900 Concrete Restoration and Cleaning

Division 4—Masonry
04050 Basic Masonry Materials and Methods
04200 Masonry Units
04400 Stone
04500 Refractories
04600 Corrosion-Resistant Masonry
04700 Simulated Masonry
04800 Masonry Assemblies
04900 Masonry Restoration and Cleaning

Division 5—Metals
05050 Basic Metal Materials and Methods
05100 Structural Metal Framing
05200 Metal Joists
05300 Metal Deck
05400 Cold-Formed Metal Framing
05500 Metal Fabrications
05600 Hydraulic Fabrications
05650 Railroad Track and Accessories
05700 Ornamental Metal
05800 Expansion Control
05900 Metal Restoration and Cleaning

Division 6—Wood and Plastics
06050 Basic Wood and Plastic Materials and Methods
06100 Rough Carpentry
06200 Finish Carpentry
06400 Architectural Woodwork
06500 Structural Plastics
06600 Plastic Fabrications
06900 Wood and Plastic Restoration and Cleaning

Division 7—Thermal and Moisture Protection

07050 Basic Thermal and Moisture Protection Materials and Methods
07100 Damp-Proofing and Waterproofing
07200 Thermal Protection
07300 Shingles, Roof Tiles, and Roof Coverings
07400 Roofing and Siding Panels
07500 Membrane Roofing
07600 Flashing and Sheet Metal
07700 Roof Specialties and Accessories
07800 Fire and Smoke Protection
07900 Joint Sealers

Division 8—Doors and Windows

08050 Basic Door and Window Materials and Methods
08100 Metal Doors and Frames
08200 Wood and Plastic Doors
08300 Specialty Doors
08400 Entrances and Storefronts
08500 Windows
08600 Skylights
08700 Hardware
08800 Glazing
08900 Glazed Curtain Wall

Division 9—Finishes

09050 Basic Finish Materials and Methods
09100 Metal Support Assemblies
09200 Plaster and Gypsum Board
09300 Tile
09400 Terrazzo
09500 Ceilings
09600 Flooring
09700 Wall Finishes
09800 Acoustical Treatment
09900 Paints and Coatings

Division 10—Specialties

10100 Visual Display Boards
10150 Compartments and Cubicles
10200 Louvers and Vents
10240 Grilles and Screens
10250 Service Walls
10260 Wall and Corner Guards
10270 Access Flooring
10290 Pest Control
10300 Fireplaces and Stoves
10340 Manufactured Exterior Specialties
10350 Flagpoles
10400 Identification Devices
10450 Pedestrian Control Devices

10500 Lockers
10520 Fire Protection Specialties
10530 Protective Covers
10550 Postal Specialties
10600 Partitions
10670 Storage Shelving
10700 Exterior Protection
10750 Telephone Specialties
10800 Toilet, Bath, and Laundry Accessories
10880 Scales
10900 Wardrobe and Closet Specialties

Division 11—Equipment

11010 Maintenance Equipment
11020 Security and Vault Equipment
11030 Teller and Service Equipment
11040 Ecclesiastical Equipment
11050 Library Equipment
11060 Theater and Stage Equipment
11070 Instrumental Equipment
11080 Registration Equipment
11090 Checkroom Equipment
11100 Mercantile Equipment
11110 Commercial Laundry and Dry Cleaning Equipment
11120 Vending Equipment
11130 Audio-Visual Equipment
11140 Vehicle Service Equipment
11150 Parking Control Equipment
11160 Loading Dock Equipment
11170 Solid Waste Handling Equipment
11190 Detention Equipment
11200 Water Supply and Treatment Equipment
11280 Hydraulic Gates and Valves
11300 Fluid Waste Treatment and Disposal Equipment
11400 Food Service Equipment
11450 Residential Equipment
11460 Unit Kitchens
11470 Darkroom Equipment
11480 Athletic, Recreational, and Therapeutic Equipment
11500 Industrial and Process Equipment
11600 Laboratory Equipment
11650 Planetarium Equipment
11660 Observatory Equipment
11680 Office Equipment
11700 Medical Equipment
11780 Mortuary Equipment
11850 Navigation Equipment
11870 Agricultural Equipment
11900 Exhibit Equipment

Division 12—Furnishings

12050 Fabrics
12100 Art
12300 Manufactured Casework
12400 Furnishings and Accessories
12500 Furniture
12600 Multiple Seating
12700 Systems Furniture
12800 Interior Plants and Planters
12900 Furnishings Restoration and Repair

Division 13—Special Construction

13010 Air-Supported Structures
13020 Building Modules
13030 Special-Purpose Rooms
13080 Sound, Vibration, and Seismic Control
13090 Radiation Protection
13100 Lightning Protection
13110 Cathodic Protection
13120 Pre-Engineered Structures
13150 Swimming Pools
13160 Aquariums
13165 Aquatic Park Facilities
13170 Tubs and Pools
13175 Ice Rinks
13185 Kennels and Animal Shelters
13190 Site-Constructed Incinerators
13200 Storage Tanks
13220 Filter Underdrains and Media
13230 Digestor Covers and Appurtenances
13240 Oxygenation Systems
13260 Sludge Conditioning Systems
13280 Hazardous Material Remediation
13400 Measurement and Control
         Instrumentation
13500 Recording Instrumentation
13550 Transportation Control
         Instrumentation
13600 Solar and Wind Energy Equipment
13700 Security Access and Surveillance
13800 Building Automation and Control
13850 Detection and Alarm
13900 Fire Suppression

Division 14—Conveying Systems

14100 Dumbwaiters
14200 Elevators
14300 Escalators and Moving Walks
14400 Lifts
14500 Material Handling
14600 Hoists and Cranes
14700 Turntables
14800 Scaffolding
14900 Transportation

Division 15—Mechanical

15050 Basic Mechanical Materials and
         Methods
15100 Building Services Piping
15200 Process Piping
15300 Fire Protection Piping
15400 Plumbing Fixtures and Equipment
15500 Heat-Generation Equipment
15600 Refrigeration Equipment
15700 Heating, Ventilating, and Air
         Conditioning Equipment
15800 Air Distribution
15900 HVAC Instrumentation and Controls
15950 Testing, Adjusting, and Balancing

Division 16—Electrical

16050 Basic Electrical Materials and Methods
16100 Wiring Methods
16200 Electrical Power
16300 Transmission and Distribution
16400 Low-Voltage Distribution
16500 Lighting
16700 Communications
16800 Sound and Video

Acknowledgements

The authors and publisher would like to thank the following individuals and companies for their assistance and contributions.

20-20 Computerized Design
A. O. Smith Water Products Company
AFM Corporation
AGS&R Studios
Alpine Structures
Alside
American ConForm Industries, Inc.
American Institute of Steel Construction
Andersen Corporation
Aqua Glass
Arcways, Incorporated
Armstrong World Industries, Inc.
ART, Inc.
Arthur Rutenberg Homes, Inc.
Associated Foam Manufacturers, Inc.
Atlas Roll-Lite Door Corporation
American Olean Tile Company
Autodesk, Inc.
Belden Electronics Division
Berol USA
Boise Cascade Corporation
Broan-NuTone, A Nortek Company
Brownlee, David
California Redwood Association
Campbell, Larry
Caradco
Carrier Corporation
Cathedralite Domes
CertainTeed Corporation
Cor-A-Vent, Inc.
CPI Plastics Group, Ltd.
Crane Co.
Craycroft Brick Company
Cultured Stone by Stucco Stone Products, Inc.
DesignJet Division, Hewlett-Packard
Domes and Homes, Inc.
Donley Brothers Company
Elk Corporation

Eneco Corporation
Federal Emergency Management Agency (FEMA)
Fegan, Ed
First Alert®
Floor Seal Technology, Inc.
Focal Point, Inc.
Formica Corporation
Four Seasons Sunrooms
Fowler, Darlana
Geiser, Helmuth A.; member AIBD
General Electric Company
Georgia-Pacific Corporation
Greyfox Systems
Hawk, Ken
Heatilator, Inc.
Hexadome of America
Home Automation, Inc.
Honeywell, Inc.
International Conference of Building Officials
James Hardie® Siding Products
Jeff Burgin Builders
K & S Testing and Engineering, Inc.
Kemeny, William
Kicklighter, Brad L.
King, Lis
Koh-I-Noor Rapidograph, Inc.
Kohler Co.
KraftMaid Cabinetry
Kurta
Lennox Industries, Inc.
Leviton Manufacturing Co., Inc.
Lindal Cedar Homes, Inc., Seattle, Washington
Lindeman, Linda
Lite-Form, Inc.
Logan Company
Lutron Electronics, Inc.
Manufactured Housing Institute
Marathon Water Heater Company
Marvin Windows

Midwestern Consulting, Inc.
Monterey Domes
Morgan Products, Ltd.
National Forest Products Association
National Solar Heating and Cooling
    Information Center
NMC/Focal Point
Norandex/Reynolds Building Products
Northern Energy Homes
OnQ Technologies, Inc.
Osmose Wood Products
Peachtree Doors, Inc.
Pella/Rolscreen Company
Pittsburgh Corning Corporation
Portland Cement Association
Potlatch Forests, Inc.
Pozzi Wood Windows
President Benjamin Harrison Memorial Home
Preway, Inc.
Prime Computer, Inc.
Progress Lighting
Radiant Electric Heat, Inc.
Radiant Heat, Inc.; Uecker, E.
Red Cedar Shingle and Handsplit Shake
    Bureau
Rolatape Corporation
Sater Design Collection, Inc.
Sauder Woodworking Co.
Schulte Corporation
Sewell, A.
Shouldice
SoftPlan Systems, Inc.
Sowa, Donald F.; ARA
Square D Company
Staedtler Mars GmbH & Co.
Stanley Hardware
Stone Products Corporation
Summitville Tile
Superior Fireplace Company
The Aladdin Co.
The Atrium Door and Window Corporation

The Engineered Wood Association
The Garlinghouse Company
The Oshkosh, WI private residence of
    Chancellor Richard H. Wells and family—
    formerly the Alberta Kimball Home
The Panel Clip Company
The Williamson Company
Thermal Industries, Inc.
Therma-Lock Products, Inc.
Therma-Tru, Division of LST Corporation
TimberTech Limited
Trex Co.
Trus Joist
TrusWal Systems, Inc.
United States Gypsum Company
United Technologies Carrier
Universal-Rundle Corporation
US Department of Commerce Weather
    Bureau
Vanguard Plastics, Inc.
Vemco Corporation
Vermont Castings
Veterans Affairs, Department of
WCI Communities, Inc.
Weather Shield Mfg., Inc.
Western Pennsylvania Conservancy
Western Wood Products Association
Whirlpool Corporation
Wilsonart International
Wood-Mode Cabinetry

The authors would like to express a special acknowledgment to Eric K. Augspurger, technical illustrator and technical writer, for his revision of the CADD material that appears in Chapter 5 and Chapter 6 of the text. His computer expertise was also invaluable in the revision of other computer-related sections in the text.

—Clois and Joan Kicklighter

Glossary

1/2 Bath: Typically has only a water closet and lavatory.

3/4 Bath: Contains only a lavatory, water closet, and shower.

3D Modeling: "True" 3D computer modeling where objects are created with a width, depth, and height.

9-12-15 Unit Method: These proportions define a right triangle and establish a 90° angle corner. Measure 9 units along one leg of the corner and 12 units along the other leg. The distance between these two endpoints should be 15 units. Adjust the legs of the angle until the distance is exactly 15 units.

A

Absorber Plate: Designed to absorb heat from solar radiation.

Access Hole: Allows entry into the attic or crawl-space.

Accordion Door: Frequently used to close large openings where bi-fold or sliding doors are not acceptable.

Acre: A plot of land comprising a total area of 43,560 square feet.

Activated Carbon System: A water treatment device in which the line pressure forces water through one or more canisters filled with activated carbon granules. These granules trap contaminates such as chlorine, organic chemicals, and pesticides.

Active Solar Space Heating: Involves collecting heat from solar radiation and then using pumps, fans, or other devices to distribute the heat to desired locations.

Adaptive Reuse: The process of changing the function of a building.

Addition: New space built onto a house.

Adhesive: A natural or synthetic material, generally in paste or liquid form, used to fasten or glue boards together, lay floor tile, fabricate plastic laminates, etc.

AEC Specific CADD Packages: Software that typically has most, if not all, of the same functions as a general purpose program, but also has functions that would typically only be useful to an architect or construction technologist/engineer.

Air-Dried Lumber: Lumber that has been piled in yards or sheds for a length of time; the minimum moisture content is usually 12% to 15%.

Alarm Functions: Performed by devices that alert the home owner or a home security agency to potential dangers based on a signal from a monitoring device.

Alcove: A recessed opening off a wall of a larger room; often used as a sitting area, coat room, or storage area.

Alphabet of Lines: The standardized collection of line types used in drafting, both manual and CADD.

Americans with Disabilities Act (ADA): A law that makes it illegal to discriminate against disabled persons in the areas of employment, public and private transportation, and access to public and commercial buildings.

Ampere (amp): The unit of current used to measure the amount of electricity flowing through a conductor per unit of time.

Analog Data: Always received with noise added into the content.

Anchor: Usually any metal fastener used to attach parts, such as joists, trusses, posts, etc., to masonry or masonry materials.

Anchor Bolt: A threaded rod inserted in masonry construction to anchor the sill plate to the foundation.

Animation: A series of still images played sequentially at a very fast rate, such as 30 frames per second; the brain mistakes the small differences as movement; a type of presentation drawing that shows motion, either through the movement of objects or the viewer's point of view.

Animation Key: Stores data related to animated movement in an animation; each keyframe has at least one animation key.

ANSI: Abbreviation for the American National Standards Institute.

Apartment: A rental unit that is a part of a larger complex.

Apron: Trim used under the stool on interior windows. Also, the concrete area in front of a garage door opening.

Arcade: A series of arches supported by columns or piers to provide an open passageway.

Arch: A curved structure that will support itself and the weight above its curved opening by mutual pressure.

Architect: A person who designs structures by working closely with the client in making preliminary drawings, sketches, and suggestions for materials to be used; must have creativity and sensitivity to form.

Architectural Drafter: Draws the details of working drawings and makes tracings from original drawings that the architect or designer has prepared.

Architectural Illustrator: Prepares drawings, sketches, renderings, and illustrations to present ideas to potential clients and as advertisements for commercial catalogs and publications.

Architectural Model: A physical, scaled model of the actual house and lot that provides the ultimate means of showing how the finished home will look in all three dimensions; computer models can also be used as architectural models.

Areaway: Below-grade recessed area around the foundation to allow light and ventilation into a basement window.

Aromatic Red Cedar: A wood primarily used in construction for chests and closet linings for its moth-proof value; has similar characteristics to Western red cedar.

Arris: A sharp edge formed when two planes or surfaces meet; found on edges of moldings, doors, shelves, and in cabinet construction.

ASCII: American Standard Code for Information Interchange; an industry standard used in transmitting information between computers, printers, and peripheral devices.

Ash Dump: The cavity or pit below the fireplace where ashes can collect and be removed.

Ashlar Stonework: Type of stonework in which dressed, cut, or squared stones are generally rectangular in shape, a specific size, and fit in an exact place in the pattern.

Asphalt Shingles: Composition roof shingles made from asphalt-impregnated felt covered with mineral granules.

Assessment: The levy of a tax or charge on property, usually according to established rates.

Assessor: A public official responsible for the evaluation of property for the purposes of taxation.

Assignee: A person to whom a transfer of interest is made in connection with a mortgage or contract for a home or piece of property.

Assignor: A person who makes an assignment for a mortgage or contract for a home or piece of property.

ASTM: Abbreviation for the American Society of Testing and Materials.

Atrium: A central hall or open court within a structure.

Atrium Design: An earth-sheltered house that places living areas around a central courtyard with all windows opening into the courtyard.

Attached Greenhouse: A type of isolated gain system; also called a sun space.

Attachment: The legal seizure of property to require payment of a debt.

Attic: The space between the ceiling and roof of a structure.

Attic Ventilators: Screened openings provided to ventilate an attic space; can also consist of power-driven fans used as an exhaust system.

Attribute: Text information saved with the block when it is inserted into a drawing.

Autoclave: A device that can treat a product in a vessel under high temperature and pressure.

Awning Window: Has sashes that are hinged at the top, swings out at an angle, and resembles an awning when open.

B

Bachelor's Degree: A college or university degree that generally requires four years of full-time study.

Backfill: The replacement of excavated earth into a trench around and against a basement foundation.

Balcony: A deck projecting from the wall of a building; above ground level.

Balloon Framing: A method of framing in which the wall studs rest directly on the sill plate and each floor "hangs" from the studs.

Balsa: A very soft wood (not a conifer) available in a wide variety of sizes and used for architectural model construction; easy to cut with a sharp knife, can be sawed, is easy to finish, and can be sanded and scored to represent exterior materials.

Balusters: Vertical members that support the handrail on open stairs.

Balustrade: A series of balusters connected by a rail; generally used for porches and balconies.

Banister: A handrail with supporting posts used alongside a stairway.

Baseboard: The finish board covering the interior wall where the wall and floor meet.

Basement: The lowest level of the house that is mostly below the grade level.

Basement Plan: A combination foundation and floor plan; includes the information commonly shown on the foundation plan and, at the same time, shows interior walls, stairs, windows, and doors in the basement.

Base Shoe: A molding used next to the floor in interior baseboards.

Basic Unit Size: The overall dimensions of a window or door unit.

Batt: A roll or sheet of insulation designed to be installed between the members of frame construction.

Batten: Narrow strips of wood used to cover joints or as decorative vertical members over plywood or wide boards.

Batter Board: One of a pair of horizontal boards nailed to posts set at the corners of an excavation; used to indicate the desired level and to retain the location of the foundation during excavation and construction; also used for fastening stretched strings to indicate outlines of foundation walls.

Bay Window: Any window space projecting outward from the walls of a building, either square or polygonal in plan; has a double-hung window on either side of a fixed center window; the side windows are normally placed at 45° to the exterior wall.

Beam: A structural member that supports the joists and effectively reduces the span.

Beam Ceiling: A ceiling in which the ceiling beams are exposed to view.

Bearing Partition: A partition that supports any vertical load in addition to its own weight.

Bearing Wall: A wall that supports any vertical load in addition to its own weight; designed to support part of the load of the structure.

Beech: A whitish- to reddish-brown hardwood used especially in construction for interior and exterior cabinet parts; blends well with birch for stained kitchen cabinets and vanities.

Benchmark: A permanent object used by surveyors to establish points of reference.

Bi-Fold Door: A door made of two parts that together form the door.

Birch: Hard and heavy, light-reddish-brown hardwood; the most widely used hardwood veneer for flush doors, cabinetwork, and paneling; mill products include interior trim, flooring, sash, and trim.

Blind Nailing: A method of nailing so that the nail is not visible.

Blocks: Special CADD objects that can best be thought of as symbols inserted into a drawing; often have *attributes.*

Board Foot: A method of lumber measurement using nominal dimensions of 1″ thick, 12″ wide, and 12″ long, or the equivalent.

Border Lines: Very heavy lines used to form a boundary for the drawing.

Bow Window: A combination of four to seven windows that form an arc extending outside the wall.

Box Bay: Combines a picture window parallel to the wall with two casement windows placed at 90° to the wall; also called garden windows.

Box Cornice: A cornice that has the space between the end of a projecting rafter and the wall enclosed with a soffit board.

Box Sill: Consists of a 2″ × 6″ plate called a sill or mudsill and a header that is the same size as the floor joists.

Branch Circuit: One of several individual electrical circuits from the distribution panel that is routed to similar devices.

Branch Main: Connects each plumbing fixture to the stack; these pipes must slope toward the stack to facilitate drainage.

Brick: A solid masonry unit composed of clay or shale; formed into a rectangular prism while soft and burned or fired in a kiln.

Brick Ledge: The portion of the foundation wall on which the brick veneer rests.

Brick Mold: Casing for a masonry wall.

Brick Veneer: A facing of brick laid against and fastened to sheathing of a frame wall or tile wall construction.

Bridging: Small wood or metal members that are inserted in a diagonal position between the floor joists at midspan to act both as tension and compression members for the purpose of bracing the joists and spreading the action of loads.

British Thermal Unit (Btu). One Btu is the quantity of heat required to increase the temperature of one pound of water one degree Fahrenheit.

Brown Coat: The second stucco layer in the three-coat process; covers any visible lath, adds strength to the shell, trues up the surface, and provides an appropriate surface for the final decorative finish coat.

Building Codes: Specify requirements for construction methods and materials for plumbing, electrical, and general building construction.

Building Main: The water supply pipe that enters the house.

Built-Up Roof: A roofing composed of three to five layers of asphalt felt laminated with coal tar, pitch, or asphalt; top is finished with crushed slag or gravel; generally used on flat or low-pitched roofs.

Bundled Cable: A cable that has several types of conductors inside one PVC jacket.

Bureau of Land Management: The branch of government in charge of surveying public lands.

C

Cable Pair: The two wires of a telephone line.

CADD: Acronym for computer-aided drafting and design.

CADD Workstation: A computer "system" that generally consists of a computer or processor, monitor, graphics adapter, input and pointing device, and hardcopy device.

Cantilevered Joists: Required when the floor joists are parallel to the overhanging (cantilevered) area; run perpendicular to the floor joists.

Cape Ann: An early Colonial house with a central chimney, gambrel roof, and attic rooms.

Cape Cod: One of the earliest and best known of the traditional Colonial styles.

Carbon Monoxide (CO): An odorless, tasteless, invisible gas that is potentially deadly; produced wherever there is incomplete combustion.

Carbon Monoxide (CO) Detector: A device that detects dangerous concentrations of carbon monoxide.

Carport: A garage not fully enclosed.

Cartesian Coordinates: X,Y,Z absolute coordinates used to locate position in space.

Casement Window: Has sashes hinged at the side so the window swings outward.

Casing: The trim that covers the space between the jamb and rough framing.

Caulk: A waterproof material used to seal cracks.

Cavity Walls: Concrete block walls; walls built of masonry units arranged to provide a continuous air space 2″ to 3″ thick.

Cement: Composed of a mixture of lime, silica, alumina, iron components, and gypsum.

Cement Mortar Mix: A mixture of one part Portland cement and six parts sand.

Centerlines: Indicate the center of holes and symmetrical objects such as windows and doors.

Central Processing Unit (CPU): Contains the processor, RAM, and input/output interfaces; the "box" found on most PCs.

Chain: A unit of land measurement 66′ in length.

Chamfer: A beveled edge on a board formed by removing the sharp corner; generally used on moldings, edges of drawer fronts, and cabinet doors.

Chase: A slot or continuous groove built in a masonry wall to accommodate ducts, pipes, or conduits.

Chimney: A vertical flue for passing smoke from a heating unit, fireplace, or incinerator.

Chipped Grain: Wood surface that has been roughened by the action of cutting tools; considered a defect when surfaces are to be smoothly finished.

Chords: The horizontal flanges at the top and bottom of a truss.

Circle Top Window: Circular windows typically installed above another window; available in quarter circles, half circles, ellipses, or full circles.

Circuit: A path through which electricity flows from a source to one or more devices and then returns to the source.

Circuit Breaker: A safety device designed to open and close a circuit by nonautomatic means, and to open the circuit automatically on a predetermined overload of current.

Circular Stairs: A set of stairs with trapezoidal steps that rise along an irregular curve or arc.

Circulating Stove: A stove that uses air flow and radiant heat to distribute warmth throughout a room.

Cleanout: In a fireplace, a door to allow access for removal of ashes from the ash dump; in plumbing system, permits the use of a cable to free waste from the house drain or sewer.

Clear Span: The horizontal distance from the inside of one exterior stud wall to the inside of the opposite exterior stud wall.

Clear Title: A title to property that is free of any defects.

Cleat: A piece of wood fastened to another member to serve as a brace or support; normally used in frame construction.

Clerestory Window: A window placed high on a wall.

Climate Control Equipment Schedule: Provides an orderly means of specifying equipment to be used in the climate control system.

Climate Control Plan: Shows the location, size, and type of heating, cooling, ventilating, humidification, and air cleaning equipment and the required piping or ducts.

Close Cornice: A cornice in which the rafter does not project beyond the wall.

Closed Plan: Rooms are in "cubicles" with little chance for overflow into other rooms.

Clothes Care Center: Provides an area for washing, drying, pressing, folding, storing, and mending clothes; intended to be more than a "utility" room.

Cold Water Branch Lines: Run from the cold water main to each of the fixtures.

Cold Water Main: Extends to various parts of the house to provide unheated water to the fixtures.

Collar Beam: Nominal 1″ or 2″ thick members connecting opposite roof rafters; serve to stiffen the roof structure.

Combination Systems: Home automation systems that "pick and choose" from hard-wired systems, power line technology, and structured wiring systems providing the opportunity to design a very high tech, custom system.

Combination Window: A window that is a mixture of two or more types of windows.

Command Line: Where a computer command can be typed to activate it.

Commands: Instructions to computer software, such as instructions given to a CADD program.

Common Brick: Not as uniform in size and color as face brick; may have a lip on one or more edges.

Common Method: The most common of several methods for drawing two-point perspectives; also called the office method.

Communication/Recording Functions: Performed by devices that allow voice, video, or data communication; record voice, video, or data communication; or both.

Computer-Aided Drafting and Design (CADD): The process of using computer software for drafting and design functions.

Concrete: The result of combining cement, sand, aggregate (usually stone or gravel), and water.

Condensation: Water vapor that has returned to a liquid state; generally forms on cool or cold surfaces.

Conditions and Restrictions: The phase used to designate any conditions to which the use of land may not be put and the penalties for failure to comply.

Condominium: Dwelling where the owner buys an apartment and a share of the common ground.

Conduction: The flow of heat through an object by transferring heat from one molecule to another.

Conductor: A material, such as copper, that permits the flow of electricity; usually refers to a wire.

Conduit, Electrical: A pipe, usually metal, in which wire is installed.

Cone of Vision: The angle between opposite sides of the object with its vertex at the station point.

Construction Details: Drawn where more information is needed to fully describe how the construction is to be done.

Construction Lines: Very light lines (in manual drafting) or temporary lines (in CADD) used in the process of constructing a drawing; they are to help the drafter and should not reproduce when a print is made.

Construction Technologist: Specializes in areas of construction technology such as managing construction, purchasing, expediting, specification writing, estimating and bidding, quality control, and site supervision.

Contemporary: Modern house styles not directly related to the styles of the past.

Contour Interval: The vertical distance between two adjacent contour lines.

Contour Lines: Help describe the topography of a site by depicting shape and elevation of the land; connect points that have the same elevation.

Contract: An agreement between a seller and purchaser; the title is withheld from the purchaser until all required payments to the seller have been completed.

Contract Specification Sheet: A document prepared by the architect that contains details of the responsibilities of the parties involved in a construction project.

Contraction Joints: Grooves cut into concrete to minimize or control cracking due to temperature changes.

Convection: Refers to the transfer of heat by a moving fluid, such as liquids and gases.

Convenience Outlet: A contact device attached to a circuit to allow electricity to be drawn off for appliances or lighting.

Cooperative: An apartment building that is managed and run as a corporation.

Coping: A cap or top course of a masonry wall used to protect areas beneath it from water penetration.

Corbel: A ledge or shelf constructed by laying successive courses of masonry out from the face of the wall.

Core: The inner layer(s) of plywood; may consist of veneer, solid lumber, or composition board.

Corner Braces: Diagonal braces at the corners of frame structure to stiffen and strengthen the wall.

Cornice: The overhang of the roof at the eave line that forms a connection between the roof and side walls.

Cornice Return: The portion of the cornice that returns on the gable end of a house.

Corridor Kitchen: A style of kitchen where work centers are located on two walls opposite each other; usually small to medium in size and are ideal for long, narrow rooms.

Counterflashing: A flashing used under the regular flashing.

Counterflow Furnace: The plenum is on the bottom and the warm air is forced downward.

Coursed Rubble: Type of rubble stonework in which the stones are generally flat and rectangular, and the result may look like courses (rows) of stone.

Courts: Similar to porches and patios and may have characteristics of both; totally or at least partially enclosed by walls or roof.

Cove: Molded trim of a concave shape used around cabinet construction and other built-ins.

Crawl Space: The shallow space below the floor of a house built above the ground; generally surrounded with the foundation wall.

Creep: Horizontal movement of a permanent object, such as pavers or concrete slabs.

Cricket: See *saddle.*

Cripples: Structural members that are not full length due to a wall opening.

Cross Bracing: Boards nailed diagonally across studs or other boards to make framework rigid.

Cross Bridging: Used to stiffen the floor and spread the load over a broader area.

Crosshatch Lines: Used to show that the feature has been sectioned; also called section lines.

Crown Molding: A decorative molding used at the top of cabinets, at ceiling corners, and under a roof overhang.

Cubic Foot Method: Produces an estimate of the building cost based on the volume of the house.

Cul-de-Sac: A street or court with no outlet, which provides a circular turnaround for vehicles.

Cull: Building material (especially boards) that is rejected because of defects or below usable grade.

Cupola: A small, decorative structure built on the roof of a house; often placed over an attached garage and may also be used for ventilation purposes.

Curtain Walls: The walls of a post and beam building; do not support much weight.

Cutting-Plane Lines: Heavy lines used to show where the object is to be sectioned.

D

Dado Joint: A groove cut across the face of a piece of stock to receive the end of another board; often used in quality shelf and cabinet construction.

Damper: A movable plate that regulates air flow in the fireplace and prevents downdraft.

Dead Loads: Static or fixed weights of the structure itself; examples of dead loads are the weights of roofing, foundation walls, siding, joists, etc.

Decks: Porches that are not under roof.

Deed: A legal document through which ownership of the property is transferred.

Dehumidifier: A device that removes water vapor from the air.

Dehumidifying System: Removes moisture vapor from the air to reduce the relative humidity in the space.

Design Temperature Difference: The difference between the outside design temperature and the inside design temperature.

Digital Data: Refers to information that is converted to only a few specific values, commonly described as "1s and 0s."

Digitizer Puck: A variation of a mouse; it is moved around like a mouse, but can have several buttons to activate a variety of functions.

Dimension Lines: Used to show size and location.

Dimensional Lumber: Lumber that is available in common nominal widths and thicknesses, i.e. 2″ × 4″, 1″ × 6″, and 2″ × 12″; available in various lengths.

Dimmer Switch: A special switch that allows the light to be adjusted to the desired brightness.

Direct Gain Systems: Solar heating systems that incorporate large areas of south-facing glazing (glass or other material) that permit large amounts of sunlight to enter the interior space of the dwelling to directly heat the air inside.

Display Controls: Software commands that allow you to change the magnification factor of the view and change the view itself.

Display Grid: In CADD, a visual guideline in the viewport, much like the lines on graph paper.

Disposal Field: One of the two components of a septic system; receives sewage in liquid form from the septic tank and allows it to seep into the soil.

Distillation System: A water treatment device in which water is heated to make steam, which is then condensed in a coil to produce distilled water.

Distribution Panel: This is where the electricity is received from the meter and is distributed to various points in the house through branch circuits; also called a service panel.

Dome: A roof used over an entryway or a complete structure in the form of a hemisphere.

Dome Structures: Structures incorporating design elements of the geodesic dome or triangular space frames.

Doorjamb: The frame that fits inside the rough opening for a door.

Door Schedule: A list of doors identified on the foundation/basement plan and floor plan with their specifications.

Doorstop: The strips on the doorjamb against which the door closes.

Dormers: Allow in natural light and increase the amount of usable space in an attic by adding headroom.

Double-Action Door: A door that is hinged in such a way that it can swing through an arc of 180°.

Double Glazing: A pane of two pieces of glass sealed with an air space between to provide insulation.

Double Header: Two or more timbers joined for strength.

Double-Hung Window: Has two sashes; the weight of each sash is usually counterbalanced or friction devices can be used to hold the sashes in the desired positions.

Double-L: A set of stairs that have two 90° turns and two landings along the flight, but are not U shaped.

Douglas Fir: A yellow to pale reddish softwood; the leading veneer wood primarily converted into plywood and widely used in building and construction; lumber used in general construction; mill products used for sash, flooring, and doors.

Downspout: A vertical pipe that receives the water from the gutter outlet.

Drawing Aids: CADD commands and functions that help you locate position on screen and on existing objects; make the task of drawing easier, faster, and more accurate.

Drawing Commands: Allow you to create objects on the computer screen.

Dressed Size: The actual size of lumber after jointing and surfacing.

Drip Cap: Used over the top piece of door trim in frame construction to shed water.

Drywall: Interior covering material, such as gypsum board or plywood, that is applied in large sheets or panels.

Dry Well: A pit located on porous ground and walled up with rock that allows water to seep through; used for the disposal of rainwater or the effluent from a septic tank.

Ducts: Used in a forced-air system to move large quantities of air for heating or cooling; can be round or rectangular; also called ductwork.

Duplex Outlet: Electrical wall outlet having two plug receptacles.

Dutch Door: A door composed of two parts—an upper and lower section—that may be opened independently.

Dwarf Wall: A low wall built to retain an excavation or embankment.

E

Earnest Money: A partial payment made as part of the purchase price to bind a contract for property.

Earthquake Zone: An area that is prone to earthquakes.

Earth-Sheltered Dwelling: A structure that uses soil to reduce heat loss or gain.

Easement: An area of a piece of property to which another has certain rights for the purpose of placing power lines, drains, and other specified uses.

Eastern Fir: A softwood similar to spruce in its general characteristics; used for siding, moldings, and general construction.

Eaves: The lower portion of the roof that overhangs the wall.

Editing Commands: CADD commands that allow you to modify drawings in several ways.

Electric Radiant System: A heating system that uses resistance wiring to produce heat.

Electrical Plan: Identifies the type and location of electrical equipment to be used in a house, such as switches, convenience outlets, ceiling outlet fixtures, television jacks, service entrance location, and the panel box.

Elevations: Drawn for each side of the structure, typically as orthographic projections, showing the exterior features of the building.

Ell: An extension or wing of a building at a right angle to the main section.

Enclosed Stairs: Stairs that have a wall on both sides; also known as closed, housed, or box stairs.

Engineered Wood Products (EWPs): Wood veneers and fibers are combined with adhesives to form beams, headers, joists, and panels that have uniformly high quality and strength.

Entourage: Surroundings, such as trees, shrubs, cars, people, and terrain.

Entrepreneur: A person who starts, manages, and assumes the risks of a new business.

Escutcheon: Door hardware that accommodates the knob and keyhole.

Equity: The amount the house is worth minus the amount owed.

Estimating: An organized effort to determine the total cost of materials, labor, and other services required to build a house.

Estimator: The person who calculates the costs of materials and labor for a building structure.

Excavation: A cavity or pit produced by digging the earth in preparation for construction.

Expansion Joint: A bituminous fiber strip used to separate blocks or units of concrete to prevent cracking due to expansion as a result of temperature changes.

Expansion Plan: Shows how the structure has been designed to accommodate future expansion.

Expansive Clay: A type of soil that swells when wet and produces very high pressure against underground walls.

Extended Plenum System: A system of ductwork in a forced-air system where a large rectangular duct (plenum) is the main supply and round ducts extend from the main supply to each register.

Extension Lines: Used to denote the termination point of a dimension line.

Exterior Insulation Finish Systems (EIFS): Synthetic stucco.

F

Facade: The front elevation or the face of a structure.

Face Brick: Usually uniform in size and has sharp corners and lines; of better quality and used on the face of a wall.

Face Size: The exposed width of a molded piece of lumber after installation.

Face Veneer: Veneer selected for exposed surfaces in plywood; especially selected for fancy paneling.

Facing: Any material attached to the outer portion of a wall used as a finished surface.

Fascia: A vertical board nailed onto the ends of the rafters.

Fiberboard: A building board made with fibrous material and used as an insulating board.

Fill: Sand, gravel, or loose earth used to bring a subgrade up to a desired level around a house.

Filled Insulation: A loose insulating material poured from bags or blown by machine into walls.

Fillet: A smoothly fitted internal arc of a specified radius between two lines, arcs, or circles

Finish Coat: The third stucco layer in the three-coat process; the decorative layer and is where texture or design patterns are applied to the surface.

Firebrick: A brick that is especially hard and heat resistant; used in fireplaces.

Fire Chamber: Where the fire is contained in a fireplace.

Fireclay: A fire-resistant, refractory mortar used as a bonding agent between the firebrick in a fireplace.

Firecut: A cut at an angle on the ends of floor joists for use with a solid masonry wall; prevents toppling the wall if the house should catch fire.

Firestop: A solid, tight closure of a concealed space; placed to prevent the spread of fire and smoke through such a space.

Firewall: Any wall designed to resist the spread of fire between sections of a house or other structure; commonly used between the main structure and an attached garage.

Flagstone: Flat stone used for floors, steps, walks, or walls.

Flash Floods: A high volume of fast-moving water that can appear suddenly.

Flashing: Sheet metal or other material used in roof and wall construction to shed water away from areas of potential leakage.

Flexible Paving System: Consists of a well-compacted subgrade beneath a layer of crushed stone, a sand setting bed, and fine sand between the pavers.

Float: A short board, about a foot long, with a handle attached to one of the flat sides and used to embed the large aggregate just beneath the surface; remove any slight imperfections, lumps, and voids to produce a flat surface; and consolidate mortar at the surface in preparation for final steel-troweling.

Floodplains: Identified throughout the US according to the average number of years between flooding, such as a 100-year floodplain or a 500-year floodplain.

Floor Framing Plan: Shows direction of joists and major supporting members.

Floor Plan: Identifies the location and dimensions of exterior and interior walls, windows, doors, major appliances, cabinets, fireplaces, and other fixed features of the house; section view taken about halfway up the wall.

Floor Trusses: Consist of a top chord, bottom chord, and web; often used in place of floor joists in residential structures.

Flue: The path for smoke to pass up the chimney.

Flue Lining: Used for the inner lining of chimneys.

Fluorescent Light: Has a tube, not a bulb, and is often used in schools and businesses.

Flush Door: A door that is smooth on both sides and usually made of wood.

Fly Rafters: End rafters of the gable overhang supported by roof sheathing and lookouts.

Footing: A masonry section, usually concrete, in a rectangular form; increase the supporting capacity of the foundation wall by spreading the load over a larger area.

Forced-Air System: Heats air in a furnace and forces it through pipes or ducts to all parts of the house; also distributes cooled air when the air conditioner is operating.

Form, Concrete: A temporary structure built to contain concrete during placement and initial hardening.

Foundation: The supporting portion of a structure below the first-floor construction, or below grade, including the footings.

Foundation Plan: A plan view drawing, in section, that provides all of the information necessary to construct the foundation; illustrates the foundation size and material.

Foyer: Functions as a place to greet guests and, in colder climates, remove overcoats and boots.

Free-Form Roof: A roof that offers complete freedom of design; urethane foam is a popular choice of material for this roof.

Freehand Sketching: A method of making a drawing without the use of instruments.

Frieze: In house construction, a horizontal member connecting the top of the siding with the soffit of the cornice.

French Doors: Panel doors with the panels made from glass.

Front Elevation: In architectural drawing, the front view of an object.

Frost Line: The depth of frost penetration in soil below which footings are placed to prevent movement; varies in different parts of the country.

Full Bath: Contains a lavatory, water closet, and tub or tub/shower combination.

Furniture Plan: Identifies the furniture to be used and its placement in each area of the house.

Furring Strips: Usually 2″ × 2″ or 1″ × 3″ lumber affixed to the wall to provide a nailing surface.

Fuse: A safety device that breaks (opens) the circuit when it is overloaded by melting a fusible link.

G

Gable End: The extension of a gable roof beyond the end wall of the house; also called the rake.

Gain: (a) A recess or notch into which a door hinge fits flush with the surface. (b) Refers to the way heat is extracted from solar radiation.

Garrett: An attic or unfinished part of a house just under the roof.

Garrison: A house style that has a distinguishing overhanging second story and narrow siding.

Gazebo: A roofed structure, similar to a porch, that is detached from the house; typically has open sides.

General Purpose CADD Packages: Software that is usually designed for making typical mechanical drawings and other general drafting applications.

Geodesic Dome: An engineered system of triangular spaceframes based on mathematically precise divisions of a sphere; designed by R. Buckminster Fuller.

Girder: A large or principle beam of wood or steel used to support concentrated loads at isolated points along its length.

Glass Size: The dimension of unobstructed glass.

Glazing: Placing of glass in windows or doors.

Glulam Beams: Glue-laminated members that consist of 1× or 2× lumber glued in stacks to the desired shape and size.

Grade: The surface of the ground around a building.

Grade, Wood: A designation given to the quality of manufactured lumber.

Grade Line: The spot where the soil surface strikes the building; the reference point for most elevations.

Gravel Stop: A strip of metal with a vertical lip used to retain the gravel around the edge of a built-up roof.

Grid Snap: Uses an invisible grid; when grid snap is turned on, the cursor "jumps" to the closest snap grid point.

Grids: Available in a wide variety of sizes and forms, they have many uses in manual architectural drafting; some grids are designed to be used under a sheet of tracing paper while others are designed to be drawn on directly.

Gross Annual Income: The amount of money you earn before taxes and other deductions.

Ground Fault Circuit Interrupter (GFCI): A safety device that continually monitors the amount of current going to the load and compares it to that coming back; if the amount of current returning is less than it should be, the GFCI will trip (open) the circuit.

Ground Line: In a perspective drawing, represents the horizontal ground plane, which is the plane on which the object rests.

Ground-Source Heat Pump: A heat pump that uses an antifreeze solution, instead of air, for the heat source and heat sink.

Grout: A plaster-like material used to seal between ceramic and other tile in kitchens, showers, and baths.

Guardrails: Rails that keep people from falling over the edge of a balcony or off the side of a staircase.

Guidelines: Used for hand lettering a drawing in manual drafting.

Gussets: Used to fastened the members of a wood truss together.

Gutters: Collect the water from the roof and direct it to an outlet.

H

Handrails: Horizontal members that help people steady themselves as they traverse areas like stairs and ramps where they might slip, trip, or fall.

Hanger: A metal strap used to support piping or the ends of joists.

Hard-Coat EIFS: EIFS that is usually greater than 1/4" thick and mechanically attached.

Hard-Wired Systems: Home automation systems that are dedicated (stand-alone) systems that are self-contained and part of the infrastructure of the building.

Hardwood: Wood produced from broadleaved trees or trees that lose their leaves annually; examples include oak, maple, walnut, and birch.

Header: (a) A beam placed perpendicular to joists and to which joists are nailed in framing for chimney, stairway, or other opening. (b) A wood lintel.

Headroom: The shortest clear vertical distance measured between the nosing of the treads and the ceiling; minimum headroom is 6'-6".

Hearth: The inner or outer floor of a fireplace; protects the floor in front of a fireplace from sparks.

Heat Exchanger: A device for removing heat from water or air and transferring the heat to another medium.

Heat Loss: The amount of heat that passes to the outside and is a function of the amount of surface area through which heat can escape.

Heat Pump: Serves the dual purpose of heating and cooling; essentially a refrigeration unit that "pumps" or transfers natural heat from air or water to heat or cool the house.

Heating and Cooling Plan: Illustrates components of the climate control system of the house.

Hexadome: One structural variation of the geodesic dome.

Hickory: A hard and heavy brown to reddish-brown hardwood; used as face veneer for decorative interior plywood paneling and as solid lumber in special flooring applications. Pecan, a variety of the hickory family, has similar properties and construction applications.

Hidden Lines: Represent an edge that is behind a visible surface in a given view in the drawing.

Hip Rafter: The diagonal rafter that extends from the plate to the ridge to form the hip.

Hip Roof: A roof that rises by inclined planes from all four sides of a building.

Historic Preservation: Involves returning a building to its original condition while maintaining traditional styles, materials, and, in some cases, furnishings.

Hopper Window: A window that is hinged at the bottom and swings to the inside of the house.

Horizon Line: In a perspective drawing, represents the place where the ground and sky meet.

Horizontal Furnace: Requires minimum clearance and can be suspended from ceilings and floor joists or installed on a concrete slab; installed in the attic or crawl space.

Horizontal Sliding Window: Has two sashes; a track attached to the head jamb and sill provides for horizontal movement.

Hose Bib: A water faucet made for the threaded attachment of a hose.

Hot Water Branch Lines: Run from the hot water main to each fixture.

Hot Water Main: Supplies heated water to the fixtures that require it.

House Drain: A drain line into which all stacks empty.

House Sewer: The house drain outside of the house that empties into the city sanitary sewer or a private septic system.

Housed Stringer: A stringer that has been routed or grooved to receive the treads and risers.

Humidifier: A device used to increase the moisture level (water vapor) in air.

Humidistat: A controlling device to regulate or maintain the desired degree of humidity (water vapor) in a house.

Hurricane: A tropical storm (cyclone) with winds that have reached a sustained speed of 74 miles per hour (64 knots) or more.

Hurricane Codes: Building codes establishing standards of construction designed to reduce damage to property during a hurricane.

Hydronic System: Heating system that consists of a boiler, water pipes, and radiators or radiant panels; also called a hot water system.

I

I-beam: A steel beam with a cross section resembling the letter I; used for long spans as basement beams or over wide wall openings, such as a double garage door when wall and roof loads are imposed on the opening.

Improvements: Any additions to property that tend to increase its value, such as buildings, streets, sewers, etc.

Incandescent Light: Traditional screw-in "lightbulb."

Indirect Gain Systems: Solar heating systems that heat the interior space by storing heat in a thermal mass, then releasing the heat into the interior space; a large thermal mass is placed between the sun and the living space.

Individual Appliance Circuits: Circuits that serve single, permanently installed appliances; each appliance will have its own circuit.

Industrialized Housing: Houses built in a factory.

Infiltration: Heat lost through spaces around windows and doors.

Inkjet Printers/Plotters: These are raster devices that are fast, quiet, and easy to use like a laser printer; produce very good color and are inexpensive to purchase.

Inlets: Required for forced-air heating and cooling systems, they receive air to be returned to the furnace or air conditioning coil; also called cold air returns.

Inner Hearth: The floor of the fireplace.

Input Device: A way to provide the computer with information; most common input device is the keyboard; second most common input device is the mouse.

Inquiry Commands: Designed to list the database records for selected objects; calculate distances, areas, and perimeters; and convert points on the screen to absolute coordinates (or the reverse).

Inside Design Temperature: The desired room temperature level.

Insulated Concrete Block System: Consists of conventional concrete block filled with plastic inserts or specially designed blocks with plastic cores.

Insulated Concrete Wall System: A panel of plastic foam insulation between two conventional metal or wood forms.

Insulated Wall Forms: Concrete cast between two rigid polystyrene foam panels or interlocking blocks of plastic foam insulation that are stackable and whose hollow cores are filled with concrete.

Insulating Board: Any board suitable for insulating purposes; usually manufactured board, such as fiberboard, made from vegetable fibers.

Insulation: Prevents or reduces the transfer of heat or sound from one location to another.

Intermediate Level: The next level up from the basement in a split-level house design.

Interior Trim: General term for all the finish molding, casing, baseboard, and cornice applied within the building by finish carpenters.

Ion Exchange: Causes the hard calcium and magnesium ions to be dissolved and exchanged for soft ions in the resin within a water softener.

Island Kitchen: May be a modification of the straight-line, L-shaped, or U-shaped style; island may house the sink, cooking center, or food preparation area.

ISO: The abbreviation for the International Standards Organization.

Isolated Gain Systems: Solar heating systems that collect and store solar energy in an area outside of the living space.

J

Jack Rafter: A rafter that spans the distance from the wall plate to a hip or from a valley to a ridge.

Jalousie Window: Has a series of narrow, horizontal glass slats that are held in metal clips, which in turn are fastened to an aluminum frame.

Jamb: The side and head lining of a doorway, window, or other opening.

Job Site Safety: The safety of all of those individuals involved at a construction site; the primary concern for every employer and employee.

Joists: Provide support for the floor.

K

Keyframe: A frame in an animation on which an important action takes place.

Kiln-Dried Lumber: Lumber that has been kiln-dried, generally to a moisture content of 6% to 12%.

King Post: The center upright piece in a roof truss.

Kip: A unit of weight measurement; one kip is one thousand pounds.

Knee Wall: A low wall resulting from one-and-one-half-story construction.

L

Lally Column: A steel column used as a support for girders and beams.

Laminated Beam: A beam made of superimposed layers of similar materials by joining them with glue and pressure.

Laminated Veneer Lumber (LVL): An engineered wood product in which veneers of wood are stacked in parallel and glued under pressure.

Landing: The floor area at either end of the stairs and possibly at some point between, as in the case of an L stairs; a platform between flights of stairs or at the termination of a flight of stairs.

Land Surveyor: Establishes areas and boundaries of real estate property.

Landscape Plan: Locates and identifies plants and other elements included in landscaping the site.

Laser Printers/Plotters: These devices produce an output in much the same way as an office copy machine; drawing is produced as a raster image, which is a series of dots.

L-Shaped Kitchen: A style of kitchen with work centers located along two adjacent walls; results in an efficient workspace.

L Stairs: A set of stairs that have one landing and turn at some point along the flight of stairs.

Lath: Affixed to the wall to provide support and attachment for the layers of stucco and to connect the stucco to the structure.

Lattice: A framework of crossed wood or metal strips.

Layer: A virtual piece of paper on which CADD objects are placed; similar to a transparent drawing sheet.

Leader: A vertical pipe or downspout that carries rainwater from the gutter to the ground or storm sewer.

Lease: A contract for the use of land for a period of years with a designated payment of a monthly or annual rental.

Ledger Strip: A strip of lumber nailed along the bottom of the side of a girder on which joists rest.

Left Side Elevation: In architectural drawing, the left side view of an object.

Legal Description: A written indication of the location and boundaries of a parcel of land; reference is generally made to a recorded plat of survey.

Light Pens: These devices work with a tablet menu, like a puck; some can also be used to select menu items directly on the monitor.

Lighting Circuits: Circuits that serve permanently installed lighting fixtures, as well as receptacle outlets into which lamps, radios, television, clocks, and similar 120 volt devices, other than kitchen appliances, are plugged.

Lighting Fixture Schedule: Identifies the fixtures to be used in a house.

Lighting Outlet: An outlet intended for a lighting fixture.

Lintel: A horizontal structural member that supports the load over an opening such as a door or window.

Live Loads: Fixed or moving weights that are not a structural part of the house; examples include furniture, occupants, snow on the roof, wind, etc.

Living Area: Where the family relaxes, entertains guests, dines, and meets together.

Living Level: The next level up from the intermediate level in a split-level house.

Long Break Line: Used to show a break when the break is two or three inches in length.

Longitudinal Method: A method of post and beam construction where the beams are placed at right angles to the roof slope and the roof decking is laid from the ridge pole to the eaves line.

Lookout: A short wooden framing member used to support an overhanging portion of a roof; extends from the wall to the underside surfacing of the overhang.

Lot: A measured amount of property (land) having fixed boundaries.

Lot Line: The line forming the legal boundary of a piece of property.

Louver: An opening with a series of horizontal slats so arranged as to permit ventilation but to exclude rain, sunlight, or vision. See *Attic Ventilators.*

M

Main Entry: Entry opens to the living area of the house, usually the foyer; should be centrally located to provide easy access to various parts of the house.

Mainframe: Computer system that consists of a common processing unit centrally-located that is connected, or networked, to many remote terminals; each terminal basically consists of a monitor, keyboard, and mouse or other input device, but a terminal does not have a central processing unit.

Main Stack: A plumbing stack that has a water closet draining into it.

Main Stairs: A stairway from the first floor to the second floor or from a split foyer to the first floor.

Major Module: In modular construction, a 4'-0" cube or 12 standard modules on each side.

Mantel: The shelf above a fireplace; also used in referring to the decorative trim around a fireplace opening.

Maple: Both hard and soft maple are generally light tan and used in construction where hardness is a major factor; used for expensive cabinetwork, flooring, doors, trim, interior railings, posts, and furniture.

Masonry: Stone, brick, concrete, hollow tile, concrete block, gypsum block, or other similar building units or materials or a combination of the same, bonded together with mortar to form a wall, pier, buttress, or similar mass.

Masonry Wall: Constructed entirely of brick, concrete block, stone, clay tile, terra cotta, or a combination of these materials.

Mastic: A flexible adhesive for joining building materials.

Material Hatch Patterns: A type of shorthand for the drafter used to indicate a material rather than trying to describe each material with words; also called material symbols.

Material Specifications: Criteria governing the types of materials, fixtures, and other physical items.

Material Symbols: See *Material Hatch Patterns.*

Material Takeoff: A method of estimating building cost that is accurate and obtained by determining the quantity, quality, and cost of materials to be used, and cost of labor required by installation.

Mean Sea Level: A standardized elevation.

Metal Wall Ties: Strips of corrugated metal used to tie a brick veneer wall to a framework.

Miniframe: Similar to a mainframe computer but generally smaller.

Millwork: Lumber that is shaped to a given pattern or molded form; includes dressing, matching, and machining; examples include casing, base, panel door parts, and stair rails.

Minor Module: In modular construction, a 16" cube or 24" cube.

Miter Joint: A joint made with the ends or edges of two pieces of lumber cut at a 45° angle and fitted together.

Model Ethics Code: List of objectives for ethical practices in the business environment.

Modular Components: Building parts that have been preassembled either in a plant or on-site.

Modular Construction: Construction in which the size of all the building materials is based on a common unit of measure.

Modules: Different size increments in which construction materials are available.

Moisture Barrier: A membrane that retards the flow of moisture vapor and reduces condensation.

Mold: A type of fungus that reproduces through the production of spores.

Monitor: The display device or "screen" used on a computer system.

Monitoring Functions: Performed by devices that examine certain aspects of the house to determine their status.

Mortar: A mixture of cement, sand, and water; used by a mason as a bonding agent for brick and stone.

Mortgage: A document used to hold property as security for a debt.

Mortise: A slot cut into a board, plank, or timber, usually edgewise, to receive the tenon of another board, plank, or timber to form a joint.

Motion Detectors: Detect the movement of an intruder that is inside the home after bypassing the perimeter system.

Mudsill: The sill in box sill construction.

Mullions: Large horizontal or vertical members that are placed between window units.

Muntins: Small vertical and horizontal bars that separate the total glass area into smaller units.

N

Narrow Box Cornice: A cornice that is usually between 6" and 12" wide; the soffit board is nailed directly to the bottom side of the rafters.

Narrow U Stairs: A set of U stairs that have little or no space between the flights.

Network: Several computers connected that can share information through the network wiring, however, the "computing power" is contained in each individual machine; typically allows devices such as printers and plotters to be shared among the computers.

New England Gambrel: Colonial style that includes a gambrel roof with pitch change between the ridge and eaves.

Newel: The main posts of the handrail at the top, bottom, and points where the stairs change direction.

Nominal Size: The size of lumber before dressing, rather than its actual size.

Nonbearing Wall: A wall supporting no load other than its own weight.

Nosing: The rounded projection of the tread that extends past the face of the riser.

O

Oak, Red: Hard and tough hardwood rich light to medium brown in color and used for flooring, interior trim, stair treads, and railings; popular as a face veneer plywood for paneling and cabinetwork; white oak has similar characteristics and applications.

Oak, White: See *Oak, Red.*

Object: The basic element used to create CADD drawings; include items such as lines, points, circles, arcs, and boxes.

Object Lines: Show the outline of the main features of the object.

Object Snap: Allows the cursor to "jump" to certain locations on existing objects.

Office Method: See *Common Method.*

Ohm: The unit of measure of electrical resistance in a circuit.

On-Center (OC): The measurement of spacing for studs, rafters, joists, and other framing members from the center of one member to the center of the next.

One-and-One-Half Story: A house design that is essentially a one-story house with a steeper roof that allows for expansion of the attic; sometimes called a Cape Cod.

One-Pipe System: A hydronic heating system that uses radiators, or convectors as they are sometimes called, connected in series.

One-Story Ranch: A house design that has all regular living space on one level.

Open Cornice: A cornice that may be used with exposed-beam construction, contemporary, or rustic designs.

Open Plan: Rooms are not closed off from each other; minimal walls.

Open Stairs: Stairs that have no wall on one or both sides.

Oriented Strand Board (OSB): An engineered wood product in which long strands of wood are mixed with resin, placed in layers, and pressed and cured.

Orthographic Projection: A means of representing the height, width, and depth of a three-dimensional object on two-dimensional paper.

Outlet: Any type of electrical box allowing current to be drawn from the electrical system for lighting or appliances.

Output Device: A means of obtaining information from a computer; the monitor is the most common output device.

Outside Design Temperature: The average outdoor temperature for the winter months.

Overall Dimensions: Provide the total length and width of the structure or feature.

Overhang: The projecting area of a roof or upper story beyond the wall of the lower part.

Overhead Sectional Door: A type of garage door.

P

Pallet: An inexpensive wood skid used to stack and ship construction materials such as brick or concrete block.

Panel: In residential construction, a thin flat piece of wood, plywood, or similar material, framed by stiles and rails, as in a door, or fitted into grooves of thicker material with molded edges for decorative wall treatment.

Panel Door: A door with a heavy frame around the outside and generally at least one cross member; the frame and cross members form small panels.

Panic Button: Permits a silent alarm to be sent to a monitoring station or to set off an audible alarm siren.

Paper, Building: A general term for paper, felt, or similar sheet materials used in buildings without reference to their properties or uses.

Parallel Strand Lumber (PSL): An engineered wood product in which thin strands of wood are glued together under pressure.

Parametric: The quality of an object in CADD where you can change the base size or any other parameter.

Parapet: A low wall or railing around the edge of a roof.

Parasol Roof: A roof that looks like an upturned parasol (umbrella); usually constructed from concrete.

Parge Coat: A thin coat of plaster over the foundation wall for refinement of the surface or for dampproofing.

Particleboard: A composition board made of wood chips or particles bonded together with an adhesive under high pressure.

Partition: A wall that subdivides spaces within any story of a building.

Passive Solar Space Heating: Involves capturing, storing, and using solar radiation to heat a dwelling without the use of fans or pumps to circulate the heat.

Patios: Usually near the house but not structurally connected; ordinarily located at ground level and constructed for durability.

Paving: The use of brick to cover exterior traffic areas such as driveways, patios, and sidewalks; may be installed either as a rigid or flexible system.

Pecan: See *Hickory.*

Pen Plotter: An output device that moves paper around under a pen to trace the object lines in the drawing; plots vectors.

Penetrational Design: An earth-sheltered house that provides window openings and access at various points around the structure facing different directions.

Peninsula Kitchen: A style of kitchen that is popular because it provides plenty of workspace; attractive and can easily join with the dining area using the peninsula as a divider.

Percolation Test: A soil test that determines the suitability of the soil for a septic disposal field.

Perimeter System: A home security system in which all doors and windows are wired with magnetic switches inside the frame; an alarm is activated when a switch is disturbed by opening a door or window.

Periphery: The boundary or the complete outside edge of a parcel of land or an object on a drawing.

Perspective: A type of pictorial drawing that provides a realistic image of the object.

Phase Change Material: A material capable of storing large amounts of heat as they change from solid to liquid; slow to release the stored heat and are, therefore, interesting as possible thermal mass materials.

Pictorial Presentation: Often included to show how the finished structure will appear.

Picture Plane: A transparent plane onto which a drawing is projected.

Picture Window: A fixed-glass unit that is usually rather large; the term "picture window" is used because the view is framed, like a picture.

Pier: A masonry pillar usually below a building to support the floor framing; piers are shorter than columns.

Pier Foundation: Consists of piers and footings on which the piers bear.

Pilaster: A rectangular column that projects from a wall; also used for additional girder or beam support.

Pine, Ponderosa: Light reddish-colored softwood used especially for sash, doors, and screens in the softer grades; harder grades are used for joists, rafters, studs, sills, sheathing, porch columns, posts, balusters, and stair rails.

Pine, White: Softwood of light tan color used for door, sash, interior and exterior trim, siding, and panels; lower grades are used for sheathing subflooring and roofing.

Pine, Yellow: Softwood of medium texture, moderately hard, and a yellow to reddish-brown color; used for joists, rafters, studs, and general construction where extra strength and stiffness are required.

Pipes: Used in a hydronic system to distribute hot water or steam from the boiler to radiators, baseboard units, or radiant panels.

Pitch: The slope of a roof; usually expressed as a ratio.

Plain Stringer: A stringer that has been cut or notched to fit the profile of the stairs.

Plan View: The top view of a house or other object.

Plaster: A mortar-like composition used for covering walls and ceilings; usually made of Portland cement mixed with sand and water.

Plat: A drawing of surveyed land indicating the location, boundaries, and dimensions of the parcel; also contains information as to easements, restrictions, and lot number.

Plate: Sill plate is a horizontal member anchored to a masonry wall; sole plate is bottom horizontal member of a frame wall; top plate is top horizontal member of a frame wall supporting ceiling joists, rafters, or other members.

Platform Framing: A method of framing where the floor joists form a platform on which the walls rest.

Plenum: The chamber where warmed air is collected for distribution.

Plot Plan: A plan view drawing that shows the site and location/orientation of the buildings on the property.

Plumb: Exactly perpendicular; vertical.

Plumbing Fixture: Any device, such as a bathtub, shower, water closet, sink, dishwasher, etc., that requires water.

Plumbing Fixture Schedule: Shows identifying symbols, names of plumbing fixtures, number required, pipe connection sizes, and includes a space for remarks.

Plumbing Plan: Shows the location, size, and type of all plumbing equipment to be used.

Plywood: A piece of wood made of three or more layers of veneer joined with glue and usually laid with the grain of adjoining plies at right angles.

Pocket Door: A variation of the sliding door where the door slides into the wall; usually the flush style.

Porches: Generally structurally connected to the house; raised above grade level; usually covered while patios are not; typically smaller than patios, but can be larger.

Portico: A covered entryway attached to house, usually open on three sides and supported by posts or columns.

Post and Beam Construction: Uses posts, beams, and planks as framing members that are larger and spaced farther apart than conventional framing members.

Post Foundation: Consists of columns (posts) and footings on which the column bears; columns are taller than piers.

Postmodern Architecture: Combines traditional and contemporary influences.

Power Line Technology: Sending home automation signals over existing electrical wiring to control almost any electrical device.

Precast: Concrete shapes that are made before being placed into a structure.

Prefabricated Houses: Houses that are built in sections or component parts in a plant and then assembled at the site.

Prefabricated Metal Fireplace: Constructed of metal with the firebox and internal components assembled.

Preframed Panels: Fabricated panels consisting of precut lumber and plywood manufactured to standard dimensions ready for structural use.

Prehung Units: Jambs assembled with the door hung and ready for installation.

Presentation Drawing: Shows the finished structure and may also present various parts of the building in a form that is more meaningful to consumers than construction drawings.

Presentation Model: The purpose of this type of model is to show the appearance of the finished building as realistically as possible; most architectural models for residential use are of this type.

Preservative: Any substance that, for a reasonable length of time, will prevent the action of wood-destroying fungi, various kinds of borers, and similar destructive agents when the wood has been properly coated or impregnated with it.

Program: A set of computer instructions that, when executed, results in the computer performing an operation.

Programming Functions: Performed by devices that can control a sequence of events.

Projecting Corner Fireplace: See *Two-Face Adjacent Fireplace.*

Property Lines: Define the site boundaries; length and bearing (direction) of each line must be identified on the plot plan.

Proportion: The relation of one part to another, or to the whole object.

Pull-Down Menus: Appear at the top of Windows-based software; used to activate commands.

Purlins: Horizontal roof members laid over trusses to support rafters.

Q

Quarter Round: A small molding that has the cross section of a quarter circle.

Quarter-Sawed Lumber: Lumber that has been sawed so that the medullary rays showing on the end grain are nearly perpendicular to the face of the lumber.

Quoins: Stone or other building materials set in the corners of masonry sections of a house for appearance.

R

Rabbet: A groove cut along the edge of a board producing an L-shaped strip; used as trim and for jointery in cabinet construction.

Radial System: A system of ductwork in a forced-air system where round ducts radiate out in all directions from the furnace.

Radiant Heat: Heat that passes through the air with no assistance from airflow.

Radiant Heating: A method of heating usually consisting of a forced hot water system with pipes placed in the floor, wall, or ceiling; electrically heated panels may also be used.

Radiant Stove: A stove that warms a room only through radiant heat.

Radiant System: A hydronic heating system that utilizes copper pipes or other type of tubing embedded in a concrete floor or plastered ceiling.

Radiation: The flow of heat from a warm source through space in waves of infrared or visible light energy; this energy travels in straight lines from the source; sometimes called isolation.

Radio Grade 6 (RG-6) Cable: A type of coaxial cable composed of a core of solid copper wire surrounded by insulation and copper braiding that is capable of high speed digital data transmission in high bandwidths between the 50 MHz and 500 MHz.

Radon: An invisible, odorless, tasteless, radioactive gas that comes from the natural decay of uranium found in soil, rock, and water.

Rafter: The most basic member of roof framing; designed to support roof loads.

Rails: Horizontal members on a panel door.

Rake: The extension of a gable roof beyond the end wall of the house; also called the gable end.

Ranch: A long, low, one-story house that developed from the homes built by ranchers in the southwestern US.

Random Rubble: Stonework having irregular shaped units and no indication of systematic courses.

Rear Elevation: In architectural drawing, the rear view of an object.

Receptacle: A contact attached to a circuit to allow electricity to be drawn off for appliances or lighting; the same as a convenience outlet.

Red Cedar: A reddish to dull brown softwood; premier wood for shingles used in the United States because of its durability, ease of working, and lightweight; also used for interior and exterior trim, sash, doors, and siding.

Redwood: Light to deep reddish-brown softwood; mill products include sash, doors, blinds, siding, and trim; extensively used for garden furniture and exterior decking.

Register: The outlet in a forced-air system.

Regular Polygon: An object with sides of equal length and included angles.

Reinforced Concrete: Concrete with steel bars or webbing embedded for strength.

Relative Humidity: The ratio (percentage) of water vapor in the atmosphere to the amount required to saturate it at a given temperature.

Relays: Electrically operated switches.

Remodeling: Changing an existing space into a new form.

Rendering: The process of representing or depicting an object or scene in an artistic form by adding colors and shading; also, shading or coloring a 3D model or drawing with shadows, colors, and textures.

Renovation: Returning an old home to its previous condition, not necessarily its original condition, without changing the spaces.

Residential Designer: A specialist familiar with the complex process of planning and designing a residential structure, codes, ordinances, design options, and product choices.

Resistivity: The ability of a material to resist the transfer of heat or cold is its resistivity; commonly known as the R factor.

Resolution: Refers to the sharpness of the display on a computer monitor.

Restoration: Returning a structure to its original condition.

Retaining Wall: A wall that holds back an earth embankment.

Reveal: The side of an opening for a window or door, between the frame and the outer surface of the wall.

Reverse Osmosis System: A water treatment device in which the line pressure forces water through a thin, semipermeable membrane; the purified water is slowly collected in a small storage tank, while the contaminants that were unable to pass through the membrane are drained away.

Rheostat: An instrument used for regulating electric current.

Ribbon Windows: Wide, short windows often used on the first-floor level to provide added privacy.

Ridge: The top edge of the roof where two slopes meet.

Ridge Board: The board placed on edge at the ridge of the roof into which the upper ends of the rafters are fastened.

Right Side Elevation: In architectural drawing, the right side view of an object.

Rigid Paving System: Consists of a well-compacted subgrade, a properly prepared base, a reinforced concrete slab, a mortar setting bed, and brick paving with mortar joints between the pavers.

Riprap: A sustaining wall or foundation of random stone that is used to prevent erosion on an embankment.

Rise: The vertical distance of a roof measured from the top of the wall plate to the underside of the rafters; also, distance from the top surface of one tread to the same position on the next tread.

Riser: The vertical face of a step.

Riser Walls: A short wall that supports the entire dome structure while providing additional headroom on the second floor.

Roof Framing Plan: Drawn to clarify construction aspects associated with the roof; included if the roof is complicated and not clearly shown by the other standard drawings.

Roof Sheathing: Placed over the rafters to support the roofing material.

Roof Slope: The slant of the roof.

Roof Truss: An assembly of members that form a rigid framework of triangular shapes.

Rough Opening: The rough framed space in a wall required to install the window or door.

Round: A smoothly fitted external arc of a specified radius between two lines, arcs, or circles.

Rubble Stonework: Type of stonework in which the pattern is made up of undressed stones of irregular shapes.

Run: One-half the distance of the clear span of a roof; in stairs, the distance from the face of one riser to the face of the next.

S

Saddle: Built onto the roof on the high side of the chimney to shed water away from the chimney and down the roof; also called a cricket.

Safe Room: A room within the house that has been constructed to withstand tornado-force winds.

Salt Box: A Colonial style house patterned after early cracker, coffee, tea, and salt boxes.

Sash: Part of a window that slides up and down in grooves formed in the window frame; contains one or more lights of glass.

Sash Opening: The size of the opening inside the frame or the outside dimensions of the sash.

Scratch Coat: The first stucco layer in the three-coat process; embeds the reinforcement in stucco and provides support for the next coat; also called the foundation coat.

Screed: A long straightedge, usually a board, that is worked back and forth across the surface of concrete; this action brings excess water to the surface and settles the aggregate.

Scuttle: A small opening in a ceiling that provides access to an attic or roof.

Secondary Stacks: Plumbing stacks that do not drain water closets.

Section: A rectangular area of land used in the survey system that is approximately one mile square.

Section Lines: Used to show that the feature has been sectioned; also called crosshatch lines.

Septic Systems: Private sewage disposal systems that are used for rural and isolated home sites that cannot be connected to public sewers.

Septic Tank: One of the two components of a septic system; removes about 75% of the solids from the sewage by bacterial action before discharging the sewage into the disposal field; also provides storage space for the settled solids while they undergo digestive action.

Service Area: Supplements the living and sleeping areas of the house; includes the kitchen, clothes care center, garage or carport, utility, and storage.

Service Drop: The overhead service conductors between the last utility pole and the first point of attachment to the house; may be overhead or underground.

Service Entrance: The fittings and conductors that bring electricity into the building.

Service Entry: Usually connected to the kitchen; overall design may be improved by placing a mudroom or utility room between the kitchen and service entry.

Service Panel: The main distribution box that receives the electricity and distributes it to various points in the house through branch circuits; contains the main disconnect switch fuse or breaker that supplies the total electrical system of the house.

Service Stairs: A stairway intended for frequent, heavy use.

Setback Lines: Lines that indicate the required distances of the location of a structure in relation to the boundaries of the property.

Sheathing: The structural covering, usually wood boards or plywood, used over studs or rafters of a structure.

Shed Roof: A flat roof, slanting in only one direction.

Shiplap: Wood sheathing that is rabbeted so that the edges of the boards make a flush joint.

Shoe Mold: The small mold (trim) against the baseboard at the floor.

Short Break Lines: Used where part of the object is shown broken away to reveal an underlying feature or part of the object removed for some other reason.

Siding: The finish covering of the outside wall of a frame building, whether made of horizontal weatherboards, vertical boards with battens, shingles, or other material.

Signaling Circuits: Supply the electrical power to buzzers, doorbells, chimes, signal lights, or warning devices.

Sill: The lowest member of the frame of a structure, it rests on the foundation and supports the floor joists or the uprights (studs) of the wall; designed to drain water away and provide support for the side jambs.

Single-Face Fireplace: Has a single opening on one face.

Single-Pole Switch: A light switch that simply opens and closes the circuit.

Site: The plot of land on which a house sits and the larger community in which the plot is located.

Skylight: A window located on the roof.

Slab Foundation: An extension of a slab floor; it is placed at the same time the floor is cast and is not a separate unit.

Slab-on-Grade Construction: Construction with a slab foundation.

Sleeper: Usually a wood member embedded in concrete, as in a floor, that serves to support and to fasten subfloor or flooring.

Sleeping Area: Includes bedrooms, bath, dressing rooms, and nurseries.

Sleeping Level: The highest level in a split-level house.

Sliding Doors: Doors that slide in front of one another; popular where there are large openings; also called bypass doors.

Slope Design: An earth-sheltered house that maximizes earth cover around the dwelling by placing all windows and doors on one side of the structure—usually the south side; also called elevational design.

Small Scale Solid Model: An architectural model that shows only the exterior of the building and is not hollow.

Smoke Chamber: The area in the chimney just above the smoke shelf and damper.

Smoke Detector: A small appliance that gives a loud warning signal when it detects smoke in the house.

Smoke Shelf: Causes downdrafts in the chimney to be deflected upward.

Snap: A function that allows the cursor to "grab on to" certain locations on the screen.

Soffit: Usually the underside of an overhanging cornice.

Soft-Coat EIFS: EIFS that is typically thin (about 1/8″), adhesively attached, and flexible.

Software: Instructions that makes the computer hardware perform the intended tasks.

Softwood: Wood produced from coniferous trees or trees that bear cones; includes fir, pines, spruce, redwood, and cedar.

Soil Stack: A vertical drain pipe that collects waste from one or more fixtures.

Solar Collector: Device for trapping the sun's energy.

Solar Orientation: How the house is located on the lot in relation to the sun.

Solar Radiation: Energy from the sun.

Sole Plate: The bottom horizontal member of the wall on which studs rest.

Solid Blocking: A method of framing headers in which the header size is increased to completely fill the space from the top of the rough opening to the top plate; also, solid member placed between adjacent floor joists near the center of the span to prevent joists from twisting.

Solid Modeling: CADD object-creation method that creates 3D objects by generating a volume.

Southern Colonial: The largest and most gracious of all the Colonial styles, it features a front colonnade and giant portico.

Special Appliance Circuits: Located in the kitchen or workshop, usually above the countertop; designed for electric fry pans, mixers, blenders, toasters, and similar appliances that require large amounts of current.

Special-Purpose Entries: Those providing access to patios, decks, and courts.

Special-Purpose Rooms: May include a dedicated home office, sunroom or atrium, greenhouse, ham radio room, and so on.

Special-Shape Window: A fixed window that is in a made-to-order shape and size.

Specifications: Describe the quality of work and materials.

Specifications Writer: Prepares all the written information needed to describe materials, methods, and fixtures to be used in the structure.

Spiral Stairs: A set of stairs with steps that rise in a circle about a center point.

Split Bedroom Plan: Separates the master bedroom from the remaining bedrooms to provide even greater privacy.

Split-Level: A house design developed to solve the problem of a sloping site by shifting floor level areas to accommodate the site.

Spruce: Pale yellowish softwood used for general building purposes as planks, dimension stock, and joists; millwork products include doors, sash, casing, and trim.

Square: A unit of measurement of 100 square feet; usually applied to roofing material.

Square Foot Method: Produces an estimate of the building cost based on the total area in the house.

Stachybotrys atra: Commonly called "black mold," it is a greenish-black mold that can grow on material with a high cellulose and low nitrogen content.

Stack Wall: A wall framed with 2" × 6" studs and housing a plumbing stack.

Stairway: A series of steps that is installed between two or more floors of a building.

Standard Module: In modular construction, a 4" cube.

Station Point: The location of the observer's eye for a perspective drawing.

Steel Framing: The use of steel instead of wood for the complete framework of a residential structure.

Stepped Footings: Frequently necessary when building on hilly terrain.

Stick-Built: Residential structures that have been built by fastening together thousands of small pieces, such as boards, bricks, etc., on the job site.

Stiles: Vertical members on a panel door.

Stool: The horizontal ledge or strip as part of the frame below an interior window.

Storage Devices: Saves computer data for later use by placing the data on storage media; the computer hard drive in your home PC is a storage device with self-contained media.

Storm Surge: A dome of ocean water fueled by a hurricane that can be 20' at its highest point and up to 100 miles wide.

Straight Run Stairs: A set of stairs that have no turns; most common type in home construction.

Straight-Line Kitchen: A style of kitchen with all work centers on one wall; frequently used in small houses, cottages, and apartments; little space is required for this style and it usually provides for an efficient arrangement of kitchen facilities.

Stretcher Course: A row of masonry in a wall with the long side of the units exposed to the exterior.

Stringer: A structural member that supports the treads and risers in stairs; also called the carriage.

Structural C: The predominant shape used in steel framing for floor joists, wall studs, roof rafters, and ceiling joists; also called a C-section.

Structural Foam Sandwich Panels: Structural members made of two strong, stiff skins adhered to a foam core that is 3-1/2" to 11-1/4" thick.

Structural Model: An architectural model frequently used to show construction features of a residence.

Structured Wiring: An organized arrangement of high-quality cables and connections that distribute services throughout the home.

Structured Wiring Systems: Provide for complete home security and home automation in one package.

Stucco: A coating applied to the outside of a structure; most commonly refers to an outside plaster made with Portland cement as its base.

Stud: A vertical wall framing member.

Subfloor: Affixed to the floor joists; provides the surface on which the underlayment for the final finished floor will rest.

Subgrade: A fill or earth surface on which concrete is placed.

Sump: A pit in a basement floor that collects water and into which a sump pump is placed to remove the water.

Sun Space: A type of isolated gain system; also called an attached greenhouse.

Superinsulation: Aims to reduce heat transmission through the building envelope by increasing R values to achieve better thermal performance.

Surface Modeling: CADD object-creation method that creates 3D objects by drawing a skin, often over a wireframe.

Survey: A description of the measure and marking of land, including maps and field notes that describe the property.

Suspended Ceiling: A ceiling system supported by hanging from the overhead structural framing.

Switching Functions: Performed by devices that initiate an action based on an input.

Symbols Library: A collection of drafting symbols saved to a file that can be quickly inserted into a CADD drawing.

T

Take-Home Pay: Earnings after taxes and other deductions have been subtracted.

Tail Beam: A relatively short beam or joist supported in a wall on one end and by a header at the other.

Templates: Serve as a guide in drawing special lines or symbols.

Termite Shield: A shield, usually of noncorrosive metal, placed in or on a foundation wall or other mass of masonry or around pipes to prevent passage of termites.

Terrazzo Flooring: Wear-resistant flooring made of marble chips or small stones embedded in concrete and polished smooth.

T-Foundation: The most common type of foundation; the name is derived from the shape of the foundation and footing, which look like an inverted T.

Thermal Lag: The principle where structures with a large thermal mass, such as concrete structures, are able to delay the transfer of heat due to the heat storage capacity of the building mass; the basis for passive solar systems.

Thermal Mass: Materials that can store large amounts of heat such as stone, masonry, or concrete.

Thermosiphoning: The result of a fluid expanding and rising.

Thermostat: An automatic sensing device that sends a signal to the furnace or air conditioner at a temperature set by the homeowner.

Three-Coat Stucco System: The stucco material, which consists of Portland cement, lime, sand, and water, is applied in three coats; the traditional stucco system that has been in use for many years.

Three-Face Fireplace: A fireplace that is open on three sides; also known as a three-way fireplace.

Three-Way Fireplace: See *Three-Face Fireplace*.

Three-Way Switch: A light switch that allows a fixture to be turned on and off from two locations.

Threshold: A strip of wood or metal with beveled edges used over the finish floor and the sill of exterior doors.

Title: Provides evidence of property ownership and is where any liens, easements, or restrictions on the property are listed.

Toolbars: Software functions that contain buttons; picking a button activates a particular command.

Topographical Features: Include trees, shrubs, streams, roads, utilities, fences, and similar features; these features are represented on drawings by symbols.

Topography: The characteristics of the land on the site.

Tornado: A swirling column of air extending from a thunderstorm cloud down to the ground.

Total Rise: The total floor-to-floor vertical height of the stairs.

Total Run: The total horizontal length of the stairs.

Tract: A specified area of land.

Tradework Specifications: Criteria governing the work to be completed and its quality.

Traffic Circulation: The movement of people from one area or room to another.

Transom: A window placed above a door or permanent window that is hinged for ventilation purposes.

Transom Bar: A horizontal divider in an awning window.

Transverse Method: A method of post and beam construction where the beams follow the roof slope and the roof decking runs parallel to the roof ridge.

Trap: Installed below each fixture to prevent gases from escaping through the fixture drain into the house.

Tread: The horizontal member of each step on which a person steps.

Trim: The finish materials in a building, such as moldings, applied around openings (window trim, door trim) or at the floor and ceiling of rooms (baseboard, cornice).

Trimmers: Studs that support the header over an opening in the wall.

Trombe Wall: A massive wall that is dark colored on the outside to absorb more heat and located inside the structure immediately behind a large glazed area; vents at the top and bottom of the wall permit cool air to enter the space between the wall and glazing at the bottom, become heated, rise by convection to the top of the wall, and return to the dwelling interior.

Trowel: A rectangular tool used in a circular motion to further harden the surface of concrete and develop a very smooth finish.

Troweling: The finishing operation that produces a smooth, hard surface on concrete slab.

True Length Line: Established where the object touches the picture plane, this line is used to project heights to the perspective drawing; also called the true height line.

True Window R-value: The total window R-value plus a value consideration of the material used in the frame and the way the glass is sealed at the edges.

Truss: Structural members arranged and fastened in triangular units to form a rigid framework for support of loads over a long span.

Tweens: The frames inbetween keyframes in an animation.

Twisted-Pair Wire: A product in which each pair of wires is twisted together to preserve signal quality.

Two-Face Adjacent Fireplace: A fireplace that is open on the front and one side; also known as a projecting corner fireplace.

Two-Face Opposite Fireplace: A fireplace that is open on both the front and back sides.

Two-Story: A house design that has living space on two full levels.

Typical Wall Section: An orthographic projection where a portion of the wall has been removed to reveal interior detail.

U

U Factor: The number of Btus transmitted in one hour through one square foot of a building material for each degree of temperature difference; commonly called the U.

Uncoursed Cobweb: Type of stonework in which the stones are dressed with relatively straight edges to fit a particular place in the pattern; however, the finished stonework has a rubble, not ashlar, appearance; also called polygonal rubble.

Underlayment: A material placed under finish coverings, such as floor or shingles, to provide a smooth, even surface for applying the finish.

Unshielded Twisted-Pair (UTP) Cable: Designed to reject interference from other cable current as well as maximize the speed of data transmission; has eight conductors of Number 24 wire bundled inside a PVC jacket; conductors are twisted together into pairs to reduce electrical interference; also known as "Category 5" or "Cat 5."

Upflow Furnace: Designed for basement installation because the plenum is on top of the furnace.

U-Shaped Kitchen: A style of kitchen that is probably the most popular and one of the most attractive; has a highly efficient workspace; the work triangle is compact and functional.

U Stairs: A set of stairs that have two flights of steps parallel to each other with a landing between.

V

Valley: The internal angle formed by the junction of two sloping sides of a roof.

Valley Rafter: The diagonal rafter at the intersection of two intersecting sloping roofs.

Vanishing Points: The points in a perspective drawing at which all lines on the object will converge if extended.

Veneer: Extremely thin sheets of wood produced by slicing or rotary cutting a log.

Veneer Construction: Type of wall construction in which frame or masonry walls are faced with other exterior surfacing materials.

Vent Stack: A vertical soil pipe connected to the drainage system to allow ventilation and pressure equalization.

Ventilation: Reduces the temperature and moisture content in the house, crawl space, and attic by replacing the air in a space with fresh outside air.

Video Card: The device that transmits data from the CPU to the monitor.

Voltage: Pressure that forces current through a wire; one volt is the force that causes one ampere of current to flow through a wire that has one ohm of resistance.

W

Wainscot: Surfacing on the lower part of an interior wall when finished differently from the remainder of the wall.

Walkthrough Animation: Shows an animated view of how a building would appear to a person actually walking through it.

Wall Stack: A vertical duct designed to fit between the studs; usually 12″ × 3-1/4″.

Wall Tie: A small metal strip or steel wire used to bind tiers of masonry in cavity wall and veneer construction.

Warm Air Solar System: An active solar heating system that contains an array or group of collectors, called a bank; a heat storage box filled with stones or other thermal mass; and one or more blowers with controls for operating the system.

Warm Water Solar System: An active solar heating system that is composed of a bank of collectors, a warm water storage tank, a pump to circulate the water, some form of heat exchange device in the living space, and controls for operating the system.

Warped Roof: Limitless in design; these roofs may be constructed from concrete, molded plywood, or plastics.

Water Conditioner: A device used to remove dissolved minerals from water to make it soft; generally used in houses supplied by well water, which may contain calcium, magnesium, and other minerals, to remove hardness that causes scale buildup in plumbing.

Water Softener: A water treatment device that uses the line pressure to push hard water through a canister filled with a synthetic resin where a process called ion exchange is performed; ion exchange causes the hard calcium and magnesium ions to be dissolved and exchanged for soft ions in the resin.

Water Storage Wall: A type of indirect gain solar heating system where drums, fiberglass tubes, and large pipes are typical storage containers; the containers are located just behind a south-facing glazed area and are generally painted black.

Water Supply: Begins at the city water main or private water source.

Water Vapor: Invisible moisture contained in all air.

Watt: A unit of measure of work in a circuit; one watt is equal to one ampere under one volt of pressure (amp × volts = watts); most appliances are rated in watts.

Weatherstripping: Seals small cracks around doors and windows to reduce heat loss.

Web: The framework between the chords.

Weep Hole: An opening at the bottom of a wall that allows the drainage of water.

Welded-Wire Sandwich Panels: Provide the framework and structural reinforcement for a panel construction system; each sandwich panel consists of a three-dimensional, welded-wire spaceframe that is integrated with a foam plastic insulation core.

Well Hole: The space between flights in wide U stairs.

Wide Box Cornice with Lookouts: A cornice that normally requires additional support members, called lookouts, for fastening the soffit.

Wide Box Cornice without Lookouts: A cornice that has a sloped soffit; the soffit material is nailed to the underside of the rafters.

Wide U Stairs: A set of U stairs that have a well hole between each flight.

Winder Stairs: Stairs that have pie-shaped steps substituted for a landing.

Window Schedule: Provides information about all windows in a structure such as type of window, size, identifying symbol, manufacturer's number, and installation.

Wing Walls: Walls on either side of riser walls in a dome structure.

Wireframe: A group of lines that represent the edges of a 3D model, but does not have a skin or "thickness."

Wiring Cabinet: All cables from the speakers, computers, security sensors, video cameras—all the elements of a high-tech security system—are routed to this single location.

Wiring Closet: The central hub of a structured wiring installation.

Wood Foundations: A below grade, plywood-sheathed, pressure-treated stud wall; known by several names: permanent wood foundation (PWF), all-weather wood foundation (AWWF), and treated wood foundation.

Wood I-Beams: Typically made from 2" × 4" machine-stressed lumber or LVL flanges grooved to receive a 3/8" OSB or plywood web that is glued in place.

Work Centers: Areas where work is performed in the kitchen; includes the food preparation center, cleanup center, and cooking center.

Work Ethic: Includes enthusiasm for the work, willingness to work late to meet deadlines, and whether you are on site and prepared to work at starting time.

Work Triangle: A measure of kitchen efficiency, it is determined by drawing a line from the front-center of the range to the refrigerator to the sink and back to the range.

Wythe: Pertaining to a single-width masonry wall.

Z

Zoning: Creates areas that have certain building requirements for the size, location, and type of structure.

Index

1/2 bath, 137
3/4 bath, 138
3D animation and rendering commands, 125–126
3D capability, 102–103
3D drawing and viewing commands, 123–125
3D modeling, 124
3D models, 607, 630–631, 647
  entourage, 647
  rendering, 631
3DORBIT command, 125
3ds max, 652
3D vehicle symbols, 107
3D views, 125
9-12-15 unit method, 233–234

A
AARP, 129
absorber plate, 554, 556
access hole, 306
accordion doors, 324
activated carbon system, 495
active solar space heating, 554
active solar systems, 554–559
  warm air, 554, 556–558
  warm water, 558–559
ADA. *see* Americans with Disabilities Act (ADA)
adaptive reuse, 710
adding on, 703–706
  ground-level addition, 704–705
  second-story addition, 705–706
addition, 703
adhesives, for EWPs, 283–284
adjustable triangles, 72
AEC specific CADD package, 100, 103–107
A-frame roof, 411
airbrush rendering, 643
air circulation and cleaning, 520
air compression chamber, 494
Air Freezing Index, 591
air infiltration, 534
alarm functions, 466
all-weather wood foundation (AWWF), 240
Alphabet of Lines, 83, 101, 122
American Forest & Paper Association (AF&PA), 245, 285

American Institute of Architects (AIA), 121, 676
  layer naming standards, 121
  standard specifications forms, 676
American Institute of Building Design (ABID), 743
American Society for Testing and Materials, 289
American Society of Civil Engineers, 742
Americans with Disabilities, 1997 report, 129
Americans with Disabilities Act (ADA), 34–35
Ames Lettering Guide, 75
ampere (amp), 449
analog data, 469–470
ANGULAR command, 119
angular dimension, 119
angular perspective, 609
angular units of measure, 102
ANIMATE command, 126
animations, 96–97, 126, 653, 655
  file types, 655
  key, 653
apartment, 34
appliance requirements, 454
appliqué rendering, 643
ARC command, 111
architect, 739–740
architect's scale, 73
architectural drafter, 740
architectural drafting, teaching, 743
Architectural Graphic Standards, 647
architectural illustrator, 740–741
architectural lettering, 87–88
architectural model, 661–672
  constructing a balsa model, 664, 666–668, 670
  landscaping details, 668
  laser-cut parts, 670
  materials used in construction, 663–664
  types, 661–663
architectural styles, 17–29
  Colonial, 19–24
  contemporary structures, 24–29
  development of, 17–18
arcs, sketching, 78–79
AREA command, 117
areas of a residence, 129
ARRAY command, 116

ash dump, 370, 372
ashlar stonework, 310
asphalt shingles, 425–426
    asphalt laminate shingles, 426
atrium design, 570
attached greenhouse, 553
ATTDEF command, 123
attic, 419, 422, 702–703
    remodeling, 702–703
    ventilation, 419, 422
attribute, 122–123
autoclave, 595
automatic garage door opener, 326–327
AVI file, 655
awning windows, 334

B

bachelor's degree, 740
backfilling, 245
back-to-front split-level design, 46
balloon framing, 274–275
balsa model, constructing, 664, 666–668, 670
balsa wood, 664
balusters, 356, 366
    spacing, 366
base cabinets, 197–198
basement, adding on, 706
basement plan, 261–262, 265–267, 269
    basement/foundation plan, 262, 265
    drawing,
        CADD, 267, 269
        manual drafting, 265–267
    scale, 261
basement walls, 245–247
    concrete and masonry, 245–247
    damp-proofing, 246–247
bathrooms, 137–146, 699
    accessibility, 139–140
    accessibility for wheelchair users, 139–140,
        142–145
        bathtubs/showers, 143–145
        door size, 140
        sinks, 142
        size, 139
    bathtubs and showers, 143
    décor, 145
    electricity, 144
    lavatories, 141–142
    mirror, 140–141
    number, location, and size, 137–139
    primary fixtures, 140–143
    remodeling, 699
    safety, 144–145
    sink cabinets and vanities, 141
    ventilation, 144
    water closets, 142–143

bathtubs, 143
batter boards, 234–235
bay window, 346
    framing, 306
beam, 276
    calculations, 250–251
    types, 291
beam compass, 74
beams and girders, 248–252
bearing angles, 218
bearing wall, 248
bedrooms, 131–137
    arranging furniture for the disabled, 134
    closets, 135
    colors and finishing, 136–137
    doors and windows, 135–136
    door sizes to accommodate wheelchair, 136
    size and furniture, 131–134
bell wire, 468
benchmark, 218
BHATCH command, 112
bidet, 143
bi-fold doors, 321, 323
bird's eye view, 616
black mold, 725
blocks, 122–123
block walls, 306
border lines, 84
bow window, 346
box bay, 346
box cornice, 414
box sill, 273
bracing, 299, 301
branch circuits, 452–454, 487
    electrical plan, 487
branch main, 496
break lines, 85
brick, 312
brick bonds, 312
brick ledge, 261
brick mold, 328
bridging boards, 278
British thermal unit (Btu), 531, 560–562
    calculation of, 560–562
brown coat, 316
budgeting for housing, 57
building codes, 54
Building Construction Cost Data Book, 687
building main, 491
Building Officials and Code Administrators
    International (BOCA), 364
built-up beams, 248
bundled cable, 477
butterfly roof, 410–411

C

cabinets, 197–198
cable, 467–469, 472, 476–478
  bundled, 477
  Category 5, 468–469, 472, 476–477
  Category 5E, 478
  RG-6 quad shield, 469, 472, 477
  telephone, 467
  unshielded twisted-pair (UTP), 468
cable pair, 467
cable/wiring standards, 468–469
CAD, 91–92. *see also* computer-aided drafting and design (CADD)
CAD Layer Guidelines, 121
CADD. *see* computer-aided drafting and design (CADD)
cantilevered joists, 282
Cape Ann, 19–20
Cape Cod, 19, 41–42
Cape Colonial, 19–20
carbon monoxide (CO), 530–531, 717–719
  detection, 717–719
  detector, 530–531, 718–719
  poisoning, 718
cardboard, 664
career opportunities, 739–748
  architect, 739–740
  architectural drafter, 740
  architectural illustrator, 740–741
  construction technologist, 743
  entrepreneurship, 745–746
  estimator, 741–742
  keeping a job and advancing a career, 743–745
  residential designer, 743
  specifications writer, 741
  surveyor, 742
  teaching architectural drafting, 743
carport, 207–213
  applications, 211
  design, 208–210
  handicapped accessible, 208
  size and location, 208
case instruments, 75
casement windows, 334
casing, 328
Category 5 cable, 468, 469, 472, 476–478
  color-coding, 468
  Category 5E cable, 478
caulk, 316
cavity walls, 306
ceiling, 306
  construction, 306
  joists, 306
cement, 253, 283
  cement mortar mix, 283

centerline method, 78–79
centerlines, 84
center-of-glass R-value, 536
center-wheel compass, 74
central air conditioner, 522
central processing unit (CPU), 97
central station monitoring, 472
Certified Professional Building Designer (CPBD), 743
CHAMFER command, 115–116
CHANGE command, 122
chimney/fireplace, 237, 370, 375–376
  footing, 237
  framing around, 375–376
  terms, 370
chords, 279
CIRCLE command, 110–111
circle top windows, 344
circles, sketching, 78–79
circuit, 449
circuit breaker, 449, 452
circuit requirement calculations, 454
circular objects, drawing in perspective, 632
circular stairs, 355
circulating stove, 380
cleanout, 370, 497
clear span, 414
clerestory window, 346–347
climate control, 515–538
  air circulation and cleaning, 520
  cooling systems, 522
  equipment schedule, 543
  heating systems, 523–530
  heat loss calculations, 531–532, 534–536
  humidity control, 518–520
  programmable thermostats, 520–522
  temperature control, 515–518
  true window R-value, 536
climate control plan, 539–547
  distribution system, 539–542
  ductwork, 540–542
  hydronic system piping, 542
  outlet and inlet locations, 540
  procedure for drawing, 543–544
    CADD, 543–544
    manual drafting, 543
  required information, 539
  schedules, calculations, and notes, 543
  thermostats and climate control equipment, 542–543
close cornice, 417
closed plan, 158
closets, 135
clothes care center, 205–207
  wheelchair accessibility, 206–207
coal-burning stove, 380, 385
coat closet, 168
cold-rolled channel, 305

cold-rolled Z members, 305
cold water branch lines, 491
cold water main, 491
Colonial styles, 19–24
colonnade, 23
COLOR command, 122
colored pencil rendering, 640, 642
colors, 101, 122
    CADD software capabilities, 101
    object display colors, 122
combination scale, 73
combination system, 478
combination windows, 346
command line, 109
commands, 102, 110–119, 123–126
    3D animation and rendering, 125–126
    3D drawing and viewing, 123–125
    dimensioning, 119
    display control, 117–119
    drawing, 110–112
    editing and inquiry, 113–117
common brick, 312
common method, 616, 625
communication/recording functions, 466
community, 52
compass, 74–75
compressor-cycle system, 522
computer components, 97
computer-aided drafting and design (CADD), 81–83,
    88, 91–100, 102–103, 109–127, 130, 133–134, 150,
    189, 225–226, 229, 267, 269, 319, 359, 371, 402,
    404–407, 442–443, 445, 488, 511, 513, 543–544
    3D capability, 102–103
    architectural applications, 95–97
    bedroom and bathroom, 130, 133–134
    climate control plan, 543–544
    commands and functions, 109–127
    doors and windows, 319
    electrical plan, 488
    elevation, 442–443, 445
    fireplace, 371
    flexibility, 94
    floor plan, 402, 404–407
    foundation plan, 267, 269
    hardware, 82
    introduction to, 91–92
    living area, 150
    plumbing plan, 511, 513
    procedure for drawing plot plan, 225–226, 229
    productivity, 93
    program customization, 102
    reasons for using, 92–95
    scale, 94–95
    selecting a CADD package, 99–100
    service area, 189
    software, 82
    stairs, 359
    symbols library, 88, 93
    uniformity, 94
    workstation, 97–99
computer-generated perspectives, 630–631
computer-generated rendering, 643, 645
concrete, composition of, 253
concrete and masonry, 245–247, 253–254
    basement walls, 245–247
concrete blocks, 254–255
concrete masonry units (CMU), 589–591
concrete slab, 254
concrete wall systems, 584–589
condensation, 722–724
    avoiding, 723–724
condominium, 33–34
conduction, 550
conductors, 449, 450–452, 468–470
    data and video, 468–470
    for buzzers, bells, and chimes, 468
    sizes and designations, 452
cone of vision, 613–614
construction, introduction to products and methods,
    579–580
construction details, 62, 107
construction lines, 85
construction materials, standard sizes, 58
construction technologist, 743
Consumer Electronic Bus (CEBus), 473
contemporary, 24–29, 412
    roof types, 412
    structures, 24–29
    style, 24–25
contour interval, 219, 224
contour lines, 219–220, 224, 229
contract specification sheet, 676
contraction joints, 254
contractor, 712
convection, 550
convenience outlets, 449, 455–456
    electrical plan, 485
cooling systems, 522
cooperative, 33
coordinate entry, 102
copper pipe, for hydronic system, 542
copper tubing, 493, 508
COPY command, 114
corner bracing, 299, 301
cornice, 414–415
corridor kitchen, 194
corrosion prevention, 461–462
cost and restrictions, 53–54
cost of housing, 57
Council of American Building Officials (CABO), 364
counterflow furnace, 525
coursed rubble, 310

court, 177, 179, 184
crawl space, keeping dry, 723–724
creep, 255
cricket, 376
cripples, 299
cross bridging, 278
crosshatch lines, 85
C-section, 304–305
cubic foot method, 686
curing, 253
curtain walls, 291
curved panel roof, 412
cutting-plane line, 85

D

damper, 370, 374
data and video conductors, 468–470
data exchange, 103
dead loads, 248
deck, 180
deck materials, 592–595
　synthetic, 593–595
　tropical hardwoods, 592–593
　weather-resistant, 592–595
decking planks, 293
deed, 53, 54
degradation, 94
dehumidifier, 520
dehumidifying system, 701
dense residential dwellings, 32
Department of Veterans Affairs (VA), 676
Description of Materials form, 676, 678–683
design temperature difference, 531
designing with CADD, 130, 150, 189, 319, 359, 371
　bedroom and bathroom, 130
　doors and windows, 319
　fireplace, 371
　living area, 150
　service area, 189
　stairs, 359
DIAMETER command, 119
diameter dimension, 119
digital data, 469–470
digitizer puck, 97, 98
DIM command, 119
dimensioning, 100, 393, 395
　floor plan, 393
　metric, 395
　with general purpose CADD packages, 100
dimensioning commands, 119
dimension lines, 84–85
dimmer switch, 458
dining rooms, 158–164
　décor, 163–164
　location, 162–163
　planning, 158, 160

size, 160–162
wheelchair accessibility, 162
direct gain system, 550–551
display control commands, 117–119
display controls, 102
display device, 98
display grid, 120, 599
disposal field, 501–502
DIST command, 117
DISTANCE command, 117
distillation system, 495
distribution panel, 450–452
distribution system, climate control plan, 539–542
dividers, 74
dome structures, 31–32, 571–576
　advantages, 576
　disadvantages, 576
　typical construction, 574–575
　variations, 573–574
door jamb, 327, 329
door schedule, 327
doorbell, 457, 468
　circuits, 468
　wiring to signaling device, 457
doors, 106, 136, 166–167, 319, 320–330
　bedroom, 136
　designing with CADD, 319
　details, 327–330
　entryway, 166–167
　exterior, 325–327
　interior, 320–324
　specifying, 327
　standard symbols, 106
　symbols, 319
dormers, 41, 703
double-action doors, 323–324
double headers, 306
double-hung windows, 334
double joist framing, 276, 278
DOUBLE LINE command, 110, 391, 402
double-L stairs, 354–355
downspout, 424
drafting equipment, 68–76
drainage network, 495
drain locations, plumbing plan, 507
drain tile, 247
drawing aids, 102, 119–121
drawing boards, 71
drawing commands, 110–112
drawing instruments and techniques, 67–90
Drawing Interchange Format (DXF), 103
drawing sheet sizes, 71
drawing units, 102
drawings included in a set of plans, 58–64
Dream® Deck, 593
drip cap, 328

driveway, 211
drum wall, 552
ducts, 539
ductwork, 539–542
    planning, 540–542
Dutch doors, 324
Dutch hip roof, 410
DWV, 508

E

earthquake, 726–727
    reducing damage, 726–727
    zone, 726
earth-sheltered dwellings, 565–571
    advantages, 571
    atrium design, 570
    cost, 569–570
    design variations, 570–571
    disadvantages, 571
    energy conservation, 568
    orientation on the site, 566–567
    penetrational design, 570–571
    roof systems, 569
    site considerations, 565–570
    slope design, 570
    soil and groundwater, 567–568
    structural system, 568–569
    topography, 567
Echelon®, 473–474
editing, CADD software capabilities, 101
editing commands, 113–117
electrical, 106, 449–450, 452–462, 483
    box, 455
    branch circuits, 452–454
    circuit requirement calculations, 454
    ground-fault circuit interrupter (GFCI), 458–459
    low voltage exterior lighting, 459–462
    outlets, 455–457
    service entrance and distribution panel, 450–452
    switches, 457–458
    symbols, 106, 483
    terms, 449–450
electrical plan, 62, 483–490
    branch circuits, 487
    convenience outlets, 485
    lighting, 485–486
    other devices, 486
    procedure for drawing (CADD), 488
    procedure for drawing (manual drafting), 487–488
    required information, 483–487
    service entrance, 483–485
    split-level house, 487–488
    switches, 485
    telephone and jacks, 486
electric meter, 485
electric radiant heating system, 528, 530

Electronics Industries Association (EIA), 468
elevation drawing, 609
elevations, 59, 62, 431–447, 650
    dimensions, notes, and symbols, 436
    doors, 434
    floor-to-ceiling height, 434
    grade line, floors, and ceilings, 434
    identification, 434
    procedure for drawing (CADD), 442–443, 445
    procedure for drawing (manual drafting), 439–440
    rendered, 650
    required information, 431–436
    roof features, 436
    typical wall section, 436–438
    walls, 434
    windows, 434
elevator, 366
ellipses, sketching, 79
enclosed stairs, 356
enclosing square method, 79
engineered floor trusses, 278–280
Engineered Wood Association (APA), 245, 285
engineered wood products (EWPs), 283–290
    advantages and disadvantages, 284
    glue-laminated lumber, 287–289
    laminated veneer lumber (LVL), 286–287
    oriented strand board (OSB), 284–285
    parallel strand lumber (PSL), 285–286
    wood I-beams, 289–290
engineer's scale, 73
entourage, 643, 646–647
    symbols, 647
entrepreneur, 745–746
entryway, 164, 166–167
    handicapped accessible, 167
Environmental Protection Agency (EPA), 720–722
EON™, 594
equity, 57
ERASE command, 113
erasers, 70
erasing shields, 71
estimating building cost, 685–693
    cubic foot method, 686
    labor, 687
    material takeoff, 686–687
    materials, 686
    more accurately, 686–687, 692
    square foot method, 685–686
estimator, 741–742
EWPs. see engineered wood products (EWPs)
excavation, 235
expanded polystyrene (EPS), 586, 591
expansion plan, 64, 396
EXTEND command, 116
extended plenum system, 540–542
extension lines, 84

exterior doors, 325–327
exterior insulation finish system (EIFS), 312, 314, 580–581
   advantages, 580–581
   disadvantages, 581
   installation/application, 581
exterior perspective, 650
exterior wall corners, 299, 301

F

face brick, 312
factory-built homes. *see* industrialized housing
family needs, 54–55, 57
family recreation room, 169, 173–175
   applications, 175
   décor, 175
   location, 169
   size, 173
   wheelchair accommodation, 173
Federal Fair Housing Act of 1988, 35
felt-tipped rendering, 642
fillet, 115
FILLET command, 115
finish coat, 316–317
fire, 471, 715–717
   causes, 715–716
   prevention, 716
   protection, 471
   safety code requirements, 717
fire chamber, 372
fireclay, 370
firecut, 306
fire extinguisher, 717
fireplace, 369–372, 377–380
   design considerations, 369–370
   designing with CADD, 371
   inserts, 380
   prefabricated metal, 380
   prefabricated steel, heat circulating, 372, 380
   single-face, 377
   specifications, 377–380
   three-face, 380
   two-face adjacent, 380
   two-face opposite, 377
fireplace/chimney, 307, 375–376
   framing around, 375–376
   terms, 370
fixed windows, 340, 344, 346
flash floods, 728–729
flashing, 308, 315–316, 422–424
   repair, 316
   roofs, 422–424
flat roof, 410
flexibility, 94
flexible curve, 75
flexible paving system, 255

float, 253
floodplains, 729
floods, 728–729
   mitigation, 729
floor framing plan, 64
floor joists, 275–278
   composition, 275
   size, 275
   spacing, 276
   span data, 276–277
   steel, 276
floor plan, 59, 68, 389–408
   cabinets, appliances, and permanent fixtures, 392
   dimensioning, 393
   drawing, 396–397, 401–402, 404–407
   drawing procedure, 396–397, 401–402, 404–407
      CADD, 402, 404–407
      manual drafting, 396–397, 401
   fireplaces, 392
   material symbols, 393
   presentation, 650
   required information, 391–395
   room names, 393
   scale and sheet identification, 393, 395
   split-level house, 396
   stairs, 392
   two-story house, 396
   walls, 391
   walks, patios, and decks, 392
   windows and doors, 391–392
floor trusses, 276, 278–280
flue, 370, 374–375
fluorescent light, 486
flush doors, 320–321, 325
flyby animation, 652
foam board, 663–664
folded plate roof, 411–412
footings, 235–237
   excavation for, 235
   for fireplaces and chimneys, 237
   shapes and specifications, 236–237
   stepped, 237
footprint, 45
forced-air heating system, 523, 525
foundation plan, 59, 259
   drawing, 261–262, 267, 269
      CADD, 267, 269
      manual drafting, 261–262
   preliminary steps to drawing, 260–261
   scale, 261
foundation walls, 237–245
   pier and post foundations, 240
   slab foundations, 238, 240
   T-foundations, 238
   wood foundations, 240, 242–245
four-wire telephone cable, 467

foyer, 168
frame wall construction, 297–302
    CADD software, 298
    exterior corners and bracing, 299, 301
    headers, 299
    interior walls, 301–302
    plates, 299
framing, 274–276, 278, 283, 302–306
    balloon, 274–275
    bay window, 306
    double joist, 276, 278
    special situations, 306
    steel, 302–305
    under slate or tile, 283
free-circle method, 79
free-form roof, 412
freehand sketching, 77–81
French doors, 324
frontage, 53
front elevation, 68
front view, 68
front-to-back split-level design, 46
frost depth, 235, 262
frost-protected shallow foundation, 591–592
full bath, 137
furniture and appliance symbols, 107
furniture plan, 64
furring strips, 308
fuse, 449

G

gable end, 418
gable roof, 409
gambrel roof, 410
garage, 207–213, 699, 701
    applications, 211
    design, 208–210
    doors, 211
    handicapped accessible, 208
    remodeling, 699, 701
    roof, 211
    siding, 211
    size and location, 208
garage doors, 326–327
Garrison, 20
gazebo, 177, 179, 184
general purpose CADD package, 100–103
geodesic dome, 572
GFCI. *see* ground-fault circuit interrupter (GFCI)
girders, 276
glider windows, 334
glue-laminated lumber, 287–289
glulam beams, 287
grab bars, 144–145
grade line, 434
green space requirements, 706

grid, 76, 120, 631
    display, 120
    perspective, 631
GRID command, 120
grid lines, 599, 600
grid snap, 120
grommets, 305
gross annual income, 57
ground-fault circuit interrupter (GFCI), 144,
    458–459, 461
ground-level addition, 704–705
ground line (GL), 609, 611
ground-source heat pump, 530
groundwater, 568
guardrails, 364, 366
    code requirements, 364, 366
guidelines, hand lettering, 85
gusset, 419
gutters, 424

H

hand pivot method, 79
handrails, 361, 364, 366–367
    code requirements, 364, 366
    for ramps, 367
hard-coat EIFS, 580
hard-wired systems, 474–475
HATCH command, 112
hatching, 100, 112
hatch patterns, 100, 104, 259
    AEC CADD programs, 104
    general purpose CADD packages, 100
    on a foundation plan, 259
headers, 299
headroom, 356
health and safety, designing for, 715–738
hearth, 370, 371–372
heat loss, 531, 568
    earth-sheltered dwellings, 568
heat loss calculations, 531–532, 534–536
    air infiltration, 534, 535–536
    ceiling, 532, 535
    example, 534–536
    final calculations, 534, 536
    floor, 532, 534, 535
    procedure, 531–532, 534
    using CADD software, 536
    walls, 531–532, 534–535
heating and cooling plan, 64
heating systems, 523–530
    electric radiant system, 528, 530
    forced-air, 523, 525
    heat pump, 530
    hydronic, 525–528
heat pump, 530
Hebel wall system, 595

Hexadome, 573–574, 575
hidden lines, 84
HIDE command, 125
high-efficiency stove, 385
hip roof, 409
historic preservation, 695, 707–712
    adaptive reuse, 710
    motivation for, 707–709
    preparing plans, 710–712
    restoration, 709
    through remodeling, 709
home automation, 472–478
    combination system, 478
    hard-wired system, 474–475
    power line technology, 475–476
    structured wiring system, 476–478
    summary questions, 478
    types, 474–478
hopper windows, 336
horizon line (HL), 611, 614, 616
    vertical height of, 614, 616
horizontal furnace, 525
horizontal lines, sketching, 77–78
horizontal sliding windows, 334
hot-rolled channel, 305
hot water branch lines, 492
hot water main, 492
hours of sunshine, calculation procedure, 560–561
house design, 37–50
house drain, 496, 506
    location, 506
house sewer, 496–497
housed stringer, 356, 360
housing cost, 57
humidifier, 518–519
humidity control, 518–520
hurricane, 732–735
    building to resist hurricanes, 734–735
    codes, 732–734
    mitigation, 732–734
    warnings, 735
HVAC symbols, 106–107
hydronic heating system, 525–528, 542
    planning piping, 542

I
I-beams, ASTM standard, 289
illustration board, 664
incandescent light, 486
inclined lines and angles, sketching, 78
indirect gain system, 551–552
individual appliance circuit, 453–454
Indoor Radon Abatement Act, 720
industrialized housing, 600–603
    module sizes, 601
    quality, 602

versatility, 603
infiltration, 531
information, communication, and security wiring, 465–482
in-house water treatment devices, 495
inkjet plotter, 99
inkjet printer, 83, 99
ink rendering, 638–639
inlets, 540
inner hearth, 370
input devices, 97, 98
inquiry commands, 113–117
INSERT command, 123
inside design temperature, 531
insulated concrete block systems, 589–591
insulated concrete wall forms, 585–587
insulated concrete wall systems, 587–588
insulation, 515–516, 549
Integra™, 589–590
Integrated Networks, 473–474
interior designer, 711
interior doors, 320–324
    minimum width, 320
interior walls, 301–302
intermediate level, 45–46
International Conference of Building Officials (ICBO), 364
ion exchange, 495
ionization smoke detector, 716
ipe, 592
irregular curves, 75, 81
    sketching, 81
island kitchen, 196, 203
isolated gain system, 552–554
isometric drawing, 124, 607

J
jacks, 468–469
jalousie windows, 336, 340
jambs, 327, 329
job site safety, 744–745
joists, 275–278, 282, 306
    cantilevered, 282
    ceiling, 306
    floor, 275–278

K
keyboard, 97, 98
keyframe, 653
kip, 248
kitchen, 189–205, 698–699
    applications, 203
    cabinets and appliances, 196–201
    corridor, 194
    décor, 202

kitchen, *(Continued)*
    eating areas, 203, 205
    handicapped accessible, 191, 193, 197–198, 205
    island, 196, 203
    location, 202
    L-shaped, 193–194
    peninsula, 195
    planning, 191–193
    remodeling, 698–699
    straight-line, 193
    U-shaped, 194–195, 203
    ventilation, 202
Kraft paper, 315

L

laminated veneer lumber (LVL), 286–287
laminates, 426
landing, 356
landscape plan, 64, 224–225
land surveyor, 742
laser-cut model parts, 670
laser printer, 83, 99
lath, 316
lavatories, 141–142
LAYER command, 121–122
layers, 101, 121–122
    CADD software capabilities, 101
leader, 119
LEADER command, 119
leadership, 745
left side elevation, 68
left vanishing point (LVP), 613
lettering devices, 76
lettering guides, 75
letter size, 88
letter spacing, 88
Leviton Integrated Networks™ (LIN), 474
light pens, 98
light sources, placing and adjusting, 643–644
lighting, 449, 453, 485–486
    circuit, 453
    electrical plan, 485–486
    fixture schedule, 486
    interior, 485–486
    outdoor, 486
    outlet, 449
LINEAR command, 119
linear dimension, 119
LINE command, 110–111, 121
    setting midpoint object snap, 121
    to draw a square or rectangle, 111
lines used in architectural drawing, 83–87
linetypes, 85–87, 101, 122
    application, 85–87
    CADD software capabilities, 101
    managing, 122

lintel, 252, 376
    fireplace, 376
LIST command, 116
Lite-Form™, 585–586
live load, 248, 276
living area, 129, 149–169, 173–175, 177–186
    designing with CADD, 150
    dining rooms, 158–164
    entryway and foyer, 164–168
    family recreation room, 169, 173–175
    living rooms, 150–158
    patios, porches, courts, and gazebos, 177–186
    special-purpose rooms, 175, 177
living level, 46
living rooms, 150–158
    décor, 155, 158
    location, 154–155
    size, 151, 154
    wheelchair accessibility, 154
    windows and doors, 155
load-bearing wall, 276
load calculation figures, 248
long break line, 85
longitudinal method, 292–293
LONWorks®, 474
louvered openings, 419, 422
low-efficiency stove, 380
low voltage exterior lighting, 459–462
    planning, 459–461
    wiring considerations, 461–462
low-voltage switching, 479
L-shaped kitchen, 193–194
L stairs, 354

M

main entry, 166
mainframe, 97
main stack, 496
main stairs, 353
major module, 598
mansard roof, 410
masonry veneer, 311
masonry wall, 306, 308–311
    construction, 306, 308–311
mass property analysis, 103
material and tradework specifications, 675–684
MATERIAL command, 125
material hatch patterns, 393
material specifications, 675, 676
material symbols, 393
material takeoff, 686–687
materials list, 686, 688–692
mean sea level, 220
mean solar radiation, 560
mechanical pencil, 70
medium-efficiency stove, 380, 385

meranti, 592
meridian arrow, 217, 224, 229
metal roofing, 426, 428
metric dimensioning, 395
miniframe, 97
minor module, 598
MIRROR command, 114
mirrors, 140–141
MLINE command, 110
model ethics code, 744
modern style, 24–25
modular applications, 597–605
    industrialized housing, 600–603
    modular components, 600
    standardization, 597–600
modular aspects, 57–58
modular components, 600
modular grid, 599
modular panel components, 598–599
modular planning and dimensioning, 599–600
modules, 57–58
modules within modules, 603
moisture and mold problems, 722–726
moisture barrier, 315, 699, 701
mold, 724–726
    health hazards of, 724–726
    health problems, 725
    prevention and removal, 725–726
    types, 725
monitor, 97, 98
monitoring functions, 465–466
mortar joints, 312
mortgage lenders, 57
motion detector, 466, 470, 471
mouse, 97, 98
MOVE command, 113–114
MOV file, 655
MTEXT command, 112
mudsill, 273
mullions, 334
multifamily housing, 32–34
muntins, 334

N

narrow box cornice, 414
narrow U stairs, 355
National Association of Home Builders (NAHB), 744
National Council of Building Designer Certification (NCBDC), 743
National Electrical Code (NEC), 452–454, 456, 459, 467–468, 483–484
    appliance circuit specifications, 454
    branch circuit specifications, 453
    classes of signaling circuits, 467–468
    GFCI regulations, 459
    minimum amp service recommendation, 452
    placement of outlets, 456
    service entrance requirements, 483–484
National Energy Policy Act, 499
National Plumbing Code, 505
National Radon Safety Board, 722
National Safety Council, 722
network, 97, 473
newel, 356
New England Gambrel, 20
nonhousing expenses, 57
nontraditional structures, 565–578
    dome structures, 571–576
    earth-sheltered dwellings, 565–571
nosing, 356

O

object display colors, 122
object lines, 84
objects, available with general purpose CADD packages, 100
object snap, 121
oblique drawing, 607
oblique perspective, 609
Occupational Safety and Health Administration (OSHA), 744–745
office method, 616, 625
OFFSET command, 391, 402
ohm, 450
one-and-one-half-story design, 41–42
    advantages, 41
    heating and cooling, 42
one-pipe system, 525–526
one-point perspective, 609, 623, 624–630
    drawing sequence, 625, 627–630
one-story ranch, 37–41
    advantages, 38
    disadvantages, 38–39, 41
    heating, 39
open cornice, 414
open plan, 158
open riser stairs, 359
open stairs, 356
open web construction, 279
OPTIONS command, 120
oriented strand board (OSB), 284–285
ORTHO command, 121
orthographic projection, 67
orthographic views, 67–68
outdoor lighting, 459–462, 486
outlets, 455–457
output devices, 82–83, 97, 98–99
outside design temperature, 531
overall dimensions, 393
overcurrent protection, 450, 452
overhead sectional door, 326

P

PAN command, 118
panel doors, 321, 325
panic button, 471
paper, 71
parallel perspective, 609
parallel strand lumber (PSL), 285–286
parasol roof, 412
parge coat, 247
partition walls, 276, 278
passive solar systems, 549–554
 direct gain system, 550–551
 indirect gain system, 551–552
 isolated gain system, 552–554
 space heating, 549–550
 summary of principles, 554
patio, 177, 179–180, 184
Pau Lope®, 592
paving, 255–256
pencil rendering, 638
pencils, 70
penetrational design, 570–571
peninsula kitchen, 195
pen plotter, 82, 99
people and their structures, 17–18
percolation tests, 502
perimeter system, 470–471, 540
permanent wood foundation (PWF), 240
Perma-Poly™, 593
perspective, 607
perspective drawing, 609
perspective drawing vs. orthographic drawing, 609
perspective grid, 76, 631
perspectives, 609–633
 computer-generated, 630–631
 drawing circular objects, 632
 drawing complex features, 632–633
 ground line, 609, 611
 horizon line, 611
 picture plane (PP), 610–612
 station point (SP), 609, 612
 terminology, 609–613
 true length line (TL), 612
 two-point, 613–614, 616
 vanishing points, 612–613
phase-change material, 552
Philippine mahogany, 592
photoelectric smoke detector, 716
pictorial presentation, 62
picture plane (PP), 610, 611–614
 distance from station point, 613–614
 position of object with respect to, 614
picture window, 340
pier foundation, 240
pilaster, 245

pin colors, 469
pipes, 539
pipe sizes and types, plumbing plan, 507–508
plain stringer, 356, 360
plan drawing, 609
plan view, 68
planked roof, 293
plans, brief descriptions of, 59, 62
plant symbols, 225
plates, 299
platform framing, 273–274
plot plan, 59, 217–232, 650
 contour lines, 219–220
 location of the structure on the site, 222–223
 presentation, 650
 procedure for drawing, 223–226, 229
  CADD, 225–226, 229
  manual drafting, 223–224
 property lines, 217–218
 scale, 223, 226
 topographical features, 220–222
plotter, 82–83
plotting, 102
plumbing, 106, 491–504
 fixtures, 498
 fixture schedule, 508
 in-house water treatment devices, 495
 private sewage disposal system, 499–502
 septic system, 499–502
 symbols, 106, 508
 water and waste removal, 495–498
 water conservation, 498–499
 water supply system, 491–495
plumbing plan, 64, 505–514
 drain locations, 507
 notes, 508–509
 pipe sizes and types, 507–508
 plumbing fixture schedule, 508
 procedure for drawing (CADD), 511, 513
 procedure for drawing (manual drafting), 509, 511
 required information, 505–509
 symbols and legend, 508
 waste lines and vent stacks, 506
 water supply lines, 506–507
pocket doors, 323
polygonal rubble, 310–311
POLYGON command, 111–112
POLYLINE command, 485, 488
polymer-based (PB) system, 580
polymer-modified (PM) system, 580
porch, 177, 179–180, 184, 699, 701
 remodeling, 699, 701
portico, 23–24
Portland cement stucco, 313
post and beam construction, 290–294
 beam types, 291

roof beam placement, 293
post calculations, 251–252
post (column) foundation, 240
post-modern architecture, 30
post sizes, 291
power line technology, 475–476
prefabricated metal fireplace, 380
prefabricated metal stove, 380
prefabricated steel, heat circulating fireplace, 372, 380
prehung units, 327
presentation drawings, 95, 637–660
    rendering, 637–645
    shading and shadows, 645–646
    types, 647, 650, 652–653, 655
    walkthrough animation, 650, 652–653, 655
presentation elevation, 650
presentation floor plan, 650
presentation model, 663
presentation plot plan, 650
principal orthographic views, 67–68
printing, 102
private mortgage insurance (PMI), 57
private sewage disposal system, 499–502
productivity, 93
program customization, 102
programming functions, 466
projecting corner fireplace, 380
PROPERTIES command, 116, 122
property lines, 217–218, 223–224, 226
property protection, 470
protractors, 72
PSL. *see* parallel strand lumber (PSL)
pull-down menu, 109
PVC jacket, 468–469
    color, 469

Q

quality of living, 58

R

R factor, 531
radial system, 540
radiant heat, 380
radiant stove, 380
radiant system, 526
radiation, 550
radiator, 525–526
radio grade 6 (RG-6) cable, 469–470, 472, 477
RADIUS command, 119
radius dimension, 119
radon, 719–722
    and lung cancer, 719
    detection, 719–722
    in the home, 720

    mitigation, 721–722
    testing, 720–721
rafter, 413–414
rails, 321
rake, 418
RAM, 97, 98
ramp, 184, 366–367
    handrails, 367
ranch home, 25, 28–29, 37–41
    advantages, 38
    disadvantages, 38–39, 41
    heating, 39
    one-story design, 37–41
rear elevation, 68
receptacle, 450
recessed lighting fixtures, 486
recreation room. *see* family recreation room
RECTANGLE command, 111
REDRAW command, 118–119
REGEN command, 119
REGENERATE command, 119
register, 540
regular polygon, 111
rehab, 695
relative humidity, 518
relays, 479
remodeling, 695–699, 701–706, 710–712
    adding on, 703–706
    architect, 711–712
    attic, 702–703
    bathroom, 699
    buying to remodel, 706
    changing lived-in areas, 698–699
    contractor, 712
    costs, 697
    for historic preservation, 709
    garage, 699, 701
    interior designer, 711
    kitchen, 698–699
    making unused space livable, 699, 701–703
    other rooms, 699
    porch, 699, 701
    preparing plans, 710–712
    reasons for choosing, 696–697
    types of, 697–706
    unfinished basement, 701–702
RENDER command, 125, 126
rendered elevation, 650
rendered section, 650
rendering, 95, 125, 631, 637–645
    3D model, 631
    airbrush, 643
    appliqué, 643
    CADD, 95
    colored pencil, 640, 642
    computer-generated, 95, 643, 645

rendering, *(Continued)*
  felt-tipped, 642
  ink, 638–639
  pencil, 638
  placing and adjusting light sources, 643–644
  presentation drawings, 637–645
  scratchboard, 642
  tempera, 639–640
  watercolor, 639
renovation, 30–31, 695, 707, 710–712
  preparing plans, 710–712
rental apartment, 34
residential designer, 743
resistivity, 531
restoration, 709
reverse osmosis system, 495
RG-6 quad shield cabling, 469–470, 472, 477
ribbon windows, 136
ridge ventilators, 419
right side elevation, 68
right vanishing point (RVP), 613
rigid paving system, 255
rise, 356, 413–414
  roof, 413–414
  stairs, 356
risers, 356, 360–363
  determining number of, 362–363
riser walls, 575
RJ-11 jack, 468
RJ-45 jack, 468–469
roof, 62, 64, 292–293, 306, 409–430
  asphalt shingles, 425
  beam placement, 292
  cornice, 414–415
  decking, 293
  designs, 409–430
  flashing, 422–424
  framing plan, 62, 64
  gutters and downspouts, 424
  metal roofing, 426, 428
  new roofing materials, 426, 428
  plan, 62
  rafters, 413–414
  rake or gable end, 418
  rise, 413–414
  run, 414
  sheathing, 424–425
  slope, 414
  traditional frame construction, 413–425
  trusses, 306, 418–419
  types, 409–412
room air conditioning units, 522
room planning, 129–147, 149–187, 189–214
  living area, 149–187
  service area, 189–214
  sleeping area and bath facilities, 129–147

ROTATE command, 114–115
round, 115
rubble stonework, 310
run, 356, 414
  roof, 414
  stairs, 356
R-value, 536, 584
  concrete wall systems, 584
  true window R-value, 536

S

saddle, 376
safe room, 731
safety, 715–722, 726–736, 744–745
  carbon monoxide (CO) detection, 717–719
  fire safety code requirements, 717
  general home safety, 736
  job site, 744–745
  radon detection, 719–722
  smoke and fire detection, 715–717
  weather- and nature-related, 726–735
safety and health, designing for, 715–738
Salt Box, 20–21, 23
sashes, 334
sauna, 143
S-beams, 248
scale, 94–95, 223, 226, 261, 265, 393, 395, 664
  basement plan, 265
  floor plan, 393, 395
  foundation plan, 261
  plot plan, 223, 226
  residential models, 664
SCALE command, 115, 442
scales, 73
schedule automation, 95, 103–104, 123
  using AEC CADD program, 103–104
scratchboard rendering, 642
scratch coat, 316
screed, 253
screed board, 244
secondary stack, 496
second-story addition, 705–706
section lines, 85
security wiring, 470–472
seismic zone map, 726
septic system, 54, 499–502
septic tank, 500–501
service area, 129, 189–214
  room planning, 189–214
service drop, 450–451
service entrance, 450–452, 483–485
  electrical plan, 483–485
service entry, 167
service panel, 450
service stairs, 353
set of plans, drawings included in, 58–64

SETTINGS command, 120
shading and shadows, 645–646
sheathing, 424–425
shed roof, 410
short break line, 85
shower stall, 143
shutoff valve, 493
sick house syndrome, 722
side-by-side split-level design, 46
signaling circuits, 467–468
sill, 273–296, 329
    and floor construction, 273–296
    construction, 274–275
    sill plate, 274
single-face fireplace, 377
single-pole switch, 458
site, 51–52, 54, 222–223
    considerations, 51–52
    location of structure on, 222–223
    shape, 54
sketching, 77–81
    circles and arcs, 78–79
    ellipses, 79
    freehand, 77–81
    horizontal lines, 77–78
    inclined lines and angles, 78
    irregular curves, 81
    proportion in, 81
    technique, 77
    vertical lines, 78
skylight, 346–347
slab foundation, 238, 240
slab-on-grade construction, 591
slate floor, framing under, 283
sleeping area and bath facilities, 129–147
sleeping level, 46
sliding and swinging glass doors, 326
sliding doors, 323
sliding windows, 332, 334
slope, 361
slope angle, 361
slope design, 570
slope triangle, 436
small scale solid model, 661
SmartBlock™, 586–587
Smart House®, 473–474
smoke and fire detection, 715–717
smoke chamber, 370
smoke detector, 471, 716–717
smoke shelf, 370, 374
snap, 120–121
soft-coat EIFS, 580
software, 91
soil stack, 496–497
solar collector, 554, 556–557
    efficiency, 554

tilt and orientation, 556–557
solar greenhouse, 553–554
solar orientation, 517
solar radiation, 549
solar space heating, 549–564
    active solar systems, 554–559
    advantages, 559
    calculation of Btus, 560–562
    disadvantages, 560
    passive solar systems, 549–554
sole plate, 299
solid beams, 248
solid blocking, 299
solid modeling, 124
solid models, 102–103
solid sill construction, 274–275
solid wire, 467
Southern Building Code Conference International
    (SBCCI), 364
Southern Colonial, 23–24
space diagram, 104, 402
    generation, using AEC CADD program, 104
special appliance circuit, 453–454
special-purpose entries, 167
special-purpose rooms, 175, 177
special-shape windows, 246
specification guides, 676
specifications, 62, 675–684
    examples, 676
    formats, 676
    information to be included, 676
    material and tradework, 675–684
    purpose of, 675–676
specification sheets, 675
specifications writer, 741
spiral ribbon wire, 467
spiral stairs, 355
SPLINE command, 485, 488
split bedroom plan, 131
split-entry house, 47
split-level design, 44–47
    advantages, 44, 46
    disadvantages, 46
    efficient use of space, 44–45
    variations, 46–47
split-level house, floor plan, 396
square foot method, 685–686
square grid, 76
Stachybotrys atra, 725
stack wall, 497
stair generation, using AEC CADD program, 104
stairlift, 366
stairs, 353–368
    adaptations for special needs, 366
    calculations and drawing procedure, 362–363
    design, 359–361

stairs, *(Continued)*
  designing with CADD, 359
  slope, 360–361
  structural details, 363
  terminology, 355–356
  types, 353–355
stairway, 353
staking out house location, 233–235
standardization, 597–600
standard module, 598
station point (SP), 609, 612–614, 616
  distance from picture plane, 613–614
  moving to improve viewing position, 614
  vertical height of, 614, 616
steel beams, 248
steel framing, 302–305
  advantages, 303
  components, 304–305
  disadvantages, 303–304
  environmental benefits, 303
  roofs, 305
  standard dimensions, 305
  thermal performance, 304
  wall construction, 302–305
  walls, 305
steel, workability of, 304
stepped footings, 237
stick-built, 597
stiles, 321
stonework, 310–311
storage devices, 97
storm surge, 732
stove, 380, 385
  circulating, 380
  prefabricated metal, 380
  wood- or coal-burning, 380, 385
straight-line kitchen, 193
straight run stairs, 353–354
stranded wire, 467
stringers, 356, 360
structural C, 304–305
structural foam sandwich panels, 581–584
  advantages, 582–583
  disadvantages, 583
  installation/application, 583–584
structural model, 661
structural symbols, 106
structured wiring, 469, 476–478
stucco, 312–317
  brown coat, 316
  finish coat, 316–317
  lath (reinforcement), 316
  moisture barrier and flashing, 315–316
  preparing for, 314–315
  scratch or foundation coat, 316
Styrofoam®, 663–664

subfloor, 280
sump pump, 243, 247, 497–498
sun angle chart, 555
sun space, 553
superinsulation, 584
surface modeling, 124
surface models, 102
surveyor, 742
swinging windows, 334, 336, 340
switches, 457–458, 485
  electrical plan, 485
switching (activating) functions, 466
symbols, 104, 106–107
  HVAC, 106–107
  in AEC drawings, 104
  title, 107
  tree and plant, 107
symbols library, 88, 93, 106–107, 123
  door and window symbols, 106
  electrical symbols, 106
  furniture and appliance symbols, 107
  plumbing symbols, 106
  structural symbols, 106
  vehicle symbols, 107
synthetic decking, 593–595
synthetic stucco, 312, 580

T
T568A standard, 468–469
T568B standard, 468–469
take-home pay, 57
technical pens, 76
Telecommunications Industry Association (TIA), 468
telephone cable, 467
telephone lines, 467
tempera rendering, 639–640
temperature control, 515–518
templates, 76
termite shields, 308–309
text, CADD software capabilities, 100–101
TEXT command, 112, 406
T-foundation, 238
thermal lag, 584
thermal mass, 550–551, 584
ThermaLock™, 590–591
Thermomass™, 587–588
thermosiphoning, 552
thermostat, 520–522, 542–543
  climate control plan, 542–543
  programmable, 520–522
three-coat stucco system, 312–317
three-face fireplace, 380
three-point perspective, 609
three-way fireplace, 380
three-way switch, 458
tile floor, framing under, 283

TimberTech®, 593–594
title, 53–54
title search, 54
title symbols, 107
toolbar, 109
top view, 68
topographical drawings, 54, 222
    colors, 222
topographical features, 220–222, 224, 229
topography, 52, 54
tornado, 729–732
    building to resist, 730–731
    season, 730
    warnings, 731–732
Tornado Alley, 729
total rise, 356, 362
    determining, 362
total run, 356, 363
    determining, 363
total solar radiation available in Btus, calculation
        procedure, 561–562
trackball, 98
track lighting, 486
tradework specifications, 675–676
traffic circulation, 47
transformer, 461, 468
transom bar, 334
transverse method, 293
trap, 497
treads, 356, 360–361, 363
    determining size, 363
treated wood foundation, 240
tree and plant symbols, 107
trends in architecture, 29–32
Trex®, 593
triangle lighting, 643
triangles, 72
trimmers, 299
Trombe wall, 551–552
tropical hardwoods, 592–593
trowel, 253–254
true length line (TL), 612
true window R-value, 536
trusses, 276, 278–280, 418–419
    floor, 276, 278–280
    roof, 418–419
T-sill construction, 275
T-square, 71–72
tweens, 653
twisted-pair wire, 467
two-face adjacent fireplace, 380
two-face opposite fireplace, 377
two-point perspective, 609, 613–614, 616–623
    distance between station point and picture plane,
        613–614
    drawing sequence, 616–623

position of object with respect to picture plane, 614
    vanishing points, 613
    vertical height of station point or horizon line,
        614, 616
two-story design, 42–44
    exterior maintenance, 44
    heating and cooling, 42
    popularity, 43
two-story house, floor plan, 396
typical wall section, drawing, 436–438

U
U factor, 531
uncoursed cobweb, 310–311
UNDO command, 113
unfinished basement, remodeling, 701–702
uniformity, 94
unshielded twisted-pair (UTP) cable, 468
upflow furnace, 525
U-shaped kitchen, 194–195, 203
U stairs, 355
utility room, 205

V
valley flashing, 423
vanishing points, 612–613
vehicle symbols, 107
veneer, masonry, 311
ventilation, 144, 202, 419, 422, 516–517, 724
    attic, 419, 422
    bathroom, 144
    kitchen, 202
    to reduce excessive humidity, 724
vent stack, 497
vertical lines, sketching, 78
video card, 98
VIEW command, 118
viewpoint, 630
voltage, 450

W
walkthrough animation, 650, 652–653, 655
    length of, 653
    purpose of, 650
    rendering time, 655
wall construction, frame, 297–302
wall framing lumber, 298
walls, 104, 305
    generating with AEC CADD programs, 104
    steel framing, 305
wall stack, 540
wall stiffeners, 245
warm air solar system, 554, 556–558
warm water solar system, 558–559
warped roof, 412

waste lines and vent stacks, 506
water and waste removal, 495–498
    pipe materials, 495
water closets, 142–143, 498–499
    water conservation regulations, 498–499
water conservation, 498–499
water heater, on-demand, 494–495
water softener, 495
water storage wall, 552
water supply, 506
water supply lines, 506–507
water supply system, 491–495
    air compression chamber, 494
    building main, 491
    cold water main and branch lines, 491, 494
    hot water main and branch lines, 492, 494
    pipe materials, 492–493
    shutoff valves, 493
water treatment devices, 495
water vapor, 722–724
    migration, 722–723
    preventative measures, 723–724
    sources, 723
watercolor rendering, 639
watt, 450
W-beams, 248
WBLOCK command, 123
weather- and nature-related safety, 726–735
    earthquakes, 726–727
    floods, 728–729
    hurricanes, 732–735
    tornadoes, 729–732
weather-resistant deck materials, 592–595
    advantages and disadvantages, 594
    list of manufacturers, 594–595
weather-resistant tropical hardwoods, 592–593
weatherstripping, 517
web, 279–280
weight calculations, 250
welded-wire sandwich panels, 588–589
well hole, 355
whirlpool, 143
wide box cornice with lookouts, 414, 417
wide box cornice without lookouts, 417

wide U stairs, 355
winder stairs, 355
windows, 106, 135–136, 319, 330–349
    bedroom, 135–136
    clerestory, 346–347
    combination, 346
    designing with CADD, 319
    fixed, 340, 344, 346
    functions of, 330
    guidelines for selecting, 330–332
    R-values, 536
    sliding, 332, 334
    swinging, 334, 336, 340
    symbols, 106, 319
    types, 332–349
window schedule, 349
winged gable roof, 409
wing walls, 575
wireframe, 124
wiring cabinet, 472
wiring closet, 469
wiring for security, 472
wood beams, 248
wood-burning stove, 380, 385
wood foundation, 240–245
    for structure with basement, 243–244
    for structure with crawl space, 241–242
    standards for, 245
wood I-beams, 289–290
wood pencil, 70
word spacing, 88
work centers, 191
work ethic, 744
working drawings, 675
work triangle, 191
worm's eye view, 616

X

X10 system, 475–476

Z

zoning, 54
ZOOM command, 118